Klett's German Dictionary

ENGLISH-GERMAN / GERMAN-ENGLISH

by
Professor Erich Weis

*Originally published in the
Federal Republic of Germany by*
Ernst Klett Verlag, Stuttgart

NTC Publishing Group

PONS

In German, the best, by definition.

This edition first published in 1982 by NTC Publishing Group,
4255 West Touhy Avenue , Lincolnwood (Chicago),
Illinois 60646-1975 U.S.A., which has been granted
exclusive publishing rights throughout the United
States of America, its territories and possessions,
and Canada. All rights reserved. No part of this
publication may be reproduced, stored in a retrieval
system, or transmitted in any form or by any means,
electronic, mechanical, photocopying, recording,
or otherwise, without the prior written permission
of the publisher. Original copyright ©1981
by Ernst Klett Verlag, Stuttgart, Federal Republic
of Germany.

The ISBN of NTC Publishing Group is 0-8442-2873-7
The ISBN of Ernst Klett Verlag is 3-12-517110-5

9 0 DP 19 18 17 16 15 14 13 12 11

Explanations

Arrangement and Subdivision of Entries

All boldface words are in alphabetical order.

The *Roman numerals* serve to distinguish the various parts of speech to which a base word can belong.

Example: **dwarf** [dwɔːf] **I** *s* Zwerg *m;*
II *adj* winzig, klein;
III *v fig* in den Schatten stellen.

Radically different meanings of an entry are indicated by means of *Arabic numerals.*

Example: **mistress** ['mɪstrɪs] 1. (Haus-)
Herrin *f;* 2. Lehrerin *f;*
3. Geliebte *f;* 4. *abgekürzt:*
Mrs ['mɪsɪz] Frau *f.*

The Tilde, or Sign of Repetition (∼)

The tilde replaces:

a) the boldface base word.

Example: **maraud** [məˈrɔːd] (aus)plündern;
∼**er** [-ə] Plünderer *m.*

b) the part of a base word up to the vertical stroke (|).

Example: **myster|ious** [mɪˈstɪərɪəs] geheimnisvoll; ∼**y** ['mɪstərɪ] Geheimnis,
Rätsel *n.*

c) the preceding boldface word, in practical examples of expressions.

Example: **operat|ive** ['ɒpərətɪv] 1. wirksam;
become ~ in Kraft treten;
2. *med* operativ; ~ **or** ['ɒpəreɪtə]
Techniker *m; telephone* ~ Tele-
fonist(in *f*) *m*.

Grammatical Notes

The gender is given for German nouns. If several German words of the same gender are listed together, the gender-indicator (*m, f* or *n*) will appear only after the last of these nouns. The gender is indicated once more, after an Arabic numeral.

Example: **advertisement** [əd'vɜːtɪsmənt]
1. (Zeitungs-)Anzeige *f*, Inserat *n;*
2. Reklame, Werbung *f*.

With irregular English verbs, the root forms are given. The principal parts of irregular verbs are marked *irr,* and the basic form of the verb is indicated.

Example: **cling** [klɪŋ] *irr clung, clung* [klʌŋ] sich
klammern (*to* an).
undo [ˌʌn'duː] *irr s. do …*

Pronunciation

With every boldface entry that is not a compound of base words presented phonetically elsewhere, the pronunciation and stress marks are given in brackets following the base word.

Pronunciation Key

Vowels and Diphthongs

[ɑ:] plant, arm, father
[aɪ] life
[aʊ] house
[æ] man, sad
[e] get, bed
[eɪ] name, lame
[ə] ago, better
[ɜ:] bird, her
[eə] there, care
[ʌ] but, son
[ɪ] it, wish
[i:] bee, see, me, beat, belief
[ɪə] here
[əʊ] no, low
[ɒ] not, long
[ɔ:] law, all
[ɔɪ] boy, oil
[ʊ] push, look
[u:] you, do
[ʊə] poor, sure

Consonants

[b] been, blind
[d] do, had
[ð] this, father
[f] father, wolf
[g] go, beg
[ŋ] long, sing
[h] house
[j] youth
[k] keep, milk
[l] lamp, oil, ill
[m] man, am
[n] no, manner
[p] paper, happy
[r] red, dry
[s] stand, sand, yes
[ʃ] ship, station
[t] tell, fat
[tʃ] church, catch
[v] voice, live
[w] water, we,
[z] zeal, these, gaze
[ʒ] pleasure
[dʒ] jam, object
[θ] thank, death

The phonetic symbols of the International Phonetic Association (IPA) are used in the transcription of the pronunciation.

List of Abbreviations

a.	auch *also*	*e-e*	
acc	Akkusativ *accusative case*	*e-m*	eine(m, n, r, s) *(of, to) a(n)*
		e-n	
adj	Adjektiv *adjective*	*e-r*	
adv	Adverb *adverb*	*e-s*	
aero	Luftfahrt *aeronautics*	*el*	Elektrizität *electricity*
agr	Landwirtschaft *agriculture*	*ent*	Entomologie *entomology*
allg	allgemein *commonly*	*etc.*	usw. *and so on*
Am	amerikanische Ausdrucksweise *Americanism*	*etw*	etwas *something*
		f	weiblich *feminine*
anat	Anatomie *anatomy*	*fam*	familiär *colloquial*
arch	Architektur *architecture*	*fig*	bildlich *figuratively*
		film	Film *film*
astr	Astronomie *astronomy*	*fin*	Finanz *finance*
		gen	Genitiv *genitive*
attr	als Attribut gebraucht *attributively*	*geog*	Geographie *geography*
aux	Hilfsverb *auxiliary (verb)*	*geol*	Geologie *geology*
		gram	Grammatik *grammar*
		hist	Geschichte *history*
biol	Biologie *biology*	*hum*	humoristisch *humorously*
bot	Botanik *botany*		
Br	Britisches Englisch *in British usage only*	*inf*	Infinitiv *infinitive*
		interj	Interjektion *interjection*
chem	Chemie *chemistry*		
com	Handel *commerce*	*iron*	ironisch *ironical*
comp	Komparativ *comparative*	*irr*	unregelmäßig *irregular*
conj	Konjunktion *conjunction*	*jem*	jemand(em, en, es) *someone,*
		jdm	
dat	Dativ *dative case*	*jdn*	*somebody*
ea.	einander *one another, each other*	*jds*	
		jur	Rechtswissenschaft *jurisprudence*
EDV	elektronische Datenverarbeitung *electronic data processing*	*ling*	Linguistik *linguistics*
		lit	literarisch *literary*
		m	männlich *masculine*

kommen - kam - gekommen
können - konnte - gekonnt
kriechen - kroch - gekrochen
laden - lud - geladen
lassen - ließ - gelassen
laufen - lief - gelaufen
leiden - litt - gelitten
leihen - lieh - geliehen
lesen - las - gelesen
liegen - lag - gelegen
lügen - log - gelogen
mahlen - mahlte - gemahlt
meiden - mied - gemieden
melken - melkte, molk -
  gemelkt, gemolken
messen - maß - gemessen
mißlingen - mißlang -
  mißlungen
mögen - mochte - gemocht
müssen - mußte - gemußt
nehmen - nahm - genommen
nennen - nannte - genannt
pfeifen - pfiff - gepfiffen
preisen - pries - gepriesen
quellen *itr* - quoll - gequollen
reiben - rieb - gerieben
reißen - riß - gerissen
reiten - ritt - geritten
rennen - rannte - gerannt
riechen - roch - gerochen
ringen - rang - gerungen
rinnen - rann - geronnen
rufen - rief - gerufen
salzen - salzte - gesalzen,
  gesalzt
saufen - soff - gesoffen
schaffen (= erschaffen) -
  schuf - geschaffen
schallen - scholl - geschallt
scheinen - schien -
  geschienen
scheißen *vulg* - schiß -
  geschissen

schelten - schalt - gescholten
scheren - schor - geschoren
schieben - schob - geschoben
schießen - schoß - geschossen
schinden - schund -
  geschunden
schlafen - schlief - geschlafen
schlagen - schlug - geschlagen
schleichen - schlich -
  geschlichen
schleifen (= schärfen) -
  schliff - geschliffen
schleißen - schliß, schleißte
  - geschlissen, geschleißt
schließen - schloß -
  geschlossen
schlingen - schlang -
  geschlungen
schmeißen *fam* - schmiß -
  geschmissen
schmelzen - schmolz -
  geschmolzen
schnauben - schnaubte,
  schnob - geschnaubt,
  geschnoben
schneiden - schnitt -
  geschnitten
schreiben - schrieb -
  geschrieben
schweigen - schwieg -
  geschwiegen
schwellen *itr* - schwoll -
  geschwollen
schwimmen - schwamm -
  geschwommen
schwinden - schwand -
  geschwunden
schwingen - schwang -
  geschwungen
schwören - schwor, schwur
  - geschworen
sehen - sah - gesehen
sein - war - gewesen

senden - sandte - gesandt, gesendet
sieden - siedete, sott - gesiedet, gesotten
singen - sang - gesungen
sinken - sank - gesunken
sinnen - sann - gesonnen
sitzen - saß - gesessen
sollen - sollte - gesollt
spalten - spaltete - gespalten, gespaltet
speien - spie - gespie(e)n
spinnen - spann - gesponnen
spleißen - spliß - gesplissen
sprechen - sprach - gesprochen
sprießen - sproß - gesprossen
springen - sprang - gesprungen
stechen - stach - gestochen
stecken - stak, steckte - gesteckt
stehen - stand - gestanden
stehlen - stahl - gestohlen
steigen - stieg - gestigen
steben - starb - gestorben
stieben - stob, stiebte - gestoben, gestiebt
stinken - stank - gestunken
stoßen - stieß - gestoßen
streichen - strich - gestrichen
streiten - stritt - gestritten
tragen - trug - getragen
treffen - traf - getroffen
treiben - trieb - getrieben
treten - trat - getreten

triefen - triefte, troff - getrieft, getroffen
trinken - trank - getrunken
trügen - trog - getrogen
tun - tat - getan
verderben - verdarb - verdorben
verdrießen - verdroß - verdrossen
vergessen - vergaß - vergessen
verlieren - verlor - verloren
wachsen - wuch - gewachsen
wägen - wog - gewogen
waschen - wusch - gewaschen
weben - wob, webte - gewoben
weichen (= nachgeben) - wich - gewichen
weisen - wies - gewiesen
wenden - wandte, wendete - gewendet, gewandt
werben - warb - geworben
werden - wurde - geworden, *aux* worden
werfen - warf - geworfen
wiegen - wog - gewogen
winden - wand - gewunden
winken - winkte - gewinkt
wissen - wußte - gewußt
wollen - wollte - gewollt
wringen - wrang - gewrungen
zeihen - zieh - geziehen
ziehen - zog - gezogen
zwingen - zwang - gezwungen

List of irregular German Verbs

Sequence;
Infinitive - Imperfect - Past
  Participle

backen - backte, buk -
  gebacken
befehlen - befahl - befohlen
beginnen - begann -
  begonnen
beißen - biß - gebissen
bergen - barg - geborgen
bersten - barst - geborsten
bewegen (= veranlassen) -
  bewog - bewogen
biegen - bog - gebogen
bieten - bot - geboten
binden - band - gebunden
bitten - bat - gebeten
blasen - blies - geblasen
bleiben - blieb - geblieben
braten - briet - gebraten
brechen - brach - gebrochen
brennen - brannte - gebrannt
bringen - brachte - gebracht
denken - dachte - gedacht
dingen - dingte, dang -
  gedungen
dreschen - drosch -
  gedroschen
dringen - drang - gedrungen
dünken - dünkte, deuchte -
  gedünkt, gedeucht
dürfen - durfte - gedurft
empfehlen - empfahl -
  empfohlen
essen - aß - gegessen
fahren - fuhr - gefahren
fallen - fiel - gefallen
fangen - fing - gefangen
fechten - focht - gefochten

finden - fand - gefunden
flechten - flocht - geflochten
fliegen - flog - geflogen
fliehen - floh - geflohen
fließen - floß - geflossen
fragen - fragte, frug - gefragt
fressen - fraß - gefressen
frieren - fror - gefroren
gären - gor, gärte - gegoren,
  gegärt
gebären - gebar - geboren
geben - gab - gegeben
gedeihen - gedieh - gediehen
gehen - ging - gegangen
gelingen - gelang - gelungen
gelten - galt - gegolten
genesen - genas - genesen
genießen - genoß - genossen
geschehen - geschah -
  geschehen
gewinnen - gewann -
  gewonnen
gießen - goß - gegossen
gleichen - glich - geglichen
gleiten - glitt - geglitten
glimmen - glomm, glimmte
  - geglommen, geglimmt
graben - grub - gegraben
greifen - griff - gegriffen
haben - hatte - gehabt
halten - hielt - gehalten
hängen *itr* - hing - gehangen
hauen - hieb - gehauen
heben - hob - gehoben
heißen - hieß - geheißen
helfen - half - geholfen
kennen - kannte - gekannt
klimmen - klomm, klimmte
  - geklommen, geklimmt
klingen - klang - geklungen
kneifen - kniff - gekniffen

mar	Schiffahrt *marine*	*ppr*	Partizip Präsens *present participle*
math	Mathematik *mathematics*	*pred*	prädikativ *predicative*
med	Medizin *medicine*	*pref*	Vorsilbe *prefix*
m-e		*pret*	Präteritum *preterite*
m-m	meine(m, n, r, s)	*prn*	Pronomen *pronoun*
m-n	*to, of my*	*prp*	Präposition *preposition*
m-r			
m-s		*psych*	Psychologie *psychology*
metal	Hüttenwesen *metallurgy*	*radio*	Rundfunk *radio*
mete	Meteorologie *meteorology*	*rail*	Eisenbahn *railway*
mil	Militär *military*	*rel*	Religion *religion*
min	Bergbau, Mineralogie *mining, mineralogy*	*S*	Sache *thing*
		s	Substantiv *substantive*
mot	Kraftfahrwesen *motoring*	*s.*	siehe *see*
mus	Musik *music*	*s-e*	
n	sächlich *neuter*	*s-m*	seine(m, n, r, s)
od	oder *or*	*s-n*	*(to) his, (to) one's*
opt	Optik *optics*	*s-r*	
orn	Ornithologie *ornithology*	*s-s*	
		sing	Singular *singular*
o.s.	sich *oneself*	*sl*	Slang *slang*
parl	parlamentarisch *parliamentary*	*s.o.*	jemand *someone*
		sport	Sport *sport*
pej	herabsetzend *pejorative*	*s.th.*	etwas *something*
		tech	Technik *technics*
pharm	Pharmazie *pharmacy*	*tele*	Telegrafie, Telefonie *telegraphy, telephony*
philos	Philosophie *philosophy*	*theat*	Theater *theatre*
phot	Fotografie *photography*	*TV*	Fernsehen *television*
		typ	Buchdruck *printing*
phys	Physik *physics*	*u.*	und *and*
physiol	Physiologie *physiology*	*v*	Verb *verb*
		Wz	Warenzeichen *registered trademark*
pl	Plural *plural*		
pol	Politik *politics*	*z. B.*	zum Beispiel *for example*
pp	Partizip Perfekt *past participle*	*zoo*	Zoologie *zoology*
		Zs-, zs-	zusammen *together*

A

a [ə, eɪ] ein, eine.

aback [ə'bæk] *he was taken ~ at the news* er war über die Nachricht bestürzt.

abandon [ə'bændən] 1. aufgeben, preisgeben; 2. verlassen, im Stich lassen; 3. *he ~ed himself to despair* er war völlig verzweifelt.

abate [ə'beɪt] 1. vermindern; 2. *(Sturm)* nachlassen; 3. *jur* beseitigen.

abbey ['æbɪ] Abtei *f.*

abbreviate [ə'briːvɪeɪt] ab-, verkürzen; **~ion** [ə,briːvɪ'eɪʃn] Abkürzung *f.*

ABC [,eɪbiː'siː] Abc *n.*

abdicate ['æbdɪkeɪt] aufgeben; abdanken.

abdomen ['æbdəmen] Unterleib *m.*

abhor [əb'hɔː] verabscheuen.

ability [ə'bɪlətɪ] Fähigkeit *f; to the best of my ~* so gut ich kann.

able ['eɪbl] 1. fähig, imstande; *are you ~ to help me?* können Sie mir helfen? 2. tüchtig, geschickt.

aboard [ə'bɔːd] an Bord; im Zug, Omnibus, Flugzeug; *go ~* an Bord gehen; sich einschiffen; *all ~!* alle Mann an Bord! *Am rail* einsteigen!

abode [ə'bəud] *with no fixed ~* ohne festen Wohnsitz.

abolish [ə'bɒlɪʃ] abschaffen, aufheben.

abomina|ble [ə'bɒmɪnəbl] scheußlich, widerwärtig; *(Wetter)* abscheulich; **~te** [-neɪt] *I ~ it* es ist mir ein Greuel.

abortion [ə'bɔːʃn] 1. Fehlgeburt *f;* 2. Abtreibung *f.*

abound [ə'baund] im Überfluß vorhanden sein; wimmeln (*with* von).

about [ə'baut] 1. *(räumlich)* um, um ... herum, über ... hin; *a fence ~ the garden* ein Zaun um den Garten herum; 2. *(Zeit, Maß)* um, ungefähr; *~ five o'clock* gegen 5 Uhr; *~ ten* etwa zehn; 3. bei sich, an sich; *have you any money ~ you?* haben Sie Geld bei sich? 4. *(hinweisend, bezüglich)* von, über, in bezug auf, betreffend, wegen; *what ~ dinner?* wie wär's mit Abendessen? 5. *be ~* im Begriffe sein; auf den Beinen sein; im Umlauf sein; 6. *just ~ enough* gerade noch genug.

above [ə'bʌv] **I** *adv* oben, droben, oberhalb; weiter oben; *(Rang, Bedeutung, Stellung)* höher; *as (mentioned) ~* wie oben erwähnt; **II** *prp* über; mehr als; *~ all* vor allem; *~ a ton* über eine Tonne; *he is ~ it* er ist darüber weg; *it is ~ me* das geht über meinen Horizont; *he's ~ the age of 18* er ist über 18; **III** *adj* obig; obenerwähnt.

abreast [ə'brest] nebeneinander; *keep ~ of, with* (fig) Schritt halten mit.

abridge [ə'brɪdʒ] (ab-, ver-) kürzen.

abroad [ə'brɔːd] 1. auswärts; im *od* ins Ausland; *live ~* im Ausland leben; 2. (weit)verbreitet; *it is all ~* es ist allgemein bekannt.

abrupt [ə'brʌpt] 1. plötzlich, unerwartet; 2. *(Verhalten)* schroff, barsch.

abscess ['æbsɪs] Geschwür *n*.

absen|ce ['æbsəns] 1. Abwesenheit *f (from* von); Fernbleiben, Fehlen *n*; 2. *(~ of mind)* Zerstreutheit *f*; **~t** [-t] 1. abwesend, fehlend; 2. *(~-minded)* geistesabwesend, unaufmerksam.

absolute ['æbsəluːt] 1. völlig, absolut; 2. *(Wahrheit)* rein, voll; 3. unumschränkt.

absorb [əb'sɔːb] 1. aufsaugen; 2. *fig* fesseln, ganz in Anspruch nehmen; *~ed in thought* in Gedanken versunken.

abstain [əb'steɪn] sich enthalten *(from s.th.* e-r S); verzichten *(from* auf).

abstention [əb'stenʃn] Stimmenthaltung *f*.

abstinen|ce ['æbstɪnəns] Enthaltsamkeit *f (from* von); **~t** [-t] enthaltsam.

abstract I *adj* ['æbstrækt] abstrakt; schwer verständlich; **II** *s* ['-] *(Buch)* Auszug, Abriß *m*; **III** *v* [æb'strækt] 1. e-n Auszug machen *(from* von); zs.fassen; 2. *fam* entwenden.

absurd [əb'sɜːd] sinn-, vernunftwidrig; unsinnig, lächerlich; **~ity** [-əti] Unsinn *m*, Ungereimtheit *f*.

abundan|ce [ə'bʌndəns] Überfluß *m (of* an); *live in ~* alles haben, was das Herz begehrt; **~t** [-t] reichlich.

abuse I *v* [ə'bjuːz] 1. mißbrauchen; 2. beschimpfen, beleidigen; **II** *s* [ə'bjuːs] 3. Mißbrauch *m*; 4. Beschimpfung *f*.

acade|mic [ˌækə'demɪk] 1. akademisch; 2. theoretisch; **~my** [ə'kædəmɪ] Akademie *f*.

accelerat|e [ək'seləreɪt] beschleunigen; **~or** [-tə] Gaspedal *n*.

accent ['æksənt] **I** *s* Ton *m*; Betonung *f*; Akzent *m*; **II** *v* betonen; **~uate** [æk'sentjʊeɪt] betonen.

accept [ək'sept] 1. annehmen; 2. glauben *(s.th.* an etw) *(Tatsache)* anerkennen, gelten lassen; **~able** [-əbl] annehmbar *(to* für); **~ance** [-əns] Annahme *f*;

find ~ gut aufgenommen werden.
access [ˈækses] 1. Zutritt *m* (*to* zu); 2. Zufahrt *f;* 3. *fig* Zugang *m;* ~**ible** [əkˈsesəbl] zugänglich (*to* für).

accessory [əkˈsesərɪ] Zubehörteil *n; motor-car accessories pl* Autozubehör *n;*

accident [ˈæksɪdənt] 1. Unglücksfall, Unfall *m; by* ~ zufällig; *in an* ~ bei e-m Unfall; ~ *insurance* Unfallversicherung *f;* 2. Zufall *m;* ~**tal** [-ˈdentl] zufällig.

accl|aim [əˈkleɪm] mit Beifall begrüßen; ~**amation** [ˌækləˈmeɪʃn] Zustimmung *f.*

acclimat|e [ˈæklɪmeɪt], *Br* ~**ize** [əˈklaɪmətaɪz] sich (an)gewöhnen (*to* an); akklimatisieren.

accomodat|e [əˈkɒmədeɪt] 1. (sich) anpassen (*to* an); 2. beherbergen, unterbringen; ~**ing** [-ɪŋ] gefällig, entgegen-, zuvorkommend; ~**ion** [əˌkɒməˈdeɪʃn] 1. Anpassung *f* (*to* an); 2. Unterkunft, Unterbringung *f;* Hotelzimmer *n.*

accompan|iment [əˈkʌmpənɪmənt] 1. Begleiterscheinung *f;* 2. *mus* Begleitung *f;* ~**y** [-nɪ] begleiten *a. mus.*

accomplice [əˈkʌmplɪs] Komplize *m.*

accomplish [əˈkʌmplɪʃ] 1. vollbringen, erledigen;

aus-, durchführen; (*Plan*) verwirklichen; (*Arbeit*) verrichten; 2. (*Zweck*) erfüllen; ~**ed** [-t] 1. vollendet; 2. kultiviert, gebildet; ~**ment** [-mənt] 1. Vollendung, Leistung *f;* 2. *pl* Fähigkeiten, Fertigkeiten *f pl.*

accord [əˈkɔːd] **I** *v* 1. übereinstimmen; im Einklang stehen (*with* mit); 2. gewähren; **II** *s* 3. Übereinstimmung *f; with one* ~ einstimmig, einmütig; *I did it of my own* ~ ich habe es aus eigenem Antrieb getan; 4. Abkommen *n;* ~**ance** [-dəns] *in* ~ *with* in Übereinstimmung mit; ~**ing** [-ɪŋ] gemäß; entsprechend (*to* dat); ~**ingly** [-ɪŋlɪ] dementsprechend; ~**ion** [-jən] Ziehharmonika *f.*

account [əˈkaʊnt] **I** *s* 1. Rechnung *f;* 2. Konto *n* (*with* bei); 3. *call to* ~ zur Rechenschaft ziehen (*for* wegen); 4. *give an* ~ *of s.th.* von etw Bericht erstatten; 5. Erwägung *f; take* ~ *of s.th.* etw berücksichtigen; *take into* ~ in Betracht ziehen; 6. Grund *m,* Ursache *f; on no* ~ unter keinen Umständen; *on* ~ *of* wegen, auf Grund *gen; on this* ~ aus diesem Grunde; 7. Gewinn, Nutzen *m; turn s. th. to* ~ sich etw zunutze machen; **II** *v* 8. erklären, begründen (*for s. th.* etw); *that* ~*s for it* das ist die Erklärung dafür; 9. Rechenschaft ablegen (*for* für); 10. ansehen, betrachten als; **~able** [-əbl] verantwortlich; **~ant** [-ənt] Buchhalter *m*; *(Am) certified public* **~**, *(Br) chartered* **~** Wirtschaftsprüfer *m*.

accumulat|e [ə'kju:mjʊleɪt] 1. auf-, anhäufen; 2. sich (an)sammeln; **~ion** [ə,kju:mjʊ'leɪʃn] Anhäufung *f*; **~or** [-ə] Akku(mulator) *m*.

accura|cy ['ækjʊrəsɪ] Genauigkeit *f*; **~te** ['ækjʊrət] genau, richtig.

accusation [,ækju:'zeɪʃn] Anklage *f*.

accusative [ə'kju:zətɪv] *gram* Akkusativ *m*.

accuse [ə'kju:z] anklagen, beschuldigen (*of having done s.th.* etw getan zu haben); **~d** [-d] Angeklagte(r *m*) *f*.

accustom [ə'kʌstəm] gewöhnen (*to* an); *get* **~ed** sich gewöhnen (*to* an).

ace [eɪs] Eins *f (auf Würfeln); (Spielkarten)* As *n; within an* **~** beinahe, um ein Haar.

ache [eɪk] **I** *v* schmerzen, weh tun; **II** *s: have* **~s** *and pains* Schmerzen haben.

achieve [ə'tʃi:v] 1. ausführen, zustande bringen; 2. *(Ziel)* erreichen; *(Erfolg)* erzielen; **~ment** [-mənt] 1. Ausführung *f*; 2. Leistung *f*.

acid ['æsɪd] **I** *adj* sauer; **II** *s* Säure *f*.

acknowledg|e [ək'nɒlɪdʒ] 1. anerkennen; 2. zugeben, (ein)gestehen; 3. bestätigen; *this is to* **~** *receipt of* ich bestätige hiermit den Empfang gen; **~(e)ment** [-mənt] 1. Anerkennung *f*; 2. Bestätigung, Quittung *f*.

acorn ['eɪkɔ:n] Eichel *f*.

acoustic [ə'ku:stɪk] **I** *adj* akustisch; **II** *s pl* Akustik *f*.

acquaint [ə'kweɪnt] bekannt machen (*with* mit); *be* **~ed** *with s.th.* mit etw bekannt, vertraut sein; *get* **~ed** *with s.o.* mit jdm bekannt werden; **~ance** [-əns] 1. Bekanntschaft *f*; 2. Bekannte(r *m*) *f*.

acquire [ə'kwaɪə] erlangen, erwerben.

acquisition [,ækwɪ'zɪʃn] 1. Erwerbung *f*; 2. Errungenschaft *f*.

acquit [ə'kwɪt] *jur* freisprechen (*of a charge* von e-r Anklage); **~tal** [-l] *jur* Freispruch *m*.

acre ['eɪkə] Morgen *m (4046 qm).*

acrid ['ækrɪd] *(Geruch)* scharf.

acrobat ['ækrəbæt] Akrobat *m*.

across [ə'krɒs] **I** *adv* hinüber, herüber; (quer) durch; **II** *prp* 1. quer über, quer durch; 2. auf der anderen Seite, jenseits.

act [ækt] **I** s 1. Handlung, Tat f; in the ~ auf frischer Tat; 2. theat Akt, Aufzug m; 3. jur Gesetz n; **II** v 4. theat (e-e Rolle) spielen; 5. tätig sein (as als); handeln, tun; 6. ~ for s.o. jdn vertreten; 7. ~ on einwirken auf.

action ['ækʃn] 1. Handlung, Tätigkeit f; take ~ Schritte unternehmen; 2. (jur) bring an ~ against s.o. gegen jdn e-e Klage einreichen; 3. mil Gefecht n.

activ|e ['æktɪv] tätig, aktiv, rührig, regsam; lebhaft; ~ity [æk'tɪvətɪ] Tätigkeit, Geschäftigkeit, Betätigung f.

act|or ['æktə] theat Schauspieler m; ~ress ['æktrɪs] Schauspielerin f.

actual ['æktʃʊəl] 1. wirklich, tatsächlich; eigentlich; 2. gegenwärtig.

acute [ə'kjuːt] 1. spitz; 2. scharfsinnig; 3. (Schmerz) heftig; 4. (Sinne) scharf; 5. (Winkel) spitz; 6. med akut.

ad [æd] fam Zeitungsanzeige f.

adapt [ə'dæpt] 1. anpassen (to an); be well ~ed sehr geeignet sein (for für); 2. (Roman) bearbeiten; ~ation [ædæp'teɪʃn] 1. Anpassung f (to an); 2. theat Bearbeitung f.

add [æd] 1. hinzusetzen, -fügen (to zu); 2. math (~ up) zs.zählen, addieren; 3. fig

beitragen (to zu); vermehren (to s.th. etw).

addict ['ædɪkt] drug ~ Rauschgiftsüchtige(r m) f.

addition [ə'dɪʃn] 1. Zugabe f; Zusatz m; in ~ außerdem (noch); in ~ to (zusätzlich) zu; 2. math Addition f; ~al [-ʃənl] zusätzlich.

address [ə'dres] **I** v 1. (Brief) adressieren, absenden, schicken (to an); 2. (Person) anreden; 3. (Anfrage) richten (to an); 4. ~ o.s. to sich widmen; **II** s 5. Anrede, Ansprache f; 6. Anschrift, Adresse f; 7. Geschicklichkeit, Gewandtheit f; ~ee [ædre'siː] Empfänger, Adressat m.

adequate ['ædɪkwət] angemessen, ausreichend (for für); entsprechend (to dat).

adhesive [əd'hiːsɪv] ~ tape, plaster Heftpflaster n.

adjacent [ə'dʒeɪsənt] in der Nähe (to von); benachbart.

adjoin [ə'dʒɔɪn] angrenzen an; ~ing [-ɪŋ] benachbart.

adjourn [ə'dʒɜːn] vertagen (for a week um e-e Woche).

adjust [ə'dʒʌst] 1. (sich) anpassen; 2. (richtig) einstellen; berichtigen; ~able [-əbl] regulierbar.

administ|er [əd'mɪnɪstə] 1. verwalten; 2. (Hilfe) leisten; ~ justice Recht sprechen; 3. (Medizin) verabreichen; ~ration [əd,mɪnɪ'streɪʃn] 1. Verwaltung(sbehörde), Regierung *f;* 2. *(Medizin)* Verabreichung *f;* 3. *(Eid)* Abnahme *f;* ~**rator** [-treɪtə] 1. Verwalter *m;* 2. Testamentsvollstrecker *m.*

admirable ['ædmərəbl] wunderbar; bewundernswert.

admir|ation [,ædmə'reɪʃn] Bewunderung *f (of, for* für); ~**e** [əd'maɪə] bewundern (*for* wegen); ~**er** [əd'maɪrə] Bewunderer *m.*

admission [əd'mɪʃn] 1. Einlaß, Zutritt *m;* ~ **free** Eintritt frei; *no* ~ Eintritt verboten! 2. Ein-, Zugeständnis *n.*

admit [əd'mɪt] 1. (her)einlassen, Zutritt gewähren; 2. zulassen, aufnehmen (*to a club* in e-n Klub); 3. zugeben, eingestehen; 4. gestatten, erlauben (*of no doubt* keinen Zweifel); ~**tance** [-əns] Einlaß, Zutritt *m.*

ado [ə'du:] *without more* ~ ohne weitere Umstände.

adolescent [,ædəʊ'lesnt] Jugendliche(r *m*) *f.*

adopt [ə'dɒpt] 1. adoptieren; 2. *(Antrag)* annehmen; 3. *(Gedanken)* sich zu eigen machen; ~**ion** [ə'dɒpʃn] 1. Adoption *f;* 2. Annahme *f.*

ador|able [ə'dɔ:rəbl] reizend, entzückend; ~**e** [ə'dɔ:] 1. anbeten, verehren; 2. *fam* sehr gern haben.

adult ['ædʌlt] **I** *adj* erwachsen; **II** *s* Erwachsene(r *m*) *f.*

adultery [ə'dʌltərɪ] Ehebruch *m.*

advance [əd'va:ns] **I** *v* 1. vorrücken; 2. *(im Rang)* befördern; 3. *(Preis)* erhöhen, steigen; 4. *(Geld)* vorschießen; 5. Fortschritte machen; **II** *s* 6. Vorrücken *n;* 7. Fortschritt *m;* 8. *(Preis)* Erhöhung *f;* 9. Vorschuß *m;* 10. *(Beamter)* Beförderung *f;* 11. *in* ~ im voraus, zuvor; ~ **booking** Vorbestellung *f;* ~ **notice** Voranzeige, Voranmeldung, -kündigung *f;* ~ **payment** Vorauszahlung *f.*

advantage [əd'va:ntɪdʒ] Vorteil, Nutzen, Gewinn *m; take* ~ *of* ausnutzen.

adventur|e [əd'ventʃə] Abenteuer *n;* ~**er** [-rə] Abenteurer *m;* ~**ous** [əd'ventʃərəs] abenteuerlich.

advers|ary ['ædvəsərɪ] Gegner *m;* ~**e** ['ædvɜ:s] ungünstig, nachteilig; *(Umstände)* widrig.

advertise ['ædvətaɪz] 1. ankündigen; inserieren (*for* nach); 2. Reklame, Propaganda machen; ~**ment** [əd'vɜ:tɪsmənt] 1. (Zeitungs-)Anzeige *f,* Inserat *n;* 2. Reklame, Werbung *f;* ~**r** [-ə] Inserent *m.*

advice [əd'vaɪs] 1. Rat(schlag) *m; ask s.o.'s* ~ jdn um Rat fragen; *take medical* ~ e-n Arzt aufsuchen; 2. Benachrichtigung *f.*

advis|able [əd'vaizəbl] ratsam, empfehlenswert; **~e** [əd'vaiz] 1. (an)raten, empfehlen; *what do you ~ me to do?* was soll ich Ihrer Ansicht nach tun? 2. *com* benachrichtigen; **~er** [-ə] Ratgeber *m*.

advocate ['ædvəkət] **I** *s* Fürsprecher, Verfechter *m*; **II** *v* eintreten (*s.th.* für etw); befürworten.

aerial ['eəriəl] Antenne *f*.

aero|drome ['eərədrəum] Flughafen *m*; **~nautics** [,eərə'nɔːtiks] Luftfahrt *f*; **~plane** [-plein] Flugzeug *n*.

affair [ə'feə] Geschäft *n*; Angelegenheit, Sache *f*.

affect [ə'fekt] 1. beeinflussen, in Mitleidenschaft ziehen, einwirken (*s.th.* auf etw); 2. (*Gesundheit*) angreifen; 3. vorgeben; so tun, als ob; **~ation** [,æfek'teiʃn] Affektiertheit *f*; **~ion** [ə'fekʃn] (Zu-)Neigung, Liebe *f* (*for, towards* zu); **~ionate** [-ʃnət] liebevoll, zärtlich.

affidavit [,æfi'deivit] *jur* eidesstattliche Versicherung *f*.

affiliated [ə'filieitid] angegliedert, angeschlossen.

affinity [ə'finəti] 1. Verwandtschaft *f*; 2. Zuneigung *f*.

affirm [ə'fɜːm] behaupten, versichern; **~ation** [,æfə'meiʃn] Bestätigung *f*;

~ative [-mətiv] bejahend; bestätigend.

afflict [ə'flikt] betrüben; **~ion** [ə'flikʃn] Leiden *n*; Kummer *m*, Betrübnis *f*.

affluen|ce ['æfluəns] Reichtum *m*; Überfluß *m*; **~t** [-ənt] wohlhabend.

afford [ə'fɔːd] 1. die Mittel aufbringen für; sich erlauben; *I can't ~ it* ich kann es mir nicht leisten; 2. (*Vergnügen*) bereiten; gewähren.

affront [ə'frʌnt] **I** *v* beleidigen; **II** *s* Beleidigung *f*.

afield [ə'fiːld] *go far ~* weit weg gehen.

afraid [ə'freid] *be ~* (sich) fürchten, Angst haben (*of* vor); *I am ~ I have to go* ich muß leider gehen; *don't be ~ to . . .* scheuen Sie sich nicht zu . . .!

Africa ['æfrikə] Afrika *n*; **~n** [-n] **I** *s* Afrikaner *m*; **II** *adj* afrikanisch.

after ['ɑːftə] **I** *adv* hinterher, darauf, danach; **II** *prp* (*räumlich*) hinter, nach, hinter . . . her; (*zeitlich*) nach; *day ~ day* Tag für Tag; *day ~ tomorrow* übermorgen; *~ all* schließlich u. endlich, letzten Endes; **III** *conj* nachdem; **~noon** [,ɑːftə'nuːn] Nachmittag *m*; *in the ~* nachmittags (*at* um); **~wards** [-wədz] danach, darauf; nachher, später.

again [ə'gen] wieder, noch

einmal, nochmals; *as much ~* noch einmal soviel; *time and (time) ~, ~ and ~* immer wieder.

against [ə'genst] gegen; *I'm not ~ it* ich habe nichts dagegen.

age [eɪdʒ] **I** *s* Alter, Zeitalter *n; at the ~ of* im Alter von; *what's your ~?* wie alt sind Sie? **II** *v* alt werden, altern; **~d** [eɪdʒd] bejahrt.

agency ['eɪdʒənsɪ] Geschäftsstelle; Agentur *f; tourist, travel(ling) ~* Reisebüro *n*.

agenda [ə'dʒendə] *be on the ~* auf der Tagesordnung stehen.

agent ['eɪdʒənt] 1. Mittel *n;* 2. Vertreter *m*.

aggravate ['ægrəveɪt] 1. verschlimmern; 2. *fam* ärgern.

aggregate ['ægrɪgət] *~ amount* Gesamtbetrag *m*.

aggress|ion [ə'greʃn] Angriff *m;* **~ive** [ə'gresɪv] aggressiv; **~or** [ə'gresə] Angreifer *m*.

aghast [ə'gɑːst] entsetzt, bestürzt (*at* über).

agile ['ædʒaɪl] flink, gewandt.

agitat|e ['ædʒɪteɪt] 1. schütteln, rütteln; 2. beunruhigen (*about* wegen); 3. agitieren (*against* gegen; *for* für); **~ion** [,ædʒɪ'teɪʃn] 1. Auf-, Erregung *f;* 2. Agitation *f;* **~or** ['ædʒɪteɪtə] Agitator *m*.

ago [ə'gəʊ] vor; *three months ~* vor drei Monaten; *not long ~* vor kurzem, unlängst; *a while ~* vor e-r Weile.

agony ['ægənɪ] 1. Todeskampf *m;* 2. Qual *f*.

agree [ə'griː] 1. zustimmen (*to* zu), einverstanden sein (*to* mit); 2. übereinstimmen; 3. übereinkommen (*with* mit); sich einigen, einig sein (*on* über); 4. zuträglich sein, bekommen; *pepper doesn't ~ with me* Pfeffer bekommt mir nicht; **~able** [ə'grɪəbl] angenehm; **~ment** [-mənt] 1. Übereinkommen *n;* Vertrag *m; reach an ~* eine Vereinbarung treffen; 2. *be in ~* sich einig sein; übereinstimmen.

agricultur|al [,ægrɪ'kʌltʃərəl] landwirtschaftlich; **~e** ['ægrɪkʌltʃə] Landwirtschaft *f*.

aground [ə'graʊnd] *go, run ~* stranden.

ah [ɑː] ach! ah! **aha** [ɑː'hɑː] aha!

ahead [ə'hed] vor, voraus; vorn; vorwärts; *~ of* vor; *~ of time* vorzeitig; *get ~* vorwärtskommen; *go ~ and tell her* sag's ihr doch! *straight ~* gerade aus.

aid [eɪd] **I** *v* helfen; **II** *s* Hilfe *f; first ~* erste Hilfe.

aim [eɪm] **I** *v* 1. zielen (*at* auf, nach); *that's ~ed at me (fig)* das gilt mir; 2. beabsichtigen, bezwecken (*at doing,*

(Am) to do zu tun); **II** *s*
3. Ziel *n;* 4. Zweck *m,* Absicht *f;* **~less** ['eımlıs] ziellos, zwecklos, planlos.

air [eə] **I** *s* 1. Luft *f; by ~* auf dem Luftwege; *in the open ~* im Freien; 2. Aussehen *n,* Miene *f;* 3. *be on the ~* im Rundfunk sprechen; **II** *v* (aus-, durch)lüften.

air|conditioned ['eəkən-ˌdıʃnd] mit Klimaanlage; **~-cooled** ['-ku:ld] luftgekühlt; **~craft** ['-krɑ:ft] Flugzeug *n; ~ carrier* Flugzeugträger *m;* **~crew** ['-kru:] (Flugzeug-)Besatzung *f;* **~drome** ['-drəum] *Am* Flughafen *m;* **~field** ['-fi:ld] Flugplatz *m; ~* **force** Luftstreitkräfte *f pl;* **~freight** ['-freıt] Luftfracht *f; ~* **hostess** Stewardeß *f;* **~ing** ['eərıŋ] *go for an ~* an die frische Luft gehen; *~* **jacket** *Br* Rettungsweste *f; ~* **letter** Luftpostbrief *m; ~* **lift** Luftbrücke *f;* **~line** ['-laın] Fluglinie, -gesellschaft *f;* **~liner** ['-ˌlaınə] Verkehrsflugzeug *n;* **~mail** ['-meıl] Luftpost *f;* **~plane** ['-pleın] *Am* Flugzeug *n; ~* **port** ['-pɔ:t] Flughafen *m; ~* **raid** Luftangriff *m;* **~ship** ['-ʃıp] Luftschiff *n;* **~sick** ['-sık] luftkrank; **~tight** ['-taıt] luftdicht; **~way** ['-weı] Fluglinie *f;* **~y** ['eərı] 1. luftig; 2. leichtfertig.

aisle [aıl] 1. *arch* Seitenschiff

n; 2. *Am* Gang *m (zwischen Sitzreihen).*

alarm [ə'lɑ:m] **I** *s* 1. Alarm *m; false ~* blinde(r) Alarm; 2. Schreck *m;* **II** *v* 3. alarmieren; 4. erschrecken (*at* über); **~-clock** [-klɒk] Wecker *m.*

alas [ə'læs] ach! leider!

Albania [æl'beınıə] Albanien *n.*

alcohol ['ælkəhɒl] Alkohol, Spiritus *m;* **~ic** [ˌælkə'hɒlık] **I** *adj* alkoholisch; **II** *s* Alkoholiker *m.*

alder ['ɔ:ldə] *bot* Erle *f.*

alderman ['ɔ:ldəmən] Ratsherr *m.*

ale [eıl] Ale *n (Bier).*

alert [ə'lɜ:t] **I** *adj* 1. wachsam; 2. munter, lebhaft; **II** *s* Alarmbereitschaft *f; on the ~* auf der Hut, alarmbereit; **III** *v* alarmieren; **~ness** [-nıs] 1. Wachsamkeit *f;* 2. Aufgewecktheit *f.*

algebra ['ældʒıbrə] Algebra *f.*

Algeria [æl'dʒıərıə] Algerien *n.*

alien ['eıljən] Ausländer *m.*

alight [ə'laıt] **I** *adj* brennend; erhellt (*with* von); *catch ~* aufflammen; **II** *v* ab-, aussteigen.

alike [ə'laık] **I** *adj: be ~* gleich, ähnlich sein; **II** *adv* ebenso; *treat ~* gleich behandeln.

alive [ə'laıv] 1. lebend(ig); 2. *he is ~ to the danger* er

ist sich der Gefahr bewußt;
3. *look* ~ auf! beeil dich!
4. *be* ~ *with s.th.* von etw
wimmeln.

all [ɔːl] **I** *adj* ganz, gesamt; alle *pl;* ~ *day long* den ganzen
Tag hindurch; **II** *prn* alle, alles; *above* ~ vor allem; *after*
~ trotzdem; schließlich (und
endlich); *(not) at* ~ überhaupt (nicht); *for* ~ trotz;
once (and) for ~ ein für allemal; ~ *in* ~ alles in allem;
III *adv* ganz u. gar; ~ *along*
schon immer; ~ *at once*
plötzlich; zugleich; ~ *right*
in Ordnung; einverstanden;
~ *the time* die ganze Zeit;
it's ~ *one to me* es ist mir
egal.

allegedly [ə'ledʒdlɪ] angeblich.

alleviate [ə'liːvɪeɪt]
(Schmerz) lindern.

alley ['ælɪ] Gasse *f; blind* ~
Sackgasse *f.*

alliance [ə'laɪəns] Bündnis *n.*

allied [ə'laɪd] verbündet.

allocate ['æləʊkeɪt] an-, zuweisen.

allot [ə'lɒt] zuweisen, verteilen; **~ment** [-mənt] Parzelle *f.*

allow [ə'laʊ] 1. erlauben, gestatten *(s.o. to do, doing
s.th.);* bewilligen; *will you* ~
me? darf ich? 2. ~ *for s.th.*
etw berücksichtigen; **~ance**
[ə'laʊəns] 1. Zuschuß *m;*
2. Nachlaß, Rabatt *m;*

3. *make* ~*(s) for s.th.* etw
berücksichtigen.

allude [ə'luːd] anspielen (*to*
auf); sich beziehen (*to* auf).

allure [ə'ljʊə] ködern, verführen.

allusion [ə'luːʒn] *make an* ~
to auf etw anspielen.

ally ['ælaɪ] **I** *s* Verbündete(r
m) f; **II** *v* (sich) verbünden.

almond ['ɑːmənd] Mandel *f.*

almost ['ɔːlməʊst] fast, beinahe.

alms [ɑːmz] *sing od pl* Almo-
sen *n.*

alone [ə'ləʊn] **I** *adj* allein,
einsam; *let me* ~! laß mich
in Ruhe! *let* ~ ganz abgesehen von; geschweige denn;
II *adv* nur, bloß.

along [ə'lɒŋ] **I** *prp* entlang,
längs; an … entlang; ~ *here*
in dieser Richtung; **II** *adv*
weiter; vorwärts; ~ *with* zusammen mit; *come* ~ mit-
kommen; *take* ~ mitneh-
men; *how are you getting*
~? wie geht es Ihnen denn?
~side [-'saɪd] Seite an Seite; längsseits.

aloof [ə'luːf] *stand, hold o.s.*
~ *from s.th.* mit etw nichts
zu tun haben wollen.

aloud [ə'laʊd] laut; *read* ~
vorlesen.

alphabet ['ælfəbɪt] Alphabet, Abc *n;* **~ical**
[ˌælfə'betɪkl] alphabetisch.

already [ɔːl'redɪ] schon, bereits.

also ['ɔːlsəʊ] auch, ebenfalls, gleichfalls; ferner, dazu.

altar ['ɔːltə] Altar *m*.

alter ['ɔːltə] 1. (ab-, um-, ver)ändern; 2. sich ändern; **~ation** [ˌɔːltə'reɪʃn] Änderung *f*.

alternat|e I *adj* [ɔːl'tɜːnət] abwechselnd; **II** *v* ['ɔːltəneɪt] abwechseln (lassen); **~ing** [-ɪŋ] abwechselnd; ~ *current* Wechselstrom *m;* **~ion** [ˌɔːltə'neɪʃn] Wechsel *m*, Abwechslung *f;* **~ive** [ɔːl'tɜːnətɪv] **I** *adj* abwechselnd; **II** *s* Alternative *f; there is no* ~ es gibt keine andere Möglichkeit.

altho(ugh) [ɔːl'ðəʊ] obgleich, obschon.

altitude ['æltɪtjuːd] Höhe *f*.

altogether [ˌɔːltə'geðə] 1. gänzlich, ganz und gar, völlig; 2. alles in allem.

always ['ɔːlweɪz] immer, stets.

amaz|e [ə'meɪz] verblüffen, sehr überraschen; *be* ~*d at* erstaunt sein über; **~ing** [-ɪŋ] erstaunlich, verblüffend.

ambassador [æm'bæsədə] Botschafter *m*.

ambiguous [æm'bɪgjʊəs] 1. zweideutig; 2. unklar; unsicher.

ambit|ion [æm'bɪʃn] Ehrgeiz *m; ~***ious** [æm'bɪʃəs] ehrgeizig.

ambulance ['æmbjʊləns] Kranken-, Sanitätswagen *m;* ~ **station** Unfallstation *f*.

ambush ['æmbʊʃ] Hinterhalt *m*.

amend [ə'mend] 1. (sich) bessern; 2. abändern; **~ment** [-mənt] Verbesserung, Änderung *f; ~***s** *pl make* ~ Schadenersatz leisten.

America [ə'merɪkə] Amerika *n; ~***n** [-n] **I** *s* Amerikaner *m;* **II** *adj* amerikanisch.

amid, ~**st** [ə'mɪd, -st] mitten unter.

amiss [ə'mɪs] *take s.th.* ~ etw übelnehmen; *there's s.th.* ~ da ist etw nicht in Ordnung.

ammunition [ˌæmjʊ'nɪʃn] Munition *f*.

amnesty ['æmnɪstɪ] Amnestie *f*.

among(st) [ə'mʌŋ(st)] mitten unter, zwischen; ~ *other things* unter anderem.

amount [ə'maʊnt] **I** *s* 1. Betrag *m*, Summe *f;* 2. Menge *f;* **II** *v* 3. sich belaufen (*to* auf), betragen, ausmachen (*to s.th.* etw); 4. hinauslaufen (*to* auf).

ample ['æmpl] 1. geräumig, ausgedehnt; weit; 2. reichlich.

amplify ['æmplɪfaɪ] 1. verstärken *a. el;* 2. (*Thema*) näher ausführen.

amputate ['æmpjʊteɪt] amputieren.

amulet ['æmjʊlɪt] Amulett *n*.

amuse [ə'mjuːz] belustigen,

amüsieren, unterhalten; **~ment** [-mənt] Unterhaltung *f*, Zeitvertreib *m*.

analogous [ə'næləgəs] analog, entsprechend.

analy|se, ~ze ['ænəlaɪz] analysieren, zergliedern, zerlegen; **~sis** [ə'næləsɪs] *pl -ses* [-iːz] Analyse *f*.

anarchy ['ænəkɪ] Anarchie *f*.

anatomy [ə'nætəmɪ] Anatomie *f*.

ancestor ['ænsestə] Vorfahre *m*.

anchor ['æŋkə] Anker *m*; *cast ~* Anker werfen.

anchovy ['æntʃəvɪ] Sardelle *f*.

ancient ['eɪnʃənt] sehr alt; antik.

and [ænd] und; *~ so forth, on* usw.

anecdote ['ænɪkdəʊt] Anekdote *f*.

angel ['eɪndʒəl] Engel *m a. fig.*

anger ['æŋgə] **I** *s* Ärger, Zorn *m*; **II** *v* erzürnen.

angle ['æŋgl] **I** *v* angeln (*for* nach) *a. fig*; **II** *s* Winkel *m*; *consider s.th. from all ~s (fig)* etw von allen Seiten betrachten.

angler ['æŋglə] Angler *m*.

Anglo-Saxon [ˌæŋgləʊ'sæksən] **I** *s* Angelsachse *m*; **II** *adj* angelsächsisch.

angry ['æŋgrɪ] ärgerlich, zornig (*at s.th.* über etw; *with s.o.* auf jdn); *what are you ~*

about? worüber ärgern Sie sich?

anguish ['æŋgwɪʃ] Schmerz *m*, Qual *f*.

angular ['æŋgjʊlə] wink(e)lig; eckig.

animal ['ænɪml] Tier *n*.

animat|e ['ænɪmeɪt] beleben, anregen; aufmuntern; **~d** *cartoon* Zeichentrickfilm *m*; **~ion** [ˌænɪ'meɪʃn] Lebhaftigkeit; Munterkeit *f*.

animosity [ˌænɪ'mɒsətɪ] Feindseligkeit *f* (*against* gegen; *between* zwischen).

ankle ['æŋkl] Fußknöchel *m*; *sprain one's ~* sich den Fuß verstauchen.

annex ['æneks] **I** *s* 1. Nebengebäude *n*; 2. Nachtrag, Zusatz *m* (*to* zu); **II** *v* 3. *pol* annektieren; 4. anhängen, beifügen.

annihilate [ə'naɪəleɪt] vernichten, ausrotten.

anniversary [ˌænɪ'vɜːsərɪ] Jahrestag *m*.

announce [ə'naʊns] ankündigen; ansagen; bekanntgeben; **~ment** [-mənt] Ankündigung, Bekanntmachung; *radio* Durchsage *f*; **~r** [-ə] *radio* Ansager *m*.

annoy [ə'nɔɪ] belästigen, ärgern; *be ~ed* sich ärgern (*at s.th.* über etw; *with s.o.* über jdn); **~ing** [-ɪŋ] ärgerlich.

annual ['ænjʊəl] **I** *adj* jährlich; **II** *s* Jahrbuch *n*.

annul [ə'nʌl] annullieren; außer Kraft setzen.

anomalous [əˈnɒmələs]
anomal.

anonymous [əˈnɒnɪməs]
anonym.

another [əˈnʌðə] 1. ein anderer; ~ *time* ein andermal;
2. noch ein; 3. *one* ~ einander, sich.

answer [ˈɑːnsə] **I** *s* Antwort
f; **II** *v* 1. antworten; ~ *the
door, (tele)phone* an die
Tür, ans Telephon gehen;
2. verantwortlich sein, bürgen (*for* für); 3. entsprechen
(*to a description* e-r Beschreibung).

ant [ænt] Ameise *f*.

antagoni|sm
[ænˈtægənɪzəm] Feindseligkeit *f*; ~**st** [-st] Gegner *m*.

antelope [ˈæntɪləʊp] *zoo*
Antilope *f*.

ant-hill [ˈænthɪl] Ameisen-
haufen *m*.

anticipat|e [ænˈtɪsɪpeɪt]
1. erwarten; 2. zuvorkom-
men; 3. voraussehen, ahnen;
~**ion** [ænˌtɪsɪˈpeɪʃn] *in* ~ im
voraus; in Erwartung (*of*
gen).

anticyclone [ˌæntɪˈsaɪkləʊn]
Hoch(druckgebiet) *n*.

antidote [ˈæntɪdəʊt] Gegen-
gift *n* (*against, for, to* gegen).

anti-freeze [ˈæntɪfriːz]
Frostschutzmittel *n*.

antipathy [ænˈtɪpəθɪ] Abneigung *f* (*to, towards, against*
gegen).

antiqu|ated [ˈæntɪkweɪtɪd]

altmodisch; ~**e** [ænˈtiːk] alt,
antik; ~**ity** [ænˈtɪkwətɪ] Al-
tertum *n*.

antlers *pl* [ˈæntləz] Geweih
n.

anxi|ety [æŋˈzaɪətɪ] Besorg-
nis, Angst *f* (*for, about* um);
~**ous** [ˈæŋkʃəs] 1. besorgt,
beunruhigt (*about* wegen);
2. bemüht (*for* um); *be* ~
darauf aus sein (*to do s.th.*
etw zu tun).

any [ˈenɪ] **I** *adv* irgend(wie);
überhaupt; ein wenig; *it isn't
~ good* es nützt nichts;
II *adj* 1. irgendein(e, s), ir-
gendwelche(r, s); *not* ~ kein;
have you ~ *other ques-
tions?* haben Sie noch e-e
Frage? 2. jede(r, s) beliebige; irgendein(e, s); *come at
~ time* kommen Sie jeder-
zeit; *in* ~ *case, at* ~ *rate* auf
jeden Fall.

any|body [ˈenɪˌbɒdɪ] 1. ir-
gend jemand; 2. jeder (beliebige), jedermann; ~ *can do
that* jeder kann das machen;
~**how** [ˈ-haʊ] 1. irgendwie;
2. auf jeden Fall, immerhin; *I
would have gone* ~ ich wäre
sowieso gegangen; ~**one**
[ˈ-wʌn] *s. anybody;* ~**thing**
[ˈ-θɪŋ] 1. (irgend) etwas, je-
des beliebige; *is there* ~
new? gibt es etwas Neues?
not for ~ um keinen Preis;
2. ~ *but* alles andere als;
~**way** [ˈ-weɪ] 1. irgendwie,
in irgendeiner Weise; 2. ohnehin, sowieso; trotzdem;

~where ['-weə] 1. irgend-wo(hin); *that won't get you ~* damit erreichen Sie gar nichts; *~ from (fam)* belie-big zwischen *(five to six* fünf u. sechs); 2. überall(hin).

apart [ə'pɑːt] 1. einzeln, (ab)gesondert; *~ from* abge-sehen von; *live ~* getrennt leben; 2. (in einzelne Teile) zerlegt; *take ~* ausea.neh-men; *tell ~* unterscheiden; 3. abseits, beiseite; *joking ~* Scherz beiseite; **~ment** [-mənt] *Am* (Miet-)Woh-nung *f; Br* Zimmer *n; pl* Wohnung *f; ~ house (Am)* Miethaus *n.*

apathy ['æpəθɪ] Teilnahms-losigkeit *f (to* gegen).

ape [eɪp] **I** *s* Affe *m a. fig;* **II** *v* nachäffen.

apiece [ə'piːs] je Stück; pro Kopf.

apolog|ize [ə'pɒlədʒaɪz] sich entschuldigen *(to s.o. for s.th.* bei jdm wegen etw); **~y** [ə'pɒlədʒɪ] Entschuldigung *f.*

apostle [ə'pɒsl] Apostel *m.*

apostrophe [ə'pɒstrəfɪ] Apostroph *m.*

appal(l) [ə'pɔːl] erschrecken; **~ling** [-ɪŋ] schrecklich.

apparatus [ˌæpə'reɪtəs] Ap-parat *m,* Gerät *n,* Vorrich-tung *f.*

apparent [ə'pærənt] 1. of-fensichtlich, einleuchtend; 2. scheinbar, vermeintlich; **~ly** [-lɪ] anscheinend.

appeal [ə'piːl] **I** *s* 1. dringen-de Bitte *f (for* um); 2. Reiz *m,* Anziehungskraft *f;* 3. *jur* Berufung *f (from* gegen); **II** *v* 4. sich wenden *(to* an); 5. gefallen; Anklang finden *(to* bei); 6. *jur* Berufung ein-legen; **~ing** [-ɪŋ] flehentlich.

appear [ə'pɪə] 1. erscheinen; 2. scheinen, den Anschein haben; **~ance** [ə'pɪərəns] 1. Erscheinen, Auftreten *n; make an ~* sich zeigen, er-scheinen; 2. Anschein *m,* Aussehen *n;* Äußere(s) *n.*

appease [ə'piːz] beruhigen, beschwichtigen; *(Hunger)* stillen.

appendicitis [əˌpendɪ'saɪtɪs] Blinddarmentzündung *f.*

appetite ['æpɪtaɪt] Appetit *m (for* auf).

applau|d [ə'plɔːd] applaudie-ren *(s.o.* jdm); **~se** [ə'plɔːz] Beifall *m.*

apple ['æpl] Apfel *m; ~ of discord* Zankapfel *m; ~ pie* [ˌ-'paɪ] Apfelkuchen *m; ~ sauce* [ˌ-'sɔːs] Apfelmus *n.*

appliance [ə'plaɪəns] Gerät *n;* Vorrichtung *f; household ~s pl* Haushaltsgeräte *n pl.*

applic|able ['æplɪkəbl] an-wendbar *(to* auf); **~cant** ['æplɪkənt] Bewerber *m (for* um); **~cation** [ˌæplɪ'keɪʃn] 1. Verwendung *f,* Gebrauch *m (to* für, auf); 2. Umschlag *m,* Kompresse *f;* 3. Bewer-bung *f (for* um); *~ form* Be-

werbungs-, Antragsformular
n; 4. Fleiß, Eifer *m.*

apply [ə'plaɪ] 1. anwenden
(*to* auf); verwenden; *(Pflaster)* auflegen; *(Bremse)* betätigen; 2. gelten (*to* für);
3. sich wenden (*to* an).

appoint [ə'pɔɪnt] 1. ernennen, berufen; 2. festlegen,
-setzen, verabreden; **~ed**
[-ɪd] *at the ~ time* zum vereinbarten Zeitpunkt;
~ment [-mənt] 1. Ernennung *f;* Anstellung *f (in a firm* bei e-r Firma); 2. *have an ~* e-e Verabredung haben (*with* mit); bestellt sein
(*at the dentist's* zum Zahnarzt).

apprais|al [ə'preɪzl] Schätzung, Bewertung *f;* **~e**
[ə'preɪz] abschätzen, bewerten.

appreciat|e [ə'pri:ʃɪeɪt]
1. schätzen, würdigen; anerkennen; 2. im Wert steigen;
~ion [ə,pri:ʃɪ'eɪʃn] Würdigung *f,* Verständnis *n (of* für); Anerkennung *f.*

apprehen|d [,æprɪ'hend]
1. verhaften; 2. begreifen,
erfassen; 3. (be)fürchten;
~sion [,æprɪ'henʃn] 1. Verhaftung *f;* 2. Verständnis *n;*
3. *oft pl* Befürchtung *f;*
~sive [,æprɪ'hensɪv] besorgt (*for* um; *of* wegen).

apprentice [ə'prentɪs] Lehrling *m;* **~ship** [-ʃɪp] Lehrzeit, Lehre *f.*

approach [ə'prəʊtʃ] **I** *v*

1. sich nähern *a. fig;* 2. sich
wenden (*s.o. about s.th.* an
jdn wegen etw); **II** *s* 3. (Heran-)Nahen *n;* 4. *fig* Annäherung, Ähnlichkeit *f;* 5. Zugang *m,* Zufahrt *f.*

appropriate I *adj*
[ə'prəʊprɪət] geeignet, angemessen (*to, for* dat); **II** *v*
[ə'prəʊprɪeɪt] 1. sich aneignen; 2. *(Geld)* bestimmen
(*for* für).

approv|al [ə'pru:vl] 1. Zustimmung, Billigung *f; does it meet with your ~?* sind
Sie damit einverstanden?
2. *on ~* zur Ansicht; **~e**
[ə'pru:v] billigen; einverstanden sein (*of* mit).

approximately
[ə'prɒksɪmətlɪ] ungefähr, etwa.

apricot ['eɪprɪkɒt] Aprikose
f.

April ['eɪprəl] April *m; ~
Fools' Day* 1. April.

apt [æpt] 1. fähig, geschickt
(*at* in); begabt; 2. *(Bemerkung)* treffend; 3. neigend
(*to* zu); *~ to break* leicht
zerbrechlich; **~itude**
['æptɪtju:d] Fähigkeit; Geschicklichkeit, Begabung *f*
(*for* für); *~ test* Eignungsprüfung *f.*

aquarium [ə'kweərɪəm]
Aquarium *n.*

Aquarius [ə'kweərɪəs] *astr*
Wassermann *m.*

aquatic [ə'kwætɪk] *~ sports
pl* Wassersport *m.*

Arab ['ærəb] Araber *m;* ~**ian** [ə'reɪbɪən] arabisch.

arbitra|ry ['ɑ:bɪtrərɪ] willkürlich, eigenmächtig; ~**te** ['ɑ:bɪtreɪt] schlichten; ~**tion** [ˌɑ:bɪ'treɪʃn] Schiedsspruch *m.*

arch [ɑ:tʃ] **I** *s arch* Bogen *m;* Gewölbe *n;* **II** *v* (sich) wölben.

archaeology [ˌɑ:kɪ'ɒlədʒɪ] Archäologie *f.*

archbishop [ˌɑ:tʃ'bɪʃəp] Erzbischof *m.*

archery ['ɑ:tʃərɪ] Bogenschießen *n.*

architect ['ɑ:kɪtekt] Architekt *m;* ~**ure** ['ɑ:kɪtektʃə] Architektur *f.*

arctic ['ɑ:ktɪk] arktisch.

ardent ['ɑ:dənt] glühend, feurig, begeistert.

ardour ['ɑ:də] Eifer *m;* Begeisterung (*for* für) *f.*

arduous ['ɑ:djuəs] anstrengend; mühsam, schwierig.

area ['eərɪə] Gebiet *n,* Bereich *m* a. *fig;* Fläche *f.*

Argentin|a, ~**e** [ˌɑ:dʒən'ti:nə, '--taɪn] Argentinien *n.*

argu|e ['ɑ:gju:] 1. sich streiten (*about* über); 2. argumentieren (*for* für, *against* gegen); 3. überreden (*s.o. into doing s.th.* jdn etw zu tun); 4. erörtern; ~**ment** ['ɑ:gjumənt] 1. Argument *n;* Beweis *m;* 2. Erörterung *f* (*about* über).

arid ['ærɪd] 1. trocken; 2. *fig* uninteressant.

Aries ['eəri:z] *astr* Widder *m.*

arise [ə'raɪz] *irr arose* [ə'rəuz], *arisen* [ə'rɪzn] entstehen (*from, out of* aus).

aristocra|cy [ˌærɪ'stɒkrəsɪ] Aristokratie *f;* ~**t** ['ærɪstəkræt] Aristokrat *m.*

arithmetic [ə'rɪθmətɪk] Rechnen *n.*

arm [ɑ:m] **I** *s* 1. Arm *m;* 2. *meist pl* Waffen *pl; be up in* ~*s* empört sein (*over* über); **II** *v* (sich) bewaffnen; ~**istice** ['ɑ:mɪstɪs] Waffenstillstand *m;* ~**o(u)r** ['ɑ:mə] Panzer *m;* ~**y** ['ɑ:mɪ] Armee *f.*

aroma [ə'rəumə] Aroma *n.*

around [ə'raund] **I** *adv* ringsherum, rundherum; nach, auf allen Seiten; **II** *prp* um ... herum; rings um.

arouse [ə'rauz] 1. (auf)wecken; 2. ~ *suspicion* Verdacht erregen.

arrange [ə'reɪndʒ] 1. (an)ordnen; 2. organisieren; 3. verabreden, vereinbaren; *as* ~*d* wie vereinbart; ~**ment** [-mənt] 1. (An)Ordnung *f;* 2. *pl* Vorkehrungen *f pl; make* ~*s* Vorbereitungen treffen; 3. Abmachung, Vereinbarung *f; come to an* ~ zu e-r Einigung kommen.

arrears [ə'rɪəz] Schulden *f pl;* Rückstände *m pl.*

arrest [ə'rest] **I** *v* 1. anhalten; hemmen; 2. (*Aufmerksamkeit*) fesseln; 3. *jur* verhaften; **II** *s* Verhaftung *f; under* ~ in Haft.

arriv|al [ə'raɪvl] 1. Ankunft *f; on ~* bei Ankunft; *~s and departures (rail)* Ankunfts- und Abfahrtszeiten *f pl;* 2. Ankömmling *m; ~e* [ə'raɪv] 1. ankommen (*at, in* in); 2. *fig* gelangen, kommen (*at a decision* zu e-r Entscheidung).

arrogan|ce ['ærəgəns] Anmaßung *f; ~t* ['ærəgənt] anmaßend.

arrow ['ærəu] Pfeil *m.*

arson ['ɑːsn] Brandstiftung *f.*

art [ɑːt] 1. Kunst; Geschicklichkeit *f;* 2. Verschlagenheit, List *f;* 3. *pl* Geisteswissenschaften *f pl; ~s and crafts* Kunstgewerbe *n pl.*

artery ['ɑːtəri] 1. Schlagader *f;* 2. Verkehrsader *f.*

artful ['ɑːtful] verschlagen, listig.

artic|le ['ɑːtɪkl] 1. Gegenstand *m; com* Ware *f;* 2. (Zeitungs-)Artikel *m;* 3. Abschnitt, Paragraph *m;* 4. *gram* Geschlechtswort *n; ~ulate* I *adj* [ɑː'tɪkjulət] 1. gegliedert; 2. deutlich, artikuliert; II *v* [-leɪt] 3. gliedern; 4. artikulieren; deutlich aussprechen.

artificial [ˌɑːtɪ'fɪʃl] künstlich; *~ leg* Beinprothese *f; ~ respiration* künstliche Atmung *f.*

artisan [ˌɑːtɪ'zæn] Handwerker *m.*

artist ['ɑːtɪst] Künstler(in *f*)

m; ~ic [ɑː'tɪstɪk] künstlerisch.

as [æz] I *adv* wie (zum Beispiel); (ebenso) wie; ~ *yet* bis jetzt; soweit; ~ *well* auch; ~ *far* ~ bis (zu); soviel, soweit; II *conj* da, weil; als, während; (in der Art) wie, genauso wie; als (ob); ~ *it were* sozusagen; ~ *if, though* als ob; ~ *soon* ~ sobald (als); ~ *you like* nach Belieben; III *prp* (in der Eigenschaft) als; ~ *for,* ~ *to* was ... anbetrifft; hinsichtlich; IV *prn* welche(r, s); was, wie; *in proportion* ~ in dem Maße wie.

Ascension (Day) [ə'senʃn(deɪ)] Himmelfahrtstag *m.*

ascent [ə'sent] Anstieg *m.*

ascertain [ˌæsə'teɪn] feststellen, ermitteln.

ascetic [ə'setɪk] asketisch.

ascribe [ə'skraɪb] zuschreiben.

aseptic [æ'septɪk] aseptisch, keimfrei.

ash [æʃ] 1. *bot* Esche *f;* 2. Asche *f; ~-bin, Am ~ can* Mülleimer *m; ~-tray* Aschenbecher *m; Ash Wednesday* Aschermittwoch *m.*

ashamed [ə'ʃeɪmd] *I feel ~* ich schäme mich; *you should be ~ of yourself* du solltest dich schämen.

ashore [ə'ʃɔː] ans Ufer; am Ufer; *go ~* an Land gehen.

Asia ['eɪʃə] Asien *n; ~n* ['eɪʃn] **I** *s* Asiat *m;* **II** *adj* asiatisch.

aside [ə'saɪd] beiseite; *joking* ~ Spaß beiseite; *lay* ~ beiseite legen; *put* ~ zurücklegen.

ask [ɑːsk] 1. fragen; sich erkundigen (*after, for* nach); ~ *s.o.'s advice* jdn um Rat fragen; ~ *s.o. his name* jdn nach s-m Namen fragen; 2. ~ *s.o. for s. th.* jdn um etw bitten; 3. fordern, verlangen; *how much do you* ~ *for it?* wieviel wollen Sie dafür?

asleep [ə'sliːp] *be fast* ~ fest schlafen; *fall* ~ einschlafen.

asparagus [ə'spærəgəs] Spargel *m.*

aspect ['æspekt] 1. Aussehen *n,* Anblick *m;* 2. Aussicht *f,* Ausblick *m;* 3. Aspekt, Gesichtspunkt *m.*

aspire [ə'spaɪə] streben (*to* nach).

ass [æs] Esel *m.*

assassinate [ə'sæsɪneɪt] ermorden.

assault [ə'sɔːlt] **I** *s* Angriff, Überfall *m* (*upon* auf); **II** *v* tätlich angreifen.

assemble [ə'sembl] 1. (sich) versammeln; 2. *tech* montieren; ~**y** [ə'semblɪ] 1. Versammlung *f;* 2. *tech* Montage *f;* ~ *line* Fließ-, Montageband *n.*

assent [ə'sent] **I** *v* einwilligen (*to* in); zustimmen (*to*

dat); **II** *s* Zustimmung, Einwilligung *f.*

assert [ə'sɜːt] 1. behaupten; 2. (*Recht*) verteidigen; ~**ion** [ə'sɜːʃn] Behauptung *f.*

assets *pl* ['æsets] Vermögenswerte *m pl.*

assign [ə'saɪn] 1. an-, zuweisen; 2. beauftragen.

assimilate [ə'sɪmɪleɪt] 1. angleichen; 2. assimilieren, aufnehmen.

assist [ə'sɪst] helfen (*s.o.* jdm), unterstützen (*s.o.* jdn); ~**ance** [ə'sɪstəns] Hilfe, Unterstützung *f;* ~**ant** [-t] Assistent, Gehilfe *m; shop-*~ Verkäufer(in *f*) *m.*

associat|e I *s* [ə'səʊʃɪət] *com* Teilhaber *m;* **II** *v* [-ʃɪeɪt] 1. vereinigen, verbinden; 2. sich zs.tun, sich zs.schließen (*with* mit); ~**ion** [ə,səʊsɪ'eɪʃn] 1. Vereinigung *f; in* ~ *with* zusammen mit; 2. Verein *m;* Gesellschaft *f;* 3. (*A*~ *football*) (europäisches) Fußballspiel *n.*

assort|ed [ə'sɔːtɪd] 1. (*Waren*) gemischt; 2. *well* ~ gut zs.passend; ~**ment** [-mənt] Auswahl *f,* Sortiment *n.*

assume [ə'sjuːm] 1. annehmen; *let's* ~ *that* nehmen wir an, daß; 2. (*Verantwortung*) übernehmen.

assur|ance [ə'ʃʊərəns] 1. Versicherung *f; life* ~ Lebensversicherung *f;* 2. Zusicherung *f;* 3. (Selbst-)Sicherheit *f;* ~**e** [ə'ʃʊə] versichern.

asthma ['æsmə] *med* Asthma *n.*

astonish [ə'stonɪʃ] in Erstaunen setzen; *be ~ed* erstaunt sein (*at* über); **~ing** [-ɪŋ] erstaunlich; *it's ~ to me* das überrascht mich; **~ment** [-mənt] Verwunderung *f* (*at* über).

astray [ə'streɪ] *go ~* in die Irre gehen.

astride [ə'straɪd] rittlings.

astro||logy [ə'strolədʒɪ] Astrologie *f;* **~naut** ['æstrənɔːt] Astronaut *m;* **~nomer** [ə'stronəmə] Astronom *m;* **~nomic(al)** [ˌæstrə'nomɪk(l)] astronomisch; **~nomy** [ə'stronəmɪ] Astronomie *f.*

asylum [ə'saɪləm] Asyl *n.*

at [æt] 1. *(Ort)* in, bei, an, auf, zu; *~ Oxford* in Oxford; *~ a distance* in e-r Entfernung; *~ the dentist's* beim Zahnarzt; *~ home* zu Hause; 2. *(Art u. Weise)* in, zu; *be ~ a loss* in Verlegenheit sein; *not ~ all* durchaus nicht; 3. *(Veranlassung)* auf ... hin; *~ his request* auf s-e Bitte (hin); 4. *(Zeit)* um; in; zu; *~ night* in der Nacht; *~ the age of* im Alter von; 5. *(Zustand)* in; *~ peace* in Frieden; *~ work* bei der Arbeit; 6. *(Richtung)* nach, gegen, zu, an, auf; über; *aim ~* zielen nach; *he is mad ~ me* er ist wütend auf mich; 7. *(bei Zahlangaben)* zu;

buy ~ a pound zu (je) e-m Pfund kaufen.

athlete ['æθliːt] Athlet *m;* **~ic** [æθ'letɪk] **I** *adj* athletisch; **II** *s pl* (Leicht-)Athletik *f.*

atlas ['ætləs] *geogr* Atlas *m.*

atmosphere ['ætmə‚sfɪə] Atmosphäre *f.*

atom ['ætəm] *chem* Atom *n;* **~ic** [ə'tomɪk] atomar; **~izer** ['ætəumaɪzə] Zerstäuber *m.*

atone [ə'təun] wiedergutmachen (*for s.th.* etw).

atroc||ious [ə'trəuʃəs] scheußlich; **~ity** [ə'trosətɪ] Scheußlichkeit *f.*

attach [ə'tætʃ] 1. anheften, befestigen (*to* an); 2. *be very ~ed to* (*fig*) sehr hängen an; 3. (*fig*) *~ importance to* Wert beimessen.

attaché case [ə'tæʃɪkeɪs] Aktentasche *f*, -koffer *m.*

attachment [ə'tætʃmənt] Anhänglichkeit *f.*

attack [ə'tæk] **I** *v* angreifen *a. fig;* **II** *s* 1. Angriff *m* (*on* auf, gegen); 2. *(Krankheit)* Anfall *m.*

attempt [ə'tempt] **I** *v* versuchen; **II** *s* Versuch *m.*

attend [ə'tend] 1. *(Schule)* besuchen; beiwohnen (*a meeting* e-r Versammlung); 2. sich befassen (*to* mit); 3. *med* behandeln; 4. bedienen (*to a customer* e-n Kunden); **~ance** [-əns] 1. Besuch *m;* 2. (Zu-)Hörerschaft *f* (*at* bei); 3. *be in ~* Dienst haben, anwesend sein; **~ant** [-ənt] Diener(in *f*), Wärter, Aufseher *m.*

attent|ion [ə'tenʃn] Aufmerksamkeit *f; (auf Briefen)* zu Händen von; *pay* ~ aufpassen; **~ive** [ə'tentıv] aufmerksam (*to* auf).

attest [ə'test] bestätigen, bescheinigen.

attic ['ætık] Dachkammer *f.*

attitude ['ætıtjuːd] 1. (Körper-)Haltung *f;* 2. Einstellung *f (towards* gegenüber).

attorney [ə'tɜːnı] *jur* Bevollmächtigte(r); Rechtsanwalt *m; power of* ~ Vollmacht *f.*

attract [ə'trækt] 1. anziehen *a. fig;* 2. *fig* fesseln, reizen; **~ion** [ə'trækʃn] 1. Anziehung *f a. phys;* 2. *fig* Reiz *m;* **~ive** [ə'træktıv] anziehend.

attribute I *v* [ə'trıbjuːt] zuschreiben, beimessen (*to s.th.* e-r S); **II** *s* ['ætrıbjuːt] Merkmal; Symbol *n.*

auburn ['ɔːbən] kastanienbraun.

auction ['ɔːkʃn] **I** *s* Versteigerung *f;* **II** *v* versteigern.

audaci|ous [ɔː'deıʃəs] 1. kühn; 2. frech; **~ty** [ɔː'dæsətı] 1. Kühnheit *f;* 2. Frechheit *f.*

audible ['ɔːdəbl] hörbar.

audience ['ɔːdjəns] 1. Zuhörer(schaft *f*) *m pl;* 2. Audienz *f (of. with* bei).

augment ['ɔːgmənt] vermehren, vergrößern.

August ['ɔːgəst] August *m.*

aunt [ɑːnt] Tante *f.*

auspices *pl* ['ɔːspısız] *under the* ~ *of* s.o. unter jds Schirmherrschaft.

auster|e [ɒ'stıə] streng; herb; **~ity** [ɒ'sterətı] Strenge; Einfachheit *f.*

Australia [ɒ'streıljə] Australien *n;* **~n** [-n] **I** *s* Australier *m;* **II** *adj* australisch.

Austria ['ɒstrıə] Österreich *n;* **~n** [-n] **I** *s* Österreicher *m;* **II** *adj* österreichisch.

authentic [ɔː'θentık] authentisch, echt; **~ate** [-keıt] beglaubigen.

author ['ɔːθə] Verfasser; Urheber *m.*

authorit|arian [ɔː;θɒrı'teərıən] autoritär; **~y** [ɔː'θɒrətı] 1. Autorität *f;* 2. Vollmacht *f;* 3. Sachverständige(r) *m;* 4. *pl* Behörde *f.*

authoriz|ation [ɔː;θəraı'zeıʃn] Bevollmächtigung; Genehmigung *f;* **~e** ['ɔːθəraız] bevollmächtigen, ermächtigen; **~ed** bevollmächtigt, berechtigt.

autograph ['ɔːtəgraːf] Autogramm *n.*

automatic [ɔːtə'mætık] automatisch, selbsttätig.

automobile ['ɔːtəməʊbiːl] *Am* Auto(mobil) *n.*

autonomy [ɔː'tɒnəmı] Autonomie *f.*

autumn ['ɔːtəm] Herbst *m.*

auxiliary [ɔːg'zıljərı] Hilfs-.

avail [ə'veıl] **I** *v:* ~ (*o.s.*) *of*

s.th. sich einer S bedienen; etw benutzen; **II** ~ Nutzen *m; of no* ~ nutzlos; ~**able** [ə'veɪləbl] 1. verfügbar; 2. vorrätig, erhältlich.

avalanche ['ævəlɑːnʃ] Lawine *f a. fig.*

avaric|e ['ævərɪs] Habsucht *f;* Geiz *m;* ~**ious** [ˌævə'rɪʃəs] habsüchtig; geizig.

avenge [ə'vendʒ] ~ *o.s. on* sich rächen an.

avenue ['ævənjuː] 1. *fig* Zugang *m;* 2. Allee *f;* 3. *Am* Pracht-, Hauptstraße *f.*

average ['ævərɪdʒ] **I** *s* Durchschnitt *m; on (the* od *an)* ~ durchschnittlich, im Durchschnitt; **II** *v* im Durchschnitt betragen.

avers|e [ə'vɜːs] abgeneigt (*to* gegen); ~**ion** [ə'vɜːʃn] Widerwille *m* (*to, from* gegen).

avert [ə'vɜːt] abwenden (*from* von).

aviation [ˌeɪvɪ'eɪʃn] Luftfahrt *f.*

avid ['ævɪd] gierig (*for, of* nach); ~**ity** [ə'vɪdətɪ] Begierde; Gier *f* (*of, for* nach).

avoid [ə'vɔɪd] meiden; vermeiden (*doing s.th.* etw zu tun).

await [ə'weɪt] erwarten.

awake [ə'weɪk] *be* ~ 1. wach sein; 2. *fig* sich klar sein (*to a difficulty* über e-e Schwierigkeit).

award [ə'wɔːd] **I** *s* Preis *m;* Auszeichnung *f;* **II** *v* (*Preis*) verleihen.

aware [ə'weə] *I'm* ~ *of that* ich bin mir dessen bewußt.

away [ə'weɪ] weg, fort; entfernt, abseits; abwesend; *far and* ~ bei weitem; *go* ~ weggehen; *send* ~ wegschicken; *take* ~ wegnehmen; *right, straight* ~ auf der Stelle; sofort, gleich.

awe [ɔː] Ehrfurcht *f (of* vor).

awful ['ɔːful] furchtbar, schrecklich.

awkward ['ɔːkwəd] 1. unangenehm, gefährlich; 2. linkisch, ungeschickt.

axe, *Am* **ax** [æks] Axt *f;* Beil *n.*

axis ['æksɪs] *pl axes phys pol* Achse *f.*

axle ['æksl] (Rad-)Achse *f.*

ay(e)s *pl* [aɪz] *the* ~ *have it* die Mehrzahl ist dafür.

B

babble ['bæbl] 1. plappern; *(Geheimnis)* ausplaudern; 2. plätschern.

baby ['beɪbɪ] Säugling *m*, (kleines) Kind *n*; ~**(-)sitter** ['-ˌsɪtə] Babysitter *m*.

bachelor ['bætʃələ] Junggeselle *m*.

back [bæk] **I** *s* 1. Rücken *m*; Rück-, Unterseite *f*; *at the* ~ hinten; 2. *(Stuhl)* Rückenlehne *f*; 3. *(Fußball)* Verteidiger *m*; **II** *v* (unter)stützen; **III** *adj* rückwärtig; hinter; **IV** *adv* rückwärts; zurück; *come* ~ zurückkommen; *get* ~ wiederbekommen; *give* ~ zurückgeben.

back|bone ['bækbəʊn] Rückgrat *n*; ~**ground** ['-graʊnd] Hintergrund *m*; ~**wards** ['-wədz] rückwärts, zurück; rücklings.

bacon ['beɪkən] Speck *m*; *eggs and* ~ Spiegeleier mit Speck.

bad [bæd] schlecht, böse, schlimm; *go* ~ schlecht werden; *that's too* ~! *(fam)* das ist zu dumm! *he feels* ~ *about it (fam)* es tut ihm leid; *I have a* ~ *cold* ich habe eine böse Erkältung; ~**ly** ['-lɪ] 1. *that's* ~ *done* das ist schlecht gemacht; 2. *she wants it* ~ sie braucht es dringend.

badge [bædʒ] Abzeichen *n*.

baffle ['bæfl] verwirren.

bag [bæg] 1. Beutel; Sack *m*; Tüte *f*; 2. *(handbag)* (Hand-)Tasche *f*.

baggage ['bægɪdʒ] (Reise-)-Gepäck *n*; ~ **office** Gepäckabfertigung *f*; ~ **rack** Gepäcknetz *n*.

bail [beɪl] Bürgschaft *f*; *put up* ~ Kaution stellen.

bait [beɪt] Köder *m*.

bak|e [beɪk] backen; ~**er** ['-ə] Bäcker *m*; *at the* ~*'s* beim Bäcker; ~**ing-powder** ['-ɪŋˌpaʊdə] Backpulver *n*; ~**ery** ['-ərɪ] Bäckerei *f*.

balance ['bæləns] **I** *s* 1. Waage *f*; 2. Gleichgewicht *n a. fig*; 3. Bilanz *f*; Rest *m*; **II** *v* 4. abwägen; 5. balancieren.

balcony ['bælkənɪ] Balkon *m*.

bald [bɔːld] kahl.

bale [beɪl] Ballen *m*, Bündel *n*.

ball [bɔːl] 1. Ball *m*; *play* ~ Ball spielen; *fam* zs.arbeiten; 2. Knäuel *n*; 3. *(Tanzveranstaltung)* Ball *m*; ~**-bearing(s** *pl*) Kugellager *n*.

ballet ['bæleɪ] Ballett *n*.

balloon [bə'luːn] Ballon *m*.

ballot ['bælət] 1. Wahl-, Stimmzettel *m*; 2. Wahl *f*.

ball|-pen ['bɔːlpen] , **~point-pen** [ˌbɔːlpɔɪnt'pen] Kugelschreiber *m*.

bamboo [bæm'buː] Bambus(rohr *n*) *m*.

ban [bæn] 1. verbieten; ~ *smoking* das Rauchen verbieten; 2. *(Sport)* sperren.

banana [bə'nɑːnə] Banane *f*.

band [bænd] 1. Band *n*; 2. Bande; Schar *f*; ~ *of robbers* Räuberbande *f*; 3. *dance* ~ Tanzkapelle *f*.

bandage ['bændɪdʒ] Binde *f*; Verband *m*.

bang [bæŋ] **I** *s* Knall *m*; **II** *v* he ~ed the door er schlug die Tür zu.

bangle ['bæŋgl] Armreif *m*.

banisters *pl* ['bænɪstəz] Treppengeländer *n*.

bank [bæŋk] 1. Ufer *n*; Böschung *f*; *river* ~ Flußufer; 2. *(sand~)* (Sand-)Bank *f*; 3. *(~ of clouds)* (Wolken-)Bank *f*; 4. Bank(haus *n*) *f*; *you can change your money at the* ~ Sie können Ihr Geld auf der Bank umtauschen; *open a* ~ *account* ein Bankkonto eröffnen.

banker [bæŋkə] Bankier *m*.

bank|note ['bæŋknəʊt] Banknote *f*; **~rupt** ['bæŋkrʌpt] go ~ in Konkurs gehen.

banner ['bænə] Banner *n*, Fahne *f*, Spruchband *n*.

banns [bænz] Aufgebot *n*.

banquet ['bæŋkwɪt] Bankett *n*, Festessen *n*.

bapt|ism ['bæptɪzəm] Taufe *f*; **~ize** [bæpt'taɪz] taufen.

bar [bɑː] **I** *s* 1. Schranke *f*, Barriere *f*; 2. *(Seife, Schokolade)* Riegel *m*, Stange *f*; 3. *fig* Hindernis *n*; 4. *(Farbe, Licht)* Streifen, Strahl *m*; 5. *mus* Taktstrich *m*, Takt *m*; 6. *jur* Gericht *n*; (Gerichts-) Schranke *f*; 7. Schanktisch *m*, Bar, Theke *f*; **II** *v* verriegeln; ab-, ver-, zusperren; **~maid** ['-meɪd] Kellnerin *f*; **~man** ['-mən] Kellner *m*.

barbarian [bɑː'beərɪən] **I** *s* Barbar *m*; **II** *adj* barbarisch.

barbed wire [bɑːbd 'waɪə] Stacheldraht *m*.

barber ['bɑːbə] Friseur *m*.

bare [beə] **I** *adj* nackt, bloß, kahl, leer; *(Raum)* unmöbliert; **II** *v* entblößen, bloßlegen; **~footed** [ˌ-'fʊtɪd] barfuß; **~headed** [ˌ-'hedɪd] barhäuptig; **~ly** ['-lɪ] kaum; gerade (genug); bloß.

bargain ['bɑːgɪn] **I** *s* 1. Handel *m*; Geschäft(sabschluß *m*) *n*; Kauf(vertrag) *m*; *into the* ~ obendrein; noch dazu; *it's a* ~ abgemacht! 2. günstige(r) Kauf *m*; ~ *price* herabgesetzter Preis; **II** *v* handeln, feilschen *(with s.o. for s.th.* mit jdm um etw); verhandeln.

barge [bɑːdʒ] Last-, Schleppkahn *m*.

bark [bɑːk] **I** *s* (Baum-)Rinde, Borke *f*; **II** *v* bellen *a. fig*.

barley ['bɑːlɪ] Gerste f.

barn [bɑːn] Scheune f.

barometer [bə'rɒmɪtə] Barometer n.

baron ['bærən] Baron m; ~**ess** [-ɪs] Baronin f.

baroque [bə'rɒk] Barock(stil m) n od. m.

barracks pl ['bærəks] Kaserne f.

barrel ['bærəl] 1. Faß n, Tonne f; 2. (Gewehr-)Lauf m; ~**-organ** [-ˌɔːɡən] Drehorgel f.

barren ['bærən] unfruchtbar.

barrier ['bærɪə] 1. Schranke, Sperre, Barriere f; 2. fig Hindernis n (to für).

barrister ['bærɪstə] Anwalt m.

base [beɪs] I s Fundament n; Basis f; Stützpunkt m; II adj niedrig, gemein, niederträchtig; III v gründen, stützen (on auf); ~**ball** ['-bɔːl] Baseball m; ~**ment** ['-mənt] arch Fundament n; Kellergeschoß n; ~**ness** ['-nɪs] Niedrigkeit, Gemeinheit f.

bashful ['bæʃful] schüchtern.

basic ['beɪsɪk] grundlegend.

basin ['beɪsn] Becken n, Schale, Schüssel f, Bassin n.

basis ['beɪsɪs] Basis, Grundlage f.

bask [bɑːsk] sich sonnen.

basket ['bɑːskɪt] Korb m.

bass [bæs] Baß m.

bastard ['bɑːstəd] Bastard m.

bat [bæt] 1. Fledermaus f;

2. sport Schlagholz n, Schläger m.

bath [bɑːθ] 1. Bad n; have od take a ~ baden; 2. Badewanne f; 3. Badezimmer n; 4. swimming ~ Schwimmbad n.

bathe [beɪð] I v baden, schwimmen; II s Bad n (im Freien); let's go for a ~ gehen wir doch zum Schwimmen.

bathing ['beɪðɪŋ] Baden n; go ~ schwimmen gehen; ~ **costume** [- kɒstjuːm] Badeanzug m.

bath|robe ['bɑːθrəub] Bademantel m; ~**room** ['-rʊm] Badezimmer n; ~**tub** ['-tʌb] Badewanne f.

batter ['bætə] heftig schlagen; zerschlagen.

battery ['bætərɪ] Batterie f.

battle ['bætl] Schlacht f; ~**field** [-fiːld] Schlachtfeld n.

bawl [bɔːl] brüllen.

bay [beɪ] 1. Bai, Bucht f; 2. Erker m.

be [biː] irr was [wɒz] , been [biːn] sein; 1. I want to ~ quite sure ich möchte ganz sicher sein; 2. is that all right? stimmt das? 3. what shall you ~ doing tomorrow? was tust du morgen? 4. where am I to write my name? wo soll ich meinen Namen hinschreiben? 5. how are you? wie geht es

Ihnen? 6. *how much will that ~?* wieviel macht das?

beach [bi:tʃ] Strand *m; sandy ~* Sandstrand *m.*

beacon ['bi:kən] Leuchtfeuer *n.*

bead [bi:d] Perle *f.*

beak [bi:k] Schnabel *m.*

beam [bi:m] I *s* 1. Balken *m;* 2. *~ of light* (Licht-)Strahl *m; ~s of sunlight* Sonnenstrahlen *f pl;* II *v* strahlen *a. fig.*

bean [bi:n] Bohne *f.*

bear [beə] I *s* Bär *m;* II *v irr* bore [bɔ:] , borne (bei Geburt: born) [bɔ:n] 1. tragen; 2. (hervor)bringen; *(Kind)* zur Welt bringen; 3. (v)ertragen, aushalten; 4. *how does this ~ on the question?* was hat das mit der Frage zu tun? 5. *~ (to the) right, left* sich rechts, links halten; nach rechts, links gehen.

bearable ['beərəbl] erträglich.

beard [bɪəd] Bart *m; ~ed* ['-ɪd] bärtig.

bearer ['beərə] Träger, Überbringer *m.*

bearing [beərɪŋ] 1. Benehmen, Verhalten *n;* 2. Bedeutung *f;* Einfluß *m* (on auf); 3. Zs.hang *m; what ~ does that have on our work?* was hat das mit unserer Arbeit zu tun? 4. Ertragen *n;* Nachsicht *f;* 5. *tech* Lager(ung *f*) *n;* 6. Richtung, Lage *f; take o.s. ~s* sich orientieren.

beast [bi:st] 1. Tier *n;* 2. *agr* Vieh *n;* 3. *fig* Biest *n; ~ly* ['-lɪ] 1. viehisch; 2. scheußlich.

beat [bi:t] I *v irr* beat, beaten ['-n] 1. schlagen; 2. *(Teppich)* klopfen; 3. verhauen, prügeln; 4. *sport* besiegen; II *s* 5. Rundgang *m,* Runde; *(Polizei)* Streife *f;* 6. *~ of the heart* Schlagen *n* des Herzens.

beautiful ['bju:təfʊl] schön; *~ly* [-flɪ] *that will do ~* das genügt völlig.

beauty ['bju:tɪ] Schönheit *f; ~-parlo(u)r* [-pɑ:lə] Schönheitssalon *m; ~ queen* Schönheitskönigin *f.*

beaver ['bi:və] Biber *m.*

because [bɪ'kɒz] I *conj* weil, da; II *prp: ~ of* wegen, infolge *gen.*

beckon ['bekən] (zu)winken; *he ~ed me in* er winkte mir, hereinzukommen.

become [bɪ'kʌm] *irr* became [-'keɪm] , become 1. werden; *~ famous* berühmt werden; 2. (gut) stehen, kleiden; 3. *that does not ~ you* das schickt sich nicht für dich.

bed [bed] 1. Bett *n; go to ~* zu Bett gehen; *a room with two ~s* ein Zimmer mit zwei Betten; 2. Blumenbeet *n; ~-clothes* *pl* ['-kləʊðz] Bettwäsche *f; ~-ding* ['-ɪŋ] Bettzeug *n; ~room* ['-rʊm] Schlafzimmer *n; ~side table* ['-saɪd teɪbl] Nachttisch *m;* ~**time** ['-taɪm] Schlafenszeit *f.*

bee [biː] Biene *f;* ~**hive** ['-haɪv] Bienenstock *m;* ~**line** ['-laɪn] Luftlinie *f;* make a ~ for auf dem kürzesten Weg auf etw losgehen.

beech [biːtʃ] Buche *f.*

beef [biːf] Rindfleisch *n;* ~**steak** [ˌ-'steɪk] Beefsteak *n;* ~ **tea** Fleisch-, Kraftbrühe *f.*

beer [bɪə] Bier *n.*

beet [biːt] Rübe; *bes. Am* Rote Bete *f.*

beetroot ['biːtruːt] *Br* Rote Bete *f.*

beetle ['biːtl] Käfer *m.*

before [bɪ'fɔː] **I** *prp* vor; früher als; *the day* ~ *yesterday* vorgestern; ~ *long* bald; *you must be back* ~ *5* du mußt vor 5 Uhr zurück sein; **II** *adv* 1. *(örtl.)* vorn, voran; 2. *(zeitl.)* vorher; *the day* ~ am Tage vorher; **III** *conj* bevor, eher als; ~**hand** [-hænd] im voraus; (schon) vorher.

beg [beg] 1. bitten; *I* ~ *your pardon* Verzeihung! wie bitte? 2. betteln; 3. *we* ~ *to inform you* wir gestatten uns, Ihnen mitzuteilen.

beggar ['begə] Bettler *m; no* ~*s allowed* Betteln verboten!

begin [bɪ'gɪn] *irr began* [-'gæn], *begun* [-'gʌn] beginnen, anfangen; *it's begin-*

ning to rain es fängt zu regnen an; *to* ~ *with* erstens; ~**ner** [-ə] Anfänger *m;* ~**ning** [-ɪŋ] Beginn, Anfang *m; from the* ~ von Anfang an; *in the* ~ anfangs, im *od* am Anfang.

behalf [bɪ'hɑːf] *on, in* ~ *of* im Interesse *gen;* an Stelle von; für.

behave [bɪ'heɪv] sich verhalten, sich benehmen; ~ *yourself!* benimm dich!

behavio(u)r [bɪ'heɪvjə] Betragen, Benehmen *n.*

behind [bɪ'haɪnd] **I** *prp* hinter; ~ *the house* hinter dem Haus; **II** *adv* 1. hinten; dahinter, hinterher; *stay* ~ bleiben Sie zurück; 2. zurück; im Rückstand; *my watch is ten minutes* ~ meine Uhr geht zehn Minuten nach.

being ['biːɪŋ] 1. (Da-)Sein *n; in* ~ existierend, vorhanden; *come into* ~ entstehen; 2. *human* ~ menschliche(s) Wesen *n.*

Belgian ['beldʒən] **I** *s* Belgier *m;* **II** *adj* belgisch; **Belgium** ['beldʒəm] Belgien *n.*

belief [bɪ'liːf] 1. Glaube(n) *m;* 2. Vertrauen *n; I have no great* ~ *in him* ich habe nicht viel Vertrauen zu ihm; 3. Überzeugung *f.*

believe [bɪ'liːv] 1. glauben (*in* an); *I* ~ *not* ich glaube, nein; 2. vertrauen (*in* auf).

bell [bel] Glocke, Klingel *f.*

belly ['belɪ] Bauch *m; with an empty ~* mit hungrigem Magen.

belong [bɪ'lɒŋ] 1. gehören (*to s.o.* jdm); 2. *I ~ here* ich bin von hier; *~ings pl* [-ɪŋz] Eigentum *n;* Habe *f.*

beloved [bɪ'lʌvd] geliebt.

below [bɪ'ləʊ] I *prp* unter, unterhalb; *it's ~ zero* es ist unter null Grad; II *adv* unten, abwärts, hinunter; *she's down ~ somewhere* sie ist irgendwo unten.

belt [belt] Gürtel, Riemen *m.*

bench [bentʃ] 1. (Sitz-)Bank *f;* 2. Werkbank *f.*

bend [bend] I *v irr* bent, bent [-t] 1. biegen, beugen; 2. sich bücken; 3. sich biegen; sich krümmen; 4. *he is bent on going home* er ist entschlossen, nach Hause zu gehen; II *s* Biegung, Kurve *f.*

beneath [bɪ'niːθ] unter, unterhalb; *that's ~ him* das ist unter s-r Würde.

benefit ['benɪfɪt] I *s* 1. Nutzen, Vorteil; Gewinn *m;* 2. Wohltat *f;* 3. Beihilfe; Unterstützung *f;* II *v* von Nutzen, Vorteil sein (*s.o.* für jdn); *the sea air will ~ you* die Seeluft wird dir guttun.

bent [bent] 1. Neigung *f,* Hang *m;* 2. Begabung *f (for* zu, für).

benzene ['benziːn] Benzol *n.*

bequeath [bɪ'kwiːð] vererben.

beret ['bereɪ] Baskenmütze *f.*

berry ['berɪ] Beere *f.*

berth [bɜːθ] 1. Ankerplatz *m;* 2. Koje *f;* (*Zug, Schiff*) Bett *n.*

beside [bɪ'saɪd] 1. (*örtlich*) neben; 2. *fig* außer(halb); *he is ~ himself with rage* er ist vor Wut außer sich; *that is ~ the point* das hat nichts mit der Sache zu tun; 3. im Vergleich zu; *~s* [-z] I *prp* außer, neben; II *adv* außerdem, ferner; übrigens.

best [best] I *adj* beste(r, s); *the ~ part of* der größte Teil (*gen*); II *s* der, die, das Beste; *at ~* bestenfalls, höchstens; *to the ~ of my knowledge* soviel ich weiß; III *adv* am besten, aufs beste, bestens; *like ~* am liebsten mögen; *do as you think ~* tun Sie, was Sie für richtig halten.

bet [bet] I *v irr* bet(ted), bet(ted) wetten (*on* auf); *I ~ you a pound* ich wette mit dir um 1 Pfund; *you ~ (fam)* da können Sie sicher sein; II *s* Wette *f; lose a ~* e-e Wette verlieren.

betray [bɪ'treɪ] verraten; *~al* [-əl] Verrat *m.*

better ['betə] I *adj* besser (*than* als); *the ~ part* der größere Teil; II *s* (das) Bessere; *get the ~ of s.o.* jdn besiegen, übertreffen, übervorteilen; III *adv:* all the *~* um so, desto besser; *you had ~ go* du tätest besser daran, zu gehen; **IV** v (ver)bessern; besser werden; ~ o.s. sich verbessern, vorwärtskommen.

between [bɪ'twiːn] **I** prp zwischen, unter; ~ 9 o'clock and 10 o'clock zwischen 9 und 10 Uhr; ~ you and me unter uns (gesagt); **II** adv dazwischen, darunter; houses are few and far ~ Häuser sind dünn gesät.

beverage ['bevərɪdʒ] Getränk n.

beware [bɪ'weə] ~ of the dog! Achtung! bissiger Hund!

bewilder [bɪ'wɪldə] in Verlegenheit bringen.

beyond [bɪ'jɒnd] **I** prp jenseits, über ... hinaus; außerhalb, später als, mehr als; ~ doubt über jeden Zweifel erhaben; ~ hope hoffnungslos; that's ~ me das ist mir zu hoch; **II** adv jenseits, darüber hinaus.

biased ['baɪəst] voreingenommen, parteiisch (against gegen).

Bible ['baɪbl] Bibel f.

bicycle ['baɪsɪkl] (Fahr-)Rad n; ride a ~ radfahren.

bid [bɪd] **I** v irr bid, bid 1. (Preis) bieten; 2. ~ good bye, good night Lebewohl, gute Nacht sagen; **II** s Angebot n.

big [bɪg] groß; erwachsen; wichtig; talk ~ prahlen; ~ **toe** große Zehe f.

bike [baɪk] fam (Fahr-)Rad n.

bilberry ['bɪlbərɪ] Heidelbeere f.

bile [baɪl] Galle f.

bilious ['bɪljəs] ~ attack Gallenkolik f.

bilingual [baɪ'lɪŋgwəl] zweisprachig.

bill [bɪl] **I** s 1. Rechnung f; the ~ please bitte, zahlen; 2. Plakat n; Liste f; ~ of fare Speisekarte f; 3. Gesetzesvorlage f; ~ of rights (pol) Grundrechte n pl; 4. Am Banknote f; 5. com Wechsel m; 6. Schnabel m; **II** v: ~ me for that stellen Sie mir das in Rechnung; ~**board** ['-bɔːd] Anschlagbrett n; ~**fold** ['-fəuld] Am Brieftasche f.

billiard ['bɪljəd] a game of ~s e-e Partie Billard; ~-**ball** [-bɔːl] Billardkugel f.

billion ['bɪljən] Billion f; Am Milliarde f.

billow ['bɪləu] Woge f.

bin [bɪn] Behälter, Kasten m.

bind [baɪnd] irr bound, bound [baund] 1. (an-, fest-, ver)binden; 2. (Buch) (ein)binden; 3. fig verpflichten; a ~ing agreement ein bindender Vertrag.

biography [baɪ'ɒgrəfɪ] Biographie f.

biology [baɪ'ɒlədʒɪ] Biologie f.

birch [bɜːtʃ] Birke f.

bird [bɜːd] Vogel m; ~ of

prey Raubvogel *m;* ~**'s-eye
view** Vogelperspektive *f.*

birth [bɜːθ] 1. Geburt *f; give
~ to* zur Welt bringen; *date,
place of ~* Geburtsdatum *n,*
-ort *m;* 2. Herkunft *f,* Ursprung *m; by ~* von Geburt;
~**-control** ['-kən‚trəʊl]
Geburtenregelung, -be-
schränkung *f;* ~**day** ['-deɪ]
Geburtstag *m; happy ~ to
you* ich gratuliere Ihnen
herzlich zum Geburtstag;
~**place** ['-pleɪs] Geburtsort
m.

biscuit ['bɪskɪt] Keks *m.*

bishop ['bɪʃəp] Bischof *m.*

bit [bɪt] Stückchen, Bißchen
n; a ~ of ein wenig.

bit|e [baɪt] **I** *v irr* bit, bit(ten)
[bɪt, ('-n)] 1. beißen; stechen
a. fig; 2. *fig* anbeißen; **II** *s*
3. Biß; *(Insekt)* Stich *m;*
4. Bissen *m;* ~**ing** *(Kälte)*
schneidend.

bitter ['bɪtə] 1. bitter *a. fig;*
2. *(Wind)* scharf; ~**ness**
[-nɪs] Bitterkeit *f a. fig.*

black [blæk] schwarz; dun-
kel *a. fig;* ~**berry** ['-bərɪ]
Brombeere *f;* ~**bird** ['-bɜːd]
Amsel *f;* ~**board** ['-bɔːd]
Wandtafel *f.*

bladder ['blædə] *anat* Blase
f.

blade [bleɪd] 1. *bot* Blatt *n;*
~ *of grass* Grashalm *m;*
2. (Messer-)Klinge *f.*

blame [bleɪm] **I** *v* tadeln (*for
doing* für, wegen); die
Schuld geben (*s.o. for s.th.*

jdm wegen etw); *who's to ~
for that?* wer ist daran
schuld? **II** *s* Tadel *m; don't
put the ~ on her* schieb die
Schuld nicht auf sie.

blank [blæŋk] **I** *adj* leer, un-
beschrieben; **II** *s* 1. Lücke;
leere Stelle *f; fill in the ~s*
füllen Sie die leeren Stellen
aus; 2. *Am* Formblatt *n;*
3. Niete *f (Lotterielos);
draw a ~ (fig)* kein Glück
haben).

blanket ['blæŋkɪt] (Woll-,
wollene) Decke *f.*

blast [blɑːst] **I** *s* 1. plötzlicher, heftiger Windstoß *m;*
2. Explosion *f;* Knall *m;*
Druckwelle *f;* 3. Hornsignal
n; 4. *at full ~ (fam)* in vollem Betrieb, auf vollen Tou-
ren; **II** *v* 5. sprengen; 6. *(sl)*
~ *it* verflucht!

blaze [bleɪz] **I** *s* 1. Flamme,
Glut *f;* 2. Glanz; helle(r)
Schein *m;* **II** *v* 3. flammen,
lodern; 4. leuchten, strahlen
a. fig.

blazer ['bleɪzə] leichte Sport-
jacke *f.*

bleach [bliːtʃ] **I** *v* bleichen;
II *s* Bleichmittel *n.*

bleak [bliːk] 1. öde; kahl;
2. windig, rauh; 3. ~ *pros-
pects* trübe Aussichten *f pl.*

bleat [bliːt] *(Schaf)* blöken.

bleed [bliːd] *irr* bled, bled
[bled] bluten.

blend [blend] **I** *v (Tee)* mischen; **II** *s* Mischung *f.*

bless [bles] segnen; **~ing** ['blesɪŋ] Segen *m.*

blind [blaɪnd] **I** *adj* blind *a. fig (to* für*);* ~ *alley* Sackgasse *f;* **II** *v* blind machen *a. fig (to* gegen*);* **III** *s* Jalousie *f;* **~ness** ['-nɪs] Blindheit *f a. fig (to* gegen*).*

blink [blɪŋk] blinzeln, zwinkern.

bliss ['blɪs] Wonne, Seligkeit *f.*

blister ['blɪstə] **I** *s med* Blase *f;* **II** *v* Blasen bekommen.

blizzard ['blɪzəd] Schneesturm *m.*

block [blɒk] **I** *s* 1. (Holz-) Klotz *m;* (Stein-, Fels-) Block *m;* 2. Häuserblock *m;* **II** *v* (ver)sperren; **~head** ['-hed] Dummkopf *m;* ~ **letters** Blockschrift *f.*

blood [blʌd] Blut *n; in cold* ~ kaltblütig; ~ **bank** Blutbank *f;* ~ **count** Blutbild *n;* **~-curdling** ['-ˌkɜːdlɪŋ] haarsträubend; **~-donor** ['-ˌdəʊnə] Blutspender *m;* **~-group** ['-gruːp] *biol* Blutgruppe *f;* **~less** ['-lɪs] blutleer; **~-poisoning** ['-ˌpɔɪznɪŋ] Blutvergiftung *f;* ~ **pressure** Blutdruck *m;* **~shed** ['-ʃed] Blutvergießen *n;* **~-vessel** ['-ˌvesl] *anat* Blutgefäß *n;* **~y** ['-ɪ] 1. blutig; 2. *vulg* verdammt.

bloom [bluːm] **I** *s* Blüte *f a. fig; be in full* ~ in voller Blüte stehen; **II** *v* blühen *a. fig.*

blossom ['blɒsəm] (Baum-)- Blüte *f.*

blot [blɒt] Fleck, Klecks *m;* **~ter** ['-ə] Löschblatt *n.*

blouse [blaʊz] Bluse *f.*

blow [bləʊ] **I** *v irr blew* [bluː], *blown* [bləʊn] 1. *(Wind)* wehen, blasen; 2. ~ *o's. nose* sich die Nase putzen; 3. ~ *up* sprengen, in die Luft jagen; 4. ~ *a whistle* pfeifen; **II** *s* Schlag, Hieb *m.*

blue [bluː] **I** *adj* blau; *light, dark* ~ hell-, dunkelblau; **II** *s* 1. blaue Farbe *f;* 2. *out of the* ~ aus heiterem Himmel; **~berry** ['-bərɪ] Heidelbeere *f.*

bluff [blʌf] **I** *v* bluffen; **II** *s* Bluff *m.*

bluish ['bluːɪʃ] bläulich.

blunder ['blʌndə] **I** *v* e-n Fehler machen; **II** *s* Fehler, Schnitzer *m.*

blunt [blʌnt] **I** *adj* 1. stumpf; 2. *fig* offen; einfach; 3. derb; **II** *v* abstumpfen; **~ly** ['-lɪ] frei heraus, unverblümt.

blur [blɜː] **I** *v* trüben; **II** *s* Fleck *m;* Trübung *f.*

blush [blʌʃ] erröten, rot werden (*at* bei; *with* od *for* vor).

bluster ['blʌstə] toben, poltern.

board [bɔːd] **I** *s* 1. Brett *n;* 2. (Anschlag-)Tafel *f;* 3. Ausschuß *m,* Behörde *f;* 4. ~ *and lodging* Unterkunft u. Verpflegung; 5. *go on* ~ an Bord gehen; **II** *v* 6. an Bord gehen; ~ *a bus* in e-n Bus einsteigen; 7. beköstigen, verpflegen; 8. in Pension sein (*with* bei); ~**er** ['-ə] Pensionsgast *m*; ~**ing-house** ['-ɪŋhaʊs] Pension *f*; ~**ing-school** ['-ɪŋsku:l] Internat *n*.

boast [bəʊst] **I** *s* Stolz *m*; Prahlerei *f*; **II** *v* sich rühmen (*of s.th.* e-r S); ~**ful** ['-fʊl] prahlerisch.

boat [bəʊt] Boot *n*, Kahn *m*; Schiff *n*; ~*s for hire* Bootsverleih *m*; ~**-race** ['-reɪs] Wettrudern *n*; ~ **train** Schiffszug *m*.

bobby ['bɒbɪ] Polizist *m*.

bodily ['bɒdɪlɪ] körperlich; ~ *injury* Körperverletzung *f*.

body ['bɒdɪ] 1. Körper *m*; 2. Leiche *f*; 3. Körperschaft; Gruppe *f*; *they left the room in a* ~ sie verließen geschlossen das Zimmer; 4. Ansammlung, Masse *f*; 5. (*Schiff, Flugzeug*) Rumpf *m*; *mot* Karosserie *f*; ~**guard** [-gɑ:d] Leibwache *f*.

bog ['bɒg] Sumpf, Morast *m*.

boil [bɔɪl] **I** *v* 1. kochen, sieden; 2. *he's* ~*ing with rage* er kocht vor Wut; **II** *s* Furunkel *m*; ~**ed eggs** *pl* gekochte Eier *n pl*; ~**er** ['-ə] Kessel *m*.

boisterous ['bɔɪstərəs] heftig, stürmisch.

bold [bəʊld] 1. kühn, tapfer, mutig; 2. dreist, frech;

~**ness** ['-nɪs] 1. Kühnheit *f*, Mut *m*; 2. Frechheit, Dreistigkeit *f*.

Bolivia [bə'lɪvɪə] Bolivien *n*.

bolt [bəʊlt] **I** *s* Riegel, Bolzen *m*; **II** *v* 1. (*Pferd*) durchgehen; 2. (*Speise*) rasch hinunterwürgen; 3. verriegeln.

bomb [bɒm] Bombe *f*.

bond [bɒnd] 1. Band *n*; 2. *com* Schuldverschreibung *f*.

bone [bəʊn] Knochen *m*; (*Fisch*) Gräte *f*; ~ *of contention* Zankapfel *m*.

bonfire ['bɒn‚faɪə] (Freuden-)Feuer *n*.

bonnet ['bɒnɪt] 1. (Damen-)Hut *m*; 2. *mot* Motorhaube *f*.

bonny ['bɒnɪ] gesund aussehend, hübsch.

bonus ['bəʊnəs] Gratifikation, Prämie *f*; *cost-of-living* ~ Teuerungszulage *f*.

bony ['bəʊnɪ] knochig, knöchern.

book [bʊk] **I** *s* Buch, Heft *n*; Block *m*; ~ *of tickets* Fahrscheinheft *n*; **II** *v* 1. vorbestellen; buchen; (*fully*) ~*ed up* (Hotel) besetzt; (Theater) ausverkauft; 2. eintragen, notieren; ~**case** Bücherschrank *m*; ~**ing office** ['-ɪŋ‚ɒfɪs] Fahrkartenschalter *m*; ~**-keeper** ['-‚ki:pə] Buchhalter *m*; ~**seller** ['-‚selə] Buchhändler *m*; ~**shelf** ['-ʃelf] Bücherregal *n*; ~**stall** ['-stɔ:l] Zeitungs-

kiosk *m*, Bahnhofsbuch-
handlung *f.*
boom [bu:m] *com* (Hoch-)
Konjunktur *f*; wirtschaftli-
che(r) Aufschwung *m.*
boost [bu:st] fördern, unterstützen.
boot [bu:t] 1. Stiefel *m*;
2. *mot* Kofferraum *m*;
~**lace** ['-leɪs] Schnürsenkel
m.
booth [bu:ð] (Markt-)Bude *f*;
polling, voting ~ Wahlzelle
f; *telephone* ~ Telefonzelle
f.
booty ['bu:tɪ] Beute *f.*
border ['bɔ:də] **I** *s* 1. Rand,
Saum *m*; 2. (Landes-)Grenze
f; **II** *v* grenzen (*on* an);
~**line** [-laɪn] Grenzstreifen
m; *fig* -gebiet *n.*
bore [bɔ:] **I** *v* 1. (aus-,
durch-)bohren; 2. langweilen; *be* ~*d* sich langweilen;
II *s* langweilige(r) Mensch
m, Nervensäge *f.*
boredom ['bɔ:dəm] Langeweile *f*; Stumpfsinn *m.*
boring [bɔ:rɪŋ] langweilig.
born [bɔ:n] *when were you*
~? wann sind Sie geboren?
~ *in* gebürtig aus.
borough ['bʌrə] Stadt(gemeinde) *f.*
borrow ['bɒrəʊ] borgen; ent-
lehnen *a. fig* (*of, from* von).
bosom ['buzəm] 1. Busen *m*
a. fig; 2. *fig* Schoß *m.*
boss [bɒs] **I** *s fam* Chef *m*;
II *v:* ~ *s.o. around* jdn herum-
kommandieren.

botanic(al) [bə'tænɪk(l)]
botanisch; ~**y** ['bɒtənɪ]
Botanik *f.*
both [bəʊθ] **I** *prn u. adj:* ~ *of*
them alle beide; *on* ~ *sides*
auf beiden Seiten; **II** *adv:*
~ ... *and* sowohl ... als
auch.
bother ['bɒðə] **I** *s* Mühe,
Schwierigkeit *f*, beläl-
stigen; plagen; 2. *don't* ~
machen Sie sich keine Um-
stände!
bottle ['bɒtl] Flasche *f*; ~**neck**
[-nek] *fig* 1. verengte Fahrbahn *f*; 2. Engpaß *m.*
bottom ['bɒtəm] Boden;
Grund *m a. fig*; *at the* ~ *of*
the page unten auf der Seite; ~**less** [-lɪs] grund-, bo-
denlos.
bough [baʊ] Ast, Zweig *m.*
boulder ['bəʊldə] Felsblock;
Findling *m.*
bounce [baʊns] **I** *v* springen,
hochschnellen; auf-, zurückprallen; **II** *s* Aufprall *m.*
bound [baʊnd] **I** *s* 1. Grenze,
Schranke *f*; 2. Sprung, Satz
m; **II** *v* 3. begrenzen;
4. (hoch)springen, hüpfen;
(auf)prallen (*against* gegen);
III *adj* 5. ~ *for* bestimmt für,
unterwegs nach; 6. *be* ~ *to*
etw tun müssen; *he's* ~ *to*
come er kommt sicher.
boundary ['baʊndərɪ] Grenze *f.*
bounty ['baʊntɪ] 1. Freige-
bigkeit *f*; 2. Prämie *f.*
bouquet [bu'keɪ] 1. (Blu-

men-)Strauß *m;* 2. *(Wein)* Blume *f.*

bout [baʊt] ~ *of malaria* Malariaanfall *m.*

bow [baʊ] **I** *v* (sich) bücken; sich verbeugen *(to, before* vor); **II** *s* 1. Verbeugung *f (to* vor); 2. *mar* Bug *m;* 3. [bəʊ] Knoten *m,* Schleife *f.*

bowels ['baʊəlz] Eingeweide *pl.*

bowl [bəʊl] Schüssel *f,* Napf *m,* Schale *f.*

box [bɒks] **I** *s* 1. Schachtel *f,* Behälter *m;* 2. *theat* Loge *f;* **II** *v* boxen; ~ *s.o.'s ears* jdn ohrfeigen; ~**er** ['-ə] Boxer *m;* ~-**office** ['-ɒfɪs] (Theater-)Kasse *f.*

boy [bɔɪ] Knabe, Junge, Bub *m;* ~**friend** ['-frend] Freund, Liebste(r) *m;* ~**hood** ['-hʊd] Knabenalter *n;* ~ **scout** Pfadfinder *m.*

bra [brɑː] *fam* Büstenhalter *m.*

brace [breɪs] **I** *s* 1. Klammer, Strebe, Stütze *f;* 2. *(pair of* ~*s)* Hosenträger *m pl;* **II** *v:* ~ *o.s. up* s-e Kräfte zs.nehmen.

bracelet ['breɪslɪt] Armband *n.*

bracket ['brækɪt] 1. Klammer *f;* 2. *income* ~ Einkommensgruppe *f.*

brag [bræg] prahlen.

braid [breɪd] Borte *f,* Besatz *m.*

brain [breɪn] 1. (Ge-)Hirn *n;* 2. Verstand *m; rack o.'s* ~*(s)*

sich den Kopf zerbrechen; ~-**washing** ['-wɒʃɪŋ] Gehirnwäsche *f;* ~-**wave** ['-weɪv] *fam* Geistesblitz *m.*

brake [breɪk] **I** *s* Bremse *f; put on the* ~*s* die Bremsen betätigen; **II** *v* bremsen.

bramble ['bræmbl] Brombeerstrauch *m.*

branch [brɑːntʃ] **I** *s* 1. Zweig, Ast *m;* 2. Abzweigung *f;* 3. Gebiet, Fach *n;* 4. *(~ office)* Zweiggeschäft *n,* Filiale *f;* **II** *v* 5. *(~ out, forth)* sich verzweigen, sich ausbreiten; 6. *(~ off)* abzweigen.

brand [brænd] Warenzeichen *n,* Marke, Sorte *f.*

brandy ['brændɪ] Weinbrand *m.*

brass [brɑːs] Messing *n;* ~ **band** Blaskapelle *f.*

brassière ['bræsɪə] Büstenhalter *m.*

brave [breɪv] tapfer, mutig.

brawl [brɔːl] Streit, Zank *m.*

brazen ['breɪzn] unverschämt.

Brazil [brə'zɪl] Brasilien *n.*

breach [briːtʃ] 1. *fig* Bruch *m;* 2. *step into the* ~ in die Bresche springen.

bread [bred] Brot *n; earn o.'s* ~ s-n Lebensunterhalt verdienen; *a slice of* ~ e-e Scheibe Brot; ~ *and butter* Butterbrot *n;* ~**winner** ['-wɪnə] Ernährer *m (e-r Familie).*

breadth [bredθ] Breite, Weite *f a. fig.*

break [breɪk] **I** s 1. Bruch, Sprung m; 2. ~ of day Tagesanbruch m; 3. Unterbrechung, Pause f; **II** v irr broke [brəuk], broken ['-ən] 4. (zer)brechen; 5. (sein Wort) nicht halten; 6. (Unwetter) los-, hereinbrechen; (Tag) anbrechen; ~ **down** zusammenbrechen; ~ **up** entzweigehen; (Versammlung) auflösen.

break-down ['breɪkdaʊn] 1. Zs.bruch m; 2. (Betriebs-)Störung, Panne f; 3. Aufgliederung f (der Kosten).

breakfast ['brekfəst] Frühstück n; have ~ frühstücken.

breast [brest] Brust f, Busen m; ~**stroke** ['-strəuk] Brustschwimmen n.

breath [breθ] Atemzug m; out of ~ außer Atem, atemlos; catch o.'s ~ den Atem anhalten.

breathe [bri:ð] 1. (ein-, aus)atmen; ~ again aufatmen; 2. flüstern; don't ~ a word verrate kein Wort.

breathless ['breθlɪs] außer Atem, atemlos.

breed [bri:d] **I** v irr bred, bred [bred] 1. sich fortpflanzen; 2. züchten; 3. erziehen; 4. fig verursachen; **II** s Zucht, Rasse, Art f; ~**er** ['-ə] Züchter m; ~**ing** ['-ɪŋ] 1. agr Zucht f; 2. Erziehung f.

breeze [bri:z] Brise f.

brew [bru:] (Bier) brauen; ~**ery** ['bruərɪ] Brauerei f.

bribe [braɪb] **I** s Bestechung(sgeld n) f; **II** v bestechen.

brick [brɪk] Ziegel m; ~**layer** ['brɪkˌleɪə] Maurer m.

bride [braɪd] Braut f; ~**groom** ['-grʊm] Bräutigam m; ~**smaid** ['-zmeɪd] Brautjungfer f.

bridge [brɪdʒ] **I** s 1. Brücke f a. mar; 2. Bridge n (Kartenspiel); **II** v (~ over) überbrücken a. fig.

bridle ['braɪdl] Zaum, Zügel m.

brief [bri:f] kurz, knapp, gedrängt; in ~ in Kürze, kurz; be ~ sich kurz fassen; ~-**case** ['-keɪs] Aktentasche, -mappe f; ~**ly** ['-lɪ] kurz, in Kürze.

brier ['braɪə] Heckenrose f.

brigade [brɪ'geɪd] fire ~ Feuerwehr f.

bright [braɪt] 1. klar, hell; glänzend; 2. aufgeweckt, klug; ~**en** ['-n] (Himmel) sich aufhellen.

brilliant ['brɪljənt] funkelnd, strahlend, glänzend.

brim [brɪm] Rand m; (Hut) Krempe f.

bring [brɪŋ] irr brought, brought [brɔ:t] 1. (mit-, her)bringen; 2. hervorbringen; einbringen; 3. ~ s.o. to do s.th. jdn dazu bringen, etw zu tun; 4. ~ to an end zu Ende bringen; ~ **about** herbeiführen; ~ **along** mitbringen; ~ **back** zurückbringen; ~ **forth** hervorbringen; ~ **on** verursachen; ~ **to** *(Ohnmächtigen)* wieder zu sich bringen; ~ **up** 1. auf-, erziehen; 2. zur Sprache bringen, vorbringen.

brink [brɪŋk] 1. Rand *m*; 2. (steiles) Ufer *n*.

brisk [brɪsk] lebhaft, munter.

bristle ['brɪsl] **I** *s* Borste *f*; **II** *v (Haar)* (sich) sträuben.

British ['brɪtɪʃ] britisch.

brittle ['brɪtl] zerbrechlich, spröde.

broad [brɔːd] breit, weit; ~ *day* helle(r) Tag *m*.

broadcast ['brɔːdkɑːst] **I** *s* Rundfunk(sendung *f*) *m*; **II** *v* senden, übertragen; ~**ing** [-ɪŋ] Rundfunk-, Fernsehübertragung *f*; ~**-station** (Rundfunk-)Sender *m*.

broaden ['brɔːdn] (sich) verbreitern, (sich) erweitern.

broad-minded [ˌbrɔːd'maɪndɪd] großzügig.

brocade [brəʊ'keɪd] Brokat *m*.

brochure ['brəʊʃə] Broschüre *f*.

broil [brɔɪl] grillen.

broke [brəʊk] *sl* pleite.

broken ['brəʊkən] 1. zerbrochen; 2. *(Gesundheit)* zerrüttet.

broker ['brəʊkə] Makler *m*.

bronze [brɒnz] Bronze *f*.

brooch [brəʊtʃ] Brosche *f*.

brood [bruːd] **I** *s* Brut *f*; **II** *v* brüten *(on, over* über).

brook [brʊk] Bach *m*.

broom [bruːm] Besen *m*; *a new ~ sweeps clean* neue Besen kehren gut; ~**stick** ['brʊmstɪk] Besenstiel *m*.

broth [brɒθ] *(Fleisch)* Brühe *f*.

brothel ['brɒθl] Bordell *n*.

brother ['brʌðə] Bruder *m*; ~(s) *and sister(s)* Geschwister *pl*; ~**-in-law** [-rɪnlɔː] Schwager *m*; ~**ly** [-lɪ] brüderlich.

brow [braʊ] Augenbraue *f*; *knit o.'s ~s* die Stirn runzeln.

brown [braʊn] **I** *adj* braun; **II** *v* (sich) bräunen; ~ **paper** Packpapier *n*.

browse [braʊz] 1. grasen, weiden; 2. *(Buch)* durchblättern.

bruise [bruːz] **I** *s* Quetschung *f*; **II** *v* quetschen.

brush [brʌʃ] **I** *s* Bürste *f*; Pinsel *m*; **II** *v* (ab)bürsten; ~ *aside, away (fig)* beiseite schieben; ~ *up (Kenntnisse)* auffrischen.

Brussels ['brʌslz] Brüssel *n*; ~ **sprouts** [ˌbrʌsl'spraʊts] *pl* Rosenkohl *m*.

brutal ['bruːtl] roh, brutal; ~**ity** [bruː'tælətɪ] Roheit *f*, Brutalität *f*.

brute [bruːt] 1. Vieh *n*; 2. Rohling *m*.

bubble ['bʌbl] **I** *s* 1. (Luft-, Seifen-)Blase *f*; 2. Sprudeln *n*; **II** *v* sprudeln.

buck [bʌk] 1. Bock m; 2. Am sl Dollar m.

bucket ['bʌkɪt] Eimer, Kübel m.

buckle ['bʌkl] I s Schnalle f; II v 1. an-, um-, zuschnallen; 2. ~ *down to work* sich an die Arbeit machen.

bud [bʌd] I s Knospe f, Auge n; II v knospen, keimen.

budget ['bʌdʒɪt] Haushalt(splan) m, Budget n.

buffalo ['bʌfələʊ] Büffel m.

buffet ['bʌfɪt] Bufett n, Theke, Bar f; ~ **supper** kalte(s) Büfett n.

bug [bʌg] Wanze f (a. Abhörgerät); Am Käfer m.

bugle ['bju:gl] Wald-, Signalhorn n.

build [bɪld] irr built built [-t] bauen, errichten; (Brücke) schlagen; ~ *up* (allmählich) aufbauen; sich entwickeln zu; ~er ['-ə] Baumeister m.

building ['bɪldɪŋ] 1. Bauen n; ~-society Bausparkasse f; 2. Bau m; Gebäude n.

built [bɪlt] ~-in eingebaut; Einbau-; ~-up area bebaute(s) Gelände n; (Verkehr) geschlossene Ortschaft f.

bulb [bʌlb] 1. Zwiebel, Knolle f; 2. (Glüh-)Birne f.

Bulgaria [bʌl'geərɪə] Bulgarien n; ~n [-n] I s Bulgare m; II adj bulgarisch.

bulge [bʌldʒ] I s Ausbuchtung, Wölbung f; II v ausbauchen, anschwellen.

bulk [bʌlk] 1. Masse f; Umfang m, Volumen n, Größe f; in ~ unverpackt, lose; 2. Hauptteil m.

bull [bʊl] Stier, Bulle m; ~dog ['-dog] Bulldogge f; ~dozer ['-dəʊzə] Planierraupe f.

bullet ['bʊlɪt] Gewehrkugel f; Geschoß n.

bulletin ['bʊlɪtɪn] Tagesbericht m.

bully ['bʊlɪ] einschüchtern, bange machen.

bumble-bee ['bʌmblbi:] Hummel f.

bump [bʌmp] I v stoßen (against, into gegen, an); in die Arme laufen (into s.o. jdm); II s i. Stoß, Schlag m; 2. Beule f; ~er ['-ə] 1. volle(s) Glas n; 2. ~ *crop* Rekordernte f; 3. mot Stoßstange f.

bun [bʌn] Rosinenkuchen m.

bunch [bʌntʃ] Büschel, Bündel, Bund n; (Blumen) Strauß m; ~ *of grapes* Weintraube f; ~ *of keys* Schlüsselbund m.

bundle ['bʌndl] I s Bündel n; II v bündeln.

bungle ['bʌŋgl] I v verpfuschen; II s Pfuscherei f.

bunk [bʌŋk] mar Koje f.

buoy [bɔɪ] Boje f; Rettungsring m.

bur [bɜ:] Klette f.

burden ['bɜ:dn] I s 1. Last f; be a ~ *to s.o.* jdm zur Last fallen; 2. Kehrreim, Refrain m; II v belasten.

bureau ['bjʊərəʊ] 1. *Br* Schreibtisch *m*; 2. Behörde *f*; *information* ~ Auskunftsstelle *f*; 3. *Am* Kommode *f.*

burglar ['bɜːglə] Einbrecher *m*; ~**y** [-rɪ] Einbruch(sdiebstahl) *m.*

burial ['berɪəl] Begräbnis *f.*

burly ['bɜːlɪ] stämmig, kräftig.

burn [bɜːn] *irr burnt, burnt* [-t] (ver-, an)brennen; ~ *down* ab-, niederbrennen; ~**ing** ['-ɪŋ] brennend, glühend.

burrow ['bʌrəʊ] I *s (Kaninchen)* Bau *m*; II *v* sich eingraben.

burst [bɜːst] I *v irr burst, burst* 1. bersten, (zer)platzen; 2. ~ *out crying (laughing)* in Weinen (Gelächter) ausbrechen; ~ *into tears* in Tränen ausbrechen; 3. zum Bersten voll sein (*with* von); 4. *he* ~ *into the room* er stürzte ins Zimmer; II *s* 5. Bersten *n*; Explosion *f*; 6. *fig* (plötzlicher) Ausbruch *m.*

bury ['berɪ] 1. begraben, beerdigen; 2. vergraben.

bus [bʌs] Omnibus *m*; *go by* ~ mit dem Bus fahren.

bush [bʊʃ] Busch, Strauch *m*, Gebüsch *n.*

bushel ['bʊʃl] Scheffel *m* (35,36 l).

bushy ['bʊʃɪ] buschig.

business ['bɪznɪs] 1. Geschäft *n*, Handel *m*; *on* ~ geschäftlich; 2. Angelegenheit *f*, Sache *f*; *mean* ~ *(fam)* es ernst meinen; *that's none of your* ~ das geht Sie nichts an; ~ **hours** *pl* Geschäftszeit *f*; ~**man** [-mæn] Geschäftsmann *m.*

bus stop ['bʌs stɒp] Omnibushaltestelle *f.*

bust [bʌst] 1. Brust *f*; Busen *m*; 2. *(Kunst)* Büste *f.*

bus terminal ['bʌs,tɜːmɪnl] Omnibusbahnhof *m.*

bustle ['bʌsl] I *v* sich tummeln; II *s* Geschäftigkeit *f*, Hetze *f.*

busy ['bɪzɪ] 1. fleißig, geschäftig; 2. beschäftigt (*at, in, with* mit); 3. *(Straße)* belebt; 4. *(Tag)* voll ausgefüllt; 5. *tele* besetzt.

but [bʌt] I *conj* aber, jedoch; *not only . . .* ~ *also* nicht nur . . . sondern auch; II *prp* außer; *nothing* ~ nichts als; *the last* ~ *one* der vorletzte; *all* ~ *one* alle bis auf einen; III *adv* nur; *all* ~ beinahe, fast, nahezu.

butcher ['bʊtʃə] Metzger, Fleischer *m*; ~**'s (shop)** Metzgerei *f.*

butt [bʌt] I *s* 1. (~*-end*) stumpfe(s), dicke(s) Ende *f*; 2. Zigaretten-, Zigarrenstummel *m*; 3. Zielscheibe *f* (*a. fig* des Spottes); II *v* 4. (mit dem Kopf) stoßen; 5. *(fam)* ~ *in* sich einmischen in.

butter ['bʌtə] I *s* Butter *f*; II *v* mit Butter bestreichen;

~**cup** [-kʌp] Butterblume *f;*
~**fly** [-flaɪ] Schmetterling
m; ~**milk** [-mɪlk] Butter-
milch *f.*

buttocks *pl* ['bʌtəks] Hinterteil, Gesäß *n.*

button ['bʌtn] **I** *s* Knopf *m;*
II *v* zuknöpfen; ~**hole**
[-həʊl] Knopfloch *n.*

buttress ['bʌtrɪs] Strebepfei-
ler *m.*

buy [baɪ] *irr bought, bought*
[bɔːt] 1. kaufen (*from* von);
(Fahrkarte) lösen; ~ *up* auf-
kaufen; 2. *fig* erkaufen; ~**er**
['-ə] Käufer, Abnehmer *m;*
~**ing** ['-ɪŋ] ~ *capacity,
power* Kaufkraft *f.*

buzz [bʌz] **I** *v* summen, surren; **II** *s* Summen, Brummen
n.

buzzard ['bʌzəd] *orn* (Mäu-
se-)Bussard *m.*

by [baɪ] **I** *prp* 1. *(örtlich)* bei,
an, neben; *sit* ~ *me* setz dich
zu mir; 2. *(örtlich)* durch,
über; *I went* ~ *Paris* ich bin

über Paris gefahren; 3. *I
walked* ~ *the post-office* ich
bin an der Post vorbeige-
gangen; 4. *(zeitlich)* während, in, an; ~ *day* tagsüber;
day ~ *day* Tag für Tag;
5. *(zeitlich)* bis; ~ *now* bis
jetzt; ~ *the time* inzwischen;
6. von, durch, mit, (ver)mit-
tels; ~ *car, rail, bus, boat,
plane* mit dem Wagen, der
Bahn, dem Bus, dem Schiff,
im Flugzeug; ~ *chance* zufällig; ~ *no means* auf keinen Fall; **II** *adv* 7. vorbei; *I
can't get* ~ ich kann, komme
nicht vorbei; 8. dabei; *stand*
~ in der Nähe, bereit sein;
9. ~ *and large* im ganzen
(gesehen).

by|gone ['baɪgɒn] vergan-
gen; ~**(e)-law** ['-lɔː] Sat-
zung *f;* ~~**pass** ['-pɑːs] Um-
gehungsstraße *f;* ~~**product** ['-ˌprɒdʌkt] Nebenpro-
dukt *n;* ~**stander**
['-ˌstændə] Zuschauer *m.*

C

cab [kæb] Taxi n.

cabbage ['kæbɪdʒ] Kohl m.

cabby ['kæbɪ] fam Taxifahrer m.

cabin ['kæbɪn] 1. Hütte f; 2. mar Kabine, Kajüte f; ~ **boy** mar Kabinensteward m; ~ **class** mar 2. Klasse f.

cabinet ['kæbɪnɪt] 1. Schrank m; 2. pol Kabinett n; 3. radio Gehäuse n.

cable ['keɪbl] I s 1. mar Tau, Seil n; 2. (Übersee) Telegramm n; II v telegraphieren.

cabstand ['kæbstænd] Taxistand m.

cackle ['kækl] gackern; schnattern.

caddie ['kædɪ] Golfjunge m.

caddy ['kædɪ] Teebüchse f.

café ['kæfeɪ] Café n.

cage [keɪdʒ] Käfig m.

cake [keɪk] 1. Kuchen m; 2. ~ of soap Stück n Seife.

calamity [kə'læmətɪ] Unglück n.

calculat|e ['kælkjuleɪt] 1. aus-, be-, errechnen; 2. Am denken, meinen; 3. Am fest rechnen (on mit); ~**ing** [-ɪŋ] berechnend; ~ **machine** Rechenmaschine f; ~**ion** [ˌkælkju'leɪʃn] 1. Berechnung f; 2. Überlegung f.

calendar ['kælɪndə] Kalender m.

calf [kɑːf] pl calves 1. Kalb n; 2. Wade f.

call [kɔːl] I s 1. Ruf m; 2. (kurzer) Besuch m; 3. tele Anruf m; 4. Aufforderung f; 5. no ~ to keine Notwendigkeit zu; II v 6. rufen; 7. kurz besuchen (on s.o. jdn); 8. nennen; 9. betrachten als; halten für; 10. aufwecken; holen; anrufen; ~ **for** (dringend) erfordern; to be called for postlagernd; ~ **off** (Veranstaltung) absagen; ~**box** ['-bɒks] Telephonzelle f; ~**ing** ['-ɪŋ] Beruf m.

callous ['kæləs] gefühllos.

calm [kɑːm] I adj ruhig; still; friedlich; II s Ruhe f; III v: ~ down sich beruhigen; ~**ness** ['-nɪs] Ruhe f.

calumniate [kə'lʌmnɪeɪt] verleumden.

calumny ['kæləmnɪ] Verleumdung f.

camel ['kæml] Kamel n.

camera ['kæmərə] Kamera f, Fotoapparat m.

Cameroon ['kæməruːn] Kamerun n.

camomile ['kæməʊmaɪl] Kamille f.

camp [kæmp] I s (Zelt-)Lager n; II v (~ out) kampieren; zelten; ~**er** ['-ə] Zeltler m; ~-**fire** ['-faɪə] Lagerfeuer n.

camping| ground ['kæmpɪŋ graʊnd] , **~ site** [- saɪt] Camping-, Zeltplatz *m.*

campus ['kæmpəs] *Am* Universitätsgelände *n.*

campaign [kæm'peɪn] Feldzug *m a. fig, bes. pol; electoral* ~ Wahlkampagne *f.*

can [kæn] **I** *s* 1. Kanne *f;* 2. Konservendose *f;* **II** *v irr pret could* [kʊd] können; *you can't go* du darfst nicht gehen; *I cannot allow this* ich kann das nicht erlauben; *could I look at it?* darf ich es mir ansehen?

Canad|a ['kænədə] Kanada *n; ~ian* [kə'neɪdʒən] **I** *s* Kanadier *m;* **II** *adj* kanadisch.

canal [kə'næl] Kanal *n; ~ize* ['kænəlaɪz] kanalisieren.

cancel ['kænsl] 1. (aus-, durch)streichen; *(bes. Briefmarke)* entwerten; 2. *(Veranstaltung)* absagen; *(Zimmer, Fahr-, Flugkarte)* abbestellen.

cancer ['kænsə] *med* Krebs *m; C~ astr* Krebs *m.*

candid ['kændɪd] aufrichtig, ehrlich.

candidat|ure ['kændɪdətʃə] Kandidatur *f; ~e* [-dət] Kandidat, Bewerber *m.*

candied ['kændɪd] *(Früchte)* kandiert.

candle ['kændl] Kerze *f; ~light* [-laɪt] Kerzenlicht *n; ~stick* [-stɪk] Leuchter *m.*

candy ['kændɪ] 1. Kan-

dis(zucker) *m;* 2. *Am* Süßigkeiten *f pl.*

cane [keɪn] Rohr *n,* Stock *m.*

cann|ed [kænd] **~** *meat* Büchsenfleisch *n;* **~** *milk* Büchsenmilch *f;* **~ery** ['kænərɪ] Konservenfabrik *f.*

cannibal ['kænɪbl] Kannibale *m.*

cannon ['kænən] Kanone *f.*

canoe [kə'nu:]· Kanu, Paddelboot *n.*

cant [kænt] 1. Jargon *m;* 2. Heuchelei *f.*

canteen [kæn'ti:n] 1. Kantine *f;* 2. (Eß-)Geschirr *n.*

canvas ['kænvəs] Segeltuch *n; (Malerei)* Leinwand *f.*

canvass ['kænvəs] *com pol* werben *(for* für).

cap [kæp] 1. Mütze *f;* 2. Kapsel *f;* Verschluß *m.*

capab|ility [ˌkeɪpə'bɪlətɪ] Fähigkeit *f; ~le* ['keɪpəbl] tüchtig; fähig *(of* zu).

capacity [kə'pæsətɪ] 1. Inhalt *m;* Fassungsvermögen *n;* 2. Leistung(sfähigkeit) *f;* 3. *fig* Auffassungsgabe *f;* 4. *in my* ~ *as* (in meiner Eigenschaft) als.

cape [keɪp] 1. Umhang *m;* 2. Kap, Vorgebirge *n.*

caper ['keɪpə] **I** *v* herumtollen; **II** *s* Kaper *f.*

capital ['kæpɪtl] **I** *adj* 1. hauptsächlich; Haupt-; 2. vortrefflich; 3. ~ *punishment* Todesstrafe *f;*

II s 4. Kapital n; 5. Hauptstadt f; 6. Großbuchstabe m.

capital|ism ['kæpɪtəlɪzəm] Kapitalismus m; ~**ist** [-st] Kapitalist m; ~**ize** [-laɪz] 1. kapitalisieren; 2. (mit) groß(en Anfangsbuchstaben) schreiben.

capricious [kə'prɪʃəs] launisch, launenhaft.

Capricorn ['kæprɪkɔ:n] astr Steinbock m.

capsize [kæp'saɪz] kentern.

capsule ['kæpsju:l] Kapsel f.

captain ['kæptɪn] 1. Kapitän m; 2. mil Hauptmann m; 3. sport Mannschaftsführer m.

caption ['kæpʃn] (Bild-)Unterschrift f; film Untertitel m.

capt|ivate ['kæptɪveɪt] faszinieren; ~**ivity** [kæp'tɪvətɪ] Gefangenschaft f; ~**ure** [kæptʃə] **I** s Gefangennahme f; **II** v gefangennehmen.

car [ka:] 1. Auto n; 2. (Straßenbahn-)Wagen; Am Eisenbahnwagen m.

caravan ['kærəvæn] 1. Karawane f; 2. mot Wohnwagen m.

carbohydrate [‚ka:bəʊ'haɪdreɪt] Kohle(n)-hydrat n.

carbon ['ka:bən] 1. chem Kohlenstoff m; 2. (~-paper) Kohlepapier n; 3. (~ copy) Durchschlag m.

carburet(t)or [‚ka:bju'retə] mot Vergaser m.

carcass, carcase ['ka:kəs] Kadaver m.

card [ka:d] Karte f; on the ~s wahrscheinlich; have a ~ up o.'s sleeve etw in petto haben; put o.'s ~s on the table (fig) s-e Karten aufdecken; ~**board** ['-bo:d] Pappe f.

cardigan ['ka:dɪgən] Wolljacke f.

cardinal ['ka:dɪnl] Kardinal m; ~ **number** Grund-, Kardinalzahl f.

care [keə] **I** s 1. Sorgfalt f; 2. Pflege, Fürsorge f; ~ of (= c/o) bei, per Adresse; take ~ sorgen (für), sich kümmern (of um), achtgeben (of auf); 3. Sorge, Besorgnis f; 4. meist pl Sorgen f pl; **II** v 5. sich Sorgen, sich Gedanken machen (about über); 6. ~ for sorgen für, aufpassen auf, sich kümmern um; 7. ~ for Interesse haben an, wünschen.

career [kə'rɪə] 1. Laufbahn f; 2. in full ~ mit Höchstgeschwindigkeit.

care|ful ['keəfʊl] 1. sorgfältig; 2. vorsichtig; be ~ to write vergiß nicht zu schreiben; ~**less** ['keəlɪs] unvorsichtig; nachlässig.

caress [kə'res] **I** s Liebkosung f; **II** v liebkosen.

caretaker ['keə‚teɪkə] Hausverwalter m.

car-ferry ['ka:‚ferɪ] Autofähre f.

cargo [ˈkaːgəʊ] *mar aero* Ladung *f*.

caricature [ˈkærɪkəˌtjʊə] Karikatur *f*.

carnation [kɑːˈneɪʃn] Nelke *f*.

carnival [ˈkɑːnɪvl] Karneval *m*, Rummel *m*.

carol [ˈkærəl] *(Christmas ~)* Weihnachtslied *n*.

carp [kɑːp] **I** *s* Karpfen *m*; **II** *v* etw auszusetzen haben (*at* an).

car-park [ˈkaːpaːk] Parkplatz *m*.

carpenter [ˈkɑːpəntə] Zimmermann *m*.

carpet [ˈkɑːpɪt] Teppich *m*.

carriage [ˈkærɪdʒ] 1. Wagen *m*; 2. Transport *m*; 3. Frachtkosten *pl*; ~ *free* frachtfrei; 4. (Körper-)Haltung *f*.

carrier [ˈkærɪə] 1. Spediteur *m*; 2. *med* Keimträger *m*.

carrot [ˈkærət] Mohrrübe *f*.

carry [ˈkærɪ] 1. tragen *a. arch, tech*; transportieren; 2. bei sich haben; 3. *(Ertrag, Geld)* (ein)bringen; 4. *fig* mit sich bringen; ~ **away** wegtragen; *fig* mitreißen; ~ **off** *(Preis)* gewinnen; ~ **on** fortsetzen; ~ **out** *(Arbeit)* ausführen.

cart [kaːt] Karren *m*, Wagen *m*.

cartoon [kɑːˈtuːn] Karikatur *f*; *animated* ~ Trickfilm *m*.

cartridge [ˈkɑːtrɪdʒ] Patrone *f*.

carv|e [kaːv] 1. schnitzen; 2. meißeln; 3. *(Fleisch)* (zer)schneiden, tranchieren; ~**ing** [ˈ-ɪŋ] Schnitzerei *f*.

case [keɪs] 1. Fall *m a. jur med*; Sache, Angelegenheit *f*; *in ~ falls; in any ~* auf alle Fälle; *in this, that ~* in d(ies)em Fall; 2. Behälter *m*; Kästchen *n*, Kiste *f*.

cash [kæʃ] **I** *s* Bargeld *n*; ~ *on delivery* gegen Nachnahme; **II** *v* einlösen; ~ **desk** Kasse *f*; ~**ier** [kəˈʃɪə] Kassierer *m*; ~ **price** Preis *m* bei Barzahlung.

casing [ˈkeɪsɪŋ] *tech* Umkleidung *f*; Gehäuse *n*.

cask [kaːsk] Faß *n*; ~**et** [ˈkaːskɪt] 1. (Schmuck-)Kästchen *n*; 2. *Am* Sarg *m*.

cast [kaːst] **I** *s* 1. Wurf *m*; 2. *tech* Guß(form *f*) *m*; *(plaster ~)* Gipsverband *m*; 3. *theat* (Rollen-)Besetzung *f*; **II** *v irr* cast, cast 4. (fort-, aus-, ab)werfen; 5. ~ *a vote* s-e (Wahl-)Stimme abgeben; 6. *tech* gießen; ~ **iron** Gußeisen *n*.

castle [ˈkaːsl] Burg *f*; Schloß *n*; *(Schach)* Turm *m*.

casual [ˈkæʒjʊəl] 1. zufällig, gelegentlich, beiläufig; *(Bekanntschaft)* flüchtig; 2. nachlässig, gleichgültig; ~ **labour(er)** Gelegenheitsarbeit(er *m*) *f*; ~**ty** [-tɪ] 1. Unfall *m*; 2. Verunglückte(r *m*) *f*; *pl mil* Verluste *m pl*; C~

Ward Unfallstation *f (in e-m Krankenhaus).*

cat [kæt] Katze *f;* ~**'s eye** *(tech)* Rückstrahler *m.*

catalogue ['kætəlɒg] Katalog *m;* Verzeichnis *n.*

catapult ['kætəpʌlt] Schleuder *f.*

cataract ['kætərækt] 1. Wasserfall *m;* 2. *med* graue(r) Star *m.*

catarrh [kə'tɑː] Katarrh *m.*

catastrophe [kə'tæstrəfɪ] Katastrophe *f.*

catcall ['kætkɔːl] *theat* Pfeifen, Zischen *n.*

catch [kætʃ] I *v irr caught, caught* [kɔːt] 1. (auf-, ein)fangen; ~ *hold of* ergreifen; 2. *(Menschen, Zug)* (noch) erreichen; 3. ertappen *(at* bei); 4. *(Krankheit)* sich holen; 5. begreifen; 6. ~ *s.o.'s eye* jds Aufmerksamkeit auf sich ziehen; 7. ~ *fire* Feuer fangen; II *s* 8. Fang *m; (Ball)* Fangen *n;* 9. *fig* Trick *m;* ~**-as-**~**-can** Freistilringen *n;* ~**ing** ['-ɪŋ] *med* ansteckend; ~**word** ['-wɜːd] Schlagwort *n.*

category ['kætɪgərɪ] Kategorie *f.*

cater ['keɪtə] ~ *for* 1. beliefern; 2. *fig* sorgen für; ~**er** [-rə] Lebensmittellieferant *m.*

caterpillar ['kætəpɪlə] *tech zoo* Raupe *f.*

cathedral [kə'θiːdrəl] Kathedrale *f.* Dom *m.*

catholic ['kæθəlɪk] *rel* I *adj* katholisch; II *s* Katholik *m.*

cattle ['kætl] Rindvieh *n; raise* ~ Vieh züchten.

cauliflower ['kɒlɪˌflaʊə] Blumenkohl *m.*

cause [kɔːz] I *s* 1. Ursache *f;* Grund, Anlaß *m (for* zu); 2. Sache *f;* II *v* verursachen.

caustic ['kɔːstɪk] ätzend; *fig* beißend.

caut|ion ['kɔːʃn] I *s* 1. Vorsicht *f;* 2. Warnung *f;* II *v* warnen *(against* vor); ~**ious** ['kɔːʃəs] vorsichtig.

cav|e [keɪv] Höhle *f;* ~**ity** ['kævətɪ] Höhlung *f; (Zahn)* Loch *n.*

cease [siːs] aufhören; ~**less** ['-lɪs] unaufhörlich.

ceiling ['siːlɪŋ] 1. *(Zimmer)* Decke *f;* 2. oberste Grenze *f;* 3. Höchstpreis *m.*

celebrat|e ['selɪbreɪt] feiern; ~**ed** [-ɪd] berühmt; ~**ion** [ˌselɪ'breɪʃn] Feier *f.*

celebrity [sɪ'lebrətɪ] Berühmtheit *f.*

celery ['selərɪ] *bot* Sellerie *m* od *f.*

celestial [sɪ'lestjəl] *(astr)* ~ *body* Himmelskörper *m.*

cell [sel] Zelle *f.*

cement [sɪ'ment] I *s* Zement, Kitt *m;* II *v* (ver)kitten.

cemetery ['semɪtrɪ] Friedhof *m.*

censure ['senʃə] I *v* tadeln; II *s* Tadel *m;* Kritik *f.*

cent [sent] 1. *Am* Cent *m;*

2. *per* ~ Prozent *n;* **~igrade** ['sentigreid] *(Thermometer)* Celsius-; **~imetre** ['senti,mi:tə] Zentimeter *n.*

central ['sentrəl] 1. zentral; ~ *heating* Zentralheizung *f;* 2. Haupt-; **~ize** ['sentrəlaiz] zentralisieren.

centre ['sentə] **I** *s* 1. Mitte(lpunkt *m*) *f; shopping* ~ Einkaufszentrum *n;* 2. *(~ forward) sport* Mittelstürmer *m;* **II** *v:* be ~d on sich drehen, kreisen um.

century ['sentʃuri] Jahrhundert *n.*

cereals *pl* ['siəriəlz] Getreide *n.*

ceremon|ial [,seri'məunjəl] zeremoniell; **~y** ['seriməni] Zeremonie *f.*

certain ['sɜ:tn] bestimmt, gewiß, sicher; *a* ~ ein(e) gewisse(r, s); *for* ~ bestimmt, (ganz) sicher; **~ly** [-li] sicher(lich), gewiß; unbedingt; **~ty** [-ti] Gewißheit *f.*

certif|icate [sə'tifikət] Zeugnis *n;* Bescheinigung *f;* **~y** ['sɜ:tifai] *this is to* ~ hiermit wird bescheinigt; *certified copy* beglaubigte Abschrift *f.*

Chad [tʃæd] Tschad *m.*

chafe [tʃeif] 1. wundreiben; 2. sich ärgern (*at* über).

chaff [tʃɑ:f] Spreu *f;* Häcksel *m* od *n.*

chaffinch ['tʃæfintʃ] Buchfink *m.*

chain [tʃein] **I** *s* Kette *f;* **II** *v* (an)ketten.

chair [tʃeə] 1. Stuhl *m;* 2. *take the* ~ den Vorsitz übernehmen; **~man** ['-mən] Vorsitzende(r) *m.*

chalk [tʃɔ:k] Kreide *f.*

challenge ['tʃælindʒ] **I** *s* Herausforderung *f;* **II** *v* herausfordern.

chamber ['tʃeimbə] ~ *of commerce* Handelskammer *f;* **~maid** [-meid] Zimmermädchen *n (im Hotel);* ~ **music** Kammermusik *f.*

champagne [,ʃæm'pein] Champagner *m.*

champion ['tʃæmpjən] 1. Verfechter *m;* 2. *sport* Meister *m;* **~ship** [-ʃip] *(sport)* Meisterschaft *f.*

chance [tʃɑ:ns] **I** *s* 1. Zufall *m; by* ~ zufällig; *take o.'s* ~ sein Glück versuchen; 2. Möglichkeit, Gelegenheit *f;* **II** *v* 3. ~ *it (fam)* es riskieren; 4. *I* ~*d to be there* zufällig war ich dort.

chancellor ['tʃɑ:nsələ] Kanzler *m.*

chandelier [,ʃændə'liə] Kronleuchter *m.*

change [tʃeindʒ] **I** *s* 1. Änderung *f;* Wechsel *m; for a* ~ zur Abwechslung; 2. Kleingeld *n; can you give me* ~ *(for a pound note)?* können Sie (e-e Pfundnote) wechseln? 3. Geldwechsel *m;* **II** *v* 4. (sich) (ab-, um-, ver)ändern; *I've* ~*d my mind* ich

hab's mir anders überlegt;
5. (aus-, um)tauschen; *(Geld)*
(um)wechseln; 6. ~ *trains*
etc umsteigen; *all* ~*! (rail)*
alles um-, aussteigen! 7. *(~
o.'s clothes)* sich umziehen;
~able ['-əbl] veränderlich.
channel ['tʃænl] Kanal *m;*
the English C~ Ärmelkanal
m; through official ~*s* auf
dem Dienst-, Instanzenweg.
chaos ['keɪɒs] Chaos *n.*
chap [tʃæp] *fam* Kerl, Bursche *m.*
chapel ['tʃæpl] *rel* Kapelle *f.*
chaplain ['tʃæplɪn] Kaplan
m.
chapter ['tʃæptə] Kapitel *n.*
character ['kærəktə] 1. Charakter *m;* 2. Beschaffenheit;
Eigenschaft *f;* 3. *theat* Rolle
f; 4. Name, Ruf *m;* 5. Schrift-
zeichen *n;* **~istic** [‚-'rɪstɪk]
I *adj* charakteristisch; **II** *s*
Kennzeichen *n;* **~ize** [-raɪz]
charakterisieren.
charge [tʃɑːdʒ] **I** *s* 1. (Un-)
Kosten *pl; free of* ~ gratis;
2. Obhut *f; be in* ~ *of;* die
Verantwortung haben für;
3. Anklage *f;* 4. Angriff *m;*
5. *tech* Ladung *f;* **II** *v* 6. berechnen *(too much* zu viel);
7. beauftragen *(with* mit);
8. beschuldigen, anklagen;
9. angreifen; 10. *(Batterie)*
aufladen.
charit|able ['tʃærətəbl]
wohltätig; **~y** ['tʃærətɪ]
Nächstenliebe *f;* Wohltätig-
keit *f.*

charm [tʃɑːm] **I** *s* Reiz, Zauber *m;* **II** *v* bezaubern, ent-
zücken; **~ing** ['-ɪŋ] bezaubernd.
chart [tʃɑːt] 1. *mar* Seekarte
f; 2. Diagramm *n.*
charter flight ['tʃɑːtə flaɪt]
Charterflug *m.*
chase [tʃeɪs] **I** *v* verfolgen;
(~ away) weg-, verjagen;
II *s* Jagd *f.*
chasm ['kæzəm] Abgrund *m,*
Kluft *f.*
chassis ['ʃæsɪ] *mot* Fahrgestell *n.*
chast|e [tʃeɪst] 1. keusch;
2. schmucklos, einfach; **~ise**
[tʃæ'staɪz] (körperlich)
züchtigen; **~ity** ['tʃæstətɪ]
Keuschheit *f.*
chat [tʃæt] **I** *s* Unterhaltung
f; **II** *v* plaudern, sich unterhalten; **~ter** ['-ə] **I** *v* plappern, quasseln; **II** *s* Geplapper, Geschwätz *n.*
cheap [tʃiːp] billig, preiswert;
hold ~ geringschätzen.
cheat [tʃiːt] **I** *v* betrügen; **II** *s*
1. Betrug *m;* 2. Betrüger *m.*
check [tʃek] **I** *v* 1. hindern,
zurückhalten, eindämmen;
2. prüfen, kontrollieren; ~
up genau überprüfen *(on*
s.th. etw); 3. ~ *in (Hotel)* sich
eintragen; ~ *out* weggehen;
abreisen; **II** *s* 4. Hindernis *n;*
5. Kontrolle *f (on* über);
6. Gepäckschein *m,*
Garderobenmarke *f;*
7. *(Textil)* Karo *n;* **III** *interj*
Schach! **~mate** ['-meɪt]

mattsetzen; **~point** ['-pɔɪnt] Kontrollpunkt *m;* **~room** ['-ru:m] *Am* Garderobe *f;* **~up** ['-ʌp] genaue Prüfung *f.*

cheek [tʃi:k] 1. Backe, Wange *f;* 2. *fam* Unverschämtheit *f;* **~y** ['-ɪ] *fam* frech.

cheer [tʃɪə] **I** *s* 1. (gute) Stimmung *f;* 2. *give three ~s for s.o.* ein dreifaches Hoch auf jdn ausbringen; **II** *v* 3. laut Beifall zollen (*s.o.* jdm); 4. ~ up froh werden, Mut fassen; ~ *s.o.* (*up*) jdn aufheitern; **~ful** ['-fʊl] froh, vergnügt; *(Zimmer)* freundlich; **~io(h)** [,tʃɪərɪ'əʊ] *interj fam* leb wohl; **~less** ['-lɪs] freudlos.

cheese [tʃi:z] Käse *m.*

chemlical ['kemɪkl] **I** *adj* chemisch; **II** *s* Chemikalie *f;* **~ist** ['kemɪst] Chemiker; Drogist *m; dispensing ~* Apotheker *m;* **~istry** ['kemɪstrɪ] Chemie *f.*

cheque, *Am* **check** [tʃek] Scheck *m; cash a ~* e-n Scheck einlösen; *traveller's ~* Reisescheck *m;* **~-book** ['-bʊk] Scheckbuch *n.*

chequered, *Am* **checkered** ['tʃekəd] 1. kariert; 2. *fig* bunt, mannigfaltig.

cherry ['tʃerɪ] Kirsche *f.*

chess [tʃes] Schach(spiel) *n;* **~-board** ['-bɔ:d] Schachbrett *n;* **~man** ['-mæn] Schachfigur *f.*

chest [tʃest] Kiste *f,* Kasten *m,* Truhe *f;* ~ *of drawers* Kommode *f.*

chestnut ['tʃesnʌt] **I** *s* Kastanie *f;* **II** *adj* kastanienbraun.

chew [tʃu:] kauen.

chicken ['tʃɪkɪn] Küken; Hühnchen *n;* **~pox** [-pɒks] Windpocken *pl.*

chief [tʃi:f] **I** *s* 1. Chef, Leiter *m;* 2. Häuptling *m (e-s Stammes);* 3. *in ~* ganz besonders; **II** *adj* hauptsächlich; **~ly** ['-lɪ] hauptsächlich.

chilblain ['tʃɪlbleɪn] Frostbeule *f.*

child [tʃaɪld] *pl children* ['tʃɪldrən] Kind *n;* **~hood** ['-hʊd] Kindheit *f;* **~ish** ['-ɪʃ] kindisch; **~like** ['-laɪk] kindlich; **~'s play** *fig* Kinderspiel *n.*

chill [tʃɪl] **I** *s* 1. Frost *m,* Kälte *f;* 2. Schüttelfrost *m; catch a ~* sich erkälten; **II** *v* kalt stellen; *I'm ~ed to the bone* ich bin ganz durch(ge)froren; **~y** ['-ɪ] kühl; *fig* frostig; *feel ~* frösteln.

chime [tʃaɪm] **I** *s meist pl* Geläut, Glockenspiel *n;* **II** *v (Stunde)* schlagen.

chimney ['tʃɪmnɪ] Schornstein *m;* **~-sweep** [-swi:p] Schornsteinfeger *m.*

chimpanzee [,tʃɪmpən'zi:] Schimpanse *m.*

chin [tʃɪn] Kinn *n;* ~ *up* Kopf hoch.

China ['tʃaɪnə] China *n.*

china ['tʃaɪnə] Porzellan *n.*

Chinese [ˌtʃaɪˈniːz] **I** s Chinese m; **II** adj chinesisch.

chink [tʃɪŋk] 1. Ritze f, Spalt m; 2. (Gläser) Klang m.

chip [tʃɪp] 1. Splitter m; 2. pl (potato ~s) Chips pl; **~ped** [-t] (Porzellan, Glas) angestoßen, angeschlagen.

chirp [tʃɜːp] **I** v zirpen, zwitschern; **II** s Gezirp, Gezwitscher, Geträller n; **~y** [ˈ-ɪ] lebhaft, munter.

chisel [ˈtʃɪzl] Meißel m.

chivalrous [ˈʃɪvlrəs] ritterlich.

chlorine [ˈklɔːriːn] Chlor n.

chocolate [ˈtʃɒkələt] Schokolade f; Praline f.

choice [tʃɔɪs] **I** s (Aus-)Wahl f; I have no ~ es bleibt mir nichts anderes übrig; **II** v (aus)gewählt, ausgesucht.

choir [ˈkwaɪə] Chor m.

choke [tʃəʊk] **I** v (er)würgen, ersticken; ~ back (Ärger) unterdrücken; **II** s mot Starterklappe f.

choose [tʃuːz] irr chose [tʃəʊz], chosen [ˈ-n] 1. (aus)wählen, aussuchen; 2. sich entscheiden für.

chop [tʃɒp] **I** v (zer)hacken; **II** s Kotelett n; **~per** [ˈ-ə] Hackmesser n.

chord [kɔːd] 1. math Sehne f; 2. mus Saite f; 3. mus Akkord m; 4. (anat) spinal ~ Rückenmark n; vocal ~ Stimmband n.

chorus [ˈkɔːrəs] 1. Chor m; 2. Refrain m.

Christ [kraɪst] Christus m.

christen [ˈkrɪsn] taufen; **~ing** [-ɪŋ] Taufe f.

Christian [ˈkrɪstjən] **I** adj christlich; **II** s Christ m; **~ity** [ˌkrɪstɪˈænəti] Christentum n; **~ name** Vorname m.

Christmas, Xmas [ˈkrɪsməs] Weihnachten n; Father ~ der Weihnachtsmann; **~ Day** der 1. Weihnachtstag (25. Dez.); **~ Eve** der Heilige Abend (24. Dez.); **~tree** [-triː] Christbaum m.

chromium [ˈkrəʊmjəm] chem Chrom n.

chronic(al) [ˈkrɒnɪk(l)] med chronisch.

chronicle [ˈkrɒnɪkl] Chronik f; **~ologic(al)** [ˌkrɒnəˈlɒdʒɪk(l)] chronologisch; in ~ order in zeitlicher Folge.

chuck [tʃʌk] fam werfen.

chuckle [ˈtʃʌkl] kichern.

chum [tʃʌm] **I** s Kamerad m; **II** v: ~ up with sich eng anschließen an; **~my** [ˈ-ɪ] eng befreundet.

chunk [tʃʌŋk] Klumpen m.

church [tʃɜːtʃ] Kirche f; go to ~ in die Kirche gehen; **~goer** [ˈ-ˌgəʊə] Kirchgänger m; **~yard** [ˈ-jɑːd] Kirchhof m.

cigar [sɪˈgɑː] Zigarre f; **~ette** [ˌsɪgəˈret] Zigarette f.

cinder [ˈsɪndə] Schlacke f.

Cinderella [sɪndəˈrelə] Aschenputtel n.

cinema ['sɪnəmə] Kino n.
cinnamon ['sɪnəmən] Zimt m.
cipher, cypher ['saɪfə] I s 1. Null f; 2. Ziffer f; 3. Chiffre f; II v chiffrieren.
circle ['sɜːkl] I s 1. Kreis m; 2. theat Rang m; II v kreisen.
circuit ['sɜːkɪt] 1. Rundgang m, -fahrt f, -flug m (of um); Rundreise f; 2. Stromkreis m; Schaltung f.
circular ['sɜːkjʊlə] I adj kreisförmig; II s Rundschreiben n; ~ saw Kreissäge f.
circulate ['sɜːkjʊleɪt] zirkulieren (a. Blut); ~ing library Leihbücherei f; ~ion [ˌsɜːkjʊ'leɪʃn] 1. Kreislauf m; 2. put into ~ in Umlauf bringen; 3. (Zeitung) Auflage f.
circumference [sə'kʌmfərəns] (Kreis-)Umfang m.
circumstance ['sɜːkəmstəns] meist pl (nähere) Umstände m pl; under the ~s unter diesen Umständen.
circus ['sɜːkəs] 1. Zirkus m; 2. Br runde(r) Platz m.

citizen ['sɪtɪzn] Bürger m; ~ship [-ʃɪp] Staatsangehörigkeit f.
city ['sɪtɪ] (Groß-)Stadt; Altstadt f; Zentrum; Geschäftsviertel n; the C~ die (Lon-

doner) City; ~ hall Rathaus n; ~ map Stadtplan m.
civil ['sɪvl] 1. bürgerlich; 2. zivil; 3. korrekt; höflich; ~ engineer Bauingenieur m; ~ian [sɪ'vɪljən] Zivilist m; ~ization [ˌsɪvɪlaɪ'zeɪʃn] Zivilisation, Kultur f; ~ize ['sɪvɪlaɪz] zivilisieren; ~ law bürgerliche(s) Recht n; ~ marriage standesamtliche Trauung f; ~ rights pl Bürgerrechte n pl; ~ servant (Staats-)Beamte(r) m; C~ Service Staatsdienst m.
claim [kleɪm] I s Anspruch m (to auf); II v 1. Anspruch erheben auf, fordern; 2. behaupten, versichern.
clairvoyant [kleə'vɔɪənt] Hellseher m.
clamo|rous ['klæmərəs] lärmend; ~(u)r ['klæmə] I s Geschrei n, Lärm m; II v schreien; laut fordern.
clamp [klæmp] Klammer f.

clan [klæn] (Schottland) Sippe f.
clang [klæŋ] I s Klang m, Klirren n; II v klirren, rasseln.
clap [klæp] I v 1. (Beifall) klatschen; ~ o.'s hands in die Hände klatschen; 2. klopfen (on the back auf die Schulter); II s: ~ of thunder Donnerschlag m.
clari|fy ['klærɪfaɪ] (sich) klären; ~ty ['klærətɪ] Klarheit f a. fig.

clarinet [ˌklærɪ'net] *mus* Klarinette *f.*

clash [klæʃ] **I** *v* 1. klirren, rasseln; 2. aufea.prallen (*with* mit); 3. nicht zs.passen (*with* mit); **II** *s* 4. Klirren *n;* 5. Zs.prall, -stoß *m.*

clasp [klɑ:sp] **I** *v* 1. einhaken; 2. umklammern, umfassen; **II** *s* 3. Haken *m,* Klammer, Schnalle *f;* 4. Umklammerung *f,* Umarmung *f.*

class [klɑ:s] 1. Klasse *f;* 2. (Gesellschafts-)Schicht *f.*

classic ['klæsɪk] **I** *adj* 1. erstklassig; 2. klassisch; **II** *s* Klassiker *m;* ~**al** [-l] klassisch.

classification [ˌklæsɪfɪ'keɪʃn] Einteilung *f.*

clatter ['klætə] **I** *s* Klappern *n,* Rattern *n;* **II** *v* klappern, rattern.

clause [klɔ:z] 1. *gram* Satz *m;* 2. *jur* Klausel *f.*

claw [klɔ:] Kralle, Klaue *f.*

clay [kleɪ] Lehm, Ton *m.*

clean [kli:n] **I** *adj* rein, sauber; **II** *v* reinigen, säubern, putzen; **(dry)** ~**ers** ['-əz] *(Geschäft)* Reinigung *f;* ~**ing** ['-ɪŋ] Reinigung, Säuberung *f;* ~**liness** ['klenlɪnɪs] Reinlichkeit *f;* ~**ly** ['klenlɪ] reinlich, sauber; ~**se** [klenz] *fig* läutern, reinigen.

clear [klɪə] **I** *adj* 1. klar; hell; rein; 2. *(Straße)* frei; 3. *com* netto; **II** *v* 4. (sich auf)klären; aufhellen; 5. säubern; *(Tisch)* abräumen; 6. *(Hindernis)* springen über; 7. abfertigen; verzollen.

clearance ['klɪərəns] 1. (Auf-)Räumung(sarbeiten *f pl) f;* 2. *(Brücke)* lichte Höhe *f;* 3. Zollabfertigung *f.*

clearing ['klɪərɪŋ] Rodung, Lichtung *f;* ~-**house** [-haʊs] Verrechnungsstelle *f.*

cleavage ['kli:vɪdʒ] Spalte *f.*

cleft [kleft] Spalt(e *f);* Riß, Sprung *m.*

clemency ['klemənsɪ] Milde; Nachsicht *f.*

clench [klentʃ] ~ *o.'s fist* die Faust ballen; ~ *o.'s teeth* die Zähne zusammenbeißen.

clergy ['klɜ:dʒɪ] Geistlichkeit *f;* ~**man** [-mən] Geistliche(r) *m.*

clerk [klɑ:k] 1. Büroangestellte(r) *m;* 2. *Am* Verkäufer(in *f) m.*

clever ['klevə] klug, gescheit; gewandt (*at* in); ~**ness** [-nɪs] Klugheit, Gewandtheit *f.*

click [klɪk] **I** *s* Klicken *n; (Schloß)* Einschnappen *n;* **II** *v* klicken, zuschnappen.

client ['klaɪənt] 1. *jur* Klient *m;* 2. Kunde *m,* Kundin *f.*

cliff [klɪf] Klippe *f.*

climate ['klaɪmɪt] Klima *n.*

climax ['klaɪmæks] Höhepunkt *m.*

climb [klaɪm] steigen, klettern (*a tree* auf e-n Baum);

~er [-ə] Kletterer, Bergsteiger m.

clinch [klɪntʃ] *(Boxen)* Clinch m, Umklammerung f.

cling [klɪŋ] *irr clung, clung* [klʌŋ] sich klammern *(to* an).

clinic ['klɪnɪk] Klinik f.

clink [klɪŋk] klinge(l)n (lassen).

clip [klɪp] **I** s (Büro-, Wäsche-)Klammer f; Spange f; **II** v 1. *(~ together)* zs.klammern, -heften; 2. *(Haar)* schneiden; *(aus e-r Zeitung)* ausschneiden; **~pers** pl ['-əz] Haarschneidemaschine f; **~ping** ['-ɪŋ] (Zeitungs-)-Ausschnitt m.

cloak [kləʊk] **I** s Umhang m; *under the ~* unter dem Vorwand; **II** v fig verbergen; **~room** ['-rʊm] Garderobe; rail Gepäckaufbewahrung f.

clock [klɒk] (Wand-)Uhr f; *4 o'clock* 4 Uhr; *alarm ~* Wecker m; **~wise** ['-waɪz] im Uhrzeigersinn; **~work** ['-wɜːk] Uhrwerk n; *like ~* *(fig)* wie am Schnürchen.

clod [klɒd] Erdklumpen m.

clog [klɒg] **I** s Holzschuh m; **II** v verstopfen.

cloister ['klɔɪstə] 1. Kloster n; 2. Kreuzgang m.

close [kləʊs] **I** adv dicht, nahe *(by* dabei; *to* bei); dicht, eng beisammen; **II** adj 1. nah, dicht(gedrängt), eng(stehend); *that was a ~ call* das ist noch einmal gut abgegangen; *he is a ~*

friend of mine wir sind eng mitea. befreundet; 2. geizig; 3. zurückhaltend, verschlossen; 4. *(Luft)* stickig; 5. genau, gründlich; *after ~ consideration* nach reiflicher Überlegung; **III** v 6. (zu-, ver)schließen, zumachen; 7. beenden; *(Versammlung)* schließen; 8. ~ *in (on, upon) (Nacht)* hereinbrechen; **IV** s (Ab-)Schluß m; *bring to a ~* zu Ende bringen; *draw to a ~* zu Ende gehen; **~-fisted** ['-fɪstɪd] geizig; ~ **season** *(Jagd)* Schonzeit f; **~-up** ['-ʌp] Nah-, Großaufnahme f.

closet ['klɒzɪt] Am eingebaute(r) (Wand-)Schrank m.

closing ['kləʊzɪŋ] *early-~ day* Tag m mit frühem Ladenschluß.

clot [klɒt] Klümpchen n.

cloth [klɒθ] Tuch m; Stoff m; *lay the ~* den Tisch decken; *dish ~* Geschirr-, Spültuch n.

clothes [kləʊðz] 1. Kleider n pl, Kleidung f; 2. Bettwäsche f; **~-brush** ['-brʌʃ] Kleiderbürste f; **~-line** ['-laɪn] Wäscheleine f; **~-peg** ['-peg], **~-pin** ['-pɪn] Wäscheklammer f.

clothing ['kləʊðɪŋ] Kleidung f.

cloud [klaʊd] **I** s 1. Wolke f; 2. ~ *of flies* Fliegenschwarm m; **II** v *(~ over)* (sich) be-

wölken; **~-burst** ['-bɜːst]
Wolkenbruch *m;* **~ed** ['-ɪd]
bewölkt; **~less** ['-lɪs] wol-
kenlos; **~y** ['-ɪ] 1. wolkig, bewölkt; 2. *(Wasser)* trübe.

clove [kləuv] (Gewürz-)Nel-
ke *f.*

clover ['kləuvə] Klee *m; live
in ~* wie die Made im Speck
leben; **~-leaf** [-liːf] *tech*
Kleeblatt *n.*

club [klʌb] **I** *s* 1. Keule *f;*
(Golf-)Schläger, (Gummi-)
Knüppel *m;* 2. Klub, Verein
m; 3. *pl (Spielkarten)* Kreuz
n; **II** *v* 4. verprügeln; 5. *~ together* sich zusammentun.

clue [kluː] Anhaltspunkt,
Schlüssel *m (to* zu).

clumsy ['klʌmzɪ] schwerfällig, ungeschickt.

cluster ['klʌstə] **I** *s* Traube *f;*
Büschel, Bündel *n;* **II** *v* sich
scharen *(round* um).

clutch [klʌtʃ] **I** *s* 1. Griff *m;*
2. *in the ~es of* in der Ge-
walt von; 3. *mot* Kupplung
f; **II** *v* greifen *(at* nach); festhalten, umklammern.

coach [kəutʃ] **I** *s* 1. (Eisen-
bahn-)Wagen *m;* 2. Reisebus
m; 3. Nachhilfelehrer *m;*
sport Trainer *m;* **II** *v* aufs
Examen vorbereiten; *sport*
trainieren.

coagulate [kəu'ægjʊleɪt] gerinnen (lassen).

coal [kəul] Kohle *f; carry ~s
to Newcastle (fig)* Eulen
nach Athen tragen; **~field**
['-fiːld] Kohlenrevier, -ge-

biet *n;* **~-pit** ['-pɪt] Kohlen-
bergwerk *n.*

coarse [kɔːs] 1. rauh, grob;
2. *fig* roh, ungebildet.

coast [kəust] Küste *f; on the
~* an der Küste; **~guard**
['-gɑːd] Küstenwache *f.*

coat [kəut] **I** *s* 1. Jacke *f;*
Mantel *m;* 2. *zoo* Fell *n;*
3. Anstrich *m;* **II** *v* überziehen *(with* mit); anstreichen,
verputzen; **~ed** ['-ɪd] bedeckt *(with* mit); *med
(Zunge)* belegt; **~-hanger**
['-,hæŋə] Kleiderbügel *m;*
~ing ['-ɪŋ] Schicht *f;* Anstrich; Überzug *m; ~ of
arms* Wappen *n.*

coax [kəuks] überreden *(s.o.
to do, into doing s.th.* jdn
etw zu tun); schmeicheln.

cob [kɒb] Maiskolben *m.*

cobweb ['kɒbweb]
Spinn(en)gewebe *n.*

cock [kɒk] **I** *s* Hahn *m;*
II *v (~ up)* aufrichten; **~pit**
['-pɪt] *aero* Cockpit *n,* Kanzel *f;* **~scomb** ['-skəum]
Kamm *m (des Hahnes);*
~sure [,-'ʃuə] todsicher; von
sich überzeugt.

cockney ['kɒknɪ] (gebürti-
ger) Londoner *m.*

cockroach ['kɒkrəutʃ] *ent*
Küchenschabe *f.*

cocoa ['kəukəu] Kakao(pulver *n) m.*

coconut ['kəukənʌt] Kokosnuß *f.*

cod [kɒd] Kabeljau *m,*

Dorsch *m;* ~**-liver oil**
[ˌ-lɪvərˈɔɪl] Lebertran *m.*
coddle [ˈkɒdl] verzärteln.
code [kəʊd] **I** *s* 1. Gesetz-
buch *n;* 2. Kode *m;* **II** *v*
(ver)schlüsseln, chiffrieren.
coexistence [ˌkəʊɪgˈzɪstəns]
pol Koexistenz *f.*
coffee [ˈkɒfɪ] Kaffee *m.*
coffin [ˈkɒfɪn] Sarg *m.*
cogwheel [ˈkɒgwiːl] Zahn-
rad *n.*
coherent [kəʊˈhɪərənt]
zs.hängend.
coil [kɔɪl] **I** *s* Spirale, Rolle,
Spule *f;* **II** *v* (~ *up*) (auf)wik-
keln, -rollen.
coin [kɔɪn] **I** *s* Münze *f;*
II *v* (*Geld, Wort*) prägen.
coincid|e [ˌkəʊɪnˈsaɪd]
1. (*zeitlich*) zs.fallen, -tref-
fen; 2. *fig* übereinstimmen;
~**ence** [kəʊˈɪnsɪdəns]
1. Zs.treffen *n;* 2. Übereinstimmung *f.*
coke [kəʊk] 1. Koks *m;* 2. *sl*
Kokain *n;* 3. *fam* Coca-Cola
n.
cold [kəʊld] **I** *adj* 1. kalt; *be*
~ frieren; 2. *fig (Empfang)*
frostig; *give s.o. the* ~ *shoulder* jdm die kalte Schulter
zeigen; **II** *s* 3. Kälte *f;* 4. Erkältung *f; catch a)* ~ sich
erkälten; ~**-blooded** kaltblütig *a. zoo;* ~**ness** Kälte *f.*
colic [ˈkɒlɪk] Kolik *f.*
collaborat|e [kəˈlæbəreɪt]
zs.arbeiten (*with* mit); ~**ion**
[kəˌlæbəˈreɪʃn] Zs.arbeit *f;*
~**or** [-ə] Mitarbeiter *m.*

collaps|e [kəˈlæps] **I** *s*
Zs.bruch *m;* **II** *v* zs.brechen;
~**ible** [kəˈlæpsəbl] zs.klapp-
bar.
collar [ˈkɒlə] **I** *s* 1. Kragen *m;*
2. (*Hund*) Halsband *n;* **II** *v*
(*beim Kragen*) packen;
~**bone** [ˈkɒləbəʊn] Schlüs-
selbein *n.*
colleague [ˈkɒliːg] Kollege *m.*
collect [kəˈlekt] 1. (ein)sam-
meln; einkassieren; 2. (*Brief-
marken*) sammeln; 3. (sich)
versammeln; 4. abholen;
~**ed** [-ɪd] gesammelt, gefaßt; ~**ion** [kəˈlekʃn]
1. Sammlung *f;* 2. (*Brief-
kästen*) Leerung *f;* ~**or** [-ə]
Sammler *m.*
collide [kəˈlaɪd] zs.stoßen.
colliery [ˈkɒljərɪ] Kohlen-
bergwerk *n.*
collision [kəˈlɪʒn] Zs.stoß *m.*
colloquial [kəˈləʊkwɪəl] um-
gangssprachlich.
Colombia [kəˈlɒmbɪə] Ko-
lumbien *n.*
colon [ˈkəʊlən] Doppelpunkt
m.
colonel [ˈkɜːnl] Oberst *m.*
colon|ial [kəˈləʊnjəl] Kolo-
nial-; ~**y** [ˈkɒlənɪ] Kolonie *f.*
colo(u)r [ˈkʌlə] **I** *s* 1. Farbe *f;*
2. Gesichtsfarbe *f;* 3. Vor-
wand *m;* 4. *pl* Abzeichen *n;*
Fahne *f;* 5. *man, woman of*
~ Farbige(r *m*) *f;* **II** *v* 6. färben, (an)streichen; 7. (sich)
färben; erröten; 8. *fig* e-n
Anstrich geben; ~**-bar**
[-bɑː] Rassenschranke *f;*

~**ed** [-d] farbig; ~**ful** [-fʊl] farbenprächtig *a. fig;* ~**ing** [-rɪŋ] Färbung *f;* ~**less** [-lɪs] farblos.

column ['kɒləm] 1. Säule *f;* 2. *typ* Spalte, Rubrik *f.*

comb [kəʊm] **I** *s* Kamm *m;* **II** *v* 1. kämmen; 2. *fig* durchkämmen, -suchen.

combat ['kɒmbæt] Kampf *m.*

combin|ation [ˌkɒmbɪ'neɪʃn] Zs.setzung, Kombination *f; in ~ with* in Verbindung mit; ~**e I** *v* [kəm'baɪn] verbinden, vereinigen, kombinieren; **II** *s* ['kɒmbaɪn] 1. Verband *m;* Kartell *n;* 2. (~ *harvester*) Mähdrescher *m.*

combust|ible [kəm'bʌstəbl] (ver)brennbar; ~**ion** [kəm'bʌstʃən] Verbrennung *f.*

come [kʌm] *irr* came [keɪm], *come* 1. (an-, her-, herbei)kommen; ~ *into sight* in Sicht kommen; ~ *what may!* komme, was (da) wolle! 2. sich belaufen (*to* auf); 3. (der Ordnung nach) kommen, folgen; 4. ~ *home to s.o.* jdm einleuchten, klarwerden; 5. ~ *to nothing* zunichte werden; sich zerschlagen; 6. ~ *true* wahr, Wirklichkeit werden; ~ **about** passieren; ~ **across** (zufällig) begegnen (*s.o.* jdm); ~ **along!** los! vorwärts! ~ **back** zurückkehren; ~ **by** erhalten, erwerben, kommen zu; ~ **down** herunterkommen; (*Preis, Temperatur*) fallen; ~ **forward** sich freiwillig melden; ~ **in** hereinkommen; Mode, modern werden; ~ **off** 1. (*Knopf*) abgehen; 2. stattfinden; 3. Erfolg haben; ~ **on!** los! vorwärts! ~ **out** 1. bekannt-, offenkundig werden; 2. (*Zeitung, Druckschrift*) erscheinen; ~ **round** (*e.r Auffassung*) sich anschließen (*to* an); 2. sich wieder erholen; ~ **through** durchkommen, überstehen; ~ **to** (wieder) zu sich kommen; ~ **up** zur Sprache kommen; *come up to (Erwartungen)* entsprechen *dat;* ~-**back** ['-bæk] Comeback.

comedy ['kɒmɪdɪ] Lustspiel *n,* Komödie *f.*

comet ['kɒmɪt] *astr* Komet *m.*

comfort ['kʌmfət] **I** *s* 1. Trost *m* (*to* für); 2. Bequemlichkeit *f;* **II** *v* trösten; ~**able** [-əbl] behaglich; *make yourself* ~ machen Sie es sich bequem; ~**er** [-ə] 1. Tröster *m;* 2. wollene(r) Schal *m.*

comic ['kɒmɪk] **I** *adj* komisch, spaßig; **II** *s* 1. *pl* Zeitschrift *f* mit Comic strips; 2. Komiker *m;* ~**al** [-əl] komisch; sonderbar.

comma ['kɒmə] Komma *n;*

inverted ~s *(pl)* Anführungszeichen *n pl.*

command [kə'mɑːnd] **I** *s* 1. Befehl *m;* 2. Oberbefehl *m;* 3. Herrschaft *f (of* über); **II** *v* 4. befehlen; 5. befehligen; 6. beherrschen; ~**er** [-ə] Befehlshaber *m;* ~*-in--chief* Oberbefehlshaber *m;* ~**ment** [-mənt] *the Ten C~s* die Zehn Gebote *pl.*

commemorate [kə'meməreɪt] gedenken *(s.o., s.th.* jds, e-r Sache); feiern.

commend [kə'mend] (an)empfehlen; ~**able** [-əbl] empfehlens-, lobenswert.

comment ['kɒment] **I** *s* Bemerkung *f (on, about* über); **II** *v* Bemerkungen machen *(on* über); ~**ary** ['kɒməntəri] Kommentar *m (on* zu); (Rundfunk-)Reportage *f;* ~**ator** [-eɪtə] (Rundfunk-)Kommentator *m.*

commerc|e ['kɒmɜːs] Handel *m;* ~**ial** [kə'mɜːʃl] geschäftlich, kaufmännisch; ~ *television* Werbefernsehen *n;* ~ *traveller (Br)* Handlungsreisende(r) *m;* ~**ialize** [kə'mɜːʃəlaɪz] kommerzialisieren, vermarkten.

commission [kə'mɪʃn] **I** *s* 1. Kommission *f,* Ausschuß *m;* 2. *com* Provision *f;* 3. *by* ~ im Auftrag; **II** *v* 4. beauftragen; 5. bevollmächtigen; ~**er** [-ə] 1. Bevollmächtigte(r) *m;* 2. Kommissar *m.*

commit [kə'mɪt] 1. übergeben; 2. *(Verbrechen)* begehen; 3. ~ *o.s.* sich festlegen, sich verpflichten *(to do* od *to doing s.th.* etw zu tun); ~**ment** [-mənt] Verpflichtung *f;* ~**tee** [-ɪ] Ausschuß *m,* Kommission *f; appoint,* *set up a* ~ e-n Ausschuß, e-e Kommission einsetzen; *standing* ~ ständige(r) Ausschuß *m; working* ~ Arbeitsausschuß *m;* ~ *meeting* Ausschußsitzung *f.*

commodious [kə'məʊdjəs] geräumig.

commodity [kə'mɒdəti] (Gebrauchs-)Artikel *m; bes.* *pl* Waren *f pl.*

common ['kɒmən] **I** *adj* 1. gemeinsam; 2. allgemein, alltäglich; 3. gewöhnlich, ordinär; **II** *s* 4. *have in* ~ gemein haben *(with* mit); 5. *the House of C~s* das (Britische) Unterhaus; ~ *law* Gewohnheitsrecht *n;* **C~ Market** Gemeinsame(r) Markt *m;* ~**place** [-pleɪs] **I** *s* Gemeinplatz *m;* **II** *adj* alltäglich; ~ *rights pl* Menschenrechte *n pl;* ~ *sense* gesunde(r) Menschenverstand *m.*

commotion [kə'məʊʃn] Aufregung *f;* Aufruhr *m.*

communic|ate [kə'mjuːnɪkeɪt] 1. mitteilen; 2. in Verbindung stehen *(with* mit); ~**ation** [kə,mjuːnɪ'keɪʃn] 1. Mitteilung *f;* 2. Verbindung *f;* 3. *pl*

Nachrichten-, Verkehrsmittel *n pl; ~ cord (rail)* Notbremse *f; ~ satellite* Nachrichtensatellit *m;* ~**ative** [kə'mju:nɪkətɪv] gesprächig.

communion [kə'mju:njən] 1. (Glaubens-)Gemeinschaft *f;* 2. *Holy C~* Abendmahl *n.*

commun|ism ['kɒmjʊnɪzəm] Kommunismus *m;* ~**ist** ['kɒmjʊnɪst] **I** *s* Kommunist *m;* **II** *adj* kommunistisch.

community [kə'mju:nətɪ] 1. Gemeinschaft *f;* 2. Gemeinde *f a. rel.*

commute [kə'mju:t] 1. *jur (Strafe)* umwandeln *(to* in); 2. pendeln; ~**r** [-ə] Pendler *m.*

compact I *s* ['kɒmpækt] 1. Vertrag *m;* 2. Puderdose *f;* **II** *adj* [kəm'pækt] dicht, fest, knapp, gedrängt.

companion [kəm'pænjən] Gefährte *m;* ~**ship** [-ʃɪp] Gesellschaft *f.*

company ['kʌmpənɪ] 1. Gesellschaft *f; keep s.o. ~* jdm Gesellschaft leisten; 2. (Handels-)Gesellschaft, Firma *f.*

comparable ['kɒmpərəbl] vergleichbar.

comparative [kəm'pærətɪv] 1. verhältnismäßig; 2. vergleichend.

compar|e [kəm'peə] 1. vergleichen (*with, to* mit); 2. sich vergleichen (lassen); ~**ison** [kəm'pærɪsn] Ver-

gleich *m; in, by ~ with* im Vergleich zu.

compartment [kəm'pɑ:tmənt] 1. Abteilung *f,* Fach, Feld *n;* 2. *rail* Abteil *n.*

compass ['kʌmpəs] 1. Bereich *m;* 2. Kompaß *m;* 3. *pl (pair of ~es)* Zirkel *m.*

compassion [kəm'pæʃn] Mitleid *n (for* mit); ~**ate** [kəm'pæʃənət] mitleidig.

compatible [kəm'pætəbl] vereinbar (*with* mit).

compatriot [kəm'pætrɪət] Landsmann *m.*

compel [kəm'pel] zwingen.

compensat|e ['kɒmpenseɪt] entschädigen; ~**ion** [ˌkɒmpen'seɪʃn] Entschädigung *f (for* für).

compete [kəm'pi:t] 1. teilnehmen (*in a contest* an e-m Wettbewerb); 2. konkurrieren, sich messen (*against, with s.o.* mit jdm).

competent ['kɒmpɪtənt] 1. qualifiziert; tüchtig; 2. angemessen, ausreichend; 3. zuständig.

competit|ion [ˌkɒmpɪ'tɪʃn] Wettbewerb *m;* ~**or** [kəm'petɪtə] Konkurrent *m.*

complain [kəm'pleɪn] sich beklagen (*to s.o.* bei jdm; *about, of* über); klagen (*of pains* wegen Schmerzen); ~**t** [-t] 1. Klage, Beschwerde *f;* 2. *med* Leiden *n.*

complet|e [kəm'pli:t] **I** *adj* vollständig; **II** *v* vervollständigen; beenden; ~**ion** [kəm'pli:ʃn] Vervollständigung *f;* Abschluß *m.*

complexion [kəm'plekʃn] (Haut-, Gesichts-)Farbe *f.*

compliance [kəm'plaɪəns] *in* ~ *with* in Übereinstimmung mit.

complicate ['kɒmplɪkeɪt] *that* ~*s matters* das macht die Sache noch schwieriger.

compliment ['kɒmplɪmənt] 1. *pay a* ~ *to s.o.* jdm ein Kompliment machen (*on s.th.* über etw); 2. *pl* (*in Briefen*) Grüße *m pl;* ~**ary** [ˌkɒmplɪ'mentərɪ] ~ *ticket* Freikarte *f.*

comply [kəm'plaɪ] nachkommen, entsprechen (*with s.o.'s wishes* jds Wünschen).

component [kəm'pəʊnənt] Bestandteil *m.*

compos|e [kəm'pəʊz] 1. bilden; *be* ~*d of* bestehen aus; 2. ab-, verfassen; komponieren; 3. ~ *o.s.* sich beruhigen, sich fassen; ~**ed** [-d] ruhig, gelassen; ~**er** [-ə] Komponist *m;* ~**ition** [ˌkɒmpə'zɪʃn] 1. *mus* Komposition *f;* 2. (Schul-)Aufsatz *m.*

compound I *s* ['kɒmpaʊnd] Zs.setzung, Verbindung *f;* II *adj* ['-] zs.gesetzt; III *v* [kəm'paʊnd] zs.setzen.

comprehend [ˌkɒmprɪ'hend] 1. verstehen, begreifen; 2. umfassen, einschließen.

comprehens|ible [ˌkɒmprɪ'hensəbl] verständ-

lich; ~**ion** [ˌkɒmprɪ'henʃn] Verständnis *n* (*of* für); ~**ive** [-sɪv] umfassend; ~ *school* Einheitsschule *f.*

compress I *v* [kəm'pres] zs.drücken, zs.pressen; II *s* ['kɒmpres] *med* Kompresse *f.*

comprise [kəm'praɪz] umfassen.

compromise ['kɒmprəmaɪz] I *s* Kompromiß *m;* II *v* e-n Kompromiß schließen.

compuls|ion [kəm'pʌlʃn] *under* ~ unter Zwang; ~**ory** [kəm'pʌlsərɪ] obligatorisch, zwingend.

compute [kəm'pju:t] (aus-, be-, er)rechnen; ~**r** [-ə] elektronische Rechenanlage *f.*

comrade ['kɒmreɪd] Kamerad *m.*

conceal [kən'si:l] 1. verstecken, verbergen; 2. verheimlichen, verhehlen.

concede [kən'si:d] einräumen (*that* daß); zugestehen.

conceit [kən'si:t] Einbildung *f;* ~**ed** [-ɪd] eingebildet.

conceiv|able [kən'si:vəbl] denkbar, vorstellbar; ~**e** [kən'si:v] 1. aus-, erdenken; 2. schwanger werden.

concentrat|e ['kɒnsəntreɪt] 1. zs.ziehen, konzentrieren; 2. sich konzentrieren (*upon, on* auf); ~**ion** [ˌkɒnsən'treɪʃn] Konzentration *f.*

concept ['kɒnsept] Begriff

m; ~**ion** [kən'sepʃn] 1. Vorstellung(svermögen *n*) *f;* 2. *physiol* Empfängnis *f;* ~ *control* Empfängnisverhütung *f.*

concern [kən'sɜːn] **I** *v* 1. betreffen; *as far as I am* ~*ed* was mich angeht; *to whom it may* ~ an die zuständige Stelle; *to be* ~*ed about* in Sorge sein um; **II** *s* 3. Sorge, Besorgnis *f;* 4. Angelegenheit, Sache *f; that is no* ~ *of yours* das geht Sie nichts an; 5. Geschäft *n;* ~**ing** [-ɪŋ] betreffend, in bezug auf.

concert ['kɒnsət] Konzert *n.*

concession [kən'seʃn] Konzession *f;* Zugeständnis *n.*

conciliate [kən'sɪlɪeɪt] versöhnen; ~**ion** [kən‚sɪlɪ'eɪʃn] ~ *board* Schlichtungsausschuß *m.*

concise [kən'saɪs] kurz, knapp, gedrängt.

conclude [kən'kluːd] 1. (be-, ab)schließen; 2. folgern (*that* daß; *from* aus).

conclus|ion [kən'kluːʒn] 1. *in* ~ zum Schluß; 2. Schluß(folgerung *f*) *m;* ~**ive** [kən'kluːsɪv] entscheidend.

concrete ['kɒnkriːt] **I** *adj* konkret; **II** *s* Beton *m.*

concur [kən'kɜː] 1. zs.kommen, -treffen; 2. übereinstimmen (*with* mit).

concussion [kən'kʌʃn] Gehirnerschütterung *f.*

condemn [kən'dem] 1. verurteilen.

condense [kən'dens] verdichten, eindicken; ~*d milk* Büchsenmilch *f.*

condescend [‚kɒndɪ'send] sich herablassen, geruhen (*to do* zu tun).

condition [kən'dɪʃn] 1. Bedingung *f* (*of* für); *on* ~ (*that*) unter der Voraussetzung *od* Bedingung (daß); *on no* ~ unter keinen Umständen; 2. Zustand *m; in good* ~ in gutem Zustand; *be in no* ~ nicht in der Lage sein (*to* zu).

conduct I *v* [kən'dʌkt] 1. führen; 2. *el* leiten; 3. ~ *o.s.* sich benehmen; **II** *s* ['kɒndʌkt] Betragen, Benehmen *n;* ~**or** [kən'dʌktə] 1. *mus* Dirigent *m;* 2. Schaffner *m;* 3. *el* Leiter *m.*

cone [kəʊn] 1. Kegel *m;* 2. (*ice cream* ~) Eistüte *f;* 3. (*pine* ~) Tannenzapfen *m.*

confectioner [kən'fekʃnə] Konditor *m;* ~**y** [-rɪ] 1. Süßwaren *f pl;* 2. Konditorei *f.*

conference ['kɒnfərəns] Tagung *f; hold a* ~ e-e Konferenz abhalten.

confess [kən'fes] 1. ein Geständnis ablegen; 2. *rel* beichten; ~**ion** [kən'feʃn] 1. Bekenntnis *n;* 2. Geständnis *n;* 3. *rel* Beichte *f.*

confide [kən'faɪd] 1. anvertrauen (*s.th. to s.o.* jdm etw); 2. vertrauen (*in s.o.* jdm).

confiden|ce ['kɒnfɪdəns] Vertrauen *n* (*in* zu); ~**t**

['kɒnfɪdənt] sicher, überzeugt; **~tial** [ˌkɒnfɪ'denʃl] vertraulich.

confirm [kən'fɜːm] 1. bestätigen; 2. *rel* konfirmieren; **~ation** [ˌkɒnfə'meɪʃn] 1. Bestätigung *f*; 2. *rel* Konfirmation *f*.

confiscate ['kɒnfɪskeɪt] beschlagnahmen.

conflict ['kɒnflɪkt] I *s* Streit, Konflikt *m*; II *v* im Widerspruch stehen (*with* zu).

confus|e [kən'fjuːz] 1. verwechseln (*with* mit); 2. verwirren; **~ion** [kən'fjuːʒn] Verwirrung *f*, Durcheinander *n*.

congestion [kən'dʒestʃən] *traffic* ~ Verkehrsstauung *f*.

congratulat|e [kən'grætjʊleɪt] beglückwünschen, gratulieren (*s.o.* jdm; *on* zu); **~ion** [kənˌgrætjʊ'leɪʃn] *meist pl* Glückwunsch *m*.

congregat|e ['kɒŋgrɪgeɪt] sich versammeln; **~ion** [ˌkɒŋgrɪ'geɪʃn] *rel* Gemeinde *f*.

congress ['kɒŋgres] Kongreß *m*.

conjecture [kən'dʒektʃə] I *s* Vermutung *f*; II *v* vermuten.

conjur|er, ~or ['kʌndʒərə] Zauberkünstler *m*.

conker ['kɒŋkə] Roßkastanie *f*.

connect [kə'nekt] 1. verbinden (*with* mit) *a. fig tele*; 2. (*Zug*) Anschluß haben

(*with* an); **~ion,** *Br a.* **connexion** [kə'nekʃn] 1. Verbindung *f a. tele*; 2. 1. Anschluß *m a. tele rail*; 3. Zusammenhang *m*; *in this* ~ in diesem Zs.hang; *in* ~ *with* im Zs.hang mit, in bezug auf.

connotation [ˌkɒnəʊ'teɪʃn] weitere Bedeutung *f*.

conquer ['kɒŋkə] erobern, überwinden *a. fig*.

conquest ['kɒŋkwest] Eroberung *f*.

conscience ['kɒnʃəns] Gewissen *n*; *have on one's* ~ auf dem Gewissen haben.

conscientious [ˌkɒnʃɪ'enʃəs] gewissenhaft; ~ **objector** Wehrdienstverweigerer *m*.

conscious ['kɒnʃəs] 1. bewußt; *be* ~ *of s.th.* sich über etw im klaren sein; 2. bei (vollem) Bewußtsein; **~ness** [-nɪs] Bewußtsein *n*.

consecutive [kən'sekjʊtɪv] aufea.folgend.

consent [kən'sent] I *v* einwilligen (*to* in); II *s* Einwilligung *f* (*to* in); *by mutual* ~ in gegenseitigem Einvernehmen *n*.

consequen|ce ['kɒnsɪkwəns] Folge *f*; *in* ~ *of* infolge *gen*; *of no* ~ belanglos; **~tly** ['kɒnsɪkwəntlɪ] folglich.

conservative [kən'sɜːvətɪv] konservativ *a. pol*.

consider [kən'sɪdə] 1. erwägen, bedenken; 2. berücksichtigen; *all things* ~*ed* wenn man alles in Betracht zieht; 3. betrachten als, halten für; ~**able** [-rəbl] beträchtlich, erheblich; ~**ate** [-rət] rücksichtsvoll; ~**ation** [kən‚sɪdə'reɪʃn] 1. Überlegung f, Erwägung f; take into ~ berücksichtigen; 2. Rücksicht f; in ~ of in Anbetracht gen, mit Rücksicht auf.

consign [kən'saɪn] 1. (ver)senden; 2. liefern; ~**ment** [-mənt] 1. Versand m; 2. Lieferung f.

consist [kən'sɪst] bestehen (of aus); ~**ent** [-ənt] 1. in Übereinstimmung f (with mit); 2. konsequent, folgerichtig.

consolation [‚kɒnsə'leɪʃn] Trost m; ~ prize Trostpreis m; ~**e** [kən'səʊl] trösten (for über).

consolidate [kən'sɒlɪdeɪt] (sich) festigen.

conspicuous [kən'spɪkjʊəs] deutlich sichtbar; auffallend (by, for durch, wegen).

conspiracy [kən'spɪrəsɪ] Verschwörung f.

constable ['kʌnstəbl] Polizist m.

constant ['kɒnstənt] beständig; fortwährend, dauernd.

constellation [‚kɒnstə'leɪʃn] astr Sternbild n.

consternation [‚kɒnstə'neɪʃn] Entsetzen n, Bestürzung f.

constipation [‚kɒnstɪ'peɪʃn] med Verstopfung f.

constituent [kən'stɪtjʊənt] Bestandteil m; ~ **part** Hauptbestandteil m.

constitute ['kɒnstɪtjuːt] 1. (Person) einsetzen, ernennen; 2. bilden, ausmachen.

constitution [‚kɒnstɪ'tjuːʃn] 1. (Mensch) Konstitution f; 2. jur Verfassung f.

construct [kən'strʌkt] bauen, errichten; ~**ion** [kən'strʌkʃn] Bau m, Konstruktion f; under ~ im Bau.

consulate ['kɒnsjʊlət] Konsulat n.

consult [kən'sʌlt] zu Rate ziehen; (Buch) nachschlagen; ~**ant** [kən'sʌltənt] Berater m; ~**ation** [‚kɒnsəl'teɪʃn] med Konsultation f; ~ hours Sprechstunden f pl; ~**ing** [-ɪŋ] beratend; ~ room (med) Sprechzimmer n.

consume [kən'sjuːm] verzehren, ver-, aufbrauchen; ~**r** [-ə] Verbraucher m.

consumption [kən'sʌmpʃn] Verbrauch m.

contact ['kɒntækt] I s Berührung f; Kontakt m; be in ~ with in Verbindung stehen mit; II v in Verbindung treten mit.

contagious [kən'teɪdʒəs] med ansteckend.

contain [kən'teɪn] 1. enthalten; 2. (Gefühl) zügeln; ~**er** [-ə] Behälter m.

contaminate
[kən'tæmıneıt] verunreinigen; verseuchen.

contemplate ['kontempleıt]
1. betrachten; 2. beabsichtigen.

contemporary
[kən'tempərərı] I *adj* zeitgenössisch, modern; II *s*
1. Altersgenosse *m;* 2. Zeitgenosse *m.*

contempt [kən'tempt] Verachtung, Geringschätzung *f;*
~**uous** [-juəs] verächtlich, geringschätzig.

content [kən'tent] I *adj* zufrieden (*with* mit); II *s* 1. *to o.'s heart's* ~ nach Herzenslust; 2. *pl* Inhalt *m a. fig.*

contest I *v* [kən'test] 1. bestreiten; anfechten; 2. konkurrieren, kämpfen um; II *s* ['kontest] Wettkampf *m.*

context ['kontekst] (Satz-, Sinn-)Zs.hang *m.*

continent ['kontınənt] Festland *n;* ~**al** [,kontı'nentl] kontinental.

continu|al [kən'tınjuəl] fortwährend, unaufhörlich;
~**ation** [kən,tınju'eıʃn] Fortsetzung *f;* ~**e** [kən'tınju:]
1. fortsetzen; *to be* ~d Fortsetzung folgt; 2. fortdauern; (*Hitze*) anhalten; ~**ous**
[kən'tınjuəs] ständig, dauernd, ununterbrochen.

contour [kon,tuə] Umriß(linie *f*) *m,* Kontur *f.*

contraception
[,kontrə'sepʃn] Empfängnis-

verhütung *f;* ~**ive** [-'septıv]
empfängnisverhütend(es
Mittel *n*).

contract I *v* [kən'trækt]
1. zs.ziehen; 2. (*Krankheit*) sich zuziehen; 3. (*Ehe*) eingehen; (*Verpflichtung*) übernehmen; II *s*
['kontrækt] Vertrag *m; by* ~ vertraglich; *make a* ~ einen Vertrag abschließen; ~**or**
[-ə] Unternehmer *m.*

contradict [,kontrə'dıkt] widersprechen (*s.o.* jdm); ~**ion**
[,kontrə'dıkʃn] Widerspruch *m;* ~**ory** [-ərı] (sich) widersprechend.

contrary ['kontrərı] I *adj*
entgegen(gesetzt); unvereinbar (*to* mit); II *s* Gegenteil *n* (*to* von); *on the* ~ im Gegenteil; *to the* ~ gegenteilig.

contrast I *v* [kən'tra:st]
1. gegenüberstellen (*with* dat); 2. sich abheben (*with* von); II *s* ['kontra:st] Gegensatz (*to* zu); Kontrast *m.*

contribut|e [kən'trıbju:t] beitragen, -steuern; ~**ion**
[,kontrı'bju:ʃn] Beitrag *m.*

contrive [kən'traıv] 1. ersinnen; 2. fertigbringen; 3. haushalten, auskommen.

control [kən'trəul] I *v* 1. beherrschen; 2. lenken, dirigieren; 3. überwachen, kontrollieren; II *s* 4. Herrschaft, Macht *f* (*of* über); *he lost* ~ *of the car* er hat die Herrschaft über den Wagen verloren); 5. Leitung *f (of, over* über); 6. Überwachung, Kontrolle *f;* ~**ler** [-ə] 1. Leiter, Aufseher; Kontrolleur *m;* 2. Rechnungsprüfer *m.*

controvers|ial [ˌkɒntrə'vɜːʃl] strittig; ~**y** ['kɒntrəvɜːsɪ] 1. Streitfrage *f;* 2. (Meinungs-)Streit *m.*

convalescen|ce [ˌkɒnvə'lesns] Genesung *f;* ~**t** [-nt] **I** *adj* genesend; ~ *home* Erholungsheim *n;* **II** *s* Genesende(r) *m.*

convene [kən'viːn] 1. sich versammeln; 2. *(e-e Versammlung)* einberufen.

convenien|ce [kən'viːnjəns] 1. Bequemlichkeit *f;* Komfort *m; at your earliest* ~ sobald es Ihnen möglich ist *od* paßt; 2. *(public* ~*)* Bedürfnisanstalt *f;* ~**t** [kən'viːnjənt] passend, bequem; praktisch.

convent ['kɒnvənt] (Nonnen-)Kloster *n.*

convention [kən'venʃn] 1. Versammlung *f,* Kongreß *m;* 2. Abkommen *n;* ~**al** [kən'venʃənl] konventionell, üblich.

convers|ation [ˌkɒnvə'seɪʃn] Gespräch *n,* Unterhaltung *f;* ~**ational** [ˌkɒnvə'seɪʃənl] Gesprächs-, Unterhaltungs-; ~**e** ['kɒnvɜːs] sich unterhalten *(with s.o. on, about s.th.* mit jdm über etw); ~**ion** [kən'vɜːʃn] 1. Umwandlung *f*

(from, into von, in); 2. *rel* Bekehrung *f.*

convert I *v* [kən'vɜːt] 1. ver-, umwandeln *(into* in); 2. bekehren *(to* zu); **II** *s* ['kɒnvɜːt] *rel* Konvertit *m,* Bekehrte(r) *m;* ~**ible** [kən'vɜːtəbl] **I** *adj (Geld)* konvertierbar, einlösbar; **II** *s mot* Kabriolett *n.*

convey [kən'veɪ] 1. befördern, transportieren; 2. mitteilen; *(Nachricht)* übermitteln; ~**ance** [kən'veɪəns] 1. Beförderung *f,* Transport *m;* 2. Übermittlung *f,* Mitteilung *f;* 3. Beförderungsmittel *n;* ~**er,** ~**or** [-ə] 1. Spediteur *m;* 2. (~*-belt)* Förderband *n.*

convict I *s* ['kɒnvɪkt] Sträfling *m;* **II** *v* [kən'vɪkt] schuldig befinden *(of a crime* e-s Verbrechens); ~**ion** [kən'vɪkʃn] 1. *jur* Verurteilung *f;* 2. Überzeugung *f.*

convince [kən'vɪns] überzeugen *(of* von).

convoke [kən'vəʊk] *(Versammlung)* einberufen.

convoy ['kɒnvɔɪ] **I** *v* geleiten; **II** *s* Geleit *n,* Konvoi *m.*

convuls|e [kən'vʌls] erschüttern; *be* ~*d with laughter* sich vor Lachen krümmen; ~**ions** *pl* [kən'vʌlʃnz] Krämpfe *m pl;* (Nerven-)Zuckungen *f pl.*

cook [kʊk] **I** *v* kochen; **II** *s* Koch *m,* Köchin *f;* ~**book** ['-bʊk] *Am* Kochbuch *n;*

~ery ['kʊkərɪ] Kochen n; **~-book** (Br) Kochbuch n; **~ie, ~y** ['kʊkɪ] Keks m.

cool [ku:l] **I** adj kühl; keep ~ Ruhe bewahren; **II** v abkühlen (lassen); ~ down (fig) (sich) beruhigen; **~ness** [-nɪs] Kühle f.

co-op, coop ['kəʊɒp] fam Konsum(verein) m.

co-operat|e [kəʊ'ɒpəreɪt] zs.arbeiten (with mit); **~ion** [kəʊˌɒpə'reɪʃn] Mitwirkung f; in ~ with in Zs.arbeit mit; **~ive** [kəʊ'ɒpərətɪv] **I** adj zs.arbeitend; **II** s (~ association, society) Genossenschaft f; **~or** [-ə] Mitarbeiter m.

cop [kɒp] sl Polizist m.

cope [kəʊp] es aufnehmen, fertigwerden (with mit).

copious ['kəʊpjəs] reich(lich).

copper ['kɒpə] Kupfer n.

copy ['kɒpɪ] **I** s 1. Kopie, Abschrift f, Durchschlag m; 2. (Buch) Exemplar n; (Zeitung) Nummer f; **II** v kopieren, abschreiben; **~right** [-raɪt] Urheberrecht n.

cord [kɔ:d] 1. Bindfäden m, Schnur f; 2. el Kabel n; 3. anat Band n; Strang m.

cordial ['kɔ:djəl] **I** adj herzlich; **II** s Magenlikör m; **~ity** [ˌkɔ:dɪ'ælətɪ] Herzlichkeit f.

corduroy ['kɔ:dərɔɪ] 1. Kord m; 2. pl Kordhose f.

core [kɔ:] 1. (Apfel) Kernge-

häuse, -haus n; 2. fig Kern(stück n) m.

cork [kɔ:k] **I** s Kork(en) m; **II** v (~ up) ver-, zukorken; **~-screw** ['-skru:] Kork(en)zieher m.

corn [kɔ:n] 1. Korn, Getreide n; Am Mais m; 2. Hühnerauge n.

corner ['kɔ:nə] **I** s Ecke f, Winkel m; **II** v in die Enge treiben a. fig; **~stone** [-stəʊn] Grundstein m.

cornet ['kɔ:nɪt] 1. mus Kornett n; 2. Eistüte f.

coronation [ˌkɒrə'neɪʃn] Krönung f.

coroner ['kɒrənə] (amtlicher) Leichenbeschauer m.

corporal ['kɔ:pərəl] **I** adj körperlich; **II** s Unteroffizier m.

corporation [ˌkɔ:pə'reɪʃn] Körperschaft f; Am Aktiengesellschaft f.

corpse [kɔ:ps] Leiche f.

corpulent ['kɔ:pjʊlənt] beleibt.

correct [kə'rekt] **I** adj richtig, korrekt, genau; **II** v 1. verbessern, korrigieren, richtigstellen; 2. zurechtweisen; **~ion** [kə'rekʃn] Verbesserung, Korrektur f.

correspond [ˌkɒrɪ'spɒnd] 1. entsprechen (to dat); 2. korrespondieren (with mit); **~ence** [-əns] 1. Übereinstimmung f; 2. Briefwechsel m; **~ent** [-ənt] Korrespondent, Berichterstatter *m;* **~ing** [-ɪŋ] entsprechend (*to* dat).

corridor ['kɒrɪdɔ:] Gang, Korridor *m.*

corrode [kə'rəʊd] 1. zerfressen; 2. rosten.

corrupt [kə'rʌpt] **I** *adj* 1. verdorben, verkommen; 2. bestechlich; **II** *v* 3. verderben; 4. bestechen; **~ion** [kə'rʌpʃn] 1. Verdorbenheit *f;* 2. Bestechlichkeit, Käuflichkeit *f.*

cost [kɒst] **I** *v irr* cost, cost kosten; **II** *s* 1. Preis *m; at all* ~*s* um jeden Preis; ~ *of living* Lebenshaltungskosten *pl;* 2. *pl* Spesen *pl;* **~ly** [-lɪ] kostspielig, teuer.

costermonger ['kɒstə‚mʌŋgə] *Br (Gemüse, Früchte)* Straßenverkäufer *m.*

costume ['kɒstju:m] Kostüm *n.*

cosy ['kəʊzɪ] **I** *adj* gemütlich, behaglich; **II** *s* Tee-, Kaffeewärmer *m.*

cot [kɒt] Kinderbett *n.*

cottage ['kɒtɪdʒ] kleine(s) Landhaus *n.*

cotton ['kɒtn] 1. Baumwolle *f;* 2. Nähfaden *m;* **~-wool** [-'wʊl] Watte *f.*

cough [kɒf] **I** *v* husten; **II** *s* Husten *m;* **~-drop** ['-drɒp] Hustenbonbon *n.*

council ['kaʊnsl] Rat(sversammlung *f*) *m; works* ~ Betriebsrat *m.*

counsel ['kaʊnsl] **I** *s*

1. (Rechts-)Anwalt *m;* 2. Rat(schlag) *m;* **II** *v* raten, empfehlen; **~(l)or** [-ə] Berater, Ratgeber *m.*

count [kaʊnt] **I** *v* 1. zählen; ~ *out* nicht rechnen ein; *(Boxen)* auszählen; ~ *me in* ich mache mit; 2. ~ *on* rechnen mit; sich verlassen auf; 3. *you can* ~ *yourself lucky* Sie können sich glücklich schätzen; **II** *s* 4. (Zs.-)Zählung, (Be-)Rechnung *f;* 5. *take no* ~ *of s.th.* etw nicht berücksichtigen; **~-down** ['-daʊn] Countdown *m.*

countenance ['kaʊntənəns] *put out of* ~ aus der Fassung bringen.

counter ['kaʊntə] Laden-, Zahltisch *m;* Theke *f;* (Bank-)Schalter *m.*

counterfeit ['kaʊntəfɪt] nachgemacht, unecht, falsch; ~ *money* Falschgeld *n.*

counterfoil ['kaʊntəfɔɪl] (Kontroll-)Abschnitt *m.*

counterpane ['kaʊntəpeɪn] Steppdecke *f.*

counterpart ['kaʊntəpɑ:t] Gegenstück (*of* zu); Duplikat *n.*

countless ['kaʊntlɪs] zahllos, unzählig.

country ['kʌntrɪ] 1. Land *n;* 2. *(native* ~*)* Heimat *f;* 3. Gegend *f;* 4. *live in the* ~ auf dem Lande leben; **~man** [-mən] 1. Bauer *m;* 2. Landsmann *m.*

county ['kaʊntɪ] Grafschaft f; Am (Verwaltungs-)Bezirk m.

couple ['kʌpl] Paar n; (married ~) Ehepaar n; a ~ of zwei, ein paar.

coupling ['kʌplɪŋ] tech (starre) Kupp(e)lung f.

courage ['kʌrɪdʒ] Mut m; lose ~ den Mut verlieren; take ~ sich ein Herz fassen; ~ous [kə'reɪdʒəs] mutig.

course [kɔːs] 1. Kurs(us), Lehrgang m; 2. Rennbahn f; Sportplatz m; 3. (Fluß) Verlauf m; 4. (Speisen) Gang m; 5. of ~ natürlich, selbstverständlich; 6. in ~ of construction im Bau (befindlich); in the ~ of time im Laufe der Zeit.

court [kɔːt] I s 1. Hof m; 2. (Tennis-)Platz m, Spielfeld n; 3. Gericht(shof m) n; II v den Hof machen (s.o. jdm); ~eous ['kɜːtjəs] höflich; ~esy ['kɜːtɪsɪ] Höflichkeit f; ~yard ['-jɑːd] Hof m.

cousin ['kʌzn] Cousin(e f) m.

cover ['kʌvə] I v 1. be-, zudecken; überziehen (with mit); 2. (finanziell) decken; 3. (Strecke) zurücklegen; 4. umfassen, einschließen; 5. (Gebiet) bearbeiten; II s 6. Decke f; 7. Deckel; Umschlag m; from ~ to ~ (Buch) von Anfang bis zu Ende (lesen); 8. Deckung f a. fin; 9. (fig) under ~ of im Schutz gen, unter dem Deckmantel, Vorwand gen; 10. Gedeck n; ~ing [-rɪŋ] I s Decke f, Überzug m; II adj: ~ letter Begleitbrief m; ~let [-lɪt] Bettdecke f.

covet ['kʌvɪt] begehren; ~ous [-əs] begierig (of nach).

cow [kaʊ] Kuh f.

coward ['kaʊəd] Feigling m; ~ice [-ɪs] Feigheit f; ~ly [-lɪ] feige.

cowslip ['kaʊslɪp] Schlüsselblume; Am Sumpfdotterblume f.

coy [kɔɪ] scheu, schüchtern.

crab [kræb] Krabbe f.

crack [kræk] I v 1. (Glas) springen; bersten; 2. knakken, krachen; 3. (auf)knakken; 4. ~ down (fam) scharf anfassen (on s.o. jdn); vorgehen (on gegen); II s 5. Sprung, Riß m; 6. Knall, Krach m; ~ of thunder Donnerschlag m; 7. Schlag m; 8. have a ~ at s.th. (sl) etw versuchen; ~er ['-ə] 1. Knallbonbon m od n; 2. (ungesüßter) Keks m; ~le ['-l] knistern, prasseln, knattern.

cradle ['kreɪdl] Wiege f.

craft [krɑːft] 1. Geschick(lichkeit f) n; (Hand-)Fertigkeit f; 2. Handwerk, Gewerbe n; 3. List f; 4. Schiff, Fahrzeug n; ~sman ['-smən] Handwerker m; ~y ['-ɪ] schlau.

crag [kræg] Felsspitze, Klippe f.

cram [kræm] 1. hineinstopfen, (voll)stopfen; 2. *(Schule)* büffeln; **~-full** [ˌ-ˈfʊl] vollgepropft, übervoll.

cramp [kræmp] **I** s 1. (Muskel-)Krampf m; 2. (Eisen-)Klammer f; **II** v fig hindern, einengen.

cranberry ['krænbərɪ] Preiselbeere f.

crane [kreɪn] **I** s 1. Kranich m; 2. tech Kran m; **II** v (den Hals) recken *(for* nach).

crank [kræŋk] 1. Kurbel f; 2. komische(r) Kauz m; **~shaft** ['-ʃɑːft] Kurbelwelle f; **~y** ['-ɪ] verschroben.

crash [kræʃ] **I** v 1. mot zs.-stoßen; *~ into* krachen gegen; *(Flugzeug)* abstürzen; 2. zerbrechen; 3. rasen, brechen *(through* durch); 4. zerschmettern; **II** s 5. Krach m; 6. (Ein-)Sturz; Aufprall; Zs.stoß; aero Absturz m; **~-helmet** ['-ˌhelmɪt] mot Sturzhelm m; **~-landing** ['-lændɪŋ] aero Bruchlandung f.

crate [kreɪt] Lattenkiste f.

crater ['kreɪtə] geol Krater m.

crave [kreɪv] sehnlichst wünschen, sich sehnen *(for* nach).

crawl [krɔːl] 1. kriechen, krabbeln; 2. be *~ing with*

wimmeln von; 3. sport kraulen.

crayfish ['kreɪfɪʃ] Krebs m.

crayon ['kreɪən] Farb-, Zeichenstift m.

crazy ['kreɪzɪ] 1. wahnsinnig; 2. fam versessen *(about* auf).

creak [kriːk] knarren, quietschen.

cream [kriːm] **I** s 1. Sahne f, Rahm m; 2. Creme(speise) f; *chocolate ~* Schokoladencreme f; *~ cheese* Schmelzkäse m; 3. (Haut-)Creme f; 4. *(the ~)* das Beste; **II** v 5. absahnen; 6. Sahne zugießen; **III** adj cremefarben; **~ery** ['-ərɪ] Molkerei f; Milchgeschäft n; **~y** ['-ɪ] sahnig.

crease [kriːs] **I** s (Bügel-)Falte f; **II** v falten, knittern.

creat|e [kriːˈeɪt] 1. (er)schaffen; 2. verursachen; **~ion** [kriːˈeɪʃn] Schöpfung f; **~ive** [kriːˈeɪtɪv] schöpferisch; **~or** [kriːˈeɪtə] (Mode-)Schöpfer m.

creature ['kriːtʃə] Geschöpf n, Kreatur f.

credentials pl [krɪˈdenʃlz] 1. Empfehlungs-, Beglaubigungsschreiben n; 2. Zeugnisse n pl.

credible ['kredəbl] glaubwürdig, -haft.

credit ['kredɪt] **I** s 1. Glaube(n) m, Vertrauen n; 2. (guter) Ruf m; 3. Kredit(würdigkeit f) m; 4. Guthaben n;

II v 5. com gutschreiben;
6. zutrauen (s.o. with s.th.
jdm etw); ~**able** [-əbl]
rühmlich, ehrenvoll (to für);
~ **card** Kreditkarte f; ~**or**
[-ə] Gläubiger m.

credulous ['kredjʊləs]
leichtgläubig.

creed [kri:d] (Glaubens-)Be-
kenntnis n.

creep [kri:p] irr crept, crept
[krept] 1. kriechen, krabbeln, schleichen; 2. it made
my flesh ~, (fam) it gave
me the ~s es überlief mich
(eis)kalt; ~**er** [-ə] Schling-,
Kletterpflanze f.

cremat|e [krɪ'meɪt] (Leiche)
einäschern; ~**orium**
[,kremə'tɔ:rɪəm] , ~**ory**
['kremətərɪ] Krematorium
n.

crescent ['kresnt] Mond-
sichel f.

cress [kres] bot Kresse f.

crest [krest] 1. (Hühner)
Kamm m; 2. Bergkamm,
-rücken m; 3. Wellenkamm
m; ~**fallen** ['-,fɔ:lən] niedergeschlagen.

crevice ['krevɪs] Spalt m,
Ritze f, Riß m.

crew [kru:] 1. Besatzung f;
2. Mannschaft f.

crib [krɪb] **I** s 1. Krippe f;
2. Kinderbett n; **II** v
(Schule) abschreiben.

cricket ['krɪkɪt] 1. zoo Grille
f; 2. sport Kricket n.

crime [kraɪm] Verbrechen n.

criminal ['krɪmɪnl] **I** adj ver-
brecherisch; **II** s Verbrecher
m; ~ law Strafrecht n.

crimson ['krɪmzn]
karm(es)inrot.

cringe [krɪndʒ] sich (ängstlich) ducken (to vor); kriechen.

crinkle ['krɪŋkl] (zer)knittern.

cripple ['krɪpl] **I** s Krüppel m;
II v 1. verkrüppeln; 2. lähmen, schwächen.

crisis ['kraɪsɪs] pl crises
[-si:z] Krise f.

crisp [krɪsp] **I** adj 1. knus-
perig; 2. (Luft) frisch;
3. (Haar) kraus; 4. (Rede)
klar, knapp; **II** s pl Br Kartoffelchips pl.

critic ['krɪtɪk] Kritiker m; ~**al**
[-l] kritisch; ~**ism**
['krɪtɪsɪzəm] 1. Kritik f (of
an, über); 2. Rezension f;
~**ize** ['krɪtɪsaɪz] kritisieren,
tadeln.

croak [krəʊk] (Frosch) quaken; (Rabe) krächzen.

crochet ['krəʊʃeɪ] häkeln.

crockery ['krɒkərɪ] Geschirr
n.

crocodile ['krɒkədaɪl] zoo
Krokodil n.

crook [krʊk] 1. Haken m;
2. fam Schwindler, Gauner
m; ~**ed** ['-ɪd] 1. krumm;
2. fig unehrlich.

crop [krɒp] **I** s 1. Ernte f;
2. Haufen m, Menge f;
3. Kropf m; **II** v 4. ab-, kahl-
fressen; 5. ~ up auftauchen.

cross [krɒs] **I** s 1. Kreuz n;

2. *biol* Kreuzung *f*; **II** *v*
3. durch-, überqueren, überschreiten; ~ *s.o.'s path* jdm begegnen; 4. (~ *off*, ~ *out*) (durch)streichen; 5. *I'll keep my fingers* ~*ed* ich halte den Daumen; 6. *biol* kreuzen; **III** *adj fam* böse (*with* mit, auf); ~-**examination** ['-ɪɡˌzæmɪ'neɪʃn] Kreuzverhör *n*; ~**ing** ['-ɪŋ] 1. Kreuzung *f*; 2. *mar* Überfahrt *f*; 3. (*Fußgänger*) Überweg *m*; ~**roads** ['-rəʊdz] *sing* Wege-, Straßenkreuzung *f*; *at the* ~ (*fig*) am Scheideweg *m*; ~-**section** [ˌ-'sekʃn] Durch-, Querschnitt *m*; ~**word** ['-wɜːd] (~ *puzzle*) Kreuzworträtsel *n*.

crouch [kraʊtʃ] sich ducken.
crow [krəʊ] **I** *s* Krähe *f*; *as the* ~ *flies* (in) gerade(r Linie); **II** *v* krächzen, krähen; ~**bar** ['-bɑː] Brecheisen *n*.
crowd [kraʊd] **I** *s* (Menschen-)Menge *f*, Gedränge *n*; **II** *v* zs.strömen; (sich) drängen (*round* um; *into* in); *be* ~*ed with* wimmeln von; ~**ed** ['-ɪd] überfüllt.
crown [kraʊn] **I** *s* Krone *f*; **II** *v* krönen.
crucial ['kruːʃl] entscheidend, kritisch.
crucify ['kruːsɪfaɪ] kreuzigen.
crude [kruːd] roh, unbearbeitet.
cruel ['kruːəl] grausam; ~**ty** ['kruːəltɪ] Grausamkeit *f*.
cruise [kruːz] **I** *v mar aero*

kreuzen; **II** *s* Kreuzfahrt *f*; ~**r** ['-ə] *mar* Kreuzer *m*.
crumb [krʌm] Krume *f*; ~**le** ['-bl] zerbröckeln, zerfallen.
crumple ['krʌmpl] zerknittern.
crunch [krʌntʃ] 1. zerbeißen; 2. (*Schnee*) knirschen.
crusade [kruː'seɪd] *hist* Kreuzzug *m*.
crush [krʌʃ] **I** *v* 1. (zer-, zs.-)drücken; ~ *out* (*Frucht*) auspressen; ~ *up* zermahlen, zerstampfen; 2. zerknittern; 3. *fig* vernichten; 4. sich drängen (*into* in, *through* durch); **II** *s* Gedränge *n*.
crust [krʌst] (Brot-)Kruste, Rinde *f*; ~**y** ['krʌstɪ] 1. verkrustet; 2. *fig* mürrisch.
crutch [krʌtʃ] Krücke *f*; *go on* ~*es* an Krücken gehen.
cry [kraɪ] **I** *v* 1. schreien (*for help* um Hilfe); 2. weinen; ~ *o.'s heart out* bitterlich weinen; 3. (aus)rufen, ankündigen; 4. ~ *down* schlechtmachen; ~ *up* überschwenglich loben; **II** *s* 5. Schrei, Ruf *m*; 6. *have a good* ~ sich ausweinen; ~**ing** ['-ɪŋ] (him-mel)schreiend; dringend.
crypt [krɪpt] Gruft *f*.
crystal ['krɪstl] Kristall *m*; ~**lize** ['krɪstəlaɪz] Kristalle bilden.
cub [kʌb] Junge(s) *n* (*e-s Raubtieres*).
Cuba ['kjuːbə] Kuba *n*.
cube [kjuːb] Würfel *m*.
cubicle ['kjuːbɪkl] Kabine *f*.

cuckoo ['kuku:] Kuckuck *m*.

cucumber ['kju:kʌmbə] Gurke *f*.

cuddle ['kʌdl] (~ *up*) sich zs.kuscheln.

cudgel ['kʌdʒəl] I *s* Keule *f*; Knüppel *m*; II *v*: ~ *o.'s brains* sich den Kopf zerbrechen (*about* über).

cue [kju:] 1. *theat* Stichwort *n*; *take o.'s* ~ *from s.o.* sich nach jdm richten; 2. (Billard-)Queue *n*.

cuff [kʌf] Manschette *f*; Ärmel-, *Am* Hosenaufschlag *m*; ~-link Manschettenknopf *m*.

culminate ['kʌlmɪneɪt] gipfeln (*in* in).

culprit ['kʌlprɪt] Missetäter, Übeltäter *m*.

cultivate ['kʌltɪveɪt] 1. an-, bebauen; 2. *fig* kultivieren, pflegen; ~**ion** [ˌkʌltɪ'veɪʃn] *agr* Anbau *m*.

cultural ['kʌltʃərəl] kulturell; ~**e** ['kʌltʃə] 1. *agr* Anbau *m*; 2. Bildung, Kultur *f*.

cumbersome ['kʌmbəsəm] lästig, beschwerlich.

cunning ['kʌnɪŋ] schlau, listig.

cup [kʌp] 1. Tasse *f*; *a* ~ *of ... e-e* Tasse ...; 2. *sport* Pokal *m*; ~**board** ['kʌbəd] Schrank *m*.

curable ['kjuərəbl] heilbar.

curate ['kjuərət] Vikar *m*.

curb [kɜ:b] I *s* 1. (*Pferd*) Zaum(zeug *n*) *m*; 2. *fig* Zügel *m pl*; II *v fig* zügeln.

curdle ['kɜ:dl] 1. gerinnen; 2. *my blood* ~*d* mir standen die Haare zu Berge.

cure [kjuə] I *s* 1. Heilung *f*; 2. Heilmittel *n*; II *v* 3. heilen; 4. pökeln, einsalzen, konservieren.

curfew ['kɜ:fju:] Sperrstunde *f*.

curi|osity [ˌkjuərɪ'ɒsətɪ] 1. Neugier(de) *f*; 2. Rarität *f*; ~**ous** ['kjuərɪəs] 1. neugierig, wißbegierig; 2. merkwürdig, sonderbar.

curl [kɜ:l] I *s* Locke *f*; II *v* 1. (sich) kräuseln; 2. ~ *up* (sich) zs.rollen; ~**y** ['kɜ:lɪ] gelockt, lockig.

currant ['kʌrənt] 1. Korinthe *f*; 2. Johannisbeere *f*.

curren|cy ['kʌrənsɪ] *fin* Währung *f*; ~**t** ['kʌrənt] I *adj* laufend, geläufig, aktuell; ~ *events pl* Tagesgeschehen *n*; II *s* 1. Strom *m a. el*; 2. *fig* Tendenz, Richtung *f*.

curriculum [kə'rɪkjuləm] *pl a. -la* Lehrplan *m*; ~ **vitae** [-'vi:taɪ] Lebenslauf *m*.

curse [kɜ:s] I *s* Fluch *m*; II *v* (ver)fluchen.

curt [kɜ:t] kurz, knapp, barsch (*to* gegen); ~**ail** [kɜ:'teɪl] (ab)kürzen.

curtain ['kɜ:tn] 1. Gardine *f*, Vorhang *m*; 2. *safety-*~ (*theat*) eiserne(r) Vorhang *m*; 3. ~ *of smoke* Rauchschleier *m*.

curts(e)y ['kɜ:tsɪ] *make,*

drop a ~ e-n Knicks machen (*to* vor).
curve [kɜ:v] **I** *s* Kurve *a. math;* Biegung, Krümmung *f;* **II** *v* e-n Bogen machen.
cushion [ˈkʊʃn] **I** *s* Kissen, Polster *n;* **II** *v* polstern.
custard [ˈkʌstəd] Eiercreme *f; (Art)* Pudding *m.*
custody [ˈkʌstədɪ] 1. Aufsicht, Obhut *f;* 2. Haft *f.*
custom [ˈkʌstəm] 1. Sitte *f,* Brauch *m;* 2. *com* Kundschaft *f;* 3. *pl* Zoll *m;* ~**ary** [-ərɪ] üblich, gebräuchlich; ~**er** [-ə] Kunde *m;* ~ **house** Zollamt *n.*

cut [kʌt] **I** *s* 1. Schnitt, Hieb, Stich *m;* 2. (Schnitt-)Wunde *f;* 3. Scheibe *f;* 4. *(Kleidung)* (Zu-)Schnitt *m;* 5. *(short-~)* (Weg-)Abkürzung *f;* 6. *fig* Verringerung, Kürzung *f;* **II** *v irr cut, cut* 7. (sich) schneiden; 8. *(Stoff)* zuschneiden; ~ *o.'s coat according to o.'s cloth (fig)* sich nach der Decke strecken; 9. ~ *it fine (fam)* es gerade (so) schaffen; 10. *fig* verringern; *(Gehalt)* kürzen; *(Preise)* herabsetzen; ~ *short* abkürzen; unterbrechen; ~ **in** 1. unterbrechen, in die Rede fallen; 2. *mot* nach dem Überholen zu schnell einbiegen; ~ **off** ab-

schneiden, plötzlich unterbrechen; ~ **out** 1. ausschneiden; 2. *(Licht)* ausschalten; 3. *be cut out for* geschaffen sein für; ~ **up** zerschneiden, -legen.
cute [kju:t] 1. *fam* gewitzt, hell(e); 2. *Am* nett, hübsch.
cutlery [ˈkʌtlərɪ] Besteck *n.*
cutlet [ˈkʌtlɪt] Kotelett *n.*
cutting [ˈkʌtɪŋ] **I** *s* 1. *tech* Einschnitt; Durchstich *m;* 2. *film* Schnitt *m;* 3. *(Zeitungs-)*Ausschnitt *m;* 4. *agr* Steckling *m;* **II** *adj* 5. *(Kälte, Wind)* schneidend; 6. *fig* beißend, verletzend.
cycle [ˈsaɪkl] **I** *s* 1. Kreis(lauf); Zyklus *m;* 2. (Fahr-)Rad *n;* **II** *v* radeln; ~**ist** [-ɪst] Radfahrer *m.*
cyclone [ˈsaɪkləʊn] Wirbelsturm *m.*
cylinder [ˈsɪlɪndə] Zylinder *m.*
cynic [ˈsɪnɪk] Zyniker *m;* ~**al** [-l] zynisch.
cypress [ˈsaɪprəs] *bot* Zypresse *f.*
Cyprus [ˈsaɪprəs] Zypern *n.*
cyst [sɪst] *med* Zyste *f.*
Czechoslovakia [ˌtʃekəʊsləʊˈvækɪə] Tschechoslowakei *f;* ~**(ian)** [ˌtʃekəʊˈsləʊvæk (ˌtʃekəʊsləʊˈvækɪən)] **I** *s* Tschechoslowake *m;* **II** *adj* tschechoslowakisch.

D

dab [dæb] ab-, betupfen (*with s.th.* mit etw).

dabble ['dæbl] sich abgeben (*at, in* mit); (herum)stümpern (*at, in* in).

dad(dy) ['dædɪ] *fam* Papa, Vati *m*.

daffodil ['dæfədɪl] *bot* Narzisse *f*.

dagger ['dægə] Dolch *m*.

daily ['deɪlɪ] **I** *adj* täglich; **II** *s* (~ *paper*) Tageszeitung *f*.

dainty ['deɪntɪ] 1. *(Person)* niedlich; 2. zart; 3. wählerisch (*about* in); 4. lecker.

dairy ['deərɪ] Molkerei *f*.

daisy ['deɪzɪ] Gänseblümchen *n*.

dam [dæm] **I** *s* Damm *m*; **II** *v* (~ *up*) (auf)stauen, eindämmen.

damage ['dæmɪdʒ] **I** *s* 1. Schaden *m; what's the* ~ *(fam)* was kostet's? 2. *pl* Schadenersatz *m;* **II** *v* beschädigen; schaden.

damn [dæm] **I** *v* verdammen; **II** *s: (fam) not care, not give a* ~ sich e-n Dreck machen aus.

damp [dæmp] **I** *adj* feucht; **II** *v* 1. an-, befeuchten; 2. *fig (Eifer)* dämpfen; ~**er** ['-ə] Dämpfer *m;* ~**ness** ['-nɪs] Feuchtigkeit *f*.

dance [dɑːns] **I** *v* tanzen; **II** *s* Tanz *m; may I have*

the next ~? darf ich um den nächsten Tanz bitten? ~**r** ['-ə] Tänzer(in *f*) *m*.

dandelion ['dændɪlaɪən] *bot* Löwenzahn *m*.

dandy ['dændɪ] Stutzer *m*.

Dane [deɪn] Däne *m;* Dänin *f*.

danger ['deɪndʒə] Gefahr *f; at* ~ *(Signal)* auf Halt; ~**ous** [-rəs] gefährlich.

dangle ['dæŋgl] baumeln (lassen).

Danish ['deɪnɪʃ] dänisch.

dar|e [deə] wagen; sich getrauen; *I* ~ *say* ich darf wohl sagen; ich glaube wohl; ~**ing** ['-rɪŋ] wagemutig.

dark [dɑːk] **I** *adj* dunkel; finster; **II** *s* Dunkelheit, Finsternis *f;* ~**en** ['-ən] (sich) verdunkeln; ~**ness** ['-nɪs] Dunkelheit *f*.

darling ['dɑːlɪŋ] Liebling *m*.

darn [dɑːn] stopfen, ausbessern.

dart [dɑːt] **I** *v* 1. schleudern, werfen; 2. stürzen, (los)stürmen; **II** *s* 3. Wurfspieß *m;* 4. Satz, Sprung *m*.

dash [dæʃ] **I** *v* 1. schleudern, werfen; 2. laufen, (sich) stürzen, rasen; **II** *s* 3. (heftiger) Schlag, Stoß *m;* 4. Prise *f;* 5. Gedankenstrich *m;* 6. *sport* Kurzstreckenlauf *m;* ~**board** ['-bɔːd] *mot* Armaturenbrett *n;* **~ing** ['-ɪŋ] schneidig.

data *pl, oft sing* ['deɪtə] Daten *pl;* **~ processing** Datenverarbeitung *f.*

date [deɪt] 1. Datum *n;* Termin, Zeitpunkt *m; up-to-~* zeitgemäß, modern; 2. *fam* Verabredung *f;* 3. Dattel *f.*

daughter ['dɔ:tə] Tochter *f;* **~-in-law** [-ɪnlɔ:] Schwiegertochter *f.*

daunt [dɔ:nt] entmutigen.

dawdle ['dɔ:dl] trödeln.

dawn [dɔ:n] **I** *s* 1. (Morgen-)-Dämmerung *f;* 2. *fig* Beginn *m;* **II** *v* dämmern.

day [deɪ] Tag *m; (three times) a ~* (dreimal) täglich; *by ~* am Tag(e), bei Tage; *the other ~* kürzlich, neulich; *the ~ after tomorrow* übermorgen; *the ~ before yesterday* vorgestern; *call it a ~ (fam)* Feierabend machen; **~break** ['-breɪk] *at ~* bei Tagesanbruch; **~light** ['-laɪt] Tageslicht *n.*

daze [deɪz] **I** *s: in a ~* verwirrt; **II** *v: he was ~d* er war benommen.

dazzle ['dæzl] blenden *a. fig.*

dead [ded] **I** *adj* 1. tot; *(Ast)* dürr; 2. unempfindlich *(to* gegen); 3. öde, langweilig; 4. *come to a ~ stop* plötzlich stehenbleiben; **II** *adv* (voll u.) ganz, völlig, vollständig; *~ slow!* Schritt fahren! **III** *s: the ~* die Toten *m pl;* **~beat** völlig erschöpft; **~en** ['-n]

unempfindlich machen; dämpfen; **~line** ['-laɪn] letzte(r) Termin, Stichtag *m;* **~lock** ['-lɒk] *be at a ~* auf dem toten Punkt angekommen sein.

deaf [def] taub *(to* für, gegen); *be ~ in one ear* auf e-m Ohr taub sein; **~ness** ['-nɪs] Taubheit *f.*

deal [di:l] **I** *v irr* dealt, dealt [delt] 1. *(~ out)* aus-, verteilen; 2. handeln *(in* mit); 3. sich befassen *(with* mit); **II** *s* 4. Handel *m,* Geschäft *n;* 5. *(Karten) whose ~ is it?* wer ist am Geben? 6. *a good, great ~ (of)* sehr viel, e-e Menge; **~er** ['-ə] Händler *m;* **~ings** *pl* ['-ɪŋz] (Geschäfts-)Beziehungen *f pl (with* zu).

dear [dɪə] **I** *adj* teuer; lieb; *(in der Briefanrede)* liebe(r); (sehr) geehrte(r); **II** *s* Liebling, Schatz *m.*

death [deθ] 1. Tod *m;* 2. Todesfall *m;* 3. *fig* Ende *n;* **~ly** ['-lɪ] tödlich.

debate [dɪ'beɪt] **I** *s* Diskussion *f;* **II** *v* diskutieren *(with s.o. on s.th.* mit jdm über etw).

debt [det] *fin com* Schuld *f; be in ~* verschuldet sein; **~or** ['-ə] Schuldner *m.*

decad(e) ['dekeɪd] Jahrzehnt *n.*

decay [dɪ'keɪ] **I** *v* verfaulen; verfallen; **II** *s* Verfall *m.*

decease [dɪ'si:s] (ver)sterben.

deceit [dɪ'si:t] Täuschung f, Betrug m; ~**ful** [-fʊl] (be)trügerisch.

deceive [dɪ'si:v] täuschen, hintergehen.

December [dɪ'sembə] Dezember m.

decen|cy ['di:snsɪ] Anstand m; ~**t** ['di:snt] anständig.

deception [dɪ'sepʃn] Täuschung f.

decide [dɪ'saɪd] beschließen; (sich) entscheiden (*between* zwischen; *for, in favour of* zugunsten; *against* gegen); ~**d** [-ɪd] entschieden.

decipher [dɪ'saɪfə] entziffern.

decis|ion [dɪ'sɪʒn] Entschluß m; *come to a* ~ eine Entscheidung treffen; ~**ive** [dɪ'saɪsɪv] entscheidend.

deck [dek] *mar* Deck n; ~ **chair** Liegestuhl m.

declar|ation [,deklə'reɪʃn] Erklärung f; ~**e** [dɪ'kleə] 1. erklären; 2. behaupten; 3. *have you anything to* ~? haben Sie etwas zu verzollen?

decline [dɪ'klaɪn] **I** v 1. nachlassen, abnehmen; 2. ablehnen; **II** s Abnahme f, Niedergang, Verfall m; *be on the* ~ abnehmen, nachlassen; *(Preise)* fallen.

decompose [,di:kəm'pəʊz] 1. zerlegen; 2. sich zersetzen, zerfallen.

decorat|e ['dekəreɪt] schmücken, dekorieren; ~**ion** [,dekə'reɪʃn] 1. Ausschmückung; Verzierung f; 2. Auszeichnung f; Orden m.

decrease I v [dɪ'kri:s] abnehmen, (sich) vermindern; **II** s ['di:kri:s] Abnahme, Rückgang m (*in* an).

decree [dɪ'kri:] **I** s Erlaß m; **II** v anordnen, verfügen.

dedicat|e ['dedɪkeɪt] widmen; ~**ion** [,dedɪ'keɪʃn] Widmung f.

deduce [dɪ'dju:s] folgern, schließen (*from* aus).

deduct [dɪ'dʌkt] abziehen; ~**ion** [dɪ'dʌkʃn] Abzug m.

deed [di:d] 1. Tat f; 2. Urkunde f.

deep [di:p] **I** adj tief; **II** s Tiefe f; ~**en** ['-ən] vertiefen a. fig; ~**-freeze** [,-'fri:z] Tiefkühltruhe f; ~**ly** ['-lɪ] (zu)tief(st); sehr stark.

deer [dɪə] pl deer Reh n, Hirsch m.

deface [dɪ'feɪs] entstellen.

defeat [dɪ'fi:t] **I** v besiegen; *(Antrag)* ablehnen; **II** s Niederlage f.

defect ['di:fekt] Fehler m, Störung f (*in* an); ~**ive** [dɪ'fektɪv] fehlerhaft, defekt.

defence, *Am* **defense** [dɪ'fens] Verteidigung f; ~**less** [-lɪs] wehr-, schutzlos.

defend [dɪ'fend] verteidigen (*against* gegen); ~**ant** [-ənt] Ange-, Beklagte(r) m.

defensive [dɪ'fensɪv] *on the* ~ in der Defensive.

defer [dɪ'fɜ:] auf-, hinaus-, verschieben.

defian|ce [dɪ'faɪəns] Herausforderung *f;* ~**t** [-t] herausfordernd, trotzig.

deficien|cy [dɪ'fɪʃnsɪ] Mangel *m;* ~**t** [-t] mangelhaft; *mentally* ~ schwachsinnig.

deficit ['defɪsɪt] Fehlbetrag *m.*

define [dɪ'faɪn] näher bestimmen, definieren.

definit|e ['defɪnɪt] endgültig; ~**ely** [-lɪ] sicherlich, bestimmt; ~**ion** [ˌdefɪ'nɪʃn] Definition *f.*

deform|ed [dɪ'fɔ:md] entstellt, mißgestaltet; ~**ity** [dɪ'fɔ:mətɪ] Mißgestalt *f.*

defraud [dɪ'frɔ:d] betrügen.

defrost [ˌdi:'frɒst] abtauen.

defy [dɪ'faɪ] sich widersetzen, trotzen (*s.o.* jdm).

degenerate I *v* [dɪ'dʒenəreɪt] entarten; **II** *adj* [dɪ'dʒenərət] entartet.

degree [dɪ'gri:] Grad *m; by* ~*s* nach und nach, allmählich; *to a certain* ~ bis zu einem gewissen Grade; ~ *of latitude, longitude* Breiten-, Längengrad *m.*

delay [dɪ'leɪ] **I** *v* 1. auf-, hinausschieben; 2. auf-, zurückhalten; *be* ~*ed* sich verzögern, sich verspäten; **II** *s* Verzögerung *f;* Aufschub *m; without* ~ unverzüglich.

delegate I *v* ['delɪgeɪt] 1. abordnen; 2. (*Befugnisse*) übertragen (*to s.o.* jdm); **II** *s* ['delɪgət] Abgeordnete(r) *m.*

deliberate I *v* [dɪ'lɪbəreɪt] beraten (*upon* über); **II** *adj* [dɪ'lɪbərət] überlegt; beabsichtigt; ~**ly** [dɪ'lɪbərətlɪ] vorsätzlich, absichtlich.

delica|cy ['delɪkəsɪ] 1. Zartgefühl *n,* Takt *m;* 2. Leckerbissen *m;* ~**te** ['delɪkət] 1. lecker; 2. fein, zart; 3. heikel, schwierig.

delicious [dɪ'lɪʃəs] köstlich.

delight [dɪ'laɪt] **I** *v* erfreuen; **II** *s: to the* ~ *of* zur (großen) Freude *gen;* ~**ed** [-ɪd] (hoch)erfreut; ~**ful** [-fʊl] entzückend.

delinquent [dɪ'lɪŋkwənt] Straffällige(r), Missetäter *m.*

deliver [dɪ'lɪvə] 1. befreien (*from* von); 2. (ab-, aus)liefern; 3. (*Post*) zustellen; 4. (*Rede*) halten; ~**y** [-rɪ] 1. Zustellung *f; on* ~ bei Lieferung; 2. Vortrag(sweise *f*) *m.*

delude [dɪ'lu:d] täuschen, irreführen.

deluge ['delju:dʒ] Sintflut *f a. fig.*

delus|ion [dɪ'lu:ʒn] Täuschung, Wahnvorstellung *f;* ~**ive** [dɪ'lu:sɪv] irreführend.

demand [dɪ'mɑ:nd] **I** *v* 1. fordern, verlangen; 2. erforderlich machen; **II** *s* 3. Anspruch *m* (*on* auf); *on* ~ auf Verlangen; 4. *com* Nachfrage *f* (*for* nach); *in* ~ begehrt, gefragt.

democra|cy [dɪ'mɒkrəsɪ] Demokratie *f;* **~t** ['deməkræt] Demokrat *m;* **~tic(al)** [,demə'krætɪk(l)] demokratisch.

demol|ish [dɪ'mɒlɪʃ] (*Gebäude*) niederreißen; zerstören; **~ition** [,demə'lɪʃn] Abbruch *m;* Zerstörung *f.*

demon ['diːmən] Dämon, Teufel *m.*

demonstrat|e ['demənstreɪt] 1. erklären; vorführen; 2. demonstrieren; **~ion** [,demən'streɪʃn] 1. Vorführung *f* (*to* vor); 2. *pol* Kundgebung, Demonstration *f.*

demure [dɪ'mjuə] ruhig; zurückhaltend.

den [den] Höhle *f.*

denial [dɪ'naɪəl] 1. Ablehnung *f;* 2. Verneinung *f.*

Denmark ['denmaːk] Dänemark *n.*

denominate [dɪ'nɒmɪneɪt] (be)nennen.

denote [dɪ'nəʊt] kennzeichnen, benennen.

dens|e [dens] dicht; **~ity** ['-ətɪ] Dichte *f;* ~ *of population* Bevölkerungsdichte *f.*

dent [dent] **I** *s* Beule, Delle *f;* **II** *v* verbeulen.

dentifrice ['dentɪfrɪs] Zahnpasta *f.*

dentist ['dentɪst] Zahnarzt *m.*

deny [dɪ'naɪ] 1. leugnen; ab-, bestreiten; 2. ablehnen.

depart [dɪ'paːt] 1. abreisen, -fahren (*from* von; *for* nach); 2. ~ *from o.'s principles* von s-n Grundsätzen abweichen; **~ment** [-mənt] 1. Abteilung *f;* ~ *store* Warenhaus *n;* 2. Fach, Gebiet *n;* 3. *D~ (Am)* Ministerium *n;* **~ure** [-fə] Abreise, -fahrt *f,* -flug *m* (*from* von; *for* nach).

depend [dɪ'pend] 1. abhängig sein (*on* von); *that ~s* das kommt darauf an; 2. sich verlassen (*on, upon* auf); **~able** [-əbl] zuverlässig; **~ence** [-əns] Abhängigkeit *f;* **~ent** [-ənt] **I** *adj* abhängig (*on* von); **II** *s a.* **~ant** (Familien-)Angehörige(r) *m.*

depict [dɪ'pɪkt] abbilden; beschreiben.

deplor|able [dɪ'plɔːrəbl] bedauernswert; **~e** [dɪ'plɔː] bedauern.

deposit [dɪ'pɒzɪt] **I** *v* 1. (nieder)legen; 2. *com* einzahlen, hinterlegen (*with* bei); 3. *geol* ablagern (*on* auf); **II** *s* 4. Pfand *n;* 5. Einlage *f;* 6. *geol* Ablagerung *f;* **~or** [-ə] Einzahler *m.*

depot ['depəʊ] 1. Lagerhaus *n;* 2. *Am* Bahnhof *m.*

depreciat|e [dɪ'priːʃɪeɪt] an Wert verlieren; **~ion** [dɪˌpriːʃɪ'eɪʃn] Wertminderung *f.*

depress [dɪ'pres] 1. nieder-,

herunterdrücken; 2. deprimieren; **~ed** [-t] deprimiert, niedergeschlagen; **~ing** [-ɪŋ] bedrückend, deprimierend; **~ion** [dɪ'preʃn] 1. *(Gelände)* Vertiefung *f;* 2. *com* Depression, Flaute, Krise *f;* 3. *mete* Tief(druckgebiet) *n;* 4. Niedergeschlagenheit *f.*

deprive [dɪ'praɪv] nehmen *(s.o. of s.th.* jdm etw); entziehen *(s.o. of s.th.* jdm etw).

depth [depθ] Tiefe *f; in the ~ of winter* mitten im Winter.

deputy ['depjʊtɪ] *pol* Abgeordnete(r) *m.*

derail [dɪ'reɪl] *be ~ed* entgleisen.

derange [dɪ'reɪndʒ] in Unordnung bringen.

derive [dɪ'raɪv] 1. ab-, herleiten *(from* von); 2. gewinnen, erhalten *(from* von).

derogatory [dɪ'rogətərɪ] nachteilig *(to* für).

derrick ['derɪk] 1. Kran *m;* 2. Bohrturm *m.*

descend [dɪ'send] 1. herab-, hinabsteigen; *(Straße)* hinabführen; 2. *(be ~ed)* ab-, herstammen *(from* von); **~ant** [-ənt] Nachkomme *m.*

descent [dɪ'sent] 1. Abstieg *m;* 2. Abhang *m;* 3. Abstammung *f.*

describe [dɪ'skraɪb] beschreiben, schildern.

description [dɪ'skrɪpʃn] Beschreibung *f.*

desegregate [ˌdiː'segrɪgeɪt] die Rassentrennung aufheben in.

desert I *v* [dɪ'zɜːt] 1. im Stich lassen; 2. desertieren; II *s* ['dezət] Wüste, Einöde *f.*

deserve [dɪ'zɜːv] verdienen.

design [dɪ'zaɪn] I *s* 1. Zeichnung *f;* Entwurf *m;* 2. Muster *n;* 3. Absicht *f; have ~s on* es abgesehen haben auf; II *v* 4. entwerfen; 5. bestimmen *(for* zu); **~er** [-ə] (Muster-)Zeichner; Formgestalter *m.*

designat|e ['dezɪgneɪt] 1. kennzeichnen; 2. ernennen; **~ion** [ˌdezɪg'neɪʃn] Bezeichnung *f.*

desir|able [dɪ'zaɪərəbl] wünschenswert; **~e** [dɪ'zaɪə] I *v* wünschen; II *s* Wunsch *m.*

desist [dɪ'zɪst] Abstand nehmen *(from* von).

desk [desk] Pult *n.*

desolate ['desələt] trostlos.

despair [dɪ'speə] I *v* verzweifeln *(of* an); die Hoffnung aufgeben *(of* auf); II *s* Verzweiflung *f.*

desperat|e ['despərət] verzweifelt; **~ion** [ˌdespə'reɪʃn] Verzweiflung *f.*

despise [dɪ'spaɪz] verachten.

despite [dɪ'spaɪt] trotz, ungeachtet *gen.*

dessert [dɪ'zɜːt] Nachtisch *m.*

destin|ation [ˌdestɪ'neɪʃn] Reiseziel *n;* Bestimmung(sort *m) f;* **~e** ['destɪn] *be ~d* bestimmt sein *(for* für); **~y** ['destɪnɪ] Schicksal *n.*

destroy [dɪ'strɔɪ] zerstören.

destruct|ion [dɪ'strʌkʃn] Zerstörung *f;* **~ive** [dɪ'strʌktɪv] zerstörerisch.

detach [dɪ'tætʃ] 1. losmachen; abtrennen; 2. *mil* (ab)kommandieren; **~ed** [-t] 1. (*Haus*) einzeln (stehend); 2. unvoreingenommen; **~ment** [-mənt] 1. Abtrennung *f (from* von); 2. *mil* Abteilung *f;* 3. Objektivität *f.*

detail ['di:teɪl] **I** *s* Einzelheit *f; in ~* im einzelnen; **II** *v* einzeln aufführen; **~ed** [-d] ausführlich.

detain [dɪ'teɪn] zurückhalten.

detect [dɪ'tekt] entdecken; **~ion** [dɪ'tekʃn] Entdeckung *f;* **~ive** [-ɪv] Detektiv *m.*

detention [dɪ'tenʃn] *jur* Haft *f;* Arrest *m.*

deter [dɪ'tɜ:] abschrecken, zurückhalten (*from* von).

deteriorate [dɪ'tɪərɪəreɪt] (sich) verschlechtern.

determin|ation [dɪˌtɜ:mɪ'neɪʃn] 1. Bestimmung *f;* 2. Entschluß *m;* Entschlossenheit *f;* **~e** [dɪ'tɜ:mɪn] 1. bestimmen, festlegen; 2. beschließen (*to do, on doing* zu tun).

deterrent [dɪ'terənt] Abschreckungsmittel *n.*

detest [dɪ'test] verabscheuen, hassen; **~able** [-əbl] abscheulich.

detour ['di:ˌtuə] 1. Umweg *m;* 2. Umleitung *f.*

detriment ['detrɪmənt] *to s.o.'s ~* zu jds Nachteil, Schaden.

devaluation [ˌdi:væljuˈeɪʃn] *fin* Abwertung *f.*

devastat|e ['devəsteɪt] verwüsten; **~ion** [ˌdevəˈsteɪʃn] Verwüstung *f.*

develop [dɪ'veləp] (sich) entwickeln; **~ment** [-mənt] Entwicklung *f.*

deviat|e ['di:vɪeɪt] abweichen (*from* von); **~ion** [ˌdi:vɪˈeɪʃn] Abweichung *f.*

device [dɪ'vaɪs] 1. Plan *m;* 2. *tech* Vorrichtung *f;* Gerät *n;* 3. Sinnbild *n.*

devil ['devl] Teufel *m; between the ~ and the deep sea* in der Klemme.

devious ['di:vjəs] *by ~ ways* (*fig*) auf krummen Wegen.

devoid [dɪ'vɔɪd] *~ of* (völlig) ohne.

devot|e [dɪ'vəut] widmen; **~ed** [-ɪd] ergeben; **~ion** [dɪ'vəuʃn] Hingabe *f; pl* Gebet(e *pl*) *n.*

devour [dɪ'vauə] verschlingen.

devout [dɪ'vaut] fromm.

dew [dju:] Tau *m;* **~y** ['-ɪ] taufeucht.

dext|erity [dek'sterətɪ] Geschicklichkeit *f;* **~(e)rous** ['dekstərəs] geschickt.

diagnos|e ['daɪəgnəuz] *med* diagnostizieren; **~is**

[ˌdaɪəg'nəʊsɪs] *pl -noses*
[-iːz] Diagnose *f.*

dial ['daɪəl] **I** *s* Zifferblatt *n;*
Skalen-, Nummernscheibe *f;*
II *v tele* wählen.

dialect ['daɪəlekt] Mundart *f.*

diameter [daɪ'æmɪtə]
Durchmesser *m.*

diamond ['daɪəmənd] Diamant *m.*

diaper ['daɪəpə] *Am* Windel
f.

diaphragm ['daɪəfræm]
1. *anat* Zwerchfell *n;* 2. *phot*
Blende *f.*

diary ['daɪərɪ] Tagebuch *n.*

diarrh(o)ea [ˌdaɪə'rɪə]
Durchfall *m.*

dice [daɪs] **I** *s pl, sing: die*
[daɪ] Würfel *m pl; the die is
cast* die Würfel sind gefallen; **II** *v* würfeln; ~ *with
death (fam)* mit dem Leben
spielen; **~-box** ['-bɒks]
Würfelbecher *m.*

dictate [dɪk'teɪt] 1. diktieren;
2. befehlen; **~ion** [dɪk'teɪʃn]
Diktat *n;* **~or** [-ə] Diktator
m.

dictionary ['dɪkʃənrɪ] Wörterbuch *n.*

die [daɪ] 1. sterben (*of* an);
(*Motor*) absterben; 2. *I'm
dying to, for* ich möchte
furchtbar gerne; ~ **away,
down** schwächer werden;
~ **out** aussterben.

diet ['daɪət] Nahrung, Kost;
Diät *f; he is on a* ~ er lebt
diät.

differ ['dɪfə] 1. sich unter-

scheiden (*from* von); 2. entgegengesetzter Meinung
sein (*on* über); **~ence**
['dɪfrəns] 1. Unterschied *m;*
2. Meinungsverschiedenheit
f; **~ent** ['dɪfrənt] verschieden.

difficult ['dɪfɪkəlt] schwer,
schwierig; **~y** [-ɪ] Schwierigkeit *f.*

diffuse [dɪ'fjuːz] aus-, verbreiten.

dig [dɪg] *irr dug, dug* [dʌg]
1. (aus-, um)graben; 2. ernten (*potatoes* Kartoffeln);
3. ~ *in (beim Essen)* zugreifen.

digest I *v* [dɪ'dʒest] verdauen; **II** *s* ['daɪdʒest] Zs.fassung *f,* Übersicht *f;* **~ion**
[dɪ'dʒestʃən] Verdauung *f.*

digit ['dɪdʒɪt] Ziffer *f.*

dignified ['dɪgnɪfaɪd] würdevoll; **~y** ['dɪgnɪfaɪ] auszeichnen, ehren.

dignity ['dɪgnətɪ] Würde *f.*

digress [daɪ'gres] abschweifen (*from* von).

dike [daɪk] Deich; Damm *m.*

dilapidated [dɪ'læpɪdeɪtɪd]
baufällig.

diligence ['dɪlɪdʒəns] Fleiß
m; **~t** [-t] fleißig.

dilute [daɪ'ljuːt] verdünnen.

dim [dɪm] **I** *adj* trübe, matt,
verschwommen; **II** *v:* ~ *your
lights!* Abblenden!

dimension [dɪ'menʃn] Dimension, Ausdehnung *f,*
Umfang *m.*

diminish [dɪ'mɪnɪʃ] sich vermindern; abnehmen (*in* an).
dimple ['dɪmpl] Grübchen *n*.
din [dɪn] Lärm *m*, Getöse *n*.
dine [daɪn] (zu) Mittag essen; ~**r** ['-ə] *rail* Speisewagen *m*.
dinghy ['dɪŋgɪ] *rubber* ~ Schlauchboot *n*.
dingy ['dɪndʒɪ] schmutzig, unansehnlich.
dining ['daɪnɪŋ] ~-*car (rail)* Speisewagen *m*; ~-*room* Eß-, Speisezimmer *n*.
dinner ['dɪnə] (Mittag-, Abend-)Essen *n*; ~-**jacket** [-ˌdʒækɪt] Smoking *m*.
dint [dɪnt] *by* ~ *of* (ver)mittels, mit Hilfe.
dip [dɪp] **I** *v* 1. (ein)tauchen, (ein)tunken (*in* in);
2. *(Fahne)* senken; 3. *mot (Licht)* abblenden; **II** *s*
4. (Wasser-, Farb-) Bad *n*;
5. Neigung *f*; Gefälle *n*.
diphteria [dɪf'θɪərɪə] *med* Diphtherie *f*.
diploma [dɪ'pləumə] Diplom *n*.
diplomacy [dɪ'pləuməsɪ] *pol* Diplomatie *f*.
direct [dɪ'rekt] **I** *adj*
1. g(e)rade, direkt; 2. offen, klar; **II** *v* 3. richten (*towards* auf); 4. den Weg zeigen (*to* nach); 5. anordnen, befehlen;
6. *(Worte)* richten (*to* an);
7. *(Brief)* schicken (*to* an);
8. leiten; ~ **current** *el* Gleichstrom *m*; ~**ion** [dɪ'rekʃn] 1. Richtung *f*;
2. *under the* ~ *of* unter Leitung *gen;* 3. *pl* Richtlinien *f pl;* ~**ive** [dɪ'rektɪv] Vorschrift *f;* ~**ly** [-lɪ] direkt, geradewegs, unmittelbar; sofort; ~**or** [-ə] Direktor; *theat film* Regisseur *m;* ~**ory** [-ərɪ] Adreß-, Telefonbuch *n.*
dirt [dɜːt] Schmutz *m;* ~-**cheap** [ˌ-'tʃiːp] spottbillig; ~**y** ['-ɪ] 1. schmutzig;
2. *(Wetter)* scheußlich.

disabled [dɪs'eɪbld] körperbehindert.
disadvantage [ˌdɪsəd'vɑːntɪdʒ] Nachteil *m.*
disagree [ˌdɪsə'griː] 1. nicht übereinstimmen (*with* mit);
2. anderer Meinung sein;
3. *(Nahrung)* schlecht bekommen; ~**able** [ˌdɪsə'grɪəbl] unangenehm.
disappear [ˌdɪsə'pɪə] ent-, verschwinden.
disappoint [ˌdɪsə'pɔɪnt] enttäuschen; ~**ment** [-mənt] Enttäuschung *f.*
disapprov|al [ˌdɪsə'pruːvl] Mißbilligung *f;* Mißfallen *n* (*of* über); ~**e** [ˌdɪsə'pruːv] mißbilligen (*of s.th.* etw.).
disarm [dɪs'ɑːm] entwaffnen; ~**ament** [dɪs'ɑːməmənt] Abrüstung *f.*
disast|er [dɪ'zɑːstə] Unglück *n*, Katastrophe *f* (*to* für); ~**rous** [dɪ'zɑːstrəs] verheerend, katastrophal.
disbelief [ˌdɪsbɪ'liːf] Unglaube *m*, Zweifel *m pl* (*in* an).

disbelieve [ˌdɪsbɪ'liːv] nicht glauben (wollen) (*in* an).

disc [dɪsk] s. *disk.*

discern [dɪ'sɜːn] wahrnehmen.

discharge [dɪs'tʃɑːdʒ] I *v* 1. *(Fahrzeug)* entladen; ab-, ausladen; 2. *(Schuß)* abfeuern; 3. entlassen; *(Angeklagten)* freisprechen; 4. *(Pflicht)* erfüllen; 5. absondern; II *s* 6. Entladen *n;* 7. (Ab-)Schuß *m;* 8. Entlassung *f;* 9. Absonderung *f.*

disciple [dɪ'saɪpl] Schüler; Jünger *m.*

discipline ['dɪsɪplɪn] Disziplin *f.*

disclaim [dɪs'kleɪm] ab-, bestreiten.

disclose [dɪs'kləʊz] 1. aufdecken; 2. bekanntmachen.

discoloured [dɪs'kʌləd] verfärbt.

discomfort [dɪs'kʌmfət] Mißbehagen *n;* Verdruß *m.*

disconcerted [ˌdɪskən'sɜːtɪd] beunruhigt; verwirrt, verlegen.

disconnect [ˌdɪskə'nekt] trennen, unterbrechen.

disconsolate [dɪs'kɒnsələt] untröstlich.

discontented [ˌdɪskən'tentɪd] unzufrieden (*with* mit, über).

discontinue [ˌdɪskən'tɪnjuː] unterbrechen, aufhören (*doing* zu tun).

discord ['dɪskɔːd] 1. Uneinigkeit *f;* 2. *mus* Mißklang *m.*

discount ['dɪskaʊnt] 1. Rabatt *m* (*on* auf); 2. Diskont *m.*

discourage [dɪs'kʌrɪdʒ] entmutigen; abhalten (*from* von; *from doing s.th.* etw zu tun).

discover [dɪs'kʌvə] entdecken; ~y [-rɪ] Entdeckung *f.*

discredit [dɪs'kredɪt] I *v* in Mißkredit bringen (*with* bei); II *s* 1. schlechter Ruf *m;* 2. Zweifel *m,* Mißtrauen *n.*

discreet [dɪs'kriːt] verschwiegen, diskret.

discretion [dɪs'kreʃn] Klugheit, Besonnenheit *f; it is within your own* ~ es liegt bei Ihnen.

discriminate [dɪ'skrɪmɪneɪt] 1. unterscheiden (*between* zwischen); 2. benachteiligen (*against s.o.* jdn).

discuss [dɪ'skʌs] diskutieren, erörtern; ~ion [dɪ'skʌʃn] Diskussion, Erörterung *f.*

disdain [dɪs'deɪn] I *v* verachten, verschmähen; II *s* Verachtung, Geringschätzung *f.*

disease [dɪ'ziːz] Krankheit *f;* ~d [-d] krank.

disembark [ˌdɪsɪm'bɑːk] ausschiffen, landen.

disengage [ˌdɪsɪn'geɪdʒ] (sich) los-, freimachen; ~ment [-mənt] *pol* Ausea.rücken *n.*

disentangle [ˌdɪsɪn'tæŋgl] entwirren; ordnen.

disfigure [dɪs'fɪgə] entstellen, verunstalten.

disgrace [dɪsˈgreɪs]
  I s Schande f (to für);
  II v Schande bringen über;
  ~ful [-fʊl] beschämend,
  schändlich.
disguise [dɪsˈgaɪz] I v verkleiden; (Stimme) verstellen; II s Verkleidung f; in ~
  verkleidet, maskiert.
disgust [dɪsˈgʌst] Ekel, Wi-
  derwille m; in ~ voller Ekel,
  angewidert; ~ed [-ɪd] angewidert (at, by, with von);
  ~ing [-ɪŋ] ekelhaft.
dish [dɪʃ] I s 1. Schüssel f;
  2. Gericht n; 3. pl Geschirr
  n; II v: ~ up auftragen;
  ~washer [ˈ-ˌwɒʃə] Ge-
  schirrspülmaschine f.
dishearten [dɪsˈhɑːtn] entmutigen.
dishevel(l)ed [dɪˈʃevld]
  (Kleidung) in Unordnung;
  (Haare) wirr, zerzaust.
dishonest [dɪsˈɒnɪst] unred-
  lich, unehrlich.
dishonour [dɪsˈɒnə] I s
  Schande f (to für); II v
  1. Schande bringen über;
  2. fin (Wechsel) nicht hono-
  rieren; ~able [dɪsˈɒnərəbl]
  schimpflich, schändlich.
disinclined [ˌdɪsɪnˈklaɪnd]
  abgeneigt (for gegen, to do
  s. th. etw zu tun).
disinfect [ˌdɪsɪnˈfekt] med
  desinfizieren; ~ant
  [ˌdɪsɪnˈfektənt] Desinfek-
  tionsmittel n.
disinherit [ˌdɪsɪnˈherɪt] enterben.

disintegrate [dɪsˈɪntɪgreɪt]
  zerfallen.
disk [dɪsk] 1. Scheibe f;
  2. Schallplatte f.
dislike [dɪsˈlaɪk] I v nicht leiden können; II s Abneigung
  f.
dislocate [ˈdɪsləʊkeɪt]
  1. med aus-, verrenken;
  2. (Verkehr) (empfindlich)
  stören.
dismal [ˈdɪzməl] düster; trübselig.
dismantle [dɪsˈmæntl] aus-
  ea.nehmen; demontieren.
dismay [dɪsˈmeɪ] I s Bestürzung f, Schrecken m; II v
  bestürzen, entsetzen.
dismiss [dɪsˈmɪs] 1. wegschicken; 2. (aus e-r Stellung) entlassen; ~al [-l] Entlassung f.
dismount [ˌdɪsˈmaʊnt] 1. absteigen; 2. abmontieren.
disobedien|ce
  [ˌdɪsəˈbiːdjəns] Ungehorsam
  m (to gegen); ~t [-t] ungehorsam (to gegen).
disobey [ˌdɪsəˈbeɪ] nicht gehorchen.
disorder [dɪsˈɔːdə] 1. Unordnung f; 2. pol Aufruhr m;
  3. med Unpäßlichkeit f; ~ly
  [-lɪ] 1. unordentlich; 2. aufrührerisch.
disown [dɪsˈəʊn] verleugnen.
disparaging [dɪˈspærɪdʒɪŋ]
  abschätzig.
disparity [dɪˈspærətɪ] Ungleichheit f (in in, bei).
dispatch [dɪˈspætʃ] I v 1. ab-

schicken, -senden; 2. schnell erledigen; **II** *s* 3. Versand *m;* 4. *with* ~ eiligst.

dispens|ary [dɪ'spensərɪ] Apotheke *f;* ~**e** [dɪ'spens] 1. austeilen; 2. ~ *with* verzichten auf; überflüssig machen.

disperse [dɪ'spɜ:s] (sich) zerstreuen; ausea.gehen.

displace [dɪs'pleɪs] 1. versetzen, -lagern; 2. ersetzen.

display [dɪ'spleɪ] **I** *v* zeigen, zur Schau stellen; **II** *s* 1. (Schaufenster-)Auslage *f;* 2. Ausstellung, Vorführung, Schau(stellung) *f.*

displeas|e [dɪs'pli:z] mißfallen *(s.o.* jdm); ~**ure** [dɪs'pleʒə] Mißfallen *n.*

dispos|al [dɪ'spəʊzl] 1. Beseitigung, Veräußerung *f;* 2. Verfügungsrecht *n; be at s.o.'s* ~ zu jds Verfügung stehen; ~**e** [dɪ'spəʊz] 1. ~ *of* beseitigen; veräußern; erledigen; 2. (an)ordnen; ~**ed** [-d] geneigt, bereit *(to* zu); ~**ition** [ˌdɪspə'zɪʃn] 1. Anordnung *f;* 2. Veranlagung *f;* 3. Verfügungsrecht *n.*

disproportionate [ˌdɪsprə'pɔ:ʃnət] unverhältnismäßig (groß *od* klein) *(to* im Vergleich zu).

dispute [dɪ'spju:t] **I** *v* 1. streiten *(with, against* mit; *about* über); 2. bestreiten; **II** *s* Streit *m; beyond, past* ~ unbestritten; *in* ~ strittig, fraglich.

disqualif|ication [dɪsˌkwɒlɪfɪ'keɪʃn] Disqualifizierung *f;* ~**ied** [dɪs'kwɒlɪfaɪd] *sport* disqualifiziert.

disregard [ˌdɪsrɪ'gɑ:d] **I** *v* nicht beachten, sich hinwegsetzen *(s.th.* über etw); **II** *s* Nichtbeachtung *f.*

disreputable [dɪs'repjʊtəbl] verrufen.

dissatis|faction [ˈdɪsˌsætɪs'fækʃn] Unzufriedenheit *(with* mit); ~**fy** [ˌdɪs'sætɪsfaɪ] nicht befriedigen; nicht genügen *(s.o.* jdm).

dissimilar [ˌdɪ'sɪmɪlə] verschieden *(to* von).

dissipate ['dɪsɪpeɪt] 1. zerstreuen; 2. verschwenden; ~**d** [-ɪd] ausschweifend.

dissociate [dɪ'səʊʃɪeɪt] trennen *(from* von).

dissolution [ˌdɪsə'lu:ʃn] Auflösung, Beendigung *f.*

dissolve [dɪ'zɒlv] (sich) (auf)lösen.

dissuade [dɪ'sweɪd] abraten *(from* von).

distan|ce ['dɪstəns] Abstand *m,* Entfernung; Strecke *f; at a* ~ von fern, von weitem; *in the* ~ in der Ferne; *keep o.'s* ~ Distanz halten; ~**t** [-t] 1. (ent)fern(t) *(from* von); 2. zurückhaltend.

distasteful [dɪs'teɪstfʊl] widerwärtig.

disti(l) [dɪ'stɪl] destillieren.

distinct [dɪ'stɪŋkt] 1. ver-

schieden (*from* von);
2. deutlich; **~ion** [dɪ'stɪŋkʃn]
1. Unterschied *m;* 2. Auszeichnung *f;* **~ive** [-tɪv] charakteristisch, spezifisch (*of* für).

distinguish [dɪ'stɪŋgwɪʃ]
1. unterscheiden (*from* von);
2. ~ *o.s.* sich auszeichnen; sich hervortun; **~ed** [-t] hervorragend.

distort [dɪ'stɔːt] 1. verzerren;
2. entstellen, verzerrt darstellen; **~ion** [dɪ'stɔːʃn]
1. Verzerrung *f;* 2. Entstellung *f.*

distract [dɪ'strækt] ablenken (*from* von); **~ion** [dɪ'strækʃn] 1. Ablenkung, Zerstreuung *f;* 2. *to* ~ bis zum Wahnsinn.

distress [dɪ'stres] 1. Kummer *m;* Not *f,* Elend *n;* 2. *in* ~ (*Schiff*) in Not; **~ing** [-ɪŋ] betrüblich, schmerzlich.

distribute [dɪ'strɪbjuːt]
1. ver-, austeilen; 2. (*Waren*) vertreiben; **~ion** [ˌdɪstrɪ'bjuːʃn] 1. Verteilung *f;* 2. *com* Vertrieb *m.*

district ['dɪstrɪkt] 1. Gebiet *n;* 2. Bezirk *m.*

distrust [dɪs'trʌst] mißtrauen (*s.o.* jdm).

disturb [dɪs'stɜːb] 1. stören;
2. in Unordnung bringen; **~ance** [-əns] Störung; Unruhe *f;* Aufruhr *m.*

disuse [ˌdɪs'juːs] *fall into* ~ außer Gebrauch kommen.

ditch [dɪtʃ] (Wasser-)Graben

m; dull as ~ *water* stinklangweilig.

dive [daɪv] **I** *v* 1. (unter)tauchen (*into* in; *for* nach); e-n Kopfsprung machen; 2. verschwinden (*into* in); rasch hineingreifen (*into* in); **II** *s*
3. Kopfsprung *m;* 4. *aero* Sturzflug *m;* **~r** [-ə] Taucher *m.*

diverge [daɪ'vɜːdʒ] ausea.gehen, -laufen.

diverse [daɪ'vɜːs] verschieden(artig); **~ion** [daɪ'vɜːʃn]
1. (Verkehrs-)Umleitung *f;* 2. Ablenkung *f;* **~ity** [-əti] Verschiedenheit *f.*

divert [daɪ'vɜːt] 1. (*Verkehr*) umleiten; 2. ablenken, zerstreuen.

divide [dɪ'vaɪd] 1. dividieren (*by* durch; *2 into 6* 6 durch 2); 2. auf-, verteilen (*among* unter); 3. trennen; 4. (*Weg*) sich teilen.

divine [dɪ'vaɪn] göttlich; **~ity** [dɪ'vɪnəti] 1. Gottheit *f;*
2. Theologie *f.*

division [dɪ'vɪʒn] 1. Teilung *f;*
2. *mil math* Division *f.*

divorce [dɪ'vɔːs] **I** *s* (Ehe-)-Scheidung *f;* **II** *v* sich scheiden lassen, trennen (*from* von).

dizzy ['dɪzɪ] schwind(e)lig.

do [duː] *irr did* [dɪd] , *done* [dʌn] 1. tun, machen; *what can I* ~ *for you?* womit kann ich Ihnen dienen?
2. bewirken; ~ *no good* nichts nützen; 3. ausführen,

erledigen; *have done with* fertig sein mit; 4. ~ *well* Erfolg haben; 5. sich befinden; *how do you* ~? wie geht es Ihnen? guten Tag! 6. *(Essen)* zubereiten; 7. *(Aufgabe, Problem)* lösen; 8. *(Entfernung)* zurücklegen; *fam (Land)* besichtigen; 9. ausreichen; *that will* ~ das genügt; 10. *(verstärkend) I* ~ *feel better* ich fühle mich wirklich besser; 11. *(Umschreibung)* ~ *you go?* gehen Sie? *I don't go* ich gehe nicht; ~ **away** *with* abschaffen; beseitigen; ~ **with** *I could do with* ich könnte gut gebrauchen; ~ **without** auskommen ohne.

docile ['dəʊsaɪl] folgsam, fügsam.

dock [dɒk] 1. *(jur) in the* ~ auf der Anklagebank; 2. *mar* Dock *n; pl* Hafenanlagen *f pl;* ~**er** ['-ə] Dockarbeiter *m;* ~**yard** ['-jɑːd] Werft *f.*

doctor ['dɒktə] Doktor, Arzt *m.*

document ['dɒkjʊmənt] Urkunde *f,* Dokument *n;* ~**ary** [,dɒkjʊ'mentəri] dokumentarisch.

dodge [dɒdʒ] I *v* 1. ausweichen *(s.th.* e-r S); 2. sich drücken *(s.th.* um etw); II *s* List *f,* Kniff, Trick *m.*

dog [dɒg] Hund *m; not stand (even) a* ~'s *chance* nicht die geringsten Aussichten

haben; *a* ~ *in the manger* Neidhammel *m;* ~-**days** *pl* ['-deɪz] Hundstage *m pl;* ~**ged** ['-ɪd] verbissen, hartnäckig.

doings *pl* ['duːɪŋz] Taten, Handlungen *f pl;* Ereignisse *n pl.*

dole [dəʊl] I *v:* ~ *out* austeilen; II *s: (fam) be on the* ~ Arbeitslosenunterstützung erhalten.

doll [dɒl] Puppe *f.*

dolphin ['dɒlfɪn] *zoo* Delphin *m.*

dome [dəʊm] *arch* Kuppel *f.*

domestic [dəʊ'mestɪk] 1. häuslich; 2. einheimisch, inländisch; 3. *(Tier)* zahm.

domicile ['dɒmɪsaɪl] Wohnsitz *m.*

dominate ['dɒmɪneɪt] beherrschen.

donat|e [dəʊ'neɪt] schenken, spenden; ~**ion** [dəʊ'neɪʃn] Spende, Schenkung *f.*

done [dʌn] 1. getan; erledigt; 2. *jur* ausgefertigt; 3. fertig, gar; 4. erschöpft.

donkey ['dɒŋkɪ] Esel *m.*

donor ['dəʊnə] *blood* ~ Blutspender *m.*

doom [duːm] I *s* Schicksal *m;* II *v* verurteilen *(to death* zum Tode).

door [dɔː] Tür *f;* Tor *n; out of* ~s im Freien; *two* ~s *off* zwei Häuser weiter; ~**keeper** ['-,kiːpə] Pförtner *m;* ~**way** ['-weɪ] Eingang *m.*

dope [dəup] **I** s Narkotikum n; **II** v dopen.

dorm|ant ['dɔːmənt] schlafend; (Vulkan) untätig; **~itory** ['dɔːmɪtrɪ] (Studenten-)Wohnheim n.

dose [dəus] Dosis f.

dot [dɒt] **I** s Punkt m; right on the ~ (fam) auf die Minute; **II** v durch Punkte markieren.

dote [dəut] ~ on vernarrt sein in.

double ['dʌbl] **I** adj doppelt; zweimal; **II** s 1. Doppelte n; 2. Zweitschrift f; 3. Doppelgänger m; film Double n; **III** v 4. verdoppeln; 5. zs.falten; 6. mar umsegeln; **~-breasted** [ˌ-'brestɪd] (Mantel) zweireihig; **~-cross** [ˌ-'krɒs] betrügen, hintergehen.

doubt [daut] **I** v (be)zweifeln; **II** s Zweifel m (of, about an); beyond (all) ~, without (a) ~ ohne Zweifel; **~ful** ['-ful] zweifelhaft; be ~ im Zweifel sein (about über); **~less** ['-lɪs] zweifellos.

douche [duːʃ] **I** s Dusche f; **II** v spülen; (sich) duschen.

dough [dəu] Teig m; **~nut** Krapfen m.

dove [dʌv] Taube f.

down [daun] **I** s Daunen f pl; Flaum m; **II** prp her-, hinunter; go ~ town in die Stadt(mitte) gehen; **III** adv her-, hinab; nieder; unten;

up and ~ auf u. ab; ~ and out (fam) erledigt, ruiniert; **IV** v (fam) niederschlagen, -strecken; ~ a glass of beer ein Glas Bier runterkippen.

down|cast ['daunkaːst] niedergeschlagen; **~hearted** [ˌ-'haːtɪd] niedergeschlagen; **~hill** [ˌ-'hɪl] bergab, abwärts; ~ **payment** Anzahlung f; **~pour** ['-pɔː] Platzregen m; **~right** ['-raɪt] **I** adj (Mensch) aufrecht, gerade, offen; **II** adv völlig; ganz u. gar; **~stairs** [ˌ-'steəz] go ~ die Treppe hinuntergehen.

dowry ['dauərɪ] Mitgift f.

doze [dəuz] (vor sich hin)dösen; ~ **off** einnicken.

dozen ['dʌzn] Dutzend n.

draft [drɑːft] **I** s 1. Skizze f, Entwurf m; 2. fin Wechsel m; **II** v skizzieren, entwerfen.

drag [dræg] 1. (hinter sich her)ziehen, schleppen, schleifen; 2. (mit e-m Schleppnetz) absuchen (for nach); 3. (Zeit) schleichen.

dragon ['drægən] Drache m; **~fly** [-flaɪ] Libelle f.

drain [dreɪn] **I** v 1. ~ away, off abfließen; 2. entwässern; 3. berauben, entblößen (of von); **II** s 4. Abfluß(rinne f, -rohr n) m; 5. Belastung f; (on für); **~age** ['-ɪdʒ] Entwässerung(sanlage) f.

drama ['drɑːmə] Schauspiel n; **~tist** ['dræmətɪst] Dramatiker m.

drapery ['dreɪpərɪ] Tuch-, Textilgeschäft n.

draught [drɑːft] 1. (Luft-)Zug m; 2. Schluck m; drink at a ~ in einem Zug austrinken; 3. (Fisch-)Fang m; ~s [-s] pl mit sing Damespiel n; ~y ['-ɪ] zugig.

draw [drɔː] I s 1. (Lotterie) Ziehung f; 2. Anziehung(skraft) f; 3. end in a ~ unentschieden ausgehen; II v irr drew [druː], drawn [drɔːn] 4. (auf-, zu)ziehen; 5. Anziehungskraft ausüben auf; 6. (Geld) abheben; 7. ~ a deep breath tief Atem holen; 8. zeichnen; ~ **near** sich nähern; ~ **up** abfassen, aufsetzen.

drawback ['drɔːbæk] Nachteil m; ~**bridge** [-brɪdʒ] Zugbrücke f; ~**er** ['drɔːə] 1. Schublade f; 2. pl Unterhose f.

drawing ['drɔːɪŋ] 1. Zeichnen n; 2. Zeichnung, Skizze f; ~**-board** [-bɔːd] Reißbrett n; ~**-pin** [-pɪn] Br Reißnagel m; ~**-room** [-rum] Empfangszimmer n, Salon m.

dread [dred] I v sich fürchten, Angst haben; II s Furcht, Angst f; Grauen n (of vor); ~**ful** ['-fʊl] schrecklich; scheußlich.

dream [driːm] I s Traum m; II v a. irr dreamt, dreamt [dremt] träumen (of von); I wouldn't ~ of doing it es fiele mir nicht im Traume ein, das zu tun.

dreary ['drɪərɪ] trüb(e), düster.

drench [drentʃ] durchnässen.

dress [dres] I v 1. (sich) anziehen; 2. (Wunde) verbinden; 3. (Salat) anmachen; II s Kleidung f; (Damen-)-Kleid n; ~ **circle** theat Br erste(r) Rang m; ~**er** ['-ə] Anrichte f.

dressing ['dresɪŋ] 1. Ankleiden n; 2. med Verband m; 3. (Salat-)Soße; (Geflügel) Füllung f; ~**-gown** [-gaʊn] Morgenrock m.

dressmaker ['dres,meɪkə] Schneiderin f.

drift [drɪft] I s 1. Strömung; Tendenz f; 2. (Schnee-)Verwehung f; II v treiben (lassen); ~**-ice** ['-aɪs] Treibeis n.

drill [drɪl] I s 1. Bohrer m; 2. Drill m; 3. agr Furche, Rille f; II v 4. bohren; 5. drillen.

drink [drɪŋk] I v irr drank [dræŋk], drunk [drʌŋk] trinken; II s Getränk n; ~**able** ['-əble] trinkbar; ~**er** ['-ə] Trinker.

drinking ['drɪŋkɪŋ] Trinken n; ~**-fountain** [-,faʊntɪn] (öffentlicher) Trinkwasserspender m; ~**-water** [-,wɔːtə] Trinkwasser n.

drip [drɪp] I v tropfen (from von); II s Tropfen m; ~**-dry** [,-'draɪ] bügelfrei; ~**ping** ['-pɪŋ] Bratenfett n.

drive [draɪv] **I** *s* 1. Fahrt *f;* 2. Fahrweg *m;* 3. Antrieb, Schwung *m,* Tatkraft *f;* **II** *v* *irr* drove [drəʊv], driven ['drɪvn] 4. antreiben; 5. *(Fahrzeug)* fahren, lenken; ~ **at** *what are you driving at?* worauf wollen Sie hinaus? ~ **in** *(Nagel)* einschlagen; ~**r** ['-ə] Fahrer, Chauffeur *m;* ~*'s license, permit (Am)* Führerschein *m.*

driving| licence *Br* Führerschein *m;* ~ **school** Fahrschule *f;* ~ **test** Fahrprüfung *f.*

drizzle ['drɪzl] **I** *v* nieseln; **II** *s* Sprühregen *m.*

drone [drəʊn] 1. *zoo* Drohn(e *f) m;* 2. Faulenzer *m;* 3. Summen *n.*

droop [druːp] den Kopf hängen lassen.

drop [drɒp] **I** *s* 1. Tropfen *m;* 2. Fall, (Ab-)Sturz *m;* 3. *com* Rückgang *m, f;* 4. *pl* Drops *pl;* **II** *v* 5. tropfen; 6. fallen(lassen); ~ *anchor* Anker werfen; 7. nachlassen; *(Wind)* abflauen; *(Temperatur)* sinken; 8. *(Fahrgäste)* absetzen, aussteigen lassen; 9. *(Brief)* einwerfen; 10. ~ *a line* ein paar Zeilen schreiben; ~ **behind** zurückbleiben (hinter); ~ **in** auf e-n Sprung vorbeikommen; ~ **off** 1. weg-, ausbleiben; 2. einnicken, -schlafen.

drought [draʊt] Trockenheit, Dürre *f.*

drown [draʊn] ertränken; *be* ~ed [-d] ertrinken.

drowsy ['draʊzɪ] schläfrig.

drudgery ['drʌdʒərɪ] Plackerei *f.*

drug [drʌg] Droge *f,* Rauschgift *n;* ~**gist** ['-ɪst] Drogist; *Am* Apotheker *m;* ~**store** ['-stɔː] *Am* Drugstore *m;* Apotheke *f.*

drum [drʌm] **I** *s* Trommel *f;* **II** *v* trommeln; ~**mer** ['-ə] Trommler *m.*

drunk [drʌŋk] betrunken; *get* ~ sich betrinken; ~**ard** ['-əd] Trunkenbold *m.*

dry [draɪ] **I** *adj* 1. trocken; 2. langweilig; **II** *v* (ab)trocknen; ~-**cleaner('s)** [ˌ-ˈkliːnə(z)] chemische Reinigungsanstalt *f;* ~-**cleaning** [ˌ-ˈkliːnɪŋ] chemische Reinigung *f.*

dual ['djuːəl] zweifach, doppelt.

dubious ['djuːbjəs] zweifelhaft; ungewiß; unsicher.

duchess ['dʌtʃɪs] Herzogin *f.*

duck [dʌk] **I** *s* Ente *f;* **II** *v* 1. sich ducken; 2. (kurz) untertauchen.

due [djuː] 1. *after ~ consideration* nach reiflicher Überlegung; 2. ~ *to an oversight* durch ein Versehen; 3. *be ~ to* sollen, müssen; *be ~ to s.o.* jdm zustehen, gebühren; 4. *become,* *fall* ~ fällig werden; 5. *the train is* ~ *at* ... die planmäßige Ankunft(szeit) des Zuges ist ...

duel ['dju:əl] Zweikampf *m*.

duke [dju:k] Herzog *m*.

dull [dʌl] 1. dumm; 2. langweilig; 3. *(Geschäft)* flau; 4. *(Messer)* stumpf; 5. *(Wetter)* trüb(e); ~**ness** [-nɪs] 1. Dummheit *f*; 2. Stumpfheit *f*; 3. Trübheit *f*.

duly ['dju:lɪ] 1. ordnungsgemäß; 2. pünktlich.

dumb [dʌm] 1. stumm; *be struck* ~ sprachlos sein; *deaf and* ~ taubstumm; 2. *Am fam* doof.

dummy ['dʌmɪ] I *s* Attrappe *f*; II *adj* nachgemacht.

dump [dʌmp] I *v* (hin)werfen, fallen lassen; II *s* Müllhaufen, -abladeplatz *m*.

dumpling ['dʌmplɪŋ] Kloß, Knödel *m*.

dune [dju:n] Düne *f*.

dung [dʌŋ] Mist, Dünger *m*.

duplicate ['dju:plɪkət] I *s* Duplikat *n*; II *v* 1. kopieren; 2. verdoppeln.

dur|able ['djuərəbl] dauerhaft; ~**ation** [djuə'reɪʃn] Dauer *f*.

during ['djuərɪŋ] während.

dusk [dʌsk] (Abend-)Dämmerung *f*.

dust [dʌst] I *s* Staub *m*; II *v* abstauben; ~**bin** ['-bɪn] Mülleimer, -kasten *m*; ~**-cart** ['-kɑ:t] Müllwagen *m*; ~**y** ['-ɪ] staubig.

Dutch [dʌtʃ] holländisch; ~**man** ['-mən] Holländer *m*.

dutiful ['dju:tɪfʊl] pflichtgetreu; gehorsam.

duty ['dju:tɪ] 1. Pflicht *f* (*to* gegenüber); 2. *off* ~ außer Dienst; dienstfrei; *on* ~ im Dienst; 3. Zoll *m*; ~**-free** [,-'fri:] abgaben-, zollfrei.

dwarf [dwɔ:f] I *s* Zwerg *m*; II *adj* winzig, klein; III *v fig* in den Schatten stellen.

dwell [dwel] *irr* dwelt, dwelt [-t] 1. wohnen; 2. ~ *on* sich abgeben mit; Nachdruck legen auf; ~**ing** ['-ɪŋ] Wohnung *f*.

dwindle ['dwɪndl] schwinden.

dye [daɪ] I *s* Farbe *f*; II *v* färben; ~**ing** ['-ɪŋ] Färben *n*.

dying [daɪŋ] sterbend.

dynamite ['daɪnəmaɪt] Dynamit *n*.

dynast ['dɪnəst] Herrscher, *m*; ~**y** ['-ɪ] Dynastie *f*.

dysentery ['dɪsntrɪ] *med* Ruhr *f*.

E

each [iːtʃ] jede(r, s); ~ *other* einander, sich (gegenseitig).

eager [iːgə] eifrig, ungeduldig, begierig (*for* auf, nach; *to do s.th.* etw zu tun); ~**ness** [-nɪs] Eifer *m*, Ungeduld, Begierde *f*.

eagle [iːgl] Adler *m*.

ear [ɪə] 1. Ohr *n* (*for* für); *I'm all ~s* ich bin ganz Ohr; 2. Schlaufe *f*, Henkel *m*; 3. Ähre *f*; ~**ache** ['-reɪk] Ohrenschmerzen *m pl*; ~**drum** ['-drʌm] Trommelfell *n*.

earl [ɜːl] (englischer) Graf *m*.

early ['ɜːlɪ] früh(zeitig); ~ *vegetables* (*pl*) Frühgemüse *n*.

earmark ['ɪəmɑːk] vormerken; zweckbestimmen (*for* für).

earn [ɜːn] verdienen; ~**ings** *pl* ['-ɪŋz] Verdienst *m*, Einkommen *n*, Lohn *m*.

earnest ['ɜːnɪst] ernst(haft); *in ~* im Ernst; ~**ly** [-lɪ] ernstlich.

ear|phones *pl* ['ɪəfəʊnz] *tele radio* Kopfhörer *m pl*; ~**rings** *pl* ['ɪərɪŋz] Ohrringe *m pl*; ~**shot** ['ɪəʃɒt] *within, out of* ~ in, außer Hörweite.

earth [ɜːθ] **I** *s* Erde *f*; **II** *v el* erden; ~**en** ['-n] irden; ~**enware** ['-nweə] irdene(s) Geschirr *n*; ~**ly** ['-lɪ] irdisch;

(*sl*) *not an* ~ (*chance*) (*fam*) nicht die geringste Aussicht; ~**quake** ['-kweɪk] Erdbeben *n*; ~**worm** ['-wɜːm] Regenwurm *m*.

earwax ['ɪəwæks] Ohrenschmalz *n*.

ease [iːz] **I** *s* Leichtigkeit, Mühelosigkeit *f*; *with ~* mit Leichtigkeit; *be* (*ill*) *at ~* sich (nicht) wohl fühlen, (nicht) in s-m Element sein; **II** *v* 1. (*Schmerz*) lindern, mildern; 2. ~ *down* (*Fahrt*) vermindern; 3. ~ *off* (*Lage*) sich entspannen.

easel ['iːzl] Staffelei *f*, Gestell *n*.

easily ['iːzɪlɪ] 1. leicht, mühelos; 2. zweifellos, bei weitem.

east [iːst] **I** *s* Ost(en) *m*; **II** *adj* östlich; **III** *adv* nach Osten.

Easter ['iːstə] Ostern *n*.

eastern ['iːstən] östlich.

Easter Sunday Ostersonntag *m*.

eastward(s) ['iːstwəd(z)] ostwärts.

easy ['iːzɪ] **I** *adj* 1. leicht; nicht schwierig; 2. sorglos, unbekümmert; 3. bequem, behaglich; 4. zwanglos, ungezwungen; **II** *adv*: *take it ~* nur (immer) mit der Ruhe; ~

chair Lehnstuhl m; ~**going** [-ˌɡəʊɪŋ] *fig* leichtlebig.

eat [iːt] *irr* ate [et], eaten ['iːtn] essen; (auf)fressen; ~**able** ['-əbl] genießbar.

eaves *pl* [iːvz] Dachrinne, Traufe f; ~**dropper** ['-drɒpə] Horcher m.

ebb [eb] (~ tide) Ebbe f.

ebony ['ebənɪ] Ebenholz n.

eccentric [ɪk'sentrɪk] I adj exzentrisch, überspannt; II s Sonderling m.

ecclesiastical [ɪˌkliːzɪ'æstɪkl] kirchlich, geistlich.

echo ['ekəʊ] I s Echo n; II v 1. widerhallen (with von); 2. wiederholen.

eclipse [ɪ'klɪps] ~ of the moon, sun Mond-, Sonnenfinsternis f.

economic [ˌiːkə'nɒmɪk] (volks)wirtschaftlich; ~**ical** [-l] wirtschaftlich, sparsam (of mit); ~**ize** [ɪ'kɒnəmaɪz] sparen; ~**y** [ɪ'kɒnəmɪ] Sparsamkeit f; ~ class Touristenklasse f.

ecstasy ['ekstəsɪ] Ekstase f.

eddy ['edɪ] Wirbel, Strudel m.

edge [edʒ] 1. (Klinge) Schneide f, (scharfe) Kante f; 2. Rand, Saum m; 3. on ~ nervös, reizbar; ~**ways** ['-weɪz] not get a word in ~ nicht zu Wort kommen.

edible ['edɪbl] eß-, genießbar.

edit ['edɪt] (Buch) herausgeben; ~**ion** [ɪ'dɪʃn] 1. (Buch) Auflage f; 2. pocket ~ Ta-

schenausgabe f; ~**or** [-ə] 1. Herausgeber m; 2. Schriftleiter m; ~**orial** [ˌedɪ'tɔːrɪəl] I adj redaktionell; II s (Zeitung) Leitartikel m.

educate ['edjuːkeɪt] erziehen, unterrichten; ~**ion** [ˌedju:'keɪʃn] Erziehung f; adult ~ Erwachsenenbildung f.

eel [iːl] Aal m.

effect [ɪ'fekt] I s 1. Wirkung f (on auf); come into ~ in Kraft treten; take ~ wirksam werden; in Kraft treten; 2. Eindruck, Effekt m; 3. pl (bewegliches) Eigentum n, Effekten pl; II v aus-, durchführen; ~**ive** [-ɪv] 1. wirksam, wirkungs-, eindrucksvoll; 2. tatsächlich, wirklich.

effeminate [ɪ'femɪnət] verweichlicht.

efficiency [ɪ'fɪʃənsɪ] Leistungsfähigkeit f; ~**t** [-t] leistungsfähig; (Mensch) tüchtig; wirksam.

effort ['efət] 1. Anstrengung, Mühe f; make an ~ sich bemühen; 2. Versuch m; ~**less** [-lɪs] mühelos.

egg [eg] Ei n; put all o.'s ~s in one basket alles auf eine Karte setzen; scrambled, boiled, fried ~s (pl) Rührei n, gekochte Eier, Spiegeleier n pl; ~-**cup** ['-kʌp] Eierbecher m; ~-**plant** ['-plɑːnt] Aubergine f; ~-**shell** ['-ʃel] Eierschale f.

egois|m ['egǝuɪzǝm] Egoismus *m;* **~t** [-ɪst] Egoist *m.*

Egypt ['iːdʒɪpt] Ägypten *n;* **~ian** [ɪ'dʒɪpʃn] **I** *s* Ägypter *m;* **II** *adj* ägyptisch.

eiderdown ['aɪdǝdaʊn] Daunendecke *f.*

eight [eɪt] acht; **~h** [eɪtθ] achte(r, s); **~y** ['eɪtɪ] achtzig.

Eire ['eǝrǝ] Irland *n.*

either ['aɪðǝ] ein(e, er, es); jede(r, s) von beiden, beide(s); *not ...* ~ kein(e, er, es) von beiden, auch nicht; *I shall not go* ~ ich gehe auch nicht; ~ *... or* entweder ... oder.

ejaculate [ɪ'dʒækjʊleɪt] ausrufen, -stoßen.

eject [ɪ'dʒekt] *(Menschen)* hinauswerfen *(from* aus).

elaborate I *adj* [ɪ'læbǝrǝt] 1. genau ausgearbeitet; 2. kompliziert; **II** *v* [ɪ'læbǝreɪt] 3. sorgfältig ausarbeiten; 4. genau darlegen.

elapse [ɪ'læps] *(Zeit)* vergehen.

elastic [ɪ'læstɪk] **I** *adj* biegsam, dehnbar, elastisch; **II** *s* Gummiband *n.*

elbow ['elbǝʊ] **I** *s* Ellbogen *m;* **II** *v* sich bahnen *(o.'s way through* e-n Weg durch); ~ **room** Bewegungsfreiheit *f,* Spielraum *m.*

elder ['eldǝ] **I** *adj* älter; **II** *s bot* Holunder *m;* **~ly** [-lɪ] ältlich.

eldest ['eldɪst] älteste(r).

elect [ɪ'lekt] wählen *(president* zum Präsidenten).

election [ɪ'lekʃn] Wahl *f;* ~ **campaign** Wahlkampf *m.*

elector [ɪ'lektǝ] 1. *Br* Wähler *m;* 2. *Am* Wahlmann *m.*

electri|c(al) [ɪ'lektrɪk(l)] elektrisch; **~cian** [ˌɪlek'trɪʃn] Elektriker *m;* **~city** [ˌɪlek'trɪsǝtɪ] Elektrizität *f;* **~fy** [ɪ'lektrɪfaɪ] elektrifizieren.

elegan|ce ['elɪgǝns] Eleganz *f;* **~t** [-t] elegant, geschmackvoll.

element ['elɪmǝnt] 1. Element *n,* Grundstoff, (Grund-)Bestandteil *m;* 2. *pl* Anfangsgründe *m pl;* 3. *pl* Natur(gewalten *f pl)* *f;* **~ary** [ˌelɪ'mentǝrɪ] elementar.

elephant ['elɪfǝnt] Elefant *m.*

elevat|e ['elɪveɪt] (hoch)heben; **~ion** [ˌelɪ'veɪʃn] 1. Erhöhung, Erhebung *f;* 2. *geog* (Meeres-)Höhe *f;* 3. *arch* Aufriß *m;* **~or** [-ǝ] *Am* Aufzug, Fahrstuhl *m.*

eleven [ɪ'levn] elf.

elicit [ɪ'lɪsɪt] ent-, hervorlocken, herausholen *(from* aus).

eligible ['elɪdʒǝbl] 1. qualifiziert *(for* für); 2. geeignet, passend.

eliminat|e [ɪ'lɪmɪneɪt] ausscheiden, -schalten, beseitigen *(from* aus); *math* eliminieren; **~ion** [ɪˌlɪmɪ'neɪʃn] Beseitigung, Streichung;

med sport chem Ausscheidung *f.*

elm [elm] *bot* Ulme *f.*

elongate ['iːlɒŋgeɪt] verlängern.

elope [ɪ'ləʊp] entlaufen; sich (heimlich) davonmachen.

eloquent ['eləkwənt] beredt.

else [els] sonst, außerdem, noch, anders; *anybody ~?* sonst noch jemand? *anything ~* sonst noch etwas? *nothing ~* nichts weiter; *or ~* sonst, andernfalls; *somebody ~* jemand anders; **~where** [,-'weə] anders-, sonstwo, woanders.

elucidate [ɪ'luːsɪdeɪt] erklären, erläutern.

elude [ɪ'luːd] umgehen, ausweichen.

elusive [ɪ'luːsɪv] 1. ausweichend; 2. schwer zu begreifen(d).

embalm [ɪm'bɑːm] (ein)balsamieren.

embankment [ɪm'bæŋkmənt] Uferbefestigung *f,* Damm *m.*

embark [ɪm'bɑːk] 1. (sich) einschiffen; verladen (*for* nach); 2. sich einlassen (*on* auf); **~ation** [,embɑː'keɪʃn] Einschiffung; Verladung *f.*

embarrass [ɪm'bærəs] 1. in Verlegenheit bringen; 2. (be)hindern; **~ing** [-ɪŋ] peinlich.

embassy ['embəsɪ] *pol* Botschaft *f.*

embezzle [ɪm'bezl] veruntreuen, unterschlagen.

emblem ['embləm] Symbol, Emblem *n.*

embody [ɪm'bɒdɪ] 1. verkörpern; 2. (in sich) vereinigen.

embrace [ɪm'breɪs] 1. umarmen; 2. *(Gelegenheit, Beruf)* ergreifen; 3. *fig* enthalten, umfassen.

embroider [ɪm'brɔɪdə] 1. sticken; 2. *(Erzählung)* ausschmücken.

emerald ['emərəld] Smaragd *m.*

emerge [ɪ'mɜːdʒ] 1. hervorkommen, auftauchen; 2. bekanntwerden.

emergency [ɪ'mɜːdʒənsɪ] Notfall *m;* kritische Situation *f; in an ~, in case of ~* im Not-, im Ernstfall; **~ brake** Notbremse *f; ~ exit* Notausgang *m.*

emigr|ant ['emɪgrənt] Auswanderer *m;* **~ate** ['emɪgreɪt] auswandern (*from* aus; *to* nach); **~ation** [,emɪ'greɪʃn] Auswanderung *f.*

eminent ['emɪnənt] hervorragend, bedeutend.

emit [ɪ'mɪt] ausströmen, ausstrahlen.

emotion [ɪ'məʊʃn] (innere) Bewegung, Erregtheit *f;* (starkes) Gefühl *n;* Rührung *f;* **~al** [ɪ'məʊʃənl] 1. gefühlsmäßig; 2. gefühlvoll.

emperor ['empərə] Kaiser *m.*

empha|sis ['emfəsɪs] *pl* -*ases* Nachdruck *m*, Betonung *f*; *put, lay* ~ *on s.th.* großes Gewicht auf etw legen; **~size** ['emfəsaɪz] hervorheben; **~tic** [ɪm'fætɪk] nachdrücklich.

empire ['empaɪə] Reich *n*.

employ [ɪm'plɔɪ] 1. benutzen, an-, verwenden; 2. beschäftigen; einstellen; **~ee** [,emplɔɪ'i:] Arbeitnehmer *m*, Angestellte(r) *m;* **~er** [-ə] Arbeitgeber *m;* **~ment** [-mənt] Beschäftigung, Anstellung, Arbeit *f;* ~ *agency* Stellenvermittlung *f.*

empress ['emprɪs] Kaiserin *f.*

empty ['emptɪ] **I** *adj* 1. inhaltslos; leer; 2. nichtssagend; **II** *v* 3. sich leeren, ent-, ausleeren; 4. *(Fluß)* münden.

enable [ɪ'neɪbl] 1. in den Stand setzen *(to do* zu tun); 2. ermöglichen, möglich machen.

enamel [ɪ'næml] Emaille *f;* Lack; (Zahn-)Schmelz *m;* Glasur *f.*

enchant [ɪn'tʃɑ:nt] bezaubern; **~ing** [-ɪŋ] faszinierend, bezaubernd.

encircle [ɪn'sɜ:kl] ein-, umschließen; umgeben.

enclose [ɪn'kləʊz] 1. umgeben, einschließen *(in* in); 2. *(e-m Brief)* beilegen.

encounter [ɪn'kaʊntə] **I** *v* (unerwartet) treffen, stoßen auf; **II** *s* 1. Begegnung *f;* 2. Zs.prallen *n*, -stoß *m.*

encourage [ɪn'kʌrɪdʒ] 1. ermutigen, aufmuntern; 2. unterstützen, bestärken in; **~ment** [-mənt] 1. Ermutigung *f;* 2. Unterstützung; Förderung *f.*

encroach [ɪn'krəʊtʃ] (unberechtigt) übergreifen *(on, upon* auf); eingreifen *(on, upon* in).

encyclop(a)edia [en,saɪkləʊ'pi:djə] Enzyklopädie *f.*

end [end] **I** *s* 1. Ende *n;* Schluß *m; in the* ~ am Ende, schließlich; *no* ~ *of (fam)* unendlich viel(e); *on* ~ ohne Unterbrechung; *(Kiste)* hochkant; *stand on* ~ *(Haare)* zu Berge stehen, sich sträuben; *make an* ~ *of, put an* ~ *to* ein Ende, Schluß machen mit; *make (both)* ~*s meet* gerade (mit s-m Gelde) auskommen; *odds and* ~*s* alles mögliche; Kleinkram *m;* 2. Zweck *m*, Ziel *n*, Absicht *f;* **II** *v* (be)end(ig)en; *to* ~ *up with* zum Schluß; **~less** ['-lɪs] endlos, ohne Ende.

endanger [ɪn'deɪndʒə] in Gefahr bringen.

endeavo(u)r [ɪn'devə] **I** *v* sich bemühen *(to do* zu tun); **II** *s* Bemühung *f.*

endorse [ɪn'dɔ:s] 1. *(Scheck)* indossieren; 2. billigen, gutheißen.

endow [ɪn'daʊ] ausstatten; stiften; **~ment** [-mənt] 1. Stiftung f; 2. *meist pl* Begabung f.

endur|ance [ɪn'djʊərəns] Ausdauer f; **~e** [ɪn'djʊə] ertragen, aushalten, erdulden.

enemy ['enəmɪ] Feind m.

energ|etic [ˌenə'dʒetɪk] energisch, tatkräftig; **~y** ['enədʒɪ] 1. Arbeitskraft, Tatkraft f; 2. *phys* Energie f.

enforce [ɪn'fɔːs] erzwingen (*upon s.o.* von jdm); *(mit Gewalt)* durchsetzen.

engage [ɪn'geɪdʒ] 1. an-, einstellen; 2. sich verpflichten (*to do* zu tun); 3. sich einlassen (*in* auf); sich abgeben (*with* mit); 4. in Anspruch nehmen; **~ed** [-d] 1. beschäftigt; 2. *tele* besetzt; 3. *get* ~ *to* sich verloben mit; **~ement** [-mənt] 1. Verpflichtung f; 2. Verlobung f (*to* mit); 3. Abmachung f; **~ing** [-ɪŋ] einnehmend, gewinnend.

engine ['endʒɪn] 1. Motor m; 2. Lokomotive f; ~ *driver* Lok(omotiv)führer m.

engineer [ˌendʒɪ'nɪə] 1. Ingenieur, Techniker m; 2. *Am* Lok(omotiv)führer m; **~ing** [-rɪŋ] Ingenieurwesen n, Maschinenbau m.

England ['ɪŋglənd] England n.

English ['ɪŋglɪʃ] **I** *adj* englisch; **II** *s (Sprache)* Englisch n; **~man** [-mən] pl ~men Engländer m; **~woman** [-ˌwʊmən] pl ~women Engländerin f.

engraving [ɪn'greɪvɪŋ] (Kupfer-, Stahl-)Stich m; *(wood* ~) Holzschnitt m.

enhance [ɪn'hɑːns] steigern, vergrößern.

enigma [ɪ'nɪgmə] Rätsel n.

enjoy [ɪn'dʒɔɪ] genießen, sich erfreuen (*s.th.* an etw); ~ *o.s.* sich gut unterhalten, sich amüsieren; ~ *good health* sich e-r guten Gesundheit erfreuen; *how are you* ~*ing London?* wie gefällt es Ihnen in London? **~able** [-əbl] angenehm, erfreulich; **~ment** [-mənt] Vergnügen n.

enlarge [ɪn'lɑːdʒ] (sich) vergrößern; **~ment** [-mənt] Vergrößerung f.

enlighten [ɪn'laɪtn] aufklären (*on, as to* über); **~ment** [-mənt] Aufklärung f.

enlist [ɪn'lɪst] sich freiwillig melden (*in the navy* zur Marine).

enmity ['enmɪtɪ] Feindschaft f; Haß m (*of, against* gegen).

enormous [ɪ'nɔːməs] riesig, ungeheuer; gewaltig.

enough [ɪ'nʌf] genug, genügend; *sure* ~ gewiß; *surprisingly* ~ überraschenderweise; *well* ~ ganz gut.

enraged [ɪn'reɪdʒd] wütend, aufgebracht (*at, by* über).

enrich [ɪn'rɪtʃ] bereichern.

enrol(l) [ɪnˈrəʊl] (in e-e Liste) eintragen, registrieren.

ensign [ˈensaɪn] *white ~* Flagge *f* der britischen Kriegsmarine.

ensue [ɪnˈsjuː] sich ergeben (*from* aus).

ensure [ɪnˈʃʊə] sicherstellen, garantieren.

entail [ɪnˈteɪl] zur Folge haben.

entangle [ɪnˈtæŋgl] verwikkeln, verwirren, verstricken (*in* in).

enter [ˈentə] 1. betreten, einsteigen, -treten, -fahren in; 2. eindringen in; 3. einschreiben, -tragen; *~ o.'s name* sich eintragen, -schreiben (lassen); *~ into details* auf Einzelheiten eingehen.

enterpris|e [ˈentəpraɪz] Unternehmen *n;* **~ing** [-ɪŋ] unternehmend.

entertain [,entəˈteɪn] 1. unterhalten; 2. bewirten, einladen (*to dinner* zum Essen); *they ~ a great deal* sie haben sehr oft Gäste; 3. *(Hoffnung, Zweifel)* hegen; *(Vorschlag)* in Erwägung ziehen; **~er** [-ə] Unterhaltungskünstler *m;* **~ment** [-mənt] Unterhaltung *f.*

enthus|iasm [ɪnˈθjuːzɪæzəm] Begeisterung *f;* **~iastic** [ɪn,θjuːzɪˈæstɪk] begeistert (*about* von).

entic|e [ɪnˈtaɪs] (an-, ver)locken, verführen, verleiten

(*into doing* zu tun); **~ing** [-ɪŋ] verführerisch.

entire [ɪnˈtaɪə] ganz, gesamt; **~ly** [-lɪ] gänzlich; *~ different* grundverschieden.

entitle [ɪnˈtaɪtl] 1. betiteln; 2. *be ~d to* Anspruch haben auf; berechtigt sein zu.

entrance [ˈentrəns] 1. Eintritt *m;* 2. Eingang *m;* Einfahrt *f;* 3. *~ examination* Aufnahmeprüfung *f;* **~-fee** [-fiː] Eintrittsgeld *n.*

entreat [ɪnˈtriːt] dringend bitten.

entrust [ɪnˈtrʌst] 1. betrauen *(s.o. with s.th.* jdn mit e-r S.); 2. anvertrauen *(s.th. to s.o.* jdm etw).

entry [ˈentrɪ] 1. Eintritt *m,* Einfahrt *f;* 2. Vermerk, Eintrag(ung *f*) *m;* Stichwort *n;* 3. Anmeldung *f.*

enumerate [ɪˈnjuːməreɪt] (auf)zählen.

envelop [ɪnˈveləp] einwikkeln, -hüllen; **~e** [ˈenvələʊp] (Brief-)Umschlag *m.*

envious [ˈenvɪəs] neidisch (*of* auf).

environment [ɪnˈvaɪərənmənt] 1. Umgebung *f;* 2. *biol* Umwelt *f;* **~al** [ɪn,vaɪərənˈmentl] *~ conditions* Umweltbedingungen *pl f.*

envoy [ˈenvɔɪ] *pol* Gesandte(r) *m.*

envy [ˈenvɪ] **I** *s* Neid *m;* **II** *v* beneiden *(s.o. s.th.* jdn um etw).

epidemic [ˌepɪˈdemɪk] Epidemie f.

episode [ˈepɪsəʊd] Episode f.

epoch [ˈiːpɒk] Epoche f.

equal [ˈiːkwəl] I adj 1. gleich; 2. be ~ to the occasion der Lage gewachsen sein; II v (Leistung) erreichen, gleichkommen (s.o. jdm); III s: he has no ~ er hat nicht seinesgleichen; ~ity [iːˈkwɒlətɪ] Gleichheit f; ~ize [ˈiːkwəlaɪz] 1. gleichmachen; 2. ausgleichen; ~ly [-lɪ] gleich, ebenso, genauso.

equation [ɪˈkweɪʒn] Gleichung f.

equator [ɪˈkweɪtə] Äquator m.

equilibrium [ˌiːkwɪˈlɪbrɪəm] Gleichgewicht n.

equip [ɪˈkwɪp] ausrüsten, -statten (with mit); ~ment [-mənt] Ausstattung, Ausrüstung f.

equity [ˈekwətɪ] Billigkeit, Gerechtigkeit f.

equivalent [ɪˈkwɪvələnt] I s Gegenwert m; II adj gleichwertig.

era [ˈɪərə] Zeitrechnung f.

erase [ɪˈreɪz] ausradieren, -wischen, -löschen (from aus); ~r [-ə] Radiergummi m.

erect [ɪˈrekt] I adj aufrecht, senkrecht; II v aufrichten; (Gebäude) errichten; ~ion [ɪˈrekʃn] Errichtung f.

erosion [ɪˈrəʊʒn] geol Erosion f.

erotic [ɪˈrɒtɪk] erotisch.

err [ɜː] (sich) irren.

errand [ˈerənd] Botengang m, Besorgung f; ~-boy [-bɔɪ] Laufbursche m.

erratic [ɪˈrætɪk] (adv ~ally) unbeständig, unberechenbar.

erratum [eˈrɑːtəm] Druckfehler m.

erroneous [ɪˈrəʊnjəs] irrig.

error [ˈerə] Irrtum, Fehler m.

erupt [ɪˈrʌpt] (Vulkan) ausbrechen; ~ion [ɪˈrʌpʃn] (Vulkan-)Ausbruch m.

escalator [ˈeskəleɪtə] Rolltreppe f.

escapade [ˌeskəˈpeɪd] dumme(r) Streich m.

escape [ɪˈskeɪp] I v 1. entfliehen, entkommen (from aus); 2. sich retten, davonkommen; 3. (Flüssigkeit, Gas) ausströmen, auslaufen (from aus); 4. (dem Gedächtnis) entfallen (s.o. jdm); II s: have a narrow ~ mit knapper Not davonkommen; fire-~ Feuerleiter f.

escort I s [ˈeskɔːt] Begleiter m; II v [ɪˈskɔːt] begleiten, eskortieren.

Eskimo [ˈeskɪməʊ] pl ~(e)s Eskimo m.

especial [ɪˈspeʃl] besonder; ~ly [-əlɪ] insbesondere.

espionage [ˌespɪəˈnɑːʒ] Spionage f.

essay [ˈeseɪ] Aufsatz m.

essen|ce [ˈesns] 1. das Wesentliche; 2. Essenz f, Duft m; ~tial [ɪ'senʃl] I adj wesentlich (to für); unentbehrlich; II s pl [-z] das Wesentliche; Hauptsache f.

establish [ɪ'stæblɪʃ] 1. er-, einrichten, gründen; 2. (Beziehung) anknüpfen; (Verbindung) herstellen; 3. (Rekord) aufstellen; 4. feststellen, nachweisen; 5. ~ o.s. sich niederlassen;
~ment [-mənt] 1. Gründung f; 2. Firma f, Unternehmen n.

estate [ɪ'steɪt] 1. Besitz m, Vermögen n; 2. Grundbesitz m; Landgut n; 3. Nachlaß m; ~ agent Br Grundstücksmakler m.

esteem [ɪ'sti:m] I v hoch-, sehr schätzen; II s Wertschätzung f; hold in great ~ hochachten.

estimat|e I v ['estɪmeɪt] 1. abschätzen, veranschlagen (at auf); 2. beurteilen; II s ['estɪmət] Kostenvoranschlag m; ~ion [,estɪ'meɪʃn] 1. (Ein-)Schätzung f; 2. Meinung f; 3. Achtung f.

estuary ['estjʊərɪ] Flußmündung f (ins Meer).

etern|al [i:'tɜ:nl] ewig; ~ally [-əlɪ] 1. für immer, für ewig; 2. fam ununterbrochen, fortwährend; ~ity [i:'tɜ:nətɪ] Ewigkeit f.

Ethiopia [,i:θɪ'əʊpjə] Äthiopien n.

etymology [,etɪ'mɒlədʒɪ] Etymologie f.

Europe ['jʊərəp] Europa n; ~an [,jʊərə'pi:ən] I s Europäer m; II adj europäisch.

evacuate [ɪ'vækjʊeɪt] 1. (aus)leeren; 2. räumen, fortschaffen; 3. (Bevölkerung) evakuieren.

evade [ɪ'veɪd] ausweichen (s.th. e-r S); vermeiden (doing s.th. etw zu tun).

evaluate [ɪ'væljʊeɪt] (ab)schätzen.

evangelic(al) [i:væn'dʒelɪk(l)] evangelisch.

evaporate [ɪ'væpəreɪt] verdampfen; ~d milk Dosenmilch f.

evasive [ɪ'veɪsɪv] ausweichend.

eve [i:v] Vorabend, -tag m.

even ['i:vn] I adj 1. eben, flach; 2. (Mensch) ausgeglichen; 3. (Zahl) gerade; 4. (Zahlen, Maßangabe) genau; 5. get ~ abrechnen (with s.o. mit jdm); heimzahlen (with s.o. jdm); II adv sogar, selbst, noch; not ~ nicht einmal; ~ if, though selbst wenn; obgleich; ~ now sogar jetzt.

evening ['i:vnɪŋ] Abend m; in the ~ am Abend; on Sunday ~ Sonntag abend; this, yesterday, tomorrow ~ heute, gestern, morgen abend; ~ **dress** Gesellschaftsanzug *m;* Abendkleid *n;* ~ **paper** Abendzeitung *f.*

event [ɪ'vent] 1. Ereignis *n;* 2. *sport* Programmnummer *f;* 3. *at all* ~*s, in any* ~ auf alle Fälle; *in the* ~ *of* im Falle, daß; ~**ful** [-fʊl] ereignisreich.

eventual [ɪ'ventʃʊəl] etwaig, möglich; schließlich; ~**ly** [-ɪ] schließlich.

ever ['evə] je(mals); *for* ~ für immer; ~ *after* seitdem (immer); ~**green** [-gri:n] immergrün(e) Pflanze *f;* ~**lasting** [,evə'lɑ:stɪŋ] ewig, dauernd.

every ['evrɪ] jede(r, s); ~ *day* täglich; ~ *hour* stündlich; ~ *time* jedesmal; ~ *now and then* von Zeit zu Zeit; ~ *other day* jeden zweiten Tag; ~ *other week* alle zwei Wochen; ~**body** [-,bɒdɪ], ~**one** [-wʌn] jeder, alle, jedermann; ~**day** [-deɪ] alltäglich; ~**thing** [-θɪŋ] alles; ~**where** [-weə] überall.

evidence ['evɪdəns] Beweise *pl m; give* ~ *of* zeugen von.

evident ['evɪdənt] offenkundig, -sichtlich; augenscheinlich.

evil ['i:vl] **I** *adj* böse, übel; **II** *s* Übel, Unglück *n; the lesser* ~ das kleinere Übel; ~-**doer** [,i:vl'du:ə] Übeltäter *m.*

evolution [,i:və'lu:ʃn] Entwicklung *f.*

ewe [ju:] (Mutter-)Schaf *n.*

exact [ɪg'zækt] genau, exakt,

pünktlich; ~**itude** [ɪg'zæktɪtju:d], ~**ness** [-nɪs] Genauigkeit, Pünktlichkeit *f;* ~**ly** [-lɪ] 1. *(als Antwort)* so ist es, allerdings. 2. genau; 3. eigentlich.

exaggerat|e [ɪg'zædʒəreɪt] übertreiben; ~**ion** [ɪg,zædʒə'reɪʃn] Übertreibung *f.*

exam [ɪg'zæm] *fam* Prüfung *f,* Examen *n.*

examin|ation [ɪg,zæmɪ'neɪʃn] 1. Prüfung *f,* Examen *n (in* in); *oral, written* ~ mündliche, schriftliche Prüfung *f;* 2. Untersuchung, Überprüfung *f; (up)on* ~ bei näherer Prüfung; 3. *jur* Vernehmung *f;* ~**e** [ɪg'zæmɪn] 1. prüfen; 2. untersuchen, (über)prüfen; 3. verhören.

example [ɪg'zɑ:mpl] Beispiel *n; for* ~ zum Beispiel.

exasperate [ɪg'zæspəreɪt] erbittern.

excavate ['ekskəveɪt] ausgraben.

exceedingly [ɪk'si:dɪŋlɪ] außerordentlich.

excel [ɪk'sel] übertreffen; ~**lence** ['eksələns] 1. hervorragende Leistung *f (at, in* in); 2. Vorzug *m;* ~**lent** ['eksələnt] ausgezeichnet, hervorragend.

except [ɪk'sept] außer, ausgenommen; ~ *for* bis auf; ~**ion** [ɪk'sepʃn] Ausnahme *f;* ~**ional(ly)** [ɪk'sepʃənl, -ʃnəlɪ] außergewöhnlich.

excess [ɪk'ses] 1. Übermaß *n*, Überschuß *m* (*of* an); *to* ~ im Übermaß; *be in* ~ *of* übersteigen; 2. Maßlosigkeit *f*; *meist pl* Ausschreitungen *f pl*; ~ **fare** *rail* Zuschlag *m*; ~ **luggage** Übergepäck *n*; ~**ive** [ɪk'sesɪv] übermäßig.

exchange [ɪks'tʃeɪndʒ] I *v* 1. (aus-, ein-, um)tauschen; 2. (um)wechseln (*for* gegen); II *s* 3. (Aus-, Um-)Tausch *m*; *in* ~ *for* als Entschädigung für; 4. (*Geld*) Wechseln *n*; *rate of* ~ Wechselkurs *m*; 5. (*foreign* ~) ausländische Zahlungsmittel *n pl*; 6. Börse *f*; 7. Fernsprechvermittlung *f*; 8. *labo(u)r* ~ Arbeitsamt *n*.

excit|able [ɪk'saɪtəbl] reizbar; ~**e** [ɪk'saɪt] aufregen; (*Interesse*) erregen; (*Neid*) wecken; ~**ed** [-ɪd] erregt, aufgeregt; ~**ement** [-mənt] Erregung, Aufregung *f*; ~**ing** [-ɪŋ] spannend.

exclaim [ɪk'skleɪm] (aus)rufen.

exclamation [ˌeksklə'meɪʃn] Ausruf *m*; ~ **mark** Ausrufezeichen *n*.

exclude [ɪk'sklu:d] ausschließen.

exclus|ion [ɪk'sklu:ʒn] Ausschluß *m*; ~**ive** [-sɪv] ausschließlich, -schließlich, exklusiv; *prices are* ~ *of meals* Mahlzeiten sind im Preis nicht inbegriffen.

excursion [ɪk'skɜ:ʃn] Ausflug *m*; ~**ist** [-ɪst] Ausflügler *m*.

excus|able [ɪk'skju:zəbl] entschuldbar; ~**e** [ɪk'skju:s] I *v* entschuldigen (*for* wegen); verzeihen (*s.o.* jdm); ~ *me, please!* entschuldigen Sie bitte; II *s* Entschuldigung, Ausrede *f*; Vorwand *m*; *make, offer an* ~ sich entschuldigen.

execute ['eksɪkju:t] 1. (*Arbeit, Befehl, Auftrag*) ausführen; 2. hinrichten; 3. (*Dokument*) ausfertigen; 4. *mus* vortragen; *theat* spielen, aufführen.

execution [ˌeksɪ'kju:ʃn] 1. Aus-, Durchführung *f*; 2. Hinrichtung *f*; 3. Ausfertigung *f*; 4. *mus* Vortrag *m*.

executive [ɪg'zekjutɪv] I *adj pol* ausführend, vollziehend; (*Stellung*) leitend; II *s* 1. *pol* Exekutive *f*; 2. Geschäftsleitung *f*; 3. leitende(r) Angestellte(r) *m*.

exempt [ɪg'zempt] I *v* befreien, freistellen (*from* von); II *adj* befreit, ausgenommen (*from* von).

exercise ['eksəsaɪz] I *s* 1. Übung; (Schul-)Aufgabe *f*; 2. *pl* (Leibes-)Übungen *f pl*; II *v* 3. (*Sorgfalt*) anwenden; 4. (*Macht*) ausüben; 5. sich Bewegung verschaffen; trainieren.

exert [ɪg'zɜ:t] (*Kraft*) anwenden; (*Druck*) ausüben; ~**ion** [ɪg'zɜ:ʃn] Anstrengung *f*.

exhale [eks'heɪl] 1. ausatmen; 2. verdunsten, verdampfen; 3. ausströmen (*from* von).

exhaust [ɪg'zɔːst] I *s mot* Auspuff *m*; II *v* erschöpfen; ~**ed** [-ɪd] 1. ver-, aufgebraucht; 2. erschöpft, ermüdet; 3. *(Buch)* vergriffen; ~**ing** [-ɪŋ] anstrengend, ermüdend; ~**ion** [ɪg'zɔːstʃən] Erschöpfung *f*; ~**ive** [-ɪv] erschöpfend; ~ **pipe** Auspuff *m*.

exhibit [ɪg'zɪbɪt] I *v* 1. ausstellen; 2. zeigen, an den Tag legen; II *s* 3. Ausstellungsstück *n*; 4. *jur* Beweisstück *n*; ~**ion** [,eksɪ'bɪʃn] Ausstellung *f*.

exhilarate [ɪg'zɪləreɪt] auf-, erheitern.

exile ['eksaɪl] I *s* 1. Verbannung *f*; 2. Verbannte(r) *m*; II *v* verbannen.

exist [ɪg'zɪst] bestehen, existieren; vorkommen, vorhanden sein; ~**ence** [ɪg'zɪstəns] Dasein, Bestehen *n*, Existenz *f*; *be in* ~ bestehen; ~**ing** [-ɪŋ] bestehend.

exit ['eksɪt] 1. *theat* Abgang *m*; 2. Ausgang *m*.

exorbitant [ɪg'zɔːbɪtənt] übertrieben, maßlos.

exotic [ɪg'zɒtɪk] exotisch.

expand [ɪk'spænd] sich (aus)dehnen; vergrößern, erweitern (*into* zu); ~**sion** [ɪk'spænʃn] Ausdehnung *f*.

expect [ɪk'spekt] 1. erwarten; 2. verlangen (*from s.o.* von jdm); 3. annehmen, meinen; ~**ation** [,ekspek'teɪʃn] Erwartung(en *pl*) *f*; *contrary to* ~(*s*) wider Erwarten; *beyond* ~ über Erwarten; *fall short of, not come up to s.o.'s* ~*s* jds Erwartungen nicht entsprechen.

expedient [ɪk'spiːdjənt] I *adj* zweckmäßig (*to* für); II *s* Ausweg, (Not-)Behelf *m*.

expedite ['ekspɪdaɪt] beschleunigen.

expedition [,ekspɪ'dɪʃn] Expedition *f*.

expel [ɪk'spel] ausweisen, ausschließen (*from* aus).

expend [ɪk'spend] 1. *(Geld)* ausgeben; 2. *(Zeit)* verwenden (*on* auf); 3. verbrauchen; ~**iture** [ɪk'spendɪtʃə] (Geld-)Ausgabe *f*; Aufwand *m* (*of* an).

expense [ɪk'spens] (Geld-)-Ausgabe *f*; *pl* Auslagen *f pl*, (Un-)Kosten *pl*; *at s.o.'s* ~ auf jds Kosten *a. fig*, zu jds Lasten.

expensive [ɪk'spensɪv] kostspielig; teuer.

experience [ɪk'spɪərɪəns] I *s* 1. Erfahrung *f* (*in, of* in); *professional* ~ Berufserfahrung *f*; 2. Erlebnis *n*; II *v* erfahren, erleben, durchmachen; ~**d** [-t] erfahren.

experiment [ɪk'sperɪmənt] I *s* Versuch *m*, Experiment *n*; II *v* experimentieren (*on*

an; *with* mit); **~al**
[ek͵sperɪ'mentl] versuchs-
weise, experimentell.

expert ['ekspɜ:t] I *adj* erfahren, sachkundig; II *s* Sach-
verständige(r), Experte *m*
(*in a field* auf e-m Gebiet);
~ opinion Sachverständi-
gengutachten *n*.

expire [ɪk'spaɪə] 1. *lit* sterben; 2. ablaufen, verfallen,
die Gültigkeit verlieren.

explain [ɪk'spleɪn] 1. erklären; 2. begründen.

explanation [͵eksplə'neɪʃn]
Erklärung, Begründung *f* (*of*
für).

explicable [ɪk'splɪkəbl] er-
klärbar.

explicit [ɪk'splɪsɪt] eindeutig,
klar, bestimmt.

explode [ɪk'spləʊd] 1. explodieren; 2. ausbrechen (*with
laughter* in ein Gelächter).

exploit I *s* ['eksplɔɪt] Heldentat *f;* II *v* [ɪk'splɔɪt] aus-
beuten; auswerten.

explor|ation [͵eksplə'reɪʃn]
Erforschung *f;* **~e** [ɪk'splɔ:]
er-, durchforschen; **~ every
possibility** jede Möglichkeit
genau prüfen; **~er** [-rə] Forscher *m*.

explos|ion [ɪk'spləʊʒn] Ex-
plosion *f;* **~ive** [-sɪv] I *adj*
explosiv; II *s* Sprengstoff *m*.

export I *v* [ek'spɔ:t] ausführen, exportieren; II *s*
['ekspɔ:t] Ausfuhr *f,* Export
m; **~er** [ek'spɔ:tə] Expor-

teur *m;* **~ trade** Export-
handel *m*.

expos|e [ɪk'spəʊz] 1. ausset-
zen (*to a danger* e-r Gefahr); 2. enthüllen; 3. (*Person*) bloßstellen; 4. *phot* belichten; **~ed** [-d] 1. ausgesetzt, ungeschützt; 2. *phot*
belichtet; **~ition**
[͵ekspəʊ'zɪʃn] Ausstellung,
Schau *f.*

exposure [ɪk'spəʊʒə] 1. Aus-
gesetztsein *n* (*to the rain*
dem Regen); 2. Enthüllung *f;*
3. *phot* Belichtung(szeit) *f;*
Aufnahme *f.*

express [ɪk'spres] I *v* ausdrücken, aussprechen; **~ o.s.**
sich äußern; II *adj* ausdrücklich, klar, deutlich; III *s*
1. *by* ~ durch Eilboten; als
Eilgut; 2. (~ *train*) Schnell-,
D-Zug *m;* **~way** [-weɪ] *Am*
Autobahn *f;* **~ion**
[ɪk'spreʃn] 1. Ausdruckswei-
se *f;* 2. Ausdruck *m;* 3. (~ *on
o.'s face*) Gesichtsausdruck
m; **~ive** [ɪk'spresɪv] aus-
drucksvoll.

exquisite ['ekskwɪzɪt] vorzüglich, ausgesucht; ausgezeichnet.

extend [ɪk'stend] 1. verlängern, erweitern, verbreitern;
2. (*Sympathie*) zeigen;
(*Glückwünsche, Einladung*)
aussprechen; 3. sich erstrek-
ken (*to* bis); (hinaus)reichen
(*beyond* über).

extension [ɪk'stenʃn] 1. Ver-
längerung *f;* 2. Fristverlän-

gerung f; 3. tele (Neben-) Anschluß m; 4. An-, Erweiterungsbau m.

extensive [ik'stensiv] ausgedehnt, umfassend.

extent [ik'stent] Ausdehnung, Größe f; Umfang m; to a certain ~ bis zu e-m gewissen Grade.

exterior [ek'stiəriə] I adj außer, Außen-; II s das Äußere.

exterminate [ik'stɜ:mineit] ausrotten.

external [ek'stɜ:nl] äußerlich.

extinct [ik'stiŋkt] (Vulkan) erloschen; (Tier) ausgestorben.

extinguish [ik'stiŋgwiʃ] 1. (Feuer) (aus)löschen; 2. ausmerzen; ~er [-ə] (fire ~) Feuerlöscher m.

extirpate ['ekstɜ:peit] ausrotten, ausmerzen.

extra ['ekstrə] I adj extra, zusätzlich; II s 1. Extrablatt n; Sondernummer f; 2. film Statist m; 3. oft pl Nebenausgaben f pl.

extract I s ['ekstrækt] Extrakt m; II v [ik'strækt] 1. (her)ausziehen, herauslösen; 2. herausbekommen (from aus jdm); (Geständnis) erpressen; 3. (Zitat) entnehmen; ~ion [ik'strækʃn] 1. (Zahn) Ziehen n; 2. Abstammung f.

extraordinary [ik'strɔ:dnri] außerordentlich; außer-, ungewöhnlich.

extravagan|ce [ik'strævəgəns] Verschwendung(ssucht) f; ~t [-t] extravagant; verschwenderisch.

extrem|e [ik'stri:m] I adj 1. äußerst, höchst; 2. extrem, radikal; II s Extrem n, das Äußerste; go to ~s bis zum äußersten gehen; ~ely [-li] äußerst, höchst; ~ity [ik'streməti] 1. äußerste(s) Ende n; 2. höchste Not f; 3. pl Extremitäten f pl.

extricate ['ekstrikeit] befreien (from von, aus).

exuberant [ig'zju:bərənt] üppig, verschwenderisch, überschwenglich.

exult [ig'zʌlt] frohlocken, jubeln (at, over, in über).

eye [ai] I s 1. Auge n; with the naked ~ mit bloßem Auge; catch s.o.'s ~ jds Aufmerksamkeit auf sich lenken; keep an ~ on (lit, fig) aufpassen, achtgeben auf; 2. Öse f, Öhr n; II v ins Auge fassen; anschauen, mustern; ~ball ['-bɔ:l] Augapfel m; ~brow ['-brau] Augenbraue f; ~lash ['-læʃ] Wimper f; ~let ['-lit] Öse f; ~lid ['-lid] Augenlid n; ~-shadow ['-ʃædəu] Lidschatten m; ~sight ['-sait] Sehkraft, -schärfe f; ~sore ['-sɔ:] Schandfleck, Dorn m im Auge; ~-tooth ['-tu:θ] Eckzahn m; ~-witness [,-'witnis] Augenzeuge m.

F

fable ['feɪbl] Fabel *f.*

fabric ['fæbrɪk] 1. Gebäude *n*; 2. Struktur *f*; 3. Gewebe *n*, Stoff *m.*

fabulous ['fæbjʊləs] 1. erdichtet; 2. *fam* phantastisch.

face [feɪs] **I** *s* 1. Gesicht *n*; *in (the) ~ of* angesichts *gen*; trotz *gen*; *have the ~* die Frechheit besitzen; *make ~s* Grimassen schneiden; 2. Vorder-, Stirnseite *f*; 3. Zifferblatt *n*; 4. *das* Äußere; *on the ~ of it* auf den ersten Blick; **II** *v* 5. ins Gesicht sehen; *~ it out* durchhalten; nicht nachgeben; *~ up to* es aufnehmen mit; 6. gehen nach, liegen nach; 7. *fig* gegenübertreten; *(e-r Gefahr)* ins Auge sehen.

facetious [fə'siːʃəs] scherz-, spaßhaft.

facilitate [fə'sɪlɪteɪt] erleichtern; **~y** [fə'sɪlətɪ] 1. Leichtigkeit *f*; 2. *pl* Gelegenheit *f (for* für); Einrichtungen *f pl.*

facing ['feɪsɪŋ] 1. Besatz, (Ärmel-)Aufschlag *m*; 2. *arch* Verputz *m.*

fact [fækt] Tatsache *f*; *as a matter of ~, in ~* in der Tat; in Wirklichkeit; tatsächlich.

factory ['fæktərɪ] Fabrik, Betriebsanlage *f*, Werk *n.*

factual ['fæktʃʊəl] sachlich.

faculty ['fæklti] 1. Fähigkeit,

Befähigung *f (for* für); 2. *(Universität)* Fakultät *f.*

fade [feɪd] 1. schwinden, nachlassen; 2. vergehen, (ver)welken; 3. *(Farbe)* verblassen; 4. *(Ton) ~ away, out* verklingen.

fail [feɪl] 1. fehlschlagen, scheitern, mißlingen; 2. schwächer werden, nachlassen, abnehmen; 3. *(im Examen)* durchfallen (lassen); 4. Bankrott machen; 5. unterlassen; *~ to appear* nicht erscheinen; **~ure** ['feɪljə] 1. Versagen, Scheitern, Mißlingen *n*; 2. Fehlschlag, Mißerfolg *m*; 3. *(Schule)* Durchfallen *n*; 4. Konkurs, Bankrott *m*; 5. *(Mensch)* Versager *m*, Niete *f.*

faint [feɪnt] **I** *adj* schwach; *(Farbe)* matt; *I haven't the ~est idea* ich habe keine Ahnung; **II** *v* ohnmächtig werden *(from, with hunger* vor Hunger); **~ness** ['-nɪs] Schwäche, Mattigkeit *f.*

fair [feə] **I** *adj* 1. sauber; 2. hell, blond; 3. *(Wetter)* schön; 4. gerecht; *(Spiel)* fair; *(Preis)* angemessen; 5. mittelmäßig, leidlich; 6. *~ and square* offen u. ehrlich; **II** *s* (Jahr-)Markt *m*, Messe *f*; *world ~* Weltausstellung *f*; **~ly** ['-lɪ] ziemlich; **~ness**

['-nɪs] 1. Redlichkeit; Unparteilichkeit, Vorurteilslosigkeit *f*; 2. Blondheit *f*.

fairytale ['feərɪteɪl] Märchen *n*.

faith [feɪθ] 1. Glaube(n) *m* (*in* an); 2. Vertrauen *n* (*in* zu); *in good ~* gutgläubig; *lose ~ in s.o.* das Vertrauen zu jdm verlieren; **~ful** ['-fʊl] 1. treu (*to s.o.* jdm); 2. gewissenhaft; **~fully** ['-fʊlɪ] *Yours ~* hochachtungsvoll.

fake [feɪk] Fälschung *f*.

falcon ['fɔ:lkən] *orn* Falke *m*.

fall [fɔ:l] **I** *s* 1. Fall, Sturz *m*; 2. Sinken, Fallen *n* (*der Preise)*; 3. Untergang *m*, Niederlage *f*; 4. *Am* Herbst *m*; 5. *meist pl* Wasserfall *m*; **II** *v irr fell* [fel], *fallen* ['-ən] 6. (herab-, hinunter)fallen; 7. (*Temperatur, Preise*) sinken; 8. *~ ill* krank werden; *~ in love with s.o.* sich verlieben in; *~ asleep* einschlafen; *~* **back** zurückweichen, sich zurückziehen; *~* **behind** zurückbleiben; in Verzug geraten; *~* **in** einfallen, -stürzen; *fall in with s.o.* jdn zufällig treffen; jdm beipflichten.

false [fɔ:ls] falsch; unecht; **~hood** ['-hʊd] Unwahrheit, Lüge *f*.

falsify ['fɔ:lsɪfaɪ] (ver)fälschen.

falter ['fɔ:ltə] 1. stolpern, straucheln; 2. zögern, zaudern; 3. stammeln.

fame [feɪm] Ruhm *m*.

familiar [fə'mɪljə] 1. vertraut (*with* mit, *to s.o.* jdm); 2. vertraulich; **~ity** [fəmɪlɪ'ærətɪ] 1. Vertrautheit *f*; 2. Vertrautheit *f* (*with* mit); **~ize** [fə'mɪljəraɪz] vertraut machen (*with* mit).

family ['fæməlɪ] Familie *f*; **~ name** Familienname *m*; **~ planning** Familienplanung *f*.

famine ['fæmɪn] Hungersnot *f*.

famous ['feɪməs] berühmt (*for* durch).

fan [fæn] 1. Fächer *m*; 2. Ventilator *m*; 3. (*fam*) begeisterte(r) Anhänger, Fan *m*.

fanatic(al) [fə'nætɪk(l)] fanatisch.

fancy ['fænsɪ] **I** *s* 1. Einbildungskraft, Phantasie *f*; 2. Einfall *m*, Laune *f*; 3. Neigung, Vorliebe *f*; *have a ~ for s.th.* etw gern haben; *take a ~ to* Gefallen, Geschmack finden an; **II** *adj* 4. bunt; 5. extravagant; 6. *Am* erstklassig; **III** *v* sich vorstellen, sich einbilden; *just ~!* denken Sie mal! *~* **goods** *pl* Luxus-, Geschenkartikel *m pl*.

fantastic [fæn'tæstɪk] phantastisch.

far [fɑ:] weit entfernt; *as ~ as* soweit; *by ~* bei weitem; *so ~* so weit; bis jetzt; *so ~ as* so weit, soviel; *~ from* lange nicht, keineswegs; *go* ~ es weit bringen.

farce [fɑːs] Komödie *f.*

fare [feə] 1. Fahrgeld *n,* -preis *m;* 2. Fahrgast *m;* 3. *bill of* ~ Speisekarte *f;* ~**well** [ˌ-'wel] I *interj* lebe(n Sie) wohl; II *s:* ~ *party* Abschiedsfeier *f.*

farm [fɑːm] I *s* Bauernhof *m,* Farm *f;* II *v (Land)* bestellen; ~**er** [-ə] Bauer, Landwirt *m;* ~**house** ['-haʊs] Bauernhaus *n;* ~**ing** ['-ɪŋ] Landwirtschaft *f.*

farth|er ['fɑːðə] weiter; ferner; ~**est** [-ɪst] weitest.

fascinat|e ['fæsɪneɪt] fesseln, faszinieren; ~**ing** [-ɪŋ] spannend; ~**ion** [ˌfæsɪ'neɪʃn] Zauber *m.*

fashion ['fæʃn] I *s* 1. Mode *f; come into* ~ Mode werden; *go out of* ~ unmodern werden; 2. Art, Weise, Art und Weise *f;* II *v* gestalten, anfertigen; ~**able** ['fæʃnəbl] modern, modisch.

fast [fɑːst] I *adj* 1. fest; 2. *(Farben)* (licht- u. wasch)echt; 3. rasch, schnell; *be 5 minutes* ~ 5 Minuten vorgehen; ~ *train* Schnellzug *m;* II *v* fasten; III *s* Fasten *n.*

fasten ['fɑːsn] 1. befestigen; 2. zumachen, (ver)schließen; ~**er** ['fɑːsnə] Verschluß *m.*

fastidious [fə'stɪdɪəs] wählerisch.

fat [fæt] I *adj* fett; dick; II *s* Fett *n.*

fatal ['feɪtl] verhängnisvoll; ~ *accident* tödliche(r) Unfall *m.*

fate [feɪt] 1. Schicksal *n;* 2. Verhängnis, Verderben *n.*

father ['fɑːðə] Vater *m;* ~**hood** [-hʊd] Vaterschaft *f;* ~**-in-law** ['fɑːðərɪnlɔː] Schwiegervater *m;* ~**land** [-lænd] Vaterland *n;* ~**less** [-lɪs] vaterlos; ~**ly** [-lɪ] väterlich.

fathom ['fæðəm] I *s* Faden *m* (1,83 m); II *v* ergründen.

fatigue [fə'tiːg] I *s* Ermüdung, Erschöpfung *f;* II *v* ermüden.

fault [fɔːlt] Fehler; Defekt; Mangel; Irrtum *m;* Schuld *f; find* ~ etw auszusetzen haben (*with* an); *it's not my* ~ es ist nicht meine Schuld; ~**less** ['-lɪs] tadellos; ~**y** ['-ɪ] fehler-, mangelhaft.

favo(u)r ['feɪvə] I *s* 1. Gunst *f;* Wohlwollen *n; be in* ~ *of s.th.* für etw sein; 2. *do s.o. a* ~ jdm e-n Gefallen tun; 3. Begünstigung *f;* II *v* 4. bevorzugen; 5. begünstigen; ~**able** ['feɪvərəbl] günstig, vorteilhaft (*to* für); ~**ite** ['feɪvərɪt] I *s sport* Favorit *m;* II *adj:* ~ *book,* ~ *pastime* Lieblingsbuch *n,* -beschäftigung *f.*

fawn [fɔːn] I *s* Rehkitz *n;* II *adj* rehfarben.

fear [fɪə] I *s* Angst, Furcht *f;*

for ~ of aus Angst vor; **II** *v*
(be)fürchten, sich fürchten
vor; **~ful** ['-fʊl] ängstlich;
besorgt (*about* wegen);
~less ['-lɪs] furchtlos (*of*
vor).

feasible ['fi:zəbl] aus-, durchführbar.

feast [fi:st] Festmahl *n.*

feat [fi:t] Heldentat, Leistung
f.

feather [feðə] **I** *s* Feder *f; as
light as a ~* federleicht; *a ~
in o.'s cap* Leistung, auf die
man stolz sein kann; **II** *v: ~
o.'s nest* sein Schäfchen ins
trockene bringen.

feature ['fi:tʃə] **I** *s* 1. *pl* (Ge-
sichts-)Züge *m pl;* 2. Charakterzug *m*, Merkmal *n;*
3. Hauptfilm *m;* 4. (*Zeitung*)
Sonderbericht *m;* **II** *v* (groß)
heraus-, zur Schau stellen;
featuring X (film) mit X in
der Hauptrolle.

February ['februərɪ] Februar
m.

feder|al ['fedərəl] bundes-
staatlich; **~ation**
[ˌfedə'reɪʃn] Bund; Verband
m.

fee [fi:] *a. pl* Gebühr(en *pl*) *f;*
Honorar *n.*

feeble ['fi:bl] schwach.

feed [fi:d] **I** *v irr fed, fed*
[fed] 1. füttern (*on* mit);
verköstigen; *be fed up with
s.th.* etw satt haben; 2. *tech
(Material)* zuführen; **II** *s*
3. Fütterung *f;* 4. Futter *n;*
5. *tech* Zuführung; Speisung

f; **~er** ['-ə] 1. (Saug-)Flasche
f; 2. (*~ road*) Zubringerstra-
ße *f;* **~ing-bottle** ['-ɪŋˌbɒtl]
(Saug-)Flasche *f.*

feel [fi:l] *irr felt, felt* [felt]
1. (be)fühlen, betasten;
2. spüren, empfinden; *~ for
s.o.* mit jdm Mitgefühl haben; *~ cold, hungry, tired*
frieren, hungrig, müde sein;
~ sure, certain sicher sein;
I'm ~ing much better es
geht mir viel besser; **~er**
['-ə] *zoo* Fühler *m;* **~ing**
['-ɪŋ] **I** *adj* mitfühlend; **II** *s*
Gefühl *n* (*of* gen); Sinn *m*
(*of* für).

feign [feɪn] vortäuschen.

fell [fel] (*Baum*) fällen.

fellow ['feləu] 1. Gefährte,
Kamerad *m;* 2. *fam* Bursche, Kerl *m;* **~-citizen**
[ˌ-'sɪtɪzn] Mitbürger *m;*
~- traveller [ˌ-'trævələ]
Reisegefährte *m.*

felt [felt] Filz *m.*

female ['fi:meɪl] **I** *adj* weiblich; **II** *s zoo* Weibchen *n.*

feminine ['femɪnɪn] weiblich.

fenc|e [fens] **I** *s* Zaun *m;*
(*iron ~*) Gitter *n;* **II** *v* 1. ein-,
umzäunen; 2. fechten; 3. ausweichen (*with a question*
e-r Frage); **~ing** ['-ɪŋ] Fechten *n.*

ferment [fə'ment] gären *a.
fig.*

fern [fɜ:n] Farn(kraut *n*) *m.*

feroci|ous [fə'rəuʃəs] wild,
grausam; **~ty** [fə'rɒsɪtɪ]
Wildheit, Grausamkeit *f.*

ferry ['ferɪ] (~-boat) Fähre f.
fertile ['fɜ:taɪl] fruchtbar a.
fig; ~ity [fə'tɪlətɪ] Fruchtbarkeit f; ~izer ['fɜ:tɪlaɪzə]
Kunstdünger m.
fester ['festə] eitern.
festival ['festəvl] 1. Fest n;
Feier f; 2. mus theat Festspiele n pl; ~e ['festɪv] festlich; ~ity [fe'stɪvətɪ] Fest n;
pl Festlichkeiten f pl.
festoon [fe'stu:n] Girlande f.
fetch [fetʃ] 1. holen, (her-,
herbei)bringen; 2. (Preis) erzielen.
feud [fju:d] Fehde f.
fever ['fi:və] Fieber n; in a ~
of excitement in fieberhafter Aufregung; ~ish
['fi:vərɪʃ] 1. fiebernd; 2. fig
fieberhaft.
few [fju:] wenig(e); a ~ einige, ein paar; quite a ~ ziemlich viele.
fiancé [fɪ'ɑːŋseɪ] Verlobte(r)
m; ~e Verlobte f.
fibre, Am **fiber** ['faɪbə] Faser f.
fickle ['fɪkl] wankelmütig.
fiction ['fɪkʃn] 1. Fiktion f;
2. Romanliteratur f.
fiddle ['fɪdl] I s Geige f; play
second ~ (fig) die zweite
Geige spielen; II v fiedeln.
fidelity [fɪ'delətɪ] Treue f.
fidget ['fɪdʒɪt] (herum)zappeln; ~y [-ɪ] zappelig.
field [fi:ld] 1. Feld n;
2. (Spiel-)Feld n; 3. fig
(Fach-)Gebiet n; ~
glass(es) pl Feldstecher m.

fierce [fɪəs] 1. wild, unbändig; 2. heftig; 3. wütend.
fiery ['faɪərɪ] feurig, glühend,
heiß.
fifth [fɪfθ] I adj fünft;
II s Fünftel n.
fifty ['fɪftɪ] fünfzig.
fig [fɪg] Feige f.
fight [faɪt] I v irr fought,
fought [fɔ:t] 1. kämpfen
(against, with gegen; on the
side of, with auf Seiten gen);
~ it out bis zur Entscheidung kämpfen; 2. streiten;
II s Kampf m (for um); put
up a good ~ sich wacker
schlagen; ~er ['-ə] 1. Kämpfer, Streiter m; 2. (prize ~)
Berufsboxer m; 3. aero
Jagdflugzeug n.
figure ['fɪgə] I s 1. Figur, Gestalt f; cut a fine, poor ~ e-e
gute, schlechte Figur machen; 2. Zahl, Summe f; at a
low, high ~ billig, teuer; be
good at ~s ein guter Rechner sein; II v 3. (figürlich)
darstellen; 4. e-e Rolle spielen; erscheinen; ~ on a list
auf e-r Liste stehen; ~ out
aus-, berechnen; verstehen;
ausdenken.
file [faɪl] I s 1. Feile f;
2. (Brief-)Ordner m; Akten
pl; on ~ bei, in den Akten;
3. Reihe f; in single, in Indian ~ im Gänsemarsch;
II v 4. feilen; 5. (Briefe,
Papiere, Akten) abheften,
einordnen; 6. (Antrag) einreichen (with bei).

fill [fɪl] 1. (an-, auf-, aus)füllen; (Zahn) plombieren; 2. (Stellung) bekleiden; 3. (Stelle) besetzen; 4. (Auftrag) erledigen; ~ **in** (Formular) ausfüllen; (Namen) einsetzen; ~ **up** tanken.

fillet ['fɪlɪt] Filet, Lendenstück n.

filling ['fɪlɪŋ] Füllung; (Zahn) Plombe f; ~ **station** Tankstelle f.

film [fɪlm] **I** s 1. Häutchen n, Belag m; Schicht f; 2. phot, film Film m; **II** v (ver)filmen.

filter ['fɪltə] **I** s Filter m; **II** v filtern; ~ **through** durchsickern a. fig.

filth [fɪlθ] Schmutz, Dreck m; ~**y** ['-ɪ] schmutzig, dreckig.

fin [fɪn] Flosse f.

final ['faɪnl] **I** adj letzt, abschließend, endgültig; **II** s 1. (Ab-)Schlußprüfung f; 2. pl sport Finale n; ~**ly** ['faɪnəlɪ] zuletzt, schließlich.

finance [faɪ'næns] **I** s Finanz f; **II** v finanzieren; ~**ial** [faɪ'nænʃl] finanziell.

finch [fɪntʃ] orn Fink m.

find [faɪnd] irr found, found [faʊnd] 1. finden; 2. begegnen (s.o. jdm); (an)treffen; 3. (jur) ~ guilty für schuldig erklären; 4. ~ s.o. out jdn ertappen; ~**ings** pl ['-ɪŋs] Befund m; jur Urteil n.

fine [faɪn] **I** adj 1. fein, schön (a. Wetter); 2. zart, dünn; 3. I'm feeling ~ mir geht's

bestens; **II** s Geldstrafe f; **III** v mit e-r Geldstrafe belegen.

finger ['fɪŋgə] Finger m; burn o.'s ~s (fig) sich die Finger verbrennen; have a ~ in the pie die Hand im Spiel haben; twist s.o. round o.'s (little) ~ jdn um den kleinen Finger wickeln; keep your ~s crossed! halten Sie mir den Daumen! ~-**nail** [-neɪl] Fingernagel m; ~**print** [-prɪnt] Fingerabdruck m; ~**tip** [-tɪp] Fingerspitze f; have s.th. at o.'s ~s etw wie am Schnürchen können.

finish ['fɪnɪʃ] **I** v 1. beenden; aufhören mit (doing s.th. etw zu tun); 2. vollenden; fertigmachen; **II** s 3. Ende n, Schluß m; 4. sport Endkampf m; 5. Politur f; letzter Schliff m.

Finland ['fɪnlənd] Finnland n.

Finn [fɪn] Finne m; Finnin f; ~**ish** ['fɪnɪʃ] finnisch.

fir [fɜː] Tanne f.

fire ['faɪə] **I** s Feuer n; Brand m; be on ~ in Flammen stehen; set on ~ in Brand stecken; anzünden; **II** v 1. anzünden; 2. (Ziegel) brennen; 3. fig anfeuern; 4. (Feuerwaffe) abfeuern; 5. fam rausschmeißen, entlassen; ~-**alarm** [-ə‚lɑːm] Feuermelder m; ~**arms** pl [-rɑːmz] Schußwaffen f pl; ~-**brigade** [-brɪ‚geɪd] Br

Feuerwehr f; **~-engine** [-ˌendʒɪn] Feuerwehrauto n; **~-escape** [-rɪˌskeɪp] Nottreppe f; **~-extinguisher** [-rɪkˌstɪŋgwɪʃə] Feuerlöscher m; **~man** [-mən] Feuerwehrmann m; **~place** [-pleɪs] Kamin m; **~proof** [-pruːf] feuerfest.

firm [fɜːm] **I** adj fest, hart; hold ~ to festhalten an; **II** s Firma f; **~ness** ['-nɪs] Festigkeit f.

first [fɜːst] **I** adj erst; ~ name Vorname m; at ~ sight auf den ersten Blick; **II** adv erstens, zunächst; ~ of all zu allererst; vor allem; zunächst; **III** s: at ~ (zu)erst, zunächst; from the ~ von Anfang an; ~ aid ['-eɪd] med Erste Hilfe f; **~-class** ['-klɑːs] erstklassig; ~ night theat Erstaufführung f; **~-rate** ['-reɪt] erstklassig.

firth [fɜːθ] Förde f.

fish [fɪʃ] **I** s (pl ~ od ~es) Fisch m; a pretty kettle of ~ (iron) eine schöne Bescherung; **II** v fischen, angeln (for nach); **~erman** ['fɪʃəmən] Fischer m; **~ing** ['-ɪŋ] Fischen n; **~-line** Angelschnur f; **~-rod** Angelrute f; **~-tackle** Angelgerät n; **~monger** ['-ˌmʌŋgə] Br Fischhändler m; **~y** ['fɪʃɪ] fam verdächtig.

fission ['fɪʃn] (phys) (Kern-) Spaltung f.

fissure ['fɪʃə] Spalt(e f) m.

fist [fɪst] Faust f.

fit [fɪt] **I** s 1. med Anfall m; ~ of coughing Hustenanfall m; 2. Anwandlung, Laune f; ~ of anger Wutausbruch m; **II** adj 3. tauglich, passend; ~ to eat genießbar; ~ for a position für e-e Stelle geeignet; ~ for work arbeitsfähig; 4. keep ~ in Form bleiben; **III** v 5. (Kleidung) passen; gut sitzen (s.o. jdm); 6. sich eignen, taugen; ~ in in Übereinstimmung sein (with mit); ~ out ausrüsten, ausstaffieren; **~ness** ['-nɪs] Tauglichkeit f; **~ter** ['-ə] Monteur, Installateur m; **~ting** ['-ɪŋ] **I** adj passend; **II** s 1. (Kleider) Anprobe f; 2. Montage f; 3. pl Einrichtung(sgegenstände m pl) f; Zubehör(teile n pl) n.

five [faɪv] fünf.

fix [fɪks] **I** v 1. festmachen, befestigen (to an; in in); 2. heften, richten (the eyes den Blick; on auf); 3. festsetzen; ~ a date sich verabreden; 4. phot fixieren; 5. fam (her)richten; (wieder) in Ordnung bringen; ~ the bed das Bett machen; **II** s (fam) be in a ~ in e-r Klemme sein.

fizz [fɪz] zischen, sprudeln.

flabby ['flæbɪ] schlaff.

flag [flæg] **I** s 1. Flagge, Fahne f; 2. (~stone) Steinplatte f; 3. bot Schwertlilie f;

II v schlaff werden; fig ermatten, erlahmen.

flagrant ['fleɪgrənt] offenkundig.

flak|e [fleɪk] **I** s Flocke f; **II** v: ~ off abblättern, abschuppen; ~**y** ['fleɪkɪ] ~ pastry Blätterteig m.

flame [fleɪm] **I** s Flamme f; be in ~s in Flammen stehen; **II** v flammen, lodern.

flank [flæŋk] **I** s Flanke f; **II** v flankieren.

flannel ['flænl] 1. Flanell m; 2. pl Flanellhose f.

flap [flæp] **I** s 1. Schlag, Klaps m; 2. Flügelschlag m; 3. Klappe f; 4. aero Landeklappe f; **II** v flattern; lose herabhängen.

flare [fleə] **I** v 1. (auf)flakkern, (auf)lodern; 2. ~ up (fig) aufbrausen; **II** s 3. fig Aufbrausen; 4. (kurzes) Aufleuchten, Aufflackern n; 5. Leuchtkugel f.

flash [flæʃ] **I** v 1. (auf)blitzen; 2. sausen, flitzen; **II** s Blitz m; fig Aufblitzen n (e-s Gedankens); ~ of lightning Blitzstrahl m; in a ~ im Nu; ~**light** ['-laɪt] 1. Taschenlampe f; 2. phot Blitzlicht n.

flask [flɑːsk] vacuum ~ Thermosflasche f.

flat [flæt] **I** adj 1. flach; 2. (Absage) glatt; 3. (Getränk) schal; 4. langweilig; 5. (Reifen) platt; **II** s 6. (Tief-)Ebene f; 7. Am Reifenpanne f; 8. (Etagen-)

Wohnung f; ~**ten** ['flætn] einebnen, abflachen.

flatter ['flætə] 1. schmeicheln (s.o jdm); 2. ~ o.s. sich einbilden (that daß); ~**ing** [-rɪŋ] schmeichelhaft; ~**y** [-rɪ] Schmeichelei f.

flavo(u)r ['fleɪvə] **I** s 1. (Wohl-)Geschmack m, Aroma n; 2. fig Beigeschmack m; **II** v würzen.

flaw [flɔː] 1. Sprung, Riß m; 2. fig Fehler m; ~**less** ['-lɪs] fehlerlos.

flax [flæks] Flachs m.

flea [fliː] Floh m; ~ **market** Flohmarkt m.

flee [fliː] irr fled, fled [fled] (ent)fliehen.

fleece [fliːs] **I** s Vlies n; **II** v: be ~d of o.'s money um sein Geld beschwindelt werden.

fleet [fliːt] Flotte f; ~ of cars Wagenpark m.

flesh [fleʃ] Fleisch n; ~**y** ['fleʃɪ] fleischig, dick.

flex [fleks] (Anschluß-, Leitungs-)Schnur f; ~**ible** ['fleksəbl] 1. biegsam, elastisch; 2. anpassungsfähig.

flicker ['flɪkə] (Flamme) flakkern.

flier ['flaɪə] s. flyer.

flight [flaɪt] 1. Flug m; 2. Schwarm m (Vögel, Insekten); 3. ~ of stairs Treppe f; 4. Flucht f; put to ~ in die Flucht schlagen; take (to) ~ fliehen, weglaufen.

flimsy ['flɪmzɪ] 1. dünn, zerbrechlich; 2. *fig* fadenscheinig.

flinch [flɪntʃ] (zurück)weichen; *without* ~*ing* ohne e-e Miene zu verziehen.

fling [flɪŋ] **I** *v irr* flung, flung [flʌŋ] schleudern, werfen; **II** *s* 1. Wurf *m*; 2. *have a* ~ *at* sich versuchen an; *have o.'s* ~ sich austoben.

flint [flɪnt] Feuerstein, Kiesel *m*.

flip [flɪp] schnipsen, schnellen.

flippant ['flɪpənt] vorlaut, frech.

flipper ['flɪpə] Flosse *f*.

flirt [flɜːt] kokettieren, flirten; liebäugeln; ~**ation** [flɜːˈteɪʃn] Flirt *m*.

flit [flɪt] 1. flattern; 2. huschen, flitzen.

float [fləʊt] **I** *s* 1. *tech* Schwimmer *m*; 2. Floß *n*; **II** *v* 3. (obenauf) schwimmen; (dahin)treiben; 4. schweben, gleiten; 5. *(Schiff)* wieder flott machen; 6. in Umlauf bringen.

flock [flɒk] **I** *s* 1. Herde *f*; *(Vögel)* Schwarm *m*; 2. Menge, Schar *f*, Haufen *m*; **II** *v* zs.kommen, sich scharen *(round s.o.* um jdn).

floe [fləʊ] Eisscholle *f*.

flog [flɒg] verprügeln; ~**ging** ['-ɪŋ] Prügel *m pl.*

flood [flʌd] **I** *s* Flut *a. fig;* Überschwemmung *f*; **II** *v* überschwemmen, überfluten; ~**lights** ['-laɪts] Flut-

licht *n*; ~**lit** ['-lɪt] angestrahlt, angeleuchtet.

floor [flɔː] **I** *s* 1. Fußboden *m*; 2. Stockwerk *n*, Etage *f*; 3. *take the* ~ das Wort ergreifen; **II** *v* 4. *(Haus)* dielen; 5. zu Boden strecken; 6. verwirren *(s.o.* jdn).

floral ['flɔːrəl] ~ *design* Blumenmuster *n*; ~**ist** ['flɒrɪst] Blumenhändler *m*.

flounce [flaʊns] ~ *out* verärgert hinausstürzen *(of a room* aus e-m Zimmer).

flounder ['flaʊndə] **I** *v* sich abmühen, sich abquälen; **II** *s* Flunder *f*, Butt *m (Fisch).*

flour ['flaʊə] Mehl *n.*

flourish ['flʌrɪʃ] **I** *v* 1. sich gut entwickeln, gedeihen, blühen; 2. *(Waffe)* schwingen; **II** *s* 3. Schnörkel *m*, Floskel *f*; 4. *mus* Tusch *m.*

flow [fləʊ] **I** *v* fließen, münden *(into the lake* in den See); **II** *s* Fließen *n*; Flut *f*; Strom *m.*

flower ['flaʊə] **I** *s* Blume, Blüte *f*; **II** *v* blühen; ~**y** ['flaʊərɪ] blumenreich *a. fig.*

flu [fluː] *(influenza) fam* Grippe *f.*

fluctuate ['flʌktjʊeɪt] schwanken, fluktuieren.

flue [fluː] Rauchfang *m.*

fluency ['fluːənsɪ] (Rede-)Fluß *m*, Geläufigkeit *f*; ~**t** [-t] fließend; *(Redner)* gewandt.

fluff [flʌf] *(Staub)* Flocke *f*, Flaum *m*; ~**y** ['-ɪ] flaumig.

fluid ['flu:ɪd] I *adj* flüssig;
II *s* Flüssigkeit *f.*

flurry ['flʌrɪ] I *s* 1. (~ *of
wind*) Windstoß *m;* 2. *in a
~ (of alarm, of excitement)*
in (großer) Aufregung; II *v*
beunruhigen.

flush [flʌʃ] I *v* 1. rot werden
(*with anger* vor Wut); erröten; 2. (aus-, durch)spülen;
II *s* Erröten *n;* III *adj* reichlich; übervoll.

flute [flu:t] Flöte *f.*

flutter ['flʌtə] flattern.

flux [flʌks] Fluß *m*, Fließen,
Strömen *n.*

fly [flaɪ] I *v irr flew* [flu:],
flown [fləʊn] 1. fliegen;
2. eilen, stürzen; ~ *into a
rage* wütend werden; ~ *off
the handle (fig)* außer sich
geraten; 3. im Flugzeug befördern; II *s* 4. *zoo* Fliege *f;*
5. (Hosen-)Schlitz *m.*

flyer, flier ['flaɪə] Flieger *m.*

flying ['flaɪɪŋ] fliegend; ~-
boat Flugboot *n;* ~ **saucer**
fliegende Untertasse *f;*
~-**squad** [-skwɔd] *Br*
Überfallkommando *n.*

fly-over ['flaɪˌəʊvə] (Straßen-, Eisenbahn-) Überführung *f.*

foal [fəʊl] Fohlen *n.*

foam [fəʊm] I *s* Schaum *m;*
II *v* schäumen (*with rage*
vor Wut); ~-**rubber**
['-ˌrʌbə] Schaumgummi *m*
od *n;* ~**y** ['-ɪ] schaumig.

focus ['fəʊkəs] I *s pl -cuses*
od *foci* ['fəʊsaɪ] Brennpunkt

m; in (out of) ~ *(phot)*
(un)scharf eingestellt; II *v*
konzentrieren (*on* auf) *a. fig.*

fodder ['fɔdə] Trockenfutter
n.

fog [fɔg] (dicker) Nebel *m;*
~**gy** ['fɔgɪ] neb(e)lig; ~**horn**
['-hɔ:n] Nebelhorn *n;*
~**lamp** ['-læmp] *mot* Nebellampe *f,* -scheinwerfer *m.*

foil [fɔɪl] I *v (Plan)* vereiteln;
II *s* (Metall-)Folie *f.*

fold [fəʊld] I *v* 1. (zs.)falten,
zs.legen; 2. ~ *in o.'s arms* in
die Arme schließen; 3. einwickeln, -schlagen; II *s*
4. Falte *f;* 5. (Schaf-)Hürde *f;*
~**er** ['-ə] 1. Schnellhefter *m;*
2. Faltprospekt *m;* ~**ing**
['-ɪŋ] zs.klappbar; ~ *boat*
Faltboot *n;* ~ *chair* Klappstuhl *m.*

foliage ['fəʊlɪɪdʒ] Laubwerk
n.

folk *pl* [fəʊk] Volk *n;* Leute
pl; (o.'s ~s) fam Familie *f;* ~
song Volkslied *n.*

follow ['fɔləʊ] 1. folgen *(s.o.*
jdm); 2. *(Laufbahn)* einschlagen; 3. *(Regel)* befolgen; 4. *(mit Interesse)* verfolgen; 5. *as* ~*s* wie folgt,
folgendermaßen; 6. ~ *up*
(e-r S) nachgehen; *(Vorteil)*
weiterverfolgen; ~**er** [-ə]
Anhänger *m.*

folly ['fɔlɪ] Torheit *f.*

fond [fɔnd] zärtlich, vernarrt
(of in); *be* ~ *of* gern haben,
mögen, lieben; ~**le** ['fɔndl]

(zärtlich, liebevoll) streicheln.

food [fu:d] 1. Nahrung f, Es-
sen n; Speise f; 2. (Tiere)
Futter n; ~-**stuff** ['-ʃtʌf]
Nahrungsmittel n.

fool [fu:l] **I** s Dummkopf,
Narr m; make a ~ of o.s.
sich lächerlich machen; All
~s' Day der 1. April; **II** v
Spaß machen, zum Narren
halten; ~ away (Zeit) ver-
trödeln; ~**hardy** ['-ˌhɑːdɪ]
tollkühn; ~**ish** ['-ɪʃ] dumm,
albern; ~**proof** ['-pru:f] nar-
rensicher.

foot [fʊt] **I** s pl feet [fi:t]
1. Fuß m; on ~ zu Fuß; fig
im Gange; put o.'s ~ down
(fig, fam) energisch werden;
2. (Bett) Fußende n; 3. Fuß
m (30,5 cm); **II** v: ~ the bill
(fam) für die Rechnung aufkommen; ~-**and-mouth
disease** Maul- und Klauen-
seuche f; ~**ball** ['-bɔːl] Fußball m; ~**hold** ['-həʊld] Halt
m a. fig.

footing ['fʊtɪŋ] 1. Halt m;
Grundlage, Basis f; 2. be on
a friendly ~ with s.o. mit
jdm auf freundschaftlichem
Fuß stehen.

foot|lights pl ['fʊtlaɪts] theat
Rampenlicht n; ~**note**
['-nəʊt] Fußnote, Anmer-
kung f; ~**path** ['-pɑːθ] Fuß-
weg, -pfad m; ~**step**
['-step] Schritt, Tritt m;
~**wear** ['-weə] Fußbeklei-
dung f.

for [fɔː] **I** prp 1. (Zeitangabe)
I haven't been there ~ three
years ich bin seit 3 Jahren
nicht dort gewesen;
2. (räuml. Ausdehnung) ~ 2
miles 2 Meilen weit; 3. (Ursache, Grund) ~ joy vor
Freude; ~ fear of aus
Furcht vor; 4. ~ all I know
soviel ich weiß; 5. (Absicht,
Zweck) come ~ dinner zum
Essen kommen; what ~? zu
welchem Zweck?
6. (Wunsch, Erwartung)
hope, wait ~ hoffen, warten
auf; 7. (Richtung) leave ~
Paris nach Paris abreisen,
-fahren; 8. (Bestimmung) ~
a joke (nur) zum Spaß;
II conj denn.

forbid [fəˈbɪd] irr forbad(e)
[fəˈbæd], forbidden
[fəˈbɪdn] verbieten; God ~!
Gott behüte!

force [fɔːs] **I** s 1. Stärke, Gewalt, Macht f; by ~ mit Ge-
walt; 2. be in ~ in Kraft, gültig sein; put into ~ in Kraft
setzen; **II** v 3. zwingen; ~
open auf-, erbrechen; 4. aufzwingen (on s.o. jdm); ~d
landing Notlandung f; ~**ful**
['-fʊl] kraftvoll, energisch.

forcible ['fɔːsəbl] gewaltsam.

ford [fɔːd] Furt f.

fore [fɔː] **I** adj vordere(r, s);
II s: come to the ~ in den
Vordergrund treten.

fore|arm ['fɔːrɑːm] Unterarm
m; ~**boding** [fɔːˈbəʊdɪŋ]
schlimme Ahnung f; ~**cast**

['fɔːkɑːst] **I** v a. irr forecast, forecast vorhersagen, vorhersehen; **II** s: weather ~ (Wetter-)Vorhersage f; ~**finger** ['fɔːfɪŋgə] Zeigefinger m; ~**ground** ['fɔːgraʊnd] Vordergrund m; ~**hand** ['fɔːhænd] (Pferd, Tennis) Vorhand f; ~**head** ['fɒrɪd] Stirn f.

foreign ['fɒrən] fremd, ausländisch; ~ currency Devisen pl; ~**er** [-ə] Ausländer m; ~ **language** Fremdsprache f; the **F~ Office** Br das Außenministerium n; ~ **policy** Außenpolitik f; ~ **trade** Außenhandel m.

fore|man ['fɔːmən] pl -men Vorarbeiter, Werkmeister m; ~**most** ['fɔːməʊst] **I** adj vorderst, erst; **II** adv zuerst; first and ~ zuallererst; ~**runner** ['fɔːˌrʌnə] Vorläufer m; ~**see** [fɔːˈsiː] irr foresaw [-ˈsɔː] , foreseen [-ˈsiːn] vorhersehen; ~**sight** ['fɔːsaɪt] Weitblick m.

forest ['fɒrɪst] Wald, Forst m; ~**er** [-ə] Förster m; ~ **fire** Waldbrand m; ~**ry** [-rɪ] Forstwirtschaft f.

foretaste [fɔːˈteɪst] Vorgeschmack m.

foretell [fɔːˈtel] irr foretold, foretold [fɔːˈtəʊld] prophezeien.

forever [fəˈrevə] für immer.

forfeit ['fɔːfɪt] **I** s verwirkte(s) Pfand n; Strafe f; **II** v verlieren, einbüßen.

forge [fɔːdʒ] **I** s Schmiede f; **II** v 1. schmieden; 2. nachmachen, fälschen; ~**r** [-ə] Fälscher m; ~**ry** ['fɔːdʒərɪ] Fälschung f.

forget [fəˈget] irr forgot [fəˈgɒt], forgotten [fəˈgɒtn] vergessen; ~ about it! denk nicht mehr daran! ~**ful** [-fʊl] vergeßlich; ~**-me-not** [-mɪnɒt] bot Vergißmeinnicht n.

forgiv|e [fəˈgɪv] irr forgave [fəˈgeɪv], forgiven [fəˈgɪvn] vergeben, verzeihen (s.o. s.th. jdm etw); ~**ing** [-ɪŋ] nachsichtig, versöhnlich.

fork [fɔːk] **I** s 1. Gabel f; 2. Gabelung, Abzweigung f; **II** v sich gabeln.

form [fɔːm] **I** s 1. Form, Gestalt, Figur f; in due ~ vorschriftsmäßig; 2. Formular n, Vordruck m; fill out, in a ~ ein Formular ausfüllen; 3. (körperliche) Verfassung f; 4. Bank f (ohne Lehne); 5. Br (Schul-)Klasse f; **II** v: ~ a judg(e)ment, an opinion sich ein Urteil, e-e Meinung bilden; ~**al** [-l] förmlich; ~**ality** [fɔːˈmælətɪ] Förmlichkeit, Formsache f; ~**ation** [fɔːˈmeɪʃn] 1. Bildung f; 2. geol mil Formation f; ~**ative** ['fɔːmətɪv] ~ years (pl) Entwicklungsjahre n pl.

former ['fɔːmə] früher; vorhergehend, vergangen, ehemalig; ~**ly** [-lɪ] früher, ehemals.

formidable ['fɔːmɪdəbl] furchtbar.

formula ['fɔːmjʊlə] 1. Formel f; 2. Rezept n; ~**te** ['fɔːmjʊleɪt] formulieren.

forsake [fə'seɪk] irr forsook [fə'sʊk], forsaken [fə'seɪkən] im Stich lassen.

forth [fɔːθ] and so ~ und so weiter; ~**coming** [ˌ-'kʌmɪŋ] bevorstehend; (Buch) herauskommend.

fortify ['fɔːtɪfaɪ] befestigen, verstärken.

fortnight ['fɔːtnaɪt] 14 Tage m pl; ~**ly** ['fɔːtˌnaɪtlɪ] vierzehntägig.

fortuitous [fɔː'tjuːɪtəs] zufällig.

fortunate ['fɔːtʃnət] glücklich; ~**ly** [-lɪ] glücklicherweise.

fortune ['fɔːtʃuːn] 1. Glück n; 2. Vermögen n; ~ **teller** Wahrsager(in f) m.

forty ['fɔːtɪ] vierzig.

forward ['fɔːwəd] **I** v 1. (be)fördern; 2. nachsenden; weiterleiten; please ~! bitte nachsenden! **II** adj 3. vorder; 4. frühzeitig; 5. fortschrittlich; 6. vorlaut; **III** adv vorwärts, nach vorn; look ~ sich freuen (to s.th. auf etw); **IV** s (Fußball) Stürmer m.

foster ['fɒstə] fördern; ~**-child** [-tʃaɪld] Pflegekind n; ~**-parents** pl [-ˌpeərənts] Pflegeeltern pl.

foul [faʊl] **I** adj 1. übelrie-

chend; 2. dreckig, schmutzig; 3. (Wetter) schlecht; 4. gemein, schändlich; 5. sport unfair; **II** v 6. verschmutzen; 7. sport foulen; **III** s sport Foul n.

found [faʊnd] 1. (sich) gründen (on, upon auf); 2. (Einrichtung) stiften; 3. metal gießen.

foundation [faʊn'deɪʃn] 1. Gründung f; 2. Stiftung f; 3. Fundament n; 4. fig Grundlage f.

founder ['faʊndə] **I** s (Be-)Gründer m; **II** v 1. (Pferd) lahmen; 2. (Schiff) sinken; 3. (Plan) scheitern.

fountain ['faʊntɪn] 1. Quelle f; 2. Springbrunnen m; ~**-pen** [-pen] Füll(feder-halt)er m.

four [fɔː] vier; ~**th** [fɔːθ] **I** adj viert; **II** s Viertel n.

fowl [faʊl] Geflügel; Huhn n.

fox [fɒks] Fuchs m.

fraction ['frækʃn] Bruch(stück n, -teil) m.

fracture ['fræktʃə] **I** s (Knochen-)Bruch m; **II** v brechen.

fragile ['frædʒaɪl] zerbrechlich, schwach; ~**ity** [frə'dʒɪlətɪ] Zerbrechlichkeit f.

fragment ['frægmənt] Bruchstück n.

fragrance ['freɪgrəns] Duft m; ~**t** [-t] wohlriechend.

frail [freɪl] gebrechlich, schwächlich.

frame [freɪm] **I** v 1. gestalten, bilden; 2. in Worte fassen; 3. (ein)rahmen; **II** s 4. Gerüst, Gestell n; 5. Rahmen m; 6. Körperbau m, Figur, Gestalt f; 7. ~ of mind Veranlagung f, Temperament n; ~**work** ['-wɜːk] 1. Gerüst n; 2. fig Gefüge n, System n.

France [frɑːns] Frankreich n.

franchise ['fræntʃaɪz] Wahlrecht n.

frank [fræŋk] frei(mütig), offen.

frantic ['fræntɪk] rasend, wütend (with vor).

fratern|al [frə'tɜːnl] brüderlich; ~**ity** [frə'tɜːnətɪ] 1. Bruderschaft f; 2. Brüderlichkeit f.

fraud [frɔːd] Betrug, Schwindel m; ~**ulent** ['frɔːdjʊlənt] betrügerisch.

fray [freɪ] (sich) verschleißen, (sich) abnutzen.

freckle ['frekl] Sommersprosse f.

free [friː] **I** adj 1. frei; set ~ freilassen; 2. freigebig; 3. reichlich; 4. freimütig; 5. kostenlos; **II** v befreien, freilassen; ~**dom** ['-dəm] Freiheit f; ~ **kick** sport Freistoß m; ~**lance** ['-lɑːns] freiberuflich; ~**mason** ['-ˌmeɪsn] Freimaurer m; ~**wheel** [ˌ-'wiːl] (Fahrrad) Freilauf m.

freez|e [friːz] irr froze [frəʊz], frozen ['frəʊzn] 1. (ge-, ein)frieren; 2. erstarren a.

fig; 3. I'm ~ing ich friere, mich friert; 4. (Lebensmittel) tiefkühlen; ~**ing-point** ['-ˌpɔɪnt] Gefrierpunkt m.

freight [freɪt] Fracht, Ladung f.

French [frentʃ] **I** adj französisch; **II** s: the ~ die Franzosen pl; ~**man** ['-mən] Franzose m; ~**woman** ['-ˌwʊmən] Französin f.

frenzied ['frenzɪd] wahnsinnig.

frequen|cy ['friːkwənsɪ] Häufigkeit; el Frequenz f; ~**t I** adj ['friːkwənt] häufig; **II** v [frɪ'kwent] häufig besuchen.

fresh [freʃ] 1. frisch; neu; 2. munter, gesund; 3. erfrischend; 4. (Wasser) nicht salzhaltig; 5. Am fam unverschämt; ~**en** ['-n] 1. erfrischen; 2. (Wind) auffrischen; ~**ness** ['-nɪs] 1. Frische, Kühle f; 2. Neuheit f; ~**water** ['-ˌwɔːtə] Süßwasser-.

fret [fret] 1. (sich) ärgern; 2. (herum)nörgeln, quengeln; ~**ful** ['-fʊl] gereizt, verdrießlich.

friar ['fraɪə] (Bettel-)Mönch m.

friction ['frɪkʃn] Reibung f.

Friday ['fraɪdɪ] Freitag m; Good ~ Karfreitag m.

fridge [frɪdʒ] Br fam Kühlschrank m.

fried [fraɪd] gebraten; ~ **egg** Spiegelei n.

friend [frend] Freund(in *f*)
m; *be* ~s befreundet sein;
~**liness** ['-lɪnɪs] Freundlichkeit *f;* ~**ly** ['-lɪ] freundlich;
~**ship** ['-ʃɪp] Freundschaft *f.*

fright [fraɪt] Schreck(en) *m;*
~**en** ['-n] erschrecken; ~
away verjagen; ~**ful** ['-fʊl]
schrecklich.

frigid ['frɪdʒɪd] 1. kalt; 2. *fig*
eisig, kühl.

frill [frɪl] Krause, Rüsche *f.*

fringe [frɪndʒ] 1. Franse *f;*
2. Saum, Rand *m.*

frisky ['frɪskɪ] ausgelassen,
munter.

frivolous ['frɪvələs] leichtfer-
tig, -sinnig.

fro [frəʊ] *to and* ~ hin und
her, auf und ab.

frock [frɒk] 1. (Mönchs-)Kut-
te *f;* 2. Kleid *n.*

frog [frɒg] Frosch *m;* ~**man**
['-mən] Froschmann *m.*

frolicsome ['frɒlɪksəm] lustig; ausgelassen.

from [frɒm] 1. *(Orts-
veränderung) fly* ~ *London
to Paris* von London nach
Paris fliegen; 2. *(zeitl.)* von
(. . . ab, an); seit; ~ *morning
to night* von früh bis spät;
3. *(Absender, Herkunft) a
letter* ~ *John* ein Brief von
John; *where are you* ~*?* wo
sind Sie her? 4. wegen, infolge; ~ *experience* aus Erfahrung.

front [frʌnt] Vorderseite,
Front *f a. arch, mil, meteo;
in* ~ *of* vor, gegenüber;

come to the ~ *(fig)* hervortreten; ~ **door** Haustür *f.*

frontier ['frʌnˌtɪə] Grenze *f.*

front-wheel drive
['frʌntwiːl draɪv] Vorderrad-
antrieb *m.*

frost [frɒst] 1. Frost *m;*
2. Reif *m;* Eisblumen *f pl;*
~**-bite** ['-baɪt] Erfrierung *f;*
~**-bitten** ['-ˌbɪtn] erfroren;
~**ed glass** ['-ɪd glɑːs]
Milchglas *n;* ~**y** ['-ɪ] frostig.

froth [frɒθ] **I** s Schaum *m;*
II *v* schäumen; ~**y** ['-ɪ]
schaumig.

frown [fraʊn] 1. die Stirn
runzeln; 2. mißbilligen (*on
s.th.* etw); 3. böse anschauen
(*at s.o.* jdn).

frozen food ['frəʊzn fuːd]
Tiefkühlkost *f.*

frugal ['fruːgl] sparsam, ge-
nügsam.

fruit [fruːt] 1. Frucht *f,* Früchte *f pl;* Obst *n;* 2. *fig* Ergebnis, Resultat *n;* ~**erer** ['-ərə]
Obsthändler *m;* ~**ful** ['-fʊl]
fruchtbar *a. fig;* ~**less** ['-lɪs]
ergebnislos, erfolglos.

frustrate [frʌˈstreɪt] zunichte machen, vereiteln; ~**ion**
[frʌˈstreɪʃn] Vereitelung;
Enttäuschung *f.*

fry [fraɪ] braten; ~**ing-pan**
['-ɪŋpæn] Bratpfanne *f.*

fuel ['fjʊəl] Brenn-, Treib-,
Kraftstoff *m.*

fugitive ['fjuːdʒɪtɪv] **I** *adj*
flüchtig; **II** *s* Flüchtling *m.*

fulfil(l) [fʊlˈfɪl] *(Wunsch)* erfüllen; *(Versprechen)* einlö-

sen; *(Verpflichtung)* einhalten; **~ment** [-mənt] Erfüllung, Ausführung *f.*

full [fʊl] 1. voll, (voll)gefüllt *(of* mit); (voll)besetzt; 2. voll(zählig, ständig); *in ~* voll; ganz, ungekürzt; voll ausgeschrieben; *in ~ swing* in vollem Gange; *come to a ~ stop* plötzlich stehen bleiben; **~-grown** [ˌ-ˈɡrəʊn] ausgewachsen; **~-length** [ˌ-ˈleŋkθ] in Lebensgröße; **~ moon** Vollmond *m;* **~ stop** Punkt *m;* **~-time** [ˈ-taɪm] ganztägig; hauptamtlich, vollberuflich; **~y** [ˈ-ɪ] völlig; ganz, vollständig; durchaus.

fumble [ˈfʌmbl] 1. umhertasten, -suchen *(for* nach); 2. ungeschickt umgehen *(s.th.* mit etw).

fume [fjuːm] **I** *s meist pl* Rauch, Dampf, Dunst *m;* **II** *v* 1. rauchen, dampfen; 2. *fig* sich aufregen, sich ärgern; **~igate** [ˈfjuːmɪɡeɪt] ausräuchern.

fun [fʌn] Spaß, Scherz *m; (only) for ~* (nur) zum Spaß; *make ~ of s.o.* sich über jdn lustig machen.

function [ˈfʌŋkʃn] **I** *s* Funktion *(a. math);* Tätigkeit; Pflicht *f;* **II** *v* funktionieren; arbeiten, tätig sein *(as* als); **~ary** [-ərɪ] Beamte(r) *m.*

fund [fʌnd] *fin* Fonds *m,* Kapital *n; pl* Gelder, Geldmittel *n pl.*

funeral [ˈfjuːnərəl] Beerdigung *f.*

funicular railway [fjuːˈnɪkjʊlə reɪlweɪ] Seilbahn *f.*

funnel [ˈfʌnl] 1. Trichter *m;* 2. *mar rail* Schornstein *m.*

funny [ˈfʌnɪ] 1. lustig, spaßig, ulkig; 2. komisch, sonderbar.

fur [fɜː] 1. Fell *n,* Pelz *m;* 2. Belag *m* (auf der Zunge); **~ coat** Pelzmantel *m.*

furious [ˈfjʊərɪəs] wütend, wild.

furnace [ˈfɜːnɪs] Heizkessel; (Hoch-)Ofen *m.*

furnish [ˈfɜːnɪʃ] 1. versehen, ausstatten *(with* mit); 2. *~ed flat* möblierte Wohnung *f;* 3. liefern; **~ings** *pl* [-ɪŋz] Einrichtungsgegenstände *m pl;* Mobiliar *n.*

furniture [ˈfɜːnɪtʃə] Möbel *n pl.*

furrier [ˈfʌrɪə] Kürschner *m.*

furrow [ˈfʌrəʊ] 1. Furche *f;* 2. Runzel *f.*

further [ˈfɜːðə] **I** *adj u. adv* weiter, ferner, entfernter; *till ~ notice* bis auf weiteres; **II** *v* fördern, unterstützen; **~more** [ˌ-ˈmɔː] überdies.

furtive [ˈfɜːtɪv] verstohlen, heimlich.

fury [ˈfjʊərɪ] 1. Wut, Raserei *f; fly into a ~* in Wut geraten; 2. *(Sturm)* Heftigkeit *f.*

fuse [fjuːz] **I** *v* 1. schmelzen; 2. *el (Sicherung)* durchbrennen; 3. *fig* fusionieren; **II** *s el* Sicherung *f.*

fuselage ['fju:zɪlɑ:ʒ] *aero* Rumpf *m.*

fusion ['fju:ʒn] 1. Schmelzen *n;* 2. Fusion, Verschmelzung *f a. fig.*

fuss [fʌs] **I** *s* Aufregung *f,* Getue *n;* **II** *v* sich aufregen (*about, over* über); ~**y** ['-ɪ]

1. aufgeregt, nervös; 2. kleinlich.

futile ['fju:taɪl] nutzlos, vergeblich.

future ['fju:tʃə] **I** *adj* (zu)künftig; **II** *s* Zukunft *f.*

fuzzy ['fʌzɪ] 1. flockig; 2. undeutlich, verschwommen.

G

gab [gæb] *have the gift of the ~ (fam)* ein gutes Mundwerk haben.

gable ['geɪbl] Giebel *m*.

gag [gæg] **I** *s* 1. Knebel *m*; 2. witzige(r) Einfall *m*; **II** *v* knebeln; mundtot machen.

gaiety ['geɪətɪ] Heiterkeit, Fröhlichkeit *f*.

gain [geɪn] **I** *s* Gewinn; Nutzen *m*; **II** *v* 1. gewinnen; erlangen; ~ *time* Zeit gewinnen; 2. erreichen; **~ful** [-'ful] einträglich.

galaxy ['gæləksɪ] *astr* Milchstraße *f*.

gale [geɪl] Sturm *m*.

gall [gɔːl] 1. Galle *f*; 2. Bitterkeit *f*, Haß *m*.

gallant ['gælənt] 1. tapfer; 2. stattlich; 3. galant.

gallery ['gælərɪ] *arch, theat* Galerie *f*; *play to the ~* Effekthascherei treiben.

gallon ['gælən] Gallone *f (Br* 4,54 l, *Am* 3,78 l).

gallop ['gæləp] **I** *s* Galopp *m*; *at a ~* im Galopp; **II** *v* galoppieren.

gallows ['gæləuz] *pl mit sing* Galgen *m*.

gamble ['gæmbl] 1. spielen; 2. spekulieren; 3. ~ *away* verspielen; **~r** [-ə] Spieler *m*; **~ing** [-ɪŋ] Spielen *n (um Geld)*.

gambol ['gæmbl] *meist pl* Umhertollen *n*.

game [geɪm] 1. Spiel *n*; *play the ~* fair spielen; *the Olympic ~s* die Olympischen Spiele *n pl*; 2. Wild *n*; *big ~* Großwild *n*; *fair ~* jagdbare(s) Wild *n*; **~keeper** ['-,kiːpə] Wildhüter *m*.

gander ['gændə] Gänserich *m*.

gang [gæŋ] Clique; *(Arbeiter)* Kolonne; *(Verbrecher)* Bande *f*.

gangway ['gæŋweɪ] 1. Gang *m*; 2. *mar* Laufplanke *f*.

gaol [dʒeɪl] *s. jail.*

gap [gæp] Lücke *f*, Spalt(e *f*) *m*.

gape [geɪp] 1. gaffen; gähnen; 2. anstarren (*at* s.o. jdn).

garage ['gærɑːdʒ] Garage; Tankstelle; Autowerkstatt *f*.

garbage ['gɑːbɪdʒ] Abfälle *m pl*; Müll *m*; **~can** [-kæn] *Am* Mülleimer *m*.

garden ['gɑːdn] Garten *m*; *pl* Anlagen *f pl*, Park *m*; **~er** [-ə] Gärtner *m*.

gargle ['gɑːgl] **I** *v* gurgeln; **II** *s* Mundwasser *n*.

garland ['gɑːlənd] Kranz *m*; Girlande *f*.

garlic ['gɑːlɪk] *bot* Knoblauch *m*.

garment ['gɑːmənt] Kleidungsstück *n*.

garnish ['gɑːnɪʃ] garnieren.
garrison ['gærɪsn] *mil* Garnison *f.*
gas [gæs] 1. Gas *n;* 2. *Am* Benzin *n; step on the ~ (Am) mot* Gas geben; **~-cooker** ['-ˌkʊkə] Gaskocher *m;* **~-fitter** ['-ˌfɪtə] Gasinstallateur *m.*
gash [gæʃ] lange, klaffende Wunde *f.*
gas|holder ['gæsˌhəʊldə] Gasometer *m;* **~-mask** ['-mɑːsk] Gasmaske *f;* **~-meter** ['-ˌmiːtə] Gasuhr *f;* **~oline, ~olene** ['gæsəuliːn] *Am* Benzin *n.*
gasp [gɑːsp] keuchen.
gastric ulcer ['gæstrɪk 'ʌlsə] Magengeschwür *n.*
gas-works *pl* ['gæswɜːks] Gaswerk *n.*
gate [geɪt] 1. Tor *n;* 2. (Tor-, Bahn-)Schranke; Sperre *f;* **~way** ['-weɪ] 1. Torweg; Durchgang *m;* 2. *fig* Weg *m (to* zu).
gather ['gæðə] 1. (sich) versammeln; 2. (ein)sammeln; pflücken; 3. *fig* entnehmen (*from* aus); 4. ~ *speed* an Geschwindigkeit zunehmen; **~ing** [-rɪŋ] Versammlung *f.*
gaudy ['gɔːdɪ] auffällig; geschmacklos.
ga(u)ge [geɪdʒ] **I** *s* 1. Eichmaß *n;* 2. Lehre *f;* Zollstock *m;* 3. *rail* Spurweite *f;* **II** *v* exakt (aus)messen; eichen.
gaunt [gɔːnt] hager; hohlwangig.

gauntlet ['gɔːntlɪt] *hist* Fehdehandschuh *m; take up the ~* die Herausforderung annehmen.
gauze [gɔːz] Gaze *f; (wire ~)* feine(s) Drahtgeflecht *n.*
gay [geɪ] *adv* gaily 1. lustig, vergnügt, fröhlich; 2. bunt; prächtig; 3. *fam* homosexuell.
gaze [geɪz] **I** *v* starren (*at, on, upon* auf); anstarren; **II** *s* starre(r) Blick *m.*
gear [gɪə] 1. Getriebe *n;* 2. *mot* Gang *m; low, second, top, reverse ~ (mot)* erste(r), zweite(r), dritte(r), Rückwärtsgang *m;* **~ lever, ~ shift** Schalthebel *m.*
gem [dʒem] Edelstein *m.*
Gemini ['dʒemɪnaɪ] *astr* Zwillinge *m pl.*
gender ['dʒendə] *gram* Geschlecht *n.*
general ['dʒenərəl] **I** *adj* 1. allgemein; *in ~* im allgemeinen; 2. *consul(ate) ~* Generalkonsul(at *n*) *m;* **II** *s mil* General *m;* **~ize** [-aɪz] 1. verallgemeinern; 2. allgemein verbreiten; **~ knowledge** Allgemeinbildung *f;* **~ly** [-ɪ] (im) allgemein(en), gewöhnlich; **~ practitioner** *Br* praktische(r) Arzt *m;* **~ strike** Generalstreik *m.*
generate ['dʒenəreɪt] erzeugen; hervorbringen, -rufen.
generation [ˌdʒenə'reɪʃn] 1. Erzeugung *f;* 2. Generation *f.*

gener|osity [ˌdʒenəˈrɒsətɪ]
1. Großmut f; 2. Freigebig-
keit f; **~ous** [ˈdʒenərəs]
1. großmütig 2. freigebig
(*with* mit).

genial [ˈdʒiːnjəl] liebenswür-
dig, freundlich, herzlich.

genius [ˈdʒiːnjəs] pl -ses
1. Eigenart f, Wesen n; Anlage, Fähigkeit f (*for* zu);
2. geniale(r) Mensch m.

gentian [ˈdʒenʃɪən] bot Enzian m.

gentle [ˈdʒentl] adv gently
1. vornehm; 2. freundlich;
3. mild, zart; (*Abhang*) sanft
ansteigend; (*Brise*) leicht;
~man [-mən] pl gentlemen
Gentleman; Herr m;
(*Ladies and*) *gentlemen*
meine (Damen und) Herren!

genuine [ˈdʒenjuɪn] echt.

geography [dʒɪˈɒgrəfɪ] Geographie f.

geology [dʒɪˈɒlədʒɪ] Geologie f.

geometry [dʒɪˈɒmətrɪ] Geometrie f.

germ [dʒɜːm] med Keim m.

German [ˈdʒɜːmən] I adj
deutsch; **II** s 1. (das)
Deutsch(e); 2. Deutsche(r)
m; **~y** [ˈdʒɜːmənɪ] Deutsch-
land n.

germinate [ˈdʒɜːmɪneɪt] keimen (lassen).

gestation [dʒeˈsteɪʃn]
Schwangerschaft f.

gesture [ˈdʒestʃə] Geste f.

get [get] irr got, got [gɒt]
1. bekommen; **~** *even with*

s.o. mit jdm abrechnen; **~**
hold of zu fassen kriegen;
2. holen, beschaffen; 3. fam
verstehen; *I* ~ *it* ich begreife
schon; *I've got it* ich hab's!
4. veranlassen, (dazu) bewegen; 5. *have got* haben, besitzen; 6. *have got to do s.th*
etw tun müssen; 7. gelangen
(*to* nach); 8. werden; **~** *married* sich verheiraten; 9. anfangen (*doing* zu tun);
10. lassen, bewirken; **~** *o.'s
hair cut* sich die Haare
schneiden lassen; 11. **~** *to
know* in Erfahrung bringen;
~ about 1. herumkommen;
2. (*Nachricht*) sich verbreiten; **~ along** sich vertragen
(*with s.o.* mit jdm); *how are
you getting along?* wie
geht's Ihnen? **~ at** *s.th.* an
etw herankommen; etw her-
ausfinden; **~ away** entkommen; **~ down** 1. entmutigen; 2. hinuntersteigen
(*from* von); **~ in** 1. herein-
holen; 2. hereinkommen;
einsteigen; (*Zug*) einfahren;
~ off ab-, aussteigen; **~ on**
1. Erfolg haben; 2. es gut
verstehen (*with* mit); **~ out**
herausbringen, -bekommen,
-holen; aussteigen; **~ round**
1. (*Sache*) umgehen; 2. (*Person*) umstimmen; **~
through** 1. (*Geld*) ausgeben; 2. (*Prüfung*) bestehen;
3. tele Anschluß bekommen;
~ together zs.kommen;
sich treffen; **~ up** aufstehen;

get o.s. up sich herausputzen.

geyser ['giːzə] *Br* Durchlauferhitzer, Boiler *m.*

ghastly ['gɑːstlɪ] grausig, entsetzlich.

ghost [gəʊst] Geist *m*, Gespenst *n.*

giant ['dʒaɪənt] **I** *s* Riese *m;* **II** *adj* riesenhaft, riesig.

gidd|iness ['gɪdɪnɪs] Schwindel(gefühl *n*) *m;* ~**y** ['gɪdɪ] schwind(e)lig.

gift [gɪft] 1. Geschenk *n;* 2. *fig* Veranlagung *f*, Talent *n* (*for* für); ~**ed** ['-ɪd] begabt, talentiert.

gigantic [dʒaɪ'gæntɪk] riesig; ungeheuer, gewaltig.

giggle ['gɪgl] **I** *v* kichern; **II** *s* Gekicher *n.*

gild [gɪld] vergolden.

gills *pl* ['gɪlz] *zoo* Kiemen *f pl.*

gilt-edged [ˌgɪlt'edʒd] *fin* mündelsicher.

ginger ['dʒɪndʒə] **I** *s* Ingwer *m;* **II** *v* (~ *up*) aufmöbeln, in Schwung bringen; ~ **ale,** ~ **beer** (alkoholfreies) Ingwerbier *n;* ~**bread** [-bred] Pfefferkuchen *m.*

gingerly ['dʒɪndʒəlɪ] vorsichtig.

gipsy, gypsy ['dʒɪpsɪ] Zigeuner(in *f*) *m.*

giraffe [dʒɪ'rɑːf] *zoo* Giraffe *f.*

girder ['gɜːdə] Tragbalken *m.*

girdle ['gɜːdl] Gürtel *m.*

girl [gɜːl] Mädchen *n;* Toch-

ter; Hausgehilfin *f; shop* ~*s* Verkäuferinnen *f pl;* ~**friend** ['-frend] Freundin *f.*

girth [gɜːθ] Gürtel-, Taillenweite *f.*

give [gɪv] *irr gave* [geɪv]. *given* [gɪvn] 1. geben; schenken; 2. hervorbringen, liefern; ~ *an example to s.o.* jdm ein Beispiel geben; 3. veranlassen, verursachen; ~ *s.o. trouble* jdm Unannehmlichkeiten bereiten; 4. (*Vorschlag*) machen; (*Grund*) angeben; (*Antwort*) geben; (*Blick*) zuwerfen; *theat mus* aufführen; 5. ~ *birth to* zur Welt bringen; *fig* hervorbringen; 6. ~ *notice* ankündigen, anzeigen; ~ **away** 1. verschenken; verteilen; 2. (*Gelegenheit*) verpassen; 3. verraten; ~ **back** zurückgeben; ~ **in** nachgeben; ~ **out** 1. verteilen; 2. bekanntgeben; 3. aus-, zu Ende gehen; ~ **up** aufgeben.

glacier ['glæsjə] Gletscher *m.*

glad [glæd] froh; glücklich (*of* über); ~**ly** ['-lɪ] gern(e).

glam|orous ['glæmərəs] bezaubernd (schön); ~**o(u)r** ['glæmə] Glanz, Zauber *m.*

glance [glɑːns] **I** *v* e-n flüchtigen Blick werfen (*at* auf); **II** *s* flüchtige(r) Blick *m; at a* ~ auf e-n Blick, mit e-m Blick.

gland [glænd] *anat* Drüse *f.*

glar|e [gleə] I *v* 1. hell glänzen, leuchten; 2. (an)starren (*at s.o.* jdn); wütend, böse anblicken (*at s.o.* jdn); II *s* blendende(r) Glanz *m;* ~**ing** ['-rɪŋ] 1. grell *a. fig;* 2. *a* ~ *injustice* ein schreiendes Unrecht.

glass [glɑːs] Glas *n;* ~**es** *pl* ['-ɪz] Brille *f;* ~**house** ['-haʊs] Treibhaus *n.*

glaz|e [gleɪz] 1. verglasen; 2. glasieren; 3. (*Augen*) glasig werden; ~**ier** ['gleɪzjə] Glaser *m.*

gleam [gliːm] Lichtstrahl; Schimmer *m.*

glee [gliː] (frohe) Stimmung *f.*

glen [glen] enge(s) Tal *n,* Klamm *f.*

glide [glaɪd] gleiten; schweben; ~**er** ['-ə] Segelflugzeug *n.*

glimmer ['glɪmə] I *v* flimmern; schimmern; II *s* Schimmer *m.*

glimpse [glɪmps] flüchtige(r) Blick *m; catch a* ~ *of s.th.* etw flüchtig zu sehen bekommen.

glisten ['glɪsn] schimmern.

glitter ['glɪtə] glitzern.

gloat [gləʊt] sich weiden (*over* an).

globe [gləʊb] 1. Globus *m;* 2. Glaskugel *f.*

gloom [gluːm] 1. Dunkel(heit *f*) *n;* 2. Schwermut *f;* ~**y** ['-ɪ] 1. düster; 2. trübselig.

glor|ify ['glɔːrɪfaɪ] rühmen, verherrlichen; ~**ious** ['glɔːrɪəs] 1. ruhmreich; 2. prachtvoll, herrlich; ~**y** ['glɔːrɪ] 1. Ruhm *m;* 2. Herrlichkeit *f;* Glanz *m.*

gloss [glɒs] 1. Glanz, Schimmer *m;* 2. *fig* Anstrich *m;* ~**y** ['-ɪ] glänzend, spiegelblank.

glove [glʌv] 1. Handschuh *m;* 2. *be hand in* ~ (*with*) ein Herz und eine Seele sein.

glow [gləʊ] glühen; ~**-worm** ['-wɜːm] Glühwürmchen *n.*

glue [gluː] I *s* Leim *m;* II *v* leimen; kleben (*to* an) *a. fig.*

glut [glʌt] (über)sättigen.

glutton ['glʌtn] Vielfraß *m.*

gnash [næʃ] knirschen (*o.'s teeth* mit den Zähnen).

gnat [næt] (Stech-)Mücke *f.*

gnaw [nɔː] nagen (*at* an).

go [gəʊ] *irr* went [went], gone [gɒn] 1. gehen; (~ *on horseback*) reiten; fahren (*by train* mit dem Zug); (~ *by air*) fliegen; ~ *to see* besuchen; 2. (*Maschine*) in Betrieb sein; funktionieren; 3. sich erstrecken, reichen (*to* bis zu); (*Weg*) führen (*to* nach); 4. (*Zeit*) vergehen; 5. weggehen, abreisen; 6. zu Ende gehen; verschwinden; 7. *let o.s.* ~ sich gehenlassen; 8. ~ *bad* (*Speise, Getränk*) verderben; 9. ~ *to sleep* einschlafen; ~ *for a walk* spazierengehen; ~ *shopping* einkaufen; 10. *one, two,* *three* — ~; *(sport)* Achtung — fertig — los! ~ **about** 1. *(Gerücht)* im Umlauf sein; 2. sich abgeben mit; ~ **away** weggehen; verreisen; ~ **back** zurückgehen; ~ **down** 1. *(Schiff)* untergehen; 2. *(Wind, Preise)* nachlassen; 3. Beifall finden *(with* bei); ~ **in** *for* sich interessieren für; teilnehmen an *(e-r Prüfung);* ~ **off** 1. einschlafen; das Bewußtsein verlieren; 2. *(Feuerwaffe)* losgehen; 3. *(Milch)* sauer werden; ~ **on** weitermachen *(with* mit); ~ **through** durchgehen, überprüfen; ~ **up** 1. *(im Preis)* steigen; 2. in die Luft fliegen; ~ **without** entbehren müssen; *that goes without saying* das ist selbstverständlich.

goal [gəʊl] 1. Ziel *n;* 2. *score a* ~ ein Tor schießen; *win by three* ~s *to one* 3 : 1 gewinnen; ~**keeper** ['-ˌkiːpə] Torwart *m.*

goat [gəʊt] Ziege *f.*

gobble ['gɒbl] gierig essen.

go-between ['gəʊbɪˌtwiːn] Vermittler *m.*

goblet ['gɒblɪt] Kelch(glas *n) m.*

god [gɒd] (heidnischer) Gott *m; G~* Gott *m;* ~**child** ['-tʃaɪld] Patenkind *n;* ~**dess** ['gɒdɪs] Göttin *f;* ~**less** ['-lɪs] gottlos; ~**like** ['-laɪk] göttlich.

go-getter ['gəʊˌgetə] *fam* Draufgänger *m.*

goggles *pl* ['gɒglz] Schutzbrille *f.*

going ['gəʊɪŋ] 1. *be* ~ *to* im Begriff sein zu; vorhaben zu; 2. ~! ~! *gone!* (*Versteigerung)* zum ersten! zum zweiten! zum dritten! 3. *a* ~ *concern* ein gutgehendes Geschäft; ~**s-on** *pl* [-zˈɒn] *fam* Treiben *n.*

gold [gəʊld] **I** *s* Gold *n;* **II** *adj* golden; ~**digger** ['-ˌdɪgə] Goldsucher *m;* ~**en** ['-ən] golden; *the* ~ *mean* die goldene Mitte.

golf [gɒlf] Golf(spiel) *n;* ~**course** ['-kɔːs], ~**links** *pl mit sing* ['-lɪŋks] Golfplatz *m.*

good [gʊd] **I** *adj* 1. gut; geeignet, passend *(for* für); 2. zuträglich; 3. tüchtig, geschickt; 4. lieb; brav; 5. *a* ~ *deal* ziemlich viel; *a* ~ *many* ziemlich viele; 6. *be* ~ *enough to* so gut sein und; 7. *have a* ~ *time* sich gut unterhalten; 8. *make* ~ es schaffen; 9. *make s.th.* ~ aufkommen für, gutmachen; **II** *s* 10. das Gute; *be no* ~ nichts nützen; nichts wert sein; 11. *for* ~ für immer; 12. *pl com* Güter *n pl;* Waren *f pl;* ~**bye** [ˌ-ˈbaɪ] Lebewohl *n;* auf Wiedersehen! ~**-for-nothing** ['-fəˌnʌθɪŋ] Taugenichts *m;* **G~ Friday** Karfreitag *m;* ~**-natured**

[ˌ-'neɪtʃəd] gutmütig; **~ness** ['-nɪs] Güte *f;* ~ *gracious!* (ach) du meine Güte! *for* ~' *sake* um Himmels willen! **~will** [ˌ-'wɪl] 1. Wohlwollen *n;* 2. Firmenwert *m.*

goose [guːs] *pl geese* [giːz] Gans *f;* **~berry** ['guzbərɪ] Stachelbeere *f;* **~-flesh** ['guːsfleʃ] Gänsehaut *f (beim Menschen).*

gorge [gɔːdʒ] **I** *s* Schlucht *f;* **II** *v* 1. vollstopfen; 2. gierig verschlingen.

gorgeous ['gɔːdʒəs] prächtig, prachtvoll.

go-slow strike [ˌgəu'sləu straɪk] Bummelstreik.

gospel ['gɔspl] Evangelium *n.*

gossip ['gɔsɪp] **I** *s* 1. Schwätzer *m,* Klatschbase *f;* 2. Geschwätz *n;* **II** *v* schwatzen; klatschen.

gourd [guəd] Kürbis *m.*

gout [gaut] Gicht *f.*

govern ['gʌvn] 1. regieren; 2. bestimmen; **~ment** [-mənt] Regierung *f;* **~or** ['gʌvənə] 1. Gouverneur; Direktor, Präsident *m;* 2. *tech* Regler *m.*

gown [gaun] 1. (Damen-)Kleid *n;* 2. Robe *f,* Talar *m.*

grab [græb] ergreifen, pakken.

grace [greɪs] 1. Anmut, Grazie *f;* 2. Gefälligkeit *f;* 3. *rel* Gnade *f;* 4. Tischgebet *n;* **~ful** ['-ful] anmutig.

gracious ['greɪʃəs] gütig;

good(ness) ~*!* ~ *me!* ach du meine Güte.

grad|e [greɪd] **I** *s* 1. Grad; Rang *m;* 2. Klasse, Qualität *f;* 3. *Am* (Schul-)Klasse *f;* 4. *(Schule)* Zensur *f;* 5. *Am* Steigung *f;* **II** *v* ab-, einstufen, sortieren; ~ **crossing** *(Am)* schienengleiche(r) Bahnübergang *m;* **~ient** ['-jənt] Steigung *f;* Gefälle *n.*

gradual ['grædʒuəl] stufen-, schrittweise; allmählich.

graduate I *s* ['grædʒuət] *(Universität)* Graduierte(r) *m;* **II** *v* ['grædʒueɪt] 1. e-n akademischen Grad erlangen; *Am* absolvieren *(from high school* die höhere Schule); 2. mit Maßeinteilung versehen; 3. abstufen.

graft [grɑːft] **I** *s* 1. Pfropfreis *n;* 2. *med* Transplantat *n;* 3. Schiebung, Korruption *f;* **II** *v* 4. *bot* pfropfen; 5. *med* verpflanzen.

grain [greɪn] 1. Korn; Getreide *n;* 2. Gran *n* (0,065 g); 3. *(Leder, Holz, Marmor)* Struktur, Maserung *f; (Leder)* Narbe *f;* 4. *it goes against my* ~ das geht mir gegen den Strich.

grammar ['græmə] Grammatik *f;* ~ **school** *Br* höhere Schule *f.*

gram(me) [græm] *(Masse)* Gramm *n.*

gramophone ['græməfəun] Plattenspieler *m.*

grand [grænd] 1. groß; 2. vornehm; 3. prachtvoll; ~**child** ['grænt∫aild] Enkelkind n; ~**daughter** ['græn,dɔ:tə] Enkelin f; ~**eur** ['grændʒə] 1. Größe; Erhabenheit f; 2. Vornehmheit f; 3. Pracht f; ~**father** ['grænd,fɑ:ðə] Großvater m; ~**mother** ['græn,mʌðə] Großmutter f; ~**parents** pl ['græn,peərənts] Großeltern pl; ~ **piano** mus Flügel; ~**son** ['grænsʌn] Enkel m.

granite ['grænɪt] min Granit m.

grant [grɑ:nt] I v 1. gewähren; bewilligen; 2. zugeben; take for ~ed als erwiesen annehmen; als selbstverständlich betrachten; II s Zuschuß m.

grape [greip] Weinbeere f; pl Weintrauben f pl; ~**fruit** ['-fru:t] Pampelmuse f; ~-**sugar** ['-,∫ugə] Traubenzucker m.

grapple ['græpl] 1. ergreifen, packen; 2. sich herumschlagen (with mit).

grasp [grɑ:sp] I v 1. (er)greifen, fassen; 2. fig begreifen, verstehen; II s 3. (Zu-)Griff m; 4. Verständnis n.

grass [grɑ:s] Gras n; ~-**hopper** ['-,hɔpə] Heuschrecke f; ~**roots** pl ['-,ru:ts] große Masse f; Volk n; ~ **widow(er)** Strohwitwe f(, -witwer m).

grate [greit] I v 1. reiben; 2. knirschen; II s (Feuer-)-Rost m.

grateful ['greitful] dankbar (to s.o. jdm); ~**ness** [-nɪs] Dankbarkeit f.

gratify ['grætɪfai] 1. erfreuen; 2. befriedigen.

gratitude ['grætɪtju:d] Dankbarkeit f.

gratuit|ous [grə'tju:itəs] 1. unentgeltlich; 2. unbegründet; ~**y** [grə'tju:əti] Trinkgeld n; Gratifikation f.

grave [greiv] I adj ernst; schwerwiegend; II s Grab n; ~**stone** ['-stəun] Grabstein m; ~**yard** ['-jɑ:d] Friedhof m.

gravel ['grævl] Kies m.

gravit|ate ['græviteit] fig tendieren (to, towards zu); ~**y** ['grævəti] 1. phys Schwerkraft f; 2. fig Schwere f, Ernst m.

gravy ['greivi] (Braten-)Soße f.

gray [grei] s. grey.

graze [greiz] 1. weiden, grasen; 2. streifen; abschürfen.

greas|e I s [gri:s] Fett n; Schmiere f; II v [gri:z] schmieren, (ein)fetten; ~**y** ['gri:zi] 1. fettig; schlüpfrig; 2. fig aalglatt.

great [greit] 1. groß; 2. bedeutend, berühmt; 3. (Freund) eng, intim; 4. fam großartig, prima; 5. a ~ deal e-e (ganze) Menge, viel.

Great Britain [ˌgreɪtˈbrɪtn] Großbritannien n.

great|ly [ˈgreɪtlɪ] sehr; **~ness** [ˈ-nɪs] Größe f.

Greece [griːs] Griechenland n.

greed [griːd] Gier f; **~y** [ˈ-ɪ] gierig (for nach).

Greek [griːk] **I** s Grieche m; Griechin f; **II** adj griechisch.

green [griːn] **I** adj 1. grün; 2. unreif; 3. unerfahren (at in); 4. he was ~ with envy er platzte vor Neid; **II** s 5. Grün n; 6. Grünfläche f; 7. pl Gemüse n; **~grocer** [ˈ-ˌgrəʊsə] (Obst- u.) Gemüsehändler m; **~horn** [ˈ-hɔːn] Grünschnabel; Anfänger m; **~house** [ˈ-haʊs] Gewächshaus n.

greet [griːt] (be)grüßen; **~ing** [ˈ-ɪŋ] Gruß m.

grey, gray [greɪ] grau; **~hound** [ˈ-haʊnd] Windhund m.

grid [grɪd] 1. Gitter n; 2. el Überlandleitungsnetz n.

grief [griːf] Kummer, Gram m; come to ~ Schaden erleiden.

griev|ance [ˈgriːvns] Beschwerde f; **~e** [griːv] bekümmern, betrüben; **~ous** [ˈgriːvəs] 1. schmerzlich; bedauerlich; 2. (Verletzung) schwer.

grill [grɪl] **I** s 1. Bratrost, Grill m; 2. gegrilltes Fleisch n; **II** v rösten, grillen.

grim [grɪm] grimmig.

grimace [grɪˈmeɪs] **I** s Grimasse f; **II** v Grimassen schneiden.

grime [graɪm] Schmutz m.

grin [grɪn] **I** v grinsen; ~ and bear it gute Miene zum bösen Spiel machen; **II** s Grinsen n.

grind [graɪnd] **I** v irr ground, ground [graʊnd] 1. mahlen, zerreiben; 2. schleifen, wetzen; 3. knirschen (o.'s teeth mit den Zähnen); **II** s fam Schufterei, Büffelei f.

grip [grɪp] **I** s Griff m; **II** v 1. (er)greifen, packen; 2. (Aufmerksamkeit) fesseln.

grizz|led [ˈgrɪzld] grauhaarig; **~y** [ˈgrɪzlɪ] zoo Grislybär m.

groan [grəʊn] **I** v seufzen, stöhnen; **II** s Seufzen n.

grocer [ˈgrəʊsə] Gemischtwarenhändler m; **~'s shop, ~y** [-rɪ] Gemischtwarenhandlung f.

grog [grɒg] Grog m; **~gy** [ˈ-ɪ] benommen, schwindlig.

groin [grɔɪn] anat Leiste(ngegend) f.

groom [gruːm] 1. Reitknecht m; 2. Bräutigam m.

groove [gruːv] 1. Furche f; 2. get into a ~ (fig) in e-e Gewohnheit verfallen.

grope [grəʊp] tappen; suchen; tasten (for nach).

gross [grəʊs] 1. dick, fett; 2. grob, rauh; 3. (Fehler) schwer; 4. com brutto.

ground [graund] **I** s 1. Grund, Boden m; cover (much) ~ e-e (große) Strecke zurücklegen; viel umfassen; fall to the ~ (fig) versagen, scheitern; hold, keep, stand o.'s ~ s-n Platz, sich behaupten; 2. (Beweg-)Grund m (for für, zu); on the ~s of auf Grund gen, wegen; 3. sport (Spiel-)Feld n; 4. pl Grundstück; Gelände n; Anlagen f pl; **II** v 5. (Schiff) auf Grund auflaufen (lassen); 6. fig gründen, basieren (on auf); 7. el erden; ~ **floor** Erdgeschoß n; ~**less** ['-lɪs] grundlos, unbegründet; ~**nut** ['-nʌt] Erdnuß f; ~ **staff** aero Bodenpersonal n.

group [gru:p] **I** s Gruppe f; **II** v (sich) gruppieren.

grove [grəuv] Wäldchen, Gehölz n.

grow [grəu] irr grew [gru:], grown [grəun] 1. wachsen a. fig; ~ up auf-, heranwachsen; fig sich entwickeln; 2. werden (into zu); dahin kommen (to do zu tun); 3. züchten, (an)bauen.

growl [graul] knurren, brummen.

grown-up I adj [ˌgrəun'ʌp] erwachsen; **II** s ['--'] Erwachsene(r) m.

growth [grəuθ] 1. Wachstum n a. fig; 2. Wuchs m; 3. med Tumor m.

grudge [grʌdʒ] **I** v mißgönnen (s.o. s.th. jdm etw); **II** s: bear s.o. a ~ etw gegen jdn haben.

gruel [gruəl] Schleim-, Mehlsuppe f.

gruesome ['gru:səm] grausig.

gruff [grʌf] schroff; barsch.

grumble ['grʌmbl] 1. murren (at, about, over über); 2. (Donner) (g)rollen.

grunt [grʌnt] grunzen.

guarantee [ˌgærən'ti:] **I** s Garantie; Bürgschaft f; **II** v garantieren; bürgen für.

guard [gɑ:d] **I** v 1. beschützen (against vor); 2. bewachen; 3. sich hüten (against vor); **II** s 4. Wache f; 5. Wachsamkeit, Vorsicht f; be on (off) o.'s ~ (nicht) auf der Hut sein.

guardian ['gɑ:djən] Vormund m; ~ **angel** Schutzengel m.

guer(r)illa war [gə'rɪlə] Partisanenkrieg m.

guess [ges] **I** v 1. (er)raten, vermuten; 2. Am fam glauben, meinen; **II** s Vermutung f; at a ~ schätzungsweise.

guest [gest] Gast m.

guidance ['gaɪdns] Leitung, Führung f.

guide [gaɪd] **I** s (Fremden-)Führer m; **II** v führen, leiten; ~-**lines** pl ['-laɪnz] Richtlinien f pl; ~**post** ['-pəust] Wegweiser m.

g(u)ild [gɪld] Gilde, Innung f.

guilt [gɪlt] Schuld f; ~**less**

['-lɪs] schuldlos, unschuldig
(of an); ~**y** ['-ɪ] 1. schuldig;
plead ~ sich schuldig bekennen; 2. schuldbewußt.

guinea-pig ['gɪnɪpɪg]
1. Meerschweinchen n;
2. fig Versuchskaninchen n.

guitar [gɪ'tɑ:] Gitarre f.

gulf [gʌlf] 1. Meerbusen,
Golf m; 2. Abgrund m a. fig.

gull [gʌl] (sea~) Möwe f.

gullet ['gʌlɪt] anat Speise-
röhre f.

gulp [gʌlp] **I** v (hinunter)schlucken; würgen;
II s Schluck m; at one ~ in
einem Zug.

gum [gʌm] **I** s 1. Gummi;
Klebstoff m; 2. pl Am
(~boots) Gummistiefel m pl;
3. Zahnfleisch n; **II** v gum-
mieren; (an)kleben.

gun [gʌn] 1. Kanone f, Ge-

schütz n; 2. Gewehr n;
3. Am Revolver m; ~**pow-
der** ['-,paʊdə] Schießpulver
n; ~**shot** ['-ʃɒt] within, out
of ~ in, außer Schußweite.

gurgle ['gɜ:gl] gurgeln.

gust [gʌst] 1. Bö f; 2. fig
Ausbruch m; ~**y** ['gʌstɪ]
stürmisch.

gut [gʌt] **I** s 1. pl fam Eingeweide n pl; 2. pl mit sing
(fam) Mut m; **II** v 3. auswei-
den; 4. ausplündern; ~ted by
fire ausgebrannt.

gutter ['gʌtə] 1. Dachrinne f;
2. Rinnstein m, Gosse f.

guy [gaɪ] sl Kerl, Bursche m.

gymn|asium [dʒɪm'neɪzjəm]
Turnhalle f; ~**astics** pl
[dʒɪm'næstɪks] Leibesübun-
gen f pl.

gypsy ['dʒɪpsɪ] s. gipsy.

gyrate [,dʒaɪə'reɪt] kreise(l)n.

H

haberdasher [ˈhæbədæʃə] Kurzwarenhändler m.

habit [ˈhæbɪt] Angewohnheit f; be in the ~ die Gewohnheit haben, pflegen (of doing s.th. etw zu tun).

habitual [həˈbɪtjʊəl] gewohnt, gewöhnlich.

hack [hæk] (zer)hacken (to pieces in Stücke).

haddock [ˈhædək] Schellfisch m.

h(a)emorrhage [ˈhemərɪdʒ] (schwere) Blutung f; **~orrhoids** pl [ˈhemərɔɪdz] med Hämorrhoiden f pl.

hag [hæg] Hexe f.

haggard [ˈhægəd] übernächtigt; verhärmt.

hail [heɪl] **I** s 1. Hagel m a. fig (of von); 2. Gruß, An-, Zuruf m; within ~ in Rufweite; **II** v 3. hageln; 4. zujubeln (s.o. jdm); 5. zurufen (s.o. jdm).

hair [heə] Haar n; his ~ stood on end die Haare standen ihm zu Berge; **~brush** [ˈ-brʌʃ] Haarbürste f; **~cut** [ˈ-cʌt] Haarschnitt m; **~dresser** [ˈ-dresə] Friseur m; **~pin** [ˈ-pɪn] Haarnadel f; ~ bend Haarnadelkurve f; **~raising** [ˈ-reɪzɪŋ] haarsträubend.

half [hɑ:f] **I** s pl halves [hɑ:vz] Hälfte f; cut in ~, into halves halbieren; **II** adj halb; ~ an hour e-e halbe Stunde; at ~ price zum halben Preis; **III** adv: ~ as much again noch mal soviel; ~ past three halb vier (Uhr); **~-brother** [ˈ-ˌbrʌðə] Halb-, Stiefbruder m; **~-time** [ˌ-ˈtaɪm] 1. be on ~ halbtags arbeiten; 2. at ~ (sport) bei Halbzeit; **~-way** [ˌ-ˈweɪ] **I** adj auf halbem Wege liegend; **II** adv: meet ~ (fig) auf halbem Weg entgegenkommen (s.o. jdm).

hall [hɔ:l] 1. Halle f, Saal m; City H~ Rathaus n; 2. Diele, (Eingangs-)Halle f.

halo [ˈheɪləʊ] pl ~(e)s 1. astr Hof m; 2. Heiligenschein m; 3. phot Lichthof m.

halt [hɔ:lt] **I** s 1. kurze Rast f; 2. Haltestelle f; 3. come to a ~ zum Stillstand kommen; **II** v (an)halten; stoppen.

halter [ˈhɔ:ltə] Halfter f.

halve [hɑ:v] halbieren.

ham [hæm] Schinken m.

hammer [ˈhæmə] **I** s Hammer m; ~ and tongs mit aller Kraft; **II** v 1. hämmern (auf); 2. fig (s.th. into s.o. jdm etw) einhämmern, -bleuen; 3. ~ (away) unermüdlich arbeiten (at an).

hammock [ˈhæmək] Hängematte f.

hamper ['hæmpə] **I** s (großer) Deckelkorb *m;* **II** *v* behindern, hemmen.
hamster ['hæmstə] *zoo*
Hamster *m.*

hand [hænd] **I** s 1. Hand *f;*
~s *off!* Hände weg! ~s *up!*
Hände hoch! *at first, second*
~ aus erster, zweiter Hand
od Quelle; *on* ~ vorrätig;
lend, give s.o. a ~ jdm helfen, behilflich sein (*in, with*
bei); *change* ~s den Besitzer
wechseln; *have a* ~ *in s.th.*
bei e-r S die Hand im Spiel
haben; *shake* ~s *with s.o.*
jdm die Hand drücken; *be* ~
in glove (with) ein Herz u.
eine Seele sein; 2. Seite;
Richtung *f;* 3. Handfertig-
keit *f,* Geschick *n;* 4. Arbeiter *m; be a poor* ~ ungeschickt sein (*at* bei, in);
5. Handschrift; Unterschrift
f; 6. (Uhr-)Zeiger *m;* **II** *v*
aushändigen; übergeben,
-reichen; ~ **down** herunter-
reichen; *fig* überliefern; ~
on weiterreichen, -geben; ~
out ausgeben, verteilen; ~
over übergeben.
hand|bag ['hændbæg]
Handtasche *f;* ~**brake**
['-breɪk] Handbremse *f;*
~**cuff** ['-kʌf] *meist pl* Hand-
schellen *f pl;* ~**ful** ['-fʊl] *a* ~
of e-e Handvoll; ein paar
(Leute).
handicraft ['hændɪkrɑːft]
Handwerk *n.*

handkerchief ['hæŋkətʃɪf]
Taschentuch *n.*
handl|e ['hændl] **I** s Griff *m,*
Klinke *f; fly off the* ~ *(fam)*
aufbrausen, wütend werden;
II *v* 1. anfassen; *glass!* ~
with care! Vorsicht! Glas!
2. erledigen; *(Thema)* abhandeln; 3. behandeln; ~**ing**
[-ɪŋ] Handhabung *f.*
hand-made ['hændmeɪd]
handgearbeitet; Hand-.
handsome ['hænsəm]
hübsch; gutaussehend;
schön.
handwriting ['hænd,raɪtɪŋ]
Handschrift *f.*
handy ['hændɪ] 1. greifbar,
zur Hand; 2. handlich; *come
in* ~ sich als nützlich erweisen; gerade gut passen;
3. geschickt.
hang [hæŋ] **I** *v irr* hung,
hung [hʌŋ] (auf)hängen;
aufgehängt sein; ~ **about,**
~ **(a)round** sich herumtrei-
ben; ~ **back** zögern, sich
zurückhalten; ~ **on** sich
(fest)halten (an); durchhalten; *tele* am Apparat bleiben; ~ **up** *tele* (den Hörer)
auflegen; aufhalten, verzögern.
hanger ['hæŋə] Aufhänger;
Haken; Bügel *m.*
hang|man ['hæŋmən] Hen-
ker *m;* ~**over** [-,əʊvə] Kater; Katzenjammer *m.*
happen ['hæpən] 1. sich ereignen; ~ *to s.o.* jdm zustoßen; 2. ~ *to do* zufällig tun;

~ing [-ɪŋ] Ereignis, Geschehnis *n*.

happiness ['hæpɪnɪs] Glück *n*; **~y** ['hæpɪ] glücklich; **~ birthday!** herzlichen Glückwunsch zum Geburtstag!

harass ['hærəs] stören, beunruhigen.

harbo(u)r ['hɑːbə] **I** *s* 1. Hafen *m*; 2. Unterschlupf *m*; **II** *v* beherbergen, Unterschlupf gewähren.

hard [hɑːd] **I** *adj* 1. hart, fest; 2. heftig; 3. anstrengend; 4. schwierig; **~ to believe** kaum zu glauben; **~ to please** schwer zu befriedigen(d); 5. *(Winter)* streng; *(Zeiten)* schlecht; 6. hart(herzig), gefühllos; *(Worte)* hart, grob; 7. fleißig; 8. **~ and fast** *(Regel)* unumstößlich; 9. **~ of hearing** schwerhörig; 10. **~ luck** Pech *n*; **II** *adv*: **try ~** sich große Mühe geben; **work ~** fleißig arbeiten; **~-boiled** [ˌ-'bɔɪld] *(Ei)* hartgekocht; **~en** ['hɑːdn] (ab-, ver)härten; **be ~ed to s.th.** an etw gewöhnt sein; **~-headed** [ˌ-'hedɪd] nüchtern, praktisch; **~-hearted** [ˌ-'hɑːtɪd] hartherzig; **~ly** ['-lɪ] schwerlich, kaum; **~ any** fast kein; **~ ever** kaum je(mals), fast nie; **~ness** ['-nɪs] Härte; Strenge *f*; **~ship** ['-ʃɪp] Mühsal, Plage *f*; **~top** ['-top] *mot* Limousine *f*; **~ware** ['-weə] 1. Eisen-,

Stahlwaren *f pl*; 2. *EDV* Hardware *f*; **~y** ['-ɪ] 1. kühn, unerschrocken; 2. *bot* winterfest.

hare [heə] Hase *m*; **~-brained** ['-breɪnd] gedankenlos; **~lip** ['-lɪp] *med* Hasenscharte *f*.

harm [hɑːm] **I** *s* Schaden *m*; Unrecht *n*; **mean no ~** es nicht böse meinen; **I** *v* ein Leid zufügen (*s.o.* jdm); **~ful** ['-fʊl] schädlich; **~less** ['-lɪs] harmlos.

harmony ['hɑːmənɪ] Harmonie *f*; **be in ~** übereinstimmen (*with* mit).

harp [hɑːp] Harfe *f*.

harpoon [hɑː'puːn] **I** *s* Harpune *f*; **II** *v* harpunieren.

harsh [hɑːʃ] 1. *(Stimme, Stoff)* rauh; 2. streng, hart; **~ness** ['-nɪs] Strenge, Härte *f*.

harvest ['hɑːvɪst] **I** *s* Ernte *f*; **II** *v* ernten; **~er** [-ə] Mähdrescher *m*.

hash [hæʃ] 1. Ragout *n*; 2. *fam* Haschisch *n*; 3. **make a ~ of** *(fig)* verhunzen.

haste [heɪst] Eile *f*; **make ~** sich beeilen; **~en** ['heɪsn] 1. beschleunigen; 2. (sich) be)eilen; **~ily** ['-ɪlɪ] eilig, hastig; **~y** ['-ɪ] überstürzt, übereilt.

hat [hæt] Hut *m*.

hatch [hætʃ] **I** *s mar* Luke *f*; **II** *v* 1. ausbrüten; 2. aushecken.

hatchet ['hætʃɪt] Beil *n*.

hat|e [heɪt] 1. hassen; 2. *fam* bedauern, sehr ungern tun; **~red** ['heɪtrɪd] Haß *m*.

haughty ['hɔːtɪ] hochmütig.

haul [hɔːl] **I** *v* ziehen; schleppen; **II** *s* 1. Fang *m*, Beute *f*; 2. Strecke *f*, Weg *m*.

haunt [hɔːnt] *(Gespenst)* umgehen in.

have [hæv] *irr* had, had [hæd] 1. haben; besitzen; 2. erleben, erleiden; ~ *a cold* erkältet sein; ~ *a good time* sich amüsieren; 3. bekommen, erhalten; 4. ~ *to* müssen; 5. ausführen, machen; ~ *a bath* ein Bad nehmen; ~ *a try* e-n Versuch machen; ~ *a walk* spazierengehen; 6. essen, trinken; ~ *tea* Tee trinken; 7. ~ *in mind* im Sinn haben; 8. *you had better* es wäre besser, wenn du; *I had rather... than* ich möchte lieber ... als; 9. zulassen; *I wouldn't ~ you do that* das dürfen Sie nicht tun! 10. *what would you ~ me do?* was soll ich machen?

havoc ['hævək] Verwüstung *f*.

hawk [hɔːk] **I** *s* Habicht *m*; Falke *m*; **II** *v* hausieren *(s.th. mit etw)*; **~er** ['-ə] Hausierer *m*.

hay [heɪ] Heu *n*; ~ **fever** Heuschnupfen *m*; **~rick** ['-rɪk], **~stack** ['-stæk] Heuhaufen *m*.

hazard ['hæzəd] **I** *s* 1. Risiko *n*; 2. Zufall *m*; **II** *v* wagen,

riskieren; **~ous** ['hæzədəs] gewagt, riskant.

haze [heɪz] Dunst *m*.

hazel-nut ['heɪzlnʌt] Haselnuß *f*.

hazy ['heɪzɪ] dunstig, diesig.

he [hiː] er; ~ *who* derjenige, welcher.

head [hed] **I** *s* 1. Kopf *m*; *a* ~ pro Kopf; *be off o.'s* ~ den Verstand verloren haben; *keep o.'s* ~ die Ruhe bewahren; *lose o.'s* ~ den Kopf verlieren; 2. Verstand *m*; Begabung *f*; 3. ~ *of the government* Regierungschef *m*; 4. Spitze *f*, Gipfel *m*; *at the* ~ *of* an der Spitze gen; 5. *(pl* ~*)* *(Vieh)* Stück *n*; 6. ~s *or tails?* Kopf oder Wappen *(e-r Münze)?* 7. (Kapitel-) Überschrift *f*; **II** *v* 8. (an)führen, an der Spitze stehen; 9. *sport (Ball)* köpfen; 10. *be ~ing for* auf dem Wege sein nach; Kurs nehmen auf; 11. ~ *off* abdrängen; verhindern; **~ache** ['hedeɪk] Kopfweh *n*; **~er** ['-ə] Kopfball; Kopfsprung *m*; **~ing** ['-ɪŋ] Überschrift *f*; *(Zeitung)* Schlagzeile *f*; **~light** ['-laɪt] Scheinwerferlicht *n*; **~line** ['-laɪn] Schlagzeile *f*; **~long** ['-lɒŋ] 1. kopfüber; 2. unüberlegt; ungestüm; **~master** [ˌ-'mɑːstə] *(Schule)* (Di-)Rektor *m*; **~-on** ['-ɒn] frontal; ~ *collision* Frontalzs.stoß *m*; **~phones** *pl* ['-fəʊnz] Kopf-

hörer m pl; ~**quarters** pl
['-ˌkwɔːtəz] Hauptquartier n;
Zentrale f; ~**rest** ['-rest]
Kopfstütze f; ~**way** ['-weɪ]
make ~ vorankommen.

heal [hiːl] heilen; ~ *up, over*
zuheilen.

health [helθ] Gesundheit f;
drink s.o.'s ~ auf jds Gesundheit trinken; ~**y** ['-ɪ] gesund.

heap [hiːp] I s Haufen m; ~**s**
(fam) ein Haufen, e-e Menge *(of money* Geld); II v (~
up) an-, auf-, zs.häufen.

hear [hɪə] *irr heard, heard*
[hɜːd] 1. hören; 2. zuhören;
3. erfahren; *let me* ~ *from
you* lassen Sie von sich hören; 4. *jur* vernehmen *(Fall)*
verhandeln; ~**er** ['hɪərə]
(Zu-)Hörer m; ~**ing** ['-rɪŋ]
1. Hören; Gehör(sinn m) n;
hard of ~ schwerhörig; *his*
~ *is poor* er hört schlecht;
~*-aid* Hörgerät n; 2. *jur*
Verhör n; 3. *within, out of* ~
in, außer Hörweite f.

heart [hɑːt] Herz n; *by* ~
auswendig; *take* ~ sich ein
Herz fassen; *have o.'s* ~ *in
o.'s mouth* zu Tode er-
schrocken sein; *don't lose* ~!
verlier den Mut nicht! I ~ **attack** *med* Herzanfall m;
~**beat** ['-biːt] Herzschlag m;
~**breaking** ['-breɪkɪŋ] herz-
zerreißend; ~**burn** ['-bɜːn]
Sodbrennen n; ~**en** ['hɑːtn]
ermutigen.

hearth [hɑːθ] Herd m.

heart|less ['hɑːtlɪs] herzlos;
~**y** ['-ɪ] 1. herzlich, innig;
aufrichtig; 2. *(Essen)* reichlich.

heat [hiːt] I s 1. Hitze, Wärme f; 2. Erregung f, Zorn,
Eifer m; 3. *dead* ~ unent-
schiedene(s) Rennen n; II v
4. heizen; 5. ~ *up* erhitzen;
(Speise) aufwärmen; ~**er**
['-ə] Heizkörper m; -gerät n.

heath [hiːθ] Heide(kraut n) f.

heather ['heðə] Heide(kraut
n), Erika f.

heating ['hiːtɪŋ] Heizung f.

heat|stroke ['hiːtstrəuk]
Hitzschlag m; ~**wave**
[-weɪv] Hitzewelle f.

heave [hiːv] 1. (an-, hoch)he-
ben; 2. wogen; (an)schwel-
len; 3. ~ *ho!* hau ruck!

heaven ['hevn] *rel* Himmel
m; ~**ly** [-lɪ] himmlisch.

heavy ['hevɪ] 1. schwer *(von
Gewicht)*; 2. müde, schläfrig;
langsam; schwerfällig;
3. *(Speise)* schwer; 4. *(Himmel)* bedeckt; 5. *(Regen)*
heftig; 6. *(Verkehr)* stark; ~
current Starkstrom m;
~**weight** [-weɪt] *sport*
Schwergewichtler m.

hectic ['hektɪk] hektisch.

he'd [hiːd] = *he had; he
would.*

hedge [hedʒ] I s Hecke f;
II v (~ *in)* einhegen, -frie-
den; ~**hog** ['-hɒg] Igel m.

heed [hiːd] *(give, pay* ~ *to,
take* ~ *of)* (be)achten; aufpassen auf; ~**ful** ['-fʊl] auf-

merksam; **~less** ['-lɪs] un-aufmerksam; sorglos.

heel [hi:l] Ferse *f; (Schuh)* Absatz *m; at, on s.o.'s ~s* jdm auf den Fersen; *head over ~s* Hals über Kopf; *come to ~* klein beigeben; *take to o.'s ~s* das Weite suchen.

height [haɪt] 1. Höhe *f; he is six feet in ~* er ist 6 Fuß groß; 2. Höhepunkt *m;* 3. Anhöhe *f;* **~en** ['haɪtn] *fig* erhöhen.

heir [eə] Erbe *m;* **~ess** ['eərɪs] Erbin *f.*

helicopter ['helɪkɒptə] *aero* Hubschrauber *m.*

hell [hel] Hölle *f; what the ~ are you doing here? (fam)* was zum Teufel machen Sie denn hier? *a ~ of a lot (fam)* e-e Unmenge.

he'll [hi:l] = *he will.*

helm [helm] Steuer(ruder) *n.*

helmet ['helmɪt] Helm *m; crash ~* Sturzhelm *m.*

help [help] **I** *v* 1. helfen *(s.o.* jdm); *~ out* aushelfen; *I can't ~ it* ich kann nichts dafür; *so ~ me God!* so wahr mir Gott helfe! 2. *~ yourself!* bedienen Sie sich! **II** *s* 3. Hilfe *f;* 4. (Haus-)Gehilfe *m;* Gehilfin *f;* **~er** ['-ə] Helfer *m;* **~ful** ['-ful] behilflich, nützlich; **~ing** ['-ɪŋ] Portion *f (e-r Speise);* **~less** ['-lɪs] hilflos.

hem [hem] **I** *s* Saum *m;* **II** *v* säumen.

hen [hen] Henne *f,* Huhn *n.*

hence [hens] folglich, deshalb; **~forth** [ˌ-'fɔ:θ] , **~forward** [ˌ-'fɔ:wəd] nunmehr, in Zukunft.

her [hɜ:] *give it to ~* gib es ihr; *it's ~ book* es ist ihr Buch.

herald ['herəld] **I** *s* 1. Herold *m;* 2. *fig* (Vor-)Bote *m;* **II** *v* ankündigen.

herb [hɜ:b] Kraut *n.*

herd [hɜ:d] **I** *s* Herde *f;* **II** *v* (hinein)treiben *(into* in).

here [hɪə] da; hier(her); *~ and there* hier und da; *come ~!* komm her! *~ he comes!* da kommt er (ja)! *~ you are!* da haben Sie es! *~'s to your health!* auf Ihr Wohl! **~after** [ˌ-'ɑ:ftə] später, in Zukunft.

hereditary [hɪ'redɪtərɪ] (ver)erblich.

heresy ['herəsɪ] Ketzerei *f.*

heritage ['herɪtɪdʒ] Erbschaft *f.*

hero ['hɪərəʊ] *pl* **-roes** Held *m;* **~ic(al)** [hɪ'rəʊɪk(l)] heroisch; **~ine** ['herəʊɪn] Heldin *f;* **~ism** ['herəʊɪzəm] Heldenmut *m.*

herring ['herɪŋ] *pl* **~(s)** Hering *m.*

hers [hɜ:z] *a friend of ~* ein Freund von ihr; *it's ~* es gehört ihr.

herself [hɜ:'self] *she hurt ~* sie hat sich verletzt; *(all) by ~* allein; ohne Hilfe.

hesitat|e ['hezɪteɪt] zögern

(*about doing, to do* zu tun);
~**ion** [ˌhezɪˈteɪʃn] *without a
moment's* ~ ohne e-n Augenblick zu zögern.
hibernate [ˈhaɪbəneɪt] überwintern.
hiccup [ˈhɪkʌp] Schluckauf
m.
hide [haɪd] **I** *v irr* hid [hɪd],
hidden [ˈhɪdn] (sich) verstecken, verbergen (*from*
vor); **II** *s* Haut *f*, Fell *n.*
hideous [ˈhɪdɪəs] scheußlich,
gräßlich.
hiding [ˈhaɪdɪŋ] *give s.o. a* ~
jdn verprügeln; ~**-place**
[-pleɪs] Versteck *n.*
high [haɪ] 1. hoch; 2. *fig*
hochgestellt; hervor-, überragend; 3. anmaßend, stolz;
4. *in* ~ *spirits* in guter Laune; 5. *it is* ~ *time* es ist höchste Zeit.
high|brow [ˈhaɪbraʊ] intellektuell; ~**-grade** [ˈ-greɪd]
hochwertig, erstklassig; ~
jump *sport* Hochsprung *m;*
~**land** [ˈ-lənd] Hochland *n;*
~**light** [ˈ-laɪt] **I** *s* Glanz-,
Höhepunkt *m;* **II** *v fig* hervorheben; ~**ly** [ˈ-lɪ] in hohem Maße, höchst, sehr, äußerst; ~**-pitched** [ˈ-pɪtʃt]
(*Ton*) hoch, schrill;
~**-pressure area** [ˈ-ˌpreʃə
ˈeərɪə] Hochdruckgebiet *n;*
~**road** [ˈ-rəʊd] Hauptstraße
f; ~**-tension** [ˈ-ˌtenʃn] *el*
Hochspannung *f;* ~**way**
[ˈ-weɪ] Landstraße *f;* ~ *code*
Straßenverkehrsordnung *f.*

hijack [ˈhaɪdʒæk] (*Flugzeug*)
entführen.
hike [haɪk] (*fam*) **I** *s* Wanderung *f;* **II** *v* wandern.
hilarious [hɪˈleərɪəs] fröhlich,
lustig; ausgelassen.
hill [hɪl] 1. Hügel, Berg *m;*
2. Steigung *f;* ~**side** [ˈ-saɪd]
(Berg-, Ab-)Hang *m;* ~**y** [ˈ-ɪ]
hüg(e)lig.
him [hɪm] *I saw* ~ ich habe
ihn gesehen; *give it to* ~ gib
es ihm; *that's* ~ (*fam*) das ist
er; ~**self** [-ˈself] (er) selbst;
sich (selbst); (*all*) *by* ~
(ganz) allein; ohne (fremde)
Hilfe; *he ist quite beside* ~
er ist ganz außer sich.
hind|er [ˈhɪndə] hindern; aufhalten; ~**rance** [ˈhɪndrəns]
Hindernis *n* (*to* für).
hinge [hɪndʒ] **I** *s* (Tür-)Angel
f; Scharnier *n;* **II** *v* 1. *fig* abhängen (*on, upon* von);
2. sich drehen (*on, upon* um).
hint [hɪnt] **I** *s* Hinweis, Wink,
Fingerzeig *m* (*at* auf); **II** *v*
andeuten, anspielen (*at* auf).
hip [hɪp] *anat* Hüfte *f.*
hippopotamus
[ˌhɪpəˈpɒtəməs] Nilpferd *n.*
hire [ˈhaɪə] **I** *s* Miete *f; for* ~
(*Taxi*) frei; **II** *v* 1. mieten;
engagieren; 2. ~ *out* vermieten; ~ **purchase** Ratenkauf
m.
his [hɪz] sein(e, r); *a friend of*
~ ein Freund von ihm; *the
book is* ~ das Buch gehört
ihm.
hiss [hɪs] **I** *v* 1. zischen; 2. ~

s.o. *off* jdn auszischen, -pfeifen; **II** s Zischen n.

histor|ian [hɪˈstɔːrɪən] Historiker m; **~ic(al)** [hɪˈstɒrɪk(l)] geschichtlich, historisch; **~y** [ˈhɪstərɪ] Geschichte f.

hit [hɪt] **I** v irr hit, hit 1. schlagen; treffen, stoßen an; 2. e-n Schlag versetzen (s.o. jdm); ~ *s.o. below the belt* (*Boxen u. fig*) jdm e-n Tiefschlag versetzen; 3. *how did you ~ on that?* wie sind Sie darauf gekommen? 4. ~ *it off* gut mitea. auskommen (*with s.o.* mit jdm); **II** s 5. Treffer m; 6. (Bomben-) Erfolg m; mus Schlager, Hit m; 7. *that was a ~ at me* das galt mir. •

hitch [hɪtʃ] **I** v 1. ~ *up* hochziehen; 2. festhaken, -binden (*to* an); **II** s Haken m fig; Schwierigkeit f; **~hike** [ˈ-haɪk] per Anhalter fahren; **~hiker** [ˈ-haɪkə] Anhalter m.

hive [haɪv] Bienenstock, -korb m.

hoard [hɔːd] **I** s Vorrat m; **II** v (~ *up*) horten.

hoarding [ˈhɔːdɪŋ] Bau-, Bretterzaun m.

hoarfrost [ˌhɔːˈfrɒst] Rauhreif m.

hoarse [hɔːs] rauh; heiser.

hoax [həʊks] Streich, Schabernack m.

hobble [ˈhɒbl] humpeln.

hoe [həʊ] Hacke f.

hoist [hɔɪst] **I** v auf-, hochziehen; mar hissen; **II** s Winde f, Flaschenzug m.

hold [həʊld] **I** s 1. Griff; Halt m; 2. fig Gewalt; Macht f; 3. mar Laderaum m; **II** v irr held, held [held] 4. (fest)halten; tragen; ~ *o.s ground* sich behaupten; ~ *the line (tele)* am Apparat bleiben; 5. besitzen; 6. (Amt) innehaben; bekleiden; 7. (Versammlung) abhalten; 8. (Ansicht) vertreten; 9. (Raum, Gefäß) fassen; 10. fig ansehen, betrachten als; ~ **back** (sich) zurückhalten; ~ **on** 1. durchhalten; 2. festhalten (*to* an); ~ **out** aushalten, -standhalten; ~ **together** zs.halten; ~ **up** 1. (hoch-, aufrecht)halten; 2. preisgeben (*to ridicule* der Lächerlichkeit); 3. überfallen (und ausrauben); 4. *be held up* aufgehalten werden; **~all** [ˈ-ɔːl] Reisetasche f; **~er** [ˈ-ə] Inhaber, Besitzer m; **~ing** [ˈ-ɪŋ] Pachtgut n; pl Besitz m; **~-up** [ˈ-ʌp] 1. (*traffic ~*) Verkehrsstörung f; 2. (bewaffneter) Raubüberfall m.

hole [həʊl] 1. Loch n; 2. Elendsquartier n.

holiday [ˈhɒlɪdɪ] 1. Feiertag m; 2. pl Ferien pl, Urlaub m; *on ~* in Urlaub; **~-maker** [-ˌmeɪkə] Urlauber m.

Holland [ˈhɒlənd] Holland n; **~er** [-ə] Holländer m.

hollow [ˈhɒləʊ] **I** adj hohl a.

fig; **II** *s* Höhlung, Vertiefung *f;* **III** *v* (~ *out*) aushöhlen.

holy ['həʊlɪ] heilig; **H~ Week** Karwoche *f.*

home [həʊm] **I** *s* 1. Wohnung, Heimat *f;* 2. Zuhause *n; Familie f; be, feel at ~ (fig)* sich zu Hause fühlen; 3. Heim *n;* Anstalt *f;* **II** *adj* heimisch, häuslich; **III** *adv: go ~* heimgehen; *see s.o.* ~ jdn nach Hause begleiten; **~less** ['-lɪs] obdachlos; **~-made** ['-meɪd] selbstgemacht; **H~ Office** Innenministerium *n;* **~sick** ['-sɪk] *be ~* Heimweh haben; **~ward(s)** ['-wəd(z)] heim, nach Hause; **~work** ['-wɜːk] *(Schule)* Hausaufgaben *f pl.*

homicide ['hɒmɪsaɪd] Totschlag; Mord *m.*

honest ['ɒnɪst] ehrlich, aufrichtig; **~ly** [-lɪ] wirklich; offengestanden; **~y** [-ɪ] Ehrlichkeit *f.*

honey ['hʌnɪ] 1. Honig *m;* 2. *fam* Liebling *m;* **~moon** [-muːn] Flitterwochen *f pl.*

hono(u)r ['ɒnə] **I** *s* Ehre, Auszeichnung *f; in s.o.'s ~* zu jds Ehren; **II** *v* ehren ~ **~able** ['-rəbl] ehrenhaft.

hood [hʊd] 1. Kapuze *f;* 2. *Am mot* Kühlerhaube *f;* **~wink** ['-wɪŋk] täuschen.

hoof [huːf] *pl a.* **hooves** [huːvz] Huf *m.*

hook [hʊk] **I** *s* Haken *m;* **II** *v* 1. einhaken; 2. angeln *a. fig;* 3. biegen, krümmen.

hooping-cough ['huːpɪŋkɒf] Keuchhusten *m.*

hoot [huːt] 1. schreien; 2. hupen.

hop [hɒp] **I** *v* hüpfen; **II** *s* 1. Sprung *m;* 2. *pl* Hopfen *m.*

hope [həʊp] **I** *s* Hoffnung *f* (*of* auf); **II** *v* hoffen (*for s.th.* etw); *I ~ not* hoffentlich nicht; **~ful** ['-fʊl] hoffnungsvoll; **~less** ['-lɪs] hoffnungslos.

horizon [hə'raɪzn] Horizont *m;* **~tal** [ˌhɒrɪ'zɒntl] horizontal.

horn [hɔːn] 1. Horn *n;* 2. *mot* Hupe *f.*

hornet ['hɔːnɪt] *zoo* Hornisse *f.*

horoscope ['hɒrəskəʊp] *cast a ~* ein Horoskop stellen.

horrid ['hɒrɪd] schrecklich, furchtbar.

horrify ['hɒrɪfaɪ] entsetzen; schockieren.

horror ['hɒrə] Entsetzen, Grauen *n.*

hors d'œuvres *pl* [ɔː'dɜːvrəz] Vorspeise *f.*

horse [hɔːs] Pferd *n;* **~back** ['-bæk] *on ~* zu Pferde; **~-chestnut** [ˌ-'tʃesnʌt] Roßkastanie *f;* **~racing** ['-reɪsɪŋ] Pferderennen *n;* **~shoe** ['hɔːʃuː] Hufeisen *n.*

hose [həʊz] Schlauch *m.*

hosiery ['həʊzɪərɪ] Strumpfwaren *f pl.*

hospitable ['hɒspɪtəbl] gastlich.

hospital ['hɒspɪtl] Kranken-haus n.

hospitality [ˌhɒspɪ'tælətɪ] Gastfreundschaft f.

host [həʊst] Gastgeber, Wirt m.

hostage ['hɒstɪdʒ] Geisel f.

hostel ['hɒstl] youth ~ Ju-gendherberge f.

hostess ['həʊstɪs] Gastge-berin; Wirtin; aero Stewar-deß f.

hostil|e ['hɒstaɪl] feindlich (to gegen); ~**ity** [hɒ'stɪlətɪ] Feindseligkeit f.

hot [hɒt] 1. heiß; 2. (Gewürz) scharf; 3. fig hitzig; ~ **dog** heiße(s) Würstchen n (mit Brötchen).

hotel [həʊ'tel] Hotel n.

hot-headed ['hɒtˌhedɪd] hitzköpfig.

hound [haʊnd] Jagdhund m.

hour ['aʊə] Stunde f; a quar-ter of an ~ e-e Viertelstun-de; half an ~ e-e halbe Stunde; at the eleventh ~ in letzter Minute; for ~s stun-denlang; ~**ly** [-lɪ] stündlich.

house [haʊs] pl houses ['haʊzɪz] **I** s Haus n; the H~ of Commons (parl) das Un-terhaus; **II** v unterbringen; ~**breaker** ['-ˌbreɪkə] Ein-brecher m; ~**hold** ['-həʊld] Haushalt m; ~**wife** ['-waɪf] Hausfrau f.

housing ['haʊzɪŋ] Unterbrin-gung f; ~ **estate** Siedlung f.

hover ['hɒvə] schweben;

~**craft** [-krɑːft] mot Luft-kissenfahrzeug n.

how [haʊ] wie; ~ about ...? wie steht es mit ...? ~ many? wie viele? ~ much? wieviel? ~ are you? ~ do you do? wie geht's? Guten Tag! (bei e-r Vorstellung) sehr erfreut! ~**ever** [-'evə] jedoch.

howl [haʊl] **I** v heulen; schreien; **II** s Geheul n.

huddle ['hʌdl] **I** v (~ to-gether) sich zs.drängen; **II** s: go into a ~ (fam) die Köpfe zs.stecken.

hue [hjuː] 1. Farbe f; Schat-tierung f; 2. ~ and cry lau-te(s) Geschrei n.

hug [hʌg] **I** v umarmen; **II** s Umarmung f.

huge [hjuːdʒ] riesig, gewal-tig.

hull [hʌl] 1. bot Hülse f; 2. mar Rumpf m.

hum [hʌm] **I** v 1. summen; 2. geschäftig, betriebsam sein; **II** s Summen n.

human ['hjuːmən] mensch-lich; ~ being Mensch m; ~**e** [hjuː'meɪn] gütig, human; ~**ity** [hjuː'mænətɪ] 1. Menschheit f; 2. Mensch-lichkeit f.

humble ['hʌmbl] bescheiden; demütig.

humid ['hjuːmɪd] feucht; ~**ity** [hjuː'mɪdətɪ] Feuchtig-keit f.

humili|ate [hjuː'mɪlɪeɪt] demütigen; **~ty** [hju:'mɪlətɪ] Demut *f.*

humorous ['hju:mərəs] drollig, komisch.

humo(u)r ['hju:mə] **I** *s* 1. Humor *m;* 2. Laune, Stimmung *f; in a good, bad* ~ gut, schlecht aufgelegt; **II** *v:* ~ *s.o.* jdm s-n Willen tun *od* lassen.

hump [hʌmp] 1. *(Kamel)* Höcker *m;* 2. *(Mensch)* Bukkel *m.*

hunchback ['hʌntʃbæk] Bucklige(r) *m.*

hundred ['hʌndrəd] hundert; **~weight** [-weɪt] *(etwa)* Zentner *m.*

Hungar|ian [hʌŋ'geərɪən] **I** *s* Ungar *m;* **II** *adj* ungarisch; **~y** ['hʌŋgərɪ] Ungarn *n.*

hunger ['hʌŋgə] **I** *s* Hunger *m; die of* ~ verhungern; **II** *v* hungern; **~ry** ['hʌŋgrɪ] hungrig.

hunt [hʌnt] **I** *v* 1. jagen; 2. suchen *(for* nach); **II** *s* 3. Jagd *f;* 4. Suche *f;* **~er** ['-ə] Jäger *m;* **~ing** ['-ɪŋ] Jagen *n.*

hurdle ['hɜ:dl] Hürde *f;* **~-race** [-reɪs] Hürdenlauf *m.*

hurl [hɜ:l] schleudern *(at* auf, gegen).

hurricane ['hʌrɪkən] *bes. Am* Orkan *m.*

hurry ['hʌrɪ] **I** *v* (~ *up*) sich beeilen; *don't* ~ immer mit

der Ruhe! **II** *s* Eile *f; be in a* ~ es eilig haben.

hurt [hɜ:t] *irr hurt, hurt* 1. schmerzen; 2. verletzen, wehtun *(s.o.* jdm); 3. ~ *s.o.'s feelings* jdn kränken.

husband ['hʌzbənd] (Ehe-)-Mann, Gatte *m.*

hush [hʌʃ] 1. zum Schweigen bringen; 2. ~ *up* vertuschen.

husk [hʌsk] **I** *s bot* Hülse *f;* **II** *v* schälen; **~y** ['-ɪ] heiser.

hustle ['hʌsl] stoßen; drängen.

hut [hʌt] Hütte *f.*

hydroelectric power--station [ˌhaɪdrəʊ'lektrɪk 'pauəˌsteɪʃn] Wasserkraftwerk *n.*

hydrogen ['haɪdrədʒən] Wasserstoff *m.*

hyena [haɪ'i:nə] Hyäne *f.*

hygien|e ['haɪdʒi:n] Hygiene *f;* **~ic(al)** [haɪ'dʒi:nɪk(l)] hygienisch.

hymn [hɪm] Hymne *f.*

hyphen ['haɪfn] Bindestrich *m.*

hypno|sis [hɪp'nəʊsɪs] *pl -ses* Hypnose *f;* **~tize** ['hɪpnətaɪz] hypnotisieren.

hypo|crisy [hɪ'pɒkrəsɪ] Heuchelei *f;* **~crite** ['hɪpəkrɪt] Heuchler *m;* **~critical** [ˌhɪpəʊ'krɪtɪkl] heuchlerisch.

hysteri|a [hɪ'stɪərɪə] Hysterie *f;* **~cal** [hɪ'sterɪkl] hysterisch.

I

I [aɪ] ich.

ice [aɪs] **I** s 1. Eis n; on thin ~ in einer gefährlichen Situation; cut no ~ keine Wirkung haben; 2. Speiseeis n; 3. Zuckerguß m; **II** v 4. gefrieren lassen; mit Eis kühlen; 5. (~ up, ~ over) gefrieren, zufrieren, vereisen a. aero; 6. glasieren; ~ **age** Eiszeit f; ~**-cream** ['-kriːm] Speiseeis n; ~ parlo(u)r Eisdiele f; ~**d** [aɪst] 1. eisgekühlt; 2. glasiert.

Iceland ['aɪslənd] Island n; ~**er** [-ə] Isländer m; ~**ic** [aɪs'lændɪc] isländisch.

ic|icle ['aɪsɪkl] Eiszapfen m; ~**ing** ['aɪsɪŋ] Zuckerguß m, Glasur f; ~**y** ['aɪsɪ] 1. (Straße) vereist; 2. eisig a. fig.

I'd [aɪd] fam = I had; I would.

idea [aɪ'dɪə] 1. Gedanke m, Idee f; 2. Meinung f; 3. Plan; Zweck m; Absicht f; 4. vage Vorstellung f; 5. what an ~! das ist doch nicht möglich!

ideal [aɪ'dɪəl] **I** adj 1. ideal, vorbildlich; 2. eingebildet, unwirklich; **II** s Ideal n; ~**ize** [-aɪz] idealisieren.

identi|cal [aɪ'dentɪkl] identisch; ~**fication** [aɪˌdentɪfɪ'keɪʃn] 1. Identifizierung f; 2. Legitimation f, Ausweis m; ~**fy** [aɪ'dentɪfaɪ] identifizieren; ~**ty** [aɪ'dentəti] Identität f; prove o.'s ~ sich ausweisen; ~ card (Personal-)Ausweis m.

ideology [ˌaɪdɪ'ɒlədʒɪ] Ideologie f.

idiom ['ɪdɪəm] 1. ling Idiom n, Dialekt m; 2. (idiomatische) Redewendung f.

idiot ['ɪdɪət] 1. med Schwachsinnige(r) m; 2. (fam) what an ~ I am! was bin ich doch für ein blöder Kerl.

idle ['aɪdl] **I** adj 1. nutzlos; vergeblich; 2. leer, eitel, hohl; 3. untätig; 4. tech nicht in Betrieb; **II** v (~ about) herumtrödeln; untätig sein; ~**r** [-ə] Müßiggänger, Faulpelz m.

idol ['aɪdl] 1. Götzenbild n; 2. fig Abgott m; Idol n; ~**ize** ['aɪdəlaɪz] fig vergöttern.

idyll ['ɪdɪl] 1. lit mus Idylle f; 2. Idyll n; ~**ic** [aɪ'dɪlɪk] idyllisch.

if [ɪf] **I** conj wenn, falls; wenn auch; ob; as ~ als ob; even ~ auch wenn; ~ only! wenn ... nur ...! **II** s: without ~s or ans ohne Wenn und Aber.

igloo ['ɪgluː] Iglu m od n.

ignition [ɪg'nɪʃn] mot Zündung f; ~ key Zündschlüssel m.

ignor|amus [ˌɪgnəˈreɪməs] *pl* *-muses* [-ɪz] Ignorant *m;* **~ance** [ˈɪgnərəns] Unwissenheit *f; be in complete ~* keine Ahnung haben; **~ant** [ˈɪgnərənt] *be ~ of* nicht wissen, nicht kennen; **~e** [ɪgˈnɔ:] keine Beachtung schenken (*s.th.* e-r S).

ill [ɪl] **I** *adj* 1. krank; *be taken ~, fall ~* krank werden; 2. schlecht; *in ~ health* bei schlechter Gesundheit; *in an ~ temper* in schlechter Laune; **II** *adv* 3. schlecht, übel, böse; *be ~ at ease* sich in s-r Haut nicht wohl fühlen; 4. kaum, schwerlich; **III** *s* 5. Übel, Böse(s) *n;* 6. Unglück, Mißgeschick *n.*

I'll [aɪl] *fam = I will; I shall.*

ill|-advised [ˌɪləˈvaɪzd] 1. schlecht beraten; 2. unklug, unvernünftig; **~-bred** [ˈ-bred] schlecht erzogen; ungebildet.

illegal [ɪˈliːgl] ungesetzlich.

illegible [ɪˈledʒəbl] unleserlich.

illegitimate [ˌɪlɪˈdʒɪtɪmət] 1. unehelich; 2. ungesetzlich.

illicit [ɪˈlɪsɪt] unerlaubt, verboten.

illiter|acy [ɪˈlɪtərəsɪ] 1. mangelnde Bildung *f;* 2. Analphabetentum *n;* **~ate** [ɪˈlɪtərət] **I** *adj* ungebildet; **II** *s* Analphabet, Ungebildete(r) *m.*

ill|-judged [ˈɪldʒʌdʒd] unüberlegt, unklug;

~-natured [ˈɪlˌneɪtʃəd] (*Mensch*) unfreundlich.

illness [ˈɪlnɪs] Krankheit *f.*

ill|-timed [ˈɪltaɪmd] ungelegen, unpassend; **~-treat** [ˌ-ˈtri:t] mißhandeln.

illuminate [ɪˈljuːmɪneɪt] 1. be-, erleuchten; 2. *fig* erläutern; **~ion** [ɪˌljuːmɪˈneɪʃn] Beleuchtung *f.*

illus|ion [ɪˈluːʒn] Illusion; (Sinnes-)Täuschung *f;* **~ive** [ɪˈluːsɪv], **~ory** [ɪˈluːsərɪ] täuschend, trügerisch.

illustrat|e [ˈɪləstreɪt] 1. erläutern; 2. (*Buch*) illustrieren; **~ion** [ˌɪləˈstreɪʃn] 1. Erläuterung *f;* 2. Abbildung *f;* **~ive** [ˈɪləstrətɪv] erläuternd.

illustrious [ɪˈlʌstrɪəs] berühmt.

I'm [aɪm] *fam = I am.*

image [ˈɪmɪdʒ] **I** *s* 1. Bild *n;* 2. Ebenbild *n;* 3. Image *n;* **II** *v* 4. abbilden, (*bildlich*) darstellen; 5. reflektieren.

imagin|able [ɪˈmædʒɪnəbl] vorstellbar; denkbar; **~ation** [ɪˌmædʒɪˈneɪʃn] Einbildung; Phantasie *f;* **~e** [ɪˈmædʒɪn] sich vorstellen, sich ausdenken.

imbecile [ˈɪmbɪsiːl] 1. schwachsinnig; 2. sehr dumm.

imitat|e [ˈɪmɪteɪt] nachahmen; **~ion** [ˌɪmɪˈteɪʃn] **I** *s* Nachahmung *f; beware of ~s* vor Nachahmungen wird gewarnt; **II** *adj:* ~ *leather* Kunstleder *n;* **~ive**

['ɪmɪtətɪv] 1. nachahmend; 2. *ling* lautmalend.
immature [ˌɪməˈtjʊə] unreif.
immeasurable [ɪˈmeʒərəbl] unermeßlich, grenzenlos.
immediate [ɪˈmiːdjət] 1. unmittelbar, direkt; 2. *(zeitlich od räumlich)* (unmittelbar) folgend, nächst; 3. sofortig; **~ly** [-lɪ] sofort.
immense [ɪˈmens] ungeheuer (groß), gewaltig.
immers|e [ɪˈmɜːs] 1. ein-, untertauchen; 2. *(fig)* ~d *in thought* in Gedanken versunken; **~ion** [ɪˈmɜːʃn] Ein-, Untertauchen *n*; ~ *heater* Tauchsieder *m*
immigr|ant ['ɪmɪgrənt] Einwanderer *m*; **~ate** ['ɪmɪgreɪt] einwandern (*into* in, nach); **~ation** [ˌɪmɪˈgreɪʃn] Einwanderung *f.*
imminent ['ɪmɪnənt] *(Gefahr)* drohend; *(Unglück)* nahe bevorstehend.
immoderate [ɪˈmɒdərət] unmäßig, maßlos, übertrieben.
immodest [ɪˈmɒdɪst] unbescheiden.
immoral [ɪˈmɒrəl] unmoralisch; **~ity** [ˌɪməˈrælətɪ] Sittenlosigkeit *f.*
immortal [ɪˈmɔːtl] **I** *adj* unsterblich; unvergänglich; **II** *s* Unsterbliche(r) *m*; **~ity** [ˌɪmɔːˈtælətɪ] Unsterblichkeit *f.*
immovable [ɪˈmuːvəbl] 1. un-

beweglich; 2. *fig* unerschütterlich.
immun|e [ɪˈmjuːn] *med* immun (*against, from* gegen); **~ity** [ɪˈmjuːnətɪ] 1. *med, jur* Immunität *f*; 2. *jur* Befreiung *f (from* von); **~ize** ['ɪmjuːnaɪz] immunisieren (*against* gegen).
impair [ɪmˈpeə] beeinträchtigen; schädigen.
impalpable [ɪmˈpælpəbl] 1. unfühlbar; 2. *fig* unbegreiflich, unfaßbar.
impart [ɪmˈpɑːt] geben, übermitteln.
impartial [ɪmˈpɑːʃl] unparteiisch.
impassable [ɪmˈpɑːsəbl] unwegsam.
impasse [æmˈpɑːs] Sackgasse *f a. fig.*
impassive [ɪmˈpæsɪv] ruhig; teilnahmslos.
impatien|ce [ɪmˈpeɪʃns] Ungeduld *f*; **~t** [-t] 1. ungeduldig; 2. begierig (*to do* zu tun); 3. unduldsam (*of* gegen).
impeach [ɪmˈpiːtʃ] 1. anklagen (*of, for* wegen); 2. anfechten; in Zweifel ziehen.
impediment [ɪmˈpedɪmənt] 1. Behinderung *f*; 2. Hindernis *n.*
impel [ɪmˈpel] zwingen, nötigen.
impending [ɪmˈpendɪŋ] (nahe) bevorstehend; drohend.
impenetrable [ɪmˈpenɪtrəbl] undurchdringlich.

imperative [ɪm'perətɪv] **I** *adj* 1. gebieterisch; 2. zwingend; **II** *s gram* Imperativ *m*.

imperceptible [ˌɪmpə'septəbl] unmerklich.

imperfect [ɪm'pɜ:fɪkt] **I** *adj* 1. unvollständig; 2. unvollkommen; **II** *s* (~ *tense*) *gram* Imperfekt *n*.

imperial [ɪm'pɪərɪəl] kaiserlich.

imperil [ɪm'perəl] in Gefahr bringen.

impermeable [ɪm'pɜ:mjəbl] undurchlässig.

impersonal [ɪm'pɜ:snl] unpersönlich.

impertinen|ce [ɪm'pɜ:tɪnəns] Unverschämtheit *f*; ~**t** [-t] frech; unverschämt.

impervious [ɪm'pɜ:vjəs] 1. undurchdringlich (*to* für *acc*); 2. *fig* unempfindlich (*to* gegen).

impetuous [ɪm'petjʊəs] ungestüm.

impetus ['ɪmpɪtəs] Antrieb, Impuls *m*.

implant ['ɪmplɑ:nt] *fig* einpflanzen.

implement ['ɪmplɪmənt] Gerät, Werkzeug *n*.

implicat|e ['ɪmplɪkeɪt] verwickeln; ~**ion** [ˌɪmplɪ'keɪʃn] 1. Verwick(e)lung *f*; 2. Bedeutung; Folgerung *f*.

implore [ɪm'plɔ:] anflehen.

imply [ɪm'plaɪ] 1. enthalten, einschließen, 2. bedeuten; 3. schließen lassen auf.

impolite [ˌɪmpə'laɪt] unhöflich.

import I *v* [ɪm'pɔ:t] *com* einführen, importieren; **II** *s* ['ɪmpɔ:t] 1. Einfuhr *f*, Import *m*; 2. Bedeutung, Sinn *m*; ~**ance** [ɪm'pɔ:tns] Wichtigkeit *f*; *of no* ~ bedeutungslos; ~**ant** [ɪm'pɔ:tnt] wichtig (*to* für).

impos|e [ɪm'pəʊz] 1. auferlegen (*on, upon s.o.* jdm); 2. aufdrängen (*on s.o.* jdm); 3. ausnützen (*upon s.o.* jdn); ~**ing** [-ɪŋ] eindrucksvoll; ~**ition** [ˌɪmpə'zɪʃn] 1. Aufbürdung *f*; 2. auferlegte Pflicht *f*; 3. Übervorteilung *f*.

impossib|ility [ɪmˌpɒsə'bɪlətɪ] Unmöglichkeit *f*; ~**le** [ɪm'pɒsəbl] unmöglich.

impostor [ɪm'pɒstə] Betrüger *m*.

impracticable [ɪm'præktɪkəbl] 1. undurchführbar; 2. ungangbar.

impregnate ['ɪmpregneɪt] 1. schwängern *a. fig*; 2. imprägnieren (*with* mit).

impress [ɪm'pres] 1. beeindrucken (*s.o.* jdn); 2. (*Worte*) einprägen (*on o.'s memory* im Gedächtnis); 3. auf-, eindrücken; ~**ion** [ɪm'preʃn] 1. *fig* Eindruck *m*; 2. *typ* Druck *m*; Auflage *f*; ~**ive** [ɪm'presɪv] eindrucksvoll.

imprint [ɪm'prɪnt] 1. aufdrucken; 2. einprägen (*on s.o.'s memory* in jds Gedächtnis).

imprison [ɪmˈprɪzn] einsperren; ~**ment** [-mənt] Haft *f.*

improbable [ɪmˈprɒbəbl] unwahrscheinlich.

improper [ɪmˈprɒpə] 1. unpassend; 2. ungehörig.

improve [ɪmˈpruːv] 1. (ver)bessern; 2. sich bessern; 3. ~ *(up)on* übertreffen, überbieten; ~**ment** [-mənt] Verbesserung *f;* Fortschritt *m.*

improvise [ˈɪmprəvaɪz] 1. improvisieren; 2. behelfsmäßig herstellen.

imprudent [ɪmˈpruːdənt] unüberlegt; unklug.

impudent [ˈɪmpjʊdənt] unverschämt; frech.

impulse [ˈɪmpʌls] 1. Impuls *m;* 2. Drang *m,* Regung *f.*

impunity [ɪmˈpjuːnɪtɪ] *with* ~ straffrei.

impure [ɪmˈpjʊə] unrein *a. fig.*

imput|ation [ˌɪmpjuːˈteɪʃn] 1. Unterstellung *f;* 2. Anschuldigung *f (on* gegen); ~**e** [ɪmˈpjuːt] zuschreiben, zur Last legen.

in [ɪn] **I** *prp* 1. *(räumlich)* in; ~ *the house* im Hause, ins Haus; 2. *(zeitlich)* in; im Verlauf *gen,* innerhalb *gen;* ~ *the evening* am Abend; ~ *all my life* in meinem ganzen Leben; 3. *(Umstände, Art u. Weise)* ~ *difficulties* in Schwierigkeiten; ~ *a storm* bei Sturm; 4. *(Richtung)* ~ *this direction* in die-

ser Richtung; 5. ~ *my opinion* meiner Meinung nach; 6. *(Beteiligung)* have a hand ~ *s.th.* bei e-r S die Hand im Spiel haben; **II** *adv* hin-, herein; (dr)innen; daheim, zu Hause; *be* ~ *for an examination* vor e-r Prüfung stehen; *summer is* ~ der Sommer ist da.

inability [ˌɪnəˈbɪlətɪ] Unfähigkeit *f.*

inaccessible [ˈɪnækˈsesəbl] unzugänglich *(to* für).

inaccurate [ɪnˈækjʊrət] ungenau.

inactive [ɪnˈæktɪv] untätig.

inadequate [ɪnˈædɪkwət] unzureichend.

inadmissible [ˌɪnədˈmɪsəbl] unzulässig.

inane [ɪˈneɪn] töricht, dumm.

inanimate [ɪnˈænɪmət] leblos.

inapplicable [ɪnˈæplɪkəbl] nicht anwendbar *(to* auf); nicht zutreffend *(to* für).

inappropriate [ˌɪnəˈprəʊprɪət] unangemessen, unangebracht.

inapt [ɪnˈæpt] 1. unpassend, 2. ungeschickt.

inarticulate [ˌɪnɑːˈtɪkjʊlət] undeutlich.

inattentive [ˌɪnəˈtentɪv] unaufmerksam.

inaudible [ɪnˈɔːdəbl] unhörbar.

inaugurat|e [ɪˈnɔːgjʊreɪt] (feierlich) eröffnen, einweihen; ~**ion** [ɪˌnɔːgjʊˈreɪʃn] (feierliche) Eröffnung, Einweihung *f.*

incalculable [ɪnˈkælkjʊləbl] unberechenbar.

incandescent [ˌɪnkænˈdesns] weißglühend.

incapable [ɪnˈkeɪpəbl] unfähig (*of doing* zu tun).

incendiary [ɪnˈsendjərɪ] **I** *adj* aufrührerisch; **II** *s* 1. Brandstifter *m;* 2. *fig* Aufwiegler *m.*

incense I *s* [ˈɪnsens] Weihrauch *m;* **II** *v* [ɪnˈsens] erzürnen.

incentive [ɪnˈsentɪv] Antrieb, Anreiz *m* (*to* zu).

incessant [ɪnˈsesnt] unaufhörlich, ununterbrochen.

inch [ɪntʃ] Zoll *m* (2,54 cm); *every ~* durch und durch; *within an ~ (of)* um ein Haar, fast.

incident [ˈɪnsɪdənt] Vorfall *m,* Ereignis *n.*

incinerate [ɪnˈsɪnəreɪt] einäschern.

incis|e [ɪnˈsaɪz] (ein)schneiden; **~ion** [ɪnˈsɪʒn] Einschnitt *m;* **~or** [ɪnˈsaɪzə] Schneidezahn *m.*

incite [ɪnˈsaɪt] aufhetzen (*to* zu).

inclin|ation [ˌɪnklɪˈneɪʃn] Neigung *f* (*a. fig*); **~e** [ɪnˈklaɪn] 1. (sich) senken; 2. dazu neigen (*to* zu); *be ~d to* geneigt sein, Lust haben zu.

include [ɪnˈkluːd] einschließen, umfassen.

inclusive [ɪnˈkluːsɪv] einschließlich (*of* gen).

incoherent [ˌɪnkəʊˈhɪərənt] zs.hanglos.

income [ˈɪŋkʌm] Einkommen *n;* **~-tax** [ˈɪnkəmtæks] Einkommensteuer *f.*

incomparable [ɪnˈkɒmpərəbl] 1. nicht vergleichbar (*to, with* mit); 2. unvergleichlich.

incompatible [ˌɪnkəmˈpætəbl] unvereinbar (*with* mit).

incompetent [ɪnˈkɒmpɪtənt] 1. unfähig; 2. unbefugt, unzuständig.

incomplete [ˌɪnkəmˈpliːt] unvollständig.

incongruous [ɪnˈkɒŋgrʊəs] 1. unvereinbar; 2. widersinnig.

inconsider|able [ˌɪnkənˈsɪdərəbl] bedeutungslos, unwichtig; **~ate** [ˌɪnkənˈsɪdərət] rücksichtslos.

inconsistent [ˌɪnkənˈsɪstənt] 1. unvereinbar (*with* mit); 2. widerspruchsvoll.

inconsolable [ˌɪnkənˈsəʊləbl] untröstlich.

inconvenien|ce [ˌɪnkənˈviːnjəns] **I** *s* Unbequemlichkeit; Unannehmlichkeit *f;* **II** *v* belästigen; **~t** [-t] unbequem, lästig.

incorporate [ɪnˈkɔːpəreɪt] 1. (sich) einverleiben; 2. (amtlich) eintragen.

incorrect [ˌɪnkəˈrekt] unrichtig.

incorrigible [ɪnˈkɒrɪdʒəbl] unverbesserlich.

incorruptible [ˌɪnkəˈrʌptəbl] unbestechlich.

increase I v [ɪnˈkriːs] (an)wachsen, (an)steigen, zunehmen; (sich) vergrößern, (sich) vermehren; **II** s [ˈɪnkriːs] Wachstum n, Vergrößerung; Steigerung; Zunahme f; *be on the* ~ im Steigen begriffen sein; ~ *in population* Bevölkerungszuwachs m.

incredible [ɪnˈkredəbl] 1. unglaubhaft; 2. unglaublich.

incredulous [ɪnˈkredjʊləs] ungläubig, skeptisch.

increment [ˈɪnkrɪmənt] 1. Zuwachs m, Zunahme f; 2. Mehreinnahme f.

incriminate [ɪnˈkrɪmɪneɪt] an-, beschuldigen.

incubator [ˈɪnkjʊbeɪtə] Brutapparat, -kasten m.

incur [ɪnˈkɜː] sich zuziehen; ~ *heavy expenses* sich in große Unkosten stürzen.

incurable [ɪnˈkjʊərəbl] unheilbar.

indebted [ɪnˈdetɪd] 1. verschuldet (*to* bei); 2. *be* ~ *to s.o. for s.th.* jdm etw zu verdanken haben.

indecency [ɪnˈdiːsnsɪ] Unanständigkeit f; ~**t** [-t] 1. unpassend, ungebührlich; 2. unanständig.

indecision [ˌɪndɪˈsɪʒn] Unentschlossenheit f.

indeed [ɪnˈdiːd] 1. in der Tat, allerdings; 2. wirklich? so? nicht möglich! 3. *(verstärkend) thank you very much* ~ vielen herzlichen Dank!

indefinite [ɪnˈdefnət] 1. unbegrenzt; 2. undeutlich; 3. unbestimmt.

indelible [ɪnˈdeləbl] untilgbar, unauslöschlich.

indelicate [ɪnˈdelɪkət] 1. unfein; 2. taktlos.

indemnify [ɪnˈdemnɪfaɪ] entschädigen (*for* für); ~**ty** [ɪnˈdemnətɪ] Schadenersatz m, Entschädigung f.

indent [ɪnˈdent] **I** v 1. (ein)kerben, auszacken; 2. *(Zeile)* einrücken; **II** s (Auslands-)Auftrag m; ~**ure** [ɪnˈdentʃə] Vertrag m.

independence [ˌɪndɪˈpendəns] Unabhängigkeit f; ~**t** [-t] unabhängig (*of* von).

indescribable [ˌɪndɪˈskraɪbəbl] unbeschreiblich.

indestructible [ˌɪndɪˈstrʌktəbl] unzerstörbar.

indeterminate [ˌɪndɪˈtɜːmɪnət] unbestimmt.

index [ˈɪndeks] *pl -es, math indices* [ˈɪndɪsiːz] 1. (Namens-, Sach-)Register n; 2. *math* Exponent m; 3. *cost-of-living* ~ Lebenshaltungsindex *m;* 4. *fig* Zeichen *n;* ~ **finger** Zeigefinger *m.*

India ['ɪndjə] Indien *n;* ~**n** [-n] **I** *s* 1. Inder *m;* 2. Indianer *m;* **II** *adj* 1. indisch; 2. indianisch.

India-rubber [,ɪndjə'rʌbə] Radiergummi *m.*

indicate ['ɪndɪkeɪt] hinweisen, zeigen, deuten auf; ~**ion** [,ɪndɪ'keɪʃn] 1. Hinweis *m;* 2. Angabe *f;* 3. Anzeichen *n.*

indict [ɪn'daɪt] *jur* anklagen (*for* wegen); ~**ment** [-mənt] *jur* Anklage *f.*

indifference [ɪn'dɪfrəns] Gleichgültigkeit *f* (*to, towards* gegen); ~**t** [-t] 1. gleichgültig (*to, towards* gegenüber); 2. mittelmäßig.

indigestion [,ɪndɪ'dʒestʃən] Magenverstimmung *f.*

indignant [ɪn'dɪgnənt] aufgebracht, empört (*at s.th.* über etw); ~**ation** [,ɪndɪg'neɪʃn] Entrüstung *f.*

indiscreet [,ɪndɪ'skri:t] 1. unklug; 2. taktlos; ~**etion** [,ɪndɪ'skreʃn] 1. Unklugheit *f;* 2. Taktlosigkeit *f;* 3. Indiskretion *f.*

indiscriminate [,ɪndɪ'skrɪmɪnət] wahllos; unkritisch.

indispensable [,ɪndɪ'spensəbl] unbedingt notwendig; unentbehrlich (*to* für).

indisposed [,ɪndɪ'spəuzd] 1. unpäßlich; 2. abgeneigt (*to* dat); ~**ition** [,ɪndɪspə'zɪʃn] 1. Unpäßlichkeit *f;* 2. Abneigung *f* (*to* gegen).

indisputable [,ɪndɪ'spju:təbl] unbestreitbar.

indistinct [,ɪndɪ'stɪŋkt] undeutlich.

individual [,ɪndɪ'vɪdjuəl] **I** *adj* persönlich, individuell; **II** *s* Individuum *n.*

indivisible [,ɪndɪ'vɪzəbl] unteilbar.

indolent ['ɪndələnt] lässig, träge.

indoors [,ɪn'dɔ:z] zu, im Hause; drinnen; *stay* ~ zu Hause bleiben.

indorse [ɪn'dɔ:s] *s. endorse.*

indubitable [ɪn'dju:bɪtəbl] unzweifelhaft.

induce [ɪn'dju:s] 1. veranlassen, überreden; 2. bewirken, verursachen; ~**ment** [-mənt] Anreiz *m.*

indulge [ɪn'dʌldʒ] 1. nachgeben (*a desire* e-m Verlangen); nachsichtig sein (*s.o.* jdm gegenüber); 2. ~ *in sth.* sich etw gönnen; ~**nce** [-əns] 1. Nachsicht, Nachgiebigkeit *f;* 2. Befriedigung *f;* Schwelgen *n;* ~**nt** [-ənt] nachsichtig; nachgiebig.

industrial [ɪn'dʌstrɪəl] gewerblich, industriell; ~ *area* Industriegebiet *n;* ~**ist** [-ɪst] Industrielle(r) *m;* ~**ize** [-aɪz] industrialisieren.

industrious [ɪn'dʌstrɪəs] fleißig.

industry ['ɪndəstrɪ] 1. Fleiß *m;* 2. Industrie(zweig *m*) *f; mining ~* Montanindustrie *f;* Bergbau *m; tourist ~* Fremdenverkehr *m.*

inebriated [ɪ'niːbrɪeɪtɪd] betrunken.

inedible [ɪn'edɪbl] ungenießbar.

ineffect|ive [ˌɪnɪ'fektɪv] , **~ual** [ˌɪnɪ'fektʃʊəl] 1. unwirksam; 2. untauglich.

inefficient [ˌɪnɪ'fɪʃnt] 1. unwirksam; 2. unfähig.

ineligible [ɪn'elɪdʒəbl] *be ~* nicht in Frage kommen.

inept [ɪ'nept] 1. unpassend; 2. dumm.

inequality [ˌɪnɪ'kwɒlətɪ] Ungleichheit *f.*

inequitable [ɪn'ekwɪtəbl] unbillig, ungerecht.

inertia [ɪ'nɜːʃjə] 1. *phys* Trägheit *f;* 2. *fig* Faulheit *f.*

inestimable [ɪn'estɪmbl] unschätzbar.

inevitable [ɪn'evɪtəbl] unvermeidlich.

inexhaustible [ˌɪnɪg'zɔːstəbl] 1. unerschöpflich; 2. unermüdlich.

inexpedient [ˌɪnɪk'spiːdjənt] unzweckmäßig.

inexpensive [ˌɪnɪk'spensɪv] preiswert.

inexperienced [ˌɪnɪk'spɪərɪənst] unerfahren.

inexplicable [ˌɪnɪk'splɪkəbl] unerklärlich.

inexpress|ible [ˌɪnɪk'spresəbl] unaussprechlich; **~ive** [ˌɪnɪk'spresɪv] ausdruckslos.

infallible [ɪn'fæləbl] unfehlbar.

infam|ous ['ɪnfəməs] berüchtigt; **~y** ['ɪnfəmɪ] Schande *f.*

infancy ['ɪnfənsɪ] 1. (frühe) Kindheit *f;* 2. *jur* Minderjährigkeit *f;* 3. *fig* Anfänge *m pl.*

infant ['ɪnfənt] 1. (Klein-)-Kind *n;* 2. *jur* Minderjährige(r) *m;* **~ile** ['ɪnfəntaɪl] 1. kindlich; 2. kindisch.

infatuated [ɪn'fætjʊeɪtɪd] vernarrt (*with* in).

infect [ɪn'fekt] *med* infizieren; anstecken (*with* mit); **~ion** [ɪn'fekʃn] Ansteckung *f;* **~ious** [ɪn'fekʃəs] ansteckend.

infer [ɪn'fɜː] den Schluß ziehen; **~ence** ['ɪnfərəns] *draw an ~ from* e-n Schluß, e-e Folgerung ziehen aus.

inferior [ɪn'fɪərɪə] **I** *adj* 1. untergeordnet, untergeben (*to* dat); 2. minderwertig; **II** *s* Untergebene(r) *m;* **~ity** [ɪnˌfɪərɪ'ɒrətɪ] Minderwertigkeit *f.*

infernal [ɪn'fɜːnl] 1. *fig* unmenschlich; 2. *fam* scheußlich.

infest [ɪn'fest] 1. *be ~ed with* wimmeln von; 2. heimsuchen.

infiltrate ['ɪnfɪltreɪt] 1. einsickern (*into* in); 2. *pol* unterwandern.

infinite ['ɪnfɪnət] 1. unendlich, unbegrenzt; 2. unermeßlich.

infirm [ɪn'fɜ:m] kraftlos; altersschwach; **~ary** [ɪn'fɜ:mərɪ] Krankenhaus n; **~ity** [ɪn'fɜ:mətɪ] Gebrechlichkeit f.

inflame [ɪn'fleɪm] entzünden a. fig.

inflammlable [ɪn'flæməbl] 1. leicht entzündbar, feuergefährlich; 2. fig reizbar; **~ation** [ˌɪnflə'meɪʃn] med Entzündung f.

inflatle [ɪn'fleɪt] 1. aufblasen, aufpumpen; 2. (Preise) hochtreiben; **~ion** [ɪn'fleɪʃn] fin Inflation f.

inflexible [ɪn'fleksəbl] 1. fig unbeugsam; 2. unelastisch.

inflict [ɪn'flɪkt] (Schmerz) zufügen; (Schlag) versetzen; (Strafe) verhängen (on, upon über).

influenlce ['ɪnfluəns] **I** s Einfluß m ((up)on auf); **II** v beeinflussen; **~tial** [ˌɪnflu'enʃl] einflußreich.

influenza [ˌɪnflu'enzə] Grippe f.

inform [ɪn'fɔ:m] 1. benachrichtigen, informieren (of über); keep s.o. ~ed jdn auf dem laufenden halten; 2. jur anzeigen (against s.o. jdn); **~al** [-l] zwanglos; **~ation** [ˌɪnfə'meɪʃn] 1. Auskunft f; give ~ Auskunft erteilen (on, about über); 2. Information;

Nachricht; Mitteilung f; **~er** [-ə] Spitzel m.

infringe [ɪn'frɪndʒ] (Gesetz) übertreten, verletzen.

infuse [ɪn'fju:z] 1. (Tee) aufgießen, -brühen; 2. fig einflößen (into s.o. jdm).

ingenlious [ɪn'dʒi:njəs] geistreich; **~uity** [ˌɪndʒɪ'nju:ətɪ] Genialität f.

ingot ['ɪŋgət] (Metall) Barren m.

ingratitude [ɪn'grætɪtju:d] Undank(barkeit f) m.

ingredient [ɪn'gri:djənt] Bestandteil m; pl (Küche) Zutaten f pl.

inhabit [ɪn'hæbɪt] bewohnen; **~able** [-əbl] bewohnbar; **~ant** [-ənt] Be-, Einwohner m.

inhale [ɪn'heɪl] einatmen.

inherent [ɪn'hɪərənt] innewohnend, anhaftend.

inherit [ɪn'herɪt] erben; **~ance** [-əns] 1. Erbschaft f; 2. biol Vererbung f.

inhibit [ɪn'hɪbɪt] psychol hemmen; **~ion** [ˌɪnhɪ'bɪʃn] psychol Hemmung f.

inhospitable [ɪn'hɒspɪtəbl] ungastlich.

inhuman [ɪn'hju:mən] unmenschlich.

initial [ɪ'nɪʃl] **I** adj Anfangs-; **II** s (großer) Anfangsbuchstabe m.

initiatle [ɪ'nɪʃɪeɪt] 1. einweihen (into in); 2. ins Leben rufen; beginnen; **~ion** [ɪˌnɪʃɪ'eɪʃn] Einführung, Ein-

weihung f; ~**ive** [ɪ'nɪʃɪətɪv]
Initiative f; on o.'s own ~
aus eigenem Antrieb.

inject [ɪn'dʒekt] med ein-
spritzen; ~**ion** [ɪn'dʒekʃn]
Injektion f.

injunction [ɪn'dʒʌŋkʃn] ge-
richtliche Anordnung f.

injur|e ['ɪndʒə] verletzen a.
fig; ~**y** [-rɪ] Verletzung f a.
fig; ~ to property Sachscha-
den m.

injustice [ɪn'dʒʌstɪs] Unge-
rechtigkeit f.

ink [ɪŋk] 1. Tinte f; 2. Druk-
kerschwärze f; ~-**pad**
['-pæd] Stempelkissen n.

inkling ['ɪŋklɪŋ] have no ~ of
s.th. von etw keine Ahnung
haben.

inland ['ɪnlənd] inländisch;
Binnen-; einheimisch.

inlet ['ɪnlet] 1. (kleine) Bucht
f; 2. (Stoff) Einsatz m.

inmate ['ɪnmeɪt] 1. Hausge-
nosse m; 2. Insasse m; 3. Be-
wohner m.

inmost ['ɪnməust] innerst.

inn [ɪn] Gasthaus n; -hof m.

innate [ˌɪ'neɪt] angeboren.

inner ['ɪnə] inner; ~ **tube**
mot Schlauch m.

innocen|ce ['ɪnəsəns] 1. Un-
schuld f; 2. Harmlosigkeit f;
~**t** [-t] 1. unschuldig (of an);
2. harmlos.

innovation [ˌɪnəu'veɪʃn]
Neuerung f.

innumerable [ɪ'nju:mərəbl]
unzählig, zahllos.

inoculate [ɪ'nɒkjuleɪt] med
impfen (against gegen).

inoffensive [ˌɪnə'fensɪv]
harmlos.

input ['ɪnput] 1. (Energie-,
Strom-)Zufuhr f; 2. EDV
(Daten-)Eingabe f.

inquest ['ɪnkwest] gerichtli-
che Untersuchung f.

inquir|e [ɪn'kwaɪə] 1. sich er-
kundigen (about, after nach;
of bei); fragen (for s.o. nach
jdm); 2. ~ into untersuchen;
~**y** [-rɪ] 1. An-, Nachfrage f
(for nach); on ~ auf Anfrage; make inquiries Erkundi-
gungen einziehen (about
über); 2. Untersuchung f.

inquisitive [ɪn'kwɪzətɪv] wißbegierig, neugierig.

inroad ['ɪnrəud] Überfall m
(into in; upon auf).

insan|e [ɪn'seɪn] 1. geistes-
krank; 2. unsinnig; ~**ity**
[ɪn'sænətɪ] Geisteskrank-
heit f.

inscription [ɪn'skrɪpʃn]
1. Einschreibung f; 2. Auf-
schrift f.

insect ['ɪnsekt] Insekt n.

insecure [ˌɪnsɪ'kjuə] 1. unsicher; 2. ungewiß.

insens|ible [ɪn'sensəbl]
1. unempfindlich (to gegen);
2. bewußtlos; 3. unmerklich;
~**itive** [ɪn'sensətɪv] gefühllos, unempfindlich (to gegen).

inseparable [ɪn'sepərəbl]
1. untrennbar; 2. unzertrennlich.

insert [ın'sɜ:t] 1. einsetzen, -fügen; 2. aufgeben (*an advertisement* e-e Anzeige); **~ion** [ın'sɜ:ʃn] 1. Einfügung *f;* 2. Inserat *n.*

inside [ın'saıd] **I** *s* 1. Innen-, innere Seite *f;* 2. Innere *n; know ~ out* in- u. auswendig kennen; **II** *adj* inner, inwendig; Innen-; **III** *adv* innen; *~ of a week* innerhalb e-r Woche; **IV** *prp* im Innern *gen.*

insight ['ınsaıt] 1. Einblick *m* (*into* in); 2. Verständnis *n* (*into* für).

insignificant [,ınsıg'nıfıkənt] bedeutungslos.

insincere [,ınsın'sıə] unaufrichtig, falsch.

insinuate [ın'sınjʊeıt] 1. zu verstehen geben; 2. *~ o.s. into s.o.'s favo(u)r* sich bei jdm einschmeicheln.

insipid [ın'sıpıd] geschmacklos.

insist [ın'sıst] 1. bestehen (*on* auf); 2. nachdrücklich betonen (*on s.th.* etw).

insolen|ce ['ınsələns] Unverschämtheit, Frechheit *f;* **~t** [-t] unverschämt, frech.

insoluble [ın'sɒljʊbl] 1. un(auf)löslich; 2. unlösbar.

insolvent [ın'sɒlvənt] zahlungsunfähig.

insomnia [ın'sɒmnıə] Schlaflosigkeit *f.*

inspect [ın'spekt] 1. genau untersuchen; 2. be(auf)sichtigen; **~ion** [ın'spekʃn] 1. Untersuchung *f;* 2. Besichti-

gung, Inspektion *f;* **~or** [-ə] Inspektor *m.*

inspir|ation [,ınspə'reıʃn] Eingebung *f,* Inspiration *f;* **~e** [ın'spaıə] 1. anregen; 2. (*Gefühl*) einflößen; 3. erfüllen (*with* mit); 4. inspirieren.

install [ın'stɔ:l] 1. (*in ein Amt*) einsetzen; 2. *tech* installieren, einbauen; 3. *~ o.s.* sich einrichten, sich niederlassen; **~ation** [,ınstə'leıʃn] Anlage *f.*

instal(l)ment [ın'stɔ:lmənt] Rate, Abschlagszahlung *f; by ~s* ratenweise; *monthly ~* Monatsrate *f.*

instance ['ınstəns] 1. Bitte *f; at s.o.'s ~* auf jds Veranlassung; 2. *for ~* zum Beispiel; *in the first ~* in erster Linie, vor allem.

instant ['ınstənt] **I** *adj* 1. sofortig, augenblicklich; 2. *~ coffee* lösliche(r) Kaffee *m;* **II** *s* Augenblick, Moment *m; in an ~* sofort; im Nu; *on the ~, this ~* sofort; **~aneous** [,ınstən'teınjəs] augenblicklich; **~ly** ['ınstəntlı] sofort, augenblicklich.

instead [ın'sted] 1. statt dessen, dafür; 2. *~ of* (an)statt *gen,* an Stelle *gen.*

instep ['ınstep] *anat* Spann, Rist *m.*

instigat|e ['ınstıgeıt] anstiften; **~ion** [,ınstı'geıʃn] Anstiftung *f.*

instinct ['ɪnstɪŋkt] Instinkt *m;* ~**ive** [ɪn'stɪŋktɪv] instinktiv.

institut|e ['ɪnstɪtjuːt] **I** *v* 1. einrichten; einführen; 2. *(Untersuchung)* einleiten; **II** *s* Institut *n;* ~**ion** [ˌɪnstɪ'tjuːʃn] 1. Einrichtung *f;* 2. Institut *n.*

instruct [ɪn'strʌkt] 1. unterrichten, unterweisen; 2. anweisen; ~**ion** [ɪn'strʌkʃn] 1. Unterricht *m;* 2. *pl* Vorschrift *f;* ~*s for use* Gebrauchsanweisung *f;* ~**ive** [-ɪv] lehrreich.

instrument ['ɪnstrʊmənt] 1. Werkzeug *n;* 2. (Musik-)Instrument *n;* 3. *fig* Mittel *n;* 4. *jur* Urkunde *f.*

insufficient [ˌɪnsə'fɪʃnt] ungenügend.

insular ['ɪnsjʊlə] Insel-.

insulat|e ['ɪnsjʊleɪt] isolieren; ~**ion** [ˌɪnsjʊ'leɪʃn] Isolierung *f.*

insult I *s* ['ɪnsʌlt] Beleidigung *f;* **II** *v* [ɪn'sʌlt] beleidigen.

insuperable [ɪn'sjuːpərəbl] unüberwindlich.

insur|ance [ɪn'ʃʊərəns] Versicherung *f; liability* ~ Haftpflichtversicherung *f;* ~**e** [ɪn'ʃʊə] versichern (*against theft* gegen Diebstahl).

insurrection [ˌɪnsə'rekʃn] Aufruhr, Aufstand *m.*

intact [ɪn'tækt] unbeschädigt, intakt.

integr|ate ['ɪntɪgreɪt] 1. vervollständigen; 2. integrieren, eingliedern; ~**ity** [ɪn'tegrətɪ] 1. Vollständigkeit *f;* 2. Rechtschaffenheit *f.*

intellect ['ɪntəlekt] Verstand *m;* ~**ual** [ˌɪntə'lektjʊəl] **I** *adj* intellektuell; **II** *s* Intellektuelle(r) *m.*

intelligen|ce [ɪn'telɪdʒəns] 1. Intelligenz *f;* Verstand *m;* 2. Nachricht *f;* ~ *service* Nachrichtendienst *m;* ~**t** [-t] 1. intelligent, klug; 2. verständig, vernünftig.

intelligible [ɪn'telɪdʒəbl] verständlich.

intemperate [ɪn'tempərət] unmäßig.

intend [ɪn'tend] 1. beabsichtigen, planen; 2. bestimmen (*for* für, zu).

intens|e [ɪn'tens] 1. stark, heftig; 2. angestrengt, intensiv; ~**ify** [-ɪfaɪ] intensivieren; ~**ity** [-ətɪ] Intensität *f;* ~**ive** [-ɪv] intensiv.

intent [ɪn'tent] *with* ~ absichtlich; ~**ion** [ɪn'tenʃn] Absicht *f;* ~**ional** [ɪn'tenʃənl] absichtlich.

intercede [ˌɪntə'siːd] vermitteln.

intercept ['ɪntəsept] 1. abfangen; 2. *tele* abhören.

interchange [ˌɪntə'tʃeɪndʒ] **I** *v* austauschen; auswechseln; **II** *s* Austausch *m.*

intercourse ['ɪntəkɔːs] Verkehr, Umgang *m* (*with* mit).

interest ['ɪntrɪst] **I** *s* 1. Interesse *n;* 2. *com* Beteiligung *f;* 3. Zins(en *pl*) *a. fig;* Zinssatz *m;* **II** *v* interessieren; *be ~ed in* sich interessieren für; **~ing** [-ɪŋ] interessant.

interfere [ˌɪntəˈfɪə] 1. sich einmischen (*in* in); 2. (*~ with*) stören; **~nce** [-rəns] 1. Einmischung *f;* 2. Störung *f.*

interior [ɪnˈtɪərɪə] **I** *adj* inner; **II** *s* das Innere.

interlude [ˈɪntəluːd] Zwischenspiel *n.*

intermedi|ary [ˌɪntəˈmiːdjərɪ] Vermittler *m;* **~ate** [ˌɪntəˈmiːdjət] dazwischenliegend.

interminable [ɪnˈtɜːmɪnəbl] endlos.

intermission [ˌɪntəˈmɪʃn] Unterbrechung, Pause *f.*

intermittent [ˌɪntəˈmɪtənt] zeitweilig aussetzend; *~ fever* Wechselfieber *n.*

intern [ɪnˈtɜːn] internieren; **~al** [-l] 1. inner; 2. inländisch.

international [ˌɪntəˈnæʃənl] international.

interpret [ɪnˈtɜːprɪt] 1. interpretieren; 2. dolmetschen; **~er** [-ə] Dolmetscher *m.*

interrogat|e [ɪnˈterəʊgeɪt] 1. aus-, befragen; 2. verhören; **~ion** [ɪnˌterəʊˈgeɪʃn] 1. Befragung *f; ~ mark* Fragezeichen *n;* 2. Verhör *n;* **~ive** [ˌɪntəˈrɒgətɪv] fragend.

interrupt [ˌɪntəˈrʌpt] unterbrechen; **~ion** [ˌɪntəˈrʌpʃn] Unterbrechung *f.*

interval [ˈɪntəvl] 1. Zwischen-

raum *m;* 2. Pause *f; after a week's ~* eine Woche später.

interven|e [ˌɪntəˈviːn] 1. eingreifen; intervenieren; 2. (*Ereignis*) eintreten; 3. (*zeitlich*) dazwischenliegen; **~tion** [ˌɪntəˈvenʃn] Eingreifen *n; pol* Intervention *f.*

interview [ˈɪntəvjuː] **I** *s* Unterredung *f;* Interview *n;* **II** *v* interviewen.

intestines [ɪnˈtestɪnz] Eingeweide *pl.*

intim|acy [ˈɪntɪməsɪ] Intimität; Vertrautheit *f; ~ate* [ˈɪntɪmət] 1. vertraut, intim; 2. (*Kenntnisse*) gründlich.

intimidate [ɪnˈtɪmɪdeɪt] einschüchtern.

into [ˈɪntə] in *acc;* in … hinein.

intoler|able [ɪnˈtɒlərəbl] unerträglich; **~ant** [ɪnˈtɒlərənt] unduldsam (*of* gegenüber).

intoxicate [ɪnˈtɒksɪkeɪt] berauschen *a. fig.*

intrepid [ɪnˈtrepɪd] unerschrocken.

intricate [ˈɪntrɪkət] kompliziert.

intrigue [ɪnˈtriːg] **I** *v* 1. intrigieren; 2. neugierig machen, fesseln; **II** *s* Intrige *f.*

introduc|e [ˌɪntrəˈdjuːs] 1. einführen *a. fig;* einleiten; 2. (*Menschen*) vorstellen (*to s.o.* jdm); **~tion** [ˌɪntrəˈdʌkʃn] 1. Einführung, Einleitung *f;* 2. Vorstellung *f* (*e-s Menschen*).

intru|de [ɪn'truːd] ~ *upon s.o.* jdn stören; ~**der** [-ə] Eindringling; Störenfried *m;* ~**sive** [ɪn'truːsɪv] zudringlich.

inundate ['ɪnʌndeɪt] überschwemmen *a. fig.*

invade [ɪn'veɪd] 1. einfallen in; *(Menschen)* strömen in; 2. *(Rechte)* antasten, verletzen; ~**r** [-ə] Eindringling *m.*

invalid 1. ['ɪnvælɪd] kränklich, gebrechlich; 2. [ɪn'vælɪd] ungültig; ~**ate** [ɪn'vælɪdeɪt] ungültig machen.

invaluable [ɪn'væljʊəbl] unschätzbar.

invariable [ɪn'veərɪəbl] unveränderlich, gleichbleibend.

invasion [ɪn'veɪʒn] 1. Invasion *f;* 2. *jur* Über-, Eingriff *m (of* in); 3. *med* Anfall *m.*

invent [ɪn'vent] erfinden; ~**ion** [ɪn'venʃn] Erfindung *f a. fig;* ~**or** [-ə] Erfinder *m.*

inverse [ˌɪn'vɜːs] umgekehrt.

invert [ɪn'vɜːt] umkehren; ~*ed commas (pl)* Anführungszeichen *n pl.*

invest [ɪn'vest] 1. ausstatten (*with* mit); 2. *(Geld)* anlegen, investieren (*in* für).

investigat|e [ɪn'vestɪgeɪt] erforschen, untersuchen; ~**ion** [ɪnˌvestɪ'geɪʃn] Untersuchung *f.*

investment [ɪn'vestmənt] (Geld-, Kapital-)Anlage *f.*

inveterate [ɪn'vetərət] eingefleischt.

invigorate [ɪn'vɪgəreɪt] stärken, kräftigen, beleben.

invincible [ɪn'vɪnsəbl] unüberwindlich.

invisible [ɪn'vɪzəbl] unsichtbar.

invit|ation [ˌɪnvɪ'teɪʃn] Einladung *f (to* an; zu); ~**e** [ɪn'vaɪt] 1. einladen; 2. auffordern, ermuntern zu.

invoice ['ɪnvɔɪs] (Waren-)-Rechnung *f.*

invoke [ɪn'vəʊk] 1. *rel* anrufen; 2. *(Geist)* beschwören.

involuntary [ɪn'vɒləntərɪ] unfreiwillig.

involve [ɪn'vɒlv] 1. zur Folge haben; 2. verwickeln, hineinziehen.

invulnerable [ɪn'vʌlnərəbl] 1. unverwundbar; 2. *fig* unanfechtbar.

inward ['ɪnwəd] **I** *adj* inner(lich); **II** *adv* nach innen; ~**s** [-z] einwärts; nach innen.

iodine ['aɪədiːn] Jod *n.*

Ireland ['aɪələnd] Irland *n;* **Northern** ~ Nordirland *n.*

iris ['aɪərɪs] 1. *anat* Iris *f;* 2. *bot* Schwertlilie *f.*

Irish ['aɪərɪʃ] **I** *s: the* ~ (*pl*) die Iren, die Irländer; **II** *adj* irisch, irländisch; ~**man** [-mən] Ire, Irländer *m;* ~**woman** [-wʊmən] Irin, Irländerin *f.*

iron ['aɪən] **I** *s* 1. Eisen *n; wrought* ~ Schmiedeeisen *n;* 2. *(flat-*~*)* Bügeleisen *n;* 3. *pl* Fesseln *f pl;* **II** *adj* eisern;

III v bügeln; **~ lung** med eiserne Lunge f; **~monger** [-ˌmʌŋgə] Eisenwarenhändler m; **~ ore** Eisenerz n; **~works** [-wɜːks] pl mit sing (Eisen-)Hütte f.
irony ['aɪərənɪ] Ironie f.

irrational [ɪ'ræʃənl] unvernünftig; vernunftwidrig.
irreconcilable [ɪ'rekənsaɪləbl] 1. unversöhnlich; 2. unvereinbar.
irrefutable [ɪ'refjʊtəbl] unwiderlegbar.
irregular [ɪ'regjʊlə] unregelmäßig; **~ity** [ɪ'regjʊ'lærətɪ] Unregelmäßigkeit f.
irreparable [ɪ'repərəbl] unersetzlich.
irreproachable [ˌɪrɪ'prəʊtʃəbl] untadelig.
irresistible [ˌɪrɪ'zɪstəbl] unwiderstehlich.
irresponsible [ˌɪrɪ'spɒnsəbl] 1. unverantwortlich; 2. jur unzurechnungsfähig.
irreverent [ɪ'revərənt] respektlos.
irrevocable [ɪ'revəkəbl] unwiderruflich.
irrigat|e ['ɪrɪgeɪt] bewässern; **~ion** [ˌɪrɪ'geɪʃn] Bewässerung f.
irritable ['ɪrɪtəbl] reizbar.
irritat|e ['ɪrɪteɪt] reizen a. med; ärgern; **~ion** [ˌɪrɪ'teɪʃn] Reizung a. med; Erbitterung f.
island ['aɪlənd] Insel f; **~er** [-ə] Inselbewohner ɪn.

isn't ['ɪznt] = is not.
isolat|e ['aɪsəleɪt] absondern, isolieren; **~ion** [aɪsə'leɪʃn] Absonderung, Isolierung f.
issue ['ɪʃuː] **I** s 1. Folge f, Ergebnis n; 2. jur Nachkommenschaft f; 3. at ~ zur Debatte stehend; strittig; 4. Herausgabe; Ausgabe f; 5. Ausfließen n; **II** v 6. herausgehen, -kommen; (her)ausfließen (from aus); 7. (Dokument) ausstellen; 8. (Buch) veröffentlichen; 9. austeilen; beliefern (with mit).
it [ɪt] 1. es; 2. er, sie; ihm, ihr, ihn.
Italian [ɪ'tæljən] **I** s Italiener m; **II** adj italienisch.
italics [ɪ'tælɪks] Kursivschrift f.
Italy ['ɪtəlɪ] Italien n.
itch [ɪtʃ] **I** v jucken; **II** s 1. Jucken n; 2. Gelüst n (for nach).
item ['aɪtəm] 1. Gegenstand; Posten; (Programm-)Punkt m; 2. (Presse-)Notiz f.
itinerary [aɪ'tɪnərərɪ] Reiseroute f; -plan m.
it'll [ɪtl] = it will.
its [ɪts] sein, ihr; dessen, deren.
it's [ɪts] = it is; it has.
itself [ɪt'self] (es) selbst; sich (selbst); (all) by ~ (ganz) allein.
I've [aɪv] = I have.
ivory ['aɪvərɪ] Elfenbein n.
ivy ['aɪvɪ] Efeu m.

J

jabber ['dʒæbə] **I** v daherreden; **II** s Geplapper n.

jack [dʒæk] **I** s 1. every man ~ Hinz und Kunz; 2. (lifting-~) Wagenheber m; 3. el Steckdose f; 4. (Kartenspiel) Bube m; **II** v: ~ up (mot) aufbocken.

jackal ['dʒækɔːl] zoo Schakal m.

jack|ass ['dʒækæs] Esel m a. fig; ~daw ['-dɔː] Dohle f.

jacket ['dʒækɪt] 1. Jacke f, Jackett n; 2. (Kartoffel) Pelle, Schale f; 3. tech Mantel m; 4. (Buch) Schutzumschlag m.

jack|knife ['dʒæknaɪf] Klappmesser n; ~pot ['-pɒt] Hauptgewinn m.

jaded ['dʒeɪdɪd] abgearbeitet, erschöpft.

jag [dʒæg] **I** s Zacke(n m) f; **II** v auszacken; ~gy ['dʒægɪ] zackig; gezahnt.

jail (Am nur so) **gaol** [dʒeɪl] **I** s Gefängnis n; **II** v ins Gefängnis stecken; ~er, ~or, **gaoler** ['-ə] Gefängniswärter m.

jam [dʒæm] **I** v 1. ein-, festklemmen; 2. quetschen; 3. versperren, verstopfen; 4. tech blockieren; 5. radio stören; **II** s 6. Marmelade f; 7. Gedränge n; 8. Verkehrsstockung f; 9. tech Blockieren n; 10. (fam) be in a ~ in der Klemme sitzen; ~-pot ['-pɒt] Marmeladeglas n.

janitor ['dʒænɪtə] 1. Pförtner m; 2. Am Hausmeister m.

January ['dʒænjuərɪ] Januar m.

Japan [dʒə'pæn] Japan n; ~ese [,dʒæpə'niːz] **I** s Japaner m; **II** adj japanisch.

jar [dʒɑː] **I** v knarren; **II** s Knarren, Quietschen n.

jaundice ['dʒɔːndɪs] 1. Gelbsucht f; 2. Neid m.

jaunt [dʒɔːnt] **I** v e-n Ausflug machen; **II** s Ausflug m.

jaunty ['dʒɔːntɪ] übermütig.

javelin ['dʒævlɪn] throwing the ~ Speerwerfen n.

jaw [dʒɔː] 1. anat Kiefer m; 2. tech Backe f.

jazz [dʒæz] Jazz m; ~ band Jazzkapelle f.

jealous ['dʒeləs] eifersüchtig, neidisch (of auf); ~y [-ɪ] Eifersucht f; Neid m.

jeans pl [dʒiːnz] Arbeitshose f, Jeans pl.

jeer [dʒɪə] **I** v verspotten; **II** s Spott, Hohn m.

jelly ['dʒelɪ] Sülze f; Gelee n; ~-fish [-fɪʃ] Qualle f.

jeopardize ['dʒepədaɪz] in Gefahr bringen.

jerk [dʒɜːk] **I** v (heftig) ziehen (an), reißen; **II** s 1. Ruck, Stoß m; by ~s ruckweise;

2. Zuckung *f;* ~**y** ['-ɪ] ruckartig.

jersey ['dʒɜːzɪ] wollene Strickjacke *f;* Pullover *m.*

jest [dʒest] **I** *s* Scherz, Spaß *m;* **II** *v* scherzen (*about* über); ~**er** ['-ə] Witzbold *m.*

jet [dʒet] **I** *v* hervorsprudeln; **II** *s* 1. (*Wasser*) Strahl *m;* 2. *mot* Düse *f.*

jetblack ['dʒetblæk] pechschwarz.

jetfighter ['dʒet,faɪtə] Düsenjäger *m.*

jetty ['dʒetɪ] Hafendamm *m.*

Jew [dʒuː] Jude *m,* Jüdin *f.*

jewel ['dʒuːəl] Juwel *n a. fig;* ~(**l)er** [-ə] Juwelier *m;* ~(**le)ry** ['dʒuːəlrɪ] Juwelen *n pl,* Schmuck *m.*

jib [dʒɪb] störrisch sein, scheuen.

jigsaw ['dʒɪgsɔː] Laubsäge *f.*

jingle ['dʒɪŋgl] **I** *v* klirren, klimpern; **II** *s* Geklingel *n.*

job [dʒɒb] **I** *s* 1. Arbeit(sleistung) *f; do odd* ~s Gelegenheitsarbeiten verrichten; *make a good, bad* ~ *of s.th.* etw gut, schlecht erledigen; 2. *fam* Arbeitsplatz *m; be out of a* ~ arbeitslos sein; 3. Aufgabe, Mühe *f;* **II** *v* 4. Gelegenheitsarbeit verrichten; 5. vermitteln; ~**ber** ['-ə] 1. Börsenmakler *m;* 2. Gelegenheitsarbeiter *m.*

jockey ['dʒɒkɪ] Jockei *m.*

jog [dʒɒg] 1. anstoßen; 2. ~ *along,* ~ *on* sich fortschlep-

pen; 3. e-n Dauerlauf machen.

joggle ['dʒɒgl] schütteln, rütteln.

join [dʒɔɪn] 1. zs.bringen, verbinden *a. math;* vereinigen (*to* mit); ~ *hands (fig)* gemeinsame Sache machen; 2. sich gesellen (*s.o.* zu jdm); 3. eintreten in; 4. ~ *in* mitmachen; ~**er** ['-ə] Tischler, Schreiner *m.*

joint [dʒɔɪnt] **I** *s* 1. Verbindungsstelle *f;* 2. *anat* Gelenk *n;* 3. (*Küche*) Keule *f;* **II** *adj* gemeinsam; **III** *v* verbinden; ~ **ownership** Miteigentum *n;* ~-**stock company** Aktiengesellschaft *f; Am* Offene Handelsgesellschaft *f* auf Aktien.

joke [dʒəʊk] **I** *s* Scherz, Spaß *m;* **II** *v* Witze machen; ~**r** ['-ə] Witzbold *m.*

jolly ['dʒɒlɪ] **I** *adj* 1. lustig; 2. angeheitert; **II** *v fam* (~ *along*) gut zureden (*s.o.* jdm).

jolt [dʒəʊlt] rütteln, stoßen.

jostle ['dʒɒsl] anrempeln.

jot [dʒɒt] **I** *s: not a* ~ nicht das geringste; **II** *v:* ~ *down* schnell aufschreiben, notieren.

journal ['dʒɜːnl] 1. Tagebuch *n;* 2. (Tages-)Zeitung, Zeitschrift *f;* ~**ism** ['dʒɜːnəlɪzəm] Journalismus *m;* ~**ist** ['dʒɜːnəlɪst] Journalist *m.*

journey ['dʒɜːnɪ] Reise *f.*

jowl [dʒaʊl] Unterkiefer *m*.
joy [dʒɔɪ] Freude *f*; Vergnügen *n*; **~ful** ['-fʊl] freudig.
jubil|ant ['dʒuːbɪlənt] frohlockend; **~ee** ['dʒuːbɪliː] Jubiläum *n*.
judge [dʒʌdʒ] **I** *s* 1. Richter *m*; 2. Sachverständige(r) *m* (*of* in); **II** *v* 3. richten, aburteilen; 4. beurteilen; *judging from what you say* aufgrund dessen, was Sie sagen.
judg(e)ment ['dʒʌdʒmənt] 1. Urteil *n* (*on* über); *the Day of J~* der Jüngste Tag; 2. Meinung, Ansicht *f*; *in my ~* meiner Ansicht nach; 3. Urteilsvermögen *n*.
judicial [dʒuːˈdɪʃl] gerichtlich.
judicious [dʒuːˈdɪʃəs] vernünftig.
jug [dʒʌg] Krug *m*.
juggle ['dʒʌgl] 1. jonglieren; 2. betrügen; **~r** [-ə] 1. Jongleur *m*; 2. Betrüger *m*.
juic|e [dʒuːs] Saft *m*; **~y** ['-ɪ] saftig.
jukebox ['dʒuːkbɒks] Musikautomat *m*
July [dʒuːˈlaɪ] Juli *m*.
jumble ['dʒʌmbl] (*~ up*) durchea.bringen; **~-sale** [-seɪl] Wohltätigkeitsbasar *m*.
jumbo ['dʒʌmbəʊ] riesig; **~ jet** *aero* Jumbo-Jet *m*.
jump [dʒʌmp] **I** *s* 1. Sprung *m a. sport;* 2. (*Preise*) Emporschnellen *n*; **II** *v* 3. springen; 4. auf-, hochfahren; 5. sich stürzen (*at* auf); *~ to*

conclusions voreilige Schlüsse ziehen.
jumper ['dʒʌmpə] 1. Pullover *m*; 2. Springer *m*.
junct|ion ['dʒʌŋkʃn] 1. Verbindung *f*; 2. Knotenpunkt *m*; **~ure** ['dʒʌŋktʃə] Zeitpunkt *m*; *at this ~* in diesem Augenblick.
June [dʒuːn] Juni *m*.
jungle ['dʒʌŋgl] Dschungel *m*.
junior ['dʒuːnjə] **I** *adj* jünger; **II** *s* Jüngere(r), Junior *m*.
junk [dʒʌŋk] Trödel *m*.
juridical [ˌdʒʊəˈrɪdɪkl] 1. gerichtlich; 2. juristisch.
juris|diction [ˌdʒʊərɪsˈdɪkʃn] Rechtsprechung, Gerichtsbarkeit *f*, -bezirk *m*; **~prudence** [-ˈpruːdəns] Rechtswissenschaft *f*.
juror ['dʒʊərə] 1. Geschworene(r) *m*; 2. Preisrichter *m*.
jury ['dʒʊərɪ] 1. die Geschworenen *m pl*; 2. Jury *f*.
just [dʒʌst] **I** *adj* 1. gerecht; 2. richtig; genau; **II** *adv* 3. gerade, eben; *~ now* eben erst; 4. nur, bloß; 5. *~ as* ebenso, geradeso . . . wie.
justice ['dʒʌstɪs] 1. Gerechtigkeit *f*; 2. Recht *n*; *court of ~* Gericht(shof *m*) *n*; 3. Richter *m*;
justif|ication [ˌdʒʌstɪfɪˈkeɪʃn] Rechtfertigung *f*; **~y** ['dʒʌstɪfaɪ] rechtfertigen.
juvenile ['dʒuːvənaɪl] **I** *adj* jugendlich; **II** *s* Jugendliche(r) *m*.

K

kangaroo [ˌkæŋgə'ruː], pl ~s [-z] Känguruh n.

keel [kiːl] mar Kiel m.

keen [kiːn] 1. (Messer, Senf, Augen, Verstand) scharf; 2. fam (Mensch) stark interessiert (on an).

keep [kiːp] I s (Lebens-)Unterhalt m; II v irr kept, kept [kept] 1. (be)halten, haben; ~ in mind im Auge behalten; sich merken; 2. einhalten, befolgen; ~ a promise ein Versprechen halten; ~ silence Stillschweigen bewahren; 3. aufbewahren; 4. sorgen für; 5. (Waren, Tagebuch) führen; 6. (~ waiting) warten) lassen; 7. aufhalten; abhalten; 8. ~ doing s.th. immer wieder etw tun; ~ going (fig) weitermachen; ~ smiling! Kopf hoch! ~ **on** 1. (Hut) aufbehalten; 2. weitermachen; keep on talking weiterreden; ~ **out** 1. nicht hereinlassen; 2. keep out! Eintritt verboten! ~ **to** 1. festhalten an; 2. keep o.s. to o.s. für sich bleiben; ~ **up** 1. fortfahren mit, weitermachen; keep up appearances den Schein wahren; 2. beibehalten, bewahren; 3. keep up with Schritt halten mit a. fig.

keeping ['kiːpɪŋ] 1. in safe ~ in sicherer Hut; 2. in ~ with in Übereinstimmung, in Einklang mit.

kennel ['kenl] Hundehütte f.

kernel ['kɜːnl] Kern m a. fig.

kettle ['ketl] Kessel m.

key [kiː] 1. Schlüssel m a. fig; 2. mus (a. Schreibmaschine) Taste f; 3. all in the same ~ (fig) monoton, ausdruckslos; ~**board** ['-bɔːd] Klaviatur; Tastatur f; ~**hole** ['-həʊl] Schlüsselloch n; ~**note** ['-nəʊt] 1. mus Grundton m; 2. fig Grundgedanke m; ~**stone** ['-stəʊn] 1. arch Schlußstein m; 2. fig Grundlage f.

kick [kɪk] I s 1. (Fuß-)Tritt, Stoß m; 2. (fam) get a big ~ out of s.th. viel Spaß an etw haben; II v (mit dem Fuß) treten.

kid [kɪd] 1. Zicklein n; 2. Ziegenleder n; 3. sl Kind n.

kidney ['kɪdnɪ] anat Niere f; ~ **machine** künstliche Niere f.

kill [kɪl] töten; ~**er** ['-ə] Mörder m.

kilo|gram(me) ['kɪləʊgræm] Kilogramm n; ~**metre, ~meter** ['kɪləʊˌmiːtə] Kilometer m; ~**watt** ['kɪləʊwɒt] Kilowatt n.

kin [kɪn] die Verwandten pl.

kind [kaɪnd] I s 1. Gattung f;

2. Sorte; Art (und Weise) *f;*
a ~ of e-e Art (von); *of a ~*
gleich(artig, -wertig); 3. *pay-*
ment in ~ Natural-, Sachlei-
stung *f;* **II** *adj* gütig, freundlich.

kindle ['kɪndl] 1. anzünden;
2. *fig* erwecken, erregen;
3. sich entzünden.

kind‖ly ['kaɪndlɪ] *will you ~*
tell me the time? würden
Sie mir bitte sagen, wieviel
Uhr es ist? **~ness**
['kaɪndnɪs] 1. Freundlichkeit
f; 2. Gefälligkeit *f.*

kindred ['kɪndrɪd] **I** *s* (Bluts-)
Verwandtschaft *f;* **II** *adj*
verwandt *a. fig.*

king [kɪŋ] König *m a. fig;*
~dom ['kɪŋdəm] (König-)
Reich *n a. fig.*

kipper ['kɪpə] Räucherhering
m.

kiss [kɪs] **I** *v* (sich) küssen;
II *s* Kuß *m; ~ of life* Mund-
-zu-Mund-Beatmung *f.*

kit [kɪt] Ausrüstung *f.*

kitchen ['kɪtʃɪn] Küche *f.*

kite [kaɪt] (Papier-)Drachen
m.

kitten ['kɪtn] Kätzchen *n.*

knack [næk] Kniff, Trick *m;*
have the ~ of it den Bogen
raushaben.

knave [neɪv] Schurke *m.*

knead [ni:d] kneten.

knee [ni:] Knie *n;* **~cap**
['-kæp] *anat* Kniescheibe *f.*

kneel [ni:l] *irr knelt, knelt*

[nelt] *(~ down)* (nie-
der)knien *(to* vor).

knell [nel] Totenglocke *f.*

knife [naɪf] **I** *s pl* knives [-vz]
Messer *n;* **II** *v* erstechen.

knight [naɪt] Ritter *m.*

knit [nɪt] *a. irr* knit, knit
1. stricken; 2. *fig* (mitea.)
verknüpfen, verbinden; 3. *~*
o.'s brows die Stirn runzeln.

knob [nɒb] (Griff-)Knopf *m.*

knock [nɒk] **I** *s* 1. Schlag,
Stoß *m;* 2. Klopfen *n;* **II** *v*
3. schlagen, prallen *(on,*
against gegen); 4. klopfen
(at an); *~* **down** 1. niederschlagen; 2. *(Preis)* drücken;
~ **out** (Boxen) k.o. schlagen.

knock‖er ['nɒkə] Türklopfer
m; ~-**kneed** [,nɒk'ni:d]
X-beinig; **~-out** ['nɒkaʊt]
(Boxen) K.-o.-Schlag *m.*

knot [nɒt] **I** *s* 1. Knoten *m;*
2. *mar* Knoten *m (1,853 km/*
h); **II** *v* (sich) verknoten.

know [nəʊ] *irr* knew [nju:],
known [nəʊn] 1. wissen,
kennen; *make o.s. ~n* sich
bekannt machen, sich vor-
stellen; 2. können; 3. erfahren; erleben; **~-how** ['-haʊ]
Erfahrung *f,* (Fach-)Wissen
*n; ~***ing** ['-ɪŋ] klug, einsich-
tig; **~ingly** ['-ɪŋlɪ] absichtlich.

knowledge ['nɒlɪdʒ] Kenntnis *f (of* von); *to (the best*
of) my ~ soviel ich weiß.

knuckle ['nʌkl] (Finger-)
Knöchel *m.*

L

label ['leɪbl] **I** s Etikett n; **II** v mit e-m Etikett versehen.

laboratory [lə'bɒrətəri] Labor(atorium) n.

laborious [lə'bɔːriəs] 1. (Arbeit) schwer; 2. (Mensch) arbeitsam, fleißig.

labo(u)r ['leɪbə] **I** s 1. Arbeit, Mühe f; casual ~ Gelegenheitsarbeit f; 2. Arbeiter(schaft f) m pl; 3. med Wehen f pl; **II** v arbeiten; sich (ab)mühen; **~er** [-rə] (un)skilled ~ (un)gelernte(r) Arbeiter m; **L~ Exchange** Arbeitsamt n; **L~ Party** (engl.) Arbeiterpartei f; **~union** Am Gewerkschaft f.

lace [leɪs] **I** s 1. Schnur f; (Schuh-)Senkel m; 2. (Textil) Spitze f; **II** v (~ up) (Schuhe) (zu)schnüren.

lack [læk] **I** s Mangel m (of an); **II** v nicht haben; be ~ing fehlen.

lacquer ['lækə] **I** s (Farb-)Lack; Firnis m; **II** v lackieren.

lad [læd] Junge; Bursche m.

ladder ['lædə] 1. Leiter f; 2. Laufmasche f; **~-proof** [-pruːf] (Strumpf) maschenfest.

lad|en ['leɪdn] 1. beladen (with mit); 2. fig bedrückt; **~ing** ['leɪdɪŋ] Ladung f.

ladle ['leɪdl] **I** s Schöpflöffel m; **II** v (~ out) fig großzügig verteilen.

lady ['leɪdɪ] Dame f; Ladies and Gentlemen meine Damen und Herren! Ladies Damentoilette f; young ~ Fräulein n; **~bird** [-bɜːd] Marienkäfer m; **~like** [-laɪk] damenhaft.

lake [leɪk] See m.

lamb [læm] Lamm n.

lame [leɪm] **I** adj lahm a. fig; **II** v lähmen.

lament [lə'ment] klagen (for s.o. um jdn); beklagen (over s.o.'s death jds Tod); **~able** ['læməntəbl] beklagens-, bejammernswert; **~ation** [,læmen'teɪʃn] Wehklage f.

lamp [læmp] Lampe f; **~-post** ['-pəust] Laternenpfahl m.

lance [lɑːns] **I** s Lanze f, Speer m; **II** v med aufstechen.

land [lænd] **I** s 1. Land n; 2. Grund und Boden m; **II** v landen.

landholder ['lænd,həuldə] Gutsbesitzer m.

landing ['lændɪŋ] 1. mar aero Landung f; 2. Treppenabsatz m; **~-field** [-fiːld] , **~-strip** [-strɪp] Landebahn f; **~-gear** [-gɪə] aero Fahrgestell n; **~-stage** [-steɪdʒ] mar Landungsbrücke f.

land|lady ['læn,leɪdɪ] (Haus-, Gast-)Wirtin *f;* **~lord** ['lænlɔːd] (Haus-, Gast-)Wirt; Gutseigentümer *m;* **~mark** ['lændmɑːk] Grenzstein *m;* **~scape** ['lænskeɪp] Landschaft *f;* **~slide** ['lændslaɪd] Erdrutsch *m (a. fig pol).*

lane [leɪn] 1. Gasse *f;* 2. *mot* Fahrspur *f.*

language ['læŋgwɪdʒ] Sprache *f a. fig.*

langui|d ['læŋgwɪd] 1. kraftlos; 2. *(Markt)* flau; **~sh** ['læŋgwɪʃ] 1. ermatten, dahinsiechen; 2. sich sehnen *(for* nach).

lank [læŋk] 1. lang und dünn; 2. *(Haar)* glatt, schlicht; **~y** ['-ɪ] schlaksig.

lantern ['læntən] Laterne *f.*

lap [læp] **I** *s* Schoß *m; on o.'s* **~** auf dem Schoß; **II** *v* 1. auflecken; 2. plätschern.

lapel [lə'pel] (Rock-)Aufschlag *m.*

lapse [læps] **I** *s* 1. Versehen *n,* Fehler *m;* 2. *(Zeit)* Verlauf *m;* **~** *of time* Zeitspanne *f;* **II** *v* 3. e-n Fehltritt tun; 4. *jur* verfallen.

lard [lɑːd] **I** *s* (Schweine-)Schmalz *m;* **II** *v (Fleisch)* spicken *a. fig;* **~er** ['lɑːdə] Speisekammer *f.*

large [lɑːdʒ] **I** *adj* 1. groß; 2. ausgedehnt; **II** *adv: by and* **~** im großen und ganzen; **III** *s: at* **~** auf freiem Fuß; ausführlich; im allge-

meinen; **~-scale** ['-skeɪl] Groß-.

lark [lɑːk] 1. *orn* Lerche *f;* 2. Spaß, Scherz *m.*

larynx ['lærɪŋks] Kehlkopf *m.*

lash [læʃ] **I** *s* 1. Peitsche(nschnur) *f;* Peitschenhieb *m (a. fig);* 2. *(eye~)* Wimper *f;* **II** *v* 3. (aus)peitschen; 4. **~** *out (fig)* ausfallend werden *(at* gegen).

last [lɑːst] **I** *adj* 1. letzt, neuest; 2. vorig; **~** *night* gestern abend; heute nacht; **~** *but one* vorletzte(r, s); 3. äußerst, höchst; **II** *adv* 4. zuletzt; 5. zum letzten Mal; **III** *v* 6. (an)dauern; 7. (aus)reichen *(for* für); **IV** *s* der, die, das Letzte; Ende *n; at* **~** schließlich; zuletzt; **~ing** ['-ɪŋ] 1. beständig; 2. haltbar; **~ly** ['-lɪ] zuletzt.

latch [lætʃ] Klinke *f;* **~key** ['-kiː] Hausschlüssel *m.*

late [leɪt] 1. spät; *at a* **~** *hour* zu später Stunde; 2. *be* **~** sich verspäten; 3. (jüngst) verstorben; **~ly** ['-lɪ] vor kurzem; *of* **~** *on* später; *sooner or* **~** früher oder später; **~st** ['-ɪst] *at the* **~** spätestens.

lateral ['lætərəl] seitlich.

lath [lɑːθ] *pl* **~s** [-s] Latte *f.*

lathe [leɪð] Drehbank *f.*

lather ['lɑːðə] **I** *s* (Seifen-)Schaum *m;* **II** *v* einseifen.

Latin ['lætɪn] **I** *s* Latein *n;* **II** *adj* lateinisch.

latitude ['lætɪtjuːd] 1. *geog* Breite *f*; 2. *fig* Spielraum *m*.

latter ['lætə] 1. später, neuer; 2. *der, die, das* letztere; **~-day** [-ˌdeɪ] modern; **~ly** [-lɪ] neuerdings.

lattice ['lætɪs] Gitter(werk) *n*.

laugh [lɑːf] **I** *v* lachen (*at* über) *a. fig*; auslachen (*at s.o.* jdn); **II** *s* Lachen *n*; *have the last* ~ am Ende triumphieren; **~able** ['-əbl] lächerlich; **~ter** ['-tə] Gelächter *n*.

launch [lɔːntʃ] **I** *v* 1. *(Schiff)* vom Stapel lassen; 2. *(Rakete)* abschießen; **II** *s* Stapellauf *m*.

laundry ['lɔːndrɪ] 1. Wäscherei *f*; 2. *the* ~ die Wäsche.

laurel ['lɒrəl] Lorbeer *m*.

lavatory ['lævətərɪ] 1. Waschraum *m*; 2. Toilette *f*.

lavish ['lævɪʃ] **I** *adj* verschwenderisch *(of* mit); **II** *v* verschwenden.

law [lɔː] 1. Gesetz *n*; 2. Recht *n*; 3. *go to* ~ *against s.o.* jdn verklagen; **~court** Gerichtshof *m*; **~ful** ['-fʊl] 1. gesetzlich; 2. rechtmäßig.

lawn [lɔːn] Rasen *m*.

lawsuit ['lɔːsuːt] Rechtsstreit *m*.

lawyer ['lɔːjə] 1. Jurist *m*; 2. Rechtsanwalt *m*.

lax [læks] locker, (nach)lässig; **~ative** ['læksətɪv] Abführmittel *n*.

lay [leɪ] *irr* laid, laid [leɪd] 1. (hin-, nieder-, um)legen *(on* auf); setzen, stellen; 2. ~ *the table* den Tisch decken; 3. ~ *hands on* in s-n Besitz bringen; ~ **down** 1. niederlegen; 2. aufgeben; 3. entwerfen, planen; *(Grundsatz)* aufstellen; ~ **on** *tech* installieren, verlegen; ~ **up** 1. sammeln, horten; lagern; sparen; 2. *be laid up* das Bett hüten (müssen) *(with* wegen).

lay|by ['leɪbaɪ] *Br mot* Rastplatz *m*; **~er** ['leɪə] Schicht *f*.

laz|iness ['leɪzɪnɪz] Faulheit *f*; **~y** ['-ɪ] faul, träge.

lead [liːd] **I** *s* 1. Führung *f*; *take the* ~ die Führung übernehmen; 2. *el* Kabel *n*; 3. (Hunde-)Leine *f*; **II** *v irr* led, led [led] führen, leiten; ~ *the way* den Weg zeigen; vorangehen; ~ *up to* hinführen, überleiten zu.

lead [led] 1. Blei *n*; 2. Lot *n*; 3. (Bleistift-)Mine *f*.

leader ['liːdə] 1. (An-)Führer *m*; 2. *Br (Zeitung)* Leitartikel *m*; **~ship** [-ʃɪp] Führung, Leitung *f*.

leading ['liːdɪŋ] **I** *adj* leitend; **II** *s* Führung, Leitung *f*.

leaf [liːf] *pl* **leaves** [liːvz] 1. Blatt *n*; *turn over a new* ~ e-n neuen Anfang machen; 2. Tischklappe *f*; **~let** ['-lɪt] Prospekt *m*.

league [li:g] I s Bund m;
II v (sich) verbünden.
leak [li:k] I v 1. leck sein;
2. (~ in, out) durchsickern a.
fig; II s Leck n.
lean [li:n] I adj mager; II v a.
irr leant, leant [lent] (sich)
lehnen (against gegen, an);
(sich) stützen (on, upon auf);
~ness ['-nɪs] Magerkeit f a.
fig.
leap [li:p] I v a. irr leapt,
leapt [lept] (über)springen;
II s Sprung m; ~-year ['-jɜ:]
Schaltjahr n.
learn [lɜ:n] a. irr learnt,
learnt [lɜ:nt] 1. (er)lernen; ~
by heart auswendig lernen;
2. erfahren, hören; 3. entnehmen (from aus); ~ed
['-ɪd] gelehrt; ~er ['-ə]
1. Anfänger m; 2. mot Fahr-
schüler m.
lease [li:s] I s Pacht, Miete f;
II v 1. verpachten, vermieten; 2. pachten, mieten.
leash [li:ʃ] (Hunde-)Leine f.
least [li:st] I adj kleinst, ge-
ringst, wenigst; II adv: ~ of
all am allerwenigsten; III s:
at ~ mindestens; not in the
~ nicht im geringsten.
leather ['leðə] Leder n; ~y
[-rɪ] ledern; zäh.
leave [li:v] I s 1. Erlaubnis f;
2. take ~ sich verabschie-
den; 3. ~ of absence (mil)
Urlaub m; II v irr left, left
[left] 4. (ver-, zurück-, üb-
rig-, hinter)lassen; ~ alone
sich nicht kümmern um; be

left übrigbleiben; 5. anheim-
stellen; ~ it to me überlassen Sie es mir; 6. abreisen
(for nach).
lecture ['lektʃə] I s 1. Vorlesung f; 2. Strafpredigt f; II v
3. e-e Vorlesung halten (on
über; to s.o. vor jdm); 4. e-e
Strafpredigt halten (s.o. jdm;
for wegen); ~r ['lektʃərə]
Dozent m.
ledger ['ledʒə] com Haupt-
buch n.
leer [lɪə] schielen (at nach).
left [left] I adj linke(r, s); II s
linke Seite f; III adv (nach)
links; on the ~ zur Linken;
to the ~ nach links; links (of
von); ~-handed [,-'hændɪd]
1. linkshändig; 2. unaufrichtig.
leg [leg] 1. Bein n; pull s.o.'s
~ jdn aufziehen; stretch o.'s
~s sich die Beine vertreten;
2. (Küche) Keule f.
legacy ['legəsɪ] Vermächtnis
n a. fig.
legal ['li:gl] gesetzlich; ~ize
['li:gəlaɪz] legalisieren.
legation [lɪ'geɪʃn] Gesandtschaft f.
legend ['ledʒənd] Legende f;
~ary [-ərɪ] sagenhaft.
legible ['ledʒəbl] leserlich.
legion ['li:dʒən] Legion f.
legislation [,ledʒɪs'leɪʃn]
Gesetzgebung f; ~ive
['ledʒɪslətɪv] gesetzgebend;
~or [-ə] Gesetzgeber m.
legitimacy [lɪ'dʒɪtɪməsɪ] Le-
gitimität f; ~ate [lɪ'dʒɪtɪmət]

I *adj* rechtmäßig; **II** *v u.*
~atize [lɪˈdʒɪtɪmətaɪz] legiti-
mieren.
leisure [ˈleʒə] Muße, Freizeit
f (for zu); **~ly** [-lɪ] gemäch-
lich.
lemon [ˈlemən] Zitrone *f;* **~
squash** Zitronenwasser *n.*
lend [lend] *irr lent, lent*
[lent] 1. (aus-, ver)leihen; ~
a (helping) hand mit Hand
anlegen; 2. *(Eigenschaft)*
verleihen; 3. ~ *o.s. to s.th.*
sich zu etw hergeben.
length [leŋθ] Länge; Strek-
ke; Dauer *f; at (great)* ~
sehr ausführlich; **~en**
[ˈleŋθən] 1. verlängern;
2. länger werden; **~ways**
[ˈ-weɪz], **~wise** [ˈ-waɪz] der
Länge nach.
lens [lenz] *opt phot anat*
Linse *f.*
Lent [lent] Fastenzeit *f.*
lentil [ˈlentl] *bot* Linse *f.*
Leo [ˈliːəʊ] *astr* Löwe *m.*
leprosy [ˈleprəsɪ] *med* Lepra
f; Aussatz *m.*
less [les] **I** *adj* kleiner, geringer; ~ *than* weniger als;
II *adv* weniger; *none the* ~
nichtsdestoweniger; **III** *prp*
abzüglich *gen;* **~en** [ˈ-n]
1. vermindern; 2. abnehmen,
nachlassen.
lesson [ˈlesn] 1. *(Schule)*
Lektion *f;* 2. Unterrichts-
stunde *f;* 3. *let this be a* ~ *to
you* laß dir das e-e Lehre
sein!
lest [lest] damit nicht.

let [let] *irr let, let* 1. lassen;
mit inf zulassen, daß; 2. vermieten; sich vermieten lassen; *this house is to be* ~
dieses Haus ist zu vermieten; ~ **down** im Stich lassen; ~ **in** *let o.s. in for s.th.*
sich auf etw einlassen; ~
into einweihen in; ~ **up**
nachlassen; aufhören.
letter [ˈletə] 1. Buchstabe *m;
to the* ~ wörtlich; 2. *typ*
Type *f;* 3. Brief *m (to* an);
4. *pl* Literatur *f;* **~-box**
[-bɒks] Briefkasten *m.*
lettuce [ˈletɪs] *bot* Lattich,
Kopfsalat *m.*
level [ˈlevl] **I** *s* 1. Ebene *f a.
fig;* 2. Höhe *f;* Niveau *n a.
fig; on the* ~ *(fam)* offen
und ehrlich; *sea* ~ Meeresspiegel *m;* **II** *adj* 3. eben;
flach; 4. *do o.'s* ~ *best* sein
möglichstes tun; 5. *have a* ~
head ausgeglichen sein;
III *v* eben machen; ~ *up*
(Niveau) anheben.
lever [ˈliːvə] Hebel *m a. fig.*
levy [ˈlevɪ] **I** *s* 1. Abgabe;
Steuer *f;* 2. *mil* Aushebung
f; **II** *v* 3. *(Steuer)* erheben;
4. *mil* ausheben.
liab|ility [ˌlaɪəˈbɪlətɪ] 1. Ver-
bindlichkeit, Verpflichtung
f; 2. Haftpflicht *f;* **~le**
[ˈlaɪəbl] 1. verpflichtet *(for*
zu); haftbar *(for* für); 2. *be*
~ *to* ausgesetzt sein; neigen
zu.
liar [ˈlaɪə] Lügner *m.*
libel [ˈlaɪbl] Schmähschrift *f.*

liberal ['lɪbərəl] 1. freigebig (*of* mit); 2. tolerant.

liberat|e ['lɪbəreɪt] befreien (*from* von); **~ion** [ˌlɪbə'reɪʃn] Befreiung *f.*

liberty ['lɪbətɪ] Freiheit *f; be at ~ to do* tun dürfen; *set at ~* freilassen; *take the ~ of doing, to do s.th* sich die Freiheit nehmen, etw zu tun.

Libra ['laɪbrə] *astr* Waage *f.*

librar|ian [laɪ'breərɪən] Bibliothekar *m;* **~y** ['laɪbrərɪ] Bibliothek *f.*

licen|ce, ~se ['laɪsəns] **I** *s* 1. Lizenz, Konzession *f; driving ~* Führerschein *m;* 2. Zügellosigkeit *f;* **II** *v* (*meist: ~se*) genehmigen; e-e Lizenz erteilen (*s.o.* jdm).

lick [lɪk] 1. (auf-, ab-, be)lecken; 2. *fam* verdreschen.

lid [lɪd] 1. Deckel *m;* 2. (Augen-)Lid *n.*

lie [laɪ] **I** *s* 1. Lage *f;* 2. Lüge *f; tell a ~* lügen; *white ~* Notlüge *f;* **II** *v irr lay* [leɪ], *lain* [leɪn] 3. liegen; *~ down* sich hinlegen; *how the land ~s* wie die Sache steht; 4. lügen; *~ to s.o.* jdn anlügen.

lieu [ljuː] *in ~ of* anstatt *gen.*

lieutenant [lef'tenənt] Leutnant *m.*

life [laɪf] *pl lives* [laɪvz] Leben *n; as large as ~* in Lebensgröße; *not for the ~ of me* beim besten Willen nicht; **~belt** ['-belt] Rettungsgürtel *m;* **~boat** ['-bəʊt] Rettungsboot *n;*

~-jacket ['-ˌdʒækɪt] Schwimmweste *f;* **~less** ['-lɪs] leblos *a. fig;* **~-size(d)** ['-saɪz(t)] lebensgroß; **~time** ['-taɪm] Lebenszeit *f.*

lift [lɪft] **I** *v* 1. (auf-, er-, hoch)heben; *~ up o.'s voice* die Stimme erheben; 2. (*~ off*) abheben (*Raumschiff*); 3. (*Nebel*) sich auflösen; **II** *s* 4. Br Fahrstuhl *m;* 5. *fig* Auftrieb *m;* 6. *give s.o. a ~* jdn mit dem Auto mitnehmen.

light [laɪt] **I** *s* 1. Licht *n a. fig; come to ~* an den Tag kommen; *shed, throw (a) ~ on* (*fig*) ein Licht werfen auf; 2. Streichholz; Feuer *n;* **II** *v a. irr lit, lit* [lɪt] 3. (*Feuer, Licht*) anzünden; 4. be-, erleuchten; 5. leuchten (*s.o.* jdm); 6. *~ upon* (zufällig) stoßen auf; **III** *adj* 7. hell; blond; *it's beginning to get ~* es wird hell; 8. leicht *a. fig; make ~ of s.th.* etw bagatellisieren.

lighten ['laɪtn] 1. erleuchten; 2. (sich) aufhellen; 3. blitzen; 4. leichter machen.

lighter ['laɪtə] (Taschen-) Feuerzeug *n.*

lighthouse ['laɪthaʊs] Leuchtturm *m.*

light-minded ['laɪtˌmaɪndɪd] gedankenlos.

lightness ['laɪtnɪs] 1. Leichtigkeit *f;* 2. Leichtfertigkeit *f.*

lightning ['laɪtnɪŋ] Blitz *m;*

~-**conductor** [-kən₁dʌktə], ~-**rod** [-rɒd] Blitzableiter m.

like [laɪk] I v 1. gern haben, (gern) mögen; 2. wollen; as you ~ wie Sie wollen; if you ~ wenn Sie wollen; II adj gleich; ähnlich; wie; III prp: it is just ~ him das sieht ihm ähnlich; it looks ~ snow es sieht nach Schnee aus; what is he ~? wie ist er? wie sieht er aus? ~**lihood** ['laɪlɪhʊd] Wahrscheinlichkeit f; ~**ly** ['-lɪ] I adj wahrscheinlich; not ~ schwerlich, sicherlich nicht; II adv: as ~ as not wahrscheinlich; ~**ness** ['-nɪs] 1. Ähnlichkeit f; 2. (Ab-)Bild n; ~**wise** ['-waɪz] ebenso.

liking ['laɪkɪŋ] 1. Gefallen n (for an); 2. Zuneigung f.

lilac ['laɪlək] I s Flieder(strauch) m; II adj lila.

lily ['lɪlɪ] Lilie f; ~ of the valley Maiglöckchen n.

limb [lɪm] 1. (Körper-)Glied n; 2. Ast m.

lime [laɪm] 1. Kalk m; 2. bot Linde f; ~**light** ['-laɪt] in the ~ im Mittelpunkt des öffentlichen Interesses.

limit ['lɪmɪt] I s Grenze f; that's the ~ (fam) das ist doch die Höhe! off ~s! (Am) Zutritt verboten! (to für); II v begrenzen, be-, einschränken (to auf); ~**ation** [₁lɪmɪ'teɪʃn] Begrenzung f; ~**ed** [-ɪd] ~ liability company (Ltd) Gesellschaft f mit beschränkter Haftung (GmbH).

limp [lɪmp] I v hinken; II s: walk with a ~ hinken; III adj schlaff, weich.

line [laɪn] I s 1. Leine f; Schnur f; 2. Telephon-, Telegraphenleitung f; 3. Bahnstrecke f; 4. Linie f; Strich m; 5. (Menschen-)Schlange f; 6. Zeile f; drop s.o. a ~ (fam) jdm ein paar Zeilen schreiben; 7. (Fach-)Gebiet n; 8. come, fall into ~ sich anschließen, fam mitmachen (with mit); II v 9. lin(i)ieren; 10. (~ up) (sich) in e-r Reihe aufstellen; 11. (Kleidungsstück) füttern; tech auskleiden.

linen ['lɪnɪn] 1. Leinwand f; 2. (Bett-)Wäsche f.

liner ['laɪnə] mar Passagierdampfer m; (air-~) Verkehrsflugzeug n.

linger ['lɪŋgə] 1. (~ about) (noch) verweilen; 2. (~ on) sich hinziehen.

lining ['laɪnɪŋ] 1. (Kleider-)Futter n; 2. tech Belag m.

link [lɪŋk] I s 1. (Ketten-)Glied n; 2. fig (Binde-)Glied n; II v (sich) verbinden.

links pl [lɪŋks] 1. Dünen f pl; 2. Golfplatz m.

linseed ['lɪnsiːd] Leinsamen m; ~-**oil** [-'ɔɪl] Leinöl n.

lion ['laɪən] Löwe m; ~**ess** ['-es] Löwin f.

lip [lɪp] Lippe f a. bot; lower,

upper ~ Unter-, Oberlippe; ~**stick** ['-stɪk] Lippenstift *m*.

liquefy ['lɪkwɪ'faɪ] (sich) verflüssigen.

liquid ['lɪkwɪd] **I** *adj* 1. flüssig *a. fin*; 2. *(Luft)* klar; **II** *s* Flüssigkeit *f*; ~**ate** ['lɪkwɪdeɪt] liquidieren *a. fig*.

liquor ['lɪkə] 1. alkoholische(s) Getränk *n*; 2. *(Fleisch)* Saft *m*.

lisp [lɪsp] **I** *v* lispeln; **II** *s* Lispeln *n*.

list [lɪst] **I** *s* 1. Liste *f*; 2. *mar* Schlagseite *f*; **II** *v* in e-e Liste eintragen; aufführen.

listen ['lɪsn] 1. horchen, hören *(to auf)*; ~ *in (tele)* mithören; 2. gehorchen *(to s.o. jdm)*; ~**er** ['-ə] *radio* Hörer *m*.

listless ['lɪstlɪs] teilnahmslos.

litany ['lɪtənɪ] *rel u. fig* Litanei *f*.

literal ['lɪtərəl] wörtlich; ~**ature** ['lɪtərətʃə] Literatur *f*.

litre, *Am* **liter** ['liːtə] Liter *n* od *m*.

litter ['lɪtə] **I** *s* Abfall *m*; **II** *v* *(~ up)* in Unordnung bringen.

little ['lɪtl] **I** *adj* klein; *(Zahl)* gering; *(Weg)* kurz; wenig; *the* ~ *ones* die Kleinen; **II** *adv* wenig; **III** *s: a* ~ ein (klein) wenig; ~ *by* ~ nach u. nach, allmählich.

live I *adj* [laɪv] 1. lebend(ig), am Leben; 2. lebhaft;

II *v* [lɪv] 3. leben; 4. über-, weiterleben; ~ *to see* erleben; 5. leben *(on* von); auskommen *(on* mit); 6. wohnen *(with* bei; *at* in); ~ **down** wiedergutmachen; ~ **through** er-, überleben.

livelihood ['laɪvlɪhud] *earn, gain o.'s* ~ s-n Lebensunterhalt verdienen.

liveliness ['laɪvlɪnɪs] Lebhaftigkeit *f*; ~**ly** ['laɪvlɪ] lebhaft.

liven ['laɪvn] ~ *up* in Schwung, in Stimmung bringen, kommen.

liver ['lɪvə] Leber *f*.

livery ['lɪvərɪ] Livree *f*; (Amts-) Tracht *f*.

livid ['lɪvɪd] 1. bleifarben, aschgrau; 2. ~ *with rage* wütend.

living ['lɪvɪŋ] **I** *adj* 1. lebend(ig) *a. fig*; 2. *be the* ~ *image of s.o.* jdm aus dem Gesicht geschnitten sein; **II** *s* 3. (Lebens-)Unterhalt *m*; *make a* ~ sein Auskommen haben *(as* als); 4. Lebensstandard *m*, -weise *f*; ~-**room** [-rum] Wohnzimmer *n*.

lizard ['lɪzəd] Eidechse *f*.

load [ləud] **I** *s* 1. (Trag-)Last, Ladung *f*; 2. *fig* Bürde *f*; **II** *v* 3. (be-, auf)laden; 4. *fig* überhäufen *(with* mit).

loaf [ləuf] **I** *s pl* **loaves** [-vz] *(bes. Brot)* Laib *m*; **II** *v* herumbummeln.

loam [ləum] Lehm *m*.

loan [ləʊn] **I** s 1. (Aus-, Ver-) Leihen n; on ~ leihweise; 2. Darlehen n; **II** v (aus-, ver)leihen.

loath, loth [ləʊθ] mit inf: be ~ to do nur mit Widerwillen tun; ~**e** [ləʊð] 1. sich ekeln vor; 2. verabscheuen; ~**ing** ['ləʊðɪŋ] Ekel, Abscheu m (at vor); ~**some** ['ləʊðsəm] ekelhaft, abscheulich.

lobby ['lɒbɪ] (Vor-)Halle, Wandelhalle f, Foyer n.

lobe [ləʊb] anat bot Lappen m; ~ of the ear Ohrläppchen n; ~ of the lung Lungenflügel m.

lobster ['lɒbstə] Hummer m.

local ['ləʊkl] **I** adj 1. örtlich; 2. ortsansässig; **II** s Ortsansässige(r) m; ~**ity** [ləʊ'kælətɪ] Örtlichkeit f; Standort m; ~**ize** ['ləʊkəlaɪz] lokalisieren; ~ **time** Ortszeit f.

locat|e [ləʊ'keɪt] 1. (örtlich) festlegen; 2. ausfindig machen, feststellen; 3. be ~d liegen, sich befinden; ~**ion** [ləʊ'keɪʃn] Lage, Stelle f; Platz; Standort m.

lock [lɒk] **I** s 1. (Tür-)Schloß n; under ~ and key hinter Schloß und Riegel; 2. mar Schleuse f; 3. (Haar-)Locke f; **II** v ver-, zuschließen, -sperren; ~ **in** einschließen; ~ **up** abschließen.

locker ['lɒkə] Schließfach n.

locket ['lɒkɪt] Medaillon n.

lock-out ['lɒkaʊt] Aussperrung f (von Arbeitern).

locksmith ['lɒksmɪθ] Schlosser m.

locomotive ['ləʊkə‚məʊtɪv] Lokomotive f.

locust ['ləʊkəst] (Wander-) Heuschrecke f.

lodge [lɒdʒ] **I** s Pförtner-, Portiersloge f; **II** v 1. wohnen (with bei); 2. beherbergen; 3. (Beschwerde) einreichen; 4. (Kugel) steckenbleiben (in in); ~**r** ['-ə] Untermieter; Pensionsgast m.

lodgings pl ['lɒdʒɪŋz] Wohnung, Unterkunft f.

loft [lɒft] 1. (Dach-, Heu-) Boden m; 2. (Orgel-)Chor m; ~**y** ['-ɪ] 1. hoch(ragend); 2. arrogant.

log [lɒg] 1. (Holz-)Klotz m; sleep like a ~ wie ein Murmeltier schlafen; 2. mar Log n.

logic ['lɒdʒɪk] Logik f; ~**al** [-l] logisch.

loin [lɔɪn] 1. (Küche) Lendenstück n; 2. pl Lenden f pl (des Menschen).

loiter ['lɔɪtə] herumbummeln; trödeln.

loll [lɒl] (~ about, around) sich rekeln.

lollipop ['lɒlɪpɒp] (Dauer-) Lutscher m.

lone [ləʊn] alleinig; allein; ~**liness** ['-lɪnɪs] Einsamkeit f; ~**ly** ['-lɪ] verlassen, einsam.

long [lɒŋ] **I** v sich sehnen (for

nach); **II** *adj* 1. lang;
2. *(Weg)* weit; *in the* ~ *run*
auf die Dauer; *take the* ~
view auf lange Sicht planen;
III *adv: as, so* ~ *as* vorausgesetzt, daß; **IV** *s: before* ~
bald.

long-distance ['lɒŋ,dɪstəns]
~ *call (Am tele)* Ferngespräch *n;* ~ *lorry driver*
Fernfahrer *m.*

longing ['lɒŋɪŋ] Sehnsucht *f,*
Verlangen *n (for* nach).

longitude ['lɒndʒɪtju:d] (geographische) Länge *f.*

long-range [,lɒŋ'reɪndʒ]
weitreichend; Langstrecken-; ~**-sighted** [,-'saɪtɪd]
weitsichtig; ~**-standing**
['-,stændɪŋ] seit langer Zeit
bestehend; ~**-term** ['-,tɜːm]
fin langfristig; ~ **wave**
radio Langwelle *f.*

loo [lu:] *fam* Toilette *f.*

look [lʊk] **I** *s* 1. Blick *m (at*
auf, nach); 2. *pl* Aussehen *n;*
II *v:* 3. sehen, schauen, blicken *(at* auf); 4. nachsehen;
5. suchen *(for s.o., s.th.* jdn,
etw); 6. sich kümmern *(after*
um); 7. aussehen; *it* ~*s like
rain* es sieht nach Regen
aus; ~ **down** *on* hochmütig
herabsehen auf; ~ **forward**
to sich freuen auf; ~ **in** e-n
kurzen Besuch abstatten *(on
s.o.* jdm); ~ **into** untersuchen, nachgehen *(s.th.* e-r S);
~ **out!** Vorsicht! ~ **to**
1. achten auf; 2. *look to s.o.
for s.th.* sich verlassen auf

jdn wegen etw; ~ **up**
1. *(Wort)* nachschlagen;
2. aufsuchen *(s.o.* jdn);
3. *things are (he is) looking
up* es geht (ihm) besser; ~
up and down prüfend betrachten *(s.o.* jdn).

looker-on [,lʊkər'ɒn]
pl lookers-on Zuschauer *m*
(at bei).

looking-glass ['lʊkɪŋglɑ:s]
Spiegel *m.*

look-out ['lʊkaʊt] 1. *be on
the* ~ Ausschau halten *(for*
nach); 2. Wache *f;* 3. Aussicht(en *pl) f.*

loom [lu:m] **I** *s* Webstuhl *m;*
II *v:* ~ *large* drohend vor
Augen treten.

loop [lu:p] **I** *s* Schlinge,
Schleife *f;* **II** *v* Schlingen,
Schleifen bilden; ~**hole**
['-həʊl] 1. Guckloch *n;* 2. *fig*
Ausweg *m; a* ~ *in the law*
e-e Gesetzeslücke.

loose [lu:s] **I** *adj* 1. frei, ungebunden; 2. lose, unverpackt; 3. locker; *(Kleidung)*
weit; *come* ~ *(Band, Knoten)* aufgehen; *(Knopf)* abgehen; 4. *(Lebenswandel)*
ausschweifend; **II** *v* los-,
freilassen.

loosen ['lu:sn] (sich) lösen;
(sich) lockern.

loot [lu:t] **I** *s* Beute *f;*
II *v* plündern.

lop-sided [,lɒp'saɪdɪd] schief.

lord [lɔːd] 1. Herr(scher) *m*
(of über); 2. Lord *m; the
House of L*~*s* das (Brit.)

Oberhaus; 3. *the L~* der Herr(gott), Gott.

lorry ['lɒrɪ] *Br* Last(kraft)wagen *m*, -auto *n*.

lose [lu:z] *irr lost, lost* [lɒst] 1. verlieren; *~ o.'s head (fig)* den Kopf verlieren; *~ o.'s way* sich verirren; 2. *(Zug)* verpassen; 3. vergeuden; 4. *(Uhr)* nachgehen; ~r ['-ə] Verlierer *m*.

loss [lɒs] Verlust *m; at a ~* in Verlegenheit *(for* um); außerstande *(to do* zu tun).

lost [lɒst] *a ~ cause* e-e aussichtslose Sache; **~-property office** ['lɒst'prɒpətɪ ˌɒfɪs] Fundbüro *n*.

lot [lɒt] 1. Los *n a. fig; draw, cast ~s* losen; 2. *com* Posten *m*; 3. *a ~, ~s (of)* e-e Menge *od* Masse, ein Haufen.

lotion ['ləʊʃn] *hair, shaving ~* Haar-, Rasierwasser *n*.

lottery ['lɒtərɪ] Lotterie *f*.

loud [laʊd] 1. laut; 2. *(Farbe)* schreiend, grell; **~-speaker** [ˌ-'spi:kə] Lautsprecher *m*.

lounge [laʊndʒ] **I** *v* herumlungern; **II** *s* (Hotel-)Halle *f*; Foyer *n*; Gesellschaftsraum *m*; **~-suit** ['-su:t] *Br* Straßenanzug *m*.

louse [laʊz] *pl lice* [laɪs] Laus *f*.

lout [laʊt] Flegel *m*.

lovable ['lʌvəbl] liebenswert.

love [lʌv] **I** *s* 1. Liebe, Zuneigung *f (of, for, to, towards s.o.* zu jdm); *be in ~ with s.o.*

in jdn verliebt sein; *fall in ~ with s.o.* sich in jdn verlieben; *give, send ~ to s.o.* jdn herzlich grüßen; 2. Liebste(r *m*) *f*, Liebling *m*; 3. *sport* null, nichts; **II** *v* lieben, (gern) mögen *(a. Speisen)*; **~-affair** ['-əˌfeə] Liebschaft *f*; **~ly** ['-lɪ] lieblich, reizend; schön, hübsch; **~r** ['-ə] 1. Liebhaber, Geliebte(r) *m*; 2. *pl* Liebespaar *n*, die Liebende(n) *pl*; 3. *a ~ of good music* ein Freund guter Musik.

loving ['lʌvɪŋ] liebevoll.

low [ləʊ] 1. niedrig, nieder; 2. tief, tief(er)liegend; 3. *(Gewässer)* flach; 4. *(Stimmung)* gedrückt; 5. klein, gering(fügig, -wertig); 6. einfach, niedrig *(a. Herkunft, Stand, Rang)*; 7. *(Meinung)* schlecht; 8. *(Luftdruck, Puls)* schwach; 9. *(Vorrat, Bestand)* erschöpft, verbraucht; 10. *(biol, Kultur)* primitiv; 11. *(Stimme, Laut)* leise.

lower ['ləʊə] 1. hinunter-, herunterlassen; 2. *(die Augen)* niederschlagen; 3. (ab)schwächen; senken; ermäßigen.

lowly ['ləʊlɪ] bescheiden.

low-spirited [ˌləʊ'spɪrɪtɪd] niedergeschlagen.

low tide Ebbe *f*.

loyal ['lɔɪəl] loyal, (pflichtge)treu; **~ty** [-tɪ] Loyalität, Treue *f* (*to* zu, gegen).

lozenge ['lozɪndʒ] *cough* ~ Hustenbonbon *n*.

lubric|ant ['lu:brɪkənt] Schmiermittel *n*; **~ate** [-keɪt] (ein-, ab)schmieren *a. fig.*

lucid ['lu:sɪd] klar; **~ity** [lu:'sɪdətɪ] Klarheit *f.*

luck [lʌk] Glück *n*; *bad* ~ Pech *n*; *good* ~! viel Glück! **~ily** ['-ɪlɪ] glücklicherweise; **~y** ['-ɪ] glücklich; *be* ~ Glück haben.

lucrative ['lu:krətɪv] einträglich.

ludicrous ['lu:dɪkrəs] spaßig.

lug [lʌg] schleppen, zerren.

luggage ['lʌgɪdʒ] (Reise-)Gepäck *n*; *left-*~ *office* (*rail*) Gepäckaufbewahrung *f*; **~-rack** [-ræk] Gepäcknetz *n*.

lugubrious [lu:'gu:brɪəs] tieftraurig.

lukewarm ['lu:kwɔ:m] 1. lauwarm; 2. *fig* lau, gleichgültig.

lull [lʌl] **I** *v* einlullen; **II** *s* Windstille *f*; **~aby** ['lʌləbaɪ] Wiegenlied *n*.

lumbago [lʌm'beɪgəu] *med* Hexenschuß *m*.

lumber ['lʌmbə] 1. Gerümpel *n*; 2. Nutzholz *n*; **~jack** [-dʒæk] Holzfäller *m*.

luminous ['lu:mɪnəs] leuchtend.

lump [lʌmp] **I** *s* 1. Klumpen *m*; Stück *n* (*Zucker*); *in the* ~ im ganzen; 2. *med* Beule *f*; Knoten *m*; **II** *v* (~ *together*) zs.fassen; ~ **sum** Pauschalbetrag *m*; **~y** ['-ɪ] klumpig.

lunacy ['lu:nəsɪ] Verrücktheit *f.*

lunar ['lu:nə] ~ *module* Mondfähre *f.*

lunatic ['lu:nətɪk] **I** *s* Wahnsinnige(r) *m*; **II** *adj* wahnsinnig.

lunch(eon) [lʌntʃ ('lʌntʃən)] Mittagessen *n.*

lung [lʌŋ] Lungenflügel *m*; *pl* Lunge *f.*

lurch [lɜ:tʃ] **I** *v* taumeln, torkeln; **II** *s*: *leave in the* ~ im Stich lassen.

lure [ljuə] **I** *s* Köder *m a. fig*; *fig* Zauber, Reiz *m*; **II** *v* (~ *on*) ködern *a. fig*; verlocken.

lurk [lɜ:k] auf der Lauer liegen.

luscious ['lʌʃəs] köstlich.

lush [lʌʃ] saftig; üppig *a. fig.*

lust [lʌst] 1. Gelüst *n*, Gier *f*; 2. (*geschlechtliche*) Begierde *f* (*for* nach).

lustre, *Am* **luster** ['lʌstə] Glanz *m.*

lute [lu:t] Laute *f.*

luxur|iant [lʌg'zjuəriənt] üppig; **~ious** [-iəs] luxuriös; **~y** ['lʌkʃərɪ] Luxus *m.*

lynch [lɪntʃ] lynchen.

lynx [lɪŋks] *zoo* Luchs *m.*

lyric ['lɪrɪk] **I** *adj* lyrisch *a. mus*; **II** *s* Lyrik *f*; *pl* Text *m* (*e-s Liedes*); **~al** ['-l] lyrisch; *become* ~ *over s.th.* über etw in Begeisterung geraten.

M

mac [mæk] *Br fam* = *mackintosh*.

macaroon [ˌmækəˈruːn] Makrone *f.*

mace [meɪs] 1. (Amts-)Stab *m;* 2. Muskatblüte *f.*

machine [məˈʃiːn] Maschine *f a. fig; ~ry* [-əri] 1. Maschinerie *f a. fig;* 2. Mechanismus *m.*

mackerel [ˈmækrəl] Makrele *f.*

mackintosh [ˈmækɪntoʃ] Regenmantel *m.*

mad [mæd] 1. geisteskrank; 2. *fig* verrückt (*with* vor); 3. *Am fam* wütend (*at, about* über).

madam [ˈmædəm] gnädige Frau *f.*

madden [ˈmædn] verrückt, rasend, toll machen.

mad|man [ˈmædmən] Geisteskranke(r) *m; ~ness* [ˈmædnɪs] 1. Geisteskrankheit *f;* 2. *fig* Verrücktheit *f.*

magazine [ˌmægəˈziːn] 1. Vorratslager *n;* 2. Zeitschrift *f.*

maggot [ˈmægət] *ent* Made *f.*

magic [ˈmædʒɪk] I *s* Magie, Zauberei *f;* II *adj, a. ~al* [-əl] magisch; ~ian [məˈdʒɪʃn] Zauberer *m.*

magistrate [ˈmædʒɪstreɪt] Friedensrichter *m.*

magnanim|ity [ˌmægnəˈnɪmətɪ] Großmut *f; ~ous* [mægˈnænɪməs] großmütig.

magnet [ˈmægnɪt] Magnet *m a. fig.*

magnificen|ce [mægˈnɪfɪsns] Pracht *f; ~t* [-t] prächtig; großartig *a. fig.*

magnify [ˈmægnɪfaɪ] vergrößern; ~ing glass Vergrößerungsglas *n.*

magnitude [ˈmægnɪtjuːd] 1. Größe *f;* 2. Wichtigkeit *f.*

magpie [ˈmægpaɪ] 1. *orn* Elster *f;* 2. *fig* Schwätzer *m.*

mahogany [məˈhogənɪ] Mahagoni *n.*

maid [meɪd] Hausangestellte *f.*

maiden [ˈmeɪdn] unverheiratet; ~ **name** Mädchenname *m.*

mail [meɪl] I *s* Post *f; by, via air* ~ mit Luftpost; II *v* mit der Post (ver)senden; ~**box** [ˈ-boks] *Am* Briefkasten *m;* ~ **carrier, ~man** [ˈ-mən] *Am* Briefträger *m; ~-order business* Versandgeschäft *n.*

maim [meɪm] verstümmeln *a. fig.*

main [meɪn] I *adj* hauptsächlich, größt, wichtigst; II *s pl* Hauptleitung *f; ~land*

['-lənd] Festland *n; ~***ly** ['-lı]
hauptsächlich.
maintain [meın'teın] 1. aufrechterhalten; 2. instand halten, warten; 3. *(Familie, Beziehungen)* unterhalten;
4. *(Stellung)* behaupten.
maintenance ['meıntənəns]
1. Wartung *f;* 2. *claim for ~*
Unterhaltsanspruch *m.*
maize [meız] Mais *m.*
majestic(al) [mə'dʒestık(l)]
majestätisch; *~***y**
['mædʒəstı] Majestät *f.*
major ['meıdʒə] **I** *adj* größer; **II** *s* Major *m; ~***ity**
[mə'dʒorətı] 1. Mehrheit *f;*
2. Volljährigkeit *f; reach o.'s
~* mündig werden.
make [meık] **I** *s* Fabrikat *n;*
(Mach-)Art *f;* **II** *v irr* made,
made [meıd] 1. machen; *~
o.s. comfortable* es sich gemütlich machen; 2. herstellen; 3. veranlassen; 4. erner-
nen zu; 5. sich belaufen auf;
6. *(den Zug)* noch kriegen,
erreichen; 7. *(Strecke)* zurücklegen; 8. *~ certain, sure*
sich vergewissern (*of* s.th.
e-r S; *that* daß); 9. *~ a living*
sich sein Brot verdienen; *~*
for sich auf den Weg machen nach; *~* **out** 1. verstehen; 2. ausfertigen; *(Formular)* ausfüllen; 3. zurecht-
kommen (*with* s.o. mit jdm);
~ **up** 1. *(Geschichte)* erfinden; 2. *(Gesicht)* schminken;
3. *(Streit)* beilegen; 4. als Ersatz dienen (*for* für);

5. *make up o.'s mind* sich
entschließen.
make-believe ['meıkbı͟li:v]
Vorwand *m.*
maker ['meıkə] *com* Hersteller *m.*
makeshift ['meıkʃıft] Notbe-
helf *m.*
make-up ['meıkʌp] 1. Auf-
machung *f;* 2. Make-up *n.*
male [meıl] **I** *adj* männlich;
II *s* 1. Mann *m;* 2. *zoo* Männchen *n.*
malice ['mælıs] Bosheit;
Böswilligkeit *f; ~***ious**
[mə'lıʃəs] boshaft, böswillig.
malign [mə'laın] **I** *adj* schädlich; **II** *v* verleumden; *~***ant**
[mə'lıgnənt] bösartig.
malinger [mə'lıŋgə] sich
krank stellen.
malleable ['mælıəbl] 1. *(Metall)* verformbar; 2. *fig* anpassungsfähig.
mallet ['mælıt] Schlegel *m.*
malnutrition [ˌmælnju:'trıʃn]
Unterernährung, falsche Ernährung *f.*
malt [mɔ:lt] Malz *n.*
mammal ['mæml] Säugetier
n.
mammoth ['mæməθ] **I** *s zoo*
Mammut *n;* **II** *adj* ungeheuer (groß).
man [mæn] **I** *s pl* **men** [men]
1. Mensch *m; to a ~, to the
last ~* bis auf den letzten
Mann; 2. die Menschheit;
3. Mann *m;* 4. Arbeiter *m;*
II *v* bemannen.
manage ['mænıdʒ] 1. hand-

haben; 2. leiten; 3. zustande
bringen; 4. auskommen
(*with* mit); ~**able** [-əbl]
1. handlich; 2. lenksam;
~**ment** [-mənt] 1. Handhabung *f*; 2. (Geschäfts-)Füh-
rung; Direktion *f*; ~**r** [-ə]
Direktor; Geschäftsführer
m.

mandatory ['mændətərɪ]
zwingend, verbindlich.

mane [meɪn] Mähne *f*.

manful ['mænfʊl] mannhaft.

manger ['meɪndʒə] (Futter-)
Krippe *f*.

mangle ['mæŋgl] entstellen
(*beyond recognition* bis zur
Unkenntlichkeit).

manhood ['mænhʊd]
1. Mannesalter *n*; 2. Männ-
lichkeit *f*.

mania ['meɪnjə] Manie; Be-
sessenheit *f*; *have a* ~ *for*
verrückt sein auf; ~**c**
['meɪnɪæk] Wahnsinnige(r)
m.

manicure ['mænɪˌkjʊə] **I** *s*
Maniküre *f*; **II** *v* maniküren.

manifest ['mænɪfest] **I** *adj*
offen (zutage liegend); augenscheinlich; **II** *v* 1. enthüllen; darlegen; 2. bekunden;
3. (*Geist*) erscheinen;
~**ation** [ˌmænɪfeˈsteɪʃn]
1. Kundgebung *f*; 2. deutli-
ches Anzeichen *n*.

manifold ['mænɪfəʊld] mannigfaltig.

manipulate [məˈnɪpjʊleɪt]
1. handhaben; bedienen;
2. *fig* manipulieren.

man|kind [mænˈkaɪnd] die
Menschheit; ~**ly** ['mænlɪ]
beherzt, tapfer.

manner ['mænə] 1. Art (u.
Weise) *f*; 2. *pl* Benehmen *n*.

manœuvre [məˈnuːvə] **I** *s*
Manöver *n a. fig*; **II** *v* ma-
növrieren *a. fig*.

manor ['mænə] Landgut *n*;
~-**house** [-haʊs] Herren-
haus *n*.

man-power ['mænˌpaʊə]
Arbeitspotential *n*.

mansion ['mænʃn] (herr-
schaftliches) Wohnhaus *n*.

manslaughter ['mænslɔːtə]
Totschlag *m*, fahrlässige Tötung *f*.

mantelpiece ['mæntlpiːs]
Kaminsims *m*.

mantle ['mæntl] **I** *s fig* Mantel *m*, Hülle *f*; **II** *v* ver-, einhüllen.

manual ['mænjʊəl] **I** *adj* ma-
nuell; **II** *s* Handbuch *n*.

manufacture
[ˌmænjuˈfæktʃə] **I** *s* 1. Herstellung *f*; 2. *pl* Erzeugnisse
n pl; **II** *v* herstellen; ~**r** [-rə]
Hersteller *m*.

manure [məˈnjʊə] **I** *s* Dünger *m*; **II** *v* düngen.

many ['menɪ] viel(e); *a great*
~ *times* sehr oft; *as* ~ *again*
noch mal so viele; ~ *a* man-
che(r, s), manch ein(e).

map [mæp] **I** *s* (Land-)Karte
f; (Stadt-)Plan *m*; **II** *v* 1. kar-
tographisch darstellen; 2. (~
out) einteilen; planen.

maple ['meɪpl] *bot* Ahorn *m*.

mar [mɑ:] verderben; beeinträchtigen.

maraud [məˈrɔ:d] (aus)plündern; **~er** [-ə] Plünderer *m.*

marble [ˈmɑ:bl] 1. Marmor *m;* 2. Murmel *f.*

March [mɑ:tʃ] März *m.*

march [mɑ:tʃ] I *v* marschieren; II *s* Marsch *m a. mus.*

mare [meə] Stute *f.*

margin [ˈmɑ:dʒɪn] 1. Rand *m;* 2. *com (profit ~)* Gewinnspanne *f;* 3. *by a narrow ~* mit knapper Not.

marine [məˈri:n] Marine *f; mercantile, merchant ~* Handelsmarine *f;* **~r** [ˈmærɪnə] Seemann *m.*

marital [ˈmærɪtl] ehelich.

maritime [ˈmærɪtaɪm] See-, Küsten-.

mark [mɑ:k] I *s* 1. Spur *f;* Fleck *m;* 2. Merkmal *n;* 3. (An-, Kenn-)Zeichen *n (of* von); 4. Zensur *f;* 5. *sport* Startlinie *f;* 6. *beside the ~* nicht zur Sache gehörig; *hit, miss the ~ (fig)* ins Schwarze treffen; das Ziel verfehlen; 7. *below the ~* unter dem Durchschnitt; II *v* 8. kennzeichnen, markieren; *(Ware)* auszeichnen; 9. sich merken; **~ off** abgrenzen; **~ out** 1. abgrenzen, -stecken; 2. aussuchen, -wählen *(for* für).

marked [mɑ:kt] merklich; auffällig.

market [ˈmɑ:kɪt] I *s* Markt *m;* II *v (auf dem Markt)* ver-, einkaufen.

marmalade [ˈmɑ:məleɪd] (Orangen-)Marmelade *f.*

marriage [ˈmærɪdʒ] Heirat *f (to* mit).

married [ˈmærɪd] verheiratet *(to* mit); *get ~* (sich ver)heiraten; **~ couple** Ehepaar *n.*

marrow [ˈmærəʊ] (Knochen-)Mark *n.*

marry [ˈmærɪ] 1. trauen; vermählen *(to s.o.* mit jdm); 2. heiraten *(s.o.* jdn).

marsh [mɑ:ʃ] Sumpf, Morast *m;* **~y** [ˈ-ɪ] sumpfig.

marshal [ˈmɑ:ʃl] I *s mil* Marschall *m;* II *v* (an)ordnen.

martial [ˈmɑ:ʃl] kriegerisch.

martyr [ˈmɑ:tə] I *s* Märtyrer *m a. fig;* II *v* martern.

marvel [ˈmɑ:vl] I *s* Wunder *n a. fig;* II *v* sich wundern *(at* über); **~(l)ous** [ˈmɑ:vələs] wunderbar.

mascot [ˈmæskət] Maskottchen *n.*

masculine [ˈmæskjʊlɪn] männlich *a. gram.*

mash [mæʃ] I *s* Brei *m;* II *v* (zer)mahlen, zerstoßen; **~ed potatoes** *pl* Kartoffelbrei *m.*

mask [mɑ:sk] I *s* Maske *f a. fig;* II *v* 1. maskieren; 2. *fig* verhüllen.

mason [ˈmeɪsn] Maurer *m.*

masquerade [ˌmæskəˈreɪd] I *s* Maskenball *m;* II *v* sich verkleiden *(as* als).

mass [mæs] I *s* 1. Masse *f a. phys;* 2. *the ~es* *pl* das Volk;

II *v* (sich) anhäufen; ~ **media** Massenmedien *n pl.*

Mass [mæs] *rel mus* Messe *f.*

massacre ['mæsəkə] Blutbad *n.*

massage ['mæsɑːʒ] I *s* Massage *f;* II *v* massieren.

massive ['mæsɪv] massiv, gediegen.

mast [mɑːst] Mast *m.*

master ['mɑːstə] I *s* 1. Meister *m; be o.'s own* ~ sein eigener Herr sein; 2. Hausherr *m;* 3. Lehrer *m;* II *v* meistern; beherrschen; ~**ly** [-lɪ] meisterhaft; ~**piece** [-piːs] Meisterstück *n; ~*y [-rɪ] 1. Herrschaft *f (over* über); 2. Beherrschung *f (of the violin* des Geigenspiels).

masticate ['mæstɪkeɪt] (zer)kauen.

mat [mæt] Matte *f a. sport.*

mat(t) [mæt], *Am* **matte** matt, glanzlos, stumpf.

match [mætʃ] I *s* 1. Streichholz *n; strike a* ~ ein Streichholz anzünden; 2. Gleich(wertig)e(r, s) *m f n; be more than a* ~ *for s.o.* jdm überlegen sein; 3. Gegenstück *n;* 4. Heirat *f; make a* ~ *(of it)* einander heiraten; 5. (Ehe-)Partner *m;* 6. Wettkampf *m; football* ~ Fußballspiel *n;* II *v* 7. ebenbürtig sein; 8. passen zu; 9. abstimmen auf; 10. *(im Wettstreit)* messen *(with, against* mit); ~**-box** ['-bɒks]

Streichholzschachtel *f;* ~**less** ['-lɪs] unübertroffen.

mate [meɪt] 1. Kamerad *m;* 2. *(Tiere)* Männchen, Weibchen *n.*

material [mə'tɪərɪəl] I *adj* 1. materiell, körperlich; 2. *jur* erheblich; II *s* Material *n,* Stoff *m (for* für); ~**ize** [-aɪz] Wirklichkeit werden.

matern|al [mə'tɜːnl] mütterlich; ~**ity** [mə'tɛːnətɪ] Mutterschaft *f.*

mathematics [ˌmæθə'mætɪks] *Abk* maths *pl mit sing* Mathematik *f.*

matri ['meɪtrɪ] *in Zssgen* Mutter-; ~**mony** ['mætrɪmənɪ] Ehe(stand *m,* -leben *n) f.*

matron ['meɪtrən] Hausdame, Vorsteherin, Oberin *f;* ~**ly** ['-lɪ] gesetzt.

matt, matte *s. mat.*

matter ['mætə] I *s* 1. Stoff *m,* Material *n;* 2. *phys* Materie *f;* 3. Thema *n;* 4. Wichtigkeit *f; it doesn't* ~ das macht nichts; 5. Angelegenheit *f; as a* ~ *of fact* tatsächlich; *what's the* ~? was ist (denn) los? 6. *printed* ~ Drucksache *f;* 7. *med* Eiter *m;* II *v* von Bedeutung sein *(to* für); *what does it* ~? was macht das (schon)? ~**-of-course** [ˌmætərəu'kɔːs] selbstverständlich; ~**-of-fact** [ˌmætərəu'fækt] realistisch.

mattress ['mætrɪs] Matratze *f.*

mature [məˈtjʊə] **I** adj 1. reif a. fig; 2. fin fällig; **II** v 3. reif werden; 4. fin fällig werden; ~**ity** [-rətɪ] 1. Reife f a. fig; 2. fin Fälligkeit f.

Maundy Thursday [ˈmɔːndɪ ˈθɜːzdɪ] Gründonnerstag m.

mauve [məʊv] malvenfarben.

maxim [ˈmæksɪm] Grundsatz m; ~**um** [-əm] **I** s pl a. -ma [-ə] Maximum n, Höchstmenge f; **II** adj: ~ amount Höchstbetrag m.

May [meɪ] Mai m; ~ **Day** 1. Mai m.

may [meɪ] (pret: might) mögen, können; dürfen; be that as it ~ wie dem auch sei; it ~ be too late es ist vielleicht zu spät; ~**be** [ˈmeɪbiː] vielleicht.

mayor [meə] Bürgermeister m.

maze [meɪz] Irrgarten m.

me [miː, mɪ] mich; mir; that's ~ (fam) ich bin's.

meadow [ˈmedəʊ] Wiese f.

meagre, Am **meager** [ˈmiːgə] 1. mager; 2. fig ärmlich.

meal [miːl] 1. Mahl(zeit f) n; 2. Mehl n.

mean [miːn] **I** v irr meant, meant [ment] 1. meinen, denken; 2. beabsichtigen; ~ business (fam) es ernst meinen; ~ mischief Böses im Schilde führen; 3. bedeuten; 4. ~ well es gut meinen (by s.o. mit jdm); **II** adj 5. durch-

schnittlich; 6. gemein; 7. schäbig, armselig.

meaning [ˈmiːnɪŋ] Zweck m; Bedeutung f.

meanness [miːnnɪs] 1. Gemeinheit f; 2. Armseligkeit f; 3. Knauserigkeit f.

means [miːnz] 1. pl a. mil sing Mittel n; by ~ of (ver)mittels; by all ~ auf alle Fälle; by no ~ auf keinen Fall; 2. pl Geldmittel n pl.

meantime [ˈmiːntaɪm] in the ~, ~**while** [ˈ-waɪl] inzwischen, mittlerweile.

measles [ˈmiːzlz] Masern pl.

measure [ˈmeʒə] **I** s 1. Maß n; 2. fig Maßstab m (of für); 3. Maßnahme f; take ~s against Maßnahmen ergreifen gegen; 4. mus Takt m; **II** v (ab-, aus-, ver)messen; ~**ment** [-mənt] 1. Messung f; 2. meist pl Maße n pl.

meat [miːt] Fleisch n.

mechanic [mɪˈkænɪk] 1. Mechaniker m; 2. pl mit sing phys tech Mechanik f; ~**al** [-l] mechanisch.

mechanism [ˈmekənɪzəm] Mechanismus m a. fig; ~**ize** [ˈmekənaɪz] mechanisieren.

medal [ˈmedl] Denkmünze f.

meddle [ˈmedl] sich einmischen (with, in in).

media [ˈmiːdjə] pl mit sing Massenkommunikationsmittel n pl; Medien pl.

mediate [ˈmiːdɪeɪt] vermitteln (between zwischen); ~**ion** [ˌmiːdɪˈeɪʃn] Vermitt-

lung *f;* ~**or** ['mi:dɪeɪtə]
(Ver-)Mittler *m.*

medic|al ['medɪkl] medizi-
nisch, ärztlich; ~**ament**
[me'dɪkəmənt] Arznei *f;*
~**ine** ['medsɪn] 1. Medizin,
Heilkunde *f;* 2. Arznei *f;*
~**-chest** Hausapotheke *f;*
3. *take o.'s* ~ *(fig)* in den
sauren Apfel beißen.

mediocr|e [ˌmiː'drəʊkə] (mit-
tel)mäßig; ~**ity**
[ˌmiː'drɒkrətɪ] Mittelmäßig-
keit *f.*

meditat|e ['medɪteɪt] grü-
beln *(on, upon* über); ~**ion**
[ˌmedɪ'teɪʃn] Nachdenken *n;*
Meditation *f.*

Mediterrannean
[ˌmedɪtə'reɪnjən] Mittel-
meer.

medium ['miːdjəm] **I** *s pl a.*
media [miː'djə] 1. Mittel *n;*
2. *(Spiritismus)* Medium *n;*
3. Mitte *f;* **II** *adj* durchschnittlich; mäßig.

medley ['medlɪ] Gemisch *n.*

meek [miːk] *as* ~ *as a lamb*
sanft wie ein Lamm.

meet [miːt] *irr met, met*
[met] 1. treffen, begegnen
(s.o. jdm); 2. bekannt werden
mit; 3. *(Rechnung)* bezahlen; ~ *s.o. half-way* jdm auf
halbem Wege entgegen-
kommen; 4. erfahren, erleben *(with s.th.* etw); ~ *with*
an accident verunglücken;
5. *make both ends* ~ (gerade) (mit s-m Gelde) auskommen.

meeting ['miːtɪŋ] Begegnung; Versammlung, Ta-
gung *f.*

melancholy ['melənkəlɪ]
I *s* Melancholie *f;* **II** *adj* me-
lancholisch; traurig.

mellow ['meləʊ] **I** *adj*
1. *(Frucht)* reif, süß; *(Farbe)*
satt; 2. *(Mensch)* abgeklärt;
II *v* reif, süß werden.

melod|ic [mɪ'lɒdɪk], ~**ious**
[mɪ'ləʊdjəs] melodisch; ~**y**
['melədɪ] Melodie *f.*

melon ['melən] *bot* Melone *f.*

melt [melt] 1. schmelzen;
2. sich auflösen.

member ['membə] Mitglied
n; ~**ship** [-ʃɪp] Mitglied-
schaft *f.*

memorable ['memərəbl]
denkwürdig.

memorandum
[ˌmemə'rændəm] *pl a. -da*
[-ə] 1. Notiz *f;* 2. kurze Mitteilung *f.*

memorial [mɪ'mɔːrɪəl] *war* ~
Gefallenen-, Kriegerdenk-
mal *n.*

memorize ['meməraɪz] sich
einprägen.

memory ['memərɪ] 1. Gedächtnis *n;* 2. *in* ~ *of* zur Erinnerung an.

menace ['menəs] **I** *s* Drohung *f;* **II** *v* (be)drohen.

mend [mend] ausbessern, reparieren.

mendacious [men'deɪʃəs]
unwahr.

mental ['mentl] geistig; ~
arithmetic Kopfrechnen *n;*

~ illness Geisteskrankheit *f;* **~ity** [men'tæləti] Mentalität *f.*

mention ['menʃn] **I** *s* Erwähnung *f;* **II** *v* erwähnen; *not to ~, without ~ing* ganz zu schweigen von; *don't ~ it!* keine Ursache (zu danken!).

menu ['menju:] Speisekarte *f,* Menü *n.*

mercantile ['mɜ:kəntaıl] **~ marine** Handelsmarine *f.*

mercenary ['mɜ:sınərı] **I** *adj (Person)* käuflich; gewinnsüchtig; **II** *s* Söldner *m.*

merchandise ['mɜ:tʃəndaız] Ware(n *pl*) *f.*

merchant ['mɜ:tʃənt] Kaufmann *m.*

merci|ful ['mɜ:sıfʊl] gnädig; barmherzig (*to* zu); **~less** ['-lıs] unbarmherzig.

mercury ['mɜ:kjʊrı] Quecksilber *n.*

mercy ['mɜ:sı] Gnade *f,* Erbarmen *n; at the ~ of* in der Gewalt *gen.*

mere [mıə], **~ly** ['-lı] bloß, nur.

merge [mɜ:dʒ] übergehen (*into* in); *com* fusionieren; **~r** ['-ə] *com* Fusion *f.*

meridian [mə'rıdıən] 1. *geog* Meridian *m;* 2. *fig* Gipfel *m.*

merit ['merıt] **I** *s* Verdienst *n;* **II** *v* verdienen.

merry ['merı] fröhlich; **~-go-round** [-gəʊ,raʊnd] Karussell *n.*

mesh [meʃ] 1. Masche *f;* 2. *pl* Netz(werk) *n.*

mess [mes] **I** *s* 1. *mil mar* Messe *f;* 2. (wüstes) Durcheinander *n; make a ~ of* verpfuschen; 3. *fam* Patsche, Klemme *f;* **II** *v* 4. (~ *up*) durchea.bringen; 5. *~ about* herumtrödeln.

message ['mesıdʒ] Botschaft; Nachricht *f.*

messenger ['mesındʒə] Bote *m.*

metal ['metl] 1. Metall *n;* 2. *Br* (*road-~*) Schotter *m;* **~lic** [mı'tælık] metallen; (*Glanz*) metallisch; **~lurgy** [me'tælədʒı] Hüttenkunde *f.*

meteorolog|ist [,mi:tjə'rɒlədʒıst] Meteorologe *m;* **~y** [-'rɒlədʒı] Meteorologie *f.*

meter ['mi:tə] 1. *gas, parking, water ~* Gas-, Park-, Wasseruhr *f;* 2. *Am s.* metre.

method ['meθəd] Methode *f;* **~ic(al)** [mı'θɒdık(l)] methodisch.

meticulous [mı'tıkjʊləs] peinlich genau.

metre, *Am* **meter** ['mi:tə] Meter *n od m.*

metropolis [mı'trɒpəlıs] Hauptstadt *f.*

mettle ['metl] Mut *m.*

micro|phone ['maıkrəfəʊn] Mikrophon *n;* **~scope** [-skəʊp] Mikroskop *n.*

midday ['mıdeı] Mittag *m.*

middle ['mıdl] 1. Mitte *f;* Mittelpunkt *m; in the ~ of the night* mitten in der

Nacht; 2. Taille *f; the* **M~ Ages** das Mittelalter; ~ **class** Mittelstand *m.*

middling ['mɪdlɪŋ] (mittel)mäßig.

midge [mɪdʒ] Mücke *f;* ~**t** ['-ɪt] Knirps, Zwerg *m.*

midnight ['mɪdnaɪt] Mitternacht *f.*

midst [mɪdst] *in the ~ of* mitten in.

mid|summer ['mɪd,sʌmə] Hochsommer *m;* ~**way** ['-weɪ] auf halbem Wege; ~**wife** ['-waɪf] *pl* midwives [-vz] Hebamme *f.*

might [maɪt] Macht, Kraft *f;* ~**y** ['-ɪ] mächtig, gewaltig.

migr|ant ['maɪgrənt] 1. Auswanderer, Nomade *m;* 2. *zoo* Zugvogel *m;* ~**ate** [maɪ'greɪt] (aus)wandern; ~**ation** [maɪ'greɪʃn] Wanderung *f.*

mild [maɪld] mild, sanft.

mildew ['mɪldjuː] Mehltau(pilz) *m.*

mile [maɪl] Meile *f (1,61 km); nautical ~* Seemeile *f (1,852 km);* ~**age, milage** ['-ɪdʒ] 1. zurückgelegte Strecke *f;* 2. Kilometergeld *n.*

military ['mɪlɪtərɪ] **I** *adj* militärisch; **II** *s: the ~ (mit pl)* das Militär.

milk [mɪlk] **I** *s* Milch *f a. bot;* **II** *v* melken; ~**man** ['-mən] Milchmann *m;* ~**y** ['-ɪ] milchig; *the M~ Way (astr)* die Milchstraße.

mill [mɪl] **I** *s* 1. Mühle *f;* 2. *(bes. Textil-)*Fabrik *f;* **II** *v (Korn)* mahlen; ~**er** ['-ə] Müller *m.*

millet ['mɪlɪt] Hirse *f.*

milliner ['mɪlɪnə] Modistin *f;* ~**y** ['-rɪ] Modewaren *f pl,* -geschäft *n.*

million ['mɪljən] Million *f.*

mimic ['mɪmɪk] **I** *s* Mime, Imitator *m;* **II** *v* nachahmen, -machen.

mince [mɪns] **I** *v* 1. *(Fleisch)* (zer)hacken, zerkleinern; 2. *not to ~ matters, o.'s words* kein Blatt vor den Mund nehmen; **II** *s* Hackfleisch *n;* ~**meat** ['-miːt] (süße) Pastetenfüllung *f.*

mind [maɪnd] **I** *s* 1. Gedächtnis *n; bring, call to s.o.'s ~* jdn erinnern an *a.* 2. Meinung *f; speak o.'s ~* offen s-e Meinung sagen; *to my ~* meines Erachtens; *change o.'s ~* s-e Meinung ändern; *make up o.'s ~* zu e-m Entschluß kommen; 3. Absicht *f; have a good ~ to* große Lust haben zu; 4. *absence, presence of ~* Geistesabwesenheit, -gegenwart *f;* 5. Gefühl *n,* Sinn *m,* Herz *n;* **II** *v* 6. bedenken, beachten; 7. ~ *the dog!* Warnung vor dem Hund! ~ *the step!* Achtung, Stufe! 8. ~ *your own business!* kümmern Sie sich um Ihre (eigenen) Angelegenheiten! 9. etw einzuwenden haben gegen; *never ~!*

macht nichts! schon gut! *I don't* ~ meinetwegen!

mindful ['maɪndful] *be* ~ *of* achten auf.

mine [maɪn] **I** *prn* der, die, das mein(ig)e; *a friend of* ~ e-r meiner Freunde; **II** *s* 1. Bergwerk *n;* 2. *mil mar* Mine *f;* **III** *v* 3. graben (*for* nach); 4. *mil* Minen legen; ~**r** ['-ə] Bergmann *m.*

mineral ['mɪnərəl] **I** *s* Mineral *n;* **II** *adj* mineralisch.

mingle ['mɪŋgl] (sich) mischen (*with* unter).

miniature ['mɪnətʃə] Miniatur *f;* ~ **camera** Kleinbildkamera *f.*

minimum ['mɪnɪməm] *pl a.* -**ma** ['-ə] **I** *s* Minimum *n;* **II** *adj:* ~ **wage** Mindestlohn *m.*

mining ['maɪnɪŋ] Bergbau *m.*

minister ['mɪnɪstə] 1. Minister *m;* 2. Gesandte(r) *m;* 3. Geistliche(r) *m.*

ministry ['mɪnɪstrɪ] Ministerium *n.*

mink [mɪŋk] *zoo* Nerz *m (a. Pelz).*

minor ['maɪnə] **I** *adj* kleiner, gering(fügig)er; **II** *s* 1. *mus* Moll *n;* 2. Minderjährige(r) *m;* 3. *Am (Univ.)* Nebenfach *n;* ~**ity** [maɪˈnɒrətɪ] Minderheit *f.*

mint [mɪnt] **I** *s* 1. *bot* Minze *f;* 2. Münz(stätt)e *f;* **II** *v* (*Geld*) prägen.

minuet [ˌmɪnjuˈet] Menuett *n.*

minus ['maɪnəs] **I** *prp* weniger, minus; **II** *s* 1. (~ *sign*) Minuszeichen *n;* 2. Fehlbetrag *m.*

minute **I** *s* ['mɪnɪt] 1. Minute *f; in a* ~ sofort; *to the* ~ pünktlich; 2. *pl* Protokoll *n;* **II** *adj* [maɪˈnjuːt] 3. sehr klein; *fig* unbedeutend; 4. genau; ~**ly** [maɪˈnjuːtlɪ] ganz genau.

miracle ['mɪrəkl] Wunder *n a. fam fig;* ~**ulous** [mɪˈrækjuləs] wunderbar.

mirror ['mɪrə] **I** *s* Spiegel *m a. fig;* **II** *v* (wider)spiegeln.

mirth [mɜːθ] Freude *f,* Frohsinn *m.*

misadventure [ˌmɪsədˈventʃə] Mißgeschick *n;* Unglück(sfall *m*) *n.*

misapprehend ['mɪsˌæprɪˈhend] mißverstehen.

misbehave [ˌmɪsbɪˈheɪv] sich schlecht benehmen.

miscalculate [ˌmɪsˈkælkjuleɪt] falsch (be)rechnen.

miscarriage [ˌmɪsˈkærɪdʒ] 1. Mißlingen *n;* 2. Fehlgeburt *f.*

miscellaneous [ˌmɪsɪˈleɪnjəs] 1. ge-, vermischt; 2. mannigfaltig; vielseitig.

mischance [ˌmɪsˈtʃɑːns] Mißgeschick *n.*

mischie|f ['mɪstʃɪf] 1. Schaden *m; do s.o. a* ~ jdm schaden; 2. Unfug *m;* ~**vous**

['mɪstʃɪvəs] boshaft, mutwillig.

misconduct [ˌmɪs'kɒndʌkt]
1. schlechte Geschäftsführung f; 2. schlechte(s) Benehmen n.

misdeed [ˌmɪs'di:d] Missetat f.

miser ['maɪzə] Geizhals m.

miserable ['mɪzərəbl]
1. elend (from vor); 2. unglücklich; 3. erbärmlich.

miserly ['maɪzəlɪ] geizig.

misery ['mɪzərɪ] Elend n.

misfortune [mɪs'fɔ:tʃən] Mißgeschick n.

misgiving [mɪs'gɪvɪŋ] (oft pl) Befürchtung f.

misguide [ˌmɪs'gaɪd] irreführen.

mishap ['mɪshæp] Unfall m; mot Panne f.

misinterpret [ˌmɪsɪn'tɜ:prɪt] mißdeuten.

misjudge [ˌmɪs'dʒʌdʒ] falsch (be)urteilen.

mislead [ˌmɪs'li:d] irr misled, misled [-'led] irreführen.

misplace [ˌmɪs'pleɪs] verlegen, verlieren.

misprint ['mɪsprɪnt] Druckfehler m.

miss [mɪs] I v 1. (Ziel) verfehlen; (Gelegenheit, Zug) verpassen; 2. übersehen, -hören; nicht verstehen; 3. (sehr) entbehren; 4. be ~ing fehlen; II s Fehlschuß, -schlag m.

Miss [mɪs] Fräulein n.

misshapen [ˌmɪs'ʃeɪpən] mißgestalt(et).

missile ['mɪsaɪl] guided ~ ferngesteuerte Rakete f.

missing ['mɪsɪŋ] 1. fehlend; 2. mil vermißt.

mission ['mɪʃn] 1. Aufgabe f; 2. rel Mission f; 3. pol Gesandtschaft f; ~ary [-ərɪ] Missionar m.

mist [mɪst] (feiner) Nebel m.

mistake [mɪ'steɪk] I v irr mistook [-tʊk], mistaken [-teɪkən] 1. mißverstehen; 2. verwechseln (for mit); II s Fehler m; by ~ irrtümlich; ~n [-ən] be ~ sich irren (about s.th. in e-r S).

mister ['mɪstə] (Mr) Herr m.

mistletoe ['mɪsltəʊ] bot Mistel f.

mistress ['mɪstrɪs] 1. (Haus-) Herrin f; 2. Lehrerin f; 3. Geliebte f; 4. abgekürzt: Mrs ['mɪsɪz] Frau f.

mistrust [ˌmɪs'trʌst] mißtrauen (s.o., s.th. jdm, e-r S).

misty ['mɪstɪ] neblig.

misunderstand [ˌmɪsʌndə'stænd] irr misunderstood, misunderstood [-'stʊd] mißverstehen; ~ing [-ɪŋ] Mißverständnis n.

misuse I v [ˌmɪs'ju:z] mißbrauchen; II s [ˌmɪs'ju:s] Mißbrauch m.

mite [maɪt] zoo Milbe f.

mitigate ['mɪtɪgeɪt] mildern.

mitten ['mɪtn] Fausthandschuh m.

mix [mɪks] 1. (ver)mischen;

2. verkehren (*with* mit); 3. ~
up in (*fig*) verwickeln in;
~**ture** ['-tʃə] Mischung *f.*
moan [məun] **I** *s* Stöhnen *n*
(a. d. Windes); **II** *v* stöhnen,
ächzen.
mob [mɒb] **I** *s* Pöbel *m;* **II** *v*
herfallen über (*s.o.* jdn).
mobil|ity [məu'bɪlətɪ] Be-
weglichkeit *f;* ~**ize**
['məubɪlaɪz] mobilisieren.
mock [mɒk] **I** *v* 1. verspotten; sich lustig machen (*at*
über); 2. trotzen (*s.o.* jdm);
II *adj* nachgemacht; ~**ery**
['-ərɪ] 1. Spott *m;* 2. Gespött
n; ~-**up** ['-ʌp] Modell *n.*
mode ['məud] 1. Art u. Weise *f;* 2. Mode *f.*
model ['mɒdl] **I** *s* Modell *n;*
II *v* modellieren; **III** *adj* bei-
spielhaft.
moderat|e I *adj* ['mɒdərət]
(ge)mäßig(t); **II** *v* ['-reɪt]
(sich) mäßigen; ~**ion**
[ˌmɒdə'reɪʃn] Mäßigung *f.*
modern ['mɒdən] modern,
neuzeitlich; ~**ize** [-aɪz] mo-
dernisieren.
modest ['mɒdɪst] bescheiden; ~**y** [-ɪ] Bescheidenheit
f.
modi|fication [ˌmɒdɪfɪ'keɪʃn]
(Ab-)Änderung *f;* ~**fy**
['mɒdɪfaɪ] 1. abändern;
2. abschwächen.
module ['mɒdjuːl] *(Raum-
fahrt)* Kapsel *f; lunar* ~
Mondfähre *f.*
moist [mɔɪst] feucht; ~**en**

['mɔɪsn] befeuchten; ~**ure**
['-ʃə] Feuchtigkeit *f.*
molar ['məulə] Back(en)zahn
m.
mold *s. mould.*
mole [məul] 1. Muttermal *n;*
2. Maulwurf *m;* 3. Hafendamm *m.*
molest [məu'lest] belästigen.
molt *s. moult.*
moment ['məumənt] 1. Augenblick *m; to the* ~ pünktlich; *(just) a* ~, *please!* e-n
Augenblick, bitte! 2. *of* ~
von Bedeutung (*to* für);
~**ary** ['məuməntərɪ] flüchtig; ~**ous** [məu'mentəs] fol-
genschwer.
monarch ['mɒnək] Monarch
m; ~**y** [-ɪ] Monarchie *f.*
monastery ['mɒnəstərɪ]
Kloster *n.*
Monday ['mʌndɪ] Montag *m.*
monetary ['mʌnɪtərɪ] Wäh-
rungs-.
money ['mʌnɪ] Geld *n; get
o.'s* ~*'s worth* auf s-e Kosten
kommen; ~-**order** [-ˌɔːdə]
Postanweisung *f.*
mongrel ['mʌŋɡrəl] *zoo*
Mischling *m.*
monitor ['mɒnɪtə] **I** *s*
1. *(Schule)* Klassenordner
m; 2. *radio TV* Kontroll-
empfänger *m;* **II** *v* abhören.
monk [mʌŋk] Mönch *m.*
monkey ['mʌŋkɪ] Affe *m;*
~-**wrench** [-rentʃ] Univer-
salschraubenschlüssel *m.*
monologue ['mɒnəlɒɡ] Mo-
nolog *m.*

monopol|ize [mə'nɒpəlaɪz] monopolisieren; **~y** [-lɪ] Monopol n a. fig.

monoton|ous [mə'nɒtənəs] monoton; **~y** [mə'nɒtənɪ] Monotonie f.

monster ['mɒnstə] Ungeheuer n.

monstr|osity [mɒn'strɒsətɪ] Ungeheuerlichkeit f; **~ous** ['mɒnstrəs] 1. riesig; 2. scheußlich.

month [mʌnθ] Monat m; **~ly** ['-lɪ] **I** adj monatlich; **~** season ticket Monatsfahrkarte f; **II** s Monatsschrift f.

monument ['mɒnjʊmənt] Denkmal n; **~al** [ˌmɒnjʊ'mentl] gewaltig.

mood [muːd] Stimmung, Laune f; **~y** [-ɪ] launisch.

moon [muːn] Mond m; **~light** ['-laɪt] Mondschein m; **~lit** ['-lɪt] mondbeschienen, -hell.

moor [mʊə] **I** s Heide(land n) f; **II** v (Schiff) vertäuen.

moose [muːs] inv zoo Amerikanische(r) Elch m.

moot [muːt] **I** v diskutieren; **II** adj: **~** point strittige(r) Punkt m.

mop [mɒp] **I** s Mop m; **II** v (~ up) auf-, abwischen.

moral ['mɒrəl] **I** adj moralisch; **II** s Moral f; **~e** [mɒ'rɑːl] Stimmung f; **~ity** [mə'rælətɪ] Sittlichkeit f.

morbid ['mɔːbɪd] krank(haft).

more [mɔː] **I** adj mehr; **II** adv: once **~** noch einmal;

~ or less mehr oder weniger; **~** and **~** immer mehr; **III** s: what **~**? was noch?; **~over** [mɔː'rəʊvə] überdies.

morning ['mɔːnɪŋ] Morgen; Vormittag m; in the **~** am Morgen, morgens; this **~** heute morgen; tomorrow **~** morgen früh; good **~**! guten Morgen!

Morocco [mə'rɒkəʊ] Marokko n.

morose [mə'rəʊs] mürrisch.

morph|ia ['mɔːfɪə], **~in(e)** ['mɔːfiːn] Morphium n.

morsel ['mɔːsl] Bissen m.

mortal ['mɔːtl] **I** adj 1. sterblich; 2. tödlich; **II** s Sterbliche(r) m; **~ity** [mɔː'tælətɪ] Sterblichkeit(sziffer) f.

mortar ['mɔːtə] 1. Mörser m; 2. Mörtel m.

mortgage ['mɔːgɪdʒ] **I** s Hypothek f; **II** v verpfänden; **~e** [ˌmɔːgə'dʒiː] Hypothekengläubiger m; **~r, mortgagor** [ˌmɔːgə'dʒɔː] Hypothekenschuldner m.

mortific|ation [ˌmɔːtɪfɪ'keɪʃn] Demütigung, Kränkung f; **~y** ['mɔːtɪfaɪ] demütigen, beschämen, kränken.

mortuary ['mɔːtjʊərɪ] Leichenhalle f.

mosque [mɒsk] rel Moschee f.

mosquito [mə'skiːtəʊ] pl -toes Moskito m.

moss [mɒs] Moos n; **~y** ['-ɪ] moosig.

most [məʊst] **I** adj meist; **~**

people die meisten Leute;
II *adv* am meisten; **III** *s: at
(the)* ~ höchstens; **~ly** ['-lɪ]
meist(ens); im wesentlichen.
moth [mɒθ] *clothes-~* Klei-
dermotte *f;* **~-eaten** ['-,iːtn]
mottenzerfressen.
mother ['mʌðə] Mutter *f;*
~hood [-hʊd] Mutterschaft
f; **~-in-law** [-rɪnlɔː] *pl* ~s-
-in-law Schwiegermutter *f;*
~ly [-lɪ] mütterlich; **~-of-
-pearl** [,-rəʊˈpɜːl] Perlmut-
ter *f;* ~ **tongue** Muttersprache *f.*
motion ['məʊʃn] 1. Bewegung *f; put, set in* ~ in Gang
bringen; 2. *parl* Antrag *m;*
~less [-lɪs] bewegungs-,
reglos; ~ **picture** Film *m.*
motiv|ate ['məʊtɪveɪt] moti-
vieren; **~e** ['məʊtɪv] **I** *s* Be-
weggrund *m (for* zu); **II** *adj:*
~ **power** Triebkraft *f a. fig.*
motor ['məʊtə] **I** *s* Motor *m;*
II *v* (mit einem Auto) fahren; **~-bike** [-baɪk],
~-cycle [-,saɪkl] Mofa, Moped *n;* **~-boat** [-bəʊt] Mo-
torboot *n;* **~e** [-kə] Au-
to(mobil) *n;* **~ing** [-rɪŋ] Mo-
torsport *m;* **~ist** [-rɪst]
Kraft-, Autofahrer *m;* **~ize**
[-raɪz] motorisieren;
~-scooter [-,skuːtə] Mo-
torroller *m;* **~-vehicle**
[-,viːɪkl] Kraftfahrzeug *n;*
~way [-weɪ] *Br* Autobahn,
Schnellstraße *f.*
mottle ['mɒtl] sprenkeln.
mo(u)ld [məʊld] **I** *s* 1. (Guß-)

Form *f;* 2. Schimmel *m;* **II** *v*
formen; (be-, ver)modern; **~y** ['-ɪ] schimm(e)lig.
mo(u)lt [məʊlt] sich mau-
sern.
mount [maʊnt] **I** *v* 1. (be-,
auf-, hinauf)steigen; 2. *tech*
montieren; **II** *s: M~ (in Ei-
gennamen)* Berg *m.*
mountain ['maʊntɪn] 1. (hoher) Berg *m;* 2. *fig* (großer)
Haufen *m;* 3. *pl* Gebirge *n;*
~eer [,maʊntɪˈnɪə] Bergsteiger *m;* **~ous** [-əs] gebirgig.
mourn [mɔːn] trauern (*for,
over* um); **~er** ['-ə] Leidtra-
gende(r) *m;* **~ful** ['-fʊl] traurig; **~ing** ['-ɪŋ] Trauer *f; go
into* ~ Trauer(kleidung) anlegen.
mouse [maʊz] *pl* mice
[maɪs] Maus *f;* **~-trap**
['maʊstræp] Mausefalle *f.*
m(o)ustache [məˈstɑːʃ]
Schnurrbart *m.*
mouth [maʊθ] *pl* ~s [-ðz]
1. Mund *m a. fig; by word
of* ~ mündlich; 2. Maul *n,*
Schnauze *f;* 3. *(Fluß)* Mündung *f;* **~ful** ['-fʊl] Bissen *m;*
~-organ ['-,ɔːgən] Mund-
harmonika *f;* **~piece** ['-piːs]
1. *(Blasinstrument)* Mundstück *n;* 2. *fig* Sprachrohr *n.*
movable ['muːvəbl] beweglich *a. jur* (Habe).
move [muːv] **I** *v* 1. (sich) bewegen; ~ *on* weitergehen;
2. *be* ~d *to tears* zu Tränen
gerührt sein; 3. umziehen; ~
in, out ein-, ausziehen;

4. *(Brettspiel)* ziehen; **II** *s*
5. Bewegung *f;* Schritt *m fig (zu e-m Ziel); on the* ~ in Bewegung; 6. Umzug *m;*
7. *(Brettspiel)* Zug *m;*
~**ment** ['-mənt] Bewegung *f.*

movie ['mu:vɪ] *fam* Film *m; go to the* ~s ins Kino gehen.

moving ['mu:vɪŋ] 1. beweglich; 2. bewegend; 3. *fig* rührend.

mow [məʊ] *a. irr mowed, mown* [-n] mähen.

Mr ['mɪstə] Herr *m (vor Namen).*

Mrs ['mɪsɪz] Frau *f (vor Namen).*

much [mʌtʃ] **I** *adj* viel; **II** *s* viel(es); *make* ~ *of* viel Aufhebens machen von; *I thought as* ~ das dachte ich mir schon; **III** *adv* sehr; viel; oft; (so) ziemlich, beinahe, fast, ungefähr.

mucous ['mju:kəs] *physiol* schleimig; ~ *membrane* Schleimhaut *f.*

mud [mʌd] Schlamm; Schmutz *m;* ~**dy** ['-ɪ] 1. schlammig; 2. trübe; ~**guard** ['-ga:d] *(Auto)* Kotflügel *m; (Fahrrad)* Schutzblech *n.*

muddle ['mʌdl] **I** *v* in Unordnung bringen; *fig* verwirren; **II** *s* Durcheinander *n.*

muffle ['mʌfl] 1. *(~ up)* einmumme(l)n; verhüllen;
2. *(Schall)* dämpfen; ~**r** ['-ə]

1. Schal *m;* 2. *tech Am* Schalldämpfer *m.*

mug [mʌg] Krug *m*, Becher *m.*

muggy ['mʌgɪ] schwül.

mule [mju:l] Maulesel *m.*

mulled wine [mʌld waɪn] Glühwein *m.*

multi|- ['mʌltɪ] *pref* viel-, mehr-; ~**farious** [,-'feərɪəs] vielfältig; ~**ple** ['mʌltɪpl] viel-, mehrfach *a. el;* ~**plication** [,mʌltɪplɪ'keɪʃn] *math* Multiplikation *f;* ~**ply** ['mʌltɪplaɪ] (sich) vervielfältigen; *math* multiplizieren *(by* mit); ~**tude** ['mʌltɪtju:d] 1. große Menge *f;* 2. *the* ~ die große Masse *(Menschen).*

mum [mʌm] **I** *adj: keep* ~ den Mund halten; **II** *s fam* Mama *f.*

mumble ['mʌmbl] 1. murmeln; 2. mummeln.

mummy ['mʌmɪ] 1. Mumie *f a. fig;* 2. *fam* Mama *f.*

mumps [mʌmps] Mumps *m.*

munch [mʌntʃ] mampfen.

mundane [,mʌn'deɪn] 1. irdisch, weltlich; 2. alltäglich.

municipal [mju:'nɪsɪpl] städtisch; Gemeinde-; ~**ity** [mju:,nɪsɪ'pælətɪ] 1. Stadt *f* mit Selbstverwaltung;
2. Stadtverwaltung *f.*

mural ['mjʊərəl] *(~ painting)* Wandgemälde *n,* -malerei *f.*

murder ['mɜ:də] **I** *s* Mord *m (of* an); **II** *v* (er)morden; ~**er**

[-rə] Mörder *m;* **~ous**
[-rəs] mörderisch *a. fig.*

murmur ['mɜ:mə] **I** *s* Murmeln *n;* **II** *v* murmeln.

musc|le ['mʌsl] Muskel *m;*
~ular ['mʌskjʊlə] muskulös.

muse [mju:z] (nach)sinnen,
grübeln (*on, over, upon*
über).

museum [mju:'zɪəm] Museum *n.*

mushroom ['mʌʃrʊm] **I** *s*
(eßbarer) Pilz *m;* **II** *v* wie
Pilze aus dem Boden schießen.

music ['mju:zɪk] 1. Musik *f;*
2. Noten *f pl;* **~al** [-l] Mu-
sik-; musikalisch; **~-hall**
[-hɔ:l] *Br* Varieté(theater) *n;*
~ian [mju:'zɪʃn] Musiker *m.*

muslin ['mʌzlɪn] Musselin *m.*

mussel ['mʌsl] (Mies-, Fluß-)
Muschel *f.*

must [mʌst] **I** *v* 1. müssen;
2. dürfen; *you ~ not* du
darfst nicht; **II** *s: (fam) this
book is a ~* dieses Buch
muß man gelesen haben.

mustard ['mʌstəd] Senf *m a.
bot.*

muster ['mʌstə] 1. (sich
ver)sammeln; 2. *~ (up)
courage* allen Mut zs.neh-
men.

musty ['mʌstɪ] muffig.

mutable ['mju:təbl] 1. veränderlich; 2. unbeständig.

mutation [mju:'teɪʃn] (Ver-)
Änderung *f.*

mute [mju:t] **I** *adj* stumm;
II *s* Stumme(r) *m.*

mutilat|e ['mju:tɪleɪt] ver-
stümmeln *a. fig;* **~ion**
[ˌmju:tɪ'leɪʃn] Verstümme-
lung *f.*

mutin|eer [ˌmju:tɪ'nɪə] Meu-
terer *m;* **~y** ['mju:tɪnɪ] **I** *s*
Meuterei *f;* **II** *v* meutern.

mutter ['mʌtə] (vor sich
hin)murmeln.

mutton ['mʌtn] Hammel-
fleisch *n;* **~ chop** Hammel-
kotelett *n.*

mutual ['mju:tʃʊəl] 1. gegen-,
wechselseitig; 2. gemeinsam.

muzzle ['mʌzl] **I** *s* 1. Schnauze *f,* Maul *n;* 2. Maulkorb *m;*
II *v* e-n Maulkorb anlegen
(*an animal* e-m Tier).

my [maɪ] mein(e).

myopic [maɪ'ɒpɪk] kurzsichtig.

myrtle ['mɜ:tl] Myrte *f.*

myself [maɪ'self] 1. ich
(selbst); 2. mich, mir.

mysterious [mɪ'stɪərɪəs] ge-
heimnisvoll; **~y** ['mɪstərɪ]
Geheimnis, Rätsel *n.*

mystif|ication
[ˌmɪstɪfɪ'keɪʃn] 1. Irreführung
f; 2. Verwirrung *f;* **~y**
['mɪstɪfaɪ] 1. täuschen; fop-
pen; 2. verwirren.

myth [mɪθ] Mythos *m a. fig.*

N

nag [næg] **I** herumnörgeln.
nail [neɪl] **I** s Nagel m; **II** v
fest-, annageln; **~-varnish**
['-ˌvɑːnɪʃ] , **~-polish** ['-ˌpɒlɪʃ]
Nagellack m.
naïve, naive [nɑː'iːv, neɪv]
naiv, unbefangen.
naked ['neɪkɪd] 1. nackt,
bloß; 2. kahl; **~ness** [-nɪs]
Nacktheit f.
name [neɪm] **I** s 1. Name m;
call s.o. ~s jdn beschimpfen;
2. (good ~) gute(r) Ruf m;
II v 3. (be)nennen (after
nach); 4. ernennen (for zu);
~less ['-lɪs] namenlos; **~ly**
['-lɪ] nämlich; **~sake** ['-seɪk]
Namensvetter m.
nap [næp] have, take a ~ ein
Nickerchen machen.
napkin ['næpkɪn] 1. Serviette
f; 2. Windel f.
narcotic [nɑː'kɒtɪk] 1. Betäu-
bungsmittel n; 2. Rausch-
gift(süchtiger m) n.
narrate [nə'reɪt] erzählen;
~ion [nə'reɪʃn] Erzählung f;
~ive ['nærətɪv] **I** adj erzäh-
lend; **II** s Erzählung f; **~or**
[nə'reɪtə] Erzähler m.
narrow ['nærəʊ] **I** adj 1. eng,
schmal; 2. fig beschränkt;
II s Enge f; **III** v (sich) verengen; **~-minded**
[-ˌmaɪndɪd] engstirnig.
nasty ['nɑːstɪ] 1. schmutzig;
2. scheußlich; 3. gefährlich.

nation ['neɪʃn] Volk n, Nation f; **~al** ['næʃənl] **I** adj
national; staatlich; **II** s
Staatsangehörige(r) m; **~al-
ity** [ˌnæʃə'næləti] Staatsangehörigkeit f; **~alize**
['næʃnəlaɪz] 1. verstaatlichen; 2. einbürgern.
native ['neɪtɪv] **I** adj 1. angeboren, natürlich; 2. einheimisch; 3. Heimat-; ~ country Vaterland n; ~ tongue
Muttersprache f; **II** s Einhei-
mische(r) m.
natural ['nætʃrəl] 1. natürlich; 2. angeboren; ~ gas
Erdgas n; **~ize** [-aɪz] einbürgern a. fig.
nature ['neɪtʃə] Natur f.
naught, nought [nɔːt] Null
f.
naughty ['nɔːtɪ] ungezogen.
nausea ['nɔːsɪə] Übelkeit f;
Brechreiz m; **~ous** [-s]
ekelhaft.
nautical ['nɔːtɪkl] nautisch; ~
mile Seemeile f.
naval ['neɪvl] See-, Marine-;
~ base Flottenstützpunkt
m.
nave [neɪv] 1. (Kirche) Schiff
n; 2. (Rad-)Nabe f.
navel ['neɪvl] Nabel m.
navigable ['nævɪgəbl]
schiffbar; **~ate** ['nævɪgeɪt]
1. navigieren; 2. (mit dem
Schiff) fahren; **~ation**

[ˌnævɪˈgeɪʃn] 1. Schiffahrt f; 2. Navigation f a. aero; ~ator [ˈnævɪgeɪtə] 1. Seefahrer m; 2. Steuermann m.

navy [ˈneɪvɪ] (Kriegs-)Marine f, Seestreitkräfte f pl.

near [nɪə] I adj nahe; the ~est way der kürzeste Weg; II adv in der Nähe; ~ at hand bei der Hand; kurz bevorstehend; III prp nahe an dat, nahe bei; IV v sich nähern; ~by [ˈ-baɪ] in der Nähe (befindlich); ~ly [ˈ-lɪ] beinahe; ~-sighted [ˌ-ˈsaɪtɪd] kurzsichtig.

neat [niːt] 1. ordentlich, sauber; 2. hübsch, nett.

necess|ary [ˈnesəsərɪ] notwendig; ~itate [nɪˈsesɪteɪt] erfordern; ~ity [nɪˈsesɪtɪ] Notwendigkeit f.

neck [nek] Hals m; Genick n; ~lace [ˈ-lɪs] Halskette f; ~tie [ˈ-taɪ] Krawatte f.

need [niːd] I s 1. Notwendigkeit f (for zu); 2. pl Bedürfnisse n pl; 3. Not f; II v 4. brauchen, benötigen; 5. ~ to do tun müssen; he ~ not do it er braucht es nicht zu tun; ~ful [ˈ-fʊl] notwendig.

needle [ˈniːdl] Nadel f.

needless [ˈniːdlɪs] unnötig.

needy [ˈniːdɪ] bedürftig, arm.

negat|ion [nɪˈgeɪʃn] Verneinung f; ~ive [ˈnegətɪv] I adj 1. verneinend; 2. negativ; II s 3. Verneinung f; 4. phot Negativ n.

neglect [nɪˈglekt] I v vernachlässigen; II s Vernachlässigung f; ~ful [-fʊl] nachlässig.

neglig|ence [ˈneglɪdʒəns] Nachlässigkeit f; ~ent [ˈ-t] nachlässig (of gegen); ~ible [ˈneglɪdʒəbl] geringfügig.

negoti|able [nɪˈgəʊʃjəbl] com verkäuflich; übertragbar; ~ate [nɪˈgəʊʃɪeɪt] 1. verhandeln (über); 2. (Hindernis) überwinden; ~ation [nɪˌgəʊʃɪˈeɪʃn] Verhandlung f.

Negr|ess [ˈniːgrɪs] Negerin f; ~o [ˈniːgrəʊ] pl -groes Neger m.

neigh [neɪ] wiehern.

neighbo(u)r [ˈneɪbə] Nachbar(in f) m; ~hood [-hʊd] 1. Nachbarschaft f; 2. in the ~ of in der Nähe von; ~ing [ˈ-rɪŋ] benachbart.

neither [ˈnaɪðə] I adj, prn keine(r) (von beiden); II conj auch nicht; ~ ... nor weder ... noch.

nephew [ˈnevjuː] Neffe m.

nerve [nɜːv] 1. Nerv m; 2. Mut m; 3. fam Frechheit f.

nervous [ˈnɜːvəs] 1. ~ breakdown Nervenzusammenbruch m; 2. nervös; ~ness [-nɪs] Nervosität f.

nest [nest] I s Nest n; II v nisten; ~le [ˈnesl] 1. (~ down) es sich bequem machen; 2. ~ up sich anschmiegen (to, against an).

net [net] I s Netz n; II adj netto.

Netherlands, *the* [neðələndz] Niederlande *pl.*

network ['netwɜ:k] (Straßen-)Netz *n a. fig.*

neur|osis [ˌnjuə'rəusɪs] Neurose *f;* **~otic** [-'rɒtɪk] neurotisch.

neutral ['nju:trəl] neutral; **~ity** [nju:'træləti] Neutralität *f.*

never ['nevə] nie(mals); ~ *mind* das macht nichts; **~theless** [ˌ-ðə'les] trotzdem.

new [nju:] neu; *(Brot)* frisch; **~ly** ['-lɪ] neulich.

news [nju:z] *pl mit sing* Neuigkeit(en *pl*); (Zeitungs-, Radio-)Nachricht(en *pl*) *f;* **~agent** ['-ˌeɪdʒənt], *Am* **~dealer** ['-ˌdi:lə] Zeitungshändler *m;* **~paper** ['-ˌpeɪpə] Zeitung *f;* **~reel** ['-ri:l] *film* Wochenschau *f.*

New Year's |Day Neujahrstag *m;* ~ **Eve** Silvesterabend *m.*

New Zealand [ˌnju:'zi:lənd] **I** *s* Neuseeland *n;* **II** *adj* neuseeländisch; **~er** [-ə] Neuseeländer *m.*

next [nekst] **I** *adj* nächst, folgend; ~ *door* nebenan; ~ *to* neben; **II** *adv* dann, darauf; *what* ~? was nun, was noch? **III** *s:* der, die, das Nächste.

nibble ['nɪbl] knabbern.

nice [naɪs] 1. nett, schön, hübsch *(a. iron)*; 2. fein.

nick [nɪk] 1. Kerbe *f;* 2. *in the*

~ *of time* gerade im richtigen Augenblick.

nickname ['nɪkneɪm] Spitzname *m.*

niece [ni:s] Nichte *f.*

niggardly ['nɪgədlɪ] knauserig, geizig.

night [naɪt] Nacht *f a. fig;* (später) Abend *m; at* ~*, by* ~ abends; *have a* ~ *out* ausgehen; **~club** ['-klʌb] Nachtlokal *n;* **~-dress** ['-dres], **~gown** ['-gaʊn] (Damen-)Nachthemd *n;* **~fall** ['-fɔ:l] Einbruch *m* der Nacht.

nightingale ['naɪtɪŋgeɪl] Nachtigall *f.*

night|ly ['naɪtlɪ] (all)nächtlich; **~mare** ['-meə] Alptraum *m a. fig.*

nil [nɪl] Nichts *n;* Null *f.*

nimble ['nɪmbl] wendig, flink.

nine [naɪn] **I** *adj* neun; **II** *s* Neun *f;* **~ty** ['naɪntɪ] neunzig.

ninth [naɪnθ] **I** *adj* neunt; **II** *s* 1. Neuntel *n;* 2. Neunte(r) *m.*

nip [nɪp] **I** *v* 1. kneifen; 2. ~ *in the bud* im Keim ersticken; **II** *s* 3. *(Kälte)* Schneiden *n;* 4. Schlückchen *n.*

nipple ['nɪpl] Brustwarze *f.*

nitrogen ['naɪtrədʒən] Stickstoff *m.*

no [nəʊ] **I** *adv* nein; nicht; **II** *adj* kein(e); ~ *one* keiner, niemand; *in* ~ *time* im Nu; ~ *smoking!* Rauchen verboten! **III** *s pl* noes Nein *n.*

nobility [nəʊ'bɪlətɪ] Adel *m.*

noble ['nəubl] 1. adlig; 2. *fig* edel; ~**man** ['-mən] Adlige(r) *m.*

nobody ['nəubədɪ] niemand.

nod [nɒd] **I** *v* (zu)nicken (*to s.o.* jdm); **II** *s* Nicken *n.*

noise [nɔɪz] Geräusch *n;* Lärm *m;* ~**y** ['-ɪ] laut; lärmend.

nominal ['nɒmɪnl] nominell, dem Namen nach; ~**ate** ['nɒmɪneɪt] ernennen (*to* zu); ~**ation** [,nɒmɪ'neɪʃn] Ernennung *f.*

non- [nɒn] *pref* Nicht-, nicht-.

none [nʌn] **I** *prn* kein; *mit pl* niemand; **II** *adv* in keiner Weise; ~ *the less* nichtsdestoweniger.

non-polluting [,nɒnpə'lu:tɪŋ] umweltfreundlich.

nonsense ['nɒnsəns] Unsinn *m.*

non-stop [,nɒn'stɒp] (*Zug*) durchgehend; ~ *flight* Nonstopflug *m.*

noodle ['nu:dl] Nudel *f.*

nook [nʊk] Winkel *m.*

noon [nu:n] Mittag *m a. fig.*

noose [nu:s] Schlinge *f a. fig.*

nor [nɔ:] und (auch) nicht; *neither ... * ~ weder ... noch.

norm [nɔ:m] Richtschnur *f;* ~**al** ['-l] normal; ~**ally** ['-əlɪ] normalerweise.

north [nɔ:θ] **I** *s* Nord(en) *m;* **II** *adj* nördlich; **III** *adv* nach, im Norden; ~**ern** ['nɔ:ðn] nördlich; **N~ Pole** Nordpol *m;* ~**ward(s)** ['-wəd(z)] nach Norden.

Norway ['nɔ:weɪ] Norwegen *n;* ~**wegian** [nɔ:'wi:dʒən] **I** *s* Norweger *m;* **II** *adj* norwegisch.

nose [nəuz] 1. Nase *f;* Schnauze *f;* 2. Vorsprung *m;* ~**bleed** ['-bli:d] Nasenbluten *n;* ~**dive** ['-daɪv] Sturzflug *m.*

nostalgia [nɒ'stældʒɪə] Heimweh *n.*

nostril ['nɒstrəl] Nasenloch *n,* Nüster *f.*

nosy ['nəuzɪ] neugierig.

not [nɒt] nicht; ~ *a* kein; ~ *at all* gar nicht; keine Ursache! ~ *even* nicht einmal; ~ *yet* noch nicht.

notable ['nəutəbl] bemerkenswert.

notary ['nəutərɪ] Notar *m.*

notch [nɒtʃ] **I** *s* Kerbe *f;* **II** *v* (ein)kerben.

note [nəut] **I** *s* 1. Notiz *f;* 2. kurze Mitteilung *f;* 3. Banknote *f;* **II** *v* 4. bemerken, beachten; 5. notieren; ~**book** ['-bʊk] Notizbuch *n;* ~**d** ['-ɪd] berühmt (*for, as* wegen); ~**worthy** ['-,wɜ:ðɪ] bemerkens-, beachtenswert.

nothing ['nʌθɪŋ] Nichts *n;* *for* ~ umsonst; ~ *but* nichts als; ~ *else* sonst nichts; *next to* ~ fast nichts.

notice ['nəutɪs] **I** *s* 1. Anzeige, Mitteilung *f;* 2. Kündigung *f;* 3. *take* ~ *of s.th.* etw zur Kenntnis nehmen; **II** *v* 4. bemerken; 5. beachten;

~**able** [-əbl] auffällig; beachtlich; ~**board** [-bɔ:d] Schwarze(s) Brett n.

notif|ication [,nəʊtɪfɪ'keɪʃn] Mitteilung f; ~**y** ['nəʊtɪfaɪ] (offiziell) unterrichten (*of* von).

notion ['nəʊʃn] Begriff m, Vorstellung f.

notorious [nəʊ'tɔ:rɪəs] stadtbekannt, berüchtigt.

notwithstanding [,nɒtwɪθ'stændɪŋ] **I** *prp* trotz; **II** *adv* dennoch; **III** *conj* (~ that) obgleich.

nought s. naught.

noun [naʊn] *gram* Hauptwort, Substantiv n.

nourish ['nʌrɪʃ] nähren a. fig; ~**ing** [-ɪŋ] nahrhaft; ~**ment** [-mənt] Nahrung n f.

novel ['nɒvl] **I** *adj* neu; **II** *s* Roman m; ~**ist** ['nɒvəlɪst] Romanschriftsteller m; ~**ty** ['-tɪ] Neuheit f.

November [nəʊ'vembə] November m.

novice ['nɒvɪs] Neuling m.

now [naʊ] jetzt, nun; eben; *in a week from* ~ heute in e-r Woche; ~ *and again*, ~ *and then* ab und zu; ~**adays** ['-ədeɪz] heutzutage.

nowhere ['nəʊweə] nirgends.

nozzle ['nɒzl] *tech* Düse f.

nuclear ['nju:klɪə] *phys* Kern-; Atom-; ~ *energy* Kernenergie f; ~ *power* Kernkraft f; ~ *reactor* Kernreaktor m; ~ *warheads* pl Atomsprengköpfe m pl.

nucleus ['nju:klɪəs] pl nuclei ['nju:klɪaɪ] (Zell-, Atom-) Kern m a. fig.

nude [nju:d] **I** *adj* nackt; **II** *s* (Kunst) Akt m.

nuisance ['nju:sns] Ärgernis n; Plage f.

null [nʌl] ~ *and void* null und nichtig.

numb [nʌm] 1. (er)starr(t) (*with* vor); 2. fig betäubt.

number ['nʌmbə] **I** *s* 1. Nummer f; 2. Zahl f; **II** *v* 3. numerieren; 4. zählen; ~**plate** [-pleɪt] *mot* Nummernschild n.

numer|al ['nju:mərəl] 1. Ziffer f; 2. Zahlwort n; ~**ous** ['nju:mərəs] zahlreich.

nun [nʌn] *rel* Nonne f.

nurse [nɜ:s] **I** *s* 1. Kinderfrau f; 2. (Kranken-)Schwester f; **II** *v* 3. (Kranke) pflegen; 4. (Kind u. fig) nähren; ~**ry** ['-ərɪ] Kinderhort m; ~ *school* Kindergarten m.

nut [nʌt] 1. Nuß f; 2. (Schrauben-)Mutter f; ~**crackers** pl ['-,krækəz] Nußknacker m.

nutri|tion [nju:'trɪʃn] 1. Ernährung f; 2. Nahrung f; ~**tious** [nju:'trɪʃəs] nahrhaft.

nutshell ['nʌtʃel] Nußschale f; *in a* ~ kurz, mit wenigen Worten.

nylons pl ['naɪlɒnz] Nylonstrümpfe m pl.

O

o [əʊ] *tele* Null *f.*
oak [əʊk] Eiche(nholz *n*) *f.*
oar [ɔ:] Ruder *n.*
oasis [əʊ'eɪsɪs] *pl* oases [-i:z] Oase *f a. fig.*
oat [əʊt] *meist pl* Hafer *m.*
oath [əʊθ, *pl* əʊðz] Eid, Schwur *m; swear, take an ~* schwören.
oatmeal ['əʊtmi:l] 1. Haferflocken *f pl;* 2. Haferschleim *m.*
obedien|ce [ə'bi:djəns] Gehorsam *m (to* gegen); **~t** [-t] gehorsam; folgsam.
obey [ə'beɪ] gehorchen.
obituary [ə'bɪtjʊərɪ] Todesanzeige *f.*
object I *s* ['ɒbdʒɪkt] 1. Gegenstand *m;* 2. Ziel *n;* II *v* [əb'dʒekt] Einspruch erheben; protestieren (*to* gegen).
objection [əb'dʒekʃn] Einwand *m (to* gegen); **~able** [-əbl] 1. nicht einwandfrei; 2. unangenehm.
objective [əb'dʒektɪv] I *adj* objektiv; II *s* Ziel *n.*
objector [əb'dʒektə] *conscientious ~* Kriegsdienstverweigerer *m.*
obligation [ˌɒblɪ'geɪʃn] Verpflichtung *f; no, without ~* unverbindlich; **~ory** [ə'blɪgətərɪ] verbindlich.
obli|ge [ə'blaɪdʒ] 1. verpflichten; 2. *be ~d to do* tun müs-

sen; 3. *I'm much ~d to you* ich bin Ihnen zu großem Dank verpflichtet; **~ing** [-ɪŋ] hilfsbereit.
oblique [ə'bli:k] 1. schräg; 2. indirekt; versteckt.
obliterate [ə'blɪtəreɪt] 1. ausradieren; 2. entwerten.
obliv|ion [ə'blɪvɪən] *sink into ~* in Vergessenheit geraten; **~ious** [-ɪəs] vergeßlich.
oblong ['ɒblɒŋ] länglich.
obnoxious [əb'nɒkʃəs] widerwärtig; verhaßt.
obscure [əb'skjʊə] I *adj* 1. dunkel; 2. *fig* unbekannt; II *v* verdunkeln.
observ|able [əb'zɜ:vəbl] wahrnehmbar; **~ation** [ˌɒbzə'veɪʃn] 1. Wahrnehmung *f;* 2. Bemerkung *f;* **~atory** [əb'zɜ:vətrɪ] Sternwarte *f.*
observe [əb'zɜ:v] 1. be(ob)achten, befolgen; 2. bemerken; 3. äußern.
obsolete ['ɒbsəli:t] veraltet.
obstacle ['ɒbstəkl] Hindernis *n (to* für).
obstin|acy ['ɒbstɪnəsɪ] Hartnäckigkeit *f;* **~ate** ['-nət] starr-, eigensinnig.
obstruct [əb'strʌkt] (ver)sperren; **~ive** [-ɪv] hinderlich.
obtain [əb'teɪn] erlangen; **~able** [-əbl] erhältlich.

obtru|de [əb'tru:d] aufdrängen (*upon s.o.* jdm); **~sive** [-sɪv] aufdringlich.

obtuse [əb'tju:s] stumpf.

obviate ['ɒbvɪeɪt] 1. beseitigen; 2. verhindern.

obvious ['ɒbvɪəs] offenbar, -sichtlich.

occasion [ə'keɪʒn] 1. Gelegenheit *f* (*of zu*); *on the ~ of* anläßlich; 2. Grund *m;* **~al** [-l] gelegentlich; **~ally** [-əlɪ] gelegentlich.

Occident ['ɒksɪdənt] Westen *m,* Abendland *n.*

occup|ant ['ɒkjupənt] Inhaber *m;* **~ation** [ɒkju'peɪʃn] 1. Besetzung *f;* 2. Beschäftigung *f,* Beruf *m; without ~* arbeitslos; **~ational** [ˌɒkju'peɪʃənl] beruflich; **~ied** ['ɒkjupaɪd] besetzt *a. mil;* **~y** ['ɒkjupaɪ] 1. *mil* besetzen; 2. bewohnen; 3. *(Stellung)* innehaben; 4. *(Zeit)* beanspruchen.

occur [ə'kɜː] 1. vorkommen; 2. einfallen (*to s.o.* jdm); **~rence** [ə'kʌrəns] Vorkommnis *n.*

ocean ['əuʃn] Ozean *m,* (Welt-)Meer *n.*

o'clock [ə'klɒk] *at three ~* um drei Uhr.

October [ɒk'təubə] Oktober *m.*

odd [ɒd] 1. einzeln; 2. ung(e)rade; 3. überzählig; 4. gelegentlich; 5. sonderbar.

odds *pl* [ɒdz] 1. (Gewinn-)Chancen *pl;* 2. *be at ~* uneins sein; 3. *~ and ends* Reste *m pl;* alles mögliche.

odious ['əudjəs] 1. verhaßt; 2. ekelhaft.

odo(u)r ['əudə] Geruch *m.*

of [ɒv, əv] von; *a friend ~ mine* ein Freund von mir; *the City ~ Manchester* die Stadt M.; *~ gold* golden; *a cup ~ tea* e-e Tasse Tee.

off [ɒf] **I** *adv* 1. weg, fort; *keep ~!* bleib weg! 2. *el* aus; 3. vorbei, aus; 4. entfernt, weit (weg); 5. *be well, badly ~* reich, arm sein; **II** *prp* (herunter) von.

offal ['ɒfl] Innereien *pl.*

offence, *Am* **-se** [ə'fens] 1. Vergehen *n;* 2. Kränkung *f; no ~!* nichts für ungut!

offend [ə'fend] 1. zuwiderhandeln (*against* gegen); 2. beleidigen.

offensive [ə'fensɪv] 1. Angriffs-; 2. unangenehm.

offer ['ɒfə] **I** *v* 1. (an)bieten; 2. *~ resistance* Widerstand leisten; 3. *(Gelegenheit)* sich bieten; **II** *s* Angebot *n;* **~ing** ['-rɪŋ] Angebot *n.*

office ['ɒfɪs] 1. Amt *n;* 2. Büro *n.*

officer ['ɒfɪsə] 1. Beamte(r) *m;* 2. Offizier *m.*

official [ə'fɪʃl] **I** *adj* amtlich; offiziell; **II** *s* Beamte(r) *m.*

officious [ə'fɪʃəs] übereifrig.

offspring ['ɒfsprɪŋ] *(pl unverändert)* Nachkomme(n *pl*) *m,* Nachkommenschaft *f.*

often ['ɒfn] oft(mals), häufig.

oil [ɔɪl] **I** s Öl n; fuel ~ Heizöl n; **II** v (ein)ölen; **~cloth** ['-klɒθ] Wachstuch n; ~ **level** ['-,levl] tech Ölstand m; **~-painting** ['-,peɪntɪŋ] Ölgemälde n; **~y** ['-ɪ] 1. ölig; 2. fig aalglatt.

ointment ['ɔɪntmənt] Salbe f.

O. K., okay [,əʊ'keɪ] (geht) in Ordnung.

old [əʊld] 1. alt; 2. bejahrt; the ~ die alten Leute; ~ **age** (hohes, Greisen-)Alter n; **~-fashioned** [,-'fæʃnd] altmodisch.

olive ['ɒlɪv] Olive f.

Olympic [əʊ'lɪmpɪk] the ~ Games die Olympischen Spiele n pl.

omen ['əʊmen] Omen n.

ominous ['ɒmɪnəs] unheilvoll; bedrohlich.

omission [ə'mɪʃn] 1. Auslassung f; 2. Unterlassung f.

omit [ə'mɪt] 1. aus-, weglassen; 2. versäumen (doing, to do zu tun).

on [ɒn] **I** prp auf, an; bei; ~ the table auf dem Tisch; ~ Sunday am Sonntag; ~ entering beim Eintritt; ~ the whole im ganzen; **II** adv: have nothing ~ nichts an haben; put a hat ~ e-n Hut aufsetzen; the light is ~ das Licht ist an; Hamlet is ~ Hamlet wird gespielt; come ~! mach weiter! and so ~ und so weiter, usw.

once [wʌns] 1. einmal; ~ a day einmal am Tag; 2. ~ more noch (ein)mal; ~ upon a time (es war) einmal; 3. at ~ sofort; gleichzeitig.

one [wʌn] **I** adj eine(r, e, es); ~ day eines Tages; **II** prn eine(r, s); jemand; man; etwas; another ~ ein anderer; ~ another einander; no ~ niemand; **III** s: ~ after another e-r nach dem andern; ~ by ~ einzeln, jeder für sich; ~self [-'self] man selbst; sich; by ~ (ganz) allein; **~-way street** ['-weɪ striːt] Einbahnstraße f.

onion ['ʌnjən] Zwiebel f.

only ['əʊnlɪ] **I** adj einzig; **II** adv nur, bloß; ~ just, ~ yesterday eben, gestern erst.

onward ['ɒnwəd] vorwärts, weiter.

ooze [uːz] **I** v (~ away) auslaufen; **II** s Schlick m.

opaque [əʊ'peɪk] undurchsichtig.

open ['əʊpən] **I** adj 1. offen a. fig; 2. öffentlich; **II** v 3. öffnen; 4. beginnen, eröffnen; **III** s: in the ~ (air) im Freien.

opener ['əʊpənə] bottle-~ Flaschenöffner m.

opening ['əʊpənɪŋ] 1. Öffnung f; 2. Beginn, Anfang m; ~ time Öffnungszeit f.

opera ['ɒprə] Oper f; **~-glasses** pl [-glɑːsɪz]

Opernglas n; ~-**house** [-haus] Opernhaus n.

operat|e ['ɒpəreɪt] 1. (Maschine) bedienen; 2. in Betrieb sein; 3. med operieren (on s.o. jdn); ~**ing** [-ɪŋ] ~ theatre Operationssaal m.

operation [ˌɒpə'reɪʃn] 1. Arbeit(sweise) f; 2. Wirkung f; come into ~ in Kraft treten; 3. Operation f allg mil med; ~**al** [ˌɒpəreɪʃənl] ~ costs Betriebskosten pl.

operat|ive ['ɒpərətɪv] 1. wirksam; become ~ in Kraft treten; 2. med operativ; ~**or** ['ɒpəreɪtə] Techniker m; telephone ~ Telefonist(in f) m.

operetta [ˌɒpə'retə] Operette f.

opinion [ə'pɪnjən] Meinung, Ansicht f; in my ~ nach meiner Meinung.

opponent [ə'pəunənt] Gegner, Gegenspieler m.

opportun|e ['ɒpətju:n] 1. günstig; 2. rechtzeitig; ~**ity** [ˌɒpə'tju:nətɪ] (gute) Gelegenheit f (of doing, to do zu tun; for s.th. zu etw).

oppos|e [ə'pəuz] 1. entgegensetzen; 2. entgegentreten; ~**ed** [-d] as ~ to im Gegensatz zu; ~**ite** ['ɒpəzɪt] I adj 1. gegenüberliegend; 2. entgegengesetzt; in the ~ direction in der Gegenrichtung; II s Gegenteil n; ~**ition** [ɒpə'zɪʃn] 1. Gegen-

satz m (to zu); 2. Opposition f; 3. Widerstand m.

oppress [ə'pres] 1. bedrükken; 2. unterdrücken; ~**ion** [ə'preʃn] 1. Bedrücktheit f; 2. Unterdrückung f; ~**ive** [ə'presɪv] 1. ungerecht; 2. (be-, er)drückend.

opt [ɒpt] sich entscheiden (for für).

optic|(al) ['ɒptɪk(l)] optisch; ~**ian** [ɒp'tɪʃn] Optiker m.

optimism ['ɒptɪmɪzəm] Optimismus m.

option ['ɒpʃn] Wahl f.

opulence ['ɒpjuləns] Reichtum; Überfluß m.

or [ɔ:] oder; either ... ~ entweder ... oder; ~ else sonst, andernfalls.

oral ['ɔ:rəl] mündlich.

orange ['ɒrɪndʒ] Orange f.

orator ['ɒrətə] Redner m.

orbit ['ɔ:bɪt] Umlaufbahn f.

orchard ['ɔ:tʃəd] Obstgarten m.

orchestra ['ɔ:kɪstrə] Orchester n.

ordain [ɔ:'deɪn] verfügen.

order ['ɔ:də] I s 1. Ordnung f; in (good) ~ in gutem Zustand; out of ~ kaputt; 2. ~ of the day Tagesordnung f; 3. mil Befehl m; by ~ auf Befehl; 4. com Auftrag m; 5. in ~ to um zu; 6. Orden m; II v 7. (an)ordnen; befehlen; 8. (com) bestellen; ~ in advance vorbestellen; ~**ly** [-lɪ] I adj ordentlich, geordnet; II s mil Ordonnanz f.

ordinary ['ɔ:dnrɪ] gewöhnlich.

ore [ɔ:] *min* Erz *n.*

organ ['ɔ:gən] 1. Organ *n a.
fig;* 2. Orgel *f.*

organ|ic [ɔ:'gænɪk] orga-
nisch; **~ism** ['ɔ:gənɪzəm]
biol fig Organismus *m.*

organiz|ation [,ɔ:gənaɪ'zeɪʃn]
1. (Auf-)Bau *m,* Anordnung
f; 2. Organisation *f;* **~e**
['ɔ:gənaɪz] organisieren; **~er**
['ɔ:gənaɪzə] Organisator *m.*

orient ['ɔ:rɪənt] Orient *m;*
~al [,ɔ:rɪ'entl] östlich.

orientat|e ['ɔ:rɪenteɪt] orien-
tieren *a. fig;* **~ion**
[ɔ:rɪen'teɪʃn] Orientierung *f
a. fig.*

orifice ['ɒrɪfɪs] Öffnung *f.*

origin ['ɒrɪdʒɪn] 1. Ursprung
m; 2. Herkunft *f;* **~al**
[ə'rɪdʒənl] *I adj* 1. ursprünglich; 2. originell; **II** *s* Original
n; **~ate** [ə'rɪdʒəneɪt] 1. hervorbringen; 2. entstehen
(*from,* in aus; *with, from s.o.*
bei, durch jdn).

ornament I *s* ['ɔ:nəmənt]
Verzierung *f;* **II** *v* ['-ment]
verzieren; **~al** [,ɔ:nə'mentl]
ornamental, dekorativ.

orphan ['ɔ:fn] **I** *s* Waise *f;*
II *adj* verwaist *a. fig.*

orthography [ɔ:'θɒɡrəfɪ]
Rechtschreibung *f.*

oscillation [,ɒsɪ'leɪʃn]
Schwingung *f.*

osten|sible [ɒ'stensəbl] an-
geblich, scheinbar; **~tation**
[ɒsten'teɪʃn] Zurschaustel-
lung *f;* **~tatious** [-'teɪʃəs]
prahlerisch; auffällig.

ostrich ['ɒstrɪtʃ] *orn* Strauß
m.

other ['ʌðə] **I** *adj* ander; *the
~ day* neulich; *every ~ day*
jeden zweiten Tag; **II** *prn:
the ~* der, die, das andere;
each ~ einander; **~wise**
[-waɪz] 1. sonst; 2. anders.

ought [ɔ:t] sollte, müßte; *you
~ to have done it* du hättest
es tun sollen.

ounce [aʊns] Unze *f*
(= 28,35 g).

our ['aʊə] unser(e); **~s** [-z]
der, die, das unsrige,
uns(e)re; **~selves** [,-'selvz]
uns (selbst).

oust [aʊst] hinauswerfen.

out [aʊt] **I** *adv* 1. *allg* aus;
2. her-, hinaus; 3. (dr)außen;
4. nicht daheim; 5. *(Feuer,
Licht)* aus; *(Gerät)* abge-
stellt; 6. aus der Mode;
II *prp (meist: ~ of)* 7. aus
(... heraus); 8. außer, ohne;
~ of breath außer Atem;
9. außerhalb *gen;*
10. *(Grund)* aus, vor.

out|board ['aʊtbɔ:d] *~ motor*
Außenbordmotor *m;*
~break ['-breɪk], **~burst**
['-bɜ:st] Ausbruch *m a. fig;*
~cast ['-ka:st] Ausgestoße-
ne(r) *m;* **~cry** ['-kraɪ] Auf-
schrei *m;* **~do** [,-'du:] *irr (s.
do)* übertreffen; **~door**
['-dɔ:] draußen; **~doors**
[,-'dɔ:z] im Freien.

outer ['autə] äußere(r, s); Außen-; ~ *space* Weltraum m.

out|fit ['autfɪt] Ausstattung f; ~**grow** ['-grəu] *irr (s. grow)* herauswachsen aus.

outing ['autɪŋ] Ausflug m.

out|last [,aut'lɑ:st] überdauern; ~**law** ['-lɔ:] Geächtete(r) m; ~**lay** ['-leɪ] (Geld-)Ausgabe f; ~**let** ['-let] 1. Abfluß m; 2. fig Ventil n; ~**line** ['-laɪn] **I** s Umriß m; **II** v skizzieren; ~**live** [,-'lɪv] überleben; ~**look** ['-luk] Aussicht f a. fig; ~**number** [,-'nʌmbə] zahlenmäßig überlegen sein; ~**put** ['-put] 1. Leistung f; 2. Produktion f.

outrage ['autreɪdʒ] **I** s Greuel-, Gewalttat f; **II** v gröblich beleidigen; ~**ous** [aut'reɪdʒəs] unerhört; schändlich.

out|right ['autraɪt] geradeheraus; ~**set** ['-set] Beginn m.

outside ['autsaɪd] **I** s 1. Außenseite f; 2. at the (very) ~ (aller)höchstens; **II** adj Außen-; **III** adv (dr)außen; **IV** prp außerhalb; ~**r** [,aut'saɪdə] Außenseiter m.

out|size ['autsaɪz] übergroß; ~**skirts** pl ['-skɜ:ts] Stadtrand m; ~**standing** [,-'stændɪŋ] 1. fig hervorragend; 2. (Schulden) ausstehend.

outward ['autwəd] **I** adj äußer, äußerlich; **II** adv ~ u. ~**s** [-z] nach außen.

out|weigh [,aut'weɪ] mehr wiegen als; ~**worn** ['-wɔ:n] abgenutzt.

oven ['ʌvn] Backofen m.

over ['əuvə] **I** adv 1. hin-, herüber; drüben; ~ *there* dort, da drüben; 2. (vorn-, hinten)über; 3. vorbei; 4. übrig; 5. ~ *again* noch (ein)mal; ~ *and* ~ (*again*) immer wieder; 6. *vor adj:* über-, (all)zu, übermäßig; **II** prp über; all ~ the town in der ganzen Stadt; ~ *night* über Nacht.

over|all ['əuvərɔ:l] **I** adj gesamt; **II** s Arbeitsanzug m; ~**cast** ['-kɑ:st] bewölkt; ~**charge** [,-'tʃɑ:dʒ] zu hoch berechnen; ~**coat** ['-kəut] Überzieher m; ~**come** [,-'kʌm] *irr (s. come)* 1. besiegen; 2. *be* ~ (fig) ergriffen sein (*by one*); ~**crowded** [,-'kraudɪd] überfüllt; ~**do** [,-'du:] *irr (s. do)* übertreiben; ~**draw** ['-drɔ:] *irr (s. draw)* (*sein Konto*) überziehen; ~**due** ['-dju:] überfällig; ~**flow** [,-'fləu] *irr (s. flow)* überfluten a. fig; ~**grow** [,-'grəu] überwuchern; ~**haul** [,-'hɔ:l] *tech* überholen; ~**head** ['-hed] 1. oberirdisch; 2. ~ *expenses* allgemeine Unkosten pl; ~**hear** [,-'hɪə] *irr (s. hear)* zufällig (mit)hören, belauschen; ~**lap** [,-'læp]

sich überschneiden; **~load** [ˌ-'ləʊd] überladen; **~look** [ˌ-'lʊk] 1. überschauen; 2. *(Fehler)* übersehen; **~power** [ˌ-'paʊə] überwältigen *a. fig;* **~rate** [ˌ-'reɪt] überschätzen; **~seas** [ˌ-'siːz] nach, in Übersee; **~see** [ˌ-'siː] *irr (s. see)* überwachen; **~seer** ['-sɪə] Aufseher *m;* **~sight** ['-saɪt] Versehen *n;* **~sleep** [ˌ-'sliːp] *irr (s. sleep)* verschlafen; **~spill** ['-spɪl] (Bevölkerungs-)Überschuß *m;* **~take** [ˌ-'teɪk] *irr (s. take)* überholen; **~throw** [ˌ-'θrəʊ] *irr (s. throw)* pol stürzen; **~time** ['-taɪm] Überstunden *f pl.*
overture ['əʊvətjʊə] 1. *mus* Ouvertüre *f;* 2. Vorspiel *n.*
over|turn [ˌəʊvə'tɜːn] umwerfen; **~weight I** *s* ['-weɪt]

Übergewicht *n a. fig;* **II** *adj* [ˌ-'weɪt] zu schwer; **~whelm** [ˌ-'welm] überwältigen.
ow|e [əʊ] 1. schulden *a. fig;* 2. verdanken; **~ing** ['-ɪŋ] ~ *to* infolge, wegen.
owl [aʊl] Eule *f.*

own [əʊn] **I** *adj* eigen; **II** *v* 1. besitzen; 2. zugeben; **III** *s:* on o.'s ~ auf eigene Faust; **~er** ['-ə] Eigentümer *m;* **~ership** ['-əʃɪp] Eigentum(srecht) *n.*
ox [ɒks] *pl* oxen ['-n] Ochse *m;* Rind *n.*
oxygen ['ɒksɪdʒən] *chem* Sauerstoff *m;* ~ **mask** Sauerstoffmaske *f.*
oyster ['ɔɪstə] *zoo* Auster *f.*
ozone ['əʊzəʊn] *chem* Ozon *n.*

P

pace [peɪs] **I** s 1. Schritt m; 2. Gang(art f) m; 3. Tempo n; keep ~ Schritt halten (with mit); set the ~ das Tempo angeben; **II** v 4. abschreiten, durchmessen; 5. (einher)schreiten; ~ up and down auf u. ab schreiten; ~-**maker** ['-ˌmeɪkə] Schrittmacher m.

paci|fic [pə'sɪfɪk] friedlich, friedliebend; ~**fist** ['pæsɪfɪst] Pazifist m; ~**fy** ['pæsɪfaɪ] besänftigen.

pack [pæk] **I** s 1. Ballen m, Bündel n; 2. Haufen m, Menge f; that's a ~ of lies das sind lauter Lügen; 3. (Hunde) Meute f; 4. Am (Zigaretten) Packung f; **II** v 5. be-, ver-, einpacken; (Koffer) packen; ~ up (fam) einpacken; 6. (Menschen) zs.drängen, einpferchen; 7. ~ (o.s.) off (schleunigst) abhauen; ~**age** ['-ɪdʒ] **I** v verpacken; **II** s Packen, Ballen m; Bündel n; Packung f; ~ tour Pauschalreise f; ~**er** ['-ə] Packer m; ~**et** ['-ɪt] (Post-)Paket, Päckchen n; (Zigaretten) Packung f; ~**ing** ['-ɪŋ] 1. Verpackung f; 2. Packen n.

pact [pækt] Vertrag, Pakt m.

pad [pæd] **I** s 1. Kissen, Polster n; 2. (writing-~) Schreibblock m; 3. (stamp ~) Stempelkissen n; 4. (Rakete) Abschußrampe f; **II** v (aus)polstern; ~**ding** ['-ɪŋ] Polsterung f.

paddle ['pædl] **I** s Paddel n; **II** v paddeln; ~-**wheel** Schaufelrad n.

padlock ['pædlɒk] Vorhängeschloß n.

pagan ['peɪgən] **I** s Heide m, Heidin f; **II** adj heidnisch.

page [peɪdʒ] 1. (Buch) Seite f; 2. (Hotel-)Page, Boy m.

pageant ['pædʒənt] Parade, Schau f.

pail [peɪl] Eimer, Kübel m.

pain [peɪn] **I** s 1. Schmerz(en pl) m; 2. Qual f; 3. pl Mühe f; take ~s sich (große) Mühe geben; **II** v schmerzen, weh tun (s.o. jdm); ~**ful** ['-fʊl] 1. schmerzhaft; 2. schmerzlich; 3. mühsam; ~**less** ['-lɪs] schmerzlos; ~**staking** ['-ˌzteɪkɪŋ] gewissenhaft, sorgfältig.

paint [peɪnt] **I** v (be)malen; anstreichen; **II** s 1. Farbe f; Anstrich m; wet ~! frisch gestrichen! 2. Schminke f; ~-**box** ['-bɒks] Malkasten m; ~**er** ['-ə] Maler m; ~**ing** ['-ɪŋ] 1. Malen n; 2. Gemälde n.

pair [peə] Paar n; a ~ of gloves ein Paar Handschuhe; *a ~ of scissors* e-e Schere.

pajamas *s.* pyjamas.

pal [pæl] *fam* Kumpel *m.*

palace ['pælɪs] Palast *m.*

palat|able ['pælətəbl] schmackhaft; **~e** ['pælət] Gaumen *m.*

pale [peɪl] **I** *adj* 1. bleich, blaß; *turn ~* blaß, bleich werden; 2. *fig* matt, farblos; **II** *v* erbleichen, erblassen; **III** *s* Pfahl, Pfosten *m.*

palette ['pælət] Palette *f.*

pall [pɔːl] **I** *v* langweilig werden (*on, upon s.o.* jdm); **II** *s* Leichentuch *n.*

palliative ['pælɪətɪv] **I** *adj* lindernd; **II** *s* Linderungsmittel *n.*

pall|id ['pælɪd] blaß, bleich; **~or** ['pælə] Blässe *f.*

palm [pɑːm] 1. Handfläche *f; grease, oil s.o.'s ~* jdn bestechen; 2. Palme *f;* 3. *bear, carry off the ~* den Sieg davontragen; **P~ Sunday** Palmsonntag *m.*

palpable ['pælpəbl] fühlbar; offenbar.

palpitat|e ['pælpɪteɪt] *(Herz)* klopfen (*with* vor); **~ion** [ˌpælpɪ'teɪʃn] Herzklopfen *n.*

paltry ['pɔːltrɪ] 1. belanglos; 2. erbärmlich.

pamper ['pæmpə] verwöhnen, verhätscheln.

pamphlet ['pæmflɪt] Broschüre; Flugschrift *f.*

pan [pæn] 1. Pfanne *f;* 2. (fla-

che) Schüssel, Schale *f;* 3. Waagschale *f;* **~cake** ['-keɪk] Pfannkuchen *m.*

pane [peɪn] Fensterscheibe *f.*

panel ['pænl] 1. *(Wand, Tür)* Füllung *f;* 2. *mot* Armaturenbrett *n;* 3. *jur* Geschworenenliste *f;* 4. *~ discussion* Podiumsgespräch *n.*

pang [pæŋ] stechende(r) Schmerz *m.*

panic ['pænɪk] **I** *s* Panik *f;* **II** *v* in Panik geraten.

pansy ['pænzɪ] *bot* Stiefmütterchen *n.*

pant [pænt] keuchen.

panther ['pænθə] Panther; *Am* Puma *m.*

panties *pl* ['pæntɪz] (Damen-)Slip *m.*

pantry ['pæntrɪ] Vorrats-, Speisekammer *f.*

pants *pl* [pænts] 1. *Br* (lange) Unterhose *f;* 2. *Am* Hose *f.*

paper ['peɪpə] 1. Papier *n; sanitary, toilet-~* Toilettenpapier *n;* 2. Abhandlung *f* (*on* über); 3. Zeitung *f; daily, evening, sports ~* Tages-, Abend-, Sportzeitung *f; illustrated ~* Illustrierte *f;* 4. *pl* Ausweispapiere *pl;* **~-hanger** [-ˌhæŋə] Tapezierer *m;* **~-weight** [-weɪt] Briefbeschwerer *m.*

par [pɑː] *fin* Pari *n.*

parachut|e ['pærəʃuːt] **I** *s* Fallschirm *m;* **II** *v* (mit dem Fallschirm) abspringen; **~ist** [-ɪst] Fallschirmspringer *m.*

parade [pə'reɪd] **I** s Parade f; **II** v 1. vorbeimarschieren; 2. zur Schau stellen.

paradise ['pærədaɪs] Paradies n.

paragraph ['pærəgrɑ:f] typ Absatz, Abschnitt m.

parallel ['pærəlel] **I** adj parallel (with, to mit) a. fig; **II** s Parallele f a. fig (to zu); without ~ unvergleichlich; draw a ~ between e-n Vergleich anstellen zwischen; **III** v 1. parallel (ver)laufen zu; 2. entsprechen; ~ **bars** pl sport Barren m.

paraly|se, Am ~**ze** ['pærəlaɪz] lähmen a. fig; ~**sis** [pə'ræləsɪs] pl -ses [-si:z] med Lähmung f a. fig.

paramount ['pærəmaʊnt] wichtigst, höchst, oberst.

paraphrase ['pærəfreɪz] **I** v umschreiben; **II** s Umschreibung f.

parasite ['pærəsaɪt] Schmarotzer m.

parasol ['pærəsɒl] Sonnenschirm m.

paratroops pl ['pærətru:ps] Fallschirmtruppen f pl.

parcel ['pɑ:sl] **I** s 1. Paket n; 2. (Land) Parzelle f; **II** v: ~ out aufteilen; ~ **post** Paketpost f.

parch [pɑ:tʃ] 1. dörren; 2. austrocknen.

parchment ['pɑ:tʃmənt] Pergament n.

pardon ['pɑ:dn] **I** v 1. begnadigen; 2. vergeben (s.o. jdm); **II** s 3. Begnadigung f; 4. Vergebung f; I beg your ~! entschuldigen Sie bitte! Verzeihung! I beg your ~? wie bitte? ~**able** [-əbl] verzeihlich.

pare [peə] 1. schälen; 2. (Nägel) schneiden.

parent ['peərənt] 1. Elternteil m; 2. pl Eltern pl; ~**s-in-law** Schwiegereltern pl; ~**age** [-ɪdʒ] Abstammung f; ~**al** [pə'rentl] elterlich.

parenthesis [pə'renθɪsɪs] pl -eses [-si:z] runde Klammer f.

parish ['pærɪʃ] (Kirchen-)Gemeinde f; ~ **church** Pfarrkirche f.

parity ['pærətɪ] 1. Gleichheit f; 2. com Parität f.

park [pɑ:k] **I** s 1. Park m, (Park-)Anlagen f pl; 2. mot Parkplatz m; **II** v mot parken, abstellen; ~**ing** ['-ɪŋ] Parken n; ~ **lot** (Am) Parkplatz m; ~ **meter** Parkuhr f.

parliament ['pɑ:ləmənt] Parlament n; ~**arian** [,pɑ:ləmən'teərɪən] Parlamentarier m; ~**ary** [,pɑ:lə'mentərɪ] parlamentarisch.

parlo(u)r ['pɑ:lə] 1. Empfangszimmer n; 2. beauty ~ (Am) Schönheitssalon m; ~**-car** [-kɑ:] Am Salonwagen m.

parole [pə'rəʊl] on ~ auf Bewährung f.

parquet ['pɑ:keɪ] Parkett n.

parrot ['pærət] Papagei *m.*

parsimon|ious
[,pɑːsɪ'məʊnjəs] knauserig;
~**y** ['pɑːsɪmənɪ] Geiz *m.*

parsley ['pɑːslɪ] Petersilie *f.*

parson ['pɑːsn] Pfarrer, Pastor *m;* ~**age** [-ɪdʒ] Pfarrhaus *n,* Pfarrei *f.*

part [pɑːt] **I** *s* 1. Teil *m u. n; the greater* ~ der größte Teil; *for the most* ~ meist(ens); *in* ~ teilweise; 2. Bestandteil *m; spare* ~ Ersatzteil *n a. m;* 3. Anteil *m; take* ~ teilnehmen (*in* an); 4. *theat* Rolle *f;* 5. *mus* Stimme *f;* 6. (*Rechtsstreit*) Partei *f; for my* ~ was mich betrifft; *on the* ~ *of* von seiten; *take s.o.'s* ~ für jdn, jds Partei ergreifen; 7. *pl* Gegend *f;* **II** *v* 8. teilen, trennen; 9. (*das Haar*) scheiteln; 10. sich trennen (*with* von); scheiden (*friends* als Freunde); 11. aufgeben (*with s.th.* etw); **III** *adv* teils, teilweise.

partial ['pɑːʃl] 1. parteiisch, voreingenommen; 2. *be* ~ *to s.th.* für etw e-e Vorliebe haben; 3. partiell; ~**ity** [,pɑːʃɪ'ælətɪ] 1. Voreingenommenheit *f;* 2. Vorliebe *f* (*for* für); ~**ly** ['pɑːʃəlɪ] teilweise.

particip|ant [pɑː'tɪsɪpənt] Teilnehmer *m;* ~**ate** [-eɪt] teilnehmen (*in* an); ~**ation** [pɑː,tɪsɪ'peɪʃn] Teilnahme *f.*

particle ['pɑːtɪkl] Teilchen *n*

a. phys; not a ~ *of sense* kein Fünkchen Verstand.

particular [pə'tɪkjʊlə] **I** *adj* 1. besonder, einzeln, speziell; *in* ~ insbesondere; 2. anspruchsvoll (*about* in bezug auf); 3. sehr genau; **II** *s* 4. Einzelheit *f; go into* ~*s* ins einzelne gehen; *for* ~*s apply to . . .* Auskünfte durch . . .; 5. *pl* Personalien *pl;* ~**ity** [pə,tɪkjʊ'lærɪtɪ] 1. Besonderheit *f;* 2. Ausführlichkeit *f;* ~**ize** [pə'tɪkjʊləraɪz] einzeln angeben; ~**ly** [pə'tɪkjʊləlɪ] im besonderen.

parting ['pɑːtɪŋ] 1. Scheitel *m;* 2. Abschied *m,* Trennung *f* (*with* von).

partisan [,pɑːtɪ'zæn] 1. Anhänger *m;* 2. *mil* Widerstandskämpfer *m.*

partition [pɑː'tɪʃn] 1. Teilung *f;* 2. Trennwand *f.*

partly ['pɑːtlɪ] teilweise.

partner ['pɑːtnə] (Ehe-, Tanz-, Spiel-)Partner *m; sleeping* ~ stille(r) Teilhaber *m;* ~**ship** [-ʃɪp] Teilhaberschaft *f.*

partridge ['pɑːtrɪdʒ] Rebhuhn *n.*

part|-time [pɑː'taɪm] Halbtags-; ~**-timer** [-ə] Halbtagskraft *f.*

party ['pɑːtɪ] 1. (politische) Partei *f a. jur;* 2. Party *f;* 3. Gesellschaft *f.*

pass [pɑːs] **I** *s* 1. Bestehen *n* (*e-r Prüfung*); 2. Passier-

schein m; 3. (Gebirge) Paß;
II v 4. durchfahren; 5. vorbei-, vorüber-, weitergehen;
6. vorbeigehen, -fahren an;
7. (Auto) überholen; 8. übergehen, -wechseln (from ... to von ... zu); 9. hinausgehen über; 10. (Zeit) vergehen; verbringen;
11. (Prüfung) bestehen;
12. gelten, gehalten werden (for für); 13. sich ereignen;
14. (Gesetz) verabschieden;
15. ~ o.'s hand mit der Hand fahren (over über; through durch); 16. weiterreichen; ~ (me) the sugar, please reichen Sie mir bitte den Zucker! 17. (Urteil) sprechen (on über); 18. (Ball) zuspielen; ~ **away** verscheiden; ~ **by** unbeachtet lassen; ~ **for** gelten als; ~ **off** vorbei-, vorübergehen; pass o.s. off as sich ausgeben als; ~ **over** stillschweigend übergehen.

passable ['pɑ:səbl] 1. passierbar; 2. leidlich.

passage ['pæsɪdʒ] 1. Vorbei-, Vorübergehen n;
2. Durchgang m; 3. mar Überfahrt f; 4. Korridor m;
5. (Text-)Stelle f.

passbook ['pɑ:sbʊk] Bankbuch n.

passenger ['pæsɪndʒə] Passagier, Reisende(r) m; ~ **train** Personenzug m.

passer-by [ˌpɑ:sə'baɪ] pl passers-by [ˌpɑ:səz'baɪ] Vorübergehende(r) m.

passing ['pɑ:sɪŋ] vorübergehend a. fig.

passion ['pæʃn] 1. Leidenschaft f (for für); 2. Zorn m; fly into a ~ e-n Wutanfall bekommen; ~**ate** ['pæʃənət] leidenschaftlich.

passive ['pæsɪv] passiv, teilnahmslos.

passport ['pɑ:spɔ:t] (Reise-) Paß m.

password ['pɑ:swɜ:d] Losung(swort n) f.

past [pɑ:st] **I** adj vergangen, früher; for some time ~ seit einiger Zeit; **II** s Vergangenheit f; in the ~ früher; **III** prp 1. (zeitl.) nach, später als; half ~ three (o'clock) halb vier (Uhr); 2. (räuml.) an vorbei; 3. über ... hinaus; ~ belief unglaublich; **IV** adv: go ~ vorübergehen.

paste [peɪst] **I** s 1. Teig m; 2. Paste f; 3. Kleister m; **II** v: ~ up (auf-, über)kleben; ~**board** ['-bɔ:d] Pappe f, Karton m.

pastime ['pɑ:staɪm] Zeitvertreib m.

pastry ['peɪstrɪ] 1. Kuchenteig m; 2. Pasteten f pl; 3. Gebäck n; ~-**cook** [-kʊk] Konditor m.

pasture ['pɑ:stʃə] **I** s Weide f; **II** v weiden.

pasty I adj ['peɪstɪ] fig bleich, blaß, käsig; **II** s ['pæstɪ] Br (Fleisch-)Pastete f.

pat [pæt] **I** s Klaps m;

II v tätscheln; ~ *s.o. on the back* jdm auf die Schulter klopfen; *fig* jdn loben.

patch [pætʃ] I s 1. Flicken, Fleck m; 2. Pflaster n; 3. (Farb-)Fleck m; 4. Stück n Land; 5. *strike a bad ~* e-e Pechsträhne haben; II v 6. flicken; 7. ~ *up* zs.flicken; *fig (Streit)* beilegen.

patent ['peɪtənt] I adj 1. offenkundig; 2. *jur* patentiert; II v patentieren lassen; III s *(Letters ~* ['pæ-]) Patent n; ~**ee** [,peɪtən'tiː] Patentinhaber m; ~ **leather** Lackleder n; **P~ Office** ['pæ-] Patentamt n.

patern|al [pə'tɜ:nl] väterlich; ~**ity** [pə'tɜ:nətɪ] Vater-, Urheberschaft f.

path [pɑ:θ] pl -s [pɑ:ðz] 1. Pfad, Weg m; 2. *astr sport* Bahn f; ~**way** ['-weɪ] Pfad, Weg m.

patien|ce ['peɪʃns] Geduld f; *have no ~ with* nicht vertragen, nicht leiden können; ~**t** ['peɪʃnt] I adj geduldig; II s Patient m.

patriot ['pætrɪət] Patriot m.

patrol [pə'trəul] I s *mil* Patrouille f; II v abpatrouillieren; ~**man** [-mæn] pl -men [-men] patrouillierende(r) Polizist m.

patron ['peɪtrən] Gönner m; ~**ize** ['pætrənaɪz] fördern; ~**izing** ['pætrənaɪzɪŋ] herablassend.

pattern ['pætən] I s 1. Vorbild n; 2. Modell n; 3. Muster n; II v formen (*upon, after* nach).

pause [pɔ:z] I s (Ruhe-)Pause f; II v e-e Pause machen.

pave [peɪv] pflastern; ~ *the way for s.o. (fig)* jdm den Weg ebnen; ~**ment** ['-mənt] 1. *Br* Gehweg m; 2. *Am* Fahrbahn f.

paw [pɔ:] I s Pfote, Tatze f; II v stampfen, scharren.

pawn [pɔ:n] I s Pfand n; II v verpfänden; ~**broker** ['-,brəukə] Pfandleiher m; ~**shop** ['-ʃɒp] Pfandhaus n.

pay [peɪ] I s 1. (Be-)Zahlung f; 2. Lohn m, Gehalt n; II v *irr* paid, paid [-d] 3. (be)zahlen *a. fig*; ~ *cash* bar zahlen; ~ *duty on* verzollen; ~ *damages* Schadenersatz leisten; 4. sich lohnen; *that doesn't ~* das lohnt sich nicht; 5. ~ *attention* achten (*to* auf); ~ *a call, a visit* e-n Besuch machen; ~ **back** zurückzahlen; ~ **off** *(Schulden)* tilgen; ~ **out** aus(be)zahlen; abfinden.

payable ['peɪəbl] zahlbar.

pay-day ['peɪdeɪ] Zahltag m.

payee [peɪ'iː] Zahlungsempfänger m.

payer ['peɪə] (Ein-)Zahler m.

pay|-load ['peɪləud] Nutzlast f; ~**master** ['peɪ,mɑ:stə] Zahlmeister m.

payment ['peɪmənt] 1. Bezahlung f; 2. Zahlung f; 3. *fig* Lohn m.

pay|-off ['peɪɒf] *fam* Abrechnung *f;* **~-phone** [-fəʊn] , *Am* **~-station** [-steɪʃn] Münzfernsprecher *m.*

pea [pi:] Erbse *f.*

peace [pi:s] 1. Friede(n) *m; (be) at ~* in Frieden (leben) (*with* mit); *make ~* Frieden schließen; 2. Friedensvertrag *m;* 3. Ruhe (u. Ordnung) *f; breach of the ~* Ruhestörung *f;* **~ful** ['-fʊl] friedlich.

peach [pi:tʃ] Pfirsich(baum *m,* -farbe *f*) *m.*

peacock ['pi:kɒk] Pfau *m.*

peak [pi:k] 1. Spitze *f,* Gipfel *m;* 2. Mützenschirm *m;* 3. Höhepunkt *m; ~* **hours** *pl* Hauptverkehrszeit *f.*

peal [pi:l] **I** *s* 1. (Glocken-) Läuten *n;* 2. Dröhnen *n;* **II** *v* 3. läuten; 4. dröhnen.

peanut ['pi:nʌt] Erdnuß *f; ~* **butter** Erdnußbutter *f.*

pear [peə] 1. Birne *f;* 2. (*~-tree*) Birnbaum *m.*

pearl [pɜ:l] Perle *f; cast ~s before swine* Perlen vor die Säue werfen.

peasant ['peznt] Bauer *m.*

peat [pi:t] Torf *m; ~-bog* ['-bɒg] Torfmoor *n.*

pebble ['pebl] Kiesel(stein) *m.*

peck [pek] **I** *v* picken, hakken; **II** *s* (Schnabel-)Hieb *m.*

peculiar [pɪ'kju:ljə] 1. besonder; 2. eigentümlich (*to* für); 3. sonderbar, seltsam; **~ity**

[pɪˌkju:lɪ'ærɪti] 1. Besonderheit *f;* 2. Eigentümlichkeit *f.*

pedal ['pedl] **I** *s* Pedal *n;* **II** *v* treten, radfahren.

peddle ['pedl] hausieren.

pedestal ['pedɪstl] Sockel *m.*

pedestrian [pɪ'destrɪən] Fußgänger *m; ~ crossing* Fußgängerübergweg *m.*

pedigree ['pedɪgri:] Stammbaum *m a. zoo.*

pedlar ['pedlə] Hausierer *m.*

pee [pi:] *fam* pinkeln.

peel [pi:l] **I** *v* 1. schälen; 2. (*~ off*) sich häuten, sich schälen; **II** *s* Schale *f;* **~ings** *pl* ['-ɪŋz] (Kartoffel-)Schalen *f pl.*

peep [pi:p] **I** *v* 1. piepsen; 2. (verstohlen) gucken (*at* nach); **II** *s* 3. Piepsen *n;* 4. flüchtige(r), heimliche(r) Blick *m; ~-hole* ['-həʊl] Gucklock *n.*

peer [pɪə] **I** *v* spähen (*at* auf; *into* in); **II** *s* 1. Ebenbürtige(r) *m;* 2. *Br* Angehörige(r) *m* des hohen Adels; *~ of the realm* Pair *m;* **~ess** ['-rɪs] Frau *f* e-s Pairs, weibliche(r) Pair *m;* **~less** ['-lɪs] unvergleichlich.

peevish ['pi:vɪʃ] übelgelaunt.

peg [peg] **I** *s* 1. Pflock, Dübel, Haken *m; be a square ~ in a round hole* am falschen Platz sein; 2. (*clothes-~*) Wäscheklammer *f;* 3. (Zelt) Hering *m;* **II** *v* 4. festpflokken; 5. abgrenzen.

pelt [pelt] **I** *s* Fell *n,* Pelz *m;*

II *v* 1. bewerfen (*with* mit); 2. (*Regen*) prasseln (*against the roof* auf das Dach).

pelvis ['pelvɪs] *pl* **pelves** [-iːz] *anat* Becken *n*.

pen [pen] **I** *s* 1. (Schreib-)Feder *f*; *ball(-point)* ~ Kugelschreiber *m*; *fountain-*~ Füllfeder(halter *m*) *f*; 2. Pferch *m*; **II** *v* 3. schreiben, abfassen; 4. (~ *up, in*) einpferchen, -sperren.

penal ['piːnl] strafbar; ~ **code** Strafgesetzbuch *n*; ~**ize** ['piːnəlaɪz] bestrafen; ~ **law** Strafrecht *n*; ~ **offence** strafbare Handlung *f*; ~ **servitude** Zuchthausstrafe *f*; ~**ty** ['penltɪ] 1. Strafe *a. fig*, Geldbuße *f*; *under* ~ *of death* bei Todesstrafe; 2. *sport* Strafpunkt *m*.

penance ['penəns] Buße *f*.

pencil ['pensl] (Blei-, Augenbrauen-)Stift *m*; ~-**sharpener** [-ʃɑːpnə] Bleistiftspitzer *m*.

pendant ['pendənt] Gehänge *n*, Anhänger *m*.

pending ['pendɪŋ] **I** *adj* 1. *fig* unentschieden; 2. *jur* anhängig; **II** *prp* 3. während *gen*; 4. bis zu *gen*; ~ *further notice* bis auf weiteres.

pendulum [pendjʊləm] Pendel *n*.

penetrate ['penɪtreɪt] 1. eindringen in; 2. *fig* ergründen (*into s.th.* etw); ~**ing** [-ɪŋ] 1. durchdringend; 2. scharfsinnig; ~**ion** [ˌpenɪ'treɪʃn]

1. Ein-, Durchdringen *n*; 2. Scharfsinn *m*.

pen-friend ['penfrend] Brieffreund *m*.

penguin ['peŋgwɪn] *orn* Pinguin *m*.

peninsula [pɪ'nɪnsjʊlə] Halbinsel *f*.

peniten|ce ['penɪtəns] Reue *f*; ~**t** [-t] reu(müt)ig; ~**tiary** [ˌpenɪ'tenʃərɪ] Strafanstalt *f*.

pen-name ['penneɪm] Schriftstellername *m*.

penniless ['penɪlɪs] völlig mittellos.

penny ['penɪ] *pl* **pence** [pens] (*Wert*) *u.* **pennies** [-z] (*Anzahl Münzen*) Penny *m*; *cost a pretty* ~ e-e schöne Stange Geld kosten.

pension ['penʃn] **I** *s* Rente; Pension *f*; **II** *v* (~ *off*) pensionieren; ~**er** ['penʃənə] Ruhegehaltsempfänger *m*.

pensive ['pensɪv] nachdenklich.

penthouse ['penthaʊs] Dachterrassenwohnung *f*.

people ['piːpl] **I** *s* 1. *pl* die Menschen, die Leute; 2. Bevölkerung *f*; 3. *the common* ~ das einfache Volk; 4. *fam* Angehörige *m pl*; 5. *sing (pl* ~*s)* Volk *n*, Nation *f*; **II** *v* bevölkern.

pep [pep] *sl* Schwung *m*.

pepper ['pepə] **I** *s* Pfeffer *m*; **II** *v* pfeffern; ~**mint** [-mɪnt] *bot* Pfefferminze *f*.

per [pɜː] per, pro; ~ *annum* jährlich; ~ *capita* pro Kopf.

perambulator [pə'ræmbjʊleɪtə] Kinderwagen *m*.

perceive [pə'si:v] wahrnehmen, erkennen.

percentage [pə'sentɪdʒ] 1. Prozentsatz *m*; 2. Anteil *m*.

percept|ible [pə'septəbl] wahrnehmbar; ~**ion** [pə'sepʃn] Wahrnehmung *f*.

perch [pɜːtʃ] 1. Hühnerstange *f*; 2. (*Fisch*) Barsch *m*.

percussion [pə'kʌʃn] 1. Stoß *m*, Erschütterung *f*; 2. *mus* Schlagzeug *n*.

peremptory [pə'remptərɪ] bestimmt, entschieden.

perennial [pə'renjəl] beständig, immerwährend.

perfect I *adj* ['pɜːfɪkt] 1. vollendet, vollkommen; 2. vollständig; 3. *he is a ~ stranger to me* er ist mir völlig unbekannt; **II** *v* [pə'fekt] vervollkommnen, vervollständigen; ~**ion** [pə'fekʃn] 1. Vervollkommnung *f*; 2. Vollkommenheit *f*; ~**ly** ['pɜːfɪktlɪ] vollkommen.

perforate ['pɜːfəreɪt] durchstechen, lochen.

perform [pə'fɔːm] 1. durch-, ausführen, leisten; 2. *theat* aufführen; ~**ance** [-əns] 1. Ausführung *f*; 2. Leistung *f*; 3. *theat* Aufführung *f*; ~**er** [-ə] Künstler *m*.

perfume I *s* ['pɜːfjuːm] Duft *m*, Parfüm *n*; **II** *v* [pə'fjuːm] parfümieren.

perhaps [pə'hæps, *fam* præps] vielleicht.

peril ['perəl] Gefahr *f*; *in ~ of o.'s life* in Lebensgefahr; ~**ous** [-əs] gefährlich.

period ['pɪərɪəd] 1. Periode *f* *a. geol*, Zeitraum *m*; *~ of validity* Gültigkeitsdauer *f*; 2. Epoche *f*; 3. Punkt *m*; 4. Schulstunde *f*; ~**ic(al)** [,pɪərɪ'ɒdɪk(l)] periodisch; ~**ical** [,pɪərɪ'ɒdɪkl] Zeitschrift *f*.

perish ['perɪʃ] 1. umkommen (*by* durch; *of, with* an); 2. (*Waren*) verderben; ~**able** [-əbl] (*Ware*) leicht verderblich.

perjur|e ['pɜːdʒə] *~ o.s.* falsch schwören; ~**y** [-rɪ] *commit ~* e-n Meineid leisten.

perk [pɜːk] (*~ up*) lebhaft, munter werden; ~**y** ['-ɪ] 1. frech; 2. munter.

perm [pɜːm] *fam* Dauerwelle *f*.

permanen|ce ['pɜːmənəns] Dauer, Dauerhaftigkeit *f*; ~**t** [-t] dauernd, ständig; *~ residence* feste(r) Wohnsitz *m*.

permea|ble ['pɜːmjəbl] durchlässig (*to* für); ~**te** ['pɜːmɪeɪt] durchsickern, -dringen (*through, among* in).

permiss|ible [pə'mɪsəbl] zulässig; ~**ion** [pə'mɪʃn] Bewilligung, Erlaubnis *f*; *without ~* unbefugt; *ask s.o.'s ~, s.o. for ~* jdn um Erlaubnis bitten; *grant ~* genehmigen.

permit I *v* [pə'mɪt] erlauben, gestatten, zulassen; *weather ~ting* bei günstigem Wetter; **II** *s* ['pɜːmɪt] 1. Genehmigung *f;* 2. Passierschein *m.*

pernicious [pə'nɪʃəs] schädlich (*to* für).

perpetrat|e ['pɜːpɪtreɪt] 1. *(Fehler)* begehen; 2. *(Verbrechen)* verüben; **~or** [-ə] (Übel-)Täter *m.*

perpetu|al [pə'petʃʊəl] 1. dauernd, ewig; 2. unaufhörlich; **~ity** [ˌpɜːpɪ'tjuːətɪ] Ewigkeit *f.*

perplex [pə'pleks] 1. verwirren; 2. *(Sache)* verkomplizieren; **~ity** [-ətɪ] 1. Bestürzung *f;* 2. Verwirrung *f.*

persecut|e ['pɜːsɪkjuːt] 1. verfolgen; 2. quälen (*with* mit); **~ion** [ˌpɜːsɪ'kjuːʃn] Verfolgung *f;* **~or** [-ə] Verfolger *m.*

persever|ance [ˌpɜːsɪ'vɪərəns] Ausdauer, Beharrlichkeit *f;* **~e** [ˌpɜːsɪ'vɪə] aus-, durchhalten, festhalten (*in, with* an); **~ing** [-rɪŋ] ausdauernd, beharrlich.

Persian ['pɜːʃn] **I** *s* Perser *m;* **II** *adj* persisch.

persist [pə'sɪst] 1. beharren (*in* auf, bei), bestehen (*in* auf); 2. fortdauern, -bestehen; **~ence** [-əns] Beharrlichkeit *f;* **~ent** [-ənt] 1. beharrlich; 2. anhaltend.

person ['pɜːsn] Person *f; in ~* persönlich; **~able** [-əbl]

gutaussehend; **~age** [-ɪdʒ] Persönlichkeit *f;* **~al** [-l] persönlich; privat; *~ affair* Privatangelegenheit *f; ~ hygiene* Körperpflege *f;* **~ality** [ˌpɜːsə'nælətɪ] 1. Persönlichkeit, Person *f;* 2. *pl* Anzüglichkeiten *f pl;* **~alize** ['pɜːsnəlaɪz] personifizieren; **~ification** [ˌpɜːsɒnɪfɪ'keɪʃn] Verkörperung *f;* **~ify** [pɜː'sɒnɪfaɪ] verkörpern; **~nel** [ˌpɜːsə'nel] Personal *n; ~ manager* Personalchef *m.*

perspir|ation [ˌpɜːspə'reɪʃn] Schweiß *m;* **~e** [pə'spaɪə] schwitzen.

persua|de [pə'sweɪd] 1. überreden (*of s.th.* zu e-r S); 2. dazu bringen (*to do, into doing* zu tun); 3. überzeugen (*of s.th.* von e-r S); **~sion** [pə'sweɪʒn] 1. Überredung *f;* 2. Überzeugung(skraft) *f;* **~sive** [pə'sweɪsɪv] überzeugend.

pert [pɜːt] vorlaut, keck.

pertinac|ious [ˌpɜːtɪ'neɪʃəs] beharrlich; **~ty** [-'næsətɪ] Hartnäckigkeit *f.*

pertinent ['pɜːtɪnənt] zur Sache (gehörig), relevant.

perturb [pə'tɜːb] beunruhigen.

peruse [pə'ruːz] (genau, sorgfältig) durchlesen.

perva|de [pə'veɪd] durchdringen *a. fig;* **~sive** [pə'veɪsɪv] durchdringend.

pervert [pə'vɜːt] 1. verdrehen; 2. verderben.

pessim|ism ['pesɪmɪzəm] Pessimismus *m;* ~**ist** [-ɪst] Pessimist *m.*

pest [pest] 1. Plagegeist *m;* 2. Schädling *m;* ~ **control** Schädlingsbekämpfung *f.*

pesticide ['pestɪsaɪd] Schädlingsbekämpfungsmittel *n.*

pester ['pestə] belästigen; quälen, plagen.

pet [pet] **I** *s* 1. Lieblingstier *n;* 2. Liebling *m;* **II** *v* (ver)hätscheln; liebkosen.

peter ['piːtə] ~ **out** allmählich zu Ende gehen.

petition [pɪ'tɪʃn] **I** *s* 1. Gesuch *n;* 2. *jur* Antrag *m;* **II** *v* 3. bitten, ersuchen (*s.o.* jdn); 4. nachsuchen (*for* um); ~**er** [-ə] Antragsteller *m.*

pet name Kosename *m.*

petrify ['petrɪfaɪ] 1. versteinern *a. fig;* 2. *fig* erstarren lassen.

petrol ['petrəl] Benzin *n;* ~**eum** [pɪ'trəuljəm] Petroleum *n;* ~ **station** Tankstelle *f.*

petticoat ['petɪkəut] Unterrock *m.*

pettifogging [petɪfogɪŋ] kleinlich.

pettish ['petɪʃ] launisch.

petty ['petɪ] 1. geringfügig, unbedeutend; 2. kleinlich.

petulant ['petjulənt] ungeduldig.

pharmacy ['fɑːməsɪ] Apotheke *f.*

phase [feɪz] Phase *f.*

pheasant ['feznt] Fasan *m.*

phenomen|al [fə'nomɪnl] phänomenal; ~**on** [fə'nomɪnən] *pl* -**ena** [-ə] 1. Erscheinung *f;* 2. Phänomen, Genie *n.*

philatelist [fɪ'lætəlɪst] Briefmarkensammler *m.*

philosoph|er [fɪ'losəfə] Philosoph *m;* ~**ic(al)** [ˌfɪlə'sofɪk(l)] philosophisch; ~**y** [fɪ'losəfɪ] Philosophie *f.*

phone [fəun] **I** *s fam* Telefon *n; be on the* ~ am Apparat sein; **II** *v* telefonieren; ~**booth** ['-buːð] Telefonzelle *f;* ~**call** ['-kɔːl] Anruf *m.*

phonograph ['fəunəgrɑːf] Plattenspieler *m.*

photo ['fəutəu] *fam* Foto *n;* Aufnahme *f;* ~**copy** [-ˌkopɪ] **I** *s* Fotokopie *f;* **II** *v* fotokopieren; ~**graph** ['fəutəgrɑːf] **I** *s* Fotografie *f;* **II** *v* fotografieren; *take a* ~ eine Aufnahme machen; ~**grapher** [fə'togrəfə] Fotograf *m;* ~**graphy** [fə'togrəfɪ] Fotografie *f.*

phrase [freɪz] **I** *s* 1. (Rede-) Wendung *f;* 2. *gram* Satzteil *m;* 3. *mus* Satz *m;* **II** *v* ausdrücken; ~**ology** [ˌfreɪzɪ'olədʒɪ] Phraseologie *f.*

phys|ical ['fɪzɪkl] 1. körperlich, physisch; ~ **education** Leibesübungen *f pl;* 2. physikalisch; ~**ician** [fɪ'zɪʃn] Arzt *m;* ~**icist** ['fɪzɪsɪst] Physiker *m;* ~**ics** ['fɪzɪks] *pl* *mit sing* Physik *f;* ~**ique** [fɪˈziːk] Körperbau *m;* Konstitution *f.*

pian|ist [ˈpɪənɪst] Pianist *m;* ~**o** [pɪˈænəʊ] *pl -nos; play (on) the* ~ Klavier spielen; *grand* ~ Flügel *m;* ~**forte** [ˌpjænəʊˈfɔːtɪ] Klavier *n.*

pick [pɪk] **I** *s* Pickel *m,* Spitzhacke *f;* **II** *v* 1. (auf)hacken, zerpflücken; stochern; *have a bone to* ~ *with s.o.* mit jdm ein Hühnchen zu rupfen haben; 2. auswählen; 3. *(Obst, Blumen)* pflücken; 4. *(Vogel)* picken; 5. ~ *at* widerwillig essen; ~ **out** (aus)wählen; ausfindig machen; ~ **up** 1. aufpicken, -heben, -lesen; 2. *pick s.o. up* jdn *(in einem Fahrzeug)* mitnehmen; jdn zufällig kennenlernen; 3. *(Kenntnisse)* sich aneignen; 4. *pick up health* wieder gesund werden; 5. *pick up speed* schneller werden.

pickaxe [ˈpɪkæks] Spitzhacke *f.*

picket [ˈpɪkɪt] **I** *s* 1. Pfosten *m;* 2. Streikposten *m;* **II** *v* 3. einzäunen; 4. Streikposten stehen.

pickle [ˈpɪkl] **I** *s* 1. (Salz-)Lake *f;* 2. *pl* eingelegte(s) Gemüse *n;* **II** *v* (ein)pökeln.

pickpocket [ˈpɪkˌpɒkɪt] Taschendieb *m.*

pick-up [ˈpɪkʌp] 1. Tonabnehmer *m;* 2. kleine(r) Lieferwagen *m.*

picnic [ˈpɪknɪk] **I** *s* Picknick *n;* **II** *v (pp -ck-)* picknicken.

pictorial [pɪkˈtɔːrɪəl] **I** *adj* bebildert; **II** *s* Illustrierte *f.*

picture [ˈpɪktʃə] **I** *v* 1. abbilden; malen; 2. sich vorstellen; **II** *s* 3. Bild *n; phot* Aufnahme *f;* 4. bildschöne Sache *od* Person *f;* 5. Verkörperung *f;* 6. *pl* Kino *n; go to the* ~*s* ins Kino gehen; 7. *put s.o. in the* ~ jdn ins Bild setzen; ~**-book** [-bʊk] Bilderbuch *n;* ~**-gallery** [-ˌgælərɪ] Gemäldegalerie *f;* ~ **postcard** Ansichtskarte *f.*

picturesque [ˌpɪktʃəˈresk] malerisch.

pie [paɪ] Pastete *f; have a finger in the* ~ die Hand im Spiel haben.

piece [piːs] **I** *v:* ~ *together* zs.setzen; **II** *s* 1. Stück *n;* ~ *by* ~ Stück für Stück; *in* ~*s* entzwei; *a* ~ *of advice* ein Rat *m; a* ~ *of news* e-e Neuigkeit; 2. *(*~ *of money)* Geldstück *n;* 3. Teil *n (e-s Services);* ~**-work** [ˈ-wɜːk] Akkordarbeit *f.*

pier [pɪə] 1. Brückenpfeiler *m;* 2. Landungsbrücke *f.*

pierc|e [pɪəs] 1. eindringen in; durchbohren; 2. dringen *(through* durch); ~**ing** [ˈ-ɪŋ] durchdringend.

piety [ˈpaɪətɪ] Frömmigkeit *f.*

pig [pɪg] Schwein *n; buy a* ~ *in a poke* die Katze im Sack kaufen; ~**-breeding** [ˌ-ˈbriːdɪŋ] Schweinezucht *f.*

pigeon ['pɪdʒɪn] orn Taube f; homing ~ Brieftaube f; **~hole** ['pɪdʒɪnhəʊl] I s (Ablege-)Fach n; II v (Papiere) ablegen.

pig|gish ['pɪgɪʃ] schweinisch; **~-headed** ['pɪg,hedɪd] störrisch; **~sty** ['pɪgstaɪ] Schweinestall m.

pike [paɪk] 1. Spieß m; 2. zoo Hecht m.

pile [paɪl] I s 1. Pfahl, Pfeiler m; 2. Stoß, Stapel m; 3. (funeral ~) Scheiterhaufen m; 4. Trockenbatterie f; 5. (atomic ~) Reaktor m; II v (~ up) aufhäufen, -stapeln; **~-up** Massenkarambolage f.

pilgrim ['pɪlgrɪm] Pilger m; **~age** [-ɪdʒ] Pilgerfahrt f.

pill [pɪl] Pille, Tablette f; be on the ~ die (Anti-Baby-)Pille nehmen.

pillar ['pɪlə] Pfeiler m, Säule f a. fig; **~-box** [-bɒks] Briefkasten m.

pillion ['pɪljən] Soziussitz m.

pillory ['pɪlərɪ] I s Pranger m; II v fig anprangern.

pillow ['pɪləʊ] Kopfkissen n; **~-case** [-keɪs] , **~-slip** [-slɪp] Kopfkissenbezug, -überzug m.

pilot ['paɪlət] I s mar Lotse; aero Pilot m; II v lotsen; steuern; III adj Versuchs-; ~ lamp Warnlampe f; **~-light** [-laɪt] Zündflamme f.

pimpl|e ['pɪmpl] Pickel m; **~y** [-ɪ] pick(e)lig.

pin [pɪn] I s 1. (Steck-)Nadel f; ~s and needles Kribbeln n; I don't care a ~ das ist mir (ganz) egal; 2. Anstecknadel f; 3. tech Stift m; II v 4. (an)heften, anstecken; 5. einklemmen; 6. ~ s.o. down jdn festlegen.

pin-ball ['pɪnbɔːl] (Spielautomat) Flipper m.

pincers pl ['pɪnsəz] 1. Zange f; 2. med Pinzette f.

pinch [pɪntʃ] I v 1. kneifen, zwicken; 2. (Schuh) drücken; 3. knausern; 4. (fam) klauen; 5. be ~ed with hunger Hunger leiden; II s 6. Kneifen n; give s.o. a ~ jdn kneifen; 7. Prise f; 8. fig Qual, Not f; at a ~, if it comes to the ~ im Notfall.

pincushion ['pɪn,kʊʃn] Nadelkissen n.

pine [paɪn] I s Kiefer, Föhre, Pinie f; II v 1. umkommen (from hunger vor Hunger); 2. sich sehnen (for nach).

pine-apple ['paɪn,æpl] Ananas f.

ping [pɪŋ] I s (Kugel) Pfeifen n; II v (Kugel) pfeifen, aufschlagen.

ping-pong ['pɪŋpɒŋ] Tischtennis n.

pinion ['pɪnjən] I s Schwungfeder f; II v 1. die Flügel beschneiden; 2. fig fesseln (to an).

pink [pɪŋk] I s 1. bot Nelke f; 2. Blaßrot n; in the ~ (fam) in bester Verfassung; **II** adj blaßrot.

pinnacle ['pɪnəkl] 1. Zinne f; 2. Bergspitze f; 3. fig Höhepunkt m.

pin-point ['pɪnpɔɪnt] **I** s Nadelspitze f; **II** v (Ziel) genau treffen.

pint [paɪnt] Pinte f (⅛ Gallone; Br 0,568 l, Am 0,473 l).

pioneer [ˌpaɪə'nɪə] **I** s Pionier m a. fig; **II** v fig Pionierarbeit leisten.

pious ['paɪəs] fromm, gottesfürchtig.

pip [pɪp] 1. (Obst-)Kern m; 2. (Würfel) Auge n; 3. Piepen n, Piepton m.

pipe [paɪp] **I** s 1. Rohr n; 2. Flöte f; 3. (Vogel) Ruf m; 4. anat Röhre f; 5. (Gas, Wasser) Leitung f; 6. (Tabaks-)Pfeife f; **II** v 7. pfeifen; 8. (durch ein Rohr) leiten.

pipe|dream ['paɪpdriːm] Luftschloß n; ~**line** ['-laɪn] Pipeline, Rohrleitung f; in the ~ im Kommen.

piping ['paɪpɪŋ] **I** s Rohrnetz n, -leitung f; **II** adv: ~ hot siedend heiß.

pirate ['paɪərət] **I** s Pirat m; **II** v unerlaubt nachdrucken.

Pisces pl ['pɪsiːz] astr Fische pl.

pistol ['pɪstl] Pistole f.

piston ['pɪstən] tech Kolben m; ~-**engine** Kolbenmotor m.

pit [pɪt] **I** s 1. Grube f;

2. theat Parterre n; **II** v Gruben graben in.

pitch [pɪtʃ] **I** v 1. errichten; (Zelt) aufschlagen; 2. werfen, schleudern; 3. mus (Ton) angeben, (Instrument) stimmen; 4. hinfallen; 5. (Schiff) stampfen; 6. ~ in sich ins Zeug legen; ~ into loslegen, zupacken; **II** s 7. Pech n; 8. Wurf m; 9. mus Tonhöhe f; 10. fig Höhe f, Grad m; 11. Neigung(swinkel m) f; 12. (Schiff) Stampfen n; ~-**dark** [ˌ-'dɑːk] stockfinster; ~**er** ['-ə] 1. Krug m; 2. sport Werfer m; ~**fork** ['-fɔːk] Heugabel f.

piteous ['pɪtɪəs] kläglich, jämmerlich.

pitfall ['pɪtfɔːl] Fallgrube f.

pith [pɪθ] 1. Mark n a. fig; 2. fig Kern m; ~ **helmet** Tropenhelm m; ~**y** ['-ɪ] 1. markig; 2. fig (Stil) prägnant.

piti|able ['pɪtɪəbl] 1. bemitleidenswert; 2. erbärmlich; ~**less** ['pɪtɪlɪs] mitleid-, erbarmungslos.

pity ['pɪtɪ] **I** s Mitleid n; out of ~ aus Mitleid; take ~ on Mitleid haben mit; what a ~! wie schade! it's a ~ that es ist schade, daß; **II** v bemitleiden, bedauern.

pivot ['pɪvət] **I** s 1. Drehpunkt m; 2. fig Angelpunkt m; **II** v sich drehen (on um) a. fig.

placard ['plækɑːd] **I** s Plakat n, Anschlag(zettel) m; **II** v plakatieren.

place [pleɪs] **I** s 1. Platz, Ort m, Stelle f a. fig; 2. Ortschaft f; 3. Stätte f; 4. in ~ of anstelle von; in my ~ an meiner Stelle, in meiner Lage; in the first ~ in erster Linie; out of ~ nicht am (rechten) Platz; unangebracht; give ~ Platz machen (to für); take ~ stattfinden; 5. (An-)Stellung f; 6. Wohnung f; **II** v 7. (auf)stellen, legen, setzen a. fig; 8. (Geld) anlegen; 9. unterbringen; 10. (Bestellung) aufgeben; (Auftrag) erteilen; ~**ment** ['-mənt] Plazierung f; ~**-name** ['-neɪm] Ortsname m.

placid ['plæsɪd] ruhig, gelassen.

plague [pleɪg] **I** s 1. (Beulen-) Pest f; 2. fig (Land-)Plage f; **II** v quälen, plagen.

plaice [pleɪs] pl ~ zoo Scholle f.

plain [pleɪn] **I** adj 1. klar; 2. einfach, schlicht; 3. flach, eben, glatt; **II** s (weite) Ebene, freie Fläche f; ~**spoken** ['-ˌspəʊkən] freimütig, offen.

plaint|**iff** ['pleɪntɪf] jur Kläger m; ~**ive** ['pleɪntɪv] traurig, kläglich.

plait [plæt] Flechte f, Zopf m.

plan [plæn] **I** s Entwurf, Plan m a. fig; **II** v 1. planen (for s.th. etw); entwerfen; 2. beabsichtigen; ~**ner** ['-ə] Planer m; ~**ning** ['-ɪŋ] Planung, Ausarbeitung f; family ~ Geburtenkontrolle f.

plane [pleɪn] **I** adj flach, eben a. math; **II** s 1. (glatte) Fläche, Ebene f a. fig; on the same ~ auf der gleichen Ebene (as wie); 2. aero fam Flugzeug n; 3. Hobel m; 4. bot Platane f; **III** v 5. aero gleiten; 6. ebnen, (ab)hobeln.

planet ['plænɪt] astr Planet m.

plank [plæŋk] Planke, Bohle f.

plant [plɑːnt] **I** s 1. bot Pflanze f; 2. Fabrik f, Werk(sanlage f) n; power ~ Kraftwerk n; **II** v 3. (an-, be-, ein)pflanzen; 4. fig (im Gedächtnis) einprägen; ~**ation** [plænˈteɪʃn] (An-)Pflanzung, Plantage f; ~**er** ['plɑːntə] Pflanzer m.

plaster ['plɑːstə] **I** s 1. arch (Ver-)Putz m; (~ of Paris) Gips m; 2. Pflaster n; sticking-~ Heftpflaster n; **II** v 3. verputzen; 4. bepflastern a. fig; ~ cast Gipsverband m; ~**er** [-rə] Stukkateur m.

plastic ['plæstɪk] **I** adj 1. formend, gestaltend; 2. plastisch; **II** s pl Kunststoff m; ~ **arts** pl bildende Kunst f; ~**s industry** Kunststoffindustrie f.

plate 217 **pliable**

plate [pleɪt] **I** s 1. Teller m, Platte f; 2. Silbergeschirr n; 3. Tafel f; 4. Schild n; **II** v (mit Metall) überziehen.

platform ['plætfɔ:m] 1. Plattform f; 2. Bahnsteig m; 3. (Redner-)Tribüne f.

platinum ['plætɪnəm] Platin n.

play [pleɪ] **I** s 1. Spiel n, a. fig, tech; in full ~ in vollem Gange; 2. (Theater-)Stück, Schauspiel n; 3. Spielraum m; **II** v spielen a. fig, mus, theat; ~ at cards Karten spielen; ~ at chess Schach spielen; ~ football Fußball spielen; ~ **down** herunterspielen; ~ **out** zu Ende spielen; played out erledigt, erschöpft.

play|back ['pleɪbæk] Abspielen n, Wiedergabe f; ~**er** ['-ə] Spieler; theat Darsteller m; ~**ground** ['-graʊnd] Spielplatz m; ~**ing** ['-ɪŋ] ~-card Spielkarte f; ~-field Sportplatz m; ~**mate** ['-meɪt] Spielgefährte m; ~**thing** ['-θɪŋ] Spielzeug n; ~**wright** ['-raɪt] Dramatiker m.

plea [pli:] 1. Vorwand m; 2. jur Plädoyer n; 3. Gesuch n (for um).

plead [pli:d] 1. jur plädieren; ~ guilty sich schuldig bekennen; 2. ~ for s.th. um etw ersuchen (with s.o. bei jdm); 3. einwenden, geltend machen; 4. vorschützen; 5. ~

the case for s.th. sich für etw einsetzen.

pleasant ['pleznt] 1. angenehm, erfreulich; 2. (Wetter) freundlich; ~**ry** ['plezntrɪ] 1. Ausgelassenheit f; 2. Scherz, Spaß m.

pleas|e [pli:z] **I** interj bitte; **II** v 1. gefallen (s.o. jdm); 2. zufriedenstellen; be ~d erfreut, zufrieden sein (with mit); ~ yourself, do as you ~ tun Sie ganz nach Belieben! 3. if you ~ wenn ich bitten darf; ~**ing** ['pli:zɪŋ] angenehm; gefällig; ~**ure** ['pleʒə] 1. Vergnügen n, Freude f; take ~ in Gefallen finden an; 2. at ~ nach Belieben.

pleat [pli:t] **I** s (Zier-)Falte f; **II** v in Falten legen.

pledge [pledʒ] 1. Pfand n; 2. fig Unterpfand n; 3. Versprechen n; under the ~ of secrecy unter dem Siegel der Verschwiegenheit; **II** v 4. verpfänden; 5. (sich) verpflichten; 6. ~ s.o. jdm zutrinken.

plenipotentiary [ˌplenɪpəʊ'tenʃərɪ] Bevollmächtigte(r) m.

plent|iful ['plentɪfʊl] reichlich; ~**y** ['plentɪ] **I** s Reichtum, Überfluß m; ~ of e-e Menge . . . ; in ~ in Hülle u. Fülle; **II** adv: (fam) it's ~ big enough already es ist schon reichlich groß.

pliable ['plaɪəbl] 1. biegsam,

geschmeidig *a. fig;* 2. *fig* leicht zu beeinflussen(d).

pliers *pl* ['plaɪəz] (Draht-) Zange *f.*

plight [plaɪt] Notlage *f; be in a terrible ~* in e-r schrecklichen Lage sein.

plod [plɒd] mühsam gehen.

plop [plɒp] plumpsen.

plot [plɒt] **I** *s* 1. Fleck(chen n) *m* Erde; *building ~* Bauplatz *m;* 2. Verschwörung *f;* 3. Handlung *f;* **II** *v* 4. aufzeichnen; 5. *(Plan)* schmieden; 6. sich verschwören.

plough, *Am meist* **plow** [plaʊ] **I** *s* Pflug *m;* **II** *v* 1. pflügen; 2. *~ through (Weg)* bahnen.

pluck [plʌk] **I** *v* 1. (ab-, aus)reißen; 2. *(Geflügel)* rupfen; 3. *(Blume)* pflücken; 4. *~ up courage* Mut fassen; **II** *s* Mut *m,* Tapferkeit *f;* **~y** ['-ɪ] mutig.

plug [plʌg] **I** *s* 1. Pflock, Pfropfen *m;* 2. *el* Stecker *m;* 3. *mot (spark-~)* Zündkerze *f;* 4. *(fire-~)* Hydrant *m;* 5. *med* Plombe, Füllung *f;* **II** *v* 6. *(~ up)* zustopfen, -stöpseln; 7. *(Zahn)* plombieren; 8. *~ away at (fam)* sich abquälen mit; 9. *~ in (el)* hineinstecken, einschalten.

plum [plʌm] Pflaume *f.*

plumage ['pluːmɪdʒ] Gefieder *n.*

plumb [plʌm] **I** *s (~-line)* Lot, Senkblei *n;* **II** *v* (aus)loten, sondieren *a. fig;* **~er** ['-ə] Klempner *m;* **~ing** ['-ɪŋ] Rohrleitungen *f pl.*

plume [pluːm] **I** *s* 1. Feder *f;* 2. *(~ of smoke)* Rauchfahne *f;* **II** *v* 3. *(Gefieder)* putzen; 4. *~ o.s. on s.th.* sich mit etw brüsten.

plump [plʌmp] **I** *adj* rundlich, mollig; **II** *v* 1. *(~ up, out)* dick machen *od* werden; 2. *~ down* (sich) fallen lassen.

plunder ['plʌndə] **I** *v* (aus)plündern; **II** *s* 1. Plünderung *f;* 2. Diebesgut *n;* **~er** [-rə] Plünderer, Dieb *m.*

plunge [plʌndʒ] **I** *v* 1. tauchen; 2. (sich) stürzen *(into* in); **II** *s* 3. Tauchen *n; take the ~ (fig)* den Sprung wagen; 4. Sturz *m.*

plural ['plʊərəl] *gram* Mehrzahl *f.*

plushy ['plʌʃɪ] *sl* luxuriös, elegant.

ply [plaɪ] **I** *s* 1. Schicht, Lage *f;* 2. Strang *m;* **II** *v* 3. *(Arbeitsgerät)* handhaben; 4. regelmäßig verkehren *(between* zwischen); 5. *~ s.o. with* jdn versorgen mit; **~wood** ['-wʊd] Sperrholz *n.*

pneumatic [njuːˈmætɪk] pneumatisch; *~ tube* Rohrpost *f.*

pneumonia [njuːˈməʊnjə] Lungenentzündung *f.*

poach [pəʊtʃ] wildern.

pock [pɒk] Pockennarbe *f.*

pocket ['pɒkɪt] I *s* Tasche *f;* II *v* 1. in die Tasche stecken; 2. *fig* einstecken; **~-book** [-bʊk] 1. Taschen-, Notizbuch *n;* 2. *Am* Handtasche *f;* ~ **calculator** Taschenrechner *m;* **~-knife** [-naɪf] Taschenmesser *n;* **~-money** [-ˌmʌnɪ] Taschengeld *n.*

pod [pɒd] *bot* Schote, Hülse *f.*

poem ['pəʊɪm] Gedicht *n.*

poet ['pəʊɪt] Dichter *m;* **~ry** [-rɪ] Dichtkunst, Dichtung *f.*

point [pɔɪnt] I *s* 1. Punkt *m a. sport; on* ~s nach Punkten; *boiling-*~ Siedepunkt *m; freezing-*~ Gefrierpunkt *m; turning-*~ Wendepunkt *m;* ~ *of view* Standpunkt *m;* 2. Grad *m;* 3. (Zeit-)Punkt, Augenblick *m; on the* ~ im Begriff (*of doing* zu tun); 4. Thema *n,* der springende Punkt; *off the* ~ nicht zur Sache gehörend; *come to the* ~ zur (Haupt-)Sache kommen; *I don't see your* ~ ich weiß nicht, worauf Sie hinauswollen; *make o.'s* ~ ein Argument anbringen; 5. *fig* Seite, Eigenschaft *f;* 6. Spitze *f;* 7. *pl* Weichen *pl;* II *v* 8. zeigen, richten (*to* auf), gerichtet sein; 9. (~ *out*) zeigen, das Interesse richten (*at* auf); 10. (*Waffe*) richten (*at* auf); 11. (an)spitzen.

point|ed ['pɔɪntɪd] 1. (zu-ge)spitz(t); 2. *fig* scharf, beißend; **~er** ['pɔɪntə] 1. Zeiger, Pfeil *m;* 2. Zeigestock *m;* **~less** ['-lɪs] bedeutungs-, zwecklos.

pointsman ['pɔɪntsmən] Weichensteller *m.*

poise [pɔɪz] I *s* 1. Gleichgewicht *n,* Haltung *f;* 2. *fig* (innere) Ausgeglichenheit *f;* II *v* balancieren.

poison ['pɔɪzn] I *s* Gift *n a. fig* (*to* für); II *v* Gift geben (*s.o.* jdm), vergiften *a. fig;* **~ous** [-əs] giftig.

poke [pəʊk] I *v* 1. (an)stoßen; 2. (*ein Loch*) bohren; 3. wühlen, stochern (*in* in); ~ *o.'s nose into* (*fam*) s-e Nase stecken in; II *s* Stoß *m;* **~r** ['-ə] 1. Feuerhaken *m;* 2. (*Spiel*) Poker *n.*

Poland ['pəʊlənd] Polen *n.*

polar ['pəʊlə] polar; ~ **bear** Eisbär *m;* ~ **circle** Polarkreis *m;* ~ **lights** *pl* Nordlicht *n.*

Pole [pəʊl] Pole *m.*

pole [pəʊl] 1. *geol* Pol *m a. phys u. fig; be* ~s *apart* himmelweit voneina. verschieden sein; 2. Stange *f; sport* Stab *m;* (Ski-)Stock *m;* **~-star** ['-sta:] Polarstern *m;* **~-vault** ['-vɔ:lt] Stabhochsprung *m.*

police [pə'li:s] Polizei *f;* **~man** [-mən] Polizist *m;* **~-office** [-ɒfɪs] Polizeipräsidium *n;* **~-officer** [-ɒfɪsə] Polizeibeamte(r) *m;*

~-station [-steɪʃn] Polizei-
revier n, -wache f.
policy ['pɒləsɪ] 1. Politik f;
politische Linie f; he makes
it a ~ to er hat es sich zum
Grundsatz gemacht; 2. (Ver-
sicherungs-)Police f.
polio(myelitis)
['pəʊlɪəʊ(maɪə'laɪtɪs)] Kin-
derlähmung f.
Polish ['pəʊlɪʃ] polnisch.
polish ['pɒlɪʃ] I v 1. polieren;
(Schuhe) putzen; 2. fig verfeinern; II s 3. Politur f;
4. fig Schliff m; ~ed [-t] fig
fein, elegant.
polite [pə'laɪt] höflich;
~ness [-nɪs] Höflichkeit f.
politic ['pɒlɪtɪk] diplomatisch,
klug; ~al [pə'lɪtɪkl] politisch,
staatspolitisch; for ~ reasons aus politischen Gründen; ~ economy Volkswirt-
schaft f; ~ian [,pɒlɪ'tɪʃn]
Politiker m; ~s ['pɒlɪtɪks] pl
mit sing Politik f; talk ~
politisieren.
poll [pəʊl] I s 1. Wahl, Abstimmung f; 2. Wahlbeteili-
gung f; 3. fig Wahllokal n; go
to the ~s zur Wahl gehen;
4. public opinion ~ Mei-
nungsumfrage f; II v Stimmen auf sich vereinigen;
~ing ['-ɪŋ] Stimmabgabe f;
~-booth Wahlzelle f.
pollut|e [pə'lu:t] verunreini-
gen; ~ion [pə'lu:ʃn] Um-
weltverschmutzung; Verun-
reinigung f.
pomp [pɒmp] Pomp, Prunk

m; ~ous ['pɒmpəs] prunk-
voll, pompös.
pond [pɒnd] Teich, Weiher
m.
ponder ['pɒndə] nachdenken, grübeln (over über);
~ous ['pɒndərəs] 1. schwer,
massig; 2. fig schwerfällig.
pony ['pəʊnɪ] Pony n; ~-tail
[-teɪl] Pferdeschwanz m
(Frisur).
poodle ['pu:dl] zoo Pudel m.
pool [pu:l] 1. kleine(r) Teich
m, Lache f; 2. (swimming-~)
Schwimmbecken n;
3. (Spiel-)Einsatz m; 4. ge-
meinsame(r) Fonds m;
5. com Kartell n, Pool m.
poor [pʊə] I adj 1. arm; ärmlich; 2. (Ernte) mager,
schlecht; 3. bedauernswert;
II s: the ~ die Armen; ~ly
['-lɪ] I adv 1. schwach, unzulänglich; 2. be ~ off übel
dran sein; II adj (fam): feel
~ sich nicht wohl fühlen.
pop [pɒp] I s 1. Knall(en n)
m; 2. Am fam Papa m; 3. (~
music) Popmusik f; (~ song)
Schlager m; II v 4. knallen,
platzen; ~ the question (sl)
e-n Heiratsantrag machen;
5. ~ in hereinplatzen; ~corn
['-kɔ:n] Am Puffmais m.
Pope [pəʊp] Papst m.
poplar ['pɒplə] Pappel f.
poppy ['pɒpɪ] Mohn-
(blume f) m.
popul|ace ['pɒpjʊləs] Pöbel,
Mob m; ~ar ['pɒpjʊlə]
1. Volks-; 2. volkstümlich,

populär; **~arity**
[ˌpɒpjuˈlærəti] Popularität,
Beliebtheit f; **~arize**
[ˈpɒpjuləraɪz] populär, beliebt machen; **~ate**
[ˈpɒpjuleɪt] bevölkern, be-
siedeln; **~ation**
[ˌpɒpjuˈleɪʃn] Bevölkerung f;
rural, urban ~ Land-, Stadt-
bevölkerung f; **~ous**
[ˈpɒpjuləs] dicht besiedelt.

porcelain [ˈpɔːsəlɪn] Porzellan n.

porch [pɔːtʃ] 1. Vorhalle f;
Portal n; 2. *Am* Veranda f.

porcupine [ˈpɔːkjupaɪn] Sta-
chelschwein n.

pore [pɔː] **I** v brüten (*over*
über); **II** s biol Pore f.

pork [pɔːk] Schweinefleisch
n; **~ chop** Schweinskotelett
n.

porous [ˈpɔːrəs] durchlässig.

porridge [ˈpɒrɪdʒ] Haferflok-
kenbrei m.

port [pɔːt] 1. (See-)Hafen m;
reach ~ in den Hafen einlaufen; 2. Hafenstadt f; *free*
~ Freihafen m; 3. Zuflucht-
sort m; 4. Luke f; 5. Backbord n; 6. Portwein m.

portable [ˈpɔːtəbl] tragbar; ~
type-writer Reise(schreib)-
maschine f; ~ *radio* Koffer-
radio n.

portal [ˈpɔːtl] Portal n.

porter [ˈpɔːtə] 1. (Gepäck-)
Träger m; 2. *Am* Schlafwa-
genschaffner m; 3. Pförtner
m.

portfolio [ˌpɔːtˈfəuljəu]
1. Aktentasche f; 2. Ge-
schäftsbereich m (e-s Mini-
sters).

portion [ˈpɔːʃn] **I** s 1. (An-)
Teil m (*of* an); 2. Portion f;
3. Schicksal n; **II** v (~ *out*)
zu-, austeilen.

portly [ˈpɔːtlɪ] stattlich.

portmanteau
[ˌpɔːtˈmæntəu] pl a. -x
Handkoffer m.

portr|ait [ˈpɔːtrɪt] 1. Bild(nis),
Porträt n; 2. *fig* Schilderung
f; **~ay** [pɔːˈtreɪ] 1. porträtie-
ren; 2. *fig* schildern.

Portug|al [ˈpɔːtjugl] Portugal
n; **~uese** [ˌpɔːtjuˈgiːz] **I** s
Portugiese m; **II** adj portu-
giesisch.

pose [pəuz] **I** v 1. (*Frage*)
aufwerfen; 2. posieren; 3. ~
as sich ausgeben als; **II** s
Stellung; Pose f a. *fig*; **~r**
[ˈ-ə] knifflige Frage f.

position [pəˈzɪʃn] 1. Stellung
a. *fig*, Lage f; *in, out of* ~
am rechten, falschen Platz;
be in a ~ *to do* in der Lage
sein zu tun; 2. Haltung, Einstellung f, Standpunkt m;
3. (Arbeits-)Platz m; *hold,
occupy a* ~ e-e Stelle haben,
ein Amt bekleiden.

positive [ˈpɒzətɪv] 1. genau;
2. sicher; *be* ~ ganz sicher
sein; 3. positiv; 4. konstruk-
tiv; 5. *fam* vollkommen, absolut.

possess [pəˈzes] 1. besitzen,
(inne)haben; 2. (*Sprache*)
beherrschen; **~ed** [-t] beses-

sen (*with* von); **~ion** [pə'zeʃn] Besitz *m*; Eigentum *n*; *be in* ~ *of s.th.* etw in Besitz haben; *take* ~ *of* Besitz ergreifen von; **~or** [-ə] Besitzer *m*.

possib|ility [ˌpɒsə'bɪlətɪ] Möglichkeit *f* (*of doing* zu tun; *of* zu, für); **~le** ['pɒsəbl] 1. möglich; *make* ~ ermöglichen; 2. denkbar, geeignet; **~ly** ['pɒsəblɪ] 1. möglicherweise; 2. *if I* ~ *can* wenn ich irgend kann; *I cannot* ~ *come* ich kann unmöglich kommen.

post [pəʊst] **I** *s* 1. Pfosten *m*; 2. *mil* Posten *m*; 3. (Arbeits-) Platz *m*; 4. Post(sendung) *f*; *by* ~ mit der Post; *by return of* ~ postwendend; 5. (*~-office*) Post(amt *n*) *f*; **II** *v* 6. in den Briefkasten werfen, aufgeben; 7. (*Plakat*) ankleben; ~ *no bills* (Zettel-)Ankleben verboten! **~age** ['-ɪdʒ] Porto *n*; ~ *stamp* Briefmarke *f*; **~al** ['-əl] postalisch; ~ *cheque* Postscheck *m*; **~-box** ['-bɒks] Briefkasten *m*; **~card** ['-kɑːd] Postkarte *f*; *picture* ~ Ansichtskarte *f*; **~code** ['-kəʊd] Postleitzahl *f*.

poster ['pəʊstə] Plakat *n*, Anschlag *m*.

poste restante [ˌpəʊst 'restɑ:nt] postlagernd.

poster|ior [pɒ'stɪərɪə] 1. (*zeitl.*) später (*to* als); 2. hinter; **~ity** [pɒ'sterətɪ]

1. Nachkommen(schaft *f*) *pl*; 2. Nachwelt *f*.

post|-free [ˌpəʊst'friː] portofrei; **~man** ['-mən] Briefträger *m*; **~mark** ['-mɑːk] **I** *s* Poststempel *m*; **II** *v* (ab)stempeln; ~ **office** Postamt *n*; *post office box* Postschließfach *n*; **~-paid** [-peɪd] frankiert, freigemacht.

postpone [ˌpəʊst'pəʊn] aufverschieben, zurückstellen.

postscript ['pəʊsskrɪpt] Nachschrift *f*.

posture ['pɒstʃə] 1. Stellung, Haltung *f*; 2. Einstellung *f*.

post-war ['pəʊstwɔː] Nachkriegs-.

pot [pɒt] **I** *s* Topf, Kessel *m*; *flower-~* Blumentopf *m*; *tea* ~ Teekanne *f*; **II** *v* eintopfen; einmachen.

potable ['pəʊtəbl] trinkbar.

potato [pə'teɪtəʊ] *pl -toes* Kartoffel *f*; *mashed ~es (pl)* Kartoffelbrei *m*; ~ **chips** *pl* Kartoffelchips *pl*.

pot-bellied ['pɒt,belɪd] dickbäuchig.

poten|cy ['pəʊtənsɪ] Stärke, Macht *f*; **~t** [-t] stark, mächtig.

pothole ['pɒthəʊl] Schlagloch *n*.

potted ['pɒtɪd] eingemacht.

potter ['pɒtə] Töpfer *m*; **~y** ['-rɪ] 1. Keramik *f*; Tonwaren *pl*; 2. Töpferei *f*.

pouch [paʊtʃ] **I** *s* Beutel *m*;

II *v* 1. in e-n Beutel stecken;
2. (sich) bauschen.

poultice ['pəʊltɪs] Umschlag,
Wickel *m.*

poultry ['pəʊltrɪ] Geflügel *n.*

pounce [paʊns] sich stürzen
(*on, at* auf).

pound [paʊnd] **I** *s* Pfund *n;*
by the ~ pfundweise; **II** *v*
1. (zer)stoßen, (zer)stamp-
fen; 2. schlagen, stampfen.

pour [pɔː] 1. gießen, schütten
(*out of, from* aus; *into* in; *on*
auf; *over* über); 2. *(Getränk)*
eingießen; 3. heftig regnen;
it's ~ing with rain es gießt
in Strömen; 4. *fig (Men-
schen)* strömen (*out of*
aus).

pout [paʊt] schmollen.

poverty ['pɒvətɪ] Armut *f.*

powder ['paʊdə] **I** *s* 1. Puder
m; 2. Pulver *n;* **II** *v* (ein)pu-
dern (*with* mit); **~ed** [-d] *~
milk* Milchpulver *n.*

power ['paʊə] 1. (Hand-
lungs-, Leistungs-)Fähigkeit
f; 2. Kraft *f;* 3. Gewalt *f*
(*over* über); Einfluß *m;*
4. Berechtigung, Befugnis *f;*
5. *pol* Macht *f; in ~* an der
Macht; im Amt; *come into
~* an die Macht gelangen;
6. *phys tech el* Energie, Leistung, (Strom-)Stärke *f;*
7. *buying, purchasing ~*
Kaufkraft *f.*

powerful ['paʊəfʊl] mächtig,
einflußreich; **~less** ['-lɪs]
kraft-, machtlos; **~-station**
['-,steɪʃn] Kraftwerk *n; ~*

supply Energie-, Stromver-
sorgung *f.*

practic|able ['præktɪkəbl]
1. aus-, durchführbar;
2. *(Straße)* befahrbar; **~al**
['præktɪkl] 1. praktisch;
2. brauchbar; **~ally**
['præktɪklɪ] beinahe, fast.

practi|ce ['præktɪs] 1. Praxis
*f (a. e-s Arztes); put in(to)
~* in die Tat umsetzen; 2. Gewohnheit, Sitte *f; make a ~
of s.th.* sich etw zur Gewohnheit machen; *in (out
of) ~* in (aus der) Übung;
~ise, *Am meist* **~ice**
['præktɪs] 1. ausüben, betreiben; *~ medicine* e-e ärztli-
che Praxis haben; 2. (sich)
üben; 3. praktizieren;
~itioner [præk'tɪʃnə] *general ~* praktische(r) Arzt *m.*

praise [preɪz] **I** *v* preisen, loben (*for* wegen); **II** *s* Lob *n;*
Anerkennung *f;* **~worthy**
['-,wɔːðɪ] lobenswert.

pram [præm] *fam* Kinderwagen *m.*

prance [prɑːns] 1. *(Pferd)*
sich aufbäumen; 2. *fig* stol-
zieren.

prank [præŋk] *play ~s on
s.o.* jdm e-n Streich spielen.

prattle ['prætl] plappern.

pray [preɪ] beten (*to* zu; *for*
um); **~er** [preə] Gebet *n;
say o.'s ~s* beten; *the Lord's
P~* das Vaterunser.

preach [priːtʃ] predigen; **~er**
['-ə] Prediger *m.*

precarious [prɪˈkeərɪəs] unsicher.

precaution [prɪˈkɔːʃn] Vorsicht(smaßnahme) *f; take ~s* Vorsichtsmaßnahmen treffen.

preced|e [ˌpriːˈsiːd] voraus-, vorangehen (*s.o., s.th.* jdm, e-r S); **~ence** [-əns] Vorrang, -tritt *m;* **~ent** [ˈprɪsɪdənt] vorher-, vorausgehend.

precept [ˈpriːsept] Gebot *n;* Regel *f.*

precinct [ˈpriːsɪŋkt] 1. *Am* (Stadt-)Bezirk *m;* 2. *pl* Umgebung *f;* 3. *pedestrian ~* Fußgängerzone *f.*

precious [ˈpreʃəs] wertvoll, kostbar; **~ metal** Edelmetall *n;* **~ stone** Edelstein *m.*

precip|ice [ˈpresɪpɪs] Abgrund *m a. fig;* **~itate** [prɪˈsɪpɪteɪt] 1. (kopfüber) hinabstürzen; 2. *fig* beschleunigen; 3. *chem mete* kondensieren; **~itation** [prɪˌsɪpɪˈteɪʃn] 1. Hast *f;* 2. *mete* Niederschläge *m pl;* **~itous** [prɪˈsɪpɪtəs] steil.

précis [ˈpreɪsiː] *pl ~* [-siːz] Zs.fassung, Übersicht *f.*

precis|e [prɪˈsaɪs] genau, exakt; **~ely** [-lɪ] genau; stimmt so, so ist es; **~ion** [prɪˈsɪʒn] Genauigkeit *f.*

preclude [prɪˈkluːd] ausschließen.

preconception [ˌpriːkənˈsepʃn] vorgefaßte Meinung *f.*

precursor [ˌpriːˈkɜːsə] Vorläufer *m.*

predecessor [ˈpriːdɪsesə] Vorgänger *m.*

predicament [prɪˈdɪkəmənt] mißliche Lage *f.*

predict [prɪˈdɪkt] vorhersagen; **~ion** [prɪˈdɪkʃn] Prophezeiung *f.*

predilection [ˌpriːdɪˌlekʃn] Vorliebe *f.*

predomin|ant [prɪˈdɒmɪnənt] vorherrschend, überwiegend; **~ate** [-eɪt] vorherrschen.

prefab [ˈpriːfæb] Fertighaus *n;* **~ricate** [ˌpriːˈfæbrɪkeɪt] vorfabrizieren.

preface [ˈprefɪs] **I** *s* Vorwort *n;* **II** *v* einleiten (*with* mit).

prefer [prɪˈfɜː] vorziehen, bevorzugen; **~able** [ˈprefərəbl] vorzuziehen(d); **~ably** [ˈprefərəblɪ] vorzugsweise; **~ence** [ˈprefərəns] Bevorzugung; Vorliebe *f (for* für); *in ~ to* lieber als; *have a ~ for* e-e Vorliebe haben für; *give ~ to s.o.* jdm den Vorzug geben; *what is your ~?* was ziehen Sie vor? **~ential** [ˌprefəˈrenʃl] *~ price* Vorzugs-, Sonderpreis *m.*

pregnan|cy [ˈpregnənsɪ] Schwangerschaft(sdauer) *f;* **~t** [ˈ-t] *(Frau)* schwanger.

prejudic|e [ˈpredʒʊdɪs] 1. Vorurteil *n (against* gegen); Voreingenommenheit *f (in favo(u)r of* für);

2. Schaden, Nachteil *m; to s.o.'s* ~ zu jds Nachteil; *without* ~ ohne Gewähr; ~**ial** [‚predʒʊˈdɪʃl] nachteilig (*to* für).

preliminary [prɪˈlɪmɪnərɪ] **I** *adj* 1. einleitend; 2. vorläufig; **II** *s* Vorbereitung *f* (*to* zu); *as a* ~, *by way of* ~ einleitend, vorbereitend.

prelude [ˈpreljuːd] Einleitung *f* (*to* zu); *mus* Vorspiel *n.*

premature [‚preməˈtjʊə] vorzeitig, zu früh; ~ *birth* Frühgeburt *f.*

premier [ˈpremjə] Premier(minister) *m.*

premises *pl* [ˈpremɪsɪz] Gelände; Gebäude *n;* Räumlichkeiten *pl; on the* ~ an Ort u. Stelle; *business* ~ Geschäftsräume *m pl.*

premium [ˈpriːmjəm] 1. *com* Prämie *f,* Bonus *m;* 2. (Versicherungs-)Prämie *f;* 3. Belohnung *f; put a* ~ *on* e-e Belohnung setzen auf.

premonition [priːməˈnɪʃən] Vorahnung *f.*

preoccupied [‚priːˈɒkjʊpaɪd] gedankenverloren.

prepaid [‚priːˈpeɪd] porto-, gebührenfrei.

preparation [‚prepəˈreɪʃn] 1. Vorbereitung *f; make* ~s Vorbereitungen treffen (*for* für); 2. Haus-, Schularbeit *f;* 3. *pharm* Präparat *n;* ~**e** [prɪˈpeə] 1. vorbereiten (*for s.th.* auf etw; *to do* zu tun); 2. (*Essen*) zubereiten; 3. sich

gefaßt machen (*for* auf); ~**ed** [prɪˈpeəd] *be* ~ *to* bereit, in der Lage sein zu; *I'm* ~ *to help you* ich will Ihnen gern helfen; 2. *be* ~ *for the worst* auf das Schlimmste gefaßt sein.

prepay [‚priːˈpeɪ] *irr (s. pay)* vorauszahlen.

preponderance [prɪˈpɒndərəns] Übergewicht *n a. fig.*

prepossession [‚priːpəˈzeʃn] Voreingenommenheit *f* (*in favo(u)r of* für; *against* gegen).

prescribe [prɪˈskraɪb] 1. vorschreiben (*to s.o.* jdm); 2. *med* verordnen (*s.th. for s.o.* jdm etw); ~**d** [-d] *as* ~, *in the* ~ *form* vorschriftsmäßig.

prescription [prɪˈskrɪpʃn] *med* Verordnung *f,* Rezept *n.*

presence [ˈprezns] Gegenwart, Anwesenheit *f; in the* ~ *of* in Gegenwart von; ~ *of mind* Geistesgegenwart *f.*

present I *adj* [ˈpreznt] 1. anwesend, zugegen; *be* ~ *at s.th.* bei e-r S anwesend sein; 2. vorhanden; 3. gegenwärtig; **II** *s* [ˈ-] 4. *the* ~ die Gegenwart *f; at* ~ im Augenblick; *for the* ~ vorläufig, einstweilen; 5. Geschenk *n; make s.o. a* ~ *of s.th.* jdm etw schenken; **III** *v* [prɪˈzent] 6. (*Person*) vorstellen (*to s.o.* jdm); 7. ~ *s.th. to s.o.* jdm etw schenken, überreichen; 8. vorlegen, präsentieren; 9. (*Gelegenheit*) sich bieten, sich ergeben; 10. *theat* zeigen, aufführen.

presentation [ˌprezən'teɪʃn] 1. Vorlage *f; on* ~ gegen Vorzeigung; 2. *theat* Aufführung *f;* 3. Überrreichung *f.*

present-day ['prezntˈdeɪ] gegenwärtig, zeitgenössisch.

presentiment [prɪˈzentɪmənt] (Vor-)Ahnung *f.*

presently ['prezntlɪ] 1. bald; 2. zur Zeit.

preserv|ation [ˌprezə'veɪʃn] Erhaltung, Konservierung *f;* ~**ative** [prɪˈzɜːvətɪv] Konservierungsmittel *n* (*from* gegen); ~**e** [prɪˈzɜːv] **I** *v* 1. bewahren, schützen (*from* vor); 2. einmachen, konservieren; **II** *s* meist *pl* Eingemachte(s) *n.*

preside [prɪˈzaɪd] den Vorsitz führen (*over* über; *at* bei).

president ['prezɪdənt] Vorsitzende(r), Präsident *m;* ~**ial** [prezɪ'denʃl] ~ *election* Wahl *f* des Präsidenten.

press [pres] **I** *v* 1. drücken (*the button* auf den Knopf); pressen; ~ *s.o.'s hand* jdm die Hand drücken; 2. ausdrücken, -pressen; 3. zs.drücken, -pressen;

4. bügeln; 5. bestürmen, bitten (*to do* zu tun); 6. aufdrängen, -nötigen, (*s.th. on s.o.* jdm etw); 7. *be* ~ed *for* knapp dran sein (*time, money* an Zeit, Geld); **II** *s* 8. Druck *m a. fig;* 9. (Frucht-)Presse *f;* 10. (*printing-*~) Druckpresse; (Buch-)Druck *m;* 11. Presse *f,* Zeitungen *f pl;* 12. Gedränge *n;* ~**-agency** ['-ˌeɪdʒənsɪ] Presseagentur *f;* ~**-button** ['-ˌbʌtn] Druckknopf *m;* ~**ing** ['-ɪŋ] dringend.

pressure ['preʃə] 1. Druck *m; atmospheric* ~ Luftdruck *m; blood* ~ Blutdruck *m; tyre* ~ Reifendruck *m;* 2. *fig* Druck, Zwang; Streß *m; under the* ~ *of necessity* notgedrungen; *bring, put* ~ Druck, Zwang ausüben (*on* auf); ~ *group* Interessengruppe *f;* ~**-cooker** [-ˌkʊkə] Dampfkochtopf *m.*

presum|able [prɪˈzjuːməbl] vermutlich; ~**e** [prɪˈzjuːm] 1. annehmen, vermuten; 2. sich herausnehmen; ~**ing** [-ɪŋ] anmaßend.

presumpt|ion [prɪˈzʌmpʃn] 1. Vermutung *f a. jur; on the* ~ *that* in der Annahme, daß; 2. Unverschämtheit *f;* ~**ive** [-tɪv] mutmaßlich; ~**uous** [-tjʊəs] anmaßend.

presuppose [ˌpriːsəˈpəʊz] 1. von vornherein annehmen; 2. voraussetzen.

preten|ce, *Am* **pretense**
['pri'tens] 1. Vorwand *m;*
make a ~ of s.th. etw vorschützen, -täuschen; 2. Ver-
stellung *f; false ~s* Vorspie-
gelung falscher Tatsachen;
3. Anspruch *m;* **~d** [-d]
1. vorgeben, -schützen, so
tun, als ob; *he's just ~ing* er
tut nur so; 2. Anspruch erheben (*to* auf); **~sion**
[pri'ten∫n] 1. Anspruch *m*
(*to* auf); 2. Anmaßung *f;*
~tious [-∫əs] anmaßend,
überheblich.

pretext ['pri:tekst] Ausrede,
Ausflucht *f; on, under the ~*
unter dem Vorwand (*of doing* etw zu tun).

pretty ['prɪtɪ] 1. hübsch, nett;
reizend; 2. *fam* ziemlich; ~
bad ziemlich mies; ~ *much*
so ziemlich; *I'm ~ well* es
geht mir ganz gut.

prevail [pri'veɪl] 1. sich
durchsetzen (*against* gegen); 2. vorherrschen, überwiegen (*in* bei); **~ing** [-ɪŋ]
(vor)herrschend; *under the
~ circumstances* unter den
gegebenen Umständen.

prevalent [prevələnt] vor-
herrschend.

prevent [pri'vent] 1. abhalten (*from doing s.th.* etw zu
tun); 2. verhindern; **~ion**
[pri'ven∫n] 1. Verhinderung
f; 2. *med* Vorbeugung *f;*
~ive [pri'ventɪv] vorbeugend; *~ custody* Vorbeuge-
haft *f.*

previous ['pri:vjəs] 1. vor-
aus-, vorhergehend; 2. voreilig; 3. ~ *to* vor; ~ **conviction** Vorstrafe *f;* **~ly** [-lɪ]
früher, vorher.

pre-war ['pri:wɔ:] Vor-
kriegs-.

prey [preɪ] **I** *s* Beute(tier *n*) *f;*
Opfer *n fig; fall a ~ to* zum
Opfer fallen *dat;* **II** *v* 1. ~
(up)on Jagd machen auf;
2. plündern; 3. *fig* lasten (*on,
upon* auf).

price [praɪs] **I** *s* Preis *m a.
fig; beyond, without ~ (fig)*
unbezahlbar; *at any ~ (fig)*
um jeden Preis; *at a ~* zum
entsprechenden Preis; **II** *v*
e-n Preis festsetzen; (*Waren*) auszeichnen; **~-con-
trol** ['-kəntrəʊl] Preiskon-
trolle *f;* **~less** ['-lɪs] unbezahlbar, unschätzbar; ~ **tag**
Preisschild *n.*

prick [prɪk] **I** *s* 1. Stich *m;*
2. stechende(r) Schmerz *m;*
~*s of conscience* Gewis-
sensbisse *m pl;* **II** *v* 3. stechen; 4. ~ *up o.'s ears* die
Ohren spitzen; **~ly** ['-lɪ]
stach(e)lig.

pride [praɪd] 1. Stolz *m; take
(a) ~ in* stolz sein auf;
2. Hochmut *m;* 3. *zoo* Rudel
n.

priest [pri:st] Priester, Geist-
liche(r) *m.*

prim [prɪm] 1. (über)korrekt;
2. steif, geziert.

primary [praɪmərɪ] **I** *adj*
1. primär, hauptsächlich(st),

wesentlich; *of ~ importance* von größter Wichtigkeit; 2. *~ colo(u)r* Grundfarbe *f;* *~ education* Grundschulunterricht *m;* **II** *s Am pol* Vorwahl *f.*

prime [praɪm] **I** *adj* 1. erst, wichtigst; 2. erstklassig; **II** *v* 3. *(Bombe)* scharf machen; 4. instruieren; 5. grundieren; **III** *s* Blüte(zeit) *f,* Höhepunkt *m; in o.'s ~* in der Blüte des Lebens; *~* **minister** Premierminister *m.*

primer ['praɪmə] Fibel *f.*

primitive ['prɪmɪtɪv] 1. ursprünglich; 2. primitiv.

primrose ['prɪmrəʊz] *bot* Primel, Schlüsselblume *f.*

prince [prɪns] 1. Fürst *m;* 2. Prinz *m; P~ of Wales (Titel des englischen Thronfolgers).*

princess [prɪn'ses] 1. Fürstin *f;* 2. Prinzessin *f.*

principal ['prɪnsəpl] **I** *adj* bedeutendst; Haupt-; **II** *s* 1. Vorsteher; *Am* Schulleiter *m;* 2. Auftraggeber *m;* 3. *jur* Haupttäter *m;* 4. Kapital *n.*

principle ['prɪnsəpl] Grundsatz *m,* Prinzip *n; in ~* im Prinzip; *on ~* aus Prinzip; *as a matter of ~* grundsätzlich, prinzipiell.

print [prɪnt] **I** *s* 1. (Ab-)Druck *m;* 2. *typ* Druck *m;* 3. *phot* Abzug *m;* **II** *v* 4. *(Papier)* (be)drucken; 5. *(Text)* veröffentlichen; 6. *phot* abziehen; *~er* ['-ə] (Buch-)Drucker *m;*

~ing [-ɪŋ] Drucken *n; ~ink* Druckerschwärze *f.*

prior ['praɪə] **I** *adj* früher *(to* als); **II** *prp: ~ to* vor; **III** *s rel* Prior *m; ~ity* [praɪ'ɒrətɪ] 1. Priorität *f,* Vorrang *m (over, to* vor); *give ~ to s.th.* etw vordringlich behandeln; 2. Dringlichkeit *f; of first ~* von größter Dringlichkeit.

prison ['prɪzn] Gefängnis *n; be sentenced to go to ~* zu Gefängnis verurteilt werden; *~er* ['-ə] Häftling *m; ~ of war* Kriegsgefangene(r) *m.*

privacy ['prɪvəsɪ] Intimsphäre *f; in strict ~* im engsten Kreise.

private ['praɪvɪt] **I** *adj* 1. privat, persönlich; *for ~ use* für den eigenen Gebrauch; 2. vertraulich; *keep ~* geheimhalten; **II** *s* (einfacher) Soldat *m.*

privation [praɪ'veɪʃn] 1. Not *f,* Mangel *m (of* an); 2. *pl* Entbehrungen *f pl.*

privilege ['prɪvɪlɪdʒ] Privileg, Vorrecht *n.*

prize [praɪz] **I** *s* Preis *m a. fig;* Gewinn *m; carry off the ~* den Preis davontragen; **II** *v* (hoch)schätzen; *~-***fighter** ['-faɪtə] Berufsboxer *m; ~-***winner** ['-wɪnə] Preisträger *m.*

pro [prəʊ] *pl ~s* Ja-Stimmen *f pl; the ~s and cons* das Für u. Wider.

probability [ˌprɒbə'bɪlətɪ]

Wahrscheinlichkeit *f; in all* ~ aller Wahrscheinlichkeit nach; **~le** ['probəbl] wahrscheinlich.

probation [prə'beɪʃn] 1. Probezeit *f; on* ~ auf Probe; 2. *jur* Bewährung *f.*

probe [prəʊb] **I** *s* 1. *med* Sonde *f;* 2. Nachforschung *f (into* über); **II** *v* 3. sondieren; 4. erforschen.

problem ['probləm] 1. Problem *n,* Schwierigkeit *f;* 2. *math* Aufgabe *f.*

procedure [prə'si:dʒə] Verfahren *n,* Handlungsweise *f.*

proceed [prə'si:d] 1. weitermachen, fortfahren (*with, in* mit); 2. in Angriff nehmen (*to s.th.* etw); 3. **~from** herrühren von; 4. verfahren (*on a principle* nach e-m Grundsatz); 5. gerichtlich vorgehen (*against s.o.* gegen jdn); **~ings** *pl* [-ɪŋz] (Gerichts-)Verfahren *n,* Verhandlungen *f pl;* **~s** ['prəʊsi:dz] Erlös *m (from* aus).

process ['prəʊses] **I** *s* 1. Ab-, Verlauf *m; in* ~ *of time* im (Ver-)Lauf der Zeit; 2. (Arbeits-)Verfahren *n;* 3. *jur* Prozeß *m;* **II** *v* 4. (chemisch) behandeln, veredeln; 5. *phot* entwickeln.

procession [prə'seʃn] Prozession *f;* Umzug *m.*

proclaim [prə'kleɪm] proklamieren, verkünden.

proclamation

[ˌproklə'meɪʃn] Verkündung *f; issue, make a* ~ e-n Aufruf erlassen.

procure [prə'kjʊə] beschaffen, besorgen.

prodigious [prə'dɪdʒəs] erstaunlich; **~y** ['prodɪʒɪ] Wunder *n; infant* ~ Wunderkind *n.*

produce I *v* [prə'dju:s] 1. *(Papiere)* vorzeigen; *(Nachweis)* erbringen; 2. *agr* hervorbringen; 3. erzeugen, produzieren, herstellen; **II** *s* ['prodju:s] *agr* Ertrag *m;* Erzeugnis(se) *n (pl);* **~r** [prə'dju:sə] Produzent *m,* Erzeuger *m.*

product ['prodʌkt] 1. Erzeugnis, Produkt *n; national* ~ Sozialprodukt *n;* 2. *fig* Ergebnis, Resultat *n;* **~ion** [prə'dʌkʃn] 1. Herstellung, Produktion *f;* 2. Leistung, Kapazität *f;* **~ive** [prə'dʌktɪv] produktiv.

profane [prə'feɪn] weltlich, profan.

profess [prə'fes] 1. bekennen; 2. *(Beruf)* ausüben.

profession [prə'feʃn] 1. Beruf *m; by* ~ von Beruf; *take up a* ~ e-n Beruf ergreifen; 2. Bekenntnis *n;* **~al** [prə'feʃənl] **I** *adj* 1. beruflich; ~ *experience* Berufserfahrung *f;* ~ *training* Berufsausbildung *f;* 2. fachmännisch; **II** *s* Fachmann *m.*

professor [prə'fesə] Professor *m.*

proficiency [prə'fiʃnsɪ] Fertigkeit, Tüchtigkeit *f.*

profile ['prəufaɪl] Profil *n.*

profit ['profɪt] **I** *s* 1. Gewinn *m; bring, yield a ~* e-n Gewinn abwerfen; 2. Nutzen *m;* **II** *v* Nutzen ziehen (*by* aus, *durch*); **~able** [-əbl] gewinnbringend; vorteilhaft (*to* für); *be ~* sich rentieren.

profound [prə'faund] 1. tief; 2. gründlich.

profus|e [prə'fju:s] verschwenderisch; **~ion** [prə'fju:ʒn] Überfluß *m.*

prognosis [prog'nəusɪs] *pl -ses* [-si:z] *med* Prognose *f.*

program(me) ['prəugræm] **I** *s* 1. Programm *n; what's on your ~* was haben Sie vor? 2. *radio TV* Sendung *f;* **II** *v tech* programmieren.

progress I *s* ['prəugres] *nur sing* Fortschritt(e) *m (pl); make ~* Fortschritte machen; **II** *v* [prəu'gres] weiter-, fortschreiten; **~ive** [prəu'gresɪv] 1. zunehmend; 2. fortschrittlich.

prohibit [prə'hɪbɪt] verbieten (*s.o. from doing s.th.* jdm, etw zu tun); **~ion** [‚prəuɪ'bɪʃn] (Alkohol-)Verbot *n;* **~ive** [prə'hɪbɪtɪv] (*Preis*) unerschwinglich.

project I *s* ['prodʒekt] Projekt *n*, Plan *m;* **II** *v* [prə'dʒekt] 1. projizieren (*on* auf); 2. entwerfen, planen; 3. vorspringen, hervorstehen.

project|ion [prə'dʒekʃən] 1. Wurf *m;* 2. Vorsprung *m;* 3. *opt film* Projektion *f;* **~or** [prə'dʒektə] *film* Vorführgerät *n.*

proli|ferate [prəu'lɪfəreɪt] *med* wuchern; **~fic** [prəu'lɪfɪk] fruchtbar *a. fig.*

prolog(ue) ['prəulog] Prolog *m.*

prolong [prəu'loŋ] verlängern.

prominent ['promɪnənt] 1. vorstehend, -springend; 2. *fig* prominent; 3. führend.

promis|e ['promɪs] **I** *s* 1. Versprechen *n; keep o.'s ~* sein Versprechen halten; 2. *show ~* vielversprechend sein; **II** *v* versprechen *a. fig; the P~d Land* das Gelobte Land; **~ing** [-ɪŋ] vielversprechend.

promot|e [prə'məut] 1. (*im Rang*) befördern; 2. fördern, unterstützen; 3. (*Geschäft*) gründen; 4. *com* werben für (*e-n Artikel*); **~er** [-ə] 1. (Geschäfts-)Gründer *m;* 2. *sport* Veranstalter *m;* **~ion** [prə'məuʃn] 1. Förderung *f;* 2. Beförderung *f;* 3. *com* Verkaufsförderung, Werbung *f.*

prompt [prompt] **I** *adj* 1. unverzüglich; 2. pünktlich; **II** *v* veranlassen (*to* zu).

promulgate ['promlgeɪt] (*Gesetz*) verkünden.

prone [prəun] 1. *fall ~* flach fallen; 2. *be ~ to* neigen zu.

prong [proŋ] *(Gabel)* Zinke *f.*

pronounce [prə'naʊns] 1. erklären für; 2. *(Urteil)* verkünden; 3. (richtig) aussprechen; **~d** [-t] 1. deutlich; 2. ausgeprägt.

pronunciation [prə‚nʌnsɪ'eɪʃn] Aussprache *f.*

proof [pruːf] **I** *s* 1. Beweis *m;* 2. Nachweis *m;* 3. Probe *f; put to (the) ~* auf die Probe stellen; **II** *adj* 4. sicher *(against* gegen); undurchlässig *(to, against* für); *water~* wasserdicht; 5. *fig* unempfindlich *(against* für); **~-read** ['-‚riːd] Korrektur lesen.

prop [prop] **I** *s* 1. Pfosten *m;* 2. *fig* Stütze, Säule *f;* **II** *v:* **~ up** stützen.

propaganda [‚propə'gændə] Propaganda *f.*

propagate ['propəgeɪt] 1. fortpflanzen; 2. verbreiten; **~ion** [‚propə'geɪʃn] 1. Fortpflanzung *f;* 2. Vermehrung *f.*

propel [prə'pel] antreiben; **~ler** [-ə] Propeller *m.*

proper ['propə] 1. passend, angebracht, geeignet *(for* für); 2. richtig, ordnungsgemäß; 3. charakteristisch *(to* für); 4. *(nachgestellt)* eigentlich.

property ['propətɪ] 1. Besitz *m,* Eigentum *n; man of ~*

begüterter Mann; 2. Gut *n;* 3. Eigenschaft *f.*

prophe|cy ['profɪsɪ] Prophezeiung, Weissagung *f;* **~sy** ['profɪsaɪ] 1. prophezeien *(s.th. for s.o.* jdm etw); 2. vorhersagen.

propitious [prə'pɪʃəs] günstig *(to, for* für).

proportion [prə'poːʃn] 1. (An-)Teil *m;* 2. Proportion *f a. math; out of ~* in keinem Verhältnis *(to* zu); **~al** [prə'poːʃənl] im (richtigen) Verhältnis *(to* zu).

propos|al [prə'pəʊzl] 1. Vorschlag *m;* 2. (Heirats-)Antrag *m;* **~e** [prə'pəʊz] 1. vorschlagen *(s.th. to s.o.* jdm etw, *doing s.th.* etw zu tun); 2. e-n Heiratsantrag machen *(to s.o.* jdm); 3. beabsichtigen; **~ition** [‚propə'zɪʃn] 1. Vorschlag *m;* 2. Plan *m,* Absicht *f.*

propriet|or [prə'praɪətə] Eigentümer *m;* **~y** [-tɪ] Schicklichkeit *f,* Anstand *m.*

prose [prəʊz] Prosa *f.*

prosecut|e ['prosɪkjuːt] verfolgen *a. jur; trespassers will be ~d* unbefugtes Betreten bei Strafe verboten; **~ion** [‚prosɪ'kjuːʃn] Verfolgung *f a. jur; the ~* die Staatsanwaltschaft; *liable to ~* strafbar; **~or** ['prosɪkjuːtə] *(public ~)* Staatsanwalt *m.*

prospect I *s* ['prospekt] 1. Aussicht *f a. fig; have in*

~ in Aussicht haben; 2. *com* Kunde *m;* **II** *v* [prə'spekt] *min* nach Bodenschätzen suchen; **~ive** [prə'spektɪv] voraussichtlich, möglich.

prospectus [prə'spektəs] Prospekt *m.*

prosper ['prɒspə] gedeihen, blühen; *he is ~ing* es geht ihm gut; **~ity** [prɒ'sperətɪ] Wohlstand *m;* **~ous** ['prɒspərəs] 1. erfolgreich; 2. *fig* blühend.

prostitute ['prɒstɪtjuːt] Prostituierte *f.*

prostrate I *adj* ['prɒstreɪt] 1. hingestreckt; 2. *fig* kraftlos; **II** *v* [prɒ'streɪt] ~ *o.s.* sich niederwerfen.

protect [prə'tekt] beschützen, verteidigen (*against* gegen); **~ion** [-'tekʃn] Schutz *m* (*from* vor); **~ive** [-ɪv] schützend; ~ *clothing* Schutzkleidung *f;* **~or** [-ə] Beschützer *m.*

protest I *v* [prə'test] 1. beteuern; 2. protestieren (*against* gegen); **II** *s* ['prəutest] Einspruch, Protest *m* (*against* gegen); *enter, lodge, make a* ~ Protest erheben (*against s.th.* gegen etw).

Protestant ['prɒtɪstənt] *rel* **I** *s* Protestant *m;* **II** *adj* protestantisch.

protestation [ˌprəute'steɪʃn] Beteuerung, Erklärung *f.*

protocol ['prəutəkɒl] Protokoll *n.*

protract [prə'trækt] in die Länge ziehen.

protrude [prə'truːd] herausragen, vorstehen.

proud [praud] 1. stolz (*of* auf); 2. hochmütig.

prov|able ['pruːvəbl] beweisbar; **~e** [pruːv] 1. be-, nachweisen; ~ *o.'s identity* sich ausweisen; 2. sich herausstellen als; ~ *(to be) false (true)* sich als falsch (richtig) herausstellen.

proverb ['prɒvɜːb] Sprichwort *n; he is a* ~ *for idleness* s-e Faulheit ist sprichwörtlich.

provide [prə'vaɪd] 1. sorgen (*for s.o.* für jdn); 2. be-, versorgen, ausstatten (*with* mit); 3. vorsorgen (*against* für); **~d** [-ɪd] ~ *(that)* vorausgesetzt, daß.

Providence ['prɒvɪdəns] die Vorsehung.

provident ['prɒvɪdənt] vorsorglich, vorsorgend.

provinc|e ['prɒvɪns] 1. Provinz *f a. fig;* 2. (Aufgaben-, Tätigkeits-)Bereich *m; fall within s.o.'s* ~ zu jds Aufgabenbereich gehören; **~ial** [prə'vɪnʃl] 1. provinziell; 2. *fig* eng(stirnig).

provision [prə'vɪʒn] 1. Vorsorge *f; make* ~ *for, against* Vorkehrungen treffen für, gegen; 2. *jur* Vorschrift *f; fall within the ~s of the law* unter die gesetzlichen Bestimmungen fallen; 3. *pl*

Proviant *m;* ~**al** [-ʒənl] provisorisch.

provocat|ion [ˌprovəˈkeɪʃn] Herausforderung *f;* ~**ive** [prəˈvɒkətɪv] herausfordernd (*of s.th.* etw).

provoke [prəˈvəʊk] 1. provozieren, herausfordern; 2. aufreizen, -stacheln.

prowl [praʊl] Streifzug *m; be on the* ~ herumschleichen.

proximity [prɒkˈsɪmətɪ] Nähe *f.*

proxy [ˈprɒksɪ] Vollmacht *f; by* ~ in Vertretung.

pruden|ce [ˈpruːdns] Um-, Vorsicht, Klugheit *f;* ~**t** [-t] um-, vorsichtig, klug.

prudish [ˈpruːdɪʃ] prüde.

prune [pruːn] I *v* 1. (*Strauch*) beschneiden; 2. *fig* zs.streichen, kürzen; II *s* (Back-)Pflaume *f.*

pry [praɪ] (~ *about*) herumschnüffeln; s-e Nase stecken (*into* in).

psalm [sɑːm] Psalm *m.*

psych|iatrist [saɪˈkaɪətrɪst] Psychiater *m;* ~**iatry** [saɪˈkaɪətrɪ] Psychiatrie *f;* ~**ic(al)** [ˈsaɪkɪk(l)] übersinnlich; ~ *research* Parapsychologie *f.*

psycholog|ical [ˌsaɪkəˈlɒdʒɪkl] psychisch; psychologisch; ~**ist** [saɪˈkɒlədʒɪst] Psychologe *m;* ~**y** [saɪˈkɒlədʒɪ] Psychologie *f.*

pub [pʌb] *fam* Kneipe *f,* Wirtshaus *n.*

puberty [ˈpjuːbətɪ] Pubertät *f.*

public [ˈpʌblɪk] I *adj* 1. öffentlich, allgemein; *become* ~ bekanntwerden; *make, render* ~ öffentlich bekanntgeben, -machen; 2. staatlich; II *s: the* ~ die Öffentlichkeit, die Allgemeinheit; *in* ~ öffentlich; ~**ation** [ˌpʌblɪˈkeɪʃn] Veröffentlichung *f; in course of* ~ im Erscheinen begriffen, im Druck; ~ *house Br* Gaststätte *f.*

publicity [pʌbˈlɪsətɪ] 1. Publizität *f;* 2. Reklame *f; give s.th.* ~ für etw Reklame machen, werben.

public| opinion öffentliche Meinung *f;* ~ **prosecutor** Staatsanwalt *m;* ~ **relations** *pl* Öffentlichkeitsarbeit *f;* ~ **spirit** Gemeinsinn *m.*

publish [ˈpʌblɪʃ] 1. publik machen, verbreiten; 2. (*Buch*) veröffentlichen; ~**er** [-ə] Verleger *m.*

pudding [ˈpʊdɪŋ] 1. Pudding *m;* 2. *black* ~ Blutwurst *f.*

puddle [ˈpʌdl] (Wasser-)Lache, Pfütze *f.*

puff [pʌf] I *s* 1. Schnaufen *n;* Windstoß *m;* 2. (*powder-*~) Puderquaste *f;* 3. ~ *pastry* Blätterteig *m;* II *v* 4. (stoßweise) blasen; Rauch ausstoßen; 5. schnaufen, keuchen; 6. (*Raucher*) paffen (*at* an).

pull [pʊl] I *s* 1. Ziehen *n,*

Ruck, Zug *m*; 2. Anstieg *m*;
3. Beziehungen *pl* (*with* zu);
II *v* 4. ziehen (*the hair* an
den Haaren); 5. ~ *s.o.'s leg*
jdn auf den Arm nehmen
(*fig*); 6. ~ *to pieces* in Stücke
reißen, zerreißen; 7. (*Zahn*)
(aus)ziehen; 8. rudern; ~ *o.'s
weight* sich ins Ruder legen;
fig sich anstrengen; 9. ~ *at,
on* ziehen an; 10. (*Muskel*)
zerren; ~ **down** nieder-,
einreißen; ~ **in** 1. (*Zug*) einfahren; 2. *fig* (*Zuschauer*)
anziehen; 3. (*Geld*) verdienen; ~ **out** 1. (her)auszie-
hen, -reißen; herausstrennen;
2. (*Zug*) abfahren; ~
through (hin)durchziehen;
(*Kranken*) durchbringen; ~
o.s. together sich zs.rei-
ßen.
pulley ['puli] *tech* Rolle *f*.
pulp [pʌlp] 1. breiige Masse
f; 2. *bot* Fruchtfleisch *n*.
pulpit ['pulpit] Kanzel *f*.
pulse [pʌls] Puls *m a. fig*;
feel, take s.o.'s ~ jdm den
Puls fühlen.
pulverize ['pʌlvəraiz] pulve-
risieren.
pump [pʌmp] **I** *s* Pumpe *f*;
II *v* pumpen; ~ **out** auspum-
pen *a. fig*; ~ **up** aufpumpen.
pumpkin ['pʌmpkin] *bot*
Kürbis *m*.
pun [pʌn] Wortspiel *n*.
punch [pʌntʃ] *v* 1. durchbohren, lochen; ~*ed card*
Lochkarte *f*; 2. mit der
Faust schlagen; **II** *s* 3. Lo-

cher *m*; 4. Faustschlag *m*;
5. *fam* Schwung *m*;
6. Punsch *m*.
Punch [pʌntʃ] Kasperle *n*;
~-**and-Judy show** Kas-
perletheater *n*.
punctual ['pʌŋktjuəl] pünktlich (*in* bei).
puncture ['pʌŋktʃə] Loch *n*;
have a ~ (*mot*) e-e (Reifen-)
Panne haben.
pungent ['pʌndʒənt] scharf,
beißend *a. fig*.
punish ['pʌniʃ] (be)strafen
(*for* für; *with* mit); ~**able**
[-əbl] strafbar; ~**ment**
[-mənt] Bestrafung; Strafe
f; *capital* ~ Todesstrafe *f*.
pupil [pju:pl] 1. Schüler *m*;
2. *anat* Pupille *f*.
puppet ['pʌpit] Puppe, Marionette *f a. fig*.
purchas|e ['pɜ:tʃəs] **I** *v* (an-,
auf-, ein)kaufen; **II** *s* 1. (An-,
Auf-, Ein-)Kauf *m*; Anschaf-
fung *f*; *hire*-~ Ratenkauf *m*;
2. *nur sing* Halt *m*; ~**er** [-ə]
Käufer *m*; ~**ing** [-ɪŋ] ~
power Kaufkraft *f*.
pure [pjuə] 1. rein; 2. unver-
fälscht; unvermischt;
3. *that's* ~ *nonsense* das ist
reiner Unsinn.
purg|ative ['pɜ:gətiv] Ab-
führmittel *n*; ~**e** [pɜ:dʒ] **I** *v*
1. reinigen, säubern *a. fig*;
2. *fig* befreien (*of, from*
von); 3. *med* abführen; **II** *s*
pol Säuberung(saktion) *f*.
purify ['pjuərifai] 1. reinigen,
läutern (*of, from* von) *a. fig*

rel; 2. säubern (*of, from* von).

purity ['pjʊərətɪ] Reinheit *f a. fig.*

purple ['pɜ:pl] purpur(farbe)n.

purpose ['pɜ:pəs] **I** *s* 1. Absicht *f,* Vorhaben *n; on ~* absichtlich; *jur* vorsätzlich; 2. Zweck, Sinn *m; for that ~* zu diesem Zweck; *to little ~* mit geringer Wirkung; *to the ~* relevant; *answer, serve o.'s ~* dem Zweck entsprechen; 3. Zielsetzung *f;* **II** *v* beabsichtigen; **~ful** [-fʊl] entschlossen; bedeutungsvoll; **~less** [-lɪs] ziellos; sinnlos; **~ly** [-lɪ] absichtlich, bewußt.

purr [pɜ:] schnurren.

purse [pɜ:s] **I** *s* Geldbeutel *m;* **II** *v* (*Lippen*) schürzen.

pursuance [pə'sjuəns] *in ~ of* auf Grund von.

pursue [pə'sju:] 1. verfolgen, jagen; 2. (*Plan, Zweck*) verfolgen; 3. (*Tätigkeit*) ausüben; **~er** [-ə] Verfolger *m;* **~it** [-t] Verfolgung, Jagd *f* (*of* auf).

push [pʊʃ] **I** *s* 1. Stoß *m;* 2. Anstrengung *f;* 3. Schwung *m;* 4. *at a ~* notfalls; **II** *v* 5. schieben, stoßen; 6. durchsetzen; 7. drängen (*for s.th.* zu etw); *be ~ed for time* in Zeitdruck sein; *~ o.s.* sich abmühen; 8. drücken; **~ around** herumstoßen; **~ off** (*fam*) abhauen; **~ over** um-

stoßen; **~ through** durchsetzen.

push button *el* Druckknopf *m,* -taste *f.*

pushing ['pʊʃɪŋ] tatkräftig; zudringlich.

puss [pʊs] (Mieze-)Katze *f;* **~yfoot** ['-fʊt] *fam fig* wie die Katze um den heißen Brei schleichen.

put [pʊt] *irr put, put* 1. setzen, stellen, legen; *~ to account* in Rechnung stellen; *~ the blame on s.o.* jdm die Schuld zuschieben; *~ o.'s foot down* energisch auftreten; *~ in force* in Kraft setzen; *~ it to s.o.* es jdm überlassen; *~ a stop to* ein Ende machen mit; 2. stecken (*into* in; *at* an); anbringen (*to* an); 3. *fig* (in e-e Lage) bringen, versetzen; 4. hineinlegen *a. fig* (*into* in); 5. (Frage) stellen; 6. stoßen, werfen, schleudern; *~ the shot* (*sport*) die Kugel stoßen; **~ aside** 1. (Geld) auf die Seite legen; 2. nicht berücksichtigen; **~ back** 1. (*an s-n Platz*) zurücklegen; 2. (Uhr) zurückstellen; 3. aufhalten, hemmen; **~ by** (*für später*) zurücklegen; **~ down** 1. niedersetzen, -stellen, -legen; 2. nieder-, aufschreiben; **~ forward** 1. vorschlagen; unterbreiten; 2. (Uhr) vorstellen; **~ in** 1. hineinbringen, einführen, -stellen; 2. einreichen; 3. (Zeit) zubringen;

verwenden; 4. *put in for* sich bewerben um; 5. *put s.o. in for* jdn vorschlagen für; ~ **off** 1. verschieben; 2. *put s.o. off* jdn hinhalten; 3. ausziehen, ablegen; 4. *(jdn)* abhalten; ~ **on** 1. *(Kleidung)* anziehen; *(Hut, Miene)* aufsetzen; 2. *(an Gewicht)* zunehmen; ~ **out** 1. hinauswerfen; 2. *(Licht, Feuer)* ausmachen, löschen; 3. ausstrecken; 4. *put s.o. out* jdn aus der Fassung bringen; ~ **through** 1. durchführen; 2. *tele* verbinden (*with* mit); ~ **together** zs.setzen, -stellen, -stecken; ~ **up** 1. hoch-

heben, -halten; *(Flagge)* hissen; 2. errichten; 3. aufhängen; 4. erhöhen; 5. *(Widerstand)* leisten; 6. *(Geld)* aufbringen; 7. absteigen (*at* in); wohnen (*with* bei); 8. sich abfinden (*with s.th.* mit etw).

putrid ['pju:trɪd] faul(ig).

putty ['pʌtɪ] Kitt *m*.

puzzle ['pʌzl] **I** *v* 1. verblüffen; 2. sich den Kopf zerbrechen (*about, over* über); **II** *s* Rätsel *n*; Puzzle *n*.

pyjamas, *Am* **pajamas** *pl* [pə'dʒɑːməz] Schlafanzug, Pyjama *m*.

pyramid ['pɪrəmɪd] Pyramide *f*.

Q

quack [kwæk] **I** v quaken a.
fig; **II** s 1. Quaken n;
2. Quacksalber m.

quadrangle ['kwɒdræŋgl]
Viereck n.

quadruped ['kwɒdrʊped]
zoo Vierfüß(l)er m.

quadruple ['kwɒdrʊpl] **I** adj
vierfach; **II** v (sich) vervier-
fachen.

quail [kweɪl] **I** v zurückschrecken (at, before vor);
II s orn Wachtel f.

quaint [kweɪnt] malerisch;
kurios.

quake [kweɪk] 1. (Boden)
(er)beben; 2. zittern (with
cold, fear vor Kälte, Angst).

quali|fication [ˌkwɒlɪfɪˈkeɪʃn]
Befähigung, Qualifikation f;
~ test Eignungsprüfung f;
~fied ['kwɒlɪfaɪd] 1. befä-
higt; qualifiziert (for für);
2. eingeschränkt, bedingt;
~fy ['-faɪ] 1. befähigen (for
für); 2. berechtigen (for zu);
3. einschränken; 4. sich qualifizieren (for für); **~ty**
['kwɒlətɪ] 1. (hohe) Qualität
f; 2. Eigenschaft f.

qualm [kwɑːm] Bedenken n;
Zweifel m.

quantity ['kwɒntətɪ] Quanti-
tät, Menge f.

quarantine ['kwɒrəntiːn]
med Quarantäne f.

quarrel ['kwɒrəl] **I** s Streit m,
Ausea.setzung f (against,
with mit); pick a ~ with s.o.
mit jdm Streit anfangen;
II v 1. streiten; (sich) zanken
(with s.o. mit jdm; about
über); 2. etw auszusetzen
haben (with an); **~some**
[-səm] streitsüchtig.

quarry ['kwɒrɪ] Steinbruch
m.

quarter ['kwɔːtə] **I** s 1. Viertel n; 2. Quartal n; 3. (Uhr)
Viertel(stunde f) n; at a ~ to
(Am of) three um Viertel
vor drei; ~ of an hour Vier-
telstunde f; 4. (Stadt-)Viertel
n; 5. pl mil Unterkunft f;
6. at close ~s dicht zs.(gedrängt); dicht dabei; **II** v mil
einquartieren; **~ly** [-lɪ] **I** adj
vierteljährlich; **II** s Viertel-
jahresschrift f.

quartz [kwɔːts] Quarz m.

quaver ['kweɪvə] zittern.

quay [kiː] Kai m.

queen [kwiːn] 1. Königin f a.
fig ent; 2. (Schach, Kartenspiel) Dame f.

queer [kwɪə] **I** adj sonderbar; eigenartig, merkwürdig;
II v: ~ s.o.'s pitch jds Pläne
durchkreuzen.

quench [kwentʃ] (Durst,
Feuer) löschen.

querulous ['kwerʊləs] nör-
gelnd.

query ['kwɪərɪ] **I** s Frage f;

Zweifel *m;* **II** *v* in Frage
stellen.

question ['kwestʃən] **I** *s*
1. Frage *f; answer a ~* e-e
Frage beantworten; *ask,
put, raise a ~* e-e Frage stellen; *without ~* fraglos, ohne
Zweifel; *be out of the ~*
nicht in Frage kommen;
2. (Streit-)Frage *f;* Problem
n; what is the ~? worum
geht es? *~ of money* Geld-
frage *f;* **II** *v* 3. (aus-, be)fra-
gen, verhören; 4. in Zweifel
ziehen; **~able** [-əbl] zweifelhaft; fragwürdig; **~-mark**
[-ma:k] Fragezeichen *n;*
~naire [ˌkwestɪə'nɛə] *fill in
a ~* e-n Fragebogen ausfüllen.

queue [kju:] **I** *s fig* Schlange
f; stand in a ~ Schlange stehen; **II** *v (~ up)* sich anstellen; Schlange stehen.

quick [kwɪk] **I** *adj* 1. schnell,
rasch, flink; *be ~ about it!*
beeil dich! 2. aufgeweckt;
munter, lebhaft; *be ~ at figures* gut rechnen können;
II *s: cut s.o. to the ~ (fig)* jdn
tief verletzen, kränken; **~en**
['-ən] 1. auf-, ermuntern; an-

regen; 2. (sich) beschleunigen; **~-frozen** ['-ˌfrəuzn]
schockgefrostet; **~ly** ['-lɪ]
schnell, rasch, in Eile; **~wit-
ted** [ˌ-'wɪtɪd] schlagfertig.

quiet ['kwaɪət] 1. leise; ruhig,
still; 2. geräuschlos.

quill [kwɪl] Federkiel *m.*

quilt [kwɪlt] Steppdecke *f.*

quince [kwɪns] *bot* Quitte *f.*

quinine [kwɪ'ni:n] Chinin *n.*

quit [kwɪt] *a. irr* quit, quit
1. verlassen; *(Stellung)* aufgeben; *notice to ~* Kündigung *f;* 2. aufhören.

quite [kwaɪt] 1. ganz, völlig,
vollständig; 2. *(~ so)* allerdings; ganz recht! 3. *fam*
ziemlich, recht; *~ a few*
ziemlich viele.

quiver ['kwɪvə] **I** *v* zittern
(with vor); **II** *s* 1. Zittern *n;*
2. Köcher *m.*

quota ['kwəutə] Anteil *m,*
Quote *f.*

quotation [kwəu'teɪʃn] 1. Zitat *n; ~ marks pl* Anführungszeichen *n pl;* 2. Kurs-,
Preisnotierung *f.*

quote [kwəut] 1. zitieren
(from aus); 2. *(Preis)* nennen, veranschlagen.

R

rabbi ['ræbaɪ] Rabbi(ner) *m.*

rabbit ['ræbɪt] Kaninchen *n.*

rabble ['ræbl] *the* ~ der Mob.

rabid ['ræbɪd] 1. toll(wütig); 2. fanatisch.

rac|e [reɪs] **I** *s* 1. (Menschen-) Rasse *f;* 2. (Wett-)Rennen *n;* 3. *(Wasser)* Strömung *f;* **II** *v* 4. um die Wette laufen *(against, with* mit); 5. rennen, jagen, rasen; ~**ing** ['-ɪŋ] 1. Rennen *n;* 2. Rennsport *m.*

rack [ræk] **I** *s* 1. Gestell, Gerüst *n;* Ständer *m;* 2. go to ~ *and ruin* völlig zugrunde gehen; **II** *v* 3. auf die Folter spannen *a. fig.;* 4. ~ *o.'s brains (fig)* sich den Kopf zerbrechen.

racket ['rækɪt] 1. Lärm, Tumult *m;* 2. *fam* Schwindel(geschäft *n) m;* 3. *(a. racquet* (Tennis-)Schläger *m;* ~**eer** [,rækə'tɪə] Erpresser, Gangster *m.*

radar ['reɪdɑː] Radar *m od n;* ~ **trap** Radarfalle *f.*

radial tyre ['reɪdjəl taɪə] *mot* Gürtelreifen *m.*

radiant ['reɪdjənt] glänzend; strahlend *(with* vor, von) *a. fig.*

radiat|e ['reɪdɪeɪt] 1. *(Licht, Wärme, Glück)* (aus)strahlen *(from* von); 2. sich strahlenförmig ausbreiten; ~**ion**

[,reɪdɪ'eɪʃn] (Aus-)Strahlung *f;* ~**or** ['reɪdɪeɪtə] 1. Heizkörper *m;* 2. *mot* Kühler *m.*

radical ['rædɪkl] radikal.

radio ['reɪdɪəʊ] *pl -dios* 1. Rundfunk *m;* 2. Radio(apparat *m) n;* 3. Funkspruch *m;* ~**graph** [-grɑːf] Röntgenaufnahme *f.*

radish ['rædɪʃ] Rettich *m.*

radium ['reɪdjəm] *chem* Radium *n.*

radius ['reɪdjəs] *pl radii* ['-dɪaɪ] 1. Radius *m;* 2. *within a* ~ *of* im Umkreis von.

raffle ['ræfl] Tombola *f.*

raft [rɑːft] Floß *n.*

rag [ræg] 1. Lumpen; Putzlappen *m;* 2. *pl* Lumpen *pl (altes Zeug); in* ~s *(and tatters)* zerlumpt.

rage [reɪdʒ] *s* 1. Wut *f,* Toben *n a. fig (d. Elemente); fly into a* ~ in Wut geraten; 2. Gier *f (for* nach); 3. *be (all) the* ~ *(fam)* große Mode sein; **II** *v* wüten, rasen, toben *a. fig.*

ragged ['rægɪd] zerlumpt, schäbig.

raid [reɪd] **I** *s* 1. (feindlicher) Überfall *m (upon* auf); 2. (Polizei-)Razzia *f (on* auf); 3. ~ *on a bank* Bankükberfall, -raub *m;* **II** *v* überfallen; plündern.

rail [reɪl] 1. Geländer *n;*

2. Handlauf *m;* 3. *rail* Gleis *n; by ~* mit der (Eisen-)Bahn; *run off the ~s* entgleisen; **~ing** ['-ɪŋ] Geländer *n; mar* Reling *f.*

railway ['reɪlweɪ] , *Am* **railroad** ['-rəʊd] Eisenbahn *f;* **~ station** Bahnhof *m.*

rain [reɪn] **I** *s* Regen *a. fig; the ~s* Regenzeit *f; it looks like ~* es sieht nach Regen aus; **II** *v* regnen *a. fig;* herabfließen *(on* auf); *~ cats and dogs* in Strömen regnen; **~coat** ['-kəʊt] Regenmantel *m;* **~drop** ['-drɒp] Regentropfen *m;* **~y** ['-ɪ] regnerisch.

raise [reɪz] **I** *v* 1. (auf-, er-, hoch)heben; *~ one's glass to s.o.* auf jds Wohl trinken; 2. auf-, errichten *(a. ein Gebäude);* 3. vergrößern, erhöhen, anheben *(a. Preis);* 4. *fig (Gefühl, Hoffnung)* erwecken; 5. *(Geld)* auf-, zs.bringen; 6. *(Frage)* stellen, aufwerfen; *~ an objection to s.th.* gegen etw e-n Einwand vorbringen; 7. *agr* anbauen, ziehen; *(Kinder)* groß-, aufziehen; *(Tier)* züchten; **II** *s (~ in wages) Am* (Lohn-, Gehalts-) Erhöhung *f.*

raisin ['reɪzn] Rosine *f.*

rake [reɪk] **I** *s* Rechen *m;* **II** *v* 1. (zs.)harken, -rechen; *~ in (Geld)* scheffeln; 2. *(~ through)* durchstöbern *(for*

nach); 3. *~ up* aufstöbern, wieder ans Licht bringen.

rally ['rælɪ] **I** *v* 1. versammeln, zs.bringen; (sich) scharen *(round* um); 2. *fig (Kräfte)* sammeln; 3. sich (wieder) erholen *(from* von); **II** *s* 4. Versammlung, Zs.kunft *f;* 5. *mot* Sternfahrt, Rallye *f.*

ram [ræm] **I** *s* 1. *zoo* Widder *m;* 2. Ramme *f;* **II** *v* rammen *(into* in).

ramble ['ræmbl] **I** *v* 1. umherschweifen, (umher)streifen; 2. *bot* wuchern; **II** *s* Bummel *m.*

ramification [ˌræmɪfɪ'keɪʃn] Verzweigung, Verästelung *f.*

ramp [ræmp] Rampe *f.*

rampant ['ræmpənt] 1. *bot* wuchernd; 2. *be ~* überhandnehmen.

ramshackle ['ræmˌʃækl] baufällig.

ranch [rɑːntʃ] Viehfarm, Ranch *f.*

rancid ['rænsɪd] ranzig.

random ['rændəm] **I** *adj* zufällig; wahllos; **II** *s: at ~* aufs Geratewohl.

range [reɪndʒ] **I** *v* 1. aufstellen; (systematisch) ordnen; 2. durchstreifen; 3. sich erstrecken, reichen bis, e-e Reichweite haben *(over* von); 4. sich bewegen *(from . . . to* zwischen . . . und); **II** *s* 5. Reihe *f; ~ of mountains* Bergkette *f;* 6. Schuß-, Reichweite *f; out of ~* außer

Hör-, Reich-, Schußweite;
7. *(rifle-~)* Schießplatz *m;*
8. (Verbreitungs-) Gebiet *n;*
~ *of transmission (radio)*
Sendebereich *m;* 9. *(kit-chen-~)* (Koch-, Küchen-)
Herd *m.*

ranger ['reɪndʒə] Förster *m.*

rank [ræŋk] **I** *s* 1. Reihe *f;*
2. Stellung *f,* Rang *m;* **II** *v*
3. einreihen, klassifizieren;
zählen *(among, with* zu);
4. rangieren *(above* über;
below unter *dat)*; **III** *adj*
5. *(Pflanzen)* wuchernd;
6. stinkend; 7. kraß.

ransack ['rænsæk] 1. durch-wühlen *(for* nach);
2. (aus)plündern.

ransom ['rænsəm] Lösegeld
n.

rap [ræp] **I** *v* klopfen *(at* an);
II *s* Klaps *m; give s.o. a ~ on
the knuckles (fig)* jdm auf
die Finger klopfen.

rape [reɪp] **I** *s* Vergewalti-gung *f;* **II** *v* vergewaltigen.

rapid ['ræpɪd] **I** *adj* schnell,
flink, eilig; **II** *s pl* Strom-schnellen *f pl;* ~**ity**
[rə'pɪdətɪ] Schnelligkeit *f.*

rapt [ræpt] hingerissen; ent-zückt; ~**ure** ['ræptʃə] Ent-zücken *n.*

rare [reə] 1. selten, unge-wöhnlich; 2. *(Luft)* dünn.

rarity ['reərətɪ] 1. Seltenheit
f; 2. Kostbarkeit *f.*

rascal ['rɑːskəl] Schuft *m.*

rash [ræʃ] **I** *adj* vorschnell,
übereilt, unbesonnen;

II *s* Hautausschlag *m;*
heat-~ Hitzebläschen *n pl.*

rasher ['ræʃə] Speckschnitte
f.

rasp [rɑːsp] **I** *v* raspeln;
II *s* Raspel *f;* Reibeisen *n.*

raspberry ['rɑːzbərɪ] Him-beere *f.*

rasping ['rɑːspɪŋ] krächzend;
kratzend; rauh.

rat [ræt] Ratte *f; like a
drowned ~* patschnaß;
smell a ~ (fig) Lunte, *fam*
den Braten riechen.

rate [reɪt] **I** *s* 1. Quote; Rate
f; birth ~ Geburtenziffer *f;
death ~* Sterbeziffer *f;*
2. Gebührensatz, Tarif *m;* ~
of exchange Wechselkurs
m; 3. *pl Br* Gemeindesteuer
f; 4. *at any ~* auf jeden Fall;
II *v* 5. einschätzen, taxieren
(at auf); 6. einstufen, rech-nen *(among* zu); *be ~d as*
angesehen werden, gelten
(as als).

rather ['rɑːðə] 1. lieber; eher;
I would, I had ~ ich würde,
hätte lieber, eher; 2. *or ~*
oder vielmehr; 3. ziemlich.

ratif|ication [ˌrætɪfɪ'keɪʃn]
1. Bestätigung *f;* 2. *pol* Rati-fizierung *f;* ~**y** ['rætɪfaɪ]
1. bestätigen; 2. ratifizieren.

ration ['ræʃn] **I** *s* Ration *f;*
II *v* rationieren.

rational ['ræʃənl] vernunft-gemäß, vernünftig; ~**ization**
[ˌræʃnəlaɪ'zeɪʃn] Rationali-sierung *f.*

rattle ['rætl] **I** *v* 1. klappern,

rattern, rasseln, knarren;
2. ~ *off* herunterleiern; **II** *s*
3. Rattern *n;* 4. (Kinder-)
Rassel *f;* ~-**snake** [-sneɪk]
Klapperschlange *f.*

ravage [ˈrævɪdʒ] **I** *s* Zerstö-
rung *f; the* ~*s of time* der
Zahn *m* der Zeit; **II** *v* 1. verwüsten; 2. plündern.

rave [reɪv] 1. *med* phantasie-
ren; 2. wüten, toben (*about,
at* über; *against* gegen); 3. ~
about schwärmen von.

raven [ˈreɪvn] (Kolk-)Rabe
m.

ravenous [ˈrævənəs] heiß-
hungrig (*for* nach).

ravine [rəˈviːn] Schlucht,
Klamm *f.*

ravish [ˈrævɪʃ] *be* ~*ed by*
entzückt sein von; ~**ing**
[-ɪŋ] hinreißend.

raw [rɔː] 1. *(Nahrung)* roh;
(Material) unbearbeitet;
2. *(Haut)* abgeschürft, wund;
~ **material** Rohmaterial *n,*
-stoff *m.*

ray [reɪ] (Licht-)Strahl *m a.
fig; X-*~*s (pl)* Röntgenstrah-
len *m; a* ~ *of hope* ein
Hoffnungsschimmer *m.*

rayon [ˈreɪɔn] Kunstseide *f.*

raze, rase [reɪz] ~ *to the
ground* dem Erdboden
gleichmachen.

razor [ˈreɪzə] Rasiermesser *n;*
-apparat *m;* ~-**blade**
[-bleɪd] Rasierklinge *f.*

reach [riːtʃ] **I** *v* 1. ~ *(out) for*
greifen nach; 2. reichen, ge-
ben; 3. erreichen; 4. ankom-

men in; 5. sich erstrecken;
as far as the eye can ~ soweit das Auge reicht; **II** *s*
Reichweite *f a. fig; out of* ~,
beyond ~ unerreichbar;
within ~ in Reichweite;
within easy ~ *of* nicht weit
(entfernt) von.

react [rɪˈækt] 1. zurückwirken (*on, upon* auf); 2. reagieren (*to* auf); ~**ion** [rɪˈækʃn]
1. Rück-, Gegenwirkung *f;*
2. Reaktion *f* (*to* auf); ~**or**
[rɪˈæktə] *nuclear* ~ Kernreaktor *m.*

read [riːd] *irr* read, read
[red] 1. lesen; vorlesen (*to
s.o.* jdm); ~ *between the
lines* zwischen den Zeilen
lesen; 2. *(Meßgerät)* anzeigen; ~**able** [ˈ-əbl] lesbar;
~**er** [ˈ-ə] 1. Leser *m;* 2. Lese-
buch *n.*

readily [ˈredɪlɪ] bereitwillig;
ohne weiteres; ~**ness**
[ˈredɪnɪs] Bereitschaft *f.*

reading [ˈriːdɪŋ] 1. Lesen *n;*
2. Belesenheit *f;* 3. Lesart *f.*

readjust [ˌriːəˈdʒʌst] wieder
in Ordnung bringen.

ready [ˈredɪ] 1. bereit, fertig
(*for, to* zu); *make* ~ vorbereiten, fertigmachen; 2. *he's
always* ~ *with an excuse* er
ist immer mit e-r Entschuldigung bei der Hand; 3. bereit, willens (*to* zu); 4. griff-
bereit; ~ *money* Bargeld *n;*
~-**made** [-meɪd] Konfek-
tions-; Fertig-.

real [rɪəl] 1. wirklich, tatsächlich; 2. echt; ~ **estate** Grundbesitz *m;* ~**istic** [ˌrɪəˈlɪstɪk] realistisch; ~**ity** [rɪˈælətɪ] Wirklichkeit *f;* ~**ization** [ˌrɪəlaɪˈzeɪʃn] 1. Verwirklichung *f;* 2. Einsicht *f,* Verständnis *n (of* gen); ~**ize** [ˈrɪəlaɪz] 1. verwirklichen; 2. einsehen, verstehen; ~**ly** [ˈrɪəlɪ] wirklich, tatsächlich.

realm [relm] Reich *n.*

reap [riːp] ernten *a. fig;* ~**er** [ˈ-ə] Mähmaschine *f.*

reappear [ˌriːəˈpɪə] wieder erscheinen.

rear [rɪə] **I** *s* rückwärtige(r) Teil *m;* **II** *v* 1. *(Kind)* aufziehen; 2. *(Pferd)* sich aufbäumen; ~-**view mirror** [ˈ-ˌvjuːˈmɪrə] Rückspiegel *m.*

reason [ˈriːzn] **I** *s* 1. Vernunft *f;* Verstand *m; bring to* ~ zur Vernunft bringen; *listen to* ~ Vernunft annehmen; *without rhyme or* ~ ohne Sinn u. Verstand; 2. Ursache *f;* Grund *m; for this* ~ aus diesem Grund; *the* ~ *why* weswegen; deswegen; **II** *v* 3. vernünftig urteilen; 4. diskutieren *(with* mit); ~**able** [-əbl] 1. vernünftig; 2. *(Preis)* angemessen.

reassur|e [ˌriːəˈʃʊə] beruhigen; ~**ing** [-rɪŋ] beruhigend.

rebel I *s* [ˈrebl] Rebell *m;* **II** *v* [rɪˈbel] sich empören *(against* gegen) *a. fig;* ~**lion** [rɪˈbeljən] Rebellion *f,* Auf-

stand *m (against* gegen); ~**lious** [rɪˈbeljəs] aufrührerisch.

rebound I *v* [rɪˈbaʊnd] 1. ab-, zurückprallen; 2. *fig* zurückfallen *(on, upon s.o.* auf jdn); **II** *s* [ˈriːbaʊnd] Rückprall *m (from* von).

rebuild [ˌriːˈbɪld] *irr (s.* build) wieder auf-, zs.bauen.

rebuke [rɪˈbjuːk] **I** *v* tadeln *(s.o. for s.th.* jdn wegen etw); **II** *s* Tadel *m.*

recall [rɪˈkɔːl] 1. zurückrufen; 2. sich (wieder) erinnern an; 3. widerrufen.

recede [rɪˈsiːd] zurückweichen.

receipt [rɪˈsiːt] 1. Empfang *m; on* ~ bei Empfang, nach Eingang; 2. Quittung *f;* Beleg *m; give a* ~ quittieren.

receive [rɪˈsiːv] 1. erhalten, bekommen; 2. *(Besucher)* empfangen; 3. an-, auf-, einnehmen; ~**r** [-ə] 1. Empfänger *m;* 2. *tele* Hörer *m;* 3. *radio TV* Empfänger *m.*

recent [ˈriːsnt] neu, modern; *(Nachrichten)* letzt; ~**ly** [-lɪ] neulich, kürzlich.

reception [rɪˈsepʃn] Aufnahme *f,* Empfang *m a. radio;* ~**ist** [-ʃənɪst] Empfangsdame *f.*

receptive [rɪˈseptɪv] aufnahmebereit; empfänglich *(of* für).

recess [rɪˈses] 1. *arch* Nische *f;* 2. *pl fig* geheime Winkel *m pl (of the mind* des Herzens); **~ion** [rɪˈseʃn] Rezession f.

recipe [ˈresɪpɪ] Rezept n.

reciprocal [rɪˈsɪprəkl] gegen-, wechselseitig.

recit|**al** [rɪˈsaɪtl] mus (Solo-) Vortrag m; **~e** [rɪˈsaɪt] vortragen, rezitieren.

reckless [ˈreklɪs] 1. sorglos, unbekümmert (of um); 2. rücksichtslos, fahrlässig.

reckon [ˈrekən] 1. (er)rechnen; be-, anrechnen; **~** up zs.rechnen; 2. zählen (among zu); 3. sich verlassen (on, upon auf); 4. Am fam denken, meinen, annehmen, vermuten.

reclaim [rɪˈkleɪm] 1. (Ödland) kultivieren; (Neuland) gewinnen; 2. zurückfordern.

reclamation [ˌrekləˈmeɪʃn] Reklamation f.

recline [rɪˈklaɪn] (sich) zurücklehnen.

recogn|**ition** [ˌrekəɡˈnɪʃn] 1. Erkennen n; 2. Anerkennung f; **~ize** [ˈrekəɡnaɪz] 1. wieder(er)kennen; 2. anerkennen.

recoil [rɪˈkɔɪl] zurückfahren, -prallen.

recollect [ˌrekəˈlekt] sich erinnern an; **~ion** [-ˈlekʃn] Erinnerung f (of an).

recommend [ˌrekəˈmend] (an)empfehlen; **~ation** [ˌrekəmenˈdeɪʃn] Empfehlung f.

recompense [ˈrekəmpens]

I s 1. Belohnung f; 2. Entschädigung f; **II** v 3. belohnen; 4. entschädigen.

reconcile [ˈrekənsaɪl] 1. ver-, aussöhnen; 2. in Einklang bringen.

recondition [ˌriːkənˈdɪʃn] (wieder) instand setzen; **~ed** engine Austauschmotor m.

reconsider [ˌriːkənˈsɪdə] überdenken.

reconstruct [ˌriːkənˈstrʌkt] 1. wieder aufbauen; 2. rekonstruieren; **~ion** [-ˈstrʌkʃn] 1. Wiederaufbau m a. fig; 2. (Verbrechen) Rekonstruktion f.

record I v [rɪˈkɔːd] 1. auf-, verzeichnen; 2. aufnehmen; **II** s [ˈrekɔːd] 3. Aufzeichnung f; off the **~** (fam) nicht für die Öffentlichkeit (bestimmt); 4. (Schall-)Platte f; 5. Rekord m; break a **~** e-n Rekord brechen; **~ing** [rɪˈkɔːdɪŋ] (Ton-)Aufnahme f; **~-player** [ˈrekɔːdˌpleɪə] Plattenspieler m.

recourse [rɪˈkɔːs] have **~** to Zuflucht suchen bei.

recover [rɪˈkʌvə] 1. zurückbekommen, -erhalten; 2. sich erholen (from von); **~y** [-rɪ] 1. Wiedererlangung f; 2. Genesung, Erholung f.

recreation [ˌrekrɪˈeɪʃn] Erholung f.

recruit [rɪˈkruːt] **I** v rekrutieren; **II** s mil Rekrut m.

rectangle [ˈrekˌtæŋɡl] Rechteck n.

rector ['rektə] 1. Pfarrer *m;* 2. *(College)* Direktor *m;* ~**y** ['rektəri] Pfarrhaus *n.*

recur [rɪ'kɜ:] wiederkehren.

recurren|ce [rɪ'kʌrəns] Wiederauftreten *n;* ~**t** [-t] wiederkehrend.

red [red] **I** *adj* 1. rot; 2. gerötet (*with* von); **II** *s* 3. Rot *n;* 4. *be in the* ~ in den roten Zahlen stecken; *the* **R~ Cross** das Rote Kreuz; ~ **current** Johannisbeere *f.*

reddish ['redɪʃ] rötlich.

redeem [rɪ'di:m] 1. ein-, ablösen; 2. los-, freikaufen; 3. *rel* erlösen; 4. *(Versprechen)* einlösen.

redemption [rɪ'dempʃn] 1. Ein-, Ablösung *f;* 2. Los-, Freikauf *m;* 3. *beyond, past* ~ unrettbar verloren.

red|-handed [,red'hændɪd] *be caught* ~ auf frischer Tat ertappt werden; ~**head** ['-hed] rothaarige(r) Mensch; ~**-hot** [,-'hot] rotglühend; ~**-letter day** [,-'letə'deɪ] *fig* Glückstag *m.*

redress [rɪ'dres] **I** *v* wiedergutmachen; **II** *s* Wiedergutmachung *f.*

red tape Bürokratismus *m.*

reduce [rɪ'dju:s] 1. verringern; *(Preis)* ermäßigen; 2. ~ *to nothing* zunichte machen; ~ *s.o. to silence* jdm den Mund stopfen.

reduction [rɪ'dʌkʃn] Verringerung; (Preis-)Ermäßigung *f.*

reef [ri:f] (Felsen-)Riff *n.*

reek [ri:k] stinken (*of* nach).

reel [ri:l] **I** *s* Rolle, Spule *f; off the* ~ *(fig, fam)* wie am Schnürchen; **II** *v* 1. rollen, spulen, wickeln; 2. schwanken, taumeln.

re-election [,ri:ɪ'lekʃn] Wiederwahl *f.*

refer [rɪ'fɜ:] 1. verweisen (*to s.o.* an jdn); 2. sich beziehen (*to* auf); 3. sich wenden (*to* an); ~**ee** [,refə'ri:] *sport jur* Schiedsrichter *m;* ~**ence** ['refrəns] 1. Bezug(nahme *f*) *m; in, with* ~ *to* in bezug, mit Bezug auf; ~ *book* Nachschlagewerk *n;* ~*-number* Aktenzeichen *n;* 2. Referenz *f.*

refill [,ri:'fɪl] nachfüllen.

refine [rɪ'faɪn] 1. raffinieren; 2. *fig* (sich) verfeinern; ~**ment** [-mənt] 1. *tech* Raffination *f;* 2. *fig* Kultiviertheit *f;* ~**ry** [-əri] Raffinerie *f.*

reflect [rɪ'flekt] 1. widerspiegeln *a. fig;* 2. *fig* nachdenken (*on, upon* über); ~**ion,** *Br a.* **reflexion** [-'flekʃn] 1. Reflexion; (Wider-)Spiegelung *f;* 2. *fig* Nachdenken *n* (*on* über); *on* ~ nach gründlicher Überlegung.

reform [rɪ'fɔ:m] **I** *v* 1. um-, neugestalten; 2. *(Menschen)* (sich) bessern; **II** *s* Reform *f;* ~**ation** [,refə'meɪʃn] (Ver-)Besserung *f;* ~**er** [rɪ'fɔ:mə] Reformer *m.*

refract [rɪˈfrækt] *phys (Strahlen)* brechen; **~ory** [-ərɪ] 1. widerspenstig (*to* gegen); 2. hitzebeständig.

refrain [rɪˈfreɪn] (sich) zurückhalten (*from doing s.th.* etw zu tun).

refresh [rɪˈfreʃ] 1. ~ *one's memory* sein Gedächtnis auffrischen; **~er course** [-ə kɔːs] Wiederholungskurs *m*; **~ing** [-ɪŋ] erfrischend, belebend; **~ment** [-mənt] Erfrischung *f*; ~ *room* Erfrischungsraum *m*.

refrigerate [rɪˈfrɪdʒəreɪt] kühlen; **~or** [-ə] Kühlschrank *m*.

refuel [ˌriːˈfjʊəl] auftanken.

refuge [ˈrefjuːdʒ] Zuflucht(sort *m*) *f*; *seek, take* ~ Zuflucht suchen (*in a place* an e-m Ort; *from* vor).

refugee [ˌrefjʊˈdʒiː] Flüchtling *m*.

refund I *v* [riːˈfʌnd] zurückzahlen; -erstatten; II *s* [ˈriːfʌnd] (Rück-)Erstattung *f*.

refus|al [rɪˈfjuːzl] Ablehnung; Absage *f*; **~e** I *v* [rɪˈfjuːz] 1. ablehnen, zurückweisen; 2. sich weigern; II *s* [ˈrefjuːs] Abfall, Müll *m*.

refute [rɪˈfjuːt] widerlegen.

regain [rɪˈgeɪn] zurück-, wiederbekommen.

regard [rɪˈgɑːd] I *v* 1. betrachten (*with suspicion* mit Mißtrauen); 2. berücksichti-

gen; 3. halten (*as* für); 4. *as* ~ *s* was ... betrifft; II *s* 5. (Hoch-)Achtung *f*; 6. Rücksicht *f* (*for, to* auf); *in, with* ~ *to* in bezug, mit Rücksicht auf; 7. *pl (Brief) with kind* ~*s* mit freundlichen Grüßen (*to* an); **~ful** [-fʊl] rücksichtsvoll (*of* gegen); **~less** [-lɪs] ohne Rücksicht auf.

regime [reɪˈʒiːm] Regime *n*.

regimen [ˈredʒɪmen] Diät *f*.

regiment [ˈredʒɪmənt] *mil* Regiment *n*.

region [ˈriːdʒən] Gegend *f*.

register [ˈredʒɪstə] I *s* Liste *f*, Verzeichnis, Register *n*; II *v* 1. (sich) eintragen, registrieren; 2. (sich) (an)melden (*with* bei); 3. *(Brief)* einschreiben (lassen); 4. *(Gepäck)* aufgeben; 5. *(Meßgerät)* anzeigen.

registrar [ˌredʒɪˈstrɑː] Standesbeamte(r) *m*.

registration [ˌredʒɪˈstreɪʃn] 1. Einschreibung; Anmeldung *f*; *compulsory* ~ Meldepflicht *f*; ~ *fee* Einschreibgebühr *f*; ~ *form* Anmeldeformular *n*; ~ *office* Meldestelle *f*; Einwohnermeldeamt *n*; 2. *mot* Zulassung *f*; ~ *number (mot)* polizeiliche(s) Kennzeichen *n*.

regret [rɪˈgret] I *v* 1. bedauern; 2. (schmerzlich) vermissen; II *s* Bedauern *n* (*at* über); *I have no* ~*s* es reut

mich nicht; ~**table** [-əbl]
bedauerlich.

regular ['regjulə] 1. regelmäßig; 2. geregelt; vorschriftsmäßig; 3. üblich, gebräuchlich.

regulat|e ['regjuleɪt] *tech* re-
gulieren, nach-, einstellen;
~**ation** [,regjuˈleɪʃn] 1. *tech*
Regulierung *f*; 2. Vorschrift
f; *pl* Bestimmungen *f pl*;
contrary to ~*s* unvor-
schriftsmäßig; *road, traffic*
~*s pl* Verkehrsvorschriften *f
pl*.

reign [reɪn] **I** *s* Herrschaft *f
a. fig*; **II** *v* regieren, herrschen (*over* über) *a. fig.*

reimburse [,riːɪmˈbɜːs] 1. zurückzahlen, (zurück)erstat-
ten (*s.th. to s.o.* jdm etw);
2. ~ *s.o.* (*for*) *s.th.* jdn für etw
entschädigen.

rein [reɪn] Zügel *m.*

reindeer ['reɪn,dɪə] Ren(tier)
n.

reinforce [,riːɪnˈfɔːs] verstärken *a. mil u. fig*; ~*d concrete* Stahlbeton *m.*

reinsurance [,riːɪnˈʃuərəns]
Rückversicherung *f.*

reissue [,riːˈɪʃuː] Neuausgabe,
-auflage *f.*

reiterate [riːˈɪtəreɪt] (oft)
wiederholen.

reject [rɪˈdʒekt] ablehnen,
zurückweisen; ~**ion**
[rɪˈdʒekʃn] Ablehnung *f.*

rejoin [rɪˈdʒɔɪn] erwidern,
entgegenhalten; ~**der** [-də]
Erwiderung *f.*

rejuvenate [rɪˈdʒuːvɪneɪt]
(sich) verjüngen.

relate [rɪˈleɪt] 1. berichten, erzählen; *strange to* ~ unglaublich, aber wahr; 2. verknüpfen (*to* mit); ~**d** [-ɪd] *be*
~ *to* verwandt sein mit.

relation [rɪˈleɪʃn] 1. Erzählung *f*; 2. Beziehung *f*, Verhältnis *n*; Verbindung *f*; *in,
with* ~ *to* in bezug, mit Bezug auf; *business* ~*s* Ge-
schäftsbeziehungen *f pl*;
public ~*s* (*pl*) Öffentlich-
keitsarbeit *f*; 3. Verwand-
te(r) *m*; ~**ship** [-ʃɪp] 1. Verwandtschaft *f*; 2. Beziehung
f.

relative ['relətɪv] **I** *adj*: *be* ~
to sich beziehen auf; **II** *s*
Verwandte(r) *m.*

relax [rɪˈlæks] 1. lockern;
(*Muskeln, Geist*) entspannen; 2. erschlaffen lassen;
3. sich erholen, sich entspannen, ausspannen; ~**ation**
[,riːlækˈseɪʃn] 1. Lockerung
f; 2. Entspannung *f.*

relay [rɪˈleɪ] 1. Ablö-
sung(smannschaft) *f*; 2. *sport*
(~ *race*) Staffellauf *m*;
3. *radio TV* Relais *n.*

release [rɪˈliːs] **I** *v* 1. frei-,
entlassen; 2. freigeben; los-
lassen; **II** *s* 3. Entlassung *f*
(*from* aus); 4. Freigabe *f*
(*zur Veröffentlichung*);
5. *phot* Auslöser *m.*

reliable [rɪˈlaɪəbl] zuverlässig.

relic ['relɪk] Überrest *m.*

relief [rɪˈliːf] 1. Erleichterung

f; 2. Unterstützung, Fürsorge *f*; 3. Ablösung *f a. mil*; 4. *stand out in ~ against* sich scharf abheben von; *~ works (pl)* Notstandsarbeiten *f pl*.

relieve [rɪ'liːv] 1. *(Los)* erleichtern; *(Krankheit, Schmerz, Not)* lindern, mildern; 2. befreien, entbinden *(from* von); 3. ablösen.

relig|ion [rɪ'lɪdʒən] Religion *f*; **~ious** [rɪ'lɪdʒəs] religiös.

relinquish [rɪ'lɪŋkwɪʃ] *(Plan)* aufgeben.

relish ['relɪʃ] **I** *s* Würze *f*; **II** *v* Geschmack finden an *dat*.

reluctan|ce [rɪ'lʌktəns] Widerstreben *n*; **~t** [-t] widerwillig *(to* zu).

rely [rɪ'laɪ] sich verlassen *(on, upon* auf).

remain [rɪ'meɪn] **I** *v* 1. übrigbleiben; 2. (ver)bleiben; **II** *s pl* Überbleibsel *n pl*; Reste *m pl*; **~der** [-də] Rest *m a.* math.

remark [rɪ'mɑːk] **I** *v* bemerken; **II** *s* Bemerkung *f (on* über); **~able** [-əbl] bemerkenswert.

remedy ['remɪdɪ] **I** *s* Heilmittel *n (for* gegen); **II** *v* abhelfen *(s.th. e-r* S).

rememb|er [rɪ'membə] 1. sich (wieder) erinnern an; sich merken, behalten; 2. *~ me to your father* grüßen Sie Ihren Vater von mir; **~rance** [-rəns] 1. Erinnerung *f (of* an); *in ~ of* zur

Erinnerung an; 2. *pl* Grüße *m pl (im* Brief).

remind [rɪ'maɪnd] erinnern *(s.o. of s.th.* jdn an etw); *that ~s me* dabei fällt mir ein; **~er** [-ə] Mahnung *f*.

remit [rɪ'mɪt] *(Geld)* schicken, überweisen; **~tance** [-əns] *(Geld)* Sendung, Überweisung *f*.

remnant ['remnənt] 1. Überbleibsel *n (of* gen); 2. Stoffrest *m*.

remorse [rɪ'mɔːs] *feel ~* Gewissensbisse haben; **~ful** [-fʊl] reumütig.

remote [rɪ'məʊt] 1. entfernt, abgelegen *(from* von); 2. *I haven't the ~st idea* ich habe nicht die geringste Ahnung; *~ control tech* Fernbedienung *f*.

remov|al [rɪ'mjuːvl] 1. Wegschaffen, Fortschaffen *n*; 2. Umzug *m*; **~e** [rɪ'muːv] 1. wegschaffen; 2. entlassen; 3. *(Geschäft)* verlegen; **~er** [-ə] 1. (Möbel-)Spediteur *m*; 2. *stain ~* Fleckentferner *m*.

remunerate [rɪ'mjuːnəreɪt] belohnen, entschädigen *(s.o. for s.th* jdn für etw).

render ['rendə] 1. *(~ back)* zurückgeben; 2. *(Dank)* abstatten; 3. *(e-n Dienst)* erweisen; 4. *~ an account of* Rechenschaft ablegen über; 5. machen; *~ s.o. speechless* jdn sprachlos machen; 6. übersetzen; 7. *mus* vortragen.

renew [rɪ'njuː] erneuern; ~**al** [-əl] Erneuerung f.

renounce [rɪ'naʊns] verzichten auf.

renovate ['renəʊveɪt] renovieren.

renown [rɪ'naʊn] Berühmtheit f; ~**ed** [-d] berühmt (for wegen).

rent [rent] **I** s Miete f; **II** v 1. mieten, pachten (from von); 2. vermieten (to an); ~**-a-car** Autoverleih m.

renunciation [rɪ,nʌnsɪ'eɪʃn] Verzicht m (of auf).

repair [rɪ'peə] **I** v reparieren; **II** s 1. Reparatur f; under ~ in Reparatur; 2. pl Instandsetzungsarbeiten f pl; closed during ~s wegen Renovierung geschlossen; 3. in good ~ in gutem Zustand; ~**-shop** [-ʃop] Reparaturwerkstatt f.

repay [riː'peɪ] irr (s. pay) 1. zurückzahlen; 2. vergelten; ~**ment** [-mənt] 1. Rückzahlung f; 2. Vergeltung f.

repeat [rɪ'piːt] **I** v wiederholen; **II** s Wiederholung f a. mus radio; ~**edly** [-ɪdlɪ] (zu) wiederholt(en Malen).

repel [rɪ'pel] 1. zurückschlagen, -weisen; 2. abstoßen.

repent [rɪ'pent] bereuen (of s.th. etw); ~**ance** [-əns] Reue f; ~**ant** [-ənt] reuig (of über).

repetition [,repɪ'tɪʃn] Wiederholung f.

replace [rɪ'pleɪs] 1. wieder hinsetzen, -stellen, -legen; 2. ersetzen a. tech; ~**ment** [-mənt] Ersatz m.

replenish [rɪ'plenɪʃ] (wieder) auffüllen (with mit).

reply [rɪ'plaɪ] **I** v (be)antworten (to auf); erwidern (to s.th. etw); **II** s Antwort f.

report [rɪ'pɔːt] **I** v 1. berichten (on s.th. über etw); 2. melden, anzeigen (for wegen); to the police bei der Polizei); **II** s 3. Bericht m (of, on über); weather ~ Wetterbericht m; 4. Knall m; 5. (Schul-)Zeugnis n; ~**er** [-ə] Reporter m.

represent [,reprɪ'zent] 1. darstellen, schildern; 2. com pol vertreten; ~**ation** [,reprɪzen'teɪʃn] 1. Darstellung, Schilderung f; 2. Vertretung f; ~**ative** [-'zentətɪv] com pol Vertreter m; House of ~s Abgeordneten-, (Am) Repräsentantenhaus n.

repress [rɪ'pres] 1. (Aufruhr) unterdrücken; 2. psych verdrängen; ~**ion** [-'preʃn] 1. Unterdrückung f; 2. psych Verdrängung f.

reprieve [rɪ'priːv] **I** v Strafaufschub, e-e Gnadenfrist gewähren (s.o. jdm); **II** s Strafaufschub m.

reprimand ['reprɪmɑːnd] **I** s (strenger) Verweis m; **II** v e-n (strengen) Verweis erteilen (s.o. jdm).

reprint I v [ˌriːˈprɪnt] wieder (ab)drucken; **II** s [ˈ-] Neudruck m.

reproach [rɪˈprəʊtʃ] **I** v vorwerfen (*s.o. with s.th.* jdm etw); **II** s Vorwurf; Tadel m; *above, beyond* ~ über jeden Tadel erhaben; ~**ful** [-fʊl] vorwurfsvoll.

reproduc|e [ˌriːprəˈdjuːs] 1. *biol* (sich) fortpflanzen; 2. reproduzieren; ~**tion** [ˌriːprəˈdʌkʃn] 1. *biol* Fortpflanzung f; 2. Reproduktion f.

reproof [rɪˈpruːf] Tadel m.

reprove [rɪˈpruːv] tadeln.

reptile [ˈreptaɪl] Reptil n.

republic [rɪˈpʌblɪk] Republik f *a. fig*; ~**an** [-ən] **I** *adj* republikanisch; **II** s Republikaner m.

repugnan|ce [rɪˈpʌɡnəns] Widerwille m (*to* gegen); ~**t** [-t] widerlich.

repulse [rɪˈpʌls] 1. *(Angriff)* zurückschlagen; 2. zurück-, abweisen; ~**ive** [-ˈpʌlsɪv] abstoßend.

reput|able [ˈrepjʊtəbl] angesehen; ~**ation** [ˌrepjʊˈteɪʃn] gute(r) Ruf m; ~**e** [rɪˈpjuːt] *be* ~d gelten (*to be, as* als, für); in dem Ruf stehen.

request [rɪˈkwest] **I** s 1. Bitte f; *by, on* ~ auf Wunsch; 2. Nachfrage f; **II** v bitten (*s.th. of s.o.* jdn um etw).

require [rɪˈkwaɪə] 1. fordern, verlangen (*s.th. of s.o.* etw von jdm); 2. brauchen; *if* ~d

falls nötig; ~**ment** [-mənt] (An-)Forderung f.

requisite [ˈrekwɪzɪt] **I** *adj* erforderlich (*for* für); **II** s *pl com* Bedarfsartikel m *pl*.

rescue [ˈreskjuː] **I** v (er)retten (*from* vor, aus); **II** s (Er-)Rettung f; *come to the* ~ *of s.o.* jdm zu Hilfe kommen.

research [rɪˈsɜːtʃ] **I** s Forschung(sarbeit) f; **II** v untersuchen (*into s.th.* etw); Forschungen treiben; ~ **work** Forschungsarbeit f.

resembl|ance [rɪˈzembləns] Ähnlichkeit f; ~**e** [rɪˈzembl] ähnlich sehen, gleichen (*s.o.* jdm).

resent [rɪˈzent] verübeln; sich ärgern über; ~**ful** [-fʊl] beleidigt; ~**ment** [-mənt] *bear no* ~ *against s.o.* jdm nicht böse sein.

reservation [rezəˈveɪʃn] 1. Vorbehalt m; *without* ~ vorbehaltlos; 2. *Am* Reservat(gebiet) n; 3. *Am* Vorbestellung f.

reserve [rɪˈzɜːv] **I** v 1. aufsparen (*for* für); 2. reservieren; 3. (sich) vorbehalten; **II** s 4. Reserve f; *in* ~ in Reserve; vorrätig; 5. *fig* Zurückhaltung f; 6. *without (any)* ~s ohne (jeden) Vorbehalt; ~**d** [-d] 1. zurückhaltend; 2. *all rights* ~ alle Rechte vorbehalten.

reservoir [ˈrezəvwɑː] Staubecken n, -see m.

reshuffle [,ri:'ʃʌfl] umordnen, -stellen, -gruppieren.

reside [rɪ'zaɪd] wohnen (*in, at* in).

residence ['rezɪdəns] Aufenthalt; *(place of ~)* Wohnsitz, -ort m.

resident ['rezɪdənt] **I** *adj* wohnhaft, ansässig (*in* in); **II** *s* Be-, Einwohner *m;* ~**ial area** [,rezɪ'denʃl 'eərɪə] Wohngegend *f.*

resign [rɪ'zaɪn] 1. *(e-e Stelle)* aufgeben; *pol* demissionieren; 2. ~ *o.s. to s.th.* be ~ed *to s.th.* sich mit etw abfinden; ~**ation** [,rezɪg'neɪʃn] 1. Verzicht *m;* 2. Rücktritt *m; hand in o.'s ~* sein Entlassungsgesuch einreichen; 3. Resignation *f;* ~**ed** [rɪ'zaɪnd] ergeben.

resin ['rezɪn] *bot* Harz *n.*

resist [rɪ'zɪst] widerstehen (*s.th.* e-r S; *doing s.th.* etw zu tun); ~**ance** [-əns] Widerstand *m (to* gegen); *offer ~ to s.o.* jdm Widerstand entgegensetzen; ~**ant** [-ənt] widerstandsfähig (*to* gegen).

resolute ['rezəlu:t] entschlossen; ~**ion** [,rezə'lu:ʃn] 1. Be-, Entschluß *m;* 2. Entschlossenheit *f.*

resolve [rɪ'zɒlv] 1. auflösen; analysieren; 2. beschließen (*on, upon s.th.* etw).

resort [rɪ'zɔ:t] **I** *v fig* s-e Zuflucht nehmen (*to* zu); **II** *s* 1. Ferien-, Ausflugsort *m; health ~* (Luft-)Kurort *m;*

2. Zuflucht *f; have ~ to* s-e Zuflucht nehmen zu.

resound [rɪ'zaʊnd] widerhallen (*with* von).

resources *pl* [rɪ'sɔ:sɪz] (Geld-)Mittel *n pl;* Hilfsquellen *f pl.*

respect [rɪ'spekt] **I** *v* achten, respektieren; **II** *s* 1. Achtung *f (for* vor); 2. Rücksicht *f (to, for* auf); 3. *with ~ to* was ... betrifft; ~**able** [-əbl] 1. angesehen; 2. beachtlich, ansehnlich; ~**ful** [-fʊl] respektvoll; ~**ive** [-ɪv] jeweilige; ~**ively** [-ɪvlɪ] beziehungsweise.

respiration [,respə'reɪʃn] Atmung *f.*

resplendent [rɪ'splendənt] strahlend.

respond [rɪ'spɒnd] 1. antworten (*to* auf; *with* mit); 2. reagieren, ansprechen (*to* auf).

response [rɪ'spɒns] 1. Antwort *f; in ~ to* als Antwort auf; 2. Reaktion *f (to* auf).

responsibility [rɪ,spɒnsə-'bɪlətɪ] Verantwortung *f (for, of* für); *on o.'s own ~* auf eigene Verantwortung; ~**le** [rɪ'spɒnsəbl] 1. verantwortlich; haftbar (*for* für); 2. verantwortungsvoll.

responsive [rɪ'spɒnsɪv] empfänglich (*to* für).

rest [rest] **I** *s* 1. Ruhe; Ruhepause; Erholung *f; be at ~* ruhig sein; *come to ~* stehenbleiben; 2. Rest *m; for* the ~ im übrigen; *(all) the ~ (of it)* alles andere; alles übrige; **II** *v* 3. (sich) ausruhen; 4. *(Sache, Arbeit)* ruhen; 5. stützen (*on* auf); lehnen (*against* an); 6. bleiben; ~ *a mystery* ein Geheimnis bleiben; 7. *it* ~s *with you* es liegt (ganz) bei Ihnen.

restaurant ['restərɒnt] Restaurant *n;* ~ **car** *(rail)* Speisewagen *m*.

rest-house ['resthaus] Rasthaus *n*.

restitution [,restɪ'tjuːʃn] Rückerstattung *f; make* ~ Ersatz leisten (*of* für).

restless ['restlɪs] ruhelos.

restor|ation [,restə'reɪʃn] Wiederherstellung *f;* ~**e** [rɪ'stɔː] 1. zurückerstatten; 2. wiedereinsetzen (*to an office* in ein Amt).

restrain [rɪ'streɪn] 1. ab-, zurückhalten (*from doing s.th.* etw zu tun); 2. *(Gefühle)* unterdrücken; ~**ed** [-d] zurückhaltend; beherrscht; ~**t** [-t] 1. Einschränkung *f;* 2. Zurückhaltung *f*.

restrict [rɪ'strɪkt] be-, einschränken (*to* auf); ~**ion** [rɪ'strɪkʃn] *be subject to* ~s Beschränkungen unterliegen.

result [rɪ'zʌlt] **I** *v* 1. herrühren (*from* aus); 2. hinauslaufen (*in* auf), enden (*in* in, mit); **II** *s* Ergebnis *n*, Resultat *n a. math; without* ~ ergebnislos.

resume [rɪ'zjuːm] wieder beginnen; ~ *o.'s seat* s-n Platz wieder einnehmen.

retail ['riːteɪl] Einzelhandel *m;* ~**er** [riː'teɪlə] Einzelhändler *m;* ~ **price** Ladenpreis *m*.

retain [rɪ'teɪn] (ein-, zurück)behalten.

retard [rɪ'tɑːd] verzögern; *mentally* ~ed geistig zurückgeblieben.

retch [retʃ] würgen, e-n Brechreiz haben.

retire [rɪ'taɪə] 1. sich zurückziehen; 2. sich zur Ruhe setzen; ~**d** [-d] im Ruhestand, pensioniert; ~**ment** [-mənt] Ruhestand *m*.

retort [rɪ'tɔːt] schlagfertig antworten.

retrace [rɪ'treɪs] zurückverfolgen.

retract [rɪ'trækt] *(Äußerung)* zurücknehmen.

retreat [rɪ'triːt] **I** *s* 1. Rückzug *m a. mil;* 2. Zuflucht(sort *m*) *f;* **II** *v* sich zurückziehen.

retrieve [rɪ'triːv] wiedererlangen, zurückhalten.

retroactive [,retrəʊ'æktɪv] rückwirkend.

return [rɪ'tɜːn] **I** *v* 1. zurückkehren *a. fig;* wiederkommen; 2. zurückgeben; **II** *s* 3. Rückkehr *f; by* ~ postwendend; *in* ~ als Gegenleistung (*for* für); *many happy* ~s *(of the day)!* viel Glück (zum Geburtstag)! 4. Rückgabe *f;* 5. *pl* Einnahmen *f pl;*

~ **journey, voyage** Rückreise *f;* ~ **ticket** Rückfahr-, -flugkarte *f.*

reveal [rɪ'vi:l] enthüllen.

revelation [,revə'leɪʃn]
1. (sensationelle) Enthüllung *f;* 2. *R~ (rel)* Offenbarung *f.*

revenge [rɪ'vendʒ] **I** *v* rächen; **II** *s* Rache *f; take ~ on s.o. for s.th.* sich an jdm wegen etw rächen; ~**ful** [-fʊl] rachsüchtig.

revenue ['revənju:] Einkommen *n.*

revere [rɪ'vɪə] verehren.

reverence ['revərəns] Verehrung *f (for* für).

reverend ['revərənd] Pastor, Pfarrer *m.*

reverse [rɪ'vɜ:s] **I** *adj* umgekehrt, entgegengesetzt *(to* zu); **II** *s* 1. Gegenteil *n;* 2. Rückseite *f;* 3. *mot* Rückwärtsgang *m;* **III** *v* 4. umkehren, umdrehen; 5. *mot* zurückstoßen.

revert [rɪ'vɜ:t] 1. zurückkommen *(to* auf); 2. sich zurückverwandeln *(to* zu, in).

review [rɪ'vju:] **I** *s* 1. Rückblick *m (of* auf); 2. Nachprüfung *f;* 3. Besprechung; Rezension *f;* 4. *(Zeitschrift)* Revue *f;* **II** *v* 5. kritisch durchsehen; 6. besprechen, rezensieren; ~**er** [-ə] Rezensent *m.*

revis|e [rɪ'vaɪz] durchsehen, überprüfen; ~**ion** [rɪ'vɪʒn] Überarbeitung *f.*

revival [rɪ'vaɪvl] *fig* Wiederaufleben *n.*

revoke [rɪ'vəuk] widerrufen.

revolt [rɪ'vəult] **I** *s* Aufruhr, Aufstand *m (against* gegen); **II** *v* sich empören; meutern *(against* gegen).

revolution [,revə'lu:ʃn]
1. *phys* Umdrehung *f;* 2. *fig* Umwälzung *f; pol* Revolution *f;* ~**ary** [-ʃnəri] **I** *s* Revolutionär *m;* **II** *adj* revolutionär; ~**ize** [-ʃnaɪz] revolutionieren.

revolve [rɪ'vɒlv] sich drehen *(round* um); rotieren *(about, round* um).

revue [rɪ'vju:] *theat* Revue *f.*

revulsion [rɪ'vʌlʃn] *fig* heftige Reaktion *f;* Umschwung *m.*

reward [rɪ'wɔ:d] **I** *s* Belohnung *f;* **II** *v* belohnen, vergelten *(for* für).

rheumat|ic [ru:'mætɪk] rheumatisch; ~**ism** ['ru:mətɪzəm] Rheuma(tismus *m) n.*

rhubarb ['ru:bɑ:b] *bot* Rhabarber *m.*

rhyme, *Am a. rime* [raɪm] Reim *m (to, for* auf); *without ~ or reason* ohne Sinn u. Verstand.

rhythm ['rɪðəm] Rhythmus *m;* ~**ic(al)** ['rɪðmɪk(l)] rhythmisch.

rib [rɪb] Rippe *f; dig, poke s.o. in the ~s* jdm e-n Rippenstoß geben.

ribbon ['rɪbən] Band *n.*

rice [raɪs] Reis *m*.

rich [rɪtʃ] 1. reich (*in* an);
2. (*Farben*) satt, kräftig;
3. (*Boden*) fruchtbar; ~**es** *pl*
['-ɪz] Reichtum, Wohlstand
m.

rickets ['rɪkɪts] *pl mit sing*
Rachitis *f*.

rickety [rɪkətɪ] wack(e)lig.

rid [rɪd] *a. irr* rid, rid; ~ *o.s. of*
s.o., s.th. sich jdn, etw vom
Halse schaffen; *get* ~ *of s.o.,*
s.th. jdn, etw loswerden.

riddle ['rɪdl] Rätsel *n a. fig.*

ride [raɪd] **I** *v irr* **rode** [rəʊd],
ridden ['rɪdn] 1. reiten;
2. fahren (*a bicycle* auf e-m
Rad; *in a train* mit e-m
Zug); 3. ~ *at anchor* vor
Anker liegen; **II** *s* 4. Ritt *m;*
5. Fahrt *f.*

rider ['raɪdə] Reiter *m.*

ridge [rɪdʒ] (Berg-)Rücken,
Grat *m.*

ridicul|e ['rɪdɪkjuːl] **I** *s* Spott
m; hold up to ~ lächerlich
machen; **II** *v* lächerlich machen; ~**ous** [rɪ'dɪkjʊləs] lächerlich.

rifle ['raɪfl] Gewehr *n;*
~**-range** [-reɪndʒ]
1. Schießstand *m;* 2. Schußweite *f.*

rigging ['rɪgɪn] *mar* Takelage
f.

right [raɪt] **I** *adj* 1. richtig;
korrekt; *be* ~ recht haben;
put ~ richtigstellen; *all* ~*!* in
Ordnung! 2. rechte(r, s); ~
hand rechte Hand; **II** *adv*
3. geradewegs; ~ *away, off*

gleich, sofort; 4. direkt, genau; 5. recht, richtig, ordentlich; *it serves him* ~ das geschieht ihm recht; **III** *s*
6. Recht *n;* ~ *of way* Vor-
fahrt *f;* 7. *das* Rechte, Rich-
tige; 8. *die* Rechte, rechte
Seite; ~**eous** ['raɪtʃəs]
recht(schaffen), gerecht;
~**ful** ['-fʊl] rechtmäßig.

rigid ['rɪdʒɪd] 1. steif, starr;
2. *fig* unnachgiebig; ~**ity**
[rɪ'dʒɪdətɪ] 1. Starrheit *f;*
2. *fig* Unnachgiebigkeit *f.*

rig|orous ['rɪgərəs] streng;
~**o(u)r** ['rɪgə] Härte, Strenge *f.*

rim [rɪm] 1. Rand *m;* 2. Felge
f.

rime *s. rhyme.*

rind [raɪnd] (Baum-, Käse-)
Rinde *f.*

ring [rɪn] **I** *v irr* **rang** [ræŋ],
rung [rʌŋ] 1. (*Glocke*) läu-
ten; 2. (*Person*) läuten, klin-
geln (*for* nach); 3. widerhallen (*with, of* von) *a. fig;*
4. *tele* (~ *up*) anrufen; **II** *s*
5. Geläut(e) *n;* 6. Klingelzei-
chen *n;* 7. *tele* Anruf *m; give*
s.o. a ~ (*a tele*) jdn anrufen;
8. Ring; Kreis *m; ear~* Ohr-
ring *m; wedding* ~ Ehering
m; 9. Manege *f;* (Box-)Ring
m; ~**-leader** ['-ˌliːdə] Rädelsführer *m.*

rink [rɪŋk] Eis-, Rollschuhbahn *f.*

rinse [rɪns] **I** *v* (ab-, aus)spü-
len; **II** *s* Spülen *n.*

riot ['raɪət] **I** *s* Tumult; Aufruhr *m;* **II** *v* randalieren; **~ous** [-əs] lärmend.

rip [rɪp] **I** *v* auf-, zerreißen; **II** *s* Schlitz, Riß *m.*

ripe [raɪp] reif *a. fig;* **~n** ['-ən] reifen; **~ness** ['-nɪs] Reife *f a. fig.*

ripple ['rɪpl] (sich) kräuseln.

rise [raɪz] **I** *v irr* rose [rəuz] risen ['rɪzn] 1. aufstehen, sich erheben; 2. *(Gestirn, Vorhang)* aufgehen; 3. *(Rauch)* aufsteigen; 4. *(Weg)* ansteigen; 5. *(Gebäude, Berg)* sich erheben; 6. *(Preise)* anziehen; 7. ~ *against* sich erheben gegen; **II** *s* 8. Steigung *f;* 9. Steigen *n;* Zunahme; Erhöhung *f;* ~ *in prices* Preissteigerung, -erhöhung *f;* 10. *give* ~ *to* Veranlassung geben zu; 11. *have, take o.'s* ~ *(Fluß)* entspringen.

risk [rɪsk] **I** *s* Risiko *n; at o.'s own* ~ auf eigene Gefahr; *run, take the* ~ Gefahr laufen *(of doing s.th.* etw zu tun); **II** *v* wagen, riskieren; **~y** ['-ɪ] gefährlich, gewagt.

rival ['raɪvl] **I** *s* Rivale *m;* **II** *v* rivalisieren mit; **~ry** [-rɪ] Rivalität, Konkurrenz *f.*

river ['rɪvə] Fluß; Strom *m;* **~side** [-saɪd] *by the* ~ am Fluß(ufer).

rivet ['rɪvɪt] **I** *s tech* Niet(e *f*) *m;* **II** *v* (ver)nieten.

road [rəud] (Land-)Straße *f; be on the* ~ unterwegs sein; *rule of the* ~ Straßenver-

kehrsordnung *f;* ~ **map** Straßen-, Autokarte *f;* **~side** ['-saɪd] Straßenrand *m;* **~way** ['-weɪ] Fahrbahn *f.*

roam [rəum] umherschweifen.

roar [rɔ:] **I** *v* brüllen; brausen; *(Sturm)* toben; ~ *with laughter* vor Lachen brüllen; **II** *s* Gebrüll *n.*

roast [rəust] braten, rösten; ~ **beef** Rinderbraten *m.*

rob [rɒb] ~ *s.o. of s.th.* jdm etw rauben; **~ber** ['-ə] Räuber *m;* **~bery** ['-ərɪ] Raub(überfall) *m.*

robe [rəub] Talar *m.*

robin ['rɒbɪn] Rotkehlchen *n.*

robust [rəu'bʌst] robust.

rock [rɒk] **I** *s* 1. Gestein(smasse *f*) *n;* Fels(en) *m; as firm as a* ~ unerschütterlich; 2. *on the* ~s *(Am) (Getränk)* mit Eiswürfeln; **II** *v* schaukeln; wiegen; ~ *the boat (fig)* das Unternehmen gefährden.

rocket ['rɒkɪt] Rakete *f;* **~-base** [-beɪs] Raketenabschußbasis *f.*

rocking-chair ['rɒkɪŋtʃeə] Schaukelstuhl *m.*

rocky ['rɒkɪ] felsig; steinig.

rod [rɒd] 1. Stange *f; fishing--* Angelrute *f;* 2. Rute *f.*

roe [rəu] 1. *(~ deer)* Reh *n;* 2. (Fisch-)Rogen *m.*

rogue [rəug] Schuft *m.*

role [rəul] *theat* Rolle *f.*

roll [rəul] **I** *v* 1. rollen;

2. *(Schiff)* schlingern;
3. zs.rollen, (auf-, ein)wik-
keln; **II** *s* 4. Rolle *f;* 5. Verzeichnis *n,* Liste *f; call the ~*
die Namen verlesen;
6. Brötchen *n,* Semmel *f;*
7. *(Trommel)* Wirbel *m;*
(Donner) Grollen *n.*

roller ['rəʊlə] Rolle, Walze *f;*
road ~ Dampfwalze *f;*
~-skates *pl* [-skeɪts] Roll-
schuhe *m pl.*

Roman ['rəʊmən] **I** *adj* rö-
misch; **II** *s* Römer *m.*

Romania [rə'meɪnɪə] Rumä-
nien *n;* **~n** [-n] **I** *s* Rumäne
m; **II** *adj* rumänisch.

romantic [rəʊ'mæntɪk] ro-
mantisch.

romp [rɒmp] herumtollen.

roof [ru:f] **I** *s* Dach *a. fig;*
mot Verdeck *n; ~ of the*
mouth Gaumen *m;* **II** *v*
überdachen; *~ rack mot*
Dachgepäckträger *m.*

room [ru:m] 1. Platz *m;*
make ~ for Platz schaffen
für; 2. Wohnraum *m,* Zimmer *n; living-~* Wohnzimmer *n;* 3. *fig* Raum *m,* Gelegenheit *f (for* für); *there is ~*
for improvement es ließe
sich noch manches verbes-
sern; 4. *pl* Wohnung *f;* **~y**
['-ɪ] geräumig.

rooster ['ru:stə] Hahn *m.*

root [ru:t] **I** *s* Wurzel *f a. fig;*
~ and branch (fig) mit
Stumpf und Stiel; **II** *v*
1. Wurzel schlagen;

2. (ein)pflanzen; 3. *~ out·*
ausrotten.

rope [rəʊp] **I** *s* Seil, Tau *n;*
Strick, Strang *m;* **II** *v* 1. fest-,
zs.binden; *(Bergsport)* ansei-
len; 2. *~ off* mit e-m Seil ab-
sperren; **~-dancer**
['-,dɑːnsə], **-walker**
['-,wɔːkə] Seiltänzer *m;*
~-ladder ['-,lædə] Stricklei-
ter *f.*

rosary ['rəʊzərɪ] *rel* Rosen-
kranz *m.*

rose [rəʊz] *bot* Rose *f;*
~-bud ['-bʌd] Rosenknospe
f.

rosy ['rəʊzɪ] rosig *a. fig.*

rot [rɒt] **I** *v* vermodern (lassen); verderben; **II** *s* 1. Fäul-
nis *f;* 2. *talk ~ (sl)* Unsinn
reden.

rotary ['rəʊtərɪ] rotierend.

rotate [rəʊ'teɪt] 1. rotieren
(lassen); 2. *fig* turnusmäßig
abwechseln; **~ion** [rəʊ'teɪʃn]
1. Umdrehung *f;* 2. *in ~* turnusmäßig abwechselnd.

rotten ['rɒtn] 1. (ver)faul(t);
verdorben; 2. *fig* niederträchtig, gemein.

rouge [ru:ʒ] Rouge *n.*

rough [rʌf] **I** *adj* 1. rauh, uneben; 2. rauh, heftig; *(Wet-
ter)* stürmisch; *(Meer)* bewegt; 3. grob, roh, ungeho-
belt; 4. unbearbeitet; *(Edelstein)* ungeschliffen; 5. *~
calculation* ungefähre Be-
rechnung *f;* **II** *adv: treat s.o.*
~ jdn hart anfassen; **III** *v: ~*
it primitiv leben; **~en** ['-n]

(auf)rauhen; **~ly** ['-lɪ]
1. rauh, grob; 2. (~ speaking) ungefähr, annähernd; **~ness** ['-nɪs] 1. Rauheit, Unebenheit f; 2. Grobheit f.

round [raʊnd] **I** adj 1. rund; 2. in ~ numbers rund, ungefähr; **II** s 3. Runde f; 4. (Brot) Scheibe f; **III** v herumgehen, -fahren um; **IV** adv: all (the) year ~ das ganze Jahr über; hand ~ herumreichen.

round|about ['raʊndəbaʊt] **I** adj umständlich; **II** s 1. Br Karussell n; 2. Br Kreisverkehr m; ~ **trip** Rundfahrt f; **~-up** ['-ʌp] Razzia f.

rouse [raʊz] 1. aufwecken; 2. aufregen, anstacheln.

rout [raʊt] 1. in die Flucht schlagen; 2. ~ out of bed aus dem Bett holen.

route [ru:t] Weg m, (Reise-) Route f.

row **I** s 1. [rəʊ] Reihe f; 2. [raʊ] Krawall; Krach m; kick up a ~ Krach schlagen; **II** v [rəʊ] rudern; ~ing-boat Ruderboot n.

rowdy ['raʊdɪ] Raufbold m.

royal ['rɔɪəl] königlich; **~ty** [-tɪ] Lizenz(gebühr); Tantieme f.

rub [rʌb] reiben; ~ **down** abreiben, frottieren; ~ **in** einreiben; fig eintrichtern, -pauken; rub it in jdm etw unter die Nase reiben; ~ **out** ausradieren.

rubber ['rʌbə] 1. Gummi m

od n; 2. Radiergummi m; **~-neck** [-nek] Am fam neugieriger Tourist; Gaffer m.

rubbish ['rʌbɪʃ] 1. Abfall m; 2. fig Blödsinn, Quatsch m.

ruby ['ru:bɪ] min Rubin m.

rudder ['rʌdə] mar Steuer-, aero Seitenruder n.

ruddy ['rʌdɪ] (Gesichtsfarbe) gesund; rot.

rude [ru:d] 1. roh, primitiv; 2. unhöflich; frech; 3. stark, kräftig; 4. heftig; hart; unsanft.

rudiments pl ['ru:dɪmənts] Anfangsgründe m pl.

ruff [rʌf] Halskrause f a. zoo.

ruffian ['rʌfjən] Rohling m.

rug [rʌg] 1. Läufer m, Brücke f; (bedside ~) Bettvorleger m; 2. (travelling-~) (Reise-) Decke f.

rugged ['rʌgɪd] uneben, rauh; (Landschaft) zerklüftet.

ruin ['rʊɪn] **I** s 1. Ruine f a. fig; pl Trümmer pl; 2. Ruin m; **II** v zerstören; zugrunde richten.

rule [ru:l] **I** s 1. Vorschrift; Regel f a. math; as a ~ in der Regel; ~ of thumb Faustregel f; 2. Herrschaft, Verwaltung f; 3. Lineal n; **II** v 4. anordnen, bestimmen; 5. regieren; herrschen; 6. ~ out ausschließen.

ruler ['ru:lə] 1. Herrscher m; 2. Lineal n.

rum [rʌm] Rum m.

rumble ['rʌmbl] 1. *(Donner)* rollen; 2. poltern.

rumo(u)r ['ru:mə] I *s* Gerücht *n (of* über); II *v: it is* ~ed *that* man munkelt, daß.

run [rʌn] I *s* 1. Lauf(en *n*) *m*, Rennen *n; on the* ~ auf den Beinen; auf der Flucht; 2. *theat* Spiel-, Laufzeit *f*; 3. *com* Ansturm, Run *m (on* auf); 4. *in the long* ~ auf die Dauer; II *v irr* ran [ræn], run 5. laufen, rennen, eilen; 6. *(Verkehrsmittel)* verkehren; 7. *(Gerücht)* umgehen; 8. *(Text)* lauten; 9. *(Tränen)* rinnen; *(Nase)* laufen; 10. *(Hand, Augen)* gleiten lassen *(over* über); 11. geraten *(into* an, in); ~ *the risk* Gefahr laufen *(of being arrested* verhaftet zu werden); 12. *(Geschäft)* betreiben; 13. *(Haushalt)* führen; 14. ~ *low* zur Neige, zu Ende gehen; ~ **across** (zufällig) treffen *(s.o.* jdn); ~ **away** weglaufen; ~ **into** stoßen auf; unerwartet treffen; ~ **off** weglaufen, -rennen; ~ **out** zu Ende gehen; *he ran out of supplies* die Vorräte gingen ihm aus; ~ **over** 1. *(Gefäß)* überlaufen; 2. überfahren; ~ **up** sich belaufen *(to* auf).

run|about ['rʌnəbaʊt] Kleinwagen *m*; ~**away** [-əweɪ] Ausreißer *m*.

rung [rʌŋ] Sprosse *f a. fig.*

runner ['rʌnə] Läufer *m.*

running ['rʌnɪŋ] I *adj* 1. *(Wasser)* fließend; 2. fortlaufend, ununterbrochen; II *s: make the* ~ *(fig)* den Ton angeben.

runway ['rʌnweɪ] *aero* Start-, Landebahn *f.*

rupture ['rʌptʃə] Bruch *m a. med.*

rural ['rʊərəl] ländlich.

rush [rʌʃ] I *v* 1. rasen, (daher)stürmen, stürzen; *the blood* ~ed *to his face* das Blut stieg ihm ins Gesicht; 2. sich stürzen; losstürmen *(at* auf); 3. drängen *(s.o.* jdn); 4. auf dem schnellsten Wege bringen *od* schaffen *(to the hospital* ins Krankenhaus); II *s* 5. große(r) Andrang, Ansturm *(for* auf); Hochbetrieb *m*; 6. Hast, Eile *f.*

rush-hour(s *pl*) ['rʌʃˌaʊə(z)] Hauptgeschäfts-, Hauptverkehrszeit *f.*

Russia ['rʌʃə] Rußland *n*; ~**n** ['rʌʃn] I *s* Russe *m*; II *adj* russisch.

rust [rʌst] I *s* Rost *m a. bot*; II *v* (ver)rosten.

rustic ['rʌstɪk] ländlich.

rustle ['rʌsl] 1. rascheln; knistern; 2. ~ *s.th.* up etw besorgen, auftreiben.

rusty ['rʌstɪ] rostig.

rut [rʌt] 1. (Wagen-)Spur *f*, G(e)leis(e) *n*; 2. *get into a* ~ in e-n Trott verfallen.

ruthless ['ru:θlɪs] unbarmherzig.

rye [raɪ] Roggen *m.*

S

sabre, *Am* **saber** ['seɪbə] Säbel *m.*

sack [sæk] 1. Sack *m;* 2. *give the ~ (fam)* entlassen; 3. Plünderung *f.*

sacred ['seɪkrɪd] heilig.

sacrifice ['sækrɪfaɪs] **I** *s* Opfer *n a. fig;* **II** *v* opfern (*s.th. to s.o.* jdm etw) *a. fig.*

sad [sæd] traurig; ~**den** ['-n] 1. betrüben; 2. traurig werden (*at* über).

saddle ['sædl] **I** *s* Sattel *m a. tech;* **II** *v* 1. satteln; 2. ~ *s.o. with s.th.* jdm etw aufhalsen.

safe [seɪf] **I** *adj* 1. heil, unversehrt; ~ *and sound* gesund und munter; 2. sicher (*from* vor); *be ~ in* Sicherheit sein; 3. gefahrlos; *(so as) to be on the ~ side* um ganz sicher zu gehen; *it is ~ to say* man kann ruhig sagen; **II** *s* Geld-, Panzerschrank *m;* ~**ty** ['-tɪ] Sicherheit *f; play for ~* kein Risiko eingehen wollen; ~**-belt** Sicherheitsgurt *m a. aero;* ~**-pin** Sicherheitsnadel *f.*

Sagittarius [sædʒɪ'teərɪəs] *astr* Schütze *m.*

said [sed, səd] *s. say; he is ~ to have done* er soll getan haben; *it is ~ that* es heißt, man sagt, daß.

sail [seɪl] **I** *s* Segel *n; II v* 1. segeln; 2. fahren (*for* nach); abfahren, auslaufen (*for* nach); ~**ing** ['-ɪŋ] Segeln *n; ~-boat, -ship, -vessel* Segelboot, -schiff *n;* ~**or** ['-ə] Seemann, Matrose *m.*

saint [seɪnt] Heilige(r) *m.*

sake [seɪk] *for my, your ~* meinet-, deinetwegen.

salad ['sæləd] Salat *m.*

salaried ['sælərɪd] (fest)angestellt; ~ *clerk* Büroangestellte(r) *m;* ~**y** ['sælərɪ] Gehalt *n.*

sale [seɪl] Verkauf *m; for, on ~* verkäuflich; *not for ~* unverkäuflich; *find a ready ~* sich gut verkaufen.

salient ['seɪljənt] hervorstechend.

saliva [sə'laɪvə] Speichel *m.*

sallow ['sæləʊ] fahl, gelb, bläßlich.

salmon ['sæmən] *pl ~(s)* Lachs *m.*

saloon [sə'luːn] 1. Gesellschaftsraum *m;* 2. *Am* Kneipe *f;* 3. *Br mot (~-car)* Limousine *f.*

salt [sɔːlt] **I** *s* Salz *n;* **II** *adj* salz(halt)ig; **III** *v* salzen; ~**y** ['-ɪ] salz(halt)ig.

salutary ['sæljʊtərɪ] gesund; heilsam *a. fig.*

salute [sə'luːt] **I** *s* Salut; Gruß *m;* **II** *v* (be)grüßen; salutieren.

salv|age ['sælvɪdʒ] **I** *s mar*

Bergung f; II v mar bergen; **~ation** [sæl'veɪʃn] (Er-)Rettung f; the S~ Army die Heilsarmee.

same [seɪm] I prn: the ~ der-, die-, dasselbe; it's all, just the ~ das ist, bleibt sich gleich; II adj: at the ~ time gleichzeitig; III adv: (thanks, the) ~ to you (danke,) gleichfalls.

sample ['sɑ:mpl] I s Probe f, Muster n; II v e-e Probe nehmen von.

sanction ['sæŋkʃn] I s 1. Sanktion f; 2. Genehmigung; Billigung f; II v billigen, gutheißen.

sanctuary ['sæŋktjʊərɪ] 1. Heiligtum n; 2. bird ~ Vogelschutzgebiet n.

sand [sænd] 1. Sand m; 2. pl Sandfläche f; Strand m; **~bag** ['-bæg] Sandsack m; **~stone** ['-stəʊn] Sandstein m.

sandwich ['sændwɪdʃ] Sandwich n; **~-man** [-mæn] Plakatträger m.

sane [seɪn] geistig normal.

sanguine ['sæŋgwɪn] zuversichtlich.

sanit|ary ['sænɪtərɪ] hygienisch (einwandfrei); ~ napkin, ~ towel Damen-, Monatsbinde f; **~ation** [,sænɪ'teɪʃn] sanitäre Anlagen f pl; **~y** ['sænətɪ] (geistige) Gesundheit f.

sap [sæp] bot Saft m.

sapphire ['sæfaɪə] min Saphir m.

sarcas|m ['sɑ:kæzəm] Sarkasmus m; **~tic** [sɑ:'kæstɪk] sarkastisch.

sardine [sɑ:'di:n] Sardine f; packed like ~s (dichtgedrängt) wie die Heringe.

sash [sæʃ] Schärpe f; ~ **window** Schiebefenster n.

satchel ['sætʃəl] Schultasche f.

satellite ['sætəlaɪt] astr Satellit m a. fig; ~ **town** Trabantenstadt f.

satin ['sætɪn] Satin, Atlas m.

satisfact|ion [,sætɪs'fækʃn] 1. Genugtuung f (at, with über); 2. Befriedigung, Zufriedenheit f (at, with mit); **~ory** [-'fæktərɪ] befriedigend.

satisfy ['sætɪsfaɪ] zufriedenstellen, befriedigen.

saturate ['sætʃəreɪt] chem sättigen.

Saturday ['sætədɪ] Sonnabend, Samstag m.

sauce [sɔ:s] Soße, Tunke f; **~pan** Kochtopf m.

saucer ['sɔ:sə] Untertasse f.

saucy ['sɔ:sɪ] 1. frech, unverschämt; 2. fam schick.

saunter ['sɔ:ntə] umherschlendern, -bummeln.

sausage ['sɒsɪdʒ] Wurst f.

savage ['sævɪdʒ] I adj 1. wild; 2. fig roh, grausam; II s Wilde(r) m.

save [seɪv] I v 1. (er)retten; bewahren (from vor); ~ ap-

pearances den Schein wahren; 2. *(Geld, Kosten)* sparen; **II** *prp* außer *dat*, ausgenommen *acc*; ~ *for* abgesehen von.

savings *pl* ['seɪvɪŋz] ~ *account* Sparkonto *n*; ~-**bank** Sparkasse *f*.

savo(u)r ['seɪvə] **I** *s* Geschmack *m*; **II** *v* schmecken, riechen *(of* nach) *a. fig*; ~**y** [-rɪ] appetitanregend.

savoy [sə'vɔɪ] Wirsingkohl *m*.

saw [sɔ:] **I** *s* Säge *f*; **II** *v irr* ~*ed*, *sawn* [-n] , *Am* ~*ed* sägen; ~**dust** ['-dʌst] Sägemehl *n*.

say [seɪ] *irr* said, said [sed] sagen, äußern; ~ *good-by(e) to* sich verabschieden von; *(let's)* ~ sagen wir; angenommen; *I should* ~ ich möchte annehmen; *I* ~*!* you *don't* ~*!* so! na, hör, hören Sie mal! *it goes without* ~*ing* das ist selbstverständlich; *that is to* ~ mit anderen Worten; ~**ing** ['-ɪŋ] Redensart *f*; *as the* ~ *goes* wie man zu sagen pflegt.

scab [skæb] Schorf *m*.

scaffold ['skæfəld] 1. (Bau-)Gerüst *n*; 2. Schafott *n*.

scald [skɔ:ld] verbrühen.

scale [skeɪl] **I** *s* 1. Skala *f*; Maßstab *m*; *on a large*, *small* ~ in großem, kleinem Maßstab; 2. *zoo med* Schuppe *f*; *remove the* ~*s from s.o.'s eyes (fig)* jdm die Au-

gen öffnen; 3. Waagschale *a. fig; meist pl* Waage *f*; *a pair of* ~*s* e-e Waage; **II** *v* 4. *(Schicht)* abschaben; (sich) abschuppen; 5. wiegen.

scamp [skæmp] Taugenichts, Racker *m*.

scandal ['skændl] Skandal *m*; ~**ize** ['skændəlaɪz] schockieren; ~**ous** ['skændələs] skandalös.

scanty ['skæntɪ] dürftig.

scapegoat ['skeɪpgəʊt] Sündenbock *m*.

scar [skɑ:] Narbe *f a. bot fig*.

scarc|e [skeəs] 1. selten; 2. knapp; schwer zu bekommen(d); ~**ely** ['-lɪ] kaum, schwerlich; ~ *anything* fast nichts; ~**ity** ['-ətɪ] Mangel *m*, Knappheit *f (of* an).

scare [skeə] **I** *v* er-, aufschrecken; **II** *s* Panik *f*; Schrecken *m*; ~**crow** ['-krəʊ] Vogelscheuche *f*.

scarf [skɑ:f] *pl a.* scarves Hals-, Kopftuch *n*, Schal *m*.

scarlet ['skɑ:lət] scharlachfarben, -rot; ~ *fever med* Scharlach *m*.

scathing [skeɪðɪŋ] *fig (Kritik)* scharf, verletzend.

scatter ['skætə] 1. (~ *about*) ver-, ausstreuen; 2. *(Menge)* sich zerstreuen.

scene [si:n] 1. Schauplatz *m*; 2. Szene *f a. theat; behind the* ~*s (a. fig)* hinter den Kulissen; ~**ry** ['-ərɪ] 1. *theat* Bühnenbild *n*; 2. Szenerie *f*.

scent [sent] **I** v 1. riechen; 2. parfümieren (*with* mit); **II** s Duft m; Parfüm n.

schedule ['ʃedjuːl] **I** s 1. Tabelle f; 2. Fahr-, Arbeitsplan m; **II** v aufstellen; tabellarisch zs.stellen; **~d** [-d] 1. as ~ fahrplanmäßig; 2. be ~ for vorgesehen sein für.

scheme [skiːm] **I** s 1. Schema n; 2. Projekt n; Plan m; **II** v 3. planen; 4. Ränke schmieden.

scholar ['skɒlə] 1. Gelehrte(r) m; 2. (*Univ.*) Stipendiat m; **~ship** [-ʃip] Stipendium n.

school [skuːl] Schule f a. fig; at ~ in der Schule; go to ~ zur Schule gehen; *boarding-~* Internat n; **~boy** ['-bɔi] Schüler m; **~girl** ['-gɜːl] Schülerin f; **~master** ['-ˌmɑːstə] (Schul-)Lehrer m; **~mistress** ['-ˌmistris] Lehrerin f.

scien|ce ['saiəns] Wissen(schaft f) n; ~ fiction Zukunftsromane m pl; **~tific** [ˌsaiən'tifik] wissenschaftlich; **~tist** ['saiəntist] (Natur-)Wissenschaftler m.

scissors pl ['sizəz] a pair of ~ e-e Schere.

scoff [skɒf] spotten (*at* über).

scold [skəuld] schelten, schimpfen; **~ing** ['-iŋ] give s.o. a ~ jdn schelten.

scoop [skuːp] 1. Schaufel f;

2. *at one* ~ (*fig*) mit e-m Schlag.

scooter ['skuːtə] (Motor-)-Roller m.

scope [skəup] Spielraum m.

scorch [skɔːtʃ] an-, versengen.

score [skɔː] **I** s 1. Kerbe f; 2. Markierung f; 3. fig Zeche, Rechnung f; 4. Punktzahl f; what's the ~? wie steht das Spiel? **II** v (*Punkte*) erzielen.

scorn [skɔːn] **I** s Verachtung f; **II** v verachten; **~ful** ['-fʊl] verächtlich.

Scorpio ['skɔːpiəu] astr Skorpion m.

Scot [skɒt] Schotte m, Schottin f; **~ch** [-ʃ] **I** adj schottisch; **II** s schottische(r) Whisky m; **~land** ['-lənd] Schottland n; **~sman** ['-smən] Schotte m; **~swoman** ['-ˌswumən] Schottin f; **~tish** ['-iʃ] schottisch.

scoundrel ['skaundrəl] Schurke m.

scour ['skauə] 1. scheuern, schrubben; 2. (*Gebiet*) absuchen.

scout [skaut] 1. Kundschafter m; 2. (*boy* ~) Pfadfinder m.

scramble ['skræmbl] 1. klettern; 2. sich reißen (*for* um); 3. ~d eggs (*pl*) Rührei n pl.

scrap [skræp] **I** s 1. (~ *of paper*) (Papier-)Fetzen m;

2. Schrott *m;* 3. *pl* Reste *m pl;* **II** *v* verschrotten.

scrape [skreɪp] **I** *v* 1. (ab-, auf-, zer)kratzen; 2. ~ *through* gerade noch durchkommen; **II** *s* 3. Kratzen *n;* 4. Kratzer *m;* Schramme *f;* 5. *in a* ~ in Verlegenheit, in der Klemme.

scrap iron Alteisen *n.*

scratch [skrætʃ] **I** *v* 1. (zer)kratzen; 2. sich kratzen; **II** *s* Schramme *f,* Kratzer *m.*

scrawl [skrɔːl] kritzeln.

scream [skriːm] **I** *v* (laut auf)schreien; ~ *with laughter* schallend lachen; **II** *s* (Auf-, Angst-)Schrei *m.*

screen [skriːn] **I** *s* 1. Schutzschirm *m;* 2. *mot* Windschutzscheibe *f;* 3. *film* Leinwand *f;* 4. *(Radar, TV)* Bildschirm *m;* **II** *v* abschirmen.

screw [skruː] **I** *s* Schraube *f;* **II** *v* (fest-, zu)schrauben; **~-driver** ['-ˌdraɪvə] Schraubenzieher *m.*

scribble ['skrɪbl] kritzeln.

script [skrɪpt] 1. (Hand-)-Schrift *f;* 2. Manuskript *n;* 3. *film* Drehbuch *n.*

scripture ['skrɪptʃə] *(the) Holy S~(s) (pl)* die Heilige Schrift *f.*

scrub [skrʌb] (ab)schrubben, (ab)bürsten.

scruple ['skruːpl] Bedenken *n;* **~ulous** ['skruːpjʊləs] gewissenhaft.

scrutinize ['skruːtɪnaɪz] genau prüfen.

scuffle ['skʌfl] sich balgen.

sculptor ['skʌlptə] Bildhauer *m;* **~ure** ['skʌlptʃə] 1. Bildhauerei *f;* 2. Skulptur *f.*

scum [skʌm] *fig* Abschaum *m (of the earth* der Menschheit).

scurry ['skʌrɪ] hasten *a. fig,* rennen.

scuttle ['skʌtl] Kohlenkasten *m.*

scythe [saɪð] Sense *f.*

sea [siː] *the* ~ See *f,* Meer *n; at* ~ auf (hoher) See; **~food** ['-fuːd] eßbare Meerestiere *n pl;* **~-going** ['-ˌgəʊɪŋ] seetüchtig.

seal [siːl] **I** *s* 1. Siegel *n a. fig;* 2. Seehund *m,* Robbe *f;* **II** *v* (be-, ver)siegeln; abdichten.

sea-level ['siːlevl] Meeresspiegel *m.*

seam [siːm] Saum *m,* Naht *f.*

seaman ['siːmən] *pl -men* Seemann *m.*

search [sɜːtʃ] **I** *v* 1. durchsuchen; 2. suchen *(for* nach); **II** *s* Durchsuchung; Suche *f (for* nach); *in* ~ *of* auf der Suche nach; **~light** ['-laɪt] Scheinwerfer *m.*

seasick ['siːsɪk] seekrank; **~side** [-saɪd] Küste *f; go to the* ~ an die See gehen.

season ['siːzn] **I** *s* 1. Jahreszeit *f;* 2. Saison *f a. theat;* **II** *v* 3. reifen lassen; ablagern; 4. gewöhnen *(to* an); 5. *(Speise)* würzen; **~able**

[-əbl] 1. zeitgemäß; 2. passend, angebracht; **~al** [-l] jahreszeitlich; saisonbedingt; **~-ticket** [-ˌtɪkɪt] *Br* Zeitkarte *f.*

seat [siːt] **I** *s* Sitz(gelegenheit *f,* -platz) *m; take a* ~ Platz nehmen; **II** *v:* ~ *o.s.* sich (hin)setzen; **~-belt** ['-belt] *fasten* ~*s* anschnallen!

secluded [sɪ'kluːdɪd] abgelegen.

second ['sekənd] **I** *adj* 1. zweit, nächst; *in the* ~ *place* an zweiter Stelle, zweitens; *on* ~ *thoughts* bei nochmaliger Überlegung; 2. geringer (*to* als); ~ *to none* unübertroffen; **II** *s* 3. Zweite(r), Nächste(r) *m;* 4. Sekunde *f; wait a* ~ warten Sie e-n Augenblick; **~ary** [-ərɪ] ~ *education* höhere(s) Schulwesen *n;* höhere Schulbildung *f;* **~-hand** [-hænd] gebraucht; (*Buch*) antiquarisch; **~ly** [-lɪ] zweitens; **~-rate** [-reɪt] zweitrangig; mittelmäßig.

secrecy ['siːkrəsɪ] Verschwiegenheit *f.*

secret ['siːkrɪt] **I** *adj* geheim, heimlich; *keep* ~ geheimhalten; **II** *s* Geheimnis *n* (*from* vor); *in* ~ im geheimen.

secretary ['sekrətrɪ] 1. Sekretär *m; 2. S~ of State* (*Br*) Minister *m.*

secrete [sɪ'kriːt] *physiol* absondern; **~ion** [sɪ'kriːʃn] *physiol* Absonderung *f.*

sect [sekt] *rel* Sekte *f.*

section ['sekʃn] 1. Ausschnitt *m; 2.* Abteilung *f.*

secular ['sekjʊlə] weltlich.

secure [sɪ'kjʊə] **I** *adj* sicher (*from* vor); **II** *v* 1. sichern, schützen (*from, against* vor); 2. festmachen; (*Türe*) (ver)schließen; 3. sich sichern, verschaffen; **~ity** [-rɪtɪ] 1. Sicherheit *f* (*against, from* vor); 2. *jur* Bürgschaft *f;* Pfand *n; 3. pl* Wertpapiere *n pl.*

sedate [sɪ'deɪt] gesetzt, ruhig.

sediment ['sedɪmənt] (Boden-)Satz *m.*

seduce [sɪ'djuːs] verführen; **~tion** [sɪ'dʌkʃn] Verführung *f;* **~tive** [sɪ'dʌktɪv] verführerisch.

see [siː] *irr saw* [sɔː] , *seen* [siːn] 1. sehen, erblicken; 2. einsehen, verstehen; *I* ~ ich verstehe; 3. *come, go to* ~ besuchen; ~ *you soon* (*fam*) auf Wiedersehen! 4. ~ *s.o. home* jdn nach Hause begleiten; 5. *I'll* ~ *about it* ich werde mich darum kümmern; ~ *to it that* sorgen Sie dafür, daß; ~ *s.o. off* jdn fortbegleiten; ~ *through* durchschauen; *see s.th. through* etw bis zum Ende durchhalten.

seed [siːd] 1. Same(n) *m; 2. pl fig* Saat *f.*

seek [siːk] *irr sought, sought* [sɔːt] 1. suchen; 2. trachten nach; *(much) sought after* gefragt, begehrt.

seem [si:m] scheinen; **~ing** ['-ɪŋ] anscheinend, scheinbar.

seemly [si:mlɪ] *it is not ~* es gehört sich nicht.

seethe [si:ð] sieden, kochen.

segregat|e ['segrɪgeɪt] trennen; absondern; **~ion** [ˌsegrɪ'geɪʃn] Rassentrennung *f.*

seize [si:z] 1. sich bemächtigen *(s.th.* e-r S) sich aneignen; 2. beschlagnahmen; 3. (er)greifen, fassen, packen; 4. *fig* begreifen.

seldom ['seldəm] selten.

select [sɪ'lekt] auswählen; **~ion** [sɪ'lekʃn] Auswahl *f.*

self [self] *pl* **selves** [selvz] *be o.'s former ~ again* wieder (ganz) der alte sein; **~-confidence** [ˌ-'kɒnfɪdəns] Selbstvertrauen *n;* **~-conscious** [ˌ-'kɒnʃəs] *fam* befangen; **~-control** [ˌ-kən'trəʊl] Selbstbeherrschung *f;* **~-defence** [ˌ-dɪ'fens] *in ~* in Notwehr; **~ish** ['-ɪʃ] selbstsüchtig; eigennützig; **~-righteous** [ˌ-'raɪtʃəs] selbstgerecht; **~-service** [ˌ-'sɜːvɪs] *com* Selbstbedienung *f.*

sell [sel] *irr* **sold,** *sold* [səʊld] 1. verkaufen; *sold out* ausverkauft; 2. *~ well* sich gut verkaufen.

semblance ['sembləns] *put on a ~ of gaiety* sich den Anschein geben, fröhlich zu sein.

semi|- [semɪ-] halb...; **~-circular** [ˌ-'sɜːkjʊlə] halbkreisförmig.

semolina [ˌseməʊ'li:nə] (Weizen-)Grieß *m.*

senat|e ['senɪt] Senat *m; ~or* ['senətə] Senator *m.*

send [send] *irr* **sent,** *sent* [sent] senden, schicken; *~ for s.o.* jdn kommen lassen; *~ s.o. word* jdm Nachricht geben; *~ in* einschicken; *~ off* abschicken; **~er** ['-ə] (Ab-)Sender *m; return to ~* an den Absender zurück.

senior ['si:njə] älter *(to* als).

sensation [sen'seɪʃn] 1. Empfindung *f,* Eindruck *m;* 2. Sensation *f;* **~al** [sen'seɪʃənl] aufsehenerregend.

sense [sens] 1. *physiol* Sinn *m;* 2. Gefühl *n;* 3. *fig* Sinn *m; (Wort)* Bedeutung *f; make ~ Sinn haben; talk ~* vernünftig reden; *in a ~* in gewissem Sinne; *~ pl* Verstand *m; bring s.o. to his ~s* jdn zur Vernunft bringen; **~less** ['-lɪs] 1. bewußtlos; 2. dumm; unvernünftig.

sensible ['sensəbl] vernünftig, klug.

sensitive ['sensɪtɪv] 1. sensibel; 2. empfindlich; *~ to light* lichtempfindlich.

sensual ['sensjʊəl] sinnlich.

sentence ['sentəns] **I** *s* 1. Gerichtsurteil *n; serve o.'s*

~ s-e Strafe verbüßen;
2. Satz *m;* **II** *v* verurteilen
(*to* zu).

sentiment ['sentɪmənt] Gefühl *n;* **~al** [,sentɪ'mentl]
1. Gefühls-; 2. gefühlvoll;
sentimental.

sentry ['sentrɪ] Wache *f.*

separ|able ['sepərəbl] trennbar; **~ate I** *v* ['sepəreɪt]
1. (ab)trennen; 2. (sich) trennen (*from* von); **II** *adj*
['seprət] (ab)getrennt, gesondert (*from* von); (*Zimmer*) separat; *keep* ~ auseinanderhalten; **~ation** [,sepə'reɪʃn]
Trennung *f.*

September [sep'tembə]
September *m.*

sequel ['si:kwəl] Folge *f.*

sequence ['si:kwəns] Reihe(nfolge) *f.*

serene [sɪ'ri:n] heiter, klar,
rein.

sergeant ['sɑ:dʒənt] Feldwebel; Wachtmeister *m.*

serial ['sɪərɪəl] 1. in regelmäßiger Folge erscheinend;
2. ~ *number* laufende Nummer *f.*

series ['sɪərɪz] *pl* ~ Reihe,
Serie *f.*

serious ['sɪərɪəs] 1. ernst;
(*Krankheit*) schwer; 2. (*Irrtum*) grob; **~ly** [-lɪ] im
Ernst; *take* ~ ernst nehmen.

sermon ['sɜ:mən] Predigt *f.*

serpent ['sɜ:pənt] (Gift-)-
Schlange *f.*

servant ['sɜ:vənt] 1. Diener

m; 2. *civil, public* ~ Beamte(r) *m.*

serve [sɜ:v] 1. dienen (*s.o.*
jdm); 2. (*Kunden*) bedienen;
3. (*Dienst*) ausüben;
4. (*Zweck*) erfüllen; ~ *no*
purpose zwecklos sein;
5. (*that*) ~s *you right!* das
geschieht dir recht!

service ['sɜ:vɪs] 1. Dienst *m;*
2. (*civil, public* ~) Staatsdienst *m;* 3. *tech* Wartung *f;*
Kundendienst *m;* ~ *station*
Tankstelle; Reparaturwerkstätte *f;* 4. *do s.o. a* ~
jdm helfen; *can I be of* ~ *to*
you? kann ich Ihnen behilflich sein? 5. (*bus* ~) (Bus-)
Verkehr *m;* 6. Bedienung *f*
(*bei Tisch*); 7. (*divine* ~)
Gottesdienst *m;* 8. (*Geschirr*) Service *n;* 9. *sport*
Aufschlag *m;* **~able** [-əbl]
tauglich.

session ['seʃn] *jur parl* Sitzung *f.*

set [set] **I** *s* 1. Satz *m,* Garnitur *f;* 2. (Rundfunk-)Gerät *n;*
II *adj* 3. festgesetzt, -gelegt,
bestimmt; 4. fest, starr; **III** *v*
irr set, set 5. (hin)setzen; hinlegen, aufstellen; 6. (ein-,
her)richten, zurecht-, fertigmachen; 7. ~ *on fire* anzünden; ~ *going* in Gang bringen; 8. ~ *the pace (fig)* den
Ton, das Tempo angeben;
9. ~ *to work* sich an die Arbeit machen; 10. (*Tisch*)
decken; 11. (*Edelstein*) fassen; 12. (*Uhr*) stellen; *radio*

einstellen; 13. *(Datum)* festsetzen; 14. *(Beispiel)* geben;
15. *(Sonne)* untergehen; ~
about in Angriff nehmen; ~
aside 1. beiseite stellen;
2. nicht beachten; ~ **out** aufbrechen *(for* nach*)*; ~ **up**
aufstellen, auf-, errichten;
eröffnen, gründen.

setback ['setbæk] *have a* ~
e-n Rückschlag erleiden.

setting ['setɪŋ] 1. (Sonnen-)-
Untergang *m;* 2. Fassung *f
(a. e-s Edelsteines);* 3. Szenerie *f;* 4. Vertonung *f.*

settle ['setl] 1. *(Staub)* sich
setzen; 2. erledigen; *that ~s
the matter* damit ist die Sache erledigt; 3. *(Streit)* beilegen; 4. *(Frage)* entscheiden;
5. *(Schuld)* bezahlen; ~ **up**
die Rechnung begleichen
(with s.o. bei jdm*)*; 6. sich
niederlassen; ~ *down* sich
(endgültig) niederlassen;
sich einleben.

settlement ['setlmənt]
1. Regelung; Abmachung *f;*
2. Bezahlung *f;* 3. Vergleich
m; 4. Siedlung *f;* ~**er** ['setlə]
(An-)Siedler *m.*

seven ['sevn] sieben; ~**th**
['sevnθ] siebent; ~**ty** [-tɪ]
siebzig.

sever ['sevə] 1. (ab)trennen
(from von*)*; 2. *(Beziehungen)* abbrechen.

several ['sevrəl] 1. verschiedene; 2. mehrere; ~ *times*
mehrmals.

severe [sɪ'vɪə] 1. streng, hart;

2. *(Schmerz)* heftig; 3. *(Anforderung)* streng;
4. *(Krankheit)* schwer; ~**ity**
[sɪ'verətɪ] Strenge, Härte *f.*

sew [səʊ] *irr* ~*ed* [-d] , ~*ed*
od ~**n** [-n] nähen; ~ *on* an-
nähen.

sewage ['sjuːɪdʒ] Abwässer
n pl.

sewer 1. [sjʊə] Abzugsrohr
n; 2. ['səʊə] Näher(in *f) m.*

sewerage ['sjʊərɪdʒ] Kanali-
sation *f.*

sex [seks] Geschlecht *n;*
~**ual** [-jʊəl] geschlechtlich.

shabby ['ʃæbɪ] schäbig.

shade [ʃeɪd] **I** *s* 1. Schatten
m; put into the ~ *(fig)* in
den Schatten stellen;
2. Schattierung *f;* 3. *fig* Nu-
ance *f;* 4. (Lampen-)Schirm
m; **II** *v* abschirmen.

shadow ['ʃædəʊ] **I** *s* Schatten *m a. fig; beyond a* ~ *of
doubt* ohne jeden Zweifel;
have ~*s under the eyes*
dunkle Ringe um die Augen
haben; **II** *v* beschatten; ~
cabinet *(pol)* Schattenkabi-
nett *n;* ~**y** 1. schattig;
2. schattenhaft.

shady ['ʃeɪdɪ] 1. schattig;
2. *fig* zwielichtig.

shaft [ʃɑːft] 1. Schaft *m;*
2. Deichsel *f;* 3. *min* Schacht
m.

shaggy ['ʃægɪ] zottig.

shake [ʃeɪk] **I** *v irr shook*
[ʃʊk], **shaken** ['ʃeɪkən]
1. schütteln, rütteln (an);
~ *hands with s.o.* jdm die

Hand schütteln *od* geben; 2. erschüttern; 3. *(Stimme)* (er)zittern (*with* vor); **II** *s* Schütteln *n;* ~**y** ['-ɪ] zitternd, wack(e)lig.

shall [ʃæl, ʃəl, ʃl] *irr should* [ʃʊd, ʃəd, ʃd] soll; werde; *I should say so!* das will ich meinen!

shallow ['ʃæləʊ] **I** *adj* 1. seicht; 2. *fig* oberflächlich; **II** *s meist pl* Untiefe *f.*

sham [ʃæm] **I** *s* Fälschung; Nachahmung *f;* **II** *adj* falsch, unecht.

shame [ʃeɪm] **I** *s* 1. Scham(gefühl *n*) *f;* 2. Schande *f (to* für); ~ *on you!* schäm dich! **II** *v* beschämen; ~**ful** ['-fʊl] schimpflich; ~**less** ['-lɪs] schamlos.

shampoo [ʃæm'puː] **I** *v (die Haare)* waschen; **II** *s* 1. Haar-, Kopfwäsche *f;* 2. Shampoon *n.*

shan't [ʃɑːnt] = *shall not.*

shanty ['ʃæntɪ] Hütte *f;* ~-**town** [-taʊn] Elendsviertel *n.*

shape [ʃeɪp] **I** *s* Form; Gestalt *f; be in bad* ~ in schlechter Verfassung sein; *take* ~ Gestalt annehmen; **II** *v* formen, gestalten *a. fig;* ~**less** ['-lɪs] form-, gestaltlos; ~**ly** ['-lɪ] wohlgestaltet.

share [ʃeə] **I** *s* 1. Anteil *m,* Teil *n* u. *m; have a* ~ *in s.th.* an e-r S beteiligt sein; 2. Aktie *f; hold* ~*s* Aktionär sein

(in a company e-r Gesellschaft); **II** *v* 3. (aus-, ver)teilen *(among* unter); 4. teilhaben, teilnehmen *(in* an); ~**holder** ['-ˌhəʊldə] Aktionär *m.*

shark [ʃɑːk] Hai(fisch) *m.*

sharp [ʃɑːp] **I** *adj* 1. scharf *a. fig;* 2. schneidend, stechend; **II** *adv* 3. pünktlich, genau; 4. *look* ~ sich beeilen; ~**en** ['ʃɑːpən] schärfen; *(Bleistift)* spitzen; ~**ener** ['ʃɑːpnə] *(pencil-*~) Bleistiftspitzer *m.*

shatter ['ʃætə] zersplittern.

shav|e [ʃeɪv] **I** *v a. irr* ~*d,* *shaven* ['-n] (sich) rasieren; **II** *s: give a clean, close* ~ gut, sauber rasieren; ~**er** ['-ə] Rasierapparat *m;* ~**ings** *pl* ['-ɪŋz] Späne *m pl.*

shawl [ʃɔːl] Schal *m,* Hals-, Kopftuch *n.*

she [ʃiː, ʃɪ] sie.

sheaf [ʃiːf] *pl sheaves* Garbe *f.*

shear [ʃɪə] **I** *v a. irr* ~*ed,* *shorn* [ʃɔːn] scheren; **II** *s pl* große Schere *f.*

sheath [ʃiːθ] Scheide *f.*

shed [ʃed] **I** *v irr shed, shed* aus-, vergießen; ~ *blood,* *tears* Blut, Tränen vergießen; **II** *s* Schuppen *m.*

sheep [ʃiːp] *pl sheep* Schaf *n a. fig.*

sheer [ʃɪə] 1. *fig* bloß, rein, völlig; ~ *madness* helle(r) Wahnsinn *m;* 2. *(Abhang)* steil, jäh.

sheet [ʃiːt] 1. Bettuch *n;*

2. Bogen *m* (Papier); 3. (große) Fläche *f;* 4. (*~ metal*)
Blech *n;* 5. *rain came down
in ~s* es regnete in Strömen.
she-goat ['ʃiːgəut] Ziege *f.*
shelf [ʃelf] *pl shelves*
(Wand-)Brett, Regal *n.*
shell [ʃel] **I** *s* 1. Schale, Hülse
f; 2. Schneckenhaus *n;*
3. Granate *f;* **II** *v* (*Erbsen*)
enthülsen, schälen.
shelter ['ʃeltə] **I** *s* 1. Schutz-
dach *n; (air-raid ~)* (Luft-)-
Schutzraum *m;* 2. *take ~*
Schutz suchen (*from* vor);
II *v* (be)schützen.
shelve [ʃelv] zu den Akten
legen.
shepherd ['ʃepəd] Schäfer
m.

shield [ʃiːld] **I** *s* 1. Schild *m;*
2. Schutz *m a. fig;* **II** *v* schützen (*from* vor).
shift [ʃift] **I** *v* 1. (ab-, von
sich) schieben; 2. *tech* umschalten; *~ into second gear*
in den zweiten Gang um-
schalten; **II** *s* (Arbeits-)-
Schicht *f.*
shilling ['ʃiliŋ] Schilling *m.*
shimmer ['ʃimə] schimmern.
shin [ʃin] (*~-bone*) Schienbein *n.*
shin|e [ʃain] **I** *v irr shone,
shone* [ʃon, *Am* ʃəun]
1. glänzen, scheinen, leuchten; 2. (*Schuhe*) putzen, polieren; **II** *s* Schein, Glanz *m
a. fig;* **~ing** ['ʃainiŋ] glänzend; **~y** ['ʃaini] glänzend.

shingle ['ʃiŋgl] (Dach-)Schin-
del *f.*
ship [ʃip] **I** *s* Schiff *n;* **II** *v*
(*Waren*) verschiffen,
(ver)senden; **~building**
['-ˌbildiŋ] Schiffbau *m;*
~ment ['-mənt] 1. Verschif-
fung *f (for* nach); 2. Schiffs-
ladung; Sendung *f;* **~wreck**
['-rek] Schiffbruch *m a. fig;*
~yard ['-jɑːd] (Schiffs-)-
Werft *f.*
shirt [ʃɜːt] (Ober-)Hemd *n;*
~-sleeve ['-ˌsliːv] *in o.'s ~s*
in Hemdsärmeln.
shiver ['ʃivə] **I** *v* zittern (*with
cold, fear* vor Kälte, Angst);
II *s: I got, had the ~s* (*fam*)
es lief mir eiskalt über den
Rücken.
shoal [ʃəul] Untiefe *f.*
shock [ʃok] **I** *s* 1. Stoß,
Schlag *m;* 2. *med* Nerven-
schock *m; be a great ~ to
s.o.* für jdn ein schwerer
Schlag sein; **II** *v: be ~ed at,
by* schockiert sein von; **~
absorber** Stoßdämpfer *m;*
~ing ['-iŋ] schockierend.
shoe [ʃuː] **I** *s* 1. (Halb-)Schuh
m; 2. (*horse-~*) Hufeisen *n;*
II *v irr shod, shod* [ʃod]
(*Pferd*) beschlagen; **~lace**
['-leis] Schnürsenkel *m;*
~maker ['-ˌmeikə] Schuh-
macher, Schuster *m;*
~string ['-striŋ] *Am*
Schnürsenkel *m.*
shoot [ʃuːt] **I** *v irr shot, shot*
[ʃot] 1. (dahin-, vorbei)schie-
ßen, -sausen; 2. (ab)schie-

ßen, (-)feuern; 3. erschießen; II *s bot* Schößling *m;* ~**ing** ['ʃɪŋ] Jagd(recht *n*) *f;* ~**ing star** Sternschnuppe *f.*

shop [ʃɒp] I *s* Laden *m;* Geschäft *n; go to the wrong* ~ *(fig, fam)* an die falsche Adresse geraten; *set up* ~ ein Geschäft eröffnen; *baker's* ~ Bäckerei *f;* II *v (go shopping)* einkaufen (gehen); ~**assistant** ['-ə,sɪstənt] Verkäufer(in *f*) *m;* ~**keeper** ['-,ki:pə] Ladenbesitzer *m;* ~**lifting** ['-,lɪftɪŋ] Ladendiebstahl *m;* ~**ping** ['-ɪŋ] *do o.'s* ~ Einkäufe machen; ~ **bag** Einkaufstasche *f;* ~ **centre** Geschäftszentrum *n;* ~**window** [,-'wɪndəʊ] Schaufenster *n.*

shore [ʃɔ:] Ufer *n;* Strand *m; on* ~ an Land.

short [ʃɔ:t] I *adj* 1. kurz; *a* ~ *time ago* vor kurzem; *at* ~ *notice* kurzfristig; 2. klein; 3. (zs.)gedrängt; *in* ~ (in) kurz(en, wenigen Worten); 4. knapp (*of* an); ~ *of cash* nicht bei Kasse; *be* ~ *with s.o.* mit jdm kurz angebunden sein; II *adv: stop* ~ plötzlich stehenbleiben.

short|age ['ʃɔ:tɪdʒ] Mangel *m,* Verknappung *f* (*of* an); ~**bread** ['-bred] Mürbeteig *m,* -gebäck *n;* ~ **circuit** [,-'sɜ:kɪt] *el* Kurzschluß *m;* ~**comings** *pl* ['-,kʌmɪŋz] Unzulänglichkeit *f;* ~ **cut**

(Weg) Abkürzung *f;* ~**en** ['ʃɔ:tn] (ab-, ver)kürzen); ~**hand** ['-hænd] Stenographie *f;* ~**ly** ['-lɪ] 1. in kurzem; 2. in wenigen Worten; ~**sighted** [,-'saɪtɪd] kurzsichtig *a. fig.*

shot [ʃɒt] 1. Schuß *m; like a* ~ wie der Blitz; sofort; 2. *fig* Versuch *m; have a* ~ *at s.th.* etw versuchen; 3. Kugel *f;* Geschoß *n;* 4. Schütze *m;* 5. *phot* film Aufnahme *f;* 6. *Am med* Spritze *f;* 7. *a big* ~ (*sl*) ein hohes Tier *n;* ~**gun** ['-gʌn] Schrotflinte *f.*

should [ʃʊd] *s. shall.*

shoulder ['ʃəʊldə] I *s* Schulter, Achsel *f; straight from the* ~ unverblümt; ~ *to* ~ Schulter an Schulter; *stand head and* ~*s above s.o.* jdn beträchtlich überragen; viel tüchtiger sein als jem; *give s.o. the cold* ~ *(fig)* jdm die kalte Schulter zeigen; II *v* 1. schultern; 2. *fig* auf sich nehmen (*s.th.* etw).

shout [ʃaʊt] I *s* Schrei *m;* Ruf *m;* II *v* rufen, schreien; ~ *at s.o.* jdn anschreien.

shove [ʃʌv] I *v* 1. schieben; stoßen; 2. *(fam)* hineinstopfen (*into a drawer* in e-e Schublade); 3. ~ *off* (*sl*) abhauen; II *s* Schubs, Stoß *m.*

shovel ['ʃʌvl] I *s* Schaufel *f;* *(Bagger)* Löffel *m;* II *v* schaufeln.

show [ʃəʊ] I *s* 1. Schau(stellung) *f; be on* ~ ausgestellt sein; 2. *theat* Aufführung; *radio TV* Sendung *f;* **II** *v irr showed, shown* [-n] *od showed* 3. zeigen; 4. den Weg zeigen, führen; 5. darlegen, erklären; 6. *(Gunst, Gnade)* erweisen; ~ **off** im besten Licht zeigen; angeben; ~ **up** 1. ans Licht bringen *od* kommen; 2. *fam* kommen, erscheinen.

show|-business ['ʃəʊ,bɪznɪs] Schaugeschäft *n;* ~-**case** ['-keɪs] Vitrine *f.*

shower ['ʃaʊə] **I** *s* 1. (Regen-)Schauer *m;* 2. *(~-bath)* Dusche *f;* **II** *v fig* überschütten; ~ *s.th. upon s.o.* jdn mit etw überhäufen; ~**y** [-rɪ] mit einzelnen Regenschauern.

show|-off ['ʃəʊɒf] Angeber *m;* ~**piece** ['-piːs] Schaustück *n;* ~-**room** ['-rʊm] Ausstellungsraum *m.*

shred [ʃred] **I** *s* 1. Fetzen *m;* 2. *fig* Spur *f;* ein (klein) bißchen; **II** *v* zerfetzen.

shrewd [ʃruːd] 1. gewitzt, klug; 2. *make a ~ guess* der Wahrheit sehr nahe kommen.

shriek [ʃriːk] **I** *v* kreischen, schreien; **II** *s* (Auf-)Schrei *m.*

shrill [ʃrɪl] schrill, gellend.

shrimp [ʃrɪmp] *zoo* Garnele, Krabbe *f.*

shrink [ʃrɪŋk] *irr shrank* [ʃræŋk] , *shrunk* [ʃrʌŋk] 1. (ein-, zs.)schrumpfen, eingehen; 2. zurückschrecken

(from vor); ~**age** ['-ɪdʒ] Schrumpfung *f.*

shrivel ['ʃrɪvl] schrumpeln, verwelken (lassen).

shroud [ʃraʊd] Leichentuch *n.*

Shrove Tuesday [,ʃrəʊv'tjuːzdɪ] Fastnacht(sdienstag *m*) *f.*

shrub [ʃrʌb] *bot* Strauch *m.*

shrug [ʃrʌg] 1. die Achseln zucken; 2. ~ *s.th. off* etw mit e-m Achselzucken abtun.

shudder ['ʃʌdə] (er)schaudern.

shuffle ['ʃʌfl] 1. *(Spielkarten)* mischen; 2. *(~ o.'s feet)* schlurfen.

shun [ʃʌn] ausweichen *(s.th.* e-r S).

shunt [ʃʌnt] *rail* rangieren.

shut [ʃʌt] *irr shut, shut* schließen, zumachen; ~ **down** *(Fabrik)* stillegen; ~ **off** zu-, abdrehen; ~ **up** zu-, verschließen; *(fam) ~!* halt den Mund! ~**ter** ['-ə] 1. Fenster-, Rolladen *m;* 2. *phot* Verschluß *m.*

shuttle ['ʃʌtl] 1. Weberschiff *n;* 2. ~ *service* Pendelverkehr *m.*

shy [ʃaɪ] **I** *adj* schüchtern; **II** *v* scheuen *(at* vor).

sick [sɪk] 1. krank; *be ~* sich erbrechen; 2. *(~ and tired)* überdrüssig *(of* gen); *be ~ of s.th.* etw satt haben; ~**en** ['-ən] 1. krank werden; 2. Abscheu empfinden *(at* vor); 3. überdrüssig werden (*of* gen).

sickle ['sıkl] Sichel *f*.

sick|-list ['sıklıst] *put on the* ~ krank schreiben; **~ly** ['-lı] kränklich, schwächlich; **~ness** ['-nıs] Krankheit; Übelkeit *f*; **~-pay** ['-peı] Krankengeld *n*.

side [saıd] **I** *s* Seite *f*; *at, by my* ~ an meiner Seite; ~ *by* ~ Seite an Seite; *from, on all* ~s von, auf allen Seiten; *on, from every* ~ auf, von allen Seiten; *this* ~ *up!* Vorsicht, nicht stürzen! **II** *v* Partei ergreifen (*with* für); **~board** ['-bɔːd] Anrichte *f*, Büfett *n*; **~light** ['-laıt] *fig* Streiflicht *n*; **~walk** ['-wɔːk] *Am* Gehweg *m*; **~ways** ['-weız] seitwärts.

sidle ['saıdl] ~ *up to s.o.* schüchtern zu jdm hingehen.

siege [siːdʒ] Belagerung *f*.

sieve [sıv] **I** *s* Sieb *n*; **II** *v* (durch)sieben.

sift [sıft] 1. sieben; ~ *out* aussieben, -sortieren (*from* aus); 2. sichten.

sigh [saı] **I** *v* 1. seufzen; 2. sich sehnen (*for* nach); **II** *s* Seufzer *m*.

sight [saıt] 1. (An-)Sicht *f*, (An-)Blick *m*; *at (the)* ~ *of* beim Anblick gen; *at first* ~ auf den ersten Blick; *by* ~ vom Ansehen; *be, look a* ~ (*fam*) verheerend aussehen; *catch* ~ *of s.th.* etw zu Gesicht bekommen; 2. Sehkraft

f; 3. Blickfeld *n*; *in, within* ~ in Sicht, Sehweite; *out of* ~ außer Sicht; 4. *pl* Sehenswürdigkeiten *f pl*; **~-seeing** ['-,siːıŋ] *go* ~ Sehenswürdigkeiten besichtigen.

sign [saın] **I** *s* 1. Zeichen *n*; *traffic* ~ Verkehrszeichen *n*; 2. *at the* ~ *of (the Red Lion)* im Wirtshaus zum (Roten Löwen); **II** *v* unterzeichnen.

signal ['sıgnəl] **I** *s* Zeichen *n*; Signal *n* (*for* zu); **II** *v* ein Zeichen, ein Signal geben.

signature [sıgnətʃə] 1. Unterschrift *f*; 2. *radio* (~ *tune*) Pausenzeichen *n*.

signific|ance [sıg'nıfıkəns] Bedeutung *f*; **~ant** [-t] bedeutsam, wichtig (*of* für).

signpost ['saınpəust] Wegweiser *m*.

silen|ce ['saıləns] **I** *s* 1. Stille, Ruhe *f*; 2. Schweigen *n*; *pass over in* ~ mit Stillschweigen übergehen; **II** *v* zum Schweigen bringen; **~cer** [-ə] 1. *mot* Auspufftopf *m*; 2. Schalldämpfer *m*; **~t** [-t] schweigend; still, ruhig; *be* ~ schweigen.

silk [sılk] Seide(nstoff *m*) *f*; **~y** ['-ı] seiden.

sill [sıl] Fensterbrett *n*; Sims *m*.

silly ['sılı] dumm; töricht.

silver ['sılvə] **I** *s* Silber *n*; **II** *adj* silbern; **III** *v* versilbern; ~ **paper** Stanniolpapier *n*.

similar ['sɪmɪlə] ähnlich (*to* dat); **~ity** [ˌsɪmɪˈlærətɪ] Ähnlichkeit *f*.

simmer ['sɪmə] bei schwacher Hitze kochen (lassen).

simpl|e ['sɪmpl] 1. einfach; 2. unkompliziert; 3. einfältig; **~icity** [sɪmˈplɪsətɪ] Einfachheit *f*; **~ify** ['sɪmplɪfaɪ] vereinfachen; **~y** ['-ɪ] (ganz) einfach.

simultaneous [ˌsɪməlˈteɪnjəs] gleichzeitig (*with* mit).

sin [sɪn] **I** *s rel* Sünde *f*; **II** *v* sündigen, sich vergehen (*against* gegen).

since [sɪns] **I** *adv* seitdem, -her; *ever* ~ seit der Zeit, seither; **II** *prp* seit; **III** *conj* da (. . . ja), weil.

sincer|e [sɪnˈsɪə] aufrichtig; herzlich; **~ely** [-lɪ] *Yours* ~ mit freundlichen Grüßen; **~ity** [sɪnˈserətɪ] Aufrichtigkeit; Herzlichkeit *f*.

sinew ['sɪnjuː] Sehne *f*.

sing [sɪŋ] *irr sang* [sæŋ], *sung* [sʌŋ] singen; **~er** ['-ə] Sänger *m*.

singe [sɪndʒ] anbrennen, -sengen.

singl|e ['sɪŋgl] **I** *adj* 1. einzig; 2. einzeln; *in* ~ *file* im Gänsemarsch; 3. ledig; **II** *s* 4. (~ *ticket*) einfache Fahrkarte *f*; 5. Einzelzimmer *n*; 6. (~*s*) *sport* Einzelspiel *n*.

singular ['sɪŋgjʊlə] **I** *adj* ungewöhnlich; beachtlich; **II** *s* Singular *m*, Einzahl *f*.

sinister ['sɪnɪstə] böse, unheilverkündend.

sink [sɪŋk] **I** *v irr sank* [sæŋk], *sunk* [sʌŋk] od *sunken* ['sʌŋkən] 1. (ein-, ver)sinken; untergehen; 2. (*Grube*) ausheben, (*Loch*) bohren; 3. *he's* ~*ing* s-e Kräfte nehmen ab; **II** *s* Ausguß, Spültisch *m*.

sip [sɪp] **I** *v* schlürfen, nippen (*an* dat); **II** *s* Schluck *m*.

sir [sɜː] 1. (*Anrede*) Herr *m*; 2. *S~* (*Titel*) Sir *m*.

siren ['saɪərən] Sirene *f*.

sirloin ['sɜːlɔɪn] (*Rind*) Lendenstück *n*.

sister ['sɪstə] Schwester *f a. rel; brothers and* ~*s* Geschwister *pl*; **~-in-law** ['-rɪnlɔː] Schwägerin *f*.

sit [sɪt] *irr sat, sat* [sæt] 1. sitzen *a. zoo*; 2. e-e Sitzung abhalten; 3. ~ (*for*) *an examination* sich e-r Prüfung unterziehen; **~ back** sich zurücklehnen; **~ down** sich (hin)setzen; ~ *up* 1. aufrecht sitzen; 2. aufbleiben (*late* lange); **~-down strike** Sitzstreik *m*; **~ting** ['-ɪŋ] 1. Sitzung, Tagung *f*; 2. **~-room** Wohnzimmer *n*.

site [saɪt] Lage *f*; Platz *m*.

situat|ed ['sɪtjʊeɪtɪd] *be* ~ liegen, gelegen sein; **~ion** [ˌsɪtjuˈeɪʃn] 1. Lage; Stelle *f*; 2. Situation; Lage *f*; 3. Stellung *f*; Posten *m*.

six [sɪks] sechs; **~th** [sɪksθ] sechst; **~ty** ['-tɪ] sechzig.

size [saɪz] **I** s 1. Größe f;
2. *(Kleidung, Schuhe)* Nummer f; *what ~ do you wear?*
welche Größe tragen Sie?
II v: ~ up *(fam)* richtig einschätzen.

skat|e [skeɪt] **I** s 1. *(ice-~)*
Schlittschuh m; 2. *(roller-~)*
Rollschuh m; **II** v Schlittschuh od Rollschuh laufen;
~**ing-rink** ['-ɪŋrɪŋk] Eis-,
Rollschuhbahn f.

skeleton ['skelɪtn] Skelett n;
~ **key** Dietrich m; ~ **service** Bereitschaftsdienst m.

sketch [sketʃ] **I** s Skizze f;
II v (~ out) entwerfen; skizzieren.

ski [skiː] **I** s Ski, Schi m; **II** v:
go ~ing Ski od Schi fahren.

skid [skɪd] **I** s 1. Bremsklotz
m; 2. mot Schleudern n; **II** v
mot rutschen, schleudern.

skilful, Am **skillful** ['skɪlful]
geschickt, gewandt, tüchtig
(at in).

skill [skɪl] Geschicklichkeit;
(Hand-)Fertigkeit f (in, at
in); ~**ed** [-d] geschickt;
fachlich ausgebildet; ~
worker Facharbeiter m;
~**ful** s. skilful.

skim [skɪm] 1. *(Milch)* entrahmen; 2. flüchtig lesen; ~
(through) a book ein Buch
durchblättern; ~**med-milk**
['-d mɪlk] Magermilch f.

skin [skɪn] **I** s 1. Haut f; by
the ~ of o.'s teeth mit knapper (Müh u.) Not; get under
s.o.'s ~ jdm auf die Nerven

fallen; 2. Fell n; 3. Schale,
Rinde f; **II** v 4. häuten;
5. schälen; ~**-deep** ['-diːp]
oberflächlich; ~**ny** ['-ɪ] hager, mager; ~**-tight** ['-taɪt]
hauteng.

skip [skɪp] 1. hüpfen, springen; 2. *(in e-m Buch)* überschlagen; ~**per** ['-ə] Kapitän; sport Mannschaftsführer m.

skirmish ['skɜːmɪʃ] Geplänkel n.

skirt [skɜːt] **I** s 1. Rock m;
2. pl Stadtrand m; **II** v sich
am Rande hinziehen (s.th.
e-r S).

skittles ['skɪtlz] pl mit sing
Kegeln n.

skull [skʌl] Schädel m.

sky [skaɪ] Himmel m; in the
~ am Himmel; ~**-light** ['-laɪt]
Dachluke f; ~**line** ['-laɪn]
Silhouette f; ~**scraper**
['-ˌskreɪpə] Wolkenkratzer
m.

slab [slæb] Platte, Tafel f.

slack [slæk] 1. nachlässig;
2. schlaff, locker; 3. com flau,
lustlos; *(Geschäft)* ruhig;
~**en** ['-ən] 1. nachlassen, abflauen; 2. (sich) verlangsamen; 3. schlaff, locker werden.

slag [slæg] Schlacke f.

slake [sleɪk] *(Durst, Kalk)*
löschen.

slam [slæm] *(Tür)* zuschlagen.

slander ['slɑːndə] **I** s üble

Nachrede *f;* **II** *v* verleumden.

slang [slæŋ] Slang *m.*

slant [slɑ:nt] **I** *v* 1. schräg stellen; 2. sich neigen; 3. tendieren (*towards* zu); **II** *s fig* Gesichtspunkt *m;* Einstellung *f.*

slap [slæp] **I** *s* Klaps, Schlag *m;* **II** *v* klatschen; ~ *s.o.'s face* jdn ohrfeigen; **~dash** ['-dæʃ] (*Arbeit*) schlampig.

slash [slæʃ] 1. (auf)schlitzen; 2. peitschen; 3. kritisieren.

slate [sleɪt] *geol* Schiefer *m.*

slaughter ['slɔ:tə] **I** *s* 1. Schlachten *n* (*von Vieh*); 2. Gemetzel, Blutbad *n;* **II** *v* 3. (*Vieh*) schlachten; 4. (*Menschen*) niedermetzeln.

slave [sleɪv] Sklave *m;* **~ry** ['-əri] Sklaverei *f a. fig.*

sled [sled] , **~ge** [-ʒ] Schlitten *m.*

sledge-hammer ['sledʒˌhæmə] Vorschlaghammer *m.*

sleek [sli:k] (*Fell*) glatt u. glänzend.

sleep [sli:p] **I** *s* Schlaf *m a. fig;* go to ~ einschlafen; **II** *v irr* slept, slept [slept] schlafen *a. fig;* ~ *s.th. off* etw (*Kopfweh, Rausch etc*) ausschlafen; **~er** ['-ə] 1. Schläfer *m;* 2. *Br rail* Schwelle *f;* 3. *rail* Schlafwagen *m;* **~ing** ['-ɪŋ] **~-bag** Schlafsack *m;* **~-car** (*rail*) Schlafwagen *m;* **~-pill** (*pharm*) Schlafmittel

n; **~-sickness** Schlafkrankheit *f;* **~less** ['-lɪs] schlaflos; **~-walker** ['-ˌwɔ:kə] Nachtwandler *m;* **~y** ['-ɪ] schläfrig.

sleet [sli:t] *mete* Graupeln *f pl.*

sleeve [sli:v] Ärmel *m;* have *s.th. up o.'s* ~ etw auf Lager haben; *laugh up o.'s* ~ sich ins Fäustchen lachen.

sleigh [sleɪ] (Pferde-)Schlitten *m.*

slender ['slendə] schlank. schmächtig.

slice [slaɪs] **I** *s* Scheibe, Schnitte *f;* **II** *v* aufschneiden.

slid|e [slaɪd] *irr* slid, slid [slɪd] 1. gleiten; ~ *down* herunterrutschen; *let things* ~ die Dinge laufenlassen; 2. *fig* geraten (*into* in); 3. gleiten lassen (*in, into* in); **~ing** ['-ɪŋ] ~ *door* Schiebetür *f;* ~ *roof* (*mot*) Schiebedach *n;* **~-rule** ['-ru:l] Rechenschieber *m.*

slight [slaɪt] **I** *adj* 1. schmächtig; 2. geringfügig; *not in the* ~*est* nicht im geringsten; **II** *v* vernachlässigen; zurücksetzen; **~ly** ['-lɪ] ein wenig.

slim [slɪm] **I** *adj* 1. schlank; 2. *fam* gering(fügig); **II** *v* e-e Schlankheitskur machen; abnehmen.

slim|e [slaɪm] Schleim *m;* **~y** ['-ɪ] schleimig *a. fig.*

sling [slɪŋ] **I** *s* 1. (Stein-)Schleuder *f;* 2. Schlinge;

Binde *f;* **II** *v irr* slung, slung [slʌŋ] schleudern, werfen.

slip [slɪp] **I** *v* 1. schlüpfen (*into a coat* in e-n Mantel); 2. *don't let the chance ~* lassen Sie sich die Gelegenheit nicht entgehen; 3. ausrutschen (*on the ice* auf dem Eis); 4. (*dem Gedächtnis*) entfallen; **II** *s* Versehen *n,* Schnitzer *m; ~ of the pen* Schreibfehler *m.*

slipper ['slɪpə] Hausschuh *m.*

slippery ['slɪpərɪ] schlüpfrig.

slip-road ['slɪprəʊd] *Br* (Autobahn-) Auf-, Ausfahrt *f.*

slipshod ['slɪpʃɒd] *fig* schlampig.

slit [slɪt] **I** *v irr* slit, slit (auf)schlitzen, aufschneiden; **II** *s* Schlitz *m.*

slogan ['sləʊgən] Schlagwort *n; com* Werbespruch *m.*

slop [slɒp] **I** *s pl* Spülwasser *n;* **II** *v* 1. (*~ over*) überlaufen; 2. verschütten.

slope [sləʊp] **I** *s* (Ab-)Hang *m,* Böschung *f;* **II** *v* schräg abfallen.

slot [slɒt] Schlitz *m; ~-machine* ['-məʃiːn] (Waren-, Spiel-)Automat *m.*

slouch [slaʊtʃ] krumm dastehen; sich hinflegeln.

slovenly ['slʌvnlɪ] schlampig.

slow [sləʊ] **I** *adj* 1. langsam; *be ~* (*Uhr*) nachgehen; *in ~ motion* in Zeitlupe; 2. schwerfällig; **II** *v* (*~ up,*

down) langsamer werden; (*in der Arbeit*) nachlassen.

slug [slʌg] (Weg-)Schnecke *f; ~gish* ['-ɪʃ] langsam; träge.

sluice [sluːs] Schleuse *f.*

slum [slʌm] *the ~s* Elendsviertel *n.*

slumber ['slʌmbə] Schlummer *m.*

slump [slʌmp] **I** *v* (*Preise*) (plötzlich) fallen; **II** *s* Rezession *f.*

slush [slʌʃ] (Schnee-)Matsch *m.*

slut [slʌt] Schlampe *f.*

sly [slaɪ] schlau, verschlagen.

smacking ['smækɪŋ] *a good ~* e-e tüchtige Tracht Prügel.

small [smɔːl] 1. klein, gering; 2. geringfügig, unbedeutend; 3. *in a ~ way* (in) bescheiden(em Umfang); *~ change* Klein-, Wechselgeld *n; ~pox* ['-pɒks] Pocken *pl; ~ talk* Plauderei *f.*

smart [smɑːt] **I** *v* (heftig) schmerzen; **II** *adj* 1. lebhaft, munter; 2. klug, gescheit; 3. fesch, elegant.

smash [smæʃ] 1. (*~ up*) zerschlagen; 2. (*Tennis*) schmettern; 3. *~ a record* e-n Rekord brechen.

smattering ['smætərɪŋ] oberflächliche Kenntnis *f* (*of* gen).

smear [smɪə] **I** *v* beschmieren (*with* mit); **II** *s* Fleck *m.*

smell [smel] **I** *v irr* smelt,

smelt [smelt] 1. riechen; ~ *a rat (fig)* den Braten riechen; 2. duften; ~ *of* riechen nach; **II** *s* Geruch(ssinn) *m.*

smelt [smelt] *metal* (aus)schmelzen, verhütten.

smile [smaɪl] **I** *v* 1. lächeln; 2. zulächeln (*at* s.o. jdm); **II** *s* Lächeln *n a. fig; he is all ~s* er strahlt übers ganze Gesicht.

smith [smɪθ] Schmied *m; ~y* ['smɪðɪ] Schmiede *f.*

smog [smɒg] Smog *m.*

smoke [sməʊk] **I** *s* Rauch; Qualm *m;* **II** *v* rauchen; **~er** ['-ə] Raucher *m; ~ing* ['-ɪŋ] *no ~* Rauchen verboten! *~-compartment* Raucherabteil *n; ~y* ['-ɪ] rauchig.

smooth [smuːð] **I** *adj* 1. glatt; eben; 2. weich, sanft; **II** *v* glätten; ebnen *a. fig.*

smother ['smʌðə] ersticken.

smo(u)lder ['sməʊldə] schwelen *a. fig.*

smudge [smʌdʒ] **I** *s* Schmutzfleck *m;* **II** *v* 1. beschmutzen; 2. klecksen.

smuggle ['smʌgl] schmuggeln; **~r** ['-ə] Schmuggler *m.*

smut [smʌt] 1. Schmutzfleck *m;* 2. *fig* Zoten *f pl;* 3. *bot* Brand *m.*

snack [snæk] Imbiß *m; ~-bar* ['-bɑː] , **~-counter** ['-kaʊntə] Schnellgaststätte *f.*

snail [sneɪl] Schnecke *f; at a ~'s pace* im Schneckentempo.

snake [sneɪk] Schlange *f.*

snap [snæp] **I** *v* 1. schnappen (*at* nach); 2. rasch zupacken; 3. (zer)springen; 4. *(~ out) (Worte)* hervorstoßen; 5. *phot* knipsen; 6. *~ to it! (sl)* los! an die Arbeit! **II** *s* (Zu-)Schnappen *n; ~shot* ['-ʃɒt] Schnappschuß *m.*

snare [sneə] Schlinge, Falle *f a. fig.*

snarl [snɑːl] (an)knurren (*at* s.o. jdn) *a. fig.*

snatch [snætʃ] **I** *v* rasch zugreifen; schnappen (*at* nach); **II** *s* 1. Zupacken *n;* 2. *by, in ~es* mit Unterbrechungen.

sneak [sniːk] schleichen, kriechen *a. fig (into* in).

sneer [snɪə] höhnen, spotten (*at* über); **II** *s* Spott *m.*

sneeze [sniːz] niesen; *it is not to be ~d at (fam)* das ist nicht zu verachten.

sniff [snɪf] 1. schniefen; 2. schnuppern (*at* an); 3. die Nase rümpfen (*at* über); **~y** ['-ɪ] hochnäsig.

snip [snɪp] (ab)schnippeln.

sniper ['snaɪpə] Heckenschütze *m.*

snippet ['snɪpɪt] Schnipsel *m.*

snob [snɒb] Snob *m; ~bish* ['-ɪʃ] snobistisch.

snooze [snuːz] *fam* Nickerchen *n.*

snore [snɔː] schnarchen.

snorkel ['snɔ:kl] Schnorchel m.

snort [snɔ:t] schnauben (*with rage* vor Wut).

snout [snaut] Schnauze f, Rüssel m.

snow [snəu].I s Schnee m; II v schneien; ~**ball** ['-bɔ:l] Schneeball m; ~**drift** ['-drɪft] Schneewehe f; ~**drop** ['-drɔp] bot Schneeglöckchen n; ~**fall** ['-fɔ:l] Schneefall m, -menge f; ~**flake** ['-fleɪk] Schneeflocke f; ~**man** ['-mæn] Schneemann m; ~**plough**, Am ~-**plow** ['-plau] Schneepflug m; ~**storm** ['-stɔ:m] Schneesturm m; ~**y** ['-ɪ] 1. verschneit; 2. schneeweiß.

snub [snʌb] I v anschnauzen; II adj: ~ nose Stupsnase f.

snuffle ['snʌfl] schnauben.

snug [snʌg] 1. behaglich, gemütlich; 2. (*Kleidung*) genau passend.

so [səu] I adv 1. not ~ ... as nicht so ... wie; ~ ... as to so ... daß; 2. ~ did I ich auch; 3. and ~ on, and ~ forth und so weiter; 4. be ~ kind as to sei so freundlich und ...; 5. ~ long! (fam) auf Wiedersehen! 6. I hope ~ das hoffe ich; you don't say ~! do you say ~? wirklich! I told you ~ ich sagte es doch! sagte ich es nicht? just ~! quite ~! ganz richtig!

II conj darum, deshalb, daher.

soak [səuk] 1. einweichen; ~ed to the skin naß bis auf die Haut; 2. (~ up) auf-, einsaugen.

soap [səup] I s Seife f; a cake of ~ ein Stück Seife; II v einseifen; ~ o.s. down sich abseifen; ~-**bubble** ['-ˌbʌbl] Seifenblase f.

soar [sɔ:] 1. sich (in die Luft) erheben; 2. (*Preise*) in die Höhe schnellen.

sob [sɔb] schluchzen; ~ o.'s heart out bitterlich weinen.

sober ['səubə] I adj 1. nüchtern; 2. besonnen; II v (~ up, down) (wieder) nüchtern werden.

soccer ['sɔkə] Fußballspiel n.

sociable ['səuʃəbl] gesellig.

social ['səuʃl] sozial; gesellschaftlich; ~ security soziale Sicherheit; Sozialversicherung f.

socialism ['səuʃəlizəm] Sozialismus m; ~**t** ['səuʃəlist] I s Sozialist m; II adj sozialistisch.

society [sə'saɪətɪ] 1. Gesellschaft f; 2. co-operative ~ Konsumverein m.

sock [sɔk] 1. Socke f; pull o.'s ~s up (fam) sich ins Zeug legen; 2. Einlegesohle f.

socket ['sɔkɪt] 1. el Fassung f; 2. Steckdose f; 3. anat (Augen-)Höhle f.

soda ['səʊdə] 1. Soda n;
2. Sodawasser n.
sodden ['sɒdn] durchweicht.
sofa ['səʊfə] Sofa n.
soft [sɒft] 1. weich; 2. mild,
sanft; 3. nachgiebig, gutmütig; 4. (Ton) schwach, leise;
5. (Getränk) alkoholfrei;
6. have a ~ spot for ein
Herz haben für; ~en ['sɒfn]
weich machen; ~ up aufwei-
chen, zermürben; ~-heart-
ed [,-'hɑːtɪd] weichherzig,
gutmütig.
soggy ['sɒgɪ] durchweicht.
soil [sɔɪl] I s (Erd-)Boden m;
II v 1. beschmutzen;
2. schmutzig werden.
solace ['sɒləs] I v trösten;
II s: find ~ in Trost finden
in.
solar ['səʊlə] Sonnen-; ~ cell
Sonnenzelle f; ~ energy
Sonnenenergie f.
solder ['sɒldə] I s Lötzinn n;
II v löten.
soldier ['səʊldʒə] Soldat m.
sole [səʊl] I s 1. Sohle f;
2. zoo Seezunge f; II adj
einzig, alleinig.
solemn ['sɒləm] 1. feierlich;
2. ernst.
solicit [sə'lɪsɪt] dringend bitten (for um); ~or [-ə]
Rechtsbeistand m.
solid ['sɒlɪd] 1. (Körper) fest;
massiv; be frozen ~ fest zu-
gefroren sein; be on ~
ground (a. fig) festen Boden
unter den Füßen haben;
2. solide, haltbar;

3. (Gründe) stichhaltig;
4. (Edelmetall) rein, gediegen; ~ify [sə'lɪdɪfaɪ] (sich)
verdichten, fest werden (lassen).
soliloquy [sə'lɪləkwɪ] Selbst-
gespräch n.
solitary ['sɒlɪtərɪ] 1. allein-
stehend; einsam; 2. abgelegen; ~ude ['sɒlɪtjuːd] Einsamkeit f.
solstice ['sɒlstɪs] summer,
winter ~ Sommer-, Winter-
sonnenwende f.
soluble ['sɒljʊbl] löslich;
~tion [sə'luːʃn] Lösung f.
solve [sɒlv] (Rätsel) lösen.
solvent ['sɒlvənt] zahlungs-
fähig.
some [sʌm, səm] I adj 1. (irgend)ein; (at) ~ time (or
other) (irgendwann) einmal;
2. vor pl manche; einige, ein
paar; 3. etwas, ein wenig;
4. to ~ extent bis zu e-m gewissen Grade; ~ time ei-
ne Zeitlang; II prn: ~ of
these days dieser Tage,
demnächst; ~body
['sʌmbədɪ] (irgend) jemand;
~how ['sʌmhaʊ] irgendwie;
~one ['sʌmwʌn] (irgend)
jemand; ~thing ['sʌmθɪŋ]
(irgend) etwas; ~times
['sʌmtaɪmz] manchmal;
~what ['sʌmwɒt] etwas;
~where ['sʌmweə] irgend-
wo(hin); ~ else irgendwo
anders.
son [sʌn] Sohn m.
song [sɒŋ] 1. Gesang m;

2. Lied *n;* 3. *for a (mere)* ~ für ein Butterbrot; spottbillig; **~bird** ['-bɜːd] Singvogel *m.*

son-in-law ['sʌnɪnlɔː] Schwiegersohn *m.*

soon [suːn] bald; früh, zeitig; rasch; *as* ~ *as possible* so bald wie möglich; *very* ~ demnächst; **~er** ['-ə] 1. eher, früher, zeitiger, schneller; ~ *or later* früher oder später; *the* ~ *the better* je eher desto besser; *no* ~ *... than* kaum ..., als; 2. lieber; *I had, would* ~ *leave* ich möchte lieber gehen.

soot [sʊt] Ruß *m.*

soothe [suːð] 1. beruhigen; 2. *(Schmerz)* lindern.

sophisticated [sə'fɪstɪkeɪtɪd] 1. (hoch)entwickelt; 2. kultiviert.

sorcer|er ['sɔːsərə] Zauberer *m;* **~y** [-rɪ] Zauberei, Hexerei *f.*

sordid ['sɔːdɪd] schmutzig; elend.

sore [sɔː] **I** *adj* 1. schmerzhaft; 2. wund, entzündet; *have a* ~ *throat* Halsweh haben; 3. *touch a* ~ *spot* e-n wunden Punkt berühren; **II** *s* wunde Stelle *f a. fig.*

sorrow ['sɒrəʊ] Kummer *m*, Leid *n; to my* ~ zu meinem Bedauern; **~ful** [-fʊl] bekümmert, traurig.

sorry ['sɒrɪ] betrübt, bekümmert; *I am* ~ es tut mir leid;

~*! Verzeihung! leider nicht! schade!*

sort [sɔːt] **I** *s* Sorte, Art *f; all* ~*s of things* alles mögliche; *nothing of the* ~ nichts dergleichen; *what* ~ *of ...?* was für ein ...? **II** *v* sichten, ordnen; ~ *out* aussortieren.

soul [səʊl] Seele *f a. fig.*

sound [saʊnd] **I** *s* 1. Laut, Schall, Ton *m;* **II** *v* 3. (er)tönen; 4. *(Instrument)* schlagen, blasen, spielen; 5. ~ *s.o. out* jdn aushorchen *(on, about s.th.* über etw); **III** *adj* 6. gesund; 7. *(Schlaf)* fest; 8. einwandfrei; stichhaltig; vernünftig; 9. (finanziell) gesichert; 10. tüchtig; **IV** *adv: be* ~ *asleep* fest schlafen; **~proof** ['-pruːf] schalldicht; **~-wave** ['-weɪv] Schallwelle *f.*

soup [suːp] Suppe *f; in the* ~ *(fam)* in der Patsche.

sour ['saʊə] sauer *a. fig.*

source [sɔːs] Quelle *f a. fig.*

south [saʊθ] **I** *s* Süd(en) *m;* **II** *adj* südlich; **III** *adv* nach, im Süden; **~ern** ['sʌðən] südlich; **S~ Pole** Südpol *m;* **~ward(s)** ['-wəd(z)] nach Süden.

souvenir [ˌsuːvə'nɪə] Andenken *n.*

sovereign ['sɒvrɪn] Monarch, Herrscher *m.*

Soviet ['səʊvɪət] **I** *adj* sowjetisch; **II** *s* Sowjet *m.*

sow I *s* [saʊ] *zoo* Sau *f;*

II v [səʊ] irr sowed, sown od sowed (Saat) (aus)säen.
spa [spa:] Kurort m.
space [speɪs] 1. Raum, Platz m; 2. Zwischenraum m; 3. Frist f; 4. Weltraum m; ~-capsule Raumkapsel f; ~craft, ~ship Raumschiff n; ~ious ['speɪʃəs] geräumig.
spade [speɪd] 1. Spaten m; call a ~ a ~ (fig) das Kind beim (rechten) Namen nennen; 2. pl (Kartenspiel) Pik n; Schippe f.
Spain [speɪn] Spanien n.
span [spæn] (um-, über-)-spannen.
Spaniard ['spænjəd] Spanier m; ~ish ['spænɪʃ] spanisch.
spank [spæŋk] (das Hinterteil) versohlen.
spanner ['spænə] Schraubenschlüssel m.
spare [speə] **I** v 1. (ver)schonen; 2. entbehren; erübrigen; do you have a minute to ~ haben Sie e-n Augenblick Zeit? enough and to ~ mehr als genug, reichlich; 3. ~ no expense keine Kosten scheuen; **II** adj frei, überzählig, überflüssig; ~ parts (pl) Ersatzteile pl.
spark [spa:k] 1. Funke(n) m; 2. fig Fünkchen n, Spur f; ~(ing)-plug ['-(ɪŋ)plʌg] mot Zündkerze f.
sparkle ['spa:kl] funkeln (with vor); ~ing [-ɪŋ] 1. funkelnd, glitzernd; 2. (Geist)

sprühend; 3. (Wein) moussierend.
sparrow ['spærəʊ] zoo Sperling m.
spasm [spæzəm] med Krampf m.
spatial ['speɪʃl] räumlich.
spatter ['spætə] 1. (be)spritzen (with mit); 2. (Regen) (nieder)prasseln.
speak [spi:k] irr spoke [spəʊk], spoken ['spəʊkən] sprechen (of von; about über; to mit, zu; for für); reden (of von, über); nothing to ~ of nicht der Rede wert; so to ~ sozusagen, gewissermaßen; ~er ['-ə] 1. Sprecher; Redner m; 2. (loud-~) Lautsprecher m.
spear [spɪə] Speer m.
special ['speʃl] **I** adj 1. un-, außergewöhnlich; 2. speziell; ~ delivery Eilzustellung f; **II** s Sonderausgabe, -nummer f; ~ist ['speʃəlɪst] Spezialist m; ~ize ['speʃəlaɪz] sich spezialisieren (in in, auf).
species ['spi:ʃi:z] pl ~ Art f.
specific [sprɪsɪfɪk] 1. genau festgelegt, bestimmt; 2. charakteristisch, spezifisch.
specify ['spesɪfaɪ] einzeln, genau angeben.
specimen ['spesɪmɪn] Muster n, Probe f.
speck [spek] Fleck(chen n) m; ~led ['-ld] gesprenkelt.
specs pl [speks] fam Brille f.

spectacle ['spektəkl]
1. Schauspiel *n;* 2. *pl (pair of ~s)* Brille *f.*
spectacular [spek'tækjʊlə] auffällig; eindrucksvoll.
spectator [spek'teɪtə] Zuschauer *m.*
speculate ['spekjʊleɪt]
1. nachdenken, grübeln (*upon, about* über); 2. *com* spekulieren (*in* in).
speech [spiːtʃ] 1. Sprache *f;* 2. Ansprache, Rede *f; deliver, make a ~* e-e Rede halten (*on, about* über; *to* vor); **~less** ['-lɪs] sprachlos (*with* vor).
speed [spiːd] **I** *s* 1. Schnelligkeit *f;* 2. Geschwindigkeit *f; at a ~ of* mit e-r Geschwindigkeit von; *at full, top ~* mit Höchstgeschwindigkeit; **II** *v irr* sped od *~ed,* sped [sped] od *~ed* 3. schnell fahren; 4. (*~ up*) beschleunigen; **~-limit** ['-ˌlɪmɪt] Höchstgeschwindigkeit *f;* **~ometer** [spɪ'dɒmɪtə] Geschwindigkeitsmesser *m;* **~y** ['-ɪ] schnell; unverzüglich.

spell [spel] **I** *s* 1. Schicht, Arbeitszeit *f;* 2. Periode *f; cold, hot ~* Kälte-, Hitzewelle *f;* 3. *cast a ~ over s.o.* jdn verzaubern; **II** *v a. irr* spelt, spelt [spelt] 4. buchstabieren; 5. *~ out* genau erläutern.
spellbound ['spelbaʊnd] verzaubert, fasziniert.

spelling ['spelɪŋ] Rechtschreibung *f.*
spend [spend] *irr* spent, spent [spent] 1. verbrauchen; (*Geld*) ausgeben; 2. verwenden (*on* für); 3. *('Zeit)* ver-, zubringen; **~ing money** Taschengeld *n;* **~thrift** ['-θrɪft] Verschwender *m.*
spent [spent] 1. erschöpft; 2. *tech* verbraucht.
sperm [spɜːm] Samen *m.*
sphere ['sfɪə] 1. *math* Kugel *f;* 2. *astr* Himmelskörper *m;* 3. *fig* Sphäre *f; ~ of influence* Einflußbereich *m.*
spic|e [spaɪs] **I** *s* 1. Gewürz *n;* 2. *fig* Würze *f;* **II** *v* würzen *a. fig;* **~y** ['-ɪ] 1. gewürzt; 2. *fig* pikant.
spider ['spaɪdə] *zoo* Spinne *f.*
spike [spaɪk] 1. Spitze *f;* Dorn *m;* 2. *bot* Ähre *f.*
spill [spɪl] *a. irr* spilt, spilt [-t] aus-, verschütten.
spin [spɪn] *irr* spun od span [spæn], spun [spʌn] **I** *v* 1. spinnen; 2. herumwirbeln; *my head is ~ning* mir dreht sich alles im Kopf; **II** *s: go for a ~ (mot fam)* spazierenfahren.
spinach ['spɪnɪdʒ] Spinat *m.*
spinal ['spaɪnl] ~ column Wirbelsäule *f;* ~ cord Rükkenmark *n.*
spin-drier ['spɪndraɪə] Trockenschleuder *f.*
spine [spaɪn] 1. Rückgrat *n;* 2. Dorn, Stachel *m.*

spinster ['spɪnstə] *jur* ledige Frau *f.*

spiral [spaɪərəl] Spirale *f.*

spire ['spaɪə] Turmspitze *f.*

spirit ['spɪrɪt] 1. Geist *m;* 2. *in high* ~s in gehobener Stimmung; *in poor, low* ~s niedergeschlagen; 3. Spiritus *m;* ~-**stove** Spirituskocher *m;* 4. Alkohol *m; pl* Spirituosen *pl;* ~**ed** [-ɪd] 1. lebhaft, feurig, energisch, mutig; 2. *high*-~ hochgestimmt; ~**less** [-lɪs] schlaff, kraft-, mut-, lustlos.

spiritual ['spɪrɪtjʊəl] **I** *adj* 1. geistig; 2. geistlich; **II** *s* (Neger-)Spiritual *n;* ~**ism** [-ɪzəm] Spiritismus *m.*

spit [spɪt] **I** *s* 1. Bratspieß *m;* 2. Landzunge *f;* **II** *v irr* spat, spat [spæt] 3. ausspeien, -spucken; 4. *(Worte)* heraussprudeln; 5. *(Regen)* sprühen; 6. *(Katze)* fauchen; 7. ~**ting image** Ebenbild *n;* ~**tle** ['-l] Speichel *m.*

spite [spaɪt] 1. *from, out of* ~ aus Bosheit; 2. *in* ~ *of* trotz *gen;* ~**ful** ['-fʊl] gehässig, boshaft.

splash [splæʃ] **I** *v* 1. (ver)spritzen; 2. planschen; **II** *s* 3. Plumps *m;* Plätschern *n;* 4. Spritzer *m;* 5. Farbfleck *m.*

spleen [spli:n] *anat* Milz *f.*

splendid ['splendɪd] prachtvoll; großartig; ~**o(u)r** ['splendə] Glanz *m,* Pracht *f.*

splint [splɪnt] *med* Schiene *f.*

splinter ['splɪntə] Splitter *m.*

split [splɪt] **I** *v irr* split, split 1. spalten, aufsplittern; ~ *hairs* Haarspalterei treiben; ~ *o.'s sides (with laughter)* platzen vor Lachen; 2. *fig* trennen, entzweien; **II** *s* Spalt; Sprung; Riß *m a. fig.*

splutter ['splʌtə] *(~ out)* heraussprudeln.

spoil [spɔɪl] *irr* spoilt od ~**ed,** spoilt ['spɔɪlt] od ~**ed** 1. vernichten, zerstören; 2. verderben; schlecht werden; 3. verwöhnen; 4. *be* ~*ing for s.th.* auf etw erpicht sein; ~-**sport** ['-spɔːt] Spielverderber *m.*

spoke [spəʊk] 1. Speiche *f;* 2. *(Leiter)* Sprosse *f.*

spokesman ['spəʊksmən] Sprecher, Wortführer *m.*

sponge [spʌndʒ] **I** *s* Schwamm *m; throw in the* ~ *(fig)* die Flinte ins Korn werfen; **II** *v* 1. mit e-m Schwamm abwischen; 2. *fig* schmarotzen; ~ *(up)on s.o.* auf jds Kosten leben; ~-**cake** ['-keɪk] Rührkuchen; Biskuit(kuchen) *m.*

sponsor ['spɒnsə] **I** *s* 1. Pate; Bürge *m;* 2. Förderer *m;* **II** *v* fördern, unterstützen.

spontaneous [spɒn'teɪnjəs] unmittelbar; spontan.

spool [spu:l] Spule; Rolle *f.*

spoon [spu:n] Löffel *m; dessert-, soup-, tea* ~ Dessert-, Suppen-, Teelöffel *m.*

sport [spɔːt] 1. Spaß, Scherz *m;* 2. Sport *m;* 3. *pl* Sportveranstaltung *f;* 4. *fam* prima Kerl *m; be a (good)* ~ sei ein netter Kerl! ~**s-car** ['-skɑː] Rennwagen *m;* ~**sman** ['-smən] Sportler *m.*

spot [spɔt] I *s* 1. (Ausguß-)Röhre, Schnauze *f;* 2. Fleck(en) *m;* ~ *of ink* Tintenfleck *m;* 3. *fig* Makel, (Charakter-)Fehler *m;* II *v* ausfindig machen; ~**less** ['-lɪs] flecken-, *fig* makellos; ~**light** ['-laɪt] Suchscheinwerfer(licht *n*) *m; in the* ~ im Rampenlicht der Öffentlichkeit; ~**ty** ['-ɪ] gesprenkelt.

spout [spaut] I *s* 1. (Ausguß-)Röhre, Schnauze *f;* 2. (Wasser-)Strahl *m;* II *v* herausspritzen, -schießen.

sprain [spreɪn] *he* ~*ed his ankle* er hat sich den Fuß verstaucht.

sprat [spræt] *zoo* Sprotte *f.*

sprawl [sprɔːl] sich strecken; sich räkeln.

spray [spreɪ] I *s* 1. Sprühregen; Gischt *m;* 2. Spray *m;* 3. zerstäuben; 4. besprühen; ~-**gun** ['-gʌn] Spritzpistole *f.*

spread [spred] I *v irr spread, spread* 1. entfalten, ausbreiten; 2. *(Brot)* bestreichen; 3. *(Butter)* streichen, schmieren *(on* auf); 4. aus

dehnen *(over several years* über mehrere Jahre); 5. *(Nachricht, Krankheit)* verbreiten; 6. sich ausdehnen, -breiten; *(Feuer)* um sich greifen; *(Gerücht)* bekannt werden; II *s* 7. Verbreitung *f;* 8. Umfang *m,* Spanne *f;* 9. *(bed-~)* Betttuch; Tischtuch *n;* 10. (Brot-)Aufstrich *m.*

sprig [sprɪg] Zweig(lein *n*) *m.*

sprightly ['spraɪtlɪ] munter, lebhaft.

spring [sprɪŋ] I *v irr sprang* [spræŋ] , *sprung* [sprʌŋ] 1. springen; 2. ~ *up* entstehen; 3. ~ *a leak* leck werden; 4. ~ *a surprise on s.o.* jdn überraschen; II *s* 5. Sprung, Satz *m;* 6. (Sprung-)Feder *f;* 7. Quelle *f;* 8. *fig* Ursprung, Anfang *m;* 9. Frühling *m; in (the)* ~ im Frühjahr; ~-**board** ['-bɔːd] *sport* Sprungbrett *n a. fig;* ~**time** ['-taɪm] Frühjahr *n.*

sprinkle ['sprɪŋkl] besprengen, bespritzen; ~**r** [-ə] 1. Rasensprenger *m;* 2. Feuerlöschgerät *n.*

sprint [sprɪnt] I *v* sprinten; II *s* (End-)Spurt *a. fig;* Kurzstreckenlauf *m;* ~**er** ['-ə] Kurzstreckenläufer *m.*

sprout [spraut] I *v* sprießen; II *s* 1. (junger) Trieb, Sproß *m;* 2. *pl (Brussels* ~*s)* Rosenkohl *m.*

spruce [spru:s] Fichte, Rottanne f.

spur [spз:] **I** s 1. Sporn m; 2. fig Ansporn m; on the ~ of the moment spontan; **II** v 3. die Sporen geben (a horse e-m Pferd); 4. fig anspornen.

spurt [spз:t] **I** v 1. (~ out) herausspritzen; 2. sport spurten; **II** s 3. (Wasser etc) Strahl m; 4. sport Spurt m.

spy [spaɪ] **I** v 1. genau beobachten; 2. (~ out) ausspionieren; **II** s Spion m.

squabble ['skwɒbl] sich (herum)zanken, sich streiten.

squad [skwɒd] mil Gruppe f; ~ car Am (Polizei-)Streifenwagen m; ~ron ['-rən] aero Staffel f.

squall [skwɔ:l] Bö f.

squander ['skwɒndə] verschwenden.

square [skweə] **I** s 1. Quadrat; Rechteck n; 2. (viereckiger) Platz m; öffentliche Anlage f; 3. Häuserblock m; **II** adj 4. quadratisch; viereckig; 5. meet with a ~ refusal e-e glatte Ablehnung erfahren; 6. fair, ehrlich; 7. (Mahlzeit) reichlich; **III** v 8. math ins Quadrat erheben; 9. (Schuld) begleichen; 10. in Übereinstimmung bringen (with mit); 11. bestechen; ~ **brackets** pl eckige Klammern f pl; ~ **dance** Volkstanz m.

squash [skwɒʃ] **I** v zerdrük-

ken, aus-, zs.-, zerquetschen; **II** s Fruchtsaft m.

squat [skwɒt] **I** v hocken; **II** adj untersetzt. v

squeak [skwi:k] **I** v 1. quiek(s)en; 2. quietschen, knarren; **II** s 3. Gequiek(s)e n; 4. have a narrow ~ mit knapper Not davonkommen.

squeal [skwi:l] quietschen; schrill schreien.

squeeze [skwi:z] **I** v 1. pressen, drücken, quetschen; 2. (~ out) ausdrücken, -pressen; 3. hineinquetschen (into in); **II** s 4. (fester) Händedruck m; Umarmung f; 5. Gedränge n; 6. fig (Geld-)Verlegenheit, Klemme f; be in a tight ~ in großer Verlegenheit sein.

squint [skwɪnt] **I** v schielen; **II** s 1. Schielen n; 2. take a ~ at e-n Blick werfen auf.

squire ['skwaɪə] Gutsbesitzer m.

squirm [skwз:m] sich winden.

squirrel ['skwɪrəl] Eichhörnchen n.

squirt [skwз:t] (be)spritzen.

stab [stæb] **I** v (er)stechen; **II** s Stich m; a ~ in the back (fig) Dolchstoß, hinterhältiger Angriff m.

stability [stə'bɪlətɪ] Stabilität f; ~**ize** ['steɪbɪlaɪz] tech stabilisieren.

stable ['steɪbl] **I** s Stall m;

II *adj* 1. fest, stabil; 2. *fig* (innerlich) gefestigt.

stack [stæk] **I** *s* 1. *agr* Miete *f*, Schober *m*; 2. Stapel *m*; **II** *v* (auf)stapeln.

staff [stɑːf] 1. Stange *f*; 2. *fig* (Mitarbeiter-)Stab *m*; *(teaching ~)* (Lehr-)Körper *m*; *be on the ~* zum Personal gehören.

stag [stæg] (Rot-)Hirsch *m*.

stage [steɪdʒ] **I** *s* 1. *theat* Bühne *f*; 2. *fig* Schauplatz *m*; 3. (Entwicklungs-)Stufe, Periode *f*; *at this ~* in diesem Stadium; 4. *(Rakete)* Stufe *f*; **II** *v* 5. inszenieren; 6. veranstalten; ~ **fright** Lampenfieber *n*; ~ **manager** Regisseur, Spielleiter *m*.

stagger ['stægə] 1. (sch)wanken, taumeln; 2. *fig* verblüffen; 3. staffeln; ~**ing** [-rɪŋ] unglaublich.

stagnant ['stægnənt] 1. *(Wasser)* stehend; 2. *com* flau, lustlos.

stain [steɪn] **I** *v* 1. beschmutzen; 2. färben; 3. Flecken bekommen; **II** *s* (Farb-)Fleck *m*; ~**less** ['-lɪs] 1. fleckenlos; 2. *(Stahl)* rostfrei.

stair [steə] (Treppen-)Stufe *f*; *pl* Treppe *f*; ~**case** ['-keɪs] Treppenaufgang *m*.

stake [steɪk] 1. Pfosten *m*; 2. *(Spiel)* Einsatz *m*; *be at ~* auf dem Spiele stehen; 3. *pl* Wetteinsatz *m*.

stale [steɪl] schal, abgestan-

den; *(Brot)* altbacken; *(Luft)* verbraucht.

stalk [stɔːk] **I** *v* 1. (ein-her)stolzieren; 2. sich anpirschen an; **II** *s bot* Stengel *m*.

stall [stɔːl] **I** *s* 1. Box *f*; 2. (Verkaufs-)Stand *m*; *flower-, fruit-, newspaper ~* Blumen-, Obst-, Zeitungsstand *m*; 3. *theat Br* Parkett *n*; **II** *v* 4. *mot* abwürgen; 5. *mot* aussetzen.

stammer ['stæmə] stottern.

stamp [stæmp] **I** *v* 1. (zer)stampfen; 2. stempeln *a. fig*; 3. frankieren; **II** *s* 4. Stampfen *n*; 5. Stempel(abdruck) *m*; 6. *fig* Gepräge *n*; 7. *(postage-~)* Postwertzeichen *n*, Briefmarke *f*; ~-**collector** ['-kə.lektə] Briefmarkensammler *m*.

stand [stænd] **I** *s* 1. Stillstand, Halt *m*; 2. Standort *m*; 3. (Verkaufs-)Stand *m*, Bude *f*; 4. Zuschauertribüne *f*; 5. *hat-~, coat-~* Garderobenständer *m*; 6. *make a ~* Widerstand leisten *(against* gegen); **II** *v irr stood, stood* [stʊd] 7. stehen; ~ *firm* od *fast, ~ o.'s ground* unnachgiebig sein; 8. ~ *back! aside! clear!* Vorsicht! Zurücktreten! 9. *fig* sich befinden; 10. (an)dauern; 11. bestehen *(on* auf); 12. sich einsetzen *(for, to* für); 13. darstellen, bedeuten *(for s.th.* etw); stehen *(for* für); 14. (hin)stellen, -setzen; 15. ertragen, aushalten; *(Kälte)* vertragen; 16. *(Menschen)* ausstehen, leiden können; ~ **back** zurücktreten; *(Haus)* zurückstehen; ~ **by** in Bereitschaft sein; ~ **in** einspringen *(for s.o.* für jdn); ~ **off** abseits stehen *a. fig;* sich zurück-, sich fernhalten von; ~ **out** *fig* heraus-, hervorragen *(from* aus); ~ **up** aufstehen; *stand up for* verteidigen.

standard ['stændəd] 1. Standarte *f;* 2. Standard *m; above, below* ~ über-, unterdurchschnittlich; *be up to* ~ den Anforderungen entsprechen; ~ *of living* Lebensstandard *m;* ~**ize** ['stændədaiz] normen, vereinheitlichen; ~ **lamp** Stehlampe *f;* ~ **size** Normalgröße *f;* ~ **time** Normalzeit *f.*

stand|by ['stændbai] ~ *equipment* Reserveausrüstung *f; keep on* ~ in Bereitschaft halten; ~-**in** ['-in] *film* Double *n.*

standing ['stændiŋ] **I** *adj* 1. stehend; 2. beständig; **II** *s* 3. Ansehen *n;* Stellung *f;* 4. *of long* ~ lang(dauernd); alt.

standpoint ['stændpɔint] Standpunkt *m a. fig.*

standstill ['stændstil] *come to a* ~ zum Stillstand kommen.

staple ['steipl] 1. Heftklammer *f;* 2. Haupterzeugnis *n;*

~ *food* Grundnahrungsmittel *n pl.*

star [sta:] **I** *s* 1. Stern *m; fixed* ~ Fixstern *m;* 2. (Film-)Star *m;* **II** *v* die Hauptrolle spielen.

starboard ['sta:bəd] Steuerbord *n.*

starch [sta:tʃ] **I** *s* 1. Stärke *f,* -mehl *n;* 2. *fig* Steifheit *f;* **II** *v (Wäsche)* stärken.

stare [steə] starren; anstarren *(at s.o.* jdn); fixieren.

starfish ['sta:fiʃ] *zoo* Seestern *m.*

staring ['steəriŋ] auffallend; *(Farbe)* grell.

stark [sta:k] **I** *adj* 1. starr, steif; 2. kahl; 3. *fig* rein, völlig; **II** *adv:* ~ *naked* splitternackt.

star|ring ['sta:riŋ] ~ *X.* mit X. in der Hauptrolle; ~**ry** ['sta:ri] (stern)hell.

start [sta:t] **I** *v* 1. anfangen, beginnen; *sport* starten; *(Motor)* anspringen; *(Produktion)* anlaufen; 2. aufbrechen *(on a journey* zu e-r Reise); 3. abfahren, -fliegen, -reisen *(for* nach); 4. *(Geschäft)* gründen, eröffnen; 5. auffahren, -schrecken; **II** *s* 6. Beginn, Anfang *m; from* ~ *to finish* von Anfang bis (zu) Ende; *make a fresh* ~ von neuem anfangen; 7. *ohne pl* Vorsprung *m;* 8. plötzlicher Schreck *m.*

starter ['sta:tə] 1. Teilnehmer *m* (an e-m Rennen);

2. *mot* Anlasser *m;* 3. *fam* Vorspeise *f.*

starting-point ['stɑ:tɪŋpɔɪnt] Ausgangspunkt *m.*

startl|e ['stɑ:tl] er-, aufschrecken; **~ing** [-ɪŋ] erschreckend.

starv|ation [stɑ:'veɪʃn] Hungertod *m;* **~e** [stɑ:v] verhungern; *I'm starving (fam)* ich habe e-n wahnsinnigen Hunger.

state [steɪt] **I** *s* 1. Zustand *m,* Lage *f,* Verhältnisse *n pl;* 2. *(S~)* Staat *m; federal ~* Bundesstaat *m; Secretary of S~ (Am)* Außenminister *m;* **II** *v* feststellen; erklären, darlegen; *~ full particulars* genaue Einzelheiten angeben; **~less** ['-lɪs] staatenlos; **~ly** ['-lɪ] stattlich.

statement ['steɪtmənt] 1. Aussage *f; give, make a ~* e-e Erklärung abgeben; 2. (Konto-)Auszug *m.*

statesman ['steɪtsmən] Staatsmann *m.*

station ['steɪʃn] **I** *s* 1. Standort *m;* 2. *radio* Sender *m;* 3. *rail* Bahnhof *m; goods ~* Güterbahnhof *m; main, central ~* Hauptbahnhof *m;* 4. *police ~* Polizeiwache *f,* -revier *n;* 5. *power-~* Kraftwerk *n;* 6. *weather-~* Wetterstation *f;* **II** *v* stationieren.

stationary ['steɪʃnərɪ] stationär.

stationer ['steɪʃnə] Schreibwarenhändler *m;* **~y** ['steɪʃnərɪ] Schreib-, Papierwaren *f pl.*

station-wagon ['steɪʃn,wægən] *Am mot* Kombi(wagen) *m.*

statistic|(al) [stə'tɪstɪk(l)] statistisch; **~s** [stə'tɪstɪks] *pl mit sing* Statistik *f.*

statue ['stætʃu:] Standbild *n,* Statue *f.*

stature ['stætʃə] Statur *f.*

statutory ['stætjutərɪ] gesetzlich; satzungs-, bestimmungsgemäß.

sta(u)nch [stɔ:ntʃ] zuverlässig, vertrauenswürdig.

stay [steɪ] **I** *s* 1. Aufenthalt *m;* 2. *fig* Stütze *f;* **II** *v* bleiben (*with s.o.* bei jdm); sich aufhalten; wohnen; *come to ~* (für immer) bleiben; *~ in bed* das Bett hüten; *~ put (fam)* sich nicht von der Stelle rühren; *~ in* daheim bleiben; *~ up* aufbleiben; *~ with* wohnen bei; **~-at-home** ['-əthəum] Stubenhocker *m.*

stead [sted] *in s.o.'s ~* an jds Stelle; *stand s.o. in good ~* für jdn von Nutzen, Vorteil sein; **~fast** ['-fəst] beständig; standhaft; **~y** ['-ɪ] 1. unbeweglich; 2. beständig.

steak [steɪk] Steak; (Fisch-)-Filet *n.*

steal [sti:l] *irr* stole [stəul], stolen ['stəulən] 1. stehlen;

2. ~ *away, in* sich weg-, einschleichen.

steam [sti:m] **I** *s* Dampf *m;* *full ~ ahead* (mit) Volldampf voraus; **II** *v* dampfen; ~**er** ['-ə], ~**ship** ['-ʃɪp] Dampfer *m;* ~-**roller** ['-ˌrəʊlə] Dampfwalze *f a. fig.*

steel [sti:l] Stahl *m.*

steep [sti:p] **I** *adj* 1. steil; 2. *fam* (Preis) gesalzen; **II** *v* einweichen.

steeple ['sti:pl] (Kirch-)Turm *m;* ~-**chase** [-tʃeɪs] Hindernisrennen *n.*

steer [stɪə] steuern *a. fig;* ~-**wheel** ['-rɪŋwi:l] Lenk-, Steuerrad *n.*

stem [stem] **I** *s bot* Stamm; Stiel; Stengel *m;* **II** *v* 1. hemmen; 2. herrühren (*from* von).

stench [stentʃ] Gestank *m.*

stencil ['stensl] Matrize *f.*

step [step] **I** *s* 1. Schritt, Tritt *m;* ~ *by* ~ schrittweise *a. fig;* 2. Stufe *f;* 3. *keep ~ with* Schritt halten mit; 4. *take* ~*s* Schritte unternehmen; **II** *v* schreiten, treten; gehen.

step|father ['step,fa:ðə] Stiefvater *m;* ~**mother** ['-,mʌðə] Stiefmutter *f.*

sterilize ['sterəlaɪz] sterilisieren.

stern [stɜ:n] **I** *adj* streng; **II** *s mar* Heck *n.*

stevedore ['sti:vədɔ:] *mar* Stauer *m.*

stew [stju:] **I** *v* schmoren *a. fig;* **II** *s* Eintopf(essen *n*) *m.*

steward ['stjʊəd] *mar aero* Steward *m;* ~**ess** [ˌstjʊə'dɪz] *aero* Stewardeß *f.*

stick [stɪk] **I** *v irr stuck, stuck* [stʌk] 1. durchbohren; 2. stecken (*into* in); 3. (an)kleben; ~ *no bills* (Zettel-)Ankleben verboten; 4. kleben(bleiben), haften (*to* an); 5. *fig* hängen, festhalten (*at, to* an); ~ *to o.'s promise* sein Versprechen halten; 6. (Türe) klemmen; 7. ~ *out* (Nagel) herausstehen; 8. *be stuck* (*fig*) in der Tinte, Patsche sitzen; **II** *s* 9. Stock *m;* 10. Stück *n* (Kreide etc).

sticker ['stɪkə] Klebe-, Aufklebzettel *m.*

sticking-plaster ['stɪkɪŋpla:stə] Heftpflaster *n.*

sticky ['stɪkɪ] klebrig.

stiff [stɪf] 1. steif, starr; 2. (Examen) schwierig; 3. steif, förmlich; 4. (Getränk) stark; ~**en** ['stɪfn] (sich) versteifen; ~-**necked** ['-nekt] halsstarrig.

stifl|e ['staɪfl] *fig* unterdrükken; ~**ing** [-ɪŋ] (Hitze) erstickend.

still [stɪl] **I** *adj* still, ruhig; *keep ~* stillhalten; **II** *adv* (immer) noch.

stimul|ant ['stɪmjʊlənt] Stimulans *n;* **~ate** ['stɪmjʊleɪt] anspornen (*to* zu); anregen.

sting [stɪŋ] **I** *v irr stung, stung* [stʌŋ] 1. stechen; 2. schmerzen; **II** *s* 3. Stich *m;* 4. Stachel *m.*

stingy ['stɪndʒɪ] geizig.

stink [stɪŋk] **I** *v irr stank* [stæŋk] *od stunk* [stʌŋk], *stunk* stinken (*of* nach) *a. fig;* **II** *s* Gestank *m.*

stint [stɪnt] *without* ~ ohne Einschränkung.

stipulat|e [,stɪpjuleɪt] vereinbaren; **~ion** [,stɪpju'leɪʃn] *on the* ~ *that* unter der Bedingung, daß.

stir [stɜː] 1. um-, durchea.rühren; 2. *fig* aufwühlen; 3. (~ *up*) auf-, wachrütteln; an-, aufstacheln; 4. *not* ~ *a finger* keinen Finger rühren; **~ring** ['-rɪŋ] aufregend, aufwühlend.

stirrup ['stɪrəp] Steigbügel *m.*

stitch [stɪtʃ] **I** *s* Stich *m;* **II** *v* nähen.

stock [stɒk] **I** *s* 1. Vorrat, (Lager-, Waren-)Bestand *m; in* ~ vorrätig; *out of* ~ ausverkauft; 2. (*live-*~) Viehbestand *m;* 3. *Br* (Stamm-)Kapital *n;* 4. Stamm *m;* Herkunft *f;* 5. (*Fleisch, Gemüse*) Brühe *f;* **II** *v* 6. auf Lager nehmen; 7. versehen, versorgen (*with* mit); **~-breeder** ['-,briːdə] Viehzüchter *m;* **~broker** ['-,brəʊkə] Börsenmakler *m;* **~ exchange**

Wertpapier-, Aktienbörse *f;* **~fish** ['-fɪʃ] Stockfisch *m.*

stocking ['stɒkɪŋ] Strumpf *m.*

stock-taking ['stɒk,teɪkɪŋ] Bestandsaufnahme *f.*

stoke [stəʊk] (*Feuer*) schüren; **~r** ['-ə] Heizer *m.*

stole [stəʊl] Stola *f.*

stolid ['stɒlɪd] stumpf(sinnig).

stomach ['stʌmək] 1. Magen *m;* 2. *I have no* ~ *for it* ich habe keine Lust dazu; **~-ache** [-eɪk] Magenschmerzen *m pl.*

ston|e [stəʊn] 1. Stein *m; leave no* ~ *unturned* (*fig*) alle Hebel in Bewegung setzen; *S~ Age* Steinzeit *f;* 2. (*precious* ~) (Edel-)Stein *m;* 3. (*Obst*) Kern, Stein *m;* **~y** ['-ɪ] 1. steinig; 2. *fig* kalt; 3. *sl* (~*-broke*) pleite.

stool [stuːl] 1. Schemel *m;* 2. Hocker *m.*

stoop [stuːp] sich bücken, sich beugen.

stop [stɒp] **I** *v* 1. an-, auf-, abhalten (*s.o. doing s.th.* jdn etw zu tun; *from* von); 2. zum Halten bringen; 3. unterbinden, verhindern; 4. unterbrechen (*s.o.* jdn); 5. beenden, aufhören (*doing* zu tun); 6. stehenbleiben, anhalten; 7. *fam* sich aufhalten, bleiben (*at* in); zu Besuch sein (*with* bei); absteigen (*at a hotel* in e-m Hotel); **II** *s* 8. Halt; (*Zug*) Aufenthalt; Stillstand *m;* Pause,

Unterbrechung *f; bring s.th. to a ~, put a ~ to s.th.* mit etw Schluß machen; 9. Haltestelle *f; -punkt m; get off at the next ~* bei der nächsten Haltestelle aussteigen; 10. *(full ~)* Punkt *m.*

stopgap ['stɒpgæp] (Not-)Behelf, Ersatz *m; ~-light* ['-laɪt] *mot* Stopp-, Bremslicht *n; ~-over* ['-əʊvə] (Flug-)Unterbrechung, Zwischenlandung *f.*

stopper ['stɒpə] Pfropf, Stöpsel *m.*

stop press *Br (Zeitung)* letzte Meldungen *f pl.*

stop-watch ['stɒpwɒtʃ] Stoppuhr *f.*

storage ['stɔːrɪdʒ] (Ein-)Lagerung *f.*

store [stɔː] **I** *s* 1. Vorrat, (Waren-)Bestand *m (of* an); 2. *(~-house)* Lagerhaus *n;* 3. *Br* Waren-, Kaufhaus *n; Am* Laden *m,* Geschäft *n;* 4. *have in ~ for s.o.* für jdn bereithalten, -haben; **II** *v* (ein)lagern; aufspeichern, -bewahren; *~-room* ['-rʊm] Vorratsraum *m.*

stor(e)y ['stɔːrɪ] Stockwerk *n,* Etage *f.*

stork [stɔːk] Storch *m.*

storm [stɔːm] **I** *s* Sturm *m; ~ of applause* Beifallssturm *m;* **II** *v* stürmen *a. fig; ~y* ['-ɪ] stürmisch *a. fig.*

story ['stɔːrɪ] 1. Bericht *m; that's another ~* das ist ein

Kapitel für sich; 2. Geschichte *f,* Märchen *n.*

stout [staʊt] 1. untersetzt; beleibt; 2. widerstandsfähig; 3. tapfer, beherzt.

stove [stəʊv] Ofen, Herd *m.*

stow [stəʊ] verstauen, -packen; *~away* ['-əweɪ] blinde(r) Passagier *m.*

straight [streɪt] **I** *adj* 1. g(e)rade; 2. unmittelbar, direkt; 3. offen, ehrlich; 4. *(Getränk)* unvermischt; 5. *put ~* in Ordnung bringen *a. fig;* **II** *adv* geradewegs, (schnur)stracks; *~ away, off* sofort, unverzüglich; *~ on* geradeaus; *come ~ to the point* keine Umschweife machen; **III** *s sport* (Ziel-)Gerade *f; ~en* ['-n] 1. begradigen; 2. *fig (~ out)* in Ordnung bringen.

straightforward [ˌstreɪt'fɔːwəd] offen, ehrlich; einfach.

strain [streɪn] **I** *v* 1. (aufs äußerste) anspannen; 2. (über)anstrengen; 3. *med* verstauchen; 4. durchseihen; **II** *s* 5. (An-)Spannung, Belastung *f (on* für); 6. (Über-)Anstrengung *f;* 7. *med* Verrenkung, Verstauchung *f; ~er* ['-ə] Filter *m,* Sieb *n.*

strait [streɪt] 1. *meist pl* Meerenge *f;* 2. *meist pl fig* Schwierigkeiten *f pl; ~en* ['-n] *in ~ed circumstances* in beschränkten Verhältnissen.

strand [strænd] stranden *a.*
fig.

strange [streɪndʒ]
1. fremd(artig); 2. merkwürdig, seltsam; ~**r** ['-ə] Fremde(r), Unbekannte(r) *m.*

strangle ['stræŋgl] erwürgen, erdrosseln; ~**-hold**
[-həʊld] Würgegriff *m a.*
fig.

strap [stræp] I *s* (Leder-)-Riemen, Gurt *m; (Kleid)*
Träger *m;* II *v* festschnallen;
~**less** ['-lɪs] trägerlos.

stratagem ['strætədʒəm]
Trick *m.*

strategy ['strætɪdʒɪ] Strategie; *fig* Taktik *f.*

straw [strɔ:] Stroh *n;* Strohhalm *m; not worth a ~* keinen Pfifferling wert; *not
care a ~* sich nicht das geringste daraus machen;
~**berry** ['-bərɪ] Erdbeere *f.*

stray [streɪ] I *v* 1. umherschweifen, -irren; 2. *fig* abschweifen; II *adj* 3. streunend; 4. vereinzelt; III *s*
Heimat-, Obdachlose(r) *m.*

streak [stri:k] I *s* 1. Streifen
m; like a ~ (of lightning)
blitzschnell; 2. *fig* Anflug *m;*
3. *a ~ of winning, losing*
Glücks-, Pechsträhne *f;* II *v*
4. streifen; 5. *fam* vorbeisausen; flitzen; ~**y** ['-ɪ] *(Fleisch,
Speck)* durchwachsen.

stream [stri:m] I *s* 1. Bach,
Fluß *m;* 2. Strom *m;* Flut *f a.*
fig; up, down the ~ stromauf-, -abwärts; II *v* 3. strö-

men, fließen, rinnen; 4. *(im
Wind)* flattern; ~**er** ['-ə]
Wimpel *m;* ~**-lined** ['-laɪnd]
stromlinienförmig.

street [stri:t] Straße *f; in the
~* auf der Straße; *main ~*
Hauptstraße *f; one-way ~*
Einbahnstraße *f;* ~**-car**
['-kɑː] *Am* Straßenbahn(wagen *m*) *f;* ~**-walker**
['-wɔːkə] Prostituierte *f.*

strength [streŋθ] 1. Kraft,
Stärke *f a. fig; on the ~ of*
auf Grund *gen;* 2. *up to (below)* ~ (nicht) vollzählig;
~**en** ['-n] kräftigen, stärken.

strenuous ['strenjʊəs]
1. rastlos (tätig); 2. anstrengend.

stress [stres] I *s* 1. *tech* Beanspruchung *f;* 2. *fig* Nachdruck *m (on auf);* 3. *med*
Streß *m;* 4. Betonung *f;*
II *v* betonen.

stretch [stretʃ] I *v* 1. *(Seil)*
spannen; 2. (sich) (aus)dehnen, (sich) strecken; ~ *o.'s
legs* sich die Beine vertreten; 3. sich erstrecken; reichen; 4. sich ausstrecken *(on
the bed* auf dem Bett); II *s*
5. Dehnung *f;* 6. Anstrengung, Anspannung *f;* 7. Ausdehnung, Strecke *f; at a ~*
in e-m Zuge; ~**er** ['-ə] *med*
Tragbahre *f.*

stricken ['strɪkən] *fig* bedrückt, heimgesucht *(with*
von).

strict [strɪkt] genau; streng
(with gegen); in ~ secrecy

streng vertraulich; ~*ly speaking* strenggenommen.

stride [straɪd] I *v irr* **strode** [strəʊd], *stridden* ['strɪdn] (~ *along*) (tüchtig) ausschreiten; II *s* (langer) Schritt *m*.

strike [straɪk] I *v irr* **struck, struck** [strʌk] *od stricken* ['strɪkən] 1. schlagen; *it has struck two* es hat zwei geschlagen; 2. (*Streichholz*) sich entzünden; 3. (*Münzen*) prägen; 4. ~ *s.o.* jdm auffallen; jdm einfallen; 5. streiken; 6. ~ *it lucky, oil* (*fam*) Glück haben; II *s* Streik, Ausstand *m; be, go on* ~; *go, come out on* ~ streiken, in den Ausstand treten.

strike-breaker ['straɪk,breɪkə] Streikbrecher *m*.

striking ['straɪkɪŋ] 1. treffend; 2. auffallend; beachtlich.

string [strɪŋ] I *s* 1. Schnur *f*; Bindfaden *m*; 2. *mus* Saite *f*; *have two* ~s *to o.'s bow* (*fig*) zwei Eisen im Feuer haben; 3. *pull* ~s (*fig*) der Drahtzieher sein; II *v irr* **strung, strung** [strʌŋ] 4. (*Instrument*) besaiten; 5. aufreihen; 6. ~ *up* aufhängen; ~ **band**, ~ **orchestra** Streichorchester *n*; ~**y** ['-ɪ] faserig.

strip [strɪp] I *v* 1. (sich) ausziehen; 2. abstreifen, abziehen; 3. *tech* auseinandernehmen; 4. *fig* berauben (*of s.th.*

e-r S); II *s* Streifen *m*, Band *n; (air-~, landing-~) aero* (Start- u.) Landestreifen *m*.

stripe [straɪp] Streif(en) *m*.

strive [straɪv] *irr* **strove** [strəʊv], *striven* ['strɪvn] sich anstrengen, wetteifern, streben (*for s.th., to do s.th.* nach).

stroke [strəʊk] I *s* 1. Schlag *a. fig*, Hieb *m*; 2. *med* Schlag(anfall) *m*; 3. (Schwimm-)Stoß *m*; 4. (Pinsel-, Bogen-)Strich *m*; 5. ~ *of luck* Glücksfall *m; at a, at one* ~ mit e-m Schlag; II *v* streicheln.

stroll [strəʊl] I *v* spazierengehen, umherschlendern; II *s: have a* ~ e-n Bummel machen.

strong [strɒŋ] 1. stark, kräftig; *feel* ~ *again* wieder bei Kräften sein; 2. tüchtig; *that is my* ~ *point* das ist meine Stärke; 3. (*Gegenstände*) stabil, dauerhaft; ~**hold** ['-həʊld] *fig* Hochburg *f*; ~**ly** ['-lɪ] nachdrücklich.

structure ['strʌktʃə] 1. Struktur *f*, Gefüge *n*, Aufbau *m*; 2. Bau *m*; Konstruktion *f*.

struggle ['strʌgl] I *v* kämpfen (*against* gegen; *with* mit); II *s* Kampf *m* (*for* um).

strut [strʌt] I *v* (herum)stolzieren; II *s* Stützbalken *m*.

stubble ['stʌbl] Stoppeln *f pl*.

stubborn ['stʌbən] widerspenstig, eigensinnig.

stuck-up [ˌstʌk'ʌp] *fam* überheblich.

stud [stʌd] **I** *s* 1. Kragen-, Hemdknopf *m;* 2. Beschlagnagel *m;* 3. Gestüt *n;* **II** *v:* ~ded with übersät mit.

student ['stju:dnt] Student *m.*

studio ['stju:dɪəu] *pl* ~s 1. Atelier *n;* 2. *radio* Senderaum *m.*

studious ['stju:djəs] lernbegierig.

study ['stʌdɪ] **I** *s* 1. Studium *n;* 2. Studie *f;* 3. Studier-, Arbeitszimmer *n;* **II** *v* 4. studieren; 5. (genau) prüfen.

stuff [stʌf] 1. Stoff *m,* Materie *f;* 2. *(sl)* he knows his ~ er kennt sich aus; ~ing ['-ɪŋ] Füllsel *n (a. Küche);* ~y ['-ɪ] stickig.

stumbl|e ['stʌmbl] 1. stolpern *(over* über); 2. ~ about, along, around torkeln; 3. stottern; ~ing-block ['-ɪŋblɒk] Stein *m* des Anstoßes.

stump [stʌmp] **I** *s* 1. (Baum-) Stumpf *m;* 2. Stummel *m;* **II** *v* sta(m)pfen; ~y ['-ɪ] stämmig, untersetzt.

stun [stʌn] betäuben; ~ning ['-ɪŋ] *fam* umwerfend, verblüffend.

stunt [stʌnt] *fam* Reklameschlager, Knüller *m;* ~ man *film* Double *n.*

stupendous [stju:'pendəs] gewaltig, ungeheuer.

stupid ['stju:pɪd] dumm, einfältig; ~ity [stju:'pɪdətɪ] Dummheit *f.*

sturdy ['stɜ:dɪ] stark, kräftig.

stutter ['stʌtə] stottern.

sty [staɪ] *(pig~)* Schweinestall *m a. fig.*

style [staɪl] 1. *fig* Stil *m;* 2. Mode *f.*

sub-committee ['sʌbkəˌmɪtɪ] Unterausschuß *m.*

subsconscious [ˌsʌb'kɒnʃəs] unterbewußt.

subdue [səb'dju:] 1. unterwerfen; überwinden; 2. abschwächen; dämpfen.

subject I *adj* ['sʌbdʒɪkt] abhängig *(to* von); ~ *to alteration* Änderungen vorbehalten; ~ *to duty* zollpflichtig; **II** *s* ['--] 1. *fig* Gegenstand *m,* Thema *n,* Stoff *m (for* für); 2. Fach(gebiet) *n;* 3. Unterrichtsgegenstand *m,* -fach *n;* 4. *gram* Subjekt *n;* 5. Staatsbürger, -angehörige(r) *m;* **III** *v* [səb'dʒekt] 6. unterwerfen; 7. *(e-r Prüfung)* unterziehen *(to* dat).

submarine [ˌsʌbmə'ri:n] U-Boot *n.*

submerge [səb'mɜ:dʒ] 1. untertauchen; 2. überschwemmen.

submit [səb'mɪt] 1. unterbreiten, einreichen; 2. sich

fügen (to dat); sich abfinden (to mit).

subscribe [səb'skraɪb] 1. e-n Geldbetrag zeichnen (to für); 2. abonnieren (to s.th. etw); 3. zustimmen, billigen (to s.th etw); ~**r** [-ə] Abonnent m; (telephone ~) (Fernsprech-)Teilnehmer m.

subscription [səb'skrɪpʃn] 1. (Mitglieds-)Beitrag m; 2. Abonnement n.

subsequent ['sʌbsɪkwənt] (nach)folgend; ~**ly** [-lɪ] danach, später.

subside [səb'saɪd] (Flut) sinken.

subsidiary [səb'sɪdjərɪ] **I** adj untergeordnet (to dat); **II** s (~ company) Tochtergesellschaft f.

subsid|ize ['sʌbsɪdaɪz] subventionieren; ~**y** ['sʌbsɪdɪ] Subvention f.

subsist [səb'sɪst] leben (on von); ~**ence** [-əns] (Lebens-)Unterhalt m.

substan|ce ['sʌbstəns] 1. Hauptsache f; in ~ im wesentlichen; 2. Materie f, Stoff m; ~**tial** [səb'stænʃl] 1. wesentlich; 2. solide, fest; 3. beträchtlich, bedeutend.

substitute ['sʌbstɪtjuːt] **I** s 1. Ersatz m; 2. Stellvertreter m; **II** v austauschen (for gegen); einspringen (for für); vertreten (for s.o. jdn).

subtle ['sʌtl] 1. fein; 2. kniff(e)lig, verzwickt, schwierig.

subtract [səb'trækt] abziehen (from von).

suburb ['sʌbɜːb] Vorstadt f; ~**an** [sə'bɜːbən] vorstädtisch.

subway ['sʌbweɪ] 1. Unterführung f; 2. Am U-Bahn f.

succeed [sək'siːd] 1. folgen (to auf); 2. Glück, Erfolg haben (in an examination bei e-r Prüfung); he ~ed es gelang ihm (in doing zu tun).

success [sək'ses] Erfolg m; meet with ~ erfolgreich sein; ~**ful** [-ful] erfolgreich; ~**ion** [sək'seʃn] Reihe(nfolge), (Aufea.-)Folge f (of von); in ~ der Reihe nach; ~**ive** [-ɪv] aufea.folgend; ~**or** [-ə] Nachfolger m.

succumb [sə'kʌm] erliegen (to a disease e-r Krankheit).

such [sʌtʃ, sətʃ] solch, derartig, so(lch) ein(e); no ~ thing nichts Derartiges; as ~ als solche(r, s); ~ as wie z. B., wie etwa; ~ a long time so lange (her).

suck [sʌk] 1. saugen (from, out of aus); 2. (Bonbon) lutschen (at an).

suckle ['sʌkl] säugen; stillen.

sudden ['sʌdn] plötzlich, unerwartet; all of a ~ (ganz) plötzlich; ~**ly** [-lɪ] plötzlich, auf einmal.

suds pl [sʌdz] Seifenschaum m.

sue [sjuː] verklagen (for auf); ~ for a divorce auf Scheidung klagen.

suède [sweɪd] Wildleder n.

suet ['sjuːɪt] Nierentalg m.

suffer ['sʌfə] 1. dulden, zulassen; 2. leiden (*from* an); **~ing** [-rɪŋ] Dulden; Leiden n.

suffic|e [sə'faɪs] genügen, ausreichen (*for* für); **~ient** [sə'fɪʃnt] genügend, genug (*for* für); *be ~* reichen.

suffocat|e ['sʌfəkeɪt] ersticken; **~ion** [ˌsʌfə'keɪʃn] Ersticken n.

sugar ['ʃugə] I s Zucker m; II v (über)zuckern; (ver)süßen.

suggest [sə'dʒest] 1. vorbringen, -schlagen (*doing* zu tun; *that* daß); 2. schließen lassen auf, andeuten; 3. *does this ~ anything to you?* können Sie sich etwas darunter vorstellen? **~ion** [-ʃən] 1. Vorschlag m; *at his ~* auf s-n Vorschlag hin; 2. Andeutung f; Anzeichen n; **~ive** [-ɪv] 1. anregend; 2. zweideutig.

suicide ['sjuːɪsaɪd] *commit ~* Selbstmord begehen.

suit [suːt] I s 1. (Herren-)Anzug m; (Damen-)Kostüm n; 2. *jur* Prozeß m; 3. *follow ~* (Kartenspiel) Farbe bekennen; II v 4. passend sein für, passen (*s.o.* jdm); kleiden; 5. anpassen (*to* dat *od* an); 6. *be ~ed* geeignet sein (*to, for* für); **~able** ['-əbl] passend, geeignet (*for* für);

~case ['-keɪs] Hand-, Reisekoffer m.

sulk [sʌlk] schlecht gelaunt sein; schmollen; **~y** ['-ɪ] schlecht aufgelegt, mißgestimmt.

sullen ['sʌlən] 1. verdrießlich; 2. trüb(e).

sulphur ['sʌlfə] Schwefel m.

sultry ['sʌltrɪ] schwül.

sum [sʌm] I s 1. (Geld-)Summe f, Betrag m; 2. *be good at ~s* gut im Rechnen sein; *do ~s* rechnen; II v (*~ up*) 3. zs.zählen; 4. zs.fassen; **~mary** ['sʌmərɪ] (kurze) Zs.fassung f.

summer ['sʌmə] Sommer m *a. fig; in (the) ~* im Sommer; **~-house** ['-haus] Ferienhaus n; *~* **holidays** pl Sommerferien pl; *~* **time** Sommerzeit f.

summit ['sʌmɪt] 1. Gipfel m; 2. *fig* Höhepunkt m.

summon ['sʌmən] 1. bestellen, kommen lassen; (*Sitzung*) einberufen; *jur* vorladen; 2. *~ up o.'s strength* sich zs.reißen; **~s** [-z] pl *-ses* [-zɪz] *jur* (Vor-)Ladung f.

sun [sʌn] I s Sonne f; II v sich sonnen; **~bathe** ['-beɪð] sonnenbaden; **~beam** ['-biːm] Sonnenstrahl m *a. fig;* **~burn** ['-bɜːn] Sonnenbrand m.

Sunday ['sʌndɪ] Sonntag m.

sundial ['sʌndaɪəl] Sonnenuhr f.

sundry ['sʌndrɪ] I *adj* ver-

schiedene; allerlei, -hand;
II *s: all and* ~ jedermann;
alle miteinander.
sun-glasses ['sʌnglɑːsɪz]
Sonnenbrille *f.*
sunken ['sʌŋkən] versunken.
sun|light ['sʌnlaɪt] Sonnen-
licht *n;* ~**ny** ['-ɪ] sonnig;
~**-ray** ['-reɪ] Sonnenstrahl
m; ~**rise** ['-raɪz] *at* ~ bei
Sonnenaufgang; ~**set** ['-set]
at ~ bei Sonnenuntergang;
~**shade** ['-ʃeɪd] Sonnenschirm *m;* ~**shine** ['-ʃaɪn]
Sonnenschein *m a. fig;*
~**stroke** ['-strəʊk] Sonnen-
stich, Hitzschlag *m;* ~**tan**
['-tæn] Sonnenbräune *f.*
super ['suːpə] *fam* erstklassig, prima.
superb [sjuː'pɜːb] großartig.
superficial [ˌsuːpə'fɪʃl] oberflächlich *a. fig.*
superfluous [suː'pɜːfluəs]
überflüssig.
superhuman
[ˌsuːpə'hjuːmən] über-
menschlich.
superintend [ˌsuːpərɪn'tend]
beaufsichtigen; überwachen;
~**ent** [-ənt] 1. Direktor, Manager *m;* 2. Polizeidirektor
m.
superior [suː'pɪərɪə] **I** *adj*
1. höher, ober; 2. besser (*to*
als); 3. überlegen (*to* dat); ~
in numbers zahlenmäßig
überlegen; **II** *s* Vorgesetz-
te(r) *m;* ~**ity** [suːˌpɪərɪ'ɒrətɪ]
Überlegenheit *f* (*to* über; *in*
an).

superman ['suːpəmæn]
Übermensch *m.*
supermarket ['suːpəˌmɑːkɪt]
Supermarkt *m.*
supersonic [ˌsuːpə'sɒnɪk] *fly*
at ~ *speed* mit Überschall-
geschwindigkeit fliegen.
superstit|ion [ˌsuːpə'stɪʃn]
Aberglaube *m;* ~**ious** [-əs]
abergläubisch.
supervis|e ['suːpəvaɪz] be-
aufsichtigen, kontrollieren;
~**ion** [ˌsuːpə'vɪʒn] Aufsicht,
Kontrolle *f* (*of* über); ~**or**
['suːpəvaɪzə] Aufsichtsper-
son *f;* Inspektor *m.*
supper ['sʌpə] Abendessen
n.
supple ['sʌpl] biegsam, geschmeidig.
supplement I *s* ['sʌplɪmənt]
1. Ergänzung *f,* Zusatz *m* (*to*
zu); 2. *(Buch)* Nachtrag *m;*
3. *(Zeitung)* Beilage *f;* **II** *v*
['-ment] ergänzen; ~**ary**
[ˌsʌplɪ'mentərɪ] ergänzend.
suppl|ier [sə'plaɪə] Lieferant
m; ~**y** [sə'plaɪ] **I** *v* 1. liefern;
2. versorgen (*with* mit); **II** *s*
3. Lieferung *f;* 4. *pl* Vorräte
m pl; 5. ~ *and demand* Angebot u. Nachfrage.
support [sə'pɔːt] **I** *v* 1. *arch*
(ab)stützen; 2. *fig* unterstützen; 3. sorgen für; ernähren;
II *s* 4. Stütze *f,* Träger *m;*
5. *fig* Unterstützung, Hilfe *f;*
~**er** [-ə] Verfechter, Anhänger *m.*
suppos|e [sə'pəʊz] 1. anneh-
men, meinen; *I* ~ *so* vermut-

lich, wahrscheinlich; 2. *I'm ~d to do* ich soll tun; **~ing** [-ɪŋ] angenommen; **~ition** [ˌsʌpəˈzɪʃn] *on the ~ that* unter der Annahme, daß.

suppress [səˈpres] 1. unterdrücken; 2. *(Skandal)* vertuschen; **~ion** [səˈpreʃn] Unterdrückung *f.*

suprem|acy [suˈpreməsɪ] Überlegenheit *f;* **~e** [suˈpriːm] *(rang)*höchst, oberst.

surcharge [ˈsɜːtʃɑːdʒ] Zuschlag *m;* Nachporto *n.*

sure [[ʃʊə] **I** *adj* sicher, gewiß; *be ~ of s.th.* e-r S sicher sein; *make ~* sich vergewissern *(of s.th.* e-r S; *that* daß); *he is ~ to come* er wird sicher(lich) kommen; *be ~ not to forget your book* vergessen Sie ja Ihr Buch nicht; *are you ~ you won't come?* wollen Sie wirklich nicht kommen? **II** *adv: for ~* sicherlich; *(fam) ~ enough* gewiß; **~ly** [ˈ-lɪ] sicher(lich); **~ty** [ˈʃʊərətɪ] *jur* Bürgschaft, Kaution *f.*

surf [sɜːf] Brandung *f.*

surface [ˈsɜːfɪs] Oberfläche *f a. fig.*

surf|board [ˈsɜːfbɔːd] Brett *n* zum Wellenreiten; **~ing** [ˈ-ɪŋ], **~-riding** [ˈ-ˌraɪdɪŋ] Wellenreiten *n.*

surge [sɜːdʒ] **I** *s* Welle, Woge *f a. fig;* **II** *v* wogen, branden.

surg|eon [ˈsɜːdʒən] Chirurg *m; dental ~* Zahnarzt *m;* **~ery** [sɜːdʒərɪ] 1. Chirurgie *f;* 2. Sprechzimmer *n.*

surly [ˈsɜːlɪ] schlecht-, übelgelaunt.

surmount [sɜːˈmaʊnt] überwinden.

surname [ˈsɜːneɪm] Familien-, Zuname *m.*

surpass [səˈpɑːs] übertreffen.

surplus [ˈsɜːpləs] Überschuß *m (of* an).

surpris|e [səˈpraɪz] **I** *v* überraschen; *be ~d at s.th.* sich wundern, staunen über; *I should not be ~d* es würde mich nicht überraschen; **II** *s* Überraschung *f; (much) (to) my ~* zu meiner (großen) Überraschung; **~ing** [-ɪŋ] erstaunlich, überraschend.

surrender [səˈrendə] **I** *v* 1. sich ergeben, kapitulieren; 2. *(Hoffnung)* aufgeben; **II** *s* 3. Kapitulation *f;* 4. Preisgabe; Abtretung *f.*

surround [səˈraʊnd] umgeben, -fassen; *be ~ed with, by* umringt sein von; **~ing** [-ɪŋ] **I** *adj* umliegend; **II** *s pl* Umgebung *f.*

survey I *v* [səˈveɪ] 1. besichtigen, inspizieren; 2. *(Land)* vermessen; **II** *s* [ˈsɜːveɪ] (allgemeine) Übersicht *f,* Überblick *m (of* über); **~or** [səˈveɪə] Geometer *m.*

surviv|e [səˈvaɪv] überleben, -dauern; **~or** [-ə] Überlebende(r) *m.*

susceptible [sə'septəbl]
1. leicht beeinflußbar;
2. *med* anfällig (*to* für); empfindlich (*to* gegen).

suspect I *v* [sə'spekt] 1. verdächtigen; 2. vermuten; *I ~ed as much* das dachte ich mir; **II** *s* ['sʌspekt] *jur* Verdächtige(r) *m*.

suspend [sə'spend]
1. (auf)hängen (*from* an);
2. herabhängen lassen (*from* von); 3. ver-, aufschieben; *~ payment* die Zahlungen einstellen; **~ers** *pl* [-əz] *Am* Hosenträger *m pl.*

suspense [sə'spens] Ungewißheit; Spannung *f.*

suspension [sə'spenʃn]
1. Aufhängung *f*; 2. (Zahlungs-)Aufschub *m*;
~ bridge Hängebrücke *f.*

suspic|ion [sə'spɪʃn] 1. Verdacht *m*; 2. *fig* Spur *f*;
~ious [-əs] 1. verdächtig;
2. mißtrauisch.

sustain [sə'steɪn] 1. stützen; aufrechterhalten; 2. aushalten, ertragen; 3. *(Verlust)* erleiden; 4. *jur* anerkennen.

swagger ['swægə] 1. (einher)stolzieren; 2. prahlen, angeben.

swallow ['swɒləʊ] **I** *s zoo* Schwalbe *f*; **II** *v* (hinunter-, ver)schlucken.

swamp [swɒmp] **I** *s* Sumpf, Morast *m*; **II** *v*: *be ~ed* überhäuft sein (*with work* mit Arbeit); **~y** ['-ɪ] sumpfig.

swan [swɒn] Schwan *m*.

swarm [swɔːm] **I** *s* Schwarm *m*; **II** *v* 1. *(Bienen)* schwärmen; 2. wimmeln (*with* von).

sway [sweɪ] 1. schwanken;
2. schwenken; 3. *be easily ~ed* leicht beeinflußbar sein.

swear [sweə] *irr* swore [swɔː], sworn [swɔːn]
1. schwören (*by* bei, auf);
2. *jur* beschwören (*to s.th.* etw); 3. fluchen (*at s.th.* auf etw); 4. *~ s.o. in* jdn vereidigen.

sweat [swet] **I** *v* schwitzen;
II *s* Schweiß *m*; **~er** ['-ə] Sweater, Pullover *m*.

Swed|e [swiːd] Schwede *m*;
~en ['-n] Schweden *n*; **~ish** ['-ɪʃ] schwedisch.

sweep [swiːp] **I** *v irr* swept, swept [swept] 1. *(Raum)* (aus)fegen, -kehren; *(Tisch)* abwischen; *(Schmutz)* wegfegen; 2. *be swept off o.'s feet (fig)* ganz mitgerissen, begeistert sein; **II** *s* 3. Fegen, Kehren *n*; 4. *(chimney-~)* Schornsteinfeger *m*; **~er** ['-ə] Straßenkehrer *m*; Kehrmaschine *f*; **~ing** ['-ɪŋ] **I** *adj* weitreichend, weittragend; **II** *s pl* Kehricht *m od n*; **~stake** ['-steɪk] *Art* Toto *n*.

sweet [swiːt] **I** *adj* süß *a. fig*; **II** *s* Süßigkeit; Süßspeise *f*;
~en ['-n] 1. süßen; 2. *fig* versüßen; **~heart** ['-hɑːt] Liebste *f*, Liebster *m*.

swell [swel] **I** *v irr* ~ed, ~ed od *swollen* ['swəʊlən] *(~*

up, out) (an)schwellen *(with* von); sich (auf)blähen *a. fig (with* vor); **II** *adj Am fam* flott; elegant; **~ing** ['-ɪŋ] Geschwulst, Beule *f.*

swelter ['sweltə] *~ing hot* drückend heiß.

swerve [swɜːv] aus-, abweichen.

swift [swɪft] schnell, rasch, flink, eilig.

swim [swɪm] **I** *v irr swam* [swæm], *swum* [swʌm] schwimmen *(on* auf) *a. fig*; **II** *s: go for a ~* schwimmen, baden (gehen); **~mer** ['-ə] Schwimmer *m.*

swimming|-bath ['swɪmɪŋbɑː θ], **~-pool** ['-puːl] Schwimmbad, -becken *n;* **~-costume** ['-kɒstjuːm], Badeanzug *m;* **~-trunks** *pl* ['-trʌŋks] Badehose *f.*

swim-suit ['swɪmsuːt] Badeanzug *m.*

swindle ['swɪndl] **I** *v* beschwindeln, betrügen *(s.o. out of s.th.* jdn um etw); **II** *s* Schwindel, Betrug *m; ~r* ['-ə] Schwindler *m.*

swing [swɪŋ] **I** *v irr swung, swung* [swʌŋ] 1. schwingen; schlenkern, baumeln; 2. (herum)schwenken; schaukeln; **II** *s* 3. Schwingung, Drehung *f;* 4. Schaukel *f;* 5. *in full ~* in vollem Gange.

swirl [swɜːl] **I** *v* herumwirbeln; **II** *s (Wasser)* Strudel, Wirbel *m.*

Swiss [swɪs] **I** *s* Schweizer *m; II adj* schweizerisch.

switch [swɪtʃ] **I** *s* 1. (Licht-)-Schalter *m;* 2. *rail* Weiche *f;* **II** *v* 3. *~ on, off (el)* ein-, ausschalten; 4. *rail* (um)rangieren; 5. überwechseln, übergehen *(to* zu); **~back** ['-bæk] Berg-u.-Tal-Bahn *f.*

swivel ['swɪvl] (sich) drehen.

Switzerland ['swɪtsələnd] Schweiz *f.*

swollen ['swəʊlən] geschwollen, dick.

sword [sɔːd] Schwert *n.*

syllabus ['sɪləbəs] *pl a.* **-bi** ['-baɪ] (Vorlesungs-)Verzeichnis *n;* Lehrplan *m.*

symbol ['sɪmbl] Sinnbild, Symbol *n.*

sympathetic [ˌsɪmpə'θetɪk] mitfühlend, verständnisvoll; **~ize** ['sɪmpəθaɪz] 1. sympathisieren; mitfühlen *(with* mit); 2. angetan sein *(with* von); **~izer** ['sɪmpəθaɪzə] *pol* Sympathisant *m; ~y* ['sɪmpəθɪ] Sympathie *f;* Mitgefühl, Mitleid *n (with, for* mit).

symptom ['sɪmptəm] Symptom; Anzeichen *n.*

synagogue ['sɪnəgɒg] *rel* Synagoge *f.*

synchronize ['sɪŋkrənaɪz] *film* synchronisieren.

syndicate ['sɪndɪkɪt] Syndikat *n.*

synonym ['sınənım] Synonym *n;* **~ous** [sı'nɒnıməs] gleichbedeutend (*with* mit).

synthe|sis ['sınθısıs] *pl* *-theses* ['-si:z] Synthese *f;* **~tic(al)** [sın'θetık(l)] synthetisch.

Syria ['sırıə] Syrien *n.*

syringe ['sırındʒ] *med* Spritze *f.*

system ['sıstəm] System *n;* **~atic(ally)** [sıstı'mætık(əlı)] systematisch, planmäßig.

table 302 **take**

T

table ['teɪbl] 1. Tisch *m; at ~* bei Tisch; 2. Tabelle, Liste *f; ~ of contents (Buch)* Inhaltsverzeichnis *n;* **~-cloth** [-klɒθ] Tischtuch *n;* **~spoon** [-spu:n] Eßlöffel *m.*

tablet ['tæblɪt] 1. Gedenktafel *f;* 2. Schreibblock *m;* 3. Tablette *f;* 4. *(Seife)* Stück *n.*

table tennis Tischtennis *n.*

table-ware ['teɪblweə] Tafelgeschirr *n.*

taboo [təˈbu:] Tabu *a. fig;* Verbot *n.*

tabular ['tæbjʊlə] *in ~ form* in Tabellenform.

tacit ['tæsɪt] stillschweigend.

tack [tæk] 1. *(Nagel)* Stift *m; (thumb-~)* Reißnagel *m;* 2. Heften *n;* 3. *on the wrong ~ (fig)* auf dem Holzweg.

tackle ['tækl] **I** *s* 1. Flaschenzug *m;* 2. (Werk-)Zeug *n; fishing ~* Angelgerät *n;* **II** *v (Problem)* anpacken.

tact [tækt] Fingerspitzengefühl *n;* **~ful** ['-fʊl] taktvoll; **~less** ['-lɪs] taktlos.

tadpole ['tædpəʊl] *zoo* Kaulquappe *f.*

tag [tæg] **I** *s* Anhänger *m;* Etikett *n,* Preiszettel *m;* **II** *v com* auszeichnen, etikettieren.

tail [teɪl] 1. Schwanz *m a. fig;*

turn ~ Reißaus nehmen; 2. *heads or ~s?* Kopf oder Wappen? *(e-r Münze);* **~-end** ['-end] *at the ~* ganz am Schluß.

tailor ['teɪlə] Schneider *m;* **~-made** [-meɪd] nach Maß angefertigt.

tainted [teɪntɪd] verdorben.

take [teɪk] *irr* took [tʊk], taken ['teɪkən] 1. (weg)nehmen; mitnehmen; 2. bringen, begleiten *(to* zu, nach); 3. ergreifen, packen; *~ hold of s.th.* etw ergreifen; 4. *(Arznei)* einnehmen; 5. *(Temperatur)* messen; 6. *~ s.o, s.th. for; ~ s.o., s.th* to be jdn, etw ansehen als, halten für; *~ for granted* als selbstverständlich betrachten; 7. *~ s.th. down* etw aufschreiben; 8. *be taken ill* krank werden; 9. *~ o.'s leave* sich verabschieden *(of* von); 10. *~ a liking to s.o.* sich zu jdm hingezogen fühlen; 11. *~ a look* e-n Blick werfen *(at* auf); 12. *~ offence at* sich beleidigt fühlen durch; *~ pleasure in* Vergnügen haben, finden an; 13. *~ part in* teilnehmen an; 14. *~ to pieces* ausea.nehmen; 15. *~ place* stattfinden; 16. *~ time* Zeit brauchen; *~ o.'s time* sich Zeit lassen; 17. *~ turns* (sich) abwechseln; 18. ~ *a walk* e-n Spaziergang machen; 19. ~ *it easy!* mach dir nichts daraus! 20. ~ *your seats!* (bitte) einsteigen! ~ **after** nachschlagen (*s.o.* jdm); ~ **away** weg-, mitnehmen; ~ **off** 1. (*Kleidung*) ausziehen; (*Hut*) abnehmen; 2. *aero* starten; ~ **out** 1. *take s.o. out* jdn ausführen; 2. (*Versicherung*) abschließen; 3. (*Führerschein*) machen; ~ **over** (*Geschäft, Amt*) übernehmen; ~ **to** 1. Gefallen finden an; 2. Zuflucht nehmen zu; sich verlegen auf.

taken ['teɪkən] *be* ~ *aback* überrascht sein; *be* ~ *up with* in Anspruch genommen, begeistert sein von.

take-off ['teɪkɒf] *aero* Start m.

takings pl ['teɪkɪŋz] Einnahmen f pl.

talc [tælk], ~**um** ['-əm] (~ *powder*) Körperpuder m.

tale [teɪl] Erzählung f.

talent ['tælənt] Talent n, Begabung f; ~**ed** [-ɪd] begabt.

talk [tɔ:k] **I** v 1. sprechen, reden (*about, of* von, über; *to, with s.o.* mit jdm); 2. *get o.s.* ~*ed about* ins Gerede kommen; 3. ~ *s.o. into doing s.th.* jdn zu etw überreden; **II** s Gespräch n.

talkative ['tɔ:kətɪv] gesprächig.

tall [tɔ:l] groß (u. schlank), hoch(gewachsen).

tame [teɪm] **I** adj zahm; **II** v (be)zähmen.

tan [tæn] **I** s Sonnenbräune f; **II** v 1. gerben; 2. bräunen.

tang [tæŋ] scharfe(r) Geschmack m.

tangent ['tændʒənt] Tangente f.

tangerine [,tændʒə'ri:n] Mandarine f.

tangible ['tændʒəbl] fühl-, greifbar.

tangle ['tæŋgl] (sich) verwirren.

tank [tæŋk] 1. Behälter m; 2. *mil* Tank, Panzer(wagen) m; ~**er** ['-ə] *mar* Tanker m.

tantalizing ['tæntəlaɪzɪŋ] quälend; aufreizend; verlockend.

tap [tæp] **I** s 1. Wasserhahn; Spund m; *on* ~ (*Bier*) vom Faß; 2. Klopfen n; **II** v 3. anzapfen a. el; 4. klopfen (*on, at* an, auf).

tape [teɪp] 1. Band n; Streifen m; 2. Tonband n.

taper ['teɪpə] **I** s dünne (Wachs-)Kerze f; **II** v (~ *off*) spitz zulaufen.

tape-recorder ['teɪprɪˌkɔ:də] Bandaufnahmegerät n.

tapestry ['tæpɪstrɪ] Gobelin m.

tar [tɑ:] Teer m.

target ['tɑ:gɪt] 1. Schießscheibe f; 2. Ziel n.

tariff ['tærɪf] (Zoll-)Tarif m.

tarnish ['tɑ:nɪʃ] 1. *tech* matt werden; 2. *fig* beflecken.

tarpaulin [tɑːˈpɔːlɪn] Zeltplane *f.*

tart [tɑːt] **I** *adj* scharf, herb; **II** *s* Obsttorte *f.*

tartan [ˈtɑːtən] Schottenmuster *n.*

tartar [ˈtɑːtə] 1. Weinstein *m;* 2. Zahnstein *m.*

task [tɑːsk] Aufgabe *f.*

taste [teɪst] **I** *v* 1. schmecken (*of* nach); 2. *(Speise)* kosten, probieren; 3. *fig* erleben; **II** *s* Geschmack *m;* ~**ful** [ˈ-ful] geschmackvoll; ~**less** [ˈ-lɪs] fade.

tasty [teɪstɪ] wohlschmeckend.

tatter [ˈtætə] *in* ~s in Lumpen; ~**ed** [-d] zerlumpt.

tattoo [təˈtuː] **I** *s mil* Zapfenstreich *m;* **II** *v* tätowieren.

taunt [tɔːnt] verspotten.

Taurus [ˈtɔːrəs] *astr* Stier *m.*

tax [tæks] **I** *v* besteuern; **II** *s* Steuer *f (on* auf*); income* ~ Einkommen(s)steuer *f;* ~**ation** [tækˈseɪʃn] Besteuerung *f;* ~**free** [ˈ-friː] steuerfrei.

taxi [ˈtæksɪ] Taxe *f,* Taxi *n;* ~**-driver** [-draɪvə] Taxifahrer *m;* ~ **rank** Taxistand *m.*

tax-payer [ˈtæksˌpeɪə] Steuerzahler *m.*

tea [tiː] Tee *m; have* ~ Tee trinken; ~**-bag** [ˈ-bæg] Teebeutel *m.*

teach [tiːtʃ] *irr* taught, taught [tɔːt] lehren, unterrichten; ~**er** [ˈ-ə] Lehrer(in *f*) *m.*

teacup [ˈtiːkʌp] Teetasse *f.*

team [tiːm] 1. Team *n,* Arbeitsgruppe *f;* 2. *sport* Mannschaft *f;* 3. Gespann *n;* ~**-work** [ˈ-wɜːk] Zs.-, Gemeinschaftsarbeit *f.*

teapot [ˈtiːpɔt] Teekanne *f.*

tear [teə] **I** *v irr* tore [tɔː], torn [tɔːn] 1. zerreißen; ~ *to pieces, to bits* in Stücke reißen; 2. herausreißen (*from* aus); 3. *(Haare)* sich raufen; **II** *s* 4. Riß *m;* 5. [tɪə] Träne *f; burst into* ~s in Tränen ausbrechen.

tearoom [ˈtiːruːm] Teestube *f;* Café *n.*

tease [tiːz] hänseln (*about* wegen).

teaspoon [ˈtiːspuːn] Teelöffel *m.*

teat [tiːt] 1. Schnuller *m;* 2. *zoo* Zitze *f.*

techn|ical [ˈteknɪkl] technisch; ~**ician** [tekˈnɪʃn] Fachmann *m;* ~**ique** [tekˈniːk] Technik *f.*

tedious [ˈtiːdjəs] langweilig, uninteressant.

teem [tiːm] in Strömen regnen.

teen|ager [ˈtiːnˌeɪdʒə] Teenager *m;* ~**s** [tiːns] *she is still in her* ~ sie ist noch nicht 20.

teeth [tiːθ] *s. tooth.*

teetotal(l)er [tiːˈtəutlə] Abstinenzler *m.*

telecommunications *pl* [ˈtelɪkəˌmjuːnɪˈkeɪʃnz] Fernmeldewesen *n.*

telegram ['telɪgræm] Telegramm *n*.

telegraph ['telɪgrɑːf] **I** *s* Telegraf *m*; **II** *v* telegrafieren.

telephone ['telɪfəʊn] **I** *s* Telefon *n*; ~ *booth*, ~ *box* Fernsprechzelle *f*; ~ *directory* Telefonbuch *n*; **II** *v* telefonieren.

telephoto lens [ˌtelɪ'fəʊtəʊ lenz] Teleobjektiv *n*.

teleprinter ['telɪˌprɪntə] Fernschreiber *m*.

telescope ['telɪskəʊp] **I** *s* Teleskop *n*; **II** *v* sich inea.schieben; ~**ic lens** [ˌtelɪ'skɒpɪk lenz] Teleobjektiv *n*.

televis|e ['telɪvaɪz] im Fernsehen übertragen; ~**ion** ['telɪˌvɪʒn] 1. Fernsehen *n*; *see s.th. on* ~ etw im Fernsehen sehen; 2. (~ *set*) Fernsehapparat *m*.

tell [tel] *irr* told, told [təʊld] 1. sagen; mitteilen; erzählen; 2. befehlen (*s.o.* jdm); 3. unterscheiden (*from* von); 4. *you never can* ~ man kann nie wissen.

teller ['telə] Kassenbeamte(r) *m*.

telltale ['telteɪl] verräterisch.

temper ['tempə] **I** *v* 1. mildern; 2. (*Stahl*) härten; **II** *s* (*bad* ~) schlechte Laune *f*; *get, fly into a* ~ *about* ärgerlich werden über.

temperament ['tempərəmənt] Temperament *n*.

temper|ance ['tempərəns] 1. Mäßigkeit *f*; 2. Abstinenz *f*; ~**ate** ['tempərət] 1. zurückhaltend; 2. (*Klima*) gemäßigt.

temperature ['temprətʃə] 1. Temperatur *f*; 2. *have, run a* ~ Fieber haben.

tempest ['tempɪst] Sturm *m*.

temple ['templ] 1. Tempel *m*; 2. *anat* Schläfe *f*.

temporary ['tempərərɪ] zeitweilig; vorläufig.

tempt [tempt] verlocken; in Versuchung führen; *a* ~*ing offer* ein verlockendes Angebot; ~**ation** [temp'teɪʃn] Versuchung *f*; ~**ing** ['-ɪŋ] verführerisch.

ten [ten] zehn.

tenacious [tɪ'neɪʃəs] *fig* zäh, beharrlich; (*Gedächtnis*) gut.

tenant ['tenənt] Pächter, Mieter *m*.

tend [tend] 1. neigen, tendieren (*to, towards* zu); 2. sich kümmern um; *Am* bedienen; ~**ency** ['-ənsɪ] *fig* Hang *m*, Neigung *f*.

tender ['tendə] **I** *v*: ~ *exact fare!* Fahrgeld abgezählt bereithalten! **II** *s* 1. Kosten(vor)anschlag *m*; 2. *mar* Leichter *m*; 3. *bar*~ Barmixer *m*; **III** *adj* 4. weich, zart, saftig; 5. *fig* zärtlich, liebevoll; 6. *touch s.o. on a* ~ *spot* jds wunden Punkt berühren; ~**ness** [-nɪs] 1. Zartheit *f*; 2. Zärtlichkeit *f*.

tenement ['tenɪmənt] (~-house) Mietshaus n.

tennis ['tenɪs] Tennis n; ~-court Tennisplatz m.

tens|e [tens] **I** adj 1. gespannt, straff; 2. fig spannungsgeladen; **II** v: be ~d up sehr nervös sein; **III** s gram Zeitform f; ~ion ['tenʃn] Spannung f a. fig.

tent [tent] Zelt n a. med.

tenth [tenθ] **I** adj zehnt; **II** s Zehntel n.

tent|-peg ['tentpeg] Hering m; ~-pole ['-pəʊl] Zeltstange f.

tenuous ['tenjʊəs] dünn, fein.

tepid ['tepɪd] lau(warm).

term [tɜːm] 1. Frist, Dauer; Laufzeit f; 2. (~ of office) Amtsdauer, -zeit f; 3. jur Sitzungsperiode f; 4. (Schule, Univ.) Trimester, Semester n; 5. gram Terminus m; 6. (Vertrags-, Zahlungs-)Bedingungen f pl; come to ~s sich einigen (with s.o. mit jdm); 7. pl Beziehungen f pl; be on good ~s with s.o. mit jdm auf gutem Fuße stehen.

terminal ['tɜːmɪnl] Endstation f; Terminal m od n.

terminate ['tɜːmɪneɪt] aufhören; enden.

terminology [ˌtɜːmɪ'nɒlədʒɪ] Terminologie f.

terminus ['tɜːmɪnəs] pl -nuses od -ni [-naɪ] Endstation f.

termite ['tɜːmaɪt] ent Termite f.

terrace ['terəs] Terrasse f.

terrib|le ['terəbl] fürchterlich; ~ly [-ɪ] fam furchtbar, sehr.

terrif|ic [tə'rɪfɪk] 1. schrecklich; 2. fam großartig; ~y ['terɪfaɪ] erschrecken.

territor|ial [ˌterɪ'tɔːrɪəl] ~ waters (pl) Hoheitsgewässer n pl; ~y ['terɪtərɪ] Gebiet n.

terror ['terə] Schreck(en); pol Terror m; ~ist ['-rɪst] Terrorist m; ~ize ['-raɪz] terrorisieren.

test [test] **I** s Prüfung f, Test m; put to the ~ auf die Probe stellen; blood ~ Blutprobe f; **II** v prüfen; testen.

testament ['testəmənt] Testament n.

test case jur Präzedenzfall m.

testify ['testɪfaɪ] 1. aussagen über; 2. ~ to s.th. etw bestätigen.

testimon|ial [ˌtestɪ'məʊnjəl] Zeugnis n, Beurteilung f; ~y ['testɪmənɪ] Zeugenaussage f; bear ~ Zeugnis ablegen (to für).

test tube ['test tjuːb] Reagenzglas n.

text [tekst] 1. Text m; 2. (~book) Lehrbuch n.

textiles pl ['tekstaɪlz] Textilien pl.

texture ['tekstʃə] 1. Gewebe n a. fig; 2. Beschaffenheit f.

than [ðæn, ðən] als; you are

taller ~ he (is) du bist größer als er.

thank [θæŋk] **I** *v* danken (*s.o.* jdm; *for s.th.* für etw); **II** *s pl* Dank *m;* *~s (fam)* danke; *no, ~s* nein, danke; *~s to* dank *dat; ~ful* ['-ful] dankbar; *~less* ['-lɪs] undankbar; *~sgiving* ['-s,gɪvɪŋ] *(~ Day) (Am)* Erntedankfest *n.*

that I *adj, prn* [ðæt] *pl those* [ðəʊz] jene(r, s); der-, die-, das(jenige); *at ~* (noch) obendrein; **II** *prn* [ðət] der, die, das; welche(r, s); **III** *conj* [ðət] daß; damit.

thaw [θɔ:] (auf)tauen (lassen).

the [ðə, ðɪ, ði:] der, die, das; *~ … ~* je … desto …; *all ~ better, worse* um so besser, schlimmer; *~ sooner ~ better* je eher, desto besser.

theatre, Am theater ['θɪətə] 1. Theater *n; ~-goer* Theaterbesucher *m;* 2. *operating ~* Operationssaal *m.*

theft [θeft] Diebstahl *m.*

their [ðeə] ihr(e); *~s* ['-z] der, die, das ihre, ihrige; *it's ~* es gehört ihnen.

them [ðem, ðəm] sie; *(to ~)* ihnen; *that's ~ (fam)* das sind sie.

theme [θi:m] Thema *n a. mus.*

themselves [ðəm'selvz] 1. *they … ~* sie … selbst; 2. sich (selbst); *all by ~* ganz allein.

then [ðen] **I** *adv* 1. damals;

before ~ vorher; 2. dann, darauf; *what ~?* was dann? 3. *by ~* zu der Zeit; bis dahin; *from ~ onwards* von da an; *until ~* bis dahin; *~ and there, there and ~* auf der Stelle; **II** *adj* damalig.

theoretic(al) [θɪə'retɪk(l)] theoretisch; *~y* ['θɪərɪ] Theorie *f.*

therap|eutic(al) [θerə'pju:tɪk(əl)] therapeutisch; *~y* ['θerəpɪ] Therapie *f.*

there [ðeə] **I** *adj* dort, da; *here and ~* hier u. da; gelegentlich; *over ~* dort drüben; *~ is, are* es ist, sind; *es gibt; ~ you are!* da hast du's! **II** *interj* na! na also! *~, ~!* schon gut! *~, that's enough* so, nun ist's aber genug; *~fore* ['ðeəfɔ:] deshalb.

thermometer [θə'mɒmɪtə] Thermometer *n.*

thermos ['θɜ:mɒs] *(~ flask)* Thermosflasche *f.*

thermostat ['θɜ:məʊstæt] Thermostat *m.*

these *s. this.*

they [ðeɪ] *prn* sie *pl;* man; es.

thick [θɪk] **I** *adj* 1. dick; 2. dicht; 3. *~ with* voll von; **II** *s: in the ~ of* mitten in; *~en* ['-ən] 1. dicker machen, werden; 2. dichter werden; *~ness* ['-nɪs] Dicke, Stärke *f; ~set* ['-set] 1. dicht gepflanzt; 2. untersetzt.

thief [θi:f] *pl thieves* Dieb *m.*

thigh [θaɪ] (Ober-)Schenkel *m*.

thimble ['θɪmbl] Fingerhut *m*.

thin [θɪn] 1. dünn; 2. mager; 3. spärlich, dürftig; 4. wäss(e)rig; 5. *(Ausrede)* fadenscheinig.

thing [θɪŋ] Ding *n*, Sache *f*; *first* ~ zuallererst; *that was a near* ~*!* das wäre beinahe schiefgegangen.

think [θɪŋk] *irr* thought, thought [θɔːt] 1. (nach)denken; 2. glauben, meinen; *I* ~ *so* ich denke schon; 3. beabsichtigen *(of doing s.th* etw zu tun); 4. ~ *highly, much of* viel halten von; ~ **over** überdenken, -legen; ~ **up** sich ausdenken; ~**ing** ['-ɪŋ] *to my* ~ meiner Meinung nach.

third [θɜːd] **I** *adj* dritt; **II** *s* Drittel *n*.

thirst [θɜːst] 1. Durst *m a. fig; satisfy, quench o.'s* ~ den Durst löschen; 2. *fig* Sehnsucht *f (for* nach); ~**y** ['-ɪ] durstig.

thirteen [ˌθɜːˈtiːn] dreizehn; ~**y** ['θɜːtɪ] dreißig.

this [ðɪs] *pl* these [ðiːz] **I** *adj* dies(e, er, es); ~ *day week* heute in acht Tagen; ~ *morning, evening, night* heute morgen, abend, nacht; **II** *prn: after* ~ danach; *before* ~ zuvor; **III** *adv (fam)* so; ~ *much* so viel.

thistle ['θɪsl] Distel *f*.

thorn [θɔːn] Dorn *m; that's a* ~ *in my flesh (fig)* das ist mir ein Dorn im Auge; ~**y** ['-ɪ] dornig *a. fig*.

thorough ['θʌrə] sorgfältig; ~**bred** [-bred] Vollblut(pferd) *n;* ~**fare** [-feə] Durchgangsstraße *f; no* ~*!* keine Durchfahrt! ~**ly** [-lɪ] 1. gründlich; 2. gänzlich.

those *s.* that.

though [ðəʊ] **I** *conj* 1. obgleich; 2. *as* ~ als ob; 3. *even* ~ obwohl; **II** *adv* indessen, doch.

thought [θɔːt] 1. (Nach-) Denken *n;* Überlegung *f; after serious* ~, *on second* ~*s* nach reiflicher Überlegung; 2. Gedanke *m;* 3. *have no* ~ *of* nicht die Absicht haben *(doing s.th* etw zu tun); ~**ful** ['-fʊl] 1. nachdenklich; 2. aufmerksam, rücksichtsvoll; ~**less** ['-lɪs] 1. rücksichtslos *(of* gegen); 2. unbekümmert *(of* um).

thousand ['θaʊznd] tausend.

thrash [θræʃ] (ver)prügeln; ~**ing** ['-ɪŋ] Tracht *f* Prügel.

thread [θred] **I** *s* Faden *m a. fig; lose the* ~ *(fig)* den Faden verlieren; **II** *v* 1. einfädeln; 2. *(Film)* einlegen; 3. ~ *o.'s way through* sich durchschlängeln; ~**bare** ['-beə] fadenscheinig.

threat [θret] 1. Drohung *f;* 2. Bedrohung, Gefahr *f;* ~**en** ['-n] drohen *a. fig;* ~ *s.o. with s.th* jdm mit etw drohen; **~ening** ['-nɪŋ] drohend.

three [θri:] drei.

thresh [θreʃ] dreschen.

threshold ['θreʃhəʊld] 1. (Tür-)Schwelle f; 2. fig Beginn m.

thrifty ['θrɪftɪ] sparsam.

thrill [θrɪl] I v 1. erregen, packen, aufwühlen; 2. zittern, beben (with vor); II s Schauer m, Erregung f; give s.o. a ~ jdn in Erregung versetzen; **~er** ['-ə] Thriller m.

thriv|e [θraɪv] a. irr throve [θrəʊv], **thriven** ['θrɪvn] 1. (gut) gedeihen; 2. fig Erfolg haben; **~ing** ['-ɪŋ] fig blühend.

throat [θrəʊt] 1. Kehle f; 2. Hals m.

throb [θrob] (Herz) schlagen.

throne [θrəʊn] Thron m.

throng [θroŋ] Gedränge n.

throttle ['θrotl] 1. erdrosseln, erwürgen; 2. mot (ab)drosseln.

through [θru:] I prp 1. durch; 2. infolge gen; 3. (ver)mittels gen; II adv 4. read ~ durchlesen; 5. be ~ durch, fertig sein, abgeschlossen haben (with mit); III adj durchgehend; **~out** [-'aʊt] I prp: ~ the country im ganzen Land; ~ the year das ganze Jahr hindurch; II adv 1. die ganze Zeit (über); 2. ganz (u. gar), völlig, vollständig.

throw [θrəʊ] I v irr threw [θru:], **thrown** [θrəʊn] werfen; II s Wurf m.

thrush [θrʌʃ] orn Drossel f.

thrust [θrʌst] I v irr thrust, thrust 1. stoßen; 2. sich drängen (into in; through durch); II s 3. Stoß m; 4. tech Schub m.

thud [θʌd] dumpf aufschlagen.

thug [θʌg] Mörder, Gangster, Rowdy m.

thumb [θʌm] I s Daumen m; his fingers are all ~s er hat zwei linke Hände; ~s up! bravo! II v 1. (Buch) durchblättern; 2. ~ a lift, a ride (fam) per Anhalter fahren; **~-tack** ['-tæk] Am Reißnagel m.

thump [θʌmp] I s dumpfe(r) Schlag m; II v 1. puffen, knuffen; 2. dumpf aufschlagen; 3. (Herz) laut pochen (with vor).

thunder ['θʌndə] I s Donner m a. fig; II v donnern a. fig; **~clap** [-klæp] Donnerschlag m a. fig; **~ous** [-rəs] donnernd a. fig; **~storm** [-stɔ:m] Gewitter n; **~struck** [-strʌk] fig wie vom Schlag getroffen; **~y** ['-rɪ] gewitt(e)rig.

Thursday ['θɜ:zdɪ] Donnerstag m.

thus [ðʌs] 1. so, auf diese Weise; 2. infolgedessen; 3. ~ far so weit; bis jetzt.

thwart [θwɔ:t] (Plan) durchkreuzen.

thyroid ['θaɪ(ə)rɔɪd]
(~ *gland*) Schilddrüse *f.*

tick [tɪk] **I** *v* 1. ticken; 2. abhaken; **II** *s* 3. Ticken *n; in a ~, in two ~s* gleich, sofort; 4. Häkchen *n;* 5. *ent* Zecke *f.*

ticket ['tɪkɪt] 1. (Eintritts-, Theater-, Fahr-, Flug-)Karte *f;* 2. Etikett *n;* Preiszettel *m;* 3. *fam* gebührenpflichtige Verwarnung *f;* ~**-office** [-ɒfɪs] Fahrkartenschalter *m.*

tickl|e ['tɪkl] kitzeln *a. fig;* ~**ish** ['-ɪʃ] 1. *(Mensch)* kitz(e)lig; 2. *(Sache)* heikel.

tidal wave ['taɪdl weɪv] Flutwelle *f.*

tidbit *Am* s. titbit.

tide [taɪd] Ebbe u. Flut *f,* Gezeiten *pl.*

tidy ['taɪdɪ] **I** *adj* sauber, ordentlich; **II** *v* sauber machen.

tie [taɪ] **I** *v* 1. (an-, fest-, zs-, zu)binden; *be ~d up (fig)* lahmgelegt sein; beschäftigt sein (*with* mit); 2. *sport* unentschieden spielen; punktgleich sein; **II** *s* 3. Band *n a. fig;* 4. *fig* Verpflichtung *f;* 5. *(neck~)* Krawatte *f;* 6. *the game ended in a ~* das Spiel endete unentschieden.

tier [tɪə] (Sitz-)Reihe *f; theat* Rang *m.*

tiff [tɪf] Verstimmung *f.*

tiger ['taɪgə] Tiger *m.*

tight [taɪt] **I** *adj* 1. (luft-, wasser)dicht; 2. straff, eng(anliegend); 3. *com* knapp; 4. *fam*

(betrunken) blau; **II** *adv hold* ~ festhalten; *sit* ~ sich nicht rühren; *fig* nicht nachgeben; ~**s** *pl* [-s] 1. Trikot *n;* 2. Strumpfhose *f;* ~**en** ['-n] zs.ziehen, enger machen; ~**-fisted** ['-ˌfɪstɪd] knauserig; ~**-rope** ['-rəʊp] (Draht-)Seil *n;* ~ *walker* Seiltänzer *m.*

tile [taɪl] **I** *s* 1. (Dach-)Ziegel *m;* 2. Kachel, Fliese *f;* **II** *v* kacheln.

till [tɪl] **I** *prp:* ~ *now* bis jetzt; ~ *then* bis dahin; **II** *conj* bis; **III** *v (Boden)* (be)ackern.

tilt [tɪlt] kippen; schief halten.

timber ['tɪmbə] 1. Nutzholz *n;* 2. Balken *m.*

time [taɪm] **I** *s* 1. Zeit(raum *m,* -spanne), (Zeit-)Dauer *f; all the* ~ die ganze Zeit (über); *for the* ~ *being* vorläufig; *from* ~ *to* ~ von Zeit zu Zeit; *in* ~ rechtzeitig; *on* ~ pünktlich; *once upon a* ~ *(there was)* (es war) einmal; *have a good* ~ sich gut unterhalten; *take* ~ Zeit erfordern; ~ *is up* die Zeit ist (her)um, vorbei; *local* ~ Ortszeit *f; summer* ~ Sommerzeit *f;* ~ *of arrival, of departure* Ankunfts-, Abfahrtszeit *f;* 2. Mal *n; another* ~ ein andermal; *at* ~s manchmal; *every* ~ jedesmal; *next* ~ das nächste Mal; *this* ~ diesmal; 3. *mus* Takt *m;* **II** *v* 4. zeitlich abstimmen; 5. die Zeit messen, (ab)stoppen; ~**lag** ['-læg] Verzögerung *f;* ~**ly** ['-li] 1. rechtzeitig; 2. opportun; ~**-saving** ['-ˌseɪvɪŋ] zeitsparend; ~**table** ['-ˌteɪbl] 1. *rail* Fahrplan *m; aero* Flugplan *m;* 2. *(Schule)* Stundenplan *m.*

timid ['tɪmɪd] 1. furchtsam; 2. schüchtern.

timing ['taɪmɪŋ] zeitliche Festlegung *f.*

tin [tɪn] **I** *s* 1. Zinn; Weißblech *n;* 2. Konservendose *f;* **II** *v* eindosen; ~**ned fruit** Obstkonserven *f pl;* ~**ned meat** Büchsenfleisch *n;* ~**foil** Stanniol *n.*

tinge [tɪndʒ] **I** *v* tönen (*with* mit); **II** *s* Tönung; *fig* (leichte) Spur *f (of* von).

tingle ['tɪŋgl] prickeln.

tin-opener ['tɪnəʊpənə] Dosenöffner *m.*

tinsel ['tɪnsl] Flitter(gold *n*) *m.*

tint [tɪnt] leicht färben, tönen.

tiny ['taɪnɪ] winzig.

tip [tɪp] **I** *s* 1. Spitze *f; (Zigarette)* Mundstück *n; I have it on the ~ of my tongue (fig)* es liegt mir auf der Zunge; 2. Trinkgeld *n;* 3. Tip *m;* **II** *v* 4. (leicht) berühren; 5. ein Trinkgeld geben (*s.o.* jdm); 6. ~ *s.o. off (fam)* jdm e-en Tip, Wink geben; 7. kippen; ~ *over* umkippen; ~ *the scale (fig)* den Ausschlag geben; ~~**-off** ['-ɒf] Hinweis *m;* Warnung *f.*

tipsy ['tɪpsɪ] beschwipst.

tiptoe ['tɪptəʊ] *on* ~ auf Zehenspitzen.

tire ['taɪə] **I** *v* ermüden; müde werden (*of doing s.th.* etw zu tun); ~ *out* völlig erschöpfen; **II** *s Am s.* tyre; ~**d** [-d] müde, erschöpft; *be* ~ *of s.th.* etw satt haben; ~**less** [-lɪs] unermüdlich; ~**some** [-səm] ermüdend; langweilig.

tissue ['tɪʃuː] 1. Gewebe *n a. biol;* 2. Papiertaschentuch *n;* ~ **paper** Seidenpapier *n.*

tit [tɪt] 1. *orn* Meise *f;* 2. *give* ~ *for tat* mit gleicher Münze heimzahlen.

titbit ['tɪtbɪt] , *Am* **tidbit** ['tɪdbɪt] Leckerbissen *m a. fig.*

title ['taɪtl] 1. Titel *m;* 2. *(Kapitel)* Überschrift *f.*

to [tuː, tʊ, tə] **I** *prp* zu; um zu; nach; bis zu; *I did it* ~ *help you* ich tat es nur, um dir zu helfen; *compare* ~ vergleichen mit; *go* ~ *school* zur Schule gehen; *tear* ~ *pieces* in Stücke reißen; *from beginning* ~ *end* von Anfang bis Ende; **II** *adv: walk* ~ *and fro* auf u. ab gehen; *the door blew* ~ die Tür schlug zu.

toad [təʊd] Kröte *f a. fig;* ~**stool** ['-stuːl] (Gift-)Pilz *m.*

toady ['təʊdɪ] Speichellecker *m.*

toast [təʊst] **I** *v* 1. rösten;

2. trinken auf (*s.o.* jdn); **II** *s*
3. Toast *m;* 4. Trinkspruch
m.

tobacco [təˈbækəʊ] *pl* -os
Tabak *m;* ~**nist**
[təˈbækənɪst] Tabakhändler
m.

toboggan [təˈbɒgən] Rodel(schlitten) *m.*

today [təˈdeɪ] heute; heutzutage.

toe [təʊ] **I** *s* Zehe *f;* Fußspitze *f;* **II** *v:* ~ the line (*fig*)
nicht aus der Reihe tanzen;
fam spuren; ~-**nail** [ˈ-neɪl]
Zehennagel *m.*

toffee [ˈtɒfɪ] Karamelbonbon
m od *n.*

together [təˈgeðə] zusammen; miteinander.

toil [tɔɪl] **I** *v* sich plagen,
schwer arbeiten; **II** *s* Mühe
f.

toilet [ˈtɔɪlɪt] 1. Toilette, Kleidung *f;* 2. Toilette *f,* Klosett
n; ~-**paper** [-ˌpeɪpə] Toilettenpapier *n.*

token [ˈtəʊkən] Zeichen,
Symbol *n;* Andenken *n.*

tolerabl|e [ˈtɒlərəbl] erträglich; ~**y** [-ɪ] leidlich, ziemlich.

toleran|ce [ˈtɒlərəns] Toleranz *f a.* tech; ~**t** [ˈ-ənt] tolerant.

tolera|te [ˈtɒləreɪt] dulden,
zulassen; ~**ion** [ˌtɒləˈreɪʃn]
Duldung *f.*

toll [təʊl] **I** *s* 1. Maut *f;* 2. *fig*
Zoll, Tribut *m; it took a
heavy* ~ *of life* es hat viele

Menschenleben gekostet;
II *v* (*Glocke*) läuten.

tomato [təˈmɑːtəʊ] *pl* -toes
Tomate *f;* ~ **juice** Tomatensaft *m.*

tomb [tuːm] Grab; (~*stone*)
Grabmal *n,* -stein *m.*

tomcat [ˈtɒmkæt] Kater *m.*

tomorrow [təˈmɒrəʊ] **I** *adv*
morgen; ~ *morning* morgen
früh; **II** *s* der morgige Tag.

ton [tʌn] Tonne *f;* ~**s** *of* e-e
Menge.

tone [təʊn] **I** *s* Ton *m;* **II** *v*
(ab)tönen; ~ *down* dämpfen;
~ *in* harmonieren (*with* mit).

tongs *pl* [tɒŋz] *a pair of* ~
e-e Zange.

tongue [tʌŋ] 1. *anat* Zunge *f;*
hold o.'s ~ den Mund halten;
2. *fig* Sprache *f.*

tonic [ˈtɒnɪk] *pharm* Stärkungsmittel *n.*

tonight [təˈnaɪt] heute abend,
heute nacht.

tonsil [ˈtɒnsl] *anat* Mandel *f;*
~**litis** [ˌtɒnsɪˈlaɪtɪs] Mandelentzündung *f.*

too [tuː] 1. (*vorangestellt*) zu,
allzu, gar zu; 2. (*nachgestellt*) auch, eben-, gleichfalls.

tool [tuːl] Werkzeug, Gerät
n.

toot [tuːt] tuten, hupen.

tooth [tuːθ] *pl teeth* [tiːθ]
Zahn *m a.* tech; ~**ache**
[ˈ-eɪk] Zahnschmerzen *m pl;*
~**brush** [ˈ-brʌʃ] Zahnbürste
f; ~**paste** [ˈ-peɪst] Zahnpa

sta f; **~pick** ['-pɪk] Zahnstocher m.

top [tɒp] **I** s 1. Kopf, Scheitel m; from ~ to bottom von oben bis unten; from ~ to toe von Kopf bis Fuß; 2. (Baum) Gipfel m; (Berg) Spitze f; 3. obere Seite f; on ~ oben(auf); 4. fig Gipfel, Höhepunkt m; 5. at the ~ of o.'s voice aus vollem Halse; 6. Kreisel m; sleep like a ~ wie ein Murmeltier schlafen; **II** v an der Spitze stehen (s.th. e-r S); (e-e Liste) anführen.

topic ['tɒpɪk] Thema n.

top|less ['tɒplɪs] oben ohne; **~most** ['-məust] oberst; **~ secret** streng (vertraulich u.) geheim.

topsyturvy [,tɒpsɪ'tɜ:vɪ] kopfüber; turn ~ das Oberste zuunterst kehren.

torch [tɔ:tʃ] 1. Taschenlampe f; 2. Fackel f a. fig.

torment I s ['tɔ:ment] Qual f; **II** v [tɔ:'ment] quälen.

torrent ['tɒrənt] Sturzbach m.

tortoise ['tɔ:təs] Schildkröte f.

tortuous ['tɔ:tjuəs] gewunden.

torture ['tɔ:tʃə] **I** s Folter f; **II** v foltern.

Tory ['tɔ:rɪ] (engl.) Konservative(r) m.

toss [tɒs] **I** v 1. (~ about) schleudern, werfen; 2. ~ up

(durch Werfen e-r Münze) losen (for um); **II** s Wurf m.

total ['təutl] **I** adj ganz, völlig, gesamt; **II** s Gesamtbetrag m; **III** v 1. (~ up) zs.zählen, -rechnen; 2. sich belaufen (to auf).

totter ['tɒtə] (sch)wanken; wackeln.

touch [tʌtʃ] **I** v 1. be-, anrühren, anfassen; 2. (seelisch) rühren; 3. angehen, betreffen; 4. ~ up vervollkommnen; **II** s 5. (leichte) Berührung f; 6. Pinselstrich m; 7. be, keep in ~ with in Verbindung stehen, bleiben mit; 8. it was a near ~ das wäre beinahe schiefgegangen; **~y** ['-ɪ] heikel, riskant.

tough [tʌf] 1. zäh; 2. widerstandsfähig; 3. hartnäckig; 4. schwierig; ~ **luck** fam Pech n.

tour [tuə] **I** s Rundreise f; conducted ~ Gesellschaftsreise f; **II** v e-e (Rund-)Reise machen; **~ism** ['-rɪzm] Fremdenverkehr m; **~ist** ['-rɪst] Tourist m; ~ office Verkehrsamt n.

tow [təu] **I** v mot (ab)schleppen; **II** s: take in ~ ins Schlepptau nehmen a. fig.

toward(s) [tə'wɔ:d(z)] 1. in Richtung auf a. fig; 2. gegenüber dat; auf ... hin; 3. um ... willen; 4. ~ evening gegen Abend.

towel ['tauəl] Handtuch n.

tower ['tauə] **I** s Turm m;

II *v* überragen (*above s.o.* jdn); **~ing** [-rɪŋ] *(Wut)* rasend.

town [taʊn] Stadt *f*; ~ **hall** Rathaus *n*; ~ **planning** Stadtplanung *f*.

toy [tɔɪ] I *s* Spielzeug *n*; II *v* spielen *a. fig* (*with* mit); **~shop** ['-ʃɒp] Spielwarenhandlung *f*.

trace [treɪs] I *s* Spur *f a. fig*; II *v* 1. nachspüren (*s.o.* jdm); 2. aufspüren; 3. *(Ereignisse)* (~ *back*) zurückverfolgen; 4. (~ *out*) entwerfen; 5. zeichnen; durchpausen.

track [træk] I *s* 1. Spur *f*; *cover up o.'s ~s (fig)* s-e Spur verwischen; *keep ~ of s.o.* jdn im Auge behalten; 2. Weg *m*; 3. *rail* Gleis *n*; II *v*: ~ *down* aufspüren, ausfindig machen.

trade [treɪd] I *s* 1. Handwerk *n*; *by ~* von Beruf; 2. *com* Handel *m*; II *v* Handel treiben (*in s.th.* mit e-r S; *with s.o.* mit jdm); **~-mark** ['-mɑːk] Schutzmarke *f*; **~r** ['-ə] Kaufmann *m*; **~-union** [ˌ-'juːnjən] Gewerkschaft *f*.

tradition [trə'dɪʃn] Tradition *f*; **~al** [-l] traditionell, üblich.

traffic ['træfɪk] I *s* 1. Verkehr *m*; 2. Handel *m*; II *v* handeln (*in s.th.* mit etw, *with s.o.* mit jdm); ~ **light(s)** Verkehrsampel *f*.

trag|edy ['trædʒɪdɪ] Tragödie *f a. fig*; **~ic(al)** ['trædʒɪk(l)] tragisch *a. fig*.

trail [treɪl] I *v* 1. hinter sich herschleifen; 2. aufspüren; II *s* 3. *(Rauch)* Fahne *f*; 4. Spur *f*; *(hot) on the ~ (fig)* (dicht) auf der Spur; 5. (Trampel-)Pfad *m*; **~er** ['-ə] 1. (~ *car*) Wohnwagen *m*; 2. (Film-)Vorschau *f*.

train [treɪn] I *s* (Eisenbahn-)Zug *m*; *get into, get on, (Am) board a ~* in e-n Zug einsteigen; II *v* schulen, ausbilden (*for* für); *sport* trainieren.

train|ee [treɪ'niː] Lehrgangsteilnehmer *m*; **~er** ['treɪnə] Trainer *m*.

train ferry Eisenbahnfähre *f*.

training ['treɪnɪŋ] Schulung *f*; Training *n*; *in, out of ~ (sport)* in, aus der Übung.

trait [treɪt] (Charakter-, Wesens-, Gesichts-)Zug *m*.

traitor ['treɪtə] Verräter *m*.

tram [træm] Straßenbahn *f*.

tramp [træmp] I *v* 1. zu Fuß gehen, marschieren; 2. trampeln; sta(m)pfen; II *s* Landstreicher *m*; **~le** ['-l] herumtrampeln (*on* auf).

trance [trɑːns] *fall into a ~* in Trance verfallen.

tranquil ['træŋkwɪl] ruhig; **~(l)izer** [-aɪzə] *pharm* Beruhigungsmittel *n*.

transatlantic [ˌtrænzət'læntɪk] transatlantisch.

transcribe [træn'skraɪb] 1. *(Stenogramm)* übertragen; 2. *radio* auf Band aufnehmen.

transfer I *v* ['træns'fɜ:]
1. verlegen (*from ... to* von ... nach); versetzen (*to* nach); 2. übertragen;
3. (*Geld*) überweisen; **II** *s* ['trænsfɜ:] 4. Verlegung; Versetzung *f;* 5. *jur* Übertragung *f.*

transform [træns'fɔ:m] umwandeln; **~ation** [ˌtrænsfə'meiʃn] Verwandlung *f;* **~er** [-'fɔ:mə] *el* Transformator *m.*

transfusion [træns'fju:ʒn] Blutübertragung *f.*

transit ['trænsit] Durchgang *m; in ~* unterwegs, auf dem Transport; **~ camp** Durchgangslager *n;* **~ visa** Durchreisevisum *n.*

translat|e [træns'leit] übersetzen; **~ion** [-'leiʃn] Übersetzung *f;* **~or** [-'leitə] Übersetzer *m.*

transmission [trænz'miʃn]
1. *tech* Transmission *f;*
2. *radio* Übertragung *f.*

transmit [trænz'mit] 1. übertragen; 2. *radio* senden; **~ter** [-ə] Sender *m.*

transparent [træns'pærənt] durchsichtig.

transpire [træn'spaiə]
1. schwitzen; 2. *fig* durchsickern.

transplant [træns'plɑ:nt] verpflanzen.

transport I *v* [træn'spɔ:t] befördern, transportieren;

II *s* ['trænspɔ:t] Beförderung *f,* Transport *m.*

trap [træp] Falle *f a. fig.*

trash [træʃ] 1. *Am* Abfall *m;* 2. *fig* Schund, Kitsch; Unsinn *m;* **~can** ['-kæn] *Am* Abfalleimer *m;* **~y** ['-ı] wertlos; kitschig.

travel ['trævl] **I** *v* 1. reisen *a. com;* 2. sich fortbewegen; **II** *s* Reisen *n;* **~ agency, bureau** Reisebüro *n;* **~(l)er** [-ə] Reisende(r) *m a. com;* **~'s cheque,** *(Am)* check Reisescheck *m.*

traverse ['trævəs] durch-, überqueren.

trawler ['trɔ:lə] Trawler *m.*

tray [trei] 1. Brett, Tablett *n;* 2. *in-, out-~* Ablage *f* für eingehende, ausgehende Post.

treacher|ous ['tretʃərəs] verräterisch; unzuverlässig; **~y** [-rı] Verrat *m (to* an).

treacle ['tri:kl] Sirup *m.*

tread [tred] **I** *v irr* trod [trɔd], trod *od* trodden ['trɔdn] treten (*on* auf) *a. fig;* **~** *on air (fig)* im Glück schwimmen; **II** *s* 1. Tritt, Schritt *m;* 2. (Treppen-)Stufe *f;* 3. (*Gummireifen*) Profil *n.*

treason ['tri:zn] Verrat *m (to* an).

treasur|e ['treʒə] Schatz *m a. fig;* **~er** [-rə] Schatzmeister *m;* **~y** [-rı] Finanz-. Staatskasse *f.*

treat [tri:t] 1. behandeln; 2. bewirten, freihalten (*to* *s.th.* mit etw); 3. ver-, unterhandeln (*with* mit; *for* wegen); ~**ise** ['tri:tɪz] Abhandlung *f* (*upon, on* über); ~**ment** ['tri:tmənt] Behandlung *f;* ~**y** ['-ɪ] Vertrag *m.*

treble ['trebl] **I** *s* Sopran *m;* **II** *adj* dreifach.

tree [tri:] Baum *m.*

tremble ['trembl] zittern (*with* vor; *for* um).

tremendous [trɪ'mendəs] 1. gewaltig; 2. *fam* toll.

trem|or ['tremə] Zittern *n;* ~**ulous** ['tremjʊləs] zitternd.

trench [trentʃ] Graben *m.*

trend [trend] **I** *v* sich neigen, tendieren (*towards* nach); **II** *s* Tendenz *f.*

trespass ['trespəs] widerrechtlich betreten (*on, upon s.th.* etw); *no* ~*ing!* Betreten verboten! ~**er** ['-ə] ~*s will be prosecuted!* Betreten bei Strafe verboten!

trial ['traɪəl] 1. Versuch *m;* Probe; Prüfung *f; by* ~ *and error* durch Ausprobieren; *on* ~ auf *od* zur Probe; 2. *jur* (Gerichts-)Verhandlung *f; be on* ~ vor Gericht stehen.

triang|le ['traɪæŋgl] Dreieck *n;* ~**ular** [traɪ'æŋgjʊlə] dreieckig.

trib|al ['traɪbl] ~ *chief* Stammeshäuptling *m;* ~**e** [traɪb] (Volks-)Stamm *m.*

tribunal [traɪ'bju:nl] Gericht(shof *m*) *n.*

tributary ['trɪbjʊtərɪ] Nebenfluß *m.*

tribute ['trɪbju:t] Tribut *m a. fig; pay* (*a*) ~ *to s.o.* jdm Anerkennung zollen.

trick [trɪk] **I** *s* Kniff, Trick *m; play a* ~ *on s.o.* jdm e-n Streich spielen; **II** *v:* ~ *s.o. into doing s.th.* jdn dazu verleiten, etw zu tun; ~**ery** ['-ərɪ] Gaunerei *f.*

trickle ['trɪkl] tröpfeln *a. fig.*

tricky ['trɪkɪ] 1. durchtrieben; 2. kompliziert.

trifl|e ['traɪfl] Kleinigkeit *f; a* ~ ein bißchen; ~**ing** [-ɪŋ] gering(fügig).

trigger ['trɪgə] **I** *s* 1. Drücker *m;* 2. *phot* Auslöser *m;* **II** *v:* ~ *off* (*fig*) auslösen.

trill [trɪl] Triller *m.*

trim [trɪm] **I** *v* 1. ausputzen, beschneiden, stutzen; 2. garnieren; 3. *mar* trimmen; **II** *adj* ordentlich; sauber, nett; **III** *s: in good, proper* ~ in Form; ~**ming** ['-ɪŋ] 1. Besatz *m;* 2. *pl* Zutaten *f pl.*

Trinity ['trɪnɪtɪ] *rel* Dreieinigkeit *f.*

trinket ['trɪŋkɪt] Tand *m.*

trip [trɪp] **I** *v* 1. trippeln; 2. stolpern (*over* über); 3. ~ *s.o. up* jdm ein Bein stellen *a. fig;* **II** *s* 4. Ausflug *m,* Reise *f;* 5. Stolpern *n.*

tripl|e ['trɪpl] dreifach; ~**ets** *pl* [-ɪts] Drillinge *m pl;* ~**icate** [-ɪkət] *in* ~ in dreifacher Ausfertigung.

tripod ['traɪpɒd] *phot* Stativ *n.*

trite [traɪt] abgedroschen.

triumph ['traɪəmf] **I** *s* Triumph *m;* **II** *v* triumphieren (*over* über); **~ant** [traɪˈʌmfənt] triumphierend.

trivial ['trɪvɪəl] belanglos, unbedeutend.

trolley ['trɒlɪ] 1. Handkarren *m;* 2. (~-*bus*) Obus *m;* 3. (~-*car*) *Am* Straßenbahnwagen *m.*

trombone [trɒmˈbəʊn] Posaune *f.*

troop [tru:p] **I** *s* Schar, Gruppe *f;* **II** *v:* ~ *in, out* (in Scharen) hinein-, hinausströmen.

trophy ['trəʊfɪ] Trophäe *f.*

tropic ['trɒpɪk] *geog* Wendekreis *m;* **~al** [-l] tropisch.

trot [trɒt] **I** *v* trotten, traben; **II** *s* Trab *m a. fig; keep s.o. on the* ~ (*fig, fam*) jdn in Trab halten.

trouble ['trʌbl] **I** *v* 1. beunruhigen; *be* ~*d* sich Sorgen machen; 2. belästigen; stören; 3. *may I* ~ *you?* darf ich Sie bitten (*for* um; *to do* zu tun); **II** *s* 4. Mühe *f,* Umstände *m pl;* Unannehmlichkeiten *f pl;* 5. Sorgen *f pl;* Verdruß *m; what's the* ~? was ist los? 6. *pol* Unruhen *f pl;* 7. *med* Leiden *n;* **~some** [-səm] störend, lästig.

trough [trɒf] Trog *m.*

trousers *pl* ['traʊzəz] (*pair of* ~) (lange) Hose *f.*

trout [traʊt] *pl* ~ od ~*s* Forelle *f.*

truant ['tru:ənt] *play* ~ (die Schule) schwänzen.

truce [tru:s] *mil* Waffenstillstand *m.*

truck [trʌk] 1. *Am* Lastwagen *m;* 2. *Br* offene(r) Güterwagen *m;* 3. *have no* ~ *with s.o.* mit jdm nichts zu tun haben.

true [tru:] 1. wahr; *come* ~ Wirklichkeit werden; 2. genau; 3. echt, wirklich, tatsächlich.

truly ['tru:lɪ] 1. aufrichtig; *Yours* ~ hochachtungsvoll; 2. wirklich.

trump [trʌmp] **I** *s* Trumpf(karte *f*) *m a. fig;* **II** *v:* ~ *up* erfinden.

trumpet ['trʌmpɪt] **I** *s* Trompete *f;* **II** *v* trompeten.

truncheon ['trʌntʃən] (Gummi-)Knüppel *m.*

trundle ['trʌndl] (dahin)rollen; schieben.

trunk [trʌŋk] 1. (Baum-) Stamm *m a. fig;* 2. (*Mensch*) Rumpf *m;* 3. (*Elefant*) Rüssel *m;* 4. Koffer *m;* 5. *pl* Turn-, Badehose *f;* **~-call** ['-kɔːl] *tele* Ferngespräch *n;* **~-road** ['-rəʊd] Fern-, Autostraße *f.*

trust [trʌst] **I** *s* 1. Vertrauen *n; put o.s.'s* ~ *in s.o.* auf jdn sein Vertrauen setzen; 2. Treuhand(vermögen *n*) *f;* **II** *v* 3. vertrauen (*in, to* auf); 4. erwarten, hoffen, glauben;

~ee [ˌtrʌsˈtiː] Treuhänder, Verwalter m; **~ful** [ˈ-fʊl] , **~ing** [ˈ-ɪŋ] vertrauensvoll; **~worthy** [ˈ-ˌwɜːðɪ] vertrauensgemäß.

truth [truːθ] Wahrheit f; *to tell the ~* ehrlich gesagt; *there is no ~ in it* es ist nichts Wahres daran; **~ful** [ˈ-fʊl] 1. wahrheitsliebend; 2. wahrheitsgemäß.

try [traɪ] **I** v 1. versuchen; 2. ~ *s.th. out* etw ausprobieren; 3. ~ *on (Kleidung)* anprobieren; 4. sich bemühen *(for* um); 5. *jur* unter Anklage stellen; *(Fall)* verhandeln; **II** s Versuch m; *let me have a ~ at it* laß es mich versuchen.

tub [tʌb] 1. Faß n; Kübel m; 2. *fam* (Bade-)Wanne f.

tube [tjuːb] 1. Röhre f, Rohr n, Schlauch m; 2. *(in London)* U-Bahn f; 3. *bronchial* ~s *(anat)* Bronchien f pl; **~less** [ˈ-lɪs] *mot* schlauchlos.

tuber [ˈtjuːbə] *bot* Knolle f.

tuberculosis [tjuːˌbɜːkjʊˈləʊsɪs] Tuberkulose f.

tubular [ˈtjuːbjʊlə] röhrenförmig; ~ *furniture* Stahlrohrmöbel n pl.

tuck [tʌk] **I** v 1. (weg)stecken; 2. ~ *up* aufkrempeln; 3. ~ *up* behaglich einhüllen, zudecken; 4. ~ *in* e-n Saum nähen in; 5. ~ *in (beim Es-* sen) tüchtig zugreifen; **II** s Saum, Abnäher m.

Tuesday [ˈtjuːzdɪ] Dienstag m.

tuft [tʌft] Büschel n.

tug [tʌg] **I** v 1. ziehen, zerren, reißen *(at* an); 2. *mar* schleppen; **II** s 3. Zerren n; ~ *of war (sport)* Tauziehen n a. fig; 4. *mar (~-boat)* Schlepper m.

tuition [tjuːˈɪʃn] Unterricht m.

tulip [ˈtjuːlɪp] Tulpe f.

tumble [ˈtʌmbl] **I** v (hin)purzeln, hinfallen; stürzen; **II** s Sturz m.

tumbler [ˈtʌmblə] Trink-, Becherglas n.

tumo(u)r [ˈtjuːmə] Geschwulst f.

tumult [ˈtjuːmʌlt] Tumult m; **~uous** [tjuːˈmʌltjʊəs] lärmend; stürmisch.

tune [tjuːn] **I** s Melodie f; *be in ~ with* harmonieren mit; **II** v 1. *(Musikinstrument)* stimmen; 2. ~ *in (radio)* einstellen *(to* auf); 3. *fig* (aufea.) abstimmen; harmonisieren; **~r** [ˈ-ə] 1. *(piano)* ~ Klavierstimmer m; 2. *radio* Tuner m.

Tunisia [tjuːˈnɪzɪə] Tunesien n.

tunnel [ˈtʌnl] **I** s Tunnel m; Unterführung f; **II** v untertunneln.

tunny [ˈtʌnɪ] *zoo* Thunfisch m.

turbine [ˈtɜːbaɪn] Turbine f.

turbot ['tɜːbət] *zoo* (Stein-) Butt *m*.

turbulent ['tɜːbjʊlənt] stürmisch; *(Wetter)* böig.

tureen [təˈriːn] Suppenschüssel *f*.

turf [tɜːf] Rasen *m*.

Turk [tɜːk] Türke *m*.

Turkey ['tɜːkɪ] Türkei *f*.

turkey ['tɜːkɪ] Truthahn *m*.

Turkish ['tɜːkɪʃ] türkisch.

turmoil ['tɜːmɔɪl] Tumult, Aufruhr *m*.

turn [tɜːn] **I** *s* 1. (Um-)Drehung, Rotation *f*; 2. Biegung, Kurve *f*; *at every* ~ auf Schritt u. Tritt; 3. Runde *f*; 4. *fig* Wechsel, Umschwung *m*; Wende *f* (*for the better* zum Besseren); 5. *by* ~s abwechselnd; *in* ~ der Reihe nach; *out of* ~ außer der Reihe; *take* ~s (sich, mitea.) abwechseln; *it is my* ~ ich bin an der Reihe; 6. *do s.o. a good* ~ jdm e-n Dienst erweisen; **II** *v* 7. drehen; drechseln *a. fig*; 8. (sich) drehen; 9. (sich) umdrehen; 10. umkehren; 11. ~ *(round) the corner* um die Ecke biegen; 12. *fig* abbringen (*from* von); 13. um-, verwandeln (*into* in), machen (*into* zu); 14. werden (*fifty* 50 Jahre alt; *2 o'clock* 2 Uhr); ~ **down** 1. *(Sache)* abschlagen, -lehnen; 2. *(Radio)* leiser stellen; ~ **off** 1. *(Wasser, Gas)* abstellen, abdrehen; *(Strom)* ab-, *(Licht)* aus-schalten; 2. vom Weg abbiegen; ~ **on** *(Wasser)* aufdrehen; *(el. Gerät)* einschalten; *(Licht)* anmachen; ~ **out** 1. produzieren; 2. hinauswerfen, wegjagen; 3. sich herausstellen, sich erweisen (*to be true* als wahr); ~ **over** 1. umdrehen, umwenden; umkippen; 2. übergeben (*to s.o.* jdm); 3. *com* umsetzen, verkaufen; ~ **round** (sich) umdrehen; ~ **to** sich wenden an; ~ **up** 1. erscheinen; 2. umschlagen, -klappen.

turncoat ['tɜːnkəʊt] Überläufer *m*.

turning ['tɜːnɪŋ] Abzweigung *f*.

turnip ['tɜːnɪp] Steckrübe *f*.

turnpike ['tɜːnpaɪk] *Am* (gebührenpflichtige) Autobahn *f*.

turn-table ['tɜːnˌteɪbl] Plattenteller *m*.

turret ['tʌrɪt] Türmchen *n*.

turtle ['tɜːtl] Schildkröte *f*; *turn* ~ kentern.

tusk [tʌsk] Stoßzahn *m*.

tutor ['tjuːtə] Privatlehrer; *(Univ.)* Tutor *m*.

tuxedo [tʌkˈsiːdəʊ] *pl* -os *Am* Smoking *m*.

tweezers *pl* ['twiːzəz] *(a pair of* ~*)* Pinzette *f*.

twelve [twelv] zwölf.

twenty ['twentɪ] zwanzig.

twice [twaɪs] zweimal; ~ *the amount* der doppelte Betrag; ~ *as much, many* noch einmal soviel(e).

twig [twɪg] **I** *s* Zweig *m;* **II** *v*
Br fam kapieren, begreifen.

twilight ['twaɪlaɪt] Zwielicht
n; Dämmerung *f.*

twin [twɪn] Zwilling *m;* ~
beds *pl* zwei Einzelbetten *n*
pl; ~ **brother, sister** Zwil-
lingsbruder *m,* -schwester *f.*

twine [twaɪn] **I** *s* Bindfaden
m, Schnur *f;* **II** *v* winden
(*s.th. round s.th.* etw um
etw).

twinge [twɪndʒ] stechende(r)
Schmerz *m.*

twinkl|e ['twɪŋkl] funkeln;
(*Augen*) blitzen; ~**ing** [-ɪŋ]
in the ~ *of an eye* im Nu.

twirl [twɜːl] herumwirbeln.

twist [twɪst] **I** *v* 1. flechten;
winden (*around* um); 2. sich
winden, sich krümmen;
3. verrenken; 4. *fig* verdrehen, entstellen; **II** *s* 5. (Bind-)
Faden *m,* Garn *n;* 6. Drehung *f.*

two [tuː] **I** *adj* zwei; beide;
break in ~ entzweibrechen;

in a day or ~ in ein paar
Tagen; *one or* ~ ein paar;
II *s: by, in* ~*s,* ~ *and* ~ zu
zweit, zu zweien, paarweise;
the ~ *of us* wir beide; *put* ~
and ~ *together* sich die Sache zs.reimen; ~**fold**
['-fəʊld] zweifach; ~**-piece**
[ˌ-'piːs] zweiteilig.

type [taɪp] **I** *s* 1. Typ *m;*
2. Art, Gattung *f;* 3. *typ*
Type *f;* **II** *v* mit der Maschine schreiben, tippen;
~**writer** ['-ˌraɪtə] Schreibmaschine *f.*

typhoid ['taɪfɔɪd] Typhus *m.*

typhoon [taɪ'fuːn] *mete* Tai-
fun *m.*

typic(al) ['tɪpɪk(l)] typisch (*of*
für).

typist ['taɪpɪst] Maschinen-
schreiber(in *f*) *m.*

tyranny ['tɪrənɪ] Tyrannei *f.*

tyrant ['taɪərənt] Tyrann *m*
a. fig.

tyre, *Am* **tire** ['taɪə] (Rad-,
Auto-)Reifen *m.*

U

udder [ˈʌdə] Euter *n.*

ugly [ˈʌglɪ] 1. häßlich; 2. ~ *customer (fig, fam)* üble(r) Kunde *m.*

ulcer [ˈʌlsə] Geschwür *n.*

ulterior [ʌlˈtɪərɪə] *the ~ motive* der eigentliche Grund.

ultimate [ˈʌltɪmət] 1. äußerst; 2. grundlegend; 3. ~ *consumer* Endverbraucher *m;* ~**ly** [-lɪ] schließlich.

umbrella [ʌmˈbrelə] (Regen-)Schirm *m.*

umpire [ˈʌmpaɪə] Schiedsrichter *m.*

unable [ʌnˈeɪbl] *be ~ to do s.th.* etw nicht tun können.

unaccompanied [ˌʌnəˈkʌmpənɪd] ohne Begleitung *a. mus.*

unanimity [ˌjuːnəˈnɪmətɪ] Einstimmigkeit *f;* ~**ous** [juːˈnænɪməs] einmütig; *parl* einstimmig.

unattended [ˌʌnəˈtendɪd] unbeaufsichtigt.

unaware [ˌʌnəˈweə] in Unkenntnis *(of* gen); ~**s** [-z] 1. unabsichtlich; 2. *take s.o. ~* jdn überraschen.

unbalanced [ʌnˈbælənst] unausgeglichen.

unbearable [ʌnˈbeərəbl] unerträglich.

unbelievable [ˌʌnbɪˈliːvəbl] unglaublich.

unbend [ʌnˈbend] *irr s.* bend *fig* sich entspannen; ~**ing** [-ɪŋ] *fig* unbeugsam.

unbounded [ʌnˈbaʊndɪd] unbegrenzt.

unbridled [ˌʌnˈbraɪdld] *fig* zügellos, unbeherrscht.

uncalled-for [ˌʌnˈkɔːldfɔː] unerwünscht, unnötig.

uncanny [ʌnˈkænɪ] unheimlich *a. fig.*

uncertain [ʌnˈsɜːtn] ungewiß; unbestimmt; unsicher.

uncle [ˈʌŋkl] Onkel *m.*

uncomfortable [ʌnˈkʌmfətəbl] unbequem, unbehaglich.

uncompromising [ʌnˈkɒmprəmaɪzɪŋ] unnachgiebig.

unconditional [ˌʌnkənˈdɪʃənl] bedingungs-, vorbehaltlos.

unconscious [ʌnˈkɒnʃəs] 1. unbewußt *(of s.th.* e-r S); unabsichtlich; 2. bewußtlos.

uncover [ʌnˈkʌvə] 1. auf-, abdecken; 2. *fig* enthüllen.

undecided [ˌʌndɪˈsaɪdɪd] unschlüssig.

undeniable [ˌʌndɪˈnaɪəbl] unleugbar.

under [ˈʌndə] **I** *prp* 1. unter *a. fig;* unterhalb *gen;* ~ *age* minderjährig; 2. während; ~ *construction* im Bau (befindlich); ~ *repair* in Repa-

ratur; **II** *adv* 3. unten; 4. *go*
~ untergehen.
undercarriage
['ʌndəˌkærɪdʒ] Fahrgestell,
-werk *n.*
under|clothes ['ʌndəkləʊðz],
~clothing ['-ˌkləʊðɪŋ] Unterwäsche *f.*
underdeveloped
[ˌʌndədɪ'veləpt] unterent-
wickelt.
underdog ['ʌndədɒg] *fig* Be-
nachteiligte(r) *m.*
underdone [ˌʌndə'dʌn] nicht
gar.
underestimate
[ˌʌndər'estɪmeɪt] unter-
schätzen.
underfloor heating
[ˌʌndə'flɔː hiːtɪŋ] Fußboden-
heizung *f.*
undergo [ˌʌndə'gəʊ] *irr s. go*
durchmachen; sich unterziehen (müssen) (*s.th.* e-r S).
undergraduate
[ˌʌndə'grædjʊət] Student *m*
(der ersten Semester).

underground ['ʌndəgraʊnd]
Untergrundbahn *f.*
undergrowth ['ʌndəgrəʊθ]
Unterholz *n.*
underline ['ʌndəlaɪn] unterstreichen *a. fig; fig* hervorheben.
undermine [ˌʌndə'maɪn]
1. unterminieren; 2. *fig* untergraben.
underneath [ˌʌndə'niːθ]
I *adv* unten, darunter;
II *prp* unterhalb.

underpants ['ʌndəpænts]
Unterhosen *f pl.*
underpass ['ʌndəpɑːs] Unterführung *f.*
underprivileged
[ˌʌndə'prɪvɪlɪdʒd] benachtei-
ligt.
underrate [ˌʌndə'reɪt] unterschätzen *a. fig.*
understaffed [ˌʌndə'stɑːft]
be ~ an Personalmangel leiden.
understand [ˌʌndə'stænd]
irr s. stand 1. verstehen;
make o.s. understood sich
verständlich machen; 2. annehmen, voraussetzen;
3. entnehmen, schließen
(*from* aus); *give s.o. to* ~ jdm
zu verstehen geben; *I* ~ wie
ich höre; **~able** [-əbl] verständlich; **~ing** [-ɪŋ] 1. Verstehen, Begreifen *n;* 2. Verständnis *n;* 3. *on the* ~ *that*
unter der Voraussetzung,
daß; 4. *come to, reach an* ~
zu e-r Verständigung kom-
men (*with* mit).

understatement
[ˌʌndə'steɪtmənt] Untertrei-
bung *f.*
undertak|e [ˌʌndə'teɪk] *irr s.
take* 1. sich verpflichten (*to
do* zu tun); 2. *(Arbeit, Reise)*
unternehmen; **~er** ['-ˌteɪkə]
Leichenbestatter *m;* **~ing**
[ˌ-'teɪkɪŋ] 1. Verpflichtung *f;*
2. Unternehmen *n;*
3. ['-teɪkɪŋ] Beerdigungs-
institut *n.*

underwear ['ʌndəweə] Unterwäsche f.

underworld ['ʌndəwɜːld] Unterwelt f.

undesirable [ˌʌndɪ'zaɪərəbl] unerwünscht.

undies pl ['ʌndɪz] fam (Damen-)Unterwäsche f.

undo [ʌn'duː] irr s. do 1. aufmachen; (Knoten) lösen; 2. zunichte machen; **~ne** [-'dʌn] unerledigt.

undoubted [ʌn'daʊtɪd] unbestritten; **~ly** [-lɪ] zweifellos.

undress [ʌn'dres] (sich) ausziehen.

undue [ʌn'djuː] übermäßig.

undulating ['ʌndjʊleɪtɪŋ] wellig.

uneasy [ʌn'iːzɪ] unruhig; besorgt; I feel ~ mir ist unbehaglich (zumute) (about s.th. wegen etw).

uneducated [ʌn'edjʊkeɪtɪd] ungebildet.

unemploy|ed [ˌʌnɪm'plɔɪd] arbeitslos; **~ment** [-'plɔɪmənt] Arbeitslosigkeit f.

unequal(l)ed [ʌn'iːkwəld] einzig(artig); beispiellos.

unexpected [ˌʌnɪk'spektɪd] unerwartet.

unfailing [ʌn'feɪlɪŋ] zuverlässig; nie versagend.

unfair [ʌn'feə] ungerecht; com unlauter; unfair.

unfaithful [ʌn'feɪθfʊl] untreu.

unfavo(u)rable [ʌn'feɪvərəbl] ungünstig.

unfeeling [ʌn'fiːlɪŋ] gefühl-, empfindungslos.

unfit [ʌn'fɪt] ungeeignet.

unfold [ʌn'fəʊld] 1. (sich) entfalten; 2. fig offen darlegen.

unforeseen [ˌʌnfɔː'siːn] unvorhergesehen.

unfortunate [ʌn'fɔːtʃnət] unglücklich; bedauerlich; **~ly** [-lɪ] leider.

unfounded [ʌn'faʊndɪd] unbegründet, grundlos.

unfriendly [ʌn'frendlɪ] unfreundlich.

unfurnished [ʌn'fɜːnɪʃt] unmöbliert.

ungainly [ʌn'geɪnlɪ] unbeholfen.

ungrateful [ʌn'greɪtfʊl] undankbar.

unguarded [ʌn'gɑːdɪd] unbewacht.

unhappy [ʌn'hæpɪ] unglücklich.

unhealthy [ʌn'helθɪ] kränklich; ungesund.

unheard-of [ʌn'hɜːdɒv] unerhört.

unhurt [ʌn'hɜːt] unverletzt.

unidentified [ˌʌnaɪ'dentɪfaɪd] nicht identifiziert; ~ flying object Ufo n.

uniform ['juːnɪfɔːm] I adj einheitlich; II s Uniform f.

unify ['juːnɪfaɪ] 1. verein(ig)en; 2. vereinheitlichen.

unilateral [ˌjuːnɪˈlætərəl] einseitig.

union [ˈjuːnjən] 1. Vereinigung f, Zs.schluß m; 2. in perfect ~ in voller Eintracht; 3. (Staaten-)Bund m, Union f; 4. (trade ~) Gewerkschaft f; the **U~ Jack** die britische Nationalflagge.

unique [juːˈniːk] einzig(artig).

unison [ˈjuːnɪzn] in ~ einstimmig.

unit [ˈjuːnɪt] Einheit f; **~e** [juːˈnaɪt] (sich) verein(ig)en.

United Nations Vereinte Nationen pl.

United States of America Vereinigte Staaten pl von Amerika.

unity [ˈjuːnəti] 1. Einheit f; 2. in ~ with in Übereinstimmung mit.

univers|al [ˌjuːnɪˈvɜːsl] allgemein; **~e** [ˈjuːnɪvɜːs] Welt(all n) f; **~ity** [ˌjuːnɪˈvɜːsəti] Universität f.

unjust [ʌnˈdʒʌst] ungerecht.

unkind [ʌnˈkaɪnd] unfreundlich, herzlos.

unknown [ʌnˈnəʊn] unbekannt (to s.o. jdm).

unless [ənˈles] wenn nicht; außer wenn.

unlike [ʌnˈlaɪk] **I** adj ungleich, verschieden(artig); **II** prp unähnlich (s.o. jdm); **~ly** [ʌnˈlaɪklɪ] unwahrscheinlich.

unload [ʌnˈləʊd] entladen.

unmarried [ʌnˈmærɪd] unverheiratet, ledig.

unmask [ʌnˈmɑːsk] demaskieren a. fig; fig entlarven.

unmistakable [ˌʌnmɪˈsteɪkəbl] unverkennbar.

unnecessary [ʌnˈnesəsərɪ] unnötig.

unpack [ˌʌnˈpæk] auspacken.

unparalleled [ʌnˈpærəleld] unerreicht; beispiellos.

unpleasant [ʌnˈpleznt] unangenehm.

unprecedented [ʌnˈpresɪdəntɪd] einmalig, beispiellos.

unreal [ˌʌnˈrɪəl] unwirklich.

unreasonable [ʌnˈriːznəbl] unvernünftig; übertrieben.

unrelenting [ˌʌnrɪˈlentɪŋ] unermüdlich; unerbittlich.

unrest [ʌnˈrest] Unruhe f.

unroll [ʌnˈrəʊl] aufrollen a. fig.

unruly [ʌnˈruːlɪ] widersetzlich.

unsaid [ˌʌnˈsed] unausgesprochen.

unscrupulous [ʌnˈskruːpjʊləs] skrupellos.

unsettle [ʌnˈsetld] (Wetter) unbeständig.

unsightly [ʌnˈsaɪtlɪ] unansehnlich, häßlich.

unskilled [ʌnˈskɪld] ungelernt.

unsound [ˌʌnˈsaʊnd] 1. ungesund; of ~ mind geistes-

krank; 2. anfechtbar; 3. unzuverlässig.

unspeakable [ʌn'spiːkəbl]
unaussprechlich.

unstuck [ʌn'stʌk] nicht fest;
lose; *come ~ (fam) (Plan)*
ins Wasser fallen.

unthinkable [ʌn'θɪŋkəbl] un-
denkbar.

until [ən'tɪl, ʌn'tɪl] **I** *prp* bis;
II *conj* bis (daß); *not... ~*
erst wenn.

untimely [ʌn'taɪmlɪ] 1. unpassend; 2. vorzeitig.

untold ['ʌntəʊld] unermeßlich.

unused [ʌn'juːzd] unbe-
nutzt.

unusual [ʌn'juːʒʊəl] ungewöhnlich.

unveil [ʌn'veɪl] enthüllen.

unwell [ʌn'wel] unwohl; unpäßlich.

unwieldy [ʌn'wiːldɪ] unhand-
lich, sperrig.

unwitting [ʌn'wɪtɪŋ] unabsichtlich; unwissentlich.

up [ʌp] 1. auf; hinauf; *~ and
down* auf u. ab, hin u. her *a.
fig;* ~ *to the present day* bis
heute; *be ~ to s.th.* etw im
Schilde führen; *~ to date*
modern; *~ to now* bis jetzt;
if it were ~ to him... wenn
es nach ihm ginge ...; *be
hard ~* übel d(a)ran sein;
feel ~ to s.th. sich e-r S gewachsen fühlen; *what's ~?*
(fam) was gibt's? 2. auf(gestanden); 3. vorbei, abgelaufen.

upbringing ['ʌp,brɪŋɪŋ] Erziehung *f.*

update [ʌp'deɪt] modernisie-
ren.

upgrade [ʌp'greɪd] höher
einstufen.

uphill [ʌp'hɪl] **I** *adv* bergauf;
II *adj* 1. (an)steigend; 2. *fig*
anstrengend.

uphold [ʌp'həʊld] *irr s. hold*
unterstützen; billigen.

upholstery [ʌp'həʊlstərɪ]
Polsterung; Innenausstat-
tung *f.*

upkeep ['ʌpkiːp] Instandhal-
tung *f.*

upon [ə'pɒn] auf; *once ~ a
time there was* es war einmal; *~ my word* auf mein
Wort.

upper ['ʌpə] **I** *adj* höher,
ober; **II** *s* Oberleder *n;* ~
arm Oberarm *m;* ~ **class**
Oberschicht *f;* ~**most**
[-məʊst] oberst, höchst.

upright ['ʌpraɪt] **I** *adj* 1. aufrecht, senkrecht; 2. rechtschaffen; **II** *s* Pfosten *m.*

uprising ['ʌp,raɪzɪŋ] Aufstand
m.

uproar ['ʌprɔː] Aufruhr *m.*

uproot [ʌp'ruːt] entwurzeln.

upset [ʌp'set] *irr s. set* 1. umwerfen; 2. *fig* durchea.brin-
gen; *(Magen)* verderben.

upshot ['ʌpʃɒt] Ergebnis *n.*

upside-down [ʌpsaɪd'daʊn]
turn ~ auf den Kopf stellen.

upstairs [ʌp'steəz] **I** *adv*
1. nach oben; 2. oben, im
oberen Stock(werk);

II *adj* im oberen Stockwerk (befindlich).

upstart ['ʌpstɑːt] Emporkömmling *m.*

upstream [ʌp'striːm] stromaufwärts.

uptake ['ʌpteɪk] *be quick, slow on the* ~ schnell begreifen, schwer von Begriff sein.

up-to-date [ˌʌptə'deɪt] modern; aktuell.

upturn [ʌp'tɜːn] Aufschwung *m.*

upward ['ʌpwəd] I *adj* ansteigend; nach oben (gerichtet); II *adv (a.* ~s) nach oben, aufwärts *a. fig.*

uranium [jʊ'reɪnjəm] *chem* Uran *n.*

urban ['ɜːbən] städtisch.

urge [ɜːdʒ] I *v* 1. ~ *on* an-, vorwärtstreiben; 2. ~ *s.o. to s.th* jdn zu etw drängen; 3. ~ *s.th. upon s.o.* jdm etw eindringlich nahelegen; jdm etw aufdrängen; II *s* Drang *m.*

urgen|cy ['ɜːdʒənsɪ] Dringlichkeit *f;* ~t [-ənt] dringend.

urin|ate ['jʊərɪneɪt] Wasser lassen; ~e ['jʊərɪn] Harn *m.*

urn [ɜːn] Urne *f.*

us [ʌs] uns *(dat* u. *acc); both of* ~ wir beide.

usage ['juːzɪdʒ] 1. Brauch *m;* 2. Gebrauch *m.*

use I *v* [juːz] 1. benützen; verwenden; ~d car Gebrauchtwagen *m;* 2. (~ *up)*

auf-, verbrauchen; 3. *(Menschen)* behandeln; II *s* [juːs] 4. Gebrauch *m;* Verwendung *f; in, out of* ~ in, außer Gebrauch; 5. *be no* ~ keinen Zweck haben; ~d [juːst] *be* ~ *to* gewöhnt sein an; *get* ~ *to* sich gewöhnen an; ~ful ['juːsfʊl] nützlich; ~less ['juːslɪs] nutzlos.

user ['juːzə] Benutzer *m.*

usher ['ʌʃə] Platzanweiser *m;* ~ette [ˌʌʃə'ret] Platzanweiserin *f.*

usual ['juːʒʊəl] üblich, normal; *as* ~ wie gewöhnlich; ~ly [-ɪ] gewöhnlich.

usur|er ['juːʒərə] Wucherer *m;* ~y ['juːʒʊrɪ] Wucher *m.*

utensil [juː'tensl] *cooking-, kitchen-*~s (pl) Küchengeräte *n pl,* -geschirr *n.*

uterus ['juːtərəs] *pl uteri* [-raɪ] *anat* Gebärmutter *f.*

utillity [juː'tɪlətɪ] 1. Nützlichkeit *f;* 2. *oft pl (public* ~) öffentlicher Versorgungsbetrieb *m;* Stadtwerke *n pl;* ~ize ['juːtɪlaɪz] Gebrauch machen von.

utmost ['ʌtməʊst] I *adj* äußerst *a. fig; of the* ~ *importance* von größter Wichtigkeit; II *s: do o.'s* ~ sein möglichstes tun; *to the* ~ (aufs) äußerst(e).

utter ['ʌtə] I *adj* völlig, vollständig, gänzlich; II *v* äußern.

uvula ['juːvjʊlə] *anat* Zäpfchen *n.*

V

vacan|cy ['veɪkənsɪ] 1. Leere f; 2. *(Hotel)* freie(s) Zimmer n; 3. offene Stelle f; ~**t** ['veɪkənt] 1. leer; 2. *(Zimmer)* frei; *(Haus)* unbewohnt; 3. *(Stelle)* unbesetzt, frei; 4. *fig* geistesabwesend.

vacation [və'keɪʃn] Ferien pl, Urlaub m; on ~ in Urlaub.

vaccinat|e ['væksɪneɪt] impfen *(against* gegen); ~**ion** [ˌvæksɪ'neɪʃn] Impfung f.

vacuum ['vækjʊəm] pl a. *-uua* [-jʊə] Vakuum n; ~ **cleaner** Staubsauger m.

vagina [və'dʒaɪnə] *anat* Scheide f.

vague [veɪg] vage; unklar; unbestimmt.

vain [veɪn] 1. vergeblich; 2. in ~ umsonst; vergebens; 3. eitel, eingebildet.

valid ['vælɪd] 1. (rechts)gültig; 2. *(Grund)* stichhaltig; ~**ity** [və'lɪdətɪ] Gültigkeit f.

valley ['vælɪ] Tal n.

valuable ['væljʊəbl] I adj wertvoll; II s meist pl Wertgegenstände m pl.

valuation [ˌvæljʊ'eɪʃn] Schätzung, Bewertung f.

value ['vælju:] I s Wert m; of no, little ~ nichts, wenig wert; ~**-added tax** Mehrwertsteuer f; II v 1. schätzen *(at* auf); 2. (hoch)schätzen. achten.

valve [vælv] Ventil n.

van [væn] 1. *Br rail* Güterwagen m; 2. Lieferwagen m.

vanish ['vænɪʃ] verschwinden.

vanity ['vænɪtɪ] Eitelkeit f; ~ **bag, case** Kosmetikkoffer m.

vanquish ['væŋkwɪʃ] besiegen.

vantage-point ['vɑ:ntɪdʒ pɔɪnt] *fig* günstige(r) (Ausgangs-)Punkt m.

vapo(u)r ['veɪpə] Dampf, Dunst m.

variable ['veərɪəbl] veränderlich.

variance ['veərɪəns] be at ~ uneinig sein *(with* mit).

variation [ˌveərɪ'eɪʃn] Veränderung, Abweichung f.

variety [və'raɪətɪ] 1. Abwechslung f; 2. Vielfalt f; for a ~ of reasons aus verschiedenen Gründen; 3. Art, Sorte f; 4. *theat* Varieté n.

various ['veərɪəs] 1. verschieden(artig); 2. verschiedene; mehrere.

varnish ['vɑ:nɪʃ] Firnis m.

vary ['veərɪ] variieren; (sich) (ver)ändern; abweichen *(from* von).

vase [vɑ:z] (Blumen-)Vase f.

vast [vɑ:st] weit(reichend), ausgedehnt.

vault [vɔːlt] I s 1. Gewölbe n;

2. Gruft *f*; 3. Tresor(raum) *m*; **II** *v* springen (*over* über).

veal [viːl] Kalbfleisch *n*.

veget|able ['vedʒtəbl] Gemüse(pflanze *f*) *n*; **~arian** [ˌvedʒɪ'teərɪən] Vegetarier *m*.

vehement ['viːɪmənt] heftig.

vehicle ['viːɪkl] 1. Fahrzeug *n*; 2. Medium, Mittel *n*.

veil [veɪl] **I** *s* Schleier *m* a. *fig*; **II** *v* verschleiern; *fig* verhüllen.

vein [veɪn] Ader *f*.

velocity [vɪ'lɒsətɪ] Geschwindigkeit *f*.

velvet ['velvɪt] Samt *m* a. *fig*.

vend [vend] *jur* verkaufen; **~er**, **~or** ['-ə] Verkäufer *m*; **~ing machine** Warenautomat *m*.

veneer [və'nɪə] Furnier *n*.

vener|able ['venərəbl] würdig; **~ation** [ˌvenə'reɪʃn] Verehrung *f* (*for* für).

venereal disease [və'nɪərɪəl dɪ'ziːz] Geschlechtskrankheit *f*.

venetian blind [və'niːʃn blaɪnd] Jalousie *f*.

vengeance ['vendʒəns] Rache *f*.

venison ['venzn] Wild(bret) *n*.

venom ['venəm] Gift *n*; **~ous** [-əs] giftig.

vent [vent] 1. Öffnung *f*; Belüftungsloch *n*; 2. *give* ~ *to* freien Lauf lassen *dat*.

ventilat|e ['ventɪleɪt] (aus)lüften; **~or** [-ə] Ventilator *m*.

venture ['ventʃə] **I** *s* Wagnis, Risiko *n*; **II** *v* riskieren; sich wagen (*on* an); *may I ~ my opinion* darf ich sagen, was ich darüber denke?

verb [vɜːb] *gram* Zeitwort *n*.

verbal ['vɜːbl] 1. mündlich; 2. (*Übersetzung*) wörtlich.

verdict ['vɜːdɪkt] *jur* Urteil *n*.

verge [vɜːdʒ] **I** *s* 1. Rand *m*; 2. *be on the ~ of doing* im Begriff, nahe daran sein zu tun; **II** *v* grenzen (*on* an) a. *fig*.

verify ['verɪfaɪ] 1. (über)prüfen; 2. bestätigen.

vermin ['vɜːmɪn] Ungeziefer *n*.

versatile ['vɜːsətaɪl] *fig* wendig, gewandt, vielseitig.

verse [vɜːs] Vers *m*.

versed [vɜːst] erfahren (*in* in).

version ['vɜːʃn] 1. Übersetzung *f*; 2. Version *f*.

very ['verɪ] **I** *adv* sehr; **II** *adj* 1. gerade, genau; 2. äußerst; 3. *the ~ thought* der bloße Gedanke.

vessel ['vesl] 1. Gefäß *n*; 2. *blood-~* Blutgefäß *n*; 3. *mar* Schiff *n*.

vest [vest] **I** *s* 1. *Br* Unterhemd *n*; 2. *Am* Weste *f*; **II** *v* ausstatten (*s.o. with s.th.* jdn mit etw); **~ed rights** (*pl*) verbriefte Rechte *pl*.

vestibule ['vestɪbjuːl] Eingang(shalle *f*) *m*.

vestige ['vestɪdʒ] Spur *f*.

veterinary surgeon ['vetərinəri 'sɜːdʒən], *fam*
vet [vet] Tierarzt *m.*

veto ['viːtəʊ] **I** *s pl -oes* Veto *n; put a ~ on s.th.* gegen etw Einspruch erheben; **II** *v* verbieten, untersagen.

vex [veks] ärgern.

via ['vaɪə] über; per.

vibrat|e [vaɪ'breɪt] vibrieren; ~**ion** [vaɪ'breɪʃn] Schwingung *f.*

vicar ['vɪkə] Pfarrer *m.*

vice [vaɪs] 1. Laster *n;* 2. Schraubstock *m.*

vice|-chancellor [ˌvaɪs'tʃɑːnsələ] Vizekanzler *m;* ~**-president** [ˌ-'prezɪdənt] Vizepräsident *m.*

vicinity [vɪ'sɪnəti] Nachbarschaft *f; in close ~ to* ganz nahe bei.

vicious ['vɪʃəs] tückisch, bösartig, gefährlich.

victim ['vɪktɪm] Opfer *n;* ~**ize** [-aɪz] ungerecht behandeln.

victor|ious [vɪk'tɔːrɪəs] siegreich; ~**y** ['vɪktəri] Sieg *m.*

vie [vaɪ] wetteifern (*with s.o.* mit jdm; *for* um).

view [vjuː] **I** *s* 1. (An-, Aus-) Sicht *f;* (An-, Aus-, Über-) Blick *m; in ~ of* im Hinblick auf; 2. *with a ~ to* in der Absicht zu; 3. *fig* Meinung *f;* Urteil *n; fall in with s.o.'s ~s* sich jds Auffassung anschließen; **II** *v* ansehen, betrachten; prüfen; ~**er** ['-ə] (Fern-

seh-)Zuschauer *m;* ~**-finder** ['-ˌfaɪndə] *opt phot* Sucher *m;* ~**point** ['-pɔɪnt] Standpunkt *m.*

vigilance ['vɪdʒɪləns] Wachsamkeit *f.*

vig|orous ['vɪgərəs] 1. stark, kräftig; 2. energisch; ~**o(u)r** ['vɪgə] 1. Energie *f;* 2. *fig* Nachdruck *m.*

vile [vaɪl] schlecht, verdorben.

village ['vɪlɪdʒ] Dorf *n.*

villain ['vɪlən] Schurke *m.*

vindicate ['vɪndɪkeɪt] rechtfertigen.

vindictive [vɪn'dɪktɪv] rachsüchtig.

vine [vaɪn] Weinstock *m,* Rebe *f.*

vinegar ['vɪnɪgə] Essig *m.*

vineyard ['vɪnjəd] Weinberg *m.*

vintage ['vɪntɪdʒ] 1. (Wein-) Lese *f;* 2. Jahrgang *m.*

viola [vɪ'əʊlə] Bratsche *f.*

violate ['vaɪəleɪt] 1. (*Recht*) verletzen; 2. (*Eid*) brechen.

violen|ce ['vaɪələns] 1. Heftigkeit *f;* 2. Gewalttätigkeit *f;* ~**t** [-t] 1. gewaltig, heftig; 2. *meet a ~ death* e-s gewaltsamen Todes sterben.

violet ['vaɪələt] 1. Veilchen *n;* 2. Violett *n.*

violin [ˌvaɪə'lɪn] Geige *f.*

viper ['vaɪpə] Viper, Otter *f.*

virgin ['vɜːdʒɪn] **I** *s* Jungfrau *f;* **II** *adj* jungfräulich; unberührt; ~**ity** [və'dʒɪnəti] Jungfräulichkeit *f.*

Virgo ['vɜːgəʊ] *astr* Jungfrau *f.*

virtual ['vɜːtʃʊəl] wirklich; eigentlich.

virtue ['vɜːtjuː] 1. Tugend *f;* 2. Vorzug *m;* 3. *by, in ~ of* auf Grund *gen;* kraft; **~ous** ['vɜːtʃʊəs] tugendhaft.

virulent ['vɪrʊlənt] giftig; tödlich.

visa ['viːzə] Visum *n.*

visibility [ˌvɪzɪ'bɪlətɪ] Sicht(weite) *f;* **~le** ['vɪzəbl] sichtbar.

vision ['vɪʒn] 1. Sehvermögen *n;* 2. Vision *f.*

visit ['vɪzɪt] **I** *v* auf-, besuchen; besichtigen; **II** *s* Besuch *m (to* bei); *go on a ~* verreisen; *pay a ~ to s.o.* jdm e-n Besuch abstatten; **~or** [-ə] Besucher; *(Hotel)* Gast *m.*

visual ['vɪzjʊəl] visuell; Seh-.

vital ['vaɪtl] lebenswichtig; **~ity** [vaɪ'tælətɪ] Vitalität *f.*

vitamin ['vɪtəmɪn] Vitamin *n.*

vivacious [vɪ'veɪʃəs] lebhaft; **~ty** [vɪ'væsətɪ] Lebhaftigkeit *f.*

vivid ['vɪvɪd] lebhaft, lebendig.

vocal cord ['vəʊkl kɔːd] Stimmband *n.*

vocation [vəʊ'keɪʃn] 1. Berufung *f;* 2. Beruf *m;* **~al** [-'keɪʃənl] beruflich; *~ guidance* Berufsberatung *f.*

vogue [vəʊg] *be the ~, be in ~ (in)* Mode sein.

voice [vɔɪs] **I** *s* 1. Stimme *f;*

2. Mitspracherecht *n;* **II** *v* äußern.

void [vɔɪd] **I** *adj* 1. leer; 2. *jur* ungültig; *null and ~* null u. nichtig; 3. *~ of* frei von, ohne; **II** *s* Leere *f.*

volcanic [vɒl'kænɪk] vulkanisch; **~o** [vɒl'keɪnəʊ] *pl* *-o(e)s* Vulkan *m.*

volley ['vɒlɪ] 1. Salve *f;* 2. *fig* Hagel *m;* 3. *sport* Flugball *m.*

volt [vəʊlt] *el* Volt *n;* **~age** ['-ɪdʒ] (Volt-)Spannung *f.*

volume ['vɒljuːm] 1. Band *m,* Buch *n;* 2. Volumen *n;* 3. *~ control* Lautstärkeregler *m.*

voluntary ['vɒləntərɪ] freiwillig; **~eer** [ˌvɒlən'tɪə] **I** *s* Freiwillige(r) *m;* **II** *v* sich freiwillig melden *(for* zu).

vomit ['vɒmɪt] sich erbrechen.

vote [vəʊt] **I** *s* 1. (Wahl-) Stimme *f;* 2. Stimmrecht *n;* 3. Abstimmergebnis *n;* **II** *v* abstimmen *(on s.th.* über etw); s-e Stimme abgeben *(for* für); **~r** ['-ə] Wähler *m.*

vouch [vaʊtʃ] sich verbürgen, garantieren *(for* für).

voucher ['-ə] 1. Beleg *m;* 2. Gutschein *m.*

vow [vaʊ] **I** *s* Gelübde *n;* **II** *v* geloben.

vowel ['vaʊəl] Vokal *m.*

voyage ['vɔɪɪdʒ] Reise *f.*

vulgar ['vʌlgə] gewöhnlich; vulgär.

vulnerable ['vʌlnərəbl] verwundbar *a. fig.*

W

wad [wɒd] Bündel *n*.
waddle ['wɒdl] watscheln.
wade [weɪd] waten.
wafer ['weɪfə] Waffel *f*.
wag [wæg] wedeln (mit).
wage [weɪdʒ] **I** *s meist pl* (Arbeits-)Lohn *m; living ~* Existenzminimum *n;* **II** *v: ~ war on* den Kampf aufnehmen gegen; **~-earner** ['-ˌɜːnə] Lohnempfänger *m;* **~-freeze** ['-friːz] Lohnstopp *m*.
wager ['weɪdʒə] **I** *s* Wette *f;* **II** *v* wetten.
waggle ['wægl] wedeln (mit).
wag(g)on ['wægən] Wagen; *rail* Waggon *m*.

wail [weɪl] 1. wehklagen (*for* um; *over* über); 2. *(Wind)* heulen.
waist [weɪst] Taille *f;* **~coat** ['weɪskəʊt] Weste *f;* **~-line** ['-laɪn] Taille *f*.
wait [weɪt] 1. warten (*for* auf); *keep ~ing* warten lassen; *~ o.'s turn* warten, bis man an der Reihe ist; *~ and see* abwarten; 2. *~ (up)on s.o.* jdn bedienen; *~ at table* servieren; **~er** ['-ə] Kellner *m; ~ the bill,* (*Am*) *check, please!* Ober, bitte zahlen! **~ing** ['-ɪŋ] *~-list* Warteliste *f; ~-room* Wartezimmer *n*,

-saal *m;* **~ress** ['-rɪs] Kellnerin *f*.
wake [weɪk] **I** *v a. irr* woke [wəʊk] , *woken* ['-ən] 1. (*~ up*) aufwachen; 2. (*~ up*) (auf)wecken *a. fig;* **II** *s* Kielwasser *n a. fig; in the ~ of* (*fig*) unmittelbar nach.
Wales [weɪlz] Wales *n*.
walk [wɔːk] **I** *v* (spazieren)gehen, zu Fuß gehen; wandern; **II** *s* 1. Spaziergang *m; an hour's ~* Weg von e-r Stunde; *go for a ~* e-n Spaziergang machen; 2. (Spazier-)Weg *m;* 3. Gang(art *f*) *m*.
walker ['wɔːkə] Fuß-, Spaziergänger *m*.
walkie-talkie [ˌwɔːkɪ'tɔːkɪ] tragbare(s) Sprechfunkgerät *n*.
walking ['wɔːkɪŋ] *~-stick* Spazierstock *m; ~-tour* (Fuß-)Wanderung *f*.
walk-out ['wɔːkaʊt] Streik *m*.
wall [wɔːl] **I** *s* Wand; Mauer *f a. fig; with o.'s back to the ~* (*fig*) in die Enge getrieben; **II** *v* mit e-r Mauer umgeben; *~ up* zumauern.
wallet ['wɒlɪt] Brieftasche *f*.
wallow ['wɒləʊ] sich wälzen; sich suhlen.
wallpaper ['wɔːlˌpeɪpə] Tapete *f*.

walnut ['wɔːlnʌt] Walnuß f.

waltz [wɔːls] **I** s Walzer m; **II** v Walzer tanzen.

wand [wɒnd] (Zauber-)Stab m.

wander ['wɒndə] 1. (umher)wandern; 2. ~ from the subject vom Thema abschweifen; ~**er** [-rə] Wanderer m.

want [wɒnt] **I** v 1. nötig haben; brauchen; 2. wünschen; (haben) wollen; 3. nicht haben; **II** s 4. Mangel m; for, from ~ of aus Mangel an; 5. be in ~ of s.th. etw nötig haben; 6. pl Bedürfnisse n pl.

wanton ['wɒntən] wild, unbeherrscht.

war [wɔː] Krieg m a. fig; be at ~ with Krieg führen gegen.

ward [wɔːd] **I** s 1. Mündel n; 2. med Station f; 3. (Stadt-)Bezirk m; **II** v: ~ off abwehren, fernhalten.

ward|en ['wɔːdn] Wärter, Aufseher m; ~**er** ['wɔːdə] Gefängniswärter m.

wardrobe ['wɔːdrəub] 1. Garderobe f; 2. Kleiderschrank m.

warehouse ['weəhaus] Lagerhaus n.

warfare ['wɔːfeə] Krieg(führung f) m.

warm [wɔːm] **I** adj 1. warm; 2. fig herzlich; **II** v (sich) (er)wärmen (to für); (~ up) (Speise) aufwärmen; ~**th** [wɔːmθ] Wärme f.

warn [wɔːn] warnen (of, against vor); ~**ing** ['-ɪŋ] Warnung f.

warp [wɔːp] (Holz) (sich) verziehen.

warrant ['wɒrənt] 1. Berechtigung f; 2. Haftbefehl m; ~**y** [-ɪ] be still under ~ noch unter Garantie stehen.

warrior ['wɒrɪə] Krieger m.

wart [wɔːt] Warze f.

wash [wɒʃ] **I** s Wäsche f; give s.th. a ~ etw (ab)waschen; **II** v waschen; ~ the dishes das Geschirr spülen.

washable ['wɒʃəbl] (ab)waschbar.

wash-basin ['wɒʃ,beɪsn] Waschbecken n.

washer ['wɒʃə] 1. Waschmaschine f; 2. Dichtungsring m.

washing ['wɒʃɪŋ] Wäsche f; ~-**machine** [-məˌʃiːn] Waschmaschine f; ~-**up** [ˌ-'ʌp] Geschirrspülen n.

wash-out ['wɒʃaut] fam 1. Reinfall m; 2. (Mensch) Niete f.

washroom ['wɒʃruːm] Am Toilette f.

wasp [wɒsp] Wespe f.

waste [weɪst] **I** v 1. verschwenden, vergeuden (on mit); don't ~ your breath sparen Sie sich Ihre Worte; 2. verwüsten; 3. (~ away) schwächer werden; **II** adj 4. (Land) öde, wüst; 5. Abfall-; **III** s 6. Verschwendung f; 7. (Ein-)Öde, Wildnis f; 8. Abfall m; ~**ful** ['-ful] ver-

schwenderisch; ~-**paper-
-basket** [ˌ-ˈpeɪpəˌbɑːskɪt]
Papierkorb m.

watch [wɒtʃ] **I** s 1. Wache f
a. mar; 2. Taschen-, Arm-
banduhr f; **II** v 3. zusehen,
beobachten; 4. aufpassen
auf; ~ your step! Achtung,
Stufe! ~-**dog** [ˈ-dɒg] Wachhund m a. fig; ~-**ful** [ˈ-fʊl]
wachsam; ~-**maker**
[ˈ-ˌmeɪkə] Uhrmacher m;
~**man** [ˈ-mən] Wachmann
m.

water [ˈwɔːtə] **I** s 1. Wasser
n; 2. pl Gewässer n od pl;
II v 3. bewässern; 4. (Vieh)
tränken; 5. (~ down) (mit
Wasser) verdünnen; fig ver-
wässern; 6. (Augen) tränen;
my mouth ~s mir läuft das
Wasser im Mund zusam-
men; ~-**colo(u)r** [-ˌkʌlə]
1. Wasserfarbe f; 2. Aquarell
n; ~**fall** [ˈ-fɔːl] Wasserfall m;
~**ing-can** [ˈ-rɪŋkæn] Gieß-
kanne f; ~-**level** [ˈ-ˌlevl]
Wasserspiegel m; ~-**lily**
[-ˌlɪlɪ] Seerose f; ~**melon**
[ˈ-ˌmelən] Wassermelone f;
~-**proof** [ˈ-pruːf] wasserdicht; ~**tight** [ˈ-taɪt] 1. wasserdicht; 2. fig unmißverständlich; ~**works** pl
[ˈ-wɜːks] Wasserwerk n; ~**y**
[ˈ-rɪ] wässerig.

wave [weɪv] **I** v 1. wogen;
sich wellen; 2. (Fahne) wehen, flattern; 3. (zu)winken
(to s.o. jdm); winken (a
handkerchief mit e-m Ta-

schentuch); **II** s 4. Welle f;
5. cold, heat ~ Kälte-, Hitzewelle f; 6. Winken n (of the
hand mit der Hand);
~-**length** [ˈ-leŋθ] (radio)
Wellenlänge f.

waver [ˈweɪvə] v schwanken a.
fig.

wavy [ˈweɪvɪ] wellenförmig.

wax [wæks] **I** s Wachs n;
II v 1. (ein)wachsen;
2. (Mond) zunehmen.

way [weɪ] 1. Weg m; on the
~ unterwegs (to nach); give
~ nachgeben a. fig; make ~
Platz machen (for für); right
of ~ Vorfahrtsrecht n; ~ out
Ausgang m; 2. Art u. Weise
f; one ~ or another irgendwie; ~s and means Mittel u.
Wege; 3. Richtung f; this ~
hierher; 4. Hinsicht, Beziehung f; in a ~ in gewisser
Weise; in no ~ keineswegs;
5. any ~ auf jeden Fall; 6. by
~ of über, durch; mit Hilfe
gen; 7. by the ~ (fig) neben-
bei (gesagt).

way|-**bill** [ˈweɪbɪl] Fracht-
brief m; ~**lay** [ˌ-ˈleɪ] irr s. lay
auflauern (s.o. jdm); ~**side**
[-ˌsaɪd] Straßenrand m.

wayward [ˈweɪwəd] widerspenstig.

we [wiː, wɪ] wir.

weak [wiːk] schwach; ~**en**
[ˈ-ən] 1. schwächen;
2. schwächer werden;
~**ness** [ˈ-nɪs] Schwäche f
(for für).

wealth [welθ] Reichtum m (of an); **~y** ['-ɪ] reich (in an).
weapon ['wepən] Waffe f a. fig.
wear [weə] **I** v irr wore [wɔ:], worn [wɔ:n] 1. (Kleidung) tragen; 2. (~ away) abtragen, -nutzen; ~ down zermürben; ~ out ermüden; 3. ~ well sich gut halten a. fig; II s 4. Tragen n; for hard ~ strapazierfähig; 5. Kleidung f; foot~ Schuhwerk n; men's, women's, children's ~ Herren-, Damen-, Kinder(be)kleidung f; 6. (~ and tear) Abnutzung f.
wear|iness ['wɪərɪnɪs] Müdigkeit f; **~y** ['-ɪ] 1. müde; 2. ermüdend; 3. überdrüssig (of s.th. e-r S).
weather ['weðə] **I** s Wetter n; **II** v 1. überstehen; 2. verwittern (lassen); **~-beaten** [-,bi:tn] verwittert; ~ **forecast** Wettervorhersage f.
weave [wi:v] irr wove [wəuv], woven ['wəuvən] 1. weben; 2. ~ o.'s way sich schlängeln (through durch); **~r** ['-ə] Weber m.
web [web] 1. Gewebe, Netz n; 2. Schwimmhaut f.
wed [wed] heiraten.
we'd [wi:d] fam = we had, we should, we would.

wedding ['wedɪŋ] Hochzeit f; **~-ring** Ehering m.
wedge [wedʒ] **I** s Keil m; **II** v verkeilen; be ~d between eingekeilt sein zwischen.
Wednesday ['wenzdɪ] Mittwoch m.
weed [wi:d] **I** s Unkraut n; **II** v (Garten) jäten.
week [wi:k] Woche f; this day ~ heute in od vor 8 Tagen; once a ~ (einmal) wöchentlich; **~day** ['-deɪ] Wochentag m; **~-end** ['-end] Wochenende n; **~ly** ['-lɪ] **I** adj, adv wöchentlich; **II** s Wochenzeitschrift f.
weep [wi:p] irr wept, wept [wept] weinen.
weigh [weɪ] 1. wiegen; 2. fig (~ up) abschätzen; 3. lasten (on auf); ~ down niederdrücken a. fig; 4. (mar) ~ anchor die Anker lichten.
weight [weɪt] 1. Gewicht n a. fig; 2. carry ~ (fig) wichtig sein; Einfluß haben; **~-lifting** ['-lɪftɪŋ] sport Gewichtheben n.
welcome ['welkəm] **I** adj 1. willkommen; 2. you're ~ bitte sehr, nichts zu danken! **II** v willkommen heißen; **III** s: give s.o. a warm ~ jdm e-n herzlichen Empfang bereiten.
weld [weld] tech schweißen.
welfare ['welfeə] Wohlfahrt; Fürsorge f; ~ **state** Wohlfahrtsstaat m.
well [wel] **I** s 1. Brunnen m; 2. min Bohrloch n; 3. Luft-, Licht-, Fahrstuhlschacht m; **II** adv gut; as ~ as ebenso-

gut wie; sowohl ... als auch; *pretty* ~ so ziemlich; *do* ~ wohlauf sein; **III** *adj: get* ~ gesund werden; **IV** *interj* hm! nun! gut!

we'll [wi:l] *fam* = *we shall, we will.*

well|-**being** ['wel‚bi:ɪŋ] Wohl(befinden, -sein) *n;* ~-**known** ['-nəʊn] (wohl)bekannt; ~-**meaning** [‚-'mi:nɪŋ] wohlmeinend; ~ **off,** ~-**to-do** [‚-tə'du:] wohlhabend.

Welsh [welʃ] walisisch; ~**man** ['-mən] Waliser *m.*

we're [wɪə] = *we are.*

west [west] **I** *s* West(en) *m;* **II** *adj* westlich; **III** *adv* nach Westen; ~**ern** ['-ən] westlich; ~**ward(s)** ['-wəd(z)] nach Westen.

wet [wet] naß; ~ *paint!* frisch gestrichen!

we've [wi:v] = *we have.*

whale [weɪl] Wal(fisch) *m.*

wharf [wɔ:f] *pl* ~*s* od *wharves* [wɔ:vz] Kai *m.*

what [wɒt] **I** *prn* was, wie; ~ *about, of?* wie steht es mit ...? ~ *for?* warum? ~'s *your name?* wie heißen Sie? ~ *is he like?* wie ist er? **II** *adj* welche(r, s); ~ *time is it?* wieviel Uhr ist es? ~**ever** [-'evə] was auch; alles, was; *no* ... ~ überhaupt kein.

wheat [wi:t] Weizen *m.*

wheel [wi:l] **I** *s* Rad; Steuer, Lenkrad *n;* **II** *v* rollen, schie-

ben; ~-**chair** [‚-'tʃeə] Rollstuhl *m.*

when [wen] **I** *adv, conj* 1. wann; 2. als; **II** *prn: since, until* ~ seit, bis wann? ~**ever** [-'evə] wann auch immer.

where [weə] wo; wohin; ~**abouts I** *adv* [‚weərə'baʊts] wo; **II** *s* [‚--] Aufenthalt(sort) *m;* ~**as** [weər'æz] während, wohingegen.

wherever [weər'evə] wo auch immer.

whet [wet] 1. wetzen, schleifen; 2. *(den Appetit)* anregen.

whether [weðə] ob.

which [wɪtʃ] der, die, das; welche(r, s).

whiff [wɪf] 1. (Luft-)Zug *m;* 2. Geruch *m.*

while [waɪl] **I** *s* Weile *f; for a* ~ e-e Zeitlang; *once in a* ~ gelegentlich; **II** *conj a. whilst* ['-st] während.

whim [wɪm] Einfall *m,* Laune *f.*

whimper ['wɪmpə] wimmern.

whimsical ['wɪmzɪkl] launisch.

whine [waɪn] wimmern, winseln.

whip [wɪp] **I** *v* peitschen, schlagen; **II** *s* Peitsche *f a. fig;* ~**ped cream** Schlagsahne *f.*

whirl [wɜ:l] **I** *v* wirbeln; **II** *s* Wirbel *m a. fig; in a* ~ in Verwirrung; ~**pool** ['-pu:l]

Strudel *m a. fig;* **~wind** ['-wɪnd] Wirbelwind *m.*

whisk [wɪsk] **I** *v* (*Eiweiß*) schlagen; **II** *s* Schneebesen *m.*

whiskers *pl* ['wɪskəz] Backenbart *m.*

whisper ['wɪspə] **I** *v* 1. wispern, flüstern; 2. *(Wind)* rauschen; **II** *s* Geflüster *n.*

whistle ['wɪsl] **I** *v* pfeifen; **II** *s* 1. Pfiff *m;* 2. (Signal-)Pfeife *f.*

white [waɪt] **I** *adj* weiß; **II** *s* das Weiße (*of the eye* im Auge); (*~ of egg*) Eiweiß *n;* **~-collar worker** Büroangestellte(r) *m;* **~ lie** Notlüge *f;* **~wash** ['-wɔʃ] **I** *s* Tünche *f;* **II** *v* 1. tünchen; 2. *(Sache)* beschönigen.

Whitsun ['wɪtsn] Pfingsten *pl.*

whiz [wɪz] zischen; sausen;

who [hu:] wer; der, die, das; welche(r, s); **~ever** ['-'evə] wer auch (immer).

whole [həʊl] **I** *adj* ganz; **II** *s das* Ganze, Gesamtheit *f; on the* **~** alles in allem; **~sale** ['-seɪl] Großhandel *m.*

wholesome ['həʊlsəm] gesund; zuträglich.

wholly ['həʊllɪ] gänzlich, völlig.

whom [hu:m] wen; *(to ~)* wem.

whooping-cough ['hu:pɪŋkɔf] Keuchhusten *m.*

whose [hu:z] 1. wessen; 2. dessen, deren.

why [waɪ] warum, weshalb, wofür; **~,** *yes!* natürlich!

wick [wɪk] Docht *m.*

wicked ['wɪkɪd] böse, übel; **~ness** ['-nɪs] Schlechtigkeit *f.*

wicker ['wɪkə] **~** *basket* Weidenkorb *m;* **~** *furniture* Korbmöbel *pl.*

wicket ['wɪkɪt] *(~gate)* Pförtchen.

wide [waɪd] **I** *adj* weit; breit; **II** *adv* 1. (**~** *of*) weit (weg), weitab; 2. *far and* **~** weit u. breit; **~-awake** ['-əweɪk] *fig* wachsam, aufmerksam (*to* auf); **~ly** ['-lɪ] weit; in hohem Maße, sehr; **~n** ['-n] erweitern; **~spread** ['-spred] weit verbreitet.

widow ['wɪdəʊ] Witwe *f;* **~ed** [-d] verwitwet; **~er** [-ə] Witwer *m.*

width [wɪdθ] Weite, Breite *f.*

wife [waɪf] *pl* **wives** [waɪvz] (Ehe-)Frau, Gattin *f.*

wig [wɪg] Perücke *f.*

wild [waɪld] wild; *run* **~** verwildern; **~erness** ['wɪldənɪs] Wildnis *f a. fig;* **~fire** ['-ˌfaɪə] *spread like* **~** *(fig)* sich wie ein Lauffeuer verbreiten.

wilful, *Am* **willful** ['wɪlfʊl] 1. absichtlich; 2. halsstarrig.

will [wɪl] **I** *v irr (pret)* **would** [wʊd] 1. *(Futur)* I'll come ich werde kommen; 2. wollen, willens sein; **~** *you please come in?* würden Sie bitte hereinkommen;

II *s* 3. Wille, Wunsch *m;* Verlangen *n; at* ~ nach Wunsch; 4. Testament *n;* ~**ing** ['-ɪŋ] bereitwillig.

willow ['wɪləʊ] Weide *f.*

wilt [wɪlt] (ver)welken.

win [wɪn] *irr* won, won [wʌn] 1. gewinnen; 2. siegen, Erfolg haben.

wince [wɪns] zs.-, zurückzukken.

wind I *s* [wɪnd] Wind *m;* **II** *v* [waɪnd] *irr* wound, wound [waʊnd] 1. kurbeln; (auf)wickeln; 2. umwinden, -wickeln; 3. sich schlängeln; sich winden; 4. ~ *up (Uhr)* aufziehen; 5. ~ *up* (be)enden.

windfall ['wɪndfɔ:l] 1. Fallobst *n;* 2. *fig* Glücksfall *m.*

wind instrument *mus* Blasinstrument *n.*

window ['wɪndəʊ] Fenster *n;* ~**-box** [-bɒks] Blumenkasten *m;* ~**-pane** [-peɪn] Fensterscheibe *f;* ~**-shopping** [-ʃɒpɪŋ] *go* ~ e-n Schaufensterbummel machen.

wind|pipe ['wɪndpaɪp] *anat* Luftröhre *f;* ~**screen** ['-skri:n] , *Am* ~**shield** ['-ʃi:ld] *mot* Windschutzscheibe *f;* ~ *wiper* Scheibenwischer *m;* ~**y** ['wɪndɪ] windig.

wine [waɪn] Wein *m;* ~**glass** ['-glɑ:s] Weinglas *n.*

wing [wɪŋ] Flügel *m; take* ~

davonfliegen; *take* ~s spurlos verschwinden.

wink [wɪŋk] **I** *v* blinzeln; zwinkern; **II** *s* Blinzeln, Zwinkern *n.*

winn|er ['wɪnə] 1. Gewinner *m;* 2. *sport* Sieger *m;* ~**ing** ['wɪnɪŋ] **I** *adj* gewinnend *a. fig;* **II** *s pl* (Geld-)Gewinn *m.*

winter ['wɪntə] Winter *m;* ~ **sports** *pl* Wintersport *m.*

wintry ['wɪntrɪ] winterlich.

wipe [waɪp] **I** *s: give s.th. a good* ~ etw ordentlich putzen; **II** *v* (ab)wischen, -trocknen; ~ *out (fig)* auslöschen; ~**r** ['-ə] *mot* Scheibenwischer *m.*

wire ['waɪə] **I** *s* 1. Draht *m;* 2. *fam* Telegramm *n;* **II** *v* telegrafieren.

wireless ['waɪəlɪs] **I** *adj* drahtlos; **II** *s (veraltet für:)* Radio *n.*

wisdom ['wɪzdəm] Weisheit, Klugheit *f;* ~**tooth** [-tu:θ] Weisheitszahn *m.*

wise [waɪz] klug, vernünftig.

wish [wɪʃ] **I** *v* 1. (sich) wünschen; wollen; 2. ~ *s.o. (good) luck* jdm Glück wünschen; **II** *s* Wunsch *m.*

wistful ['wɪstfʊl] sehnsüchtig.

wit [wɪt] *oft pl* 1. Verstand *m; be at o.'s* ~*s' end* mit s-r Weisheit am Ende sein; 2. Geist, Witz *m;* 3. witzige(r) Kopf *m.*

witch [wɪtʃ] Hexe *f;* ~**craft**

['-kra:ft] , **~ery** ['-əri] Hexerei, Zauberei *f.*

with [wɪð] mit; ~ *the window open* bei offenem Fenster; ~ *all his faults* trotz all s-r Fehler; *tremble ~ fear* vor Angst zittern.

withdraw [wɪð'drɔ:] *irr s. draw* 1. (sich) zurückziehen, -nehmen; 2. *(Geld)* abheben; **~al** [-əl] 1. Abhebung *f (vom Konto)*; 2. Rückzug *m.*

wither ['wɪðə] (ver)welken.

withhold [wɪð'həuld] *irr s. hold* verweigern, vorenthalten (*s.th. from s.o.* jdm etw).

within [wɪ'ðɪn] innerhalb *gen.*

without [wɪ'ðaut] ohne; *that goes ~ saying* das versteht sich von selbst.

withstand [wɪð'stænd] *irr s. stand* aus-, standhalten *dat.*

witness ['wɪtnɪs] **I** *s* 1. Zeuge *m;* 2. *bear ~* Zeugnis ablegen (*to s.th.* von e-r S); **II** *v* 3. sehen, miterleben; 4. bezeugen (*to s.th.* etw); **~-box** [-bɒks] , *Am* **~-stand** [-stænd] Zeugenstand *m.*

witty ['wɪtɪ] witzig.

wizard ['wɪzəd] Zauberer *m.*

woe [wəu] Leid *n*, Schmerz *m.*

wolf [wulf] *pl* **wolves** [wulvz] Wolf *m.*

woman ['wumən] *pl* **women** ['wɪmɪn] Frau *f.*

womb [wu:m] *anat* Gebärmutter *f.*

wonder ['wʌndə] **I** *s* 1. Wunder *n a. fig;* 2. Verwunde-

rung *f,* Erstaunen *n;* **II** *v* 3. sich (ver)wundern; verwundert sein (*at* über); 4. sich fragen; gern wissen wollen; **~ful** [-ful] wunderbar; erstaunlich.

won't [wəunt] = *will not.*

wood [wud] 1. Wald(ung *f*) *m; out of the ~ (fig)* über den Berg; 2. Holz *n;* **~ed** ['-ɪd] bewaldet; **~en** ['wudn] hölzern *a. fig;* **~pecker** ['-,pekə] Specht *m;* **~work** ['-wɜːk] 1. Holzarbeiten *f pl;* 2. Balkenwerk *n.*

wool [wul] Wolle *f;* **~(l)en** ['-ən] **I** *adj* wollen; **II** *s pl* (~ *goods)* Woll-, Strickwaren *f pl;* **~ly** ['-ɪ] wollig.

word [wɜːd] **I** *s* 1. Wort *n; by ~ of mouth* mündlich; *break, keep o.'s ~* sein Wort brechen, halten; 2. Bescheid *m,* Nachricht *f; leave ~* eine Nachricht hinterlassen; **II** *v* formulieren; **~ing** ['-ɪŋ] Formulierung *f.*

work [wɜːk] **I** *s* 1. Arbeit *f; make short ~ of* kurzen Prozeß machen mit; *set, get to ~* sich an die Arbeit machen; *skilled ~* Facharbeit *f;* 2. Werk *n;* 3. *pl* Anlage(n *pl*) *f;* Fabrik *f; water ~s (pl)* Wasserwerk *n;* **II** *v* 4. arbeiten; beschäftigt sein (*at* mit); 5. funktionieren; ~ **out** 1. ausrechnen; 2. erfinden; 3. *work out well* sich gut anlassen; 4. *work out at* sich belaufen auf; ~ **up** 1. sich

steigern (*to* zu);
2. *(Geschäft)* hochbringen;
3. *fig* aufpeitschen.

work|able ['wɜːkəbl] 1. bearbeitbar; 2. durchführbar;
~**day** ['-deɪ] Werktag *m;*
~**er** ['-ə] Arbeiter *m;* ~**ing**
['-ɪŋ] *in* ~ *order* betriebsfähig; ~ *class* Arbeiterklasse
f; ~**shop** ['-ʃɒp] Werkstatt
f.

world [wɜːld] Welt, Erde *f; a*
~, ~s *of* e-e Menge, sehr
viel; *think the* ~ *of* große
Stücke halten auf; ~ **fair**
Weltausstellung *f;* ~**ly** ['-lɪ]
weltlich, irdisch; ~**-wide**
['-waɪd] weltweit.

worm [wɜːm] Wurm *m a. fig.*

worr|ied ['wʌrɪd] beunruhigt
(*about* über); ~**y** ['wʌrɪ] **I** *v*
1. beunruhigen, Sorgen machen; ärgern, quälen;
2. beunruhigt sein (*about,
over* über); **II** *s* Ärger *m;*
Sorge *f;* Kummer *m.*

worse [wɜːs] **I** *adj* schlechter, schlimmer; *he's none
the* ~ *for it* es hat ihm nichts
geschadet; **II** *s: a change
for the* ~ eine Wendung
zum Schlechten; ~**n** ['-n]
(sich) verschlechtern.

worship ['wɜːʃɪp] **I** *s rel* Verehrung *f;* Gottesdienst *m;*
II *v* verehren; anbeten.

worst ['wɜːst] **I** *adj* schlechtest, übelst; **II** *adv* am
schlimmsten, am ärgsten;
III *s: at (the)* ~ schlimmstenfalls; *if the* ~ *comes to the* ~

im allerschlimmsten Fall; *get
the* ~ *of it* den kürzeren ziehen.

worsted ['wʊstɪd] Kammgarn *n.*

worth [wɜːθ] **I** *s* Wert *m; a
pound's* ~ *of apples* für 1 £
Äpfel; **II** *adj* wert; ~**less**
['-lɪs] wertlos; ~**while**
[,-'waɪl] der Mühe wert; ~**y**
['wɜːðɪ] würdig, wert (*of s.th.*
e-r S).

would [wʊd] *pret von will*
würde; möchte; wollte;
~**-be** ['-biː] angeblich; ~**n't**
['-nt] = *would not.*

wound [wuːnd] **I** *s* Wunde *f;*
II *v* verwunden *a. fig.*

wrangle ['ræŋgl] (sich) zanken.

wrap [ræp] 1. wickeln
(*round* um); 2. (~ *up*) einwickeln; 3. *be* ~*ped up in*
(fig) völlig in Anspruch genommen sein von; ~**per**
['-ə] *(Buch)* Schutzumschlag
m; ~**ping** ['-ɪŋ] *meist pl*
Verpackung(smaterial *n*) *f.*

wreath [riːθ] *pl* ~*s* [riːðz]
Kranz *m.*

wreck [rek] **I** *s* 1. Wrack *n;*
2. Untergang, Ruin; Schiffbruch *m;* **II** *v* zerstören *a.
fig;* ~**age** ['-ɪdʒ] Trümmer
pl.

wren [ren] *orn* Zaunkönig *m.*

wrench [rentʃ] **I** *s* 1. (heftiger) Ruck *m;* 2. *med* Verrenkung *f;* 3. *tech* Schraubenschlüssel *m;*

II *v* 4. (ent)reißen (*from* aus); 5. *med* verrenken.

wrestle ['resl] ringen.

wretch [retʃ] Schuft *m;* ~**ed** ['-ɪd] elend, erbärmlich.

wriggle ['rɪgl] ~ *(o.s.) out* sich herauswinden (*of s.th.* aus etw).

wring [rɪŋ] *irr* **wrung, wrung** [rʌŋ] 1. (~ *out*) auswringen; 2. *fig* erpressen (*from* von).

wrinkle ['rɪŋkl] I *s* Falte, Runzel *f;* II *v* (sich) runzeln; *(Stoff)* knittern.

wrist [rɪst] Handgelenk *n;* ~**watch** ['-wɒtʃ] Armbanduhr *f.*

write [raɪt] *irr* **wrote** [rəʊt], **written** ['rɪtn] schreiben; ~ *down* nieder-, aufschreiben.

writer ['raɪtə] Schriftsteller *m.*

writing ['raɪtɪŋ] 1. Schreiben *n; put down in* ~ niederschreiben; 2. (Hand-)Schrift *f;* 3. *pl* Werk *n;* ~**-desk** [-desk] Schreibtisch *m.*

wrong [rɒŋ] I *adj* verkehrt, falsch; unrecht; *be* ~ unrecht haben; sich irren; *there is s.th.* ~ da stimmt etw nicht (*with* mit); II *s* Unrecht *n;* III *v* ein Unrecht zufügen (*s.o.* jdm); ~**ly** ['-lɪ] falsch, zu Unrecht.

wrought iron [,rɔːt'aɪən] Schmiedeeisen *n.*

wry [raɪ] *(Lächeln)* gezwungen; *make a* ~ *face* das Gesicht verziehen.

X

Xmas ['krısməs] = *Christmas* Weihnachten *n.*
X-ray ['eksreı] **I** *s* 1. Rönt-
genstrahl *m;* 2. Röntgenaufnahme *f;* **II** *v* 3. röntgen; 4. durchleuchten.

Y

yacht [jɒt] *mar* Jacht *f;* **~ing** ['-ıŋ] Segelsport *m.*
yap [jæp] kläffen *a. fig.*
yard [jɑ:d] 1. Yard *n* (= 0,914 m); 2. Hof *m.*
yarn [jɑ:n] 1. Garn *n;* 2. *fig fam* Seemannsgarn *n.*
yawn [jɔ:n] gähnen *a. fig.*
year [jɜ:, jɪə] Jahr *n; all (the)* ~ *round* das ganze Jahr über; **~ly** ['-lı] jährlich.
yearn [jɜ:n] sich sehnen (*for* nach); **~ing** ['-ıŋ] Sehnsucht *f.*
yeast [ji:st] Hefe *f.*
yell [jel] **I** *v* (laut) schreien *n;* **II** *s* gellende(r) Schrei *m.*
yellow ['jeləu] **I** *adj* gelb; **II** *s* 1. gelbe Farbe *f;* 2. Eigelb *n;* ~ **fever** *med* Gelbfieber *n.*
yelp [jelp] kläffen.
yes [jes] ja, jawohl.
yesterday ['jestədı] **I** *adv* gestern; **II** *s* der gestrige Tag; *the day before* ~ vorgestern.
yet [jet] **I** *adv* noch; jetzt; schon; *as* ~ bis jetzt; *not* ~

noch nicht; **II** *conj* (je)doch; dennoch.
yield [ji:ld] **I** *v* 1. hervorbringen, liefern; 2. einbringen, abwerfen; 3. nachgeben; 4. aufgeben; **II** *s* Ertrag *m.*
yoke [jəuk] Joch *n.*
yolk [jəuk] Dotter *m od n,* Eigelb *n.*
you [ju:, ju, jə] *prn* ihr, euch; du, dir, dich; Sie, Ihnen; *fam* man; einen.
you'd [ju:d] = *you had; you would.*
you'll [ju:l] = *you will; you shall.*
young [jʌŋ] **I** *adj* jung; **II** *s* (Tier-)Junge(s) *n; with* ~ (Tier) trächtig; **~ster** ['-stə] Junge *m;* Kind *n.*
your [jɔ:, jə] euer, eu(e)re; dein(e); Ihr(e).
you're [juə] = *you are.*
yours [jɔ:z] der, die, das eu(e)re, deine, Ihre; *this book is* ~ dieses Buch gehört dir, euch, Ihnen; ~ *truly* hochachtungsvoll.
yourself [jɔ:'self] *pl your-*

selves [-'selvz] du, Sie selbst; *(all) by* ~ allein.
youth [ju:θ] 1. Jugend *f;* 2. junge(r) Mann *m;* ~**ful** ['-fʊl] jugendlich; ~ **hostel** Jugendherberge *f.*

you've [ju:v] = *you have.*
Yugoslav ['ju:gəʊslɑ:v] , ~**ian** [ˌju:gəʊ'slɑ:vɪən] **I** *s* Jugoslawe *m;* **II** *adj* jugoslawisch; ~**ia** [ˌju:gəʊ'slɑ:vɪə] Jugoslawien *n.*

Z

zeal [zi:l] Eifer *m;* Begeisterung *f (for* für); ~**ous** ['zeləs] eifrig; begeistert.
zebra ['zi:brə] Zebra *n;* ~ **crossing** Zebrastreifen *m.*
zenith ['zenɪθ] Zenit *m a. fig; at the* ~ *of (fig)* auf dem Höhepunkt *gen.*
zephyr ['zefə] Westwind *m.*
zero ['zɪərəʊ] *pl -os* Null *f; fall to* ~ auf 0 Grad fallen; ~ **hour** entscheidende(r) Augenblick *m.*
zest [zest] 1. Begeisterung *f;* 2. *fig* Würze *f;* Reiz *m.*

zigzag ['zɪgzæg] *go in a* ~ im

Zickzack gehen; ~ **path** Zickzackweg *m.*
zip [zɪp] **I** *s* 1. Zischen, Surren *n;* 2. Reißverschluß *m;* **II** *v:* ~ *up, open* mit e-m Reißverschluß schließen, öffnen; ~**er** ['-ə] , ~-**fastener** ['-ˌfɑ:snə] Reißverschluß *m.*
zodiac ['zəʊdɪæk] *astr* Tierkreis *m.*
zone [zəʊn] Zone *f;* Bezirk *m.*
zoo [zu:] Zoo *m.*
zoologic(al) [ˌzəʊə'lɒdʒɪk(l)] zoologisch; ~**y** [zəʊ'ɒlədʒɪ] Zoologie *f.*
zoom [zu:m] steil aufsteigen.

Klett's Super-Mini German and English Dictionary

GERMAN-ENGLISH

Explanations

Arrangement and Subdivision of Entries

The boldface base words are in strict alphabetical order. The umlaut does not affect word order.

Example: **Backen|bart** *m* whiskers *pl;* **~zahn** *m* molar.
Bäcker *m* baker; **~ei** *f* bakery.
Back|huhn *n* fried chicken; **~ofen** *m* oven; ...

A base word may be subdivided through the use of:

a) *Roman numerals,* when an entry can belong to various parts of speech.

Example: **verschlafen I** *irr* oversleep; **II** *adj* sleepy.

b) *Arabic numerals,* to distinguish radical differences in meaning possible for an entry.

Example: **Ballast** *m* 1. ballast; 2. *fig* burden.

c) the *semicolon,* between translations having different meanings (when Arabic numerals are not used).

Example: **Bauch** *m* belly; abdomen; ...

Tilde (∼)

The tilde replaces:

a) the boldface base word.

Example: **Brief** *m* letter; ∼**kasten** *m* letter-box; ...

b) the part of a base word up to the vertical stroke (|).

Example: **bedroh|en** threaten; ∼**lich** threatening.

c) in sayings and idiomatic expressions, the preceding boldface entry.

Example: **ersuchen** ask, request; **E**∼ *n* request; *auf sein* ∼ at his request.

Grammatical Notes

Adverbial forms are given only when they are unusual in formation or meaning.

The gender of nouns is indicated through the use of *m, f* or *n* (however, not in the case of nouns in italics, nouns in practical examples or nouns that exist only in the plural).

With irregular German verbs, *irr* is used to indicate the irregularity; however, the principal parts are not given.

A Few Special Points

Where the base word that is replaced by the tilde begins with a *lowercase* letter (whereas in itself it would begin with a *capitàl)*, the lowercase letter is put before the tilde.

Example: **erschöpf|end** exhaustive; **~t** exhausted;
E~ung *f* exhaustion.
Front *f* front; **f~al** head-on.

If a *hyphen* occurring at the end of a line must be read as a dash, the hyphen is repeated at the beginning of the next line to make it clear that the word would normally be written with a dash.

Example: **turning-**
-point (turning-point).

The *stress* of a German word is always indicated by the mark ' which in each case stands immediately before the syllable to be stressed.

Example: **'übersetzen** ...;
über'setzen ...

Differences in meaning are indicated through the use of explanatory words in italics or information relating to the subject (in italics, preceding the translation).

Example: **Aufzug** *m* 1. lift, *Am* elevator; 2. *theat* act;
3. *(Festzug)* procession.

The spelling of the German words is according to the 18th newly revised and expanded edition of Duden, *Rechtschreibung der deutschen Sprache und der Fremdwörter*, Mannheim 1980; the orthographical basis for the English is the *Oxford Advanced Learner's Dictionary of Current English*, 11th revised edition, Oxford 1980.

A

Aal *m* eel.

ab I *adv* off; from; *von da* ~ from that time forward; *von jetzt* ~ from now on; ~ *und zu* now and then; *auf und* ~ *gehen* walk up and down; **II** *prp:* ~ *Hamburg* from Hamburg; ~ *Fabrik* ex works; ~ *heute* from today.

abändern change, modify; **A~ung** *f* modification.

Abbau *m* reduction; dismantling; **a~en** 1. *(Gebäude)* dismantle; 2. *(Zölle)* reduce; 3. *(Beamte)* dismiss.

abbestellen 1. *(Auftrag)* countermand; 2. *(Abonnement)* cancel.

abbiegen *irr* bend off; *von e-r Straße* ~ turn off a road; *rechts, links* ~ turn right, left.

Abbildung *f* picture, illustration.

abblenden *mot* dip the headlights; **A~licht** *n* dipped headlights.

abbrechen *irr* 1. *(wegbrechen)* break off; 2. *(Häuser)* pull down; 3. *(beenden)* stop.

abbrennen *irr* burn down.

abbringen *irr* dissuade *(jdn von etw* s.o. from doing s.th.).

Abbruch *m* 1. *(e-s Gebäu-* *des)* demolition; 2. *fig* breaking off.

Abc *n* alphabet.

abdanken abdicate; **A~ung** *f* abdication.

abdecken *(Tisch)* clear.

abdichten make tight.

abdrehen 1. *(Gas)* turn off; 2. *(Licht)* switch off.

Abend *m* 1. evening, night; *am* ~ in the evening; *gegen* ~ towards evening; *heute a~* this evening, tonight; *gestern a~* last night; *zu ~ essen* have supper; 2. *der Heilige* ~ Christmas Eve; **~dämmerung** *f* dusk; **~kleid** *n* evening dress; **~land** *n* the Occident; **~mahl** *n* the Lord's supper.

abends in the evening.

Abendzeitung *f* evening paper.

Abenteuer *n* adventure; **a~erlich** adventurous; strange; **~rer** *m* adventurer.

aber 1. *(Gegensatz)* but; *(jedoch)* however; *oder* ~ or else, otherwise; 2. *(Erstaunen)* *nein* ~ I say.

Aberglaube *m* superstition; **a~gläubisch** superstitious.

abfahren *irr* 1. *(Person)* depart, leave; 2. *(Schiff)* sail; *(Zug)* pull out.

Abfahrt *f* 1. departure;

2. *(Schiff)* sailing; **~zeit** *f* time of departure.

Abfall *m* 1. *(Überbleibsel)* waste, refuse; 2. *(Müll)* rubbish, garbage; **~eimer** *m* dustbin.

abfallen *irr* 1. *(Blätter)* fall off; 2. *(Gewinn)* yield a profit; 3. *(schräg sein)* slope, descend; 4. *fig (Leistung)* decline, drop.

abfärben rub off.

abfassen write, draw up.

abfertig|en 1. *(Waren)* dispatch; 2. *(bedienen)* serve; deal with; **A~ung** *f* dispatch; service.

abfind|en *irr* 1. *(entschädigen)* satisfy, pay off; 2. *sich damit ~* make the best of it; **A~ung** *f* compensation, indemnity.

abfliegen *irr aero* take off.

Abflug *m* take off.

abführ|en 1. lead away; 2. *(Steuern)* pay off; **A~-mittel** *n* purgative, laxative.

abfüllen *(in Flaschen)* bottle.

Abgabe *f* 1. *(Paket)* delivery; 2. *(Steuer)* duty, rate, tax; 3. *(Gepäck)* depositing, *Am* checking; **a~nfrei** duty-free.

Abgas *n mot* exhaust gas.

abgeben *irr* 1. *(übergeben)* give up, hand over; *abzugeben bei* care of, c/o; 2. *(Gepäck)* leave; 3. *(Urteil)* pass; 4. *sich mit etw ~* occupy o.s. with; *sich mit jdm ~* associate with s.o.

abgehen *irr* 1. *(weggehen)* leave; *(Zug)* start; 2. *(sich ablösen)* come off; 3. *(ändern)* change; 4. *(abweichen)* digress; 5. *(Straße)* branch off.

abgehetzt breathless.

abgelegen remote, out-of--the-way.

abgemacht agreed; *das ist e-e ~e Sache* that's settled.

abgenutzt worn-out.

Abgeordneter *m* deputy.

abgesehen: *~ von* apart from.

abgespannt *(müde)* tired out.

abgewöhnen: *sich etw ~* break o.s. of the habit of.

abgrenzen mark off, limit.

Abgrund *m* precipice.

abhalten *irr* 1. keep away *(jdn von* s.o. from); 2. *(hindern)* prevent, hinder; 3. *(Sitzung)* hold; *(Gottesdienst)* celebrate.

abhandeln *(erörtern)* treat, discuss.

abhanden: *~ kommen* get lost.

Abhandlung *f* treatise, dissertation, paper.

Abhang *m* slope.

abhäng|en *irr fig* depend *(von* on); **~ig** dependent *(von* on); **A~igkeit** *f* dependence.

abhauen *irr* cut off.

abheben *irr* 1. *(Hörer, Deckel)* take off, lift off, remove; 2. *aero* take off;

3. *(Geld)* withdraw (money from the bank); 4. *sich* ~ distinguish o.s.

abhelfen *irr* remedy.

Abhilfe *f:* ~ *schaffen* remedy.

abholen 1. fetch, collect; 2. call for *(jdn* s.o.); *(am Bahnhof)* go to meet s.o. at the station; ~ *lassen* send for.

Abitur *n* school-leaving examination or final examination (at German secondary schools).

abkaufen buy, purchase *(von jdm* from s.o.).

abkochen boil, *(Milch)* scald.

abkommen *irr* 1. lose o.'s way; 2. give up *(von etw* s.th.); 3. *(Thema)* get off; **A~** *n* treaty, accord.

abkühlen cool.

abkürz|en 1. shorten; 2. *(Wort)* abbreviate; **A~ung** *f* 1. abbreviation; 2. *(Weg)* short cut.

abladen *irr* unload, dump.

ablassen *irr* 1. *(Wasser)* drain off; 2. *(Luft)* let off; 3. *von etw* ~ desist from s.th.

Ablauf *m* 1. *(Verlauf)* course; 2. *(e-r Frist)* expiration; *nach* ~ at the expiration; **a~en** *irr* 1. *(Frist)* expire; 2. *(Schuhe)* wear out; 3. *gut* ~ end well.

ablegen 1. *(Kleider)* take off; 2. *(Gewohnheiten)* give up; 3. *(Last)* lay down; 4. *e-n Eid* ~ take an oath; *e-e Prüfung* ~ pass an examination.

ablehn|en 1. decline, refuse; 2. *(Antrag)* vote down, defeat; **~end** negative; **A~ung** *f* refusal, rejection.

ableiten *(Wort)* derive from.

ablenk|en 1. *(Aufmerksamkeit)* divert; *(Arbeit)* distract from; 2. *(zerstreuen)* divert, amuse; 3. *(vom Thema)* change the subject; **A~ung** *f fig* distraction.

abliefer|n deliver; **A~ung** *f* delivery; *bei* ~ on delivery.

ablös|en 1. detach, remove; 2. *jdn* ~ replace s.o.; *sich einander* ~ relieve one another; **A~ung** *f* relief.

abmach|en 1. take off, detach; 2. *(vereinbaren)* arrange; *das ist abgemacht* that's settled; **A~ung** *f* settlement, arrangement, agreement.

abmühen, *sich* take pains.

Abnahme *f* 1. *com* purchase; 2. decrease, reduction; 3. *(Gewicht)* loss.

abnehm|en *irr* 1. take off; 2. *tele* remove the receiver; 3. *jdn etw* ~ take s.th. from s.o.; 4. *com* purchase; 5. *an Zahl* ~ decrease; 6. *(Kräfte)* decline; 7. *(an Gewicht)* lose weight; **A~er** *m* buyer, purchaser.

Abneigung *f* dislike, aversion *(gegen* to).

abnorm abnormal.

abnutzen 1. *(Kräfte)* use up; 2. *(Kleider)* wear out.

abonnieren *(Zeitung)* subscribe *(auf* to).

abordn|en delegate; **A~ung** *f* delegation.

abraten *irr: jdm von etw ~* dissuade s.o. from s.th.

abräumen *(Geschirr)* clear away.

abreiben *irr* rub off.

Abreise *f* departure *(nach* for); *vor der ~* before leaving; **a~n** depart, leave, set out.

abreißen *irr* 1. tear off; 2. *(Haus)* pull down.

absagen 1. cancel; 2. *jdm ~* refuse s.o.'s invitation.

Absatz *m* 1. *(Abschnitt)* break, paragraph; 2. *(Schuh)* heel; 3. *(Waren)* sale, market; 4. *(Treppe)* landing.

abschaffen abolish; get rid of.

abschalten switch off.

Abscheu *m (Ekel)* disgust *(vor* for), loathing *(vor* for); **a~lich** detestable.

abschicken *(Brief)* send off, dispatch; post, mail.

Abschied *m* departure, farewell; *~ nehmen* take o.'s leave, bid farewell.

Abschlepp|dienst *m* break-down service; **a~en** tow off; **~seil** *n* towing rope; **~wagen** *m* break-down lorry.

abschließen *irr* 1. *(Türe)* lock up; 2. *(beenden)* finish; 3. *(Vertrag)* conclude; 4. *(Geschäft)* strike (a bargain); **~d** 1. final; 2. *~ bemerkte er* in conclusion he remarked.

Abschluß *m* 1. conclusion, end, close; 2. *(geschäftlich)* deal, transaction; **~prüfung** *f* finals.

abschmieren *mot* grease.

abschneiden *irr* 1. cut off; 2. *jdm das Wort ~* cut s.o. short; 3. *gut ~* do well.

Abschnitt *m* 1. *mil* sector; 2. *(Teil)* section, segment; 3. *(Buch)* paragraph; 4. *(Entwicklung)* period.

abschrecken frighten, discourage; **~d** repulsive.

abschreiben *irr* 1. copy; *(Schule)* crib; 2. *com (Forderung)* write off.

Abschrift *f* copy, duplicate.

abseh|bar *(Zukunft)* foreseeable; **~en** *irr* 1. *(Ende)* foresee; 2. *(verzichten auf)* refrain from; 3. *davon abgesehen* apart from this.

abseits 1. aside, apart; 2. *(Fußball)* off side.

absend|en *irr* 1. *(Brief, Paket)* send off, dispatch; *Br* post, *Am* mail; 2. *(Güter)* dispatch, forward; **A~er** *m* sender.

absetz|bar 1. removable; 2. *com* sal(e)able, marketable; **~en** 1. *(Last)* put down; 2. *(Theaterstück)* withdraw; 3. *(des Amtes ent-*

heben) remove s.o.; 4. *(Waren)* sell.

Absicht *f* intention, purpose; *mit ~* on purpose; **a~lich I** *adj* intentional, wilful; **II** *adv* on purpose.

absolut absolute.

absondern separate, isolate.

absperr|en 1. *(Polizei)* cordon off; 2. *(Straße)* block, barricade; 3. *(Tür)* lock; **A~ung** *f* 1. *(Strom)* stoppage; 2. *(Straße)* barricade.

abspielen 1. *(Musik)* play; 2. *sich ~ (fig)* take place.

absprechen *irr* 1. arrange; 2. *sich mit jdm ~* come to an agreement with s.o.

abspringen *irr* 1. jump off; 2. *fig (abtrünnig werden)* desert.

abspülen *(Geschirr)* wash up.

abstamm|en be descended from; **A~ung** *f* descent.

Abstand *m* 1. distance, interval; 2. *von etw ~ nehmen* desist from s.th.

abstauben dust.

abstech|en *irr* contrast *(von* with); **A~er** *m* trip, excursion.

abstehen *irr* 1. *(Gebäude)* stand off; 2. *(Ohren)* stick out.

absteigen *irr* 1. *(Rad)* get off; *(Pferd)* dismount; *(Wagen)* alight; 2. *(Berg)* come down, descend; 3. *(Hotel)* stay at.

abstell|en 1. *(Last)* put down; 2. *(Maschine)* stop, switch off; 3. *(parken)* park; 4. *fig* put an end to, abolish; **A~platz** *m* parking place.

Abstieg *m* descent.

abstimm|en 1. *(Farbe)* harmonize, match; 2. *pol* vote, ballot; *über etw ~ lassen* put s.th. to the vote; **A~ung** *f* 1. harmonization; 2. *pol* voting.

abstoßen *irr* 1. push off; 2. *fig* repel; *~d* repulsive.

abstreiten *irr (leugnen)* deny.

Absturz *m* 1. fall; 2. *aero* crash.

abstürzen 1. fall down; 2. *(Flugzeug)* crash.

Abt *m* abbot; *~ei f* abbey.

Abteil *n* compartment.

abteil|en 1. *(abtrennen)* partition off, separate; 2. *(aufteilen)* divide; **A~ung** *f* 1. division; 2. *(Klinik)* ward; 3. *(Verwaltung)* section, department.

abtreib|en *irr* procure abortion; **A~ung** *f* abortion.

abtrennen detach, separate.

abtreten *irr* 1. *(Ansprüche, Gebiet)* cede, transfer; 2. *(Schuhe)* wipe; 3. *jdm etw ~* let s.o. have s.th.

abtrocknen *(Geschirr)* dry up; *(Hände)* wipe.

abwarten await, wait for; *das bleibt abzuwarten* that remains to be seen.

abwärts down, downwards.

abwaschen *irr* wash up.

Abwasser *n* waste, sewage.
abwechs|eln 1. alternate;
2. *miteinander* ~ take turns;
~**elnd** alternate, alternating;
A~lung *f* 1. alternation;
2. *(Unterbrechung)* change;
3. *(Zerstreuung)* distraction.
abweich|en *irr* 1. *(Richtung)*
deviate; 2. *(Meinung)* differ,
vary *(von* from); **A~ung** *f*
1. deviation, divergence;
2. difference.
abweisen *irr* refuse, reject;
~**d** unfriendly, rejecting.
abwenden *irr* 1. *(Blick)* turn
away; 2. *(Gefahr)* avert,
prevent; 3. *sich* ~ turn away
(von from).
abwert|en 1. depreciate;
2. *(Währung)* devaluate;
A~ung *f* devaluation; depreciation.
abwesen|d 1. absent; 2. *(gei-
stig)* absent-minded;
A~heit *f* absence.
abwick|eln 1. unwind; 2. *(Ge-
schäft)* settle; **A~lung** *f*
settlement.
abwiegen *irr* weigh out.
abwürgen *(Motor)* stall.
abzahlen 1. pay off; 2. *(in
Raten)* pay by instal(l)ments.
abzählen count out.
Abzahlung *f* payment by in-
stal(l)ments.
Abzeichen *n* 1. *(am Anzug)*
badge; 2. *(Merkmal)* mark,
sign.
abziehen *irr* 1. *(Hut)* take
off; 2. *(Bett)* strip; 3. *phot*
print; 4. *(Schlüssel)* take

out; 5. *math* subtract; 6. *com*
discount, deduct.
Abzug *m* 1. deduction, sub-
traction; 2. *com* discount;
nach ~ *der Kosten* expenses
deducted; 3. *typ* proof; copy;
4. *phot* print; 5. *mil* retreat.
abzüglich less, deducting.
abzweig|en branch off;
A~ung *f* 1. *(Straße)* branch,
bifurcation, junction; 2. *(Eisenbahn)* junction.
ach! oh! alas!; ~ *so!* oh, I see!
Achse *f* 1. axle; 2. *math* axis.
Achsel *f* shoulder; *die ~n
zucken* shrug o.'s shoulders.
acht eight; *alle* ~ *Tage* every
week; *heute in* ~ *Tagen* today week; *vor* ~ *Tagen* a
week ago.
Acht *f: etw außer a~ lassen*
disregard s.th.; *sich vor etw
in a~ nehmen* guard o.s.
against s.th.
achten 1. respect, esteem;
2. ~ *auf* take care of, pay attention to.
achtgeben *irr* pay attention
to.
Achtung *f* 1. respect, esteem; 2. ~*!* attention! caution! ~ *Stufe!* mind the step!
achtzig eighty.
Acker *m* arable ground, soil;
~**bau** *m* agriculture.
addieren add up.

ade goodbye, farewell.
Adel *m* aristocracy; nobility;
a~ig noble.
Ader *f* 1. vein; *(Schlag~)* ar-

tery; 2. *(Verkehr)* traffic artery.

Adler *m* eagle.

adoptieren adopt.

Adressat *m* addressee.

Adreßbuch *n* directory.

Adress|e *f* address; *per ~* care of (c/o); **a~ieren** address.

Advent *m* advent.

Affe *m* monkey.

Afrika *n* Africa; **~ner** *m,* **a~nisch** African.

After *m* anus.

Ägypt|en *n* Egypt; **~er** *m,* **ä~isch** Egyptian.

Agent *m* agent; **~ur** *f* agency.

ähneln: *jdm ~* resemble s.o.

ahnen 1. have a presentiment of, suspect; 2. *(erraten)* guess.

ähnlich like, similar; *jdm ~ sehen* look like s.o.; **Ä~keit** *f* likeness, similarity.

Ahnung *f* 1. presentiment; 2. *er hat keine ~ davon* he has no idea of it; **a~slos** unsuspecting.

Ahorn *m* maple (~tree).

Ähre *f* ear.

Akadem|ie *f* academy, college, university; **a~isch** academic.

akklimatisieren acclimatize.

Akkord *m* 1. *mus* chord; 2. *im ~ arbeiten* be on piece-work.

Akku(mulator) *m* accumulator.

Akrobat *m* acrobat.

Akt *m* 1. act, action; 2. *jur* deed; 3. *(Malerei)* nude.

Akte *f* file, dossier; *zu den ~n legen* file; **~nmappe, ~ntasche** *f* briefcase.

Aktie *f* share, *Am* stock; **~ngesellschaft** *f* joint--stock company.

Aktion *f* action.

Aktionär *m* shareholder, *Am* stockholder.

aktiv active; **A~ität** *f* activity.

Akustik *f* acoustics *pl.*

Alarm *m* alarm; **a~ieren** alarm, alert.

albern silly, absurd, foolish; **A~heit** *f* silliness.

Alge *f* alga.

Alkohol *m* alcohol; **a~frei** non-alcoholic, soft.

All *n* universe.

all 1. *(adjektivisch)* all; *vor ~en Dingen* above all; *auf ~e Fälle* in any case; 2. *(jeglich)* every, any; 3. *(Menge)* ~e *zwei Jahre* every two years; 4. *(substantivisch)* ~*e beide* both; ~*e vier* all four.

Allee *f* avenue.

allein I *adj* alone; **II** *adv* only; **~stehend** 1. isolated; 2. *(ledig)* single, unmarried.

allenfalls at the most.

aller|best best of all, very best; **~dings** though; certainly, indeed.

Allerheiligen *n* All Saints' Day.

allerlei all kinds of, various.

Allerseelen *n* All Souls' Day.

allerseits on all sides.

alles all, everything, anything; ~ *in allem* on the whole.

allgemein *a* universal, common to all, general; *im ~en* in general, generally; **A~bildung** *f* general education; **~verständlich** popular.

all|jährlich every year; **~mählich** gradual; little by little.

All|tag *m* everyday life; **a~täglich** 1. daily; 2. *(gewöhnlich)* commonplace.

Alpen *pl* Alps.

Alphabet *n* alphabet.

als 1. (*nach Komparativen u.* other, otherwise, else, rather) than; 2. *(zeitlich)* when, as; *damals ~* at the time when; 3. *(in der Eigenschaft)* as; ~ *Entschuldigung* as an excuse; 4. *(Vergleich)* as, *(bei Negation)* but; *so bald ~ möglich* as soon as possible; 5. ~ *ob* as if.

also I *conj* consequently, therefore; II *adv* so thus.

alt 1. old; aged; *wie ~ sind Sie?* how old are you? *Ich bin 20 Jahre ~* I am twenty years old; ~ *werden* grow old; 2. *(geschichtlich)* ancient; 3. *(ehemalig)* former; 4. *es bleibt alles beim ~en* everything remains as it was.

Altar *m* altar.

Alter *n* age; *im ~ von* at the age of.

älter older; *(innerhalb der Familie)* elder.

altern grow old.

Altersversorgung *f* old-age pension.

Alter|tum *n* antiquity; **~tümer** *pl* antiquties; **a~tümlich** archaic; ancient, antique.

altmodisch old-fashioned.

Alt|papier *n* waste paper; **~stadt** *f* old town, city.

Aluminium *n* aluminium.

am 1. *(räumlich) Frankfurt ~ Main* F. on the Main; 2. *(zeitlich)* ~ *1. Mai* on the first of May; ~ *Abend* in the evening; ~ *Anfang* at the beginning; ~ *Tage* by day; ~ *Leben* alive.

Ameise *f* ant; **~nhaufen** *m* ant-hill.

Amerika *n* America; **~ner** *m*, **a~nisch** American.

Amme *f* wet-nurse.

Amnestie *f* amnesty.

Ampel *f* traffic light.

Amsel *f* blackbird.

Amt *n* 1. *(Dienststelle)* office; 2. *(Tätigkeit)* office, position; *ein ~ antreten* enter on an office; 3. *(Aufgabe)* duty; 4. *tele* exchange; **a~lich** official; **~ssprache** *f* official language.

amüs|ant amusing; **~ieren,** *sich* enjoy o.s.

an I *prp* at, on in; to; against; near, about; ~ *seiner Stelle* in his place; ~ *der Tür* at the door; ~ *der Wand* on the wall; ~ *Bord* on board, aboard; ~ *der See* at the seaside; ~ *die Wand lehnen* lean against the wall; **II** *adv:* von … ~ from … on.

Ananas *f* pineapple.

Anbau *m agr* cultivation; **a~en** grow, cultivate.

anbei enclosed.

anbelangen relate to; *was mich anbelangt* as to me.

anbeten worship, adore.

Anbetracht: *in* ~ considering.

anbieten *irr* offer.

anbinden *irr* tie, fasten.

Anblick *m* 1. sight; *beim ersten* ~ at first sight; 2. (*Blick*) aspect, view; **a~en** look at, glance at.

anbrechen *irr* 1. (*beginnen*) begin; (*Tag*) break; 2. (*Flasche*) open.

anbrennen *irr* 1. catch fire; 2. (*Speise*) burn.

anbringen *irr* (*festmachen*) fix to, put up.

andauern last, continue; ~**d** continual, constant.

Andenken *n* 1. remembrance; 2. (*Gegenstand*) keepsake.

ander 1. other, another; ~*e Leute* other people; *ein ~es Buch* another book; 2. (*weitere*) further; 3. *am ~en Morgen* the next morning; 4. (*verschieden*) different; 5. *nichts ~es als* nothing

but; *unter ~em* among other things; 6. *ein ~er* someone else; *e-r nach dem ~en* one after the other; ~**enfalls** otherwise; ~**erseits** on the other hand.

ändern 1. alter, change; 2. *sich* ~ change.

anders 1. otherwise, differently; *ich weiß es* ~ I know better; 2. *jemand* ~ somebody else; ~**wo** elsewhere.

anderthalb one and a half.

Änderung *f* change, alteration.

andeut|en hint, intimate; **A~ung** *f* indication, hint, intimation.

Andrang *m* crush, rush.

andrehen (*Licht*) switch on.

aneignen: *sich etw* ~ appropriate s.th., adopt s.th.

aneinander together.

Anekdote *f* anecdote.

anerkenn|en *irr* 1. acknowledge, recognize; 2. (*loben*) appreciate; 3. (*Schuld*) admit; **A~ung** *f* acknowledg(e)ment, recognition.

anfahr|en *irr* 1. (*fahren*) start, begin to move; 2. *jdn* ~ fly at s.o.; **A~t** *f* approach, drive.

Anfall *m* 1. attack; 2. *med* fit; **a~en** *irr* attack, assault.

anfällig susceptible (*für* to).

Anfang *m* beginning, start, outset; ~ *Mai* at the beginning of May; *am* ~ at the beginning; *von* ~ *an* from the outset; **a~en** *irr* begin, set about, start; *von vorn* ~ begin again, start again; *ein Gespräch* ~ engage in a conversation with.

Anfänger *m* beginner; **a~lich I** *adj* initial, original; **II** *adv* at first.

anfangs at first, in the beginning.

Anfangsbuchstabe *m* initial letter.

anfassen touch, take hold of, grasp, seize, handle.

anfertigen 1. make; 2. *(Liste)* draw up.

anflehen implore, beseech.

anfliegen *irr aero* approach; **A~flug** *m* approach.

anfordern 1. demand; 2. *(bestellen)* order; **A~ung** *f* 1. demands *pl*; 2. *den ~en genügen* satisfy requirements.

Anfrage *f* enquire; **a~n** inquire, ask.

anfügen join, attach.

anführen 1. head, lead, command; 2. *(zitieren)* quote; 3. *(behaupten)* allege; **A~er** *m* leader; **A~ungszeichen** *pl* inverted commas.

Angabe *f* 1. indication; 2. *(Mitteilung)* statement; 3. *(Prahlerei)* boasting.

angeben *irr* 1. give, state, indicate; *e-n Grund* ~ give a reason; 2. *(darlegen)* declare, specify; 3. *(zeigen)* show; 4. *(prahlen)* boast;

A~er *m* braggart, swaggerer; **~lich** supposed.

angeboren innate, inborn.

Angebot *n* offer; ~ *und Nachfrage* offer and demand.

angebracht: ~ *sein* be in order, in place.

angehen *irr* 1. *(anfangen)* begin; 2. *(betreffen)* concern, regard; *das geht Sie nichts an* that's none of your business.

angehören belong to; *(Partei)* be a member of.

Angehöriger *m* relative.

Angeklagter *m* accused, defendant.

Angel *f* 1. *(Tür~)* hinge; 2. fishing-rod.

Angelegenheit *f* concern, affair, business.

angeln angle.

angemessen adequate, suitable, appropriate.

angenehm 1. pleasant, agreeable; 2. *(sehr)* ~! glad to meet you!

angenommen: ~, *daß* let us suppose that.

angesehen esteemed, respected.

Angesicht *n* face, countenance; *von* ~ *zu* ~ face to face; **a~s** in view of.

Angestellter *m* employee.

angewiesen depending *(auf* on).

angewöhnen: *sich etw* ~ get into the habit of s.th.;

A~wohnheit *f* habit, custom.

Angler *m* angler.

Anglo-Amerikaner *m* Anglo-American.

angreife|n *irr* 1. *(Feind)* attack, assail; 2. *(schaden)* impair; 3. *(Gesundheit)* affect; **A~r** *m* aggressor.

angrenzen border on, adjoin to; **~d** adjacent.

Angriff *m* attack, assault.

Angst *f* anxiety, fear; **~ haben** be afraid.

ängst|igen 1. frighten *(jdn* s.o.); 2. *sich ~* be frightened, be afraid *(vor* of); **~lich** anxious, timid.

anhaben *irr (Kleidung)* wear.

anhalten *irr* 1. stop; 2. *(fortdauern)* continue, last; **~d** continuous, incessant.

Anhalter *m* hitch-hiker; *per ~ fahren* hitch-hike.

Anhaltspunkt *m* clue.

Anhang *m* 1. appendix; 2. *(Vertrag)* annex.

anhäng|en 1. hang on; 2. *(hinzufügen)* annex, add; **A~er** *m* 1. adherent, follower; 2. *(Gepäck)* tag, tie-on label; 3. *(Schmuck)* locket; 4. *(an Auto)* trailer; **~lich** faithful.

anheben *irr* 1. lift up; 2. *(Preise)* raise.

anheuern hire.

anhören listen to.

Ankauf *m* purchase; **a~en** buy, purchase.

Anker *m* anchor; *vor ~ gehen* (cast) anchor; *vor ~ liegen* ride at anchor.

Anklage *f jur* charge, accusation; *~ erheben* bring an accusation against; **a~n** accuse of; *(belasten)* charge with, impeach for.

Ankläger *m* accuser; *jur* indicter; *öffentlicher ~* public prosecutor.

ankleben *(Plakate)* stick on; *A~ verboten!* stick no bills!

ankleide|n dress; **A~raum** *m* dressing-room.

anklopfen knock at.

ankommen *irr* 1. arrive, come; 2. *es ~ lassen auf* chance it, run the risk; *es kommt darauf an* it depends; 3. *(von Bedeutung sein)* matter, be important; *darauf kommt es gerade an* this is just the point.

Ankömmling *m* new-comer.

ankündig|en announce, give notice of; **A~ung** *f* announcement.

Ankunft *f* arrival; **~szeit** *f* time of arrival.

Anlage *f* 1. *(Entwurf)* plan, draft, outline, design; 2. *(e-s Gartens)* laying-out; 3. *(Beilage)* enclosure; *in der ~* enclosed; 4. *(Bau)* construction; 5. *(Geld~)* investment; 6. *(Fabrik~)* plant, installation, works *pl;* 7. *med* predisposition; 8. *(Begabung)* apitude, gift, talent (for); **~n** *pl* grounds.

Anlaß *m* 1. occasion, cause; *aus* ~ on the occasion of; 2. ~ *geben* give occasion to.

anlass|en *irr* 1. *mot* start; 2. *(nicht ausziehen)* keep on, leave on; **A~er** *m* starter.

anläßlich on the occasion of.

Anlauf *m* start, run; **a~en** *irr* 1. *(beginnen)* start; 2. *(beschlagen)* steam up, tarnish; 3. *med* swell.

anlegen 1. *(Kleid)* put on; 2. *(Leiter)* lean; 3. *(Akte)* make; 4. *(Stadt)* build; 5. *com* invest, place; 6. *(Gewehr)* point; 7. *(Verband)* apply; 8. *mar* land.

Anlegestelle *f* landing-place.

anlehnen 1. lean against; 2. *(fig) sich* ~ *an* follow.

Anleihe *f* loan.

anleit|en guide, lead, direct, instruct; **A~ung** *f* guidance, instruction.

anlernen train, teach.

Anlieg|en *n* concern; request; ~**er** *m* adjoining owner.

anmachen 1. *(Salat)* dress; 2. *(Feuer)* kindle; 3. *(festbinden)* attach, fasten *(an* on).

anmaß|en, *sich* pretend, arrogate; ~**end** arrogant; **A~ung** *f* arrogance.

Anmeldeformular *n* registration form.

anmeld|en 1. announce, give notice of; 2. *(Zoll)* declare;

3. *(polizeilich)* register; **A~ung** *f* announcement, notification; declaration; registration.

Anmerkung *f* note, annotation.

Anmut *f* grace, charm.

annäher|nd approximate, roughly; **A~ung** *f* approach.

Annahme *f* 1. acceptance; 2. *(Kinder)* adoption; 3. *(Vermutung)* assumption, supposition; 4. *(Schalter)* counter.

annehm|bar acceptable; ~**en** *irr* 1. take, accept; 2. *(Name, Kind)* adopt; 3. *(Gesetz)* pass, carry; 4. *(Besuch)* receive; 5. *(vermerken)* suppose, assume; 6. *sich jds* ~ take care of s.o.

annullieren annul, cancel.

anonym anonymous.

anordn|en dispose, order, arrange; **A~ung** *f* order, arrangement, regulation.

anpassen 1. adapt, fit; 2. *fig* adjust; 3. *sich* ~ adapt o.s. to.

anpflanz|en cultivate, plant; **A~ung** *f* plantation.

Anprobe *f* fitting; **a~ieren** try on.

anrechnen *(gutschreiben)* credit.

Anrecht *n* claim, title *(auf* to).

Anrede *f* address; **a~n** speak to, address.

anreg|en 1. stimulate; 2. *(vor-*

schlagen) hint, suggest;
~end stimulating; **A~ung** f
1. stimulation; 2. *(Vorschlag)* suggestion.
Anreiz m incitement, stimulus.
anrichten 1. *(Mahlzeit)*
serve up; 2. *(verursachen)*
cause; *(Schaden)* do damage.
Anruf m tele call; **a~en** irr
1. jdn ~ call s.o., ring s.o. up;
2. *(Gericht)* appeal to.
Ansage f announcement;
a~n announce, notify; **~r** m
radio announcer.
ansamm|eln 1. *(Vermögen)*
amass; *(aufhäufen)* heap
up, accumulate; 2. sich ~
collect, gather; **A~lung** f
1. collection, accumulation;
2. *(von Menschen)* crowd.
ansässig domiciled, resident.
anschaff|en purchase;
A~ung f buy, purchase.
anschau|en look at, take a
look at; **~lich** evident, clear;
A~ung f view, opinion.
Anschein m appearance; *allem ~ nach* to all appearances; **a~end** apparent,
seeming.
Anschlag m 1. *mus* touch;
2. *(Plakat)* poster, placard,
bill; 3. *(Bekanntmachung)*
notice, announcement;
4. *(Verschwörung)* plot,
conspiracy; **a~en** irr 1. fix,
post, put up; 2. *(Ton)* strike;
~tafel f notice-board, bulletin board.

anschließen irr 1. *(anfügen)*
join, link; 2. *el* connect;
3. *(folgen)* follow; 4. sich
jdm ~ join s.o.
Anschluß m 1. *(Gas~, Wasser~, Netz~)* supply; 2. *(Zug, Telefon)* connection; 3. *im ~
an* in connection with; 4. *(tele)* ~ erhalten get through.
anschnall|en 1. buckle on;
2. *(im Auto)* fasten o.'s seat-belt; **A~gurt** m seat-belt.
anschneiden irr 1. cut;
2. *(Frage)* broach.
anschreiben irr write down.
Anschrift f address.
anschwellen irr swell.
ansehen irr 1. look at; *(prüfend)* examine; *(sehr genau)* scan; 2. *(besichtigen)*
go to see, view; 3. *etw ~ für*
take for; ~ *als* look upon as,
regard as; **A~** n standing,
reputation, credit.
ansetzen 1. *(Preise)* fix;
2. *(Termin)* set (a date), fix.
Ansicht f 1. sight, view; 2. *fig*
opinion; *nach meiner ~* in
my opinion; *zur ~* on approval.
Ansichts|karte f picture
(post)card; **~sache** f matter
of opinion.
anspiel|en: *auf etw ~* hint at
s.th.; **A~ung** f hint, allusion.
anspornen spur, stimulate.
An|sprache f address,
speech; **a~sprechen** irr
1. jdn ~ address s.o., speak
to s.o.; 2. *(gefallen)* please;
3. *(reagieren)* react *(auf* to).

anspringen *irr mot* start.
Anspruch *m* 1. claim, demand; 2. ~ *haben auf* be entitled to; *etw in* ~ *nehmen* call upon s.th.; 3. *(Anforderung)* pretension; **a~slos** unassuming, modest; **a~svoll** 1. fastidious; 2. *(genau)* exacting.
Anstalt *f* 1. *med* asylum; 2. *(Einrichtung)* institution, establishment.
Anstand *m* decency, propriety.
anständig decent, proper, respectable.
anstands|halber for propriety's sake; ~**los** without hesitation.
anstarren gaze at, stare at.
anstatt instead of.
ansteck|en 1. *(mit Nadel)* pin on; 2. *(Ring)* put on; 3. *(med)* infect; ~**end** infectious; **A~ung** *f* contagion, infection.
anstehen *irr* queue up.
ansteigen *irr* mount, ascend.
anstell|en 1. *(in Gang setzen)* start; 2. *(Radio)* turn on; 3. *(Arbeiter)* employ, engage, appoint, hire; 4. *Betrachtungen* ~ speculate *(über on)*; *e-e Untersuchung* ~ examine s.th.; *(Versuch)* make a trial; *(Vergleich)* draw a comparison; 5. *sich* ~ behave; *sich* ~ *als ob* pretend, make believe that; 6. *(Schlange stehen)* queue up, *Am* line up; **A~ung** *f*

1. employment, appointment; 2. *(Stelle)* place, post.
Anstoß *m* 1. *fig* impulse; 2. ~ *nehmen* take offence; **a~en** *irr* 1. *(an etw)* bump against; 2. *mit den Gläsern* ~ touch glasses.
anstößig offensive, shocking.
anstreichen *irr* 1. *(Haus)* paint; 2. *(Fehler)* underline.
anstreng|en, *sich* make an effort, exert; ~**end** strenous; **A~ung** *f* exertion, effort
Ansturm *m* 1. assault; 2. *(Bank)* run.
Anteil *m* 1. share, portion, part; 2. ~ *nehmen* sympathize with; ~**nahme** *f* sympathy.
Antenne *f* aerial, antenna.
antik antique; **A~e** *f* antiquity.
Antiquar|iat *n* second-hand bookshop; **a~isch** second-hand.
Antiquitätenhändler *m* antique dealer.
Antrag *m* 1. *(Gesuch)* application; *auf* ~ on request; 2. *pol* motion; 3. *jur* petition; 4. *(Vorschlag)* proposal, proposition; ~**steller** *m* applicant, petitioner.
antreffen *irr* meet with, find.
antreiben *irr fig* urge, impel.
antreten *irr* begin, take up; *e-e Reise* ~ set out on a journey.
Antrieb *m* 1. *tech* drive, propulsion; 2. *fig* impulse, impe-

tus; *aus eigenem* ~ of o.'s own free will.
antun *irr* 1. *jdm etw* ~ do to; 2. *sich etw* ~ commit suicide.
Antwort *f* answer, reply; **a~en** answer.
anvertrauen 1. confide to, entrust; 2. *sich jdm* ~ confide in s.o.
Anwalt *m* lawyer, solicitor, advocate.
Anwärter *m* candidate.
anweis|en *irr* 1. *(Geld)* transfer, order; 2. *(anleiten)* instruct, direct; 3. *(befehlen)* order; **A~ung** *f* 1. *com* transfer; *(Post~)* money-order; 2. *(Belehrung)* instruction.
anwend|en *irr* 1. use, employ; 2. *(übertragen)* apply; **A~ung** *f* application, use.
anwesen|d present; **A~heit** *f* presence.
anwidern disgust.
Anzahl *f* number, quantity.
anzahl|en pay on account; **A~ung** *f* deposit.
Anzeichen *n* symptom, sign, omen.
Anzeige *f* 1. notice, announcement; 2. *(Zeitung)* advertisement; 3. *jur* information, denunciation; **a~n** 1. announce, give notice of; 2. *(zeigen)* indicate; 3. *jur* denounce, inform against.
anzieh|en *irr* 1. *(Kleider)* put on; 2. *(Seil, Schraube)* tighten; 3. *fig* attract; 4. *(Preise)* rise; 5. *sich* ~

dress; **~end** attractive; **A~ungskraft** *f* attraction.
Anzug *m* suit.
anzünden light, kindle, strike.
Apfel *m* apple; **~saft** *m* apple juice; **~sine** *f* orange.
Apostel *m* apostle.
Apotheke *f* chemist's shop, pharmacy; *Am* drugstore; **~r** *m* chemist, druggist.
Apparat *m* 1. *(Gerät)* apparatus, appliance; 2. *(Vorrichtung)* device; 3. *tele* phone; *bleiben Sie am* ~*!* hold the line, please!
Appetit *m* appetite (*auf etw* for s.th.); **a~lich** appetizing, delicious.
applau|dieren applaud; **A~s** *m* applause.
Aprikose *f* apricot.
April *m* April; *jdn in den* ~ *schicken* send s.o. on a fool's errand.
Arbeit *f* 1. work, labo(u)r; *ohne* ~ unemployed; *(mühselige)* toil; 2. *(Mühe)* effort; 3. *(Beschäftigung)* employment, job; 4. *(Auftrag)* task; 5. *(Prüfung)* test, paper; **a~en** 1. work *(an* at); *(schwer~)* work hard; 2. *(beschäftigt sein)* be employed; 3. *(Maschine)* function, run, operate; **~er** *m* workman, worker, labo(u)rer; *gelernter* ~ skilled worker; *angelernter* ~ semi-skilled worker; **~geber** *m* employer; **~nehmer** *m* em-

ployee; **a~sam** industrious, diligent.

Arbeits|amt n Labour Exchange; **~erlaubnis** f permit to work; **~kräfte** pl labo(u)r; **~lohn** m wages pl, pay; **a~los** out of work, unemployed; **~loser** m unemployed, Am jobless; **~losenunterstützung** f unemployment benefit, dole; **~losigkeit** f unemployment; **a~unfähig** unfit for work; (dauernd) disabled; **~zimmer** n study.

Architekt m architect; **~ur** f architecture.

Archiv n archives pl.

arg 1. bad, mischievous; 2. fam (sehr) very, awful.

Ärger m annoyance, irritation, vexation, worry; **ä~lich** 1. angry; 2. (Ärger erregend) annoying, vexing; **ä~n** 1. vex, annoy, irritate; 2. sich ~ be annoyed (über at); **~nis** n scandal, vexation.

Arg|list f craft(iness); **a~ig** crafty, cunning.

Argument n argument; **a~ieren** argue.

Arg|wohn m suspicion; **a~wöhnen** suspect; **a~wöhnisch** suspicious (gegen of).

arm 1. poor; 2. (bedürftig) indigent; 3. (ohne Geld) penniless, impecunious.

Arm m arm.

Armaturenbrett n dash-board.

Armband n bracelet; **~uhr** f wrist-watch.

Armee f army.

Ärmel m sleeve; **~kanal** m the Channel.

Armlehne f armrest.

ärmlich 1. poor; 2. (elend) miserable.

armselig wretched.

Armut f poverty, indigence; (stärker) penury.

Aroma n aroma; flavour.

Arrest m arrest, detention.

Art f 1. (Weise) way, manner; 2. (Natur, Wesen) nature, kind; 3. (Benehmen) manners pl, behaviour; 4. (Sorte) sort, type; zoo species.

Arterie f artery.

artig (Kinder) good, well-behaved.

Artikel m 1. gram article; 2. (Ware) commodity; 3. (Aufsatz) paper.

Artist m artiste.

Arznei f medicine.

Arzt m physician, doctor (praktischer ~) (general) practitioner.

Ärzt|in f lady doctor; **ä~lich** medical; **~e Verordnung** medical prescription; in ~er Behandlung sein be under medical care.

Asche f ash, ashes pl; **~nbecher** m ash-tray; **~nbrödel** n Cinderella; **~rmittwoch** m Ash Wednesday.

Asi|at m, **a~atisch** Asiatic; **~en** n Asia.

asozial asocial.

Assistent m assistant.

Ast m bough, branch.

Astro||loge m astrologer; **~logie** f astrology; **~naut** m astronaut; **~nom** m astronomer; **~nomie** f astronomy.

Asyl n asylum, refuge.

Atelier n studio.

Atem m breath; außer ~ kommen get out of breath; **a~los** breathless; **~pause** f breathing-space; **~zug** m breath; in e-m ~e in the same breath.

Athlet m athlete; **a~isch** athletic.

Atlas m atlas.

atmen breathe.

Atmosphäre f atmosphere.

Atmung f breathing.

Atom m atom; **a~ar** atomic; **~energie** f atomic energy; **~kraft** f atomic power; **~spaltung** f atomic fission.

Attent|at n attempt; **~äter** m assassin.

Attest n certificate.

auch 1. (ebenso) also, too; nicht nur.., sondern ~ not only ... but also; sowohl ... als ~ both ... and; ~ nicht not ... either, neither; 2. (selbst) even; 3. wenn ~ even if; 4. wann ~ whenever; was ~ whatever; wo ~ wherever.

auf I prp on, upon; in, into; of; at; by; for; to; about; up, upward, up to; towards; against; ~ Anfrage on inquiry; ~ dem Bahnhof at the station; ~ der Bank at (od in) the bank; ~ meine Bitte at my request; ~ den ersten Blick at first sight; ~ deutsch in German; ~ einmal (all) at once; (plötzlich) suddenly; ~ jeden Fall in any case; ~ keinen Fall by no means; ~ alle Fälle at all events, at any rate; ~ seine Gefahr at his risk; ~ immer for ever; ~ der Karte in the map; ~ dem Lande in the country; ~ Lebenszeit for life; ~ die Minute to a minute; ~ die Post gehen go to the post-office; ~ der Stelle at once; ~ der Straße in the street, Am on the street; ~ diese Weise in this manner; ~ der Welt in the world; ~ Wiedersehen! Good-by(e)! so long! see you again! bis ~ weiteres until further notice; **II** adv up, upwards; open; und ab up and down; (hin und her) to and fro; ~ und davon off and away; (offen stehen) be open; **III** conj: ~ daß in order that; ~ daß nicht lest, for fear that; **IV** interj: ~! come on! let's go!

aufatmen breathe again.

Aufbau m 1. erection; 2. (Gefüge) structure; 3. (Zusammensetzung) composition; **a~en** 1. build, erect; 2. fig base (auf on).

aufbehalten irr 1. (Hut)

keep on; 2. *(Augen)* keep open.

aufbewahren keep, preserve, store.

aufbleiben *irr* 1. stay up, sit up; 2. *(offen bleiben)* be left open.

aufblenden *mot* turn the headlights on.

aufblühen *fig* flourish.

aufbrechen *irr* 1. break open; 2. *(fortgehen)* set out, depart.

Aufbruch *m* departure.

aufdecken uncover, reveal.

aufdrängen 1. *jdm etw ~* force s.th. on; 2. *sich jdm ~* thrust o.s. upon s.o.

aufdrehen 1. *(Heizung)* turn on; 2. *(Schraube)* unscrew.

aufdringlich importunate, insistent.

aufeinander 1. one after the other; 2. *(gegeneinander)* one against the other; 3. *(nacheinander)* successively; **~folgen** succeed; **~folgend** successive; **~prallen** collide.

Aufenthalt *m* 1. stay; 2. *(Wohnort)* residence, domicile; 3. *(Zug)* stop; **~sort** *m* residence, domicile; **~sraum** *m* lounge.

auferlegen 1. impose; 2. *(Strafe)* inflict.

Auferstehung *f* resurrection.

auffahr|en *irr* 1. *mot* drive up; *(zusammenstoßen)* collide; 2. *(plötzlich)* jump up;

A~t *f* driving up; *(Zufahrt)* approach.

auffallen *irr* attract attention, be striking; **~d, auffällig** striking, conspicuous.

auffangen *irr (fassen)* catch (up).

auffass|en *(begreifen)* understand, comprehend, grasp; **A~ung** *f* comprehension, understanding, interpretation.

auffordern 1. call upon, ask, request; 2. *(einladen)* invite.

aufführ|en 1. *(Theaterstück)* perform, represent; 2. *(auf e-r Liste)* list, enter; 3. *sich ~* behave; **A~ung** *f theat* performance.

Aufgabe *f* 1. *(Arbeit)* task, job; 2. *(Pflicht)* duty; 3. *(Schularbeit)* homework, lesson; 4. *math* problem; 5. *(Auftrag)* advice; 6. *(e-r Wohnung)* giving-up; 7. *(Gepäck)* registration, *Am* checking; 8. *(Brief)* posting, *Am* mailing.

Aufgang *m* 1. *(Gestirne)* rising; 2. *(Treppe)* staircase, stairs *pl.*

aufgeben *irr* 1. *(Brief)* post, *Am* mail; 2. *(Gepäck)* register, *Am* check; 3. *(Anzeige)* insert; 4. *(Schulaufgabe)* set, assign; 5. *(Rätsel)* propose; 6. *(Wohnung)* give up; 7. *(Amt)* resign; 8. *(Plan)* abandon.

Aufgebot *n (Ehe)* banns *pl.*

aufgehen *irr* 1. *(Gestirne,*

Teig, Vorhang) rise; 2. *(Geschwür)* break up; 3. *(Saat)* come up; 4. *(sich öffnen)* open.

aufge|legt: *gut (schlecht)* ~ *sein* be in a good (bad) mood; **~regt** excited, nervous; **~sprungen** *(Lippen)* chapped; **~weckt** bright, quick-witted, clever.

aufhaben *irr* 1. *(Hut)* have on, wear; 2. *(Laden)* be open.

aufhalten *irr* 1. stop, check; 2. *(Angriff)* stem; 3. *(Tür)* keep open; 4. *sich* ~ be: stay.

aufhängen hang up; **A~er** *m (Kleider)* loop, hanger.

aufheben *irr* 1. *(hochheben)* raise, hold up, lift up; 2. *(aufbewahren)* keep, preserve; 3. *(Vertrag)* cancel, annul; *(Gesetz)* abrogate.

aufheitern 1. cheer up; 2. *sich* ~ *(Wetter)* clear up.

aufholen 1. *(Zeitverlust)* make up for; 2. *(Rückstand)* catch up.

aufhören leave off, stop.

aufklären 1. clear up; 2. *(unterrichten)* inform, instruct; 3. *(Irrtum)* set right; 4. *das Wetter hat sich aufgeklärt* the weather has cleared up.

aufkommen *irr* 1. *(Wind)* spring up, rise; 2. *(Mode)* come into fashion; 3. *(Zweifel)* arise; 4. *gegen jdn* ~ cope with s.o.; 5. *für etw* ~ be responsible for s.th.

aufladen *irr* 1. load; 2. *(Batterie)* charge up.

Auflage *f typ* edition; *(Zeitung)* circulation.

auflassen *irr* leave open.

Auflauf *m* 1. *(Menschen)* gathering, crowd; 2. *(Speise)* soufflé; **a~en** *irr* go aground.

auflegen 1. *(Buch)* publish, print; 2. *(Hörer)* replace; 3. *(Schallplatte)* put on.

auflehnen, *sich* revolt *(gegen* against).

aufleuchten light up.

auflös|en 1. *(in Flüssigkeiten)* dissolve; 2. *(Versammlung)* break up; 3. *(Verlobung)* break off; 4. *(Vertrag)* cancel; 5. *(Geschäft)* liquidate; **A~ung** *f* 1. *(in Flüssigkeiten; Versammlung)* dissolution; 2. *(Rätsel)* solution; 3. *(Vertrag)* cancellation.

aufmach|en 1. open; 2. *(aufschließen)* unlock; 3. *(Flasche)* uncork; **A~ung** *f (e-r Ware)* presentation.

aufmerksam 1. attentive; *jdn auf etw* ~ *machen* call s.o.'s attention to s.th.; 2. *(höflich)* obliging; **A~keit** *f* 1. attention; 2. *(Zuvorkommenheit)* obligingness.

aufmuntern cheer up, encourage.

Aufnahme *f* 1. *(Empfang)* reception; 2. *(Liste)* enrolment, enlistment; 3. *(Ton-*

band) recording; 4. *(in e-e Organisation)* admission, acceptance; 5. *phot (Vorgang)* taking a picture; *(Bild)* photograph; **~bedingungen** *pl* terms of admission; **~prüfung** *f* entrance examination.

aufnehmen *irr* 1. receive *(jdn* s.o.); 2. *(Tätigkeit)* start, begin; 3. *(zulassen)* admit, accept; 4. *es mit jdm ~* cope with s.o.; 5. *(fassen)* hold, take; 6. *phot* take a photograph, shoot; 7. *(Tonband)* record; 8. *(Protokoll)* draw up; 9. *(Gold)* borrow, take up.

aufpassen take care of.

Aufprall *m* impact.

aufpumpen pump up.

aufputschen stimulate.

aufräumen 1. *(Zimmer)* tidy up; 2. *(ordnen)* clear up.

aufrecht 1. upright, erect; 2. *fig* honourable; **~erhalten** *irr* maintain.

aufreg|en 1. excite, stir up; 2. *(beunruhigen)* upset; 3. *sich ~ über* get excited about; **~end** exciting; **A~ung** *f* agitation, excitement.

aufreißen *irr* 1. tear open; 2. *(Tür)* fling open.

aufricht|en 1. put upright; 2. *sich ~* straighten up; **~ig** sincere, honest, upright; **A~igkeit** *f* sincerity, honesty.

Aufruf *m* call, proclamation;

~ an appeal to; **a~en** *irr* call *(jdn* s.o.'s name).

Aufruhr *m* riot, uproar.

Aufrühr|er *m* rioter, rebel; **a~erisch** rebellious.

aufsagen recite.

Aufsatz *m* 1. *(Abhandlung)* essay, treatise; 2. *(Schule)* composition, paper.

aufschieben *irr fig* put off, defer, postpone.

Aufschlag *m* 1. *(Hose)* turn-up; 2. *(e-r Granate)* impact; 3. *(Preis~)* rise; **a~en** *irr* 1. *(Buch)* open; 2. *(Zelt)* pitch; 3. *(Betrag)* put *(auf etw* on s.th.); 4. *(auftreffen)* hit, strike.

aufschließen *irr* unlock, open.

aufschneid|en *irr* 1. cut open; 2. *(übertreiben)* boast, talk big; **A~er** *m* boaster.

auf|schreiben *irr* write down, take down, note; **A~schrift** *f* 1. *(Etikett)* label; 2. *(Inschrift)* inscription.

Aufschub *m* postponement, deferment, delay.

Aufschwung *m* rise, boom, upswing.

aufseh|en *irr* look up; **A~en** *n* sensation, stir; **A~er** *m* 1. *(im Gefängnis)* warder; 2. *(Fabrik)* overseer; 3. *(Museum)* attendant.

aufsetzen 1. *(Hut)* put on; 2. *(Brief)* draft, draw up; 3. *aero* touch down, land; 4. *sich ~* sit up.

Aufsicht f inspection, supervision, control; **~srat** m board of directors.

aufspringen irr 1. jump up; 2. (auf e-n Zug) jump on; 3. (von Haut) chap.

Aufstand m rebellion, insurrection.

aufstapeln pile up, stack up.

aufstehen irr 1. get up, rise; 2. (von Tür) be open.

aufsteigen irr 1. (hochsteigen) rise; 2. (auf e-n Berg, Ballon) ascend; 3. ~ auf get on, climb on, mount; 4. (abheben) take off; 5. (befördern) be promoted.

aufstell|en 1. (hinstellen) put up, set up; 2. (Maschine) erect; 3. (Wahl) nominate, put forward; 4. (Rekord) establish; 5. e-e Behauptung ~ make an assertion; 6. (Bilanz, Liste) make up; 7. sich ~ place o.s.; **A~ung** f 1. (Anordnung) arrangement; 2. (Darlegung) statement; 3. (Maschine) erection; 4. (Kandidat) nomination.

Aufstieg m 1. ascent; 2. fig rise; (sozialer ~) advancement.

aufstoßen irr 1. fling open; 2. (rülpsen) belch.

aufstützen, sich lean on.

auftanken mot fill up.

auftauchen 1. rise up, emerge; 2. fig appear, arise.

auftauen thaw.

aufteilen divide, partition.

Auftrag m 1. com order; im ~e von by order of; 2. (Weisung) instruction; **a~en** irr 1. serve; 2. (Farben) lay on; 3. jdm etw ~ instruct s.o. to do s.th.

auftreten irr 1. step on; 2. (benehmen) behave; 3. (im Theater) appear, perform; **A~** n 1. (Betragen) behavio(u)r; 2. (Vorkommen) occurrence.

Auftrieb m fig impetus, stimulus.

Auftritt m 1. (Erscheinen) appearance; 2. theat scene.

aufwachen wake up.

aufwachsen irr grow up.

Aufwand m expenditure, luxury.

aufwärmen warm up.

aufwärts upward(s).

aufwecken awake(n), wake up.

aufweisen irr show, exhibit.

aufwend|en irr spend; Mühe ~ take pains; **~ig** expensive.

aufwerfen irr (Frage) raise.

aufwert|en revalue; **A~ung** f revaluation.

aufwickeln 1. roll up; 2. (Haar) put in curlers.

aufwirbeln 1. (Staub) whirl up; 2. fig make a sensation.

aufzählen enumerate.

aufzeichn|en take down, record; **A~ung** f 1. record; 2. pl papers.

aufziehen irr 1. (hochziehen) pull up, haul up; 2. (Uhr) wind up; 3. (Kind) bring up; 4. *(Pflanzen)* cultivate; 5. *(necken)* tease; 6. *(Wolken)* come up, gather.

Aufzug *m* 1. lift, *Am* elevator; 2. *theat* act; 3. *(Festzug)* procession.

aufzwingen *irr* force, impose *(jdm etw* s.th. upon s.o.).

Auge *n* eye; *im ~ behalten* keep in mind; *ich sagte es ihm unter vier ~n* I told it to him in confidence.

Augenarzt *m* oculist.

Augenblick *m* moment, instant; *im ~* at the moment; **a~lich** 1. *(sofortig)* immediate, instantaneous; 2. *(gegenwärtig)* at present.

Augen|braue *f* eyebrow; **~licht** *n* eyesight; **~lid** *n* eyelid; **~schein** *m: etw in ~ nehmen* examine s.th.; **~wimper** *f* eyelash; **~zeuge** *m* eyewitness.

August *m* August.

Auktion *f* auction.

aus I *prp* 1. from; *~ dem Englischen* from the English; *~ Überzeugung* from conviction; 2. of: *~ Holz* made of wood; 3. through: *~ dem Fenster* through the window; 4. for: *~ diesem Grunde* for this reason; 5. in: *~ Scherz* in jest; 6. out of: *~ Mitleid* out of pity; 7. by: *~ Erfahrung* by experience; 8. on: *~ Grundsatz* on principle; **II** *adv*

9. *vom Fenster ~* from the window; *von Natur ~* by nature; 10. *(vorüber)* out, over, finished; 11. *es ist ~ damit* that's the end of it; *von hier ~* from here; *von mir ~* as far as I am concerned.

ausarbeiten 1. work out, elaborate; 2. *(Dokument)* prepare; 3. *(schriftlich)* write, compose.

ausatmen breathe out.

Ausbau *m* extension, completion; **a~en** 1. *fig* extend, complete; 2. *(Motor)* remove.

ausbessern mend, repair.

Ausbeute *f* profit, gain; **a~n** exploit.

ausbezahlen pay off.

ausbild|en 1. develop; 2. *(geistig)* educate, cultivate; 3. *(schulen)* train, instruct; **A~ung** *f* training, education, instruction.

ausbleiben *irr* stay away, be absent.

Ausblick *m* outlook, prospect, view.

ausbrechen *irr* 1. break out; 2. *in etw ~* burst into s.th.

ausbreiten 1. spread out; 2. *(Arme)* stretch; 3. *sich ~* spread; *(von Wiese)* extend.

Ausbruch *m* 1. escape; 2. *(Feuer)* outbreak, eruption.

Ausdauer *f* endurance, perseverance; **a~nd** persistent, persevering.

ausdehnen 1. expand, extend; 2. *(verlängern)* prolong.

ausdenken *irr* think out, conceive, devise.

Ausdruck *m* expression, term; *zum ~ bringen* express; *zum ~ kommen* find expression.

ausdrück|en 1. *(Frucht)* squeeze out; 2. *(Zigarette)* stub out; 3. *(formulieren)* express, formulate; *~lich* express, explicit.

ausdrucks|los expressionless; *~voll* expressive.

auseinander apart; *~gehen* *irr* 1. *(sich trennen)* part; 2. *(Meinung)* differ, diverge; 3. *(Versammlung)* dissolve; *~nehmen* *irr* dismantle; *~setzen* 1. *(erklären)* explain; 2. *sich ~ mit* come to an agreement with; **A~setzung** *f* argument, dispute.

auserlesen exquisite, choice.

Ausfahrt *f (Garage, Autobahn)* exit; *~ freihalten!* keep exit clear!

Ausfall *m* loss; **a~en** *irr* 1. fall out; 2. *(nicht stattfinden)* not to take place; 3. *(Maschine)* fail; *~straße* *f* arterial road.

ausfertig|en draw up, draft; **A~ung** *f* copy, draft.

ausfindig: *~ machen* discover, find out.

Ausflucht *f* evasion, excuse.

Ausflug *m* excursion, trip.

ausfragen interrogate, question.

Ausfuhr *f* export, exportation; *~zoll* *m* export duty.

ausführ|en 1. *com* export; 2. *(Plan, Aufgabe)* execute, carry out; 3. *(Idee)* explain, elaborate on; *~lich* detailed, circumstantial; **A~ung** *f* 1. *(Plan, Aufgabe)* execution; 2. *(Merkmal)* make, model; 3. *(Darlegung)* exposition.

ausfüllen 1. fill up; 2. *(Formular)* fill in.

Ausgabe *f* 1. *(Kosten)* expense, expenditure, outlay; 2. *(Buch)* edition, issue.

Ausgang *m* 1. way out, exit; 2. *(Ende)* end, close; 3. *(Ergebnis)* result, issue; *~spunkt* *m* starting-point.

ausgeben *irr* 1. give out, distribute; 2. *(Geld)* spend; 3. *(Aktien)* issue; 4. *sich für jdn ~* pretend to be s.o.

ausge|bucht booked up; *~fallen* *fig* unusual, odd, queer, strange; *~glichen* well-balanced.

ausgehen *irr* 1. go out; 2. *(enden)* end; *gut ~* turn off well; 3. *(schwinden)* run out; 4. *(Feuer)* go out; 5. *von etw ~* start out from s.th.; 6. *leer ~* get nothing.

ausgelassen frolicsome, boisterous.

ausgenommen except, with the exception of, save.

ausgeprägt distinct, marked.

ausgerechnet just, exactly.

ausgeschlossen impossible, out of the question.

ausgesprochen *fig* marked, decided.

ausgewogen well-balanced.

ausgezeichnet splendid, excellent, first-rate.

ausgiebig ample, extensive, abundant.

ausgießen *irr* pour out.

Ausgleich *m* balance, compensation; **a~en** *irr* 1. level out, balance; 2. *(Mangel)* compensate, make up for; 3. *(Konflikt, Streit)* settle, harmonize.

ausgrab|en *irr* 1. dig out; 2. *(Leiche)* exhume; **A~ungen** *pl* excavations *pl.*

Ausguß *m* sink.

aushalten *irr* 1. *(Schmerz)* bear, endure, stand; 2. *(Blick)* sustain; 3. hold out, persist, persevere.

aushandeln negotiate.

Aushang *m* notice.

aushängen 1. hang out, put up; 2. *(Tür)* unhinge.

ausharren hold out.

aus|helfen *irr:* jdm ~ help s.o. out; **A~hilfe** *f* temporary help.

auskennen *irr* 1. *fig* be well versed in; 2. *(in e-r Stadt)* know o.'s way about.

auskommen *irr* 1. mit etw ~ manage on s.th., get along with s.th.; 2. mit jdm ~ get on, get along with s.o.; **A~** *n* livelihood; sein ~ haben make o.'s living.

auskundschaften explore.

Auskunft *f* 1. information; particulars *pl;* 2. *(Büro)* information (office, desk); **~sstelle** *f* inquiry-office.

auskuppeln declutch.

auslachen laugh *(jdn* at s.o.).

ausladen *irr* unload.

Auslage *f* 1. *(Kosten)* expenses *pl;* 2. *(Waren)* display.

Ausland *n* foreign country; ins, im ~ abroad; aus dem ~ from abroad.

Ausländ|er *m* foreigner; **a~isch** foreign, alien.

Auslands|korrespondent *m* foreign correspondent; **~nachrichten** *pl* foreign news *pl.*

auslassen *irr* 1. *(Wort)* leave out, omit; 2. *(Wut)* vent.

auslaufen *irr* 1. *(Flüssigkeit)* run out; 2. *mar* put to sea; 3. *(rinnen)* leak.

auslegen 1. *(Waren)* lay out, exhibit, display; 2. *(Geld)* pay; 3. *(deuten)* interpret.

ausleihen *irr* 1. *(verborgen)* lend (out); 2. *(borgen)* borrow.

Auslese *f* choice, selection; **a~n** *irr* 1. *(aussondern)* choose, pick out; 2. *(fertiglesen)* finish (reading).

ausliefer|n 1. deliver, hand over; 2. *jur* extradite; **A~ung** *f* 1. delivery; 2. *jur* extradition.

auslös|en 1. *(Schuß)* release;

2. *(Begeisterung)* arouse, call forth; 3. *(verursachen)* cause; **A~er** *m phot* trigger.

ausmachen 1. *(Feuer)* put out; 2. *(Radio)* switch off; 3. *(Streit)* settle; 4. *(Termin)* agree upon; 5. *(Bestandteil)* constitute; 6. *(Betrag)* amount to; 7. *das macht nichts aus!* it does not matter! *würde es Ihnen etw ~, wenn ich rauche?* would you mind my (me) smoking?

Ausmaß *n* dimensions *pl*, extent, proportion.

ausmessen *irr* measure.

Ausnahme *f* exception; *mit ~ von* with the exception of, except; *e-e ~ bilden* be an exception; **~zustand** *m* state of emergency.

ausnahms|los without exception; **~weise** exceptionally.

ausnehmen *irr* 1. take out; 2. *(ausschließen)* except, exclude.

ausnutzen use, take advantage of, exploit.

auspacken unpack.

auspressen squeeze out.

ausprobieren try, test.

Auspuff *m* exhaust; **~topf** *m* silencer.

ausradieren erase.

ausräumen 1. *(Wohnung)* clear, empty; 2. *(Möbel)* remove.

ausrechnen calculate, reckon.

Ausrede *f* excuse; **a~n**

1. finish speaking; 2. *jdm etw ~* dissuade s.o. from doing s.th.

ausreichen suffice, be enough; **~d** sufficient.

Ausreise *f* departure; **a~n** leave (a country).

ausreißen *irr* tear, pull out.

ausrichten 1. *(erreichen)* accomplish; 2. *(Mitteilung)* pass on, deliver; 3. *tech* straighten.

Ausruf *m* cry, exclamation; **a~en** *irr* cry out, call out; **~ungszeichen** *n* exclamation mark.

ausruhen rest, take a rest.

ausrüst|en equip; **A~ung** *f* equipment, outfit.

ausrutschen slip.

Aussage *f* 1. declaration, statement; 2. *jur* evidence; **a~n** 1. state; 2. *jur* testify, give evidence.

ausschalten 1. *el* switch off; 2. *(Maschine)* disengage; 3. *fig* eliminate.

Ausschank *m* sale of drinks.

ausschauen: *nach jdm ~* look out for s.o.

ausscheiden *irr* 1. eliminate; 2. *med* excrete, secrete; 3. *aus etw ~* retire from s.th.

ausschlafen *irr* get enough sleep.

Ausschlag *m* 1. *med* rash; 2. *den ~ geben* be decisive; **a~en** *irr* 1. knock out; 2. *(ablehnen)* refuse; 3. *(Pferd)* lash out; *(Waage)* turn; **a~gebend** decisive.

ausschließ|en *irr* 1. exclude; 2. *(ausnehmen)* except; 3. *(Irrtum)* preclude; **~lich** exclusive.

ausschneiden *irr* cut out.

Ausschnitt *m* 1. *(e-s Kleides)* neck; 2. *(e-s Bildes)* detail.

ausschreiben *irr* 1. *(Wort)* write in full; 2. *(Quittung)* write out; 3. *(bekanntgeben)* announce, advertise.

Ausschuß *m* 1. committee, board; 2. *(Abfall)* waste; **~sitzung** *f* committee meeting.

ausschütten 1. pour out *a. fig*; 2. *(Gewinn)* distribute; 3. *(sein Herz)* unburden o.'s heart to.

ausschweif|end excessive dissolute; **A~ung** *f* excess, dissoluteness.

aussehen *irr* 1. look; *gut ~* look well; 2. *es sieht nach Regen aus* it looks like rain; **A~** *n* look, appearance.

außen outside; *nach ~* outward(s).

Außen|aufnahme *f* exterior shot; **~bordmotor** *m* outboard motor; **~handel** *m* export trade, foreign trade; **~minister** *n* Minister for Foreign Affairs; *(in England)* Secretary of State for Foreign Affairs, *(in USA)* Secretary of State; **~politik** *f* foreign policy; **~seiter** *m* outsider; **~stelle** *f* branch office.

außer I *prp* 1. out of; *~ Kraft setzen* put out of force; *~ Zweifel stehen* be beyond doubt; 2. *~ sich sein* be beside o.s.; 3. *(abgesehen)* apart from, except; 4. *(neben)* in addition to; 5. *~ Landes* out of the country; **II** *conj*: *~ wenn* unless, except when.

außerdem besides, moreover.

außerdienstlich unofficial, private.

äußere outer, outside, external; **Ä~** *n* exterior, appearance.

außer|ehelich illegitimate; **~gewöhnlich** extraordinary, unusual; **~halb** 1. beyond, outside, out of; 2. *~ wohnen* live outside the town.

äußerlich 1. external; 2. *fig (oberflächlich)* superficial.

äußern 1. utter, express; 2. *sich ~* talk, speak.

außerordentlich extraordinary, outstanding.

äußerst 1. *(räumlich)* outermost; 2. *(zeitlich)* latest, last; 3. *fig* extreme; *von ~er Wichtigkeit* of utmost importance; *im ~en Fall* at the worst; **Ä~e** *n* 1. *sein ~s tun* do o.'s very best; 2. *aufs ~ gefaßt sein* be prepared for the worst.

Äußerung *f* expression, remark, utterance.

aussetzen 1. *ein Kind ~* expose a child; 2. *(unterwerfen)* subject; 3. *(Preis)* offer; 4. *etw an jdm ~* find fault with s.o.; 5. *(Zahlung)* suspend; 6. *(unterbrechen)* pause; 7. *(Motor)* fail, stop; 8. *sich ~* expose o.s.

Aussicht *f* 1. view, outlook; 2. *fig* prospect; **a~slos** hopeless, desperate; **a~sreich** promising.

ausspannen relax, rest.

aussöhnen reconcile.

Aussprache *f* 1. pronunciation; 2. *(Gespräch)* talk.

aussprechen *irr* 1. pronounce; 2. *(Meinung)* express, utter; 3. *(beenden)* finish; 4. *sich ~* unburden o.s.; 5. *(sich äußern)* give o.'s opinion.

ausspucken spit out.

ausstatt|en fit out, equip, furnish; **A~ung** *f* 1. equipment, outfit; 2. *theat* scenery.

ausstehen *irr* 1. suffer, endure, bear; *ich kann ihn nicht ~* I can't stand him; 2. *(von Antwort)* be still expected.

aussteigen *irr* get out, alight.

ausstell|en 1. *(Ware)* exhibit, display; 2. *(Pässe)* issue; 3. *(Rechnung)* make out; 4. *(Scheck)* write out; **A~er** *m* 1. exhibitor; 2. *com* issuer; **A~ung** *f* 1. exhibition, show, exposition; 2. *(Paß)*

issue; **A~ungsgelände** *n* exhibition grounds.

aussterben *irr* become extinct.

Aussteuer *f* 1. trousseau; 2. *(Mitgift)* dowry.

Ausstieg *m* exit.

ausstoßen *irr* 1. *(ausschließen)* expel; 2. *(Schrei)* utter.

ausstrahlen 1. *(Wärme)* radiate, emit; 2. *radio* transmit.

ausstrecken stretch out, extend.

ausstreichen *irr* strike out.

ausströmen stream out, pour out.

aussuchen select, pick out, choose.

Austausch *m* exchange; **a~en** exchange, interchange.

austeilen distribute, deal out.

Auster *f* oyster.

austilgen exterminate.

austragen *irr* 1. *(Briefe)* deliver; 2. *(Streit)* deliver; 3. *(Wettkampf)* hold.

Australi|en *n* Australia; **~er** *m*, **a~sch** Australian.

austreiben *irr (Geist)* exorcize, cast out.

austreten *irr* 1. *(aus Verein)* withdraw, leave; 2. *(Schuhe)* wear out; 3. *(Zigarette)* tread out.

austrinken *irr* finish, empty.

Austritt *m (aus Verein)* withdrawal.

ausüben 1. *(Beruf)* practise, exercise; 2. *(Einfluß)* exert.

Ausverkauf *m* clearance sale; **a~t** sold out.
Aus|wahl *f* 1. choice, selection; 2. *(Warenlager)* assortment, collection; **a~wählen** choose, select.
Auswander|er *m* emigrant; **a~n** emigrate (*von* from; *nach* to); **~ung** *f* emigration.
auswärtig 1. from outside; 2. *(ausländisch)* foreign, external.
auswärts 1. *(außerhalb des Hauses)* out; 2. *(außerhalb des Landes)* abroad.
auswechseln 1. change (*gegen* for); 2. *(ersetzen)* replace, renew.
Ausweg *m* way out; **a~los** hopeless.
ausweichen *irr* 1. *(im Verkehr)* make way; 2. *jdm ~* avoid s.o.; *e-r Frage ~* evade a question; **~d** evasive.
Ausweis *m* identity card, passport; **a~en** *irr* 1. expel; 2. *sich ~* identify o.s.
ausweiten stretch.
auswendig *fig* from memory, by heart.
auswickeln unwrap.
auswirk|en, *sich* work out, have consequences; **A~ung** *f* consequences *pl*, effect.
Auswuchs *m fig (Mißstand)* abuse.
auszahlen pay out.
auszählen count out.
auszeichn|en 1. honour, award; 2. *(Waren)* mark out,

label, ticket; 3. *sich ~* distinguish o.s., excel; **A~ung** *f* 1. honour; 2. *(Orden)* decoration.
ausziehen *irr* 1. *(Kleid)* take off; 2. *(Tisch)* pull out; 3. *(Zahn)* extract; 4. *(aus Wohnung)* move; 5. *sich ~* undress.
Auszug *m* 1. *(Zusammenfassung)* outline, summary; 2. *(aus Wohnung)* removal; 3. *(Konto)* statement.
Auto *n* motor-car, car; *mit dem ~ fahren* go by car; **~bahn** *f* motorway; **~bus** *m* bus; **~bushaltestelle** *f* bus stop; **~buslinie** *f* bus line; **~fähre** *f* car ferry; **~fahrer** *m* motorist, driver; **~gramm** *n* autograph; **~karte** *f* road map.
Automat *m* automate; **~ik** *f* automatism; **a~isch** automatic.
Autonomie *f* autonomy.
Auto|nummernschild *n* licence plate; **~panne** *f* breakdown; **~parkplatz** *m* parking-place.
Autor *m* author, writer.

Auto|reifen *m* tyre, *Am* tire; **~reparaturwerkstatt** *f* repair shop.
Autorität *f* authority.
Auto|straße *f* highway, motor-road; **~verkehr** *m* motor traffic; **~vermietung** *f* car hire (service).
Axt *f* axe, hatchet.

B

Bach *m* brook, rivulet.
Backbord *n* port.
Backe *f* cheek.
backen *irr* bake.
Backen|bart *m* whiskers *pl;* ~**zahn** *m* molar.
Bäcker *m* baker; ~**ei** *f* bakery.
Back|huhn *n* fried chicken; ~**ofen** *m* oven; ~**pulver** *n* baking-powder; ~**stein** *m* brick.
Bad *n* 1. bath; 2. *(Badeort)* spa.
Bade|anzug *m* bathing-suit; ~**hose** *f* swimming-trunks *pl;* ~**mantel** *m* bathrobe; ~**meister** *m* bath attendant.
baden 1. bath; 2. *(im Freien)* bathe, go swimming.
Bade|ofen *m* geyser; ~**tuch** *n* bath-towel; ~**wanne** *f* bathtub; ~**zimmer** *n* bathroom.
Bahn *f* 1. *(Eisenbahn)* railway; *mit der* ~ by train, by rail; 2. *(Weg)* way, path; 3. *(Fahrbahn)* lane; **b~brechend** epoch-making.
bahnen *(Weg)* clear; *sich e-n Weg* ~ make a way for o.s.
Bahn|hof *m* station; **b~lagernd** to be called for; ~**linie** *f* railroad line; ~**schranke** *f* level-crossing barrier; ~**steig** *m* platform; ~**übergang** *m* level-crossing; ~**verbindung** *f* train connection.
Bahre *f* 1. stretcher; 2. *(Toten~)* bier.
Bakterie *f* bacterium.
Balance *f* balance, equilibrium; **b~ieren** balance.
bald 1. soon, in a short time; *möglichst* ~ as soon as possible; 2. *(fast)* almost, nearly; 3. *(frühzeitig)* early; ~**ig** early, speedy, quick.
Balken *m* beam.
Balkon *m* balcony.
Ball *m* 1. ball; ~ *spielen* play ball; 2. *(Tanz)* ball, dance.
Ballade *f* ballad.
Ballast *m* 1. ballast; 2. *fig* burden.
Ballen *m* 1. bale; 2. *anat* ball.
Ballett *n* ballet.
Ballon *m* balloon.
Ballungsgebiet *n* conurbation.
Balsam *m* balsam, balm.
Bambus *m* bamboo.
banal commonplace, trite; **B~ität** *f* banality.

Banane *f* banana.
Band 1. *n (pl Bänder)* ribbon; 2. *(Tonband)* recording tape; 3. *(Fließband)* assembly line; 4. *n (pl Bande)* tie, chains *pl,* fetters *pl;* 5. *m (pl Bände)* volume; 6. *f (Musiker)* band.

Bandag|e *f* bandage;
b~ieren bandage.
Bande *f* band, gang.
bändigen 1. tame; *(Pferd)*
break in; 2. *fig* subdue.
Bandit *m* bandit.
Bandwurm *m* tapeworm.
bange scared; ~ *sein* be
afraid, be anxious; **~n** 1. be
afraid of; 2. *sich* ~ *um* be
worried about.
Bank *f* 1. *(pl Bänke)* bench,
seat; 2. *(pl Banken)* bank;
~auszug *m* bank-state-
ment; **~feiertag** *m* bank
holiday; **~guthaben** *n* bank
balance; **~ier** *m* banker;
~konto *n* banking-account;
~note *f* banknote.
Bankrott *m* bankruptcy, insolvency; ~ *machen* go
bankrupt; **b~** bankrupt.
Banner *n* banner, flag.
bar in cash; ~ *zahlen* pay
cash.
Bar *f* bar.
Bär *m* bear.
Baracke *f* hut.
Barbar *m* barbarian; **b~isch**
barbarous.
barfuß barefooted.
Bargeld *n* cash, ready
money; **b~los** cashless.
Bar|hocker *m* bar stool;
~keeper *m* barkeeper.
Barock *n* baroque.
Barometer *n* barometer.
Barren *m* 1. *(Metall)* ingot;
2. *sport* parallel bars *pl.*
Barrikade *f* barricade.
barsch rough, harsh.

Bart *m* 1. beard; 2. *(Schlüssel)* bit.
bärtig bearded.
Barzahlung *f* cash payment.
Basis *f* basis.
Baß *m* bass.
Batterie *f* battery.
Bau *m* 1. building, construction; *im* ~ under construction; 2. *(Bauwerk)* building,
edifice, structure.
Bauch *m* belly; abdomen;
~weh *n* stomach-ache.
bauen build, construct.
Bauer *m* 1. *Am* peasant, *Br*
farmer; 2. *(Käfig)* bird-cage.
Bäuer|in *f* farmer's wife;
b~lich rural.
Bauern|haus *n* farm-house;
~hof *m* farm.
baufällig dilapidated.
Bau|herr *m* building owner;
~kasten *m* box of bricks;
~kunst *f* architecture.
Baum *m* tree; **~stamm** *m*
trunk; **~wolle** *f* cotton.
Bau|plan *m* building plan;
~platz *m* building site;
~sparkasse *f* building-so-
ciety; **~stein** *m* brick, building stone; **~stelle** *f*
1. building site; 2. *(Straße)*
repairs, roadworks *pl;*
~werk *n* building.
Bazillus *m* bacillus.

beabsichtigen intend, mean,
plan.
beacht|en 1. *(Rat)* pay atten-
tion to; 2. *(Gebot)* observe;
3. *(Ereignis)* take notice of;

~lich considerable; **B~ung** f notice, attention.

Beamter m civil servant, officer.

beängstigend alarming, frightening.

beanspruchen claim, demand, lay claim to.

beanstand|en complain of, object to, find fault with; **B~ung** f objection, complaint.

beantragen apply for.

beantwort|en answer, reply to; **B~ung** f answer, reply.

bearbeit|en 1. work; 2. (behandeln) treat; 3. (Thema) work on, deal with; 4. (Buch) adapt; 5. (an etw arbeiten) handle; **B~ung** f 1. (Behandlung) treatment; 2. (Buch) adaptation; 3. (Feld) cultivation.

beaufsichtigen supervise, control.

beauftrag|en 1. instruct; 2. jdn mit etw ~ charge s.o. with s.th.; **B~ter** m representative, agent.

bebauen 1. (Gelände) build on; 2. (Feld) cultivate, farm.

beben tremble, shake.

Becher m cup, mug.

Becken n 1. basin; 2. med pelvis.

Bedacht m deliberation; mit ~ with consideration; **b~:** auf etw ~ sein be mindful of s.th.

bedächtig 1. (überlegt) deliberate, thoughtful;

2. (langsam) slow, deliberate.

bedanken, sich thank (bei jdm s.o.).

Bedarf m 1. want, need; bei ~ in case of need, if required; 2. (Menge) requirements pl; **~schaltestelle** f request stop.

bedauer|lich regrettable; **~licherweise** unfortunately; **~n** 1. (Vorfall) regret; 2. (Menschen) pity, feel for; **~nswert** pitiable.

bedeck|en cover (mit with); **~t** (Himmel) overcast, cloudy.

bedenk|en irr consider, ponder; **B~en** pl doubts; ohne ~ without hesitation; **~lich** 1. (fraglich) doubtful; 2. (besorgt) serious, grave; **B~zeit** f time for reflexion.

bedeut|en mean, signify; das hat nichts zu ~ that doesn't mean anything; **~end** 1. (wichtig) important; 2. (beträchtlich) considerable; 3. (bekannt) distinguished; **B~ung** f 1. (Sinn) meaning, sense; 2. (Wichtigkeit) importance; **~ungslos** insignificant; meaningless; **~ungsvoll** 1. meaningful; 2. (wichtig) significant.

bedien|en 1. serve, attend to, wait on; 2. (Maschine) work, operate; **B~ung** f 1. service; 2. (Kellnerin) waitress; 3. tech operation.

bedingt conditioned, conditional.

Bedingung f 1. condition, stipulation; *unter der ~, daß* on condition that; 2. *com* terms pl; **b~slos** unconditional.

bedroh|en threaten; **~lich** threatening.

bedrück|en oppress; **~end** oppressive; **~t** depressed.

bedürf|en irr need, require; **B~nis** n 1. need, want; 2. *(Verlangen)* wish; **B~nisanstalt** f public convenience.

beeilen hasten, hurry up.

beeindrucken impress.

beeinflussen influence.

beeinträchtigen *(schädigen)* impair, harm, prejudice.

beendigen end, finish.

beerdig|en bury; **B~ung** f funeral.

Beere f berry.

Beet n flowerbed.

befähig|en enable, qualify *(zu* for); **~t** qualified *(für* for); **B~ung** f ability, qualifications pl.

befahr|bar practicable, passable; **~en** irr 1. *(e-e Strecke)* drive (on), travel (on); 2. *mar* navigate.

befallen irr 1. *med* attack, strike; 2. *(Furcht)* seize.

befangen embarrassed.

befassen, *sich* occupy o.s. *(mit* with), deal *(mit* with).

Befehl m order, command; *auf ~ von* on the orders of; **b~en** irr order, command.

befestigen fasten, fix *(an* on, to).

befinden, *sich* irr 1. be; 2. *(gelegen sein)* be situated; 3. *(fühlen)* feel; 4. *jur* decree; **B~** n health.

befolgen 1. *(Anweisung)* obey; 2. *(Rat)* follow.

beförder|n 1. *(transportieren)* forward, transport, carry, dispatch; 2. *fig (im Rang)* promote; **B~ung** f 1. transport, carriage; 2. *(im Rang)* promotion.

befrag|en 1. question; 2. *(Zeugen)* interrogate; **B~ung** f interrogation.

befrei|en 1. free, liberate; 2. *(von Pflichten)* dispense; **B~er** m liberator; **B~ung** f liberation.

befreundet: *gut ~ sein* be good friends.

befriedigen 1. satisfy, please, content; 2. *(Hunger)* appease; **~d** satisfactory.

befristet limited.

befruchten fertilize.

Befug|nis f authority, competence; **b~t** authorized, competent.

Befund m 1. *(Gutachten)* report; 2. *med* findings pl.

befürcht|en fear, be afraid of; **B~ung** f fear, apprehension.

befürworten recommend.

begab|t gifted, talented; **B~ung** f gift, talent, ability.

begeben, *sich irr* 1. go, set out; *sich auf Reisen ~* set out on a journey; 2. *(ereignen)* happen, occur.

begegn|en meet *(jdm s.o.);* **B~ung** *f* meeting, encounter.

begehen *irr* 1. *(Straße)* walk on; 2. *(Verbrechen)* commit; 3. *(Fehler)* make.

begehren desire, wish (for).

begeister|n 1. inspire; 2. *sich ~* get enthusiastic *(über* about); **~t** enthusiastic; **B~ung** *f* enthusiasm.

Begier|de *f* desire, longing; **b~ig** desirous, eager.

Beginn *m* beginning; *bei ~* at the beginning; **b~en** *irr* begin, start.

beglaubigen attest, certify, legalize.

begleichen *irr* pay, settle.

begleit|en accompany; **B~er** *m* 1. companion; 2. *mus* accompanist; **B~ung** *f* company; *in ~ von* accompanied by.

beglückwünschen congratulate.

begnadigen pardon.

begnügen, *sich* be satisfied *(mit* with).

begraben *irr* bury.

Begräbnis *n* burial.

begreif|en *irr* understand, comprehend; **~lich** comprehensible.

Begriff *m* 1. idea, notion, concept; 2. *im ~ sein* be on

the point *(etw zu tun)* of doing s. th.).

begründ|en 1. *(Behauptung)* give the reasons for, justify; 2. *(gründen)* found, establish; **~et** well-founded.

begrüß|en greet, welcome; **B~ung** *f* greeting, welcome.

begünstigen favour, promote.

behaart hairy.

behaglich comfortable, cosy; **B~keit** *f* comfort, cosiness.

behalten *irr* 1. keep; 2. *(im Gedächtnis)* remember.

Behälter *m* 1. container, receptacle; 2. *(Wasser, Öl)* tank.

behand|eln 1. treat, deal with; 2. *(Thema)* discuss; 3. *med* treat *(wegen* for, *mit* with); **B~lung** *f* treatment.

beharr|en persist *(auf* in), stick; **~lich** persistent, persevering.

behaupt|en 1. state, maintain, affirm; 2. *sich ~* hold o.'s own; **B~ung** *f* assertion, affirmation, statement.

beheben *irr (Schaden)* repair, mend.

Behelf *m* makeshift, expedient; **b~en,** *sich irr* manage *(mit* with), make do; **b~smäßig** improvised, temporary.

beherbergen accomodate, lodge.

beherrschen 1. *(Land)* rule over, govern; 2. *(Lage)* control, dominate; 3. *sich ~* control o.s.; **~d** dominating.

behilflich helpful.

behindern hinder, hamper, handicap.

Behörde *f* authorities *pl.*

behüten guard (*vor* from).

behutsam careful, cautious.

bei at, near, by; *~m Bäcker* at the baker's; *~ meiner Ankunft* on my arrival; *~ Tag* by day; *~ Tisch* at table; *~ alledem* for all that; *er wohnt ~ uns* he's staying with us; *sie saß ~ ihm* she sat by him; *(Adresse) ~ Meyer* care of, c/o Meyer.

beibehalten *irr* keep, maintain.

beibringen *irr* 1. *(lehren)* teach; 2. *(mitteilen)* put across.

Beichte *f* confession; **b~n** confess.

beide both; *wir ~* both of us; we two; *einer von ~n* one of the two; *keiner von ~n* neither of them; *in ~n Fällen* in either case; *~s ist richtig* both are correct.

beieinander together.

Beifahrer *m* assistant driver.

Beifall *m* 1. applause; 2. *~ finden* meet with approval.

beifügen 1. *(Brief)* enclose; 2. *(zufügen)* add.

Beihilfe *f* aid, grant.

Beil *n* axe, hatchet.

Beilage *f* 1. *(Brief)* enclosure; 2. *(Zeitung)* supplement.

beiläufig casual, passing.

Beileid *n* condolence; *jdm sein ~ bezeugen* condole with s.o.; **~sschreiben** *n* letter of condolence.

beiliegend enclosed.

beimessen *irr: Wichtigkeit ~* attach importance (to).

Bein *n* leg; *sich auf die ~e machen* set out.

beinahe nearly, almost.

beinhalten contain.

beipflichten agree (*jdm* with s.o.).

beisammen together.

Beisein *n* presence.

beiseite aside, apart.

Beispiel *n* example; *zum ~* for example; **b~haft** exemplary; **b~los** unparalleled; **b~sweise** by way of example, for instance.

beißen *irr* 1. *(Hund)* bite; 2. *(stechen)* sting; **~d** 1. biting; 2. *fig* cutting, sarcastic.

Beistand *m* assistance, help.

beistehen *irr* help, assist.

beisteuern contribute (*für* to).

Beitrag *m* 1. contribution; 2. *(Verein)* subscription; **b~en** *irr* contribute (*zu* to).

bei|treten *irr* join; **B~tritt** *m* 1. *(Klub)* joining; 2. *(zu e-m Vertrag)* accession.

beiwohnen attend, be present.

bejahen answer in the affirmative; **~d** affirmative, positive.

bejahrt aged.

bekämpfen fight, combat.
bekannt 1. known; ~ *als* kown as; ~ *werden* become known; 2. *(berühmt)* famous; 3. *(vertraut)* familiar; 4. *mit jdm* ~ *sein* be acquainted with s.o.; **B~er** *m* acquaintance; **B~gabe** *f* announcement, publication; **~geben** *irr* 1. make known; 2. *(veröffentlichen)* publish; **~lich** as is (well-)known; **B~schaft** *f* acquaintance.
bekehren convert.
bekennen *irr* admit, confess; **B~tnis** *n* 1. *(Glaube)* creed; 2. *(Konfession)* denomination.
beklagen 1. deplore; 2. *sich* ~ complain *(über* of, about); **~enswert** deplorable; **B~ter** *m* accused, defendant.
bekleiden 1. *(angezogen sein)* clothe, dress; 2. *(Amt)* hold; **B~ung** *f* clothes *pl*, garments *pl*.
beklemmend oppressive; **B~ung** *f* oppression.
bekommen *irr* 1. *(erhalten)* get, receive; 2. *(Ware)* obtain; 3. *(Sinn)* acquire; 4. *(Krankheit)* get, catch; 5. *(Klima)* agree *(jdm* with s.o.).
bekömmlich digestible, wholesome.
bekräftigen confirm.
beladen *irr (Wagen)* load *(mit* with).
Belag *m* 1. coating;

2. *(Schicht)* layer; 3. *(Fußboden)* covering; 4. *(Kuchen* ~) topping.
belagern besiege.
Belang *m* importance; **b~los** insignificant.
belasten 1. *(Wagen)* load; 2. *fig* burden; 3. *(beschuldigen)* accuse, charge; 4. *(Konto)* charge, debit.
belästigen bother, trouble, annoy; **B~ung** *f* molestation.
Belastung *f* load, burden.
belaufen *irr: sich* ~ *auf* amount to.
beleben animate, stimulate; **~t** animated, busy.
Beleg *m* 1. *(Beweis)* proof; 2. *(Quittung)* receipt, voucher; **b~en** 1. *(Boden)* cover; 2. *(Brot)* put on; 3. *(Platz)* reserve; 4. *(nachweisen)* prove; 5. *(Kurs)* enroll for; **b~t** 1. *(Platz)* taken, occupied; 2. *(reservieren)* reserved; 3. *med* coated; 4. *tele* engaged.
belehren instruct, inform; **B~ung** *f* information, instruction.
beleidigen offend, insult; **~end** insulting; **B~ung** *f* offence, insult.
beleuchten 1. light (up), illuminate; 2. *(Thema)* elucidate; **B~ung** *f* illumination, lighting.
Belgien *n* Belgium; **~ier** *m*, **b~isch** Belgian.
belichten *phot* expose.

Belieb|en *n* will, pleasure; *nach* ~ as you like; **b~ig** any; *jeder* ~*e* anybody you please; *zu jeder* ~*en Zeit* at any time.

beliebt popular; *sich* ~ *machen* make o.s. popular; **B~heit** *f* popularity.

bellen bark.

belohn|en reward; **B~ung** *f* reward, recompense; *als* ~ as a reward (*für* for).

belügen *irr* lie (*jdn* to s.o.).

belustigen amuse, divert.

bemächtigen, *sich* take possession (*e-r Sache* of s.th.), seize.

bemerk|bar 1. noticeable, apparent; 2. *sich* ~ *machen* become noticeable; ~**en** 1. notice, note, observe; 2. (*erwähnen*) remark, observe; ~**enswert** noteworthy, remarkable; **B~ung** *f* remark, observation.

bemüh|en 1. take trouble; ~ *Sie sich nicht* don't bother; 2. *sich um etw* ~ strive to obtain s.th.; **B~ung** *f* effort, trouble.

benachbart neighbouring.

benachrichtig|en inform (*von* of); **B~ung** *f* information.

benachteiligen disadvantage.

benehmen, *sich irr* behave o.s.; **B~** *n* behaviour.

beneiden envy; ~**swert** enviable.

benennen *irr* name, designate.

benötigen need, want.

benutz|en 1. (*verwenden*) use, utilize; 2. (*Gebrauch machen*) make use of; 3. (*Verkehrsmittel*) take; **B~ung** *f* use.

Benzin *n* petrol, gas(oline); ~**tank** *m* petrol tank.

beobacht|en 1. observe, watch; 2. (*wahrnehmen*) notice; **B~ung** *f* observation.

bequem 1. comfortable; 2. (*faul*) lazy; **B~lichkeit** *f* comfort, ease.

berat|en *irr* 1. give advice, advise (*jdn* s.o.); 2. *sich mit jdm* ~ deliberate, confer with s.o. (*über* about); **B~er** *m* adviser, consultant; **B~ung** *f jur med* consultation.

berechn|en 1. calculate, reckon; 2. *com* charge; ~**end** calculating; **B~ung** *f* calculation.

berechtig|en entitle (*zu* to); ~**t** 1. justified; 2. ~ *sein* be authorized (*zu* to); **B~ung** *f* authority; justification.

Bereich *m* 1. (*örtlich*) area, region; 2. *fig* range; 3. (*Gebiet*) sphere, realm.

bereichern enrich.

Bereifung *f* (set of) tyres *pl.*

bereit 1. ready; 2. (*fertig sein*) be prepared (*zu* to); ~**en** prepare; ~**s** already.

Bereitschaft *f* readiness;

~sdienst *m* emergency service.
bereitstellen 1. *(Ware)* put ready; 2. *(Geld)* provide.
bereitwillig ready, willing.
bereuen regret, repent.
Berg *m* mountain; *(kleinerer)* hill; **b~ab** downhill.
Berg|arbeiter *m* miner; **~bau** *m* mining.
bergauf uphill.
bergen *irr* rescue, save.
Bergführer *m* mountain guide.
bergig mountainous.
Bergsteiger *m* alpinist.
Bergung *f* rescue.
Bergwerk *n* mine.
Bericht *m* 1. report, account; 2. *(Kommentar)* commentary; 3. *(Überblick)* survey; **b~en** 1. report; 2. *(informieren)* inform; **~erstatter** *m* reporter, correspondent.
berichtigen correct, rectify.
berücksichtig|en 1. take into consideration, consider; 2. *(Umstände)* bear in mind; **B~ung** *f* consideration; *unter ~* taking into consideration, in view of.
Beruf *m* 1. *(freier)* profession, job; 2. *(Handwerker)* trade; 3. *(Beschäftigung)* occupation; **b~en** *irr* 1. *(ernennen)* appoint, nominate; 2. *sich auf etw ~* refer to s.th.; 3. *zu etw ~ sein* feel a vocation for s.th.; **b~lich** professional.
Berufs|ausbildung *f* profes-

sional, vocational training; **~beratung** *f* vocational guidance; **~krankheit** *f* occupational disease; **~schule** *f* vocational school.
Berufung *f* 1. *(innere)* vocation; 2. *(Ernennung)* appointment; 3. *jur* appeal; *~ einlegen* lodge an appeal.
beruhen 1. *auf etw ~* be based on s.th.; 2. *etw auf sich ~ lassen* let s.th. rest.
beruhig|en 1. calm, quiet, soothe *(jdn* s.o.*)*; 2. *sich ~* calm down; **~end** reassuring; **B~ung** *f* pacification; reassurance; **B~ungsmittel** *n med* sedative.
berühmt famous, renowned; **B~heit** *f* 1. fame, renown; 2. *(Mensch)* celebrity.
berühr|en 1. touch; 2. *fig* touch *(etw* on*)*; 3. *jdn ~ (fig)* affect s.o.; **B~ung** *f* contact, touch.
Besatzung *f mar aero* crew.
beschädig|en damage; **B~ung** *f* damage.
beschaffen 1. procure, provide; 2. *~ sein* be conditioned; **B~heit** *f* 1. state, condition; 2. *(Art)* quality.
beschäftig|en 1. *(Arbeiter)* employ; 2. *jdn ~* occupy s.o.'s mind; 3. *sich ~* occupy o.s.; concern o.s.; **~t** 1. *(Arbeiter)* employed; 2. *(beansprucht)* occupied, busy; **B~ung** *f* 1. *(Tätigkeit)* occupation; 2. *com* employment, job.

Bescheid m 1. *(Antwort)* answer, notice, notification; 2. *(Auskunft)* information; ~ *geben* inform.

bescheiden 1. modest; 2. *(einfach)* simple; 3. *(gering)* humble; **B~heit** f modesty.

bescheinig|en certify, attest; **B~ung** f certificate.

beschenken: *jdn* ~ give s.o. presents.

beschimpfen abuse, insult *(jdn* s.o.).

Beschlag m tech fittings pl; **b~en I** irr 1. *(Pferd)* shoe; 2. *sich* ~ steam up; tarnish; **II** adj 3. shoed; 4. steamed up; 5. *fam* be well versed in.

Beschlagnahme f jur seizure; **b~n** seize, confiscate.

beschleunigen speed, hasten, accelerate.

beschließen irr 1. *(sich entscheiden)* decide, resolve, determine; 2. *(enden)* end, close, finish, conclude.

Beschluß m resolution, decision.

beschmutzen dirty, soil.

beschneiden irr cut, clip.

beschränk|en 1. limit, reduce, restrict; 2. *sich* ~ *auf* confine o.s. to; ~**t** 1. limited; 2. *(geistig)* dull.

beschrankt *(Bahnübergang)* guarded.

beschreib|en irr describe; **B~ung** f description.

beschriften *(Umschlag)* letter, adress.

beschuldig|en accuse (of), charge (with); **B~ung** f accusation, charge.

beschütz|en protect, guard *(gegen, vor* against, from); **B~er** m protector.

Beschwerde f 1. complaint; 2. *jur* appeal.

beschweren 1. weight; 2. *fig* burden; 3. *sich* ~ complain.

beschwerlich arduous, tiring, tiresome.

beschwichtigen soothe, appease, calm.

beschwören irr 1. *(bitten)* implore, beseech; 2. *etw* ~ swear to s.th.

beseitigen 1. *(Schwierigkeit)* eliminate, remove; 2. *(Schutt)* clear away.

Besen m broom.

besessen obsessed.

besetz|en 1. *(Amt)* fill; 2. *(Land)* occupy; ~**t** 1. *tele* engaged; 2. *(Platz)* occupied, taken; 3. *(Bus)* full.

besichtig|en 1. *(Stadt)* visit, tour; 2. *(prüfend)* inspect; **B~ung** f sightseeing.

besiedel|n settle, colonize; ~**t**: *dicht, dünn* ~ densely, thinly populated.

besiegen defeat, conquer, win, beat.

besinn|en, *sich* irr 1. deliberate *(über* upon); 2. *(nachdenken)* remember; **B~ung** f 1. consciousness; *die* ~ *verlieren* lose consciousness; 2. *(Selbstbeherrschung)* self-control; ~**ungslos** unconscious.

Besitz m 1. possession; 2. (Eigentum) ownership; 3. (Besitztum) property, estate; **b~en** irr 1. possess, hold, own; 2. (versehen mit) be provided with; ~**er** m proprietor, owner; ~**ung** f estate, possessions pl.

besohlen sole.

besonder particular, special; **B~e** n: etwas ~s something special; **B~heit** f peculiarity, particularity.

besonders 1. particularly; 2. (sehr) specially; 3. nicht ~ not particularly.

besorgen 1. (beschaffen) procure, provide; 2. (erledigen) attend to.

Besorgnis f concern, worry, fear; **b~erregend** alarming.

besorgt worried, anxious, concerned (um about).

Besorgung f 1. procurement; 2. (Einkauf) purchase.

besprech|en irr 1. (beraten) talk over, discuss; 2. (Buch) review; **B~ung** f 1. discussion, conference; 2. (Buch) review.

besser better; um so ~ all the better; je eher, desto ~ the sooner the better.

besser|n improve, become better; **B~ung** f 1. improvement; 2. gute ~! speedy recovery!

Bestand m (Vorrat) stock.

beständig 1. (dauerhaft) permanent, lasting; 2. (andauernd) constant, continuous; **B~keit** f 1. permanence; 2. (Standhaftigkeit) steadfastness, constancy.

Bestandteil m component, part, element.

bestätig|en 1. confirm; 2. (bescheinigen) certify; 3. sich ~ prove true; **B~ung** f 1. confirmation; 2. certificate.

bestatt|en bury; **B~ung** f burial.

beste I adj best; der erste ~ the first person who one comes to; jdn zum ~n haben pull s.o.'s leg; in ~m Zustand in first-class condition; **II** adv: am ~n best; **B~** n the best thing; **B~** m best.

bestech|en irr bribe; ~**lich** corrupt; **B~ung** f bribery.

Besteck n knife, fork and spoon; cutlery.

bestehen irr 1. (vorhanden sein) exist; es ~ zwei Möglichkeiten there are two possibilities; zu Recht ~ be justified; die Tatsache besteht, daß the fact remains that; 2. aus etw ~ be composed, consist of, be made of; 3. auf etw ~ insist on s.th.; 4. (sich behaupten) stand up, hold out; 5. (Prüfung) pass; **B~** n existence; ~**d** existing.

besteigen irr 1. (Berg) climb (up); 2. (Pferd) mount; 3. (Zug, aero) board.

bestell|en 1. *(Waren)* order;
2. *(Zimmer)* book; 3. *(kommen lassen)* ask s.o. to
come; 4. *(Gruß)* give, deliver; 5. *(bebauen)* till, cultivate; **B~schein** m order-
-form; **B~ung** f com order.
besten|falls at best; **~s** as
well as possible.
bestimm|en 1. *(festsetzen)*
determine, decide *(etw* upon
s.th.), fix; 2. *(anordnen)* order; 3. *jdn zu etw ~* appoint
s.o. s.th.; 4. *etw für jdn ~* assign s.th. for s.o.; 5. *(ermitteln)* determine; 6. *über etw
~* dispose of s.th.; **~t** 1. *(festgelegt)* decided, determined;
2. *(Zeitpunkt)* given; 3. *(Absicht)* special; 4. *(sicherlich)*
for certain, surely; **B~theit**
f firmness; **B~ung** f 1. *(Festlegung)* determination;
2. *(Anordnung)* regulation,
rule; 3. *jur* term, provision;
4. *(Ernennung)* appointment; 5. *(Schicksal)* destiny.
bestraf|en punish *(jdn für
etw* s.o. for s.th.); **B~ung** f
punishment.
bestrahl|en med give radiation treatment; **B~ung** f
ray treatment.
bestreben, sich endeavour,
strive; **B~** n endeavours pl,
efforts pl.
bestreiten irr 1. *(Recht)*
contest, challenge;
2. *(Schuld)* deny; 3. *(Kosten)*
defray.
bestürzt dismayed.

Bestürzung f consternation.
Besuch m 1. visit; *jdm e-n ~
machen* pay s.o. a visit; *zu ~
sein* be on a visit *(bei* to);
2. *(Person)* visitor; 3. *(Vortrag)* attendance *(bei* at);
b~en 1. *jdn ~* visit s.o., call
on s.o.; 2. *(Vortrag)* attend;
~er m visitor, caller, guest;
~szeit f visiting hours pl.
betätig|en 1. *tech* operate,
control; 2. *sich ~* be active.
betäub|en med anaesthetize;
B~ung f med anaesthetization; **B~ungsmittel** n
1. med narcotic; 2. drug.
beteilig|en 1. *sich ~* participate *(an* in), join; 2. com
take a share; 3. *jdn ~* give
s.o. a share; **B~ung** f
participation.
beten pray *(zu Gott* to God),
say o.'s prayers.
Beton m concrete.
beton|en stress, emphasize;
B~ung f stress, emphasis.
Betracht m: *in ~ kommen*
come into question; *nicht in
~ kommen* be out of the
question; *in ~ ziehen* take
into account, into consideration; **b~en** 1. *(ansehen)*
look at, regard; 2. *(Problem)*
consider; 3. *jdn ~ als* regard
s.o. as; 4. *sich ~* look at s.o.;
5. *(halten für)* regard o.s. as.
beträchtlich considerable.
Betrachtung f 1. view; 2. fig
consideration; *bei näherer
~* on closer examination.
Betrag m amount, sum;

b~en *irr* 1. (*sich belaufen auf*) amount to; 2. *sich ~* behave o.s., conduct o.s.; **~en** *n* behaviour, conduct.
Betreff *m* (*Brief*) reference.
betreffen *irr* 1. (*angehen*) concern, regard, refer to; *was mich betrifft* as far as I am concerned; 2. (*beeinflussen*) affect, touch; **~d** concerning, regarding.
betreiben *irr* 1. (*Geschäft*) pursue, carry on; 2. (*Unternehmen*) run; 3. *tech* operate, drive.
betreten *irr* 1. (*Rasen*) step on; 2. (*Zimmer*) enter, go into; **B~** *n: das ~ des Rasens ist verboten* keep off the grass.
betreuen (*Kinder*) look after, take care of.
Betrieb *m* 1. (*Unternehmen*) enterprise, business, undertaking, works *pl;* 2. (*nur sing*) (*Maschine*) operation; *in (außer) ~ sein* be in (out of) operation; *außer ~* out of order; 3. (*nur sing*) (*Trubel*) rush; **b~sam** industrious, busy.
Betriebs|angehörige *pl* members of a firm; **~ferien** *pl: ~ machen* shut down for the holidays; **~führung** *f* management; **~rat** *m* works council; **~störung** *f* breakdown.
betrinken, *sich irr* get drunk.
betroffen 1. (*berührt*) af-

fected; 2. (*bestürzt*) perplexed.
Betrug *m* fraud, swindle, trickery.
betrüg|en *irr* 1. (*täuschen*) deceive; 2. (*hintergehen*) cheat, trick, swindle; **B~er** *m* swindler, impostor; **~erisch** deceitful; fraudulent.
betrunken drunk, tipsy.
Bett *n* bed; *zu ~ gehen* go to bed; *das ~ hüten* be confined to o.'s bed; **~decke** *f* blanket.
betteln beg (*um* for).
Bettflasche *f* hot-water bottle.
bettlägerig confined to bed.
Bettlaken *n* sheet.
Bettler *m* beggar.
Bett|ruhe *f* rest in bed; **~vorleger** *m* bedside rug; **~wäsche** *f* bedclothes *pl.*
beugen bend, bow.
Beule *f* 1. dent; 2. *med* bump

beunruhig|en 1. alarm, disturb; 2. *sich ~* worry; **~end** alarming; **B~ung** *f* anxiety, alarm.
beurkunden record, certify.
beurlauben give leave of absence.
beurteil|en judge; *etw falsch ~* misjudge s.th.; **B~ung** *f* judg(e)ment.
Beute *f* 1. booty, spoil; 2. (*Tier*) prey.
Beutel *m* bag.
bevölker|n populate; **~t** populated; *dicht, spärlich ~*

densely, sparsely populated; **B~ung** f population.

bevollmächtig|en authorize; **B~ter** m jur authorized person; **B~ung** f authorization.

bevor 1. (ehe) before; 2. until.

bevorzug|en 1. prefer (jdn vor jdm s.o. to s.o.); 2. (begünstigen) favour; **~t** preferential, privileged; **B~ung** f preference, favour.

bewach|en 1. (Gefangene) guard; 2. bewachter Parkplatz car park with an attendant; **B~ung** f guard.

bewaffn|en arm; **B~ung** f armament.

bewahren keep, preserve (vor from).

bewähr|en, sich prove o.s. (als as); **~t** proved; **B~ung** f jur probation.

bewältigen 1. (Schwierigkeiten) master, surmount; 2. (Arbeit) manage.

bewässer|n water, irrigate; **B~ung** f irrigation.

bewegen I 1. move; set in motion; 2. (Blätter) stir; 3. fig move, touch; 4. sich ~ move; **II** irr: jdn zu etw ~ make s.o. do s.th.

beweglich movable, mobile; **B~keit** f mobility.

bewegt 1. (Meer) rough; 2. fig touched.

Bewegung f 1. movement, motion; 2. (Unruhe) agitation, stir; 3. (Rührung) emotion.

Beweis m 1. proof; zum ~ by way of proof; 2. (Zeichen) token; 3. jur evidence; **b~en** irr 1. prove; 2. (zeigen) show; **~führung** f argumentation.

bewerb|en, sich irr apply (bei jdm um etw to s.o. for s.th.); **B~er** m applicant; **B~ung** f application.

bewerkstelligen manage, effect.

bewerten value, estimate.

bewillig|en grant, allow; **B~ung** f grant, allowance.

bewirken bring about, effect, cause.

bewirt|en entertain; **~schaften** (Hof) manage, run.

bewohn|bar habitable; **~en** inhabit, live in; **B~er** m inhabitant, resident.

bewölk|en, sich become overcast; **B~ung** f clouds pl.

Bewunder|er m admirer; **b~n** admire; **b~nswert** admirable; **~ung** f admiration.

bewußt 1. sich e-r Sache ~ sein be conscious of s.th.; 2. (absichtlich) deliberate; 3. (besagt) in question, mentioned.

bewußtlos unconscious; **B~igkeit** f unconsciousness.

Bewußtsein n consciousness; das ~ verlieren lose consciousness; bei ~ sein be conscious.

bezahl|en 1. pay for;

2. *(Schulden)* settle; 3. *(Leistung)* remunerate; **B~ung** f payment.

bezaubern charm, captivate; **~d** charming, delightful.

bezeichn|en 1. *(kennzeichnen)* mark; 2. *(bedeuten)* signify, mean; 3. *(beschreiben)* describe *(jdn als* s.o. as); 4. *(benennen)* designate; **~end** characteristic *(für* of), significant; **B~ung** f 1. denotation; 2. *(Angabe)* indication; 3. *(Benennung)* designation, description; 4. *(Name)* name.

bezeugen testify, attest.

bezieh|en irr 1. *(mit Stoff)* cover; 2. *(Bett)* put clean linen on; 3. *(Wohnung)* move into; 4. *(Waren)* buy, get; 5. *(Zeitung)* subscribe to; 6. *(Gehalt)* receive; 7. *(Wissen)* obtain; 8. *etw auf etw* ~ relate s.th. to s.th.; 9. *sich* ~ refer *(auf* to), relate *(auf* to); **B~er** m subscriber (to).

Beziehung f 1. relation, relationship; 2. *(Verbindungen)* connections pl; 3. *(Hinsicht)* in jeder ~ to all intents and purposes; in keiner ~ in no respect; **b~sweise** respectively.

Bezirk m district.

Bezug m 1. case; 2. *(Waren)* purchase; 3. *(Zeitung)* subscription; 4. *(Bezüge)* earnings; 5. ~ nehmen auf etw refer to s.th.; mit ~ auf in

relation to; in b~ auf with respect to.

bezüglich referring to, relating to.

Bezugsquelle f source of supply.

bezweifeln doubt.

bezwingen irr conquer, defeat.

Bibel f Bible.

Bibliothek f library; **~ar** m librarian.

bieg|en irr 1. bend; 2. um die Ecke ~ turn the corner; **~sam** flexible; **B~ung** f bend.

Biene f bee; **~nkorb** m beehive.

Bier n beer.

bieten irr 1. offer; *(bei Versteigerungen)* bid; 2. *(darbieten)* present; 3. *(zeigen)* show; 4. sich ~ present itself.

Bikini m bikini.

Bilanz f balance; die ~ ziehen strike the balance.

Bild n 1. picture; 2. *(Gemälde)* painting; 3. phot photo; 4. *(Abbild)* image; 5. *(Anblick)* scene, picture, sight; 6. fig idea, notion, conception.

bilden 1. form; 2. *(hervorbringen)* produce; 3. *(darstellen)* compose, make up; 4. *(gestalten)* shape; 5. *(Geist)* educate; 6. sich ~ form; 7. *(geistig)* cultivate o.'s mind; **~d:** die ~en Künste the Fine Arts.

Bild|erbuch *n* picture-book; **~hauer** *m* sculptor; **b~lich** *fig* figurative; **~nis** *n* likeness; **~schirm** *m* screen.

Bildung *f* 1. *(Erziehung)* education; 2. *(Entstehung)* formation, development.

Billard *n* billiards *sing.*

billig 1. *(Preis)* cheap, low-priced; 2. *(gerecht)* just, fair.

billigen approve (*etw* of s.th.).

Binde *f* 1. band; 2. *med* sling, bandage; *(Monats~)* sanitary towel; **~glied** *n* connecting link.

binden *irr* 1. *(Buch)* bind; 2. *(anbinden)* fasten up, attach, tie; 3. *sich ~* commit o.s.; **~d** binding.

Bind|estrich *m* hyphen; **~faden** *m* string; **~ung** *f* 1. *(Verpflichtung)* commitment; 2. *fig* tie, bond; 3. *(Ski)* binding.

binnen within.

Binnen|gewässer *pl* inland water(s); **~handel** *m* domestic trade; **~land** *n* inland.

Biographie *f* biography.

Biolog|ie *f* biology; **b~isch** biological.

Birke *f* birch.

Birn|baum *m* pear-tree; **~e** *f* 1. pear; 2. *el* bulb.

bis I *prep* 1. *(zeitlich)* till, until, to; *~ heute* until today; *von morgens ~ abends* from morning till night; 2. *(örtlich)* as far as, up to, to; **II** *adv* 3. *~ auf weiteres* until further notice; 4. *~ auf einen* except one; 5. *fünf ~ zehn Pfund* five to ten pounds; **III** *conj* till, until.

Bischof *m* bishop.

bisher up to now, so far; *wie ~* as before; **~ig** previous.

Biß *m* bite.

bißchen I *adj* (little) bit; *ein ~* a little; **II** *adv: das ist ein ~ zu viel verlangt* that is asking a little too much.

Bissen *m* bite, bit, morsel.

bissig 1. biting, dangerous; 2. *fig* cutting, caustic.

Bitte *f* request (*um* for); *e-e dringende ~* an urgent request; *ich habe e-e ~ an Sie* I want to ask you a favour; **b~** 1. *(Wunsch)* please; *~, sagen Sie mir* please tell me; 2. *kann ich Ihr Buch haben? ~!* may I have your book? certainly! 3. *danke schön! ~ (sehr)!* thank you — don't mention it! 4. *wie ~?* (I beg your) pardon?

bitten *irr* 1. *jdn um etwas ~* ask, beg s.o. for s.th.; *darf ich Sie um das Salz ~?* may I trouble you for the salt? 2. *(einladen)* ask, invite (*jdn zu etw* s.o. to s.th.).

bitter 1. bitter; 2. *fig* hard, bitter; **B~keit** *f* bitterness.

bizarr bizarre.

bläh|en 1. *(Segel)* belly (out); 2. *med* make flatulent; **B~ung** *f med* flatulence.

Blam|age f disgrace; **b~ie-ren,** sich make a fool of o.s.

blank 1. (glänzend) bright; 2. (sauber) polished.

blanko com in blank; **B~scheck** m blank cheque.

Blase f 1. anat bladder; 2. med blister; 3. (Wasser) bubble.

blas|en irr 1. blow; 2. mus (Flöte) play; (Trompete) sound; **B~instrument** n wind instrument.

blaß pale.

Blässe f paleness.

Blatt n 1. (Pflanze) leaf; 2. (Papier) sheet; vom ~ spielen play at sight; 3. (Zeitung) newspaper; **~gold** n gold leaf.

blau 1. blue; ~es Auge black eye; 2. ~ sein (fam) be drunk; 3. Fahrt ins B~e mystery tour.

Blech n sheet metal; **~dose** f tin, Am can.

Blei n lead.

Bleibe f lodging; **b~n** irr 1. (sich aufhalten) stay, remain; zu Hause ~ stay at home; ~ Sie am Apparat hold the line, please; 2. bei etw ~ keep to s.th.; bei der Wahrheit ~ stick to the truth; bei seiner Meinung ~ keep to o.'s opinion; 3. (in einem Zustand) remain, continue; gesund ~ keep well; 4. es bleibt dabei that's settled; **b~nd** permanent.

bleich pale.

Bleistift m pencil; **~spitzer** m sharpener.

Blende f phot diaphragm; **b~n** 1. blind, dazzle; 2. (täuschen) deceive; **b~nd** wonderful, brilliant.

Blick m 1. look, glance; (flüchtig) glimpse; 2. (Aussicht) view; 3. auf den ersten ~ at first sight; **b~en** look (auf jdn at s.o.); **~feld** n field of vision.

blind 1. blind (auf e-m Auge in one eye); 2. (Spiegel) clouded; (Glas) dim; 3. ~er Passagier stowaway.

Blinddarm m appendix; **~entzündung** f appendicitis.

Blind|gänger m dud; **~heit** f blindness; **b~lings** blindly.

blink|en signal, blink; **B~licht** n mot indicator.

Blitz m (flash of) lightning; **~ableiter** m lightning-conductor; **b~en** 1. es blitzt it is lightning; 2. (Licht) sparkle, flash; **~licht** n phot flashlight; **~schlag** m: vom ~ getroffen struck by lightning; **b~schnell** as quick as a flash.

Block m 1. (Stein, Holz) block; 2. pol bloc; **~ade** f blockade; **~flöte** f mus recorder; **b~frei** non-aligned; **~haus** n log-cabin; **b~ieren** 1. (Straße) block, obstruct; 2. (Bremsen) jam, lock.

blöd|e stupid, silly; **B~sinn** *m* nonsense; **b~sinnig** stupid, foolish.

blond fair.

bloß 1. *(nackt)* bare, naked; 2. *(nur)* only, merely, simply.

Blöße *f* nakedness.

bloßstellen expose, compromise.

blühen 1. *(Blume)* bloom, blossom; 2. *fig* flourish, prosper; **~d** 1. flowery; 2. *fig* flourishing.

Blume *f* 1. flower; 2. *(Wein)* bouquet; **~nbeet** *n* flowerbed; **~ngeschäft** *n* flowershop; **~nkohl** *m* cauliflower; **~nstrauß** *m* bunch of flowers; **~ntopf** *m* flowerpot; **~nvase** *f* vase.

Bluse *f* blouse.

Blut *n* blood; **~bad** *n* slaughter; **~bank** *f* blood bank; **~druck** *m* blood pressure.

Blüte *f* 1. bloom, blossom; 2. *fig* climax, height.

bluten bleed.

Blut|erguß *m* hemorrhage; **~gefäß** *n* blood-vessel; **~gruppe** *f* blood-group; **b~ig** bloodstained, bloody; **~kreislauf** *m* blood circulation; **~spender** *m* blood-donor; **~übertragung** *f* blood-transfusion; **~ung** *f* bleeding; **~vergiftung** *f* blood-poisoning; **~verlust** *m* loss of blood.

Bö *f* squall.

Bock *m* buck, he-goat.

Boden *m* 1. *(Erde)* soil, ground; 2. *(Erdboden)* ground; 3. *(Fußboden)* floor; 4. *(Gefäß)* bottom; 5. *(Haus)* attic; **~schätze** *pl* mineral resources *pl.*

Bogen *m* 1. bend, curve; 2. *arch* arch; 3. *(Papier)* sheet.

Bohne *f* 1. bean; 2. *grüne ~n* French beans; **~nstange** *f* beanpole *a. fig;* **~nsuppe** *f* bean soup.

bohner|n polish; **B~wachs** *n* floor polish.

bohr|en 1. *tech* drill, bore; 2. *in der Nase ~* pick o.'s nose; **~end** *(Hunger)* gnawing; **B~er** *m* drill; **B~turm** *m* drilling derrick.

Boje *f* buoy.

Bolzen *m* pin, bolt.

bomb|ardieren bomb; **B~e** *f* bomb; **B~enattentat** *n* bomb attempt *(auf jds Leben* on s.o.'s life).

Bon *m* voucher.

Bonbon *n* sweet, candy.

Boot *n* boat; **~sfahrt** *f* boating; **~shaus** *n* boat-house.

Bord *m* board; **an ~** on board, aboard; **über ~ gehen** go overboard; **~funker** *m* wireless operator; **~stein** *m* kerb *or* curb.

borgen 1. *(entleihen)* borrow *(von jdm* from s.o.); 2. *(ausleihen)* lend *(jdm* s.o.).

Börse *f* 1. *com* stock exchange; 2. *(Geldbeutel)* purse.

Borste f bristle.
Borte f border, braid.
bösartig 1. vicious; 2. med malignant.
Böschung f slope, embankment.
böse 1. bad; 2. (verrucht) evil, wicked; 3. (bösartig) malicious; 4. (unerfreulich) nasty; 5. (ärgerlich) angry, annoyed; jdn ~ machen make s.o. angry; **B~** n evil, ill; **B~wicht** m rascal.
bos|haft 1. (tückisch) vicious; 2. (bösartig) malicious; **B~heit** f wickedness, malice.
böswillig malevolent, malicious.
Botan|ik f botany; **b~isch** botanical.
Bote m messenger.
Botschaft f 1. message; 2. pol embassy; **~ter** m ambassador.
Bowle f punch.
box|en box; **B~er** m boxer; **B~kampf** m boxing-match.
boykottieren boycott.

Brand m fire, blaze; in ~ geraten catch fire; in ~ stekken set on fire.
branden break, surge.
Brand|gefahr f fire risk; **~stifter** m fire-raiser; **~stiftung** f fire-raising, arson; **~ung** f breakers pl; **~wunde** f burn.
braten irr (im Ofen) roast; (am Feuer) broil; (auf dem

Rost) grill; (in der Pfanne) fry; **B~** m roast.
Brat|huhn n roast chicken; **~kartoffeln** pl fried potatoes; **~pfanne** f frying-pan; **~wurst** f fried sausage.
Brauch m usage, custom.
brauchbar useful, practicable.
brauchen 1. (nötig haben) need, want, be in need of; 2. (Zeit) need, take; 3. ich brauche nicht zu arbeiten I don't have to work; 4. (verwenden) use; 5. das braucht Zeit it takes time.
Braue f eyebrow.
brau|en brew; **B~erei** f brewery.
braun brown; ~ werden get tanned.
Bräune f (Sonne) tan; **b~n** brown; (Sonne) tan.
Braunkohle f brown coal.
Brause f 1. shower; 2. (Getränk) fizzy lemonade; **b~n** (Wind) roar, rage.
Braut f fiancée; (am Hochzeitstag) bride.
Bräutigam m fiancé; (am Hochzeitstag) bridegroom.
Brautpaar n bride and bridegroom.
brav 1. (artig) well-behaved; 2. (ehrlich) honest.
brech|en irr 1. break; 2. jur violate, break; 3. med fracture; 4. (Blut) vomit; 5. das Eis bricht the ice breaks; 6. mit jdm ~ break with s.o.;

7. *sich* ~ break; **B~reiz** *m* nausea.

Brei *m* pulp, mash.

breit 1. broad, wide; 2. *(ausführlich)* lengthy, diffuse; **B~e** *f* 1. breadth, width; *e-e* ~ *von 5 m haben* be 5 metres in width; 2. *fig* lengthiness **B~engrad** *m* degree of latitude; **b~schulterig** broad-shouldered; **B~wand** *f* wide-screen (film).

Bremse *f* 1. brakes *pl*; 2. *(Tier)* horsefly; **b~en** brake; ~**flüssigkeit** *f* brake fluid; ~**pedal** *n* brake pedal; ~**spur** *f* skid marks *pl*; ~**weg** *m* braking distance.

brennbar inflammable, combustible; ~**en** *irr* 1. *(Feuer, Holz)* burn; *(Haus)* be on fire; *die Sonne brennt* the sun is scorching; *wo brennt's denn?* what's the matter? *alle Lichter brannten* all the lights were on; 2. *(Wunde)* smart, burn; 3. *(Kaffee)* roast; 4. *(Schnaps)* distill; ~**end** 1. *(Kerze)* burning; 2. *fig* pressing, urgent, fervent; 3. *med* caustic.

Brennessel *f* nettle.

Brennholz *n* firewood; ~**punkt** *m* focal point, focus; ~**stoff** *m* fuel; ~**weite** *f* focal length.

Brett *n* 1. board; 2. *(Regal)* shelf; 3. *Schwarzes* ~ notice-board, *Am* bulletin board.

Brezel *f* pretzel.

Brief *m* letter; ~**bogen** *m* sheet of paper; ~**geheimnis** *n* secrecy of correspondence; ~**kasten** *m* letter-box; **b~lich** by letter; ~**marke** *f* stamp; ~**markenautomat** *m* stamp-machine; ~**öffner** *m* letter-opener; ~**papier** *n* letter-paper; ~**tasche** *f* wallet; ~**träger** *m* postman, *Am* mailman; ~**umschlag** *m* envelope; ~**waage** *f* letter-balance; ~**wechsel** *m* correspondence.

Brikett *n* briquette.

Brille *f* spectacles, glasses *pl.*

bringen *irr* 1. *(herbei)* bring, fetch; 2. *(hinwegtragen)* take, get; *jdn zu Bett* ~ put s.o. to bed; 3. *(begleiten)* take, see; *jdn nach Hause* ~ take s.o. home; 4. *(verschaffen)* bring; 5. *(verursachen)* cause, produce; 6. *(Zinsen)* bear; 7. *(Film)* present; 8. *ans Licht* ~ bring to light; 9. *jdn auf etw* ~ suggest s.th. to s.o.; 10. *etw mit sich* ~ bring s.th. about; 11. *jdn um etw* ~ deprive s.o. of s.th.; 12. *jdn zu etw* ~ make s.o. do s.th.

Brise *f* breeze.

Brite *m* Briton; **b~isch** British.

Brocken *m (Stein)* lump.

Brombeere *f* blackberry.

Brosche *f* brooch.

Broschüre *f* booklet.

Brösel *m* crumb.

Brot *n* bread.
Brötchen *n* roll, bun.
Brotlaib *m* loaf of bread.
Bruch *m* 1. *(e-r Achse)* breakage; 2. *fig* break, rupture; break up; 3. *med* fracture, rupture; 4. *(Riß)* crack; 5. *math* fraction.
brüchig cracked, brittle.
Bruchteil *m* fraction.
Brücke *f* 1. bridge; 2. *(Teppich)* rug.
Bruder *m* brother.
brüderlich brotherly, fraternal; **B~keit** *f* brotherhood.
Brühe *f* broth, consommé.
brüllen 1. roar *(vor Lachen* with laughter); 2. *(Kind)* bawl, howl; 3. *(Rind)* bellow; 4. *(laut rufen)* shout.
brummen 1. hum, buzz; 2. *(Mensch)* growl, grumble.
Brunnen *m* 1. well; 2. *(Spring~)* fountain; 3. *(Heilquelle)* mineral spring.
Brust *f* 1. chest; 2. *(Busen)* breast.
brüsten, *sich* boast, brag *(mit* of); **B~ung** *f* parapet.
Brut *f* brood, hatch.
brutal brutal; **B~ität** *f* brutality.
brüten *(von Vögeln)* brood, hatch, incubate, sit.
Brutstätte *f* breeding ground.
brutto gross; **B~gewicht** *n* gross weight.
Bub *m* boy, son; ~**e** *m (Karten)* knave, jack.

Buch *n* book; ~**binder** *m* bookbinder; ~**drucker** *m* printer; ~**druckerei** *f* printing office.
Buche *f* beech.
buchen 1. *com* book, enter; 2. *(Flug)* book, reserve.
Bücher|brett *n* book-shelf; ~**ei** *f* library; ~**schrank** *m* bookcase; ~**wurm** *m fig* bookworm.
Buch|halter *m* book-keeper; ~**haltung** *f* book-keeping; ~**händler** *m* bookseller; ~**handlung** *f* bookshop.
Buchsbaum *m* box-tree.
Büchse *f* 1. *(Dose)* box, can, tin; 2. *(Gewehr)* gun, rifle; ~**nmilch** *f* tinned milk; ~**nöffner** *m* tin-opener.
Buchstab|e *m* letter; *großer, kleiner* ~ capital, small letter; *in* ~*n* in words, in full; **b~ieren** spell.
buchstäblich literal.
Bucht *f* bay, bight.
Buch|umschlag *m* jacket; ~**ung** *f* booking, reservation.
Buckel *m* hump, hunch; **b~ig** hunchbacked.
bücken, *sich* stoop, bend (down).
Bude *f* 1. *(Stand)* stall, booth, stand; 2. *(Hütte)* hut, cabin; 3. *(Student)* room, digs *pl.*
Büfett *n* 1. *(Anrichte)* sideboard, buffet; 2. *(Ausschank)* bar, buffet.
Büffel *m zoo* buffalo.
Bug *m* bow.

Bügel *m* 1. bow; 2. *(Kleider~)* hanger; **~brett** *n* ironing-board; **~eisen** *n* flatiron; **~falte** *f* crease; **b~frei** non-iron; **b~n** iron; *(Hosen)* press.

Bühne *f* 1. *theat* stage, platform; 2. *politische ~* political scene.

Bulgar|e *m* Bulgarian; **~ien** *n* Bulgaria; **b~isch** Bulgarian.

Bullauge *n* porthole.

Bulle *m* bull.

Bummel *m* stroll; *e-n ~ machen* go for a stroll; **b~n** 1. stroll; 2. *(faulenzen)* loaf, be idle; **~streik** *m* go-slow.

Bund 1. *m (Verbindung)* bond; 2. *(Pakt)* agreement; 3. *pol* alliance, union, confederacy, coalition; 4. *(Staaten)* confederation; 5. *(an Hosen)* waistband; 6. *n (Schlüssel)* bunch.

Bündel *n* 1. *(Reisig, Stroh)* bundle; 2. *(Strahlen)* beam; **b~n** bundle up.

Bündnis *n* alliance, league.

bunt 1. *(gefärbt)* coloured; 2. *(mehrfarbig)* colourful; 3. *(buntgefleckt)* variegated, spotted; 4. *(gemischt)* mixed; 5. *(abwechslungsreich)* varied, variegated; *~er Abend* variety programme; 6. *(wirr)* confused; **B~stift** *m* crayon.

Burg *f* castle.

Bürge *m* 1. guarantor; 2. *für etw. jdn ~ sein* stand security for s.th., s.o.; **b~n** guaran-

tee *(für* s.th.), vouch *(für* for).

Bürger *m* citizen; **~krieg** *m* civil war; **b~lich** 1. *jur* civic, civil, civilian; 2. *(mittelständisch)* middle-class; 3. *(einfach)* plain; **~meister** *m* mayor; **~pflicht** *f* citizen's duty; **~rechte** *pl* civic rights; **~steig** *m* sidewalk, pavement; **~tum** *n* the middle classes *pl*.

Bürgschaft *f* guarantee, security, bail.

Büro *n* office, bureau; **~klammer** *f* paper-clip.

Bürokrat|ie *f* bureaucracy, red tape; **b~isch** bureaucratic.

Bürste *f* brush; **b~n**: *sich die Haare ~* brush o.'s hair.

Bus *m (Stadt-)* bus; *(Reise-)* coach.

Busch *m* bush, shrub.

Büschel *n* 1. bunch, cluster; 2. *(Stroh)* wisp; 3. *(Haare)* tuft.

buschig bushy.

Busen *m* bosom, breast.

Buße *f* 1. *~ tun* do penance; 2. *(Geldstrafe)* fine.

büßen expiate, pay for.

Büste *f* bust; **~nhalter** *m* bra, brassière.

Butter *f* butter; *mit ~ bestreichen* butter a piece of bread; **~brot** *n* piece of bread and butter; **~dose** *f* butterdish; **~milch** *f* buttermilk.

C

Café n coffee-house, café.

camp|en camp; **C~er** m camper; **C~ing** n camping; **C~ingplatz** m campground, campsite.

Champagner m champagne.

Champignon m mushroom.

Chance f chance, opportunity.

Chao|s n chaos; **c~tisch** chaotic.

Charakter m character.

charakterisieren characterize.

Charakteristik f characterization.

charakter|istisch characteristic; **~los** without character.

Charakterzug m trait of character.

charmant charming.

Charter m charter; **~flugzeug** n charter plane; **c~n** charter; **~vertrag** m charter-party.

Chauffeur m driver, chauffeur.

Chaussee f high road.

Chef m head, boss, chief; **~arzt** m head physician;

~redakteur m chief editor.

Chem|ie f chemistry; **~ikalien** pl chemicals; **~iker** m chemist; **c~isch** chemical; **~e Reinigung** f dry-cleaning.

chiffrieren code.

Chin|a n China; **~ese** m, **c~esisch** adj Chinese.

Chinin n chem quinine.

Chirurg m surgeon; **~ie** f surgery; **c~isch** surgical.

Chlor n chem chlorine.

Cholera f med cholera.

Cholesterin n cholesterol.

Chor m choir, chorus.

Christ m Christian; **~entum** n Christianity; **c~lich** Christian.

Chrom n chrome.

Chronik f chronicle.

chronisch med chronic.

chronologisch chronological.

circa approximately.

Clique f clique, clan.

Clou m highlight, point.

Computer m computer.

Conférencier m showmaster.

Container m container.

Creme f cream.

D

da I adv 1. (dort) there; hier und ~ here and there; von ~ from there; 2. (hier) here; ist er ~? is he here? 3. sieh ~! look there! 4. (zeitlich) then, at that time; von ~ an from that time on; 5. (in diesem Fall) in that case; ~ irren Sie sich you are mistaken there; 6. (dennoch) yet; **II** conj (kausal) as, since, because.

dabei 1. (nahe) near by; 2. (angeschlossen) attached to; 3. ~ sein, etw zu tun be about to do s.th.; 4. (gleichzeitig) at the same time; 5. (überdies) moreover, into the bargain; 6. (dennoch) nevertheless; 7. (Anlaß) on the occasion; 8. es bleibt ~ that's settled.

dabeisein irr be present, take part.

dableiben irr stay, remain.

Dach n roof; ~**boden** m loft, attic; ~**decker** m tiler; ~**garten** m roof-garden; ~**kammer** f attic; ~**luke** f skylight; ~**rinne** f gutter.

Dachs m badger.

Dach|**stuhl** m roof timbers; ~**ziegel** m tile.

Dackel m dachshund.

dadurch I adv 1. by it, by that; 2. (aus diesem Grund) in this manner; **II** conj: ~,

daß because, owing to the fact that.

dafür 1. for that, for it; 2. (anstatt) instead of it; 3. (Gegenleistung) in exchange, in return for it; 4. ich kann nichts ~ it is not my fault; 5. ~ sein be in favour of; (Abstimmung) vote for.

dagegen I adv 1. against it, against that; 2. (Vergleich) in comparison with; 3. (Gegenleistung) in return (for), in exchange (for); 4. ich habe nichts ~ I have no objections; **II** conj (andererseits) on the other hand.

daheim 1. at home; 2. (in der Heimat) in one's own country.

daher 1. (von da) from there; 2. (deshalb) therefore; ~ konnte ich nicht kommen that's why I couldn't come.

dahin 1. (örtl.) there, to that place; 2. (zeitl.) bis ~ until then, by then.

dahin|**ten** back there; ~**ter** behind that.

damalig of that time, then.

damals at that time; ~, als at the time when.

Dame f 1. lady; 2. (Tanzen) partner; 3. (Karten) queen; meine ~n und Herren! ladies and gentlemen!

~nbinde f sanitary towel; **~nfriseur** m ladies' hairdresser; **~nkleidung** f ladies' wear; **~ntoilette** f ladies' room.

damit I adv with it, with that; **II** conj in order that, so that; ~ nicht lest.

Damm m 1. dam; 2. (Deich) dike; 3. (Fahr~) roadway.

dämmern: es dämmert (morgens) it is dawning; (abends) it is getting dark; **D~ung** f: in der ~ (morgens) at dawn; (abends) at dusk, at twilight.

Dampf m steam; **~bad** n steam-bath; **d~en** steam.

dämpfen 1. (Ton) deaden; 2. (Stimme) lower; 3. (Küche) steam.

Dampf|er m steamer; **d~ig** steamy; **~kessel** m boiler; **~kochtopf** m pressure-cooker; **~maschine** f steam-engine.

danach 1. after that, afterwards; 2. (später) later on; 3. (demzufolge) according to, accordingly; 4. er fragte ihn ~ he asked him about it.

Däne m Dane.

daneben 1. (örtl.) near it, next to it; 2. (außerdem) besides, moreover; **~gehen** irr (Schuß) miss.

Dän|emark n Denmark; **d~isch** Danish.

Dank m 1. thanks pl; zum ~ für as a reward for; herzlichen ~ many thanks; Gott sei ~! thank God! 2. (Dankbarkeit) gratitude; ich bin Ihnen zu großem ~ verpflichtet I am much obliged to you; **d~** thanks to, owing to; **d~bar** thankful (jdm für etw to s.o. for s.th.); **~barkeit** f gratitude; **d~en** 1. thank; nichts zu ~! don't mention it! ~ schön you're welcome! danke schön thank you very much; 2. (verdanken) thank, owe (jdm etw s.th. to s.o.); **d~end**: ~ erhalten received with thanks.

dann 1. (darauf) then, next, after that; 2. ~ und wann now and then; 3. (in diesem Fall) in that case; selbst ~, wenn even if.

daran 1. on it; to it; 2. ~ denken think of it; 3. ~ glauben believe in it; 4. nahe ~ close to it.

darauf 1. on it; to it; 2. er ist stolz ~ he is proud of it; 3. bald ~ soon after; 4. es kommt ~ an it all depends; **~hin** thereupon.

daraus from it; ~ folgt, daß hence it follows that.

darin in it, in that.

darleg|en explain; **D~ung** f explanation.

Darlehen n loan.

Darm m gut, bowels pl, intestines pl.

darstell|en 1. (zeigen) represent, describe, picture; 2. (bedeuten) mean; 3. theat perform, act; **D~er** m actor; **D~erin** f actress.

darüber 1. (örtl.) over it, above it; 2. (zeitl.) meanwhile, in the meantime; 3. ~ hinaus beyond that, in addition.

darum 1. (deswegen) therefore, for that reason; 2. (um herum) around it; 3. ~ handelt es sich that's the point.

darunter 1. (räumlich) underneath, below; 2. (weniger) less; 3. (dazwischen) among them; 4. was verstehen Sie ~? what do you understand by it?

das 1. (Artikel) the; 2. was ist ~? what's that?

dasein irr 1. (gegenwärtig) be present; 2. (vorhanden) exist; **D~** n existence.

daß 1. that; 2. es sei denn, ~ unless; kaum ~ hardly.

Daten pl data; particulars; **~verarbeitung** f data processing.

datieren date.

Dattel f date.

Datum n date.

Dauer f 1. duration; 2. (Zeitspanne) period; 3. auf die ~ in the long run; **d~haft** 1. (Friede) lasting; 2. (Material) durable, solid; **~karte** f season-ticket; **~lauf** m jogging.

dauern 1. last; 2. das wird lange ~ that will take a long time; **~d** continuous, continual, constant.

Dauerwelle f permanent wave.

Daumen m thumb.

Daune f down; **~nbett** n feather-bed.

davon 1. (räumlich) from it, away; 2. (dadurch) by it; 3. genug ~! enough of it; 4. das kommt ~ that's what happens; **~kommen** irr escape, get off; mit knapper Not ~ have a narrow escape.

davor 1. (räumlich) in front of; 2. (zeitl.) first, before it.

dazu 1. (Zweck) for that purpose; 2. (außerdem) in addition to that; 3. noch ~ into the bargain; **~gehören** belong to it; **~kommen** irr be added; **~tun** irr add.

dazwischen 1. (räumlich) between them; 2. (zeitlich) in between; 3. (darunter) amongst them; **~kommen** irr intervene, interfere; wenn nichts dazwischen kommt if nothing happens.

Debatte f debate; zur ~ stehen be under discussion; **d~ieren** debate.

Deck n mar deck.

Decke f 1. blanket, cover; 2. (Zimmer) ceiling; 3. (Tischdecke) tablecloth.

Deckel m lid, cover.

decken 1. (Dach, sport) cover; 2. den Tisch ~ set the table; 3. den Bedarf ~ meet o.'s needs; *die Kosten* ~ defray the expenses; *der Scheck ist gedeckt* the cheque is covered.

Deckname *m* pseudonym, alias.

Deckung *f com* cover; *ohne* ~ without cover, security.

defekt defective.

defini|eren define; **D~tion** *f* definition.

Defizit *n* deficit, deficiency.

dehn|bar 1. stretchable, extensible; 2. *fig* flexible; **~en** 1. stretch; 2. *(in die Länge ziehen)* extend, lengthen.

Deich *m* dike.

dein 1. your; 2. *der* ~*e* yours; 3. *die D~igen* your family; **~etwegen** for your sake.

Dekan *m* dean.

Dekor|ateur *m* decorator; window-dresser; **d~ieren** 1. decorate; 2. *(Schaufenster)* dress.

delegier|en delegate; **D~ter** *m* delegate, deputy.

delikat 1. *(lecker)* delicious; 2. *(Gesundheit)* delicate; 3. *(Frage)* awkward; **D~esse** *f* delicacy.

Delphin *m* dolphin.

dem 1. *wenn* ~ *so ist* if that is so; 2. *das ist der Mann,* ~ *ich es gab* that's the man to whom I gave it; **~entsprechend** accordingly; **~gegenüber** on the contrary; **~nächst** soon, shortly.

Demokrati|e *f* democracy; **d~sch** democratic.

Demonstr|ant *m* demonstrator; **~ation** *f* demonstration; **d~ieren** demonstrate.

Demoskopie *f* opinion poll.

Demut *f* humility.

demütig humble; **~en** humiliate; **D~ung** *f* humiliation.

denk|bar imaginable, conceivable; **~en** *irr* 1. think *(an* of); 2. *(annehmen)* suppose, imagine; 3. *(sich erinnern)* remember; 4. *(sich vorstellen)* fancy; 5. *(erwägen)* consider.

Denkmal *n* memorial; *(Statue)* monument; **~schutz** *m: unter* ~ *stehen* be classified as an historical monument.

denn I *conj* 1. because, for; 2. *mehr* ~ *je* more than ever; 3. *es sei* ~ unless; **II** *adv* then.

dennoch nevertheless.

deponieren deposit.

Depot *n* depot, deposit.

deprimieren depress.

der the; *(dieser)* this, that; *(welcher)* who; ~ *dort* that one; **~artig** such, in such a manner.

derb 1. *fig* coarse, rough; 2. *(fest)* solid, firm.

der|en whose; **~gleichen** of that kind; **~jenige** *:* ~, *welcher* he that, he who; **~maßen** so, in such a manner; **~-, die-, dasselbe** *pl* **die-**

selben the same; ~**zeitig** for the time being.

desertieren desert.

des|gleichen likewise; ~**halb I** *adv (Folge)* therefore; **II** *conj* 1. for that reason; 2. *(einschränkend)* nevertheless.

desinfizieren disinfect.

Dessert *n* dessert.

desto the more; *je größer, ~ besser* the bigger, the better.

Detektiv *m* detective.

deut|en 1. interpret; 2. *auf jdn ~* point at s.o.; ~**lich** 1. clear, distinct; 2. *(eindeutig)* obvious; 3. *(augenfällig)* evident; 4. *(lesbar)* legible.

deutsch 1. German; 2. *in das D~e übersetzen* translate into German; **D~er** *m* German; **D~land** *n* Germany.

Deutung *f* interpretation.

Devise *f* 1. *(Wahlspruch)* motto; 2. *com pl* foreign currency.

Dezember *m* December.

Dia *n phot* slide.

Diagnose *f* diagnosis.

Dialekt *m* dialect.

Dialog *m* dialogue.

Diamant *m* diamond.

Diät *f* diet; *d~ leben* live on a diet.

dich you; yourself.

dicht 1. *(Nebel, Verkehr)* dense, thick; 2. *(undurchlässig)* tight; 3. *~ beim Haus* close to the house; 4. *~ bevölkert* densely populated.

dicht|en 1. write poetry;

2. *(Fugen)* tight; **D~er** *m* poet; ~**erisch** poetic; **D~ung** *f* 1. poetry; 2. *tech* gasket.

dick 1. thick; 2. *(massig)* big; 3. *(Person)* fat, stout; 4. *fig* close, intimate.

Dickicht *n* thicket.

dickköpfig stubborn.

die *s. der.*

Dieb *m* thief; ~**stahl** *m* theft; *jur* larceny.

Diele *f* 1. *(Brett)* board, plank; 2. *(Hausflur)* hall, vestibule.

dien|en 1. serve; 2. *jdm mit etw ~* help s.o. in s.th.; *womit kann ich Ihnen ~?* can I help you? 3. *als etw ~* serve as s.th.; 4. *e-r Sache ~* be useful for s.th., serve s.th.; **D~er** *m* servant, domestic.

Dienst *m* 1. service; 2. *(beim Staat)* service, employment; 3. *(Beruf)* duty; *außer ~* off duty; 4. *(Stellung)* position, post; 5. *(Arbeit)* work; 6. *mil* service, duty; 7. *jdm e-n ~ erweisen* do s.o. a favour.

Dienstag *m* Tuesday.

Dienst|alter *n* seniority; ~**grad** *m* rank; **d~habend** on duty; ~**leistung** *f* service; **d~lich** official; ~**reise** *f* official journey; ~**stelle** *f* agency, office; ~**stunden** *pl* office hours *pl;* ~**weg** *m: auf dem ~* through official channels.

Diesel|motor *m* diesel engine; ~**öl** *n* diesel oil.

dies|er 1. this, *pl* these; 2. ~ *Tage* one of these days; 3. *(substantivisch)* this one, *pl* these; 4. ~ *und jener* some people; 5. *(letzterer)* the latter; ~**jährig** this year's; ~**mal** this time; ~**seits** on this side.

Dietrich *m* skeleton key.

Diktat *n* dictation.

Diktat|or *m* dictator; ~**ur** *f* dictatorship.

diktier|en dictate; **D~gerät** *n* dictaphone *Wz*.

Dilemma *n* dilemma.

Dimension *f* dimension.

Ding *n* 1. *(Sache)* thing; *vor allen* ~*en* first of all, above all; *guter* ~*e sein* be in high spirits; 2. *(Angelegenheit)* matter, affair.

Diphterie *f* diphteria.

Diplom *n* diploma; ~**at** *m* diplomat; ~**atie** *f* diplomacy; **d~atisch** diplomatic.

dir 1. you; 2. yourself.

direkt direct, straight.

Direkt|ion *f* management, administration; ~**iven** *pl* instructions *pl;* ~**or** *m* 1. director, head; 2. *(e-r Schule)* headmaster, principal.

Dirig|ent *m mus* conductor; **d~ieren** 1. *mus* conduct; 2. *(lenken)* direct, manage.

disharmonisch dissonant.

Diskjockey *m* disc jockey.

Diskont *m* discount; ~**satz** *m* bank rate.

Diskothek *f* disco(theque).

diskret discreet.

Disku|ssion *f* discussion, debate; *etw zur* ~ *stellen* put s.th. up for discussion; **d~tieren** discuss, debate.

Distanz *f* distance.

Distel *f* thistle.

Disziplin *f* discipline; **d~iert** disciplined.

dividieren divide *(durch* by).

doch 1. *(aber)* but, however, yet; 2. *(trotzdem, dennoch)* however, nevertheless, all the same; 3. *(gewiß)* surely.

Docht *m* wick.

Dock *n* dock.

Dogma *n* dogma; **d~tisch** dogmatic.

Doktor *m* 1. doctor; 2. *(Arzt)* doctor, physician.

Dokument *n* document; ~**arfilm** *m* documentary (film); **d~ieren** document.

Dolch *m* dagger.

dolmetsch|en interpret; **D~er** *m* interpreter.

Dom *m* cathedral.

dominieren 1. *(vorherrschen)* predominate; 2. *biol* dominate.

Domino *n* game of dominoes.

Dompteur *m* trainer.

Donner *m* thunder; **d~n** thunder; *es donnert* it's thundering.

Donnerstag *m* Thursday.

doof stupid.

Doppel *n* duplicate; ~**bett** *n* double bed; ~**gänger** *m* double; ~**punkt** *m* colon; **d~t** 1. double; 2. ~ *soviel* twice as much; **~zentner** *m* quintal; **~zimmer** *n* double room.

Dorf *n* village.

Dorn *m* thorn; **d~ig** thorny; **~röschen** *n* the Sleeping Beauty.

dörren dry.

Dörrobst *n* dried fruit.

Dorsch *m* cod.

dort there; **~ unten** down there; **~her** from there; **~hin** there; **bis ~** as far as there.

Dose *f* box; tin, *Am* can; **~nöffner** *m* tin-opener.

Dosis *f* dose, dosage.

Dotter *m* yolk.

Dozent *m* lecturer.

Drache *m* dragon.

Drachen *m* kite; *e-n ~ steigen lassen* fly a kite.

Draht *m* wire; *auf ~sein* be on the ball; **d~en** wire, telegraph, cable; **d~los** wireless.

Drama *n* drama; **~tiker** *m* dramatist; **d~tisch** dramatic; **~turg** *m* producer.

Drang *m* 1. pressure; 2. (*Trieb*) urge, drive.

drängen 1. push, press; 2. *fig* be pressing; 3. *sich ~* crowd.

drastisch drastic.

draußen 1. outside; 2. (*im Freien*) out of doors.

Dreck *m* 1. dirt; 2. (*Schlamm*) mud; **d~ig** dirty, filthy.

Drehbuch *n film* scenario,

(film-)script; **~autor** *m* scriptwriter.

drehen 1. *allg* turn; 2. (*Zigarette*) roll; 3. *film* shoot; 4. *sich ~* rotate, turn; 5. (*Wind*) shift; 6. *fig* revolve; 7. *es dreht sich darum, ob* it is a matter of.

Dreher *m* turner.

Dreh|kreuz *n* turnstile; **~orgel** *f* barrel-organ; **~scheibe** *f* 1. turn-table; 2. (*Töpfer*) potter's wheel; 3. *tele* dial; **~tür** *f* revolving door; **~ung** *f* turn; **~zahl** *f* number of revolutions.

drei three; **D~eck** *n* triangle; **~fach** threefold; **~hundert** three hundred; **~mal** three times; **D~rad** *n* tricycle.

dreißig thirty.

dreist 1. audacious; 2. (*frech*) cheeky, impertinent.

drei|viertel three quarters; **~** *Jahr* nine months; **~** *acht* a quarter to eight; **~zehn** thirteen.

dreschen *irr* thresh.

dress|ieren train; **D~ur** *f* training.

dring|en *irr* 1. *durch etw ~* break through s.th., force o.'s way through s.th., penetrate s.th.; 2. *aus etw ~* come from s.th., break out of s.th.; 3. *in etw ~* penetrate s.th., invade s.th.; 4. *auf etw ~* press for s.th., insist on s.th.; 5. *in jdn ~* press s.o.; **~end** 1. urgent, pressing; **~er** *Fall* case of emergency;

2. (*Rat*) strong; **D~lichkeit** *f* urgency.

drinnen inside.

dritt third; *zum ~en Mal* for the third time; *~en Ranges* third-rate; *zu ~* three of us; **D~el** *n* third (part); *~ens* thirdly.

Drog|e *f* drug; *~enabhängiger* *m* drug addict; *~erie* *f* chemist's shop; *Am* drugstore; *~ist* *m* druggist.

drohen threaten (*mit* with); *~d* threatening.

dröhnen (*Stimme*) roar.

Drohung *f* threat, menace.

drollig funny, comical.

Droschke *f* cab.

Drossel *f* thrush.

drosseln throttle, choke.

drüben on the other side.

Druck *m* 1. pressure; push; 2. (*Zwang*) force, compulsion; 3. (*Belastung*) burden; 4. *typ* printing; 5. (*Auflage*) edition; *~buchstabe* *m* block letter; **d~en** print.

drücken 1. press; 2. (*Knopf*) push; 3. (*Schuh*) pinch; 4. (*fig*) *jdn ~* weigh on s.o.; 5. (*Stimmung*) damp; 6. *auf etw ~* press s.th.; 7. *sich vor etw ~* shirk s.th.; *~d* oppressive.

Druck|er *m* printer; *~erei* *f* printing office, printers *pl*; *~fehler* *m* printer's error; *~knopf* *m* push-button; *~mittel* *n* *fig* lever; *~sache* *f* printed matter.

Drüse *f* gland.

Dschungel *m* jungle.

du you; *auf ~ und ~ stehen* be on intimate terms.

Dübel *m* dowel, plug.

Dudelsack *m* bagpipes *pl.*

Duell *n* duel.

Duett *n* duet.

Duft *m* smell, scent; **d~en** smell; **d~ig** filmy, frothy.

duld|en 1. (*zulassen*) allow, tolerate, permit; 2. (*leiden*) endure, suffer; *~sam* tolerant.

dumm stupid, silly, foolish; **D~heit** *f* stupidity, foolishness; **D~kopf** *m* fool.

dumpf dull, hollow.

Düne *f* dune.

düng|en manure, fertilize; **D~er** *m* fertilizer, manure.

dunkel 1. dark; 2. *sich ~ erinnern* remember vaguely; 3. *fig* obscure, doubtful; *~blond* light-brown; **D~heit** *f* darkness; **D~kammer** *f* darkroom.

dünn 1. thin; 2. (*schlank*) slender; 3. (*Gewebe*) flimsy; 4. (*Flüssigkeit*) weak.

Dunst *m* vapour, haze.

dünsten steam.

dunstig hazy, misty.

Duplikat *n* duplicate.

durch I *prp* 1. through; across; 2. (*mittels*) by means of, by; 3. (*weil*) because of, owing to; 4. *die ganze Zeit ~* all the time; **II** *adv:* *~ und ~* through and through.

durchaus 1. thoroughly;

2. *(unbedingt)* absolutely;
3. ~ *nicht* by no means.
durchblättern leaf through.
Durchblick *m* view, vista
(*auf* of); **d~en** 1. *(verste-*
hen) get (*etw* s.th.); 2. ~ *las-*
sen hint, give to understand.
durchbohren bore through.
durchbrechen *irr* 1. break
through; 2. *tech* pierce.
durchbrennen *irr el* burn
out, fuse.
durchbringen *irr* 1. get
through; 2. *(Kranke)* pull
through.
Durchbruch *m: zum* ~ *kom-*
men break through.
'**durchdringen** *irr*
1. *(Schall)* penetrate; 2. *mit*
etw ~ succeed with s.th.;
durch'dringen *irr* 1. penetrate, pierce; 2. *fig* pervade.
durcheinander in disorder,
in confusion; **D~** *n* confusion, disorder; **~bringen**
irr fig confuse.
'**durchfahren** *irr (Zug)* go
straight through;
durch'fahren *irr* travel,
pass through.
Durchfahrt *f* passage; *keine*
~ no thoroughfare.
Durchfall *m med* diarrhoea.
durchführ|en 1. lead
through; 2. *(Plan)* carry out,
execute; **D~ung** *f* execution.
Durchgang *m* 1. passage-
way, gateway; *kein* ~! private; 2. *com* transit; **~sver-**
kehr *m* through-traffic.

durchgeben *irr* 1. *(Mel-*
dung) pass on; 2. *(Radio)*
broadcast.
durchgehen *irr* 1. *(Person)*
pass through; 2. *(Straße)* go
through; 3. *fig* get through,
be accepted; **~d** 1. *(Zug)*
through; 2. *(andauernd)*
continous; ~ *geöffnet*
round-the-clock service.
durchgreifen *irr* 1. reach
through; 2. *fig* take strong
measures.
durchhalten *irr* hold out to
the end.
durchkommen *irr* 1. *(Zug)*
pass through; 2. *(Kranke)*
come through; 3. *(mit Geld)*
manage; 4. *(Prüfung)* pass
through.
Durch|laß *m* passage, open-
ing; **d~lassen** *irr: jdn* ~ let
s.o. pass through; **d~lässig**
permeable.
durchlaufen *irr (Schuhe)*
wear out.
durchlesen *irr* read through;
flüchtig ~ skim through.
durchmachen 1. go
through; 2. *(Schule)* pass
through.
Durchmesser *m* diameter.
durchnäßt wet through,
soaked.
durchnehmen *irr (Thema)*
go through, deal with.
durchqueren cross, traverse.
Durchreise *f* transit; *auf der*
~ passing through; **~nder**
m transit passenger.
Durchsage *f radio* an-

nouncement; **d~n** announce.

durchschauen see through, find out.

Durchschlag *m* carbon copy; **d~end** striking; conclusive; **~skraft** *f fig* convincing power.

durchschneiden *irr* cut through.

Durchschnitt *m* average; *über, unter dem* ~ above, below the average; *im* ~ on average; **d~lich** average, ordinary.

Durchschrift *f* carbon copy.

durchsehen *irr* look through, examine.

durchsetzen 1. *(Plan)* put through, succeed with; 2. *sich* ~ have o.'s way.

Durchsicht *f fig* inspection, examination; **d~ig** 1. transparent; 2. *(augenscheinlich)* obvious.

durchsprechen *irr (Problem)* talk over, discuss.

durchstehen *irr* go, come through.

durchstreichen *irr* strike out, cross out.

durchsuch|en, D~ung *f* search.

durchwandern walk through.

durchweg without exception, all through.

Durchzug *m* draught.

dürfen *irr* 1. *(Erlaubnis)* etw *tun* ~ be allowed to do s.th.; 2. *darf ich kommen?* may I come? 3. *(bei Verbot)* Sie ~ *nicht* you must not; 4. *es dürfte schwierig sein* it would be difficult.

dürftig 1. *(Kleidung)* poor, wretched, shabby; 2. *(Verhältnisse)* humble; 3. *(Einkommen)* meagre.

dürr 1. *(trocken)* dry; 2. *(Boden)* parched, arid; 3. *(mager)* lean, skinny; **D~e** *f* drought; dryness.

Durst *m* thirst; ~ *haben* be thirsty; **d~ig** thirsty.

Dusche *f* shower(-bath); **d~n,** *sich* take a shower.

Düse *f* 1. *tech* nozzle; 2. *aero* jet; **~nflugzeug** *n* jet (plane).

düster dark, gloomy.

Dutzend *n* dozen.

duzen, *sich* be on familiar terms with s.o.

Dynam|ik *f* dynamics *pl;* **d~isch** dynamic(al), progressive.

Dynamit *n* dynamite.

Dynamo *m* dynamo.

D-Zug *m* express train.

E

Ebbe *f* low tide, ebb.
eben I *adj (flach)* level, flat, even; **II** *adv* 1. *(gerade)* just; *er wollte ~ gehen* he was just about to leave; 2. *(genau)* exactly; 3. ~ *erst* just now; ~ *noch* just a moment ago; **E~bild** *n* likeness, image.
Ebene *f* 1. plain; 2. *fig* level; *auf der höchsten ~* at the highest level.
eben|falls also, too, likewise; **~so** just as; just so; **~sogut** just as well.
ebnen level, make even.
Echo *n* echo.
echt 1. true, real, genuine; 2. *(Urkunde)* authentic; 3. *(Farbe)* fast; 4. *fig* typical.
Eck|e *f* corner; *um die ~* round the corner; **e~ig** angular, square.
edel 1. *(wertvoll)* precious; 2. *(selbstlos)* generous; **E~mut** *m* generosity; **E~stein** *m* precious stone.
Efeu *m* ivy.
Effekt *m* effect; **e~iv** effective, actual, real.
egal equal; *das ist mir ganz ~* it's all the same to me.
Egois|mus *m* egoism; **~t** *m* egoist; **e~tisch** egoistic.
ehe before, until.
Ehe *f* marriage, matrimony; *e-e ~ schließen* marry, get

married; **~bruch** *m* adultery; **~frau** *f* wife; **e~lich** 1. matrimonial; 2. *jur* marital, conjugal; 3. *(Kind)* legitimate.
ehe|malig former; **~mals** formerly.
Ehe|mann *m* husband; **~paar** *n* married couple.
eher 1. *(früher)* earlier, sooner, before; *je ~, desto besser* the sooner the better; 2. *nicht ~, als* not until; 3. *(lieber)* rather, preferably; 4. *um so ~, als* all the more as; 5. *(wahrscheinlich)* more likely.
Ehe|ring *m* wedding-ring; **~scheidung** *f* divorce; **~schließung** *f* marriage.
ehr|bar respectable, honourable; **E~e** *f* honour; **~en** 1. honour; 2. *sehr geehrter Herr X.* dear Mr. X; **~enamtlich** honorary; **E~enbürger** *m* honorary citizen; **~enhaft** honourable; **E~enmitglied** *n* honorary member; **~envoll** honourable; **E~enwort** *n* word of honour.
Ehr|furcht *f* respect, reverence; **e~fürchtig** reverential, reverent.
Ehrgeiz *m* ambition; **e~ig** ambitious.
ehrlich 1. *(Person)* honest,

straight; 2. *(offen)* frank; 3. *(echt)* sincere; 4. *(anständig)* honourable; **E~keit** *f* honesty.

ehrwürdig 1. venerable; 2. *rel* reverend.

Ei *n* egg; *hart(weich)gekochtes ~* hard-(soft-)boiled egg.

Eiche *f* oak(-tree); **~l** *f bot* acorn; **e~n** gauge.

Eichhörnchen *n* squirrel.

Eid *m* oath; *e-n ~ ablegen* take an oath; *unter ~* on, under oath.

Eidechse *f* lizard.

eidesstattlich: *~e Erklärung* affidavit.

Eier|becher *m* egg-cup; **~kuchen** *m* omelet(te); **~löffel** *m* egg-spoon; **~schale** *f* egg-shell; **~stock** *m anat* ovary.

Eifer *m* zeal, eagerness, enthusiasm; **~sucht** *f* jealousy; **e~süchtig** jealous.

eifrig eager, zealous, keen.

Eigelb *n* yolk.

eigen 1. own; 2. *(besonderer)* particular; 3. *(seltsam)* strange, odd, peculiar.

Eigenart *f* peculiarity; **e~ig** peculiar, odd, strange.

Eigenheim *n* home of o.'s own.

eigenmächtig arbitrary.

Eigenname *m* proper name.

eigennützig selfish.

Eigenschaft *f* quality, property.

Eigensinn *m* obstinacy, stubbornness; **e~ig** stubborn, obstinate.

eigentlich 1. *(wirklich)* real, actual; 2. *(genau)* exact, precise; 3. *(in Wirklichkeit)* in reality; 4. *(genaugenommen)* strictly speaking, actually; 5. *(offen gesagt)* as a matter of fact.

Eigen|tum *n* property; **~tümer** *m* proprietor, owner.

eigen|tümlich 1. *(seltsam)* strange; 2. *(typisch)* specific; **~willig** 1. self-willed; 2. *fig* original, individual.

eignen, *sich* be qualified, suited *(für* for).

Eil|bote *m: durch ~* by express messenger; **~brief** *m* express letter; *Am* special delivery letter.

Eile *f* hurry, haste; *in aller ~* hurriedly, in great haste; **e~n** 1. *(Mensch)* hurry, hasten; 2. *(Sache)* be urgent; *eilt!* urgent!

Eilgut *n* express goods *pl.*

eilig 1. quick, hurried; *es ~ haben* be in a hurry; 2. *(dringend)* urgent.

Eilzug *m* fast train.

Eimer *m* pail, bucket.

ein I *(Artikel)* a, an; *~ jeder* each one; **II** *prn: ~er nach dem andern* one after the other; **III** *(Zahlwort)* 1. *~ für allemal* once and for all; 2. *~er von beiden* one of them; 3. *in ~em fort* incessantly; 4. *(eingeschaltet)* on;

~ander each other, one another.

einarbeiten, *sich* become familiar with.

einäschern cremate; **E~ung** *f* cremation.

einatmen inhale, breathe in.

Einbahnstraße *f* one-way street.

Einband *m (Buch)* binding.

Einbau *m* installation; **e~en** build in, install in; **~schrank** *m* built-in-cupboard.

einberufen *irr* convene.

einbiegen *irr* bend in; *in e-e Straße* ~ turn into a road.

einbilden, *sich* 1. imagine, fancy; 2. *(eingebildet sein)* be self-conceited; **E~ung** *f* imagination.

einbinden *irr (Buch)* bind.

Einblick *m* insight *(in e-e Lage* into a situation).

einbrechen *irr* 1. *(Tür)* break open; 2. *(in ein Haus)* break in; **E~er** *m* burglar.

einbringen *irr* 1. *(Gesetz)* bring in; 2. *(Gewinn)* yield; 3. *(Ernte)* gather in.

Einbruch *m* 1. burglary; *e-n* ~ *verüben* commit a burglary; 2. *bei* ~ *der Dunkelheit* at night(fall).

einbürgern 1. *jur* naturalize; 2. *(Brauch)* come into use; **E~ung** *f* naturalization.

einbüßen lose.

eindecken, *sich* stock up *(mit* with, on), lay in *(mit etw* s.th.).

eindeutig clear, plain.

eindringen *irr* 1. *(in ein Land)* invade (a country), penetrate; 2. *(von Personen)* force o.'s way in; 3. *in etw* ~ *(fig)* study s.th.

eindringlich 1. urgent; 2. *(eindrucksvoll)* impressive; 3. *(Stimme)* penetrating.

Eindringling *m* intruder.

Eindruck *m* 1. impression; *auf jdn* ~ *machen* make an impression on s.o.; 2. *(Nachwirkung)* effect.

eindrücken 1. *(Tür)* smash; 2. *(zerdrücken)* crush.

eindrucksvoll impressive.

einen unite.

einerlei *(gleichgültig)* all the same; ~, *wer* whoever; **~seits** on the one hand.

einfach 1. simple; *~e Fahrkarte* single ticket; 2. *(leicht zu tun)* easy; 3. *(schlicht)* plain, ordinary; 4. *das ist* ~ *unmöglich* that's simply impossible; **E~heit** *f* simplicity.

einfädeln *(Nadel)* thread.

einfahren *irr* 1. *(Zug)* come, pull in; 2. *(Auto)* run in; 3. *(Ernte)* bring in; **E~t** *f* entry *(in* into); ~ *verboten!* no entry! *bitte* ~ *freihalten* please keep entrance clear.

Einfall *m* 1. idea; 2. *mil* invasion; **e~en** *irr* 1. *(einstürzen)* collapse; 2. *jdm* ~ occur to s.o.; 3. *(ins Gespräch)* interrupt; 4. *mil* invade.

einfältig simple, naive.

Einfamilienhaus *n* self-contained house.

einfangen *irr* catch, capture.

einfarbig of one colour.

einfassen 1. *(Stoff)* edge, border; 2. *(umgeben)* surround.

einfetten 1. grease; 2. *(Haare)* cream.

einflößen 1. *(Flüssigkeit)* pour *(jdm etw* s.th. into s.o.'s mouth); 2. *jdm Vertrauen ~* inspire s.o.'s confidence.

Einfluß *m* influence *(auf* on); **e~reich** influential.

einförmig uniform, monotonous; **E~keit** *f* monotony, uniformity.

einfrieren *irr* freeze.

einfügen 1. insert; 2. *sich ~* adapt o.s. *(in* to), fit in.

einfühlen feel *(in jdn* with s.o.).

Einfuhr *f* import, importation; **~bestimmungen** *pl* import regulations *pl.*

einführen 1. *(Neuheit)* introduce, adopt, bring in; 2. *(vorstellen)* present; 3. *(einweihen)* initiate; 4. *(Ware)* import; **E~ung** *f* introduction.

Einfuhrzoll *m* import duty.

Eingabe *f (Gesuch)* petition, application.

Eingang *m* 1. entrance *(zu* to); *~ verboten!* no entry; 2. *nach ~ Ihres Schreibens* on receipt of your letter; **e~s** at the beginning.

eingeben *irr* 1. *med* administer *(jdm* to s.o.); 2. *(inspi-*

rieren) inspire *(mit* with); 3. *(e-m Computer)* feed.

eingebildet 1. imaginary; 2. *(eitel)* conceited.

Eingeborener *m* native.

Eingebung *f* inspiration.

eingehen *irr* 1. *in etw ~* enter into s.th.; 2. *(Post, Geld)* come in, arrive; 3. *(Tier)* perish; 4. *auf etw ~* accept s.th., comply with s.th.; 5. *(Ehe)* contract, conclude; 6. *(Risiko)* take.

eingehend 1. *(Post)* incoming; 2. *(genau)* detailed, exhaustive, circumstantial.

eingemeinden incorporate.

eingeschrieben *(Brief)* registered.

Eingeständnis *n* avowal, confession; **e~stehen** *irr* admit, confess.

eingetragen registered.

Eingeweide *pl* intestines *pl.*

eingießen *irr* pour out.

eingleisig single-track.

eingliedern incorporate.

eingraben *irr* dig in.

eingreifen *irr* 1. *fig* intervene, interfere; 2. *in etw ~* influence s.th.

Eingriff *m* 1. *med* operation; 2. *fig* intervention *(in* in).

Einhalt *m: e-r Sache ~ gebieten* put a stop to s.th.; **e~en** *irr* 1. *(Vertrag)* observe; 2. *(Versprechen)* keep.

einheimisch 1. native, indigenous, domestic; 2. *com* home, inland; **E~er** *m* native.

Einheit *f* unity, unit; **e~lich** uniform, homogeneous.

einheizen make a fire.

einhellig unanimous.

einholen 1. *(Auskunft)* ask for, seek; 2. *(Ernte)* bring in; 3. *(erreichen)* catch up *(jdn* with s.o.); 4. *(Zeit)* make up; 5. *(Fahne)* lower.

einig in agreement; *sich ~ sein (über* on); **~e** 1. *pl* several, some, a few; 2. *(ziemlich)* some.

einigen, sich 1. agree, come to terms; 2. *(Volk)* unite, unify.

einigermaßen to some extent, somewhat.

einiges something.

Einigkeit *f* 1. unity, union; 2. *(Ansicht)* unanimity.

Einigung *f* agreement, accord.

einkalkulieren take into account.

Einkauf *m* purchase; **e~en** buy, purchase **~sbummel** *m: e-n ~ machen* go shopping; **~skorb** *m* shopping-basket; **~snetz** *n* string-bag, shopping-bag; **~spreis** *m* purchase price **~szentrum** *n* shopping centre.

einkehren stop (off) at an inn.

Einklang *m* accord; *in ~ mit* in harmony with.

einkleiden clothe.

einklemmen jam.

Einkommen *n* income; **~steuer** *f* income-tax.

Einkünfte *pl* earnings, receipts.

einladen *irr* 1. *(Gast)* invite; 2. *(Waren)* load; **~end** inviting; **E~ung** *f* invitation.

Einlage *f* 1. *(im Brief)* enclosure; 2. *com* deposit; 3. *(Schuh~)* insole.

einlagern put into stock, store.

einlassen *irr* 1. let in; 2. *sich auf etw ~* go into s.th.; 3. *sich in etw ~* engage in s.th.; 4. *sich mit jdm ~* enter into relations with s.o.

einlaufen *irr* 1. *(Zug)* come in, arrive; 2. *(Stoff)* shrink.

einleben, sich accustom o.s., settle down.

einlegen 1. *(in e-n Brief)* enclose; 2. *e-n Film ~* load a camera; 3. *ein gutes Wort für jdn ~* put in a word for s.o.; 4. *jur* lodge; 5. *(Küche)* preserve, pickle.

einleiten 1. start, begin; 2. *(einführen)* introduce; 3. *(Verhandlung)* open; **~end** introductory; **E~ung** *f* introduction.

einleuchten be clear; **~d** evident.

einliefern *(Person)* take *(in* to).

einliegend enclosed.

einlösen 1. *(Versprechen)* keep, redeem; 2. *(Scheck)* cash; *(Wechsel)* honour.

einmachen preserve.

einmal 1. once; *auf* ~ all at once; *(plötzlich)* suddenly; *nicht* ~ not even; 2. *(künftig)* one day.

Einmaleins *n* multiplication table.

einmalig unique.

einmischen, *sich* interfere, meddle (*in* in).

einmünden run into.

einmütig unanimous.

Einnahme *f* 1. *com* receipts *pl;* 2. *(Steuern)* revenue; 3. *mil* capture.

einnehmen *irr* 1. *(Medizin, Mahlzeit)* take; 2. *(Geld)* receive, take; 3. *(Platz)* occupy; 4. *(innehaben)* hold; 5. *(Haltung)* assume; 6. *jdn für sich* ~ charm, captivate s.o.

Einöde *f* solitude.

einordnen 1. *(Briefe)* file; 2. *mot* get in lane.

einpacken 1. *(Sachen)* pack; 2. *(einschlagen)* wrap up.

einpräg|en, *sich* memorize; ~**sam** easily remembered.

einrahmen frame.

einräumen 1. *(Sachen)* put in order; 2. *fig (gewähren)* grant; 3. *(zugeben)* admit.

einreden*: jdm etw* ~ persuade s.o. of s.th.

einreiben *irr* rub (in).

einreichen send in, submit, present.

Einreise *f* entry; **e**~**n** enter; ~**visum** *n* entry visa.

einrichten 1. *(Zimmer)* furnish; 2. *(Geschäft)* equip; 3. *(eröffnen)* set up, establish; 4. *(ermöglichen)* arrange; 5. *sich* ~ furnish o.'s home.

Einrichtung *f* 1. *(Möbel)* furniture; 2. *(Ausrüstung)* equipment; 3. *(öffentlich)* institution; ~**sgegenstand** *m* piece of furniture.

eins 1. one; *um* ~ at one (o'clock); 2. *das läuft auf* ~ *hinaus* it all comes to the same thing.

einsam 1. lonely, lonesome, solitary; 2. *(menschenleer)* deserted; **E**~**keit** *f* solitude, loneliness.

einsammeln 1. *(Geld)* collect; 2. *(Dinge)* gather.

Einsatz *m* 1. *(Kleid)* insertion, insert; 2. *(Spiel)* stake; 3. *unter* ~ *s-s Lebens* at the risk of his life.

einschalten 1. *(Licht, Strom)* switch on, turn on; 2. *tech* start, engage; 3. *sich* ~ intervene.

einschätzen 1. *(Wert)* estimate; 2. *(beurteilen)* judge.

einschenken pour (out).

einschieben *irr* put in.

einschiffen, *sich* embark (*nach* for).

einschlafen *irr* 1. fall asleep; 2. *(Glied)* become numb.

einschläfern 1. lull to sleep; 2. *med* narcotize.

einschlagen *irr* 1. *(Nagel)* drive (*in* in); 2. *(Tür)* break, smash; 3. *(Zähne)* knock out; 4. *(Weg)* take; 5. *(ein-*

wickeln) wrap up; 6. *(Blitz)* strike; 7. *auf jdn* ~ beat s.o.

einschleichen, *sich irr* sneak, steal *(in* into).

einschleppen *(Krankheit)* bring in.

einschließ|en *irr* 1. lock *(in* in); 2. *(umgeben)* enclose; 3. *(einbeziehen)* include; ~**lich** included; *vom 6. bis 10. Januar* ~ from the sixth to the tenth of January inclusive.

einschmieren 1. smear; 2. *tech* lubricate.

einschneidend *(Maßnahme)* radical, drastic.

Einschnitt *m* cut, incision.

einschränk|en 1. restrict, limit *(auf* to); 2. *(Ausgaben)* cut down, reduce; **E~ung** *f* limitation, restriction; *ohne* ~ unreservedly.

einschreiben *irr* 1. *(in Verein)* enrol; *(Uni)* register; 2. *(Brief)* register; **E~** *n* registered letter.

einschreiten *irr* step in, intervene, take measures.

einschüchtern intimidate.

einsehen *irr* 1. *(Akten)* look into, examine; 2. *(verstehen)* see, understand.

einseitig 1. one-sided *a. fig;* 2. *(Ernährung)* unbalanced; 3. *(parteiisch)* partial, biassed; 4. *pol jur* unilateral.

einsend|en *irr* send in; **E~er** *m* sender.

einsetzen 1. put in, insert; 2. *pol* set up, establish;

3. *(Person)* instal, appoint; 4. *(Mittel)* use, employ; 5. *(Truppen)* mobilize; 6. *sich für jdn* ~ speak up for s.o.

Einsicht *f fig* insight, understanding; **e~ig** understanding.

Einsiedler *m* hermit.

einspar|en economize; **E~ung** *f* economy, cut.

einsperren lock up.

einspringen *irr: für jdn* ~ step in for s.o., take s.o.'s place.

Einspruch *m* objection, protest.

einst 1. *(früher)* once; 2. *(vor langer Zeit)* in former times; 3. *(künftig)* one day.

einstecken 1. *(in die Tasche, e-n Gewinn)* pocket; 2. *(Schlüssel)* put in.

einsteigen *irr (in ein Fahrzeug)* board, get into.

einstell|en 1. *(Arbeitskraft)* employ, engage; 2. *(aufhören)* stop, cease; *(Betrieb)* shut down; 3. *(Sender)* tune in; 4. *phot* focus; 5. *tech* adjust; 6. *(Zahlungen)* suspend; 7. *sich* ~ appear; 8. *sich auf etw* ~ be prepared for s.th.; 9. *(sich anpassen)* accommodate o.s.; **E~ung** *f* 1. *fig* attitude *(zu* towards); 2. *tech* adjustment; 3. *(Zahlungen)* suspension).

Einstieg *m* entrance.

einstimmig unanimous;
E~**keit** f unanimity.
einstufen 1. classify (in into);
2. (nach Qualität, Fähigkeit) grade.
Einsturz m collapse.
einstürzen 1. (Haus) collapse; 2. (Decke) fall in.
Einsturzgefahr f danger of collapse.
einstweilen meanwhile, for the moment.
einteil|en 1. divide; 2. (Zeit) organize; 3. (Geld) budget;
E~**ung** f 1. division, classification; 2. (nach Rang) gradation.
eintönig monotonous, dull.
einträchtig harmonious, peaceable.
eintragen irr 1. enter (in ein Buch in a book); 2. (amtlich) register; 3. (Gewinn) yield.
einträglich profitable, remunerative.
Eintragung f 1. entry;
2. (amtlich) registration.

eintreffen irr 1. (ankommen) arrive; 2. (geschehen) happen.
eintreten irr 1. enter, go in;
2. (einsetzen) set in; 3. (geschehen) happen, take place; 4. (beitreten) join;
5. für jdn ~ stand up for s.o.;
6. für etw ~ answer for s.th.
Eintritt m entry, entrance; ~ frei! admission free! ~ verboten! no entry! keep out!

~**skarte** f (admission) ticket.
einüben practise.
Einvernehmen n agreement; in gutem ~ on friendly terms (mit with).
einver|standen: ~ sein agree, consent; ~! agreed!
E~**ständnis** n assent, approval (mit of); im ~ mit in agreement with.
Einwand m objection (gegen to).
Einwander|er m immigrant;
e~**n** immigrate (in to);
~**ung** f immigration.

einwandfrei perfect, faultless; irreproachable.
einweichen soak.
einweih|en 1. (Denkmal) inaugurate; 2. jdn in etw ~ initiate s.o. into s.th.; E~**ung** f inauguration.
einweis|en irr 1. (in e-e Wohnung) assign; 2. (in ein Amt) install (in); 3. (in Aufgaben) introduce (in to);
E~**ung** f introduction, instruction.
einwend|en irr object (gegen to); dagegen ist nichts einzuwenden there is nothing to be said against it; E~**ung** f objection.
einwerfen irr 1. (Brief) post, Am mail; 2. (Fenster) break, smash; 3. (Münzen) insert.
einwickeln wrap up.
einwillig|en agree (in to);
E~**ung** f approval, consent.

einwirken influence (*auf jdn* s.o.).

Einwohner *m* inhabitant; ~**zahl** *f* number of inhabitants, population.

Einwurf *m* 1. (*Einwerfen*) insertion; 2. (*an e-m Briefkasten*) slit; 3. (*Automat*) slot.

einzahl|en pay in; **E~ung** *f* payment.

einzäun|en fence in; **E~ung** *f* fence, enclosure.

Einzel *n* (*Tennis*) single; ~**fall** *m* individual case; ~**handel** *m* retail trade; ~**händler** *m* retailer; ~**heit** *f* detail; *auf ~en eingehen* go into details.

einzeln 1. single, individual, particular; 2. *jeder ~e* each one; 3. *im ~en* in detail; 4. ~ *verkaufen* sell separately.

Einzel|stück *n* unique piece; ~**zimmer** *n* (*im Hotel*) single room.

einziehen *irr* 1. (*in ein Haus*) move in(to); 2. (*Geld*) cash; (*Steuer*) collect; 3. (*Auskünfte*) gather; 4. *aero* (*Fahrgestell*) retract; 5. (*Kopf*) duck.

einzig 1. only, sole, single; 2. ~ *und allein* simply and solely; ~**artig** unique.

Einzug *m* 1. (*in eine Wohnung*) moving in; 2. (*in e-e Stadt*) entry, entrance.

Eis *n* 1. ice; 2. (*zum Essen*) ice-cream; ~**bahn** *f* icerink; ~**bär** *m* polar bear; ~**berg**

m iceberg; ~**diele** *f* ice--cream parlour.

Eisen *n* iron.

Eisenbahn *f* railway, *Am* railroad; *mit der ~ fahren* go by train; ~**brücke** *f* railway bridge; ~**er** *m* railway employee; ~**knotenpunkt** *m* railway junction; ~**station** *f* railway station; ~**wagen** *m* railway carriage.

Eisenwarenhandlung *f* ironmonger's.

eisern 1. iron *a. fig*; 2. *fig* rigorous; 3. ~*er Bestand* emergency stock.

eisig, e~kalt icy(-cold).

Eis|krem *f* ice-cream; ~**(kunst)lauf** *m* figure skating; **e~laufen** *irr* ice--skate; ~**würfel** *m* ice cube; ~**zapfen** *m* icicle; ~**zeit** *f* Ice Age.

eitel vain (*auf* of); **E~keit** *f* vanity.

Eiter *m* pus; **e~ig** purulent; **e~n** fester.

Eiweiß *n* 1. white (of an egg); 2. albumen, protein.

Ekel *m* disgust, loathing; **e~haft** disgusting, repulsive, nasty; **e~n**: *sich vor etw ~* feel disgust at s.th.

Ekstase *f* ecstasy; *in ~ geraten* go into ecstasies.

elastisch 1. elastic; 2. *fig* flexible.

Elefant *m* elephant.

elektr|ifizieren electrify;

E~iker *m* electrician; **~isch** electric(al).
Elektrizität *f* electricity; **~swerk** *n* power station.
Elektroherd *m* electric range.
Elektronen|mikroskop *n* electronic microscope; **~rechner** *m* computer.
Elektrotechnik *f* electrical engineering.
Element *n* element; **e~ar** 1. elemental; 2. *(grundlegend)* basic, elementary.
Elend *n* misery, wretchedness; **e~** miserable, wretched; **~sviertel** *n* slums *pl.*
elf eleven.
Elfenbein *n* ivory.
elft eleventh.
Elite *f* elite, cream, pick.
Ellbogen *m* elbow.
Elster *f* magpie.
Eltern *pl* parents; **~haus** *n* parents' house; **e~los** parentless.
Email *n* enamel.
Emanzipation *f* emancipation.
Emigra|nt *m* emigrant; **~tion** *f* emigration.
Empfang *m* 1. receipt; 2. *(Begrüßung)* reception *a. radio;* **e~en** *irr* 1. receive; 2. *(begrüßen)* welcome.
Empfänger *m* 1. *(Brief)* addressee; 2. *(Gerät, Person)* receiver.
empfänglich susceptible, receptive *(für* to).
Empfängnis *f* conception;

e~verhütend contraceptive; **~verhütung** *f* contraception.
Empfangs|bescheinigung *f com* receipt; **~büro** *n (Hotel)* reception (-desk); **~chef** *m (Hotel)* reception clerk; **~zimmer** *n* reception room.
empfehl|en *irr* 1. recommend *(jdm etw* s.th. to s.o.); 2. *sich jdm* ~ give o.'s regards; 3. *es empfiehlt sich* it is recommended; **~ens-wert** recommendable; **E~ung** *f* recommendation, reference.
empfind|en *irr* be sensible of, feel; **~lich** 1. sensitive *(gegen* to); 2. *(leicht gekränkt)* touchy; **E~lichkeit** *f* sensitivity; **~sam** sentimental; **E~ung** *f (Gefühl)* feeling, sentiment.
empor up, upwards; **~arbeiten**, *sich* work o.'s way up.
empören, *sich* grow indignant; **~d** outrageous.
Emporkömmling *m* upstart.
emporragen tower up.
Empörung *f* indignation.
emsig assiduous, industrious.
Ende *n* 1. *(räuml.)* end, extremity; 2. *(zeitlich)* end, close; *am* ~ at the end; *(schließlich)* in the end; 3. *(Schluß)* conclusion; 4. *(Ausgang)* result; **e~n** 1. come to an end; 2. *(schließen)* close; 3. *(aufhören)* cease, stop.

End|ergebnis *n* final result;
e~gültig final, definitive;
e~lich at last, finally; **e~los**
interminable, endless; **~sta-
tion** *f* terminus; **~ung** *f*
gram ending.

Energie *f* energy, vigour;
~problem *n* problem of energy; **~verbrauch** *m* consumption of energy.

energisch energetic.

eng 1. narrow; 2. *(Kleidung)*
tight; *~er machen* take in;
3. *(Beziehungen)* close, intimate; **~anliegend** *(Kleidung)* tight-fitting; **E~e** *f*
1. narrowness; 2. *in die ~
treiben* drive into a corner.

Engel *m* angel.

engherzig narrow-minded.

Eng|land *n* England; **~län-
der** *m* Englishman; **e~lisch**
English.

Engpaß *m* 1. *geog* narrow
pass; 2. *fig* bottle-neck.

en gros wholesale.

Enkel *m* grandchild; *(Sohn)*
grandson; **~in** *f* grand-
daughter.

enorm enormous, huge.

Ensemble *n* ensemble, company.

entäußern: *sich e-r Sache ~*
get rid of s.th.

entbehr|en do without,
spare; **~lich** superfluous;
E~ungen *pl* privations.

entbind|en *irr* 1. *(von e-r
Verpflichtung)* release *(jdn
von etw* s.o. from s.th.)*;
2. *med* deliver of a child;

E~ung *f med* delivery, con-
finement.

entdeck|en discover, find
out; **E~ung** *f* discovery.

Ente *f* 1. duck; 2. *(Zeitung)*
canard.

entehren dishonour.

enteignen expropriate.

enterben disinherit.

entfallen *irr* 1. *(den Hän-
den)* fall, slip *(aus* from)*;
2. *auf jdn ~* fall to s.o.'s
share; 3. *(Fragebogen) ent-
fällt* not applicable, n.a.

entfalten 1. unfold; 2. *(fig)*
develop.

entfern|en 1. *(wegnehmen)*
take away; 2. *(Fleck)* remove; 3. *sich ~* go away,
leave; **~t** *(entlegen)* distant; 2. *(Verwandte)* remote; **E~ung** *f* 1. distance;
2. *(Flecken)* removal.

entflammen inflame.

entfliehen *irr* escape *(aus*
from)*.

entfremd|en alienate;
E~ung *f* alienation.

entführ|en 1. kidnap, abduct;
2. *aero* hijack; **E~er** *m*
1. kidnapper, abductor; 2. hi-
jacker; **E~ung** *f* 1. kidnap-
ping, abduction; 2. hijacking.

entgegen 1. *(Richtung)* towards, against; 2. *(Gegensatz)* contrary to; **~gehen**
irr go to meet *(jdm* s.o.)*.

entgegengesetzt opposite.

entgegen|halten *irr: jdm
etw ~* confront s.o. with s.th.;
~kommen *irr* 1. *jdm ~*

come to meet s.o.; 2. *fig* comply with; **~kommend** *fig* obliging, accomodating; **~sehen** *irr* expect, await; *(freudig)* look forward to; **~stehen** *irr: dem steht nichts entgegen* there is no objection to it.

entgegn|en reply, answer; **E~ung** *f* reply.

entgehen *irr* escape (*jdm* s.o.).

entgleisen *(Zug)* run off the rails.

enthalt|en *irr* 1. contain, hold; 2. *(umfassen)* comprise; 3. *sich ~* refrain, abstain (from doing s.th.); 4. *~ sein* be included; **~sam** abstinent; **E~samkeit** *f* abstinence.

entheben *irr (e-s Amtes)* remove (from).

enthüll|en 1. *(Denkmal)* unveil; 2. *fig* reveal, disclose; **E~ung** *f fig* revelation.

Enthusias|mus *m* enthusiasm; **e~tisch** enthusiastic.

entkommen *irr* escape (*aus* from).

entladen *irr* 1. unload; 2. *el* discharge.

entlang along; *die Straße ~* along the street; *hier ~, bitte!* this way, please! **~fahren** *irr* drive along; **~gehen** *irr* go along.

entlass|en *irr* 1. dismiss, discharge; 2. *(Gefangener)* release; **E~ung** *f* 1. dismissal,

discharge; 2. *(Beamter)* removal.

entlast|en 1. *(Angeklagter)* exonerate; 2. *(von Arbeit)* relieve (*jdn* s.o.); **E~ung** *f* 1. exoneration; 2. relief.

entlaufen *irr* run away.

entledigen, *sich* get rid of.

entlegen remote, distant.

entleihen *irr* borrow (*von* from).

entlocken: *jdm etw ~* draw, elicit s.th. from s.o.

Entlüftung *f* ventilation.

entmündigen incapacitate.

entmutigen discourage.

entnehmen *irr* 1. take (*aus* from); 2. *etw e-r Sache ~* conclude s.th. from s.th.

entrinnen *irr* escape, get away.

entrüst|en, *sich* become indignant (*über etw* at s.th.); **E~ung** *f* indignation.

entschädig|en compensate (*jdn für etw* s.o. for s.th.), indemnify; **E~ung** *f* 1. compensation, indemnification; *als ~ für* as compensation for; 2. *(Entgelt)* remuneration.

entschärfen defuse *a. fig.*

entscheid|en *irr* 1. decide, settle (*über* on); 2. *sich ~* make up o.'s mind; **~end** decisive; **E~ung** *f* decision (*über* on); *e-e ~ treffen* come to a decision.

entschieden 1. decided; 2. *(entschlossen)* decisive, resolute.

entschließen, *sich irr* make up o.'s mind, decide.

entschlossen determined, resolute.

entschlüpfen *(Wort)* slip out.

Entschluß *m* decision, resolution; *zu e-m ~ kommen* come to a decision.

entschlüsseln decipher.

entschuldig|en 1. excuse, pardon; *~ Sie!* excuse me! sorry! 2. *(rechtfertigen)* justify; 3. *sich ~* apologize *(bei jdm* to s.o.); **E~ung** *f* 1. excuse; 2. *Ich bitte um ~* I beg your pardon.

entsetzlich horrible, frightful.

entsinnen, *sich irr* remember, recall.

entspann|en, *sich* 1. *fig* relax; 2. *(Lage)* ease; **E~ung** *f* relaxation.

entspechen *irr* 1. correspond (to), agree (with); 2. *(Erwartung)* meet, answer; 3. *(Bitte)* comply (with); **~d** 1. corresponding; 2. *(passend)* appropriate.

entspringen *irr* 1. *(Fluß)* have its source; 2. *fig* spring.

entsteh|en *irr* 1. come into being, originate; 2. *(Bau)* be made; 3. *(Idee)* originate; 4. *(Streit)* arise; 5. *durch etw ~* be caused by s.th., result from s.th.; **E~ung** *f* 1. beginning, emergence; 2. *(Ursprung)* origin.

enttäusch|en disappoint; **~t** disappointed *(über* at); **E~ung** *f* disappointment.

entwaffnen disarm.

entweder: *~ ... oder* either ... or.

entweichen *irr* escape *(aus* from).

entweihen profane.

entwenden steal, pilfer.

entwerfen *irr* 1. *(Rede)* draw up; 2. *(Muster)* design.

entwert|en 1. *(Geld)* depreciate; 2. *(Briefmarken)* cancel; **E~ung** *f* 1. depreciation; 2. cancellation.

entwick|eln 1. develop *a. phot;* 2. *sich ~* develop *(aus* from; *zu* into); **E~lung** *f* 1. development; 2. *biol* evolution; **E~lungsland** *n pol* developing country.

entwirren disentangle.

entwöhnen cure *(von* of).

entwürdigend degrading.

Entwurf *m* draft, outline; sketch.

entzieh|en *irr* 1. *(wegnehmen)* jdm etw ~ take s.th. away from s.o.; 2. *(Vertrauen)* withdraw; 3. *sich e-r Sache ~* evade s.th., defy s.th.; **E~ungskur** *f* cure for drug addiction.

entziffern decipher.

entzück|end charming; **~t** delighted *(über* at).

entzünd|en, *sich* 1. catch fire; 2. *med* become inflamed; **~et** inflamed; **E~ung** *f med* inflammation.

Enzian *m bot* gentian.

Enzyklopädie f encyclop(a)edia.
Epidemie f epidemic.
Epoche f epoch, period.
Epos n epic (poem).
er 1. (Person) he; 2. (Sache) it.
Erachten n: meines ~s in my opinion.
erbarmen: sich jds ~ pity s.o.; **E~** n pity, mercy.
erbärmlich pitiable, pitiful.
erbarmungslos pitiless.
erbau|en n build up, construct; **E~er** m builder, constructor.
Erbe 1. m heir; 2. n inheritance, heritage; **e~n** inherit (von from).
erbeuten seize, capture.
Erbfolge f succession.
erbittert fierce, stubborn.
erblassen grow pale.
Erblasser m testator.
erblich hereditary, heritable.
erblicken see.
erblinden become blind.
erbrechen irr 1. (Behältnis) break open; 2. sich ~ vomit.
erbringen irr (Beweis) bring, produce, furnish.
Erbschaft f inheritance; ~**ssteuer** f death duty, Am inheritance tax.
Erbse f pea; ~**nsuppe** f pea-soup.
Erd|ball m globe; ~**beben** n earthquake; ~**beere** f strawberry; ~**boden** m ground, soil.
Erd|e f 1. earth; 2. über der ~ above ground; unter der ~ below the ground; 3. (Stück Land) soil, ground; ~**gas** n natural gas; ~**geschoß** n ground floor, Am first floor; ~**kunde** f geography; ~**nuß** f peanut; ~**öl** n mineral oil.
erdrücken crush.
Erd|rutsch m 1. landslip; 2. pol landslide; ~**teil** m continent.
erdulden suffer, endure.
ereig|nen, sich happen, take place; **E~nis** n 1. event; 2. (Vorfall) occurrence; ~**nislos** uneventful; ~**nisreich** eventful.
erfahr|en irr 1. (erleben) experience; 2. (hören) hear, learn; 3. (bewährt) experienced; **E~ung** f experience; aus ~ from experience; in ~ bringen learn.
erfassen 1. (packen) seize, grasp; 2. fig realize, grasp; 3. (registrieren) register.
erfind|en irr 1. invent; 2. (ausdenken) make up; **E~er** m inventor; **E~ung** f invention.
Erfolg m 1. success; zum ~ führen meet with success; 2. (Ergebnis) result, outcome; **e~en** 1. (geschehen) happen; 2. (Zahlung) be effected; 3. auf etw ~ follow s.th.; **e~los** unsuccessful; ineffective; ~**losigkeit** f failure; **e~reich** successful

(*in* in); **e~versprechend** promising.

erforder|lich necessary; **~n** require, demand.

erforschen 1. (*Land*) explore; 2. (*untersuchen*) inquire (*etw* into s.th.).

erfragen ask, inquire.

erfreu|en 1. please; 2. *sich e-r Sache* ~ enjoy s.th.; **~lich** pleasing; **~licherweise** fortunately.

erfrieren *irr* 1. freeze to death; 2. (*Pflanze*) be killed by frost.

erfrisch|en, *sich* refresh; **E~ung** *f* refreshment.

erfüll|en 1. fill; 2. (*Aufgabe*) fulfil; 3. (*Wunsch*) meet, comply with; 4. (*Erwartung*) come up to; 5. (*Pflicht*) carry out; 6. (*Versprechen*) keep; **E~ung** *f* 1. fulfilment; 2. *in* ~ *gehen* come true.

ergänzen 1. (*vervollständigen*) complete; 2. (*einsetzen*) supply; supplement; **~d** 1. complementary; 2. (*zusätzlich*) additional.

ergeben *irr* 1. result in; 2. (*betragen*) amount to; 3. *sich* ~ (*mil*) surrender; 4. (*auftauchen*) arise; 5. *sich aus etw* ~ be a result of s.th.; 6. *jdm* ~ *sein* be devoted to s.o.; 7. (*verfallen*) addicted; **E~heit** *f* devotion.

Ergebnis *n* result, outcome; **e~los** without result.

ergehen *irr* 1. *etw über sich*

~ *lassen* endure s.th.; 2. *sich in etw* ~ indulge in s.th.; 3. *jdm ergeht es gut* s.o. fares well, s.o. gets on well.

ergiebig 1. productive; 2. (*Boden*) fertile; 3. (*Geschäft*) profitable.

ergötzen amuse, delight.

ergreifen *irr* 1. seize, grasp; 2. (*Dieb*) capture; 3. (*Gelegenheit*) take; 4. (*Beruf*) take up; **~d** touching.

ergriffen moved, touched; **E~heit** *f* emotion.

ergründen fathom *a. fig.*

erhaben 1. *fig* sublime; 2. (*großartig*) magnificent.

erhalten *irr* 1. (*bekommen*) get, receive, obtain; 2. (*bewahren*) preserve; 3. (*Gebäude*) maintain; 4. *sich* ~ keep o.s.; 5. *gut* ~ in good condition.

erhältlich obtainable.

Erhaltung *f* preservation.

erhängen, *sich* hang o.s.

erheb|en *irr* 1. (*Hand*) lift, raise; 2. (*im Rang*) promote; 3. (*Steuern*) levy, impose; 4. *sich* ~ rise, get up; 5. (*Frage*) arise; **~lich** considerable; **E~ung** *f* 1. elevation; 2. (*Steuern*) levy; 3. (*Nachforschung*) investigation.

Erheiterung *f* amusement.

erhitzen, *sich* 1. grow hot; 2. *fig* get heated.

erhöh|en 1. raise, increase *a. fig*; 2. *sich* ~ rise; **~t** 1. increased, raised; 2. (*Puls*) raised.

erhol|en, *sich* 1. recover (*von* from); 2. (*sich entspannen*) relax; **~sam** relaxing; **E~ung** *f* recovery, relaxation.

erinner|n 1. *jdn an etw ~* remind s.o. of s.th.; 2. *sich an etw ~* remember, recall s.th.; **E~ung** *f* memory, remembrance.

erkält|en, *sich* catch (a) cold; **E~ung** *f* cold.

erkenn|bar recognizable; **~en** *irr* 1. recognize; 2. (*wahrnehmen*) perceive, discern; 3. (*einsehen*) realize; 4. *sich zu ~ geben* make o.s. known; **~tlich:** *sich ~ zeigen* show o.'s gratitude.

Erkenntnis *f* 1. knowledge; 2. (*Einsicht*) realization; 3. *pl* findings.

Erkennungszeichen *n* sign of recognition.

erklär|bar explainable; **~en** 1. (*erläutern*) explain (*etw jdm* s.th. to s.o.); 2. (*Absicht*) declare; 3. (*nennen*) pronounce; 4. *sich ~* be explained; 5. *sich für etw ~* declare o.s. for s.th.; **~lich** explicable, understandable; **E~ung** *f* explanation, declaration.

erkrank|en fall ill (*an* with); **E~ung** *f* illness, sickness.

erkundig|en: *sich nach etw ~* inquire about s.th.; **E~ung** *f* inquiry; **~en einholen** make inquiries (*über* about).

erlangen 1. (*erreichen*) attain; 2. (*sich verschaffen*) obtain; 3. (*erwerben*) acquire.

Erlaß *m* (*Verordnung*) decree.

erlassen *irr* 1. (*Befehl*) issue; 2. (*Strafe*) remit; 3. *jdm etw ~* release s.o. from s.th.

erlaub|en 1. allow, permit (*jdm etw* s.o. s.th.); 2. *sich etw ~* permit o.s. s.th.; **E~nis** *f* permission.

erläutern explain, comment on; **E~ung** *f* explanation, comment.

Erle *f bot* alder.

erleb|en 1. see, experience; 2. (*durchmachen*) go through; **E~nis** *n* 1. experience; 2. (*Ereignis*) event.

erledigen 1. (*besorgen*) do; 2. (*behandeln*) deal with, attend to; 3. (*beenden*) finish; 4. (*ordnen*) adjust; 5. (*Post*) go through.

erleichter|n 1. (*Lage*) facilitate; 2. (*Schmerzen*) relieve; **E~ung** *f* relief.

erleiden *irr* suffer, endure.

erlernen learn, acquire.

erlesen choice, select.

erleuchten light, illuminate.

erliegen *irr* (*e-r Krankheit*) succumb (to).

Erlös *m* proceeds *pl.*

erlöschen 1. go out; 2. *jur* expire.

erlös|en release; **E~ung** *f* 1. release; 2. *rel* redemption.

ermächtig|en authorize; **E~ung** *f* authorization.

ermahn|en admonish;
  E~ung *f* admonition.
ermäßigen *(Preis)* reduce,
  diminish, cut down.
ermessen *irr* 1. *fig (abschätzen)* estimate; 2. *(erfassen)*
  imagine, conceive.
ermitt|eln 1. find out, locate;
  2. *(feststellen)* ascertain;
  E~lungen *pl* investigations,
  inquiries.
ermöglichen make possible.
ermord|en 1. murder; 2. *(At-
  tentat)* assassinate; **E~ung** *f*
  1. murder; 2. assassination.
ermüd|en tire; **~end** tiring;
  E~ung *f* fatigue.
ermutigen encourage.
ernähr|en 1. nourish; 2. *(ver-
  sorgen)* support, maintain;
  3. *sich ~* live *(von* on);
  E~ung *f* 1. *med* nutrition;
  2. *(Nahrung)* food, nourishment.
ernennen *irr* appoint, name.
erneuer|n renew; **E~ung** *f*
  renewal.
erniedrigen *fig* humble,
  humiliate.
Ernst *m* seriousness; *ist es
  Ihnen ~ damit?* are you in
  earnest? *das ist mein voller
  ~* I am dead serious; **e~**
  1. serious, earnest; 2. *(gefährlich)* grave, critical; 3. *~
  bleiben* remain serious;
  ~fall *m: im ~* in case of
  emergency; **e~haft** serious,
  earnest; **e~lich** seriously.
Ernte *f* harvest, crop; **e~n**
  1. harvest; 2. *fig* reap.

erober|n conquer *a. fig;*
  E~ung *f* conquest.
eröffn|en 1. open; *(feierlich)*
  inaugurate; 2. *(Geschäft)* establish.
erörter|n discuss, debate;
  E~ung *f* discussion.
Erot|ik *f* eroticism; **e~isch**
  erotic(al).
erpress|en extort, blackmail
  (jdn s.o.); **E~er** *m* black-
  mailer; **~erisch** blackmail-
  ing; **E~ung** *f* extortion,
  blackmail.
erproben test, try, prove.
erraten *irr* guess.
errechnen calculate, work
  out, compute.
erreg|en 1. excite; 2. *(aufre-
  gen)* upset; 3. *(Haß)* arouse;
  E~er *m med* exciting agent;
  ~t excited, agitated; **E~ung**
  f excitement.
erreichen 1. reach; 2. *(Zug)*
  catch; 3. *fig (Ziel)* achieve,
  attain.
errichten build, erect.
erringen *irr* gain, win.
erröten blush *(vor* with).
Errungenschaft *f* 1. acquisition; 2. *fig* achievement.
Ersatz *m* 1. *(zeitweilig)* substitute; 2. *(dauernd)* re-
  placement; 3. *(Entschädigung)* indemnification; *als ~
  für* as compensation for;
  4. *(für Kaffee)* substitute;
  ~rad *n* spare wheel; **~rei-
  fen** *m* spare tyre; **~teil** *m
  od n tech* spare part;
  e~weise alternatively.

erschaff|en *irr* create;
E~ung *f* creation.
erschein|en *irr* 1. appear;
2. *(scheinen)* seem, look;
3. *(auftauchen)* turn up;
4. *(Buch)* be published;
E~ung *f* 1. *in* ~ *treten* become evident; 2. *(Tatsache)*
occurrence; 3. *(Aussehen)*
appearance; 4. *(Geist)* apparition.
erschießen *irr* shoot dead
(jdn s.o.).
erschlaffen become slack.
erschlagen *irr* kill *(jdn s.o.)*.

erschließen *irr* 1. *(Absatzgebiet)* open up; 2. *(Gelände)*
make accessible.
erschöpf|end exhaustive; ~**t**
exhausted; **E~ung** *f* exhaustion.
erschrecken 1. frighten,
scare; 2. *irr: sich~* be frightened *(über* at).
erschütter|n 1. shake; 2. *fig*
(Nachricht) shock, upset;
~**nd** deeply moving; **E~ung**
f 1. *tech* vibration; 2. *fig*
emotional upset.
erschweren make more difficult.
erschwinglich attainable.
ersehen *irr* learn, understand *(aus* from).
ersetz|bar replaceable *a.*
tech; ~**en** 1. *(auswechseln)*
replace *(durch* by); 2. *(ausgleichen)* compensate;
3. *(Schaden)* make up for.
ersichtlich evident, obvious.

erspar|en save up; **E~nis** *f*
1. saving; 2. *pl* savings.
erst 1. *(zuerst)* at first;
2. *(nicht eher als)* not till,
not before; 3. *(noch)* still,
yet; 4. *(verstärkend)* ~ *recht*
all the more, more than
ever; ~ *recht nicht* certainly
not, now less than ever.
erstarren 1. *(Glieder)* become numb; 2. *vor Schrekken* ~ be paralysed with
fear.
erstatten 1. pay back, reimburse; 2. *Bericht* ~ give a report.
erstaun|en be surprised;
E~en *n* astonishment, surprise; ~**lich** astonishing,
amazing.
erste I *adj* first; *in* ~*r Linie*
in the first place; *zum* ~*n!*
zum zweiten! zum dritten!
going, going, gone! **II** *adv:*
fürs ~ for the time being.
ersteigen *irr* climb, scale,
mount.
erstens in the first place.
ersticken choke, suffocate.
erstklassig 1. first-class;
2. *com* top-quality.
erstrecken extend, stretch
(bis zu to).
ersuchen ask, request; **E~** *n*
request; *auf sein* ~ at his request.
ertappen catch, surprise.
erteilen *(Rat)* give.
Ertrag *m* 1. *(Feld)* yield;
2. *com* yield, returns *pl,*
proceeds *pl;* **e~en** *irr*

1. *(Schmerz)* stand, bear, endure; 2. *(dulden)* tolerate, suffer.
erträglich bearable.
ertränken drown.
ertrinken *irr* be drowned.
erübrigen 1. save; 2. *sich ~* be superfluous.
erwachen awake, wake up.
Erwachsener *m* grown-up, adult.
erwäg|en *irr* consider; **E~ung** *f: in ~ ziehen* take into consideration.
erwähn|en mention; **E~ung** *f* mention, reference (to).
erwärmen 1. warm up; 2. *jdn für etw ~* get s.o. interested in s.th.
erwart|en 1. expect; 2. *(freudig)* look forward to; 3. *(rechnen mit)* anticipate; **E~ung** *f* expectation.
erwecken *fig* arouse, raise, provoke.
erweisen *irr* 1. *(e-n Dienst)* render (a service); 2. *sich als ... ~* prove to be.
erweitern enlarge, extend.
Erwerb *m* acquisition; **e~en** *irr* 1. acquire; 2. *(verdienen)* earn; **e~slos** unemployed, out of work.
erwidern 1. reply, answer; 2. *(Gruß)* return.
erwürgen strangle, throttle.
Erz *n min* ore.
erzähl|en tell *(jdm über etw* s.o. of, about s.th.); **E~ung** *f* story, tale.
Erzbischof *m* archbishop.

erzeug|en 1. *(Industrie)* produce, manufacture; 2. *agr* grow; 3. *(verursachen)* cause, bring about; **E~er** *m* 1. manufacturer, producer; 2. *agr* grower; **E~nis** *n* 1. product; 2. *agr* produce.
erzieh|en *irr* bring up, raise, educate; **E~er** *m* educator; **E~ung** *f* education.
erzielen 1. *(Ergebnis)* obtain, achieve; 2. *(Gewinn)* realize, make.
erzwingen *irr* force, obtain by force.
es 1. it; *(bei bekanntem Geschlecht)* he, she; 2. *~ gibt* there is, there are; 3. *ich bin ~* it's me; *ich hoffe ~* I hope so.
Esche *f* ash(-tree).
Esel *m* donkey.
Eskalation *f* escalation.
eßbar eatable, edible.
essen *irr* eat; *zu Mittag ~* have lunch; *zu Abend ~* have dinner, supper; **E~** *n* 1. *(Kost)* food; 2. *(Mahlzeit)* meal.
Essig *m* vinegar.
Eß|löffel *m* table-spoon; *~tisch* *m* dining-table; *~zimmer* *n* dining-room.
Etage *f* floor, stor(e)y.
Etappe *f* stage, period.
Etat *m* budget.
Etikett *n* 1. label; 2. *(Anhänger)* tag.
Etikette *f* etiquette.
Etui *n* case.
etwa 1. *(ungefähr)* about,

approximately; 2. *(vielleicht)* by any chance, perhaps.

etwas I *prn* something; anything; *sonst noch* ~? anything else? *das ist* ~ *anderes* that's something else; **II** *adj* a little; ~ *mehr* a little more; **III** *adv* some, a little; *kaum* ~ hardly anything.

euch 1. you; 2. yourself.

euer your; *das ist eure Sache* that's your business.

Eule *f* owl.

Europa *n* Europe; **~äer** *m*, **e~äisch** European.

Euter *n* udder.

evangelisch 1. evangelical; 2. *(Kirche)* Protestant.

eventuell possibly.

ewig I *adj* eternal, perpetual; **II** *adv* eternally, forever; *auf immer und* ~ for ever and ever; **E~keit** *f* eternity; *bis in alle* ~ to all eternity.

exakt exact, precise.

Examen *n* examination.

Exemplar *n* 1. specimen; 2. *(Buch)* copy; *(Zeitschrift)* number.

Exil *n* exile; *ins* ~ *gehen* go into exile.

Existenz *f* 1. existence; 2. *(Unterhalt)* living; **~minimum** *n* subsistence level.

existieren 1. exist; 2. *(leben können)* live (*von* on).

exklusiv exclusive.

Experiment *n* experiment; **e~ieren** make experiments.

Experte *m* expert.

explodieren explode *a. fig;* **E~sion** *f* explosion; **~siv** explosive.

Export *m* export; **~handel** *m* export trade; **e~ieren** export (*nach* to).

Expreßbrief *m* express letter; **~zug** *m* express train.

extra 1. extra, separately, apart; 2. *(zusätzlich)* in addition.

extrem extreme; **E~** *n* extreme; *bis zum* ~ to the extreme.

F

Fabel *f* fable; **f~haft** fabulous.

Fabrik *f* 1. factory, mill; *Am* plant; 2. *(Werk)* works *pl;* **~ant** *m* manufacturer, factory owner; **~arbeiter** *m* factory worker; **~at** *n* product, make, brand; **~ation** *f* production, manufacture; **f~mäßig** industrial; **~ hergestellt** manufactured.

fabrizieren manufacture, make.

Fach *n* 1. *(Regal)* shelf; *(Schreibtisch)* pigeonhole; 2. *fig* branch, field; 3. *(Unterricht)* subject; **~arbeit** *f* skilled work; **~arbeiter** *m* skilled worker; **~arzt** *m* medical specialist; **~ausdruck** *m* technical term.

Fächer *m* fan.

Fachgeschäft *n* special shop; **~mann** *m* specialist, expert (*in* at, in; *für* on); **~werkhaus** *n* half-timbered house.

Fackel *f* torch.

fade tasteless, flat.

Faden *m* thread.

fähig able, capable; **F~keit** *f* ability, capability.

fahnden: *nach jdm* **~** search for so; **F~ung** *f* search.

Fahne *f* flag.

Fahrbahn *f* 1. carriageway; 2. *(Spur)* lane.

Fähre *f* ferry.

fahren *irr* 1. *aufs Land* **~** go (in)to the country; *wie lange fährt man nach X?* how long does it take to go to X? 2. *(verkehren)* run; 3. *(abfahren)* leave; 4. *(sich bewegen)* travel; 5. *mit dem Bus (Zug)* **~** go by bus (train); *im Auto* **~** ride in a car; 6. *(mit Auto)* drive; 7. *(e-n Wagen lenken)* drive; *(befördern)* carry, convey; 8. *sich mit den Fingern durch das Haar* **~** pass o.'s fingers through o.'s hair; *was ist in ihn gefahren?* what has come over him?

Fahrer *m* driver; chauffeur; **~erflucht** *f* hit-and-run driving; **~gast** *m* passenger; **~geld** *n* fare; **~gestell** *n* 1. chassis; 2. *aero* landing-gear; **~karte** *f* ticket; **~kartenautomat** *m* automatic ticket machine; **~kartenschalter** *m* ticket-office.

fahrlässig negligent, careless; **F~keit** *f* negligence, carelessness.

Fahrlehrer *m* driving instructor.

Fährmann *m* ferryman.

Fahrplan *m* time-table; **f~mäßig** scheduled.

Fahrrad *n* bicycle.

Fahr|schein *m* ticket;
~**schule** *f* driving school;
~**stuhl** *m* lift, *Am* elevator.
Fahrt *f* 1. *(Reise)* journey,
tour, trip; 2. *(Auto)* drive,
ride; 3. *(Geschwindigkeit)*
speed; *in voller* ~ at full
speed; 4. *(Fahrpreis)* fare;
5. *freie* ~ *haben* have a
clear road; 6. *(fig) in* ~ *sein*
be in full swing.
Fährte *f* track, trail.
Fahrtrichtung *f* driving direction.
Fahrzeit *f* running time.
Fahrzeug *n* vehicle; *gesperrt
für* ~*e aller Art* closed to
vehicular traffic.
Faktor *m* factor, element.
Falke *m* falcon, hawk.
Fall *m* 1. *(Sturz, Barometer,
Preise)* fall, drop; 2. *(Zusam-
menbruch)* collapse;
3. *(Sachverhalt)* case, instance; 4. *(Umstand)* case;
auf alle Fälle at all events,
auf keinen ~ on no ac-
count; 5. *(Angelegenheit)*
matter, affair.
Falle *f* trap, snare; *e-e* ~ *stellen* set a trap.

fallen *irr* 1. fall; 2. *(hinunter-
fallen)* fall down, drop;
3. *auf die Knie* ~ fall on o.'s
knees; 4. *(Barometer, Temperatur)* fall, drop; 5. *(Preise)* decline; 6. *die Entscheidung ist noch nicht gefallen*
the decision has not yet
been taken; 7. *(Fest)* fall on;

8. *die Würfel sind gefallen*
the die is cast.
fällen fell, cut down.
fällig 1. due; 2. *(Wechsel)*
mature; ~ *werden* fall due.
Fallobst *n* windfall.
falls 1. in case, if; 2. *(vorausgesetzt)* provided (that).
Fallschirm *m* parachute.
Falltür *f* trap door.
falsch I *adj* 1. wrong; 2. *(unrichtig)* false, incorrect;
3. *(unwahr)* false, untrue;
4. *(irrig)* wrong, mistaken;
5. *(Geld)* counterfeit; II *adv:
meine Uhr geht* ~ my watch
is wrong.
fälsch|en 1. fake, forge;
2. *(Geld)* counterfeit; **F~er**
m 1. forger, faker; 2. *(Dokumente)* falsifier.
Falschheit *f* 1. *(Person)* in-
sincerity; 2. *(Aussage)* false-
ness.
fälschlich false, mistaken.
Fälschung *f* forgery, falsifi-
cation.
Faltboot *n* collapsible boat.
Falt|e *f* 1. *(Stoff)* fold;
2. *(Rock)* pleat; 3. *(Hose)*
crease; 4. *(Gesicht)* wrinkle;
f~en 1. fold; 2. *(knittern)*
wrinkle, crease; **f~ig**
wrinkled.
Faltstuhl *m* folding-chair.
familiär familiar.
Familie *f* family; ~**nan-
schluß** *m: mit* ~ live as one
of the family; ~**nname** *m*
surname; ~**nstand** *m* personal status.

Fan *m* fan.

Fanati|ker *m* fanatic; **f~sch** fanatic; **~smus** *m* fanaticism.

Fang *m* catch; **f~en** *irr* catch; *e-n Dieb* ~ capture a thief.

Farbband *n* typewriter ribbon.

Farbe *f* 1. colour; 2. *(Malfarbe)* paint; 3. *(Gesicht)* complexion.

farbecht colour-fast; **F~heit** *f* colour-fastness.

färben 1. *(Haare, Kleider)* dye; 2. *(tönen)* colour, tinge.

farbenblind colour-blind.

Färber *m* dyer; **~ei** *f* dye-works *pl*; ~ *und chemische Reinigung* dyers and cleaners.

Farb|fernsehen *n* colour television; **~fernseher** *m* colour receiver; **~film** *m* colour film; **~fotografie** *f* colour photography.

farbig 1. coloured; 2. *(Schilderung)* colourful; 3. *(Glas)* stained.

Farbiger *m* coloured person.

farblos colourless.

Farbstift *m* coloured pencil.

Färbung *f* colouring *a. fig.*

Farnkraut *n* fern.

Fasan *m* pheasant.

Fasching *m* carnival.

Faser *f* fibre, *Am* fiber.

Faß *n* barrel, cask; *Wein vom* ~ wine from the wood.

Fassade *f* façade, front.

fass|en 1. *(ergreifen)* seize, catch, grasp; 2. *e-n Beschluß* ~ take a decision; 3. *(festnehmen)* seize, apprehend; 4. *(begreifen)* conceive, grasp, understand; 5. *(räumlich)* hold, take, contain; 6. *(Edelstein)* set; 7. *sich* ~ compose o.s.; **F~ung** *f* 1. *(Beherrschung)* composure, selfpossession; *die* ~ *bewahren* keep o.'s countenance; *die* ~ *verlieren* lose o.'s self-control; 2. *(inneres Gleichgewicht)* poise; 3. *(schriftlich)* version; 4. *(Edelstein)* setting; *tech* socket.

fassungslos disconcerted.

Fassungsvermögen *n* 1. *(Saal)* capacity; 2. *(geistig)* comprehension.

fast 1. almost; 2. ~ *nie* hardly ever; ~ *gar nichts* next to nothing; ~ *niemand* hardly anyone.

fasten fast; **F~zeit** *f* 1. period of fasting; 2. *rel* Lent.

Fastnacht *f* Shrove Tuesday.

faszinieren fascinate.

fatal 1. fatal; 2. *(peinlich)* awkward.

faul 1. *(Früchte, Fleisch)* rotten, bad; 2. *(verdächtig)* dubious; 3. *(Ausrede)* lame; 4. *(Mensch)* lazy; **~en** 1. *(verfaulen)* putrefy; 2. *(Fleisch, Früchte)* rot, go bad.

faul|enzen be lazy, idle;

F~enzer m lazybones pl; **F~heit** f laziness, idleness.

Faust f fist; die ~ ballen clench o's fist.

Fäustchen n: sich ins ~ lachen laugh up o.'s sleeve.

Faustregel f rule of thumb.

Favorit m favourite, Am favorite.

Fazit n result; aus etw das ~ ziehen sum s.th. up.

Februar m February.

fecht|en fence; **F~sport** m fencing.

Feder f 1. feather; 2. (Schreib~) pen; 3. tech spring.

Federball m badminton.

Feder|bett n feather-bed; **~halter** m fountain-pen; **f~n** 1. fit with springs; 2. (elastisch sein) be elastic; 3. gut gefedert sein (Matratze) be well sprung; (Auto) have good springs; **~ung** f springs pl; **~vieh** n poultry.

Fee f fairy.

Fegefeuer n purgatory.

fegen sweep.

Fehl|anzeige f (Fragebogen) nil, not applicable; **~betrag** m deficit.

fehlen 1. be missing; 2. (ermangeln) be lacking; 3. wo fehlt's? what's the trouble? 4. es fehlten ihm 100 DM he was 100 marks short; 5. das hat mir gerade noch gefehlt! that's all we needed!

Fehler m 1. mistake; 2. (Charakter) fault; 3. (Mangel) shortcoming; 4. (Irrtum) error; **f~frei** faultless, perfect; **f~haft** defective, faulty.

Fehlgeburt f miscarriage.

Fehl|griff m mistake, blunder; **~schlag** m failure; **f~schlagen** irr fail.

Fehlzündung f backfire.

Feier f celebration, ceremony, party; **~abend** m 1. closing time; 2. nach ~ after working hours; **f~lich** solemn; **f~n** celebrate; **~tag** m holiday.

feige cowardly.

Feige f fig; **~nbaum** m fig (tree).

Feig|heit f cowardice; **F~ling** m coward.

Feile f file; **f~n** 1. file; 2. fig polish.

feilschen haggle (um etw about s.th.).

fein 1. fine; 2. (hübsch) nice; 3. (zart) delicate; 4. (gebildet) refined; 5. (elegant) smart; 6. (erlesen) choice.

Feind m enemy; **f~lich** hostile, enemy; **~schaft** f enmity, hostility.

Fein|gehalt m titre; **~gold** n refined gold.

Feinheit f fineness, delicacy.

Fein|kostgeschäft n delicatessen shop; **~mechanik** f precision engineering; **~schmecker** m gourmet.

Feld n field, enemy; durch ~ und Flur over field and meadow; **~maus** f field-vole; **~messer** m surveyor; **~stecher** m field-glasses pl; **~webel** m sergeant; **~weg** m country-lane; **~zug** m campaign.

Felge f mot rim.

Fell n 1. coat; 2. (große Tiere) hide; (kleine Tiere) skin.

Fels|en m rock; **f~ig** rocky.

Fenster n window; aus dem ~ out of the window; **~bank** f window-sill; **~laden** m shutter; **~platz** m window-seat; **~scheibe** f window-pane.

Ferien pl holidays, Am vacation; ~ haben be on holiday; **~lager** n holiday camp.

Ferkel n little pig, piglet.

fern 1. far, distant, remote; 2. von nah und ~ from far and near.

Fernblick m distant view.

Ferne f distance; aus der ~ from far away.

ferner 1. further; 2. (außerdem) moreover, besides.

Fernfahrer m long-distance lorry driver; Am long-haul truck driver.

ferngelenkt remote-controlled.

Fern|gespräch n trunk-call; **~glas** n binoculars pl; **f~halten** irr keep away (von from); **~heizung** f district heating; **~laster** m long-distance lorry; **~licht** n mot full beam; **~meldewesen** n telecommunication; **~rohr** n telescope; **~schnellzug** m long-dis-

tance express train; **~schreiber** m teleprinter, telex.

Fernseh|antenne f television aerial; **~en** n television; **f~en** irr watch television; **~er** m 1. (Person) television viewer; 2. (Gerät) television set, receiver; **~programm** n television programme; **~turm** m television tower.

Fernsicht f prospect, view.

Fernsprech|buch n telephone directory; **~er** m telephone; **~teilnehmer** m telephone subscriber; **~vermittlung** f telephone exchange; **~zelle** f telephone box, Am booth.

Fernverkehr m long-distance traffic; **~sstraße** f trunk road, highway.

Ferse f heel; jdm auf den ~n sein be at s.o.'s heels.

fertig 1. (vollendet) finished, completed, done; 2. (bereit) ready; **~bringen** irr manage, bring about.

Fertighaus n prefabricated house.

Fertigkeit f 1. (Geschicklichkeit) facility, skill; 2. (Können) proficiency.

Fertigkleidung f ready-to-wear clothing.

fertigstellen finish, complete, get ready.

Fertigung f production.

Fessel f chain, fetter; **f~n** 1. bind; 2. fig captivate.

fest 1. (nicht weich) firm;

2. *(nicht flüssig)* solid;
3. *(kräftig)* strong; 4. *fig* firm; 5. *(starr)* fixed.
Fest *n* festival, festivity; **~essen** *n* banquet.
festhalten *irr* 1. hold fast; 2. *(in Gewahrsam)* keep; 3. *fig* record; 4. *an etw ~* stick to s.th.; 5. *sich ~* hold on.
festigen strengthen.
Festland *n* continent, mainland.
festlegen 1. set, lay down; 2. *sich ~* commit o.s.
festlich festive.
fest|machen fasten, fix; **~nehmen** *irr* arrest, seize.
Festplatz *m* fairground.
festsetzen 1. *(Preis)* fix, set, settle; 2. *(Bedingung)* stipulate; 3. *(Termin)* set *(auf* for).
Festspiel *n* festival.
fest|stehen *irr* 1. *fig* be certain; 2. *es steht fest* it is a fact; **~stellen** 1. find out; 2. *(herausfinden)* establish; 3. *(bestimmen)* determine.
Festung *f* fortress.
fett fat; **F~** *n* 1. fat; 2. *chem* grease; **F~fleck** *m* grease-spot; **~ig** greasy.
Fetzen *m* 1. scrap; 2. *(Lumpen)* rag.
feucht damp; **F~igkeit** *f* dampness, humidity.
Feuer *n* 1. fire; *in ~ geraten* catch fire; 2. *haben Sie ~?* do you have a light? **f~fest** 1. fire-proof; 2. *(Glas)* heat-

-resistant; **f~gefährlich** inflammable; **~leiter** *f* fire-escape; **~löscher** *m* fire extinguisher; **~melder** *m* fire-alarm box; **~sbrunst** *f* conflagration; **~stein** *m* flint; **~wehr** *f* fire-brigade; **~wehrauto** *n* fire engine; **~wehrmann** *m* fireman; **~werk** *n* fireworks *pl;* **~zeug** *n* lighter.
feurig 1. burning; 2. *fig* fiery.
Fibel *f* primer.
Fichte *f* spruce.
Fieber *n* fever, temperature; *haben Sie ~?* have you any temperature? *jdm ~ messen* take s.o.'s temperature; **f~haft** feverish *a. fig.*
Figur *f* 1. figure; 2. *(Wuchs)* stature.
Filet(braten *m) n* roast fillet.
Filiale *f* branch office.
Film *m* 1. *phot* film; *e-n ~ einlegen* load, fill a camera; 2. *(im Kino)* picture, film, *Am* movie; **~atelier** *n* film studio.
filmen film, shoot, take.
Film|festspiele *pl* film festivals; **~schauspieler(in** *f)* *m* film screen actor, actress; **~star** *m* film-star.
Filter *m* filter; **~mundstück** *n* filter tip; **f~n** filter, strain; **~papier** *n* filter-paper; **~zigarette** *f* filter-tipped cigarette.
filtrieren filter, filtrate.
Filz *m* felt.
Finanz|amt *n* (inland) reve-

nue office; **~en** pl finances;
f~iell financial; **f~ieren** finance; **~ierung** f financing.
Findelkind n foundling.
find|en irr 1. find; 2. Beifall ~ meet with approval; 3. (entdecken) discover; 4. (feststellen) find out; **F~er** m finder; **F~erlohn** m finder's reward; **~ig** clever, ingenious.
Finger m finger; **~abdruck** m finger-print; **~hut** m thimble; **~nagel** m finger-nail; **~ring** m ring; **~spitze** f finger-tip.
Fink m finch.
Finn|e m Finn; **f~isch** Finnish; **~land** n Finland.
finster 1. dark, gloomy; 2. (Gedanken) sinister; **F~nis** f darkness, gloom.
Firma f firm, company, business.
firm|en rel confirm; **F~ung** f confirmation.
Firnis m varnish.
First m (Dach) ridge.
Fisch m 1. fish; 2. astr Pisces; **~braterei** f fried-fish shop; **f~en** fish; **~er** m fisherman; **~erboot** n fishing-boat; **~erei** f fishery; **~gabel** f fish-fork; **~geschäft** n, **~handlung** f fish-shop; **~markt** m fish-market; **~netz** n fishing-net; **~teich** m fish-pond; **~vergiftung** f fish-poisoning; **~zucht** f fish-farming.
fix 1. (fest) fixed; 2. (schnell)

quick; **~ieren** 1. fix; 2. (festlegen) fix, determine; **F~stern** m fixed star.
flach 1. flat; 2. (eben) level, plain, even.
Fläche f 1. (Ober~) surface; 2. (Gebiet) area, expanse.
Flachland n lowland.
Flachs m flax.
Flagge f flag; die ~ hissen hoist the flag.
Flamingo m flamingo.
Flamme f flame; in ~n stehen be in flames.
Flanell m flannel.
Flank|e f flank; **f~ieren** flank; **~de Maßnahmen** supporting measures pl.
Flasche f bottle; **~nbier** n bottled beer; **~nöffner** m bottle-opener; **~nzug** m pulley-block.
flatter|haft capricious, flighty; **~n** 1. (Vogel) flutter; 2. (Fahne) stream, flap.
flau 1. (Wind) slack; 2. (übel) queasy; faint.
Flaum m down, fluff; **~feder** f down.
Flaute f 1. dead calm; 2. com slackness.
Flecht|e f 1. bot lichen; 2. (Haar) plait, braid; **f~en** irr 1. (Kranz) wreathe; 2. (Haar) plait, braid; **~werk** n wickerwork.
Fleck m 1. spot, stain; 2. (Ort) spot, place; **~entferner** m stain-remover; **f~ig** spotted, stained.
Fledermaus f bat.

Flegel *m* rude fellow; **f~haft** rude, ill-mannered; **~jahre** *pl* awkward age.

flehen implore (*jdn um etw* s.o. for s.th.).

Fleisch *n* 1. (*zum Essen*) meat; 2. (*lebendes*) flesh; **~brühe** *f* broth; **~er** *m* butcher; **~erei** *f* butcher's shop; **f~farbig** flesh-coloured; **~speise** *f* meat dish.

Fleiß *m* 1. diligence, industry; 2. (*Mühe*) pains *pl*; 3. **mit ~** on purpose, intentionally; **f~ig** 1. industrious, hard-working; 2. (*sorgfältig*) painstaking.

fletschen: *die Zähne ~* show o.'s teeth.

flicken mend, patch, repair; **F~** *m* patch.

Flieder *m* lilac.

Fliege *f* 1. fly; 2. (*Schlips*) bow(-tie).

fliegen *irr* 1. fly; *aero* go by air; 2. *in die Luft ~* explode; 3. (*Haare im Winde*) stream (in the wind); 4. (*geworfen werden*) be thrown.

Fliegenfänger *m* fly-paper; **~er** *m* flyer, pilot.

fliehen *irr* 1. flee, run away; 2. (*entkommen*) escape.

Fliese *f* tile.

Fließband *n* 1. assembly line; 2. (*Förderband*) conveyor-belt.

fließen *irr* 1. flow; 2. (*in Strömen*) pour; 3. (*von Wasserhahn*) come; **~d** 1. flowing; 2. (*Wasser*) running; 3. (*Ver-*

kehr) moving; 4. *Englisch ~ sprechen* speak English fluently.

flimmern 1. glimmer, glitter; 2. (*Stern*) twinkle.

flink quick, nimble, agile.

Flinte *f* shotgun.

Flitter *m* cheap finery; **~wochen** *pl* honeymoon.

Flocke *f* flake.

Floh *m* flea; **~markt** *m* flea-market.

Flor *m* 1. (*Blüte*) blossom; 2. (*Trauer~*) crape.

Floß *n* raft, float.

Flosse *f* (*Fisch*) fin.

flößen float, raft.

Flöte *f* flute.

flott 1. (*schnell*) fast, quick, speedy; 2. (*schick*) smart.

Flotte *f* 1. fleet; 2. (*Marine*) navy.

flottmachen (*Schiff*) set afloat.

Fluch *m* curse, malediction; **f~en** swear, curse.

Flucht *f* 1. flight; *in die ~ schlagen* put to flight; 2. (*Gefangener*) escape.

flüchten 1. flee, run away; 2. (*Zuflucht*) take refuge; 3. (*entkommen*) escape.

flüchtig 1. fugitive; 2. (*eilig*) hurried; 3. (*nachlässig*) careless; 4. (*Bekanntschaft*) passing, nodding; 5. *wir kennen ihn ~* we know him casually; **F~keitsfehler** *m* careless mistake.

Flüchtling *m* 1. fugitive; 2. *pol* refugee.

Flug *m* flight; *e-n* ~*absagen* cancel a flight; ~**blatt** *n* leaflet, handbill.

Flügel *m* 1. (*Vogel, Gebäude*) wing; 2. *mus* grand piano.

Fluggast *m* (air) passenger; ~**raum** *m* passenger cabin.

flügge fully-fledged.

Flug|gesellschaft *f* airline; ~**hafen** *m* airport; ~**linie** *f* (*Strecke*) air-route; ~**personal** *n* flying personnel; ~**plan** *m* flight schedule; ~**platz** *m* airfield, airport; ~**schein** *m* 1. air-travel ticket; 2. (*Führerschein*) pilot's licence; ~**steig** *m* gate; ~**verkehr** *m* air traffic; ~**zeit** *f* flying time; ~**zeug** *n* plane, aircraft; ~**zeugentführung** *f* hijacking; ~**zeugträger** *m* aircraft carrier.

Flur *m* (*Haus*) hall, vestibule.

Fluß *m* 1. river, stream; 2. (*Fließen*) flow; **f~ab(wärts)** downstream; **f~auf(wärts)** upstream.

flüssig 1. liquid, fluid; 2. *fig* fluent; 3. (*Geld*) liquid; **F~keit** *f* 1. liquid, fluid; 2. *com* liquidity; 3. (*Rede*) fluency.

Flußschiffahrt *f* river navigation.

flüstern whisper.

Flut *f* 1. flood, tide; 2. *fig* flood; ~**licht** *n* floodlight.

Fohlen *n* foal; *männliches* ~ colt; *weibliches* ~ filly.

Föhn *m* foehn.

Folge *f* 1. (*Ergebnis*) result, consequence; 2. (*Aufeinanderfolge*) succession, sequence; 3. (*Reihenfolge*) order, series; 4. (*Fortsetzung*) continuation; 5. *in der* ~ subsequently, later on.

folgen 1. follow; 2. (*verfolgen*) pursue; 3. (*sich anschließen*) come after; *Fortsetzung folgt* be continued; 4. (*Nachfolger*) succeed; 5. ~ *aus* follow from; ~**d** 1. following, as follows; 2. *am* ~*en Tag* next day; ~**dermaßen** as follows; ~**schwer** momentous.

folger|n conclude (*aus* from), gather; **F~ung** *f* conclusion, deduction.

folglich 1. consequently; 2. (*daher*) therefore; 3. (*also*) thus.

Folter *f* torture, rack; **f~n** torture.

Fön *m* hair-dryer.

Fontäne *f* fountain.

förder|lich beneficial, useful; **f~n** 1. (*anregen*) stimulate; 2. (*ermutigen*) promote, encourage; 3. (*als Gönner*) patronize, *Am* sponsor; 4. (*Kohle*) mine.

forder|n 1. demand, require (*von jdm* of s.o.); 2. *sein Recht* ~ claim o.'s right; 3. (*erfordern*) call for; 4. (*Preis*) ask for; 5. (*herausfordern*) challenge; **F~ung** *f* 1. demand, requirement;

2. *com* debt; 3. *(Herausforderung)* challenge.

Förderung *f* promotion, advancement.

Forelle *f* trout.

Form *f* 1. *(Gestalt, Umriß)* form, shape; 2. figure; 3. *(Modell)* type; 4. *(Art und Weise)* manner, way; 5. *(Anstand)* proprieties *pl;* 6. *(Kondition) in ~ sein* be in top form; **f~al** formal; **~alitäten** *pl* formalities; **~at** *n* 1. format, size; 2. *fig* stature, calibre; **~el** *f* formula; **f~ell** formal.

formen form, shape, model.

förmlich formal, conventional.

formlos formless, shapeless.

Formul|ar *n* form, blank; **f~ieren** formulate; **~ierung** *f* wording, formulation.

forsch energetic, vigorous.

forsch|en 1. do research; 2. *(suchen)* search (for); **F~er** *m* researcher, scientist; **F~ung** *f* research, scientific investigation.

Forst *m* forest.

Förster *m* forest guard; **~ei** *f* forester's office.

Forst|haus *n* forester's house; **~wirtschaft** *f* forestry.

fort 1. *(weg)* away, gone; 2. *in einem ~* on and on; *und so ~* and so on.

Fort|bestand *m* continuation; **f~bestehen** *irr* continue (to exist).

fortbewegen move on.

fortbild|en, *sich* improve o.s.; **F~ung** *f* advanced training.

Fortdauer *f* continuance.

fortfahren *irr* 1. *(abreisen)* leave, depart; 2. *(Auto)* drive away; 3. *(fortsetzen)* continue, go on.

fortführen carry on, continue.

Fort|gang *m* progress; **f~gehen** *irr (weggehen)* leave, go away.

fortgeschritten advanced.

fortgesetzt continual, constant.

Fortkommen *n* advancement.

fortlaufend continuous, running.

fortpflanz|en, *sich* 1. *biol* propagate, reproduce; 2. *phys* be transmitted; **F~ung** *f* 1. propagation; 2. transmission.

fortschreiten *irr* proceed, advance.

Fortschritt *m* progress, advance; **f~lich** progressive.

fortsetz|en *(Arbeit, Reise)* continue; **F~ung** *f* continuation; *~ folgt* to be continued.

forttragen *irr* carry away.

fortwährend constant, perpetual.

fortziehen *irr* move (away).

Foto *n* photo, picture; **~album** *n* photo-album; **~apparat** *m* camera; **~ate-**

lier *n* studio; **f~graphieren** photograph.

Fracht *f (Ladung)* freight, load, cargo; **~brief** *m* waybill; **f~frei** carriage paid; **~gut** *n* freight, goods *pl;* **~schiff** *n* freighter.

Frack *m* dress coat, tails *pl.*

Frag|e *f* 1. question (*zu* about); 2. *(Problem)* problem; 3. *etw in ~ stellen* question s.th.; 4. *in ~ kommen* be possible; **~ebogen** *m* questionnaire; **f~en** 1. ask (*jdn nach etw* s.o. for s.th.); 2. *(sich erkundigen)* inquire (*nach* after); 3. *sich ~* ask o.s., wonder; *ich frage mich, warum* I wonder why; **~ezeichen** *n* question mark; **f~lich** doubtful; **f~los** undoubtedly.

frankieren stamp.

franko post-paid; free.

Frankreich *n* France.

Franz|ose *m* Frenchman; **f~ösisch** French.

Fratze *f* grimace.

Frau *f* 1. woman; 2. *(Ehe~)* wife; 3. *(Anrede)* Mrs; **~enarzt** *m* gynaecologist.

Fräulein *n* 1. girl, young lady; 2. *(Anrede)* Miss.

frech insolent, impudent, impertinent; **F~heit** *f* impudence, impertinence.

frei 1. free (*von* from, of); *~ sprechen* speak off-hand; *unter ~em Himmel* in the open air; 2. *(Wohnung)* vacant; 3. *(nicht beschäftigt)* not busy, free; *~e Stelle* vacancy, opening; 4. *(freimütig)* frank(ly); 5. *sich ~ fühlen* feel at ease; 6. *(Straße)* clear; 7. *(com) ~ Haus* free domicile.

Frei|bad *n* swimming pool; **~betrag** *m* allowance; **~gabe** *f* release.

freigebig generous, liberal; **F~keit** *f* generosity, liberality.

Frei|gepäck *n* free luggage; **~hafen** *m* free port.

freihalten *irr* keep free, reserve.

Freiheit *f* freedom, liberty; **f~lich** liberal; **~sstrafe** *f* (sentence of) imprisonment.

freilass|en *irr* 1. release, set free; 2. *(Formular)* leave blank; **F~ung** *f* release, liberation.

Freilicht|bühne *f* open-air stage; **~museum** *n* open--air museum.

freimachen 1. *(Weg)* clear; 2. *(Oberkörper)* strip to the waist; 3. *(Brief)* prepay.

Freimaurer *m* Freemason.

frei|sprechen *irr* 1. absolve; 2. *jur* acquit; **F~spruch** *m* acquittal.

frei|stehen *irr* 1. *(Wohnung)* be vacant; 2. *es steht Ihnen frei* it is open to you; **F~stelle** *f* scholarship; **~stellen** 1. *jdm etw ~* leave s.th. to s.o.; 2. *(Steuer)* exempt s.o. (from).

Freitag *m* Friday.

freiwillig voluntary; of o.'s own free will.

Freizeit f leisure time; **~kleidung** f leisure wear.

fremd 1. strange; 2. (ausländisch) foreign; 3. (unbekannt) unfamiliar; **~artig** strange, foreign; **F~e** f foreign country; (im Ausland) abroad.

Fremd|er m stranger; foreigner; tourist; **~enbuch** n visitor's book; **~enführer** m guide; **~enverkehr** m tourist traffic; **~enzimmer** n guest room; **~sprache** f foreign language; **~wort** n foreign word.

Freske f fresco.

fressen irr eat; dem Hund zu ~ geben feed the dog.

Freud|e f 1. joy (an in, über at); vor ~ strahlen beam with joy; 2. (Vergnügen) pleasure; **f~ig** 1. (froh) glad; 2. (Ereignis) joyful; etw ~ erwarten be looking forward to s.th.

freuen, sich be pleased (über about); es freut mich sehr, Sie kennenzulernen I'm very glad to meet you.

Freund m friend; **~in** f girl friend.

freundlich 1. friendly, kind (gegen to); ~e Grüße kind regards (an to); 2. (Raum) cheerful; 3. (Wetter) pleasant; **F~keit** f friendliness, kindness.

Freundschaft f friendship; ~ schließen make friends (mit with); **f~lich** friendly; auf ~em Fuße stehen be on friendly terms (mit with).

Frieden m peace; im ~ in peace-times; ~ schließen make peace; **~srichter** m Justice of the Peace.

Friedhof m churchyard, cemetery.

friedlich peaceful, pacific.

frieren irr 1. freeze; es friert it is freezing; 2. es friert mich I'm cold; 3. (Fluß) freeze over.

frisch 1. (Wind) fresh; 2. (Wäsche) clean; 3. (kühl) chilly; 4. ~ gestrichen! wet paint! **F~e** f freshness.

Fris|eur m hairdresser; (Herren) barber; **f~ieren** 1. do s.o.'s hair; 2. sich ~ comb o.'s hair; **~iersalon** m hairdresser's salon; **~iertisch** m dressing-table.

Frist f 1. (Zeitraum) period of time; e-e ~ einhalten observe a term; 2. (Zahlung) term; 3. (Zeitpunkt) deadline; **f~los** without notice.

Frisur f hair-style, hair-do.

froh 1. joyful, happy; über etw ~ sein be glad of, about s.th.; 2. (lustig) merry.

fröhlich cheerful, gay, merry; ~e Weihnachten Merry Christmas; **F~keit** f cheerfulness, gaiety.

fromm pious, religious.

Frömmigkeit f piety.

Fronleichnam(sfest) n Corpus Christi.

Front f front; **f~al** head-on.

Frosch m frog.

Frost m frost.

frösteln shiver; *mich fröstelt* I feel chilly.

frost|ig 1. frosty; 2. *fig* cold, frigid; **F~schutzmittel** n anti-freeze.

Frottee n towelling.

Frucht f 1. fruit; 2. *(Getreide)* corn; **f~bar** fertile; **~barkeit** f fertility; **f~los** fruitless; **~saft** m fruit-juice.

früh early; *heute ~* early this morning; *von ~ bis spät* from morning till night.

Früh|aufsteher m early bird; **~e** f dawn; *in aller ~* early in the morning.

früh|er 1. earlier; 2. *(ehemalig)* former; 3. *~ oder später* sooner or later; **~estens** at the earliest.

Früh|jahr n, **~ling** m spring; **f~reif** precocious; **~sport** m early morning exercises pl; **~stück** n breakfast; **f~stücken** have breakfast.

Fuchs m fox.

Fuge f 1. *tech* joint; 2. *mus* fugue.

fügen, *sich* submit to, comply with.

fühlbar 1. sensible; 2. *(beträchtlich)* considerable.

fühle|n 1. feel; 2. *(bewußt sein)* be conscious (of); 3. *sich gewachsen ~* feel able to cope with; *sich wohl ~*

feel well; **F~r** m feeler, antenna.

Fuhre f cart-load.

führen 1. lead *(nach, zu* to); 2. *(hinbringen)* conduct, guide; *jdn nach Hause ~* take s.o. home; 3. *ein Geschäft ~* run a business; 4. *(Bücher)* keep; *(Waren)* deal in; 5. *den Vorsitz ~* preside; 6. *(zur Folge haben)* lead to, end in; 7. *sich gut ~* conduct oneself well; *das führt zu nichts* that leads us nowhere; **~d** leading, prominent.

Führer m 1. leader; head, chief, guide; 2. *sport* captain; 3. *mot* driver; *aero* pilot; **~haus** n driver's cab; **~schein** m driving licence, *Am* driver's licence.

Führung f 1. leadership; 2. *(Museum)* guided tour; 3. *(Leitung)* guidance; 4. *(Verhalten)* conduct; **~szeugnis** n certificate of good conduct.

Fuhrwerk n cart.

Fülle f plenty, abundance; **f~n** fill.

Füll|(federhalt)er m fountain-pen; **~ung** f filling, stuffing.

Fund m find.

Fundament n 1. *arch* foundations pl; 2. *fig* basis; **f~al** fundamental, basic.

Fund|büro n lost property office; **~grube** f *fig* rich source; **~sache** f object found.

fünf five; **~hundert** five hundred; **F~tel** n fifth; **~tens** in the fifth place; **F~ter** m fifth; **~zehn** fifteen; **~zig** fifty.

Funk m radio, wireless.

Funke m spark a. fig; **f~ln** sparkle, glitter.

funk|en radio, transmit; **F~er** m radio, wireless operator; **F~haus** n broadcasting centre; **F~sprechgerät** n (tragbar) walkie-talkie; **F~spruch** m radio message; **F~streifenwagen** m radio patrol car.

Funktion f function; **~är** m functionary, official; **f~ie-ren** work, function.

Funk|turm m wireless tower; **~verbindung** f radio contact; **~verkehr** m radio communication.

für 1. for; Schritt ~ Schritt step by step; ein ~ allemal once and for all; 2. (anstatt) instead of; 3. (zugunsten) in favour of; 4. (zeitlich) ~ 14 Tage verreisen be off on a trip for two weeks; 5. was ~ ein what kind, sort of.

Furche f 1. (Wagenspur) rut; 2. (Acker, Gesicht) furrow.

Furcht f 1. fear (vor of), fright; 2. (Besorgnis) apprehension; **f~bar** terrible, frightful, horrible.

fürchten 1. fear; 2. sich ~ be afraid of; **~erlich** awful.

furcht|los fearless; **f~sam** fearful, timid.

füreinander for one another, for each other.

Furnier n veneer.

Fürsorge f care; öffentliche ~ public welfare work.

Für|sprache f intercession (für for); **~sprecher** m intercessor.

Fürst m prince; **f~lich** princely.

Fuß m foot; zu ~ on foot; zu ~ gehen walk; auf dem ~ folgen follow on the heels.

Fußball m football; Am soccer; **~spieler** m football player; **~verein** m football club.

Fuß|boden m floor; **~brem-se** f foot-brake; **~gänger** m pedestrian; **~gänger-überweg** m pedestrian crossing; **~gängerzone** f pedestrian precinct; **~note** f footnote; **~sohle** f sole of the foot; **~spitze** f point of the foot; **~stapfen** m: in jds ~ treten follow in s.o.'s footsteps; **~weg** m footpath.

Futter n 1. (für Tiere) feed, fodder; 2. (Mantel) lining.

Futteral n case, cover.

füttern 1. (Tiere) feed; 2. (Mantel) line; **F~ung** f (Tiere) feeding.

Futur n gram futur.

G

Gabe f 1. (Geschenk) gift, present; 2. (Begabung) talent, gift.

Gabel f fork; **g~n,** sich fork; **~stapler** m fork-lift truck.

Gage f salary.

gähnen yawn.

Galerie f gallery.

Galle f 1. gall; 2. (Sekret) bile; **~nblase** f gall bladder; **~nstein** m gallstone.

Galopp m gallop; im ~ at a gallop; **g~ieren** gallop.

Gammler m loafer, beatnik.

Gang m 1. (Haus) hall, corridor; 2. (Weg, Haltung) walk, gait; 3. (von Geschehen) course; 4. etw in ~ setzen put s.th. in action; in vollem ~e sein be in full swing; 5. (Sitzreihen) aisle; (Durch-) passage; 6. mot gear; **~art** f 1. walk, gait; 2. (Pferd) pace.

gängig 1. (Ausdruck) current; 2. com marketable, saleable.

Gangschaltung f gear change.

Gans f goose.

Gänse|blümchen n daisy; **~braten** m roast goose; **~haut** f gooseskin; ich bekam e-e ~ it gave me the creeps.

ganz I adj 1. whole, entire; die ~e Stadt the whole town; in der ~en Welt the world over; 2. (unbeschädigt) intact; 3. (alle) all; **II** adv 4. wholly; das ist etw ~ anderes that is quite another thing; das ist mir ~ egal that is all the same to me; e-e ~e Menge quite a lot; ~ und gar nicht not at all; ~ gewiß most certainly; 5. im großen und ~en on the whole; **~jährig** all-year.

gänzlich completely, entirely.

gar I adj (Küche) cooked; **II** adv: ~ nicht not at all, by no means; ~ nichts nothing at all; das ist besser als ~ nichts that's better than nothing; es besteht ~ kein Zweifel, daß there isn't the least doubt that; ich kenne ihn ~ nicht I don't even know him.

Garage f garage.

Garantie f guarantee; **g~ren** guarantee, warrant.

Garderobe f 1. wardrobe; 2. (Kleiderablage) cloak-, (Am) check-room; (Flur) hall-stand; **~nfrau** f cloak-room attendant; **~nständer** m hall-stand.

Gardine f curtain.

gären irr 1. (Wein) ferment; 2. es gärt im Volk the population is seething.

Garn n 1. thread, yarn; 2. jdm ins ~ gehen fall into s.o.'s snare.

garnieren 1. (Hut) trim; 2. (Fisch) garnish.

Garnison f garrison.

Garnitur f 1. (Satz) set; 2. (Besatz) trimmings pl.

garstig nasty.

Garten m garden; ~anlage f gardens pl; ~fest n garden party; ~gestaltung f garden architecture; ~haus n summer-house; ~möbel pl garden furniture; ~schau f flower show; ~schirm m garden umbrella; ~weg m garden path; ~zaun m garden fence.

Gärtner m gardener; ~ei f (Betrieb) market-, (Am) truck garden.

Gas n gas; auf ~ kochen cook by gas; ~anzünder m gas lighter; ~hahn m gas tap; ~heizung f gas-heating; ~kocher m gas-cooker; ~leitung f gas main; ~maske f gas-mask; ~ofen m gas-stove; ~pedal n accelerator, (Am) gas pedal.

Gasse f lane, narrow street.

Gast m 1. guest; bei jdm zu ~ sein stay with s.o.; 2. (Besucher) visitor; 3. (im Gasthaus) customer; ~arbeiter m foreign worker.

Gästebuch n visitors' book.

gast(freund)lich hospitable.

Gastfreundschaft f hospi-

tality; ~geber m host; ~haus n inn; ~spiel n guest performance; ~stätte f restaurant; ~wirt m inn-keeper; ~zimmer n guestroom.

Gatte m husband; ~in f wife.

Gattung f 1. (Art) type, kind, sort; 2. bot zoo species.

Gaumen m palate.

Gauner m swindler, cheat.

Gebäck n pastry.

Gebälk n framework.

Gebärde f gesture.

gebär|en irr give birth to; G~mutter f uterus.

Gebäude n building, structure.

Gebell n barking.

geben irr 1. give; 2. (schenken) present; 3. (reichen) jdm die Hand ~ shake hands with s.o.; 4. (überlassen) hand over; 5. (gewähren) jdm Kredit ~ give s.o. credit; 6. Grund zur Besorgnis ~ give reason to be anxious; 7. (Film) present; 8. (ergeben) das gibt keinen Sinn that doesn't make any sense; 9. von sich ~ utter; 10. sich Mühe~ take pains; 11. sich ~ behave; 12. es gibt Regen there will be rain; 13. was gibt's? what's the matter?

Gebet n prayer.

Gebiet n 1. region, area, territory; 2. (Fach) field, domain; 3. (Bereich) sphere, realm; g~en irr 1. (erfor-

dern) require; 2. *(befehlen)* impose, command.

Gebilde n *(Form)* form, shape.

gebildet educated.

Gebinde n *(Blumen)* spray; bundle.

Gebirg|e n mountains *pl;* **g~ig** mountainous; **~sbach** n mountain stream; **~sgegend** f mountainous region; **~spaß** m mountain pass.

Gebiß n denture.

geblümt flowered.

geboren born; **~e** Meyer née Meyer.

Gebot n 1. *rel* commandment; *die Zehn ~e* the Ten Commandments; 2. *(Erfordernis)* necessity.

Gebrauch m use; *das ist nicht mehr in ~* that's no longer in use; 2. *(Gepflogenheit)* usage, practice; **g~en** use, make use of; employ.

gebräuchlich 1. customary; 2. *nicht mehr ~* no longer used.

Gebrauchsanweisung f instructions for use.

gebraucht used; second-hand.

gebrechlich decrepit, infirm.

gebrochen broken.

Gebrüder pl brothers pl.

Gebühr f 1. charge, fee, tax; 2. *(Maut)* toll; 3. *(Tarif)* rate; 4. *über ~* excessively.

gebührend due, proper; appropriate.

Gebühren|erlaß m remis-

sion of charges; **~ermäßigung** f reduction of charges; **g~frei** free of charge; **g~pflichtig** subject to charges.

gebunden 1. *(Buch)* bound; 2. *vertraglich ~* bound by contract.

Geburt f birth; *von ~* by birth; **~enkontrolle** f birth control; **g~enschwach** with a low birth-rate; **~enüberschuß** m excess of the birth-rate; **~sdatum** n date of birth; **~sname** m maiden name; **~sort** m place of birth; **~stag** m birthday; **~surkunde** f birth certificate.

Gebüsch n bushes pl, brushwood.

Gedächtnis n *(Erinnerung)* remembrance; *aus dem ~* from memory; *im ~ behalten* keep in mind.

Gedanke m 1. thought *(an* of); *machen Sie sich keine ~n darüber* don't worry yourself about it; 2. *(Einfall)* idea; 3. *(Absicht)* intention; **~nstrich** m dash.

Gedeck n 1. *ein ~ auflegen* lay a place; 2. *(Speise)* set menu.

gedeihen irr 1. thrive; 2. fig flourish, prosper.

gedenk|en irr 1. *(sich erinnern)* remember; 2. *(denken an)* think of; 3. *(erwähnen)* mention; **G~feier** f commemoration.

Gedicht *n* poem.
Gedränge *n* 1. *(Menge)* crowd; 2. *(Ansturm)* rush *(um* for*)*.
gedrungen *(Gestalt)* stocky, thickset.
Geduld *f* patience; *mir riß die ~* I lost all patience; **g~en**, *sich* be patient; *Sie müssen sich e-n Augenblick ~* you'll have to wait a moment; **g~ig** patient.
geehrt hono(u)red; *Sehr ~er Herr!* Dear Sir.
geeignet 1. *(Person)* qualified, apt; 2. *im ~en Augenblick* at the right moment.
Gefahr *f* danger; *~ laufen* run the risk (of); *auf eigene ~* at o.'s own risk.
gefähr|den 1. endanger, imperil; 2. *(Zukunft)* jeopardize; **~det** endangered.
gefährlich 1. dangerous, perilous; 2. *(gewagt)* risky; **G~keit** *f* danger(ousness).
Gefährt *n* vehicle, carriage; **~e** *m,* **~in** *f* companion.
Gefälle *n* slope, descent; *starkes ~* steep gradient.
gefallen I *irr* 1. like; *gefällt Ihnen mein Hut?* do you like my hat? *das gefällt mir* I fancy that; 2. please; 3. *das lasse ich mir nicht ~* I won't stand (for) that; **II** *adj* killed in action.
Gefallen *m* pleasure; *~ finden an* take pleasure in; *jdm den ~ tun* do s.o. a favour.

gefällig 1. *(zuvorkommend)* obliging; 2. *(ansprechend)* pleasing, pleasant; **G~keit** *f* kindness; *jdm um e-e ~ bitten* ask a favour of s.o.
Gefangen|er *m* prisoner; **g~halten** *irr: jdn ~* keep s.o. in captivity, keep s.o. a prisoner; **g~nehmen** *irr* 1. capture, take prisoner; 2. *fig* captivate, charm; **~schaft** *f* captivity.
Gefängnis *n* 1. prison, jail; 2. *jdn zu 2 Jahren ~ verurteilen* sentence s.o. to 2 years imprisonment.
Gefäß *n* vessel, container.
gefaßt 1. calm; 2. *auf das Schlimmste ~* prepared for the worst; *sich auf etw ~ machen* prepare o.s. for s.th.; *auf etw ~ sein* be prepared for s.th.
Gefecht *n* fight, combat.
gefedert *(Sitze)* sprung.
Gefieder *n* plumage, feathers *pl;* **g~t** feathered.
Geflügel *n* poultry, fowls *pl;* **~farm** *f* poultry farm; **~handlung** *f* poultry shop.
Geflüster *n* whispers *pl.*
Gefolg|e *n (Herrscher)* retinue, suite; **~schaft** *f* followers *pl.*
gefräßig gluttonous, greedy.
Gefreiter *m* lance-corporal; *(Am)* private 1st class.
gefrieren *irr* freeze.
Gefrier|fach *n* freezing compartment; **~fleisch** *n* frozen meat; **~punkt** *m*

freezing-point; **~truhe** *f* deep-freeze.

Gefüge *n fig* structure.

gefügig flexible; docile.

Gefühl *n* 1. feeling; 2. *(Wahrnehmung)* sensation; 3. *(Sinn)* sense *(für* of); 4. *(Berührung)* touch; **g~los** 1. *(Person)* insensible *(gegen* to); 2. *(Glied)* numb; **g~voll** 1. emotional, sentimental; 2. *(zärtlich)* tender.

gegeben: *zu ~er Zeit* at the proper time; **~enfalls** 1. if necessary; 2. *(Formular)* if applicable.

gegen 1. *(Richtung)* ~ *Osten* towards the east; 2. *er lehnte sich ~ die Mauer* he leaned against the wall; 3. *(zeitlich)* ~ *Abend* towards evening; 4. *fig* against; ~ *alle Erwartung* contrary to all expectations; 5. *(im Vergleich zu)* in comparison with; *ich wette zehn* ~ *eins* I'll bet you ten to one; 6. *(für)* ~ *Kopfschmerzen* for headaches; 7. *com* in exchange for; ~ *bar* for cash.

Gegend *f* 1. region, area; 2. *(Umgebung)* environs *pl; in der ~ von* in the neighbourhood of.

gegeneinander against one another; towards one another.

Gegen|fahrbahn *f* oncoming lane; **~gewicht** *n* counterbalance; **~gift** *n* antidote;

~**licht** *n: bei ~* against the light; **~maßnahme** *f* counteraction; *(vorbeugend)* preventive measure; **~partei** *f* opposite party; *zur ~ übergehen* go over to the opposition.

Gegen|satz *m* 1. contrast *(zu* to); *im ~ dazu* in contrast with; 2. *(Meinungen)* differences *pl;* **g~sätzlich** opposite, opposing.

Gegenseite *f* opposite side.

gegenseitig 1. mutual; 2. *sich ~ helfen* help each other; **G~keit** *f* mutuality.

Gegenstand *m* 1. object; 2. *(Thema)* subject, topic; 3. *(Tagesordnung)* item; 4. *(Angelegenheit)* matter.

Gegenteil *n* contrary, reverse, opposite; *im ~* on the contrary.

gegenüber 1. opposite; 2. *(im Vergleich zu)* in comparison with; 3. *das Haus ~* the house across the road; **~liegend** opposite; **~stehen** *irr* 1. *jdm ~* face s.o.; *sich ~* face each other; 2. *e-r Sache ~* be confronted with s.th.; **~stellen** 1. *fig* confront with; 2. *(Sache)* contrast with.

Gegenverkehr *m* oncoming traffic; *Achtung! ~!* caution: two-way traffic!

Gegen|wart *f* 1. present; 2. *in meiner ~* in my presence; **g~wärtig** 1. *(jetzig)* present; *im ~en Augenblick*

at the moment being;
2. *(heutig)* present-day.

Gegenwind *m* head-wind.

Gegner(in *f***)** *m* opponent, adversary; **g~isch** 1. adverse, antagonistic;
2. *(feindlich)* hostile.

Gehalt 1. *m* content (*an* of); *(Wert)* substance, value; 2. *n* salary; *ein* ~ *beziehen* get a salary; **~serhöhung** *f* increase in salary; **~sstreifen** *m* salary slip.

gehässig spiteful, malicious; **G~keit** *f* spitefulness.

Gehäuse *n* 1. case, box, receptacle; 2. *tech* frame.

geheim 1. secret; 2. *im ~en* secretly; **G~dienst** *m* secret service; **G~nis** *n* 1. secret (*vor* from); 2. *(Rätsel)* mystery; **~nisvoll** mysterious; **G~polizei** *f* secret police.

gehemmt *(befangen)* self-conscious.

gehen *irr* **I** 1. go; *(zu Fuß)* walk; 2. *(fort~)* leave, start; 3. *(com) gut* ~ sell well; 4. *(funktionieren)* go, run, work; *die Uhr geht falsch* the clock is wrong; 5. *sich* ~ *lassen* take it easy, let o.s. go; **II** *imp: wie geht es Ihnen?* how are you? *es geht mir gut* I am well; *es geht nichts über* there is nothing better than; *es geht Sie nichts an!* that's none of your business! **III** *mit adv oder adv Bestimmungen:*

auf und ab ~ go to and fro; *auseinander* ~ separate; *aufs Land* ~ go into the country; *er geht auf die fünfzig* he is getting on for fifty; *schlafen* ~ go to sleep; *spazieren* ~ go for a walk; *das Fenster geht auf die Straße* the window looks into the street; *ich lasse es mir gut* ~ I take good care of myself.

Gehilfe *m* assistant.

Gehirn *n* brain; **~erschütterung** *f* cerebral concussion; **~hautentzündung** *f* meningitis; **~schlag** *m* stroke, apoplexy.

Gehölz *n* copse.

Gehör *n* (sense of) hearing; *nach dem* ~ by ear.

gehorchen obey.

gehören 1. belong to; 2. ~ *unter* come under; 3. ~ *zu* be a member of, form part of; 4. *das gehört sich nicht* it is bad form.

gehörlos deaf.

gehorsam obedient (*jdm* to s.o.); **G~** *m* obedience (*gegenüber jdm* to s.o.).

Gehweg *m* pavement, sidewalk.

Geier *m* vulture.

Geige *f* violin; ~ *spielen* play (on) the violin; **~r** *m* violinist.

Geisel *f* hostage.

Geißel *f* whip, lash, scourge.

Geist *m* 1. *(Verstand)* mind, intellect; 2. *(Seele, Sinn, Ge-*

sinnung) spirit; 3. *(Gespenst)* ghost; **g~esabwesend** absent-minded; **~esblitz** *m* flash of genius; **~esgegenwart** *f* presence of mind; **g~eskrank** mentally ill, insane; **~eskranker** *m* insane person; **g~esschwach** feeble-minded; **~eswissenschaften** *pl;* **~eszustand** *m* mental condition.

geistig I *adj* 1. mental; *~e Freiheit* freedom of thought; 2. *~e Fähigkeiten* intellectual abilities; 3. *(seelisch)* spiritual; **II** *adv:* ~ *beschränkt sein* be mentally limited; ~ *gesund* sane.

geistlich 1. religious, spiritual; 2. *(kirchlich)* ecclesiastical; **G~er** *m* clergyman; minister; priest; **G~keit** *f* clergy.

geist los spiritless; **g~reich, g~voll** witty; clever.

Geiz *m* stinginess, miserliness; **~hals** *m* miser, niggard; **g~ig** stingy, miserly.

gekleidet dressed.

gekonnt masterly, accomplished.

Gelächter *n* laughter; *in schallendes ~ ausbrechen* roar with laughing.

Gelage *n* banquet, feast.

gelähmt paralyzed.

Gelände *n* ground, terrain, area, country; **~fahrt** *f* cross-country drive; **~lauf** *m* cross-country race.

Geländer *n* railing, banister.

gelangen 1. get to, arrive at, reach; *ans Ziel ~* reach o.'s destination; *zur Erkenntnis ~, daß* realize that; 2. *zu etw ~* gain s.th., attain s.th.; 3. *in jds Besitz ~* come into s.o.'s possession.

gelassen calm, composed, cool; **G~heit** *f* composure.

Gelatine *f* gelatin(e).

gelaunt*: gut ~* good-humoured; *schlecht ~* ill-humoured.

gelb 1. yellow; 2. *(Verkehrslicht)* amber; **~lich** yellowish; **G~sucht** *f* jaundice.

Geld *n* 1. money; *flüssiges ~* ready money; *kleines ~* change; 2. *(Währung)* currency; 3. *(Gelder)* funds *pl;* **~anweisung** *f* money-order; **~betrag** *m* amount, sum (of money); **~beutel** *m* purse; **~geschenk** *n* donation; **~markt** *m* money-market; **~schein** *m* bank-note; **~schrank** *m* safe; **~strafe** *f* fine; **~stück** *n* coin; **~verlegenheit** *f: in ~ sein* be hard up; **~wechsel** *m* exchange of money.

Gelee *n* jelly.

gelegen I *adj* 1. situated, *Am* located; 2. *(passend)* suitable; *der Termin ist mir sehr ~* the date is very convenient for me; 3. *es ist mir viel daran ~* it matters a great deal to me; 4. *zu ~er Zeit* at an opportune moment; **II** *adv: das kommt* *mir sehr* ~ that suits me perfectly.

Gelegenheit *f* 1. *(günstige)* opportunity; 2. *(Anlaß)* occasion; *bei welcher* ~? on what occasion? ~**sarbeit** *f* odd job; ~**skauf** *m* bargain.

gelegentlich 1. occasional; 2. *(zufällig)* incidental; 3. *(bei Gelegenheit)* on occasion.

gelehrig 1. docile; 2. *(klug)* clever; **G~samkeit** *f* scholarship; ~**t** learned, scholarly; **G~ter** *m* scholar.

Geleit *n* escort; *jdm das* ~ *geben* accompany s.o.; ~**zug** *m* convoy.

Gelenk *n* 1. *anat* joint; 2. *tech* hinge; ~**entzündung** *f* arthritis; **g~ig** 1. supple; 2. *(gewandt)* nimble.

gelernt *(Arbeiter)* skilled; trained.

Geliebte(r) *m f* sweetheart, beloved.

gelingen *irr* 1. succeed; 2. *(Arbeit)* turn out; 3. *es gelingt jdm, etw zu tun* s.o. succeeds in doing s. th.; **G~** *n* success.

geloben promise solemnly.

gelten *irr* 1. *(wert sein)* be worth; 2. *(gültig sein)* be valid; 3. *(wichtig sein)* count; 4. *(fig) er gilt dort viel* he counts for much; 5. *(bestimmt sein für)* be meant, intended for; 6. *(anwendbar sein auf)* apply to,

be applicable to; 7. *es gilt!* agreed! 8. ~ *lassen* let pass; 9. *als etw* ~ be regarded as; ~**end** 1. valid, in force; 2. *s-n Einfluß* ~ *machen auf* bring all o.'s influence to bear; **G~ung** *f* 1. *(Gültigkeit)* validity; 2. *(Achtung)* respect, recognition; 3. *(Wichtigkeit)* importance; 4. *zur* ~ *kommen* be effective.

Gelübde *n: ein* ~ *ablegen* take a vow.

gelungen successful.

Gemahl *m* husband; ~**in** *f* wife.

Gemälde *n* painting, picture; ~**galerie** *f* art gallery.

gemäß *(entsprechend)* according to; *Ihrem Auftrag* ~ in compliance with your request; ~ *den Bestimmungen* under the regulations; ~**igt** 1. moderate; 2. *geol* temperate.

gemein 1. *(tückisch)* mean, nasty, rotten; vulgar; 2. *(allgemein)* common; 3. *nichts miteinander* ~ *haben* have nothing in common.

Gemeinde *f* 1. community; municipality; 2. *(Kirche)* parish; ~**verwaltung** *f* local administration.

gemeingefährlich: *er ist* ~ he is a public danger; **G~heit** *f* meanness; baseness; **G~kosten** *pl* overhead costs.

gemeinnützig for the public welfare.

gemein|sam I *adj* 1. common; 2. ~*e Bemühungen* joint efforts; 3. *(gegenseitig)* mutual; **II** *adv:* ~ *handeln mit* act together with; **G~schaft** *f* 1. community; 2. *(Gruppe)* team; ~**verständlich** generally understandable; **G~wohl** *n* public welfare.

Gemetzel *n* massacre, slaughter.

Gemisch *n* mixture *a. fig;* **g~t** mixed.

Gemse *f* chamois.

Gemurmel *n* murmer(ing).

Gemüse *n* vegetables *pl,* greens *pl;* ~**garten** *m* kitchen garden.

Gemüt *n* feeling, heart, mind; **g~lich** 1. *(behaglich)* comfortable, snug, cosy; 2. *(angenehm)* pleasant; 3. *(Mensch)* good-natured; ~**lichkeit** *f* cosiness; leisure.

genau 1. exact; 2. *(sorgfältig)* careful; 3. *(klar)* precise, definite; 4. *(im einzelnen)* detailed; 5. ~ *dasselbe* just the same; 6. *(Vorschriften)* ~ *befolgen* follow closely; 7. *er nimmt es sehr* ~ he's very particular; 8. *die Uhr geht* ~ the watch keeps perfect time; ~**genommen** strictly speaking; **G~igkeit** *f* accuracy, exactness, precision.

genauso just the same; ~ *gut* just as well.

genehmig|en 1. *(Gesuch)* approve; 2. *(bewilligen)* grant, allow; 3. *(gutheißen)* agree; **G~ung** *f* 1. approval; 2. grant; 3. assent (to); ~**ungspflichtig** requiring official approval.

geneigt inclined *a. fig.*

General *m* general; ~**direktor** *m* general manager; ~**konsul(at** *n)* *m* consul(ate)-general; ~**sekretär** *m* secretary-general; ~**überholung** *f* major overhaul.

Generation *f* generation.

Generator *m* generator.

generell general.

genes|en *irr* recover; **G~ung** *f* recovery.

genial ingenious, genius; **G~ität** *f* ingenuity, genius.

Genick *n* neck.

Genie *n* genius.

genieren, *sich* feel embarrassed.

genießen *irr* 1. *(Freiheit)* enjoy; 2. *(Nahrung)* eat, take, drink.

genormt standardized.

Genosse *m* comrade, companion; ~**nschaft** *f* com cooperative society.

genug enough, sufficient; *mehr als* ~ enough and to spare.

genüg|en 1. be sufficient; *das genügt mir* that will do; 2. *jdm* ~ satisfy s.o.; 3. *e-r*

Sache ~ meet s.th.; **~end**
1. enough, sufficient;
2. (*Zeugnis*) fair; **~sam**
modest, moderate;
G~samkeit *f* modesty.
Genugtuung *f* (*Befriedigung*) satisfaction (*über* at).
Genuß *m* 1. (*Vergnügen*) enjoyment, pleasure; 2. (*Nahrung*) consumption;
3. (*Nutznießung*) benefit.
Geographie *f* geography;
g~isch geographic(al).
Geologie *f* geology.
Geometrie *f* geometry.
Gepäck *n* luggage, *Am* baggage; **~abfertigung** *f* registration, *Am* checking of luggage; **~aufbewahrung**
f left-luggage office; **~netz**
n luggage-rack; **~schein** *m*
luggage ticket, *Am* baggage check; **~stück** *n* parcel;
~träger *m* 1. porter; 2. *mot*
luggage-rack; **~versicherung** *f* luggage insurance;
~wagen *m* luggage-van.
gepflegt 1. well-groomed;
2. (*Sache*) well cared-for.
Geplauder *n* small talk.
gerade I *adj* 1. (*Zahl*) even;
2. (*Linie*) straight; 3. (*aufrecht*) upright; 4. (*aufrichtig*) honest; **II** *adv* just,
exactly; *sie kommen* ~ *recht*
you are just in time; *er war*
~ *dort* he happened to be
there; **~aus** straight ahead;
~zu 1. (*fast*) almost;
2. (*nichts anderes als*)
sheer, downright.

Gerät *n* 1. (*Apparat*) apparatus, appliance; 2. (*Werkzeug*) tool, implement;
3. *radio* set.
geraten I *irr* 1. (*gelingen*)
turn out; 2. (*hineinkommen*) get into; 3. *an jdn* ~
come across s.o.; (*Gefahr*)
run into; *in Wut* ~ fly into a
rage; *in Brand* ~ catch fire;
II *adj* (*ratsam*) advisable,
commendable.
Geratewohl *n: aufs* ~ at
random, on the off-chance.
geräumig spacious.
Geräusch *n* noise; **g~los**
noiseless; **g~voll** noisy,
loud.
gerb|en tan; **G~er** *m* tanner.
gerecht 1. just, fair; 2. *jdm* ~
werden do justice to s.o.;
G~igkeit *f* justice.
Gerede *n* rumo(u)r, gossip;
ins ~ *kommen* get talked
about.
gereizt irritable; **G~heit** *f* irritability.
Gericht *n* 1. (*Essen*) dish;
2. (*Gang*) course; 3. *jur*
court (of justice), law-court;
vor ~ in court; *vor* ~ *bringen* take a matter to court;
ein ~ *anrufen* apply to a
court; **g~lich** 1. legal, judicial; 2. ~ *vereidigt* sworn; ~
vorgehen gegen jdn sue s.o.;
~sdiener *m* (court) usher;
~sentscheid *m* court decision; **~shof** *m* court of justice; **~skosten** *pl* costs *pl;*
~ssaal *m* court-room;

~sverhandlung f 1. judicial hearing; 2. (Strafverhandlung) trial; **~svollzieher** m bailiff.

gering 1. (Unterschied) small, slight; 2. (unbedeutend) unimportant, trifling; 3. (Entfernung) short; 4. (geringwertig) inferior, poor; 5. (bescheiden) humble, modest; 6. nicht im ~sten not in the least, by no means; **~fügig** insignificant, unimportant, **~schätzig** 1. disparaging, disdainful; 2. jdn ~ behandeln treat s.o. with contempt; **G~schätzung** f disdain, contempt.

gerinnen irr 1. (Blut) coagulate; 2. (Milch) curdle.

Gerippe n skeleton.

gern 1. gladly; herzlich ~ with great pleasure; 2. (bereitwillig) readily; das glaube ich ~ I quite believe it; ich möchte ~ wissen I should like to know; 3. ~ haben be fond of; 4. reisen Sie ~? do you like to travel?

Gerste f barley.

Gerte f switch.

Geruch m smell, odo(u)r; **~ssinn** m sense of smell; **g~los** odo(u)rless.

Gerücht n rumour; es geht das ~, daß it is rumoured that; **~emacher** m rumour-monger.

geruhen: ~, etw zu tun deign to do s. th.

Gerümpel n junk.

Gerüst n (Bau) scaffold, skeleton.

gesamt 1. all; 2. whole, entire; im ~en on the whole.

Gesamt|ansicht f general view; **~heit** f totality, the whole; **~kosten** pl total expenses pl; **~summe** f sum total.

Gesandt|er m envoy; minister; **~schaft** f legation.

Gesang m 1. song; 2. (Dichtung) canto, book; **~verein** m singing society, glee club.

Gesäß n buttocks pl.

Geschädigter m injured person.

Geschäft n 1. business; die ~e gehen gut business is good; in ~en on business; 2. (Laden) shop, store; 3. (Angelegenheit) affair; 4. (Unternehmen) transaction, deal; 5. (Beschäftigung) occupation, trade; 6. (Handel) commerce; 7. (Firma) undertaking.

geschäft|ig busy, active; **~lich** on business.

Geschäfts|brief m business letter; **~bücher** pl account books pl; **g~fähig**: voll ~ sein be fully capable (of doing s.th.); **~frau** f business woman; **~führer** m manager, managing director; **~führung** f management; **~geheimnis** n business secret; **~haus** n business house, firm; **~inhaber** m holder of a business;

~mann m businessman; **~ordnung** f 1. (Tagesordnung) agenda; 2. rules of procedure; **~reise** f business trip; **~stelle** f office, branch; **~straße** f shopping street; **~zeit** f business, office hours pl; **~zimmer** n office.

geschehen irr 1. happen, take place, occur; 2. es geschieht ihm recht it serves him right; 3. es muß etw ~ something must be done; was soll damit ~? what's to be done with it?

gescheit clever, intelligent, bright.

Geschenk n present, gift; **~korb** m gift hamper; **~packung** f gift pack.

Geschichte f 1. history; 2. (Erzählung) story, tale; 3. (Angelegenheit) affair, business; **g~lich** historical.

Geschick n 1. (Schicksal) fate, destiny; 2. (Gewandtheit) skill, dexterity; **~lichkeit** f skilfulness; **g~t** skilful, dexterous.

geschieden (Eheleute) divorced.

Geschirr n 1. dishes pl; 2. (Pferd) harness; **~spülmaschine** f dishwasher; **~tuch** n tea-towel, Am dishtowel.

Geschlecht n 1. sex; 2. (Gattung) kind, species, race; 3. kommende ~er future generations pl; 4. gram gen-

der; **g~lich** sexual; **~skrankheit** f veneral disease; **~sorgane** pl genitals; **~strieb** m sexual instinct; **~sverkehr** m sexual intercourse.

geschlossen 1. closed; 2. ~e Gesellschaft private party, meeting; 3. ~e Ortschaft built-up area.

Geschmack m 1. taste, flavo(u)r; 2. über ~ läßt sich streiten there's no accounting for tastes; **g~los** 1. tasteless; 2. fig in bad taste; **~losigkeit** f fig bad taste; **g~voll** fig tasteful, in good taste.

geschmeidig supple, soft.

Geschöpf n creature.

Geschoß n 1. missile, projectile; 2. (Stockwerk) stor(e)y, floor.

Geschrei n shouting, yelling.

Geschütz n gun.

Geschwader n 1. mar squadron; 2. aero group.

Geschwätz n idle talk, gossip, chatter; **g~ig** talkative; **~igkeit** f talkativeness.

geschweige: ~ denn say nothing of, let alone.

geschwind quick, hasty.

Geschwindigkeit f 1. quickness, speed, rapidity; 2. mit voller ~ fahren drive (at) full speed; **~sbegrenzung** f speed limit; **~skontrolle** f speed check.

Geschwister pl brother(s) and sister(s).

geschwollen 1. swollen;
2. *fig* pompous.
Geschworener *m jur* juror.
Geschwulst *f* swelling.
Geschwür *n* ulcer.
Gesell|e *m* 1. journeyman;
2. *(Bursche)* fellow; **g~ig**
sociable.
Gesellschaft *f* 1. society;
2. ~ *leisten* keep company;
3. *(Veranstaltung)* party, social gathering; 4. *(Vereinigung)* society, association;
5. *com* company, *Am* corporation; **~er** *m* 1. *com*
shareholder; partner; 2. *er
ist ein angenehmer* ~ he is a
pleasant company; **~erin** *f*
(lady) companion; **g~lich**
social; **~sanzug** *m* evening
dress; **g~sfähig** socially
acceptable; **~sreise** *f* conducted tour.
Gesetz *n* law, statute;
~buch *n* code; **~entwurf**
m parl bill; **~gebung** *f*
legislation; **g~lich** 1. legal,
lawful, statutory, legitimate;
2. ~ *geschützt* patented;
(Warenzeichen) registered;
g~mäßig lawful, legitimate.
gesetzt 1. *(ruhig)* sedate;
2. *(älter)* mature; 3. ~ *den
Fall* supposing.
gesetzwidrig illegal, unlaw-
ful.
gesichert 1. secured *(gegen*
against); 2. *(Existenz)* secure.
Gesicht *n* 1. face; *etw zu* ~
bekommen set eyes on s.th.;

er sagte ihm das ins ~ he
told him that to his face; 2.
*dadurch bekommt die Sa-
che ein anderes* ~ that puts
a different light on the matter; 3. *(Miene) er machte
ein langes* ~ he made a long
face; **~sfarbe** *f* complexion;
~skreis *m* horizon;
~spunkt *m* point of view,
aspect; *von meinem* ~ *aus*
from my point of view;
~swasser *n* face lotion;
~szüge *pl* features *pl.*
Gesindel *n* mob, rabble.
Gesinnung *f* 1. *(Ansichten)*
views *pl*, opinion; 2. *(Einstellung)* attitude.
gesittet well-mannered.
Gespann *n* team.
gespannt 1. tense, tight, taut;
2. *(Beziehungen)* strained,
tense; 3. *sehr* ~ *sein auf* be
anxious to see.
Gespenst *n* ghost, phantom.
gesperrt blocked; *Straße* ~!
road closed!
Gespräch *n* 1. conversation;
im ~ *bleiben* remain under
discussion; 2. *~e am runden
Tisch* round-table talks;
3. *(Telefon)* call; **g~ig** talkative; **~sdauer** *f* duration of
a call.
gesprenkelt spotted,
speckled.
Gespür *n* feeling.
Gestalt *f* 1. shape; 2. *(Körperbau)* build, stature; *(Person)* figure; 3. ~ *annehmen*
take shape, materialize;

g~en 1. shape, form; 2. (*einrichten*) organize, arrange; 3. (*entwerfen*) design; **~ung** f 1. organization; 2. (*Formgebung*) designing, styling; 3. (*Schaffen*) creation.

geständ|ig confessing; **G~nis** n 1. *jur* confession; 2. (*Bekenntnis*) avowal.

Gestank m stench, stink.

gestatten 1. allow, permit; *wenn Sie* ~ if you don't mind; 2. *sich* ~ take the liberty (of doing).

Geste f gesture a. fig.

gestehen irr admit, confess; *offen gestanden* to tell the truth, frankly.

Gestein n rock, stone.

Gestell n 1. (*Bücher*) shelf; 2. (*Flaschen*) rack; 3. (*Fahrrad*) frame.

gestern yesterday; ~ *früh* yesterday morning; ~ *abend* last night.

gestikulieren gesticulate.

Gestirn n star.

gestreift striped.

gestrig: *am* ~*en Tag* yesterday; *am* ~*en Abend* last night.

Gestrüpp n brushwood, undergrowth.

Gestüt n stud-farm.

Gesuch n application; *e-m* ~ *entsprechen* comply with a request.

gesucht 1. com in great demand; 2. (*Inserat*) wanted.

gesund 1. (*Aussehen, Klima*) healthy; ~ *sein* be in good health; ~ *und wohlbehalten* safe and sound; 2. (*geistig*) sane; 3. (*Lebensweise*) healthy, wholesome; 4. ~*er Menschenverstand* common sense.

Gesundheit f health; *auf jds* ~ *trinken* drink to s.o.'s health; **g~lich** hygienic, sanitary; **~sgründe** pl: *aus* ~*n* for reasons of health; **~spaß** m certificate of health; **~szustand** m state of health.

getragen (*Kleider*) worn.

Getränk n beverage, drink.

Getreide n cereals pl, grain.

getrennt separate.

Getriebe n mot gear-box, transmission.

geübt skilled, practised.

Gewächs n 1. (*Pflanze*) plant, vegetable; 2. med growth.

gewachsen 1. grown; 2. *jdm* ~ *sein* be a match for s.o.; *sich der Lage* ~ *zeigen* rise to the occasion.

Gewächshaus n greenhouse.

gewagt risky.

Gewähr f security; *ohne* ~ without guarantee; **g~en** 1. (*e-e Bitte*) grant; 2. (*Rabatt*) allow; **g~leisten** guarantee, ensure.

Gewahrsam m 1. (*Haft*) custody; 2. (*Sache*) *in* ~ *nehmen* take charge of.

Gewalt f 1. force, violence; *mit* ~ by force; ~ *anwenden* apply force; *mit aller* ~ with might and main; 2. power; *höhere* ~ act of providence; *elterliche* ~ parental authority; 3. *sich in der* ~ *haben* have o.s. under control; **g~ig** 1. huge, mighty; 2. *(Kraft)* powerful, tremendous; **g~sam** 1. violent, by force; 2. *(Maßnahme)* drastic; **g~tätig** violent, brutal.

Gewand *n* garment, robe.

gewandt 1. *(geschickt)* skilful, nimble; 2. *(tüchtig)* efficient; **G~heit** *f* skill, agility.

Gewässer *pl* waters.

Gewebe *n* 1. *(Stoff)* woven fabric; 2. *biol* tissue.

Gewehr *n* rifle.

Geweih *n* antlers *pl.*

Gewerbe *n* 1. business, occupation; *ein* ~ *betreiben* practise a trade; 2. profession; ~**schein** *m* trade licence; ~**steuer** *f* trade tax.

gewerblich commercial, trade.

Gewerkschaft *f* trade union, *Am* labor union; ~**ler** *m* trade-unionist; **g~lich**: *sich* ~ *organisieren* unionize.

Gewicht *n* weight; **g~ig** important.

gewillt willing (*zu* to).

Gewimmel *n (Menge)* crowd.

Gewinde *n (Schraube)* thread.

Gewinn *m* 1. profit, returns *pl; (Ertrag)* gains *pl;* ~ *ab-*

werfen yield a profit; *mit* ~ *verkaufen* sell at a profit; 2. winnings *pl; (Lotterie)* prize; ~**anteil** *m* dividend; **g~bringend** profitable, lucrative.

gewinn|en *irr* 1. win, gain; 2. *(erwerben)* obtain; 3. *jds Aufmerksamkeit* ~ attract s.o.'s attention; 4. *Bedeutung* ~ gain significance; 5. *(Kohle)* extract; 6. *er gewinnt bei näherer Bekanntschaft* he becomes on closer acquaintance; ~**end** winning, captivating; **G~er** *m* winner.

gewiß 1. certain; *es ist ganz* ~, *daß* it is quite sure that; 2. *ein gewisser Herr X* a certain Mr. X; *in gewissem Sinne* in a sense; 3. *er hat* ~ *recht* no doubt, he is right; 4. *interj:* ~! of course!

Gewissen *n: ein gutes/ schlechtes* ~ *haben* have a good/bad conscience; *nach bestem* ~ to the best of o.'s conscience; **g~haft** conscientious; **g~los** without conscience, unscrupulous; ~**sbisse** *pl* pricks of conscience; ~**skonflikt** *m* conflict of conscience.

gewissermaßen so to speak, in a way.

Gewißheit *f* certainty; *sich* ~ *verschaffen* make sure (*über* of).

Gewitter *n* thunderstorm; *ein* ~ *zieht herauf* a storm is gathering.

gewöhnen 1. *jdn an etw ~* accustom s.o. to s.th.; 2. *sich an etw ~* get used to s.th.

Gewohnheit *f* habit; *etw aus ~ tun* do s.th. from force of habit; **~srecht** *n* common law.

gewöhnlich 1. usual, normal, ordinary; 2. *im ~en Leben* in every-day life; 3. *für ~* as a rule.

gewohnt 1. accustomed, familiar; 2. *~ sein, etw zu tun* be used to doing s.th.

Gewöhnung *f* habituation.

Gewölbe *n* vault; **g~t** vaulted, arched.

Gewühl *n* crowd, throng.

Gewürz *n* spice; **g~t** spicy, flavoured.

Gezeiten *pl* tides *pl*; **~kraftwerk** *n* tidal power station.

geziert affected.

Gezwitscher *n* chirping.

gezwungen forced.

Gicht *f* gout.

Giebel *m* gable.

Gier *f* greed, craving (*nach* for); **g~ig** 1. greedy (*nach* for); 2. *~ lesen* read avidly.

gieß|en *irr* 1. pour; *Wein in ein Glas ~* pour wine into a glass; 2. (*Pflanzen*) water; 3. (*e-e Glocke ~*) found; 4. *es gießt in Strömen* it is pouring; **G~kanne** *f* watering-can.

Gift *n* 1. poison; 2. *zoo* venom; **g~ig** poisonous, venomous; toxic; **~pilz** *m* toadstool.

gigantisch gigantic.

Ginster *m* broom.

Gipfel *m* 1. summit, peak, top; 2. *fig (Höhepunkt)* height, peak, culmination; **~treffen** *n pol* summit meeting.

Gips *m* 1. *min* gypsum; 2. (*gebrannt*) plaster; **~er** *m* plasterer; **~verband** *m* plaster cast.

Giraffe *f* giraffe.

Girlande *f* garland.

Giro *n* endorsement; **~konto** *n* current account.

Gitarre *f* guitar.

Gitter *n* 1. lattice; 2. (*Fenster*) grating; 3. (*Käfig*) bars *pl*; 4. (*Park*) railings *pl*.

Glanz *m* 1. brightness, lustre; 2. (*Oberfläche*) polish; 3. *fig* glamour, splendour.

glänzen 1. shine; 2. (*in der Sonne*) glisten; **~d** 1. shiny; 2. (*Redner*) brilliant; 3. (*Gedanke*) splendid; 4. (*funkelnd*) sparkling; 5. (*blank*) glossy.

glanz|los dull; **~voll** splendid, magnificent.

Glas *n* 1. glass; 2. (*Brille*) (eye-)glasses; **~bläser** *m* glass-blower; **~er** *m* glazier; **~erei** *f* glazier's workshop; **~hütte** *f* glassworks *pl* (*mit sing*); **g~ieren** 1. (*Ziegel*) glaze; 2. (*Früchte*) candy; **g~ig** glassy; **~scheibe** *f* pane of glass; **~scherbe** *f* piece of broken glass; **~splitter** *m* glass splinter;

~**tür** f glass door; ~**ur** f
1. (Keramik) glaze; 2. (Kuchen) icing, Am frosting.
glatt 1. (Oberfläche) smooth,
even; 2. (glitschig) slippery;
3. ~er Unsinn utter non-
sense; das ist ~er Wahn-
sinn that is sheer madness.
Glätte f 1. smoothness;
2. (Straße) slipperiness.
Glatt|eis n slippery ice; jdn
aufs ~ führen trip s.o. up;
~**eisgefahr** f: ~! danger,
ice!
glätten smooth.
Glatze f bald head.
Glaub|e m 1. belief (an in);
jdm ~ schenken believe s.o.;
2. (Vertrauen) faith, confidence; 3. rel faith; **g~en**
1. believe; 2. (meinen) think;
3. ich glaube wohl I sup-
pose so; **g~haft** credible,
plausible.
gläubig believing; religious,
pious; **G~er** m 1. believer;
2. com creditor.
glaubwürdig reliable, trustworthy; **G~keit** f reliability.

gleich I adj 1. equal, like; von
~er Größe of equal size;
2. (ähnlich) same, identical;
3. das ist mir ganz ~ it's all
the same to me; **II** adv
4. alike; ~ groß equally
large; 5. (sofort) at once,
immediately; ~**altrig** of the
same age; ~**artig** of the
same kind; ~**berechtigt** en-
joying equal rights; **G~be-**

rechtigung f equal rights,
equality.
gleichen irr: jdm ~ look like
s.o., resemble s.o.
gleich|ermaßen likewise;
~**falls** also, as well, likewise;
danke ~! thank you, the
same to you!
Gleichgewicht n balance,
equilibrium a. fig.
gleichgültig 1. indifferent,
uninterested; 2. (unwichtig)
unimportant; es ist ~, ob it
does not matter whether;
G~keit f indifference.
Gleichheit f equality.
gleich|machen make equal;
dem Erdboden ~ level to
the ground; ~**mäßig** 1. proportional; 2. (Bewegung)
regular; ~**schalten** bring
into line.
Gleichschritt m: im ~ marschieren march in time.
gleichstellen jur assimilate.
Gleichstrom m direct current.
gleich|wertig of equal value;
~**zeitig** simultaneous; at the
same time.
Gleis n track, rails pl.
gleiten irr 1. glide, slide, slip;
2. ~de Lohnskala sliding
scale of wages.
Gleit|flug m gliding flight;
~**schutz** m anti-skid protection.
Gletscher m glacier.
Glied n 1. (Körper~) limb;
2. (Kette) link; **g~ern** 1. (anordnen) order, arrange, or-

ganize; 2. *sich* ~ *in* be divided into; **~erung** *f* division, classification;
~maßen *pl* limbs *pl.*

glimmen *irr* glow; *(Feuer)* smoulder.

glimpflich: ~ *davonkommen* get off lightly.

glitzern glitter, glister, sparkle.

glob|al world-wide, global; **G~us** *m* globe.

Glöckchen *n* small bell.

Glocke *f* 1. bell; *etw an die große* ~ *hängen* proclaim s.th. from the housetops; 2. *(Käse~)* cover; **~nblume** *f* harebell; **~nturm** *m* belfry.

Glück *n* 1. luck, fortune; *er hat* ~ he is lucky; 2. *viel* ~! good luck! *viel* ~ *im neuen Jahr!* a happy new year! 3. *(Fügung)* good fortune; 4. *(Gefühl)* happiness.

glück|en succeed, turn out well; **~lich** 1. lucky, fortunate; 2. *(zufrieden)* happy; **~licherweise** fortunately, luckily.

Glücksbringer *m* talisman.

glückselig blissful.

Glück|sfall *m* lucky chance; **~sspiel** *n* game of chance, gambling; **~streffer** *m* lucky hit; **~wunsch** *m* 1. *herzlichen* ~! congratulations! 2. good wishes *pl.*

Glüh|birne *f* electric bulb; **g~en** glow, burn; **g~end** 1. glowing; 2. *auf* ~*en Koh-*

len sitzen be on tenterhooks; **~wein** *m* mulled wine; **~würmchen** *n* glow-worm.

Glut *f* 1. *(glühende Masse)* embers *pl;* 2. *(Hitze)* scorching heat; 3. *(Leidenschaft)* ardour, fervour.

Gnade *f* 1. mercy; *um* ~ *bitten* ask, plead for mercy; 2. *rel* grace; **~ngesuch** *n* petition for mercy.

gnädig 1. merciful; 2. *(gütig)* gracious, benevolent; 3. ~ *e Frau* Madam.

Gold *n* gold; **~barren** *m* gold bar; **g~braun** golden brown.

golden of gold; *der* ~*e Mittelweg* the happy mean.

Gold|fisch *m* goldfish; **~grube** *f* gold mine *a. fig;* **~münze** *f* gold coin; **~regen** *m bot* laburnum; **~schmied** *m* goldsmith; **~stück** *n* 1. gold piece; 2. *fig* gem.

Golf 1. *m geog* gulf; 2. *n sport* golf.

Gondel *f* gondola.

gönn|en 1. *ich gönne es Ihnen* I don't begrudge it to you; 2. *sich etw* ~ allow o.s. s.th.; **G~er** *m* patron.

Gosse *f* gutter.

Got|ik *f,* **g~isch** *arch* Gothic.

Gott *m* 1. God, Lord; ~ *der Allmächtige* Almighty God; 2. *(Gottheit)* god; 3. ~ *sei Dank!* thank heavens! *um* ~*es Willen!* for heaven's sake! **~esdienst** m religious service.

Göttin f goddess.

göttlich divine.

gottlos godless.

Götze m idol.

Gouverneur m governor.

Grab n 1. grave; (~mal) tomb, 2. sepulchre.

graben irr dig (nach etw for s.th.).

Grab|rede f funeral oration; **~stein** m tombstone.

Grad m 1. degree; 2. bis zu e-m gewissen ~e to some degree; in hohem ~e to a high degree.

Graf m earl, count.

Gräfin f countess.

Gramm n gram(me).

Gramma|tik f grammar; **g~tisch** grammatical.

Grammophon n gramophone, Am phonograph; record-player.

Granat m min garnet; **~apfel** m pomegranate.

Granate f grenade, shell.

Granit m min granite.

Graph|ik f graphic arts pl; **~iker** m graphic artist; **g~isch** graphic; das ~e Gewerbe the printing trade; **~it** m min graphite; **~ologe** m graphologist.

Gras n 1. grass; 2. darüber ist schon längst ~ gewachsen it's already a thing of the past; **g~en** graze; **~halm** m blade of grass.

grassieren rage.

gräßlich 1. (Anblick) horrible, dreadful; 2. (Verbrechen) hideous.

Grat m edge, ridge.

Gräte f fish-bone.

gratis free, gratuitous; **G~probe** f free sample.

Gratul|ation f congratulation; **g~ieren**: jdm zu etw ~ congratulate s.o. on s.th.

grau 1. grey; 2. der ~e Alltag the dull monotony of daily life.

grauen: es graut mir I dread; **~haft, ~voll** horrible, ghostly.

Graupe f pearl-barley.

graupel|n: es graupelt hail is falling; **G~schauer** m shower of small hail.

grausam cruel, inhuman; **G~keit** f cruelty.

graus|en: mir graust bei diesem Anblick I shuddered at this sight; **~ig** ghastly, gruesome.

gravieren engrave.

Grazi|e f grace, charm; **g~ös** graceful.

greif|bar 1. fig tangible, palpable; 2. (Gegenstand) within reach; **~en** irr 1. seize, reach, grasp (nach for); 2. zu Maßnahmen ~ resort to measures; um sich ~ spread; unter die Arme ~ lend a helping hand.

Greis m old man; **g~enhaft** senile; **~in** f aged woman.

grell 1. (Licht) glaring,

dazzling; 2. *(Ton)* shrill; 3. *(Farbe)* loud.

Grenzbahnhof *m* frontier station.

Grenze *f* 1. *(Staat)* frontier; 2. *(Linie)* boundary, border; 3. *fig* limit; *sich über alle ~n hinwegsetzen* pass all bounds; **g~n** border (*an on*).

grenzenlos boundless, unbounded, unlimited.

Grenz|gebiet *n* 1. frontier area; 2. *fig* borderland; **~kontrolle** *f* frontier control; **~übergang** *m* frontier crossing-point; **~übertritt** *m* crossing of the frontier; **~verkehr** *m* goods traffic across the frontier; **~verletzung** *f* violation of the frontier; **~zwischenfall** *m* frontier incident.

Greuel *m* horror; **~tat** *f* atrocity.

greulich horrible, awful, terrible.

Griech|e *m* Greek; **~enland** *n* Greece; **g~isch** Greek.

griesgrämig grumbling, morose.

Grieß *m* semolina.

Griff *m* 1. handle, knob; 2. *(Zu~)* grasp, hold, grip; *etw in den ~ bekommen* get the knack of s.th.; *e-n guten ~ tun* make a good choice; **g~bereit** at hand, ready to hand.

Griffel *m* 1. slate-pencil; 2. *bot* style, pistil.

Grill *m* grill.

Grille *f* 1. *zoo* cricket; 2. *fam* whim, fancy.

Grimasse *f:* **~n schneiden** make a grimace.

grimmig 1. *(Kälte)* fierce; 2. *(Blick)* furious.

grinsen grin.

Grippe *f* influenza, flu.

grob 1. coarse *a. tech;* 2. **~er** *Irrtum* big mistake; 3. *(Manieren)* rude; 4. *(ungefähr)* rough; **G~heit** *f* 1. coarseness; 2. roughness; 3. rudeness.

Groll *m* ranco(u)r, grudge; **g~en** 1. *(zürnen) mit jdm ~* have a grudge against s.o.; 2. *(Donner)* rumble.

groß 1. *(Umfang)* large, big; 2. *(Wuchs)* tall; 3. *(hoch)* high; 4. *(Entfernung)* long; 5. *e-e ~e Auswahl* a great variety; 6. *(Kälte)* severe; 7. *(fig) ein ~er Geist* a great spirit; 8. *(Verlust)* heavy; 9. *im ~en und ganzen* on the whole; **~artig** grand, wonderful; **G~aufnahme** *f* close-up.

Großbritannien *n* Great Britain.

Großbuchstabe *m* capital (letter).

Größe *f* 1. *(Umfang)* size, largeness; 2. *(Körper)* height; 3. dimension; 4. *fig* magnitude, significance.

Großeltern *pl* grandparents.

Größenwahn *m* megalomania.

Groß|grundbesitzer *m*

landed proprietor; **~handel** m wholesale trade; **~macht** f great power; **~mut** f generosity.

Großmutter f grandmother.

Großstadt f large city.

größtenteils for the most part, mostly.

Großvater m grandfather.

großzügig generous, liberal.

grotesk grotesque.

Grotte f grotto.

Grube f mine, pit.

Grübel|ei f brooding, musing; **g~n** brood, muse.

Gruft f tomb, vault.

grün 1. green; 2. (unreif) unripe; 3. **~e Welle** (mot) linked signals (at 50 km); **G~anlage** f public parks pl.

Grund m 1. ground; (Erde) soil; (Meer, Gefäß) bottom; 2. fig (Ursache) cause, reason; im **~e** after all; aus welchem **~e** for what reason? 3. auf **~** von on account of, according to; im **~e** strictly speaking; von **~** auf completely; **~besitz** m landed property; **~buch** n register of landed property.

gründ|en found, establish, set up; **G~er** m founder, promoter.

Grund|gebühr f basic rate; **~gesetz** n pol Basic Law.

Grund|lage f 1. base, foundation; 2. fig basis, fundamentals pl; **g~legend** fundamental, basic.

gründlich thorough, careful, painstaking.

grundlos fig unfounded, baseless.

Grundmauer f foundation wall.

Gründonnerstag m Maundy Thursday.

Grundriß m 1. ground-plan; 2. outline, sketch.

Grund|satz m principle; **g~sätzlich** fundamental, basic; in principle.

Grund|schule f primary school; **~stein** m: den **~** legen zu etw lay the foundations for s.th.; **~steuer** f real-estate tax; **~stück** n plot of land; **~stücksmakler** m real-estate agent.

Gründung f foundation, establishment.

Grundwasser n ground-water.

Grün|span m verdigris; **~streifen** m grass strip.

Grupp|e f group; **~enbild** n group picture; **g~enweise** in groups; **g~ieren** group, arrange.

gruselig creepy.

Gruß m 1. greeting (aus from), salutation; 2. sagen Sie e-n **~** von mir give my regards (an to).

grüßen say hallo; **~** Sie ihn von mir give him my regards.

Gulasch n goulash.

gültig 1. valid; **~** sein be valid; 2. (jur) in **~er** Form in

due form; **G~keit** f validity;
G~keitsdauer f period of
validity.

Gummi m 1. rubber; 2. (Ra-
dier~) eraser; **~band** n rubber band; **~baum** m rubber
plant; **~boot** n rubber dinghy; **~handschuh** m rubber glove; **~knüppel** m
truncheon; **~schuhe** pl rub-
bers pl; **~stiefel** pl rubber
boot.

Gunst f favour; zu meinen
~en to my credit.

günstig favourable; im ~sten
Falle at best.

Gurgel f throat; **g~n** gurgle.

Gurke f cucumber.

Gurt m belt, strap.

Gürtel m 1. belt; den ~ enger
schnallen tighten o.'s belt;
2. geog zone; **~rose** f med
shingles pl.

Guß m 1. (Regen~) down-
pour; 2. (Wasser) gush,
stream; 3. tech casting;
~eisen n cast iron.

gut I adj 1. good; 2. capable,
efficient; 3. (freundlich)
kind, friendly; ~ zu jdm sein
be good to s.o.; 4. so ~ wie
as good as; schon ~! that's
all right! **II** adv well; es ist ~
möglich, daß it is quite
possible that.

Gut n 1. (Besitz) property;
2. (Güter) goods pl.

Gutacht|en n expert opin-
ion; **~er** m expert.

gutartig good-natured,
harmless.

Gute n good; ich ahne nichts
~s I fear the worst; alles ~!
all the best!

Güte f 1. kindness; 2. (Qualität) quality.

Güter|abfertigung f dis-
patch of goods; **~bahnhof**
m goods station; **~gemein-
schaft** f community of
property.

guterhalten in good condition.

Güter|trennung f separation
of property; **~verkehr** m
goods traffic; **~wagen** m
goods waggon, Am freight
car.

guterzogen well-bred.

Güterzug m goods train, Am
freight train.

gutgehen irr 1. be well;
2. turn out well; **~d** flourishing.

gutgelaunt in good hu-
mo(u)r.

guthaben irr com have to
o.'s credit; **G~** n credit
balance.

gütig kind, good.

gutmütig good-natured.

Gutsbesitzer m estate
owner.

Gutschein m voucher.

gut|schreiben irr: jdm etw ~
credit s.th. to s.o.;
G~schrift f credit entry.

Gutshaus n manor-house.

guttun irr do good.

Gymnastik f gymnastics
sing.

H

Haar n 1. hair; *sich die ~e schneiden lassen* have o.'s hair cut; 2. *sie hat ~e auf den Zähnen* she's a tough customer; *kein gutes ~ an jdm lassen* pull s.o. to pieces; *das ist bei den ~en herbeigezogen* that's far--fetched; ~**bürste** f hairbrush; ~**farbe** f hair colour.

haarig hairy.

Haar|nadel f hairpin; ~**öl** n hair oil; ~**schneiden** n: *bitte, ~!* hair-cut, please; ~**spalterei** f hair-splitting; **h~sträubend** scandalous; ~**trockner** m hair-dryer; ~**waschen** n shampooing; ~**wasser** n hair lotion.

Habe f 1. property, belongings pl; 2. *bewegliche ~* movables pl; *unbewegliche ~* real estate.

haben irr 1. have, possess; 2. *(bekommen)* get; 3. *es schwer ~* have a difficult time; 4. *den wievielten ~ wir heute?* what is the date today? *wir ~ Sommer* it is summer; 5. *das hast du nun davon!* see what you've done! 6. *es hat* there is.

Haben n credit.

Habgier f greediness; **h~ig** greedy.

Habicht m goshawk.

Hack|e f 1. hoe; 2. *(Ferse)* heel; **h~en** 1. hack; 2. *(Holz, Fleisch)* chop; ~**fleisch** n minced meat; ~**messer** n chopper.

Hafen m harbour, port; ~**arbeiter** m docker, Am longshoreman; ~**becken** n harbour basin; ~**stadt** f seaport.

Hafer m oat(s pl); ~**brei** m porridge; ~**flocken** pl oat flakes pl.

Haft f custody; **h~bar** liable *(für* for); *jdn ~ machen für* hold s.o. responsible for; ~**befehl** m warrant of arrest.

haften 1. *(kleben)* stick *(an* to); 2. *(verantwortlich)* be responsible *(für* for).

Haftentlassung f release (from custody).

Häftling m prisoner.

Haft|pflicht f liability; ~**pflichtversicherung** f liability insurance; ~**ung** f 1. responsibility; 2. *jur* liability; *keine ~ übernehmen* accept no liability.

Hagel m hail; ~**korn** n hailstone; **h~n**: *es hagelt* it hails.

hager lean, thin.

Hahn m 1. cock, rooster; 2. *(Wasserhahn)* tap; *den ~ auf-/zudrehen* turn the tap on/off.

Hai(fisch) *m* shark.

häkeln crochet; **H~nadel** *f* crochet-hook.

Haken *m* 1. hook; 2. *die Sache hat e-n ~* there's a snag.

halb 1. half; 2. *e-e ~e Stunde* half an hour; *ein ~es Jahr* six months; *~ soviel* half as much; *um den ~en Preis* at half-price; **~amtlich** semi-official.

halbieren cut in two.

Halb|insel *f* peninsula; **~jahr** *n* six months; **h~jährlich** half-yearly.

Halb|kreis *m* semi-circle; **~kugel** *f* hemisphere; **~messer** *m* radius; **~mond** half-moon.

halbstündlich half-hourly.

Halbtagsarbeit *f* part-time job.

halbwegs to some extent.

Halbzeit *f* sport half(-time).

Halde *f min* dump.

Hälfte *f* half; *um die ~ mehr* half as much again.

Halle *f* 1. hall; 2. *(Hotel)* lounge, lobby.

hallen sound.

Hallenbad *n* indoor swimming-pool.

hallo hallo.

Halm *m* stem, stalk.

Hals *m* 1. neck; *sich den ~ brechen* break o.'s neck; 2. *~ über Kopf* helter-skelter; *es hängt mir zum ~e heraus* I'm sick and tired of it; **~entzündung** *f* sore throat; **~kette** *f* necklace.

Hals-, Nasen- und Ohren|-Arzt *m* otolaryngologist; **~-krankheiten** *pl* diseases of the ear, nose and throat.

Halstuch *n* scarf, muffler.

Halt *m* 1. hold; 2. *(Stütze)* support; 3. *(Festigkeit)* stability; 4. *(Anhalten)* stop.

halt *interj:* ~*!* stop!

haltbar durable, hard-wearing; *~ machen* preserve; **H~keit** *f* 1. durability; 2. *(Lebensmittel)* keeping quality.

halten *irr* 1. hold; *(stützen)* support; 2. *(Niveau)* maintain; 3. *Ordnung ~* keep order; *sein Wort ~* keep o.'s word; 4. *(Rede)* deliver; 5. *(aufhalten)* stop; 6. *jdn ~ für* consider s.o.; *wofür ~ Sie mich?* what do you think I am?; 7. *(verfahren)* do, handle; 8. *etw auf sich ~* have self-respect; 9. *(dauerhaft)* last, wear; 10. *sich ~* keep, wear well; *sich ruhig ~* keep quiet; *sich an etw ~* keep to s.th.; *sich an jdn ~* turn to s.o.; *sich für etw ~* consider o.s. s.th.; *(Gleichgewicht)* keep o.'s balance.

Halter *m* 1. tech holder; 2. *(Inhaber)* holder, *(Eigentümer)* owner.

Halte|stelle *f* stop; **~verbot** *n* "no stopping".

haltlos *(Mensch)* unstable; **H~igkeit** *f* instability.

haltmachen stop, halt.

Haltung *f* 1. *(Körper~)* pos-

ture; 2. *(Stellung)* position;
3. *(Einstellung)* attitude,
opinion.
hämisch malicious, spiteful.
Hammel *m* 1. wether;
2. *(Fleisch)* mutton; **~braten** *m* roast mutton; **~keule** *f* leg of mutton.
Hammer *m* 1. hammer *a.*
sport; 2. *unter den ~ kommen* come under the hammer.
hämmern 1. hammer;
2. *(Herz)* pound, throb.
Hämorrhoiden *pl* haemorrhoids *pl.*
Hampelmann *m* jumping jack.
Hamster *m* hamster; **h~n** hoard.

Hand *f* 1. hand; 2. *(pol) die öffentliche ~* the state;
3. *an ~ von* with the help of;
das liegt auf der ~ that's obvious; *aus erster ~* first-hand; *bei der ~* handy; *jdn bei der ~ nehmen* take s.o. by the hand; *~ in ~ mit* together with; *mit der ~ gemacht* made by hand;
4. *(fig) freie ~ haben* have a free hand; *jdm die ~ geben* shake s.o.'s hand; *weder ~ noch Fuß haben* have neither rhyme nor reason; *die ~ im Spiel haben* have a finger in the pie; **~arbeit** *f*
1. made by hand; 2. *(Nadelarbeit)* needlework, fancywork; **~ball** *m* handball;

~bremse *f* handbrake;
~buch *n* handbook.
Händedruck *m* handshake.
Handel *m* 1. commerce, business, trade, traffic; *~ treiben* trade; 2. *(Geschäft)* deal, transaction.
handeln 1. act; 2. *von etw ~* deal with; 3. *com* trade;
4. *(feilschen)* bargain; 5. *es handelt sich um etw* it is about s.th., it is a question of s.th.; *worum handelt es sich?* what is it about?; *es handelt sich darum, ob* it's a question whether.
Handels|bilanz *f* trade balance; **~bücher** *pl* commercial books; **~geschäft** *n* commercial transaction;
~gesetzbuch *n* Commercial Code; **~kammer** *f* Chamber of Commerce;
~partner *m* trade partner;
~recht *n* commercial law;
~register *n* commercial register; **~schiff** *n* merchant ship; **~spanne** *f* trade margin; **~vertreter** *m* commercial representative.
Hand|fläche *f* palm; **~gelenk** *n* wrist; **~gemenge** *n* scuffle; **~gepäck** *n* hand-luggage.
handgreiflich: *~ werden* become violent.

Handgriff *m* grip, handle.
handhaben handle, operate.
Handhabung *f* handling, management.

Hand|koffer m suitcase; ~**langer** m handyman.

Händler m trader, dealer, merchant; shopkeeper.

handlich handy.

Handlung f 1. act, action, deed; 2. *jur* act; 3. (*e-s Romans*) story; ~**svollmacht** f power of attorney.

Hand|schellen pl handcuffs; ~**schlag** m handshake; ~**schrift** f handwriting; **h~schriftlich** handwritten.

Handschuh m glove; ~**fach** n glove compartment.

Hand|spiegel m hand mirror; ~**tasche** f handbag; ~**tuch** n towel; ~**tuchhalter** m towel-rack.

Handumdrehen n: im ~ in no time.

Hand|voll f handful; ~**wagen** m handcart.

Handwerk n handicraft, trade; *sein* ~ *verstehen* know o.'s business; ~**er** m craftsman, artisan.

Hanf m hemp.

Hang m 1. slope; 2. *fig* inclination, tendency (*zu* to); bent (*zu* for).

Hänge|brücke f suspension bridge; ~**lampe** f hanging lamp; ~**matte** f hammock.

hängen *irr* 1. hang; 2. *an etw* ~ cling to s.th.; *an jdm* ~ be fond of s.o.; 3. *jdn* ~ hang s.o.; *sein Herz an etw* ~ set o.'s heart on s.th.; 4. *sich an etw* ~ hang on to s. th.

hängenbleiben *irr* stick, adhere (*an* to); get caught.

hänseln tease.

Hantel f dump-bell.

hantieren be busy.

Happen m morsel, mouthful; *e-n* ~ *essen* have a bite.

Harfe f harp.

Harke f, **h~n** rake.

harmlos harmless; innocent.

Harmon|ie f harmony; **h~ieren** harmonize (*mit* with); ~**ika** f 1. (*Zieh~*) accordion; 2. (*Mund~*) mouth-organ; **h~isch** harmonious; ~**ium** n harmonium.

Harn m urine; ~**blase** f (urinary) bladder; ~**röhre** f urethra.

Harpun|e f, **h~ieren** f harpoon.

harren wait (*auf* for).

hart I *adj* 1. hard, firm, solid; 2. (*Ei*) hard-boiled; 3. (*Charakter*) hard, harsh, severe; **II** *adv*: ~ *arbeiten* work hard; *es ging* ~ *auf* ~ it was a fight to the finish.

Härte f 1. hardness; solidity, firmness; 2. *fig* severity, harshness.

Hartgeld n hard cash.

hart|herzig hard-hearted; ~**näckig** obstinate, stubborn; **H~näckigkeit** f obstinacy, stubbornness.

Harz n resin.

Hase m hare, *Am* rabbit.

Haselnuß f hazel-nut.

Hasen|braten m roast hare; ~**scharte** f harelip.

Haß *m* hate, hatred (*gegen* of, for).

hassen hate; detest.

häßlich ugly.

Hast *f* hurry; *in größter* ~ in great haste; **h~en** hurry, hasten; **h~ig** hasty.

Haube *f* bonnet; cap.

Hauch *m* 1. breath; 2. (*Parfüm*) whiff; 3. *fig* trace, touch; **h~en** breathe (*auf* on).

hauen *fam* strike, beat; *er ist übers Ohr gehauen worden* he's been stung.

Haufen *m* pile, heap.

häufen heap up, pile up, amass.

haufenweise in great quantities, in heaps.

häufig frequent, often; **H~keit** *f* frequency.

Haupt *n* head; **~bahnhof** *m* main station; **~beruf** *m* main profession; **~eingang** *m* main entrance; **~fach** *n* (*Schule*) main subject, *Am* major; **~film** *m* feature (film).

Häuptling *m* chieftain.

Haupt|mahlzeit *f* main meal; **~mann** *m* captain; **~mieter** *m* principal tenant; **~probe** *f theat* dress rehearsal; **~punkt** *m* main point; **~quartier** *n* headquarters *pl*; **~rolle** *f* leading part, lead; **~sache** *f* main thing; **h~sächlich** mainly, chiefly; **~stadt** *f* capital; **~straße** *f* main

street; **~verkehrszeit** *f* peak, rush hour(s) *pl*.

Haus *n* 1. house; 2. (*Wohnung*) home; *nach* ~e *gehen* go home; *zu* ~e *at* home; *im* ~e indoors; *frei* ~ free domicile; 3. *com* firm; **~angestellter** *m* domestic; **~arbeit** *f* housework; **~arzt** *m* family doctor; **~aufgabe** *f* homework.

Häuschen *n* 1. cottage; 2. *aus dem* ~ *sein* be beside o.s.

Haus|eigentümer *m* house-owner; **h~en** live.

Häuserblock *m* block.

Haus|flur *m* (entrance-)hall; **~frau** *f* housewife; **~halt** *m* 1. household; *den* ~ *führen* keep house; 2. (*Haushaltung*) housekeeping; 3. (*Staats*~) finances *pl*; budget; **h~halten** *irr* 1. keep house (*für jdn* for s.o.); 2. (*sparsam sein*) be economical; husband (*s-e Kräfte* o.'s resources); **~hälterin** *f* housekeeper; **~haltsgeld** *n* housekeeping money; **~haltsjahr** *n* (*Staat*) budgetary year; **~herrin** *f* mistress of the house.

haushoch: ~ *gewinnen* win hands down; ~ *verlieren* lose disastrously.

hausier|en hawk, peddle; **H~er** *m* hawker, pedlar.

Hauslehrer *m* private tutor.

häuslich 1. domestic; home-

-loving; 2. *sich ~ einrichten* settle down.

Haus|meister *m* caretaker, janitor; **~nummer** *f* house number; **~ordnung** *f* house rules *pl;* **~schlüssel** *m* front-door key; **~schuhe** *pl* slippers *pl;* **~suchung** *f* house search; **~suchungs-befehl** *m* search-warrant; **~telefon** *n* interphone *(Betrieb)* intercom(munication); **~tier** *n* domestic animal; **~tür** *f* front-door; **~wirtin** *f* landlady.

Haut *f* 1. skin; 2. *(Tier)* hide; **~arzt** *m* dermatologist.

Häutchen *n* membrane.

Hautcreme *f* skin cream.

häuten, *sich* cast o.'s skin.

Hautfarbe *f (Gesicht)* complexion.

Hebamme *f* midwife.

Hebebock *m* (lifting-)jack.

Hebel *m* lever; *alle ~ in Bewegung setzen* move heaven and earth.

heben *irr* 1. lift; 2. *(Hand)* raise; 3. *(hochwinden)* hoist; 4. *(verbessern)* improve; *(steigern)* increase; 5. *sich ~* rise.

Hecht *m* pike.

Heck *n* 1. *mar* stern; 2. *aero* tail; 3. *mot* rear.

Hecke *f* hedge; **~nschere** *f* hedge-shears *pl.*

Heckmotor *m* rear engine.

Heer *n* army.

Hefe *f* yeast.

Heft *n* 1. *(Griff)* handle;

2. copy-book; 3. *(Zeitschrift)* number; **h~en** fasten, attach *(an to)*; pin s.th.

heftig 1. violent; 2. **~e** *Schmerzen* severe pains; 3. *(jähzornig)* hot-tempered; *~ werden* lose o.'s temper; **H~keit** *f* 1. violence; 2. hot temper.

Heft|pflaster *n* adhesive plaster; **~zwecke** *f* drawing-pin, *Am* thumb-tack.

hegen 1. *(Wild)* preserve; 2. *(Zweifel)* entertain.

Hehl *n: kein ~ machen aus etw* make no secret of s.th.; **~er** *m* receiver (of stolen goods).

Heide 1. *m* heathen; 2. *f* heath.

Heidelbeere *f* bilberry, *Am* blueberry.

heidnisch heathen, pagan.

heikel *(Angelegenheit)* delicate, awkward.

Heil *n* 1. welfare; 2. *sein ~ versuchen* try o.'s luck.

heil 1. *(unverletzt)* unhurt; 2. *(ganz)* undamaged.

Heil|bad *n* health resort; **h~bar** curable.

heilen 1. cure *(von* of); 2. *(Wunde)* heal.

Heilgymnastik *f* physiotherapy.

heilig 1. sacred, holy; *der H~e Abend* Christmas Eve; **~e** *Elisabeth* Saint (St) Elisabeth; 2. *etw hoch und ~ versprechen* promise s.th.

faithfully; **H~e** f saint;
H~tum n sanctuary.

Heil|kräuter pl medicinal
herbs pl; **~mittel** n medicine, remedy; **~praktiker** m
non-medical practitioner;
~quelle f mineral spring.

heilsam 1. wholesome,
healthful; 2. (Rat) salutary;
3. med curative.

Heilung f healing, cure.

Heim n home; **~arbeit** f
home-work.

Heimat f home, homeland,
native country; **h~lich** of
o.'s native land; **h~los**
homeless; **~recht** n right of
citizenship.

heim|bringen irr: jdn ~ see
s.o. home; **~fahren** irr
1. travel, drive home; 2. jdn
~ take s.o. home (by car);
H~fahrt f return; **~gehen**
irr go home.

heimisch 1. (Erzeugnis)
domestic, home; 2. (Tier)
native, indigenous; 3. ~ werden acclimatize o.s. (in to);
4. sich ~ fühlen feel at
home.

Heim|kehr f return (home);
~leiter m warden.

heimlich 1. secret, clandes-
tine; 2. sich ~ treffen meet
secretly.

heimsuchen 1. (Unglück)
afflict, strike; 2. (Ungeziefer)
infest; 3. (Seuchen) visit.

heimtückisch insidious;
treacherous.

Heim|weg m: auf dem ~ on

the way home; **~weh** n
homesickness.

Heirat f marriage; **h~en**
marry, get married; **~sur-
kunde** f marriage certificate.

heiser hoarse; **H~keit** f
hoarseness.

heiß 1. hot; 2. fig ardent,
burning.

heißen irr 1. be called; 2. (bedeuten) mean, signify; 3. das
heißt that is; es heißt it is
said, it says; 4. wie heißen
Sie? what is your name?

heißlaufen irr tech run hot.

Heißwasserbereiter m
water heater.

heiter 1. bright, clear; 2. (vergnügt) cheerful, gay;
H~keit f brightness; cheerfulness.

heizen heat.

Heiz|kissen n heating pad;
~körper m radiator; **~ofen**
m heater; **~öl** n fuel oil;
~platte f hot-plate; **~son-
ne** f bowl-fire; **~ung** f (central) heating.

Hektar m hectare.

hektisch hectic.

Held m hero; **h~enhaft**
heroic; **~entum** n heroism.

helfen irr help, assist, aid;
(fördern) promote; (nützen)
be of use; sich zu ~ wissen
know what to do.

hell 1. bright; 2. (Stimme)
clear; 3. (Farbe) light, pale;
~blau light-blue; **~blond**
light-blond.

Helligkeit *f* clearness.
Hellseher *m* clairvoyant.
Helm *m* helmet.
Hemd *n* shirt; **~särmel** *m: in ~n* in o.'s shirt-sleeves.
hemm|en 1. check, stop; 2. *(behindern)* hamper; 3. *(verlangsamen)* slow down; **H~ung** *f* inhibition, suppression; *keine ~en haben* have no scruples; **~ungslos** without restraint.
Hengst *m* stallion.
Henkel *m* handle.
Henker *m* hangman.
Henne *f* hen.
her 1. *(zeitlich)* ago; *es ist zwei Jahre ~, daß* it is two years ago since; 2. *von weit ~* from far away; 3. *~ damit!* give it to me!
herab down, downwards; *von oben ~* from above; **~fallen** *irr* fall down; **~lassen** *irr* 1. let down; 2. *sich ~* condescend to s.th.; **~setzen** 1. *(Preis)* reduce, lower; 2. *(Personen)* belittle, disparage.
heran near, close; *~ an* near to; **~fahren** *irr* pull to; **~kommen** *irr* 1. approach, draw near; 2. *dicht an etw ~* come right up to s.th.; **~reichen** reach up *(an* to); **~treten** *irr* step up *(an* to); **~wachsen** *irr* 1. grow up; 2. *die ~de Generation* the rising generation; **H~wachsender** *m* adolescent; **~ziehen** *irr* 1. *(zur*

Hilfe) consult, call in; 2. *(Stuhl)* draw up.
herauf 1. up, upwards; 2. *die Treppe ~* upstairs; **~beschwören** *irr* 1. evoke, call up; 2. *fig (verursachen)* give rise to, provoke; **~kommen** *irr* come up.
heraus out *(aus* of); *von innen ~* from within; **~arbeiten** *fig* work out; **~bekommen** *irr* 1. get out; 2. *(Geheimnis)* find out; 3. *(Geld)* get change; **~bringen** *irr* 1. bring out; 2. *(Buch)* publish; 3. *(auf den Markt)* put on the market; **~fahren** *irr* 1. drive out; 2. *(Wort)* slip out; **~finden** *irr* find out; **~fordern** challenge; provoke; **~fordernd** challenging; provoking; **H~forderung** *f* provocation; *die ~ annehmen* accept the challenge.
herausgeb|en *irr* 1. *(Buch)* publish, edit; 2. *(Geld)* give change; 3. *(Sache)* hand over, give up, deliver; **H~er** *m* editor; publisher.
heraus|gehen *irr (Fleck)* come out; **~holen** take out *(aus* from); **~kommen** *irr* 1. come out *(aus* of); 2. *aus Schwierigkeiten ~* get out of o.'s difficulties; 3. *com* come out; 4. *es kommt nichts dabei heraus* nothing will come of it; **~nehmen** *irr* 1. *etw aus etw ~* take s.th. out of s.th.; 2. *sich etw ~*

take liberties; **~reden,** *sich* talk o.'s way out; **~reißen** *irr* tear out, pull out; **~stellen** 1. *etw* ~ put s.th. out; 2. *fig* present clearly; 3. *sich* ~ turn out (*als ein Irrtum* to be a mistake); *sich als wahr* ~ prove to be true; **~ziehen** *irr* pull, draw out.

herb 1. *(Wein)* dry; 2. *(Frucht)* tart; 3. *(streng)* austere.

herbei here; near; **~eilen** come hurrying up; **~führen** *fig* bring about, give rise to.

Herberge *f* hostel; inn.

herbringen *irr* bring here.

Herbst *m* autumn, *Am* fall; **h~lich** autumnal.

Herd *m* 1. stove; 2. *fig* home, hearth; 3. *(Zentrum)* focus, centre.

Herde *f* 1. *(Vieh~)* herd; 2. *(Schafe)* flock.

herein 1. in; 2. ~! come in! **~fallen** *irr fig* be taken in (*auf etw* by s.th.); *auf etw* ~ fall for s.th.; **~holen** fetch in; **~kommen** *irr* come in; **~lassen** *irr* let in; **~legen**: *jdn* ~ take s.o. in; **~regnen**: *es regnet herein* it is raining in.

herfallen *irr: über jdn* ~ attack s.o.

Hergang *m* course of events.

hergeben *irr* 1. give away; 2. *s-n Namen zu etw* ~ lend o.'s name to s.th.

Hering *m* herring.

herkommen *irr* 1. come here; 2. *(herstammen)* come from.

Herkunft *f* 1. origin, birth; 2. *(e-r Sache)* provenance.

hero|isch heroic; **H~ismus** *m* heroism.

Herr *m* 1. gentleman; 2. ~ *X* Mr. *X*; *mein* ~! sir! 3. *(Gebieter)* master; 4. *(rel) der* ~ God, the Lord; **~enbekleidung** *f* men's clothing; **~enfriseur** *m* barber, men's hairdresser; **~enhaus** *n* manor-house; **h~enlos** 1. *(Sache)* abandoned; 2. *(Tier)* stray.

herrichten prepare, arrange.

Herrin *f* mistress, lady.

herrisch imperious, commanding.

herrlich magnificent, wonderful; **H~heit** *f* magnificence, splendo(u)r.

Herrschaft *f* 1. rule, power (*über* over); 2. *(Monarch)* reign; 3. control; 4. *meine* ~*en!* ladies and gentlemen.

herrschen 1. rule (*über* over), govern; reign; 2. *es herrschte schlechtes Wetter* the weather was bad; 3. *(verbreitet sein)* prevail, rage.

Herrscher *m* ruler; sovereign; monarch.

herrschsüchtig greedy for power.

her|rufen *irr: jdn* ~ call s.o. over; **~rühren** come from; **~sagen** recite; **~sehen** *irr* look over; **~stellen**

1. make, produce; 2. (*Verbindungen*) establish;
H~steller *m* manufacturer, producer; **H~stellung** *f* 1. *com* manufacture, production; 2. *fig* establishment.
herüber over here, across.
herum about; (a)round; **~bummeln** stroll about; **~drehen** turn round; **~führen** show around; **~gehen** *irr* walk around; **~kommen** *irr* 1. *um etw ~* come round s.th.; 2. (*reisen*) get around; **~laufen** *irr* run about; **~liegen** *irr* lie scattered around; **~reichen** hand round; **~sprechen** *irr: sich ~* get about, be spread; **~stehen** *irr* stand about; **~treiben** *irr: sich ~* knock around, gad about.
herunter down; off; **~bringen** *irr* bring down; **~fallen** *irr* fall down; **~holen** fetch down; **~kommen** *irr* 1. come down; 2. (*Geschäft*) go to rack and ruin; **~schlucken** swallow.
hervor forth, out of; **~bringen** *irr* 1. (*erzeugen*) produce; 2. (*äußern*) utter; **~gehen** *irr* 1. come out of; 2. (*Folge*) follow; *daraus geht hervor, daß* that shows that; **~heben** *irr* 1. emphasize, stress; 2. (*sich abheben*) stand out; **~ragend** prominent, excellent, outstanding; **~rufen** *irr* (*bewirken*) cause, bring about,

evoke; **~tun**: *sich ~* distinguish o.s.
Herz *n* heart; *sich ein ~ fassen* take heart; *ein ~ und eine Seele sein* be of one and the same mind; **~anfall** *m* heart attack; **~beschwerden** *pl* heart trouble; **~enslust** *f*: *nach ~* to o.s.'s heart's content; **~infarkt** *m* cardiac infarction; **~klopfen** *n med* palpitation (of the heart).
herz|lich 1. cordial, hearty; 2. (*Brief*) *~e Grüße* kind regards; 3. *~ gern* with pleasure; **~los** heartless, unfeeling.
Herzog *m* duke; **~in** *f* duchess.
Herz|schlag *m* heartbeat; **~schrittmacher** *m* cardiac pace-maker; **h~zerreißend** heart-rending.
Hetze *f* 1. (*Eile*) hurry, rush; 2. *~ gegen jdn* agitation against s.o.; **h~n** 1. *fig* agitate (*gegen* against); 2. (*eilen*) rush, hurry; 3. *den Hund auf jdn ~* set the dog on s.o.
Heu *n* hay; *~ machen* hay; **~boden** *m* hayloft.
Heuch|elei *f* hypocrisy; **h~eln** feign, simulate; **~ler** *m* hypocrite; **h~lerisch** hypocritical.
Heu|ernte *f* hay-harvest; **~haufen** *m* haycock.
heulen 1. (*Wind*) howl, roar; 2. (*Kind*) bawl.
Heu|schnupfen *m* hay fe-

ver; **~schrecke** f grasshopper.

heut|e today; *~ früh* this morning; *~ abend* this evening, tonight; *~ in einem Jahr* a year from today; *~ vor einer Woche* a week ago today; *~ nacht* tonight; *(vergangene Nacht)* last night; **~ig** of today, today's; **~zutage** nowadays.

Hexe f witch; **~nschuß** m lumbago; **~rei** f witchcraft.

Hieb m blow, stroke.

hier 1. *(örtlich)* here; *~ und dort* here and there; *dieser ~* this one here; 2. *(zeitlich)* now; *~ und da* now and then; **~auf** hereupon, after that; **~bleiben** *irr* stay here; **~her**: *bis ~ (örtlich)* thus far; *(zeitlich)* up to now; **~mit** herewith, hereby.

hiesig local, here.

Hilfe f help, assistance; *mit ~ von* with the aid of; *jdn um ~ bitten* ask for s.o.'s help; *jdm zu ~ kommen* come to s.o.'s aid; *um ~ rufen* cry for help; *Erste ~* first aid; **~ruf** m cry for help.

hilf|los helpless; **~reich** helpful.

Hilfs|arbeiter m unskilled worker; **h~bedürftig** needy; **h~bereit** ready to help, helpful; **~dienst** m mot roadside assistance service; **~kraft** f helper, assistant; **~maßnahmen** pl remedial measure; **~mittel**

n aids pl, facility; **~motor** m: mit ~ motor-assisted.

Himbeere f raspberry.

Himmel m sky; firmament, heaven; *am ~* in the sky; *unter freiem ~* in the open air; *um ~s willen!* good heavens! **h~blau** sky-blue; **~fahrt** f: *Christi ~* Ascension Day; *Mariä ~* Assumption Day; **~srichtung** f direction, cardinal point.

himmlisch 1. heavenly; 2. *(göttlich)* divine.

hin 1. *auf die Gefahr ~* at the risk of; 2. *bis zu etw ~ (räumlich)* as far as s.th., *(zeitlich)* till s.th.; *zu etw ~* towards s.th.; 3. *~ und her* to and fro; *~ und zurück* there and back; *eine Fahrkarte ~ und zurück* a return ticket.

hinab downward(s).

hinauf upward(s); **~fahren** *irr* drive, travel up; **~gehen** *irr* 1. go, walk up; 2. *die Treppe ~* go upstairs; 3. *(Preise)* rise; **~setzen** *(Preise)* raise, mark up.

hinaus 1. out(side); *hier ~* this way out; *aufs Meer ~* out to sea; 2. *(zeitlich)* beyond; *auf Jahre ~* for years to come; **~begleiten**: *jdn ~* see s.o. out; **~gehen** *irr* 1. go out; 2. *(Fenster)* face, look out; 3. *über etw ~* go beyond s.th.; **~lassen** *irr* let out *(jdn s.o.)*; **~lehnen**: *nicht ~!* do not lean out of

the window! **~ragen**
1. tower up (*über etw* over
s.th.); 2. *fig* be far superior
(*über* to); **~schieben** *irr*
put off, postpone; **~werfen**
irr throw out; **~wollen** *irr*:
auf etw ~ be driving at s.th.

Hinblick *m: im ~ auf* in view
of, with reference to.

hinder|lich 1. impeding;
2. (*lästig*) cumbersome; 3. ~
sein be in the way; **~n** stop,
hamper, hinder.

Hindernis *n* 1. obstacle;
2. (*Schranke*) barrier;
3. (*Schwierigkeit*) difficulty;
~rennen *n* steeplechase.

hindurch 1. (*räumlich*)
through; 2. (*zeitlich*) *die
ganze Nacht ~* all through
the night.

hinein into, in; *bis in die
Nacht ~* till into the night;
~finden *irr: sich ~* familiarize o.s. with; **~gehen** *irr*
1. enter, go into; 2. (*fassen*)
hold; **~geraten** *irr: in etw ~*
get caught in s.th.; **~passen**
fit in; **~stecken** 1. put
in(to); 2. *er steckt s-e Nase
überall hinein* he pokes his
nose into everything.

Hinfahrt *f* journey there;
(*Fahrkarte*) single.

hin|fallen *irr* fall (down);
h~fällig 1. (*ungültig*) invalid; 2. (*gebrechlich*) frail.

Hinflug *m* outward flight.

hinführen lead, take (to).

Hingabe *f* devotion, dedica-
tion.

hingegen whereas, but,
however.

hin|gehen *irr* walk, go there;
~halten *irr* 1. hold out;
2. *jdn ~* keep s.o. waiting;
~hören listen.

hinken limp; **~d** (*Vergleich*)
lame.

hin|länglich sufficiently; **~le-
gen** 1. lay, put down; 2. *sich
~* lie down; **~nehmen** *irr*
take, accept.

hinreichend sufficient.

hinreißen *irr: sich ~ lassen*
let o.s. be carried away; **~d**
enchanting, captivating.

hinricht|en execute; **H~ung**
f execution.

hinsehen *irr* look over
to(wards).

Hinsicht *f: in dieser ~* in this
respect; *in jeder ~* in every
respect, in every way; *in gewisser ~* in certain ways;
h~lich with regard to, with
respect to.

hinstellen put down, place
there.

hinten 1. behind, at the back;
sich ~ anstellen queue up;
2. *nach ~* backwards; *von ~*
from behind.

hinter (*örtlich und zeitlich*)
behind; *jdn ~ sich lassen*
leave s.o. behind.

Hinter|achse *f* rear axle;
~bliebenen *pl jur* surviving
dependents.

hinter|e rear, back; **~einan-
der** 1. one behind the other;

2. *dreimal* ~ three times in succession.
Hintergedanke *m* ulterior motive.
hintergehen *irr* deceive.
Hinter|grund *m: im* ~ in the background; **~halt** *m* ambush; *im* ~ *liegen* lie in wait; **h~hältig** perfidious; **~haus** *n* house at the back.
hinterher 1. *(örtlich)* after, behind; 2. *(zeitlich)* afterwards.
Hinterkopf *m* back of the head.
hinter|lassen *irr* 1. *(Eindruck)* leave; 2. *jdm etw* ~ bequeath s.th. to s.o., leave s.o. s.th.; **~legen** deposit.
Hinterlist *f* deceit, cunning; **h~ig** deceitful, cunning.
Hinter|rad *n* backwheel; **~tür** *f* back door.
hinterziehen *irr (Steuern)* evade.
hinüber *(örtlich)* over (there); to the other side; **~gehen** *irr* go over, walk across.
Hin- und Rückfahrkarte *f* return ticket.
hinunter down; downwards; *(Treppe)* downstairs; **~bringen** *irr: etw* ~ take s.th. down; **~gehen** *irr* go, walk down; **~schlucken** swallow.
Hinweg *m* way there.
hinweg|gehen *irr: über etw* ~ pass over s.th.; **~kommen** *irr* get over *(etw* s.th.);

~setzen: *sich über etw* ~ ignore s.th.
Hinweis *m* 1. *(Rat)* hint, advice; 2. *(Wink)* tip; 3. *(Andeutung)* indication; **h~en** *irr: auf etw* ~ point to s.th., indicate s.th.; *jdn auf etw* ~ draw s.o.'s attention to s.th.
hinzu|fügen add; **~kommen** *irr* 1. come up to; 2. *(von Gegenständen)* be added; **~ziehen** *irr: e-n Spezialisten* ~ call in a specialist.
Hirn *n* brain; **~gespinst** *n* fantasy.
Hirsch *m* stag; **~kuh** *f* hind.
Hirse *f* millet.
Hirte *m* shepherd.
hissen hoist, haul up.
historisch historical.
Hitze *f* heat, hot weather; **~ewelle** *f* heat-wave; **h~ig** 1. hot-headed; 2. *(heftig)* violent; **~schlag** *m* heat-stroke.
Hobel *m*, **h~n** plane; **~späne** *pl* shavings *pl.*
hoch I *adj* 1. *(oben)* high; *50 Meter* ~ 50 metres high; 2. *(Wuchs)* tall; 3. *(Ansehen, Fieber)* high, great; 4. *ein hohes Alter* a great age; 5. *(Strafe)* heavy; **II** *adv* 6. ~ *oben* high up; ~ *liegen* lie at a high level; 7. *es ging* ~ *her* it was quite an affair; **H~** *n* 1. *ein dreifaches* ~ *für* three cheers for; 2. *(Wetter)* high(-pressure) area.
Hochachtung *f* respect, es-

teem; **h~svoll** yours faithfully.

Hoch|amt n High Mass; **~bahn** f elevated railway; **~betrieb** m great activity, rush; **h~deutsch** standard German; **~druck** m high pressure; **~ebene** f geog plateau; **h~empfindlich** highly sensitive; **~gebirge** n high mountains; **~genuß** m great delight; **~haus** n skyscraper.

Hoch|konjunktur f boom; **~leistung** f great performance; **~mut** m arrogance; **h~mütig** arrogant, haughty; **~ofen** m blast-furnace; **~parterre** n raised ground floor; **~ruf** m cheer; **~saison** f peak season; **~see** f the open sea; **~sommer** m midsummer; **~spannung** f 1. el high voltage; 2. fig high tension; **~spannungsleitung** f high-voltage transmission line; **~sprung** m high jump.

höchst 1. highest; 2. auf ~er Ebene at the highest level; es ist ~e Zeit it is high time; **H~alter** n maximum age.

Hochstapler m confidence man, swindler.

Höchste n utmost.

höchstens at the most.

Höchst|geschwindigkeit f maximum speed, speed limit; **~grenze** f maximum limit; ceiling; **~leistung** f maximum performance;

h~wahrscheinlich most probably.

Hoch|verrat m high treason; **~wasser** n flood.

Hochzeit f wedding, marriage; **~sreise** f honeymoon.

hock|en squat; **H~er** m stool.

Höcker m hump.

Hoden m testicle; **~sack** m scrotum.

Hof m 1. yard; 2. (Innenhof) courtyard; 3. agr farm; 4. (Mond) halo.

hoff|en hope (auf etw for s.th.); **~entlich** it is to be hoped; **H~nung** f hope; in der ~, daß in the hope of; sich ~en machen have hopes; **~nungslos** hopeless; **~nungsvoll** hopeful, promising.

Hofhund m watch-dog.

höflich polite, courteous; **H~keit** f politeness, courtesy.

Höhe f 1. heigh; aero altitude; 2. lichte ~ headway; 3. in die ~ up into the air; in die ~ springen jump up; 4. auf gleicher ~ abreast; 5. in ~ von to an amount of.

Hoheit f sovereignty; (Titel) Highness; **~sgewässer** pl territorial waters.

Höhen|krankheit f altitude sickness; **~kurort** m mountain health resort; **~messer** m aero altimeter; **~sonne** f: künstliche ~ sun-ray lamp.

Höhepunkt m 1. climax, height, peak; 2. *(der Macht)* peak, zenith.

höher 1. higher; 2. *immer ~* higher and higher.

hohl 1. hollow; 2. *fig* empty.

Höhle f 1. cave, cavern; 2. *(Augen~)* socket.

Hohl|maß n measure of capacity; **~raum** m cavity.

Hohn m derision, scorn.

höhnisch scornful.

holen 1. *(herbringen)* get, fetch; 2. *(herbeirufen)* call for; *~ lassen* send for; 3. *sich etw ~* catch s.th.

Holland n the Netherlands.

Holländ|er m Dutchman; **h~isch** Dutch.

Hölle f hell; inferno; *Himmel und ~ in Bewegung setzen* move heaven and earth; **~enmaschine** f time bomb; **h~isch** infernal, devilish.

holp(e)rig *(Weg)* rough, uneven.

Holunder m elder.

Holz n 1. wood; 2. *(Nutz~)* timber, *Am* lumber.

hölzern wooden.

Holz|fäller m woodcutter, *Am* lumberjack; **~faser** f wood fibre; **~hammer** m mallet; **~handlung** f timber firm; **~haus** n timber house.

holzig woody.

Holz|klotz m wooden block; **~kohle** f charcoal; **~schnitt** m woodcut; **~schuh** m clog; **~stapel** m, **~stoß** m woodpile; **~weg** m: *auf dem ~ sein* be on the wrong track; **~wolle** f wood-wool; **~wurm** m woodworm.

homosexuell homosexual.

Honig m honey.

Honor|ar n fee, royalties *pl;* **h~ieren** 1. pay a fee; 2. *com (Scheck)* honour, cash a cheque.

Hopfen m hop.

hörbar audible.

hören 1. hear; 2. *(zuhorchen)* listen to; 3. *auf den Namen ... ~* answer to the name of ...; 4. *(erfahren)* learn, understand; 5. *sich ~ lassen* sound good; 6. *etw von jdm ~* hear s.th. of s.o.

Hörensagen n: *vom ~* from hearsay.

Hör|er m 1. listener; 2. *tele* receiver; **~fehler** m error in hearing; **~funk** m sound broadcasting; **~gerät** n hearing aid.

Horizont m horizon; *am ~* on the horizon; **h~al** horizontal.

Hormon n hormone.

Horn n 1. horn; 2. *mus* horn; *(Jagd~)* bugle; **~haut** f 1. horny skin; 2. *(Auge)* cornea.

Hornisse f hornet.

Horoskop n: *ein ~ stellen* cast a horoscope.

Hör|saal m lecture hall, auditorium; **~spiel** n radio play.

Hort m 1. day-nursery;

2. *(Zuflucht)* safe retreat, shelter; **h~en** 1. hoard up; 2. *(Rohstoffe)* stockpile.

Hörweite *f: außer ~* out of earshot.

Hose *f* (a pair of) trousers *pl*, pants *pl*; *(Freizeit)* slacks *pl*; **~nanzug** *m* trouser suit; **~nbein** *n* trouser leg; **~ntasche** *f* trouser pocket; **~nträger** *n* (pair of) braces *pl*, *Am* suspenders *pl*.

Hospital *n* hospital.

Hotel *n* hotel; **~besitzer** *m* hotel owner; **~boy** *m* page(-boy), *Am* bellboy; **~zimmer** *n* hotel room.

Hubraum *m* cubic capacity.

hübsch pretty, nice, good--looking.

Hubschrauber *m* helicopter.

Huf *m* hoof; **~eisen** *n* horse-shoe.

Hüfte *f* hip; **~gelenk** *n* hip--joint; **~halter** *m* suspender belt.

Hügel *m* hill, hillock; **h~ig** hilly.

Huhn *n* chicken, hen.

Hühner|auge *n* corn; **~brühe** *f* chicken broth; **~hof** *m* chicken yard; **~stall** *m* hen--house; **~suppe** *f* chicken soup.

Huld *f* favour.

Hülle *f* 1. wrapper; 2. *(Brief~)* envelope; 3. *(Buch~)* cover; 4. *(Schallplatte)* jacket; 5. *in ~ und Fülle* in abundance, plenty of; **h~n** 1. *etw in etw ~*

wrap s.th. in s.th.; 2. *sich in Schweigen ~* wrap o.s. in silence.

Hülse *f* 1. *bot* husk, hull; 2. *tech* tube, sleeve, case, cap; **~nfrüchte** *pl* pulse.

human 1. humane; 2. *~ behandeln* treat decently; **~itär** humanitarian; **H~ität** *f* humanity; **H~medizin** *f* human medicine.

Hummel *f* bumble-bee.

Hummer *m* lobster.

Humor *m* humo(u)r; *~ haben* have a sense of humour; *etw mit ~ ertragen* take s.th. good-humouredly; **h~voll** humorous.

humpeln limp, hobble.

Hund *m* dog; *(Jagd~)* hound; **~ehütte** *f* kennel; **h~emüde** dog-tired.

hundert hundred; *etwa ~ Menschen* about a hundred people.

Hundert *n* hundred; *fünf von ~* five per cent; *zu ~en* in hundreds.

hundertfach hundredfold; a hundred times.

Hundertste *m* hundredth; **~l** *n* hundredth (part).

hunderttausend a one hundred thousand.

Hündin *f* bitch.

Hundstage *pl* dog-days, canicular days.

Hunger *m* hunger *a. fig*; *~ leiden* suffer from hunger; **h~n** starve, go hungry; **~snot** *f: es herrscht große*

~ there's a severe famine;
~**streik** *m: in den* ~ *treten*
go on hunger-strike.
hungrig*:* ~ *sein* be hungry.
Hupe *f mot* horn; **h~n** sound
the horn, hoot, honk.
hüpfen hop, skip, jump.
Hürde *f* 1. *sport* hurdle; 2. *fig*
obstacle; ~**nlauf** *m* hurdle-
race.
hurra hurrah, hooray.
huschen scurry, flit, whisk.
hüsteln cough a little.
husten cough; **H~** *m* cough;
H~mittel *n* cough remedy.
Hut 1. *m* hat; *den* ~ *aufsetzen* put on o.'s hat; 2. *f*
guard; *auf der* ~ *sein* be on
o.'s guard.

hüten 1. *(Schafe)* tend;
2. *(Geheimnis)* keep; 3. *das
Bett* ~ stay in bed; 4. *sich* ~,

etw zu tun take care not to
do s.th.; 5. *sich* ~ *vor* watch
out for, beware of.
Hutmacher *m* milliner.
Hütte *f* hut, log-cabin.
Hyäne *f* hyena.
Hyazinthe *f* hyacinth.
Hydrant *m* hydrant.
Hygiene *f* hygiene; **h~isch**
hygienic.
Hymne *f* hymn.
Hyperbel *f* hyperbola.
Hypnose *f* hypnosis; **h~ti-
sieren** hypnotize.
Hypothek *f* mortgage; *eine*
~ *auf etw aufnehmen* raise
a mortgage on s.th.; *etw mit
einer* ~ *belasten* mortgage
s.th.
Hypothese *f* hypothesis;
h~thetisch hypothetical.
Hysterie *f* hysteria; **h~isch**
hysterical.

I

ich I; ~ *selbst* I myself; ~ *bin es* it is I, it's me.

ideal ideal.

Ideal *n* ideal; **~ismus** *m* idealism; **~ist** *m* idealist; **i~istisch** idealistic.

Idee *f* 1. idea, thought; 2. *(ein wenig)* a little bit, a trifle.

ident|ifizieren identify; **~isch** identical; **I~ität** *f* identity.

Idiot *m* idiot; **i~isch** idiotic.

Idyll *n* idyll; **i~isch** idyllic.

Igel *m* hedgehog.

Ignor|ant *m* blockhead, ignoramus; **i~ieren** ignore, overlook.

ihm (to) him; *das Auto gehört ~* the car belongs to him; *ein Freund von ~* a friend of his.

ihn *(Person)* him; *(Dinge)* it.

ihnen (to) them; *das Haus gehört ~* the house is theirs; **I~** *dat von Sie* to you.

ihr I *pers prn* you; *was wollt ~?* what do you want?; **II** *pers prn (dat von sie)* 1. (to) her; *sie hat es ~ gesagt* she told her; 2. *(Sache)* (to) it; **III** *posses prn 3 sg:* 3. ~ *Vater* her father; 4. *(Sache)* its; 5. *(Brief)* your; **IV** *posses prn 3 pl* their; *einer ~er Freunde* one of their friends; **V** 6. *I~e, der, die,*

das: posses prn hers; theirs; 7. *die I ~ (ig)en* her family.

illeg|al illegal; **~itim** illegitimate.

Illus|ion *f*: *sich ~en machen* have illusions *(über* about); **i~orisch** illusory.

Illustr|ation *f* illustration; **i~iert** illustrated; **~ierte** *f* magazine.

Imbiß *m* snack; **~stube** *f* snack bar.

Imker *m* bee-keeper.

immer 1. always; 2. *(jedesmal)* every time; 3. ~ *noch* still; ~ *noch nicht* not yet; 4. ~ *wieder* again and again; 5. ~ *schwieriger* increasingly difficult; **~hin** 1. nevertheless, after all, anyway; 2. *(wenigstens)* at least; **~zu** all the time, continuously.

Immobilien *pl* immovables *pl*; real estate.

immun immune *(gegen* to, against).

impf|en inoculate; *(Pocken)* vaccinate; *sich ~ lassen* get an inoculation; **I~ung** *f* vaccination.

imponieren: *jdm ~* impress s.o.

Import *m* import; **i~ieren** import.

impotent impotent.

imprägnieren waterproof.

improvisieren improvise.

Impuls *m* impulse, impetus; **i~iv** impulsive.

imstande: *zu etw ~ sein* be capable of s.th., be in a position, be able to do s.th.

in 1. *(örtlich)* in, at; *~ der Stadt* in the town; *~ der Schule* at school; *~s Haus gehen* go into the house; *~s Bett gehen* go to bed; 2. *(zeitlich)* ~ *diesem Jahr* this year; *~ diesem Alter* at this age; *(während)* ~ *den letzten beiden Kriegen* during the last two wars; *(innerhalb)* ~ *den nächsten Monaten* within the next few months; *(nach Verlauf von)* ~ *einem Monat* in a month; *morgen* ~ *14 Tagen* a fortnight tomorrow; 3. *(Zustand)* ~ *ihrer Angst* in her anxiety; 4. *(auf bestimmte Weise)* ~ *aller Eile* quickly.

Inbegriff *m* embodiment, personification; **i~en** included, inclusive.

indem 1. *(während)* while, whilst, as; *~ er das Papier holte, sagte er* fetching the paper, he said; 2. *(Grund)* by, through (doing s.th.).

Inder *m* Indian.

indessen I *conj* whereas; **II** *adv* meanwhile; *(jedoch)* however.

Indianer *m* (American) Indian.

Indien *n* India.

indirekt indirect.

indisch Indian.

indiskret indiscreet; **I~ion** *f* tactlessness, indiscretion.

individuell individual; **I~um** *n* individual.

Indizienbeweis *m* circumstantial evidence.

industrialisieren industrialize.

Industrie *f* industry; **~anlage** *f* industrial plant; **~betrieb** *m* industrial establishment; **~erzeugnis** *n* industrial product; **~gebiet** *n* industrial district; **~land** *n* industrial country.

industriell industrial; **i~er** *m* industrialist.

Industrie|stadt *f* industrial town; **~zweig** *m* branch of industry.

ineinander in(to) one another, in(to) each other; **~schieben** *irr* fit into each other.

infam infamous, shameful, disgraceful.

Infektion *f* infection.

infizieren 1. infect *(jdn mit e-r Krankheit* s.o. with a disease); 2. *sich* ~ catch an infection.

Inflation *f* inflation; **i~är, i~istisch** inflationary.

infolge owing *(von* to), on account of, as a result of; **~dessen** in consequence, consequently.

Information *f* information *(über* on, about); *nach den neuesten* ~*en* according to

the latest informations;
i~ieren: *jdn über etw* ~ inform s.o. about s.th.; notify.
Infrastruktur *f* infrastructure.
Ingenieur *m* engineer.
Ingwer *m* ginger.
Inhaber *m* 1. *(Eigentümer)* proprietor, owner; 2. *(Besitzer)* possessor, occupant; 3. keeper; 4. *jur* bearer, holder, tenant.
Inhalt *m* 1. *(Flasche)* contents *pl a. fig;* 2. *(Gehalt)* subject matter, tenor; 3. *(Raum~)* area, volume, capacity; **~sangabe** *f* summary, outline, résumé, synopsis; **~sverzeichnis** *n* table of contents.
Initiative *f: die* ~ *ergreifen* take the initiative; *auf s-e* ~ *hin* at his instigation.
inklusive inclusive (of), including.
inkognito, I~ *n* incognito.
inkonsequen|t inconsequent(ial); **I~z** *f* inconsequence.
Inkrafttreten *n* coming into effect, into force.
Inland *n* home(land); *im* ~ *und Ausland* at home and abroad.
Inländ|er *m* national; **i~isch** 1. home, domestic, native; 2. *(Erzeugnis)* home-made, inland.
inliegend enclosed.
inmitten in the middle (midst) of.

inne|haben *irr* 1. *(Amt)* hold, occupy; 2. *(Haus)* possess; **~halten** *irr: er hielt plötzlich inne:* he suddenly stopped.
innen inside; *nach* ~ inwards; *von* ~ from within.
Innen|architekt *m* interior designer; **~ausstattung** *f* interior decoration; **~minister** *m* Secretary of State for Home Affairs; **~ministerium** *n* Home Office; **~politik** *f* domestic (home) policy.
innere 1. inner; 2. *(nicht außen)* inside; 3. *fig* internal, inward; **I~** *n* 1. inside, interior; 2. *fig* heart, soul.
Innereien *pl* innards.
innerhalb 1. *(räumlich)* within, inside; 2. *(zeitlich)* within, in.
innerlich 1. inward; 2. *med* internal.
innig close, intimate.
Innung *f* corporation, guild.
inoffiziell unofficial.
Insasse *m* 1. *(Auto)* occupant; 2. *(Gefängnis)* inmate.
insbesondere in particular, especially.
Inschrift *f* inscription.
Insekt *n* insect; **~envernichtungsmittel** *n* insecticide; **~enstich** *m* insect bite, insect sting.
Insel *f* island; *auf e-r* ~ *wohnen* live on an island.
Inser|at *n* ad(vertisement); *ein* ~ *aufgeben* put an ad-

vertisement in a paper; **i~ie-ren** advertise.

ins|geheim secretly; **~ge-samt** on the whole, in all.

insofern in this respect.

Inspekt|eur m, **~or** m inspector, superintendent.

Install|ateur m plumber, fitter; **i~ieren** fix, instal(l).

instand 1. etw ~ halten keep s.th. in good repair; 2. etw ~ setzen repair s.th.; **I~haltung** f 1. maintenance; 2. (Haus) upkeep; 3. (Kleider) care.

inständig earnest, urgent.

Instanz f jur instance; e-e höhere ~ anrufen appeal to a higher court.

Instinkt m instinct; **i~iv** instinctive.

Institut n institute.

Institution f institution; **i~oll** institutional.

instruieren: jdn ~ instruct s.o.

Instruktion f instruction.

Instrument n 1. instrument; 2. (Handwerkszeug) tool, implement.

inszenier|en theat produce; **I~ung** f theat staging, production.

intakt intact.

Intell|ekt m intellect; **i~ek-tuell** intellectual; **i~igent** intelligent; clever; bright; **~igenz** f intelligence.

Intendant m theat director.

Intens|ität f intensity, intenseness; **i~iv** 1. (Farbe) intense; 2. (Arbeit) intensive; **i~ivieren** intensify.

interess|ant interesting; **I~e** n 1. interest; er hat ein persönliches ~ daran he has a personal interest in it; 2. (Belange) interests pl; **I~ent** m interested person; **~ieren** 1. jdn für etw ~ interest s.o. in s.th.; 2. sich für etw/jdn ~ be interested in s.th./s.o.

intern internal.

Internat n boarding school.

international international.

Interner m boarder.

interpretieren interpret.

intervenieren intervene.

Interview n, **i~en** interview.

intim intimate, close, familiar; **I~ität** f intimacy.

intoleran|t intolerant; **I~z** f intolerance.

Intrig|e f intrigue, scheme; **i~ieren** plot; gegen jdn ~ scheme, intrigue against s.o.

Invalide m disabled person.

Invasion f invasion.

Invent|ar n inventory, stock; **~ur** f: ~ machen take stock.

invest|ieren invest (in in); **I~ition** f investment.

inwendig inside; on the inside.

inwie|fern, ~weit in what respect, to what extent, how far.

inzwischen in the meantime, meanwhile.

ird|en earthen; ~es Geschirr earthenware; **~isch**

1. earthly, wordly; 2. *(sterblich)* mortal.
Ire m Irishman.
irgend 1. wenn ~ *möglich* if at all possible; 2. ~ *etwas* something; anything; 3. ~ *jemand* someone, somebody; anyone, anybody; ~**ein** some; any; ~**wann** sometime; at any time; ~**wie** somehow (or other); ~**wo** somewhere; anywhere; ~**woher** from anywhere; ~**wohin** anywhere, somewhere.
irisch Irish.
Irland n Ireland.
Iron|ie f irony; **i~isch** ironical.
irre 1. mad, insane, crazy, demented; 2. *(verwirrt)* confused.
Irre m, f insane person.

irreführ|en mislead; deceive; ~**end** misleading; **I~ung** f misleading; deception.
irren 1. sich ~ be mistaken, be wrong; 2. sich in jdm ~ be wrong about s.o.; 3. *(herumstreifen)* wander, roam, rove.
Irrenhaus n lunatic asylum, mental home.
Irr|fahrt f odyssey; ~**garten** m maze, labyrinth.
irrig erroneous, mistaken.
irritieren 1. irritate, annoy *(jdn* s.o.); 2. *(verwirren)* confuse, muddle (s.o.) up.
Irr|licht n will-o'-the-wisp; ~**sinn** m insanity, madness; **i~sinnig** insane, mad; ~**tum** m error, mistake; e-n ~ *begehen* commit an error; **i~tümlich** 1. erroneous, false; 2. by mistake, in error.
Ischias m sciatica.
Islam m Islam.
Is|land n Iceland; ~**länder** m Icelander; **i~ländisch** Icelandic.
Isolation f 1. *pol* isolation; 2. *el* insulation.
isolier|en 1. isolate; 2. *tech* insulate; **I~ung** f insulation.
Italien n Italia; ~**er** m, **i~isch** Italian.

J

ja 1. yes; *ich glaube ~* I think so; 2. *(feststellend) da bist du ~!* there you are; 3. *(einleitend)* well.
Jacht *f* yacht.
Jacke *f* jacket; cardigan.
Jagd *f* 1. hunt(ing); *auf die ~ gehen* go hunting, shooting; 2. *(Verfolgung)* chase, pursuit; **~gewehr** *n* sporting gun, shotgun; **~hund** *m* hunting dog; **~schein** *m* hunting licence.
jagen 1. hunt, shoot; 2. *fig* chase, pursue.
Jäger *m* hunter.
jäh 1. *(plötzlich)* sudden, unexpected; 2. *(steil)* steep, precipitous.
Jahr *n* year; *ein halbes ~* six months; *im vergangenen ~* last year; *ein ~ darauf* a year later; *alle ~e* every year; *das ganze ~ hindurch* throughout the whole year; *heute in einem ~* a year from today; **j~elang** for many years; **~estag** *m* anniversary; **~eszahl** *f* date; **~eszeit** *f* season; **~gang** *m* 1. age-group; 2. *(Wein)* vintage; **~hundert** *n* century.

jährlich yearly, annual; *einmal ~* once a year.
Jahr|markt *m* fair; **~tausend** *n* millennium.

Jähzorn *m* violent temper; **j~ig** hot-tempered.
Jalousie *f* Venetian blind.
Jammer *m* misery, distress.
jämmerlich miserable, wretched, pitiful.
jammern moan, lament, wail *(über etw* over s.th.).
Januar *m: im ~* in January.
jäten pull out weeds.
jauchzen: *vor Freude ~* shout for joy.
jawohl yes; *mil* yes, sir!
Jawort *n* approval.
je I *adv* 1. *(jemals)* ever; 2. *wie eh und ~* as always; 3. *~ zwei* two each; 4. *(pro)* per; 5. *~ nach* according to; **II** *conj: ~ mehr, desto besser* the more the better.
jede (r,s) 1. *~r einzelne* each person; 2. *in ~r Hinsicht* in every respect; 3. *~r andere* anyone else; 4. *(ohne Ausnahme)* everybody; 5. *(jeder beliebige)* anybody.
jedenfalls in any case.
jedermann everyone, everybody.
jederzeit at any time.
jedesmal everytime; *~, wenn* whenever.
jedoch but, however, nevertheless.
jeher: *von ~* at all times.
jemand 1. someone, somebody; 2. anyone, anybody.

jen|e(r, s) that, that one; *pl* those; *in ~n Tagen* in those days; **~seitig** (*Ufer*) opposite; **~seits** on the other side, beyond; **J~seits,** *das* hereafter.

Jesus *m* Jesus (Christ).

jetzig present; current.

jetzt 1. now, at present; *bis ~* until now; *von ~ an* from now on, henceforth; 2. (*heutzutage*) nowadays.

jeweilig 1. respective; 2. (*zu einem Zeitpunkt*) at the moment.

jeweils at a time.

Joch *n* yoke.

Jod *n* iodine.

Joghurt *n od m* yogurt.

Johannisbeere *f* currant.

jonglieren (*Bälle, Zahlen*) juggle (*mit* with).

Journalist *m* journalist.

Jubel *m* jubilation, exultation, rejoicing; **j~n** cheer, rejoice, exult, jubilate.

Jubiläum *n* jubilee.

juck|en itch; *es juckt mich am ganzen Körper* I'm itching all over; **J~reiz** *m* itch.

Jude *m* Jew; **~ntum** *n* Judaism.

jüdisch Jewish.

Jugend *f* 1. youth; 2. young people; **~freund** *m* friend of o.'s youth; **~herberge** *f* youth hostel; **j~lich** young, youthful; **~licher** *m* young person, juvenile, adolescent;

~stil *m* Art Nouveau.

Jugoslaw|e *m* Yugoslavian; **~in** *n* Yugoslavia; **j~isch** Yugoslavian.

Juli *m: im ~* in July.

jung 1. young; *von ~ an* since an early age; 2. (*neu*) new.

Junge *m* boy, lad, young fellow.

Junge *n* young, kitten.

jünger 1. younger; *mein ~er Bruder* my younger brother; 2. (*zeitlich näher*) later.

Jünger *m* disciple, follower.

Jungfer *f* old maid.

Jungfrau *f* 1. virgin, maid; 2. *astr* Virgo.

Junggeselle *m* bachelor, single.

Jüngling *m* young man.

jüngst youngest; *in ~er Zeit* lately; *das J~e Gericht* the last Judg(e)ment.

Jungverheirateten *pl* the newly-weds.

Juni *m: im ~* in June.

Jura: *pl ~ studieren* read law.

Jurist *m* lawyer; legal expert; **j~isch** legal.

Jury *f* jury.

Justiz *f* 1. (*Rechtspflege*) judicature; 2. (*Gerechtigkeit*) justice, law; **~minister** *m* *Br* Lord Chancellor; *Am* Attorney General.

Juwel *n* jewel, gem *a. fig;* **~ier** *m* jeweller; **~iergeschäft** *n* jeweller's shop.

Jux *m* practical joke.

K

Kabarett n cabaret.
Kabel n cable.
Kabeljau m cod.
kabeln cable.
Kabine f 1. *mar* cabin; 2. *(Fahrstuhl)* cage; 3. *(Umkleide~)* cubicle; 4. *tele* booth; ~**nkoffer** f cabin trunk.
Kabriolett n cabriolet, convertible.
Kachel f Dutch tile; ~**ofen** m tiled stove.
Kadaver m 1. corpse; 2. *(Tier)* carcass.
Käfer m beetle.
Kaffee m coffee; *e-e Tasse ~ trinken* have, drink a cup of coffee; ~**bohne** f coffee bean; ~**haus** n café; ~**kanne** f coffee-pot; ~**mühle** f coffee-mill, grinder; ~**pause** f coffee break; ~**satz** m coffee-grounds *pl*; ~**service** n coffee-service; ~**tasse** f coffee-cup; ~**wärmer** m coffee-pot cosy.
Käfig m cage.
kahl 1. bald; 2. *(Baum)* bare; 3. *(Landschaft)* bleak, barren.
Kahn m 1. boat; 2. *(Last~)* barge.
Kai m *mar* quay, wharf.
Kaiser m emperor; ~**in** f empress; **k~lich** imperial;

~**reich** n empire; ~**schnitt** m *med* Caesarean operation.
Kajüte f *mar* cabin.
Kakao m cocoa.
Kaktus m cactus.
Kalb n calf; ~**fleisch** n veal; ~**sbraten** m roast veal; ~**sschnitzel** n veal cutlet.
Kalender m calendar.
Kaliber n *mil tech* calibre, bore.
Kalk m lime; **k~en** *(Wand)* whitewash.
kalkulieren 1. *(Preis)* calculate; 2. *fig* estimate; **K~ation** f calculation.
kalt 1. cold; *es wird ~* it is getting cold; *mir ist ~* I feel cold; 2. *fig* unfriendly; ~**blütig** *(Person)* cold-blooded.
Kälte f 1. coldness; *vor ~ zittern* shiver with cold; *es herrscht e-e bittere ~* it is bitterly cold; *drei Grad ~* three degrees below zero; 2. *fig* coldness, coolness; ~**einbruch** m cold spell.
Kalt|front f *mete* cold front; ~**luft** f cold air; ~**welle** f cold wave.
Kalvarienberg m Calvary.
Kamel n camel.
Kamera f camera.
Kamerad m comrade, mate, chum, pal; ~**schaft** f comradeship, fellowship;

k~schaftlich companionable, comradely.
Kameramann m cameraman.
Kamille f camomile.
Kamin m 1. chimney; 2. (offener) fire-place; **~kehrer** m chimney-sweep(er).
Kamm m 1. comb; 2. (Hühner) crest; 3. (Gebirge) ridge.
kämmen: sich die Haare ~ comb o.'s hair.
Kammer f 1. small room; 2. pol chamber; 3. jur court; **~diener** m valet; **~musik** f chamber music.
Kampf m 1. fight, struggle, battle; 2. der ~ ums Dasein the struggle for existence; 3. sport contest.
kämpf|en 1. fight, struggle; 2. mit Schwierigkeiten ~ contend with difficulties; **K~er** m 1. fighter, warrior; 2. fig champion.
Kampfgebiet n battle area.
kampieren camp.
Kana|da n Canada; **~dier** m, **k~disch** Canadian.
Kanal m 1. (natürlicher) channel; (künstlicher) canal; der ~ the Channel; 2. (Abzugs~) sewer; 3. radio channel; **~isation** f 1. (Fluß) canalization; 2. (e-r Stadt) sewerage.
Kanarienvogel m canary.
Kandid|at m 1. candidate; 2. (Antragsteller) applicant; **k~ieren** 1. pol be a candidate (für for), stand as a candidate; 2. (sich bewerben) apply (um for).
Kandiszucker m candy.
Känguruh n kangaroo.
Kaninchen n rabbit.
Kanister m can.
Kanne f 1. (Kaffee~) pot; 2. (Milch~) jug; 3. (Wasser~) can.
Kannibale m cannibal.
Kanone f 1. mil cannon, gun; 2. fig ace.
Kante f 1. edge; 2. (Ecke) border; **k~n** (com) nicht ~! don't tilt!
Kantine f canteen.
Kanu n canoe.
Kanzel f 1. rel pulpit; 2. aero cockpit.
Kanz|lei f office; **~er** m chancellor.
Kap n cape.
Kapazität f 1. tech capacity; 2. fig authority.
Kapelle f 1. rel chapel; 2. mus band; **~meister** m bandmaster, conductor.
kapern (Schiff) capture.
Kapital n capital; (Geldmittel) funds pl; **~ismus** m capitalism; **k~istisch** capitalistic.
Kapitän m captain, skipper, master.
Kapitel n chapter.
Kapitell n arch capital.
kapitulieren capitulate, surrender.
Kaplan m chaplain.
Kappe f cap.

Kapsel f capsule; box.
kaputt 1. (entzwei) broken, out of order; 2. (erschöpft) fagged out.
Kapuze f hood, cowl.
Karabiner m carbine; ~**haken** f snap hook.
Karaffe f carafe.
Karambolage f mot collision, crash.
Karat n carat.
Karawane f caravan.
Kardinal m cardinal; ~**zahl** f cardinal number.
Karfreitag m Good Friday.
karg meagre, poor, scanty.
kärglich frugally, poorly.
kariert 1. check(ed); 2. (Papier) squared.
Karies f caries.
Karikatur f caricature, cartoon.
Karneval m carnival.
Karo n 1. (Karten) diamond; 2. (Stoff) square.
Karosserie f mot body(work).
Karotte f carrot.
Karpfen m carp.
Karre(n m) f 1. (Schub~) cart, wheelbarrow; 2. tech trolley, truck.
Karriere f career.
Karte f 1. card; 2. (Post~) (post)card; 3. (Speise~) menu; 4. (Spiel~) (playing)-card; 5. (Fahr~, Eintritts~) ticket; 6. (Land~) map; ~**ei** f (card-)index; ~**eikarte** f filing card; ~**eikasten** m filing box; ~**enlegerin** f for-

tune-teller; ~**enspiel** n card game.
Kartoffel f potato; ~**brei** m mashed potatoes pl; ~**knödel** m potato dumpling; ~**salat** m potato salad.
Karton m 1. cardboard; 2. (Schachtel) carton.
Karussell n merry-go-round.
Karwoche f Holy Week.
Käse m cheese; ~**kuchen** m cheese-cake.
Kaserne f barracks pl.
Kasino n 1. casino; 2. mil officers' mess.
Kaskoversicherung f mot comprehensive insurance.
Kasperletheater n Punch and Judy show.
Kasse f 1. money-box; 2. (Ladenkasse) till, cash register; 3. (Theater) box--office; (Bank) teller's counter; 4. (Bargeld) cash, ready money; ~**nschalter** m (Bank) teller's counter; ~**nschlager** m box-office hit; ~**nstunden** pl business hours pl; ~**nzettel** m sales slip.
Kassette f cassette, cash-box; ~**nrecorder** m cassette recorder.
kassieren 1. (einkassieren) collect, take in; 2. (wegnehmen) confiscate; 3. (verdienen) make; **K~er** m cashier.
Kastanie f chestnut; ~**nbaum** m chestnut(-tree); **k~nbraun** chestnut-brown.
Kästchen n small box, case.

Kasten *m* box; crate, chest, trunk.

Katalog *m* catalogue.

Katasteramt *n* land-registry office.

katastroph|al disastrous; catastrophic; **K~e** *f* disaster; catastrophy.

Kater *m* 1. tomcat; 2. *(fig)* e-n ~ haben have a hang-over.

Kathedrale *f* cathedral.

Kathol|ik *m* Catholic; **k~isch** Catholic, Roman.

Kätzchen *n* kitty-cat.

Katze *f* 1. cat; 2. *die* ~ *im Sack kaufen* buy a pig in a poke; *die* ~ *aus dem Sack lassen* let the cat out of the bag; **~nsprung** *m* stone's throw; **~nwäsche** *f* cat's lick.

kauen chew, masticate.

kauern, *sich* crouch, squat.

Kauf *m* 1. purchase, buying; *(günstiger)* bargain; 2. *etw in* ~ *nehmen* accept s.th.

kaufen buy, purchase *(von* from); *etw auf Raten* ~ buy s.th. by instal(l)ments, buy s.th. on hire-purchase.

Käufer *m* buyer, purchaser.

Kauf|haus *n* department store; **~kraft** *f* purchasing power; **~mann** *m* businessman; trader, dealer; **k~männisch** 1. commercial; 2. ~ *tätig* in business; **~vertrag** *m* contract of purchase; **~zwang** *m* obligation to buy.

Kaugummi *m* chewing--gum.

Kaulquappe *f* tadpole.

kaum I *adv* scarcely, hardly, barely; ~ *jemand* hardly anyone; *das ist* ~ *zu glauben* that is scarcely believable; **II** *conj:* ~, *daß* no sooner ... than.

Kaution *f* 1. *e-e* ~ *stellen* provide a security; 2. *jur* bail.

Kautschuk *m* rubber.

Kauz *m* 1. little owl; 2. *fig* odd fellow.

Kavalier *m* gentleman; **~sdelikt** *n* petty offence.

Kaviar *m* caviar.

Kegel *m* 1. *(Spiel)* skittle; 2. *tech math* cone; 3. *mit Kind und* ~ with bag and baggage; **~bahn** *f* skittle-, *Am* bowling-alley; **k~n** play at skittles; **~spiel** *n* (game of) skittles, ninepins.

Kehl|e *f* throat; **~kopf** *m* larynx.

Kehrbesen *m* broom.

kehren 1. *er kehrte mir den Rücken* he turned his back on me; 2. *sich* ~ turn; 3. *(Zimmer)* sweep.

Kehricht *m* sweepings *pl;* **~schaufel** *f* dustpan.

Kehrseite *f (fig) das ist die* ~ *der Medaille* that's the other (reverse) side of the coin.

kehrtmachen turn back.

Keil *m* wedge.

Keim *m* 1. *bot* germ, bud;

2. *etw im* ~*e ersticken* nip s.th. in the bud; **k~en** *bot* germinate, sprout; **k~frei** sterile; *med* aseptic.

kein no, not any, not a; *ich habe* ~ *Geld* I have no money.

keine(r, s) 1. *(von Personen)* no one, nobody, none, not one; ~*r von beiden* neither of them; 2. *(von Sachen)* none, not one, not any.

keinerlei no ... at all.

keines|falls on no account, under no circumstances; ~**wegs** by no means, not in the least, not at all.

Keks *m* biscuit; *Am* cookie.

Kelch *m* 1. goblet, cup; 2. *rel* chalice.

Kelle *f* 1. scoop; 2. *(Maurer)* trowel.

Keller *m* cellar; basement; ~**fenster** *n* basement window; ~**geschoß** *n* basement (floor).

Kellner *m* waiter; ~**in** *f* waitress.

Kelten *pl* Celts *pl*.

Kelter *f* wine-press; **k~n** press.

keltisch Celtic.

kennen *irr* 1. know, be acquainted with; 2. *(erkennen)* recognize; 3. *sich* ~ know one another; know o.s.

kennenlernen 1. *jdn* ~ get to know s.o.; 2. *etw* ~ become acquainted with; 3. *sich* ~ meet.

Kenner *m* expert, authority; connoisseur.

Kennkarte *f* identity card.

kenntlich 1. recognizable (*an etw* by s.th.); 2. *sich* ~ *machen* make o.s. known.

Kenntnis *f* 1. knowledge; ~ *von etw haben* have knowledge on s.th.; 2. *(Auskunft)* information; *jdn in* ~ *setzen* inform s.o.; 3. *etw zur* ~ *nehmen* take note of s.th.; 4. *pl (Wissen)* knowledge; education; ~**nahme** *f: zur* ~ for information.

Kennzeich|en *n* 1. characteristic, sign; 2. *(mot) Br* registration number, *Am* licence number; 3. *besondere* ~ special peculiarities; **k~nen** mark, characterize; **k~nend** characteristic, typical.

Kennziffer *f* box number; index number.

kentern capsize.

Keramik *f* ceramics *pl*.

Kerbe *f* notch.

Kerker *m* jail, prison.

Kerl *m* fellow, chap, *Am* guy.

Kern *m* 1. *(Äpfel)* seed; *(Steinobst)* stone; *(Nuß)* kernel; 2. *(Zell~)* nucleus; 3. *fig* core, essence; ~**energie** *f* nuclear energy; ~**forschung** *f* nuclear research; ~**frage** *f* crucial question; ~**fusion** *f* nuclear fusion; **k~gesund** fit as a fiddle; ~**kraftwerk** *n* nuclear power station; ~**reaktor** *m* nuclear reactor; ~**spaltung**

f nuclear fission; **~stück** *f* principal item; **~teilchen** *n* nuclear particle; **~waffen** *pl* nuclear weapons.

Kerze *f* candle.

Kessel *m* 1. kettle; *(großer)* cauldron; 2. *(Dampf~)* boiler; 3. *(Tal~)* basin; **~stein** *m* scale, fur.

Kette *f* 1. chain; 2. *(Hals~)* necklace; **~nraucher** *m* chain-smoker; **~nreaktion** *f* chain reaction.

Ketzer *m* heretic.

keuchen pant, gasp.

Keuchhusten *m* whooping cough.

Keule *f* 1. club, cudgel; 2. *(Fleisch)* leg.

keusch chaste.

kichern giggle, titter.

Kiefer 1. *f bot* pine; 2. *m* jaw(bone).

Kiel *m* keel; **~wasser** *n* wake.

Kiemen *pl* gills *pl.*

Kies *m* gravel; **~el** *m* pebble; **~grube** *f* gravel pit.

Kilo(gramm) *n* kilogram(me); **~hertz** *n* kilocycle; **~meter** *m* kilometre; **~watt(stunde)** *n* kilowatt(-hour).

Kind *n* 1. child; 2. *(Klein~)* baby; **~erarzt** *m* p(a)ediatrician; **~erbett** *n* cot; **~erei** *f* childish behavior; **~ergarten** *m* nursery school; **~ergeld** *n* family allowance; **~erheim** *n* children's home; **~erkrank-**

heit *f* children's disease; **~erlähmung** *f* polio (myelitis); **~ermädchen** *n* nursemaid; **~ernahrung** *f* baby foods *pl;* **k~erreich**: *~e Familien pl* large families *pl;* **~ertagesstätte** *f* daynursery; **~erwagen** *m* pram, perambulator, *Am* baby-carriage; **~erzimmer** *n* nursery.

Kindheit *f* childhood; *von ~ an* from childhood.

kind|isch childish; **~lich** childlike.

Kinn *n* chin.

Kino *n* cinema, *Am* movie theater; *ins ~ gehen* go to the pictures, movies.

Kiosk *m* kiosk, *Am* (news) stand.

kippen 1. tip over; 2. *(Person)* lose o.'s balance.

Kirch|e *f* 1. church; 2. *(Gottesdienst)* service, chapel; **~endiener** *m* sexton; **~enfenster** *n* church window; **k~lich** 1. ecclesiastical; 2. *(geistlich)* spiritual; 3. *(~ gesinnt)* religious; **~turm** *m* steeple.

Kirsch|baum *m* cherry(-tree); **~e** *f* cherry; **~kuchen** *m* cherry tart.

Kissen *n* cushion; *(Kopf~)* pillow.

Kiste *f* crate, case; box.

Kitsch *m* kitsch, trash; **k~ig** slushy, sloppy.

Kitt *m* 1. *(Fenster~)* putty; 2. *(Porzellan)* cement *a. fig.*

Kittel m overall.

kitten 1. (*Porzellan*) cement; 2. (*Loch*) putty, fill, stop.

Kitzel m tickle; **k~ig** ticklish; **k~n** tickle.

Klage f 1. complaint; lament, wail; *Grund zur ~ haben* have cause for complaint; 2. *jur* (*Zivilrecht*) action; (*Strafrecht*) charge, indictment; **k~n** 1. complain (*über* about, of; *bei* to); (*jammern*) lament, moan; 2. *jur* bring an action (*gegen* against), sue.

Kläger(in f) m plaintiff, suitor.

kläglich 1. pitiful; 2. (*Dasein*) miserable.

Klammer f 1. peg, pin, clip; 2. (*Heftklammer*) staple; 3. brackets *pl*; 4. *tech* cramp; **k~n** 1. fasten together; 2. *sich ~ an* cling to.

Klang m 1. sound; 2. (*Glocken~*) peal; 3. (*Ton*) tone; **k~voll** 1. sonorous; 2. (*Name*) illustrious.

Klappbett n folding bed.

Klappe f 1. flap; 2. (*Luft*) air shutter; **k~n** 1. clap; fold; 2. *es wird schon ~* it will work out all right.

Klapper f rattle; **k~n** clatter, clack, click.

klapprig ramshackle; rickety.

Klapp|sitz m folding seat; **~stuhl** m folding chair.

Klaps m smack, slap.

klar 1. clear; 2. *fig* conscious, lucid; obvious; 3. *es ist mir ~, daß I* realize that; 4. *er brachte es ~ zum Ausdruck* he made it clear.

Kläranlage f sewage plant; waste-water purification plant.

klären 1. clear, clarify, purify; 2. *sich ~* become clear.

Klarheit f clearness; clarity.

Klarinette f clarinet.

klar|machen: *jdm etw ~* explain s.th. to s.o.; **~stellen**: *etw ~* clear s.th. up.

Klasse f 1. class; *Br* form, *Am* grade; 2. (*Gesellschaft*) class; 3. *erster ~ fahren* travel first-class; 4. (*Qualität*) grade, quality.

Klass|iker m classical writer; **k~isch** 1. classical; 2. (*zeitlos*) classic.

Klatsch m 1. smack; 2. (*Geschwätz*) gossip; **k~en** 1. (*schwatzen*) gossip; 2. (*Regen*) splash; 3. *in die Hände ~* clap o.'s hands; 4. *Beifall ~* clap, applaud (*jdm* s.o.).

Klaue f *zoo* hoof, claw, paw.

klauen steal, pinch, swipe.

Klausel f clause; stipulation.

Klavier n: *~ spielen* play the piano.

kleb|en 1. stick, glue; 2. *dieser Leim klebt gut* this glue sticks well; **~rig** adhesive, sticky; **K~stoff** m adhesive; (*Leim*) glue; (*Kitt*) cement; **K~streifen** m adhesive tape.

kleckern spill, make spots.

Klecks *m* blot; blob.

Klee *m* clover; **~blatt** *n* clover-leaf.

Kleid *n* 1. dress; 2. *(Bekleidung)* clothes *pl*, clothing; **k~en** 1. clothe, dress; 2. *(gut stehen)* suit; 3. *sich ~* dress o.s.; **~erablage** *f* cloakroom; **~erbügel** *m* (coat-)hanger; **~erbürste** *f* clothes brush; **~erhaken** *m* clothes hook, peg; **~erschrank** *m* wardrobe; **k~sam** becoming; **~ung** *f* clothes *pl*; clothing; **~ungsstück** *n* garment.

Kleie *f* bran.

klein 1. little, small; 2. *(Wuchs)* short; 3. *(kurze Zeit)* short, little; 4. *(unbedeutend)* slight, trifling, insignificant; 5. *(bescheiden)* humble, modest; 6. *~ schreiben* write small; *ein ~ wenig* a little bit.

Kleiner *m* little boy.

Klein|geld *n* change; **~handel** *m* retail trade; *im ~* by, *Am* at retail; **~holz** *n* firewood.

Kleinigkeit *f* little thing, trifle; *das war keine ~* that was no small matter.

Kleinkind *n* infant.

klein|laut: *~ werden* sing small; **~lich** 1. pedantic; 2. *(engstirnig)* small-minded; 3. *(geizig)* mean.

Klein|od *n* jewel, treasure; **~staat** *m* small state;

~stadt *f* small town; **~wagen** *m* minicar.

Kleister *m* paste.

Klemme *f* 1. *tech* clamp; 2. *in der ~ sitzen* be in a tight corner; **k~n** 1. stick; 2. *(von Tür)* be stuck; 3. *sich ~ pinch* o.'s finger.

Klempner *m* plumber.

Klerus *m* clergy.

kletter|n climb; **K~pflanze** *f* climber, creeper.

Klient *m* client.

Klima *n* climate; **~anlage** *f* air-conditioning plant; **k~tisch** climatic; **k~tisiert** air-conditioned.

klimpern jingle, clink.

Klinge *f* blade.

Kling|el *f* bell; **k~eln** 1. ring *(an der Tür* at the door); 2. *es klingelt* the doorbell is ringing; **k~en** *irr* ring, sound, resound.

Klin|ik *f* hospital, clinic; **k~isch** clinical.

Klinke *f* (door-)handle.

klipp: *~ und klar* clearly and concisely, clear-cut.

Klippe *f* 1. cliff, rock, crag; 2. *fig* obstacle.

klirren rattle, jingle, clink.

klitschig muddy, soggy.

klopf|en 1. knock *(an die Tür* at the door); tap *(ans Fenster* on the window); 2. *auf die Schultern ~* pat s.o. on the back; 3. *(Herz)* pound *(vor Erregung* with excitement); 4. *es klopft* s.o.

knocks; **~fest** mot knock-proof.

Klops m meatball.

Klosett n toilet, lavatory; **~bürste** f lavatory brush; **~papier** n toilet paper.

Kloß m 1. (Küche) dumpling, meatball; 2. (Erde) lump.

Kloster n (Mönche) monastery; (Nonnen) convent.

Klotz m log, block.

Klub m club; **~sessel** m club chair.

Kluft f 1. geol joint, cleft; 2. fig gulf, gap.

klug 1. clever, intelligent, bright, wise; 2. (vorsichtig) prudent; shrewd; judicious; **K~heit** f intelligence, cleverness.

Klumpen m lump, clod, clump; **~fuß** m clubfoot.

knabbern nibble.

Knabe m boy.

Knäckebrot n crispbread.

knacken (Nüsse) crack; snap, crackle.

Knall m crack, bang; **k~en** 1. crack, bang; 2. (detonieren) detonate; 3. (Korken) pop; **k~rot** bright red.

knapp 1. scanty, meagre, small, low; 2. (Vorräte) scarce, short; 3. (Kleid) tight, close-fitting; 4. (Mehrheit) narrow; 5. etw ~ zusammenfassen summarize s.th. concisely; ~ ausreichend just satisfactory; **K~heit** f scantiness, meagreness.

knarren creak.

knattern rattle, chatter.

Knäuel m ball, clew.

knauserig stingy, niggardly.

Knebel m gag; **k~n** 1. gag; 2. fig muzzle.

Knecht m farmhand; **k~en** enslave, tyrannize.

kneif|en irr pinch (in den Arm s.o.'s arm); **K~zange** f pincers pl.

Kneipe f tavern, pub, Am saloon.

kneten knead.

Knick m 1. (Weg) bend; 2. (Papier) fold, crease; 3. (Rohr) knee; **k~en** 1. bend; 2. fold, crease; bitte nicht ~! please do not bend.

Knie n 1. knee; 2. (Weg) bend; 3. tech elbow, angle; **~fall** m prostration; **~gelenk** n knee-joint; **~kehle** f hollow of the knee; **k~n** kneel; **~scheibe** f kneecap.

Kniff m 1. fig trick; 2. (Falte) fold, crease; **k~lig** tricky.

knipsen 1. phot take a snapshot; 2. (Fahrkarte) punch.

Knirps m shrimp.

knirschen 1. (Schnee) crunch; 2. mit den Zähnen ~ gnash, grind o.'s teeth.

knistern 1. (Feuer) crackle; 2. (Papier) rustle.

knitterfrei crease-resistant.

Knoblauch m garlic.

Knöchel m anat (Hand) knuckle; (Fuß) ankle.

Knoch|en m bone; **~enbau**

m bone structure;
~**enbruch** *m* fracture;
k~ig bony.
Knödel *m* dumpling.
Knolle *f bot* bulb, tuber.
Knopf *m* button; ~**loch** *n*
buttonhole.
Knorpel *m* cartilage.
Knorr|en *m* (*Holz*) knot,
gnarl; **k~ig** gnarled, knotty.
Knospe *f bot* bud.
Knoten *m* 1. knot *a. mar;*
2. *med* lump; ~**punkt** *m*
point of intersection, junction.
knüpfen 1. (*Teppich*) knot;
2. (*Netz*) tie.
Knüppel *m* 1. cudgel, club;
2. (*Polizei*) truncheon.
knurren 1. (*Hund*) growl;
2. (*Magen*) rumble; 3. (*murren*) grumble (*über* at).
knusprig crisp.
Koch *m* cook; ~**buch** *n*
cookery-book; **k~en** 1. boil;
2. (*von Speisen*) cook; 3. ~
lernen learn to cook;
4. (*Tee, Kaffee*) make; ~**er**
m cooker; **k~fest** boil-
-proof.
Köchin *f* cook.
Koch|kunst *f* culinary art;
~**löffel** *m* spoon; ~**platte** *f*
hot plate; ~**rezept** *n* (cook-
ery) recipe; ~**topf** *m* pot,
saucepan.

Köder *m* 1. bait, lure; 2. *fig*
allurement, enticement; **k~n**
bait, lure.
Koexistenz *f* coexistence.

Koffein *n* caffeine; **k~frei**
decaffeinated.
Koffer *m* 1. (*Hand~*) suitcase, case, bag, *Am* grip; *e-n*
~ *packen* pack o.'s case;
2. (*großer*) trunk; ~**raum** *m*
boot, *Am* trunk; ~**träger** *m*
porter.
Kohl *m bot* cabbage.
Kohle *f* coal; *auf glühenden*
~*n sitzen* be on tenter-
hooks; ~**hydrat** *n* carbohydrate; ~**nbergwerk** *n*
coal-mine; ~**ndioxyd** *n* carbon dioxide; ~**nhändler** *m*
coal merchant; ~**nhand-
lung** *f* coal merchant's office; ~**nherd** *m* coal-burn-
ing range; ~**nkeller** *m* coal-
-cellar; ~**nsäure** *f* carbonic
acid; ~**nschaufel** *f* coal
shovel; ~**nstoff** *m* carbon;
~**nwasserstoff** *m* hydro-
carbon; ~**papier** *n* carbon
paper; ~**zeichnung** *f* char-
coal drawing.
Kohlrabi *m* kohlrabi.
Koje *f* bunk, berth.
Kokain *n* cocaine.
Kokerei *f* coking plant.
kokett coquettish; **K~erie** *f*
coquetry; ~**ieren** flirt.
Kokosnuß *f* coconut.
Koks *m* coke.
Kolben *m* 1. (*Gewehr*) butt;
2. *tech* piston.
Kolchose *f* collective farm.
Kolik *f* colic.
Kollaps *m* collapse.
Kolleg|e *m*, ~**in** *f* colleague.
Kollektion *f* collection.

kollektiv collective.
Kollision f collision, clash, conflict.
Kolon|ie f colony; **k~isieren** colonize; settle; **~ist** m colonist; settler.
Kolonne f 1. column; 2. *(Fahrzeuge)* mil convoy.
Koloß m colossus.
kolossal colossal, gigantic.
Kombin|ation f 1. combination; 2. *(Kleidung)* union suit; **k~ieren** 1. *etw mit etw* ~ combine s.th. with s.th.; 2. *(gedanklich)* conclude, deduct, reason.
Komet m comet.
Komfort m modern conveniences pl; luxury; **k~abel** well-appointed, comfortable.
Komik f comic; humour; **~iker** m comedian.
komisch comical, funny.
Komma n comma; 5,5 five point five (5.5).
Kommand|ant m commanding officer; **k~ieren** command, order.
Kommanditgesellschaft f limited partnership.
Kommando n 1. command, order; 2. *das ~ führen* be in command.
kommen irr 1. come; *jdm nahe ~* come close to s.o.; *jdn besuchen ~* come to see s.o.; 2. *(ankommen)* arrive, come in; *wann kommt der nächste Zug?* when does the train arrive? 3. *ihr*

kamen die Tränen tears came into her eyes; *das kommt mir gerade recht* that suits me perfectly; 4. *zuerst ~* come first; *jetzt kommt die Hauptsache* now comes the main point; 5. *(geschehen)* happen, come about; *was auch immer ~ mag* come what may; 6. *etw ~ lassen* let s.th. come; *jdn ~ lassen* send for s.o.; 7. *(kosten) wie teuer kommt das?* how much does that cost? 8. *(hervortreten)* come out, appear; 9. *auf etw zu sprechen ~* come to speak of s.th.; 10. *weit ~* get far; 11. *es kommt jem* s.o. is coming; *es kam, wie es ~ mußte* it was bound to happen; *mit Präpositionen:* ~ *an* come to, get to; ~ *auf* come on, get on; ~ *aus* come out of; *(zurückkommen)* come back, return; ~ *bis* get as far as; ~ *hinter* discover, get at; ~ *in* come into; *ins Krankenhaus ~* go to hospital; *nach Hause ~* come home; *(Reihenfolge)* come after; ~ *über* come over; pass; ~ *um* come round; miss; ~ *unter* come, get under; ~ *von* come from, be from; *(herrühren)* come of, be due to, be caused by; *vor den Richter ~* come before a judge; *(Reihenfolge)* come before; *wegen e-r Sache ~* come regarding s.th.; *er kam zu mir* he came to me; *zu Geld ~* come into money; *(erreichen)* achieve, get to; *(Zeit finden)* find time for; *zu sich ~* regain consciousness; *zur Sprache ~* come up.

Kommentar *m* commentary; *kein ~!* no comment; **k~ieren** comment (*etw* upon s.th.).

Kommiss|ar *m* superintendent; **~ion** *f: in ~* on commission.

Kommode *f* chest of drawers.

kommunal local, municipal.

Kommune *f* community, commune.

Kommunikationsmittel *n* means of communication.

Kommunion *f* Communion.

Kommunis|mus *m* communism; **~t** *m,* **k~tisch** communist.

Komödie *f* comedy.

Kompaß *m* compass.

kompetent competent (*für* for), authorized.

Kompetenz *f* authority, competence; responsibility.

komplett complete.

Komplex *m* complex.

Kompli|kation *f* complication; **~ze** *m* accomplice; **k~ziert** complicated, complex.

Komplott *n: ein ~ schmieden* hatch a plot.

Komponente *f* component.

kompon|ieren *mus* compose; **K~ist** *m* composer.

Kompott *n* stewed fruit.

Kompromiß *m: e-n ~ schließen* make a compromise (*über* on).

kondens|iert condensed; **K~milch** *f* condensed milk.

Kondition 1. *com* terms *pl,* conditions *pl;* 2. *(sport)* fitness.

Konditor *m* confectioner, pastry-cook; **~ei** *f* confectionery; café; **~eiwaren** *pl* confectionery products *pl.*

Konferenz *f* conference, meeting; **~dolmetscher** *m* conference interpreter.

Konfession *f rel* confession of faith, religion, creed; **k~ell** denominational; **k~slos** non-denominational.

konfiszieren confiscate.

Konfitüre *f* preserve, jam.

Konflikt *m* conflict, dispute.

konform conforming.

konfrontieren: *jdn mit etw ~* confront s.o. with s.th.

konfus confused, mixed-up.

Kongreß *m* congress.

König *m* king; **~in** *f* queen; **~inpastete** *f* chicken vol-au-vent; **k~lich** royal, king's; **~reich** *n* kingdom.

Konjunktur *f* economic situation; **~abschwächung** *f* downswing; **~anstieg** *m* upswing.

konkret concrete, precise.

Konkurren|t *m* competitor,

rival; **~z** *f* competition, rivalry.

konkurrenz|fähig competitive; **~los** unrivalled, matchless.

Konkurs *m* bankruptcy, insolvency, failure.

können *irr* **I** *aux* 1. *(vermögen)* be able to, be capable of; *kannst du mir die Nummer sagen?* can you give me the number? 2. *(beherrschen)* know to, understand to; *sie kann reiten* she knows how to ride; 3. *(dürfen)* be permitted, allowed to; *kann ich die Butter haben?* may I have the butter? 4. *(möglich sein) der Brief könnte verlorengegangen sein* the letter could have got lost; *es kann sein, daß* it's possible that; **II** 5. *(imstande sein)* be able to do; *man tut, was man kann* one does what one can; 6. *(beherrschen)* know, understand; *kannst du die Wörter?* do you know the words? 7. *er kann nichts dafür* it isn't his fault; 8. *(vermögen)* be able to; *ich konnte nicht anders, ich mußte lachen* I could not help laughing.

konsequen|t 1. consequent, logical, consistent; 2. ~ *bleiben* stand firm; **K~z** *f* consequence; conclusion.

konservativ conservative.

Konserve *f* preserved food; **~ndose** *f* tin, can; **~nfabrik** *f* cannery.

konservieren preserve.

konstant 1. *phys* constant; 2. *(beständig)* consistent, steady.

konstatieren state, establish.

konstruieren 1. *(entwerfen)* design; 2. *(bauen)* build, construct; 3. *(erfinden)* invent, fabricate.

Konstruktion *f* 1. *(Entwurf)* design; 2. *tech* construction.

Konsul *m* consul; **~at** *n* consulate.

konsultieren: *jdn* ~ consult s.o.

Konsum *m* consumption; **~gesellschaft** *f* consumer society; **~güter** *pl* consumer goods *pl;* **k~ieren** consume.

Kontakt *m* contact, connexion; **~schalen** *pl* contact lenses *pl.*

Kontext *m: in diesem* ~ in this context.

Kontinent *m* continent, mainland; **~alklima** *n* continental climate.

kontinuierlich continuous, uninterrupted.

Konto *n* account; **~auszug** *m* statement of account; **~inhaber** *m* account-holder; **~stand** *m* state of an account.

Kontor *n* office, bureau; **~ist** *m* (office) clerk.

Kontrast *m* contrast;

k~ieren form a contrast (*mit etw* with, to s.th.).

Kontrolle f control, supervision; **k~ieren** check, control, supervise.

Konvention f convention; **k~ell** conventional.

Konversationslexikon n encyclop(a)edia.

Konzentration f concentration; **~slager** n concentration camp.

konzentrieren, sich concentrate.

Konzern m combine, group.

Konzert n concert; **~saal** m concert hall.

Konzession f 1. *jur* licence; 2. concession.

Konzil n council.

koordinieren co-ordinate.

Kopf m head; *den ~ verlieren* lose o.'s head; *klaren ~ behalten* keep a clear head; *etw auf den ~ stellen* turn s.th. upside down; *über etw den ~ schütteln* shake o.'s head about s.th.; *sich etw durch den ~ gehen lassen* think s.th. over; *von ~ bis Fuß* from head to foot; *~ an ~* neck and neck; *pro ~* per person; **~ball** m *sport* header.

köpfen: *jdn ~* behead s.o.

Kopf|ende n head; **~haut** f scalp; **~hörer** m headphone; **~kissen** n pillow; **~kissenbezug** m pillow-case; **~rechnen** n mental arithmetic; **~salat** m cabbage lettuce; **~schmerzen** pl: *~ haben* have a headache; **~sprung** m header; **~stand** m headstand; **~tuch** n head scarf; **k~über** head first, headlong; **~wäsche** f hair-wash, shampoo.

Kopie f 1. (carbon-)copy, duplicate; 2. *(Nachbildung)* copy, reproduction.

kopieren copy.

Kopilot m co-pilot.

koppeln couple.

Koralle f coral.

Korb m 1. basket; 2. *(Picknick)* hamper; 3. *jdm e-n ~ geben* turn s.o. down; **~sessel** m wicker-chair.

Kork m cork; **~en** m stopper; **~enzieher** m corkscrew.

Korn n 1. *(Getreide)* grain, corn, cereals *pl*; 2. *(Samenkorn)* grain of seed; **~blume** f cornflower; **~feld** n cornfield.

körnig grainy, granular.

Körper m body; **~bau** m structure of the body, anatomy; **k~behindert** physically disabled, handicapped; **~gewicht** n body-weight; **~größe** f weight; **k~lich** 1. physical; 2. *phys* corporeal; **~pflege** f hygiene; **~schaft** f *jur* corporation; **~teil** m part, member of the body; **~verletzung** f bodily harm.

korrekt correct, right;

K~heit f correctness; **K~ur** f correction.

Korresponden|t m correspondent; **~z** f correspondence.

korrigieren correct, improve.

Korruption f corruption; bribery.

Korse m Corsican.

Korsett n corset.

Kors|ika n Corsica; **k~isch** Corsican.

Kosename m pet name.

Kosmeti|k f cosmetics pl; **~kerin** f beautician; **k~sch** cosmetic.

kosmisch cosmic.

Kosmos m cosmos.

Kost f 1. (Nahrung) food; 2. (Verpflegung) boarding.

kostbar precious, expensive.

kosten 1. cost; wieviel kostet das? how much does it cost? 2. das hat mich viel Mühe gekostet it cost me great pains; 3. (probieren) taste, try, sample.

Kosten pl 1. costs, expenses; (Gebühren) charges, fees; laufende ~ running costs; weder Mühe noch ~ scheuen spare neither effort nor expense; 2. (fig) auf jds ~ leben live at s.o.'s expense; auf s-e ~ kommen get o.'s money's worth; **~anschlag** m estimate; **~beteiligung** f cost sharing; **~erstattung** f reimbursement of expenses; **k~los** free, gratis, gratu-

itous; **~punkt** m matter of expense.

Kost|gänger m boarder; **~geld** n board.

köstlich delicious, savoury; delightful.

Kostprobe f sample.

kostspielig expensive.

Kostüm n costume, suit; **~ball** m fancy-dress ball.

Kot m 1. (Schmutz) mud, mire; 2. (Exkremente) faeces pl, stool.

Kotelett n chop, cutlet; **~en** pl side-whiskers.

Köter m dog.

Kotflügel m wing, Am fender.

Krabbe f crab.

krabbeln crawl, creep.

Krach m 1. noise; crash; 2. fig row, quarrel; **k~en** crack, bang; creak, crash.

Kraft f 1. strength; 2. (Gewalt) force; 3. (Energie) energy; 4. (Anstrengung) effort; 5. (Fähigkeit) power; 6. treibende ~ driving force; 7. (Arbeitskraft) worker, employee; 8. in ~ sein be in force; in ~ treten come into force; außer ~ treten become invalid.

kraft: ~ s-s Amtes by virtue of his office.

Kraftfahrer m driver.

Kraftfahrzeug n motor vehicle; **~steuer** f motor vehicle tax; **~versicherung** f motor vehicle insurance.

kräftig 1. (Mensch) strong,

robust; 2. *(Händedruck)* firm; 3. *(Schlag)* heavy, powerful; 4. *(Stimme)* loud; 5. *(Mahlzeit)* nourishing; 6. *er ist ~ gebaut* he is powerfully built; **~en** strengthen; **K~ung** *f* strengthening, invigoration.

kraftlos weak, feeble; exhausted.

Kraftstoff *m* fuel, *Am* gasoline.

kraftvoll 1. strong, vigorous; 2. *fig* powerful.

Kraftwerk *n* power station.

Kragen *m* 1. collar; 2. *Kopf und ~ riskieren* stick o.'s neck out; **~weite** *f* collar size.

Krähe *f.* **k~n** crow.

Kralle *f* claw, talon.

Kram *m* trash, rubbish; things *pl.*

Krampf *m med* cramp; **~ader** *f* varicose vein; **k~haft** 1. convulsive; 2. *fig* desperate.

Kran *m* crane.

krank sick, ill; *~ sein* be ill; *sich ~ melden* report sick.

kranken*: an etw ~* suffer from s.th.

kränken hurt, wound, injure.

Kranken|geld *n* sick benefit; **~haus** *n* hospital; **~kasse** *f* health insurance scheme; **~pfleger** *m* male nurse; **~schein** *m* health insurance certificate; **~schwester** *f* nurse; **~versiche-rung** *f* health insurance; **~wagen** *m* ambulance.

Kranker *m* sick person.

krankhaft morbid, diseased.

Krankheit *f* illness, sickness, disease; *(Leiden)* affection; **~serreger** *m* agent of disease; **~sherd** *m* focus of a disease.

kränk|lich weak, sickly; **K~ung** *f* injury, offence, *Am* offense.

Kranz *m* wreath.

Krapfen *m* doughnut.

kraß 1. *(Lüge)* gross, flagrant; 2. *(Widerspruch)* absolute, extreme; 3. *(Unterschied)* huge, enormous.

Krater *m* crater.

Krätze *f med* scabies.

kratz|en scratch, scrape; **K~er** *m* 1. *tech* scraper; 2. scratch.

kraulen *sport* crawl.

kraus *(Haar)* crinkly, curly.

Kraut *n* herb, herbage.

Krawall *m* riot; row.

Krawatte *f* tie, *Am* necktie; **~nnadel** *f* tie pin.

Kreatur *f* creature.

Krebs *m* 1. *zoo* crayfish; 2. *astr* Cancer; 3. *med* cancer; *an ~ leiden* suffer from cancer; **~erreger** *m* carcinogen.

Kredit *m* credit, loan; *auf ~* on credit.

Kreide *f* 1. chalk, crayon; 2. *min* chalk; **~zeichnung** *f* chalk drawing.

Kreis *m* 1. *math* circle;

2. *(abgegrenztes Gebiet)* sphere; 3. *(von Menschen)* circle, group; 4. *el* circuit.
kreischen shriek, scream.
kreisen 1. rotate, revolve; 2. *(herumgehen)* circle, go round.
Kreislauf *m* 1. cycle, circle; 2. *med* circulation; ~**kollaps** *m* circulatory collapse.
Kreis|säge *f* circular saw; ~**stadt** *f* district town; ~**verkehr** *m* roundabout traffic.
Krematorium *n* crematorium, *Am* crematory.
Krepp *m* crape.
Kreuz *n* 1. cross *a. rel;* 2. *fig (Leiden)* suffering; 3. *med* small of the back; 4. *(Karten)* club.
kreuzen 1. cross; *die Beine ~* cross o.'s legs; 2. *bot* crossbreed; 3. *sich ~* cross.
Kreuzer *m mar* cruiser.
Kreuz|fahrer *m* crusader; ~**fahrt** *f* cruise; ~**feuer** *n* cross-fire; ~**gang** *m* cloister.
kreuzig|en crucify; **K~ung** *f* crucifixion.
Kreuz|otter *f* adder; ~**schmerzen** *pl* backache.
kreuz und quer criss-cross.
Kreuzung *f* 1. *(Straße)* intersection, crossroad; 2. *loc* crossing, junction; 3. *biol* cross-breeding.
Kreuz|verhör *n* cross-examination; ~**weg** *m* 1. crossway; 2. *rel* way of the Cross;

~**worträtsel** *n* crossword; ~**zug** *m* crusade.
kriech|en *irr* crawl, creep; **K~spur** *f* creeper lane; **K~tier** *n* reptile.
Krieg *m* war; *gegen jdn ~ führen* make war against s.o.; ~**er** *m* warrior; ~**erdenkmal** *n* war memorial.
kriegerisch warlike, martial.
Kriegerwitwe *f* war widow.
krieg|führend belligerent; **K~sführung** *f* warfare.
Kriegs|beschädigter *m* war-disabled person; ~**gefangener** *m* prisoner of war; ~**gefangenschaft** *f* captivity; ~**marine** *f* navy; ~**schiff** *n* warship.
Krimi *m* crime thriller.
Kriminal|abteilung *f* criminal investigation department; ~**ität** *f* criminality; crime; ~**polizei** *f* detective police.
kriminell criminal.
Krippe *f* 1. manger, crib; 2. *(Tagheim)* day-nursery.
Krise *f* crisis.
Kristall *m* crystal.
Kritik *f* 1. criticism, critique; 2. *(Rezension)* review; ~**er** *m* critic, reviewer.
kritiklos uncritical.
kritisch critical.
kritisieren criticize; *an jdm etw ~* find fault with s.o.
kritzeln scribble, scrawl.
Krokodil *n* crocodile.
Krone *f* 1. crown; 2. *(das Höchste)* peak, summit;

3. *(Schmuck)* coronet;
4. *(Baum)* top.
krönen 1. *jdn zum König ~* crown s.o. king; 2. *fig* crown, cap.
Kron|kolonie *f* royal colony; **~leuchter** *m* chandelier; **~prinz** *m* crown prince.
Krönung *f* 1. coronation; 2. *fig* crowning.
Kropf *m med* goitre.
Kröte *f* toad.
Krücke *f* crutch; *auf ~n gehen* walk on crutches.
Krug *m* jug, pitcher.
Krume *f agr* topsoil.
Krümel *m* crumb; **k~ig** crumbly; **k~n** crumble.
krumm crooked, bent; curved.
krümm|en 1. bend, crook; 2. *sich ~* writhe *(vor Schmerzen* with pain); *(Straße)* bend; **K~ung** *f* bend, curve, turn.
Krüppel *m* cripple.
Kruste *f* crust *a. med.*
Kruzifix *n* crucifix.
Krypta *f* crypt.
Kübel *m* bucket, vat, tub.
Kubikmeter *n* cubic metre.
Küche *f* 1. kitchen; 2. *(Speisen)* cuisine, cooking.
Kuchen *m* cake, pastry, tart.
Küchen|abfälle *pl* kitchen refuse; **~chef** *m* head cook.

Kuchengabel *f* pastry fork.
Küchen|geschirr *n* kitchen crockery; **~messer** *n* kitchen knife; **~schabe** *f*

cockroach; **~schrank** *m* cupboard.
Kuchenteller *m* cake plate.
Kuckuck *m* cuckoo; **~suhr** *f* cuckoo-clock.
Kugel *f* 1. *mil* bullet; 2. *(Erd~)* sphere, globe; 3. ball; **~lager** *n* ball-bearing; **~schreiber** *m* ball-(point-)pen; **~stoßen** *n* shot-putting.
Kuh *f* cow.
kühl 1. cool, fresh, chilly; refreshing; 2. *(Person)* reserved.
Kühle *f* coolness, freshness.
kühlen cool, chill.
Kühler *m* radiator; **~haube** *f* radiator bonnet.
Kühl|haus *n* cold-storage depot; **~raum** *m* refrigerating chamber; **~schrank** *m* refrigerator; **~wasser** *n* cooling water.
kühn brave, courageous; **K~heit** *f* bravery, courage.
Küken *n* chick.
Kulisse *f* scenery, wing; *hinter den ~n* behind the scenes.
Kult *m* cult.
kultivier|en cultivate, till; **~t** refined, cultured.
Kultur *f* culture, civilization; **k~ell** cultural.
Kümmel *m* caraway (seed).
Kummer *m* grief, sorrow; trouble, worry.
kümmerlich 1. *(Leben)* miserable, wretched; 2. *(Mahlzeit)* paltry, meagre.

kümmern 1. *sich ~ um* look after, take care of; 2. *(sich befassen)* see about, do s.th. about; 3. *(sich Gedanken machen)* care about, mind; *kümmere dich nicht darum!* never mind!

kündbar 1. terminable; 2. *(Vertrag)* subject to notice.

Kunde 1. *m* customer, patron, client; 2. *f* news *pl,* tidings *pl.*

Kundendienst *m* after-sales service.

Kundgebung *f pol* meeting, rally; demonstration.

kundig expert, experienced.

kündigen 1. give notice; 2. *(entlassen)* dismiss, discharge, remove from office; 3. *(Vertrag)* cancel.

Kündigung *f* 1. notice; 2. *(Entlassung)* dismissal, discharge; **~sfrist** *f* period of notice; **~sgrund** *m* reason for giving notice.

Kundin *f* customer.

Kundschaft *f* customers *pl,* clients *pl.*

künftig 1. from now on, in (the) future; 2. *(Ereignisse)* future, coming.

Kunst *f* 1. art; 2. *(Kunstfertigkeit)* art, skill; **~ausstellung** *f* art exhibition; **~dünger** *m* artificial fertilizer; **~geschichte** *f* history of art; **~gewerbe** *n* arts and crafts *pl;* **~händler**

m art dealer; **~handlung** *f* art dealer's shop.

Künstler *m* artist; master; **k~isch** artistic.

künstlich artificial.

Kunst|maler *m* painter; **~reiter** *m* circus rider; **~sammlung** *f* art collection; **~stoff** *m* plastic, synthetic fibre; **~stück** *n* trick, feat; **k~voll** artistic; elaborate; **~werk** *n* work of art.

Kupfer *n* copper; **~stich** *m* copper engraving.

Kuppe *f* 1. rounded mountain top; 2. *(Finger)* finger-tip.

Kuppel *f* dome, cupola.

Kuppelei *f* procuration.

kuppeln 1. *tech* couple *(etw an etw* s.th. to s.th.); 2. *(Auto)* disengage the clutch.

Kupplung *f* 1. *tech* coupling; 2. *(Auto)* clutch.

Kur *f* cure.

Kurbel *f* crank, handle; **k~n** turn a crank.

Kürbis *m* pumpkin.

Kurgast *m* visitor to a health resort.

Kurier *m* messenger.

kurieren cure.

kurios odd, curios; **K~ität** *f* oddness, curiosity.

Kur|ort *m* health resort; **~pfuscher** *m* quack, charlatan.

Kurs *m* 1. *(mar) ~ nehmen auf* set course for; 2. *fig* policy, line, course; 3. *com* rate, quotation; *hoch im ~ stehen* be in great demand; **~buch** *n* railway guide.

Kürschner *m* furrier.

kursieren circulate.

kursiv italic.

Kurs|notierung *f* quotation; **~teilnehmer** *m* participant in a study-course; **~us** *m* (study-)course; **~wagen** *m* through coach.

Kurtaxe *f* visitor's tax.

Kurve *f* 1. curve; 2. *(Straße)* bend, curve, corner; **k~n** 1. *aero* circle; 2. *(Auto)* drive round; **k~nreich** *(Straße)* winding, twisting.

kurz I *adj* 1. short; *er zog den kürzeren* he came off second-worst; 2. *(Besuch)* short, brief; *e-e ~e Zeit lang* for a short while; *in ~er Zeit* in a short time; 3. *(rasch)* quick; 4. *binnen ~em* within a short time; *bis vor ~em* until recently; **II** *adv* 5. short; *sie ist zu ~ gekommen* she got off badly; 6. *~ hinter dem Fluß* just beyond the river; 7. *(zeitlich)* short, briefly; 8. *(knapp) etw ~ zusammenfassen* recapitulate s.th. briefly.

Kurzarbeit *f* short-time work.

Kürze *f* 1. shortness; 2. *(Be-such)* briefness; *in ~* in the near future; 3. *in aller ~* very briefly; **k~n** 1. shorten, cut; 2. *math* reduce.

kurzerhand at once, without hesitation.

kurzfristig short-term; at short notice.

Kurzgeschichte *f* short story.

kürzlich lately, recently, not long ago.

Kurz|schluß *m* short circuit; **~schrift** *f* shorthand.

kurzsichtig short-sighted *a. fig;* **K~keit** *f* short-sightedness.

Kürzung *f* cut, abridgement.

Kurz|waren *pl* haberdashery; **~welle** *f* short wave.

Kusine *f* cousin.

Kuß *m* kiss.

küssen kiss.

Küste *f* coast, shore; *an der ~ liegen* lie on the coast; **~ngewässer** *pl* coastal waters *pl.*

Küster *m* sexton.

Kutsche *f* carriage, coach; **~r** *m* coachman.

Kutte *f rel* habit, cowl.

Kuvert *n* envelope.

Kybernetik *f* cybernetics *sing.*

L

Labor n lab; **~ant** m laboratory assistant; **~atorium** n laboratory.

Labyrinth n labyrinth, maze.

lächeln smile; **L~** n smile.

lachen 1. laugh (*über* at); *er hat nichts zu* ~ he has got nothing to laugh about; 2. *sich krank* ~ split o.'s sides with laughing; **L~** n laughter.

lächerlich 1. ridiculous; absurd, trifling; 2. *sich* ~ *machen* make a fool of o.s.

Lachs m salmon; **l~farben** salmon-pink; **~schinken** m smoked double loin of pork.

Lack m lacquer, varnish; paint; **l~ieren** lacquer, varnish, enamel.

Ladefläche f loading area.

laden irr 1. *etw auf etw* ~ load s.th. on s.th.; 2. *etw auf sich* ~ burden o.s. with s.th.; 3. *ein Gewehr* ~ load a gun; 4. *el* charge; 5. (*einladen*) *zu Tisch* ~ invite to dinner; 6. *vor Gericht* ~ summon before a court.

Laden m 1. shop, *Am* store; 2. (*Fenster~*) shutter; **~besitzer** m shopkeeper; **~diebstahl** m shoplifting; **~preis** m selling price; **~schluß** m closing time; **~tisch** m counter.

Laderampe f loading ramp.

Ladung f 1. load, freight, cargo; 2. *el* charge; 3. *jur* summons, citation.

Lage f 1. (*Gegenstand*) position; 2. (*Haus*) situation, site; 3. (*Umstände*) circumstances *pl; in der* ~ *sein, etw zu tun* be in a position to do s.th.; *nach* ~ *der Dinge* as matters stand; 4. (*Schicht*) layer; 5. *mus* register.

Lager n 1. bed, couch; 2. camp; 3. *com* stock; store(-room); warehouse; *Waren auf* ~ *haben* have goods in store; 4. *tech* bearing; **~bestand** m stock; **~feuer** n camp-fire; **~gebühr** f storage; **~haus** n warehouse; **~ist** m stock-keeper.

lagern 1. (*Rast*) take a rest; 2. (*aufbewahren*) store.

Lager|raum m store-room; **~schein** m warehouse receipt.

lahm lame; crippled; **L~e** m lame person; **~en** be lame.

lähmen 1. lame, cripple; 2. *fig* paralyse, petrify, immobilize.

lahmlegen paralyse.

Lähmung f 1. *med* paralysis; 2. immobilization.

Laib m loaf (of bread).

Laich m, **l~en** spawn.

Laie m layman, amateur;

l~nhaft amateurish, dilettante.

Laken n sheet.

Lakritze f liquorice.

Lamm n lamb.

Lamp|e f lamp; light; **~enfieber** n stage fright; **~enschirm** m lampshade; **~ion** m Chinese lantern.

Land n 1. land; an ~ gehen go ashore; 2. (Acker) soil, ground; 3. country; auf dem ~ wohnen live in the country; aufs ~ fahren go into the country; 4. (Staat) country.

landauf, landab all over the country.

Lande|bahn f runway; **~erlaubnis** f permission to land.

landen 1. land; 2. mar go ashore, disembark; 3. aero touch down.

Land|enge f isthmus; **~eplatz** m landing field.

Länderspiel n international match.

landesüblich customary.

Landesverrat m treason.

Land|haus n country house; **~karte** f map.

ländlich rural, rustic.

Landplage f plague, nuisance.

Landschaft f countryside, landscape, scenery; **l~lich** scenic; regional; **~sschutzgebiet** n preserve.

Landsmann m countryman, compatriot.

Land|straße f country road, B road; **~streicher** m tramp; **~strich** m region, district.

Landung f landing, touch-down.

Land|weg m: auf dem ~ by land; **~wein** m homegrown wine; **~wirt** m farmer; **~wirtschaft** f agriculture; **l~wirtschaftlich** agricultural; **~zunge** f spit.

lang I adj 1. (räumlich) long; e-e ~e Straße a long road; 2. 90 cm ~ sein be 90 centimetres long; 3. (groß) tall; 4. (zeitlich) ein ~er Winter a long winter; seit ~em for a long time; **II** adv: ~ anhaltender Beifall long applause; je länger je lieber the longer the better; etw ~ und breit erzählen tell s.th. in great detail; nicht ~e danach not long after; das war ~e vorher that was long before; wie ~e sind Sie schon hier? how long have you been here? noch ~e nicht not nearly; sie ist noch ~ nicht fertig she is far from being ready; **~atmig** long-winded, lengthy.

Länge f 1. (räumlich) length; von 10 Meter ~ 10 metres in length; 2. (Personen) length; 3. (zeitlich) length; 4. geog longitude; **~ngrad** m degree of longitude; **~nmaß** n linear measure.

Langeweile f boredom.

lang|fristig long-term; **~jäh-rig** of many years; **L~lauf** *m* cross-country running.
länglich elongated.
längs alongside.
langsam slow; ~ *fahren* slow down.
Langspielplatte *f* long-play-ing record, LP.
längst long ago; *ich hatte ihn ~ erkannt* I had recog-nized him long before; *das ist ~ bekannt* that has been known for a long time.
Langstreckenflug *m* long--distance flight.
langweil|en, *sich* be bored; **~ig** boring, tedious, dull.
Langwelle *f* long wave.
langwierig lenghty; wear-isome.
Lanze *f* spear.
Lappalie *f* trifle.
Lappen *m* cloth, rag, patch.
Lärche *f* larch.
Lärm *m* noise, din; **~be-kämpfung** *f* noise abate-ment; **l~en** make a noise, row, rocket.
Larve *f* zoo larva.
Lasche *f* 1. flap; 2. tech strap.
lassen *irr* **I** *aux* 1. *(zulassen)* let; *jdn warten ~* keep s.o. waiting; *laß ihn nur kom-men!* just let him come! 2. *jdn etw tun ~* let s.o. do s.th., allow s.o. to do s.th., make s.o. do s.th.; *jdn ent-kommen ~* let s.o. escape; 3. *etw tun ~* have s.th. done; 4. *laß dir helfen!* let me help

you! *das ließ er sich nicht zweimal sagen* he didn't have to be told twice; *laß dir ein Glas Wasser geben* have a glass of water; *sich die Haare schneiden ~* have o.'s hair cut; *es läßt sich nicht leugnen, daß* it cannot be denied that; **II** 5. *(überlassen)* let, leave; *jdm Zeit ~* give s.o. time; 6. *(unterlassen)* stop; 7. *(zu-rücklassen)* leave; *jdn zu Hause ~* leave s.o. at home; 8. *Blut ~* lose blood; 9. *(be-lassen)* leave, let; ~ *Sie mich damit in Ruhe!* don't bother me!
lässig casual; indolent; **L~keit** *f* casualness.
Last *f* 1. load; 2. *(Gewicht)* weight; 3. *(Bürde) jdm zur ~ fallen* be a burden to s.o.; 4. *com* burden, charge; *zu ~en von* to the account of; 5. *jur* encumbrance; **l~en** lie, weigh, rest *(auf* on); **~enaufzug** *m* goods lift.
Laster *n* vice; **l~haft** vicious.
lästern 1. slander, defame; 2. *(Gott)* blaspheme.
lästig troublesome, pestilent; *jdm ~ sein* be a nuisance to s.o.
Last|kahn *m* barge, lighter; **~kraftwagen** *m* lorry, *Am* truck; **~schrift** *f* debit; **~tier** *n* pack animal.
Latein *n* Latin; *mit s-m ~ am Ende sein* be at o.'s wits' end; **~amerika** *n* Latin

America; **l~isch**: *auf* ~ in Latin.

Laterne *f* lantern; **~npfahl** *m* lamp-post.

Latte *f* 1. lath, batten; 2. *sport* bar.

Latz *m* bib; **~hose** *f* dungarees *pl*.

lau lukewarm, tepid.

Laub *n* leaves *pl*, foliage; **~baum** *m* deciduous tree.

Laube *f* bower, arbour; **~ngang** *m* pergola; **~kolonie** *f* allotment gardens *pl*.

Laub|frosch *m* tree frog; **~säge** *f* fretsaw.

Lauch *m* leek.

Lauer *f*: *auf der* ~ *liegen* be on the lurk; **l~n** lie in wait (*auf* for).

Lauf *m* 1. run; 2. *sport* race, sprint; 3. *im* ~*e der Zeit* in the course of time; *im* ~*e der letzten Jahre* during the last few years; 4. *tech* motion, operation; 5. (*Fluß*) flow; 6. *astr* course; 7. *mil* barrel; **~bahn** *f* career.

laufen *irr* 1. run; 2. *tech* work, function; 3. (*gehen*) walk; 4. *theat* run, show; 5. *jur* be valid; 6. (*fließen*) flow; 7. (*sich hinziehen*) stretch, extend.

laufend 1. current; *das* ~*e Jahr* the present year; 2. *com* running, current; 3. (*regelmäßig*) regular; 4. *auf dem* ~*en sein* be up-to-date.

Läufer *m* 1. runner; 2. (*Schach*) bishop; 3. (*Teppich*) carpet.

Lauf|junge *m* errand boy; **~masche** *f* ladder, *Am* run; **~paß** *m*: *jdm den* ~ *geben* give s.o. the sack; **~stall** *m* (*Kind*) playpen; **~steg** *m* gangway; **~zeit** *f* 1. (*Wechsel*) term, currency; 2. (*Film*) running time.

Lauge *f* lye.

Laune *f* humour, temper; *gute, schlechte* ~ *haben* be in a good, bad mood; **l~nhaft** 1. moody; 2. capricious; 3. *fig* changeable, uncertain.

Laus *f* louse.

lauschen 1. listen (to s.o.); 2. (*heimlich*) eavesdrop (*an der Tür* at the door).

laut I *adj* 1. loud; 2. (*Straße*) noisy; 3. *es wurde das Gerücht* ~, *daß* the rumour spread that; **II** *adv*: ~ *sprechen* speak loudly; **III** *prp* according to; ~ *Vorschrift* by rule.

Laut *m* sound, tone.

Laute *f* lute.

lauten 1. run, go; *der Brief lautet wie folgt* the letter reads as follows; 2. (*besagen*) say; 3. *wie lautet sein Name?* what is his name? 4. *auf den Namen X* ~ be in the name of X; *das Urteil lautet auf* the sentence is.

läuten 1. ring, peal, chime; 2. *es läutet* there is a ring at the door.

lauter 1. (*Gold*) pure; 2. (*Ab-*

sichten) honest; 3. *aus ~ Vergnügen* from sheer pleasure; 4. *~ Lügen* nothing but lies.

läutern purify, purge.

Laut|schrift *f* phonetic transcription; **~sprecher** *m* loudspeaker; **~stärke** *f* sound volume.

Lava *f* lava.

Lavendel *m* lavender.

Lawine *f* avalanche.

Lazarett *n* (military) hospital.

leben 1. live; be alive; 2. *(existieren)* live, exist; 3. *einsam ~* lead a lonely life; 4. *(wohnen)* live, dwell; 5. *von etw ~* live on s.th.; *für etw ~* live for s.th.

Leben *n* 1. life; *am ~ sein* be alive; *sich das ~ nehmen* commit suicide; 2. *(Dasein) das tägliche ~* daily life; *das ~ auf dem Lande* the life in the country; 3. *(Lebensweise)* way of life; 4. *fürs ganze ~* for the rest of o.'s life; *zeit s-s ~s* during o.'s lifetime; 5. *(Treiben)* liveliness, activity; 6. *(Lebensunterhalt)* living, livelihood.

lebend living, alive.

Lebende *m* living person.

lebendig 1. living; *ein ~er Mensch* a man alive; 2. *(lebhaft)* lively, vivid.

Lebens|abend *m* old age; **~anschauung** *f* view of life; **~dauer** *f* 1. life-span; 2. *tech* durability; **~erwar-**

~tung *f* life expectancy; **l~fähig** viable; **~gefahr** *f* danger to life; *unter ~* at the risk of o.'s life; **l~gefährlich** dangerous (to life); **~gefährte** *m* companion; **~größe** *f: in ~* full-length; **~haltungskosten** *pl* cost of living; **~jahr** *n: im 70. ~* at the age of seventy; **~kunst** *f* art of living; **~künstler** *m: er ist ein ~* he makes the best of everything; **l~länglich** lifelong; **~e Rente** life annuity; **~lauf** *m* 1. *(schriftlich)* curriculum vitae; 2. course of life; **~mittel** *pl* food, provisions *pl;* groceries *pl;* **~mittelgeschäft** *n* food store,- grocery; **l~müde** tired of life; **~regel** *f* maxim; **~standard** *m* standard of living; **~unterhalt** *m* livelihood; *s-n ~ verdienen* earn o.'s living; **~versicherung** *f* life assurance; **~zeichen** *n: kein ~ von sich geben* show no sign of life; **~zeit** *f* 1. lifetime; 2. *auf ~* for life.

Leber *f* liver; **~fleck** *m* liver spot; **~tran** *m* cod-liver oil.

Lebewesen *n* living being.

lebhaft 1. lively, vivacious; 2. *(Treiben)* active, busy; **L~igkeit** *f* liveliness; briskness.

Lebkuchen *m* gingerbread.

leblos lifeless.

Leck *n* leak.

lecken 1. *(undicht)* leak, be leaky; 2. *(schlecken)* lick.
lecker delicious, tasty; **L~bissen** *m* titbit, delicacy; **L~ei** *f* candy, sweets *pl.*
Leder *n* leather; **~jacke** *f* leather jacket; **~mantel** *m* leather coat; **~waren** *pl* leather goods *pl.*
ledig single, unmarried; **~lich** only, merely, simply.
leer 1. empty; 2. *(unbesetzt)* vacant, unoccupied; 3. *fig* vain; **L~e** *f* emptiness; **~en** empty, clear.
Leergut *n* empties *pl;* **~lauf** *m tech* idling; *mot* neutral (gear); **~ung** *f (Briefkasten)* collection.
legal legal, lawful.
legen 1. lay, put, place; 2. *Eier ~* lay eggs; *sich ins Bett ~* go to bed; *der Wind hat sich gelegt* the wind has calmed down; *besonderes Gewicht ~ auf* attach particular importance to.
legendär legendary.
Legierung *f* alloy.
legitim legitimate; **L~ation** *f* proof of identity; legitimation; **~ieren** 1. *jur* legitimate; 2. *(berechtigen)* authorize.

Lehm *m* 1. loam; 2. *(Ton)* clay.
Lehne *f (Rücken~)* back (-rest); *(Arm~)* arm(-rest); **l~en,** *sich* lean *(an* against); *sich aus dem Fenster ~* lean

out of the window; **~stuhl** *m* armchair.
Lehrbuch *n* textbook.
Lehre *f* 1. teaching, doctrine; 2. *(Lehrsatz)* theory; 3. *(Warnung)* lesson; 4. *(Folgerung)* conclusion; 5. apprenticeship; **l~n** 1. teach, instruct; 2. *(zeigen)* show, prove; **~r(in** *f)* *m* teacher, instructor, master.
Lehrgang *m* course *(für* in); **~ling** *m* apprentice, trainee; **~meister** *m* teacher, master; **l~reich** instructive; **~stuhl** *m* chair; **~zeit** *f* apprenticeship.
Leib *m* 1. body; *sich jdn vom ~e halten* keep s.o. at arms length; *mit ~ und Seele* with heart and soul; 2. *(Rumpf)* trunk; *(Bauch)* belly; **~arzt** *m* personal physician; **~esübungen** *pl* physical exercise; **~gericht** *n* favourite dish; **l~haftig** incarnate; **~schmerzen** *pl* stomach-ache; **~wäsche** *f* underwear.
Leiche *f* 1. (dead) body, corpse; 2. *(Tier)* carcass; **~nhalle** *f* mortuary; **~nstarre** *f* rigor mortis; **~nwagen** *m* hearse; **~nzug** *m* funeral procession.
Leichnam *m* (dead) body, corpse.
leicht 1. light; 2. *(Krankheit)* slight; 3. *(Aufgabe)* easy; *nichts ~er als das!* nothing

easier! *es war nicht ~, etw zu tun* it was not easy task to do s.th.; *es ~ haben* have an easy life; *das ist ~er gesagt als getan* that's easier said than done.

Leichtathletik *f* athletics *pl.*

leicht|fertig 1. careless, rash; 2. frivolous; **~gläubig** credulous; **L~sinn** *m* carelessness; **~sinnig** careless, reckless, thoughtless.

leid: *etw ~ sein* be sick and tired of; *es tut mir ~!* I am sorry!

Leid *n* sorrow, grief, pain; *jdm ein ~ zufügen* do s.o. harm.

leiden *irr* 1. suffer (*an* from); endure, bear; 2. *(dulden)* allow, tolerate, permit; 3. *ich kann ihn nicht ~* I can't stand him; *wir können ihn gut ~* we like him a lot.

Leiden *n* suffering, affliction; complaint.

leidend 1. suffering; 2. *~ sein* be in poor health.

Leidenschaft *f* passion (*für* for), ardour; **l~lich** passionate, ardent.

Leidensgenosse *m* fellow--sufferer.

leid|er unfortunately, I am sorry to say, much to my regret; **~ig** troublesome, confounded; **~lich** 1. tolerable, passable; 2. *es geht mir ~ gut* I'm tolerably well.

Leih|bibliothek *f*, **~bücherei** *f* lending library; **l~en**

irr 1. *jdm etw ~* lend s.o. s.th.; rent s.th. to s.o.; 2. *sich von jdm etw ~* borrow s.th. from s.o.; **~frist** *f* lending period; **~gabe** *f* loan; **~gebühr** *f* lending fee; **~haus** *n* pawnshop; **l~weise** on loan.

Leim *m* 1. glue; 2. *aus dem ~ gehen* fall apart; *fig* break up; **l~en** glue (together).

Leine *f* line; *(Hunde~)* lead.

Lein|en *n* linen; **~tuch** *n* linen sheet; **~wand** *f* 1. *(Maler)* canvas; 2. *film* screen.

leise 1. low, soft, gentle; *mit ~r Stimme* in a low voice; *das Radio ~r stellen* turn the radio down; 2. *seien Sie bitte ~!* please keep quiet! 3. *ich habe nicht die ~ste Ahnung* I haven't the faintest idea.

Leiste *f* 1. strip; 2. *anat* groin.

leisten 1. do, work; 2. *(durchführen)* carry out, execute, perform; 3. *(vollbringen)* achieve, accomplish; 4. *Widerstand ~* offer resistance; 5. *sich etw ~* treat o.s. to s.th., afford s.th.

Leisten *m* last.

Leistung *f* 1. performance; 2. *(Arbeit)* work; 3. *(gute ~)* accomplishment, feat; 4. *(Ausstoß)* output, 5. *(Motor)* power; 6. *(Dienst ~)* service; 7. *(Beitrag)* contribution; *(e-r Krankenkasse)* benefit; **l~sfähig** 1. efficient; 2. *(körperlich)* fit; 3. *tech* powerful; **~sfähigkeit** f 1. efficiency; 2. *tech* power; 3. *(Firma)* productivity; output; 4. *(Auto)* performance.

Leitartikel m leader.

leiten 1. lead, guide, conduct; 2. *(Geschäft)* run, manage, direct; 3. *el* conduct; 4. *etw in die Wege ~* pave the way for s.th.; 5. *(Diskussion)* lead; 6. *(Versammlung)* preside (over a meeting); **l~end** 1. *(führend)* leading; 2. *(Angestellter)* executive; **L~er** 1. m leader, manage, director, head; 2. *el* conductor; 3. f ladder.

Leitgedanke m basic idea; **~satz** m guiding principle.

Leitung f 1. control, management; 2. *(Schule)* administration; 3. *(Vorsitz)* chairmanship; 4. *unter der ~ von* directed by; headed by; *mus* conducted by; 5. *tech* mains pl, pipeline; *(Rohr~)* conduit; *(Strom)* circuit; 6. *(tele) in der ~ bleiben* hold the line; **~swasser** n tap water.

Lektion f lesson; **~üre** f reading matter, book.

Lende f med loin.

lenken 1. *(Fahrzeug)* drive, steer; 2. *(führen)* guide, conduct, direct; 3. *jds Aufmerksamkeit ~ auf* call s.o.'s attention to; **L~rad** n steering

wheel; **L~stange** f *(Fahrrad)* handlebar.

Lepra f leprosy.

Lerche f lark.

lernen learn *(etw zu tun to do s.th.)*, study.

lesbar readable.

lesen irr read; **L~er** m reader; **L~erbrief** m reader's letter.

leserlich legible, readable.

Lesesaal m reading room; **~zeichen** n book-mark.

Lesung f: *(pol) in zweiter ~* on second reading.

letzt 1. last, final; *im ~en Augenblick* at the last moment; *~en Endes* after all; 2. *in der ~en Zeit* lately; *in den ~en Wochen* in recent weeks; *~e Nachrichten* latest news.

Letzt f: *zu guter ~* in the end, finally.

Letzte m last.

letztens lastly.

letztere latter.

Leuchte f light, lamp; **l~en** 1. shine; 2. *(Lampe)* light; 3. *fig* sparkle; **l~end** shining; sparkling; **~er** m candlestick; **~farbe** f luminous colour; **~turm** m lighthouse.

leugnen deny.

Leumund m reputation; **~szeugnis** n testimonial.

Leute pl people, men, persons, folk.

Leutnant m second lieutenant; *aero* pilot officer.

Lexikon *n* dictionary, ency-clop(a)edia.

Libelle *f* dragon-fly.

liberal liberal, broad-minded; **~isieren** liberalize; **L~ismus** *m* liberalism.

Licht *n* 1. light; ~ *machen* switch the light on; *das ~ ausschalten* switch the light out; *die Wahrheit ans ~ bringen* bring the truth to light; ~ *in e-e Angelegenheit bringen* throw light on a matter; 2. *(Helle)* brightness; 3. *(Beleuchtung)* illumination.

licht 1. light, bright; 2. *(Haar)* sparse; 3. **~e** *Höhe* clearance.

Licht|bild *n* lantern slide; **~blick** *m* glimmer of hope; **l~echt** light-proof; **l~empfindlich** sensitive; **l~en** 1. *(Wald)* clear; 2. *sich* ~ get thin; 3. *Anker* ~ weigh anchor; **~geschwindigkeit** *f* speed of light; **~jahr** *n* light-year; **~mast** *m* lamp-post; **~schacht** *m* light shaft; **~schein** *m* gleam of light; **~schranke** *f* light barrier; **~strahl** *m* beam of light; **~ung** *f* clearing, glade; **~wellen** *pl* light waves *pl*.

Lid *n* (eye)lid.

lieb 1. *(teuer, wert)* dear; ~*er Herr X* dear Mr. X; 2. *(freundlich)* nice, kind, good; *seien Sie so* ~ *und* will you be so kind as to;

3. *es ist mir* ~, *daß* I am glad that.

Liebe *f* 1. love *(zu* for); 2. *(Zuneigung)* affection; 3. *(Nächsten~)* charity; **~lei** *f* flirtation.

lieben 1. love, be in love *(jdn* with s.o.); 2. *(Zuneigung)* be attached (to), be fond of; like; **~swürdig** 1. charming; 2. *(zuvorkommend)* kind, obliging.

lieber I *comp von lieb* much nicer; **II** *adv* 1. *(eher)* rather, sooner; 2. *(besser)* better; 3. *etw* ~ *haben* like s.th. better, prefer s.th.

Liebes|brief *m* love letter; **~kummer** *m* lover's grief; **~paar** *n* lovers *pl*.

liebevoll affectionate, tender.

Liebhaber *m* lover, admirer; **~ei** *f* hobby, fancy; **~preis** *m* collector's price; **~wert** *m* collector's value.

lieblich lovely, charming, sweet.

Liebling *m* darling, favourite; **~saufenthalt** *m* favourite spot.

lieblos 1. unkind; 2. *(kalt)* unloving, cold.

liebst I *sup von lieb* dearest; favourite; **II** *sup von gern:* *am* **~en** most of all; *es wäre mir am* **~en**, *wenn* I would like it best, if.

Lied *n* 1. song; 2. *(Weise)* air.

liederlich 1. *(unordentlich)* slovenly, sloppy; 2. *(aus-*

schweifend) dissipated, dissolute.

Liefer|ant *m* supplier; **I~bar** available; **~frist** *f* term of delivery; **I~n** 1. deliver (*nach* to); *(beschaffen)* supply, furnish; 2. *(Ertrag)* yield; **~schein** *m* bill of delivery; **~ung** *f* delivery, supply; *zahlbar bei ~* payable on delivery; **~wagen** *m* delivery van; **~zeit** *f* time of delivery.

Liege *f* couch.

liegen *irr* 1. lie, be; 2. *(gelegen sein)* be situated, lie; 3. *(Fenster)* face (*nach Süden* south); 4. be lying (*auf dem Tisch* on the table); 5. *im Bett ~* lie in bed; 6. *der Fehler liegt bei dir* it es your fault; 7. *mir liegt nichts daran* I don't care for it; 8. *jdm ~ suit s.o.;* **~bleiben** *irr* 1. *im Bett ~* remain in bed; 2. *(Auto)* break down; 3. *(vergessen)* be forgotten; 4. *(Arbeit)* pile up; **~lassen** *irr* 1. *(vergessen)* leave; 2. *(Arbeit)* leave off.

Liege|sitz *m (Auto)* reclining seat; **~stuhl** *m* deck-chair; **~wagen** *m* couchette; **~wiese** *f* lawn for sunbathing.

Lift *m* lift, *Am* elevator; **~boy** *m* lift boy, *Am* elevator boy.

Likör *m* liqueur.

lila lilac.

Lilie *f bot* lily.

Limonade *f* lemonade.

lind mild, gentle.

Linde *f* lime.

lindern relieve, alleviate, soothe.

Lineal *n* ruler.

Linie *f* 1. line; *in erster ~* first of all, primarily; 2. *(Reihe)* alignment; 3. *fig* trend, course; 4. *(Bus)* route, line; **~nschiff** *n* liner.

liniert ruled, lined.

link 1. left; 2. *auf der ~en Straßenseite* on the left-hand side of the street; 3. *pol* left-wing

Linke *f* 1. left hand; 2. *pol* left wing.

linkisch clumsy, awkward.

links on the left; *von ~* from the left; *von ~ nach rechts* from left to right; *er kam von ~* he came from the left; **L~händer** *m* left-handed person; **~herum** to the left; **L~verkehr** *m* left-hand traffic.

Linse *f* 1. *bot* lentil; 2. *opt* lens; **~nsuppe** *f* lentil soup.

Lippe *f* lip; **~nstift** *m* lipstick.

lispeln lisp.

List *f* trickery, cunning.

Liste *f* list; register.

listig cunning, tricky, crafty.

Liter *n* litre.

Literatur *f* literature; **~geschichte** *f* literary history.

Litfaßsäule *f* advertising pillar.

Lizenz *f* licence, *Am* license.

Lob *n* praise; **l~en** praise (*jdn* s.o.); **l~enswert** praiseworthy.

Loch *n* 1. hole; 2. *ein ~ im Reifen haben* have a puncture; **l~en** 1. punch; 2. perforate; **~karte** *f* punch card; **~streifen** *m* punch tape.

Locke *f* curl.

locken lure (*in e-e Falle* into a trap), entice, tempt.

Lockenwickel *m* hair curler.

locker 1. loose; 2. (*Teig*) light; **~n** 1. loosen, untighten; 2. (*Seil*) slacken.

Lockvogel *m* decoy.

lodern blaze, flame.

Löffel *m* spoon.

Loge *f* box, loge.

Log|ik *f* logic; **l~isch** logical.

Lohn *m* 1. wage(s *pl*); 2. (*Verdienst*) earnings *pl*; 3. (*Gehalt*) salary; 4. (*Vergütung*) remuneration; 5. (*Belohnung*) reward; **l~en** 1. reward, recompense; 2. (*wert sein*) be worth; 3. *sich ~* be rewarding; *die Mühe lohnt sich* it is worth the trouble; **l~end** worthwhile; profitable; **~steuer** *f* wage tax; **~zettel** *m* pay slip.

Lokal *n* 1. restaurant, public house; 2. (*Geschäft*) business premises *pl*; **~patriotismus** *m* local patriotism.

Lokomotiv|e *f* engine; **~führer** *m* engine driver, *Am* engineer.

Lorbeer *m* 1. laurel; 2. (*Gewürz*) bay leaf.

Los *n* 1. lot; 2. (*Schicksal*) fate, destiny.

los 1. loose; *der Knopf ist ~* the button is off; 2. *etw ~ sein* be rid of s.th.; 3. *was ist ~?* what's up? *mit ihm ist nicht viel ~* he's not up to much; 4. *~!* go on!

lösbar solvable.

Löschblatt *n* blotting paper.

löschen 1. (*Feuer*) extinguish, put out; 2. (*Durst*) quench; 3. *com* cancel, liquidate; 4. (*Tonband*) erase; 5. *mar* (*Ware*) unload.

Löschfahrzeug *n* fire engine.

lose loose; unfastened.

Lösegeld *n* ransom.

losen cast lots.

lösen 1. loosen; 2. (*Knoten*) untie, unfasten; 3. (*abtrennen*) separate, detach; 4. *math* solve; 5. (*Fahrkarte*) buy; 6. *chem* dissolve; 7. *sich ~* loosen; *sich von jdm ~* break away from s.o.

los|fahren *irr* depart, start; **~gehen** *irr* 1. go off; 2. *auf jdn ~* attack s.o. go for s.o.; 3. *fam* (*beginnen*) begin, start; **~lassen** *irr* 1. let go; 2. *den Hund auf jdn ~* set the dog after s.o.

löslich soluble.

los|machen 1. detach; 2. *sich ~* disengage o.s.; **~reißen** *irr: sich ~* break away;

~sagen: *sich von etw* ~ renounce s.th.
Losung *f* password.
Lösung *f* solution, answer.
loswerden *irr*: *jdn* ~ get rid of s.o.
Lot *n* 1. *mar* lead; 2. *tech* plumb; **l~en** 1. plumb; 2. *mar* sound.
löt|en solder; **L~kolben** *m* soldering iron.
Lotse *m*, **l~n** pilot; **~nboot** *n* pilot vessel.
Lotterie *f* lottery.
Lotto *n* lotto.
Löwe *m* lion; **~nzahn** *m* dandelion.
Luchs *m* lynx.
Lücke *f* 1. gap, hole; 2. *(Auslassung)* omission; 3. *(Fragebogen)* blank; 4. *(im Gedächtnis)* slip; **~nbüßer** *m* stopgap; **l~nhaft** incomplete, fragmentary; **l~nlos** complete.
Luft *f* 1. air; *frische* ~ *schöpfen* breathe in fresh air; 2. *(Atem)* breath; *die* ~ *anhalten* hold o.'s breath; *tief* ~ *holen* take a deep breath; 3. *das ist aus der* ~ *gegriffen* that's pure imagination; **~angriff** *m* air raid; **~bad** *n* air bath; **~ballon** *m* (air-) balloon; **~bild** *n* aerial view; **~brücke** *f* airlift; **l~dicht** airtight, airproof; **~druck** *m* 1. atmospheric pressure; 2. *(Explosion)* blast; 3. *(Reifen)* inflation, pressure.
lüften 1. *(Zimmer)* air, venti-

late; 2. *(Hut)* raise, lift; 3. *(Geheimnis)* reveal.
Luft|fahrt *f* aviation; aeronautics *mit sing*; **~feuchtigkeit** *f* atmospheric humidity; **~fracht** *f* airfreight, air cargo; **~gewehr** *n* airgun; **l~ig** airy *a. fig*; **~kissen** *n* air cushion; **~kissenfahrzeug** *n* air cushion vehicle; **~korridor** *m* air corridor; **~kurort** *m* climatic health resort; **l~leer** vacuous; **~linie** *f*: *in der* ~ as the crow flies; **~loch** *n aero* air pocket; **~matratze** *f* air mattress; **~pirat** *m* hijacker; **~post** *f*: *durch* ~ by air mail; **~postbrief** *m* air mail letter; **~pumpe** *f* air pump; **~röhre** *f anat* windpipe; **~schacht** *m* air shaft; **~schiff** *n* airship; **~schlösser** *pl*: ~ *bauen* build castles in the air; **~schneise** *f* air lane; **~schutz** *m* air-raid protection; **~schutzraum** *m* air-raid shelter; **~sprung** *m* caper; *vor Freude e-n* ~ *machen* jump for joy; **~stützpunkt** *m* air base.
Lüftung *f* airing, ventilation.
Luft|veränderung *f* change of air; **~verkehrslinie** *f* air-line; **~verschmutzung** *f* air pollution; **~waffe** *f* Air Force; **~weg** *m* 1. *auf dem* ~ by air; 2. *anat pl* respiratory tracts *pl*; **~widerstand** *m* air resistance,

drag; **~zug** m draught, *Am* draught.

Lüg|e f lie; **l~en** *irr* (tell a) lie; **~endetektor** m lie detector; **~ner** m liar.

Luke f 1. *mar* hatch; 2. *(Dach~)* skylight.

Lümmel m lout, rude fellow.

Lump m scoundrel, rascal; **~en** m rag.

Lunge f *anat* lungs *pl;* **~nentzündung** f pneumonia; **~nflügel** m lobe of the lung; **~nheilstätte** f sanatorium; **l~nkrank** tuberculous; **~nkrebs** m lung cancer.

Lunte f: **~** *riechen* smell a rat.

Lupe f magnifying glass.

Lust f 1. *(Wunsch)* inclination, desire; **~** *haben, etw zu tun* be inclined to do s.th., like to do s.th.; 2. *(Vergnügen)* pleasure, delight, joy;

3. *(Interesse)* interest; 4. *(Verlangen)* longing, craving; 5. *(Begierde)* desire, lust.

Lüster m lustre.

lüstern lascivious, lustful, lecherous; **L~heit** f lasciviousness.

lustig 1. gay, merry; *sich über jdn ~ machen* make fun of s.o.; 2. *(heiter)* amusing, funny.

Lustspiel n comedy.

lutschen suck (*an etw* s.th.)

Luxemburg n Luxembourg; **~er** m Luxembourger; **l~isch** Luxembourgian.

lux|uriös luxurious; **L~us** m luxury; **L~ushotel** n luxury hotel.

Lymphdrüse f lymphatic gland.

lynch|en lynch; **L~justiz** f lynch law.

Lyrik f lyric poetry.

M

Machart f 1. *(Kleid)* style; 2. *(Möbel)* design.

machen 1. *(anfertigen, zubereiten)* make, prepare; *Feuer* ~ make a fire; 2. *(tun)* do; *was machst du da?* what are you doing there? 3. *(erreichen)* manage; 4. *etw zu etw* ~ make s.th. s.th.; 5. *(verursachen)* give, cause; *das macht Appetit* that gives you a good appetite; 6. *sich etw aus e-r Sache* ~ care about s.th.; *das macht mir nichts aus* I don't care about that; 7. *(ergeben)* be; 8. *sich* ~ *an* set to work.

Macht f 1. power, might; *aus eigener* ~ by o.'s own power; 2. *(Herrschaft)* power *(über* over), control; 3. *(Staatsmacht)* power; *an die* ~ *kommen* come into power; 4. *(Einfluß, Gewalt)* force; ~ *der Gewohnheit* force of habit; 5. *(Streitmacht)* forces *pl;* ~**befugnis** f authority; ~**haber** m ruler, dictator.

mächtig 1. powerful, mighty, strong; 2. *(erheblich)* enormous; 3. *e-r Sprache* ~ *sein* have a good command of a language.

machtlos powerless.

Mädchen n girl.

Made f maggot, grub.

Magazin n 1. *(Lagerhaus)* warehouse; 2. *(Zeitschrift)* magazine.

Magd f (female) farm-worker.

Magen m stomach, belly; *ich habe mir den* ~ *verdorben* I have an upset stomach; ~**beschwerden** pl gastric trouble; ~**geschwür** n gastric ulcer.

mager 1. lean, thin, skinny, meagre; 2. *fig* scanty, poor, spare; **M**~**keit** f 1. leanness, meagreness; 2. *(Boden)* poorness; **M**~**milch** f skim milk.

Magie f magic; **m**~**isch** magic(al).

Magistrat m town council.

Magnet m magnet; **m**~**isch** magnetic; **m**~**isieren** magnetize.

Mahagoni n mahogany.

Mähdrescher m combine; **m**~**en** mow, cut; *(Korn)* reap.

Mahl n meal.

mahlen *(Korn)* grind, mill.

Mahlzeit f: *e-e* ~ *einnehmen* have a meal.

Mähmaschine f mowing machine.

Mähne f mane.

mahnen 1. *jdn an etw* ~ remind s.o. of s.th.; 2. *(ermahnen)* admonish, warn;

M~mal n memorial;
M~ung f 1. com reminder;
2. *(Ermahnung)* admonition,
exhortation.
Mai m May; **~glöckchen** n
lily of the valley; **~käfer** m
cockchafer.
Mais m maize, Indian corn.
Majestät f majesty;
m~isch majestic.
Major m major.
Makel m 1. stain, spot *a. fig*;
2. *fig* blemish.
Makkaroni pl macaroni.
Makler m broker.
Makrele f mackerel.
Makrone f macaroon.
mal by; *zwei ~ zwei ist vier*
two times two is four.
Mal n 1. time; *das erste ~* the
first time; *mit e-m ~* all at
once; *ein anderes ~* another
time; *dieses ~* this time; *ein
für alle ~e* once and for all;
2. *(Zeichen)* mark, sign.
Malaria f malaria.
mal|en paint; draw; **M~er** m
painter; **M~erei** f painting;
~erisch picturesque.
Malz n malt.
Mama f mummy.
man 1. one, you; *~ kann nie
wissen* you never know;
2. they, people; *~ sagt, daß*
it is said that; *~ nehme ...*
take ...
manch 1. *~e haben Geld*
some people have money;
2. several, a few; *~es Mal*
many a time; **~mal** some-
times, at times.

Mandant m client.
Mandarine f bot tangerine.
Mandel f 1. bot almond;
2. anat tonsil; **~entzün-
dung** f tonsillitis.
Mangel 1. m lack, want, absence; *aus ~ an* for lack of;
2. *(Knappheit)* shortage;
3. *(Fehler)* defect, fault;
4. med deficiency; 5. f *(Wäsche ~)* mangle; **~erschei-
nung** f med deficiency
symptom; **m~haft** 1. *(fehlerhaft)* defective; 2. *(ungenügend)* deficient, insufficient; **m~n** 1. want, be
wanting, be lacking; *es man-
gelt an* there is a lack of;
2. *(Wäsche)* mangle; **m~nd**
lacking; **m~s** for lack of;
~ware f article in short
supply.
Manieren pl manners.
Manifest n manifesto.
Maniküre f manicure.
Mann m 1. man; 2. *(Ehe~)*
husband.
Männchen n zoo male.
mannigfaltig various, diverse; **M~keit** f variety, diversity.
männlich 1. male; 2. gram
masculine; 3. *fig* manly.
Mannschaft f 1. aero crew;
2. personnel; 3. sport team.
Manöv|er n, **m~rieren**
manoeuvre.
Mansarde f attic.
Manschette f 1. *(Hemd)*
cuff; 2. *(Blumentopf)* paper
frill; **~nknopf** m cuff-link.

Mantel m 1. (over)coat; 2. *tech* casing, jacket.

Manuskript n 1. manuscript; 2. *film* scenario.

Mappe f 1. (*Akten~*) portfolio, briefcase; 2. (*Schreib~*) folder.

Märchen n fairy tale, story; **m~haft** fabulous, fantastic, fairy-tale.

Marder m marten.

Margarine f margarine.

Marienkäfer m ladybird.

Marine f 1. *mil* navy; 2. (*Handels~*) marine.

Marionette f marionette.

Mark 1. f (*Währung*) mark; 2. *hist* march; 3. n *anat* marrow, medulla.

markant (*auffallend*) striking, prominent.

Mark|e f 1. *com* brand, make; type, kind; 2. (*Handels~*) trademark; 3. (*Zeichen*) mark; 4. (*Brief~*) stamp; (*Spiel~*) chip; **~enartikel** m branded article; **m~ieren** 1. mark, sign; 2. (*vortäuschen*) simulate.

Markise f awning.

Markt m 1. market; *auf den ~ bringen* put on the market; 2. (*Jahr~*) fair; **~bude** f market stall; **~flecken** m small market town; **~frau** f market women; **~halle** f covered market; **~platz** m market-place; **~tag** m market-day; **~wirtschaft** f market economy.

Marmelade f jam.

Marmor m marble.

Marone f (edible) chestnut.

Marsch m march; *sich in ~ setzen* set off.

Marschall m marshal.

marschieren march; walk.

Marter f torment, torture.

Märtyrer m martyr.

Martyrium n *rel* martyrdom.

März m March.

Marzipan n marzipan.

Masche f 1. (*Netz*) mesh; 2. (*Strick~*) stitch; 3. (*Strumpf~*) ladder; **~ndraht** m wire netting.

Maschin|e f 1. machine, engine; 2. *aero* plane; 3. *loc* locomotive; 4. *auf der ~ schreiben* type; **m~ell** mechanical; **~enbau** m mechanical engineering; **~enfabrik** f engineering works; **m~engeschrieben** typed, typewritten; **~engewehr** n machine-gun; **~enpistole** f tommy-gun; **~enschlosser** m engine fitter; **~ist** m machinist, *Am* operator.

Masern pl measles *sing*.

Maserung f (*Holz*) grain.

Mask|e f 1. mask; 2. *fig* pretence; **~enball** m masked ball; **~erade** f masquerade; **m~ieren** disguise, mask.

Maß n 1. measure; 2. (*Abmessung*) dimension; 3. (*Körpermaß*) measurement; *nach ~ gemacht* made to measure; 4. (*Ausmaß*) extent, degree, measure; *in hohem* ~*e* to a high degree; *in gewissem* ~*e* to a certain degree; 5. *(fig) über alle* ~*en glücklich sein* be exceedingly happy.

Massage *f* massage.

Massaker *n* massacre.

Maßanzug *m* tailor-made suit.

Masse *f* 1. mass *a. phys;* quantity; 2. *(Menge)* crowd; *die breite* ~ the masses; 3. *(Teig)* batter.

Maßeinheit *f* unit of measure.

Massen|artikel *m* mass-produced article; ~**demonstration** *f* mass demonstration; **m~haft** massive, enormous; heaps of; ~**medien** *pl* mass media; ~**produktion** *f* mass production; ~**versammlung** *f* mass meeting.

Maßgabe *f: nach* ~ *von* according to.

maß|gebend standard, authoritative; competent; ~**halten** *irr* be moderate.

mäßig 1. moderate, sober; 2. *(Qualität)* mediocre; ~**en** 1. moderate; 2. *sich* ~ control o.s.; **M~keit** *f* moderation.

massiv solid; massive.

Maßkleidung *f* tailor-made clothes.

maßlos 1. uncontrolled, immoderate; 2. *(übermäßig)* excessive, boundless.

Maßnahme *f* step; ~*n ergreifen* take measures.

maßregel|n reprimand; **M~ung** *f* rebuke.

Maßstab *m* 1. rule, graduation; 2. *(Karte)* scale; 3. *fig* measure; *e-n* ~ *anlegen* apply a standard.

maßvoll moderate.

Mast 1. *f* fattening; 2. *m* mast, pole; ~**darm** *m med* rectum.

mästen fatten.

Material *n* material, fabric; ~**fehler** *m* material defect; ~**ismus** *m* materialism; ~**ist** *m* materialist; **m~istisch** materialist(ic).

Materie *f* matter *a. fig;* **m~ll** material.

Mathematik *f* mathematics *mit sing.*

Matratze *f* mattress.

Matrose *m* sailor, seaman.

Matsch *m (Schlamm)* mud, slush; **m~ig** muddy.

matt 1. *(erschöpft)* exhausted; feeble, weak; 2. *(Farbe, Licht)* dull; soft, dim; 3. *(Schach)* mate.

Matte *f* mat, carpet.

Mattscheibe *f phot* focusing screen.

Mauer *f* wall.

Maul *n* 1. mouth; *(Schnauze)* muzzle, snout; 2. *halt's* ~*!* shut up!

Maul|beerbaum *m* mulberry tree; ~**esel** *m* mule; ~**korb** *m* muzzle *a. fig;* ~- **und Klauenseuche** *f* foot-and-

-mouth disease; **~wurf** *m* mole.

Maurer *m* bricklayer, mason.

Maus *f* mouse; **~efalle** *f* mousetrap; **~eloch** *n* mousehole.

maximal maximum; at the most.

Mayonnaise *f* mayonnaise.

Mechan|ik *f* mechanics *mit sing;* **~iker** *m* mechanic; **m~isch** mechanical; **~ismus** *m* mechanism.

meckern grumble, carp (*über* at).

Medaille *f* medal.

Medien *pl* media.

Medikament *n* medicine, drug.

Medizin *f* medicine; **~er** *m* physician; **m~isch** medical.

Meer *n* sea, ocean; *am* ~ at the seaside, on the sea--shore; **~busen** *m* gulf; **~enge** *f* straits *pl;* **~esboden** *m* sea-bottom; **~esspiegel** *m: über dem* ~ above sea level; **~schaum** *m* 1. sea froth; 2. *min* meerschaum; **~schweinchen** *n* guinea-pig; **~wasser** *n* sea--water.

Mehl *n* flour.

mehr 1. more; ~ *als* more than; *je* ~, *desto besser* the more the better; ~ *oder weniger* more or less; *um so* ~ *als* so much the more as; 2. (*besser*) better; 3. (*eher*) rather; 4. (*ferner*) other; 5. (*länger*) longer.

Mehrbetrag *m* surplus.

mehrdeutig ambiguous; **M~keit** *f* ambiguity.

mehrere several, various.

mehrfach multiple, repeated.

Mehrheit *f* majority; *absolute* ~ absolute majority.

mehrmals several times.

Mehrwert *m* surplus value; **~steuer** *f* valued-added tax, VAT.

Mehrzahl *f* 1. *gram* plural; 2. (*Mehrheit*) most of, majority.

meiden *irr* avoid.

Meile *f* mile.

mein my; **~e** *Damen und Herren!* Ladies and Gentlemen! *das* ~e the mine.

Meineid *m* perjury.

meinen 1. (*denken*) think, believe; *Am* guess; ~ *Sie mich?* do you mean me? 2. (*sagen wollen*) mean; 3. (*beabsichtigen*) intend; *es gut mit jdm* ~ mean well by s.o.; *er meint es nicht böse* he means no harm; 4. *das habe ich nicht gemeint* I did not mean that.

mein|erseits as for me, for my part; **~esgleichen** people like myself; **~etwegen** I don't mind; for my sake; because of me.

Meinung *f: meiner* ~ *nach* in my opinion; *ich bin der* ~, *daß* I am of the opinion that; **~sforscher** *m* opinion researcher, *Am* pollster.

Meise *f* titmouse.

Meißel *m* chisel.

meist 1. most (of); 2. *die ~en* most people; *am ~en* most; *~ens* mostly, in most cases.

Meister *m* 1. master; 2. *sport* champion; **m~haft** masterly, masterful; **m~n** master, command; **~schaft** *f* 1. *sport* championship; 2. mastership; **~werk** *n* masterpiece.

Melancho|ie *f,* **m~isch** melancholy.

Meldefrist *f* time for registration.

melden 1. report; 2. *(ankündigen)* announce; 3. *(mitteilen)* inform, notify; 4. *sich ~* report, register *(bei der Polizei* with the police); 5. *sich auf ein Inserat ~* answer an ad; *sich zu e-r Prüfung ~* enter for an examination; *sich zum Wort ~* ask leave to speak; *sich freiwillig ~* volunteer.

Meldepflicht *f* obligation to register; **m~ig** obliged to register.

Meldung *f* 1. report, news *pl;* 2. *(Mitteilung)* notification, information.

melk|en *irr* milk *a. fig;* **M~maschine** *f* milking machine.

Melod|ie *f* melody, tune; **m~isch** melodious.

Melone *f* 1. *bot* melon; 2. *(Hut)* bowler.

Memoiren *pl* memoirs *pl.*

Menge *f* 1. *(Anzahl)* quantity, amount; 2. *(Menschen)* crowd, throng; 3. *e-e ~* a lot of, lots of, a great many.

Mensch *m* human being, man, person; *jeder ~* everybody; *kein ~* nobody; **~enaffe** *m* anthropoid; **~enalter** *n* generation; **~enfreund** *m* philanthropist; **~enleben** *n* man's life; **m~enleer** empty, deserted; **~enrechte** *pl* human rights *pl;* **~enverstand** *m: gesunder ~* common sense; **~heit** *f* mankind; **m~lich** 1. human; 2. *(human)* humane; **~lichkeit** *f* 1. humanity; 2. humaneness.

Mentalität *f* mentality.

Menü *n* menu.

merk|en 1. *(wahrnehmen)* perceive, notice; 2. *(erkennen)* realize; 3. *(gewahr sein)* be aware of, know; 4. *sich etw ~* remember s.th.; 5. *jdn etw ~ lassen* let s.o. know s.th.; show s.th.; **~lich** noticeable; **M~mal** *n* 1. characteristic; 2. mark, sign; 3. *besondere ~e* distinguishing features *pl;* **~würdig** strange; curious; **~würdigerweise** strange to say.

meßbar measurable.

Messe *f* 1. *(rel) die ~ lesen* say mass; 2. *(Ausstellung)* fair; **~halle** *f* exhibition hall.

messen *irr* 1. measure; *Zeit ~* take time; 2. *med* take the temperature; 3. *sich mit jdm ~* compete with s.o.

Messer *n* knife.
Messing *n* brass.
Meßinstrument *n* measuring instrument.
Metall *n* metal; **m~isch** metallic.
Meteor *m* meteor; **~it** *m* meteorite; **~ologie** *f* meteorology.
Meter *n* metre; **~maß** *n* tape-measure.
Method|e *f* method; **m~isch** methodical.
Metropole *f* metropolis.
Metzger *m* butcher; **~ei** *f* butcher's shop.
Meute *f* pack.
Meuter|ei *f* mutiny; **~er** *m* mutineer; **m~n** mutiny, rebel.
mich 1. *pers prn* me; 2. *ref prn* myself.
Mieder *n* bodice.
Miene *f* 1. expression, look; 2. *(Gesicht)* face, countenance.
mies bad, miserable.
Miesmuschel *f* mussel.
Miet|e *f* 1. rent; hire; 2. *zur ~ wohnen* live in lodgings; **m~en** rent; hire; **~er** *m* tenant, lodger; **~vertrag** *m* lease; **~wagen** *m* hired car.
Migräne *f* migraine.
Mikro|film *m* microfilm; **~phon** *n* microphone; **~skop** *n* microscope; **m~skopisch** microscopic.
Milbe *f* mite.
Milch *f* milk; *saure ~* curdled milk; **~bar** *f* milk bar; **~ge-**

schäft *n* dairy; **m~ig** milky; **~kaffee** *m* white coffee; **~schokolade** *f* milk chocolate; **~straße** *f* Milky Way.
mild 1. *(Klima)* mild, soft, temperate; 2. *(Wesen)* gentle, kind; **M~e** *f* mildness; kindness; **~ern** 1. *(Schmerzen)* soothe, relieve; 2. *(Urteil)* moderate; 3. *(Strafe)* mitigate; **~ernd**: *~e Umstände* mitigating circumstances.
Milieu *n* environment, milieu.
Militär *n* military, army; **~dienst** *m* service; **m~isch** military; **~polizei** *f* military police, M.P.
Milliardär *m* multi-millionaire; **~arde** *f* milliard; **~on** *f* million; **~onär** *m* millionaire.
Milz *f* spleen.
Mim|ik *f* mimic art; **m~isch** mimic.
Minarett *n* minaret.
minder less; minor; inferior; **M~heit** *f* minority; **~jährig** minor, under age; **M~jährigkeit** *f* minority; **~n** 1. lessen, diminish; 2. *(Preis)* reduce; **~wertig** 1. of inferior quality; 2. *fig* second-rate; **M~wertigkeitskomplex** *m* inferiority complex.
mindest 1. least, slightest; 2. *das ~e* the least; *nicht im ~en* not in the least; **M~alter** *n* minimum age.

mindestens at least.
Mindestzahl f minimum number.
Mine f 1. *mil* mine; 2. *(Bleistift)* refill.
Mineral n mineral; ~**bad** n mineral bath; ~**ogie** f mineralogy; ~**wasser** n mineral water.
Miniatur f miniature.
Minigolf n mini-golf.
minim|al minimal; **M~algewicht** n minimum weight; **M~um** n minimum.
Minister m minister; **m~iell** ministerial; ~**ium** n ministry; ~**präsident** m Prime Minister.
Ministrant m rel server.
Minorität f minority.
minus minus; **M~zeichen** n minus sign.
Minute f minute; *auf die* ~ to the minute; *in der letzten* ~ at the last minute.
mir 1. (to) me; 2. (to) myself; 3. *ein Freund von* ~ a friend of mine; 4. ~ *ist kalt* I feel cold.
mischen 1. mix; *(Tabak)* blend; 2. *(Karten)* shuffle; 3. *sich in etw* ~ meddle with, in s.th.
Misch|ling m half-breed; ~**masch** m hotchpotch; ~**ung** f mixture; blend.

miserabel miserable.
mißachten disregard, ignore.
Mißbildung f deformity.

mißbillig|en disapprove (of); **M~ung** f disapproval.
Mißbrauch m abuse, misuse; **m~en** abuse, misuse.
mißbräuchlich wrong, improper.
mißdeuten misinterpret.
missen: *etw* ~ do without s.th.
Mißerfolg m failure.
Mißernte f bad crop.
mißfallen *irr* displease (*jdm* s.o.); **M~** n disapproval; *jds* ~ *erregen* displease s.o.
Mißgeburt f monster.
Mißgeschick n bad luck, misfortune.
mißgestimmt: ~ *sein* be in a bad mood.
mißgönnen grudge (*jdm etw* s.o. s.th.).
Mißgriff m mistake.
Mißgunst f envy.
mißhand|eln maltreat; **M~lung** f maltreatment.
Missionar m missionary.
Mißklang m dissonance, discord.
mißlich awkward, unpleasant.
mißlingen *irr* fail, be unsuccessful.
Mißmut m bad mood; **m~ig** ill-humoured.
mißraten *irr* turn out a failure.
Mißstand m bad state of affairs.
Mißstimmung f discord.
mißtrau|en distrust, mistrust; **M~en** n mistrust;

M~ensantrag *m pol* motion of no confidence; **~isch** distrustful, suspicious.
Mißverhältnis *n* disproportion.
Mißver|ständnis *n* misunderstanding; **m~stehen** *irr* misunderstand.
Mißwirtschaft *f* mismanagement.
Mist *m* dung, manure; **~haufen** *m* manure heap.
mit I *prp* 1. with; 2. *(in Begleitung von)* in the company of; 3. ~ dem Bus fahren go by bus; 4. ~ Gewalt by force; 5. *(Zeitangabe)* ~ dem Alter in old age; ~ einem Male suddenly; ~ 20 Jahren at the age of 20; **II** *adv:* ~ dabei sein take part too.
Mitarbeit *f* cooperation, collaboration; **m~en** collaborate, cooperate; **~er** *m* collaborator, assistant.
Mitbestimmung *f* co-determination.
mitbringen *irr* bring (*etw* s.th.), bring along (*jdn* s.o.).
Mitbürger *m* fellow citizen.
miteinander 1. with each other; 2. *(zusammen)* together.
Mitesser *m med* blackhead.
mitfahren *irr* travel with s.o.
mitfühlend sympathetic.
Mitgefühl *n* sympathy, compassion.
Mitgift *f* dowry.
Mitglied *n* member.

mithören 1. listen in to; 2. *(Gespräch)* overhear.
mitkommen *irr* come along (*mit jdm* with s.o.).
Mitleid *n* pity, compassion; ~ haben mit jdm take pity on s.o.; **~enschaft** *f: in ~ ziehen* affect; **m~ig** pitying, compassionate.
mitmachen 1. *(teilnehmen)* participate, take part in; 2. *(zusammenarbeiten)* cooperate.
Mitmensch *m* fellow being.
mitnehmen *irr* 1. take along, pick up (*jdn* s.o.); 2. *(im Auto)* give s.o. a lift.
Mitreisender *m* fellow passenger.
mitreißen *irr fig* drag along.
mitschreiben *irr* take notes (of).
Mitschuld *f* complicity.
mitspielen take part, participate.
Mittag *m* noon; *am ~* at noon; *zu ~ essen* have lunch; **~essen** *n* lunch; dinner; **m~s** at midday; **~spause** *f* break for lunch; **~sschlaf** *m* after-dinner nap; **~stisch** *m* lunch-table.
Mitte *f* 1. middle; ~ nächster Woche in the middle of next week; ~ Mai in mid-May; 2. *(Mittelpunkt)* centre; 3. *fig* midst.
mitteil|en tell (*jdm etw* s.o. s.th.), inform (of s.th.), communicate (to s.o.); **~sam** communicative; **M~ung** *f*

1. communication, information; 2. *(Nachricht)* message.

Mittel *n* 1. means *sing;* 2. method; measure; 3. *(Heil~)* remedy *(gegen* for*)*; 4. *(Ausweg)* expedient; 5. *(Werkzeug)* instrument; **~alter** *n* Middle Ages *pl;* **m~alterlich** medi(a)eval; **m~bar** indirect; **~gebirge** *n* low mountain range; **m~groß** medium-sized; **m~los** penniless; **m~mäßig** mediocre; **~meer** *n* the Mediterranean; **~punkt** *m* centre, central point.

mittels by means of.

Mittel|stand *m* middle class; **~streifen** *m* middle strip; **~welle** *f* medium wave.

mitten in the middle of; ~ *am Tage* in broad daylight; ~ *in der Stadt* right in the centre of the town.

Mitternacht *f* midnight; *um* ~ at midnight; **~smesse** *f* midnight mass.

mittler 1. middle; *im ~en Alter* middle-aged; 2. *(durchschnittlich)* medium, average.

Mittwoch *m* Wednesday.

mitwirk|en contribute, assist; take part; **M~ung** *f* participation; cooperation.

Mitwissen *n: ohne mein* ~ without my knowledge.

mix|en mix; **M~er** *m* mixer.

Möbel *n* furniture; **~ge-**

schäft *n* furniture shop; **~wagen** *m* furniture van.

mobil mobile.

Mobiliar *n* 1. furniture; 2. movable goods.

möblieren furnish.

Mode *f* fashion, vogue, style; *die neueste* ~ the latest fashion; *in* ~ *sein* be in fashion, in vogue; **~geschäft** *n* fashion store.

Modell *n* 1. model *(für* for*)*; 2. *tech* pattern, prototype; **m~ieren** model; **~kleid** *n* model dress.

Moder *m* decay, rot.

Moderator *m* moderator.

modern *(verfaulen)* decay, rot.

modern modern, up-to-date, progressive; **~isieren** modernize.

Mode|schau *f* fashion show; **~schöpfer** *m* fashion designer, stylist.

modisch fashionable.

mogeln cheat.

mögen *irr* 1. *(gern haben)* like, be fond of; *ich mag lieber Tee* I prefer tea; *ich möchte ein Glas Wein* I should like to have a glass of wine; *ich möchte wissen* I wonder; 2. *(wollen)* want, like; 3. *es mag sein, daß* it may be that.

möglich 1. possible; *so schnell wie* ~ as quickly as possible; *das ist schon* ~ that's quite possible; *das ist eher* ~ that's more likely;

2. *alles* ~e all sorts of things; ~**erweise** possibly, maybe; **M~keit** *f* possibility; *nach* ~ if possible; ~**st**: *sein* ~*es tun* do o.'s utmost.

Mohammedan|er *m*, **m~isch** Mohammedan.

Mohn *m* poppy.

Möhre *f* carrot.

Mokka *m* mocha.

Mole *f mar* mole.

Molekül *n* molecule.

Molkerei *f* dairy.

mollig warm, cosy.

Moment *m* moment; *e-n* ~, *bitte!* just a moment, please! **m~an** present, momentary; at the moment, for the time being; ~**aufnahme** *f* snap(shot).

Monarch *m* monarch; ~**ie** *f* monarchy.

Monat *m* month; *im* ~ *Mai* in the month of May; *am 5. dieses* ~*s* on the fifth of this month; **m~elang** for months; **m~lich** monthly; ~**sgehalt** *n* monthly salary; ~**skarte** *f* monthly ticket; ~**srate** *f* monthly instal(l)ment.

Mönch *m* monk.

Mond *m* moon; *der* ~ *scheint* the moon is shining.

mondän fashionable.

Mond|finsternis *f* lunar eclipse; ~**landung** *f* moon landing; ~**schein** *m* moonlight.

Mono|gramm *n* monogram; ~**kel** *n* monocle; ~**kultur** *f* monoculture; ~**log** *m* monologue; ~**pol** *n* monopoly; **m~ton** monotonous.

Monstrum *n* monster.

Montag *m* Monday.

Mont|age *f* mounting, installation; ~**eur** *m* fitter; **m~ieren** assemble, install.

Moor *n* bog, moor; ~**bad** *n* mud-bath.

Moos *n* moss; **m~ig** mossy.

Moped *n* moped.

Moral *f* ethics *pl;* morals *pl;* **m~isch** ethical, moral.

Morast *m* morass, marsh.

Mord *m* murder; **m~en** murder, commit a murder.

Mörder *m* murderer, killer; ~**in** *f* murderess; **m~isch** murderous.

Morgen *m* morning; *am* ~ in the morning; *am anderen* ~ the next morning; *guten* ~*!* good morning! *e-s schönen* ~*s* one fine morning.

morgen *adv* tomorrow; ~ *früh* tomorrow morning; ~ *in e-r Woche* tomorrow week; *heute* ~ this morning.

Morgen|dämmerung *f* dawn, daybreak; ~**rock** *m* dressing gown; ~**rot** *n* dawn.

morgens in the morning, a.m.

Morphium *n* morphine.

morsch rotten, decayed.

Morsezeichen *n* Morse signal.

Mörtel *m* mortar.

Mosaik *n* mosaic.

Moschee *f* mosque.
Moskito *m* mosquito; **~netz** *n* mosquito net.
Moslem *m* Moslem.
Most *m* must; cider.
Motel *n* motel.
Motiv *n* 1. motive; 2. *jur* drive, subject.
Motor *m* motor, engine; *der ~ sprang nicht an* the engine didn't start; **~boot** *n* motor-boat; **~haube** *f* bonnet, *Am* hood; **m~isieren** motorize; **~isierung** *f* motorization; **~rad** *n* motor-cycle; **~radfahrer** *m* motor-cyclist; **~radrennen** *n* motor-cycle racing; **~roller** *m* motor-scooter; **~schaden** *m* engine trouble; **~segler** *m aero* powered glider.
Motte *f* moth; **~nkugel** *f* moth-ball.
Motto *n* motto, slogan.
Möwe *f* (sea)gull.

Mücke *f* gnat, mosquito; **~nstich** *m* gnat bite.
müd|e tired, weary; **~ werden** get tired; **M~igkeit** *f* tiredness, weariness.
muffig musty.
Mühe *f* trouble, pains *pl; mit großer ~* with great effort; *keine ~ scheuen* spare no trouble; *sich ~ geben* take pains; *mit ~ und Not* with great difficulty, barely; **m~los** effortless.
Mühle *f* mill.

mühsam tiresome; troublesome, toilsome.
Mulatte *m* mulatto.
Mulde *f* 1. trough; 2. *(Vertiefung)* hollow.
Müll *m* refuse, rubbish, waste, *Am* garbage; **~abfuhr** *f* refuse collection; **~eimer** *m* dustbin; *Am* garbage-box.
Müller *m* miller.
Müll|schlucker *m* waste chute; **~wagen** *m* dust-cart.
multi|lateral multilateral; **~plizieren** multiply.
Mumie *f* mummy.
Mund *m* mouth; *den ~ voll nehmen* talk big; *halten Sie den ~!* hold your tongue! **~art** *f* dialect.
Mündel *n* ward.
munden taste good.
münden 1. flow (*in* into); 2. *(Straße)* lead into.
Mund|geruch *m* bad breath; **~harmonika** *f* mouth-organ.
mündig: *~ sein* be of age; **M~keit** *f* full age, majority.
mündlich 1. verbal; 2. *(Prüfung)* oral.
Mundstück *n (Zigarette)* tip.
Mündung *f* mouth, outlet.
Mund|wasser *n* mouthwash; **~-zu-~-Beatmung** *f* mouth-to-mouth respiration.
Munition *f* ammunition.
Münster *n* cathedral.
munter lively, cheerful, gay; **M~keit** *f* liveliness.
Münz|e *f* coin; **~einwurf** *m*

coin slot; ~**fernsprecher** m pay phone.

mürb|e 1. short, crisp; 2. (Fleisch) tender; **M~teig** m short pastry.

murmeln murmur, mutter.

murren grumble.

mürrisch morose, sullen.

Mus n puree, stewed fruit.

Muschel f zoo shell, mussel.

Muse f muse.

Museum n museum.

Musik f music; ~**alienhandlung** f music shop; **m~alisch** musical; ~**ant** m musician; ~**box** f jukebox; ~**er** m musician; ~**hochschule** f conservatoire, Am conservatory; ~**instrument** n musical instrument; ~**stück** n piece of music; ~**truhe** f radiogram, Am radio-phonograph.

musizieren make music.

Muskat m nutmeg.

Muskel m muscle; ~**kater** m: ~ haben be stiff.

muskulös muscular.

Muße f leisure.

müssen irr 1. have to; ich muß jetzt gehen I have to go now; 2. (gezwungen sein) be forced, compelled to; 3. (nötig sein) be necessary; 4. (brauchen) need; du mußt es nicht sagen you need not say it; 5. (sollen) Sie ~ nämlich wissen you ought to know; 6. (verpflichtet sein) be obliged to, be bound to; 7. er muß weinen he could not help crying; 8. sie muß wohl krank sein she must be ill; 9. (wollen) want to.

müßig 1. idle; 2. (unnütz) superfluous, futile.

Muster n 1. pattern, model; 2. com sample; 3. fig example; ~**beispiel** n model example (für for); **m~gültig, m~haft** exemplary; **m~n** examine; ~**prozeß** m test case; ~**schüler** m model pupil; ~**ung** f 1. examination; 2. mil review.

Mut m courage; jdm ~ machen encourage s.o.; den ~ verlieren lose courage; **m~ig** courageous, brave; **m~los** discouraged; ~**losigkeit** f discouragement; **m~maßlich** presumed, probable.

Mutter f 1. mother; 2. tech nut.

mütterlich maternal; ~**erseits** on the mother's side.

Mutter|mal n birthmark; **m~seelenallein** utterly forlorn; ~**sprache** f mother tongue; ~**tag** m Mother's Day.

Mut|wille m mischievousness, mischief; **m~willig** mischievous, wilful.

Mütze f cap.

mysteriös mysterious.

myth|isch mythical; **M~ologie** f mythology; **M~os** m myth.

N

Nabe *f* hub.

Nabel *m* navel; **~schnur** *f* umbilical cord.

nach I *prp* 1. to, for; *der Zug ~ London* the train for London; *~ Hause gehen* go home; 2. *(in Richtung)* towards; *~ der Straße* facing the street; *~ oben* upwards; *~ unten* downwards; *~ hinten* backwards; *~ rechts* to the right; 3. *(hinter) ~ mir* after me; next to; 4. *(zeitlich später)* after; *~ dem Essen* after dinner; *~ drei Jahren* three years later; *~ einem halben Jahr* within six months; *~ Ablauf der Frist* at the expiration of the term; *Viertel ~ drei* a quarter past three; 5. *allen Anschein ~* to all apperances; *m-r Ansicht ~* in my opinion; 6. *(entsprechend)* according to; *~ Bedarf* on request; **II** *adv:* ~ *und* ~ little by little, gradually.

nachahm|en imitate; **N~ung** *f* imitation.

Nachbar *m* neighbour; **~haus** *n: er wohnt im ~* he lives next door; **~schaft** *f* neighbourhood.

nachbestell|en 1. order additionally; 2. *com* reorder; **N~ung** *f* supplementary order.

Nachbildung *f* reproduction.

nachdem 1. *(zeitlich)* after, when; 2. *je ~* according to; *je ~ das Wetter ist* depending on the weather.

nachdenk|en *irr* 1. think *(über etw* about s.th.), reflect *(über* on); 2. *(nachsinnen)* ponder; **N~en** *n* reflexion; **~lich** thoughtful, reflective.

Nachdruck *m* 1. *(Betonung)* emphasis, stress; 2. *typ* reprint.

nachdrücklich 1. emphatic; 2. *(ausdrücklich)* explicit.

nacheifern emulate *(jdm s.o.)*.

nacheilen hurry *(jdm after s.o.)*.

nacheinander 1. one after another; 2. *(abwechselnd)* in turn; 3. *drei Wochen ~* for three weeks running.

nachempfinden *irr* feel.

Nachfolge *f* succession; **n~n:** *jdm ~* succeed s.o.; **~r** *m* successor.

nachforsch|en enquire, investigate; **N~ung** *f* investigation, enquiry.

Nachfrage *f com* demand.

nachfüllen fill up.

nachgeben *irr* 1. give in, yield *(jdm* to s.o.); 2. *(dem Druck)* concede; 3. *(Erde)* give way.

Nachgebühr f (Post) surcharge.

nachgehen irr 1. jdm ~ follow s.o.; 2. (e-m Problem) investigate; 3. s-r Arbeit ~ pursue o.'s work; 4. (Uhr) be slow.

Nachgeschmack m after-taste.

nachgiebig 1. indulgent, yielding, compliant; 2. (Material) flexible.

nachhaltig lasting, durable.

nachher 1. afterwards; 2. bis ~! see you later!

Nachhilfeunterricht m private lessons pl.

nachholen make up (etw for s.th.), catch up on.

Nachkomme m descendant; n~n irr 1. follow, come after; 2. (e-r Pflicht) meet, satisfy, fulfil; 3. (Wunsch) comply with.

Nachkur f after-treatment.

Nachlaß m 1. com discount, deduction; 2. jur inheritance, estate.

nachlassen irr 1. abate; 2. (Leistung) fall off, slacken; 3. (Schmerz) ease off; 4. com decline, drop; decrease; (Preis) deduct, make an allowance.

nachlässig careless, neglectful, sloppy.

nachlaufen irr run after.

nachlösen (Fahrkarte) pay additional fare.

nachmachen imitate, copy, duplicate.

Nachmittag m afternoon; heute n~s this afternoon; n~s in the afternoon; ~svorstellung f afternoon performance.

Nachnahme f: etw per ~ schicken send s.th. cash on delivery, C.O.D.

Nachname m surname, last name.

Nachporto n surcharge.

nachprüfen check, verify.

Nachrede f: üble ~ slander, defamation, libel.

nachreichen hand in.

Nachricht f 1. news pl; die neuesten ~en the latest news; 2. ~en hören listen to the news; 3. (Mitteilung) information; message.

Nachruf m obituary.

nachsagen repeat.

Nachsaison f off-season.

nachschlagen irr 1. (Wort) look up; 2. (Lexikon) consult.

Nachschlüssel m skeleton key.

Nachschrift f 1. transcription; 2. (Brief) postscript.

Nachschub m supply (an of).

nachsehen irr 1. look after (jdn s.o.); 2. (suchen) look and see; 3. (prüfen) examine, check; N~n: das ~ haben be left out in the cold.

nachsenden irr (Brief) forward.

Nachsicht f indulgence, forbearance; n~ig indulgent.

Nachspiel n consequence, sequel.

nachspionieren spy on (*jdm* s.o.).

nächst I *adj* 1. *(örtlich)* nearest, proximate; *(Reihenfolge)* next; 2. *(zeitlich)* next, following; *am ~en Tag* the next day; *in der ~en Zeit* in the near future; **II** *adv: am ~en* next, nearest, closest.

Nächste m 1. fellow-man; 2. *der n~, bitte* next, please.

nachstell|en 1. place after; 2. *(Uhr)* put back; 3. *jdm ~* persecute s.o.; **N~ung** *f* persecution.

Nächstenliebe *f* charity.

nächstens in the near future, soon.

Nächstliegende n: *das ~* the thing nearest at hand.

Nacht *f* night; *gute ~!* good night! *bei ~* at night; *bis spät in die ~* until late in the night; *letzte ~* last night; *heute n~* tonight; **~dienst** m *(Apotheke)* night service.

Nachteil m disadvantage, drawback; **n~ig** disadvantageous, unfavourable.

Nacht|frost m night frost; **~hemd** n nightdress.

Nachtigall *f* nightingale.

nächtigen spend the night.

Nachtisch m dessert.

nächtlich nightly, nocturnal.

Nacht|lokal n nightclub; **~portier** m night porter.

Nachtrag m supplement;

n~en *irr* 1. *(fig)* jdm etw ~ bear a grudge against s.o.; 2. *(in e-e Liste)* add (to a list); **n~end** resentful.

nachträglich supplementary, additional; later.

nachts at, by night, in the night.

Nachttisch m bedside table; **~lampe** *f* bedside lamp.

Nachttopf m chamber pot.

Nachweis m evidence; *den ~ erbringen* furnish proof; **n~en** *irr* prove.

Nachwelt *f* posterity.

nachwirk|en have after-effects; **N~ung** *f* after-effect; repercussions *pl*.

Nachwort n epilogue.

Nachwuchs m offspring; rising generation.

nachzahlen pay in addition.

nachzählen recount.

Nachzahlung *f* additional, subsequent payment.

Nachzügler m latecomer, straggler.

Nacken m neck.

nackt 1. naked; 2. *(bloß)* bare; 3. *(Kunst)* nude; **N~heit** *f* nakedness, nudity; bareness.

Nadel *f* 1. *(Näh~)* needle; 2. *(Haar~)* pin; **~öhr** n eye of a needle.

Nagel m 1. *anat tech* nail; 2. *(fig) etw an den ~ hängen* give up, chuck up *(sein Studium* o.'s studies); **~feile** *f* nail-file; **~lack** m nail-varnish; **~lackentferner** m

nail varnish remover; **n~n**
nail (*etw an* s.th. on, to);
n~neu brand-new.

nag|en gnaw (*an* at); **N~er**
m, **N~etier** *n* rodent,
gnawer.

nah I *adj* 1. near, close,
neighbouring; 2. (*zeitlich*)
imminent; *in ~er Zukunft* in
the near future; 3. *ein ~er
Verwandter* a near relation;
II *adv* near, close; *von ~
und fern* from far and near;
ein ~e gelegenes Dorf a
nearby village.

Nähe *f* nearness, closeness;
in nächster ~ in close proximity to; *in der ~ von* in the
neighbourhood of.

nahe|kommen *irr* come
near, approach; **~legen**:
jdm etw ~ urge s.th. upon
s.o.; **~liegen** *irr* suggest itself; **~liegend** obvious.

nahen approach, draw near.

nähen sew, stitch.

näher 1. nearer, closer; 2. (*ge-
nauer*) further, more detailed; *bei ~er Betrachtung* on
closer inspection; 3. *etw ~
ausführen* point out details;
4. *~ kommen* approach.

Näherin *f* sewer.

näherkommen *irr* 1. *sich ~*
get closer to each other;
2. (*e-r Sache*) come to the
point.

nähern, *sich* approach, come
near.

nahestehen *irr*: *jdm ~* be

close to s.o.; **~d** close, intimate.

nahezu almost, nearly.

Näh|garn *n* sewing cotton;
~kasten *m* sewing box;
~maschine *f* sewing machine; **~nadel** *f* needle.

nähren 1. feed, nourish;
2. (*Kind*) nurse.

nahrhaft nutritious, nourishing.

Nährmittel *pl* alimentary
pastes.

Nahrung *f* food, nourishment; **~smittel** *pl* foods *pl*,
victuals *pl*.

Nährwert *m* nutritional
value.

Nähseide *f* sewing silk.

Naht *f* seam; **n~los** seam-
less.

Nahverkehr *m* short-dis-
tance traffic.

Nähzeug *n* sewing gear.

naiv naive; **N~ität** *f* naivety.

Name *m* 1. name; *dem ~n
nach* by name; 2. (*Ruf*)
reputation; 3. *in jds ~n* in
behalf of s.o.; **n~nlos**
anonymous, unknown;
n~ns by the name of,
named; **~nstag** *m* name-
-day; **~nsvetter** *m* name-
sake; **~nszug** *m* signature;
n~ntlich 1. nominal, by
name; 2. (*insbesondere*)
particularly.

namhaft 1. well-known, re-
nownd; 2. (*beträchtlich*)
considerable.

nämlich 1. namely, (and) that

is; 2. *(begründend)* for, you
see.

Napf *m* bowl, dish.

Narbe *f* scar, cicatrice.

Narkose *f* narcosis.

Narr *m* fool; *jdn zum ~en
halten* make a fool of s.o.;
~heit *f* folly; foolishness.

närrisch foolish, silly.

Narzisse *f* narcissus.

nasch|en nibble; **~haft** fond
of dainties.

Nase *f* 1. nose; *er blutet aus
der ~* his nose is bleeding;
2. *s-e ~ in alles stecken*
poke o.'s nose into everything; **~nbluten** *n* nose-
bleed; **~nloch** *n* nostril;
n~nweis nosy; saucy.

Nashorn *n* rhinoceros.

naß 1. *~ werden* get wet;
2. *(durchnäßt)* soaked.

Nässe *f* wetness; *vor ~
schützen* keep dry.

naßkalt wet and cold.

Nation *f* nation; **n~al** national; **~alfeiertag** *m* national holiday; **~algericht** *n*
national dish; **~alhymne** *f*
national anthem; **~alitäts-
kennzeichen** *n* international registration plate.

Natron *n* bicarbonate of
soda.

Natter *f* adder.

Natur *f* 1. nature; 2. *(Wesens-
art)* disposition, character;
die menschliche ~ human
nature; 3. *(Körperbeschaf-
fenheit)* constitution; **n~ali-
sieren** naturalize; **~ell** *n*

disposition, temperament;
~erscheinung *f* natural
phenomenon; **~forscher** *m*
naturalist; **~geschichte** *f*
natural history; **~heilkunde**
f med naturopathy.

natürlich 1. natural, real,
normal, actual; 2. *(selbstverständlich)* naturally, of
course.

naturrein unadulterated.

Natur|schutz *m* nature con-
servation; **~schutzgebiet**
n nature reserve; **~wissen-
schaften** *pl* the (natural)
sciences.

Nebel *m* fog, mist.

neben 1. beside, close to,
near, next to; 2. *(außer)* in
addition to, besides; 3. *(Vergleich)* in comparison with;
~an next door.

Neben|anschluß *m tele*
branch extension; **n~bei** by
the way, incidentally; **~be-
ruf** *m* side-line; **n~beruf-
lich** as a side-line; **~buhler**
m rival; **n~einander** side
by side; **~eingang** *m* side
entrance; **~fach** *n (Schule)*
subsidiary subject; **~fluß** *m*
tributary; **~gebäude** *n* adjacent building, annexe;
~geräusch *n* background
noise; **~kläger** *m jur* co-
-plaintiff; **~kosten** *pl* additional expenses *pl;* **~pro-
dukt** *n* by-product; **~raum**
m next room; **~rolle** *f theat*
subordinate part; **~sache** *f*

minor matter; **n~sächlich** unimportant, secondary, accessory; **~satz** *m* dependent clause; **~straße** *f* by--way, by-road; **~strecke** *f* branch line; **~wirkung** *f* side-effect.

neblig misty, foggy.

nebst together with.

necken tease.

Neffe *m* nephew.

negativ negative; **N~** *n phot* negative.

Neger *m* Negro; **~in** *f* Negress.

nehmen *irr* 1. take, seize; 2. *(Hürde)* take, do; 3. *(benutzen)* use; 4. *(auffassen)* take; *er nimmt alles viel zu ernst* he takes everything much too seriously; 5. *(annehmen)* accept; 6. *etw an sich* ~ keep s.th.; *etw zu sich* ~ take s.th. to eat; *etw aus der Tasche* ~ take s.th. out of the pocket.

Neid *m* envy, jealousy; **n~isch** envious, jealous.

Neige *f: zur* ~ *gehen* draw to a close.

neigen 1. bend, incline; 2. *sich* ~ bow; 3. *zu etw* ~ tend to s.th.; **N~ung** *f* 1. *(Gefälle)* gradient, inclination; 2. *fig* inclination, tendency; 3. *(Verlangung)* disposition.

nein no.

Nelke *f* pink, carnation.

nennen *irr* 1. name, call; 2. *(bezeichnen)* designate, denominate; 3. *(erwähnen)* mention; 4. *sich* ~ be called; **~enswert** worth mentioning; **N~er** *m* denominator.

Neonröhre *f* neon tube.

Nerv *m* nerve; *die ~en verlieren* lose o.'s head; **~enarzt** *m* neurologist; **~enklinik** *f* mental hospital; **~enleiden** *n* nervous disorder; **~ensystem** *n* nervous system; **~enzusammenbruch** *m* nervous breakdown; **n~ös** nervous; **~osität** *f* nervousness.

Nerz *m* mink.

Nest *n* 1. nest; 2. *(Ort)* village.

nett 1. nice; 2. *(angenehm)* pleasant, kind; *seien Sie so* ~ *und* would you be so kind as to.

netto *com* net; **N~gehalt** *n* net salary; **N~gewicht** *n* net weight; **N~lohn** *m* net wages *pl.*

Netz *n* 1. net; 2. *(Straße, Kabel, Radio)* network; 3. *el* mains *pl;* **~anschluß** *m* mains connection; **~gerät** *n* mains receiver; **~haut** *f anat* retina.

neu 1. new; 2. *die ~este Mode* the latest fashion; 3. *ein glückliches ~es Jahr!* happy new year! 4. *(kürzlich)* recent; 5. *auf dem ~esten Stand sein* be up to date; 6. *seit ~estem* since very recently; *von ~em* again; 7. *haben Sie das N~este ge-*

hört? have you heard the latest?

Neu|bau *m* newly built house; **n~erdings** lately, recently; **~erscheinung** *f* new publication; **~erung** *f* innovation; **~gier(de)** *f* curiosity; **n~gierig** curious, inquisitive; **~heit** *f* newness, novelty; **~igkeit** *f*: *die letzten ~en* the latest news; **~jahr** *n* New Year's Day.

neulich recently, the other day.

Neu|ling *m* novice, newcomer; **~mond** *m* new moon.

neun nine; **~fach** ninefold; **~t** ninth; *am ~en Juni* on the ninth of June; **~zehn** nineteen; **~zig** ninety.

Neu|ralgie *f* neuralgia; **n~ralgisch** neuralgic; **~rose** *f* neurosis; **n~rotisch** neurotic.

Neuschnee *m* new-fallen snow.

neutral neutral; **N~ität** *f* neutrality.

neuwertig as new.

Neuzeit *f* modern times *pl;* **n~lich** modern.

nicht 1. not; *ganz und gar ~* absolutely not; 2. *(Verneinung von Verben)* ich glaube ~ I don't think so; *bitte ~ berühren!* please do not touch; 3. *ich auch ~* nor I; *noch ~* not yet; 4. *~ nur, ... sondern auch* not only ... but also.

Nichtbeachtung *f* failure to comply with, disregard.

Nichte *f* niece.

nichtig 1. futile; 2. *(jur) null und ~* null and void; **N~keit** *f* futility; triviality; invalidity.

Nicht|raucher *m* non-smoker; **n~rostend** non-rusting.

nichts nothing, not anything; *~ anderes als* nothing else but; *fast gar ~* hardly anything; *alles oder ~* it's all or nothing; *das macht ~* that does not matter, never mind; *er weiß ~ davon* he doesn't know anything about it.

Nichts *n* nothing, naught.

Nichtschwimmer *m* non-swimmer.

nichtsdestoweniger nevertheless.

nichtssagend meaningless, trivial.

Nichtstuer *m* idler.

Nichtwähler *m* abstentionist, non-voter.

Nichtzutreffende *n:* *~s streichen!* delete what does not apply.

Nickel *n* nickel.

nicken nod *(mit dem Kopf o.'s head).*

nie never, at no time; *fast ~* hardly ever; *~ wieder* never again.

nieder down; low; *auf und ~* up and down; **~fallen** *irr* fall down.

Niedergang m decline, fall.
niedergeschlagen: ~ *sein* be dejected, depressed.
niederknien kneel down.
Niederlage f 1. defeat; 2. *com* warehouse.
Nieder|lande f Netherlands *pl;* **~länder** m Netherlander, Dutchman; **n~ländisch** Dutch.
niederlass|en *irr* 1. *sich* ~ sit down; 2. *(Wohnsitz)* settle down; 3. *(Praxis)* set up, establish; **N~ung** f 1. establishment; 2. *com* branch.
niederlegen 1. lay down; 2. *(aufgeben)* resign, abdicate, give up; 3. *sich* ~ lie down.
niederreißen *irr* pull down, tear down, demolish.
Niederschlag m 1. *(Regen)* precipitation, rainfall; 2. *(radioaktiv)* fall-out; **n~en** *irr* 1. knock s.o. down; 2. *(Blick)* cast down; 3. *(Aufstand)* suppress; 4. *sich* ~ condense.
nieder|schreiben *irr* write down, record; **N~schrift** f notes *pl,* record.
Nieder|tracht f vileness, meanness; **n~trächtig** mean, low, vile.
niedertrampeln trample down.
Niederung f lowlands *pl.*
niedlich sweet, *Am* cute.
niedrig 1. low; **~er** *Blutdruck* low blood pressure; 2. *(minderwertig)* inferior; 3. *Preise*

~ *halten* keep prices low; **N~keit** f lowness.
niemals never.
niemand nobody, no one; *überhaupt* ~ no one at all; *er glaubt* ~ he doesn't believe anyone.
Niere f kidney; **~nentzündung** f med nephritis; **n~nförmig** kidney-shaped; **~nkolik** f renal colic; **~nleiden** n renal disease; **~nstein** m kidney stone.
niesel|n: drizzle; **N~regen** m drizzle.
niesen sneeze.
Niet n tech rivet.
Niete f *(Los)* blank.
nieten rivet.
Nikotin n nicotine; **n~frei** nicotine-free.
nirgends nowhere, not anywhere.
Nische f arch niche.
nist|en nest; **N~kasten** m nest(ing)-box.
Niveau n level, plane, niveau, standard.
nivellieren level.
Nixe f water nymph.
nobel noble, aristocratic.
noch I *adv* 1. still; 2. *(mit Negation)* ~ *nicht* not yet; ~ *nie* never before; 3. *(außerdem)* ~ *dazu* in addition to; *ich wartete* ~ *zwei Stunden* I waited for another two hours; *sonst* ~ *was?* anything else? 4. ~ *besser als ich dachte* even better than I imagined; 5. ~ *vor e-r Wo-*

che only a week ago;
II *conj: weder ... ~* neither
... nor; *(nach Verneinung)*
either ... or.
Nomade *m* nomad.
Nonne *f* nun.
Nord|afrika *n* North Africa;
~amerika *n* North
America.
Nord|en *m* north; *im ~* in the
north; *nach ~* northwards;
n~isch Northern, Nordic.
nördlich northern, northerly.
Nord|licht *n* northern lights
pl; **~ost(en)** *m* northeast;
~pol *m* north pole; **~see** *f*
the North Sea; **~seite** *f*
north side; **~west(en)** *m*
northwest; **~wind** *m* north
wind.
nörgeln carp, crab.
Norm *f* standard, rule; **n~al**
normal, regular; **n~en** stan-
dardize.
Norweg|en *n* Norway; **~er**
m, **n~isch** Norwegian.
Not *f* 1. need; *zur ~* if necessary, at a pinch; 2. *(Notwendigkeit)* necessity; 3. *(Mühe)*
trouble, difficulty; *mit knapper ~* barely; 4. *~ leiden* suffer want, privation; 5. *in ~
geraten* fall on hard times.
Notar *m* notary public;
n~iell authenticated by a
notary public.
Not|ausgang *m* emergency
exit; **~behelf** *m* makeshift,
expedient, temporary
measure, stopgap; **~be-
leuchtung** *f* emergency

lighting; **~bremse** *f* emergency brake; **n~dürftig**
makeshift, provisional, temporary.
Note *f* 1. *mus* note; *pl* music;
2. *(Schule)* mark; 3. (bank-)-
note; 4. *(Wesen)* character,
touch; **~nbank** *f* bank of
issue; **~nheft** *n* book of music; **~nständer** *m* music-
-stand.
Notfall *m* emergency case;
im ~ in case of need; **n~s** in
case of emergency.
notieren 1. note down, mark;
2. *(Börse)* quote.
nötig necessary, required;
wenn ~ if necessary; *etw ~
brauchen* need s.th. badly;
das N~e veranlassen ar-
range what is necessary;
~en force, compel; **~en-
falls** if need be; **N~ung** *f*
force.
Notiz *f* 1. note; *sich ~en machen* take notes; 2. *von etw
~ nehmen* take notice of
s.th.; **~buch** *n* notebook.
Notlage *f* distress, plight,
pinch.
notland|en make a forced
landing; **N~ung** *f* emergency landing.
notleidend needy, destitute,
distressed.
Notlüge *f* white lie.
notorisch notorious.
Not|ruf *m* emergency call;
~sitz *m* emergency seat;
~stand *m* state of emergency; **~standsgebiet** *n* dis-

tressed area; **~verband** *m* emergency dressing; **~wehr** *f* self-defence; **n~wendig** necessary; essential; **~wendigkeit** *f* necessity, needfulness.

Notzucht *f:* ~ *begehen* commit rape.

Novelle *f* 1. short novel; 2. *jur* amendment.

November *m: im* ~ in (the month of) November.

Nu *m: im* ~ in an instant, in a moment.

nüchtern 1. *(Magen)* empty; 2. *wieder* ~ *werden* sober up; 3. *(Raum)* bare, plain; 4. *(besonnen)* prudent; 5. *etw* ~ *betrachten* look at s.th. soberly.

Nudel|n *pl* noodles *pl;* **~suppe** *f* noodle soup.

Nugat *m, n* nougat.

null 1. zero; 2. *sport* nil; *drei zu* ~ three nil; **N~** *f* zero, nought.

numerieren number.

Nummer *f* 1. number; 2. *(Schuhe)* size; 3. *(Zeitschrift)* number, copy, issue; 4. *(Auftritt)* number, act; *(Zirkus) die große* ~ the big star; **~nscheibe** *f* telephone dial; **~nschild** *n* number (licence) plate.

nun 1. *(jetzt)* now, at present; 2. *(also)* now, well; *was* ~? what now? ~, *wie steht's?* well, how are things? *von* ~ *an* from now on; ~? well? **~mehr** from now on.

nur 1. *(bloß)* only, just; 2. *(lediglich)* merely, simply; 3. *(ausschließlich)* exclusively; 4. *(nichts als)* nothing but; 5. *wenn* ~ if only; ~ *zu!* go on! *nicht* ~, *sondern auch* not only, but also; 6. *(fragend)* just.

Nuß *f* nut; **~baum** *m* walnut-tree; **~knacker** *m* nut-cracker.

Nutz|anwendung *f* practical application; **n~bar** usable, utilizable; **n~bringend** lucrative.

Nutzen *m* 1. utility; *von* ~ *sein* be of use; 2. *(Gewinn)* profit; *aus etw* ~ *ziehen* make use of s.th.; 3. *(Vorteil)* advantage; 4. *(Ertrag)* yield.

nutzen, nützen 1. be of use, be useful; *das nützt nichts* that's useless; 2. *(vorteilhaft)* be of advantage; 3. *die Gelegenheit* ~ make use of the opportunity; *die Zeit* ~ utilize the time.

Nutzholz *n* timber.

nützlich useful; *sich* ~ *machen* make o.s. useful; **N~keit** *f* usefulness.

nutzlos useless; futile, vain; **N~igkeit** *f* uselessness, futility.

Nutznießer *m* 1. beneficiary; 2. *jur* usufructuary.

Nutzung *f* utilization, use.

O

Oase f oasis.
ob 1. if, whether; 2. *als* ~ as if, as though; 3. ~ ..., ~ ... whether ... or; 4. *na und* ~*!* I should say so!
Obdach n shelter; **o~los** homeless; **O~loser** m homeless person.
Obelisk m obelisk.
oben 1. above, up; *weiter* ~ further up; ~ *und unten* above and below; 2. *von* ~ *bis unten* from top to bottom; *(bei Personen)* from head to foot; 3. *ich gehe nach* ~ I am going upstairs; 4. ~ *auf Seite 10* at the top of page 10; *siehe* ~ see above; ~**an** at the top; ~**auf** on top; ~**drein** into the bargain; ~**genannt** above-mentioned.
ober, top; *die* ~*e Seite* the upper side; *die* ~*en Zehntausend* the upper ten.
Ober m waiter; *Herr* ~, *bitte zahlen!* waiter, the bill (*Am* check), please!
Oberarm m upper arm.
Oberdeck n upper deck.
Oberfläch|e f surface; **o~lich** superficial, cursory.
oberhalb above.
Oberhaupt n head.
Oberkellner m head waiter.
Oberkiefer m upper jaw.
Oberkörper m upper body;

mit nacktem ~ stripped to the waist.
Oberleder n upper leather.
Oberleitung f tech overhead wire.
Oberlicht n arch skylight.
Oberlippe f upper lip.
Oberschenkel m thigh.
Oberschwester f head nurse.
oberst 1. topmost, uppermost; 2. *(rangmäßig)* highest, supreme; ~*er Grundsatz* leading principle.
Oberweite f bust measurement.
obgleich although.
Obhut f care; *etw jds* ~ *anvertrauen* entrust s.o. s.th.
obig above-mentioned.
Objekt n 1. object; 2. *das* ~ *e-r Untersuchung* the subject of an investigation; **o~iv** objective, impartial.
Oblate f 1. wafer; 2. *rel* host.
obligatorisch obligatory, compulsory.
Oboe f oboe.
Obst n fruit; ~**baum** m fruit tree; ~**garten** m orchard; ~**geschäft** n fruiterer's (shop), *Am* fruit-store; ~**kuchen** m fruit tart; ~**messer** n fruit knife; ~**schale** f fruit bowl.
obszön obscene.
obwohl although.

Ochse *m* ox; **~nschwanz-suppe** *f* oxtail soup.
öde desolate, deserted.
Öde *f* wasteland.
oder 1. or; 2. *entweder . . . ~* either . . . or.
Ofen *m* 1. *(Küche)* stove; 2. *(Back~)* oven.
offen I *adj* 1. open, unclosed; 2. *(unverhüllt)* bare, naked; 3. *auf ~er See* on the open sea; *auf ~er Strecke* on the open track; 4. *(unbesetzt)* vacant; 5. *(ehrlich)* frank, sincere; 6. *(Rechnung)* outstanding; **II** *adv:* ~ *gesagt* frankly speaking; *ich will ganz ~ sprechen* I'll speak quite openly.
offenbar obvious, manifest, evident.
offenbar|en reveal, disclose; **O~ung** *f* revelation, disclosure.
offen|bleiben *irr* remain open; **~halten** *irr* keep open.
Offenheit *f* frankness.
offensichtlich evident, obvious.
offensiv offensive.
öffentlich 1. public; 2. ~ *auftreten* appear in public; **Ö~keit** *f* public; publicity; **Ö~keitsarbeit** *f* public relations work.
Offerte *f* offer.
offiz|iell official; **O~ier** *m* officer; **~iös** semi-official.
öffn|en 1. open; 2. *(Paket)* undo; 3. *(Flasche)* uncork;

Ö~nung *f* 1. *(Loch)* opening, hole; 2. *(Spalte)* gap; **Ö~nungszeit** *f* business hours *pl.*
oft often, frequently, many times.
öfter more often; repeatedly.
ohne without; ~ *Arbeit sein* be out of work; ~ *weiteres* without ceremony; **~glei-chen** matchless; unparalleled; **~hin** anyway.
Ohnmacht *f* 1. faint; 2. *fig* powerlessness.
ohnmächtig unconscious; ~ *werden* faint.
Ohr *n* ear; *ganz ~ sein* be all ears.
Öhr *n* *(Nadel)* eye.
ohrenbetäubend deafening.
Ohr|feige *f: jdm e-e ~ geben* slap s.o.'s face; **~läppchen** *n* ear lobe; **~ring** *m* earring.
ökonomisch economic(al).
Oktober *m: im ~* in October.
Öl *n* oil; **~baum** *m* olive tree.
Oleander *m bot* oleander.
ölen 1. oil; 2. *tech* lubricate.
Öl|farbe *f* oil colour; **~gemälde** *n* oil painting; **~heizung** *f* oil heating; **ö~ig** oily.
Olive *f* olive; **~nöl** *n* olive oil.
Öl|kanne *f* oil-can; **~leitung** *f* oil pipeline; **~sardinen** *pl* sardines in oil; **~stand** *m* oil level; **~tank** *m* oil tank; **~tanker** *m* oil-tanker; **~ung** 1. lubrication; 2. *die letzte ~* Extreme Unction; **~wechsel** *m* oil change.

Olympiade *f* Olympiad; *die Olympischen Spiele* Olympic Games *pl.*

Oma *f* granny.

Omelett(e *f)* *n* omelet.

Omnibus *m* bus, coach; **~bahnhof** *m* bus station; **~haltestelle** *f* bus stop; **~linie** *f* bus line.

Onkel *m* uncle.

Opa *m* grandpa.

Oper *f* opera.

Operation *f* med operation; **~ssaal** *m* med operating-theatre.

operativ *med* operative, surgical.

Operette *f* operetta.

operier|bar operable; **~en** operate (*jdn* on s.o.).

Opern|glas *n* (opera-)glasses *pl;* **~sänger** *m* opera singer.

Opfer *n* 1. sacrifice; 2. (*Unfall~*) victim; **o~n** 1. sacrifice; 2. *s-e Zeit ~* spend o.'s time.

Opium *n* opium.

Opposition *f* opposition.

optieren opt (*für* for).

Optiker *m* optician.

optimal optimum, optimal, best, highest.

Optim|ismus *m* optimism; **~ist** *m* optimist; **o~istisch** optimistic(al).

optisch optical.

Orakel *n* oracle.

Orange *f* orange.

Orchester *n* orchestra.

Orchidee *f* orchid.

Orden *m* 1. *rel* order; 2. (*Auszeichnung*) decoration, medal.

ordentlich 1. (*sauber*) tidy, neat; 2. (*exakt*) accurate, diligent; 3. (*geregelt*) orderly, proper.

ordinär 1. common; 2. (*unanständig*) vulgar.

ordn|en 1. (put in) order; 2. arrange, grade; 3. (*Akten*) file; **O~er** *m* (*Brief~*) file.

Ordnung *f* 1. order; *in ~!* all right! *etw in ~ halten* keep s.th. in order; 2. (*Sauberkeit*) neatness; 3. (*Anordnung, Reihenfolge*) arrangement; sequence, succession; 4. *öffentliche ~* public order; **~sstrafe** *f* fine.

Organ *n* anat organ *a. fig;* **~isation** *f* organization.

organ|isch organic(al); **~isieren** organize.

Organ|ismus *m* organism; **~ist** *m* organist.

Orgasmus *m* orgasm.

Orgel *f* organ.

Orient *m* the Orient; **o~alisch** Oriental, Eastern.

orient|ieren 1. *fig* inform, instruct (*jdn* s.o.); 2. *sich ~* get o.'s bearings, inform o.s.; **O~ierung** *f* 1. orientation; 2. *fig* information; **O~teppich** *m* Oriental carpet.

original original, authentic; **O~** *n* original; **O~ität** *f* originality.

originell original, ingenious.

Orkan *m* hurricane.

Ornament *n* ornament; **o~al** ornamental.

Ornat *m* 1. clerical vestments *pl;* 2. *in vollem ~* in full array.

Ort *m* 1. place, locality, spot; *an ~ und Stelle* on the spot; *am angegebenen ~* in the place sited; 2. *(Szene)* scene; 3. *(Ortschaft)* place, town.

orthodox orthodox.

Orthographie *f* orthography; **o~isch** orthographic.

orthopädisch orthop(a)edic.

örtlich local, regional; **Ö~keit** *f* locality.

Ortschaft *f* small town, village.

Orts|gespräch *n* tele local call; **o~kundig** familiar with a place; **~netz** *n* tele local exchange network;

~schild *n* place-name sign; **~zeit** *f* local time.

Öse *f* 1. eye; 2. *(Schuh)* eyelet.

Ostblock *m* Eastern Bloc.

Osten *m* east; *im ~ von* to the east of; *der Ferne ~* the Far East.

Osterei *n* Easter egg.

österlich Easter, paschal.

Ostern *n* Easter.

Österreich *n* Austria; **~er** *m*, **ö~isch** Austrian.

östlich eastern; *in ~er Richtung* eastwards.

Ost|see *f: die ~* the Baltic Sea; **~wind** *m* east wind.

oval oval.

Oxyd *n* oxide; **o~ieren** oxidize.

Ozean *m* ocean; **o~isch** oceanic.

P

Paar n 1. pair; *ein ~ Handschuhe* a pair of gloves; 2. *(Ehepaar)* couple.

paar: *ein ~* a few, some; *vor ein ~ Tagen* a few days ago.

paaren *(zoo) sich ~* mate, pair.

paar|mal: *ein ~* a few times; **~weise** in pairs.

Pacht f *jur* lease; *auf ~* by lease; **p~en**: *etw ~* take s.th. on lease.

Pächter m tenant, leaseholder.

Pachtland n leasehold land.

Pack 1. m pack, pile; 2. n rabble, riff-raff.

Päckchen n pack, packet.

packen 1. pack; *s-e Koffer ~* pack o.'s suitcases; 2. *(einwickeln)* wrap up; 3. *(ergreifen)* grab, seize, grasp; 4. *(erschüttern)* shake, upset; **~d** gripping, impressive.

Packpapier n wrapping paper.

Packung f 1. packet, package; 2. *med* compress.

Pädagog|e m p(a)edagogue, educator; **~ik** f pedagogy; **p~isch** educational, pedagogic.

Paddel n paddle; **~boot** n canoe.

Page m page.

Paket n parcel, package; **~annahme** f parcel acceptance service; **~karte** f parcel dispatch note; **~zustellung** f parcel delivery.

Palast m palace.

Palme f palm.

Pampelmuse f *bot* grapefruit.

panier|en bread; **P~mehl** n bread crumbs *pl.*

Pan|ik f panic; **p~isch** panic.

Panne f 1. *mot* breakdown; 2. *(Reifen~)* flat tyre, puncture; 3. *fig* mishap; **~ndienst** m breakdown service.

Panorama n panorama.

Panther m panther.

Pantoffel m slipper.

Pantomime f pantomime.

Panzer m 1. *mil* tank; 2. *(Ritter)* armour; 3. *zoo* shell, shield; **~glas** n bullet-proof glass; **~schrank** m safe.

Papa m daddy.

Papagei m parrot.

Papier n 1. paper; 2. *pl* papers *pl*, documents *pl*; **~geld** n paper money; **~geschäft** n stationer's shop; **~korb** m waste-paper basket; **~taschentuch** n paper handkerchief, tissue; **~waren** *pl* stationary.

Pappe f cardboard, pasteboard.

Pappel f *bot* poplar.

Pappschnee m sticky snow.

Paprika *m* red pepper, paprika.

Papst *m* Pope.

päpstlich papal.

Parade *f* parade, review.

Paradies *n* paradise; **p~isch** paradisiacal.

paradox paradoxical.

Paragraph *m* article, paragraph.

parallel parallel; **P~e** *f* parallel.

Parasit *m* parasite *a. fig.*

Parfüm *n* perfume.

Park *m* park; **p~en** park; *P~ verboten!* no parking.

Parkett *n* 1. parquet; 2. *(theat)* stalls *pl.*

Park|gebühr *f* parking fee; **~haus** *n* multi-storey car park; **~licht** *n* parking light; **~lücke** *f* gap (for parking); **~platz** *m* car park, *Am* parking lot; **~scheibe** *f* parking disc; **~streifen** *m* parking strip; **~uhr** *f* parking meter; **~verbot** *n* prohibition of parking.

Parlament *n* parliament; **p~arisch** parliamentary.

Parodie *f* parody (*auf* on).

Parodontose *f* parodontosis.

Parole *f* password, watchword.

Partei *f* 1. *pol* party; 2. *(jur)* *beklagte* ~ defending party; 3. *für jdn* ~ *ergreifen* take s.o.'s part; **~führer** *m* party leader; **p~isch** biased; **~lichkeit** *f* partiality; bias.

Parterre *n Br* ground floor, *Am* first floor; *im* ~ *wohnen* live on the ground floor.

Partitur *f* score.

Partner(in *f)* *m* partner; **~stadt** *f* twin town.

Party *f* party.

Parzelle *f* allotment.

Paß *m* 1. passport; *Ihr* ~ *ist abgelaufen* your passport has expired; 2. *geog* pass.

Passagier *m* passenger; *blinder* ~ stowaway; **~dampfer** *m* passenger steamer; **~flugzeug** *n* passenger aircraft; **~liste** *f* passenger list.

Paßbild *n* passport photograph.

passen 1. *(Kleider, Schlüssel, Deckel)* fit; 2. ~ *zu* match, suit; 3. *das paßt in m-n Plan* that fits in with my plan; 4. *(harmonieren)* suit, fit; 5. *zueinander* ~ be suited to each other; 6. *das paßt sich nicht* this is not the proper thing to do; **~d** 1. *(Kleidung)* fitting, matching; 2. *(Bemerkung)* suitable, appropriate; 3. *(angemessen)* becoming.

passieren 1. pass (through), cross; 2. *(geschehen)* happen, occur.

Passierschein *m* pass, permit.

Passionswoche *f* Passion Week.

passiv passive; **P~** *n gram* passive voice.

Paß|kontrolle f passport inspection; **~stelle** f passport office.

Paste f paste.

Pastete f (Fleisch~) pie.

pasteurisiert pasteurized.

Pastor m pastor, minister, vicar.

Pate m godfather; **~nkind** n godchild.

Patent n patent.

path|etisch pathetic; **~ologisch** pathological.

Patient m patient.

Patin f godmother.

Patri|arch m patriarch; **~ot** m patriot.

Patrone f cartridge.

Patsche f: in der ~ sitzen be in a fix, jam.

patt stalemate.

Pauke f mus kettledrum.

pauschal over-all, all-inclusive; **P~e** f lump sum; **P~reise** f package tour.

Pause f 1. stop, rest; 2. (Schule) break; 3. (Gespräch) pause; **p~nlos** incessant.

Pavillon m pavilion.

Pazifik m the Pacific (Ocean).

Pech n 1. pitch; 2. fig bad luck.

Pedal n pedal.

Pedant m pedant; **p~isch** meticulous; fussy.

Pegel m water gauge.

Pein f pain, suffering; **p~igen** torture, torment; **p~lich** 1. (Lage) embarrassing, awkward; es ist mir ~ I am very sorry; 2. (sehr sorgfältig) meticulous, painstaking.

Peitsche f whip; **p~n** lash, whip.

Pell|e f peel, skin; **p~en** peel; **~kartoffeln** pl potatoes boiled in their skin.

Pelz m fur, coat; **p~gefüttert** fur-lined; **~geschäft** n furrier's shop; **~jacke** f fur jacket; **~mantel** m fur coat.

Pendel n pendulum; **p~n** oscillate, swing to and fro; **~verkehr** m commuter traffic.

Pendler m commuter.

penetrant penetrating.

Pension f 1. pension, retirement; 2. (Haus) boarding-house; **~är** m pensioner; **p~iert** retired.

Pensum n 1. allotted task; 2. (Lehrstoff) lesson, subject.

perfekt 1. perfect; 2. (abgemacht) settled.

Pergament n parchment.

Period|e f period; **p~isch** periodic.

Peripherie f periphery.

Perl|e f pearl; **~enkette** f pearl necklace; **~mutt(er f)** n mother-of-pearl.

Person f 1. person; pro ~ per person; 2. ich für meine ~ I for my part; **~al** n personnel, staff; **~alabteilung** f personnel department; **~alausweis** m identity card;

~alien pl personal data, particulars pl; **~enbeschreibung** f personal description; **~enkraftwagen** m motor car; **~enstand** m status; **~enwaage** f scales pl; **p~ifizieren** personify.

persönlich 1. personal, private; 2. ich möchte Sie ~ sprechen I'd like to speak to you personally; **P~keit** f personality.

Perspektive f perspective.

Perücke f wig.

pervers perverted.

Pessim|ismus m pessimism; **~ist** m pessimist; **p~istisch** pessimistic.

Pest f plague, pestilence.

Petersilie f parsley.

Petroleum n petroleum, mineral oil; **~lampe** f kerosene lamp.

Pfad m path; **~finder** m boy scout.

Pfahl m stake, post.

Pfand n 1. pledge, pawn, gage; als ~ für in pledge of; 2. (Flaschen~) deposit.

pfänden: etw ~ seize s.th. as a pledge, distrain s.th.

Pfand|leihe f pawnshop; **~schein** m pawn-ticket.

Pfändung f seizure, distraint.

Pfann|e f pan; **~kuchen** m pancake.

Pfarr|amt n clergyman's office; **~ei** f parish; **~er** m 1. (anglikanisch) clergyman, vicar; 2. (katholisch) priest, pastor; **~haus** n vicarage, parsonage.

Pfau m peacock.

Pfeffer m pepper; **~minze** f peppermint; **~streuer** m pepper-pot.

Pfeife f 1. whistle; 2. (Tabaks~) pipe; 3. mus fife; **p~en** irr whistle (s-m Hund to o.'s dog).

Pfeil m arrow.

Pfeiler m pillar; (Brücke) pier.

Pferd n horse; zu ~e on horseback; vom ~ steigen dismount; **~erennen** n horse-race; **~estall** m stable.

Pfiff m whistle.

Pfifferling m bot chanterelle.

Pfingsten n Whitsun(tide).

Pfirsich m peach.

Pflanz|e f, **p~en** plant; **p~lich** vegetable.

Pflaster n 1. med adhesive plaster; 2. (Straßen~) pavement; **p~n** pave; **~stein** m paving stone.

Pflaume f plum.

Pflege f 1. care, charge; 2. tech maintenance; **~eltern** pl foster parents pl; **~kind** n foster child; **~mutter** f foster mother; **p~n** 1. (Kranke) nurse, take care of; 2. (erhalten) preserve; 3. (Kunst) cultivate; 4. etw zu tun ~ be in the habit of doing s.th.; 5. sich ~ groom o.s.; **~r** m ward attendant; **~vater** m foster father.

Pflicht f duty; **p~bewußt** dutiful.

pflücken pick.

Pflug m, **pflügen** plough.

Pforte f 1. gate, entrance; 2. *(Krankenhaus)* reception.

Pförtner m porter, doorkeeper; **~loge** f (porter's, gatekeeper's) lodge.

Pfosten m jamb, post.

Pfote f paw.

Pfropf(en) m stopper, cork.

pfropfen graft.

pfui pugh!

Pfund n pound.

pfusch|en botch; **P~er** m botcher.

Pfütze f puddle.

Phänomen n phenomenon; **p~al** phenomenal.

Phantas|ie f imagination; **p~ieren** 1. daydream, fancy, imagine; 2. *med* be delirious; **p~tisch** fantastic, fanciful, whimsical.

Phantom n phantom.

Phase f phase, stage.

Philosoph m philosopher; **~ie** f philosophy; **p~isch** philosophical.

phlegmatisch phlegmatic.

Phon n phon; **~etik** f phonetics pl; **p~etisch** phonetic.

Phosphor m phosphorus.

Photo n photo; **~apparat** m camera; **~graph** m photographer; **~graphie** f 1. photography; 2. *(Bild)* photograph; **p~graphieren** take pictures; **~kopie** photocopy.

Physik f physics pl; **p~alisch** physical; **~er** m physicist.

Pian|ist m pianist; **~o** n piano.

Pickel m 1. pick; 2. *med* pimple.

picken peck.

Picknick n picnic; **~ machen** have a picnic.

piepen cheep, chirp.

Pietät f piety; **p~los** impious; **p~voll** reverent.

Pik n *(Karten)* spades pl.

Pilger m pilgrim; **~fahrt** f pilgrimage; **p~n** go on a pilgrimage.

Pille f pill.

Pilot m pilot.

Pilz m mushroom; *(giftiger)* toadstool.

Pinguin m penguin.

Pinie f *bot* stone pine.

Pinsel m brush.

Pinzette f tweezers pl.

Pionier m *mil* engineer, pioneer.

Pirat m pirate.

Pistazie f pistachio.

Pistole f pistol, gun.

Plage f trouble, affliction; plague; **p~n** 1. trouble, torment; 2. *sich ~* struggle hard; take pains.

Plakat n poster, placard; **~e ankleben verboten!** stick no bills!

Plakette f badge.

Plan m 1. plan; 2. *(Stadt~)* map; 3. *(Absicht)* intention; 4. *(Vorhaben)* project, scheme; **p~en** plan, intend.

Planet m *astr* planet; **~arium** n planetarium.

planier|en level; **P~raupe** f bulldozer.

Planke f plank, board.

plan|los planless; **~mäßig** 1. systematic, methodical; 2. *(Zug)* scheduled.

Plansch|becken n paddling-pool; **p~en** paddle.

Plantage f plantation.

Planung f planning.

plappern chatter, babble.

Plastik n plastic(s); **~beutel** m plastic bag.

plastisch plastic.

Platane f *bot* plane(tree).

Platin n platinum.

plätschern *(Wasser)* babble.

platt flat.

Platte f 1. *(Stein~)* slab; 2. *(Kachel)* tile; 3. *(Metall)* sheet, plate; 4. *(Koch~)* hot-plate; 5. *mus* record, disc; **~nleger** m tile-setter; **~nspieler** m record player.

Platt|form f platform; **~fuß** m flat foot.

Platz m 1. *(Ort, Stelle)* place, spot; 2. *(Lage)* site, locality; 3. room; 4. *(Sitz~)* seat; 5. *(Posten)* place, post; **~anweiser** m usher.

Plätzchen n biscuit.

platzen 1. burst, split, explode; 2. *fig* fail, fall through.

Platzkarte f reservation ticket.

Plauder|ei f chat; **p~n** chat, gossip.

pleite bankrupt; **P~** f bankruptcy.

Plombe f 1. *(Zahn)* filling; 2. *com* seal; **p~ieren** *(Zahn)* fill.

plötzlich 1. sudden; 2. *(unerwartet)* unexpected; 3. *(auf einmal)* all of a sudden.

plump plump; clumsy.

plünder|n plunder, loot, pillage, sack; **P~ung** f pillage, sack.

Plus n 1. plus; 2. *com* profit; **~zeichen** n plus sign.

Pöbel m rabble, mob; **p~haft** vulgar, coarse.

pochen 1. knock *(an die Tür* on the door); 2. *(Herz)* beat, pound; 3. *auf sein Recht ~* insist on o.'s right.

Pocken pl smallpox; **~impfung** f smallpox vaccination.

Podium n podium, platform; **~sdiskussion** f panel discussion.

Poe|sie f poetry; **p~tisch** poetic.

Pokal m 1. goblet; 2. *sport* cup.

Pol m pole; **p~ar** polar; **~arkreis** m polar circle.

Pole m Pole.

Polem|ik f controversy; **p~isch** controversial, polemic.

Polen n Poland.

polieren polish.
Politik f 1. politics pl;
2. (Maßnahmen) policy;
~**iker** m politician; **p~isch**
political; **p~isieren** talk
politics.
Politur f polish.
Polizei f police; ~**beamter**
m police officer; **p~lich**:
sich ~ melden register with
the police; ~**revier** n police
district; ~**streife** f police
patrol; ~**stunde** f closing
hours pl; ~**wache** f police
station.
Polizist m policeman.
polnisch Polish.
Polster n cushion; ~**möbel**
pl upholstered furniture;
p~n upholster, pad.
poltern rumble, grumble.
Polyp m 1. zoo polyp; 2. med
adenoids pl.
Pomp m pomp, splendour;
p~ös pompous.
Pony m pony.
popul|är popular; **P~arität** f
popularity.
Por|e f pore; **p~ös** porous.
Portal n portal.
Portemonnaie n purse.
Portier m porter; ~**sloge** f
porter's lodge.
Portion f 1. portion, helping;
2. (Tee) pot.
Porto n postage; **p~frei**
post-free.
Porträt n portrait; **p~ieren**
paint a portrait of.
Portu|gal n Portugal; ~**giese**
m, **p~giesisch** Portuguese.

Portwein m port(wine).
Porzellan n china, porcelain;
~**manufaktur** f china factory.
Posaune f mus trombone.
Pos|e f, **p~ieren** pose.
Position f position.
positiv positive.
Poss|e f tomfoolery; **p~ier-
lich** amusing, funny.
Post f 1. post office; 2. (Beförderung) postal service;
per ~ by mail, post; mit ge-
trennter ~ under separate
cover; 3. (Briefe) mail, post;
4. (Austragung) delivery;
p~alisch postal; ~**amt** n
post office; ~**anweisung** f
postal order, money order;
~**auto** n mail van; ~**beamter** m post office official.
Posten m 1. mil station; auf
~ stehen stand guard;
2. (Stellung) post, position;
3. com item, entry, amount.
Post|fach n P.O. box; ~**kar-
te** f postcard; **p~lagernd**
poste restante; ~**leitzahl** f
postal code, Am zip code;
~**scheck** m postal check;
~**scheckkonto** n postal
giro account; ~**stempel** m
postmark; **p~wendend** by
return of post; ~**wurfsen-
dung** f sample packet.
poten|tiell potential; **P~z** f
1. math power; 2. med po-
tency.
Pracht f splendour, magnificence.

prächtig magnificent, splendid, gorgeous; brilliant.

prägen 1. *(Münzen)* coin, strike; 2. *etw auf etw* ~ stamp s.th. on s.th.; 3. *fig* shape, form.

prahl|en brag, boast; **P~erei** *f* boasting, bragging; **~erisch** bragging.

Prakt|ikant *m* trainee; **~ikum** *n* practical training; **p~isch** 1. practical, useful; 2. *~er Arzt* general practitioner.

Praline *f* chocolate.

prall 1. *(Arme)* stout; 2. *in der ~en Sonne* in the blazing sun; **~en** 1. *auf etw* ~ run into s.th., collide with s.th.; 2. *gegen etw* ~ bump into s.th.

Prämie *f* 1. prize, award; 2. *(Versicherung)* premium; 3. *(Zusatz)* bonus; **p~en** award a prize to.

Präparat *n med* preparation.

Präservativ *n* condom.

Präsid|ent *m* chairman, president; **p~ieren** preside over, chair; **~ium** *n* presidency.

prasseln 1. *(Regen)* patter; 2. *(Feuer)* crackle.

Praxis *f* 1. practice; 2. *(Erfahrung)* practical experience; 3. *(Arzt~)* practice, consulting rooms *pl.*

präzis precise, exakt; **~ieren** specify; **P~ion** *f* precision, exactness.

predig|en preach; **P~er** *m* preacher; **P~t** *f* sermon.

Preis *m* 1. price; *um jeden* ~ at any price; *um keinen* ~ not for anything; *zu herabgesetzten* ~*en* at reduced prices; 2. *(Ehrenpreis)* prize; **~ausschreiben** *n* competition.

Preiselbeere *f* red whortleberry, cranberry.

preisen *irr* praise, laud.

Preis|erhöhung *f* raising of prices; **p~geben** *irr* 1. *(verraten)* reveal; 2. *(aufgeben)* give up, abandon; **p~gekrönt** prize-winning; **~schild** *n* price tag, label; **~senkung** *f* price reduction; **~stopp** *m* price stop; **~träger** *m* prizewinner; **~verteilung** *f* distribution of prizes; **~verzeichnis** *n* price list; **p~wert** very reasonable, low-priced, moderate in price.

prekär delicate, precarious.

Prell|bock *m fig* buffer; **p~en**: *jdn um etw* ~ cheat, trick s.o.; **~ung** *f* contusion, bruise.

Premier(minister) *m* prime minister.

Presse *f* 1. press; 2. *(Zitronen~)* squeezer; 3. *(Zeitungswesen)* press, journalism; **~agentur** *f* news agency; **~ausweis** *m* press card; **~konferenz** *f* press conference; **~meldung** *f* press report.

pressen press, squeeze.
Priester m priest.
prima 1. first-class, first-rate;
2. (großartig) marvellous.
primitiv primitive.
Prinz m prince; ~**essin** f
princess.
Prinzip n principle; aus ~ as
a matter of principle; p~**iell**
1. in principle; 2. (aus Prinzip) on principle.
Prior m prior; ~**ität** f priority.
Prise f: e-e ~ Salz a pinch of
salt.
privat 1. private, personal;
2. (vertraulich) confidential;
kann ich Sie ~ sprechen?
can I talk to you in private?
Privatangelegenheit f personal matter; das ist m-e ~
that's my own business;
~**detektiv** m private detective; ~**eigentum** n private
property; ~**klinik** f private
hospital; ~**leben** n private
life; ~**patient** m private patient; ~**schule** f private
school; ~**unterricht** m private lessons pl.
Privileg n privilege.
pro per; ~ Jahr per year; ~
Kopf per head.
Probe f 1. trial, test; 2. etw
auf ~ kaufen buy s.th. on
approval; 3. (Ware) sample,
specimen; 4. theat rehearsal;
5. etw auf die ~ stellen put
s.th. to the test; ~**alarm** m
test alarm; ~**fahrt** f test
drive; p~**n** theat rehearse;

p~**weise** by way of trial;
~**zeit** f probation.
probieren taste, sample, try.
Problem n problem; ~**atik** f
problematic nature;
p~**atisch** problematic(al).
Produkt n product; ~**ion** f
production, output; p~**iv**
productive.
Produzent m producer;
p~**ieren** produce, manufacture.
professionell professional;
P~**or** m professor.
Profil n 1. profile; im ~ in
profile; 2. (Reifen) tread.
Profit m profit, gain; p~**ieren**: von etw ~ profit by
s.th..
Prognose f 1. prognosis;
2. mete forecast.
Programm n programme;
~**gestaltung** f programme
planning; p~**ieren** program;
~**ierer** m programmer;
~**vorschau** f: ~ für morgen
tomorrow's programme.
Projekt n project; p~**ieren**
project, plan; ~**ionsappa-
rat** m projector.
projizieren project (auf e-e
Leinwand on to a screen).

Pro-Kopf-Einkommen n
income per head.
Prokura f power of attorney; ~**ist** m authorized
signatory.
Proletariat n proletariat;
~**ier** m, p~**isch** proletarian.
Prolog m prologue.

Promenade *f* promenade; **~ndeck** *n* promenade deck.

Promille *n* per mille.

prominent prominent; **P~er** *m* prominent personality.

Propaganda *f* propaganda, publicity; **p~ieren** propagate.

Propan(gas) *n* propane.

Propeller *m* air-screw, propeller.

Prophet *m* prophet.

prophezeien prophesy; predict; **P~ung** *f* prophecy; prediction.

proportional proportional.

Prosa *f* prose; **p~isch** prosaic.

prosit cheers! cheerio!

Prospekt *m* prospectus.

Prostituierte *f* prostitute.

Protektion *f* sponsorship, patronage.

Protest *m* protest.

Protestant *m* Protestant; **~ismus** *m* Protestantism.

protestieren protest.

Prothese *f* artificial limb.

Protokoll *n* 1. minutes *pl*; 2. *jur* protocol; **p~arisch**: *etw ~ festhalten* record s.th. in the minutes.

Proviant *m* provisions *pl*, food.

Provinz *f* province; **p~iell** provincial.

Provision *f* commission.

provisorisch provisional.

provozieren provoke; **~d** provocative.

Prozent *n* per cent; **~satz** *m* percentage; **p~ual** in per cent.

Prozeß *m* 1. *jur* lawsuit, trial; *e-n ~ führen* carry on a lawsuit; 2. *(Ablauf)* process; 3. *tech* operation, procedure.

prozessieren bring an action (*gegen jdn* against s.o.).

prüde prudish; **P~rie** *f* prudishness.

prüfen 1. examine, test; 2. *(nach~)* check; 3. *(genau)* scrutinize, size up; 4. *(untersuchen)* study, enquire; **P~ung** *f* 1. examination, test; *sich e-r ~ unterziehen* sit for an examination; 2. *(Untersuchung)* study, enquiry; 3. *tech* inspection.

Prügel *m* 1. cudgel; 2. *pl* thrashing; **p~n** thrash.

Prunk *m* magnificence; **p~voll** magnificent, sumptuous.

Psalm *m* psalm.

pseudonym pseudonymous; **P~** *n* pseudonym.

Psychiater *m* psychiatrist; **p~iatrisch** psychiatric; **p~isch** psychic.

Psychoanalyse *f* psychoanalysis; **~loge** *m* psychologist; **~logie** *f* psychology; **p~logisch** psychological; **~therapie** *f* psychotherapy.

Pubertät *f* puberty.

publik public; **P~ation** *f* publication; **P~um** *n* 1. public; 2. *(Zuhörer)* audience;

3. *(Kundschaft)* customers
pl.
publizieren publish.
Pudding *m* pudding.
Puder *m* powder; **~dose** *f*
powder-box; **p~n** powder
(das Gesicht o.'s face).
Puffer *m loc* buffer.
Pullover *m* pullover, jumper,
sweater.
Puls *m* pulse; *jdm den ~ fühlen* feel s.o.'s pulse; **p~ieren**
pulse, pulsate; **~schlag** *m*
pulsation.
Pult *m* desk.
Pulver *n* powder; **~kaffee**
m instant coffee; **~schnee**
m powder snow.
Pumpe *f* pump; **p~n** pump.

Punkt *m* 1. *gram* full stop,
Am period; 2. *(Fleck)* spot,
speck; 3. *(Ort, Stelle)* point,
spot, place; 4. *(Einzelheit)*
item, detail; 5. *das ist der
springende ~* that's the crux
of the matter; *in vielen ~en*
in many respects; *ein wunder ~* a sore point; *nach*

~en siegen win on points.
pünktlich punctual(ly), on
time; *auf die Minute ~ sein*
be punctual to the minute;
P~keit *f* punctuality.
Pupille *f* pupil.
Puppe *f* 1. doll; 2. *theat* puppet; **~nhaus** *n* doll's house;
~ntheater *n* puppet theatre.
pur 1. *(rein)* pure; 2. *aus ~er
Neugierde* out of sheer
curiosity.
Püree *n* purée.
Purpur *m* purple.
Puste *f* breath; **p~n** blow.
Pute *f* turkey hen; **~r** *m* turkey.
Putsch *m* revolt; **~ist** *m* in-
surgent, rebel.
Putz *m arch* plaster; **p~en**
1. clean; 2. *(Zähne)* brush;
3. *(Schuhe)* polish; 4. *sich
die Nase ~* blow o.'s nose.
Putz|frau *f* charwoman;
~lappen *m* cleaning rag.
Pyjama *m* (pair of) pyjamas
pl.
Pyramide *f* pyramid.

Q

Quadrat n square; **q~isch**
1. square; 2. math quadratic;
~meter m square metre.
quäken screech.
Qual f 1. pain, suffering, agony; 2. (Hunger) torture,
torment.
quäl|en 1. torture, torment;
2. (bedrücken) distress,
trouble; 3. (belästigen)
pester, bother; 4. sich~ suffer pain, toil; **~end** 1. tor-
menting, agonizing; 2. (Husten) painful; **Q~erei** f torment, torture.
Qualifikation f qualification,
capability.
qualifizieren qualify (für
for).
Quali|tät f quality; **q~tativ**
qualitative.
Qualle f jellyfish.
Qualm m, **q~en** smoke.
qualvoll racking, painful, har-
rowing.

Quant|ität f quantity;
q~itativ quantitative; **~um**
n quantum, share.
Quarantäne f quarantine.
Quark m curd, cottage
cheese.
Quart|al n quarter; **~ett** n
mus quartet; **~ier** n accommodation, lodging.

Quarz m quartz.
Quaste f tassel.
Quatsch m nonsense, rubbish, junk; **q~en** talk, chat.
Quecksilber n mercury,
quicksilver.
Quelle f 1. spring, source;
2. fig (Herkunft) source;
aus guter ~ on good auth-
ority; **q~n** irr spring, well,
pour.
quer crosswise; ~ über
across; ~ durch through;
Q~e f: jdm in die ~ kommen get in s.o.'s way, upset
s.o.'s plans; **~feldein** across
country; **Q~schiff** n tran-
sept; **Q~schnitt** m cross
section a. fig; **Q~straße** f
cross street.
quetsch|en 1. squash; 2. med
contuse, bruise; **Q~ung** f
med contusion, bruise.

quietschen squeak, squeal.
quitt: mit jdm ~ sein be quits
with s.o.
Quitte f quince (tree).
quittieren 1. die Rechnung ~
receipt the bill; 2. den
Dienst ~ retire resign.
Quittung f receipt, acquit-
tance.
Quiz n quiz.
Quote f quota; dividend.

R

Rabatt *m* discount, reduction.

Rabe *n* raven.

Rache *f* revenge, vengeance; *an jdm ~ nehmen* take revenge (*an jdm* on s.o.).

Rachen *m* 1. *anat* pharynx; 2. *(Tier)* jaws *pl.*

räch|en 1. revenge; 2. *sich ~* take revenge (*an jdm* on s.o.); **R~er** *m* avenger.

Rachitis *f* rickets *pl.*

rachsüchtig revengeful.

Rad *n* wheel.

Radar *m* radar; **~anlage** *f,* **~gerät** *n,* **~station** *f* radar installation, equipment, station.

Rädelsführer *m* ringleader.

radfahr|en *irr* cycle, ride a bicycle; **R~er** *m* cyclist; **R~weg** *m* cycle track.

radier|en erase, rub out; **R~gummi** *m* rubber, eraser; **R~ung** *f (Kunst)* etching.

Radieschen *n* radish.

radikal radical; **R~ismus** *m* radicalism.

Radio *n* radio, wireless; *~ hören* listen to the radio; *ein Hörspiel im ~* a play on the radio; *das ~ abstellen* switch, turn off the radio.

radioaktiv radioactive; **R~ität** *f* radioactivity.

Radioapparat *m* radio, wireless set.

Radius *m* radius.

Rad|rennbahn *f* cycling track; **~rennen** *n* cycle race; **~tour** *f* bicycle tour.

Raffin|esse *f* 1. *(Geschmack)* finesse; 2. *(schlau)* shrewdness; **r~iert** ~ refined; 2. shrewd.

ragen tower, rise up.

Ragout *n* ragout.

Rahm *m* cream.

Rahmen *m* 1. frame; 2. *tech* chassis, rim; **r~:** *ein Bild ~* frame a painting.

Rakete *f* 1. rocket; 2. *ferngelenkte ~* guided missile.

rammen: *etw in etw ~* ram s.th. into s.th.

Rampe *f* ramp; **~nlicht** *n* 1. *tech* footlight; 2. *im ~ stehen* be in the limelight.

Ramsch *m* junk.

Rand *m* 1. edge; 2. *(Glas)* brim; *(Tasse)* rim; 3. *(Abgrund)* brink; 4. *(Papier)* margin, edge; 5. *am ~e der Stadt* on the outskirts *pl* of the town.

randalieren make a row.

rand|los *(Brille)* rimless; **R~stein** *m* kerbstone.

Rang *m* 1. *mil* rank; 2. *(Stellung)* position, status; 3. *(Stand)* class; 4. *(Güte)*

quality, order; 5. *theat* row;
~ordnung *f* order of rank.

Ränke *pl* intrigues *pl;* **~ schmieden** intrigue.

ranken, *sich* creep, climb.

ranzig rancid.

Raps *m* rape, colza.

rar rare, scarce; **R~ität** *f* rarity.

rasch quick; speedy.

rascheln rustle.

rasen 1. race; 2. *vor Wut ~* be raging.

Rasen *m* lawn.

rasend 1. scorching; 2. *(wütend)* raging, mad.

Rasen|mäher *m* lawn-mower; **~sprenger** *m* sprinkler.

Raserei *f* frenzy.

Rasier|apparat *m* safety razor; **~creme** *f* shaving cream; **r~en,** *sich* shave (o.s.); **~klinge** *f* razor blade; **~messer** *n* straight razor; **~pinsel** *m* shaving brush; **~seife** *f* shaving soap; **~spiegel** *m* shaving mirror; **~zeug** *n* shaving things *pl.*

Rasse *f* 1. (human) race; 2. *zoo* breed.

rasseln rattle, clank.

rass|ig fiery, classy; **~isch** racial.

Rast *f* repose, rest; pause; **r~en** rest; **r~los** restless, ceaseless; **~platz** *m* lay-by; **~stätte** *f* service area.

Rat *m* 1. advice, counsel; *jdn um ~ fragen* ask s.o. for advice; 2. *(Vorschlag)* sugges-

tion; 3. *(Beratung)* deliberation; 4. *(Versammlung)* council.

Rate *f* instal(l)ment; *in ~n zahlen* pay by instal(l)ments.

raten *irr* 1. *jdm ~* advise s.o., recommend s.o.; 2. *(erraten)* guess.

Ratenkauf *m* hire purchase.

Rat|geber *m* adviser, counsel(l)or; **~haus** *n* town hall.

ratifizieren ratify.

Ration *f* ration; **r~alisieren** rationalize.

rationell 1. efficient; 2. *(sparsam)* economical.

rationieren ration.

rat|los helpless, perplexed; **~sam** advisable; *für ~ halten* think s.th. advisable; **R~schlag** *m* advice, counsel.

Rätsel *n* 1. puzzle, riddle; 2. *(Geheimnis)* mystery; **r~haft** 1. mysterious; 2. puzzling.

Ratte *f* rat.

rattern rattle, clatter.

Raub *m* robbery; **r~en** 1. rob *(jdm etw* s.o. of s.th.); 2. *(Menschen)* kidnap.

Räuber *m* robber.

Raub|mord *m* murder with robbery; **~tier** *n* beast of prey; **~überfall** *m* robbery.

Rauch *m* smoke; **r~en** smoke; **R~ verboten** no smoking; **~er** *m* smoker; **~erabteil** *n* smoker.

räuchern smoke.

rauchig smoky.

Rauch|verbot n ban on smoking; **~vergiftung** f smoke poisoning; **~waren** pl tobacco products; **~wolke** f cloud of smoke.

rauf|en 1. fight; 2. sich die Haare ~ tear o.'s hair; **R~erei** f scuffle.

rauh 1. rough, coarse; 2. (Stimme) harsh; 3. (Gegend) uneven; 4. fig harsh, blunt; **R~reif** m hoar-frost.

Raum m 1. room; 2. (Gegend) area, region; 3. (Gebiet) space, expanse; 4. phys space.

räumen 1. vacate, leave; 2. (Straße) clear; 3. (entfernen) remove; 4. mil abandon.

Raum|fahrer m astronaut; **~fahrt** f space travel; **~inhalt** m volume.

räumlich spatial; **R~keit** f 1. spatiality; 2. pl rooms pl.

Raum|mangel m lack of space; **~pflegerin** f cleaner; **~schiff** n spaceship; **r~sparend** space-saving.

Räumung f 1. clearance; 2. jur eviction; **~sverkauf** m clearance sale.

Raupe f zoo caterpillar; **~nschlepper** m caterpillar tractor.

Rausch m intoxication.

rauschen 1. (Wind) rush; 2. (Bach) bubble.

Rauschgift n drug, narcotic; **~händler** m trafficker in

drugs; **~süchtiger** m drug addict.

räuspern, sich clear o.'s throat.

Razzia f raid.

reagieren react (auf to).

Reaktion f reaction; **r~är** reactionary.

Reaktor m reactor.

real (wirklich) real, actual; **~isieren** realize; **R~ität** f reality.

Rebe f shoot.

Rebell m, **r~ieren** rebel; **~ion** f rebellion, revolt; **r~isch** rebellious.

Rebhuhn n partridge.

Rechen|aufgabe f sum; **~fehler** m error in calculation; **~maschine** f calculating machine; **~schaft** f: über etw ~ ablegen give, render account of s.th.; jdn zur ~ ziehen call s.o. to account (über for); **~schaftsbericht** m report.

rechnen 1. reckon, calculate; 2. (zählen) count; 3. ~ zu number among; 4. mit etw ~ expect s.th.; auf jdn ~ count on s.o.; 5. (Aufgabe) work out; 6. (berücksichtigen) take into account; 7. sich ~ zu count o.s. among; **R~** n arithmetic.

Rechner m calculator; **r~isch** mathematical, arithmetic.

Rechnung f 1. calculation; 2. (Aufgabe) problem; 3. com account; (im Lokal) bill; 4. *jdm etw in ~ stellen* charge s.th. to s.o.'s account.

recht I *adj* 1. right; 2. *pol* right-wing; 3. *(Masche)* plain; 4. *ganz ~* quite right; *zur ~en Zeit* in time; 5. *(passend) ist es dir ~,* would you mind if; *wenn es Ihnen ~ ist* if you please; 6. *(gerecht)* just, fair; 7. *jdm ~ geben* agree with s.o.; *~ haben* be right; **II** *adv* 8. *~ gern* with pleasure; *~ handeln* do right; *es allen ~ machen* please everybody; 9. *nach dem R~en sehen* see things.

Recht *n* 1. right; *mit ~* with good reason; *im ~ sein* be in the right; *ein ~ auf etw haben* be entitled to s.th.; *von ~s wegen* by right; 2. *(Gesetz)* law; 3. *(Gerechtigkeit)* justice; 4. *(Vollmacht)* power, authority.

Rechte *f* 1. right hand; 2. *pol* right wing.

Rechteck *n* rectangle; **r~ig** rectangular.

recht|fertigen 1. *etw ~* justify s.th.; 2. *sich vor jdm ~* justify o.s. to s.o.; **~haberisch** dogmatical.

recht|lich legal, lawful; **~los** lawless; **~mäßig** lawful, rightful, legitimate.

rechts 1. on the right; *nach ~* to the right; *~ fahren* keep to the right; 2. *~ der Donau* in the right side of

the Danube; **R~abbieger** *m* vehicle turning right.

Rechts|anwalt *m* 1. *Br* lawyer, solicitor; *(vor Gericht)* barrister-at-law; 2. *Am* lawyer, attorney-at-law; **~berater** *m* legal adviser.

rechtschaffen honest, upright.

Rechtschreib|fehler *m* spelling mistake; **~ung** *f* orthography, spelling.

rechts|fähig having legal capacity; **R~geschäft** *n* legal act.

rechtshändig right-handed.

rechts|kräftig valid; *~ werden* become final; **R~mittel** *n* legal remedy; **R~pflege** *f* administration of justice.

Rechtsprechung *f* jurisdiction.

Rechts|verkehr *m* right-hand traffic; **~verletzung** *f* infringement; **~weg** *m* course of law; *auf dem ~* in court; **~wissenschaft** *f* jurisprudence.

recht|winklig rectangular; **~zeitig** 1. punctual; 2. in time.

Reck *n* horizontal bar; **r~en**: *den Hals ~* stretch o.'s neck.

Redakteur *m* editor; **~ion** *f* editorial staff; **r~ionell** editorial.

Rede *f* 1. *e-e ~ halten* make a speech; 2. *(Unterhaltung)* conversation; 3. *(Gespräch)* talk; 4. *(Redeweise)* language; 5. *(Gerücht)* rumour;

6. *(Aussprache)* address;
7. *jdn zur* ~ *stellen* call s.o.
to account; *davon ist keine*
~ that's not the point; *es ist
nicht der* ~ *wert* it is not
worth mentioning; **~freiheit** *f* freedom of speech;
r~gewandt eloquent.
reden 1. *von jdm, etw* ~ talk
of, about s.o., s.th.; 2. *mit
jdm* ~ talk to s.o.; 3. *(sprechen)* speak; discuss; 4. *mit
sich* ~ *lassen* come to terms
with s.o.; 5. *viel von sich* ~
machen be very much in
the news; **R~sart** *f* expression, phrase.
Redewendung *f* expression;
idiom.
redlich honest, upright;
R~keit *f* honesty.
Redner *m* speaker; **~pult** *n*
speaker's desk.
redselig talkative.
Reede *f mar* roads *pl;* **~r** *m*
shipowner.
reell 1. *(Person)* honest, solid;
2. *(Preis)* fair; 3. *(Firma)*
solid, respectable.
Referenz *f* reference.
reflektieren 1. *(Licht)* reflect; 2. *über ein Problem* ~
reflect on a problem.
Reflex *m* reflex, reflection.
Reform *f* reform; **~ation** *f:
die* ~ the Reformation.
Regal *n* shelf, rack.
Regatta *f* regatta.
rege 1. *(Verkehr)* busy;
2. *(Mensch)* active, alert;
lively.

Regel *f* rule; *in der* ~ as a
rule; **r~mäßig** regular; **r~n**
1. arrange, regulate, settle;
2. *tech* adjust, control;
r~recht 1. *(völlig)* downright; 2. *(richtig)* proper;
~ung *f* 1. regulation; 2. control; 3. settlement.
regen, *sich* move, stir.
Regen *m* rain; *bei strömendem* ~ in pouring rain; *es
sieht nach* ~ *aus* it looks
like rain; **~bogen** *m* rainbow; **~fälle** *pl* heavy rains
pl; **~mantel** *m* raincoat;
~schauer *m* rain shower;
~schirm *m* umbrella;
~tropfen *m* raindrop;
~wasser *n* rainwater;
~wetter *n* rainy weather;
~wurm *m zoo* earthworm;
~zeit *f* rainy season.
Regie *f film* direction; *unter
der* ~ *von* directed by.
regieren govern, rule; *(von
Königen)* reign over.
Regierung *f* government,
rule, reign; *an die* ~ *kommen* come into power;
~schef *m* head of the government.
Regiment *n mil* regiment.
Region *f* region; **r~al** regional.
Regisseur *m* 1. *theat* stage
manager; 2. *film* director.
Register *n* register; index;
~ratur *f com* filing cabinet;
r~rieren register, record.
Regler *m tech* regulator.

regne|n: *es regnet* it's raining; **~risch** rainy.

regul|är regular; **~ieren** regulate, control.

Regung *f* 1. movement; 2. *fig* feeling; **r~slos** motionless.

Reh *n* roe (-deer); **~bock** *m* roebuck; **~keule** *f* haunch of (roe-)venison; **~rücken** *m* saddle of (roe-)venison.

Reib|eisen *n* grater; **r~en** *irr* 1. rub; 2. *(Käse)* grate; 3. *(kratzen)* scratch; **~ereien** *pl* friction; **r~ungslos** *fig* smooth.

Reich *n* 1. empire; 2. *fig (Bereich)* kingdom; 3. *(Gebiet)* realm, domain.

reich 1. rich *(an* in), wealthy; 2. *(reichlich)* abundant.

reichen 1. reach, pass; 2. *jdm den Arm* ~ offer o.'s arm to s.o.; 3. *(anbieten)* offer; 4. *(genügen)* suffice, do; 5. *(sich ausdehnen)* stretch, extend.

reich|haltig rich, sumptuous; **~lich** 1. plenty; generous, ample; 2. *(gut)* a good; 3. *(mehr als)* well over, more than.

Reichtum *m* 1. wealth, fortune; 2. *fig* richness.

Reichweite *f* 1. reach; *in* ~ *sein* be within reach; 2. *mil* range.

reif 1. *(Früchte)* ripe, mature; ~ *werden* ripen, mature; 2. *die Zeit ist* ~ time is ripe.

Reif *m* 1. hoarfrost; 2. *(Ring)* ring.

Reife *f* ripeness, maturity.

reifen 1. ripen, mature; 2. *fig* take shape; 3. *es reift* there is a hoarfrost.

Reifen *m* 1. *(Faß)* hoop; 2. *(Auto)* tyre; 3. *(Armreif)* bracelet; **~druck** *m* tyre pressure; **~panne** *f* puncture; **~wechsel** *m* change of tyre.

reiflich mature, careful.

Reigen *m* round dance.

Reihe *f* 1. *(Menschen)* line, row; ranks; 2. *(Häuser)* row; 3. *(Folge)* succession; 4. *(Reihenfolge)* turn; *ich bin an der* ~ it's my turn; *der* ~ *nach* one after the other, in turn; 5. *(Anzahl)* number.

reihen 1. put in a row; 2. *sich* ~ form a row, line up.

Reihen|folge *f* succession, sequence; *in alphabetischer* ~ in alphabetical order; **~haus** *n* terraced house, *Am* row house.

Reiher *m* heron.

Reim *m* rhyme; **r~en** rhyme *(auf* with).

rein 1. *(sauber)* clean; 2. *(Wasser, Luft)* pure; 3. *(unschuldig)* innocent; 4. *(Klang)* clear; 5. *com* net, clear; 6. *~er Wahnsinn* sheer madness; 7. *(nur)* merely; 8. *ins* ~*e schreiben* make a fair copy.

Rein|emachefrau *f* charwoman; **~erlös** *m* net proceeds *pl*; **~fall** *m* failure, flop; **~gewinn** *m* net profit;

~heit f 1. purity, pureness;
2. *(Sauberkeit)* cleanness;
3. *fig* innocence.

reinig|en 1. clean; 2. *(Luft)*
purify; 3. *(Wunde)* cleanse;
4. *fig* purge; **R~ung** f
1. cleaning; 2. *(Geschäft)*
cleaner's; *chemische ~* dry
cleaning.

rein|lich clean, immaculate;
R~schrift f fair copy.

Reis m rice; **~brei** m rice
pudding.

Reise f 1. *(nach* to) journey,
trip; *e-e ~ antreten* set out
on a journey; *auf ~n gehen*
go travelling; *gute ~!* have a
nice trip! 2. *(zu Wasser)*
voyage; **~andenken** n
souvenir; **~(auto)bus** m
tourist coach; **~bekannt-
schaft** f travelling
acquaintance; **~büro** n
tourist office, travel agency;
r~fertig ready to start;
~führer m guidebook;
~gepäck n luggage, *Am*
baggage; **~gesellschaft** f
tourist party; **~koffer** m
suitcase; **~leiter** m courier;
r~n travel *(mit der Eisenbahn, dem Flugzeug, dem
Wagen* by train, by air, by
car)*, make a journey; **~nder**
m 1. passenger, tourist;
2. *com* traveller; **~paß** m
passport; **~route** f travel
route, itinerary; **~scheck** m
traveller's cheque;
~schreibmaschine f portable (typewriter); **~tasche**

f travelling bag; **~ziel** n
destination.

Reißaus m: *~ nehmen* take
to o.'s heels.

reiß|en irr 1. tear; break; *etw
in Stücke ~* tear s.th. to
pieces; 2. *etw von etw ~* pull
s.th. off s.th.; *jdn aus etw ~*
snatch s.o. out of s.th.; *etw
an sich ~* grasp s.th.; *fig*
seize s.th.; 3. *mir reißt die
Geduld* my patience is
stretched to the limit; 4. *zu
Boden ~* drag to the
ground; 5. *sich ~ um*
scramble for; **~end** 1. *(Tier)*
rapacious; 2. *(Strom)* raging;
3. *~en Absatz finden* be in
great demand; **~erisch**
sensational; **R~verschluß**
m zip(-fastener), *Am* zipper;
R~zwecke f drawing pin.

Reit|bahn f riding school;
r~en irr ride; *auf e-m Pferd
~* ride on horseback; **~en** n
equitation; **r~end** on horseback; **~er** m, **~erin** f rider,
horseman, -woman; **~hose**
f riding breeches pl, jodh-
purs pl; **~peitsche** f riding
whip; **~pferd** n riding-
horse; **~sport** m eques-
trian sport; **~stiefel** pl
riding-boots pl.

Reiz m 1. *(Zauber)* attraction, charm; 2. *(Verlockung)*
temptation; 3. *(Anreiz)*
stimulus; 4. *med* irritation;
r~bar 1. *(Nerv)* irritable;
2. *(empfindlich)* sensitive;
3. *(jähzornig)* irascible;

r~en 1. irritate, annoy; 2. *(erregen)* excite; 3. *(aufregen)* provoke; 4. *(locken)* tempt, entice; **r~end** 1. charming, delightful; 2. *(hübsch)* attractive; **~klima** *n* invigorating climate; **r~los** unattractive; **r~voll** 1. charming; 2. *(anziehend)* attractive; 3. *fig* interesting.

rekeln, *sich* 1. loll about; 2. *(sich strecken)* stretch.

Reklamation *f* complaint.

Reklame *f* advertising, publicity, advertisement, sales promotion.

reklamieren complain *(etw* about s.th.).

rekonstruieren reconstruct; **R~ktion** *f* reconstruction.

Rekord *m* record; *e-n ~ aufstellen* set up a record.

Rekrut *m,* **r~ieren** recruit.

Rektor *m* 1. *(Uni)* vice-chancellor; 2. *(Schule)* headmaster.

relativ relative; **R~itätstheorie** *f* theory of relativity.

Religion *f* 1. religion; 2. *(Konfession)* denomination.

religiös religious.

Reling *f mar* rail.

Remoulade *f* remoulade.

Renn|bahn *f* race track, racing course; **r~en** *irr* 1. run, rush, dash; hurry; 2. *gegen etw ~* knock, bump against s.th.; **~en** *n* race; **~fahrer** *m* racing driver;

~pferd *n* racehorse; **~rad** *n* racing cycle; **~sport** *m* racing; **~strecke** *f* race track; **~wagen** *m* racing car.

renovieren renovate; **R~ung** *f* renovation.

rentabel profitable.

Rente *f* 1. pension; 2. *(Jahres~)* annuity; **r~ieren,** *sich* pay, be profitable; **~ner** *m* pensioner.

Reparatur *f* repairs *pl;* **~werkstatt** *f* repair shop.

reparieren repair, mend.

Reporter *m* reporter; commentator.

repräsentieren represent.

Repressalie *f* reprisal.

Reproduktion *f* reproduction.

Reptil *n* reptile.

Republik *f* republic; **~aner** *m,* **r~anisch** republican.

Reservat *n* reservation.

Reserve *f* 1. reserve, store, supplies *pl;* 2. *mil* reserves *pl;* 3. *(Rücklagen)* reserve; **~rad** *n* spare wheel; **~tank** *m* reserve tank.

reservieren 1. reserve; 2. book *(ein Zimmer* a room); **r~iert** reserved.

Residenz *f* residence.

resignieren give up; **~t** resigned.

Resonanz *f* resonance.

Respekt *m* respect; **r~abel** respectable; **r~ieren** respect; **r~los** disrespectful; **r~voll** respectful.

Rest *m* 1. rest, remainder; 2. *pl* remains *pl*, leftovers *pl*.

Restaur|ant *n* restaurant; **r~ieren** restore; **~ierung** *f* restoration.

rest|lich remaining; **~los** complete, perfect.

Resultat *n* result.

Retorte *f* retort.

rett|en 1. save (*jds Leben* s.o.'s life), rescue; 2. *sich ~* escape (*vor* from); **R~er** *m* 1. rescuer; 2. (*Christus*) saviour.

Rettich *m* radish.

Rettung *f* 1. rescue; 2. (*Hilfe*) help; **~sboot** *n* lifeboat; **~sdienst** *m* rescue service; **~sgürtel** *m* life-belt; **r~slos** irredeemable, hopeless.

Reu|e *f* repentance (*über* for), remorse; **r~en:** *es reut mich, daß* I am sorry that; **r~mütig** remorseful, repentant.

revanchieren, *sich* take revenge.

Revier *n* 1. district, quarter; 2. (*Polizei*) ward, beat; 3. (*Jagd*) shooting ground; **~förster** *m* district forest officer.

Revol|te *f* revolt, insurrection; **r~ieren** revolt, rebel.

Revolution *f* revolution; **r~är** revolutionary.

Revolver *m* revolver.

Rezept *n* 1. *med* prescription; 2. (*Küche*) recipe.

Rhabarber *m* rhubarb.

Rheuma(tismus *m*) *n* rheumatism.

rhythm|isch rhythmic; **R~us** *m* rhythm, cadence.

richten 1. point (*auf etw* at s.th.); 2. fix, arrange; 3. (*vorbereiten*) fix up; 4. (*ordnen*) tidy up, straighten; 5. (*reparieren*) repair; 6. (*verurteilen*) sentence, judge; 7. *sich ~* get ready; *sich nach jdm ~* comply with s.o.; depend on s.o.; 8. *e-e Frage an jdn ~* address a question to s.o.; *etw gegen jdn ~* direct s.th. against s.o.

Richter *m* judge; **r~lich** judicial.

richtig 1. (*Antwort*) right, correct; 2. (*wahr*) true; 3. (*passend*) proper, appropriate; 4. *etw für ~ halten* deem s.th. right; 5. (*eigentlich*) actual, real, regular; 6. *geht deine Uhr ~?* is your watch right? 7. *im ~en Augenblick* at the proper moment; **R~keit** *f* 1. correctness, rightness; 2. (*Ordnung*) order, regularity; **~stellen** correct, put right.

Richtlinien *pl* guide-lines *pl*.

Richtung *f* 1. direction; *in ~ auf* in direction of; *aus allen ~en* from all directions; 2. (*e-r Straße*) course; 3. *fig* trend, tendency, drift; views *pl*; **~sanzeiger** *m* (*Auto*) direction indicator.

riechen *irr* 1. smell (*nach* of;

an etw s.th.) 2. *gut* ~ have a good smell.

Riegel *m* 1. bolt; 2. *(Seife)* bar; 3. *(Schokolade)* strip.

Riemen *m* strap; belt.

Riese *m* giant.

rieseln drizzle.

riesig gigantic, enormous, giant.

Riff *n* reef.

rigoros rigorous, severe, drastic.

Rille *f* 1. groove; 2. *(Furche)* furrow.

Rind *n* ox, cow.

Rinde *f* 1. *(Baum~)* bark; 2. *(Brot~)* crust; 3. *(Käse~)* rind.

Rind|erbraten *m* roast beef; ~**fleisch** *n* beef; ~**vieh** *n* cattle.

Ring *m* 1. *allg* ring, circle; 2. *com* pool, trust.

ringen *irr* 1. *sport* wrestle; 2. *(fig) um etw* ~ struggle with s.th.

Ringer *m* wrestler.

Ring|finger *m* ring finger; ~**kampf** *m* wrestling.

rings around, round about.

Ringstraße *f* ring road.

ringsum all around.

Rinne *f* gutter, drain, channel; **r~n** *irr* 1. *(fließen)* flow, run, pour, stream; 2. *(undicht sein)* leak.

Rinnsal *n* rivulet.

Rippe *f* rib; ~**nbruch** *m* rib fracture; ~**nfell** *n* costal pleura; ~**nstück** *n* rib cut.

Risiko *n* risk; *auf eigenes* ~ at o.'s own risk; *ein* ~ *eingehen* take, run a risk.

risk|ant risky, hazardous; ~**ieren** risk, dare.

Riß *m* 1. *(Kleidung)* tear, rent; 2. *(Wand, Glas)* crack; 3. *(Freundschaft)* rift.

rissig 1. *(Wand)* cracked; 2. *(Metall)* fissured.

Ritt *m* ride (on a horse).

Ritter *m* knight; **r~lich** chivalrous, gallant.

rituell ritual.

Ritus *m* rite.

Ritze *f* cleft; fissure; **r~n** *(kratzen)* scratch; carve, cut.

Rival|e *m* 1. *sport* competitor; 2. rival; **r~isieren** compete (*mit jdm* with s.o.), rival (*mit jdm* s.o.); ~**ität** *f* rivalry, competition.

Rizinusöl *n* castor oil.

Roastbeef *n* roastbeef.

Robbe *f* seal.

Robe *f* gown; robe.

Roboter *m* robot.

robust 1. *(Gesundheit)* robust; 2. *(kräftig)* strong, sturdy.

röcheln rattle.

Rock *m* 1. coat, jacket; 2. *(Damen~)* skirt.

rodel|n toboggan, sledge; **R~schlitten** *m* sledge.

roden make arable, cultivate.

Rogen *m* roe.

Roggen *m* rye.

roh 1. raw, uncooked; 2. *(Öl)* crude; 3. *(Stein, Holz)* rough; 4. *fig* rude, rough, brutal; **R~bau** *m* carcass;

R~eit f harshness, roughness, brutality; **R~kost** f raw vegetarian food; **R~ling** m brute.

Rohr n 1. *bot* cane; *(Schilf)* reed; 2. *tech* pipe, tube; **~bruch** m burst pipe.

Röhre f 1. pipe, tube; 2. *radio* valve.

Rohr|leitung f pipeline; conduit; **~post** f pneumatic post.

Rohstoff m raw material.

Rokoko n rococo.

Rolladen m sliding shutter.

Rollbahn f *aero* taxiway.

Rolle f 1. *(Papier~)* roll; 2. *(Draht)* coil; 3. *(Register)* register, list, roll; 4. *theat* role; *(film)* part; 5. *(fig)* e-e *große ~ spielen* play an important part *(bei* in); *Geld spielt keine ~* money is no object; **r~n** 1. roll; 2. *(Donner)* roar, rumble; 3. *aero* taxi; **~r** m scooter.

Roll|film m roll film; **~kragen(pullover)** m polo-neck; **~schuh** m roller-skate; **~stuhl** m wheel chair; **~treppe** f escalator.

Roman m novel.

romanisch Romance.

Roman|tik f Romanticism; **r~tisch** romantic.

Röm|er m, **r~isch** Roman.

röntgen X-ray; **R~apparat** m X-ray apparatus; **R~aufnahme** f radiograph; **R~strahlen** pl X-rays pl.

rosa pink.

Rose f *bot* rose; **~ngarten** m rose-garden; **~nkohl** m (Brussels) sprouts pl; **~nkranz** m *rel* rosary; **~nmontag** m Shrove Monday.

Rosette f *arch* rosette.

rosig rosy.

Rosine f raisin.

Roß n horse; **~haar** n horse-hair; **~kastanie** f horse-chestnut.

Rost m 1. grill, grate; 2. *(auf Eisen)* rust; **~braten** m sirloin steak.

Röstbrot n toast.

rosten rust, corrode.

rösten 1. *(Fleisch)* grill; 2. *(Brot)* toast; 3. *(Korn)* parch; 4. *(Kaffee)* roast.

Rost|fleck m rust stain; **r~frei** rustless; **r~ig** rusty.

rot 1. red; 2. *(Wangen)* ruddy; *~ werden* blush; 3. *(Haare)* carroty, red; **~blond** sandy.

Röte f 1. red; 2. *fig* flush; blush; **r~n** 1. colour red; 2. *sich ~* redden.

rothaarig red-haired.

rotieren rotate; **~d** rotary.

Rotkohl m red cabbage.

rötlich reddish.

Rot|licht n red light; **~stift** m red pencil; **~wein** m red wine; **~wild** n red deer.

Route f route.

Routine f practice; routine.

Rowdy m rowdy, hooligan.

Rübe f *bot* beet; *gelbe ~* carrot; *rote ~* beetroot.

Rubin m ruby.

Rubrik *f (Spalte)* column.
Ruck *m* jolt, jerk; *auf e-n ~* at one go; **r~artig** jerky.
Rückblick *m* retrospect.
rücken 1. move *(nach rechts* to the right), shift; 2. *näher ~* approach.
Rücken *m* 1. back; *auf den ~ fallen* fall on o.'s back; *jdm in den ~ fallen* stab s.o. in the back; 2. *(Berg~)* ridge; **~wind** *m* tail wind.
Rückerstattung *f* reimbursement.
Rückfahr|karte *f* return ticket; **~t** *f* return trip; *auf der ~* on the journey back.
Rück|fall *m* med relapse; **r~fällig** 1. *jur* recidivous; 2. *~ werden* relapse.
Rückflug *m* return flight.
Rückfrage *f* further enquiry.
Rückgabe *f: gegen ~ von* upon return of.
Rück|gang *m* 1. *(Abnahme)* decrease, decline; 2. *(Preise)* drop; *(Kurse)* fall; *(Umsatz)* let-down; *(Wirtschaft)* recession; 3. *med* regression; **r~gängig:** *~ machen* cancel, annul.
Rückgrat *n anat* backbone *a. fig.* spine.
Rückhalt *m* support, backing; **r~los** unreserved.
Rück|kehr *f* return; **~lagen** *pl com* reserves *pl.*
rückläufig retrograde, declining, falling.
Rücklicht *n* rear light.
Rucksack *m* rucksack.

Rück|schlag *m* 1. setback; 2. *med* relapse; **~seite** *f* 1. back; 2. *(Gebäude)* rear; 3. *(Stoffe)* reverse side.
Rücksicht *f* consideration; *mit ~ auf* out of consideration for; *ohne ~ auf etw* regardless of s.th.; *auf etw ~ nehmen* have regard for s.th.; **r~slos** without consideration *(gegen* for); reckless; **~slosigkeit** *f* inconsiderateness; recklessness; **r~svoll** considerate *(gegen* towards).
Rücksitz *m* back seat.
Rückspiegel *m* rear mirror.
Rücksprache *f: nach ~ mit* on consultation with.
Rück|stand *m* 1. *im ~ sein* be in arrears; 2. *pl* outstanding debts *pl;* 3. *tech* residue; **r~ständig** 1. *com* in arrears; 2. *(Land)* backward; 3. *(überholt)* outdated.
Rücktritt *m* 1. resignation; 2. *(von e-m Vertrag)* withdrawal.
rück|wärtig back, rear; **~wärts** backwards; *~ gehen* go backwards; **R~wärtsgang** *m* reverse gear.
Rückweg *m: auf dem ~* on the way back.
rückwirk|end retroactive; **R~ung** *f* 1. repercussion; 2. *jur* retroactivity.
Rückzahlung *f* 1. repayment; 2. *com* redemption.

Rückzug m retreat, retirement.

Ruder n oar; **~er** m oarsman; **r~n** 1. row; 2. (Ente) paddle; **~sport** m rowing.

Ruf m 1. shout, cry, call; 2. (Ansehen) reputation; 3. telephone (number); **r~en** irr 1. call (nach jdm for s.o.); 2. (aufrufen) summon; 3. (laut) shout, cry; **~name** m Christian name; **~nummer** f telephone number.

Rüge f reprimand, rebuke, reproach; **r~n** reprove, reproach, reprimand.

Ruhe f 1. rest, repose; 2. (Schlaf) sleep; 3. (Frieden) peace, quiet; jdn in ~ lassen leave s.o. in peace; laß mich in ~! leave me alone! in aller ~ quietly; 4. (Stille) silence; 5. (Gemütsruhe) calmness; s-e ~ bewahren maintain o.'s composure; 6. sich zur ~ setzen retire; **~gehalt** n retirement pension; **r~los** restless; **r~n** 1. rest, repose; 2. (schlafen) sleep; 3. ~ auf supported by; 4. (liegen) lie; 5. (aufhören) have ceased; 6. (einstellen) have been stopped; 7. (stoppen) be at a standstill; **~pause** f break, pause; **~stand** m retirement; **~tag** m rest day.

ruhig 1. quiet, silent, still; 2. (friedlich) peaceful; 3. (gelassen) cool; ~ werden calm down; 4. (glatt) smooth; 5. (Atem) regular.

Ruhm m fame, renown, glory.

rühm|en 1. praise, glorify; 2. sich ~ boast, brag; **~lich** praiseworthy, glorious.

ruhmvoll glorious.

Rühr|ei n scrambled eggs pl; **r~en** 1. stir, move; 2. (ergreifen) touch, move; 3. an etw ~ touch on s.th.; von etw ~ come from s.th.; 4. sich ~ move, stir; **r~end** moving, touching; **r~ig** bustling, active; **r~selig** sentimental.

Ruin m 1. ruin; 2. (finanziell) collapse; **~e** f ruin(s pl); **r~ieren** 1. ruin; 2. (Kleidung) spoil.

Rum m rum.

Rumän|e m Romanian; **~ien** n Romania; **r~isch** Romanian.

Rummel m hustle and bustle.

Rumpf m 1. trunk, body; 2. mar hull; 3. aero fuselage.

Rumpsteak n rump-steak.

rund I adj round, circular; **II** adv 1. ~um around; 2. (ungefähr) about, approximately; **R~blick** m panorama; **R~e** f 1. (Personen) group, round; 2. e-e ~ ausgeben stand a round; 3. sport round; **R~fahrt** f sight-seeing tour; **R~flug** m sight-seeing flight.

Rundfunk m 1. radio, broadcasting; im ~ sprechen speak over the radio; 2. (Ge-

sellschaft) broadcasting corporation; ~**gebühr** *f* radio licence fee; ~**gerät** *n* radio set; ~**programm** *n* radio programme; ~**sender** *m* radio, broadcasting station; ~**sprecher** *m* announcer; ~**teilnehmer** *m* listener; ~**übertragung** *f* radio, wireless transmission.

Rund|gang *m* round; **r~lich** plump; ~**reise** *f* circular tour; ~**reisefahrkarte** *f* circular tour ticket; ~**schreiben** *n* circular letter.

Runzel *f* wrinkle; **r~ig** wrinkled; **r~n** 1. wrinkle; 2. *die Stirn* ~ frown.

Rüpel *m* lout.

rupfen *(Hühnchen)* pluck.

Ruß *m* soot.

Russe *m* Russian.

Rüssel *m (Elephant)* trunk; *(Schwein)* snout.

rußig sooty.

russisch Russian.

Rußland *n* Russia.

rüst|en 1. *mil* arm; 2. *sich* ~ prepare; ~**ig** sprightly; **R~ung** *f* 1. armament, arms *pl;* 2. *(Panzer)* armour.

Rute *f* rod, switch.

Rutsch|bahn *f* chute; **r~en** 1. slip *(aus der Hand* out of o.'s hand); 2. *(Auto)* skid; ~**en** *n: ins* ~ *kommen* start slipping; **r~fest** *(Reifen)* non-skid, skid-proof; **r~ig** slippery.

rütteln 1. *(schütteln)* shake; 2. rattle *(an der Tür* the door); 3. *(Wagen)* jolt.

S

Saal *m* hall.

Saat *f* 1. seed; 2. crops *pl.*

Säbel *m* sabre.

Sabot|**age** *f* sabotage; **~eur** *m* saboteur; **s~ieren** sabotage.

Sach|**e** *f* 1. *(Ding)* thing, object; 2. *(Angelegenheit)* matter, affair, business; *das ist meine ~!* that's my affair; 3. *(Frage)* problem; 4. *(Aufgabe)* task; 5. *(Anliegen)* cause; *in eigener ~ sprechen* speak on o.'s own behalf; 6. *(Sachlage)* state of affairs; 7. *(Punkt)* point; *zur ~ kommen* come to the point; 8. *jur* matter, case; 9. *pl* property, belongings *pl*; **s~gemäß** proper, adequate; **s~kundig** expert; **s~lich** 1. relevant; 2. *(inhaltsmäßig)* substantial; 3. objective; 4. *(geschäftsmäßig)* matter-of-fact, businesslike; **~schaden** *m* material damage.

sacht 1. soft, gentle; 2. *(allmählich)* gradually.

Sach|**verhalt** *m* state of affairs; **~verständiger** *m* expert *(in, für* on); **~werte** *pl* material assets *pl.*

Sack *m* sack, bag; **~gasse** *f* blind alley, *Am* dead-end street.

sadistisch sadistic(ally).

säen sow, seed.

Safe *m* safe(-deposit box).

Saft *m* 1. *(Baum)* sap; 2. *(Obst)* juice; **s~ig** juicy, succulent.

Sage *f* legend, myth.

Säge *f* saw; **~mehl** *n* sawdust.

sagen 1. say; *etw zu etw ~* say s.th. to s.th.; *unter uns gesagt* between you and me; *wenn ich so ~ darf* if I may say so; 2. *jdn etw ~* tell s.o. s.th.; *ich habe mir ~ lassen* I have been told; 3. *(darlegen)* give state; 4. *(behaupten)* assert, claim; 5. *(besagen)* mean, say; *was wollen Sie damit ~?* what do you mean by that? 6. *die Wahrheit ~* tell the truth.

sägen saw.

sagenhaft 1. legendary; 2. *fig* incredible.

Sahn|**e** *f* cream; **s~ig** creamy.

Saison *f* season; **s~bedingt** seasonal.

Saite *f* string; **~ninstrument** *n* string instrument.

Sakko *m* lounge, sports jacket.

sakra|**l** sacral; **S~ment** *n* sacrament.

Sakristei *f* vestry.

Salat *m* salad; *grüner ~* lettuce; **~besteck** *n* salad-

-servers pl; ~**schüssel** f salad bowl.
Salbe f ointment, salve; **s~n** anoint.
Salbung f unction.
Saldo m balance.
Salmiakgeist m ammonia solution.
Salon m 1. drawing room, Am parlor; 2. mar saloon.
salopp casual.
Salpeter m saltpetre.
Salve f salve.
Salz n salt; **s~en** salt; **s~ig** salty; ~**kartoffeln** pl boiled potatoes pl; ~**säure** f hydrochloric acid; ~**streuer** m salt-cellar.
Samen m 1. bot seed; 2. med sperm; ~**korn** n grain of seed.
Samm|elfahrkarte f, ~**elfahrschein** m collective ticket; **s~eln** 1. (Briefmarken) collect; 2. (Holz) gather; 3. (anhäufen) accumulate; 4. (scharen) gather, assemble; 5. für jdn ~ collect money for s.o.; 6. sich ~ compose o.s.; ~**elpunkt** m meeting place; ~**eltransport** m collective transport; ~**ler** m collector; ~**lung** f 1. (Geld-, Münz~) collection; 2. (innere ~) composure.
Samstag m Saturday.
Samt m velvet.
sämtlich 1. (vollständig) complete; 2. (gesamt) entire; ~**e** all together.

Sanatorium n sanatorium, Am sanitarium.
Sand m sand.
Sandale f sandal.
Sand|bank f sandbank; ~**haufen** m heap of sand; **s~ig** sandy; ~**kasten** m (Kinder) sand-pit; ~**stein** m sandstone.
sanft 1. gentle; 2. (mild) mild; 3. (Stimme) soft; 4. (Steigung) gentle; ~**mütig** gentle, mild.
Sänger m, ~**in** f singer.
sanieren com reorganize.
sanitär: ~e Einrichtungen pl sanitary facilities pl; **S~ter** m first-aid man.
Sanktion f pol sanctions pl; **s~ieren** approve.
Sard|elle f anchovy; ~**ine** f sardine.
Sarg m coffin.
Sarkas|mus m sarcasm; **s~tisch** sarcastic(ally).
Satellit m satellite; ~**en-stadt** f satellite town.
Satir|e f satire (auf on); **s~isch** satiric(al).
satt 1. satisfied, full; sich ~ essen eat o.'s fill; 2. etw ~ haben be tired of s.th.
Sattel m 1. saddle; 2. (Gebirgs~) ridge; ~**schlepper** m truck tractor.
Sattler m (Polsterer) upholsterer.
Satz m 1. sentence, clause; 2. math principle, proposition; 3. mus movement; 4. typ setting-up; 5. tech set;

6. *(Kaffee)* grounds *pl;*
7. *com* rate; 8. *(Sprung)*
bound, jump; **~ung** *f* statute, by-law; **~zeichen** *n*
punctuation mark.
Sau *f* sow.
sauber 1. *(rein)* clean; 2. *(ordentlich)* neat, tidy; 3. *(genau)* neat; **~halten** *irr* keep clean; **S~keit** *f* cleanliness, tidiness.
säuber|lich *(sorgfältig)* carefully; **~n** 1. clean, cleanse;
2. *pol* purge.
sauer 1. sour, tart, acid;
2. *(Milch)* sour; 3. *fig (Arbeit)* hard; 4. ~ *werden* turn sour; *(Person)* become cross.
säuerlich 1. sourish; 2. *(Lächeln)* sour.
Sauerstoff *m* oxygen.
saufen *irr* 1. *(Tier)* drink;
2. *vulg* guzzle, tipple.
Säufer *m* drunkard.
saugen *irr* 1. suck *(an etw* s.th.); 2. *(mit Staubsauger)* vacuum.
säug|en *(Kind)* suckle, nurse;
S~etier *n* mammal; **S~ling** *m* baby; **S~lingspflege** *f* baby care.
Säule *f* 1. column; 2. *(Pfeiler)* pillar; 3. *(Zapf~)* pump.
Saum *m* 1. hem; 2. *(Naht)* seam; 3. *(Rand)* border.
säumen hem; seam.
Sauna *f* sauna.
Säure *f* 1. *chem* acid; 2. *(Magen)* acidity.
sausen 1. *(sich schnell be*

wegen) rush, dash; 2. *(brausen)* whistle, whiz.
Saxophon *n* saxophone.
schaben scrape, rasp, grate.
schäbig 1. shabby; 2. *fig* stingy, miserly.
Schablone *f* 1. *(Muster)* pattern, model; 2. *fig* routine.
Schach *n:* ~ *spielen* play (at) chess; **~brett** *n* chessboard; **~figur** *f* chessman.
Schacht *m* 1. shaft; 2. *(in der Straße)* manhole.
Schachtel *f* box, carton.
Schachzug *m* move *a. fig.*
schade 1. *es ist* ~ it's a pity, too bad; 2. *es ist* ~ *um ihn* it's a great pity about him.
Schädel *m* skull.
schaden 1. harm, do damage (to); 2. *es schadet nichts* it doesn't matter.
Schaden *m* 1. damage; ~ *nehmen* suffer damage;
2. *(körperlich)* injury;
3. *(Verlust)* loss; 4. *(Nachteil)* detriment, prejudice; *zu jds* ~ to the detriment of s.o.; 5. *(Verwüstung)* ravage;
6. *jdn* ~ *zufügen* do s.o. harm; **~sersatz** *m* damages *pl,* indemnification.
schadhaft 1. defective;
2. *(beschädigt)* damaged.
schäd|igen damage, harm, impair, injure; **~lich**
1. harmful; 2. *(nachteilig)* detrimental; 3. *(Einfluß)* bad.
schadlos*: jdn* ~ *halten* indemnify s.o.

Schaf n sheep.
Schäfer m shepherd; ~**hund** m shepherd's dog.
schaffen 1. irr create; Platz ~ make room; 2. reg (beschaffen) get, procure; 3. (bewirken) give; 4. fam manage; geschafft! we've made it! 5. (erreichen) achieve; 6. (tun) do; 7. (entfernen) jdn aus dem Weg ~ get rid of s.o.; 8. sich mit etw zu ~ machen busy o.s. with s.th.; **S~** n creative activity; **S~skraft** f creative power.
Schaffner m conductor.
Schaffung f creation.
Schafott n scaffold.
Schafpelz m sheepskin.
Schaft m shaft, staff.
Schafwolle f sheep's wool.
schal stale.
Schal m scarf, shawl.
Schale f 1. bowl, dish, vessel; basin; 2. (von Früchten) skin; 3. (abgeschält) peel; 4. (Kartoffel-) peeling; 5. (Ei) shell.
schälen 1. peel, pare; 2. (Erbsen) husk; 3. (Ei) shell; 4. sich ~ peel off.
Schall m 1. sound; 2. (Glokken) ring; 3. (Widerhall) echo; ~**dämpfer** m silencer, Am muffler; **s~dicht** soundproof; **s~en** sound, ring, resound; **s~end**: ~es Gelächter peal of laughter; ~**geschwindigkeit** f speed of sound; ~**mauer** f sound barrier; ~**platte** f record,

disc; ~**plattenmusik** f recorded music.
Schalt|brett n el switchboard; **s~en** 1. mot change, shift gears; 2. el switch, wire, connect; 3. mit etw ~ und walten manage s.th.; ~**er** m 1. tech switch; 2. (in Banken) counter, window; ~**hebel** m gear lever; ~**jahr** n leap year; ~**ung** f gear change.
Scham f shame.
schämen, sich be ashamed.
scham|haft bashful; ~**los** shameless.
Schande f 1. disgrace; 2. (Schmach) shame, dishonour; zu m-r ~ muß ich gestehen to my shame I must confess.
schänden 1. profane, violate; 2. (Ehre) dishonour.
schändlich 1. shameful, disgraceful; 2. dishonourable.
Schandtat f shameful deed, abomination.
Schanze f (Sprung~) ski--jump.
Schar f crowd, flock **s~en**: um sich ~ rally round o.s.; **s~enweise** in crowds.
scharf 1. (Messer, Zunge) sharp; 2. (Geschmack) highly seasoned; 3. (Gewürz) hot, strong; 4. (ätzend) caustic; 5. (Wind) raw, biting; 6. (Augen) sharp; 7. (Bild) distinct; 8. (Kurve) acute; 9. (Verstand) keen; 10. (Kritik) severe; 11. (Munition)

live; **S~blick** *m fig* perspicacity.

Schärfe *f* 1. sharpness; 2. *(Gewürz)* hotness, strongness; 3. *(Bild)* distinctness; 4. *(Verstand)* keenness, acuteness; **s~n** sharpen, grind, edge.

scharfsinnig keen-witted, sharp-witted.

Scharlach *m*, **s~rot** scarlet.

Scharnier *n* hinge.

Schärpe *f* sash.

scharren scrape, scratch.

Scharte *f* notch, nick.

Schatt|en *m* 1. shadow *a. fig;* 2. *(Baum; Schattierung)* shade; *im ~* in the shade; **s~enhaft** shadowy; **~enseite** *f* 1. shady side; 2. *fig (Nachteil)* drawback; **s~ig** shady.

Schatz *m* 1. treasure; 2. *fig* wealth (*an* of); 3. *(Geliebter)* sweetheart.

schätzen 1. *(Wert)* estimate, judge; *wie alt ~ Sie ihn?* how old would you estimate him? 2. *(vermuten)* reckon, *Am* guess; 3. *com* evaluate, rate, value; 4. *(hochachten)* esteem, think highly of; 5. *zu ~ wissen* appreciate; **~swert** estimable.

Schatzmeister *m* treasurer.

Schätzung *f* estimate, appraisal; **s~weise** approximately.

Schau *f* 1. *(Darbietung)* show, spectacle; *etw zur ~*

stellen display s.th.; 2. *(Aussicht)* point of view.

Schauder *m* shudder, shiver; **s~haft** horrible, ghastly; **s~n** shudder, shiver (*vor* with).

schauen 1. look; 2. *auf etw ~* take care of s.th.

Schauer *m* 1. *(Regen~)* shower; 2. *(Angst)* shudder; **s~lich** horrible, hideous.

Schaufel *f* shovel, scoop; **s~n** shovel, dig.

Schaufenster *n* shop-window; *~ ansehen* go window-shopping; **~dekoration** *f* window dressing.

Schaukel *f* swing; **s~n** 1. swing; 2. *(schwanken)* sway; 3. *mar* roll; **~stuhl** *m* rocking-chair.

Schaum *m* 1. foam; 2. *(Bier)* froth; 3. *(Seife)* lather; 4. *(Gischt)* spray.

schäumen 1. *(Seife)* lather; 2. *(Sprudel)* fizz; 3. *(Flüssigkeiten)* froth, foam; 4. *vor Wut ~* foam with rage; **~d** foamy; sparkling.

Schaum|gummi *m* foam rubber; **s~ig** frothy.

Schauplatz *m* scene.

schaurig hair-raising.

Schauspiel *n* 1. stage play, drama; 2. *fig* spectacle; **~er** *m* actor; **~erin** *f* actress.

Scheck *m* cheque, *Am* check (*über* for); **~buch** *n*, **~heft** *n* cheque-book.

Scheibe *f* 1. *(runde Platte)* disk, disc; 2. *(Fenster~)* (window) pane; 3. *(Brot)* slice (of bread); 4. *(Ziel~)* target; **~nwischer** *m* windscreen wiper.

Scheid|e *f* 1. *(Futteral)* sheath, scabbard; 2. *anat* vagina; **s~en** *irr* 1. *(trennen)* separate, part; 2. *(teilen)* divide; 3. *jur* divorce; *sich ~ lassen* get a divorce *(von* from); 4. *(weggehen)* depart; *voneinander ~* take leave of one another; **~ung** *f jur* divorce.

Schein *m* 1. *(Licht)* shine; 2. *(Sonne)* light; 3. *(äußeres Bild)* appearances *pl; der ~ trügt* appearances are deceptive; *dem ~ nach* to all appearances; 4. *(Vortäuschung)* pretence, make-believe; 5. *(Papier)* paper, slip; 6. *(Bescheinigung)* certificate; 7. *(Banknote)* banknote, *Am* bill.

schein|bar 1. apparent, seeming; 2. *(vorgetäuscht)* feigned, ostensible; **~en** *irr* 1. *(Licht)* shine; *die Sonne scheint* the sun is shining; 2. *(Anschein haben)* appear, seem; *mir scheint, daß* it seems to me that; **~heilig** hypocritical; **S~werfer** *m* 1. *mot* headlight; 2. *(Such ~)* searchlight; 3. *film* spotlight.

Scheitel *m* 1. *(höchster Punkt)* summit, peak; 2. *(Haare)* (hair-)parting.

Scheiterhaufen *m* stake.

scheitern 1. fail, miscarry;

2. *mar* wreck; **S~** *n: zum ~ verurteilt* doomed to failure.

Schellfisch *m* haddock.

Schelm *m* rogue.

schelten *irr* scold *(wegen* for).

Schema *n* pattern, scheme, system; **s~tisch** schematic.

Schemel *m* stool.

Schenkel *m* 1. thigh; 2. *(e-s Winkels)* side; **~knochen** *m* thighbone.

schenk|en give (as a present), make a present of, present; **S~ung** *f* 1. gift; 2. *jur* donation.

Scherbe *f* piece; *in ~n gehen* go to pieces.

Schere *f* 1. a pair of scissors *pl*, shears *pl;* 2. *(Krebs)* claw; **s~n** *irr* 1. *(Schafe)* shear; 2. *(Haare)* cut, trim, clip; 3. *das schert mich nicht* I don't care about it; 4. *sich um etw ~* trouble about s.th.; **~nschnitt** *m* scissors cut; **~reien** *pl* trouble, bother.

Scherz *m* joke, jest; *~ beiseite* joking apart; **s~en** joke; **s~haft** joking, jocular.

scheu 1. shy, bashful; 2. *(Tier)* timid; **S~** *f* shyness; **~en** 1. *(Pferde)* shy; 2. *sich ~ vor* be afraid of; 3. *keine Kosten ~* spare no expense; 4. *sich ~, etw zu tun* shrink from doing s.th.; **~ern** scrub, scour.

Scheune *f* barn.

Scheusal *n* monster.

scheußlich hideous, atrocious.

Schi *m s.* Ski.

Schicht *f* 1. layer; 2. *geol* stratum; 3. *(Öl)* film; 4. *(Überzug)* coat; 5. *(Gesellschaft)* class; 6. *(Arbeit)* shift; **s~en** stack, pile.

schick chic, stylish; **S~** *m* elegance, chic.

schick|en 1. send; *jdm etw ~* send s.o. s.th.; *~ nach* send for; 2. *sich ~* be good form; 3. *sich in etw ~* resign o.s. to s.th.; **~lich** fitting, seemly; 2. *(anständig)* decent.

Schicksal *n* fate, destiny, fortune; **s~haft** fateful; **~sschlag** *m* stroke of fate.

Schiebefenster *n* sliding-window.

schieben *irr* 1. push; 2. *die Schuld auf jdn ~* put the blame on s.o.; 3. *(verschieben)* put off, postpone.

Schieds|gericht *n* 1. court of arbitration; 2. *sport* jury; **~richter** *m* 1. *jur* arbitrator; 2. *sport* jury, umpire, referee; **~spruch** *m* arbitral award.

schief 1. *(schräg)* slanting, crooked; 2. *(geneigt)* sloping, inclined; *~e Ebene* inclined plane; 3. *~ hängen* be hanging crooked.

Schiefer *m* slate.

schiefgehen *irr* go wrong.

schielen *med* be cross-eyed, squint.

Schienbein *n* shinbone.

Schiene *f* rail, track, bar; **s~n** *(Bein)* splint.

schießen *irr* 1. shoot *(auf jdn* at s.o.), fire; *scharf ~* shoot with live ammunition; 2. *(Blut)* gush; 3. *(rennen)* streak; 4. *in die Höhe ~* shoot up; 5. *(ab~)* launch; 6. *ein Tor ~* score a goal.

Schieß|scheibe *f* target; **~stand** *m* shooting stand.

Schiff *n* 1. ship, boat, vessel; *mit dem ~ fahren* go by ship; 2. *arch* nave.

Schiffahrt *f* shipping, navigation.

schiff|bar navigable; **S~bau** *m* shipbuilding; **S~bruch** *m* shipwreck; *~ erleiden* be shipwrecked; **~brüchig** shipwrecked; **S~brücke** *f* pontoon bridge; **S~sschraube** *f* screw; **S~sverkehr** *m* shipping traffic.

Schikan|e *f* harassment; **s~ieren** harass.

Schild 1. *n* sign, signboard; 2. *(Firma)* nameplate; 3. *(Tür)* door-plate; 4. *(Straße)* road sign; 5. *(Preis~)* ticket, label; 6. *m mil* shield; **~drüse** *f* thyroid gland; **s~ern** describe, relate; **~erung** *f* description; **~kröte** *f* turtle; *(Land~)* tortoise; **~patt** *n* tortoise-shell.

Schilf(rohr) *n* reed.

schillern be iridescent, glit-

ter; **~d** iridescent, scintil-
lating.

Schimmel m 1. *bot* mould;
2. *zoo* white horse; **s~ig**
mo(u)ldy; **s~n** mo(u)ld.

Schimmer m glitter, glimmer, gleam (*von etw* of
s. th.); **s~n** glitter, lustre;
s~nd lustrous.

schimpf|en 1. scold (*mit
jdm; jdn* s.o.); 2. *auf jdn* ~
grumble at s.o.; **~lich** disgraceful (*für* to); **S~wort** n
abusive word.

Schinken m ham.

Schirm m 1. umbrella;
2. (*Sonnen~*) sunshade;
3. (*Lampen~*) shade;
4. (*Mützen~*) peak; 5. (*Fern-
seh~*) screen; **~herrschaft**
f protection; patronage;
~mütze f peaked cap.

Schlacht f battle; **s~en** kill,
slaughter *a. fig;* **~en-
bummler** m fan; **~er** m
butcher; **~erei** f butcher's
shop; **~feld** n battlefield;
~hof m slaughter-house,
abattoir.

Schlaf m sleep; ~ *haben* be
sleepy; **~anzug** m pyjamas
pl.

Schläfe f temple.

schlafen *irr* 1. sleep, be
asleep; ~ *gehen* go to bed;
2. (*übernachten*) spend the
night.

Schläfer m sleeper.

schlaff 1. (*Körper*) limp,
flabby; 2. (*locker*) slack.

schlaflos sleepless; **S~ig-
keit** f sleeplessness.

Schlafmittel n sleeping
drug.

schläfrig sleepy, drowsy.

Schlaf|saal m dormitory;
~sack m sleeping-bag;
~wagen m sleeping-car,
Am sleeper; **~zimmer** n
bedroom.

Schlag m 1. blow, thump,
knock; 2. (*mit der Faust*)
blow; slap, tap; 3. *mit e-m* ~
at a stroke; 4. (*Prügel*)
beating; 5. (*Schicksal*) blow;
6. (*Uhr*) stroke; 7. (*Herz*)
beat; 8. *el* shock; 9. *med*
apoplexy; 10. (*Art*) stamp,
kind; **~ader** f artery; **~an-
fall** m stroke; **~baum** m
turnpike; **s~en** *irr* 1. strike,
hit, beat; 2. (*besiegen*) defeat, beat; 3. (*Holz*) fell; 4. *zu
Boden* ~ down knock; *etw
in etw* ~ drive s.th. into s.th.;
5. (*Uhr*) strike; 6. (*Herz*)
beat; **~er** m 1. hit(-song);
2. (*theat*) smash hit; 3. (*Ver-
kaufs~*) sales hit.

Schläger m 1. rowdy;
2. (*Tennis~*) racket; **~ei** f
brawl.

schlag|fertig quick-witted;
S~instrumente *pl* percussion instruments; **S~loch** n
pot-hole; **S~sahne** f
whipped cream; **S~wort** n
slogan; **S~zeile** f headline;
S~zeug n percussion,
drums *pl;* **S~zeuger** m per-
cussionist.

Schlamm m mud; ~**bad** n mud bath; **s~ig** muddy.
Schlamp|erei f slovenliness, sloppiness; **s~ig** 1. (unordentlich) sloppy; 2. (nachlässig) untidy.
Schlange f 1. snake; (große) serpent; 2. ~ stehen stand in queue, Am in line (um for).
schlängeln, sich 1. wind; 2. worm (durch e-e Menge through a crowd).
Schlangenlinie f serpentine line.
schlank slim, slender.
schlapp (müde) listless; **S~e** f rebuff, set-back.
schlau (klug) clever, shrewd.
Schlauch m 1. (Garten~) hose; 2. (Fahrrad) tube; ~**boot** n rubber dinghy.
Schlaufe f loop.

schlecht I adj 1. bad; ~e Zeiten hard times; 2. (minderwertig) poor, rotten; 3. (unzulänglich) incompetent; 4. (unangenehm) bad, nasty; 5. (geschädigt) impaired; 6. (böse) wicked; 7. mir ist ~ I feel sick; 8. (Luft) stale; II adv: es steht ~ um ihn he is in a bad way; jdn ~ behandeln treat s.o. badly; ~**hin** purely and simply; **S~wetterfront** f bad weather front.
schlecken lick (an at).
Schlehe f sloe.
schleichen irr slink, sneak, creep; ~**d** 1. (Krankheit)

lingering; 2. (Krise) insidious.
Schleier m veil; **s~haft** mysterious.
Schleife f 1. bow; 2. (Kurve) loop, bend.
schleif|en irr 1. (Messer) sharpen; grind; 2. etw auf dem Boden ~ drag s.th.; auf dem Boden ~ trail on the ground; **S~stein** m whetstone.
Schleim m 1. slime; 2. med mucus; ~**haut** f mucous membrane; **s~ig** slimy.
schlemm|en feast; **S~er** m 1. gourmet; 2. (Fresser) glutton.
schlend|ern stroll; **S~rian** m dawdling.
Schlepp|e f (Kleid) train; **s~en** 1. drag, lug, haul; 2. sich ~ drag o.s. along; 3. (sich hinziehen) drag on; **s~end** dragging, sluggish; ~**er** m 1. mar tugboat; 2. mot tractor; ~**kahn** m lighter.
Schleuder f sling; **s~n** 1. fling, hurl; 2. mot skid; ~**sitz** m ejector seat.
schleunig speedy; ~**st** as quickly as possible.
Schleuse f 1. sluice; 2. (Kanal) lock.
Schliche pl: jdm auf die ~ kommen find s.o. out.
schlicht (einfach) plain, simple; ~**en** 1. (Streit) settle; 2. jur arbitrate.
Schlick m mud.

schließen *irr* 1. shut, close; *(ver~)* lock; 2. *(beenden)* conclude, bring to an end; 3. *etw aus etw ~* conclude s.th. from s.th.; 4. *Frieden ~* make peace; *e-n Vertrag ~* conclude a treaty; *e-n Vergleich ~* come to terms; 5. *(hinzufügen)* add s.th. to s.th.; 6. *auf etw ~ lassen* suggest s.th.; 7. *etw schließt sich an etw* s.th. is followed by s.th.

Schließfach *n* safe deposit box.

schließlich 1. *(am Schluß)* eventually, finally; 2. after all; 3. *(zu guter Letzt)* in the end, at last.

Schliff *m (Glas)* cut.

schlimm 1. *(schlecht)* bad, dreadful; *das ist nicht so ~* that's not so serious! never mind! *es steht ~ um ihn* his condition is serious; 2. *(unangenehm)* unpleasant; 3. *(böse)* wicked, evil; **S~e** *n* the bad thing; **~er**: ~ *werden* get worse; **~stenfalls** if the worst comes to the worst.

Schlinge *f* 1. noose, loop; 2. *med* sling; **s~n** *irr* 1. sling; 2. *(binden)* tie; 3. *sich um etw ~* wind round s.th.

schlingern *mar* roll.

Schlingpflanze *f* creeper.

Schlitt|en *m* 1. sledge; 2. *(Rodel)* toboggan; **~enfahrt** *f* sledging; **~schuh** *m* skate.

Schlitz *m* 1. slit, slot; 2. *(Riß)* fissure; **s~en** slit, slash.

Schloß *n* 1. *(Tür~)* lock, padlock; 2. *(Verschluß)* clasp, buckle; 3. *(Gebäude)* castle; palace, manor.

Schlosser *m* locksmith; **~ei** *f* locksmith's shop.

Schloßhof *m* castle yard.

Schlot *m* chimney.

schlottern 1. *(Kleider)* hang loosely, bag; 2. *(zittern)* tremble.

Schlucht *f* ravine, gorge.

schluchzen sob.

Schluck *m* drink, mouthful; *ein kleiner ~* a sip; **~auf** *m* hiccup; **s~en** swallow; gulp (down); **~impfung** *f* oral vaccination.

Schlummer *m*, **s~n** slumber.

Schlund *m* 1. *anat* throat, gorge; 2. *(Abgrund)* gulf.

schlüpfen 1. slip *(in ein Kleid* on a garment); 2. *(Kücken)* hatch; **S~er** *m* panties *pl*; **~rig** slippery *a. fig.*

schlürfen quaff.

Schluß *m* 1. *(Ende)* close, end; *~ machen* finish; *mit etw ~ machen* stop s.th.; *zum ~* in conclusion, finally; 2. *(Folgerung)* conclusion, deduction, consequence; *e-n ~ ziehen* draw a conclusion *(aus* from).

Schlüssel *m* 1. key; 2. *fig* cypher, code; **~bein** *n* collarbone; **~blume** *f* cowslip; **~brett** *n* keyboard; **~bund**

m bunch of keys; **~loch** *n* keyhole.
Schlußfolgerung *f* conclusion.
schlüssig 1. *(Beweis)* conclusive; 2. *sich ~ werden* make up o.'s mind.
Schluß|licht *n* tail-light; **~wort** *n* final remark.
schmächtig slender.
schmackhaft tasty.
schmal 1. narrow; 2. *(dünn)* thin; 3. *fig (gering)* scanty, meagre, slender.
schmälern *(kürzen)* curtail, cut down, reduce.
Schmalz *m* fat, dripping; *(Schweine~)* lard.
Schmarotzer *m* 1. *zoo* parasite; 2. *fig* sponger.
schmecken 1. taste *(nach* of); *wie schmeckt es?* how do you like it? 2. *(munden)* taste good.
Schmeich|elei *f* flattery; **s~elhaft** flattering *(für* to); **s~eln** flatter *(jdm* s.o.); **~ler** *m* flatterer.
schmeißen *irr* throw.

Schmelz *m* enamel; **s~en** *irr* melt *a. fig;* **~wasser** *n* melted snow.
Schmerz *m* 1. pain, ache; 2. *(Kummer)* grief, sorrow; **s~en** pain, hurt, ache; **~ensgeld** *n* sum of money for injuries suffered; **s~haft** painful; **s~lich** grievous, painful; **s~los** painless.
Schmetterling *m* butterfly.

schmettern *(werfen)* smash, dash.
Schmied *m* (black)smith; **~e** *f* smith's shop; **s~en** 1. forge; 2. *(Pläne)* make.
schmieg|en: *sich ~ an* snuggle up to; **~sam** flexible, supple.
schmier|en 1. smear, spread; 2. *tech* grease, lubricate; 3. *(kritzeln)* scribble; **~ig** greasy; **S~öl** *n* lubricating oil.
Schminke *f* make-up; **s~n** paint (o.'s face), make up.
Schmirgel *m* emery; **s~n** rub with emery; **~papier** *n* emery paper.
schmollen sulk *(mit* with).
Schmor|braten *m* *(Rinder~)* braised beef; **s~en** 1. *(Küche)* stew, braise; 2. *fig (in der Sonne)* roast.
Schmuck *m* 1. jewels *pl;* 2. *(Verzierung)* adornment.
schmücken 1. adorn; 2. *(verschönern)* embellish.
Schmuck|kästchen *n* jewel case; **s~los** plain.
Schmugg|el *m* smuggling; **s~eln** smuggle; **~ler** *m* smuggler.
schmunzeln smile.
Schmutz *m* mud, dirt, mire; **~fleck** *m* stain; **s~ig** dirty.
Schnabel *m* *zoo* bill, beak.
Schnake *f* gnat.
Schnalle *f* buckle; **s~n** fasten; *enger ~* tighten.
schnapp|en 1. *(Hund)* snap *(nach jdm* at s.o.); 2. *nach*

Luft ~ gasp for air;
S~schloß *n* snap lock.

Schnaps *m* spirits *pl,* strong,
Am hard liquor.

schnarchen snore.

schnattern cackle *a. fig.*

schnaufen 1. breathe hard;
2. *(keuchen)* pant.

Schnauze *f* snout, muzzle.

Schnecke *f* snail; **~nhaus** *n*
snail-shell.

Schnee *m* snow; **~ball** *m*
snowball; **~decke** *f* blanket
of snow; **~fall** *m* snowfall;
~flocke *f* snow-flake;
s~frei free of snow; **~ge-
stöber** *n* snow flurry;
~glöckchen *n bot* snow-
drop; **~grenze** *f* snow line;
~höhe *f* depth of snow;
~kette *f* snow chain;
~mann *m* snowman;
~pflug *m* snow-plough;
~schmelze *f* melting of
snow; **~verwehung** *f,*
~wehe *f* snow-drift.

Schneidbrenner *m* cutting
torch.

Schneide *f* edge; **s~n** *irr*
1. cut, carve; 2. *(mähen)*
mow; 3. *(kürzen)* trim, clip;
sich die Haare ~ *lassen*
have o.'s hair cut; 4. *(fig) jdn*
~ slight s.o.; 5. *sich in den
Finger* ~ cut o.'s finger;
s~nd *(Kälte)* biting.

Schneider *m* tailor; **~in** *f*
dressmaker.

Schneidezahn *m* incisor.

schneidig dashing.

schneien: *es schneit* it is
snowing.

Schneise *f* 1. *aero* lane;
2. *(Wald)* forest aisle.

schnell quick, rapid, swift,
speedy, fast; **S~bahn** *f*
high-speed railway;
S~boot *n* speedboat.

schnellen: *in die Höhe* ~
shoot up.

Schnell‖**gaststätte** *f*
snack(bar); **~igkeit** *f*
1. quickness; 2. *(Fahrzeug)*
speed; **~kochtopf** *m*
pressure-cooker; **s~stens**
as quickly as possible;
~straße *f* expressway;
~zug *m* fast train.

Schnepfe *f zoo* snipe.

Schnitt *m* 1. cut; 2. *med* incision; **~blumen** *pl* cut
flowers *pl;* **~e** *f (Brot)* slice;
~lauch *m bot* chives *pl;*
~punkt *m* intersection;
~wunde *f* cut.

Schnitzel *n* 1. escalope;
2. *(Papier)* scrap.

schnitz‖**en** whittle, carve;
S~er *m* carver.

Schnorchel *m* snorkel.

schnüffeln sniff (*an* at),
nose.

Schnuller *m* comforter, *Am*
pacifier.

schnupf‖**en** snuff; **S~en** *m*
catarrh; *den* ~ *bekommen*
catch (a) cold; **S~tabak** *m*
snuff.

schnuppern sniff.

Schnur *f* string, cord.

schnüren tie (up).

Schnurr|bart *m* moustache;
s~en purr; **s~ig** queer, odd.
Schnür|senkel *m* shoelace;
~stiefel *m* laced boot.
Schock *m,* **s~en, s~ieren**
shock.
Schöffe *m jur* lay assessor.
Schokolade *f* chocolate.
Scholle *f* 1. clod, lump;
2. *(Rasen~)* sod; 3. *(Eis~)*
floe; 4. *zoo* plaice.
schon 1. *(bereits)* already;
wie lange sind Sie ~ hier?
how long have you been
here? 2. *(verstärkend) ~*
von Anfang an from the
very beginning; 3. *(Zeit-*
punkt) ~ im Jahre 1066 as
early as 1066; 4. *ist sie ~ da?*
has she come yet? 5. *sind*
Sie ~ einmal in England ge-
wesen? have you ever been
to England? 6. *(nur)* only,
just; 7. *es wird ~ gehen* it
will be all right; 8. *(aller-*
dings) really; 9. *(ohnehin)*
as it is, anyway.
schön 1. beautiful, lovely,
nice, delightful; 2. *(Frau)*
pretty, good-looking; handsome; 3. *(gut)* good, fine;
4. *~e Literatur* belles lettres
pl; 5. *iron* nice, fine; 6. *dan-*
ke ~ thank you very much;
7. *(einverstanden)* okay, I
agree.
Schon|bezug *m* seat cover;
s~en 1. *(Nerven, Kleider)*
take care of; save; 2. *sich ~*
mind o.'s health; take a rest;
s~end careful, gentle.

Schönheit *f* beauty, loveli-
ness; **~sfehler** *m* flaw,
blemish *a. fig;* **~skönigin** *f*
beauty queen; **~spflege** *f*
beauty care.
Schon|kost *f* mild diet;
~ung *f* 1. *(Behandlung)*
good care; 2. *med* relax-
ation; 3. *(Gnade)* mercy;
4. *(Wald)* young forest plantation; **s~ungslos** merciless; **~zeit** *f (Jagd)* close
season.
Schopf *m (Haar~)* tuft.
schöpf|en 1. scoop; 2. *Luft ~*
take breath; **S~er** *m* cre-
ator, maker; **~erisch** creative; **S~ung** *f* creation.
Schorf *m med* scurf.
Schornstein *m* chimney;
~feger *m* chimney-
sweep(er).
Schoß *m* lap; *auf den ~*
nehmen take on o.'s lap.
Schotte *m* Scot, Scotsman.
Schotter *m* gravel.
schott|isch Scottish, Scotch;
S~land *n* Scotland.
schräg 1. oblique, slanting;
2. *(geneigt)* sloping.

Schramme *f* scratch.
Schrank *m* 1. cupboard,
closet; 2. *(Kleider~)* wardrobe; 3. *(Bücher~)* book-
case; 4. *(Büfett)* sideboard.
Schranke *f* 1. barrier *a. fig;*
2. *(Zug)* gate, level-crossing
gate; 3. *(Gericht)* bar; 4. *pl*
fig limits, bounds; **s~nlos**
1. *(Bahnübergang)* un-

guarded; 2. *fig* unlimited, boundless.

Schraub|e *f* screw, bolt; propeller; **s~en** screw; **~enzieher** *m* screw-driver; **~stock** *m* vice.

Schreck *m* fright, scare; **~en** *m* 1. fright, terror; *mit dem ~ davonkommen* get off with a fright; 2. *(Aufregung)* dismay, panic; 3. *(Bestürzung)* consternation; **s~en**: *jdn ~* frighten s.o.; **s~haft** fearful, timid; **s~lich** 1. terrible, dreadful, fearful, awful; 2. *(grauenhaft)* horrible.

Schrei *m* 1. cry, shout; 2. *(kreischend)* scream; 3. *(gellend)* yell.

schreiben *irr* 1. write; *etw mit Tinte ~* write s.th. in ink; 2. *lit* pen; 3. *jdm etw ~* write s.o. s.th.; 4. *(richtig ~)* spell; 5. *(berichten)* report, say; 6. *jdn krank ~* certify s.o. ill; 7. *wie ~ Sie sich?* how do you spell your name? 8. *in Deutsch ~* write in German; **S~** *n* writing; letter.

Schreiber *m* writer, author; **~fehler** *m* spelling mistake; **~heft** *n* copybook; **~maschine** *f* typewriter; **~tisch** *m* writing-desk; **~waren** *pl* stationery.

schreien *irr* cry out, scream, shout; **~d** 1. crying; 2. *(Farben)* glaring, loud.

Schreiner *m* joiner; **~ei** *f* joiner's workshop.

schreiten *irr* stride, walk.

Schrift *f* 1. writing, characters *pl*, script; 2. *(Handschrift)* handwriting; 3. *typ* type; 4. *(Werk)* publication, work; **~führer** *m* secretary; **s~lich** written, in writing; **~sprache** *f* standard language; **~steller(in** *f*) *m* writer; **~stück** *n* document, paper; **~wechsel** *m* correspondence.

schrill shrill.

Schritt *m* 1. step *a. fig*; *~ für ~* step by step; 2. *(Tempo)* pace; *mit jdm ~ halten* keep pace with s.o.; 3. *(Maßnahme)* measure, move; *~e unternehmen* take steps; **s~weise** gradually.

schroff 1. *(steil)* steep; 2. *fig* harsh, bursque.

Schrot *m od n* 1. buckshot; 2. *(Getreide)* groats *pl*.

Schrott *m* scrap.

schrubb|en scrub; **S~er** *m* scrubbing brush.

schrumpfen shrink.

Schub *m (Stoß)* push; **~karre(n** *m*) *f* wheelbarrow; **~lade** *f* drawer; **s~weise** in batches.

schüchtern bashful, shy.

Schuft *m* scoundrel.

Schuh *m* shoe; **~anzieher** *m* shoehorn; **~bürste** *f* shoe-brush; **~creme** *f* shoe cream; **~geschäft** *n* shoe shop; **~größe** *f* shoe size; **~macher** *m* shoemaker; **~putzer** *m* shoeblack.

Schul|aufgaben *pl* homework; **~ausflug** m school outing; **~bildung** f education; **~buch** n textbook.

Schuld f 1. (Fehler) fault, blame; es ist m-e ~ it is my fault; jdm die ~ geben blame s.o.; 2. jur guilt; 3. (Ursache) cause; 4. com debt; ~en machen contract debts; **s~:** ~ haben be at fault; **s~en**: jdm etw ~ owe s.o. s.th.; **s~enfrei** free from debts.

schuldig 1. guilty, culpable, responsible; jdn ~ sprechen pronounce s.o. guilty; 2. jdm etw ~ sein owe s.o. s.th.; 3. (gebührend) due; **S~keit** f duty, obligation.

schuld|los guiltless; **S~ner** m debtor; **S~schein** m certificate of indebtedness; **S~spruch** m verdict of guilty.

Schule f school; e-e ~ besuchen go to a school; nach der ~ after school; **s~n** train, school.

Schüler m 1. schoolboy, pupil; 2. (Anhänger) disciple, follower; **~austausch** m student exchange; **~in** f schoolgirl.

Schul|fernsehen n school television; **s~frei**: ein ~er Tag a holiday; **~funk** m school broadcasting; **~geld** n school fee, tuition; **~jahr** n school year; **~leiter** m headmaster; **~pflicht** f compulsory education.

Schulter f shoulder; mit den ~n zucken shrug o.'s shoulder; **~blatt** n shoulder--blade.

Schulung f training, instruction.

Schund m trash, rubbish.

Schuppe f 1. (Fisch) scale; 2. pl dandruff.

Schuppen m shed.

Schur f shearing.

schüren (Feuer) poke, stir up.

schürfen min prospect, dig (nach for).

Schurke m rascal.

Schurwolle f fleece.

Schürze f apron.

Schuß m 1. shot; e-n ~ abgeben fire a shot; 2. sport kick; 3. ein ~ Milch a dash of milk; 4. im ~ sein be in excellent order.

Schüssel f 1. bowl, dish, basin; 2. (Suppen~) tureen.

Schuß|feld n field of fire; **~waffe** f firearm; **~weite** f: außer ~ out of range.

Schuster m shoemaker.

Schutt m 1. refuse, rubbish; 2. (Trümmer) debris; **~abladeplatz** m refuse, Am garbage dump.

Schüttelfrost m shivering fit; **s~n** shake; jdm die Hand ~ shake s.o.'s hand.

schütten 1. pour; etw in etw ~ pour s.th. into s.th.; 2. (ver~) spill; 3. (werfen) throw.

Schutz m 1. protection (ge-

gen against); 2. (*Verteidigung*) defence; *jdn in ~ nehmen* defend s.o.; 3. (*Obdach*) shelter; *bei jdm ~ suchen* seek refuge with s.o.; **~blech** *n mot* mudguard, *Am* fender.
Schütze *m* shot, marksman.
schützen 1. protect (*vor* from, against); guard; 2. (*gegen Regen*) shelter; 3. (*erhalten*) preserve.
Schutz|hülle *f* protective covering; **~hütte** *f* refuge; **s~los** unprotected; **~marke** *f* trade-mark; **~umschlag** *m* (*Buch*) jacket, wrapper; **~zoll** *m* protective duty.
schwach 1. (*kraftlos*) weak, feeble; 2. (*gebrechlich*) frail; 3. (*gering*) faint, dim, dill; 4. (*mäßig*) poor; 5. (*Puls*) low.
Schwäche *f* 1. weakness, feebleness; 2. (*Charakter*) fault; 3. (*Vorliebe*) weakness, fancy; **~anfall** *m* faintness; **s~n** 1. weaken *a. fig;* 2. (*Gesundheit*) undermine, sap, impair.
schwachsinnig feeble-minded.
Schwager *m* brother-in-law.
Schwägerin *f* sister-in-law.
Schwalbe *f* swallow.
Schwamm *m* 1. sponge; 2. (*Pilz*) fungus; **s~ig** 1. spongy; 2. (*aufgedunsen*) bloated.
Schwan *m* swan.

schwanger pregnant; **~ werden** conceive, become pregnant; **S~schaft** *f* pregnancy; **S~schaftsunterbrechung** *f* interruption of pregnancy.
Schwank *m theat* farce, burlesque.
schwank|en 1. sway *a. fig;* rock; 2. (*taumeln*) stagger; 3. (*wechseln*) alternate; 4. (*variieren*) vary; 5. (*zögern*) hesitate; 6. (*unentschlossen*) waver, vacillate; 7. *com* fluctuate; **S~ung** *f* change, variation.
Schwanz *m* tail.
schwänzen (*Schule*) play truant.
Schwarm *m* 1. (*Menge*) crowd, troops *pl;* 2. (*Bienen*) swarm; 3. *fig* idol.
schwärmen 1. (*begeistert sein*) be enthusiastic (*für* about); 2. *für jdn ~* worship s.o.; 3. (*Bienen*) swarm.
schwarz 1. black; *etw ~ auf weiß haben* have s.th. in black and white; 2. (*dunkel*) dark, murky; 3. (*schmutzig*) black, dirty; 4. (*unheilvoll*) fatal, fateful, gloomy; **S~brot** *n* brown bread.
schwärzen make black.
Schwarz|fahrer *m* fare dodger; **~hörer** *m* pirate listener.
schwärzlich blackish.
Schwarz|markt *m* black market; **~wild** *n* wild boar.
schwatzen talk, chat.

Schwätzer m chatterbox.
schwatzhaft talkative.
Schwebe f: in der ~ sein be undecided; ~**bahn** f suspension railway; **s~n** 1. (Wolken) float, hover, hang; 2. (unentschieden) be pending; 3. in Gefahr ~ be in danger; **s~nd** (Verfahren) pending.
Schwede m Swede; ~**n** n Sweden.
Schwefel m sulphur.
schweifen (umherstreifen) roam, rove.
schweig|en irr 1. be silent, keep silence; 2. (nichts sagen) say nothing; 3. ganz zu ~ von not to mention; **S~en** n silence; ~**end** silent; **S~e-pflicht** f professional secrecy; ~**sam** silent; taciturn.
Schwein n 1. pig; 2. (Fleisch) pork; ~**ebraten** m roast pork; ~**efleisch** n pork; ~**estall** m pigsty; ~**sleder** n pigskin.
Schweiß m sweat, perspiration; in ~ geraten get into a sweat; ~**en** tech weld.
Schweiz f Switzerland; ~**er** m, **s~erisch** Swiss.
schwelen smoulder a. fig.
schwelgen (schlemmen) feast, regale.
Schwelle f 1. (Tür~) threshold a. fig; 2. loc sleeper.
schwellen irr 1. med swell; 2. (an~) rise.
Schwemme f 1. watering

place; (Pferde) horse-pond; 2. com glut.
schwenken wave, brandish, swing.
schwer I adj 1. heavy; wie ~ bist du? what weight are you? 2. (nahrhaft) rich; 3. (Bier) strong; 4. (lastend) burdensome; 5. ~en Herzens with a heavy heart; 6. (schwierig) hard, difficult; 7. (ernst) grave, serious; 8. (groß) gross; **II** adv 9. ~ an etw tragen be burdened with s.th.; 10. das ist ~ zu sagen that's difficult to say; 11. ~ arbeiten work hard; er ist ~ krank he is gravely ill; **S~beschädigter** m severely disabled man; ~**bewaffnet** heavily armed; **S~e** f weight, heaviness; ~**elos** weightless.
schwer|fallen irr: etw fällt jdm schwer s.th. is hard for s.o.; ~**fällig** 1. (Bewegung) ponderous; 2. (langsam) slow; ~**hörig** hard of hearing.
Schwer|industrie f heavy industry; **s~krank** seriously ill; **s~lich** hardly, scarcely; ~**punkt** m 1. phys centre of gravity; 2. fig focal point.
Schwert n sword.
Schwerverbrecher m big criminal.
schwer|verdaulich heavy, stodgy a. fig; ~**verletzt** seriously injured; ~**wiegend** serious, grave.

Schwester *f* 1. sister; 2. (Kranken~) nurse.

Schwieger|eltern *pl* parents-in-law; **~mutter** *f* mother-in-law; **~sohn** *m* son-in-law; **~tochter** *f* daughter-in-law; **~vater** *m* father-in-law.

schwierig 1. difficult; 2. (unangenehm) awkward; 3. (Mensch) hard to please; **S~keit** *f* difficulty; auf ~en stoßen meet with difficulties.

Schwimm|bad *n* swimming-pool; **s~en** *irr* 1. swim; durch e-n Fluß ~ swim across a river; 2. (treiben) float, drift; **~en** *n:* zum ~ gehen go for a swim; **s~end** floating; **~er** *m* swimmer; **~sport** *m* swimming.

Schwindel *m* 1. med vertigo, dizziness; 2. (Betrug) swindle, fraud; **~anfall** *m* dizzy spell; **s~erregend** causing dizziness; **s~frei** free from dizziness; **s~n** 1. es schwindelt mir I feel dizzy; 2. (flunkern) fib.

schwinden *irr* 1. shrink, decrease; 2. fig fade, vanish.

Schwindl|er *m* swindler; **s~ig** dizzy, vertiginous.

Schwind|sucht *f* med consumption; **s~süchtig** *med* consumptive.

Schwing|e *f* (Flügel) wing; **s~en** *irr* 1. wave, swing; 2. (Ton) vibrate, linger; 3. sich auf etw ~ swing o.s. on s.th.; **~ung** *f* vibration.

Schwips *m:* e-n ~ haben be tipsy.

schwirren 1. (Pfeil) whiz(z); 2. (Insekt) buzz.

schwitzen sweat, perspire.

schwören *irr* 1. swear (auf jdn by s.o.); 2. e-n Eid ~ take an oath.

schwül sultry, sticky.

Schwund *m* 1. (Abnehmen) diminution, shrinkage; 2. (Verlust) loss; 3. (Flüssigkeit) leakage.

Schwung *m* 1. motion; etw in ~ bringen set s.th. in motion; 2. (Pendel) swing; 3. (Anstoß) push; 4. (Elan) drive, impetus, stimulus; **s~haft** com booming, flourishing; **s~voll** full of vivacity.

Schwur *m:* e-n ~ leisten take an oath; **~gericht** *n* jury court.

sechs six; **~t:** an ~er Stelle in the sixth place; **S~tel** *n* sixth (part); **~tens** in the sixth place.

sech|zehn sixteen; **~zig** sixty.

See 1. *m* lake; 2. *f* sea, ocean; auf hoher ~ on the high seas; an der ~ at the sea; an die ~ gehen go to the seaside; **~bad** *n* seaside resort; **~fahrt** *f* 1. (Reise) voyage; 2. mar navigation; **~fisch** *m* salt-water fish; **~gang** *m* seaway; hoher ~ rough sea; **~hafen** *m* seaport; **~hund** *m* zoo seal; **~klima** *n* maritime climate; **s~krank** seasick; **~krankheit** f seasickness.

Seel|e f 1. soul; *keine ~* not a living soul; 2. *(Intellekt)* mind; *ein Herz und e-e ~ sein* be of one heart and mind; **s~isch** 1. *(geistig)* mental; 2. *(gefühlsmäßig)* emotional.

See|mann m sailor, mariner; **~meile** f nautical mile; **~not** f distress; **~reise** f voyage; **~rose** f water lily; **s~tüchtig** seaworthy; **~weg** m: *auf dem ~* by sea; **~zunge** f zoo sole.

Segel n sail; **~boot** n sailing-boat; **~flugzeug** n glider; **s~n** sail; **~schiff** n sailing-ship; **~sport** m sailing, yachting; **~tuch** n canvas.

Seg|en m 1. blessing; 2. *(Gebet)* prayers pl; 3. *(Gottesgabe)* gift; **s~nen** 1. bless; 2. *(weihen)* consecrate.

sehen irr 1. see; 2. *(betrachten)* have a look at; 3. *(beobachten)* watch, observe; 4. *(wahrnehmen)* discern, distinguish; 5. *(bemerken)* notice; 6. *es war nichts zu ~* there was nothing to be seen; *etw gern ~* like s.th.; *etw ~ lassen* show s.th.; 7. *sich bei jdm ~ lassen* let o.s. be seen; *sich ~ lassen können* not to be bad at all; 8. *(treffen)* meet; 9. *(erleben)* experience, see; 10. *(erkennen)* realize; 11. *gut ~*

have good eyes; *siehe oben* see above; 12. *(blicken) aus dem Fenster ~* look out of the window; 13. *nach jdm ~* look after s.o.; **S~** n sight; vision; **~swert** worth seeing; **S~swürdigkeit** f sight.

Sehne f med sinew.

sehnen, sich long *(nach* for); *sie sehnt sich nach ihm* she is yearning for him.

Sehnenzerrung f strained tendon.

Sehnerv m optic nerve.

sehn|lich ardent, fond; **S~sucht** f longing, hankering *(nach* for); **~süchtig** longing, wistful.

sehr 1. very; *~ viel* much; *danke ~* thank you very much; *~ viele* a great many; 2. *(höchst)* most, highly; 3. *ich vermisse ihn ~* I miss him very much; 4. *~ geehrter Herr!* dear Sir.

Sehschärfe f visual power.

Seide f silk; **~npapier** n tissue paper.

Seife f soap; **~nschale** f soap-dish; **~nschaum** m lather; **~nspender** m soap dispenser.

Seil n 1. rope; 2. *(Tau)* cable; **~bahn** f cable railway.

sein irr I 1. be; 2. *er ist Arzt* he is a doctor; 3. *(sich fühlen) mir ist schlecht* I feel sick; 4. *es ist Abend* it is evening; 5. *es ist zu hoffen* it is to be hoped; 6. *im Be-*

griff ~, *etw zu tun* be about to do s.th.; 7. *(sich befinden)* be; 8. *(sich aufhalten)* stay; 9. *(wohnen)* live; 10. *(existieren)* exist; 11. *(stattfinden)* take place; 12. *(geschehen)* happen; 13. *(sich ergeben) 2 und 2 ist 4* 2 and 2 are 4; **II** *aux* have; *ich bin beim Arzt gewesen* I have been to the doctor; **III** *prn* 14. *(männlich)* his; *(weiblich)* her; *(sächlich)* its; 15. *das* ~*e* his.

seiner him, her, it; ~**seits** on his part.

seinesgleichen his equals, his own kind.

seinetwegen for his sake.

seit I *prp* 1. *(Zeitpunkt)* since; 2. *(Zeitspanne)* for; **II** *conj* since; ~**dem** 1. since then, since that time; 2. *(seither)* ever since.

Seite *f* 1. side; 2. *(Buch)* page; *siehe* ~ *10* see page 10; 3. ~ *an* ~ side by side; 4. *(Charakter)* side, feature; 5. *(Stärke)* point; 6. *auf der* ~ *von X stehen* be on the side of X; 7. *(Aspekt)* aspect; 8. *von allen* ~*n* from all sides; *auf die* ~ aside; ~**nflügel** *m* side-wing; ~**nlehne** *f* arm-rest.

seitens on the part of.

Seiten|schiff *n* arch (side-)-aisle; ~**sprung** *m* fig escapade; ~**straße** *f* side-street; ~**wind** *m* side-wind.

seit|lich lateral; ~**wärts** sideways.

Sekret|är *m* secretary; ~**ariat** *n* secretariat(e).

Sekt *m* champagne; ~**glas** *n* champagne glass.

Sekunde *f* second; ~**nzeiger** *m* second hand.

selb same; *zur* ~*en Zeit* at the same time.

selbst 1. *ich* ~ I myself; 2. *(in eigener Person)* personally; 3. *(ohne Hilfe)* without help; 4. *von* ~ automatically; *die Tür schließt von* ~ the door shuts itself; *das versteht sich von* ~ that goes without saying; 5. *(sogar)* even.

selbständig 1. independent; 2. *com* autonomous; **S**~**keit** *f* independence.

Selbst|bedienungsladen *m* self-service store; ~**beherrschung** *f* self-control; **s**~**bewußt** self-confident; **s**~**gebacken** homemade; **s**~**gemacht** self-made; ~**kostenpreis** *m:* ~*um* ~ at cost price; **s**~**los** disinterested; ~**mord** *m,* ~**mörder** *m* suicide; ~**sucht** *f* selfishness; **s**~**süchtig** selfish; **s**~**verständlich** 1. self-evident, obvious; 2. *(natürlich)* of course, naturally; ~**vertrauen** *n* self-confidence.

selig 1. blessed; 2. *fig* happy, blissful; **S**~**keit** *f* bliss.

Sellerie *m* bot celery.

selten 1. rare, seldom; 2. *höchst* ~ very rarely; **S**~**heit** *f* rarity.

Selter(s)wasser n soda-
-water.

seltsam strange, odd, peculiar.

Semester n term.

Semikolon n semicolon.

Seminar n seminar.

Senat m senate; **~or** m sena-
tor.

send|en irr 1. (Briefe) send,
forward, dispatch; 2. (dele-
gieren) delegate; 3. (radio)
broadcast; 4. (funken)
transmit; **S~er** m broadcasting station; **S~ung** f
1. com consignment; 2. (radio) broadcast; (tele) tele-
cast.

Senf m mustard.

sengen scorch.

Senior m senior.

Senk|e f geol depression;
s~en 1. (Stimme) lower;
2. (Kopf) bow; 3. (Preise) reduce; 4. sich ~ drop; **~fuß**
m flat foot; **s~recht** verti-
cal, perpendicular.

sensationell sensational.

Sense f scythe.

sensib|el sensitive; **~ilisie-
ren** sensitize.

separat separate.

September m September.

Serie f series.

seriös 1. serious; 2. com reliable.

Ser|vice n service; **s~vieren**
serve; **~viererin** f waitress;
~viette f napkin.

Sessel m armchair; **~lift** m
chair-lift.

seßhaft sedentary; ~ werden settle.

setzen 1. (stellen) put, place;
2. (Pflanzen) plant; 3. (Segel) set; 4. (wetten) stake
(auf on); 5. e-e Anzeige in
die Zeitung ~ put an ad in
the paper; 6. (Frist) set, fix;
7. gesetzt den Fall assuming;
7. typ compose; 8. sich ~ sit
down; chem settle.

Seuche f epidemic.

seufz|en sigh (über at); **S~er**
m sigh.

sexuell sexual.

sezieren dissect a. fig.

sich I refl prn oneself; him-,
her-, itself; themselves; **II**
pers prn 1. er wäscht ~ die
Hände he is washing his
hands; 2. an ~ denken think
of oneself; außer ~ sein be
beside oneself; 3. (2 Personen) each other; (mehrere)
one another.

Sichel f sickle.

sicher 1. (ungefährlich) safe,
secure; 2. (gewiß) sure, certain; das ist ~ that is certain;
3. (überzeugt) ich bin ~, daß
I am sure that; 4. (Urteil) reliable, unfailing; 5. (geübt)
experienced, practised;
6. (bestimmt) surely; **~ge-
hen** irr be sure.

Sicherheit f 1. safety, security; jdn in ~ bringen take
s.o. to safety; 2. (Gewißheit)
certainty, sureness; 3. (Ge-
übtheit) experience; 4. com
security; **~sabstand** m safe

distance; **~snadel** f safety pin; **~sschloß** n safety lock; **~sventil** safety valve.

sicherlich 1. surely; 2. *(zweifellos)* undoubtedly.

sichern 1. secure, protect *(vor* from); 2. *(Rechte)* ensure; 3. *sich gegen etw ~* guard o.s. against s.th.

sicher|stellen 1. put in safe keeping; 2. *com* provide, secure; **S~ung** f 1. *el* fuse; 2. *(Schutz)* protection, safeguard.

Sicht f 1. sight, view; *auf lange ~* in the long run; 2. *(Ausblick)* outlook; 3. *mete* visibility; 4. *(fig) aus m-r ~* from my point of view; **s~bar** 1. visible; 2. *(wahrnehmbar)* appreciable; 3. *(offenkundig)* obvious; **s~en** *(prüfen)* examine, screen; **s~lich** evident, obvious; **~vermerk** m visa; **~weite** f: *in, außer ~* within, out of sight.

sickern seep, soak.

sie she; *(Dinge)* it; *pl* they; **S~** *(Höflichkeitsform)* you.

Sieb n 1. sieve; 2. *(für Flüssiges)* strainer; **s~en** 1. sieve, strain; 2. *fig* sift, screen.

sieben *(Zahlwort)* seven.

siebent: *am ~en Mai* on the seventh of May; **S~el** n seventh part.

sieb|zehn seventeen; **~zig** seventy.

siedeln settle.

sieden *irr* simmer, boil.

Siedepunkt m boiling point a. fig.

Sied|ler m settler; **~lung** f 1. settlement; 2. *(Wohn~)* housing-estate.

Sieg m 1. victory *(über* over); 2. *sport* win.

Siegel n seal; **~ring** m signet-ring.

siegen 1. win; *über jdn ~* gain the victory over s.o.; 2. *sport* win; **S~er** m victor, winner; **~reich** victorious, triumphant.

Signal n signal.

signieren sign.

Silbe f syllable.

Silber n, **s~n** silver.

Silvester n New Year's Eve.

Sims m od n *(Fenster~)* sill.

simulieren simulate.

Sinfonie f symphony; **~konzert** n symphony concert; **~orchester** n symphony orchestra.

sing|en *irr* sing; *falsch ~* sing out of tune; **S~vogel** m singing bird.

sinken *irr* 1. sink, fall, drop; *zu Boden ~* sink to the ground; 2. *(Schiff)* go down.

Sinn m 1. sense; 2. *(Verstand)* mind; 3. *(Bewußtsein)* consciousness; 4. *(Denken)* es kam mir in den ~ it occurred to me; *etw im ~ haben* have s.th. in mind; 5. *(Empfinden)* feeling; 6. *(Bedeutung)* sense, meaning; *übertragener ~* figurative sense; 7. *es hat* *keinen* ~ it is no use; 8. *in diesem* ~ in this direction; **~bild** *n* symbol; **s~en** *irr* meditate (*über* on), reflect; **s~gemäß** corresponding; **s~lich** sensual; **s~los** 1. senseless, meaningless; 2. *(unsinnig)* absurd; 3. *(zwecklos)* useless, futile; **s~voll** 1. meaningful; 2. *(vernünftig)* suitable.

Sintflut *f* the Flood.

Sippe *f* family, clan.

Sirene *f* siren.

Sitte *f* 1. custom; 2. *(Gepflogenheit)* convention, usage, manner, habit; *es ist* ~, *daß* it is customary that; 3. *(Manieren)* manners *pl;* **s~en-los** immoral; **s~lich** moral, ethical; **~lichkeit** *f* morality; **s~sam** demure.

Situation *f* situation.

Sitz *m* 1. seat; 2. *(Wohnsitz)* residence, domicile; 3. *(Auto)* place; 4. *com* headquarters *pl.*

sitzen *irr* 1. sit; *am Tisch* ~ sit at the table; 2. *(Vögel)* perch; 3. *(stecken)* be stuck; 4. *(passen)* sit, fit; 5. *für jdn* ~ pose for s.o.; **~bleiben** *irr* 1. remain seated; 2. *(Schule)* repeat a year.

sitzend sedentary.

sitzenlassen *irr: jdn* ~ leave s.o. in the lurch; stand s.o. up.

Sitz|platz *m* seat; **~ung** *f* 1. *pol* session, meeting;

2. conference; **~ungssaal** *m* conference room.

Skala *f* scale, graduation.

Skandal *m* scandal, outrage, uproar; **s~ös** scandalous.

Skelett *n* skeleton.

Skep|sis *f* scepticism; **~tiker** *m* sceptic; **s~tisch** sceptical.

Ski *m* ski; **~ausrüstung** *f* ski outfit; **~fahrer** *m* skier; **~lauf** *m* skiing; **~lehrer** *m* ski-instructor; **~lift** *m* ski--lift; **~springen** *n* ski-jumping; **~stiefel** *m* ski-boot; **~stock** *m* ski-stick.

Skizze *f* 1. sketch, outline; 2. *(Entwurf)* draft; **s~ieren** outline, sketch.

Sklave *m* slave.

Skonto *n od m* discount; *abzüglich* ~ less discount.

Skorpion *m zoo* scorpion.

Skrupel *m* scruple; **s~los** unscrupulous.

Skulptur *f* sculpture.

Slawe *m*, **s~isch** Slav.

Smaragd *m* emerald.

Smoking *m* dinner suit, *Am* tuxedo.

so I *adv* 1. *(Art und Weise)* so, like this, thus; *und* ~ *weiter* and so on; ~ *nicht!* that won't do! 2. like this; ~ *ist das Leben!* such is life! ~ *steht es* that's how it is; 3. *(folgendermaßen)* as follows, thus; 4. *(sehr)* ~ *weit,* ~ *gut* so far so good; 5. ~ *früh wie möglich* as early as possible; 6. ~ *gut wie* next to; 7. ~ ..., ~ ... as much as; 8. *um* ~ all the; **II** *prn:* ~ ein Mensch a man like him; **III** 9. *(nun)* well; 10. *(also)* so, then; 11. *(ungefähr)* about; 12. *ich habe* ~ *e-e Ahnung, daß* I have a feeling that; **IV** *conj* 13. *(da, als)* when; 14. *(folglich)* therefore, thus; 15. ~ *leid es mir tut, ich muß gehen* I must go now much as I regret it; **V** *interj: ach* ~! I see.

sobald: ~ *als* as soon as.

Socke *f* sock.

Sockel *m arch* socle, base.

Soda *n od f* soda.

Sodbrennen *n* heartburn.

soeben just.

Sofa *n* sofa.

sofern 1. if, provided; 2. ~ *nicht* unless.

sofort at once, immediately; ~**ig** immediate, prompt; **S~maßnahme** *f* immediate steps *pl*.

sogar even.

sogenannt 1. so-called; 2. *(angeblich)* pretended.

Sohle *f* 1. sole; 2. *(Tal~)* bottom.

Sohn *m* son.

solange as long as.

solch such, like this; ~ *einer* such a one.

Sold *m mil* pay; ~**at** *m* soldier.

Söldner *m* mercenary.

solidarisch solidary; *sich* ~ *erklären* solidarise.

solide 1. *(Sache)* solid, robust, sturdy; 2. *com (Firma)* reliable; *(Preise)* stable; 3. *(Person)* respectable, steady.

Solist(in *f)* *m* soloist.

Soll *n* 1. *com* debit; ~ *und Haben* debit and credit; 2. *(Plan~)* target.

sollen 1. be to; *er soll jetzt kommen* he is to come now; 2. *(müssen)* have to; 3. *ich weiß nicht, was ich tun soll* I don't know what to do; 4. *ich hätte hingehen* ~ I ought to have gone; 5. *man sollte lieber* one had better; 6. *sollte es wahr sein?* could it be true? 7. *(Absicht)* shall; 8. *er soll reich sein* he is said to be rich; 9. *falls er kommen sollte* in case he should come; 10. *(herausfordernd)* let; 11. *was soll ich hier?* what am I doing here?

somit consequently, therefore.

Sommer *m* summer; *im* ~ in (the) summer; ~**fahrplan** *m* summer timetable; ~**ferien** *pl* summer holidays *pl*; ~**schlußverkauf** *m* summer sale; ~**sprossen** *pl* freckles *pl*; ~**zeit** *f* summertime.

Sonder|angebot *n* bargain; **s~bar** strange, queer; ~**fall** *m* special case.

sondern I *conj* 1. but; *nicht nur,* ~ *auch* not only, but also; **II** *(absondern)* separate.

Sonder|nummer *f* special edition; **~stellung** *f* special position; **~zug** *m* special train.

Sonnabend *m* Saturday; **s~s** on Saturdays.

Sonne *f* sun; *in der ~ sitzen* sit in the sun; **s~n,** *sich* bask (in the sun); **~naufgang** *m: bei ~* at sunrise; **~nbad** *n* sunbath; **~nblume** *f* sunflower; **~nbrand** *m* sunburn; **~nbrille** *f* (a pair of) sun-glasses *pl;* **~nenergie** *f* solar energy; **~nfinsternis** *f* solar eclipse; **~nschein** *m* sunshine; **~nschirm** *m* sunshade; **~nstrahl** *m* sunbeam; **~nuntergang** *m: bei ~* at sunset.

sonnig sunny *a. fig.*

Sonntag *m* Sunday; **s~s** on Sundays.

sonst 1. otherwise, else; *wer ~?* who else? ~ *noch etwas?* anything else? 2. *(andernfalls)* or else; 3. *(im allgemeinen)* normally, usually; 4. *(früher, immer)* always; 5. *(anderweitig)* in other respects; **~ig** other.

sooft whenever.

Sopran *m* soprano.

Sorge *f* 1. worry, trouble; 2. *(Unruhe)* concern, anxiety; *um jdn* **~n** *machen* worry about s.o.; 3. *(Kummer)* sorrow; **s~n** 1. *für jdn ~* look after s.o.; *für etw ~* see to s.th.; 2. *dafür ~, daß*

take care that; 3. *sich ~* be worried; **s~nfrei** carefree.

Sorg|falt *f* 1. care; 2. *(Gewissenhaftigkeit)* conscientiousness; **s~fältig** 1. careful; 2. *(gewissenhaft)* conscientious; **s~los** 1. carefree; 2. *(gleichgültig)* unconcerned; 3. *(unachtsam)* careless.

Sort|e *f* 1. kind, sort, type; 2. *(Marke)* brand; *beste ~* prime quality; **s~ieren** sort (out), assort; **~iment** *n* assortment.

Soße *f* sauce.

soundso 1. such and such; 2. *Herr S~* Mr. so-and-so.

Souterrain *n* basement.

soviel I *adv* 1. so much; 2. *~ wie* as much as; *doppelt ~* twice as much; **II** *conj* as for as; *~ ich weiß* as for I know.

soweit I *adv* 1. *~ sein* be ready; 2. *es ist ~* it is time; 3. *~ wie* as far as; 4. *(im ganzen)* on the whole; **II** *conj* as far as.

sowenig I *adv* 1. *~ wie* as little as; 2. *noch ~* no matter how little; **II** *conj* little as.

sowie as soon as; **~so** anyway, anyhow.

sowjetisch Soviet.

Sowjetunion *f* Soviet Union.

sowohl: *~ als auch* as well as, both . . . and.

sozial social; **S~amt** *n* social welfare office; **~isieren** socialize; **~istisch** socialis(tic); **S~leistungen** pl social charges pl; **S~produkt** n national product; **S~versicherung** f social insurance, Am Social Security.

sozusagen so to speak.

spähen peer, peep.

Spalier n 1. agr espalier; 2. ~ bilden form a lane.

Spalt m 1. opening, crack, slit; 2. (Lücke) gap; 3. (Riß) fissure; **~e** f 1. (Fels) split; 2. typ column; **s~en** 1. split; 2. (Holz) chop; 3. fig divide; 4. sich ~ fission; **~ung** f 1. splitting, division; 2. (Atom) fission.

Span m shavings pl.

Spanferkel n sucking pig.

Spange f 1. clasp; 2. (an der Kleidung) clip.

Spanien n Spain; **~er** m Spaniard; **s~sch** Spanish.

Spanne f 1. (Frist) span; 2. com margin; **s~en** 1. (Seil) stretch; 2. (Bogen) bend; 3. (Muskeln) tense; 4. (Saite) tighten; 5. etw vor etw ~ harness s.th. to s.th.; 6. (von Hose) be too tight; 7. sich ~ über span; **s~end** thrilling; **~ung** f 1. tension; 2. (Erregtheit) suspense; 3. (Verhältnis) strained relation; 4. el voltage; unter ~ stehen be live; **~weite** f 1. span; 2. fig range.

Sparbuch n savings bank book; **~büchse** f money box; **s~en** 1. save; 2. (einschränken) economize; be

economical; 3. (ersparen) spare; 4. auf etw ~ save up for s.th.; mit etw ~ save on s.th.; be sparing in s.th.

Spargel m asparagus.

Sparguthaben n savings deposits; **~kasse** f savings bank; **~konto** n savings account.

spärlich 1. scanty, meagre; 2. (Haare) sparse.

sparsam 1. economical, sparing; 2. ~ umgehen mit be economical with s.th., save s.th.; **S~keit** f economy, thrift.

Sparte f branch, field, section.

Spaß m 1. (Vergnügen) fun; 2. (Witz) joke, jest; ~ beiseite! joking apart; zum ~ as a joke; keinen ~ verstehen have no sense of humour; **s~en** joke, make fun; **s~ig** funny.

spät 1. late; bis ~ in die Nacht till late at night; wie ~ ist es? what time is it? 2. zu ~ kommen be late (zu for).

Spaten m spade.

später 1. later; 2. (zukünftig) future; 3. bis ~! till later! **~estens** at the latest; **S~herbst** m late autumn.

Spatz m sparrow.

spazierenfahren irr go for a drive; **~engehen** irr go for a walk; **S~fahrt** f drive, ride; **S~gang** m walk,

stroll; **S~gänger** *m* stroller;
S~stock *m* walking-stick.
Specht *m* woodpecker.
Speck *m* bacon.
Spedit|eur *m* forwarding
agent; **~ion** *f* forwarding.
Speer *m* spear; **~werfen** *n*
javelin-throwing.
Speiche *f* 1. *tech* spoke;
2. *anat* radius.
Speichel *m* spittle.
Speicher *m* 1. (*Korn~*) gran-
ary; 2. (*Lagerhaus*) warehouse; 3. (*Dachboden*) loft,
attice; **s~n** store.
speien *irr* 1. spit; 2. (*sich erbrechen*) vomit.
Speise *f* 1. (*Nahrung*) food,
nourishment; 2. (*Mahlzeit*)
dish; **~kammer** *f* larder,
pantry; **~karte** *f* bill of fare,
menu; **s~n** 1. dine; 2. have
for dinner; 3. *el* feed, supply;
~öl *n* edible oil; **~röhre** *f*
(o)esophagus; **~wagen** *m*
dining-car.
Spektakel *m* (*Lärm*) noise,
row.
spekulieren speculate (*auf*
on).
Spend|e *f* contribution, do-
nation; **s~en** 1. give, donate; 2. (*Licht*) provide;
3. (*beitragen*) contribute;
4. (*Blut*) donate; 5. *rel* administer; **~er** *m* 1. contribu-
tor; 2. (*Blut~*) donor; **s~ie-
ren** provide (*jdm etw* s.o.
with s.o.).
Sperr|e *f* 1. barrier, *Am* gate;
2. (*Hindernis*) obstacle;

3. (*Straße*) barricade;
4. (*Verbot*) ban; **s~en**
1. (*durch Verbot*) close, bar;
2. (*Hindernis*) block;
3. (*Strom*) cut off; 4. *jdn in
etw* ~ shut s.o. in s.th.; 5. *mil*
blockade; 6. (*Konto*) block,
freeze; 7. *typ* space;
~gebiet *n* prohibited area;
~gut *n* bulky goods *pl*;
~holz *n* plywood; **s~ig** bulky; **~sitz** *m* stall, *Am* orchestra.
Spesen *pl* charges, expenses
pl.
Spezia|list *m* specialist;
~lität *f* speciality.
speziell special, particular.
spezifisch specific.
Sphäre *f* sphere.
Spiegel *m* mirror, glass;
~bild *n* reflection; **~ei** *n*
fried egg; **s~n** 1. shine,
sparkle; 2. *sich* ~ be re-
flected.
Spiel *n* 1. play; 2. (*nach Re-
geln*) game; 3. (*Wettkampf*)
match; 4. *etw ins* ~ *bringen*
bring s.th. forward;
5. (*Glücks~*) gambling; *sein
Leben aufs* ~ *setzen* jeopardize o.'s life; *auf dem* ~
stehen be at stake; 6. *theat*
play; (*Darbietung*) performance; **~automat** *m* slot machine; **~bank** *f* casino;
s~en 1. play; *Karten* ~ play
cards; 2. *theat* act, perform;
3. (*vortäuschen*) feign, pretend; 4. (*Glücksspiel*)
gamble; 5. (*geschehen*) be

set; 6. *(fig)* etw ~ *lassen* make use of s.th.; **~er** *m* 1. player; 2. *(Glücks~)* gambler; **~feld** *n sport* field; **~karte** *f* playing-card; **~marke** *f* chip; **~plan** *m* program(me); **~platz** *m* playground; **~raum** *m fig* scope, latitude; **~regel** *f* rule; **~waren** *pl* toys *pl;* **~zeug** *n* toy.

Spieß *m* 1. spear; 2. *(Brat~)* spit; **s~ig** narrow-minded.

Spinat *m* spinach.

Spinne *f* spider; **s~n** *irr* 1. spin *a. fig;* 2. *(verrückt sein)* be daft; **~nnetz** *n* cobweb; **~rei** *f* spinning-mill.

Spion *m* spy; **~age** *f* espionage; **s~ieren** spy.

Spirale *f* spiral *a. fig.*

Spiri|tuosen *pl* spirits *pl;* **~tus** *m* spirit.

spitz 1. pointed *a. fig;* 2. *(Nase)* sharp; 3. *(beißend)* biting, sharp; **S~e** *f* 1. point; *auf die ~ treiben* carry too far; 2. *(Finger)* tip; 3. *(Baum)* top; 4. *(Berg)* summit, peak; 5. *(Unternehmer)* head; 6. *(Gewebe)* lace.

Spitzel *m* informer.

spitzen 1. point, sharpen; 2. *die Ohren ~* prick up o.'s ears; **S~geschwindigkeit** *f* top speed; **S~klöpplerin** *f* lacemaker; **S~leistung** *f* 1. record; 2. *com* maximum output; **S~reiter** *m* leader.

spitz|findig hair-splitting;

S~hacke *f* pick; **S~name** *m* nickname.

Splitt *m* gravel.

Splitter *m* splinter, fragment; **s~nackt** stark naked.

spontan spontaneous.

Sport *m* sport, athletics *pl; ~ treiben* go in for sports; **~abzeichen** *n* sports badge; **~bekleidung** *f* sportswear; **~geschäft** *n* sports shop; **~halle** *f* gymnasium; **~hemd** *n* sports shirt; **~ler** *m* sportsman; **s~lich** 1. sportive; 2. *(Person)* athletic; **~nachrichten** *pl* sport news; **~platz** *m* sports field; **~veranstaltung** *f* sporting event; **~verein** *m* sports club; **~wagen** *m* sports car.

Spott *m* mockery, derision, scorn; **s~billig** dirt cheap; **s~en** mock, scorn *(über* at).

spöttisch mocking, derisive.

Sprach|e *f* 1. *(Vermögen)* speech; 2. *(e~s Volkes)* language, tongue; *alte ~n* ancient languages; 3. *(Ausdruck)* accent, pronunciation; 4. *zur ~ kommen* come up for discussion; 5. *(Ausdrucksweise)* language, parlance, words *pl;* **~kenntnisse** *pl* knowledge of languages; **~lehre** *f* grammar; **s~lich** 1. linguistic; 2. *(Fehler)* grammatical; **s~los** 1. speechless; 2. *ich war ~* I was dumbfounded.

sprech|en *irr* 1. speak; *laut ~*

speak loud; *für jdn* ~ speak in s.o.'s favour; *vieles spricht dafür* there is much to be said for it; *mit jdm* ~ speak to s.o.; 2. *(sich unterhalten)* talk; *über Politik* ~ talk politics; *über jdn* ~ talk about s.o.; 3. *auf etw zu* ~ *kommen* bring s.th. up; *auf jdn zu* ~ *kommen* come to speak about s.o.; 4. *(Rede)* speak; 5. *jur* pronounce; 6. *jdn* ~ speak to s.o.; **S~er** *m* 1. speaker, spokesman; 2. *(Ansagen)* announcer; **S~stunde** *f* 1. office hour; 2. *(Arzt)* consulting hour; **S~zimmer** *n (Arzt)* consulting room.

spreng|en 1. *(Garten)* water, sprinkle; 2. *etw in die Luft* ~ blow up s.th.; 3. *(Felsen)* blast; 4. *(Ketten)* burst; 5. *(Versammlung)* break up; **S~stoff** *m* explosive; **S~ung** *f* explosion.

Sprichwort *n* proverb.

sprießen *irr* sprout.

Spring|brunnen *m* fountain; **s~en** *irr* 1. jump; *in die Höhe* ~ jump into the air; 2. *(hüpfen)* hop; 3. *(Glas)* crack; 4. *(zerbrechen)* break; 5. *(platzen)* burst; **s~end**: *der* ~*e Punkt* the crucial point; ~**er** *m* 1. *sport* springer; 2. *(Schach)* knight.

Spritze *f* 1. syringe; 2. *jdm e-e* ~ *geben* give s.o. an injection; 3. *(Feuer)* fire engine; **s~n** 1. *(Rasen)* sprinkle, spray; 2. *med* inject; 3. *(hervorschießen)* spurt; 4. *(planschen)* splash; ~**nhaus** *n* fire-station; ~**r** *m* splash.

spritzig 1. *(Wein)* fizzy; 2. *fig* sparkling, fizzy.

spröde 1. brittle; 2. *(Haut)* chapped; 3. *fig* reserved.

Sproß *m* 1. *bot* shoot; 2. *fig* offspring.

Sprosse *f (Leiter)* rung.

Spruch *m* 1. saying; 2. *(Bibel)* text, verse; 3. *(Urteil)* sentence; ~**band** *n* banner.

Sprudel *m* mineral water; **s~n** gush, bubble up.

sprüh|en 1. *(Funken)* spark; 2. *(Wasser)* spray; 3. *fig* scintillate; **S~regen** *m* drizzle.

Sprung *m* 1. leap, jump; 2. *(Satz)* bound; *auf dem* ~ *sein zu* be on the point of; *auf e-n* ~ *vorbekommen* drop in *(bei* on); 3. *(in Glas)* crack; ~**brett** *n* springboard; ~**schanze** *f* ski-jump; ~**tuch** *n* jumping-sheet; ~**turm** *m* high-diving tower.

Spucke *f* spittle; **s~n** 1. spit; 2. *(erbrechen)* vomit.

Spuk *m* haunting; **s~en** 1. haunt; 2. *(Haus)* be haunted.

Spülbecken *n* sink.

Spule *f* spool, reel.

spül|en 1. wash up; 2. *(aus~)* rinse; **S~lappen** *m* dishcloth.

Spur f 1. (Fährte) track, trail; *auf der falschen ~ sein* be on the wrong track; 2. *jur* clue; 3. (Abdruck) print; 4. (Zeichen) mark, trace; 5. (Fahrbahn) lane; *in der ~ bleiben* keep in lane.

spür|bar 1. noticeable; 2. (deutlich) distinct; 3. (beträchtlich) considerable; ~**en** 1. feel, be conscious of; 2. (wahrnehmen) perceive.

spurlos traceless; without leaving a trace.

Spürsinn m scent, flair (*für* for).

Staat m 1. (Land) state, country; 2. *jur* government; 3. (Prunk) pomp, display; ~**enbund** m confederacy; **s~enlos** stateless; **s~lich** national, state; public.

Staats|angehöriger m citizen, subject; ~**angehörigkeit** f citizenship; ~**anwalt** m public prosecutor; **s~bürgerlich** civil, civic; ~**dienst** m civil service; ~**form** f form of government; ~**gelder** pl public funds pl; ~**gewalt** f public authority; ~**haushalt** m budget; ~**mann** m statesman; ~**präsident** m President of the State; ~**recht** n public law; ~**vertrag** m convention.

Stab m 1. rod, bar; 2. *fig* staff; 3. (Dirigent) baton; ~**hochsprung** m pole-vaulting.

stabil 1. stable; 2. (robust) solid, sturdy; ~**isieren** stabilize; **S~ität** f stability.

Stachel m 1. prick; 2. *zoo* sting; 3. (Dorn) thorn; 4. (Ansporn) goad, spur, stimulus; **S~beere** f gooseberry; ~**draht** m barbed wire.

stachelig prickly, thistly, bristly.

Stadion n sport stadium.

Stadium n stage.

Stadt f town, city; *in die ~ gehen* go to town.

Städte|bau m town planning; **s~ebaulich**: *~e Planung* town planning, urbanism; ~**er** m townsman.

Stadtgespräch n tele local call.

städtisch 1. municipal; 2. (Bevölkerung) urbain.

Stadt|mauer f town wall; ~**plan** m town map; ~**rand** m outskirts pl; ~**rat** m town council; ~**rundfahrt** f town sight-seeing tour; ~**teil** m quarter; ~**verwaltung** f municipality; ~**zentrum** n town centre.

Staffel f 1. sport relay; 2. mil aero squadron; ~**ei** f easel; ~**lauf** m sport relay race; **s~n** 1. (Löhne) grade, graduate; 2. (Zeit, sport) stagger.

stagnieren stagnate.

Stahl m steel; ~**stich** m steel engraving; ~**träger** m steel girder; ~**waren** pl steel goods pl, Am hardware; **~werk** n steel works pl.

Stall m 1. (Pferde) stable; 2. (Kuh~) cowshed; 3. (Schweine~) pigsty.

Stamm m 1. (Baum) trunk; 2. (Volk) tribe; 3. (Wort) root; 4. (Familie) line, stock; **~baum** m family tree.

stammeln stammer.

stamm|en 1. (Personen) be descended (aus from); 2. (aus einem Land) come; 3. (zeitlich) date; 4. (zurückgehen) originate; 5. (sich ableiten) derive; **S~gast** m regular customer.

stämmig sturdy, stout.

Stamm|kunde m com regular (customer); **~platz** m habitual seat; **~tisch** m round.

stampfen 1. stamp (mit dem Fuß o.'s foot); 2. mar pitch.

Stand m 1. stand, position; 2. (Barometer) reading; 3. (Niveau) level; 4. (Lage) state; 5. (Beschaffenheit) condition; 6. sport score; 7. (gesellschaftlich) rank, status; 8. (Klasse) class; 9. (Verkaufs~) stand, stall.

Standard m standard.

Ständchen n serenade.

Ständer m stand, rack.

Standes|amt n registry office; **s~amtlich**: ~e Trauung civil marriage; **~beamter** m registrar.

stand|fest stable; **~haft** 1. steadfast; 2. (unerschüt-

terlich) firm, unflinching; **~halten** irr withstand, resist.

ständig constant, continual, permanent.

Stand|licht n parking light; **~ort** m stand, position; site; **~punkt** m point of view, standpoint; den ~ vertreten take the view.

Stange f 1. pole, stick, post; 2. (Fahnen~) staff; 3. (Hühner) perch; 4. (Metall) bar; 5. (Seife) stick.

Stanniol n tinfoil.

Stapel m pile; **~lauf** m launching; **s~n** stack, pile up.

Star m 1. zoo starling; 2. film star; 3. med cataract.

stark 1. (körperlich) strong, stout; 2. (mächtig) powerful, mighty; 3. (Umfang) thick; 4. (beleibt) corpulent; 5. (mengenmäßig) heavy, great; 6. ~er Tee strong tea; 7. (Schmerz) intense, severe; 8. (Motor) powerful; 9. es regnet ~ it is raining very hard.

Stärke f 1. strength, force, power; 2. (Dicke) thickness; 3. (Beleibtheit) corpulence; 4. (starke Seite) strong point; 5. chem starch; **s~n** 1. strengthen, fortify; 2. (kräftigen) invigorate; 3. sich ~ refresh o.s.

Starkstrom m heavy current.

Stärkungsmittel n tonic.

starr 1. *(steif)* stiff; 2. *(empfindungslos)* numb; 3. *(Blick)* staring; 4. *(Regel)* rigid; **~en** 1. stare *(auf* at); 2. *vor etw* ~ be full of s.th.; **~sinnig** stubborn.

Start m 1. start a. *fig;* 2. aero take-off; *(Rakete)* launch; **~bahn** f runway; **s~bereit** ready to start; **s~en** 1. start; 2. aero take off; 3. *sport* take part; **~rampe** f *(Rakete)* launching ramp.

Station f 1. station; 2. *(Haltestelle)* stop; 3. *(Unterbrechung)* stay; 4. *(Kranken~)* ward; **s~är** 1. stationary; 2. *~e Behandlung* in-patient treatment; **~sarzt** m ward physician.

Statist m *theat* super(numerary); **~ik** f statistics *mit sing;* **s~isch** statistic(al).

statt instead of, in place of.

Stätte f place.

statt|finden *irr* take place, happen; **~lich** 1. stately; 2. *(Summe)* handsome.

Statut n statute.

Stau m *(Verkehr)* jam.

Staub m dust; **s~en** make dust; **s~ig** dusty; **~sauger** m vacuum cleaner; **~tuch** n duster; **~wolke** f cloud of dust.

Staudamm m dam.

Staude f shrub.

stauen 1. *(Wasser)* dam up; 2. *(Verkehr)* congest; 3. *sich* ~ accumulate; become jammed.

staunen be suprised, astonished *(über* at); **S~** n astonishment.

Stausee m artificial lake.

stech|en *irr* 1. stick; 2. *(Mükke)* bite; 3. *(Biene)* sting; 4. *(Spargel)* cut; 5. *sich in den Finger* ~ prick o.'s finger; **~end** 1. *(Blick)* piercing; 2. *(Schmerz)* shooting; **S~mücke** f gnat, mosquito.

Steck|brief m wanted poster; **~dose** f *el* socket, wall-plug; **s~en** 1. stick, put; 2. *(befestigen)* fix; 3. *(hinein~)* insert into; 4. *(gleiten)* slip; 5. *(hineinstopfen)* stick; 6. *(befestigen)* pin; 7. *(sich befinden)* be; **s~enbleiben** *irr* 1. be stuck, stick; 2. *(Verhandlungen)* come to a standstill.

Steckenpferd n hobby.

Steck|er m plug; **~nadel** f pin.

Stegreif m: *aus dem* ~ *sprechen* extemporize, improvise, *Am* ad-lib.

stehen *irr* 1. stand; *aufrecht* ~ stand upright; 2. *(sich befinden)* be, stand; *rechts von jdm* ~ be on s.o.'s right; *die Sache steht gut* things are going well; *auf jds Seite* ~ be on s.o.'s side; *auf der Liste* ~ be on the list; *in Flammen* ~ be on fire; *gut mit jdm* ~ be on good terms with s.o.; *über jdm* ~ be s.o.'s superior; 3. *(geschrieben* ~*)* say, be written; *hier*

steht, daß it says here that;
4. *(stillstehen)* stop; 5. *etw steht jdm* s.th. suits s.o.;
6. *(bestehen)* exist; 7. *(anzeigen) wie steht das Barometer?* what is the barometer at? 8. *zu etw* ~ stand by s.th.; *für etw* ~ stand for s.th.;
9. *zu* ~ *kommen* cost; 10. *so steht es also!* so that's the way it is! **S~** *n* 1. *zum* ~ *kommen* come to a standstill; 2. *das* ~ *fällt ihm schwer* standing is difficult for him; **~bleiben** *irr* 1. stop, halt; 2. *(zurückbleiben)* be left; 3. *(Zeit)* come to a halt; **~d** 1. upright;
2. *(Auto)* standing; 3. *(Gewässer)* stagnant; **~lassen** *irr* 1. leave; 2. *(Fehler)* overlook; 3. *jdn* ~ leave s.o. standing.

Steh|imbiß *m* stand-up snack; **~lampe** *f* standard lamp.

stehlen *irr* steal; *jdm die Zeit* ~ waste s.o.'s time.

Stehplatz *m* standing-room.

steif 1. stiff; ~ *werden* stiffen; 2. *(Kälte)* numb; 3. *(Stoff)* hard; 4. *(gestärkt)* starched; 5. *(förmlich)* stardy, formal; 6. ~ *und fest* stubbornly.

Steig|bügel *m* stirrup; **~eisen** *n* crampon; **s~en** *irr* 1. step, get; *aufs Pferd* ~ mount s.o.'s horse; *aus dem Bett* ~ get out of bed;
2. *(klettern)* climb; *auf e-n Berg* ~ climb a mountain;

3. *(Tränen)* rise; 4. *e-n Drachen* ~ *lassen* fly a kite;
5. *(Wasser)* swell, rise;
6. *(Preise)* increase; 7. *Treppen* ~ climb stairs; **s~end** increasing, rising.

steiger|n 1. *(vermehren)* increase, heighten; 2. *(verbessern)* improve; 3. *(Preise)* raise; 4. *sich* ~ intensify; **S~ung** *f* increase, rise.

Steigung *f* gradient, incline.

steil steep; **S~hang** *m* steep slope; **S~küste** *f* steep coast.

Stein *m* 1. stone; rock;
2. *(Edel~)* precious stone;
3. *(Spiel)* piece; 4. *bot* stone, kernel; **~bruch** *m* quarry; **~butt** *m zoo* turbot; **s~ig** stony; rocky; **~kohle** *f* hard-coal; **~metz** *m* stone-cutter; **~pilz** *m* yellow boletus; **~schlag** *m* falling stones *pl;* **~zeit** *f* Stone Age.

Stelldichein *n: jdm ein* ~ *geben* arrange a rendezvous with s.o.

Stelle *f* 1. place, spot; *zur* ~ *sein* be at hand; *an* ~ *von* in place of; *auf der* ~ on the spot; 2. *(Standort)* site, position; 3. *an erster* ~ in the first place; 4. *(Text)* passage; 5. *(Posten)* post, job; *e-e freie* ~ a vaccant position; 6. *(Amt)* authority, office; **s~n** 1. *(hin~)* set up, stand up; 2. put, set, place; 3. *etw unter Beweis* ~ prove s.th.;

etw in Frage ~ jeopardize s.th.; 4. *etw kalt* ~ put s.th. to cool; 5. *(anordnen)* arrange; 6. *(schalten)* turn; 7. *(Uhr, Falle)* set; *(Frage)* ask; *(Anspruch)* make; *(Arbeitskraft)* supply; 8. *tech* adjust; 9. *sich* ~ place o.s.; 10. *(Schwierigkeiten)* arise; 11. *(Verbrechen)* surrender; 12. *(e-m Gegner)* face; 13. *(sich verstellen)* pretend, feign; 14. *sich mit jdm gut* ~ get on good terms with s.o.

Stellen|angebot *n* vacancy, vacant post; **~bewerber** *m* applicant; **~gesuch** *n* application for a post; **s~weise** here and there, in places.

Stellung *f* 1. *(Arbeit)* job, position, employment; 2. *(Körperhaltung)* posture, pose; 3. *(Rang)* status, position; 4. ~ *nehmen zu* comment on; ~ *nehmen für* stand up for; **~nahme** *f* commentary, statement.

stell|vertretend acting, vicarious; **S~vertreter** *m* 1. deputy; 2. *jur* proxy; **S~werk** *n loc* signal box.

Stelze *f: auf ~n gehen* walk on stilts.

Stemm|eisen *n* crowbar; **s~en** 1. lift up, stem; 2. *sich gegen etw* ~ press o.s. against s.th.; *fig* resist s.th.

Stempel *m* 1. stamp; 2. *(Post~)* postmark; **s~n** stamp.

Stengel *m bot* stalk, stem.

Steno|graphie *f* shorthand; **s~graphieren** take down in shorthand; **~typistin** *f* stenotypist.

Steppdecke *f* quilt.

Steppe *f* steppe.

sterben *irr* die, decease; *vor Hunger* ~ starve to death; **S~** *n: im* ~ *liegen* be dying; **~skrank** sick to death.

Sterbe|urkunde *f* death certificate; **s~lich** mortal; **~lichkeit** *f* death rate.

Stern *m* star *a. fig;* **~bild** *n* 1. constellation; 2. *(Tierkreis)* sign of the zodiac; **~enhimmel** *m* starry sky; **~fahrt** *f* motor rally; **~schnuppe** *f* shooting star; **~warte** *f* observatory.

stet|ig constant; steady; **~s** always, invariably.

Steuer 1. *n* steering wheel; *am* ~ *sitzen* be at the wheel; *mar* rudder; 2. *f* tax, rate, imposition; *e-e* ~ *auf etw legen* tax s.th.; **~aufkommen** *n* inland revenue; **~berater** *m* tax adviser; **~bescheid** *m* notice of assessment; **~erklärung** *f* tax return; **~flucht** *f* tax evasion; **s~frei** tax-free; **~klasse** *f* tax group; **~knüppel** *m* stick; **s~lich** fiscal; **~mann** *m* 1. helmsman; 2. *sport* coxswain; **~marke** *f* revenue stamp; **s~n** 1. *(Auto)* drive, steer; 2. *mar* navigate; 3. *el* control, regulate; 4. *fig* head *(nach* for); **s~pflich-**

tig subject to tax; **~prüfer** *m* tax inspector; **~rad** *n* steering wheel; **~ung** *f* control.

Steward *m* steward; **~eß** *f* stewardess.

Stich *m* 1. *(Insekt)* bite, sting; 2. *(Nadel)* prick; 3. *(Wunde)* stab; 4. *(Nähen)* stitch; 5. *med* pang; 6. *(fig)* jdn im ~ lassen abandon s.o.; 7. e-n ~ haben have gone off; 8. *(Bild)* engraving; **s~eln** gibe; **~flamme** *f* darting flame; **s~haltig** sound, valid; **~probe** *f com* random sample; **~tag** *m* *(Termin)* deadline; **~wort** *n* 1. catchword; 2. *(Lexikon)* headword; 3. *theat* cue.

stick|en embroider; **S~erei** *f* embroidery.

stick|ig stuffy; **S~stoff** *m chem* nitrogen.

Stiefel *m* boot.

Stief|mutter *f* stepmother; **~vater** *m* stepfather.

Stiel *m* 1. *bot* stem, stalk; 2. *(Besen)* handle; 3. *(Glas)* stem.

Stier *m* bull; **~kampf** *m* bull-fight.

Stift 1. *m* pin, plug; 2. *n* foundation, convent; **s~en** 1. *(gründen)* found, establish; 2. *(spenden)* donate, give; 3. *Frieden ~* make peace; **~er** *m* 1. founder; 2. *(Spender)* donor; **~ung** *f* 1. foundation; 2. *(Schen-*

kung) endowment, donation.

Stil *m* style.

still 1. quiet, silent; 2. *(Gegend)* peaceful; 3. *(See)* calm, still; 4. *(zurückhaltend)* quiet; 5. *(heimlich)* secret; *im ~en* secretly; inwardly; **S~e** *f* 1. silence, stillness; 2. *(See)* calmness; 3. *in aller ~* quietly.

Stilleben *n* still life.

stillen 1. nurse; 2. *(Hunger)* appease; *(Durst)* quench; 3. *(Blut)* stop; 4. *(Verlangen)* satisfy; 5. *(Schmerz)* soothe.

still|gelegt shut down; **~halten** *irr* keep still.

stillschweigen *irr* be silent; **S~** *n: mit ~ übergehen* pass over in silence; **~d** 1. tacit, implicit; 2. in silence.

Stillstand *m* 1. *(Verhandlungen)* deadlock; 2. *zum ~ kommen* come to a standstill.

stillstehen *irr* 1. stand still; 2. *(außer Betrieb)* lie idle; 3. *(Motor)* stop.

Stimm|band *n* vocal chord; **~bruch** *m* breaking of the voice.

Stimme *f* 1. voice; *mit lauter ~* in a loud voice; 2. *pol* vote; *s-e ~ abgeben* go to the polls; **s~n** 1. *mus* tune *(auf* to); 2. *jdn ernst ~* make s.o. serious; 3. *(richtig sein)* be right, correct; 4. *das stimmt!* that's right! 5. *für*

jdn ~ vote for s.o.;
~ngleichheit *f* equality of votes.

Stimm|enthaltung *f* abstention; **~ung** *f* 1. *(Gemütslage)* mood, humour; *in guter* ~ *sein* be in a good mood; 2. *(Frohsinn)* spirits *pl; jdm die* ~ *verderben* dash s.o.'s spirits; 3. *(Atmosphäre)* atmosphere; 4. *(der Bevölkerung)* feeling, opinion; 5. *(Börse)* tendency; **~zettel** *m* ballot.

stinken *irr* stink, smell *(nach* of).

Stipendium *n* scholarship.

Stirn *f* forehead; *die* ~*e runzeln* frown; **~band** *n* headband; **~höhle** *f* anat sinus.

stöbern rummage *(in* about).

Stock *m* 1. stick; *am* ~ *gehen* walk on a stick, with a cane; 2. *(~werk)* stor(e)y, floor.

stock|en 1. *(innehalten)* pause, stop; 2. *(steckenbleiben)* stop short; 3. *(Arbeit)* come to a standstill; 4. *(stagnieren)* stagnate; **S~fisch** *m* dried cod; **S~ung** *f* 1. delay, stoppage; 2. *(Verkehr)* jam, congestion.

Stoff *m* 1. material, fabric; 2. *(Unterlagen)* material, matter; 3. *fig* subject; 4. *chem* substance; **~wechsel** *m* metabolism.

stöhnen groan, moan *(über* at).

Stollen *m* 1. *min* tunnel; 2. *(Gebäck)* fruit loaf.

stolpern stumble *(über* over), trip.

stolz 1. proud *(auf* of); 2. *(hochmütig)* haughty; **S~** *m* pride *(auf* in).

stopf|en 1. *(Strümpfe)* darn, mend; 2. *(zu~)* plug; 3. *(hinein~)* stuff, cram (into); 4. *med* constipate; **S~nadel** *f* darning-needle.

Stopp *m* 1. stop; 2. *(der Preise)* freeze; **s~!** stop! **s~en** 1. stop; 2. *(Uhr)* time; **~licht** *n* mot stoplight; **~uhr** *f* stop-watch.

Stöpsel *m* 1. stopper; 2. *(Flasche)* cork.

Storch *m* stork.

stör|en 1. disturb; *stört es Sie, wenn ich rauche?* do you mind my smoking? 2. *(unterbrechen)* interrupt; 3. *(Sendung)* jam; 4. *(ärgern)* bother; **~d** disturbing, troublesome; **S~fried** *m* troublemaker.

störrisch stubborn, obstinate.

Störung *f* 1. disturbance; 2. *(Unterbrechung)* interruption; 3. *tech* defect.

Stoß *m* 1. push; *jdm e-n* ~ *geben* give s.o. a push; 2. *(Schlag)* blow, knock; 3. *(Anstoß)* impulse; 4. *(Stapel)* pile; **s~en** *irr* 1. push, shove; *jdn von sich* ~ push s.o. off; 2. *(Waffe)* thrust; 3. *(Fuß)* kick; *(Faust)* punch;

4. *sich* ~ *an* bump against; *fig* take offence (at); 5. *(grenzen)* border *(an* on), adjoin; 6. *(Widerstand)* meet with; 7. *zu jdm* ~ join up with s.o.; **~seufzer** *m* deep sigh; **~stange** *f mot* bumper bar; **~zeit** *f* peak, rush hours *pl.*

stottern stammer, stutter.

Straf|anzeige *f* charge; **s~bar** punishable, criminal; **~e** *f* 1. punishment, penalty; *bei* ~ *von* under penalty of; 2. *(Geld~)* fine; **s~en** punish *(für* for).

straff 1. tight; 2. *(Haltung)* straight; 3. *(Zucht)* strict, rigid.

straffällig liable to a penalty.

straffen tighten.

straf|frei unpunished; **S~gefangener** *m* convict; **S~gesetzbuch** *n* penal code; **S~porto** *n* postage due; **S~prozeß** *m* criminal procedure; **S~recht** *n* criminal law; **S~tat** *f* crime.

Strahl *m* 1. ray; 2. *(Wasser)* stream; 3. *(Licht~)* beam; **s~en** 1. beam *(vor Freude* with joy); 2. *(glänzen)* shine, sparkle; **s~end** 1. radiating *a. fig;* 2. *(Wetter)* bright; **~ung** *f* radiation.

Strähne *f (Haar)* strand.

stramm 1. *(eng)* tight; 2. *(kräftig)* bouncing.

strampeln kick.

Strand *m* beach, sea-shore; **s~en** run ashore; **~gut** *n* flotsam; **~korb** *m* beach--chair; **~wärter** *m* life--guard.

Strang *m* 1. *(Seil)* rope; 2. *(Schienen)* track.

Strapaz|e *f,* **s~ieren** strain; **s~ierfähig** hard-wearing.

Straße *f* 1. *(Stadt)* street; *auf der* ~ in the street; *auf offener* ~ in the open street; 2. *(Land)* road; *~ gesperrt!* road up! 3. *(Fern~)* high-road; 4. *(Meerenge)* straits *pl;* **~nbahn** *f* tram(way); **~bahnhaltestelle** *f* tram stop; **~necke** *f* street corner; **~ngraben** *m* road ditch; **~nhändler** *m* street--hawker; **~nkarte** *f* road map; **~nkreuzung** *f* cross-roads *pl mit sing;* **~nlaterne** *f* street-lamp; **~nnetz** *n* road net; **~nübergang** *m* pedestrian crossing; **~nverkehrsordnung** *f* Highway Code; **~nzustand** *m* road condition.

Stratosphäre *f* stratosphere.

sträuben, *sich* refuse to do s.th., resist s.th.

Strauch *m* shrub, bush.

Strauß *m* 1. *(Blumen)* bunch; 2. zoo ostrich.

streb|en 1. *(sich bemühen)* endeavour o.s.; 2. ~ *nach etw* strive after s.th.; **S~en** *n* aspiration; **~sam** industrious and ambitious.

Strecke *f* 1. *(Entfernung)* distance; 2. *(Weg)* way,

stretch; 3. (*Abschnitt*) part;
4. (*Route*) route; 5. (*Zug*)
track.

streck|en 1. stretch, extend;
2. (*verdünnen*) dilute;
S~verband *m: im* ~ in high
traction.

Streich *m* 1. stroke, blow;
2. (*Scherz*) joke, trick; *jdm*
e-n bösen ~ *spielen* play s.o.
a nasty trick; **s~eln** caress,
pet; **s~en** *irr* 1. (*mit Farbe*)
paint; 2. (*Butter*) spread;
3. (*aus~*) strike out; 4. (*gleiten*) glide (*über* over);
5. (*wandern*) roam; 6. *über*
etw ~ stroke s.th.; **~holz** *n*
match.

Streif|band *n: unter* ~ in
wrappers; *f~e* *f* patrol;
s~en 1. touch; 2. (*leicht*)
graze, brush; 3. (*Thema*)
touch (on); 4. *etw von etw* ~
slip s.th. off s.th.; 5. (*Blick*)
skim over; **~en** *m* stripe,
streak, strip; **~enwagen** *m*
patrol car; **~zug** *m* scout.

Streik *m* strike; **s~en** 1. go
on strike, walk out; 2. (*Motor*) conk out; **~posten** *m*
picket.

Streit *m* 1. quarrel, row;
2. (*Wortgefecht*) dispute,
controversy; 3. (*handgreiflich*) fight; **s~en** *irr* 1. quarrel, argue; 2. dispute; 3. *für*
etw ~ fight for s.th.; 4. *sich* ~
row; **~fall** *m* dispute; **~fra-
ge** *f* point of controversy;
s~ig: *jdm etw* ~ *machen*
dispute s.o.'s right to s.th.;

~kräfte *pl* armed forces *pl*;
s~süchtig quarrelsome.

streng 1. severe, rigorous;
2. (*Vorschrift*) strict;
3. (*Kälte*) severe; 4. (*Geruch*) pungent; 5. ~ *genommen* strictly speaking; ~ *verboten!* strictly prohibited.

Streu *f* litter; **~dose** *f* castor; **s~en** 1. strew, scatter;
2. (*aus~*) spread.

Strich *m* 1. stroke; 2. (*Linie*)
line; 3. *das geht mir gegen
den* ~ that goes against my
grain; **~punkt** *m* semicolon;
s~weise: ~ *Regen* local
rainshowers.

Strick *m* cord; **s~en** knit;
~jacke *f* cardigan; **~nadel**
f knitting needle; **~waren**
pl knitwear.

strikt severe, strict.

strittig contentious, in dispute.

Stroh *n* straw; **~blume** *f*
strawflower; **~dach** *n*
thatched roof; **~halm** *m*
straw; **~hut** *m* straw hat.

Strolch *m* tramp; rascal.

Strom *m* 1. (*Fluß*) river;
2. (*Strömung*) current; *gegen den* ~ *schwimmen*
swim against the tide;
3. (*von Flüssigkeiten*)
stream, flood; 4. *el* current;
unter ~ *stehen* be live; 5. *es
regnet in Strömen* it is
raining cats and dogs;
s~abwärts downstream;
s~aufwärts upstream;
~ausfall *m* power failure.

strömen stream, flow, pour; ~**d**: *in* ~*em Regen* in the pouring rain.

Strom|netz *n* supply mains *pl;* ~**schnelle** *f* rapid.

Strömung *f* current *a. fig.*

Strudel *m* 1. whirlpool, eddy; 2. *fig* whirl.

Struktur *f* structure.

Strumpf *m* stocking; ~**halter** *m* suspender; ~**hose** *f* panty hose; ~**waren** *pl* hosiery.

struppig 1. unkempt; 2. *(Hund)* shaggy.

Stube *f* room; **s~nrein** *(Hund)* house-trained.

Stuck *m* stucco.

Stück *n* 1. piece; 2. *(Zucker)* lump; 3. *theat* play; 4. ~ *Vieh* head of cattle; 5. *(fig)* *ein starkes* ~ a bit thick; 6. *aus einem* ~ all of a piece; 7. *aus freien* ~*en* of o.'s own accord; 8. *große* ~*e halten auf* have a high opinion of; ~**gut** *n* package freight.

Student *m* student; ~**en(wohn)heim** *n* hall (of residence), *Am* dormitory.

Studie *f* study; ~**naufenthalt** *m* educational stay; ~**njahr** *n* academic year; ~**nreise** *f* study trip.

studieren 1. study; 2. *er studiert* he is at a university.

Stud|io *n* studio; ~**ium** *n* 1. studies *pl;* 2. *(Fachgebiet)* study.

Stufe *f* 1. *(Treppe)* step,

stair; 2. *(Rang)* rank, grade; 3. *(Niveau)* level; *auf der gleichen* ~ *stehen* be on the same level; ~**nleiter** *f fig* scale, gamut; **s~nweise** by steps, gradually.

Stuhl *m* 1. chair, seat; 2. *(Hocker)* stool; 3. *(Kirche)* pew; ~**gang** *m:* ~ *haben* have a bowel movement; ~**lehne** *f* back of a chair.

stumm mute, dumb.

Stummel *m (Zigarre)* end, stub.

Stummfilm *m* silent film.

Stümper *m* bungler; **s~haft** botchy, unskilful.

stumpf 1. *(Werkzeug)* dull, blunt; 2. *(Winkel)* obtuse; 3. *(gefühllos)* insensitive (to); **S~** *m* stump, stub; **S~sinn** *m* dullness, impassiveness; ~**sinnig** dull.

Stunde *f* 1. hour; *e-e halbe* ~ half an hour; 2. *(Unterricht)* lesson, class; 3. *(Moment)* moment, time; **s~n** *com* grant a respite; ~**ngeschwindigkeit** *f* speed per hour; ~**nkilometer** *m* kilometre per hour; **s~nlang** for hours (and hours); ~**nplan** *m* time-table, *Am* schedule.

stündlich hourly; every hour.

stupid(e) stupid.

stur pigheaded.

Sturm *m* 1. storm *a. fig.,*

gale; 2. *(Orkan)* hurricane; ~**bö** *f* squall.

stürm|en 1. *es stürmt* there is a storm; 2. *(Wind)* rage; 3. *mil* take by assault; **S~er** *m (Fußball)* forward.

Sturmflut *f* storm tide.

stürmisch 1. stormy *a. fig;* 2. *(See)* rough; 3. *(schnell)* rapid.

Sturz *m* 1. fall; 2. *com (Kurs)* drop; 3. *(Regierung)* overthrow.

stürzen 1. fall; 2. *(eilen)* rush; 3. *(steil abfallen)* drop abruptly; 4. *com* drop; 5. *sich in etw* ~ throw o.s. into s.th.; *sich auf jdn* ~ pounce on s.o.; 6. *sich in die Arbeit* ~ plunge into work; 7. *(stoßen)* throw.

Sturz|flug *m* nose dive; ~**helm** *m* crash helmet.

Stute *f* mare.

Stütze *f* 1. *tech* support, stay; 2. *(Beistand)* mainstay; aid; 3. *(Pfeiler)* pillar; **s~n** 1. support; 2. *(Mauer)* prop up; 3. *(Behauptung)* base; 4. *sich* ~ *auf* lean upon; *fig* be based on.

stutz|en 1. *(beschneiden)* cut, curtail; 2. *(Haare)* trim; 3. *(zögern)* wonder; become suspicious; ~**ig:** ~ *werden* be puzzled.

Stützpunkt *m* 1. point of support; 2. *mil* base.

Subjekt *n* subject; **s~iv** subjective.

Subskription *f* subscription.

Substanz *f* substance.

subtropisch subtropical.

Subvention *f* subsidy.

Such|aktion *f* search operation; ~**dienst** *m* tracing service; ~**e** *f* search, hunt; *sich auf die* ~ *machen* go and search; *auf der* ~ *nach* in search of; **s~en** 1. look for, search for, seek; 2. ~, *etw zu tun* endeavour to do s.th.; 3. *das Weite* ~ run away.

Sucht *f* 1. greed *(nach* for); 2. *med* addiction (to).

süchtig addicted (to), manic.

Süd|en *m* south; *im* ~ in the south; *im* ~ *von* to the south of; ~**früchte** *pl* tropical fruits *pl;* ~**lage** *f* southern exposure; **s~lich** south(ern); ~**ost(en)** *m* southeast; ~**pol** *m* South Pole; ~**see** *f* South Seas *pl;* ~**west(en)** *m* southwest.

sugge|rieren suggest; **S~stion** *f* suggestion.

Sühne *f* atonement; **s~n** expiate, atone for.

Sülze *f* brawn.

summarisch summary; **S~e** *f* sum, amount.

summen buzz, hum.

summieren 1. sum up; 2. *sich* ~ accumulate.

Sumpf *m* swamp, bog; **s~ig** marshy, swampy.

Sünd|e *f* sin; ~**enbock** *m* scapegoat; ~**er** *m* sinner; **s~haft** 1. sinful; 2. ~ *teuer* awfully expensive; **s~igen** sin (*gegen* against).

Super|(benzin) n super; **~markt** m supermarket.

Suppe f soup; (*Fleischbrühe*) broth, bouillon; **~nfleisch** n boiling meat; **~ngrün** n greens pl; **~nhuhn** n boiling fowl; **~nterrine** f soup tureen; **~nwürfel** m soup cube.

surren 1. (*Insekt*) buzz; 2. (*Maschine*) whir(r).

süß 1. sweet; 2. (*angenehm*) pleasant; **~en** sweeten; **S~igkeiten** pl sweets pl; **~lich** 1. sweetish; 2. *fig* sugary; **~-sauer** sour-sweet; **S~speise** f sweet, *Am* dessert; **S~waren** pl

confectionery; **S~wasser** n freshwater; **S~wein** m dessert wine.

Symbol n symbol; **s~isch** symbolic(al).

Sympa|thie f sympathy; **s~thisch** sympathetic, likable; **s~thisieren** sympathize (*mit* with).

Synagoge f synagogue.

synchronisieren 1. synchronize; 2. *film* dub.

Synthe|se f synthesis; **s~tisch** synthetic(al).

System n 1. system, method; 2. *in ein ~ bringen* systematize; **s~atisch** systematic(al).

Szene f 1. scene; 2. (*Bühne*) stage.

T

Tabak *m* tobacco; **~geschäft** *n* tobacconist's; **~sbeutel** *m* tobacco pouch.
Tabelle *f* 1. table *a. sport;* 2. (*Verzeichnis*) index; 3. (*Liste*) schedule.
Tablett *n* tray; **~e** *f* tablet.
tabu, T~ *n* taboo.
Tachometer *n* speedometer.
Tadel *m* reproach, reprimand; **t~los** irreproachable, impeccable; **t~n** 1. (*bemängeln*) find fault with, blame; 2. (*zurechtweisen*) reproach, rebuke (*wegen* for).
Tafel *f* 1. (*Wand~*) blackboard; 2. (*Anschlag~*) board; 3. (*Hinweis~*) sign; 4. (*Schokolade*) bar; 5. (*Mahlzeit*) dinner.
täfeln (*Decke, Wand*) panel, wainscot.
Tafelsilber *n* silver plate.
Tag *m* 1. day; *jeden ~* every day; *am nächsten ~* next day; *in acht ~en* in a week; *e-s ~es* one day, some day; 2. *am ~e* by day; *den ganzen ~ arbeiten* work all day; *es wird ~* day is breaking; 3. *was für ein ~ ist heute?* what date is it today? 4. *in diesen ~en* nowadays; 5. *guten ~!* how do you do? **~ebuch** *n* diary; **t~elang** 1. lasting for days; 2. day after day; **t~en** 1. *es tagt* it is

dawning; 2. (*Konferenz*) sit (in conference); **~esanbruch** *m: bei ~* at daybreak; **~esgericht** *n* day's menu; **~eslicht** *n* daylight; **~esordnung** *f: auf die ~ setzen* put on the agenda; **~esschau** *f* news *pl;* **~eszeit** *f: zu jeder ~* at any time of the day; **~eszeitung** *f* daily (paper).
täglich every day, daily.
tagsüber during the day.
Tagung *f* meeting, conference, *Am* convention.
Taille *f* waist.
Takt *m* 1. *mus* time, measure; *aus dem ~* off the beat; 2. (*Feingefühl*) tact, delicacy.
Tak|tik *f* tactics *pl;* **t~tisch** tactical.
taktlos tactless; **T~igkeit** *f* tactlessness, indelicacy.
Takt|stock *m* baton; **t~voll** tactful.
Tal *n* valley.
Talent *n* talent, gift (*für etw* for s.th.); **t~iert, t~voll** gifted.
Talg *m* suet.
Tal|kessel *m* hollow; **~sohle** *f fig* time of depression; **~sperre** *f* dam, barrage.
Tang *m bot* seaweed.
Tank *m* tank; **t~en** tank, fill up; **~er** *m* tanker; **~erflot-**

te f tanker fleet; ~**stelle** f service station; ~**wagen** m tank lorry; ~**wart** m service station attendant.
Tanne f fir; ~**nnadel** f fir-needle; ~**nzapfen** m fir-cone.
Tante f aunt.
Tantieme f 1. (Autor) royalty; 2. com bonus.
Tanz m, **t~en** dance.
Tänzer m dancer.
Tanz|fläche f dance-floor; ~**kapelle** f, ~**orchester** n dance-band; ~**schule** f dancing-school; ~**stunde** f dancing-lesson; ~**tee** m tea dance; ~**turnier** n dancing competition.
Tape|te f wallpaper; ~**tenwechsel** m change of scenery; **t~zieren** paper; ~**zierer** m paper-hanger.
tapfer brave, courageous.
Tara f com tare.
Tarif m 1. tariff, rates pl; 2. (Lohn) wage scale.
tarn|en, **T~ung** f camouflage a. fig.

Tasche f 1. pocket; 2. (Hand~) bag, purse; 3. (Reise~) bag; 4. (Akten~) briefcase; ~**nbuch** n paperback, pocket-book; ~**ndieb** m pickpocket; ~**ngeld** n pocket-money; ~**nlampe** f (electric) torch, Am flashlight; ~**nmesser** n pocketknife; ~**nrechner** m pocket calculator; ~**ntuch** n hand-

kerchief; ~**nuhr** f (pocket) watch.
Tasse f cup.
Taste f key; **t~n** 1. feel, grope (nach for); 2. tech (ab~) scan.
Tat f 1. deed, act; 2. (Handeln) action; 3. auf frischer ~ ertappen catch in the very act; 4. in der ~ indeed; ~**bestand** m jur facts pl, state of affairs.
Täter m 1. doer; 2. jur culprit.
tätig 1. active, busy; 2. ~ sein be employed; ~**en** effect, conclude; Geschäfte ~ transact business; **T~keit** f 1. activity; 2. (Arbeit) work, occupation; 3. (Dienst) service; function.
Tat|kraft f energy; **t~kräftig** energetic.
tätlich violent; gegen jdn ~ werden assault s.o.
tätowieren tattoo.
Tat|sache f fact; **t~sächlich** 1. real, actual, factual; 2. (wahrhaftig) true.
Tatze f paw.
Tau 1. m dew; 2. n rope.
taub 1. deaf; 2. (Glieder) numb.
Taube f pigeon, dove; ~**nschlag** m dovecot.
Taub|heit f deafness; **t~stumm** deaf and dumb.
tauch|en 1. dive; 2. (ein~) dip; **T~er** m diver; **T~eranzug** m diving-suit; **T~sieder** m immersion heater.

tauen *es taut* it is thawing.
Taufe *f* baptism; **t~n** baptize, christen.
taug|en be good (*für* for); *es taugt nichts* it's good for nothing; **T~enichts** *m* good-for-nothing; **~lich** 1. suitable (*für, zu* for, to); 2. (*fähig*) capable; 3. *mil* fit; **T~lichkeit** *f* 1. fitness; 2. (*Fähigkeit*) capability.
taumeln stagger.
Tausch *m* exchange; *im ~ gegen* in exchange for; **t~en** trade, swap, exchange.
täusch|en 1. deceive; 2. (*betrügen*) cheat; 3. (*enttäuschen*) disappoint; 4. *sich ~* be mistaken; **~end** (*Ähnlichkeit*) remarkable, striking; **T~ung** *f* 1. deception; 2. (*der Sinne*) illusion; 3. (*Irrtum*) error.
tausend thousand; *einige ~ Exemplare* several thousands of copies; **T~** *n* thousand; **T~stel** *n* millesimal.
Tau|tropfen *m* dew-drop, **~wetter** *n* thawing weather.
Taxe *f* (*Abgabe, Gebühr*) rate, tax, fee.
Taxi *n* cab; **t~eren** estimate, value; **~fahrer** *m* taxi-driver; **~stand** *m* taxi rank.
Tech|nik *f* 1. technology, engineering; 2. (*Verfahren*) technique; **~niker** *m* engineer; **t~nisch** 1. engineering, technical; *~e Universität f*

university of technology; 2. *aus ~en Gründen* for technical reasons.
Teddybär *m* teddy bear.
Tee *m* tea; **~beutel** *m* tea-bag; **~kanne** *f* teapot; **~löffel** *m* teaspoon.
Teer *m*, **t~en** tar.
Tee|service *n* tea-set; **~sieb** *n* tea-strainer; **~tasse** *f* teacup; **~wagen** *m* tea-wagon.
Teich *m* pond.
Teig *m* dough; **~waren** *pl* paste foods *pl.*
Teil *m* 1. part; *zum größten ~* for the most part; 2. (*e-s Volkes*) number; 3. (*Zeitung*) section; 4. (*Anteil*) share; *zu gleichen ~en* in equal shares; **~chen** *n* particle; **t~en** 1. divide; 2. (*trennen*) part; 3. *mit jdm ~* share with s.o.; 4. *sich ~* branch; 5. *sich in etw ~* share s.th.
teilhab|en *irr: an etw ~* participate in s.th.; **T~er** *m com* partner, associate.
Teilnahm|e *f* 1. participation (*an* in); 2. (*Mitarbeit*) cooperation; 3. (*Anteil*) sympathy; 4. (*Beileid*) condolence; **t~slos** 1. indifferent; 2. (*gefühllos*) impassive.
teilnehm|en *irr* 1. take part, participate (*an* in); 2. (*mitarbeiten*) cooperate **T~er** *m* 1. participant; 2. *tele* subscriber; 3. (*Mitglied*) member.

teils 1. in part; 2. ~ ... ~ some ... some, partly ... partly.

Teil|strecke f (Bus) stage; **~stück** n fragment, section; **~ung** f 1. division; 2. (Auf~) partition; **t~weise** partially, in part; ganz oder ~ wholly or in part; **~zahlung** f 1. part payment; 2. auf ~ kaufen buy on the instal(l)ment plan.

Telefon n (tele)phone; am ~ on the phone; ans ~ gehen answer the telephone; **~anruf** m phone call; **~buch** n telephone directory; **~gebühren** pl telephone charges pl; **t~ieren** phone, ring up; **t~isch** by, over the phone; **~nummer** f phone number; **~zelle** f call box.

Telegraf m telegraph; **t~ieren** wire, cable; **t~isch** by wire, by cable.

Telegramm n telegram, wire; **~adresse** f telegraphic address; **~annahme** f telegram acceptance.

Teleskop n telescope.

Teller m plate, dish.

Tempel m temple.

Temperament n 1. temperament; 2. hitziges ~ hot temper; **t~voll** 1. high-spirited; 2. (feurig) passionate.

Temperatur f temperature a. med; **~sturz** m sudden drop in temperature.

Tempo n speed, pace; in langsamem ~ at a slow

pace; bei diesem ~ at this rate.

Tendenz f tendency, trend; **t~iös** tendentious.

Tennis n tennis; **~ball** m tennis-ball; **~platz** m tennis-court; **~schläger** m tennis-racket.

Tenor m tenor.

Teppich m carpet, rug.

Termin m 1. date; e-n ~ anberaumen set a date (für for); 2. (Frist) term; letzter ~ deadline; 3. (Verabredung) appointment; **t~gemäß** in due time; **~kalender** m appointment book.

Terpentin n turpentine.

Terrasse f terrace.

Territorium n territory.

Terror m terror; **t~isieren** terrorize; **~ist** m, **t~istisch** terrorist.

Test m test.

Testament n 1. last will; 2. (Bibel) Testament; **t~arisch** 1. testamentary; 2. ~ verfügen dispose by will; **~seröffnung** f opening of the will; **~svollstrecker** m executor.

teuer 1. expensive, dear, costly; wie ~ ist das? how much is that? 2. (kostbar) precious; 3. fig dear; ~ zu stehen kommen cost dearly.

Teuf|el m devil; **~elskreis** m vicious circle; **t~lisch** devilish, diabolic.

Text m 1. text; 2. (e-s Liedes)

words *pl;* **~er** *m* text writer; copywriter.

Textil|ien *pl* textiles *pl;* **~industrie** *f* textile industry.

Theater *n* theatre; *ins ~ gehen* go to the theatre; **~karte** *f* theatre ticket; **~stück** *n* (stage-)play.

Theke *f* bar, counter.

Thema *n* subject, theme, topic; *beim ~ bleiben* stick to the point.

Theolo|ge *m* theologian; **~gie** *f* theology.

theo|retisch theoretical; **T~rie** *f* theory.

Thermo|meter *n* thermometer; **~sflasche** *f* thermos (bottle); **~stat** *m* thermostat.

These *f* thesis.

Thron *m* throne; **~folger** *m* successor to the throne.

Thunfisch *m* tuna.

ticken tick.

tief 1. *(See)* deep; 2. *(niedrig)* low; 3. *(Farbe)* strong; 4. *fig* profound, sound; *bis ~ in die Nacht* far into the night; 5. *~ atmen* breathe deeply.

Tief *n mete* depression; **~bau** *m* civil engineering; **~e** *f* depth, deepness; **~ebene** *f* lowland; **~flug** *m* low-level flight; **~gang** *m mar* draught; **~garage** *f* basement garage; **t~gekühlt** deep-frozen; **~kühlkost** *f* frozen foods *pl;* **~kühltruhe** *f* deep-freeze; **~see** *f* deep sea.

Tier *n* 1. animal; 2. *fig* brute, beast; **~art** *f* species of animal; **~arzt** *m* veterinary; **~garten** *m* zoo; **~halter** *m* keeper of animals; **~heilkunde** *f* veterinary science; **t~isch** *fig* bestial, brutish; **~kreis(zeichen** *n)* *m* (sign of the) zodiac; **~quälerei** *f* cruelty to animals; **~schutzverein** *m* Society for Prevention of Cruelty to Animals.

Tiger *m* tiger.

tilg|en 1. *(auswischen)* wipe out, strike out; 2. *com* pay off; amortize; **T~ung** *f com* discharge, amortization.

Tinte *f* ink; **~nfaß** *n* ink-pot; **~nfisch** *m* cuttlefish, octopus.

Tip *m* 1. tip; 2. *(Wink)* clue, hint.

tipp|en 1. *(berühren)* tip, hint; 2. *(wetten)* tip; 3. *(auf der Maschine)* type; **T~fehler** *m* typing error.

Tisch *m* 1. table; *bei ~* at table; *den ~ decken* set the table; 2. *(Mahlzeit) zu ~ gehen* go to table; **~bein** *n* table-leg; **~decke** *f* table-cloth; **~lampe** *f* lamp.

Tischler *m* joiner; **~ei** *f* joiner's workshop.

Tisch|ordnung *f* seating order; **~platte** *f* table-top; **~rede** *f* after-dinner speech; **~tennis** *n* table tennis; **~tuch** *n* table-cloth;

~**wein** m table-wine; ~**zeit** f: zur ~ at lunchtime.

Titel m title; ~**blatt** n title-page.

Toastbrot n toast.

tob|en 1. romp; 2. (See) rage, storm; ~**süchtig** raving mad.

Tochter f daughter; ~**firma** f subsidiary.

Tod m death, decease; ~**esanzeige** f obituary; ~**esfall** m: im ~ in the event of death; ~**eskampf** m agony; ~**esopfer** n casualty; ~**esstrafe** f capital punishment; ~**esursache** f cause of death; ~**esurteil** n death sentence.

tödlich 1. mortal, fatal, deadly; 2. ~ verunglücken be killed in an accident.

todmüde dead tired.

Toilette f 1. (Kleidung) toilet; 2. (Abort) lavatory, toilet, W. C., (öffentlich) public convenience; ~**napier** n toilet-paper.

tole|rant tolerant (gegen of); **T~ranz** f tolerance (gegen for, of); ~**rieren** tolerate.

toll 1. (verrückt) mad, crazy; 2. (großartig) fantastic; ~**kühn** foolhardy; **T~wut** f rabies.

Tomate f tomato; ~**nmark** n tomato-pulp; ~**nsuppe** f tomato-soup.

Ton m 1. geol clay; 2. mus tone, sound; den ~ angeben give the pitch; 3. (Redewei-

se) in barschem ~ in a harsh tone; 4. der gute ~ good form; 5. (Betonung) accent, stress; 6. (Farbe) colour, shade, tone; ~**abnehmer** m pick-up; ~**art** f mus key; ~**band** n tape; auf ~ aufnehmen tape-record; ~**bandgerät** n tape recorder.

tönen 1. sound, ring; 2. (färben) tinge.

Ton|fall m intonation, accent; ~**film** m sound film; ~**leiter** f mus scale.

Tonne f 1. (Gewicht) ton; 2. (Faß) tun; (klein) barrel.

Topf m 1. pot; 2. (zum Kochen) saucepan.

Töpfer m potter; ~**ei** f pottery; ~**ware** f ceramics pl, earthenware.

Topflappen m pot holder.

Tor 1. n gate, door; 2. (Fußball) ein ~ schießen score a goal; 3. m fool; ~**einfahrt** f gateway.

Torf m peat, turf; ~**mull** m peat mould.

Torheit f foolishness, silliness.

töricht foolish, silly.

torkeln reel, stagger.

Torso m torso a. fig.

Torte f fancy cake; ~**nplatte** f cake plate.

Torwart m goalkeeper.

tosen roar, thunder.

tot 1. dead; er ist schon lange ~ he has been dead for a long time; 2. (verstorben)

late; 3. *(leblos)* lifeless;
4. *(taub)* numb.
total total, complete;
T~ausverkauf *m* clearance sale; **T~schaden** *m*
total wreckage.
töten kill, put to death.
Toten|gräber *m* gravedigger; **~kopf** *m* death's head.
Toter *m* dead man.
tot|geboren still-born; **~lachen,** *sich* split o.'s sides
with laughter; **~sagen***: jdn
~* declare s.o. dead;
T~schlag *m* manslaughter;
~schlagen *irr* kill *(jdn s.o.);*
T~schläger *m* life-preserver; **~stellen,** *sich* feign
death.
Tötung *f* homicide; *fahrlässige ~* involuntary manslaughter.
Tour *f* 1. *(Ausflug)* trip, excursion; 2. *tech* turn;
3. *(Strecke)* way; 4. *(Trick)*
trick; 5. *in e-r ~* at a stretch.
Tou|rismus *m* tourism; **~rist**
m tourist; **~ristenklasse** *f*
tourist class.
Trab *m* trot.
Trabantenstadt *f* satellite
town.
traben trot.
Tracht *f* 1. *(Kleidung)* traditional costume; 2. *(fig) e-e ~
Prügel* a sound thrashing.
trachten 1. endeavour; 2. *(erstreben)* aspire *(nach* to),
strive *(nach* for); 3. *jdm
nach dem Leben ~* seek
s.o.'s life.

trächtig *(Tier)* pregnant.
traditionell traditional.
Trag|bahre *f* stretcher;
t~bar 1. *tech* portable; 2. *fig*
bearable.
träge idle, laze, sluggish.
tragen *irr* 1. carry; 2. *(hinbringen)* take; 3. *(Kleider)*
wear; 4. *(haben)* have, bear;
5. *(stützen)* support; 6. *(aushalten)* take; 7. *(Unglück)*
endure; 8. *(Zinsen)* yield;
9. *(tragfähig sein)* hold.
Träger *m* 1. porter; 2. *tech*
support; 3. *(Wäsche)* strap;
4. *fig (e-r Idee)* supporter;
5. *(Vermittler)* vehicle;
~rakete *f* launch vehicle.
tragfähig load-carrying;
T~keit *f* carrying power,
safe load.
Tragfläche *f aero* wing.
Trägheit *f* laziness, idleness.
Tra|gik *f* tragedy; **t~gisch**
tragic(al); **~gödie** *f* tragedy.
Tragweite *f* 1. range, reach;
2. *fig* importance, consequence.
Trai|ner *m* trainer, coach;
t~nieren train *(für, zu* for);
~ning *n* training; **~ningsanzug** *m* track-suit.
Traktor *m* tractor.
trampeln trample.
tram|pen hitchhike; **T~per**
m hitchhiker.
Tran *m* train-oil.
tranchieren carve.
Träne *f* tear; *in ~n ausbrechen* burst into tears;
~ngas *n* tear-gas.

Tränk|e f watering-place;
t~en 1. water; 2. (durch~)
soak.

Transfer m com transfer;
t~ieren transfer (an to).

Transformator m el transformer.

Transistor m transistor.

Transit m transit.

Transplan|tation f grafting;
t~tieren graft.

Transport m transport, carriage; **t~fähig** transportable; **~flugzeug** n transport aircraft; **t~ieren** transport, carry, convey; **~kosten** pl transport charges pl, carriage; **~unternehmen** n carriers pl; **~versicherung** f transport insurance.

Trapez n 1. (Turnen) trapeze; 2. math trapezium.

Traube f 1. grape; 2. (Büschel) bunch; **~nlese** f vintage; **~nsaft** m grape juice; **~nzucker** m grape-sugar.

trauen 1. (Brautpaar) marry, wed; 2. jdm ~ trust s.o.;
3. (glauben) believe; 4. sich
~ dare, venture.

Trauer f 1. grief, sorrow;
2. (Trauern) mourning;
~fall m death; **t~n** 1. um
jdn ~ mourn s.o., grieve for
s.o.; 2. (Trauerkleider tragen) be in mourning; **~spiel**
n tragedy; **~weide** f
weeping willow.

träufeln drip.

traulich cosy, homely.

Traum m dream; wie im ~
like in a dream.

träu|men dream; von jdm ~
dream about s.o.; **~merisch**
dreamy.

traurig 1. sad, sorrowful;
2. (betrübt) upset, grieved;
3. (trostlos) deplorable,
lamentable.

Trau|ring m wedding-ring;
~ung f marriage, wedding;
~zeuge m witness to a
marriage.

treff|en irr 1. (Schlag) hit,
strike; 2. (verletzen) hurt,
wound; 3. (heimsuchen)
strike, afflict; 4. (begegnen)
meet; 5. (antreffen) find;
6. Maßnahmen ~ take
measures; e-e Auswahl ~
make a selection; 7. auf etw
~ strike on s.th.; 8. es trifft
sich gut it is convenient;
T~en n 1. meeting; 2. sport
contest; **~end** 1. fitting, appropriate; 2. (Bild) well-
-done; **T~er** m 1. hit;
2. (Los) win; **~lich** excellent; **T~punkt** m
meeting-place.

Treib|eis n floating ice; **t~en**
irr 1. drive; 2. (antreiben)
power; 3. (mit sich führen)
drift; 4. zur Eile ~ rush;
5. jdn dazu ~ urge s.o.;
6. (Blätter) put forth, sprout;
7. (Sport) do; 8. etw zu weit
~ carry s.th. too far;
9. (Floß) drift; **~en** n activity, hustle and bustle;
t~end: ~e Kraft driving

force; **~haus** n hothouse; **~jagd** f battue; **~sand** m quicksand; **~stoff** m fuel.

trenn|en 1. separate, divide, part; 2. *(unterscheiden)* distinguish; 3. *sich von jdm ~* separate from s.o.; **T~ung** f separation, division; **T~wand** f partition.

Treppe f staircase, stairs pl; *die ~ hinaufgehen* go upstairs; **~ngeländer** n banisters pl; **~nhaus** n staircase; **~nstufe** f step.

Tresor m safe.

treten irr 1. *(mit dem Fuß)* kick; 2. *(die Füße setzen)* step, walk; 3. *(sich hinstellen)* go and stand; *auf die Seite ~* step aside; *in den Hintergrund ~* become insignificant; 4. *(rücken)* move; 5. *(hervorkommen)* come; 6. *(eintreten)* enter; 7. *jdn auf den Fuß ~* tread on s.o.'s foot.

treu 1. faithful, loyal; 2. *(ergeben)* devoted; 3. *e-r Sache ~ sein* be true to s.th.; **T~e** f 1. *(Gesinnung)* loyalty; 2. *(gegenseitig)* fidelity, faithfulness; **T~händer** m trustee, fiduciary; **~los** disloyal, faithless *(gegen* to).

Tribüne f 1. *(Redner~)* platform; 2. *(Zuschauer)* stand.

Trichter m funnel.

Trick m trick, ruse; **~film** m trick film, cartoon.

Trieb m 1. *bot* sprout; 2. *(Drang)* urge, desire,

drive, impulse; **~feder** f mainspring; **~werk** n engine, driving unit.

triefen irr 1. drip; 2. *(tröpfeln)* trickle, ooze.

triftig 1. *(stichhaltig)* valid; 2. *(überzeugend)* plausible, convincing.

trink|en irr drink, have; *Tee ~* have tea; *aus der Flasche ~* drink from the bottle; *auf jdn ~* drink to s.o.; **T~er** m drinker; **T~geld** n: *jdm ein ~ geben* tip s.o.; **T~spruch** m toast; **T~wasser** n drinking-water.

trippeln trip.

Tripper m med gonorrh(o)ea.

Tritt m 1. *(Schritt)* footstep, kick, pace; 2. *(Stufe)* step; **~brett** n *(Zug)* footboard.

Triumph m, **t~ieren** triumph *(über* over).

trocken 1. dry a. fig; 2. *im T~en sein* be out of the rain; **T~heit** f 1. dryness; 2. *(Dürre)* drought; **~legen** *(Land)* drain.

trocknen dry, become dry.

Troddel f tassel.

Tröd|el m junk, trash; **t~eln** fig dawdle; **~ler** m 1. second-hand dealer; 2. fig slowcoach.

Trog m 1. trough; 2. *(Bottich)* vat.

Tromm|el f drum; **~elfell** n anat eardrum; **t~eln** drum; **~ler** m drummer.

Trompete f trumpet; **~r** m trumpeter.

Tropen *pl* tropics.
tropfen drip, fall in drops.
Tropf|en *m* 1. drop;
2. *(Schweiß~)* bead;
~**steinhöhle** *f* stalactite cavern.
Trophäe *f* trophy.
tropisch tropical.
Trost *m* comfort, consolation.
tröst|en 1. comfort, console;
2. *sich* ~ take comfort;
~**lich** comforting, consoling.
trost|los 1. *(öde)* desolate;
2. *(jämmerlich)* miserable;
T~preis *m* consolation prize.
Trott *m* 1. trot; 2. *fig* routine;
~**el** *m* fool, idiot; **t~en** trot, jog along.
trotz in spite of, notwithstanding; ~ *allem* for all that.
Trotz *m* 1. defiance; *jdm* ~ *bieten* bid defiance to s.o.;
2. *(boshaft)* spite, malice.
trotzdem nevertheless, still, all the same.
trotz|en defy, brave; ~**ig**
1. sulky; 2. *(Antwort)* defiant.
trübe 1. cloudy; 2. *(Glas)* opaque; 3. *(Augen)* dull;
4. *(Licht)* dim; 5. *(Himmel)* overcast; 6. *(Gedanken)* gloomy.
Trubel *m* bustle.
trüb|en 1. make cloudy, trouble; 2. *(Blick)* blur, dim;
3. *(Freude)* spoil, darken;
4. *(Urteil)* obscure; 5. *der*

Himmel trübt sich the sky is becoming overcast; **T~sal** *f* sorrow, grief; ~**selig** gloomy, melancholy.
Trüffel *f* truffle.
trüg|en *irr* deceive; *der Schein trügt* appearances are deceptive; ~**erisch**
1. *(Person)* deceitful;
2. *(Glück)* deceptive;
3. *(Hoffnung)* false.
Trugschluß *m* fallacy.
Truhe *f* 1. chest; 2. *radio* cabinet, console.
Trümmer *pl* 1. ruins *pl;*
2. *(Schutt)* debris; 3. *in* ~ *gehen* go to pieces; ~**haufen** *m* heap of rubble.
Trumpf *m* trump *a. fig.*
Trunk *m* drink; ~**enbold** *m* drunkard; ~**enheit** *f* drunkenness *(am Steuer* at the wheel); ~**sucht** *f* alcoholism.
Trupp *m* 1. troop, band;
2. *(Arbeiter)* gang; ~**e** *f*
1. *theat* company; 2. *mil* troop; ~**enübungsplatz** *m* training area.
Trut|hahn *m* turkey;
~**henne** *f* turkey-hen.
tschechisch Czech.
Tschechoslowak|e *m* Czechoslovak(ian); ~**ei** *f* Czechoslovakia.
Tsetsefliege *f* tsetse-fly.
Tube *f* tube.
Tuberkulose *f* tuberculosis.
Tuch *n* 1. *(Stoff)* cloth, fabric; 2. *(Hals~)* scarf, shawl.
tüchtig 1. *(fähig)* capable,

competent; 2. *(gut)* proficient, be good; 3. ~ *arbeiten* work hard.

Tück|e *f* 1. malice; 2. *(Hinterlist)* perfidy; **t~isch** malicious, spiteful.

Tugend *f* virtue; **t~haft** virtuous.

Tüll *m* tulle.

Tulpe *f* tulip.

tummeln, *sich* romp, splash.

Tümpel *m* slough, marshy pool.

Tumult *m* tumult, riot.

tun *irr* 1. do; *jdm etw zu ~ geben* give s.o. s.th. to do; 2. *(verrichten) e-e Arbeit ~* do work; 3. *(genügen)* do; 4. *nichts mit jdm zu ~ haben* have nothing to do with s.o.; 5. *jdm Gutes ~* do s.o. a favour; 6. *zu ~ haben* have work to do; 7. *mit jdm zu ~ haben* have dealings with s.o.; 8. *~, als ob* behave as if, pretend; 9. *es tut mir leid* I am sorry; *Sie ~ gut daran zu gehen* you had better go; **T~** *n* deeds *pl*, acts *pl*, activities *pl*.

Tünche *f*, **t~n** whitewash.

Tunnel *m* tunnel.

tupfen dab.

Tür *f* 1. door; *vor jds ~* at s.o.'s doorstep; 2. *jdn vor die ~ setzen* turn s.o. out.

Turban *m* turban.

Turbine *f* turbine.

Türhüter *m* doorkeeper.

Türk|e *m* Turk; **~ei** *f* Turkey; **t~isch** Turkish.

Türklinke *f* door handle.

Turm *m* 1. tower; 2. *(Kirch~)* steeple; 3. *(Schach)* castle.

turn|en do gymnastics; **T~en** *n* gymnastics *sing;* **T~er** *m* gymnast; **T~gerät** *n* gymnastic apparatus; **T~halle** *f* gym(nasium); **T~hemd** *n* gym vest; **T~hose** *f* gym shorts *pl.*

Turnier *n* tournament.

Turnschuhe *pl* gym shoes *pl.*

Tür|schild *n* door-plate; **~schloß** *n* (door-)lock.

Tusch *m* fanfare.

Tusche *f* Indian ink.

tuscheln whisper.

Tüte *f* paper bag, cornet.

Typ *m* type, kind; **~ennummer** *f* model number.

Typhus *m med* typhoid fever.

typisch typical *(für* of).

Tyrann *m* tyrant; **~ei** *f* tyranny; **t~isch** tyrannical.

U

U-Bahn *f* underground (railway), *(London)* tube, *Am* subway.

übel 1. bad, nasty; 2. *(Person)* nasty, wicked, evil; 3. *(Streich)* mean; 4. *(Geruch)* foul; 5. *(Laune)* filthy; 6. *mir ist ~* I feel sick; 7. *es geht ihm ~* he is in a bad situation; 8. *nicht ~* quite well; 9. *~ gelaunt sein* be ill-humoured; **Ü~** *n* 1. evil; *das kleinere ~* the lesser evil; 2. *(Mißstand)* grievance; **Ü~keit** *f* sickness, nausea; **~nehmen** *irr: etw ~* take s.th. badly; *jdm etw ~* be offended at s.o. for s.th.; **~riechend** evil-smelling; **Ü~stand** *m* grievance; **Ü~täter** *m* 1. wrongdoer; 2. *(Verbrecher)* culprit.

üben 1. practise; 2. *(Gedächtnis)* exercise, train; 3. *sich ~* school o.s.

über I *prp* 1. *(oberhalb)* above, over; *zehn Grad ~ Null* ten degrees above zero; 2. *(jenseits)* across; 3. *~ dem Durchschnitt* above average; 4. *(infolge von)* over, on account of; 5. *~ die Straße gehen* go across the street; 6. *~ etw hinaus* beyond, past; *das geht ~ meine Kräfte* that is beyond my strength;

7. *(durch)* through, from; 8. *~ die Autobahn kommen* come by expressway; 9. *~ Nacht bleiben* stay for the night; 10. *(betreffend)* *~ etw sprechen* talk about s.th.; *ein Buch ~* a book on; 11. *(im Wert von)* for; **II** *adv* 12. *(während)* long; *den ganzen Tag ~* all day long; 13. *(mehr als)* more than, over; 14. *~ und ~* all over.

überall everywhere, all over.

überaltert superannuated.

überanstrengen, *sich* strain o.s.

überarbeit|en 1. *(Buch)* revise; 2. *(verbessern)* touch up; 3. *sich ~* overwork o.s.; **~et** revised, overworked.

überaus extremely.

überbacken gratinate.

überbelichtet overexposed.

überbevölkert overpopulated.

überbewertet overestimated.

überbieten *irr* 1. *(Auktion)* outbid; 2. *fig* surpass.

Überbleibsel *n* leftover; remnant *a. fig.*

Überblick *m* 1. *fig* survey *(über* of); 2. *(Zusammenfassung)* summary; 3. *den ~ verlieren* lack perspective; **ü~en** survey *a. fig.*

überbringe|n *irr* deliver; **Ü~r** *m* bringer, deliverer.

überbrücken *fig* bridge.

überdauern outlast.

überdies besides, moreover.

Über|druß *m* weariness; **ü~drüssig**: *e-r Sache ~ werden* be weary of s.th.

übereilt rash, overhasty.

übereinander one upon another.

übereinkommen *irr* agree (*über* on); **Ü~** *n* agreement, understanding.

übereinstimm|en 1. *mit jdm ~* agree with s.o.; 2. *mit etw ~* correspond with s.th., be identical with s.th.; **~end** 1. corresponding, concurrent; identical; 2. *~ mit* in accordance with; **Ü~ung** *f* accord, concurrence; *in ~ mit* in agreement with.

über|fahren *irr* 1. (*Person*) run over; 2. (*Signal*) go through; **überfahren** *irr* take across.

Überfahrt *f* crossing (*über e-n Fluß* a river).

Überfall *m* raid, hold-up; **ü~en** *irr* 1. (*e-e Bank*) hold up; 2. *mil* assault, invade.

überfällig overdue, missing.

Überfallkommando *n* flying squad.

überfliegen *irr* 1. fly over; 2. *fig* glance over.

überfließen *irr* overflow, run over.

überflügeln *fig* outstrip.

Überfluß *m* 1. abundance

(*an* of); *im ~ haben* have plenty of s.th.; 2. (*Wohlstand*) opulence.

überflüssig superfluous, unnecessary.

über|fluten 1. overflow, flood; 2. *fig* inundate.

überfordern: *jdn ~* overtax s.o.

überführ|en transport, transfer; **Ü~ung** *f* 1. transport; 2. (*Straße*) overpass.

überfüllt overcrowded, jammed.

Übergabe *f* delivery.

Übergang *m* 1. passage; 2. (*Straße*) crossing; 3. *fig* transition, change; **~szeit** *f* transition period.

übergeben *irr* 1. *jdm etw ~* deliver s.th. to s.o., hand s.th. over to s.o.; 2. *sich ~* vomit.

'**übergehen** *irr* 1. *auf jdn ~* pass over to s.o.; 2. *zu etw ~* proceed to s.th.; 3. *zu jdm ~* go over to s.o.; 4. *~ in* change to; **über'gehen** *irr* (*übersehen*) pass over, ignore, overlook.

Übergewicht *n* 1. overweight; 2. *das ~ bekommen* overbalance; 3. *fig* preponderance.

übergreifen *irr*: *auf etw ~* spread to s.th.

Übergriff *m* encroachment (*auf* on).

überhaupt 1. (*eigentlich*) actually, at all; 2. (*außerdem*) anyway; 3. *~ nicht* not at all; *~ nichts* nothing whatever.

überheblich overbearing, arrogant.

überhol|en 1. pass, overtake; 2. *tech* overhaul; 3. *Ü~ verboten* no overtaking; *~t fig* out-of-date.

überhören 1. not to hear, miss; 2. *(absichtlich)* ignore.

überkochen boil over.

überladen *irr* 1. *(Auto)* overload; 2. overburden (*mit Arbeit* with work).

überlassen *irr: jdm etw ~* leave s.o. s.th.

überlast|et overburdened; **Ü~ung** *f* 1. overcharge; 2. *fig* overwork, stress.

überlaufen *irr* 1. boil over; 2. *(übergehen)* go over (*zu* to); **über'laufen** *adj* overcrowded.

Überläufer *m* deserter.

überleben survive, outlive; **Ü~der** *m* survivor.

überleg|en I *v* 1. think over, consider; *ohne zu ~* without reflection; 2. *(nachdenken)* reflect, deliberate, ponder; **II** *adj* 3. superior (*an in*); *sich ~ fühlen* feel superior; *jdm ~ sein* be better than s.o.; 4. *(gelassen)* serene; **Ü~enheit** *f* superiority; *~t* deliberate; **Ü~ung** *f* consideration, reflexion; *bei näherer ~* on second thoughts.

überliefer|t traditional; **Ü~ung** *f* tradition.

Über|maß *n* excess (*an of*);

im ~ in excess; **ü~mäßig** excessive, immoderate.

übermitteln transmit.

übermorgen the day after tomorrow.

übermüdet overtired.

übernächst: *~e Woche* the week after next.

übernachten stay overnight.

Übernahme *f* acceptance.

übernatürlich supernatural.

übernehmen *irr* 1. take over (*von jdm* from s.o.); 2. *(Verantwortung)* take (on); 3. *(besorgen)* deal; 4. *sich ~* overdo (*bei etw* s.th.), take on too much.

überprüfen 1. *(Frage)* examine, consider, study; 2. *(kontrollieren)* inspect, scrutinize.

überqueren cross.

überragen 1. *jdn ~* tower over s.o.; 2. *etw ~* rise above s.th., overtop s.th.; *~d* outstanding, prominent.

überrasch|en surprise; *~end* 1. surprising; 2. *(unerwartet)* unexpected; **Ü~ung** *f* surprise.

überreden persuade, talk into.

überreichen hand over.

Überrest *m* 1. remains *pl*, relics *pl*; 2. *pl (Essen)* leftovers.

überrumpeln take unawares.

überrunden *sport* lap.

überschätzen overestimate.

überschauen overlook.

Überschlag *m* estimate.

'**überschlagen** *irr (Beine)* cross; **über'schlagen** *irr* 1. *(Seite)* skip; 2. *(berechnen)* calculate; 3. *(Auto)* sich ~ overturn; 4. *(Stimme)* break.

überschreiten *irr* 1. cross; 2. *(Zeit)* overrun; 3. *(Termin, Geschwindigkeit)* exceed.

Überschrift *f* heading, title.

Überschuß *m* 1. surplus; 2. *(Gewinn)* profit.

überschwemm|en inundate, flood; **Ü~ung** *f* inundation, flood.

überschwenglich effusive.

Übersee *f* overseas *pl; nach* ~ *gehen* go overseas; **ü~isch** overseas; transoceanic.

übersehen *irr* 1. overlook; 2. *(nicht beachten)* ignore; 3. *(vergessen)* omit, forget.

übersenden *irr* send, consign.

über'setzen translate *(in into; aus from)*; '**übersetz|en** ferry over; **Ü~er** *m* translator; **Ü~ung** *f* 1. translation *(aus from; in into)*; 2. *tech* gear; **Ü~ungsbüro** *n* translation agency.

Übersicht *f* 1. general view; 2. *die* ~ *verlieren* lose control; 3. *(Aufstellung)* outline, review, summary; **ü~lich** 1. easy to survey; 2. *(klar)* clear, distinct.

überspannt extravagant, eccentric, exaggerated.

'**überspringen** *irr* 1. *von etw*

~ jump from s.th.; 2. *(Funke)* spring over; **über'springen** *irr* 1. *(Zaun)* jump; 2. *(Seite)* skip.

'**überstehen** *irr (vorstehen)* project; **über'stehen** *irr* 1. *(Krankheit)* recover, get over; 2. *(Gefahr)* weather, survive.

übersteigen *irr* 1. climb over, cross; 2. *fig* exceed, go beyond.

überstimmen outvote.

Überstunden *pl* overtime.

überstürz|en 1. rush into; 2. *sich* ~ follow in rapid succession; **~t** overhasty, precipitate.

Übertrag *m com* amount brought forward; **ü~bar** 1. transferable *(auf* to); 2. *med* catching, contagious; 3. *com* negotiable; **ü~en** *irr* 1. transfer *(auf* to); 2. *(Bereich)* apply; 3. *(senden)* broadcast; 4. *jur* transfer, assign; delegate; 5. *(Sprache)* translate; 6. *med* transplant, transfuse; 7. *sich* ~ be communicated to s,o.; **~ung** *f* 1. transcription; translation; 2. *(Sendung)* broadcast; 3. *jur* assignment, transfer; 4. *med* transmission, grafting, transplantation, transfusion.

übertreffen *irr* 1. outdo, outstrip; 2. *(Bedeutung)* surpass, exceed.

übertreib|en *irr* 1. overdo;

2. *(Bericht)* exaggerate;
Ü~ung *f* exaggeration.
'**übertreten** *irr* 1. *(Fluß)*
overflow; 2. *(Partei)* go
over; 3. *(konvertieren)* convert; **über'treten** *irr (Gesetz)* break, violate, infringe;
Ü~ung *f* violation, infringement.
übertrieben exaggerated.
überwach|en supervise;
Ü~ung *f* supervision.
überwältigen 1. *jdn ~* overpower s.o.; 2. *fig* overwhelm; **~d** overwhelming.
überweis|en *irr* 1. *(Geld)*
remit, transfer; 2. *(Patient)*
refer; **Ü~ung** *f* remittance.
'**überwerfen** *irr (Mantel)*
wrap round o.'s shoulders;
über'werfen *irr: sich ~* fall
out *(mit jdm* with s.o.).
überwiegen *irr* outweigh;
~d predominant, preponderant.
überwinden *irr* 1. overcome;
2. *sich ~* bring o.s. to.
überwintern winter, hibernate.
Über|zahl *f* majority, superiority; **ü~zählig** surplus.
überzeug|en 1. convince;
2. *sich von etw ~* persuade
o.s. of s.th.; **~end** convincing, persuasive; **~t** convinced (*von* of); **Ü~ung** *f*
conviction.
'**überziehen** *irr (Kleid)* put
on; **über'ziehen** *irr* 1. *(mit
Stoff)* cover, line; 2. *tech*
plate; 3. *ein Bett ~* put clean

linen on; 4. *(Konto)* overdraw.
Überzug *m* 1. *(Bett)* cover,
case; 2. *tech* coating.
üblich 1. customary, usual;
2. *es ist allgemein ~* it is a
common practice.
U-Boot *n* submarine.
übrig 1. left over, remaining;
2. *(andere)* other; 3. *(weiter)*
further; 4. *haben Sie Zeit
für mich ~?* can you spare
me a few minutes? 5. *nichts
~ haben für jdn* think little
of s.o.; 6. *die ~en* the rest;
7. *im ~en* for the rest;
~bleiben *irr* 1. be left, remain; 2. *es blieb mir nichts
anderes übrig* I had no
other choice; **~ens** by the
way, incidentally; **~lassen**
irr 1. leave; 2. *viel zu wünschen ~* leave much to be
desired.
Übung *f* 1. practice, experience; *aus der ~ sein* be out
of practice; 2. *(Probe)* exercise.
Ufer *n* 1. *(Fluß)* bank; 2. *(See,
Meer)* shore; **u~los** *fig*
boundless; **~mauer** *f* quay.
Ufo *n* unidentified flying objekt, UFO.
Uhr *f* 1. clock; 2. *(Taschen~)*
watch; 3. *wieviel ~ ist es?*
what time is it? *es ist 12 ~* it
is 12 o'clock; **~macher** *m*
watch-maker; **~zeiger** *m*
hand.
Ulk *m* fun; **u~ig** funny.
Ulme *f* elm.

Ultra|kurzwelle f very high frequency, VHF; **~schall** m ultrasound; **u~violett** ultraviolett.

um I prp 1. (örtlich) around; 2. (zeitlich) about, at; 3. (für) for; 4. (in bezug auf) about; 5. (wegen) for; ~ Geld spielen play for money; 6. ~ so mehr all the more; **II** ~ ... willen for the sake; **III** conj: ~ zu in order to; **IV** adv: ~ und ~ all around, completely.

umarmen embrace.

umbauen rebuild, reconstruct.

umbilden 1. remodel, reshape; 2. pol reshuffle.

umbinden irr (Schürze) put on.

umblättern turn over.

umbringen irr kill, murder.

umdreh|en 1. turn; 2. (verdrehen) twist; 3. sich ~ turn round; **U~ung** f rotation.

umfallen irr fall down.

Umfang m 1. (Kreis) circumference; 2. (Volumen) size, volume; 3. (räumlich) dimension; 4. (Ausmaß) extent; **u~reich** 1. extensive; 2. (dick) voluminous.

umfassen 1. clasp; 2. (umarmen) embrace; 3. (enthalten) include, contain; **~d** extensive, comprehensive.

umform|en transform, remodel; **U~er** m el transformer.

Umfrage f 1. inquiry; 2. (Meinungs~) opinion poll.

Umgang m dealings pl; mit jdm ~ haben associate with s.o.

umgänglich sociable.

Umgangs|formen pl manners pl; **~sprache** f colloquial language.

umgeb|en irr surround, enclose; **U~ung** f surroundings pl, environs pl.

Umgegend f environs pl.

'umgehen irr 1. (verbreiten) go round; 2. (spuken) haunt; 3. mit jdm ~ deal with s.o.; mit etw ~ use s.th.; **um'geh|en** irr 1. by-pass; 2. (vermeiden) avoid, evade; 3. (Gesetz) get round; **U~ungsstraße** f by-pass.

umgekehrt 1. reverse; 2. (entgegengesetzt) opposite, reverse; 3. (dagegen) on the other hand.

umgestalten alter, modify.

umgraben irr dig up.

Umhang m cape.

umher around, about; **~irren** wander about.

Umkehr f return; **u~en** 1. turn back; 2. (Tasche) turn upside down (etw s.th.).

umkippen turn, tip over.

umkleide|n, sich change (o.'s clothes); **U~raum** m dressing-room.

umkommen irr 1. lose o.'s life; 2. (Tier) perish; 3. (Nahrungsmittel) spoil, go off.

Umkreis m: im ~ von within

a radius of; **u~en** 1. circle round; 2. *astr* revolve round.

umladen *irr* transship.

Umlage *f* rate, levy.

Umlauf *m* 1. im ~ sein be in circulation; 2. in ~ setzen spread (*ein Gerücht* a rumour); 3. (*Schreiben*) circular; **~bahn** *f* orbit; **~zeit** *f* *astr* orbital period.

umlegen 1. (*verteilen*) apportion, distribute; 2. (*e-e Straße*) divert; 3. (*umbiegen*) turn down; 4. (*umkippen*) tilt; 5. (*töten*) kill.

umleit|en divert, detour; **U~ung** *f* deviation, detour, by-pass.

'**umpflanzen** transplant; **um'pflanzen** surround with trees.

umquartieren remove to other quarters.

umrahmen frame.

umrechn|en convert (*in* into); **U~ungskurs** *m* rate of exchange.

'**umreißen** *irr* pull down; **um'reißen** *irr* (*Plan*) outline, sketch.

umringen gather round.

Umriß *m* outline.

umrühren stir up.

umsatteln change o.'s profession.

Umsatz *m com* turnover, sales *pl.*

umschalten 1. *el* switch over; 2. *tech* shift.

Umschau *f:* ~ *halten* look around; **u~en,** sich look around.

Umschlag *m* 1. (*Brief*) envelope; 2. (*Buch*) jacket; 3. *med* compress; 4. (*Witterung*) change; **u~en** *irr* 1. (*Seite*) turn over; 2. *com* (*Güter*) handle; 3. (*Wind*) change; 4. (*Kragen*) turn down; 5. (*Stimmung*) change.

'**umschreiben** *irr* 1. rewrite; 2. *jur* transfer; **um'schreib|en** *irr* paraphrase; **U~ung** *f* paraphrase, circumlocution.

umschulen retrain.

Umschweife *pl: ohne ~* bluntly, directly.

Umschwung *m* 1. change, reversal; 2. *pol* revolution.

umsehen, sich *irr* 1. look around; 2. (*zurück~*) look back.

umsetzen 1. *com* sell; 2. *in die Tat* ~ translate into action.

Umsicht *f* circumspection; **u~ig** circumspect, prudent.

umsonst 1. free of charge, gratis; 2. (*vergeblich*) in vain.

Umstand *m* circumstance.

Umstände *pl* 1. (*Lage*) conditions; *unter ~n* possibly; *unter allen ~n* at all events; *unter keinen ~n* under no circumstances; 2. *in anderen ~n sein* be expecting; 3. ~ *machen* cause inconvenience.

umständlich 1. intricate; 2. *(weitschweifig)* long-winded; 3. *(schwerfällig)* ponderous, fussy.

Umstandskleid *n* maternity dress.

umsteigen *irr (Zug)* change.

umstellen 1. rearrange; 2. *(Fabrik)* convert; 3. *sich ~* adapt, adjust o.s. (to); **um'stellen** surround.

umstimmen: *jdn ~* make s.o. change his mind.

umstoßen *irr* 1. overturn; 2. *(Urteil)* reverse.

umstritten controversial.

Umsturz *m* overthrow.

Umtausch *m* exchange; **u~en** change *(für* for).

umwälzend revolutionary.

umwandeln change, transform.

Umweg *m* 1. detour; 2. *auf ~en* in a roundabout way.

Umwelt *f* environment; **u~freundlich** ecologically, beneficial; **~schützer** *m* environmentalist; **~verschmutzung** *f* environmental pollution.

umwenden, *sich irr* turn round.

umwerfen *irr* 1. knock over, overthrow; 2. *fig (Plan)* upset; **~d** fantastic.

umwickeln *(einwickeln)* wrap up in.

umziehen *irr* 1. move *(nach* to); 2. *sich ~* change (o.'s clothes).

Umzug *m* 1. *pol* demonstration; 2. *(Wohnung)* removal.

unabhängig independent; **U~keit** *f* independence.

unabkömmlich indispensable.

unabsichtlich unintentional.

unachtsam careless.

unanfechtbar incontestable.

unangebracht inappropriate.

unangenehm disagreeable, unpleasant.

unannehmbar unacceptable; **U~lichkeiten** *pl* inconvenience.

unanständig indecent.

unappetitlich unsavoury.

Unart *f* bad habit; **u~ig** *(Kind)* naughty.

unauffällig inconspicuous, unobtrusive.

unauffindbar untraceable.

unaufhörlich incessant, continuous.

unaufmerksam inattentive.

unaufschiebbar undeferable.

unausbleiblich inevitable.

unausgeglichen unbalanced.

unbarmherzig merciless.

unbeachtet unnoticed.

unbebaut *(Grundstück)* vacant.

unbedeutend unimportant, insignificant.

unbedingt 1. unconditional, absolute; 2. *(unter allen Umständen)* by all means.

unbefangen unembarrassed.

unbefriedigend unsatisfactory.

unbefristet unlimited.

unbefugt unauthorized.

unbegreiflich incomprehensible.

unbegrenzt unlimited.

unbegründet unfounded.

Unbehagen *n* discomfort, uneasiness.

unbeholfen awkward.

unbekannt 1. unknown; 2. *(nicht vertraut)* unfamiliar.

unbeliebt unpopular.

unbemannt unmanned.

unbemerkt unnoticed.

unbequem inconvenient, uncomfortable.

unberechtigt unjustified.

unberücksichtigt unconsidered.

unbeschädigt undamaged.

unbescheiden immodest.

unbescholten of good reputation, blameless.

unbeschrankt without gates.

unbeschränkt 1. *(Vertrauen)* unrestricted; 2. absolute.

unbeschreiblich indescribable.

unbesorgt unconcerned; *seien Sie* ~ don't worry.

unbeständig 1. unsteady; 2. *(Markt)* unsettled, fluctuating.

unbestechlich incorruptible.

unbestimmt indefinite, vague.

unbestreitbar incontestable.

unbewaffnet unarmed.

unbeweglich 1. immobile; 2. *(Miene)* motionless.

unbewohn‖bar uninhabitable; ~**t** uninhabited, vacant.

unbewußt unconscious.

unbezahl‖bar priceless; ~**t** 1. unpaid; 2. *(Forderung)* outstanding.

unbrauchbar useless.

und 1. and; ~ *so weiter* and so on; 2. *(entgegengesetzt)* but; 3. *(selbst wenn)* even if.

Undank *m* ingratitude; **u**~**bar** ungrateful *(gegen* to).

undeutlich vague, indistinct.

undicht leaking, permeable, not waterproof.

unecht 1. artificial; 2. *(gefälscht)* conterfeit, false.

unehelich illegitimate.

Unehr‖e *f* dishono(u)r; **u**~**enhaft** dishono(u)rable; **u**~**lich** dishonest.

uneigennützig disinterested.

uneinig differing, disunited; **U**~**keit** *f* disagreement, discord.

unempfindlich insensitive *(für* to).

unendlich 1. endless; 2. *(grenzenlos)* infinite; **U**~**keit** *f* infinity.

unentbehrlich indispensable *(für* to).

unentgeltlich gratuitous, free of charge.

unentschieden 1. undecided; 2. *(Charakter)* indecisive; 3. *sport* drawn; **U**~ *n* draw, tie.

unentschlossen irresolute, undecided.
unerbittlich pitiless.
unerfahren inexperienced.
unerfreulich unpleasant.
unerhört *(empörend)* outrageous.
unerkannt unidentified.
unerläßlich compulsory, imperative.
unerlaubt illicit.
unermeßlich immeasurable, immense.
unermüdlich indefatigable, untiring.
unerschöpflich inexhaustible.
unerschütterlich imperturbable.
unerschwinglich *(Preis)* exorbitant.
unersetzlich irreplaceable.
unerträglich unbearable.
unerwartet unexpected.
unerwünscht undesirable.
unfähig unable (*zu* to), incapable (of), incompetent.
unfair unfair.
Unfall *m* accident; *bei diesem* ~ in this accident; ~**station** *f* first-aid station; ~**verhütung** *f* prevention of accidents; ~**wagen** *m* ambulance.
unfaßbar inconceivable.
unförmig shapeless, deformed.
unfreiwillig involuntary.
unfreundlich unfriendly, unkind.
unfruchtbar 1. *(Boden)* in-

fertile, unfruitful; 2. *bot* sterile; 3. *med* barren.
Unfug *m* mischief, nuisance.
Ungar *m*, **u~isch** Hungarian; ~**n** *n* Hungary.
ungeachtet regardless of, notwithstanding.
ungebildet uneducated.
ungebräuchlich unusual.
ungedeckt *(Scheck)* uncovered.
Ungeduld *f* impatience; **u~ig** impatient.
ungeeignet unsuitable.
ungefähr 1. approximate, rough; 2. ~ *20 Jahre alt sein* be about 20 years old.
ungefährlich harmless.
ungehalten annoyed, indignant (*über* at).
ungeheuer enormous, immense; **U~** *n* monster.
ungehindert unchecked.
ungehörig improper.
ungehorsam disobedient; **U~** *m* disobedience.
ungekürzt *(Buch)* unabridged.
ungelegen 1. *(unpassend)* inconvenient, inopportune; 2. *komme ich* ~? am I disturbing you?
ungelernt unskilled.
ungemütlich uncomfortable
ungenau inaccurate.
ungeniert unembarrassed.
ungenießbar 1. *(Speisen)* uneatable; 2. *(Person)* unbearable.
ungenügend insufficient.
ungerade *(Zahl)* odd.

ungerecht unjust; **U~igkeit** _f_ injustice.

ungern grudgingly.

ungeschickt awkward, clumsy; **U~heit** _f_ awkwardness, clumsiness.

ungestüm impetuous.

ungesund 1. _(Klima)_ unhealthy; 2. _(Nahrung)_ unwholesome.

Ungetüm _n_ monster.

ungewiß uncertain; **U~heit** _f_ uncertainty.

ungewöhnlich unusual, uncommon.

ungewohnt 1. _(unüblich)_ unusual, uncustomary; 2. _(fremdartig)_ strange.

Ungeziefer _n_ vermin.

ungezogen 1. ill-mannered; 2. _(Kind)_ naughty; **U~heit** _f_ unmannerliness; impertinence.

ungezwungen unconstrained, casual.

Unglauben _m_ unbelief.

ungläubig unbelieving.

unglaublich incredible; **~würdig** 1. _(Bericht)_ unbelievable; 2. _(Person)_ unreliable.

ungleich 1. _(Aussehen)_ unlike; 2. _(Größe)_ unequal, different; **~mäßig** irregular.

Unglück _n_ 1. misfortune, bad luck; 2. _(Elend)_ misery; 3. _(Unheil)_ disaster; 4. _(Mißgeschick)_ mishap; **u~lich** 1. unfortunate, unhappy, unlucky; 2. _(unheilvoll)_ fatal, ill-fated.

Ungnade _f: in ~ fallen bei jdm_ fall into disgrace with s.o.

ungültig 1. invalid; 2. _für ~ erklären_ declare null and void; 3. _(Geld)_ not current; 4. _(Urteil)_ void.

Ungunst _f_ disfavour; _zu jds ~en_ to s.o.'s disadvantage.

ungünstig 1. unfavourable; 2. _(Zeitpunkt)_ inopportune.

Unheil _n_ 1. mischief; 2. _(Schaden)_ harm; 3. _(Katastrophe)_ disaster; **u~bar** incurable; **u~voll** disastrous.

unheimlich 1. uncanny, weird; 2. _fig_ terrific.

unhöflich impolite; **U~keit** _f_ impoliteness.

unhygienisch insanitary.

Uniform _f_ uniform.

uninteressant uninteresting.

Universität _f_ university.

Universum _n_ universe.

unkenntlich unrecognizable.

Unkenntnis _f_ ignorance, unawareness; _aus ~_ out of ignorance; _in ~ sein über_ be unaware of.

Unkosten _pl_ costs _pl_, expenses; _allgemeine ~_ overhead(s).

Unkraut _n_ weed(s _pl_).

unlauter 1. _fig_ dishonest; 2. _com_ unfair.

unleserlich illegible.

unlogisch illogical.

Unlust _f (Abneigung)_ aversion, dislike (_gegenüber_ of).

Unmensch _m_ monster; **u~lich** inhuman.

unmißverständlich unmistakable.

unmittelbar 1. immediate; 2. ~ *bevorstehend* imminent.

unmodern unfashionable, out-of-date.

unmöglich impossible, unfeasible; **U~keit** *f* impossibility.

unmündig: ~ *sein* be a minor.

unnach\|ahmlich inimitable; **~giebig** unyielding; **~sichtig** severe.

unnatürlich unnatural *a. fig.*

unnötig 1. unnecessary; 2. *(überflüssig)* superfluous.

unnütz useless.

unord\|entlich untidy, careless; **U~nung** *f* 1. disorder, confusion; 2. *in* ~ in a mess; *in* ~ *sein* be out of order.

unparteiisch impartial.

unpassend 1. unsuitable, inappropriate; 2. *(Zeit)* inconvenient.

unpersönlich impersonal.

unpopulär unpopular.

unpraktisch unpractical.

unpünktlich unpunctual.

Unrat *m* rubbish, refuse.

unrecht 1. wrong; 2. *(ungerecht)* unjust; 3. *jdm* ~ *geben* contradict s.o.; ~ *haben* be wrong; **U~** *n* 1. injustice, wrong; *jdm ein* ~ *tun* do s.o. injustice; 2. *im* ~ *sein* be in the wrong; 3. *zu* ~ unjustly.

unregelmäßig irregular.

unreif 1. unripe; 2. *fig* immature.

Unruhe *f* 1. unrest, restlessness; 2. *(Angst)* uneasiness; *in großer* ~ *sein* be very anxious; 3. *(Aufruhr)* riots *pl;* **~herd** *m* storm centre; **~stifter** *m* trouble-maker.

unruhig 1. restless, nervous; 2. *(ängstlich)* uneasy, worried, anxious; 3. *(Zeiten)* troubled; 4. *(See)* rough.

uns I *prn* us; *ein Freund von* ~ a friend of ours; **II** *refl* ourselves; **III** *(einander)* each other.

unsachlich unobjective, irrelevant.

unsauber unclean, untidy.

unschädlich harmless, innocuous.

unscharf *(Bild)* blurred.

unschätzbar inestimable.

unscheinbar 1. insignificant; 2. *(einfach)* plain.

unschicklich improper, indecent.

unschlüssig irresolute.

Unschuld *f* innocence; *s-e* ~ *beteuern* protest o.'s innocence; **u~ig** innocent (*an* of).

unser I *pers prn* of us; **II** *poss prn* our; ours; **~eins** the likes of us; **~erseits** on our parts.

unsicher 1. unsafe, dangerous; 2. *(ungewiß)* uncertain; 3. *(unentschlossen)* irresolute; 4. *(nicht stabil)* insecure, unstable.

unsichtbar invisible.

Unsinn *m* nonsense; **u~ig**

1. unreasonable, absurd; 2. *(sehr)* terribly.

Unsitte *f* bad habit; **u~lich** immoral.

unsterblich immortal.

Unstimmigkeit *f* disagreement.

unsym|metrisch unsymmetrical; **~pathisch** disagreeable, unlikeable.

Untat *f* crime.

untätig inactive, idle.

untauglich unfit, unsuitable, unservicable.

unten 1. below, down; *von oben bis* ~ from top to bottom; 2. *(am Boden)* at the bottom; 3. *nach* ~ downwards, downstairs; 4. *von* ~ *her* from underneath; 5. *siehe* ~ see below.

unter 1. below, beneath, underneath; ~ *dem Durchschnitt* below the average; 2. ~ *jdm arbeiten* work under s.o.; 3. ~ *anderem* among other things; *mitten* ~ in the midst of; 4. ~ *uns gesagt* between you and me; 5. *was versteht man* ~? what is meant by?

Unterarm *m* forearm.

unterbelichtet underexposed.

unterbewußt subconscious; **U~sein** *n* subconscious; *im* ~ subconsciously.

unterbinden *irr fig* stop.

unterbrech|en *irr* 1. interrupt; 2. *tele* disconnect; 3. *(Reise)* break; 4. *(verta-*

gen) adjourn; **U~ung** *f* 1. break, interruption; 2. *(Verkehr)* suspension; 3. *ohne* ~ non-stop.

unterbringen *irr* 1. *(beherbergen)* accommodate, lodge; 2. *(lagern)* store.

unterdessen in the meantime, meanwhile.

unterdrück|en 1. *(Aufstand)* suppress; 2. *(Volk)* oppress, hold down; 3. *(Gefühl)* repress; **U~ung** *f* suppression; oppression.

untere lower, inferior.

untereinander 1. between each other, among one another; 2. *(gegenseitig)* mutually.

unterernährt undernourished.

Unterführung *f* subway, underpass.

Untergang *m* 1. *fig* ruin, decline; 2. *mar* shipwreck; 3. *(Sonne)* setting.

Untergebener *m* subordinate.

untergehen *irr* 1. *mar* sink, founder; 2. *(Sonne)* set; 3. *fig* perish.

Untergeschoß *n* ground, *Am* first floor.

untergliedern subdivide.

untergraben *irr* undermine.

Untergrund *m* 1. underground; 2. *geog* subsoil; 3. *(Malerei)* grounding; **~bahn** *f* underground, *Am* subway; *(London)* tube.

unterhalb 1. below, underneath; 2. *(über hinaus)* beyond, on the other side.

Unterhalt *m* 1. keep, maintenance; *s-n ~ bestreiten* support o.s.; 2. *(Lebens~)* livelihood, living.

unterhalten *irr* 1. support, maintain, keep; 2. *(Beziehungen)* maintain; 3. *(Gäste)* entertain; 4. *sich ~* enjoy o.s.; *sich mit jdm ~* talk to s.o.; *~sam* entertaining.

Unterhaltung *f* 1. entertainment; 2. *(Gespräch)* conversation, talk; *~smusik* *f* light music.

Unterhemd *n* undershirt.

Unterholz *n* undergrowth.

Unterhose *f* pants *pl;* *(Frauen~)* panties *pl.*

Unterkiefer *m* lower jaw.

unterkommen *irr (Arbeit)* find work.

Unterkunft *f* accommodation, lodings *pl.*

Unterlage *f* 1. pad; 2. *pl (Dokumente)* documents, papers; 3. *(Angaben)* data.

unterlassen *irr* 1. omit, neglect; 2. *(bleibenlassen)* stop; 3. *(sich enthalten)* refrain from.

'**unterlegen** put under; **unter'legen** *(schwächer)* inferior.

Unterleib *m* belly.

unterliegen *irr* 1. *(im Kampf)* be defeated, be beaten, lose; 2. *(Bestimmungen)* be subject; 3. *(Gebühr)* be liable.

Unterlippe *f* lower lip.

Untermieter *m* subtenant, lodger.

unternehmen *irr* undertake, do; **U~en** *n* 1. *com* business, enterprise, firm; 2. *(Vorhaben)* enterprise; **U~er** *m* employer, entrepreneur.

Unteroffizier *m* non-commissioned officer, NCO.

unterordnen, *sich* submit.

Unterricht *m* 1. instruction, teaching; 2. *(Stunden)* lessons *pl,* classes *pl;* **u~en** 1. teach *(über* on); 2. *jdn ~* inform s.o. *(über* of).

Unterrock *m* petticoat.

untersagen forbid *(jdm etw* s.o. to do s.th.).

unterschätzen underestimate.

unterscheiden *irr* 1. distinguish *(zwischen* between); 2. *sich ~* differ *(von* from); **U~ung** *f* distinction.

Unterschied *m* 1. difference; 2. *e-n ~ machen* distinguish; *zum ~ von* unlike, as opposed to; **u~lich** different, differing; **u~slos** indiscriminate.

unterschlagen *irr (Geld)* embezzle; **U~ung** *f* embezzlement.

Unterschlupf *m* 1. hiding-place; 2. *(Obdach)* refuge.

unterschreiben *irr* subscribe, sign.

Unterschrift *f* signature.

Unterseeboot *n* submarine.

untersetzt stocky, thick-set.

unterst lowest, undermost, bottom.

'**unterstehen** *irr* take shelter; **unter'stehen** *irr* 1. *jdm* ~ be subordinate to s.o., be under s.o.; 2. *(Gesetz)* be subject to; 3. *sich* ~ dare.

'**unterstellen** put, garage; **unter'stellen** 1. *jdm etw* ~ put s.th. under s.o.; 2. *etw* ~ assume s.th.; 3. *(zuschreiben)* impute.

unterstreichen *irr* 1. underline; 2. *fig* emphasize.

unterstütz|en support, assist, aid; **U~ung** *f* support, aid.

untersuch|en 1. examine, test; 2. *(e-n Fall)* investigate; 3. *(durchsuchen)* search, inspect; 4. *chem* analize; **U~ung** *f* 1. examination; 2. investigation; 3. analysis; **U~ungsgefangener** *m* prisoner on trial; **U~ungshaft** *f* remand, custody; **U~ungsrichter** *m* investigating judge.

Untertasse *f* saucer.

untertauchen 1. dive; 2. *fig* disappear.

Untertitel *m* subtitle.

Unterwäsche *f* underwear.

unterwegs on o.'s way, away.

Unterwelt *f* underworld.

unterwerfen *irr* 1. subjugate, subdue; 2. *(vorlegen)* submit.

unterwürfig obsequious.

unterzeichne|n sign; **U~ter** *m* the undersigner; subscriber.

'**unterziehen** *irr* wear underneath; **unter'ziehen,** *sich irr* 1. *(Operation)* undergo; *(e-r Prüfung)* go in for; 2. *sich der Mühe* ~ take the trouble (to).

Untiefe *f* shallow.

untreu 1. unfaithful; 2. ~ *werden* desert, give up; **U~e** *f* unfaithfulness.

untröstlich inconsolable.

untrüglich unfailing.

untüchtig incapable.

unüber|legt inconsiderate; **~trefflich** matchless; **~troffen** unsurpassed; **~windlich** *(Schwierigkeit)* unsurmountable.

ununterbrochen uninterrupted, incessant.

unveränderlich unchangeable.

unverantwortlich irresponsible.

unverbesserlich incorrigible.

unverbindlich *com* not binding, without obligation.

unverdaulich indigestible *a. fig.*

unvergänglich imperishable.

unvergeßlich unforgettable.

unvergleichlich incomparable.

unverheiratet single, not married.

unverhofft unexpected.

unverkäuflich not for sale.

unvermeid|bar, ~lich inevitable.
unvermutet unexpected.
unvernünftig unreasonable.
unveröffentlicht unpublished.
unverpackt loose.
unverschämt impudent, saucy; **U~heit** *f* impudence, impertinence.
unversehens unexpectedly.
unversehrt uninjured, intact.
unverständlich indistinct, unintelligible.
unverwüstlich indestructible *a. fig.*
unverzüglich immediately, without delay.
unvoll|endet unfinished; **~kommen** imperfect; **~ständig** incomplete.
unvorbereitet unprepared.
unvoreingenommen unbiased.
unvorhergesehen unforeseen.
unvorsichtig imprudent, careless.
unvorteilhaft 1. unprofitable; 2. *(Kleidung)* unbecoming.

unwahr untrue; **U~heit** *f* untruth; **~scheinlich** improbable, unlikely.
unwegsam impassable.
unweigerlich inevitable.
unwesentlich irrelevant *(für* to), trivial.
Unwetter *n* thunderstorm.
unwichtig insignificant.

unwider|ruflich irrevocable; **~stehlich** irresistible.
Unwill|e *m* indignation; **u~ig** indignant, angry; **u~kommen** unwelcome; **u~kürlich** involuntary, instinctively.
unwirksam ineffective.
unwissen|d ignorant; **U~heit** *f* ignorance; **~tlich** unknowingly.
unwohl unwell; **U~sein** *n* indispositon.
unwürdig unworthy (of).
unzählig countless.
Unzeit *f: zur ~* at the wrong time; **u~gemäß** old-fashioned.
unzerbrechlich unbreakable.
unzertrennlich inseparable.
unzufrieden dissatisfied, discontented; **U~heit** *f* dissatisfaction.
unzulänglich insufficient.
unzulässig inadmissible.
unzumutbar unacceptable.
unzureichend insufficient.
unzutreffend 1. unfounded; 2. *(nicht anwendbar)* inapplicable.
unzuverlässig 1. unreliable; 2. *(Gedächtnis)* treacherous.
unzweckmäßig unsuitable.
üppig 1. luxuriant; 2. *(Mahl)* opulent; 3. *(Figur)* full.
uralt ancient, very old.
Uran *n* uranium.
Uraufführung *f* première, first night.
urbar arable.

Urenkel *m* great-grandson;
~**in** *f* great-granddaughter.
Urheberrecht *n* copyright
(*für* in).
Urin *m* urine; **u~ieren** uri-
nate.
Urkunde *f* 1. document, record; 2. (*Diplom*) diploma;
~**nfälschung** *f* forgery of
documents.
Urlaub *m* 1. leave (of absence), vacation; 2. (*Ferien*)
holidays *pl; in* ~ *gehen* go
on holiday; ~**er** *m* tourist,
holiday-maker, *Am* vaca-
tionist; ~**sgeld** *n* holiday
pay.
Urne *f* 1. urn; 2. (*Wahl*~) bal-
lot-box.

Ursache *f* 1. (*Grund*) cause,
reason; 2. (*Anlaß*) motive;

3. *keine* ~! don't mention it!
you are welcome.
Ursprung *m fig* origin, beginning, source.
ursprünglich initial, original.
Urteil *n* 1. judg(e)ment;
2. (*Ansicht*) opinion; *m-m* ~
nach in my opinion; *sich ein*
~ *bilden* form an opinion;
3. *jur* sentence, verdict, decree; **u~en** judge (*über jdn*
s.o.); ~**sverkündung** *f* pro-
nouncing of judgement;
~**svollstreckung** *f* execution of sentence.

Urwald *m* virgin forest.
urwüchsig 1. original;
2. (*derb*) robust.
Utensilien *pl* utensils *pl.*
Utop|**ie** *f* utopia; **u~isch**
utopian.

V

Vagabund *m* vagabond, tramp.

Vanille *f* vanilla.

Varieté *n* music-hall.

variieren vary.

Vase *f* vase.

Vater *m* father; **~land** *n* native country.

väterlich paternal, fatherly.

Vater|schaft *f* paternity; **~unser** *n* Lord's prayer.

Vegetarier *m* vegetarian.

vegetieren vegetate.

Veilchen *n* violet.

Vene *f* vein.

Ventil *n* 1. valve; 2. *fig* outlet; **~ator** *m* ventilator; **v~ie-ren** ventilate *a. fig.*

verabred|en 1. agree on, arrange; 2. *sich ~* make an appointment, fix a date; **~et** 1. ~ *sein* have a rendezvous, an engagement; 2. *wie ~* as arranged; **V~ung** *f* appointment, date, rendezvous.

verabscheuen detest.

verabschieden 1. dismiss; 2. *(Gesetz)* pass; 3. *sich ~* say good-bye (to).

verachten 1. *jdn ~* despise s.o.; 2. *etw ~* disdain s.th.

verächtlich contemptuous, disdainful.

Verachtung *f* contempt, disdain.

verallgemeinern generalize.

veraltet 1. out-dated, anti-

quated; 2. *(Ausdruck)* obsolete.

Veranda *f* veranda(h), *Am* porch.

veränder|lich variable, changeable; **~n** 1. change, alter; 2. *er hat sich verändert* he has changed; **V~ung** *f* 1. change; 2. *(Abänderung)* alteration.

verängstigt frightened.

verankern anchor, moor.

veranlag|t talented, gifted *(für* for), inclined (to); **V~ung** *f* 1. *(Neigung)* disposition, nature; 2. *(Begabung)* talent, inclination; 3. *(Steuer)* assessment.

veranlass|en 1. *jdn zu etw ~* cause s.o. to do s.th.; 2. *etw ~* arrange for s.th.; **V~ung** *f* 1. *auf meine ~* at my suggestion, at my request; 2. *keine ~ haben zu* have no reason to.

veranschaulichen illustrate.

veranstalt|en 1. organize; 2. *(geben)* give; **V~er** *m* organizer, promotor; **V~ung** *f* 1. show, performance; 2. *sport* event.

verantwort|en 1. answer *(etw* for s.th.); 2. *sich ~* justify o.s. *(vor* before); **~lich** responsible; *jdn ~ machen für* hold s.o. responsible for; **V~ung** *f: die ~ überneh-**

men take the responsibility; *auf eigene* ~ at o.'s own risk; **~ungslos** irresponsible.

verarbeiten 1. process (*zu* into); 2. (*Eindrücke*) digest.

verärgert angry, annoyed.

veräußern sell.

Verband *m* 1. *med* bandage, dressing; 2. (*Vereinigung*) association, union, federation; **~skasten** *m* first-aid box; **~späckchen** *n* first--aid packet; **~szeug** *n* dressing.

verbann|en banish; **V~ter** *m* exile; **V~ung** *f* exile, banishment.

verbauen block up, obstruct.

verbergen *irr* conceal, hide.

verbessern 1. improve, ameliorate; 2. (*berichtigen*) correct, rectify.

verbeugen, *sich* bow (*vor* to).

verbiegen *irr* 1. bend; 2. (*Holz*) warp.

verbieten *irr* 1. forbid; 2. (*amtlich*) prohibit; 3. (*Zeitung*) proscribe; 4. *rel* interdict.

verbind|en *irr* 1. *med* bandage, dress; 2. (*Flüsse*) connect; 3. *tech* couple, connect, link; 4. (*vereinen*) unite, join; 5. (*kombinieren*) combine; 6. *tele* put through; 7. *sich* ~ be associated, be connected; **~lich** 1. (*verpflichtend*) obligatory, compulsory; 2. (*Person*) oblig-

ing; **V~lichkeit** *f* 1. obligation; 2. (*Benehmen*) obligingness, civilty; **V~ung** *f* 1. connection, link; 2. (*Kombination*) combination; 3. (*Kontakt*) contact; *sich in* ~ *setzen mit* get in touch with; 4. (*Vereinigung*) association; 5. *in* ~ *mit* in conjunction with; 6. *tele* communication; 7. *chem* compound.

verbitter|t embittered; **V~ung** *f* bitterness.

Verbleib *m* whereabouts *pl*; **v~en** *irr* 1. remain; 2. (*festhalten an*) persist.

verblüff|end amazing, astonishing; **~t** dumbfounded.

verbluten bleed to death.

verborgen 1. concealed, hidden; 2. *im* ~*en* in secret.

Verbot *n* forbiddance, prohibition, ban (on); **v~en** forbidden, prohibited; *Rauchen* ~ no smoking; *Zutritt* ~ no admittance.

Verbrauch *m* consumption (*an* of); **v~en** 1. consume, use; 2. (*erschöpfen*) exhaust; **~er** *m* consumer; **~sgüter** *pl* consumer goods *pl*; **v~t** 1. (*Material*) used, consumed; 2. (*Luft*) stale.

Verbrech|en *n* crime; **~er** *m*, **v~erisch** criminal.

verbreiten 1. (*Nachricht*) spread, circulate; 2. (*Licht*) diffuse; 3. (*ausstrahlen*) radiate, effuse; 4. (*Freude*) be the cause of.

verbreitern widen, broaden.
verbreitet common, wide-
-spread.
verbrenn|en irr 1. burn;
2. *(Leiche)* cremate; 3. *sich
die Hand* ~ burn o.'s hand;
V~ungsmotor m internal
combustion engine.
verbringen irr *(Zeit)* spend.
Verbrüderung f fraterniz-
ation.
verbrühen scald.
verbuchen book.
verbunden 1. *(Wunde)*
bound, bandaged; 2. *mit jdm
~ sein* have ties with s.o., be
connected to s.o.
verbünden, sich ally o.s.
with.
Verbundenheit f connection, *(enge)* bonds pl, ties pl.
verbündet allied.
verbürgen, sich guarantee.
verbüßen *(Strafe)* serve.
verchromt chromium-
-plated.
Verdacht m suspicion; *im ~
stehen* be suspected of.
verdächtig suspicious; ~**en**
suspect.
verdamm|en condemn,
damn; ~**t** 1. cursed, blasted;
2. *(verurteilt)* condemned.
verdampfen evaporate.
verdanken owe *(jdm etw
s.th. to s.o.)*.
verdau|en digest a. fig; ~**lich**
digestible; *leicht, schwer* ~
easy, hard to digest; **V~ung**
f digestion; **V~ungsstö-
rungen** pl indigestion.

Verdeck n 1. *(Auto)* roof,
top; 2. *mar* deck; **v~en**
cover (up), conceal, hide.
verderb|en irr 1. *(Früchte)*
spoil, ruin; 2. *(Plan)* upset;
3. *sich die Augen* ~ ruin o.'s
eyes; 4. *(Charakter)* corrupt; 5. *es mit jdm* ~ fall out
with s.o.; **V~en** n ruin, un-
doing; ~**lich** perishable.
verdienen 1. *(Geld)* earn,
make; 2. *(Strafe)* deserve,
merit.
Verdienst 1. m earnings pl,
wages pl; 2. *(Gewinn)*
profit; 3. n merit; *es ist
hauptsächlich sein* ~ it's
owing to him; ~**voll** meri-
torious.
verdient: *sich ~ machen* do
great service.
verdoppeln double a. fig.
verdorben 1. *(Ware)* spoilt;
2. *(Magen)* upset; 3. *(Luft)*
polluted; 4. fig corrupt.
verdorren wither.
verdrängen 1. displace;
2. *(aus e-r Stellung)* oust;
3. psych repress.
verdrehen 1. distort, twist a.
fig; 2. *jdm den Kopf* ~ turn
s.o.'s head.
verdreifachen treble.
verdrießlich 1. annoyed;
2. *(schlecht gelaunt)* ill-
-humo(u)red.
verdrossen vexed, morose.
Verdruß m 1. annoyance;
vexation; 2. *jdm ~ bereiten*
give s.o. trouble.
verdunkel|n 1. darken;

2. *(Luftschutz)* black out;
3. *fig* obscure; **V~ungsgefahr** *f jur* danger of collusion.

verdünnen 1. *(Farbe)* thin;
2. *(Flüssigkeit)* dilute.

verdunsten evaporate.

verdursten die of thirst.

verdutzt perplexed.

veredeln 1. ennoble; 2. *tech* refine, process.

verehr|en 1. venerate, honour; 2. *fig* adore; **V~er** *m* admirer, fan.

vereidig|en administer an oath *(jdn* to s.o.); **V~ung** *f* swearing-in.

Verein *m* 1. society, association; 2. *(kleiner)* club.

vereinbar compatible *(mit* with); **~en** 1. agree upon, settle upon; 2. *sich nicht ~ lassen* be inconsistent with; **V~ung** *f* 1. agreement, arrangement; 2. *nach ~* by appointment; *e-e ~ treffen* enter into an arrangement.

verein|fachen simplify; **~heitlichen** standardize.

vereinig|en 1. join, unite, unify; 2. *etw in sich ~* combine s.th.; 3. *(Übereinstimmung)* consistent with; 4. *(Stimmen)* collect, amass; 5. *sich ~* associate, join, unite; **~t** united; **V~ung** *f* 1. union; 2. *(Fluß)* confluence; 3. *pol* alliance, coalition.

vereinzelt isolated.

vereist ice-coated.

vereiteln *(Plan)* thwart, torpedo.

vereitern suppurate.

verenden perish.

verengen, sich narrow.

vererb|en 1. *jdm etw ~* leave s.o. s.th., bequeath s.o. s.th.; 2. *sich auf jdn ~* be transmitted to s.o.; **V~ung** *f* heredity.

verfahren *irr* 1. proceed *(nach* on); 2. *sich ~* miss the way; **V~** *n* 1. process; 2. *jur* proceedings *pl.*

Verfall *m* 1. ruin, decay;
2. *(Frist) bei ~* upon expiration; 3. *(sittlich)* corruption; **v~en I** *irr* 1. *(Haus)* dilapidate, fall into decay;
2. *(Besitz)* decay; 3. *(ablaufen)* expire, lapse; 4. *(e-r Sache)* become addicted to;
5. *auf etw ~* hit on s.th.; **II** *adj* 6. *(Haus)* dilapidated;
7. *(Rauschgift)* addicted;
8. *(abgelaufen)* expired.

verfälschen 1. falsify; 2. *(Lebensmittel)* adulterate.

verfänglich insidious, tricky.

verfärben, sich 1. become discolo(u)red; 2. *(Blätter)* turn.

verfass|en write, compose;
V~er *m* author; **V~ung** *f*
1. *(körperlich)* condition;
2. *(seelisch)* state of mind;
3. *pol* constitution.

verfaulen rot, moulder.

verfehlen *(Ziel)* miss.

verfeinden, sich become enemies, fall out (*mit jdm* with s.o.).

verfeinern refine.

verfertigen make, manufacture.

verfilm|en film; **V~ung** *f* film adaption.

verfluchen curse.

verflüchtigen evaporate, volatilize.

verfolg|en 1. pursue, persecute; 2. (*Spur*) follow; 3. *jur* prosecute; **V~er** *m* pursuer; persecutor; **V~ung** *f* 1. pursuit; 2. persecution; 3. *jur* prosecution.

verfrüht premature.

verfüg|bar available; **~en** 1. order, decree; 2. *über etw ~* dispose of s.th.; **V~ung** *f* 1. (*Erlaß*) decree, order; 2. *zur ~ stehen* be available; *er steht zu Ihrer ~* he's at your disposal.

verführ|en 1. seduce; 2. (*verlocken*) tempt, entice; **V~er** *m* seducer; **~erisch** 1. seductive, bewitching; 2. (*verlockend*) tempting.

vergammeln *fig* go to seed.

vergangen 1. bygone, past; 2. (*Woche*) last; *im ~en Jahr* last year; **V~heit** *f* past.

vergänglich passing, transitory.

Vergaser *m* carburettor.

vergeb|en *irr* 1. (*verzeihen*) forgive (*jdm* s.o.); 2. *sich etw ~* compromise o.s.; 3. (*Auftrag*) place, award; 4. (*Po-*

sten) assign; **~ens** in vain; **~lich** useless, idle, futile.

vergehen *irr* 1. (*Zeit*) go by, pass 2. (*aufhören*) go away; 3. (*Duft*) vanish; 4. *vor etw ~* be dying of s.th.; 5. *sich an jdm ~* rape, violate s.o.; **V~** *n* offence, misdemeanour.

Vergeltung *f* reprisal; *~ üben* retaliate (*an* on).

vergessen *irr* 1. forget; 2. (*übersehen*) overlook; 3. (*Pflicht*) omit, neglect; 4. *sich ~* lose o.'s head; **V~heit** *f* oblivion.

vergeßlich forgetful.

vergeuden waste, dissipate.

vergewaltig|en violate, rape; **V~ung** *f* violation.

vergewissern, *sich* make sure.

vergießen *irr* 1. (*Tränen*) shed; 2. (*verschütten*) spill.

vergiften 1. poison; 2. (*Umwelt*) pollute.

Vergißmeinnicht *n* forget-me-not.

Vergleich *m* 1. comparison; *e-n ~ ziehen* draw a comparison; *im ~ zu* compared to, with; 2. *jur* settlement, agreement; **v~bar** comparable (*mit* to); **v~en** *irr* 1. compare (*mit* with, to), put on the same level; 2. (*nachprüfen*) check; 3. *vergleiche Seite 1* confer page 1; 4. *sich ~* compare.

verglichen: *~ mit* compared to.

vergnüg|en, *sich* amuse, en-

joy o.s. (*mit* with); **V~en** *n*
1. pleasure, fun, enjoyment;
viel ~! have a good time!
mit ~ with amusement;
2. *(Unterhaltung)* entertainment; **~t** gay, merry.
Vergnügungs|park *m*
amusement park; **~reise** *f*
pleasure-trip; **~viertel** *n*
night-life district.
vergoldet gilt.
vergöttern *fig* adore.
vergraben *irr* bury.
vergreifen, *sich irr* 1. lay
hands (*an jdm* on s.o.);
2. *(an Eigentum)* misap-
propriate; 3. *(an Geld)* embezzle.
vergriffen out-of-print.
vergrößer|n 1. enlarge *a.*
phot; 2. *(Not)* increase, intensify; 3. *(ausdehnen)* extend; **V~ung** *f* enlargement,
extension; **V~ungsglas** *n*
magnifying glass.
Vergünstigung *f* privilege,
allowance.
vergüten 1. remunerate,
compensate (*jdm etw* s.o.
for s.th.); 2. *(Auslagen)* refund; 3. *(Schaden)* indemnify.
verhaft|en, V~ung *f* arrest.
verhalten, *sich irr* 1. behave,
act; *sich falsch ~* behave in-
correctly; 2. *sich ruhig ~*
keep quiet; 3. *die Sache ver-*
hält sich anders it is not as
you think; 4. *sich zu etw ~*
be to s.th. as; **V~** *n* behav-
io(u)r, conduct, demeanour.

Verhältnis *n* 1. *(zwischen*
Menschen) relationship, relations *pl; 2. (Beziehung) im*
~ zu in proportion to, in
comparison with; 3. *(Bedin-*
gungen) conditions, circumstances; 4. *er lebt über s-e*
~se he lives beyond his
means; 5. *(Liebes~)* affair;
6. *math* ratio; *im umgekehr-*
ten ~ in inverse ratio;
v~mäßig comparatively,
relatively.
verhand|eln 1. negotiate
(über on, about); 2. *(sich be-*
raten) deliberate, debate;
3. *jur* try; **V~lung** *f* 1. nego-
tiation; 2. *(Beratung)* debate, discussion; 3. *jur* trial.
verhäng|en *(Strafe)* inflict
(über on); **V~nis** *n* disaster;
~nisvoll fatal, disastrous.
verharmlosen minimize.
verhaßt hated, detested.
verheilt healed.
verheimlichen hide, conceal
(vor from).
verheiraten, *sich* marry, get
married.
verheißungsvoll promising.
verhelfen *irr* help (*jdm zu*
etw s.o. to s.th.).
verherrlichen glorify.
verhexen bewitch.
verhindern 1. prevent; 2. *ver-*
hindert sein be unable (to
do s.th.).
verhöhnen jeer, jibe (at),
mock.
Verhör *n* interrogation;
v~en 1. *jur* interrogate,

examine; 2. *sich* ~ hear wrong.

verhüllen veil *a. fig.* disguise.

verhungern die of hunger, starve.

verhüten prevent.

verirren, *sich* get lost.

verjagen chase, drive away.

verjähr|en come under the statute of limitation; **V~ungsfrist** *f* period of limitation.

verkalkt 1. *fig.* senile; 2. *med.* sclerotic.

Verkauf *m* sale; *zum* ~ for sale; **v~en** sell; *zu* ~ for sale.

Verkäuf|er *m* salesman, shop-assistant; **~erin** *f* saleswomen; **v~lich** sal(e)able, for sale.

Verkehr *m* 1. traffic; 2. *(Verkehrsmittel)* transport; 3. *(Umgang)* dealings *pl*; 4. *(Verbindung)* contact; 5. *com* trade, commerce; *(Banknoten)* circulation; **v~en** 1. *(Autobus)* run *(zwischen* between); 2. *bei jdm* ~ go to, frequent s.o.'s house; 3. *mit jdm* ~ associate with s.o.

Verkehrs|ader *f* arterial road; **~amt** *n* tourist office; **~flugzeug** *n* airliner; **~hindernis** *n* obstacle to traffic; **~insel** *f* traffic island; **~knotenpunkt** *m* junction; **~mittel** *n* (means of) transportation; **~polizei** *f* traffic police; **~polizist** *m* traffic

policeman; **~regeln** *pl* traffic regulations *pl*; **~schild** *n* traffic sign; **~störung** *f* interruption of traffic; **~teilnehmer** *m* road user; **~unfall** *m* traffic accident; **~verein** *m* tourist office; **~zählung** *f* traffic census.

verkehrt 1. *(falsch)* wrong; 2. *(entgegengesetzt)* opposite.

verkennen *irr* misjudge, underestimate.

verklagen *jur* bring an action *(jdn* against s.o.).

verkleiden 1. *tech* cover, line; 2. *sich* ~ dress up *(als* as).

verkleinern 1. reduce, make smaller; 2. *(Maßstab)* scale down.

Verknappung *f* shortage.

verknüpfen 1. knot, tie; 2. *fig* connect (with).

verkommen I *irr (Ware)* go to waste; **II** *adj* 1. dilapidated; 2. *(moralisch)* depraved.

verkörpern personify, incarnate.

verkrampfen, *sich* cramp, clench.

verkrüppelt crippled.

verkühlen, *sich* catch a (a) cold.

verkümmern *med* atrophy.

verkünd(ig)en 1. announce; 2. *jur* pronounce.

verkürzen 1. shorten; 2. *(Urlaub)* curtail.

verladen *irr* load (*auf* on to), ship.

Verlag *m* publishing firm.

verlagern 1. (*Gewicht*) shift; 2. *tech* displace.

verlangen 1. (*fordern*) demand; 2. (*erwarten*) expect; 3. (*erfordern*) require, call for; 4. (*bitten*) ask for; 5. (*berechnen*) charge; 6. *Sie werden am Telefon verlangt* you're wanted on the phone; **V~** *n* longing, desire.

verlänger|n 1. lengthen; 2. (*Frist*) extend, prolong; 3. (*Vertrag*) renew; **V~ung** *f* 1. extension, prolongation; 2. (*Ausweis*) renewal; 3. *sport* extra time.

verlangsamen slow down, slacken, reduce.

Verlaß *m: es ist kein ~ auf sie* she is not reliable.

verlassen I *irr* 1. (*weggehen*) leave; 2. (*im Stich lassen*) abandon, desert; 3. *sich ~ auf* rely on, depend on; (*vertrauen*) trust to; **II** *adj* abandoned, forsaken, deserted.

verläßlich reliable, dependable.

Verlauf *m* 1. (*Fluß*) course; 2. (*Ablauf*) run; *im ~ von* in the course of; *nach ~ von* after a lapse of; *e-n schlimmen ~ nehmen* take a bad turn; **v~en** *irr* 1. (*Fluß*) run; 2. (*Zeit*) pass; 3. (*ablaufen*) go; 4. (*enden*) end; 5. (*schmelzen*) run; 6. *sich ~*

get lost, disappear; 7. (*zerstreuen*) scatter.

verlaust lousy.

verleben spend, pass.

verlegen I 1. (*Sache*) mislay; 2. (*Wohnsitz*) move, transfer; 3. (*aufschieben*) postpone, adjourn; 4. (*veröffentlichen*) publish; 5. *sich ~ auf* take to s.th.; **II** *adj* embarrassed, confused; **V~heit** *f* 1. embarrassment, confusion; *in ~* embarrassed; 2. (*mißliche Lage*) predicament, dilemma.

Verleger *m* publisher.

Verleih *m film* distribution; **v~en** *irr* 1. lend out; (*gegen Geld*) hire out; 2. (*Recht*) bestow, vest; 3. (*Preis*) award.

verleiten 1. (*veranlassen*) lead; 2. (*verführen*) seduce.

verlernen forget.

verlesen *irr* 1. (*Namen*) call; 2. *sich ~* read wrong.

verletz|en 1. hurt, injure; 2. *fig* offend; 3. (*Pflicht*) break, violate; **~t** hurt, injured; **V~ter** *m* injured person; **V~ung** *f* 1. injury; 2. (*Beleidigung*) offence.

verleumd|en, V~ung *f* slander.

verlieb|en, *sich* fall in love (*in jdn* with s.o.); **~t** 1. amorous; 2. *~ sein* be in love.

verlieren *irr* 1. lose; 2. (*Zeit*) waste; 3. (*Hoffnung*) give up; 4. *aus den Augen ~* lose sight of; 5. *sich ~* disappear.

verlob|en, *sich* become engaged; **~t** : *~ sein* be engaged; **V~te** 1. *m* fiancé; 2. *f* fiancée; **V~ung** *f* engagement.

verlock|end tempting; **V~ung** *f* temptation.

verloren 1. lost; 2. *~ geben* give up for lost; 3. *der ~e Sohn* the prodigal son; **~gehen** *irr* get lost.

verlosen raffle.

Verlust *m* 1. loss; 2. *mit ~ verkaufen* sell at a loss.

vermachen *jur* bequeath (*jdm etw* s.th. to s.o.).

Vermächtnis *n* bequest, legacy.

vermähl|en, *sich* marry, get married (*mit* to); **V~ung** *f* marriage, wedding.

vermehren increase, multiply.

vermeid|bar avoidable; **~en** *irr* avoid.

vermeintlich alleged, supposed, pretended.

Vermerk *m* note, notice, entry.

vermess|en I *irr (ausmessen)* measure; **II** *adj* presumptuous.

vermiet|en 1. rent, let; *Zimmer zu ~* rooms for rent; 2. *(Auto)* hire; **V~er** *m* renter; hirer; **V~ung** *f* 1. letting; 2. hiring out.

vermindern diminish, lessen.

vermischen 1. mix up, mingle; 2. *(Farbe)* blend.

vermissen 1. *(Brille)* not be able to find; 2. *(Abwesenheit feststellen)* see that s.th. is not there; 3. *(schmerzlich)* miss, regret the loss.

vermißt missing; **V~er** *m* missing person.

vermitt|eln 1. mediate, intervene (*zwischen* between); 2. *(arrangieren)* arrange; 3. *(beschaffen)* procure; **~els(t)** by means of, through; **V~ler** *m* 1. mediator; 2. *(Mittelsmann)* go-between; **V~lung** *f: durch ~ von* through the intermediary of.

vermöge 1. in virtue of; 2. *(dank)* owing to; **~n** *irr* 1. *(können)* be capable of; 2. *(imstande sein)* be in a position to, be able to; **V~n** *n* 1. *(Besitz)* property, fortune, means *pl*; 2. *com* assets *pl*; **~nd** wealthy, rich; **V~nsteuer** *f* property tax.

vermut|en suppose, presume, suspect; **~lich** presumable, probable; **V~ung** *f* supposition, presumption.

vernachlässigen neglect.

vernarben heal up.

vernehm|en *irr* 1. *(hören)* hear, learn; 2. *(befragen)* question, examine; **~lich** audible; **V~ung** *f* interrogation.

verneigen, *sich* bow.

verneinen 1. answer in the negative; 2. *(leugnen)* deny.

vernicht|en destroy, annihilate; **V~ung** f destruction, annihilation.

Vernunft f 1. common sense, reason; 2. *jdn zur ~ bringen* bring s.o. to his senses.

vernünftig 1. *(Person)* sensible; 2. *(annehmbar)* reasonable.

veröffentlich|en publish; **V~ung** f publication.

verordnen 1. order, decree; 2. *med* prescribe.

verpachten lease.

verpack|en pack up, wrap up; **V~ung** f 1. packing; 2. *(Material)* packing material.

verpassen 1. *(Zug)* miss; 2. *(Gelegenheit)* let slip.

verpfänden pledge, pawn.

verpfleg|en 1. *(beköstigen)* board; 2. *(Person)* feed, supply with food; **V~ung** f 1. food; 2. *Zimmer mit ~* room and board.

verpflicht|en 1. oblige; 2. *(engagieren)* engage; 3. *sich ~* oblige o.s., bind o.s.; **~et:** *~ sein* be obliged *(jdm* to s.o.); **V~ung** f obligation, commitment.

verprügeln thrash, give a beating.

Verputz m *arch* plaster, roughcast; **v~en** *(Wand)* plaster.

Verrat m treason, betrayal; **v~en** *irr* 1. betray; 2. *(sagen)* disclose; 3. *(erkennen lassen)* reveal.

Verräter m traitor; **v~isch** treacherous.

verrechnen 1. *(ausgleichen)* balance, compensate; 2. *sich ~* make a mistake; *Sie haben sich um 10 DM verrechnet* you are 10 DM out, *Am* off.

verregnet rainy.

verreisen go on a journey, go away *(nach* to).

verrenken sprain, dislocate.

verrichten perform, do, carry out.

verriegeln bolt.

verringern diminish, lessen, reduce.

verrinnen *irr (Zeit)* elapse.

verrost|en rust; **~et** rusty.

verrückt 1. mad, crazy; 2. *~ machen* drive crazy; **V~er** m lunatic, madman.

Verruf m: *in ~ kommen* get into disrepute; **v~en** ill-reputed, notorious.

Vers m verse.

versage|n 1. *(ablehnen)* deny, refuse; 2. *(nicht funktionieren)* fail, break down; **V~n** n failure; **V~r** m *fig* failure.

versalzen oversalt.

versamm|eln 1. gather, assemble; 2. *sich ~* meet; **V~lung** f meeting, gathering, assembly.

Versand m dispatch; **~geschäft** n mail-order business.

versäumen 1. neglect;

2. *(Gelegenheit)* miss; 3. *(zu tun)* omit, fail (to do).

verschaffen 1. get, procure; 2. *sich etw* ~ gain s.th.

verschärfen 1. *(Lage)* aggravate, intensify; 2. *(Bestimmungen)* tighten up; 3. *sich* ~ mount, increase.

verschenken give away.

Verschiebe|bahnhof *m* shunting station; **v~n** *irr* 1. *(zeitlich)* postpone, put off; 2. *(in e-e andere Stellung)* shift, displace; 3. *(vertagen)* adjourn.

verschieden 1. different *(von* from); 2. *(mehrere)* various, several; ~**artig** various, diverse; ~**es** of various kinds; ~**tlich** 1. repeatedly; 2. *(gelegentlich)* now and then.

verschimmelt mouldy.

verschlafen I *irr* oversleep; **II** *adj* sleepy.

Verschlag *m* shed; **v~en I** 1. *irr (Buchseite)* lose o.'s place; 2. *es verschlug ihm die Sprache* he was struck dumb; **II** *adj* cunning.

verschlechtern 1. make worse; 2. *sich* ~ deteriorate.

verschleiern veil.

Verschleiß *m* wear and tear; **v~en** *irr* wear out.

verschleppen 1. carry off; 2. *jdn* ~ deport s.o.; 3. *(Krankheit)* spread.

verschleudern 1. *(Geld)* squander; 2. *com* sell dirt--cheap.

verschließen *irr* lock, shut.

verschlimmern aggravate, make worse.

verschlingen *irr* swallow up, devour.

verschlossen 1. closed, locked; 2. *fig* reserved.

verschlucken swallow.

Verschluß *m* 1. clasp; 2. *(Deckel)* cap; 3. *phot* shutter; 4. *unter* ~ *halten* keep under lock and key.

verschlüsselt coded.

verschmähen scorn, disdain.

verschmerzen *(Verlust)* get over.

verschmutzt 1. dirty; 2. *(Luft)* polluted.

verschnaufen, *sich* recover o.'s breath.

verschneit snow-covered.

verschnüren tie up.

verschonen spare.

verschönern embellish.

verschreiben *irr* 1. *med* prescribe; 2. *(Leben)* devote; 3. *sich* ~ make a mistake.

verschrotten scrap.

verschüchtert intimidated.

verschulde|n 1. be responsible for; 2. *(verursachen)* cause; 3. *com* become indebted; **V~n** *n* fault; ~**t** indebted.

verschütten 1. spill; 2. *(Menschen)* bury.

verschwägert related by marriage.

verschweigen *irr* conceal, hide.

verschwend|en squander,

waste; **V~er** m spendthrift; **~erisch** wasteful, extravagant; **V~ung** f waste, wastefulness, extravagance.

verschwiegen concealed, secret; **V~heit** f reticence, secrecy.

verschwinden irr disappear, vanish.

verschwommen vague.

verschwör|en, sich irr plot, conspire; **V~er** m conspirator; **V~ung** f plot, conspiracy.

versehen I irr 1. supply, furnish (mit with); 2. (besorgen) look after; 3. (innehaben) perform, hold; 4. sich ~ (versorgen) provide; 5. sich ~ (falsch sehen) make a mistake; **II** adj: mit etw ~ sein be provided with s.th.; **V~** n mistake, error; **~tlich** by mistake.

Versehrter m disabled person.

versenden irr dispatch, forward, ship.

versengen singe, scorch.

versenken sink.

versetzen 1. move, shift; transplant; 2. (Arbeitsplatz) transfer; 3. (verpfänden) pawn; 4. (im Stich lassen) let down, leave in the lurch; 5. jdm etw ~ give s.o. s.th.; 6. (vermischen) add, mix; 7. (Schüler) move up; 8. sich in jds Lage ~ put o.s. in o.'s place.

verseuchen infect, contaminate.

versicher|n 1. insure (gegen against); 2. (bestätigen) affirm, assert; 3. sich ~ lassen take out an insurance; **V~ung** f 1. insurance; 2. (Bestätigung) assurance, affirmation.

versinken irr sink, founder.

versöhn|en reconcile; **~lich** conciliatory; **V~ung** f reconciliation.

versorg|en 1. provide, supply; 2. (Kranke) care for, look after; **V~ung** f 1. (Waren) supply; 2. (Familie) support, maintenance; 3. med care, attendance.

verspät|en, sich be late, be behind time; **~et** late, belated; **V~ung** f 1. delay; 20 Minuten ~ haben be 20 minutes late; 2. (Person) being late.

verspeisen eat up.

versperren 1. lock up; 2. (Weg) block.

verspotten ridicule.

versprech|en 1. promise; 2. sich ~ make a slip of the tongue; 3. sich etw ~ von expect s.th. of; 4. ~, schön zu werden be promising; **V~en** n promise; sein ~ halten keep o.'s promise; **V~ung** f: große ~en machen make great promises.

verstaatlichen nationalize.

Verstand m 1. (Denkvermögen) mind, intellect; den ~

verlieren lose o.'s head;
2. *(Auffassung)* understanding; *das geht über meinen ~* that's beyond me; 3. *(Vernunft)* reason, sense.

verständlig sensible, reasonable; **~igen** 1. inform, notify; 2. *sich ~* come to an understanding; 3. *sich mit jdm ~* communicate with s.o.; **V~igung** *f* information, notification; communication; **~lich** 1. *(hörbar)* audible; 2. *(klar)* clear, distinct; 3. *(erfaßbar)* intelligible, comprehensible; 4. *sich ~ machen* make o.s. understood.

Verständnis *n* 1. *(Verstehen)* understanding; *für etw ~ haben* appreciate s.th.; 2. *(Begreifen)* comprehension; **v~los** unappreciative, uncomprehending; **v~voll** understanding, sympathetic.

verstärkeln 1. reinforce, strenghten; 2. *(steigern)* intensify; 3. *el* amplify; **V~r** *m* amplifier.

verstauchen sprain; *sich den Arm ~* sprain o.'s arm.

Versteck *n* hiding-place; **v~en** hide, conceal.

verstehen *irr* 1. *(deutlich hören)* hear; 2. *(geistig)* understand; *jdm zu ~ geben* give s.o. to understand; 3. *(verarbeiten)* comprehend, grasp; 4. *(Verständnis haben)* understand; 5. *(können)* have a knowledge of;

6. *es ~, etw zu tun* know how to do s.th.; 7. *(auffassen, meinen)* see, mean; 8. *sich ~* get along; 9. *sich auf etw ~* be an expert at s.th.; 10. *das versteht sich* that goes without saying.

versteigerln sell by auction; **V~ung** *f* auction.

verstelllbar adjustable; **~en** 1. *(versperren)* block, bar; 2. *(falsch stellen)* put in the wrong place; 3. *(täuschen)* disguise; 4. *sich ~* dissimulate.

versteuern pay tax on.

verstimmt 1. out of tune; 2. *(ärgerlich)* annoyed.

verstohlen furtive, stealthy.

verstopfen 1. stop up, block; 2. *(Straße)* congest; 3. *med* constipate; **V~ung** *f* 1. blockage; 2. *(Straße)* congestion; 3. *med* constipation.

verstorben deceased, late.

verstört haggard, upset.

Verstoß *m* offence, infraction; **v~en** *irr* 1. repudiate; 2. *aus etw ~* expel from s.th.; 3. *gegen etw ~* offend against s.th.

verstreichen *irr* 1. *(Butter)* spread; 2. *(Zeit)* pass, elapse.

verstreuen scatter, spill.

verstümmeln mutilate.

verstummen grow silent.

Versuch *m* 1. experiment, attempt; 2. *(Prüfung)* try, trial, test; **v~en** 1. try, attempt; 2. *(kosten)* taste, try; **~skaninchen** *n fig* guinea-pig;

v~sweise as a trial; **~ung** *f* temptation.

vertagen adjourn.

vertauschen 1. confuse; 2. *(austauschen)* change round; 3. *(Rollen)* exchange.

verteidig|en 1. defend; 2. *jur* plead *(jdn* for s.o.); **V~er** *m* 1. defender; 2. *jur* counsel for the defence; **V~ung** *f* defence.

verteil|en 1. distribute *(unter* among); 2. *(Aufstrich)* spread; 3. *sich ~* disperse, scatter; **V~r** *m* 1. *el* distributor; 2. *(Liste)* distribution list.

verteuern raise the price of.

vertief|en 1. deepen; 2. *sich ~ (fig)* become absorbed *(in* in); **V~ung** *f* depression.

vertilgen exterminate, extirpate.

Vertrag *m* 1. contract; 2. *pol* treaty; 3. *(Abkommen)* agreement; **v~en** *irr* 1. *(aushalten)* stand, endure; 2. *(nehmen)* take; *Spaß ~* take a joke; 3. *(ertragen)* bear, tolerate; 4. *sich ~* get on together, harmonize; **v~lich** contractual; by contract.

verträglich 1. *(Mensch)* peaceable; 2. *(verdaulich)* digestible; 3. *(Medizin)* well-tolerated.

Vertrags|bruch *m* breach of contract; **~schließender** *m* contractor; contracting party.

vertrauen 1. *jdm ~* trust s.o.: 2. *auf jdn ~* trust in s.o., rely upon s.o.

Vertrauen *n* confidence, trust, faith; *jds ~ genießen* enjoy s.o.'s confidence; *jdn ins ~ ziehen* take s.o. into o.'s confidence; *im ~* confidentially, between you and me; *im ~ auf* trusting in; **~smann** *m* man of confidence; **~sperson** *f* confidant; **~sposten** *m* position of trust; **~ssache** *f: das ist ~* that's a matter of confidence; **v~svoll** trustful; **v~swürdig** trustworthy.

vertraulich 1. confidential; 2. *streng ~!* strictly confidential!

vertraut 1. intimate, close; 2. *(bekannt)* familiar; *sich mit etw ~ machen* familiarize o.s. with s.th.; **V~er** *m* intimate friend.

vertreiben *irr* 1. drive away; 2. *jdn ~* expel s.o.; 3. *com* distribute, sell; 4. *sich die Zeit ~* while away o.'s time.

vertret|en *irr* 1. *(Chef)* replace; 2. *(Firma)* represent; 3. *(verantworten)* justify; 4. *(einstehen)* answer for; 5. *e-e Ansicht ~* hold a view; 6. *sich die Füße ~* stretch o.'s legs; **V~er** *m* 1. *(Chef)* substitute; *(Firma)* representative; 2. *com* commercial traveller, representative, agent; **V~ung** *f* 1. representation, substitution; *in ~* acting as deputy; 2. *com* agency.

Vertrieb *m* 1. distribution; 2. *(Absatz)* sale.

vertrocknen dry up.

vertrösten: *jdn* ~ put s.o. off.

verübeln: *jdm etw* ~ blame s.o. for s.th., be annoyed at s.o. for s.th.

verüben commit, perpetrate.

verunglücken meet with an accident; *tödlich* ~ be killed in an accident.

verunreinigen 1. dirty; 2. *(Luft)* pollute.

verunstalten disfigure, deform.

veruntreuen embezzle.

verursachen cause, bring on, give rise to, create.

verurteilen 1. sentence, condemn; 2. *(mißbilligen)* disapprove.

verviel|fachen multiply; ~**fältigen** duplicate; **V~fältigung** *f* duplication, copy.

vervoll|kommnen perfect; ~**ständigen** complete.

verwahr|en 1. keep, preserve; 2. *sich* ~ protest *(gegen* against); ~**lost** neglected.

verwaist orphaned.

verwalt|en administer, manage; **V~er** *m* administrator, manager; **V~ung** *f* administration, management.

verwand|eln 1. transform, convert, turn *(in* into); 2. *sich* ~ change; **V~lung** *f* transformation, change.

verwandt 1. related *(mit* to); *sie ist mit mir* ~ she is a relative of mine; 2. *fig* cognate; **V~er** *m* relative, kin; **V~schaft** *f* 1. relationship, kinship; 2. *fig* relation, alliance.

verwarn|en warn, caution; **V~ung** *f* warning, caution.

verwaschen washed out.

verwechs|eln 1. confuse, mix up; confound; 2. *jdn mit jdm* ~ mistake s.o. for s.o.; **V~(e)lung** *f* confusion, mistake.

verwegen bold, daring.

verweigern refuse, deny.

Verweis *m* 1. *(Tadel)* reprimand, rebuke; 2. *(Hinweis)* reference; **v~en** *irr* 1. *(hinweisen)* refer *(auf* to); 2. *von der Schule* ~ expel from school; 3. *(tadeln)* rebuke, reprimand.

verwelken fade, wither.

verwend|bar 1. applicable; 2. *(brauchbar)* usable, serviceable; ~**en** *irr* 1. use, utilize, employ; 2. *(Mühe)* spend; 3. *(Geld)* use, expend; 4. *(anwenden)* apply; 5. *sich* ~ *für* use o.'s influence for; **V~ung** *f* 1. employment; 2. *(Nutzung)* use, utilization.

verwerf|en *irr* 1. give up, reject; 2. *(Bedenken)* dismiss; ~**lich** condemnable.

verwerten 1. make use of; 2. *com* realize.

verwick|eln 1. *(Garn)*

tangle; 2. *jdn in etw* ~ involve s.o. in s.th.; **~elt** involved, complicated.

verwildert *(Garten)* overgrown.

verwirklichen 1. realize; 2. *sich* ~ materialize.

verwirr|en confuse, embarrass; **V~ung** *f* confusion, embarrassment.

verwittert weather-beaten.

verwitwet widowed.

verwöhn|en spoil; **~t** spoiled.

verworren confused.

verwund|bar vulnerable; **~en** wound *a. fig.*

verwunder|lich surprising; **~n** astonish, amaze; **V~ung** *f: zu m-r* ~ to my astonishment, surprise.

Verwundung *f* wound, injury.

verwünschen 1. curse; 2. *(verzaubern)* bewitch.

verwüsten devastate.

verzählen, *sich* miscount.

verzaubern 1. cast a spell over; 2. *fig* bewitch, charm.

Verzehr *m* consumption; **v~en** consume, eat up.

Verzeichnis *n* 1. list; 2. *(amtlich)* register; 3. *(Buch)* index.

verzeih|en *irr* pardon, excuse, forgive; **~lich** excusable; **V~ung** *f: um* ~ *bitten* beg s.o.'s pardon; **~!** I beg your pardon!

Verzerrung *f* distortion.

verzetteln, *sich* dissipate o.'s energies.

Verzicht *m* 1. renunciation *(auf* of); 2. *(Opfer)* sacrifice; 3. *jur* waiver; **v~en** 1. renounce, resign, do without; 2. *jur* waive.

verziehen *irr* 1. remove *(nach* to); *unbekannt verzogen* moved to an unknown address; 2. *das Gesicht* ~ pull a face; 3. *(verzerren)* distort; 4. *(verwöhnen)* spoil; 5. *sich* ~ *(Gesicht)* twist; *(Holz)* warp; *(Wolken)* disperse.

verzieren adorn, decorate; **V~ung** *f* decoration, ornament.

verzinsen, *sich* bear, yield interest.

verzogen *(Kind)* spoiled.

verzöger|n 1. delay; 2. *sich* ~ be delayed; **V~ung** *f* delay.

verzollen pay duty on; *haben Sie etw zu* ~? have you anything to declare?

Verzug *m* delay; *in* ~ *geraten* get into arrears; **~szinsen** *pl* interest for default.

verzweif|eln 1. despair *(an* of); 2. *es ist zum V~* it's enough to drive one to despair; **~elt** desperate; **V~lung** *f* desperation; *zur* ~ *bringen* drive to despair.

Veteran *m* veteran.

Vetter *m* cousin.

Viadukt *m* viaduct.

vibrieren vibrate.

Vieh *n* cattle; **~bestand** *m*

livestock; **~zucht** f cattle-
-breeding.
viel 1. much, a great deal of,
plenty of; ~ *Glück!* good
luck! 2. *(vor Substantiven
im pl)* many, lots of; 3. *das
ist nicht* ~ that is not much;
4. *ein bißchen* ~ a bit too
much; 5. *hat es* ~ *gekostet?*
did it cost much? 6. *(viele
Menschen)* many people;
7. *um* ~*es* much, far; 8. *in*
~*em* in many respects; 9. ~
zuviel much too much;
~fach 1. multiple, manifold;
2. *(in vielen Fällen)* in many
cases; **V~falt** f diversity.
vielleicht perhaps, maybe.
viel|mehr 1. rather; 2. *(im
Gegenteil)* on the contrary;
~seitig 1. versatile; 2. *auf
~en Wunsch* by popular request; **V~zahl** f multitude.
vier four; **V~eck** n square;
~eckig quadrangular;
V~linge pl quadruplets pl;
~t fourth; *am ~en Mai* on
May fourth.
Viertel n 1. *(Stadt~)* quarter;
2. *ein ~ drei* a quarter past
two; *drei ~ drei* a quarter to
three; **~jahr** n three
months; **v~jährlich** quar-
terly; **~stunde** f quarter of
an hour.

vier|zehn fourteen; ~ *Tage* a
fortnight; **~zehntägig** four-
teen-day, fortnightly; **~zig**
forty.
Vikar m curate.

Vill|a f villa; **~enviertel** n
residential district.
violett violet.
Violine f violin.
Virus n med virus.
Visier n *(Gewehr)* sight.
Visite f visit a. med;
~nkarte f visiting card.
Visum n visa.
Vitamin n vitamin(e);
v~reich rich in vitamins.
Vize|admiral m vice-admiral;
~präsident m vice-presi-
dent.
Vogel m bird; **~bauer** n
bird-cage; **~nest** n bird's
nest; **~perspektive** f
bird's-eye view; **~scheu-
che** f scarecrow.
Volk n 1. *(Nation)* people,
nation; 2. *(Klasse)* class;
3. *(Masse)* mass of people,
crowds pl; 4. *(Bienen)*
swarm.
Völker|kunde f ethnology;
~recht n international law.
Volks|abstimmung f, **~ent-
scheid** m plebiscite, refer-
endum; **~fest** n public festival; **~hochschule** f adult
evening classes pl; **~kunde**
f folklore; **~lied** n folk
song; **~schule** f elementary
school; **~tanz** m folk-dance;
~tracht f national costume;
v~tümlich popular; **~wirt-
schaft** f political economy;
~zählung f census.
voll 1. full; *ein ~es Glas* a full
glass; 2. *(ganz)* full; *die ~
Wahrheit* the full truth; *ein*

~es *Jahr* a whole year;
3. *(vollkommen)* complete;
4. *mit* ~*er Kraft* by might
and main; 5. ~*er Leben* full
of life; 6. *(bedeckt)* covered;
7. *aus dem* ~*en schöpfen*
draw on abundant re-
sources; 8. ~ *verantwortlich*
fully responsible; ~ *zahlen*
pay in full; ~ *und ganz* completely; 9. *man kann ihn
nicht für* ~ *nehmen* you
can't take him seriously;
~**auf** fully, abundantly;
~**automatisch** fully automatic; **V**~**bart** *m* full beard;
V~**beschäftigung** *f* full
employment; ~**bringen** *irr,*
~**enden** accomplish,
achieve; ~**endet** perfect,
accomplished; ~**ends** completely, totally; ~**füllen** fill
up; **V**~**gas** *n* full speed.

völlig 1. complete; 2. *(absolut)* absolute; full; 3. ~ *unmöglich* absolutely impos-
ible.

volljährig of age, major;
V~**keit** *f* majority.

Vollkaskoversicherung *f*
full-comprehensive insur-
ance.

vollkommen perfect;
V~**heit** *f* perfection.

Vollkornbrot *n* wholemeal
bread.

Vollmacht *f jur* power of attorney; *jdm* ~ *geben* authorize s.o.

Vollmilch *f* whole milk.

Vollmond *m* full moon.

Vollpension *f* full board and
lodging.

vollschlank rather plump.

vollständig 1. complete, full;
2. ~ *recht haben* be absolutely, quite right; **V**~**keit** *f*
integrity; *der* ~ *halber* for
the sake of completeness.

vollstopfen cram, stuff.

vollstrecken *jur* execute.

volltanken fill up.

Volltreffer *m: e-n* ~ *erzielen*
hit the jackpot.

Vollversammlung *f* plenary
session.

vollzählig complete, full.

vollziehen *irr* execute, perform, carry out.

Volontär *m* trainee.

Volumen *n* volume.

von 1. *(Richtung)* from; *der
Wind kommt* ~ *Süden* the
wind comes from the south;
2. ~ *einem Teller essen* eat
from one plate; 3. *(Bildung
des Genitives)* of; *der Bau* ~
Schulen the building of
schools; *e-r* ~ *uns* one of us;
4. *(Urheber) ein Gedicht* ~
a poem by; 5. *(Eigenschaft)
ein Kind* ~ *drei Jahren* a
child of three; 6. ~ *jdm sprechen* talk about s.o.; 7. *(infolge* ~*)* from; 8. *(Adelstitel)*
of; 9. ~ *jetzt ab* from now
on; ~ *da an* since then; ~
Grund auf completely; ~
Zeit zu Zeit from time to
time; ~**einander** from each
other; ~**statten**: ~ *gehen*
take place.

vor 1. *(räumlich)* in front of, before; ~ *dem Haus* in front of the house; 2. *(weiter vorn)* ahead of; 3. *(außerhalb)* outside; 4. *(in Gegenwart)* before, in the presence of; 5. ~ *dem Gesetz* before the law; 6. ~ *kurzem* a short time ago; 7. *(zeitlich)* before; ~ *Weihnachten* before Christmas; 8. *(Uhrzeit)* to; 9. *sicher* ~ *jdm sein* be safe from s.o.; 10. *(infolge von)* with; ~ *Neid erblassen* go green with envy; 11. ~ *allen Dingen* above all; 12. *(gegen)* against; 13. *aus Furcht* ~ for fear of.

Vorabend *m* evening before, eve.

Vorahnung *f* presentiment.

voran at the head; ~**gegangen** previous; ~**gehen** *irr* 1. go in front; 2. *fig* lead, set an example; 3. *(sich entwickeln)* come on, progress; ~**kommen** *irr* get on, advance.

Voranschlag *m* estimate.

Vorarbeiter *m* foreman.

voraus 1. ahead of; 2. *im* ~ in advance, beforehand; ~**bezahlen** pay in advance; ~**gehen** *irr* 1. lead the way, go on ahead; 2. *(zuerst geschehen)* precede; ~**haben** *irr: jdm etw* ~ have an advantage over s.o.; ~**sagen** predict, foretell, forecast; ~**sehen** *irr* foresee; ~**setzen** 1. *(annehmen)* assume,

presume, take for granted; *vorausgesetzt, daß* provided that; 2. *(erfordern)* require; **V**~**setzung** *f* supposition, assumption; *unter der* ~, *daß* on condition that; ~**sichtlich** presumable, prospective.

Vorbedacht *m* premeditation; *mit* ~ on purpose, deliberately.

Vorbedingung *f* prerequisite, precondition.

Vorbehalt *m* reservation; *unter dem* ~, *daß* provided that; **v**~**en** *irr* 1. *sich etw* ~ reserve s.th.; 2. *Änderungen* ~ subject to alterations; *alle Rechte* ~ all rights reserved; **v**~**los** unconditional.

vorbei 1. *(örtlich)* past, by; 2. *(zeitlich)* over, gone, past; ~**fahren** *irr* pass by; ~**gehen** *irr* 1. go past; 2. *an etw* ~ pass s.th.; 3. *bei jdm* ~ call on s.o.; 4. *(vergehen)* pass, go by; ~**kommen** *irr* 1. *an etw* ~ pass s.th.; 2. *(Besuch)* drop in; ~**lassen** *irr* let pass; ~**reden**: *am Thema* ~ miss the point.

vorbereit|**en** prepare *(auf, für* for), get ready (for); ~**end** preparatory; **V**~**ung** *f* preparation; ~*en treffen* make preparations.

vorbestellen *(Zimmer)* book.

vorbestraft previously convicted; *nicht* ~ *sein* be a first offender.

vorbeugen 1. prevent, preclude; 2. *sich ~* bend, lean forward; **~d** preventive.

Vorbild *n* 1. model; 2. *(Muster)* pattern; 3. *(Beispiel)* example; **v~lich** exemplary; **~ung** *f* (preparatory) training.

vorbringen *irr* 1. *(Wunsch)* express; 2. *(Argument)* bring forward; 3. *(Entschuldigung)* make.

Vorder|achse *f* front axle; **~ansicht** *f* front view.

vordere 1. *(Reihe)* front; 2. *der ~ Teil* the fore part.

Vorder|grund *m* 1. foreground; 2. *in den ~ treten* come to the fore; **~haus** *n* front building; **~rad** *n* front wheel; **~seite** *f* front side; **~sitz** *m* front seat; **v~st** foremost; **~teil** *n* front part.

vordring|en *irr* advance, penetrate; **~lich** urgent.

Vordruck *m* form, *Am* blank.

voreilig hasty, rash.

voreingenommen prejudiced, biassed *(für* in favour of).

vorenthalten *irr* withhold *(jdm* from s.o.).

vorerst for the time being.

Vorfahr *m* ancestor.

vorfahr|en *irr* 1. drive up *(vor* before); 2. *(vorausfahren)* go on ahead; **V~t** *f* right of way, priority; *~ beachten!* give way!

Vorfall *m* incident; **v~en** *irr* happen, occur.

vorfinanzieren prefinance.

Vorfreude *f* anticipated joy.

vorführ|en 1. demonstrate; 2. *film* show; 3. *e-n Zeugen ~* produce a witness; **V~raum** *m* projection room; **V~wagen** *m* demonstration car.

Vorgabe *f sport* handicap.

Vorgang *m* 1. *(Ablauf)* proceedings *pl;* 2. *(Ereignis)* event; 3. *tech* process.

Vorgänger *m* predecessor.

Vorgarten *m* front garden.

vorgeben *irr fig* pretend, allege.

Vorgebirge *n* promontory.

vorgefaßt preconceived.

vorgefertigt prefabricated.

vorgehen *irr* 1. go first; 2. *(nach vorne)* go to the front; 3. *(Uhr)* be fast; 4. *(Vorrang haben)* come first, have priority; 5. *(handeln)* act, proceed; 6. *gegen jdn ~* take actions against s.o.; 7. *(passieren)* take place; **V~** *n* action, procedure.

vorgerückt advanced, late.

vorgeschichtlich prehistoric.

Vorgeschmack *m* foretaste.

vorgeschritten advanced.

Vorgesetzter *m* superior, senior.

vorgestern the day before yesterday.

vorgreifen *irr fig* anticipate *(jdm* s.o.).

vorhaben *irr* 1. *(planen)*

plan, propose; intend; 2. *etw mit etw* ~ be going to do s.th. with s.th.; **V~** *n* intention, project.

Vorhalle *f* (entrance-)hall.

vorhalt|en *irr fig* reproach (*jdm etw* s.o. for s.th.); **V~ungen** *pl: jdm* ~ *machen* remonstrate with s.o.

vorhanden 1. existing; ~ *sein* exist; 2. *(verfügbar)* available.

Vorhang *m* curtain.

Vorhängeschloß *n* padlock.

Vorhaut *f anat* foreskin.

vorher 1. *kurz* ~ shortly beforehand; *am Abend* ~ the previous evening; 2. *(im voraus)* in advance; **~gehend, ~ig** preceding, previous.

vorherrschen prevail, predominate.

vorher|sagen *mete* forecast; **~sehen** *irr* foresee.

vorhin a short time ago.

Vorhut *f* vanguard.

vorig 1. *(früher)* former, previous; 2. *(letzt)* last.

Vorkämpfer *m fig* pioneer.

Vorkehrungen *pl:* ~ *treffen* take precautions.

Vorkenntnisse *pl* previous experience, knowledge.

vorkomm|en *irr* 1. *(sich finden)* be found; 2. *(geschehen)* happen, occur; 3. *(scheinen)* seem; 4. *(nach vorne kommen)* come forward; 5. *es kann* ~, *daß* it may happen that; **V~nis** *n* occurrence, event.

Vorkriegszeit *f* pre-war period, days *pl.*

vorlad|en *irr (Zeugen)* summon; **V~ung** *f* summons *pl*, citation.

Vorlage *f* 1. *jur* presentation; *gegen* ~ *von* on presentation on; 2. *zahlbar bei* ~ payable on presentation; 3. *(Muster)* model, pattern.

Vorläufer *m* precursor.

vorläufig 1. provisional; 2. *(nicht endgültig)* preliminary; 3. *(bis auf weiteres)* for the time being.

vorlegen 1. *(zeigen)* present; 2. *(einreichen)* submit; 3. *(Beweise)* produce.

vorles|en *irr* read out (*etw jdm* s.th. to s.o.); **V~ung** *f* lectures *pl (über* on).

vorletzt 1. *(örtlich)* last but one; 2. ~*e Woche* the week before last.

Vorlieb|e *f* preference, predilection; *e-e* ~ *haben für* have a special liking for; **v~nehmen** *irr: mit etw* ~ put up with s.th.

vorliegen *irr* 1. *(von Akten)* have come in; 2. *(dasein)* be; 3. *etw liegt gegen jdn vor* s.o. is charged with s.th.; 4. *es liegt kein Grund zur Besorgnis vor* there is no cause for worry; ~**d:** *im* ~*en Fall* in the present case.

vormachen 1. *(zeigen)* show; 2. *(täuschen)* fool.

vormerken 1. put down; 2. *(Zimmer)* reserve.

Vormittag *m* morning, forenoon; **v~s** in the morning.

Vormund *m* guardian.

vorn 1. at the front of; 2. *(im Vordergrund)* in the foreground; 3. *(am Anfang)* at the beginning; 4. *nach ~* to the front; *von ~e* from the front; 5. *von ~ anfangen* begin at the beginning; 6. *von ~e bis hinten* from beginning to end.

Vorname *m* first name.

vornehm distinguished.

vornehmen, *sich irr* make up o.'s mind (to).

vorn|herein: *von ~* from the beginning; **~über** forward.

Vorort *m* suburb; **~zug** *m* suburban train.

Vorrang *m* precedence; *~ haben* have priority.

Vorrat *m* 1. *(Waren)* stock, store, supply, provisions *pl; auf ~ kaufen* buy in stocks; 2. *(Bodenschätze)* reserve.

vorrätig available, on hand, in stock.

Vorrecht *n* privilege.

Vorrichtung *f* device, appliance.

vorrücken move up, advance.

Vorsaison *f* off-season.

Vor|satz *m* intention, resolution; **v~sätzlich** intentional, deliberate.

Vorschau *f* 1. preview *(auf* of); 2. *(Wetter)* forecast.

Vorschein *m*: *zum ~ kommen* appear, emerge.

vorschießen *irr (Geld)* advance.

Vorschlag *m* proposal, proposition, suggestion, offer; **v~en** *irr* propose, suggest.

vorschreiben *irr* prescribe, dictate.

Vorschrift *f* 1. *(Anweisung)* instruction, rule; 2. *med* prescription; **v~smäßig** according to instructions.

Vorschuß *m* advance.

vorschützen pretend, use as a pretext.

vorseh|en *irr* 1. plan; 2. *(bestimmen)* designate; 3. *sich ~* be careful; **V~ung** *f* Providence.

vorsetzen 1. serve; 2. *(anbieten)* offer.

Vorsicht *f* caution, care, precaution; *~ Stufe!* mind the step! **v~ig** 1. cautious, careful; 2. *(umsichtig)* circumspect; **v~shalber** to be on the safe side; **~smaßnahme** *f* precautionary measure.

Vorsitz *m* chairmanship; *den ~ führen* preside; **~ender** *m* president, chairman.

Vorsorg|e *f* precaution, provision; **v~en** make provisions; **~euntersuchung** *f* preventive check-up; **v~lich** precautionary.

Vorspeise *f* hors d'œuvres *pl.*

Vorspiel *n* 1. *mus* prelude; 2. *theat* prologue.

Vorsprung m (Abstand) lead, advantage a. fig; mit e-m ~ von by a margin of.

Vorstand m 1. board of directors; 2. (Verein) managing committee.

vorstehen irr 1. (Haus) project; 2. e-m Geschäft ~ manage a business; **~d** projecting.

Vorsteher m 1. superintendent, manager; 2. (Schule) headmaster; **~drüse** f prostate gland.

vorstell|en 1. (Uhr) put forward; 2. (davorstellen) put in front; 3. (darstellen) represent; 4. (bedeuten) signify, mean; 5. sich etw ~ imagine s.th., picture s.th.; stellen Sie sich das vor! fancy that! 6. sich jdm ~ introduce o.s. to s.o.; **V~ung** f 1. theat performance; 2. (Begriff) idea, conception; sich e-e ~ machen have an idea; Sie machen sich keine ~! You wouldn't believe it! 3. (Phantasie) imagination.

Vorstoß m (Versuch) attempt, try.

Vorstrafe f previous conviction.

vorstrecken 1. (Geld) advance; 2. (Kopf) put forward.

Vortag m previous day.

vortäuschen feign, pretend.

Vorteil m 1. advantage; 2. (Gewinn) profit; ~ bringen be profitable; 3. (Nutzen) benefit; ~ ziehen aus benefit from; **v~haft** advantageous, favourable, profitable.

Vortrag m 1. (Vorlesung) lecture; e-n ~ halten hold a lecture; 2. radio talk; 3. mus recital; 4. (Gedicht) recitation; **v~en** irr 1. carry forward; 2. (Vortrag halten) lecture on; 3. (hersagen) recite; 4. (darlegen) express, state.

vortrefflich excellent, splendid.

Vortritt m: jdm den ~ lassen give precedence to s.o.

vorüber 1. (örtlich) have gone past, have passed; 2. (zeitlich) be over, be past; **~gehen** irr pass; **~gehend** 1. temporary; 2. (flüchtig) passing, transitory.

Voruntersuchung f preliminary examination.

Vorurteil n prejudice, bias; **v~slos** unbiassed.

Vorverkauf m theat advance booking; **~sstelle** f booking office.

vorverlegen place on an earlier date.

Vorwahl f 1. pol preliminary, Am primary election; 2. tele preselection.

Vorwand m pretext; e-n ~ suchen look for a pretext.

vorwärts 1. forward; ~! go ahead! 2. (vorn) onwards; **V~gang** m forward gear;

~**kommen** *irr* get along, progress.

vorweg to begin with; ~**nehmen** *irr* anticipate.

vorweisen *irr* show, produce.

vorwerfen *irr* 1. *fig* reproach, rebuke; 2. *(e-m Hund)* throw to.

vorwiegend predominantly, chiefly, mainly.

Vorwort *n* preface, foreword.

Vorwurf *m* reproach; **v~svoll** reproachful.

Vorzeichen *n* 1. omen;

2. *math* sign.

vorzeigen show.

vorzeitig premature.

vorziehen *irr* 1. *fig* prefer; 2. *(bevorzugen)* favour; 3. *(nach vorn ziehen)* pull up; 4. *(Vorhang)* draw.

Vorzimmer *n* anteroom.

Vorzug *m* 1. preference; *den* ~ *geben* give preference to; 2. *(Vorteil)* advantage; 3. *(gute Seite)* merit.

vorzüglich 1. excellent, exquisite; 2. *(erstklassig)* first--rate.

Vulkan *m* volcano; ~**ausbruch** *m* volcanic eruption.

W

Waage *f* balance, scales *pl;* **w~recht** level, horizontal.
Wabe *f* honeycomb.
wach awake; ~ **werden** wake up; **W~ablösung** *f* relief.
Wache *f* 1. guard; 2. *(Posten)* sentry; 3. *(Polizei)* police-station; ~ **haben** be on guard; **w~n** 1. *(wach sein)* be awake; 2. *(Wache halten)* watch.
Wachhund *m* watchdog.
Wacholder *m* juniper.
wachrufen *irr* rouse, evoke.
Wachs *n* wax.
wachsam watchful, vigilant.
wachsen *irr* 1. grow; 2. *(anbauen)* be grown; 3. *(sich erheben)* rise up; 4. *(zunehmen)* grow, increase; 5. *(mit Wachs behandeln)* wax; ~**d** increasing.
Wachsfigurenkabinett *n* waxworks *pl;* ~**tuch** *n* oil-cloth.
Wachstum *n* 1. growth; 2. *(Entwicklung)* development; 3. *(Zunahme)* increase.
Wachtel *f orn* quail.
Wächter *m* guard, attendant.
Wachtmeister *m* constable.
wackelig wobbly, shaky.
Wackelkontakt *m* loose contact; **w~n** 1. wobble, shake; 2. *(Zahn)* be loose.

Wade *f* calf; ~**nkrampf** *m* cramp in the calf.
Waffe *f* weapon, arm.
Waffel *f* waffle; ~**eisen** *n* waffle-iron.
Waffengewalt *f: mit* ~ by force of arms; ~**händler** *m* arms dealer; ~**schein** *m* fire-arm certificate; ~**stillstand** *m* armistice *a. fig.*
Wagemut *m* daring, boldness; **w~ig** daring, bold.
wagen 1. venture, risk; 2. *(sich getrauen)* dare; 3. *sich aus dem Haus* ~ venture out of doors.
Wagen *m* 1. *(Auto)* car, automobile; 2. *(Pferde~)* waggon; 3. *(Kutsche)* carriage; ~**führer** *m* driver; ~**heber** *m* lifting jack; ~**ladung** *f* carload; ~**papiere** *pl* driving papers; ~**park** *m* car park; ~**spur** *f* wheel track; ~**tür** *f* car door.
Waggon *m* wag(g)on, truck.
waghalsig dare-devil.
Wagnis *n* venture, risk.
Wahl *f* 1. choice; *s-e* ~ *treffen* make o.'s choice; 2. *freie* ~ *haben* be free to choose; *jdn vor die* ~ *stellen* confront s.o. with the choice; 3. *(Güte)* quality; 4. *pol* election; *(geheim)* ballot; *(Abstimmung)* vote; *(Vorgang)* voting, poll.

wähl|en 1. choose; 2. *(aussuchen)* select; 3. *tele* dial; 4. *pol* elect; *jdn zum König ~ elect s.o. king; er darf schon ~* he is allowed to vote; *~ gehen* go to the polls; **W~er** *m* voter, elector.

Wahlergebnis *n* election result.

wählerisch choosy, particular.

Wahl|gang *m* ballot; **~kampf** *m* election campaign; **~liste** *f* list of candidates; **~lokal** *n* polling station; **w~los** 1. indiscriminate; 2. *(aufs Geratewohl)* at random; **~recht** *n* right to vote; *allgemeines ~* universal suffrage; **~spruch** *m* slogan; **w~weise** alternatively; **~zelle** *f* polling booth; **~zettel** *m* ballot.

Wahn *m* illusion, delusion; **~sinn** *m* madness; **w~sinnig** insane, mad, lunatic.

wahr 1. true; *es ist ~, daß* it is true that; 2. *(echt)* genuine, real; *~ werden* come true.

wahren 1. *(schützen)* protect, defend; *ein Geheimnis ~* guard a secret; 2. *(bewahren)* keep.

während 1. during; 2. *(im Verlauf von)* in the course of; 3. *(als)* while, whilst; 4. *(Gegensatz)* whereas.

wahrhaft true, real; **~ig** really, truly.

Wahrheit *f* 1. truth; *um die*

~ zu sagen to tell the truth; 2. *in ~* in reality; **w~sgetreu** truthful, faithful.

wahrnehm|bar perceptible, noticeable; **~en** *irr* 1. perceive, notice, observe; 2. *(Gelegenheit)* seize; 3. *(Termin)* observe; **W~ung** *f* perception.

wahrsage|n tell fortunes; **W~r** *m* fortune-teller.

wahrscheinlich probable, likely; **W~keit** *f* probability, likelihood.

Währung *f* currency; **~skrise** *f* monetary crisis; **~sreform** *f* currency reform.

Wahrzeichen *n* landmark.

Waise *f* orphan; **~nhaus** *n* orphanage.

Wal *m* whale.

Wald *m* wood; *(großer ~)* forest; **~brand** *m* forest fire.

Wäldchen *n* grove.

Wald|lauf *m* cross-country run; **~meister** *m* bot woodruff.

Wall *m* 1. *(Befestigung)* rampart; 2. *(Erd~)* embankment.

Wallfahrt *f* pilgrimage.

Walnuß *f* walnut.

Walze *f* 1. roller; 2. *math* cylinder; **w~n** roll.

wälzen 1. roll; 2. *(Bücher)* pore over; 3. *die Schuld auf jdn ~* lay the blame on s.o.

Walzer *m* waltz.

Wand *f* 1. wall; 2. *(Seitenfläche)* side; 3. *(Trenn~)* partition; 4. *(Fels~)* rock.

Wandel m change; **~halle** f
1. (Parlament) lobby;
2. theat lobby; **w~n,** sich
change.
Wander|ausstellung f touring exhibition; **~düne** f
shifting sand dune; **~er** m
wanderer, hiker.
wandern 1. walk, hike;
2. (ziellos) wander; 3. (Volk)
migrate; 4. (Düne) shift;
5. (Blick) roam.
Wander|ung f 1. walking-
-tour, hike; 2. (Volk) migration; **~vogel** m bird of passage; **~weg** m footpath.
Wand|karte f wall-map;
~leuchte f wall lamp.
Wandlung f 1. change; 2. rel
transsubstantiation.
Wand|schrank m wall cup-
board; **~spiegel** m pier-
-glass; **~uhr** f wall-clock.
Wange f cheek.
wankelmütig inconstant.
wanken 1. stagger; 2. (Gebäude) shake; 3. ins W~ geraten begin to stagger.
wann when; seit ~? how
long? bis ~? till when?
Wanne f 1. tub; 2. (zum Baden) bath-tub.
Wanze f bug.
Wappen n (coat of) arms pl.

Ware f merchandise, goods
pl, article; **~nbestand** m
stock on hand; **~nhaus** n
department store; **~nlager**
n 1. warehouse, depot;
2. (Vorrat) stock; **~nprobe**
f sample; **~nzeichen** n
trade-mark.
warm 1. warm; 2. sich ~ halten keep warm; mir ist ~ I
am warm; ~ machen warm
up.
Wärm|e f 1. warmth a. fig;
2. (Luft) heat; zehn Grad ~
ten degrees above zero;
w~en warm (up), heat; **~e-
regler** m thermostat; **~fla-
sche** f hot-water bottle.
Warmwasser|bereiter m
water heater; **~heizung** f
hot-water heating.
Warn|anlage f warning de-
vice; **~dreieck** n mot warning triangle.
warnen warn (vor of,
against), caution, alarm.
Warn|licht n warning light;
~schuß m warning shot a.
fig; **~signal** n warning signal; **~streik** m token strike;
~ung f warning, caution,
admonition.
Wart|eliste f waiting list;
w~en 1. wait; jdn ~ lassen
keep s.o. waiting; warte mal
wait a minute; 2. auf jdn ~
wait for s.o.; 3. (Maschine)
service, maintain.
Wärter m keeper, attendant.
Wartesaal m waiting-room.
Wartung f maintenance.
warum why; ~ nicht? why
not?
Warze f wart.
was I Frageprn 1. what; ~
hat er gesagt? what did he
say? ~ nun? what now? 2.

(wieviel) how much; 3. ~ *für* what sort of; 4. ~ *du nicht sagst!* you don't say! **II** *Relativprn* 5. what; *ich weiß,* ~ *du willst* I know what you want; ~ *auch immer geschehen mag* whatever may happen; 6. *er kam,* ~ *ich nicht erwartet habe* he came which I didn't expect; **III** *unbestimmtes prn* something; *ich muß dir* ~ *sagen* let me tell you something.

Wasch|automat *m* automatic washing machine; **w~bar** washable; **~bär** *m* racoon; **~becken** *n* wash-basin.

Wäsche *f* 1. laundry, washing, linen; 2. *(Waschen)* wash; *in die* ~ *geben* put in the wash; 3. *(Unter~)* underwear.

waschecht fast, non-shrinkable.

Wäsche|fach *n* linen shelf; **~geschäft** *n* lingerie shop; **~klammer** *f* clothes-peg; **~leine** *f* clothes-line.

waschen *irr* 1. wash; *sich das Gesicht* ~ wash o.'s face; 2. *(Haare)* shampoo; 3. *(Wäsche haben)* wash; 4. *sich* ~ wash; **W~** *n* washing.

Wäscherei *f* laundry.

Wasch|gelegenheit *f* washing facility; **~küche** *f* wash-house; **~lappen** *m* face-cloth; **~maschine** *f* washing-machine; **~mittel** *n* detergent; **~pulver** *n* washing powder; **~raum** *m* wash-room; **~schüssel** *f* wash-basin; **~tag** *m* wash-day.

Wasser *n* 1. water; ~ *holen* fetch water; 2. *fließendes* ~ running water; *ins* ~ *fallen* fall into the water; *ins* ~ *gehen* drown o.s.; *unter* ~ *stehen* be under water; *zu* ~ *und zu Land* by land and by water; 3. *das* ~ *läuft mir im Mund zusammen* my mouth waters; **~ball** *m* water polo; **~becken** *n* water basin; **w~dicht** waterproof; **~fall** *m* waterfall; **~farbe** *f* water-colour; **~flasche** *f* water-bottle; **~hahn** *m* tap, *Am* faucet.

wässerig watery.

Wasser|kraft *f* water-power; **~lauf** *m* water-course; **~leitung** *f* water pipes *pl;* **~mann** *m astr* Aquarius; **~melone** *f* watermelon; **w~n** *aero* alight on water; **~rohr** *n* water pipe; **~scheide** *f* watershed, *Am* divide; **~schlauch** *m* water-hose; **~ski** *m* water-ski; **~sport** *m* aquatic sports *pl;* **~spülung** *f* (water) flush; **~stoff** *m* hydrogen; **~stoffbombe** *f* hydrogen bomb; **~stoff-superoxid** *n* hydrogen peroxide; **~strahl** *m* jet of water; **~straße** *f* waterway, canal; **~tropfen** *m* drop of water; **~turm** *m* water-

-tower; **~waage** f spirit level; **~weg** m: auf dem ~ by water; **~werk** n waterworks pl.

waten wade.

Watt n mud flats pl.

Watt|e f cotton; **w~iert** wadded, padded.

web|en irr weave; **W~er** m weaver; **W~erei** f weaving mill; **W~stuhl** m loom.

Wechsel m 1. change; 2. alternation; 3. (Aufeinanderfolge) succession; 4. (Austausch) exchange; 5. com bill of exchange; **~geld** n (small) change; **w~haft** variable, changeable; **~jahre** pl climacterium; **~kurs** m rate of exchange.

wechseln 1. (Kleider) change; 2. (austauschen) exchange; 3. (Wohnort) move; 4. (abwechseln) alternate; **~d** changing, varied.

wechselseitig reciprocal.

Wechsel|strom m alternating current, A. C.; **~stube** f exchange office; **w~voll** eventful, varied; **~wirkung** f reciprocal action, correlation, interaction.

weck|en wake, arouse; **W~r** m alarm(-clock).

wedeln 1. wag (mit dem Schwanz its tail); 2. (Ski) wedel.

weder: ~ ... noch neither ... nor.

weg 1. (fort) gone; ~ da! get out of the way! Hände ~! hands off! 2. (abwesend) away; 3. über etw ~ sein have got over s.th.

Weg m 1. path; 2. (Wander~) track, trail; 3. (Spaziergang) walk; 4. (Wegstrecke) way; e-n ~ einschlagen take a way; jdm den ~ zeigen show s.o. the way; den ~ freigeben make way; den ~ zum Erfolg the way to success; 5. (Route) route; 6. am ~e along the way; auf dem ~e nach on the way to; auf diesem ~ (fig) this way; auf friedlichem ~ by peaceful means; auf halbem ~ halfway; auf schriftlichem ~ in writing; jdm aus dem ~ gehen step out of s.o.'s way; jdn aus dem ~ räumen get s.o. out of the way; jdm im ~e stehen be in s.o.'s way.

weg|bleiben irr stay away; **~bringen** irr 1. jdn ~ take s.o. away; 2. (Flecken) remove, take out.

wegen 1. because of; 2. (auf Grund) by reason of, on account of; 3. (um jds willen) for the sake of; 4. (infolge) due to.

weg|fahren irr 1. leave; 2. mot drive away; **~fallen** irr 1. be omitted; 2. (abschaffen) be abolished; 3. (beseitigen) clear up.

Weggabelung f road fork.

weg|geben irr give away;

~**gehen** *irr* 1. go away, leave; 2. *(von Waren)* sell;
~**jagen** chase away;
~**kommen** *irr* 1. get away; 2. *(Gegenstand)* get lost; 3. *gut, schlecht* ~ come off well, badly; ~**lassen** *irr* 1. *(Person)* let got; 2. *(auslassen)* omit, leave out;
~**laufen** *irr* run away; ~**legen** put aside; ~**nehmen** *irr* 1. take away; 2. *viel Zeit* ~ take a lot of time; 3. *(entfernen)* remove; ~**räumen** clear away, remove;
~**schicken** 1. *(Paket)* send off; 2. *(Person)* send away;
~**schließen** *irr* lock up;
~**schütten** pour away;
~**sehen** *irr* 1. look away; 2. *fig* shut o.'s eyes to;
~**stellen** put away.
Wegweiser *m* signpost.
weg|werfen *irr* throw away; ~**werfend** disparaging;
~**wischen** wipe off; ~**ziehen** *irr* pull off.
weh 1. *(wund)* sore; 2. *(schmerzend)* aching; 3. ~ *tun* be sore, ache; 4. *jdm* ~ *tun* hurt s.o.
Wehe *f:* ~*n haben* be in labour.
wehen blow.
wehleidig *(Stimme)* plaintive.
Weh|mut *f* wistfulness, nostalgia; **w~mütig** wistful.
Wehr 1. *f: sich zur* ~ *setzen* offer resistance; 2. *n* weir;
~**dienst** *m* military service;

~**dienstverweigerer** *m* conscientious objector;
w~en, *sich* resist, reject, defend o.s.; **w~los** 1. defenceless; 2. *(hilflos)* helpless; ~**pflicht** *f* compulsory military service;
w~pflichtig liable to military service; ~**pflichtiger** *m* conscript.
Weib *n* woman; ~**chen** *n* female; **w~isch** womanish, effeminate; **w~lich** 1. female; 2. *gram* feminine.
weich 1. soft; 2. *(zart)* tender; 3. *(sanft)* smooth; 4. *(Person)* tender-hearted, gentle; 5. ~ *machen* soften; **W~e** *f* 1. *anat* flank; 2. *loc* switch.
weichen *irr* 1. *(nachgeben)* yield; 2. *(Platz räumen)* give way; 3. *von jdm* ~ leave s.o.
Weichensteller *m* pointsman.
weichgekocht *(Ei)* soft-boiled.
Weichheit *f* softness, tenderness, gentleness.
weichlich flabby, soft.
Weichtiere *pl* molluscs *pl.*
Weide *f* 1. *bot* willow; 2. *(für Vieh)* pasture; **w~n** graze, pasture; ~**nkorb** *m* wicker basket.

weiger|n, *sich* refuse;
W~ung *f* refusal.
Weih|bischof *m* suffragan (bishop); ~**e** *f rel* consecration; *(Priester)* ordination;

w~en consecrate; *(Priester)* ordain.

Weiher *m* pond.

Weihnacht|en *n* Christmas; *frohe ~!* merry Christmas; **~sbaum** *m* Christmas-tree; **~sgeschenk** *n* Christmas present; **~lied** *n* Christmas carol; **~smann** *m* Father Christmas; *Am* Santa Claus.

Weih|rauch *m* incense; **~wasser** *n* holy water; **~wasserkessel** *m* font.

weil because.

Weiler *m* hamlet.

Wein *m* wine; *leichter ~* light wine; **~bau** *m* wine-growing; **~berg** *m* vineyard; **~bergschnecke** *f* edible snail; **~brand** *m* brandy.

wein|en 1. weep (*um* for), cry; 2. *(Tränen)* shed tears (*um* over); **~erlich** whining.

Wein|glas *n* wineglass; **~händler** *m* wine-merchant; **~handlung** *f* wine-store; **~karte** *f* wine-list; **~keller** *m* wine-cellar; **~lese** *f* vintage; **~stock** *m* vine; **~stube** *f* wine-tavern; **~traube** *f* grape.

weise 1. wise; 2. *(klug)* prudent.

Weise *f* 1. way, manner; *auf diese ~* in this way; *auf gleiche ~* the same way; *in der ~, daß* in such a way that; 2. *(Melodie)* air, tune.

weisen *irr* 1. show, point; 2. *etw von sich ~* repudiate s.th.

Weiser *m* wise man.

Weisheit *f* wisdom.

weismachen: *jdm etw ~* fool s.o., make s.o. believe; *das können Sie anderen ~* you can tell that to the marines.

weiß white.

Weissagung *f* prophecy.

Weiß|blech *n* tinplate; **~brot** *n* white bread; **~dorn** *m bot* whitethorn.

weißen *(tünchen)* white-wash.

Weißer *m* white man.

Weiß|gold *n* white gold; **~kohl** *m* cabbage; **w~lich** whitish; **~waren** *pl* linen goods *pl;* **~wein** *m* white wine.

weit I *adj* 1. *(Kleid)* wide; 2. *(Fläche)* broad; 3. *(Raum)* spacious; 4. *im ~eren Sinne* in the broader sense; 5. *(groß)* great; *das liegt in ~er Ferne* that is in the distant future; **II** *adv* 6. *die Tür ~ öffnen* open the door wide; 7. *~ verbreitet sein* be widespread; 8. *er ist ~ gereist* he is widely travelled; 9. *(räumlich)* far; *~er oben* farther up; *~ in der Ferne* far in the distance; *~ und breit* far and wide; *ist es noch ~?* is it far? 10. *das geht zu ~* that's going too far; 11. *so ~ ist es noch nicht* it has not come to that yet; *so ~, so gut* so far, so good; 12. *das liegt ~ zurück* that's a long way back; ~**aus** by far.

Weite *f* 1. *(Kleidung)* width; 2. *(Ebene)* vastness, immensity; distance; **w~n** 1. stretch, widen; 2. *(Fluß)* open.

weiter 1. *(zusätzlich)* further, additional; 2. ~! go on! *und so* ~ and so on; 3. *was* ~? what else? *kein Wort* ~ not another word; 4. *bis auf* ~es until further notice; *des* ~en in addition; *ohne* ~es without hesitation; ~**fahren** *irr* go on; ~**geben** *irr* pass on; ~**gehen** *irr* go on, continue; ~**hin** *(ferner)* furthermore, moreover; ~**kommen** *irr* get on; ~**leben** survive; ~**machen** continue; ~**reichen** hand on; ~**reisen** travel on.

weit|gehend to a large extent; ~**gereist** far-travelled; ~**her** from the distance; ~**hin** far away; ~**läufig** 1. spacious; 2. *(Verwandte)* distant; ~**reichend** far-reaching; ~**sichtig** *med* long-sighted; **W~sprung** *m* long jump; ~**verbreitet** widespread.

Weizen *m* wheat.

welch I *Frageprn* what, which; **II** *Relativprn* 1. *(Personen)* who, that; *derjenige, ~er* anyone who; 2. *(Sachen)* which, that; **III** *unbestimmtes prn* 3. *(etwas)* some; 4. *es gibt ~e, die ...*

there are some who ...; ~**erart** of what kind.

welk withered, faded.

Wellblech *n* corrugated iron.

Welle *f* 1. wave; 2. *tech* shaft, axle; 3. *radio* wave-length; 4. *(große)* surge; 5. *fig* trend; ~**nbrecher** *m* breakwater; ~**nlänge** *f* wave-length; ~**nsittich** *m* budgerigar.

wellig *(Haar)* wavy.

Wellpappe *f* corrugated board.

Welt *f* 1. *(Erde)* world; *e-e Reise um die* ~ a journey round the world; *bis ans Ende der* ~ to the end of the world; *aus der ganzen* ~ from all over the world; 2. *(Weltall)* universe; 3. *(Dasein)* life; *zur* ~ *kommen* come into the world; *das ist der Lauf der* ~ such is life; 4. *alle* ~ the whole world; ~**all** *n* universe; ~**ausstellung** *f* world's fair; ~**geschichte** *f* world history; ~**krieg** *m* world war; **w~lich** 1. wordly; 2. *(Geistlicher)* secular, profane; ~**literatur** *f* world literature; ~**macht** *f* world power; ~**markt** *m* world market; ~**meer** *n* ocean; ~**meister(schaft** *f)* *m* world champion(ship); ~**raum** *m* (outer) space; ~**reise** *f* world tour; ~**rekord** *m* world record; ~**stadt** *f* metropolis; **w~weit** world-wide; ~**wirtschaft** *f* world

economy; ~**wirtschafts-krise** f world depression.
wem I *Frageprn* to whom; ~ *gehört das Haus?* whom does the house belong to? **II** *Relativprn* whom; ~ *auch immer* whomever.
wen I *Frageprn* whom; *an* ~ *schreibst du?* whom are you writing to? **II** *Relativprn* whom.
Wende f turn; ~**kreis** m 1. *astr* tropic; 2. *mot* turning circle.
Wendeltreppe f winding staircase.
wenden I *irr* 1. turn; 2. *(lenken)* den Blick zur Seite ~ look aside; 3. *Zeit an etw* ~ spend time on s.th.; 4. *sich* ~ turn; *sich von jdm* ~ turn from s.o.; 5. *sich an jdn* ~ turn to s.o.; **II** 6. *reg (umdrehen)* turn; *das Auto* ~ turn the car; 7. *(sich ändern)* change.
Wendepunkt m turning--point *a. fig.*
wendig 1. *(Auto)* manœuvrable; 2. *(flink)* nimble, agile.
Wendung f 1. turn; 2. *fig* turn of events; 3. *dem Gespräch e-e* ~ *geben* change the subject.
wenig I *(adjektivisch)* 1. *(vor Substantiven im sing)* little; ~ *Geld haben* have little money; 2. *(vor Substantiven im pl)* a few; *in* ~*en Tagen bin ich zurück* I'll be back in a few days' time; 3. *das ist* ~

that is not much; **II** *(substantivisch)* 4. little; *sie ißt sehr* ~ she eats very little; 5. *(ein paar Leute)* a few people; **III** *(adverbial)* 6. little; *das interessiert mich* ~ that interests me little; 7. *ein* ~ a little, a bit; 8. *(selten)* very little.
weniger 1. less, fewer; 2. *es gefällt mir immer* ~ I like it less and less; *in* ~ *als* in less than; *je mehr ..., desto* ~ the more ... the less.
wenigst 1. least, fewest; 2. *am* ~*en* least of all; ~**ens** at least.
wenn 1. *(zeitlich)* when; *jedesmal,* ~ whenever; 2. *(falls)* if; ~ *das der Fall ist* if that is the case; ~ *nicht* unless; 3. ~ *auch, und* ~ even though; 4. *(Wunsch)* if only; 5. *wie* ~ as though, as if.
wer I *Frageprn* who; ~ *von euch beiden?* which of you two? **II** *Relativprn* who; ~ *auch immer* whoever; **III** *unbestimmtes prn* someone; *ist da* ~*?* someone there?

Werbe|berater m advertising consultant; ~**büro** n advertising agency; ~**fernsehen** n commercial television; ~**funk** m commercial radio.
werben *irr* 1. *(Mitglieder)* recruit, enlist; 2. *(Wähler)*

canvass; 3. *für etw* ~ advertise s.th., boost s.th.

Werbung f 1. com advertising, publicity, sales promotion; 2. *(Wähler)* canvassing.

werden irr **I** 1. *(anfangen)* become, get; *reich* ~ become rich; *krank* ~ become ill; *mir wird schlecht* I feel sick; 2. grow; *älter* ~ grow older; *müde* ~ grow tired; *dunkel* ~ grow dark; 3. *was ist aus ihm geworden?* what has become of him? 4. *(Beruf)* become; *Arzt* ~ become a doctor; 5. *(geschehen)* happen; 6. *(ausfallen)* turn out; 7. *(entstehen)* arise; **II** *aux* 8. shall, will; 9. *(Bildung des Passivs) geliebt* ~ be loved; 10. *ich werde es wohl verloren haben* I will have lost it; **~d**: *e-e* ~*e Mutter* a mother-to-be.

werfen irr 1. *(Ball)* throw; *nicht* ~! handle with care; 2. *Bomben* ~ drop bombs; *Schatten* ~ cast shadows; 3. *e-n Blick auf etw* ~ cast a glance at s.th.; *jdn ins Gefängnis* ~ throw s.o. into prison; 4. *sich auf jdn* ~ throw o.s. on s.o.; *sich auf den Boden* ~ throw o.s. on the floor; 5. *mit e-m Stein* ~ throw a stone.

Werft f shipyard.

Werk n 1. *(Tat)* work, deed, action; *ein gutes* ~ *tun* do a good work; 2. *(Erzeugnis)* work; 3. *(Produkt)* product; 4. *(Leistung)* achievement; 5. *sich ans* ~ *machen* set to work; 6. *(literarisch)* work, opus; 7. *(Fabrik)* works pl, factory; 8. tech mechanism; **~meister** m foreman; **~statt** f workshop; **~stoff** m material; **~tag** m workday; **w~tags** on weekdays; **~zeug** n tool, implement; **~zeugmacher** m toolmaker.

Wermut m vermouth.

wert 1. dear; 2. *(geschätzt)* esteemed; 3. *etw* ~ *sein* be worth; *e-n Versuch* ~ *sein* be worth a try; *es ist nicht der Rede* ~ it's not worth mentioning.

Wert m 1. value; *im* ~ *von* with a value of; *keinen* ~ *haben* be worthless; 2. *(Wertsache)* object of value; 3. *(Geltung)* value; 4. *(Wichtigkeit)* importance; *großen* ~ *legen* set great value; 5. *(Nutzen)* use; 6. *(Qualität)* quality; 7. com value; asset; **~angabe** f declaration of value; **w~beständig** *(Währung)* stable; **~brief** m insured letter.

werten appreciate, rate, judge.

Wertgegenstand m object of value; **w~los** worthless, of no value; **~minderung** f depreciation; **~papier** n security; **~sachen** pl valuables pl; **~schätzung** f esteem; **~steigerung** f increase in value; **~ung** f sport score, classification; **~urteil** n value judgement; **w~voll** valuable, precious.

Wesen n 1. (Art) manner, way; 2. (Natur) nature; s-m innersten ~ nach in his innermost nature; 3. (Kern) essence; 4. (Lebewesen) being, creature.

wesentlich 1. essential; 2. (wichtig) important; 3. (beträchtlich) considerable; 4. (grundlegend) fundamental; 5. (sehr viel) a great deal; 6. im ~en essentially, for the most part.

weshalb I adv why; **II** conj and ... therefore, so that.

Wespe f wasp; **~nnest** n wasp's nest.

wessen whose.

Weste f waistcoat, Am vest.

West|en m west; im ~ in the west; nach ~ westwards; der Wilde ~ the Wild West; **w~lich** 1. western; 2. ~ von west of; **~mächte** pl Western Powers pl; **~wind** m west wind.

Wettbewerb m com competition; **~steilnehmer** m competitor, contestant.

Wette f 1. bet; e-e ~ eingehen make a bet; 2. um die ~ laufen race.

Wetteifer m rivalry; **w~n** compete (with), vie (with).

wetten bet; auf ein Pferd ~ bet on a horse; ich wette darauf I bet you that.

Wetter n weather; es herrscht schönes ~ the weather is fine; wie wird das ~ morgen? what will the weather be like tomorrow? **~aussichten** pl weather outlook; **~bericht** m weather forcast; **~karte** f weather chart; **~lage** f weather situation; **~leuchten** n sheet lightning; **~vorhersage** f weather forecast; **~warte** f weather station.

Wett|kampf m 1. competition; 2. (Spiel) game, match; **~lauf** m race; **w~machen** make up for; **~streit** m contest, match.

wichsen shine, polish.

wichtig important (für to); sich ~ machen assume an air of importance; **W~keit** f: von großer ~ of great importance.

wickeln 1. wind; 2. (Haare) curl; 3. (Säugling) change; 4. etw um etw ~ tie s.th. round s.th.

Widder m 1. ram; 2. astr Aries.

wider against, contrary to.

Wider|haken m barbed hook; **~hall** m echo.

wider|legen refute; **~lich** repulsive, disgusting; **~rechtlich** illegal.

Wider|rede f contradiction; **~ruf** m 1. revocation; bis *auf* ~ until revoked; 2. *(Erklärung)* recall; 3. *com* countermand, cancellation; **w~rufen** *irr* revoke, recall; **~sacher** *m* opponent; **w~setzen,** *sich* oppose, resist *(jdm* s.o.).

wider|spenstig refractory, unruly; **~spiegeln** reflect *a. fig;* **~sprechen** *irr* contradict *(jdm* s.o.); **~sprechend** contradictory, conflicting.

Wider|spruch *m* 1. contradiction; 2. *(Protest)* protest; 3. *(Gegensatz)* contradiction; *in* ~ *zu etw geraten* contradict s.th.; *im* ~ *zu etw stehen* be contradictory to s.th.; **w~sprüchlich** contradictory; **w~spruchslos** without contradiction.

Widerstand *m* 1. resistance; ~ *leisten* offer resistance; 2. *(Ablehnung)* opposition; *auf* ~ *stoßen* meet with opposition; 3. *(Hindernis)* obstacle; **w~sfähig** resistant *(gegen* to); **w~slos** without resistance.

wider|stehen *irr* resist, withstand; **~streben** 1. *(Gefühl)* go against; 2. *es widerstrebt mir* I am reluctant (to do); **~strebend** reluctantly; **~wärtig** disagreeable, objectionable.

Widerwill|e *m* 1. aversion *(gegen* to), repugnance; 2. *(Ekel)* disgust (at); **w~ig**

with great distaste; reluctantly.

widm|en 1. *(Buch)* dedicate (to); 2. *(Zeit)* devote; 3. *sich* ~ devote o.s.; **W~ung** *f* dedication.

widrig adverse.

wie I *Frageadv* 1. how; ~ *geht es?* how are you? 2. ~ *alt ist er?* how old is he? ~ *spät ist es?* what time is it? 3. *(welcher Art)* what; ~ *bitte?* pardon; ~ *ist er?* what is he like? 4. ~ *ist dein Name?* what is your name? **II** *conj* 5. *das ist so gut* ~ *sicher* that is practically certain; 6. *(Vergleich)* like; *er sieht aus* ~ he looks like; 7. *(als Beispiel)* such as like; *ein Mann* ~ *er* a man like him; 8. *(und)* both ... and; 9. ~ *man sieht* as can be seen; ~ *man sagt* people say; ~ *so oft* as is often the case; 10. ~ *sehr* however; 11. ~ *wenn* as if; 12. *ich sah,* ~ *er fiel* I saw him falling.

wieder again; *immer* ~ again and again, over and over again; *hin und* ~ now and then; **~bekommen** *irr* get back.

Wiederbelebungsversuch *m* attempt at resuscitation.

wieder|bringen *irr* bring back; **~einfallen** *irr* come back; **~einstellen** re-employ; **~erkennen** *irr* recognize.

Wiedereröffnung f reopening.

wiederfinden irr find again.

Wieder|gabe f 1. (Bericht) account, description; 2. (Vortrag) interpretation; 3. (Bild) reproduction; 4. (Übersetzung) translation; 5. (Tonband) playback; **w~geben** irr 1. return; 2. (schildern) describe; reproduce; 3. mus interpret; **~geburt** f rebirth.

wieder|gewinnen irr regain; **~herstellen** restore.

wiederhol|en repeat; **~t** repeatedly; **W~ung** f 1. repetition; 2. film retake.

Wiederhören n: auf ~ (tele) good-bye.

wieder|kehren 1. return; 2. (sich wiederholen) recur; **~kommen** irr 1. come again; 2. (zurückkommen) come back.

wiedersehen irr see again; **W~** n: auf ~! see you again!

wiederum 1. (erneut) again; 2. (hingegen) on the other hand.

Wiege f cradle; **w~n I** irr weigh; wieviel wiegst du? what do you weigh? **II** reg 1. (Kind) rock; 2. (Kopf) shake.

wiehern neigh.

Wiese f meadow.

Wiesel n weasel.

wieso why; how.

wieviel 1. how much; ~ Uhr ist es? what is the time? 2. (vor pl) how many; **~t:** den ~en haben wir heute? what day of the month is it? zum ~en Male? how many times?

wild 1. wild; 2. (unzivilisiert) savage; 3. (wütend) furious.

Wild n game, deer, venison.

Wild|bach m torrent; **~er** m savage; **~erer** m poacher; **w~ern** poach; **~leder** n suede; **~nis** f wilderness a. fig; **~schwein** n wild boar.

Wille m 1. will; gegen jds ~n handeln act against s.o.'s will; 2. (Absicht) intention; beim besten ~n with the best will in the world; es ist mein fester ~ it is my firm intention; 3. (jur) letzter ~ the last will and testament; **w~n:** um ... ~ for the sake of; **w~nlos** irresolute; **w~ns:** ~ sein be willing (to); **~nsfreiheit** f free will.

willig willing; **~kommen** welcome; jdn ~ heißen welcome s.o.

Willkür f arbitrariness; **w~lich** arbitrary.

wimmeln swarm (von with).

wimmern whimper.

Wimpel m pennant.

Wimper f eyelash; **~ntusche** f mascara.

Wind m wind; bei ~ und Wetter in all weathers.

Winde f 1. tech winch, windlass; 2. bot bindweed.

Windel f napkin.

winden irr 1. wind; 2.

(Kranz) bind; 3. *sich ~ (Wurm)* wriggle; *(Schlange)* writhe; 4. *sich vor Schmerzen ~* writhe with pains; 5. *sich um etw ~* wind around s.th.

windgeschützt protected against the wind

Windhund *m* greyhound.

windig windy, drafty.

Wind|mühle *f* windmill; **~pocken** *pl* chickenpox; **~richtung** *f* direction of the wind; **~schutzscheibe** *f* windscreen; **~stärke** *f* wind speed; **w~still** calm; **~stoß** *m* gust, blast.

Windung *f* 1. *(Weg)* bend, turn; 2. *tech* winding.

Wink *m* 1. sign; 2. *fig* hint, tip.

Winkel *m* 1. angle; *ein rechter ~* a right angle; 2. *(Ecke)* corner; **w~ig** 1. angular; 2. *(Straße)* crooked; **~messer** *m* protractor.

winken 1. wave; *mit dem Taschentuch ~* wave o.'s handkerchief; 2. signal, beckon; *den Kellner an den Tisch ~* sign to the waiter.

Winker *m* *mot* direction indicator.

winseln whimper.

Winter *m* winter; *im ~* in winter; **~fahrplan** *m* winter timetable; **~garten** *m* winter garden; **~halbjahr** *n* winterhalf-year; **w~lich** wintry; **~reifen** *m* winter tyre; **~schlaf** *m* hiberna-

tion; *e-n ~ halten* hibernate; **~schlußverkauf** *m* winter sale; **~spiele** *pl* Winter (Olympic) Games *pl;* **~sport** *m* winter sports *pl.*

Winzer *m* wine-grower.

winzig tiny, minuscule, minute.

Wipfel *m* tree-top.

Wippe *f* seesaw; **w~n** *(schaukeln)* teeter, seesaw.

wir we; *~ alle* all of us, we all; *~ selbst* we ourselves.

Wirbel *m* 1. whirl; 2. *(im Wasser)* eddy, whirlpool; 3. *fig* fuss, stir; 4. *anat* vertebra; **w~n** 1. whirl; 2. *(Trommel)* roll; **~säule** *f* spinal column; **~sturm** *m* tornado; **~wind** *m* whirlwind.

wirken 1. *(Erfolg haben)* work; 2. *(wirksam sein)* have effect; 3. *(Wirkung erzielen)* act *(auf* on), have an effect; 4. *(Eindruck machen)* make an impression; *er wirkt gehemmt* he makes an inhibited impression; 5. *(aussehen)* look; 6. *~ als* serve as; 7. *(tätig sein)* work; **W~** *n* work.

wirklich 1. *(wahr)* real; 2. *(tatsächlich)* real, true; 3. actually, in reality; *es ist ~ wahr* it is really true; **W~keit** *f* 1. reality; 2. *in ~* as a matter of fact; *(eigentlich)* in fact.

wirksam 1. *(Mittel)* effective; 2. *(Dosis)* operative;

3. *(jur)* ~ *sein* be in force; ~ *werden* take effect; **W~keit** f 1. efficiency; 2. *jur* validity.

Wirkung f 1. effect; *ohne* ~ *bleiben* have no effect; *mit* ~ *vom* with effect from; 2. *(Eindruck)* impression; 3. *(Einfluß)* influence; 4. *(Ergebnis)* result; **w~slos** ineffectual; ~ *bleiben* produce no effect; **w~svoll** impressive.

wirr 1. confused; 2. *(Haar)* dishevelled; 3. *mir ist ganz* ~ my head is in a whirl; **W~en** pl troubles, confusion *sing;* **W~warr** m mess, jumble, chaos.

Wirt m 1. landlord; inn-keeper; 2. *(Gastgeber)* host; ~**in** f 1. landlady; 2. *(Gastgeberin)* hostess.

Wirtschaft f 1. pub, inn; *Am* saloon; 2. *com* economy; trade and industry, commerce; 3. *(Haushaltung)* housekeeping; **w~en** 1. keep house; 2. *(im Haushalt)* manage o.'s money; ~**erin** f housekeeper; **w~lich** 1. *(Volkswirtschaft)* economic; 2. *(persönlich)* financial; 3. *(Gewinn)* profitable; 4. *(sparsam)* economical, thrifty; ~**sberater** m business consultant; ~**sgeld** n housekeeping money; ~**skrise** f economic crisis; ~**slage** f economic situation; ~**swachstum** n economic growth.

Wirtshaus n pub.

Wisch m scrap of paper; **w~en** wipe, mop; *Staub* ~ dust; ~**lappen** m, ~**tuch** n dish-cloth.

wißbegierig curious, inquisitive.

wissen irr 1. know; *etw nicht* ~ be ignorant of s.th.; *etw von jdm* ~ know s.th. from s.o.; *das hättest du doch* ~ *müssen* you ought to have known that; *man kann nie* ~ you never know; 2. *etw nicht mehr* ~ have forgotten s.th.; *von etw nichts* ~ *wollen* not to want s.th.; 3. *(sich erinnern)* remember; 4. *er weiß zu leben* he knows how to live; *jdn etw* ~ *lassen* let s.o. know s.th.; 5. *etw zu schätzen* ~ appreciate s.th.; **W~** n 1. knowledge; 2. *m-s* ~*s* as far as I know; *ohne mein* ~ without my knowledge.

Wissenschaft f science; ~**ler** m 1. scientist; 2. *(Forscher)* researcher; **w~lich** scientific.

Wissen|sgebiet n field of knowledge; **w~swert** interesting; **w~tlich** knowingly.

wittern 1. smell, scent; 2. *fig* suspect; **W~ung** f: *bei dieser* ~ in this weather.

Witwe f widow; ~**r** m widower.

Witz m 1. joke; 2. *(witzige Bemerkung)* witticism;

~**bold** *m* joker; **w~ig** witty; funny; **w~los** *(zwecklos)* useless.

wo I *Frageadv* where; ~ *bist du gewesen?* where have you been? **II** *Relativadv* where; **III** *unbestimmtes adv (irgendwo)* somewhere; **IV** *conj* if; ~**anders** somewhere else; ~**bei** whereby; upon what; in the course of which.

Woche *f* week; *in e-r* ~ in a week; *unter der* ~ during the week; *vor drei* ~*n* three weeks ago; ~**nausgabe** *f* weekly edition; ~**nbett** *n* childbed; ~**nende** *n* weekend; ~**nendhaus** *n* weekend house; **w~nlang** for weeks; ~**ntag** *m* weekday; **w~ntags** on weekdays.

wöchentlich weekly; *einmal* ~ once a week.

Wöchnerin *f* woman in childbed.

wo|durch 1. *(fragend)* how, by what means; 2. *(relativ)* through which; ~**für** 1. *(fragend)* ~ *ist das gut?* what is that good for? 2. *(relativ)* for which.

Woge *f* wave, billow.

wogegen 1. *(fragend)* against what; 2. *(relativ)* which ... against; 3. *(im Austausch)* in exchange for which.

wogen surge, heave.

wo|her where ... from; ~**hin**: ~ *gehst du?* where are you

going to? ~**hingegen** whereas, whilst.

wohl 1. *(gesund)* well; *sich nicht* ~ *fühlen* be unwell; 2. *(behaglich)* happy; 3. *(ungezwungen)* at ease; 4. *sich* ~ *sein lassen* live well; 5. *(anscheinend)* no doubt; *es wird* ~ *Regen geben* I'm sure it's going to rain; *es ist* ~ *anzunehmen* it is to be expected; 6. *(ungefähr)* about; 7. *er weiß sehr* ~, *daß* he knows very well that; 8. *das mag* ~ *sein, aber* that may well be, but; **W~** *n* well-being, welfare; *auf jds* ~ *trinken* drink to s.o.'s health; *zum* ~*!* cheers! ~**auf** well.

Wohl|befinden *n* well-being; **w~behalten** 1. safe and sound; 2. *(Sache)* in good condition; ~**fahrtsstaat** *m* welfare state; **w~gemeint** well-meant; ~**geschmack** *m* flavour; **w~habend** wealthy, well-to-do; **w~ig** cosy; ~**stand** *m* prosperity; ~**tat** *f* relief, blessing, benefit; ~**täter** *m* benefactor; ~**täterin** *f* benefactress; **w~tätig** charitable; ~**tätigkeit** *f* charity.

wohl|tuend pleasant; soothing; ~**tun** *irr* do good; ~**weislich** very wisely.

Wohlwollen *n* goodwill, benevolence; **w~d** benevolent.

Wohn|anhänger *m* trailer,

Am caravan; **~block** *m* block of flats; **w~en** 1. live, dwell; *in der Stadt* ~ live in town; *im dritten Stock* ~ live on the third floor; 2. *(vorübergehend)* stay; 3. *(als Mieter)* lodge; *bei jdm zur Miete* ~ lodge with s.o.; *möbliert* ~ live in lodgings; **~fläche** *f* dwelling space; **w~haft** be resident, domiciled; **~haus** *n* residential building; **~heim** *n* *(Studenten)* hostel; *Am* dormitory; **~lage** *f* residential location; **w~lich** comfortable, homely; **~ort** *m* residence; **~raum** *m* housing space; **~sitz** *m* domicile, residence; *fester* ~ permanent abode.

Wohnung *f* 1. dwelling, flat, *Am* apartment; 2. *(Heim)* home; 3. *(Unterkunft)* lodgings *pl;* **~snachweis** *m* house-agency.

Wohn|viertel *n* residential quarter; **~wagen** *m* caravan; **~zimmer** *n* living-room.

wölben, *sich* arch, vault.

Wolf *m* wolf; **~shund** *m* Alsatian (dog).

Wolke *f* cloud; *der Himmel ist mit ~n bedeckt* the sky is cloudy; **~enbruch** *m* cloud-burst; **~enkratzer** *m* skyscraper; **w~enlos** cloudless *a. fig;* **w~ig** cloudy.

Wolle *f* wool; **w~n** wool(l)en.

wollen 1. want; *was ich sagen wollte* what I wanted to say; *er will immer alles wissen* he always wants to know everything; 2. *etw tun* ~ be going to do s.th., be about to do s.th.; 3. *er will Arzt sein* he claims to be a doctor; 4. *wir* ~ *sehen* we'll see; 5. ~ *Sie mir bitte die Milch reichen?* would you pass me the milk, please? 6. *das will nichts heißen* that doesn't mean anything; 7. *(mögen)* want, like; 8. *(gewillt sein)* be willing; 9. ~ *Sie zu mir?* do you want to see me? 10. *etw lieber* ~ prefer s.th.; 11. *(wünschen)* wish; 12. *(brauchen)* need.

wollig wool(l)y.

Woll|jacke *f* cardigan; **~sachen** *pl* wool(l)ens *pl.* **Wollust** *f* voluptuousness. **Wollwaren** *pl* wool(l)en goods.

wo|mit 1. *(relativ)* with which; 2. *(fragend)* ~ *kann ich dienen?* what can I do for you? **~möglich** possibly; **~nach** 1. ~ *suchst du?* what are you looking for? 2. *(relativ)* what . . . for; according to which.

Wonne *f* bliss, delight, joy.

wo|ran 1. ~ *denkst du?* what are you thinking about? ~ *liegt es, daß?* how is it that? *ich weiß nicht,* ~ *ich bin* I don't know where I stand; 2. *(relativ) etw,* ~ *man Freu-*

de hat s.th. that one enjoys; **~auf** 1. ~ *warten Sie?* what are you waiting for; 2. *(relativ)* whereupon; *etw. ~ er besteht* s.th. which he insists upon; **~aus** 1. ~ *ist es gemacht?* what is it made of? 2. from which; *etw. ~ man lernen kann* s.th. which one can learn from; **~in** 1. where; ~ *liegt der Unterschied?* where (what) is the difference? 2. in which, where.

Wort *n* 1. word; ~ *für* ~ word for word; *das letzte* ~ *haben* have the final say; *kein* ~ *über etw verlieren* not to mention a word about s.th.; *sie sprechen kein* ~ *mehr miteinander* they don't speak to each other anymore; *ohne ein* ~ *zu sagen* without a word; *sein* ~ *halten* keep o.'s word; *jdm das* ~ *erteilen* give s.o. leave to speak; *das* ~ *ergreifen* take the floor; 2. *bei diesen* **~en** at these words; *in* **~en** in writing; *mit anderen* **~en** in other words; *ums* ~ *bitten* request leave to speak; *jdn nicht zu* ~ *kommen lassen* not to let s.o. get a word in; *jdm ins* ~ *fallen* interrupt s.o.; **~bruch** *m* breach of promise; **w~brüchig**: ~ *werden* break o.'s word.

Wörterbuch *n* dictionary.

wort|karg taciturn; **W~laut**

m wording; *der Brief hat folgenden* ~ the letter reads as follows.

wörtlich 1. literal; 2. *etw zu* ~ *nehmen* take s.th. too literally.

Wort|schatz *m* vocabulary; **~schwall** *m* flood of words; **~wechsel** *m* dispute.

worüber 1. *(fragend)* what ... about; 2. *(relativ)* about which; **~um** 1. *da ist etw.* ~ *ich dich bitten möchte* there is s.th. which I want to ask you for; 2. ~ *handelt es sich?* what's it all about? **~unter** among, under what, which.

wo|von 1. which ... about; 2. ~ *spricht er?* what is he talking about? **~vor** 1. *etw.* ~ *sie Angst hat* s.th. she is afraid of; 2. ~ *haben Sie Angst?* what are you afraid of? **~zu** 1. for what; what ... for; 2. ~ *soll das gut sein?* what's that supposed to be good for?

Wrack *n* wreck *a. fig.*

wringen *irr* wring.

Wucher *m* usury; **~er** *m* usurer; **w~n** 1. *bot* grow rampant; 2. *med* proliferate; **~ung** *f* 1. *bot* rank growth; 2. *med* proliferation.

Wuchs *m* 1. growth; 2. *(Gestalt)* build, stature.

Wucht *f* 1. *(Gewicht)* weight; 2. *(Aufprall)* impact *a. fig;* 3. *mit voller* ~ with full force; **w~ig** 1. *(Figur)* heavy, weighty; 2. *(Mauer)* massive.

wühl|en 1. *(suchen)* rummage; 2. *(Tiere)* burrow (in into); **W~maus** *f* vole.

Wulst *m* bulge, roll; **w~ig** *(Lippen)* thick.

wund sore; *sich ~ reiben* rub o.s. sore; *sich die Füße ~ laufen* get sore feet; *e-e ~e Stelle* a sore point; **W~e** *f* 1. wound; 2. *(Verletzung)* injury, lesion.

Wunder *n* 1. miracle; *wie durch ein ~* miraculously; 2. wonder, marvel; *es ist ein ~, daß* it is a wonder that; **w~bar** wonderful, marvel(l)ous; **w~lich** queer, odd, strange; **w~n, sich** 1. wonder *(über* at); 2. *es wundert mich* I am surprised; **w~nehmen** *irr: es nimmt mich wunder, daß* I am astonished that; **w~schön, w~voll** marvel(l)ous, wonderful.

Wund|fieber *n* traumatic fever; **~salbe** *f* ointment; **~starrkrampf** *m* tetanus.

Wunsch *m* 1. wish; *haben Sie noch e-n ~?* is there anything else I can do for you? 2. *(Bitte)* request; *auf ~* by request; *auf allgemeinen ~* by popular request; *nach ~* as desired; 3. *(Glück) mit den besten Wünschen* with the best wishes.

wünschen 1. wish *(jdm etw* s.o. s.th.); *es ist zu ~, daß* it is to be hoped that; *es wäre zu ~* it would be desirable; 2. *(wollen)* want, desire; *was ~ Sie?* what can I do for you? 3. *was wünschst du dir zum Geburtstag?* what would you like for your birthday? *jdm frohe Weihnachten ~* wish s.o. merry Christmas; **~swert** desirable.

wunsch|gemäß as requested; **~los**: *~ glücklich* perfectly happy; **W~traum** *m* dream of o.'s dreams; **W~zettel** *m* list of wishes.

Würd|e *f* 1. dignity; 2. *(Rang)* rank, degree; **w~elos** undignified; **~enträger** *m* dignitary; **w~evoll** dignified; **w~ig** 1. dignified; 2. *(Wert)* worthly; **w~igen** 1. appreciate, value; 2. *(anerkennen)* acknowledge; 3. *keines Wortes ~* not to vouchsafe a word *(jdn* to s.o.).

Wurf *m* 1. throw, cast; 2. *zoo* litter.

Würfel *m* 1. die, *pl* dice; *die ~ sind gefallen* the die is cast; 2. *math* cube; **w~n** play (at) dice; **~zucker** *m* lump sugar.

würgen 1. choke; 2. *(beim Essen)* gag, retch.

Wurm *m* worm; **w~stichig** worm-eaten.

Wurst *f* sausage.

Würstchen *n: heiße* ~ hot dogs *pl.*

Wursthaut *f* sausage skin.

Würze 1. *(Gewürz)* spice, relish, condiment; 2. *(Aroma)* seasoning.

Wurzel *f* 1. root; ~ *schlagen* take root; 2. *math* radical; **w~n** be rooted, root (*in* in).

würz|en season, spice, flavour; **~ig** spicy.

Wust *m* *(Durcheinander)* mess, jumble.

wüst 1. *(öde)* waste, desert; 2. *(unordentlich)* wild; 3. *(liederlich)* dissolute; 4. *(grob)* coarse.

Wüste *f* desert, waste.

Wüstling *m* debauchee.

Wut *f* rage, fury; *in* ~ *geraten* fly into a rage; **~anfall** *m* fit of rage.

wüten 1. *(toben)* rage, foam; 2. *(Unwetter)* rage; **~d** furious, raging; ~ *werden* become furious; *auf jdn* ~ *sein* be furious at s.o.

Z

Zack|e f 1. (Fels~) jag, peak; 2. (Kamm) tooth; **z~ig** jagged, pointed.

zaghaft timid, shy.

zäh 1. tough; 2. (Fleisch) stringy; 3. (ausdauernd) tenacious; 4. (~flüssig) viscous.

Zahl f 1. number; 2. (Ziffer) figure; **z~bar** payable (bei at, with); ~ bei Lieferung cash on delivery, C. O. D; **z~en** 1. pay; 2. bitte ~ the bill, Am check, please.

zählen 1. (Geld) count; 2. jdn zu s-n Kunden ~ count s.o. as one of o.'s clients; 3. number; 4. zu etw ~ number among s.th.; 5. auf jdn ~ count on s.o.

zahlenmäßig numerical; ~ überlegen sein superiority in number.

Zahler m payer; säumiger ~ dilatory payer.

Zähler m 1. tech meter; 2. math numerator.

Zahl|karte f money-order form; **z~los** innumerable; **z~reich** 1. numerous; 2. ~ kommen come in large numbers; **~tag** m pay-day.

Zahlung f payment, settlement; ~ in Raten payment by instal(l)ments; etw in ~ geben trade s.th. in; **~sauf- forderung** f request for payment; **~sbedingungen** pl terms pl of payment; **~sbefehl** m order to pay; **~serleichterungen** pl facilities of payment; **~smit- tel** n 1. instrument of payment; 2. (Münzen) money, currency; gesetzliches ~ legal tender; **z~sunfähig** insolvent.

zahm tame a. fig.

zähmen 1. tame, domesticate; 2. (Pferd) break in; 3. fig control.

Zahn m tooth; Zähne bekommen teethe; e-n ~ ziehen lassen have a tooth pulled out; sich die Zähne putzen brush o.'s teeth; **~arzt** m dentist; **~bürste** f toothbrush; **z~en** cut o.'s teeth; **~ersatz** m dentures pl; **~fleisch** n gums pl; **~fleischbluten** n bleeding from the gums; **z~los** toothless; **~lücke** f gap (in o.'s teeth); **~pasta** f toothpaste; **~rad** n cogwheel; **~radbahn** f rack-railway; **~schmerzen** pl toothache; **~stein** m med tartar; **~stocher** m toothpick; **~techniker** m dental technician; **~wechsel** m second dentition; **~ziehen** n (tooth) extraction.

Zange f 1. pliers pl; e-e ~ a

pair of pliers, tongs *pl*, pincers *pl*; 2. *(für Fingernägel)* clippers *pl.*

Zank *m* quarrel, dispute; ~**apfel** *m* apple of discord; **z~en,** *sich* quarrel, squabble *(um* about, over).

Zäpfchen *n* 1. *anat* uvula; 2. *med* suppository.

Zapf|en *m* 1. *tech* tenon; 2. *(Pflock)* peg, pin; 3. *bot* cone; **z~en** *(Bier)* tap; ~**enstreich** *m mil* curfew, tattoo; ~**stelle** *f* filling station.

zappel|ig fidgety, ~**n** fidget, struggle.

zart 1. *(Fleisch)* tender; 2. *(Stoff, Haut)* soft, delicate; 3. *(Gesundheit)* delicate, frail; 4. *(sanft)* gentle; 5. *(Farbe)* pale.

zärtlich tender, affectionate; **Z~keit** *f* tenderness, fondness.

Zauber *m* 1. spell, charm; 2. *fig* magic, enchantment; ~**ei** *f* magic, witchcraft; ~**er** *m* sorcerer, magician; **z~haft** enchanting, charming; ~**künstler** *m* conjurer; **z~n** conjure; practise magic; ~**stab** *m* magic wand.

zaudern hesitate *(mit* about); **Z~** *n* hesitation.

Zaum *m* bridle.

Zaun *m* fence, hedge.

Zebra *n* zebra; ~**streifen** *m* zebra crossing.

Zech|e *f* 1. *(Rechnung)* bill; 2. *(Bergwerk)* coal mine;

z~en carouse; ~**er** *m* tippler; ~**preller** *m* bilk; ~**prellerei** *f* bilking.

Zeder *f bot* cedar.

Zehe *f* toe; ~**nspitze** *f: auf* ~*n* on tiptoe.

zehn ten; ~**fach** tenfold; **Z~kampf** *m* decathlon; ~**mal** ten times; **Z~te** *m* tenth; **Z~tel** *n* tenth (part).

zehren 1. live *(von* on); draw; 2. *(Kummer)* gnaw.

Zeichen *n* 1. sign; *jdm ein* ~ *geben* give s.o. a sign; 2. *(Signal)* signal; 3. *(Merk~)* mark; 4. *(An~)* sign, indication; 5. *zum* ~ as a token; 6. *(Omen)* omen; 7. *(Symbol)* symbol; ~**block** *m* sketch block; ~**papier** *n* drawing paper; ~**sprache** *f* sign language; ~**trickfilm** *m* animated cartoon.

zeichn|en 1. draw; 2. *(entwerfen)* design; 3. *(kenn~)* mark; 4. *(Anleihe)* subscribe for; **Z~en** *n* 1. drawing; 2. *(Schule)* art; **Z~er** *m* 1. draughtsman, designer; 2. *(Anleihe)* subscriber; **Z~ung** *f* drawing; sketch; design

Zeige|finger *m* forefinger, index; **z~n** 1. show; 2. *(anzeigen)* indicate, mark; *die Uhr zeigt halb drei* the clock says half past two; 3. *(zur Schau stellen)* exhibit, display; 4. *(darlegen)* demonstrate, point out; 5. *auf etw* ~ point at s.th.;

6. *sich* ~ appear, come out; 7. *sich dankbar* ~ be grateful; 8. *es zeigt sich, daß* it turns out that; **~r** *m* 1. *(Uhr)* pointer, hand; 2. *tech* indicator; **~stock** *m* pointer.

Zeile *f* 1. line; *e-e neue* ~ *anfangen* start a new line; 2. *(Reihe)* row; **~nzahl** *f* lineage.

Zeit *f* 1. *(Zeitraum)* time; *die ganze* ~ the whole time; *keine* ~ *haben* have no time; *das hat* ~ there is no hurry; *die* ~ *drängt* time is pressing; *jdm* ~ *lassen* give s.o. time; *sich* ~ *nehmen* take time; *die* ~ *vergeht* time passes; *sich die* ~ *vertreiben* pass the time; *in der* ~ *von* between; *in letzter* ~ lately; *im Laufe der* ~ in the course of time; *seit einiger* ~ for some time; *vor kurzer* ~ a short time ago; 2. *(Zeitpunkt) es ist höchste* ~ it is high time; *von* ~ *zu* ~ from time to time; *alles zu s-r* ~ one thing at a time; 3. *(Datum)* date; 4. *(Moment)* moment; 5. *(Zeitabschnitt)* times *pl; die gute alte* ~ the good old days *pl;* 6. *(Epoche)* epoch, period; 7. *(Uhrzeit)* time; **z~:** ~ *s-es Lebens* during his life; **~alter** *n* age, era, epoch; **~ansage** *f* announcement of the time; **z~gemäß** modern, up-to-date; **~genosse** *m,* **z~genössisch** contemporary;

z~ig early; **~karte** *f* season ticket; **~lang** *f: e-e* ~ for a while; **z~lebens** all o.'s life; **z~lich** 1. temporal; 2. *(chronologisch)* chronological; **~lupenaufnahme** *f* slow-motion picture; **~mangel** *m* lack of time; **~plan** *m* schedule, time-table; **~punkt** *m* 1. time; 2. *(Moment)* moment; 3. *(Datum)* date; **z~raubend** time-consuming; **~schalter** *m* time switch; **~schrift** *f* journal, periodical, magazine; **~umstände** *pl* circumstances *pl.*

Zeitung *f* 1. (news) paper, journal; 2. *(Presse)* press; **~sanzeige** *f* ad; **~sartikel** *m* newspaper article; **~sausschnitt** *m* newspaper clipping; **~skiosk** *m* newsstand; **~skorrespondent** *m* press correspondent; **~snotiz** *f* press item; **~spapier** *n* newsprint; **~sreklame** *f* press advertising; **~sverkäufer** *m* news-vendor.

Zeit|verschwendung *f* waste of time; **~vertreib** *m* pastime; *zum* ~ to pass the time; **z~weilig** 1. temporary; 2. *(gelegentlich)* occasional; **z~weise** 1. from time to time; 2. *(zeitweilig)* for a time; **~zeichen** *m* *radio* time signal.

Zelle 1. cell; 2. *tele* booth; **~stoff** *m* cellulose; **~teilung** *f* *biol* cell division.

Zellulo|id n celluloid; **~se** f cellulose.

Zelt n 1. tent; *ein ~ aufschlagen* put up a tent; 2. *(Fest~)* marquee; **~ausrüstung** f camping outfit; **~bahn** f tent square; **z~en** camp; **Z~en** n camping; **~lager** n camp; **~platz** m camping site.

Zement m, **z~ieren** cement.

Zenit m 1. zenith; *im ~ stehen* be at the zenith; 2. *fig* peak.

zens|ieren 1. censor; 2. *(Schule)* give marks; **Z~ur** f 1. censur; 2. *(Note)* mark; 3. *(Zeugnis)* report.

Zentimeter n centimetre.

Zentner m quintal.

zentral central; **Z~e** f 1. central office; 2. *(von Firmen)* headquarters pl; 3. *tele* telephone exchange; **Z~heizung** f central heating; **~isieren** centralize.

Zentrum n centre.

zerbrech|en irr 1. break; 2. *(von Glas)* break in pieces, shatter, smash; **~lich** 1. *(Porzellan)* fragile, breakable; 2. *(Person)* delicate.

zerdrücken 1. crush, squash; 2. *(Kleider)* crumple.

Zeremonie f ceremony; **z~ll**, **Z~ll** n ceremonial.

Zerfall m 1. *(Gebäude)* decay, ruin; 2. *(Moral)* decline, decadence; 3. *biol* disintegration; **z~en** irr 1. *(Mauer)* fall into ruin, decay; 2. *(Mo-*

ral) decline; 3. *phys* disintegrate.

zerfetzen 1. *(Hose)* tear to pieces; 2. *(in Stückchen)* tear to shreds.

zerfleischen mangle, lacerate.

zerfressen irr 1. *(Stoff)* eat; 2. *chem* corrode.

zergehen irr 1. *(auflösen)* dissolve; 2. *auf der Zunge ~* melt in o.'s mouth.

zergliedern *fig* analyse.

zerhacken 1. hack, chop to pieces; 2. *(Fleisch)* mince.

zerkleinern 1. *(Holz)* cut down; 2. *(Steine)* crush.

zerknittern crumple, crease.

zerkratzen scratch.

zerlassen irr melt, dissolve.

zerleg|bar detachable; **~en** 1. dismantle, detach; 2. *(Braten)* carve; 3. *fig* analyse.

zerlumpt ragged.

zermalmen crush a. fig.

zermürben wear down.

Zerrbild n caricature.

zerreiben irr grind down.

zerreißen irr 1. *(Papier)* tear to pieces; 2. *(Faden)* break; 3. *sich etw ~* tear s.th.; 4. *(Bindungen)* sever, break off.

zerren 1. drag, haul; 2. *an etw ~* tug, pull at s.th.

zerrissen torn.

Zerrung f med strain.

zerrütt|en 1. *(ruinieren)* destroy, ruin; 2. *(Gesundheit)* shatter; 3. *(Ehe)* wreck;

Z~ung f disruption, break-up.

zerschellen be smashed.

zerschlagen irr 1. break, smash a. fig; 2. (Plan) sich ~ come to nothing; 3. ich bin ganz ~ I am absolutely dead beat.

zerschmettern crush, smash.

zerschneiden irr cut up, carve.

zersetz|en 1. disintegrate; 2. fig corrupt; **Z~ung** f 1. disintegration; 2. fig corruption, corrosion.

zersplittern 1. splinter, split up; 2. fig fragment.

zerstäube|n spray, atomize; **Z~r** m atomizer.

zerstör|en 1. destroy a. fig, demolish; 2. (mutwillig) wreck; **Z~ung** f 1. destruction; 2. wreckage; **Z~ungswut** f vandalism.

zerstoßen irr crush, bray.

zerstreu|en 1. scatter, disperse; 2. fig (Bedenken) dissipate; 3. sich ~ be dissipated; **~t** 1. scattered; 2. fig absent-minded; **Z~theit** f absent-mindedness; **Z~ung** f fig amusement.

zerstückeln dismember.

zerteilen divide (in into).

zertreten irr 1. tread down, crush; 2. (Feuer) stamp out.

zertrümmern 1. demolish, smash; 2. (Atom) split.

Zerwürfnis n quarrel, disagreement.

Zettel m 1. slip, scrap (of paper); 2. (Klebe~) label; 3. (Notiz) note.

Zeug n 1. stuff; 2. (Stoff) cloth, fabric; 3. (Sachen) things pl; (Kram) junk; 4. dummes ~ rubbish, nonsense.

Zeuge m witness; **z~n** 1. (Kinder) father; 2. von etw ~ testify s.th.; **~naussage** f testimony; **~nbank** f witness-box.

Zeugnis n 1. (Schule) report; 2. (Prüfung) certificate; 3. (Führungs~) reference; 4. (Zeugenaussage) testimony.

Zickzack m zigzag.

Ziege f goat.

Ziegel m 1. brick; 2. (Dach~) tile; **~ei** f brickyard.

Ziegen|bock m billy-goat; **~leder** n kid(-leather).

zieh|en irr 1. draw, pull; 2. (Graben) dig; 3. (Mauer) build; 4. jdn an den Haaren ~ pull s.o.'s hair; die Aufmerksamkeit auf sich ~ attract attention; e-n Zettel aus der Tasche ~ pull a note out of o.'s pocket; Schlüsse ~ draw conclusions; Wurzel ~ extract the root; ins Lächerliche ~ ridicule s.th.; etw nach sich ~ have consequences; 5. (züchten) breed; 6. (Nebel) drift; 7. in den Krieg ~ go to war; 8. an etw ~ pull at s.th.; 9. (umziehen) aufs

Land ~ move to the country; 10. *(Tee)* draw; 11. *(sich erstrecken)* stretch, extend; 12. *sich in die Länge* ~ drag on; 13. *es zieht* there is a draft; **Z~harmonika** *f* concertina; **Z~ung** *f* drawing.

Ziel *n* 1. *(e-r Reise)* destination; 2. *mil* target, aim; 3. *fig* goal, end, aim; *ein* ~ *verfolgen* pursue a goal; *etw als* ~ *nehmen* aim at; *ein* ~ *erreichen* reach a goal; 4. *sport* finish, winning-post; 5. *com* credit, term; **z~en** 1. aim *(auf* at); 2. *auf jdn* ~ be directed at s.o.; **z~los** aimless; **~scheibe** *f* target; **z~strebig** purposeful, resolute.

ziemen, *sich* be suitable.

ziemlich 1. *(einigermaßen)* quite, rather; ~ *viel Leute* a fair number of people; 2. *(fast)* almost, more or less, practically.

Zier *f,* **~de** *f* ornament; **z~en** 1. adorn, decorate; 2. *sich* ~ hesitate, make a fuss; **z~lich** dainty, delicate; **~pflanze** *f* ornamental plant.

Ziffer *f* figure; *in* ~*n* in figures; **~blatt** *n* dial.

Zigarette *f* cigarette; **~nautomat** *m* cigarette slot-machine; **~netui** *n* cigarette-case; **~nspitze** *f* cigarette-holder; **~nstummel** *m* cigarette-end, butt.

Zigarre *f* cigar; **~nkiste** *f* cigar-box.

Zigeuner *m* gipsy.

Zimmer *n* room; *ein* ~ *mieten* rent a room; **~antenne** *f* indoor aerial; **~kellner** *m* room waiter; **~mädchen** *n* chambermaid; **~mann** *m* carpenter.

zimperlich 1. *(empfindlich)* sensitive; 2. *(prüde)* prudish.

Zimt *m* cinnamon.

Zink *n* zinc.

Zinke *f* prong.

Zinn *n* tin; **~geschirr** *n* pewter.

Zins *m* interest; **~en bringen** bear interest; *von den* ~*en leben* live on the interest; **z~bringend** bearing interest; **~eszins** *m* compound interest; **~fuß** *m* rate of interest; **z~los** free of interest.

Zipfel *m* 1. *(Wurst, Sack)* tip, end; 2. *(Taschentuch)* corner.

zirka approximately.

Zirkel *m* 1. a pair of compasses; 2. *fig* circle.

zirkulieren circulate.

Zirkus *m* circus.

zirpen chirp.

zischen hiss.

Zisterne *f* cistern.

Zitat *n* quotation.

Zither *f* zither.

zitieren 1. quote, cite; 2. *(vorladen)* summon.

Zitron|at *n* candied lemon peel; **~e** *f* lemon; **~enpresse** *f* lemon squeezer; **~enschale** *f* lemon peel; **~en-**

scheibe f slice of lemon; **~enwasser** n lemonade.

zitterig shaky, tremulous; **~n** shiver, tremble, shake (*vor* with).

zivil 1. civilian; 2. *jur* civil; 3. *(Preis)* reasonable; **Z~bevölkerung** f civilian population; **Z~isation** f civilization; **~isiert** civilized; **Z~ist** m civilian; **Z~klage** f civil suit; **Z~person** f civilian; **Z~prozeßordnung** f Code of Civil Procedure; **Z~recht** n civil law.

Zofe f lady's maid.

zögern hesitate, delay; **Z~** n: *ohne ~* without hesitation.

Zölibat m od n celibacy.

Zoll m 1. customs duty; *auf etw ~ erheben* levy a duty on s.th.; 2. *(Behörde)* customs *pl*; 3. *(Längenmaß)* inch; **~abfertigung** f customs clearance; **~amt** n customs office; **~beamter** m customs official; **~erklärung** f customs declaration; **z~frei** duty-free; **~gebiet** n customs district; **~kontrolle** f customs inspection; **z~pflichtig** liable to duty; **~tarif** m tariff; **~verschluß** m: *unter ~ lassen* leave in bond.

Zone f 1. *geog* zone; 2. *(Gegend)* region, area.

Zoo m zoo; **z~logisch** zoological.

Zopf m plait, braid.

Zorn m rage, anger, fury (*auf* at); **z~ig** angry; *auf etw ~ sein* be angry at (with) s.th.

Zote f filthy joke.

zottig shaggy.

zu I prp 1. *(örtlich)* to; *~r Schule gehen* go to school; *~ Bett gehen* go to bed; 2. *(Richtung)* towards; *das Zimmer liegt ~r Straße* the room looks out towards the street; *~m Fenster hinaussehen* look out of the window; 3. *~ sich kommen* regain consciousness; 4. *(Ort)* *~ Hause* at home; *~ beiden Seiten* on both sides; 5. *(zeitlich)* to; *von Tag ~ Tag* from day to day; *bis ~r Stunde* to this moment; 6. *(Zeitpunkt)* at; *~ Anfang* at the beginning; *~r Zeit* for the time being; 7. *(Übergang)* *~ Eis werden* turn into ice; 8. *(Zweck)* *~m Nutzen von* for the benefit of; *~ s-n Gunsten* in his favour; 9. *(Anlaß)* for; 10. Zucker *~m Kaffee nehmen* take sugar with o.'s coffee; 11. *(Verhältnis)* Liebe *~ Gott* love of god; 12. *(Mittel)* *~ Fuß* on foot; *~ Schiff* by ship; 13. *~m Teil* partly; *~m ersten Mal* for the first time; **II** prp (*vor Infinitiv*) to; *anstatt ~* instead of; *ohne ~* without; *was ~ beweisen wäre* which is to be proved; **III** adv 14. *das ist ~ schön* this is too good; 15. *nach Norden ~* towards the north; 16. *ab und* ~ from time to time; *Tür* ~*!* close the door!

Zubehör *n* accessories *pl;* ~**industrie** *f* accessories industry.

zubereiten prepare, make, dress.

zubring|en *irr (Zeit)* spend, pass; **Z~erstraße** *f* feeder road; **Z~erverkehr** *m* feeder service.

Zucht *f* 1. *(von Tieren)* breeding; 2. *(Rasse)* breed, stock; 3. *(Pflanzen)* cultivation, culture; 4. *(Disziplin)* discipline.

züchten 1. *(Tiere)* breed, raise; 2. *(Pflanzen)* grow, cultivate; **Z~er** *m* 1. breeder; 2. *(Anbauer)* grower.

Zuchthaus *n* penitentiary.

züchtigen punish.

zucht|los undisciplined; **Z~perle** *f* culture pearl.

zucken 1. twitch; 2. *(Blitz)* flash; 3. *mit den Achseln* ~ shrug o.'s shoulders.

Zucker *m* sugar; ~**dose** *f* sugar-basin; ~**guß** *m* icing; ~**krankheit** *f* diabetes; **z~n** sweeten; ~**rohr** *n* sugar--cane; ~**rübe** *f* sugar-beet; ~**zange** *f* sugar-tongs *pl.*

Zuckung *f* convulsion.

zudecken cover up.

zudem moreover, in addition.

zudrehen turn off.

zudringlich importunate.

zueinander to each other, to one another.

zuerst 1. *(als erster)* first; 2. *(anfangs)* at first.

Zufahrt *f* approach.

Zufall *m* 1. chance, accident; *durch* ~ by chance; *ein glücklicher* ~ a lucky chance; 2. *(Zusammentreffen)* coincidence.

zufällig 1. accidental, coincidental; 2. *rein* ~ purely by chance; *ich traf ihn* ~ I happen to meet him.

Zuflucht *f* 1. refuge, shelter; 2. *(Ausweg)* resort.

zuflüstern whisper (*jdm* to s.o.).

zufolge in consequence of, according to.

zufrieden content, satisfied; *sich* ~ *geben* be content (*mit* with); **Z~heit** *f* contentment, satisfaction; ~**stellen** satisfy; ~**stellend** satisfactory.

zufrieren *irr* freeze over.

zufügen 1. add (to); 2. *jdm etw* ~ *(Verlust)* inflict s.th. on s.o.; *(Schaden)* harm s.o.; *jdm ein Unrecht* ~ do s.o. an injustice.

Zufuhr *f* supply.

Zug *m* 1. train; *mit dem* ~ *fahren* go by train; 2. *(Fest~)* procession; 3. *(Kolonne)* line; 4. *(Vogel~)* migration; 5. *(Berg~)* mountain range; 6. *(Luft~)* draught; 7. *(Rauchen)* drag, puff; 8. *(Trinken)* draught;

9. *(Ziehen)* pull;
10. *(Schach)* move; *zum ~e kommen* get a word in; *~ um ~* one after the other;
11. *(Gesichts~)* feature;
12. *(Charakter)* trait;
13. *(Trend)* trend; 14. *(Umriß)* outline; 15. *(Neigung)* tendency.

Zugabe *f* 1. extra; 2. *theat* encore; 3. *(Prämie)* bonus.

Zugang *m* 1. entrance; 2. *(Tür)* door, entry; 3. *kein ~* no admittance.

zugänglich 1. accessible; 2. *(umgänglich)* approachable; 3. *fig* open.

Zugbrücke *f* drawbridge.

zugeben *irr* 1. *(dazu)* throw in; 2. *(gestehen)* admit, confess; 3. *(einräumen)* concede; 4. *(zulassen)* allow.

zugegen present *(bei* at).

zugehen *irr* 1. *(Türe)* close, shut; 2. *(Brief) jdm etw ~ lassen* have s.th. sent to s.o.; 3. *auf jdn ~* go towards s.o.; 4. *(Zeitpunkt)* be going on for; *dem Ende ~* be nearing the end; 5. *(geschehen)* happen; 6. *hier geht es lustig zu* you are having a good time.

zugehörig: *~e Teile* accessory parts.

Zügel *m* 1. rein; 2. *die ~ in die Hand nehmen* take the reins; **z~los** dissolute, unrestrained; **z~n** 1. *(Pferd)* rein; 2. *fig* bridle, curb.

Zuge|ständnis *n* concession; **z~stehen** *irr* 1. *(Recht)*

grant; 2. *(zugeben)* admit, confess.

Zugführer *m* chief guard.

zugießen *irr (Getränk)* give more of.

zugig draughty.

zügig *(rasch)* swift, smart, brisk.

Zug|kraft *f* 1. traction power; 2. *fig* appear, attraction; **z~kräftig** *fig* attractive.

zugleich 1. *(zeitlich)* at the same time; 2. both.

Zug|maschine *f* motor, *Am* truck tractor; **~nummer** *f* 1. train number; 2. *fig* drawing card.

zugreifen *irr* 1. grab; 2. *fig* jump at the opportunity; 3. *(bei Tisch)* help o.s.; 4. *(helfen)* give a hand.

zugrunde 1. *~ gehen* go to ruin; 2. *~ legen* take as a basis (for); 3. *~ liegen* be the basis; 4. *~ richten* ruin, destroy.

zugunsten 1. in favour of; 2. *(Nutzen)* for the benefit of.

zugute 1. *jdm etw ~ halten* make allowances for s.th.; 2. *~ kommen* be an advantage *(jdm* to s.o.).

Zug|verbindung *f* train connection; **~vogel** *m* bird of passage.

zuhalten *irr: sich die Ohren ~* stop o.'s ears; *sich die Nase ~* hold o.'s nose.

Zuhälter *m* pimp, pander.

zuhöre|n listen (to); **Z~r** *m* listener; **Z~rschaft** *f* audience.

zujubeln cheer (*jdm* s.o.).

zuknöpfen button up.

zukommen *irr* 1. *auf jdn* ~ come up to s.o.; 2. *jdm etw* ~ *lassen* let s.o. have s.th.; 3. *jdm* ~ be due to s.o.

Zukunft *f* future; *in naher* ~ in the near future; *in* ~ in future, henceforth.

zukünftig 1. future, prospective; 2. in future.

Zulage *f* extra pay, allowance, bonus.

zulassen *irr* 1. *(erlauben)* allow, permit; 2. *(akzeptieren)* admit; 3. *amtlich* ~ authorize; 4. *(Auto)* license; 5. *(Tür)* leave closed.

zulässig permissible, admissible.

Zulauf *m (Andrang)* rush, run; *e-n großen* ~ *haben* have a large clientele.

zulegen 1. *(hinzutun)* add; 2. *(Gehalt)* increase s.o.'s salary by; 3. *sich etw* ~ buy s.th.; adopt s.th.

zuleide: *jdm etw* ~ *tun* harm s.o.

zuletzt 1. *(als letzter)* last; *ganz* ~ last of all; 2. *bis* ~ to the end; 3. *(schließlich)* finally, in the end; 4. *nicht* ~ not least.

zuliebe: *jdm* ~ *etw tun* do s.th. for s.o.'s sake.

zumachen close, shut.

zumeist mostly, for the most part.

zumindest at least.

zumut|bar reasonable; ~**e**: ~ *sein* feel; ~**en**: *jdm etw* ~ expect s.th. of s.o.

zunächst 1. *(vorerst)* for the time being; 2. *(anfangs)* first; 3. *(erstens)* in the first place, to begin with.

Zunahme *f* increase, growth.

zünd|en 1. *(Streichholz)* kindle, catch fire; 2. *(Blitz)* strike; 3. *mot* ignite; **Z~flamme** *f* pilot flame; **Z~holz** *n* match; **Z~kerze** *f* spark(ing) plug; **Z~schlüssel** *m* ignition key; **Z~schnur** *f* (safety) fuse; **Z~ung** *f* ignition.

zunehmen *irr* 1. increase, grow; 2. *(Mensch)* put on weight; ~**d** 1. *(Mond)* waxing; 2. *in* ~*em Maße* increasingly.

Zuneigung *f* affection, attachment (für for).

Zunge *f* tongue; *es lag mir auf der* ~ I had it on the tip of my tongue.

zunichte: ~ *machen* wreck, ruin; *(Plan)* thwart.

zunutze: *sich etw* ~ *machen* avail o.s. of, profit from s.th.

zupfen pull, pluck (*an* at).

zurechnungsfähig sound of mind, sane; **Z~keit** *f* soundness of mind; *verminderte* ~ diminished responsibility.

zurecht|finden, *sich irr* 1. find o.'s way; 2. *fig* get along with; **~kommen** *irr: mit etw* ~ manage s.th.; **~legen**: *sich etw* ~ prepare s.th.; **~weisen** *irr* reprimand.

zureden: *jdm* ~ persuade s.o., urge s.o.

zurichten 1. prepare; 2. *jdn* ~ injure s.o. badly.

zürnen be angry (*jdm* with s.o.).

zurück 1. back; *ich bin gleich* ~ I'll be back in a minute; ~*!* go back! 2. ~ *sein* be behind the times, be late; 3. *an Absender* ~ return to sender.

zurückbehalten *irr* keep back.

zurückbekommen *irr* get back.

zurückbezahlen pay back.

zurückbleiben *irr* 1. stay behind; 2. *fig* fall behind; 3. (*geistig*) be behind, be retarded; 4. (*übrigbleiben*) be left; 5. *hinter etw* ~ fall short of s.th.

zurückbringen *irr* bring back, return.

zurückdrängen push back.

zurückfahren *irr* drive back; (*Zug*) travel back.

zurückfallen *irr* 1. fall back; 2. *fig* go down; 3. *an jdn* ~ return to s.o.

zurückfinden *irr* find o.'s way back.

zurückfordern claim back.

zurückführen 1. *jdn* ~ lead s.o. back; *in die Heimat* ~

repatriate; 2. *auf etw* ~ attribute to s.th.

zurückgeben *irr* return, give back.

zurückgeblieben (*geistig*) (mentally) retarded.

zurückgehen *irr* 1. go back, return; 2. (*Preis*) go down, decrease, diminish, drop; 3. (*Fieber*) abate, fall; 4. *fig* go back; 5. (*Ursprung*) originate (*auf* from).

zurückgezogen: ~ *leben* lead a retired life.

zurückgreifen *irr* fall back (*auf* on).

zurückhalt|en *irr* 1. hold, keep back (*von* from); 2. (*Gefühle*) restrain; 3. *sich* ~ be reserved; **~end** reserved, distant; **Z~ung** *f fig* reserve, reticence.

zurückholen fetch back.

zurückkehren return, go back (*nach* to).

zurückkommen *irr* 1. come back; 2. *auf etw* ~ refer to s.th.

zurücklassen *irr* 1. leave behind; 2. (*überholen*) outstrip.

zurücklegen 1. put back; 2. (*Entfernung*) cover; 3. (*aufheben*) keep, put aside.

zurücklehnen, *sich* lean back.

zurückliegen *irr: es liegt Jahre zurück* it is years ago.

zurücknehmen *irr* 1. take back, withdraw; 2. (*Ange-*

bot) revoke; 3. *(Ware)* reduce the price of.
zurückprallen rebound,
bounce off.
zurückreisen travel back.
zurückrufen *irr* 1. call back;
2. *ins Gedächtnis* ~ recall.

zurückschalten *mot*
change, shift down.
zurückscheuen: *vor etw* ~
shrink from s.th.
zurückschicken return,
send back.
zurückschlagen *irr* 1. strike
back, repulse; 2. *(Decke)*
fold back.
zurücksehnen, sich long
for.
zurückstehen *irr* 1. *hinter
etw* ~ be behind s.th.; 2. ~
müssen be left out.
zurückstellen 1. *(Uhr)* put
back; 2. *(an den Platz)* put
back in its place.
zurückstoßen *irr* 1. push
back; 2. *(Auto)* back.
zurückstrahlen reflect.
zurücktreten *irr* 1. step
back; 2. *pol* resign; *(Vertrag)* withdraw *(von* from);
3. *(weniger werden)* diminish; 4. *(weniger wichtig)* be
less important.
zurückverweisen *irr* refer
back *(an* to).
zurückweichen *irr*: ~ *vor*
recede before, shrink back
from.
zurückweisen *irr* reject, refuse, turn down.

zurückwerfen *irr* 1. throw
back; 2. *(Licht)* reflect.
zurückwirken react *(auf*
upon).
zurückzahlen 1. pay back;
2. *(Auslage)* reimburse.
zurückziehen *irr* 1. draw
back; 2. *(Antrag)* withdraw,
cancel; 3. *sich* ~ retire.
Zuruf *m* shout; *durch* ~ by
acclamation; **z~en** *irr* shout
(jdm etw s.th. at).
Zusage *f* 1. promise; 2. *(auf
e-e Einladung)* acceptance;
z~n 1. promise; 2. *(Einladung)* accept an invitation;
3. *es sagt mir nicht zu* it
doesn't appeal to me.
zusammen 1. together *(mit*
with); 2. *(insgesamt) das
macht* ~ *genau zehn Mark*
that comes to exactly ten
marks all together; *alles* ~
in all.
Zusammenarbeit *f* co-
-operation, teamwork.
zusammen\|brechen *irr*
break down, collapse;
Z~bruch *m* collapse, breakdown.
zusammenfahren *irr* start,
recoil.
zusammenfallen *irr* 1. collapse; 2. *(zeitlich)* coincide.
zusammenfalten fold up.
zusammenfass\|en 1. *(verei-
nigen)* unite, combine;
2. *(Text)* summarize, sum up;
Z~ung *f* summary, synopsis.
zusammen\|fügen join to-
gether; **~führen** ng to-

gether; **~gehören** 1. belong together; 2. *(von Sachen)* match; **~gesetzt**: *~ sein aus* be composed of, consist of.

zusammenhalten *irr* 1. hold together; 2. *(von Menschen)* stick together.

Zusammen|hang *m* 1. connection; *etw in ~ bringen* establish a connection between s.th.; *das steht im ~ mit* that is connected with; *in diesem ~* in this connection; 2. *(Text)* context; 3. *(Beziehung)* relation, correlation; **z~hängen** *irr* 1. be joined; 2. *fig* be connected; **z~hängend** coherent; **z~hangslos** incoherent.

zusammenklapp|bar collapsible; **~en** fold up.

zusammen|kommen *irr* 1. meet, assemble, come together; 2. *(ansammeln)* accumulate; **Z~kunft** *f* meeting, gathering, assembly.

zusammenlaufen *irr* 1. *(herbeiströmen)* gather; 2. *(Fluß)* flow together; 3. *(Linie)* intersect.

Zusammenleben *n* living together.

zusammenlegen 1. *(falten)* fold up; 2. *(in e-m Haufen)* put together, pile up; 3. *(Geld)* club together; 4. *com* consolidate, merge.

zusammennehmen *irr*

1. collect, summon up; 2. *sich ~* pull o.s. together.

zusammenpassen 1. *(farblich)* match; 2. *(Stil)* go together, harmonize; 3. *(Personen)* be suited to each other.

Zusammenprall *m* crash, collision; **z~en** collide.

zusammenrechnen add up, reckon up.

zusammen|rücken move together; **~rufen** *irr* call together.

zusammen|schlagen *irr* 1. *(Hände)* clap; 2. *jdn ~* beat s.o. up; **~schließen, sich** *irr* 1. join up, unite; 2. *com* consolidate, merge; 3. *pol* federate.

zusammensetz|en 1. put together; 2. *tech* assemble; 3. *sich ~* sit together; 4. *sich ~ aus* consist of; **Z~ung** *f* 1. composition; 2. *chem* compound; 3. *(Bestandteile)* ingredients *pl.*

zusammenstell|en 1. put together; 2. *(Liste)* compose; 3. *(Farben)* combine; 4. *(anordnen)* arrange; 5. *(Übersicht)* compile; **Z~ung** *f* 1. compositon; 2. combination; 3. arrangement.

Zusammenstoß *m* 1. collision; 2. *mot* crash; 3. *(Aufprall)* impact; **z~en** *irr* 1. collide, crash; 2. *fig* clash; 3. *(grenzen)* adjoin (*an on*).

zusammentreffen *irr* meet (*mit jdm s.o.*); **Z~** *n* 1. meeting; 2. *(Gleichzeitigkeit)* coincidence.

zusammentreten *irr* convene, assemble.

zusammen|zählen add up; ~**ziehen** *irr* 1. pull together; 2. *(Truppen)* concentrate; 3. *sich* ~ contract, shrink; 4. *mit jdm* ~ live with s.o.

Zusatz *m* 1. addition; 2. *(Nahrung)* additive; 3. *(Ergänzung)* supplement.

zusätzlich 1. additional, extra; 2. *(ergänzend)* supplementary; 3. *(außerdem)* in addition to.

Zusatzversicherung *f* supplementary insurance.

zuschaue|n watch, look on; **Z~r** *m* 1. spectator; 2. *tele* viewer; 3. *(Beobachter)* observer; **Z~rraum** *m theat* auditorium.

zuschicken: *jdm etw* ~ send, mail s.o. s.th.

Zuschlag *m* 1. *(Fahrpreis)* supplement; 2. *(Erhöhung)* increase; 3. *(Ausschreibung)* award; **z~en** *irr* 1. *(Tür)* slam; 2. *(aufschlagen)* add on; 3. *(Ausschreibung)* award *(jdm* to s.o.*)*; ~**karte** *f* extra ticket; **z~pflichtig** liable to extra payment.

zuschließen *irr* lock (up).
zuschrauben screw tight.
zuschreiben *irr* 1. *(beimessen)* attribute; 2. *(anlasten)* blame.

zuschulden: *sich etw* ~

kommen lassen make o.s. guilty (of doing s.th.).

Zuschuß *m* 1. allowance; 2. *(staatlich)* subsidy.

zuschütten fill up.

zusehen *irr* 1. watch, look on; 2. *(abwarten)* wait and see; ~**ds** visibly, noticeably.

zusetzen 1. add (to); 2. *(Geld)* lose; 3. *(bedrängen)* importune, badger *(mit Fragen* with questions*)*.

zuspitzen 1. point, sharpen; 2. *sich* ~ *(Lage)* come to a crisis.

zusprechen *irr* 1. *jdm Mut* ~ encourage s.o.; *jdm Trost* ~ comfort s.o.; 2. *(zuerkennen)* adjudge; 3. *(Essen)* do justice, eat heartily.

Zuspruch *m* 1. *(Anklang)* reception, appreciation; ~ *finden* meet with approval; 2. *(Zulauf)* popularity.

Zustand *m* 1. condition; *in gutem* ~ in good condition; 2. *(Lage)* state of affairs.

zustande 1. ~ *bringen* manage, achieve; 2. ~ *kommen* materialize, come off.

zuständig 1. responsible, appropriate; 2. *jur* competent.

zustatten: *jdm* ~ *kommen* be useful to s.o.

zustehen *irr* 1. *jdm steht etw zu* s.o. is entitled to s.th.; 2. *es steht jdm nicht zu* s.o. has no right.

zusteigen *irr* get on, board.

zustell|en 1. *(Briefe)* deliver; 2. *jur* serve; **Z~gebühr** *f* delivery charge; **Z~post-amt** *n* delivery office.

zustimm|en agree (*jdm* with s.o.; *e-r Sache* to s.th.); **Z~ung** *f* consent, agreement, approval.

zustopfen stop up.

zustoßen *irr* 1. (*Tür*) slam; 2. (*Unglück*) happen (*jdm* to s.o.).

Zustrom *m* inflow, influx.

zutage: ~ *fördern* bring to light.

Zutaten *pl* (*Speise*) ingredients.

zuteil: *jdm* ~ *werden* fall to s.o.'s share; ~ *werden lassen* grant s.o. s.th.; **~en** 1. allot, apportion; 2. (*zuweisen*) assign.

zutragen *irr* 1. (*berichten*) report; 2. *sich* ~ take place, happen.

zuträglich 1. beneficial; 2. (*Nahrung*) wholesome.

zutrauen: *jdm etw* ~ think s.o. capable of s.th.; **Z~en** *n* confidence, trust; **~lich** trusting, confiding.

zutreffen *irr* 1. apply; 2. (*passend*) fit; 3. (*stimmen*) come true, prove true; **~d** apt, appropriate.

Zutritt *m* admission, access, entry; ~ *verboten!* no admittance! *sich* ~ *verschaffen* gain admittance.

Zutun *n*: *ohne sein* ~ without his help.

zuverlässig 1. reliable, trustworthy; 2. (*Nachricht*) aus

~er *Quelle* from a reliable source.

Zuversicht *f* confidence, trust; **z~lich** confident.

zuviel too much; too many.

zuvor (*vorher*) before; *kurz* ~ shortly before; *nie* ~ never before; **~kommen** *irr*: *jdm* ~ anticipate s.o., steal a march on s.o.; **~kommend** obliging, polite.

Zuwachs *m* increase (*an* in), increment (*an* of); **~rate** *f* rate of growth.

zuwege: ~ *bringen* manage, achieve, succeed in.

zuweilen now and then, occasionally.

zuweisen *irr* assign.

zuwenden *irr* 1. (*widmen*) devote; 2. *sich jdm* ~ turn to s.o.

zuwenig too little; too few.

zuwerfen *irr*: *jdm etw* ~ (*Ball*) throw s.th. to s.o., (*Blick*) cast a glance at s.o.

zuwider: *jdm* ~ *sein* be repugnant to s.o.; **~handeln** (*e-m Gesetz*) offend against; **Z~handlung** *f* violation, offence.

zuwinken beckon (*jdm* to s.o.), wave (*jdm* to s.o.).

zuzahlen pay extra.

zuziehen *irr* 1. (*Vorhänge*) draw, pull together; 2. (*Schraube*) tighten; 3. *jdn* ~ call in s.o., consult s.o.; 4. *sich* ~ catch s.th., incur s.th.

zuzüglich plus.

Zwang *m* 1. compulsion; 2. *(Pflicht)* obligation; 3. *allen ~ ablegen* abandon all restraint; 4. *(Druck)* pressure; **z~los** 1. casual, informal, without constraint; 2. *sich ~ benehmen* have a casual manner.

Zwangs|arbeit *f* forced labour; **~handlung** *f* compulsive act; **~lage** *f* predicament, fix; **z~läufig** *fig* necessary, inevitable; **~maßnahme** *f* coercive measure; **~vollstreckung** *f* execution; **z~weise** compulsory.

zwanzig twenty; *etw ~ sein* be about twenty; *die ~er Jahre* the twenties; *Mitte der Z~er sein* be in o.'s mid twenties; **~st** twentieth; **Z~stel** *n* twentieth (part).

zwar 1. *~, aber* it is true but; 2. *und ~* namely, in fact.

Zweck *m* 1. purpose; *s-n ~ verfehlen* defeat its purpose; *zu diesem ~* for this purpose; *zu welchem ~?* what for? 2. *(Ziel)* object, aim, purpose; *e-n ~ verfolgen* pursue an object; 3. *(Sinn)* es hat keinen ~ there is no use, no point; 4. *(Absicht)* design, intention; **~bau** *m* functional building; **z~dienlich** useful, expedient, serviceable; **z~entfremdet** misappropriated; **z~entsprechend**

appropriate; **z~los** pointless, useless; **z~mäßig** appropriate, advisable; **z~s** for the purpose of.

zwei two; *alle ~* both; *zu ~t* in twos; *zu ~en* two by two; **Z~bettzimmer** *n* double room.

zweideutig ambiguous; **Z~keit** *f* ambiguity.

zwei|erlei of two kinds; **~fach** double, twofold.

Zweifel *m* 1. doubt; *es besteht kein ~, daß* there is no doubt that; *~ haben* have doubts; *außer ~* beyond doubt; *im ~ sein* be doubtful; *etw in ~ ziehen* doubt s.th.; *ohne ~* without doubt, doubtless; 2. *(Verdacht)* suspicion; **z~haft** doubtful, dubious, dubitable; **z~los** undoubtedly, doubtless; **z~n** doubt; *an etw ~* be doubtful about s.th.; *nicht ~ an* have no doubt about; **~sfall** *m: im ~* in case of doubt.

Zweig *m* branch, arm, bough.

zweigleisig double-track.

Zweigstelle *f* branch.

zweihundert two hundred.

Zweikampf *m* duel.

zwei|mal twice; *~ täglich* twice a day; **~reihig** *(Anzug)* double-breasted; **~schneidig** double-edged; **~seitig** 1. *(Vertrag)* bilateral; 2. *(Stoff)* reversible; **Z~sitzer** *m* two-seater; **~sprachig** bilangual; **~spurig** two-lane.

zweit second; *zum ~en Mal* for the second time.
Zweitaktmotor *m* two--stroke engine.
zweitausend two thousand.
zweitbest second-best.
zweiteilig two-piece.
zweitens in the second place, secondly.
Zweiter *m* 1. second; 2. *heute ist der Zweite* today is the second.
zweit|letzt last but one; ~**rangig** of secondary importance, second-rate.
Zweit|schrift *f* duplicate; ~**wohnung** *f* second home.
Zwerchfell *n* *anat* diaphragm.
Zwerg *m* dwarf.
Zwetsch(g)e *f* plum; ~**nbaum** *m* plum-tree; ~**nwasser** *n* plum brandy.
Zwickel *m* gusset.
zwick|en pinch; **Z~mühle** *f*: *in e-r ~ sein* be in a quandary, dilemma.

Zwieback *m* rusk.
Zwiebel *f* 1. onion; 2. *bot* bulb; ~**suppe** *f* onion soup.
Zwielicht *n* twilight.
Zwiespalt *m* conflict, dilemma.
Zwietracht *f* discord; ~ *säen* sow the seeds of discord.
Zwilling *m* 1. twin; 2. *astr pl* Gemini.
zwingen *irr* 1. force, compel; *jdn zu etw ~* force s.o. into

s.th.; 2. *zu etw ~* necessitate s.th.; 3. *sich ~* force o.s.; ~**d** 1. (*Grund*) urgent; 2. (*Argument*) forcible, conclusive; 3. (*Pflicht*) imperative.
zwinkern blink, twinkle.
Zwirn *m* twist.
zwischen 1. between; 2. (*mehrere*) among.
Zwischen|akt *m* entr'acte; ~**bemerkung** *f* interjection; ~**bericht** *m* interim report; ~**deck** *n* between decks *pl*; **z~durch** (*zeitlich*) in between; 1. (*gelegentlich*) occasionally; ~**ergebnis** *n* provisional result; ~**fall** *m* incident; ~**frage** *f* interposed question; ~**handel** *m* intermediate trade; ~**landung** *f* intermediate landing; *ohne ~* non-stop; ~**lösung** *f* interim solution; ~**mahlzeit** *f* snack between meals; **z~menschlich** interhuman; ~**raum** *m* 1. space between; 2. (*zeitlich*) interval; 3. (*Zeilenabstand*) spacing; ~**ruf** *m* interjection, interruption; ~**zeit** *f* meanwhile; *in der ~* in the meantime.
zwitschern twitter.
zwölf twelve; *um ~* at noon; ~**t** twelfth; **Z~tel** *n* twelfth (part).
Zyklus *m* cycle.
Zylinder *m* 1. *tech* cylinder; 2. (*Hut*) top hat; ~**kopf** *m* *mot* cylinder head.
Zypresse *f* cypress.

Cardinal Numbers

0 *null* nought, naught, zero, cipher
1 *eins* one
2 *zwei* two
3 *drei* three
4 *vier* four
5 *fünf* five
6 *sechs* six
7 *sieben* seven
8 *acht* eight
9 *neun* nine
10 *zehn* ten
11 *elf* eleven
12 *zwölf* twelve
13 *dreizehn* thirteen
14 *vierzehn* fourteen
15 *fünfzehn* fifteen
16 *sechzehn* sixteen
17 *siebzehn* seventeen
18 *achtzehn* eighteen
19 *neunzehn* nineteen
20 *zwanzig* twenty
21 *einundzwanzig* twenty-one
22 *zweiundzwanzig* twenty-two
30 *dreißig* thirty
31 *einunddreißig* thirty-one
40 *vierzig* forty
41 *einundvierzig* forty-one
50 *fünfzig* fifty
51 *einundfünfzig* fifty-one
60 *sechzig* sixty
61 *einundsechzig* sixty-one

70 *siebzig* seventy
71 *einundsiebzig* seventy-one
80 *achtzig* eighty
81 *einundachtzig* eighty-one
90 *neunzig* ninety
91 *einundneunzig* ninety-one
100 *hundert* a (*od* one) hundred
101 *hundert* (*und*)*eins* one hundred and one
200 *zweihundert* two hundred
300 *dreihundert* three hundred
400 *vierhundert* four hundred
764 *siebenhundert* (*und*)*vierundsechzig* seven hundred and sixty-four
1 000 *tausend* a (*od* one) thousand
1 001 *tausendundeins* one thousand and one
1 150 *eintausendeinhundert* (*und*)*fünfzig* one thousand one hundred and fifty
2 000 *zweitausend* two thousand
1 000 000 *eine Million* a (*od* one) million
5 000 000 *fünf Millionen* five millions
1 *Milliarde* one milliard, *Am* one billion

Ordinal Numbers

1. *erste* first	1st	
2. *zweite* second	2nd	
3. *dritte* third	3rd	
4. *vierte* fourth	4th	
5. *fünfte* fifth	5th	
6. *sechste* sixth	6th	
7. *sieb(en)te* seventh	7th	
8. *achte* eighth	8th	
9. *neunte* ninth	9th	
10. *zehnte* tenth	10th	
11. *elfte* eleventh	11th	
12. *zwölfte* twelfth	12th	
13. *dreizehnte* thirteenth	13th	
14. *vierzehnte* fourteenth	14th	
15. *fünfzehnte* fifteenth	15th	
16. *sechzehnte* sixteenth	16th	
17. *siebzehnte* seventeenth	17th	
18. *achtzehnte* eighteenth	18th	
19. *neunzehnte* nineteenth	19th	
20. *zwanzigste* twentieth	20th	
21. *einundzwanzigste* twenty-first	21st	
22. *zweiundzwanzigste* twenty-second	22nd	
23. *dreiundzwanzigste* twenty-third	23rd	
30. *dreißigste* thirtieth	30th	
31. *einunddreißigste* thirty-first	31st	
40. *vierzigste* fortieth	40th	

41. *einundvierzigste* forty-first	41st	
50. *fünfzigste* fiftieth	50th	
51. *einundfünfzigste* fifty-first	51st	
60. *sechzigste* sixtieth	60th	
61. *einundsechzigste* sixty-first	61st	
70. *siebzigste* seventieth	70th	
71. *einundsiebzigste* seventy-first	71st	
80. *achtzigste* eightieth	80th	
81. *einundachtzigste* eighty-first	81st	
90. *neunzigste* ninetieth	90th	
100. *hundertste* (one) hundredth	100th	
101. *hundert(und)erste* one hundred and first	101st	
200. *zweihundertste* two hundredth	200th	
300. *dreihundertste* three hundredth	300th	
1 000. *tausendste* (one) thousandth	1 000th	
1 001. *tausendunderste* thousand and first	1 001st	
1 150. *tausendeinhundert-(und)fünfzigste* thousand one hundred and fiftieth	1 150th	
2 000. *zweitausendste* two thousandth	2 000th	
1 000 000. *millionste* millionth	1 000 000th	
5 000 000. *fünfmillionste* five millionth	5 000 000th	